... ENSURE STUDENTS ARE "GETTING IT"

aplia™

Through **Aplia's** unique online, interactive format, students review the basics of grammar and mechanics as well as important concepts throughout the text. Aplia improves learning by increasing student effort and engagement—without requiring more work from instructors.

For more details on Aplia, visit **www.aplia.com/cengage.**

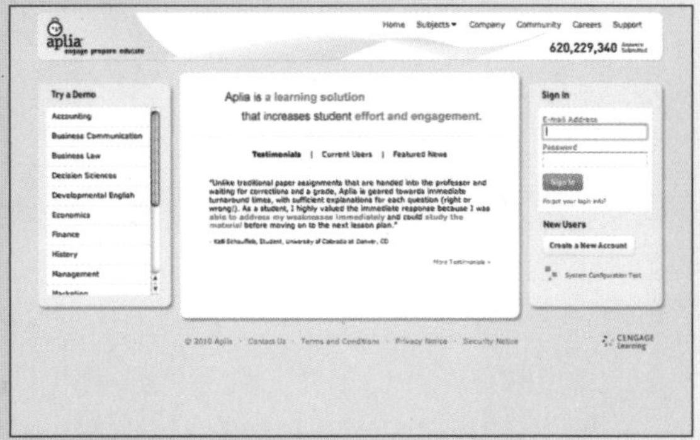

... GET STUDENTS WRITING MORE!

CENGAGE LEARNING'S writexperience POWERED BY MEASURED SUCCESS

Cengage Learning's *Write Experience* delivers. This breakthrough solution provides a new technology that scores select written work; assesses style, mechanics, and format of writing; and ensures originality of written work.

The assignments in *Write Experience* for *Business Communication* require students to demonstrate these skills in structured memos, customer service letters, complaint letters, media communication, and other messages.

Find out more at **www.cengage.com/writeexperience.**

... OFFER COST-SAVING PURCHASE OPTIONS

CENGAGE brain .com

On CengageBrain.com students will be able to save up to 60 percent on their course materials through our full spectrum of options. Students will have the option to rent their text-books, purchase print textbooks, e-textbooks, or individual e-chapters and audio books—all for substantial savings over average retail prices. CengageBrain.com also provides access to a broad range of homework and study tools, along with a selection of free content from Cengage Learning.

Find out more today at **www.CengageBrain.com**.

7th Edition

Business Communication

Process & Product

Mary Ellen Guffey
Professor Emerita of Business
Los Angeles Pierce College

Dana Loewy
Business Communication Program
California State University, Fullerton

SOUTH-WESTERN
CENGAGE Learning™

Australia • Brazil • Japan • Korea • Mexico • Singapore • Spain • United Kingdom • United States

Business Communication: Process & Product, Seventh Edition
Mary Ellen Guffey
Dana Loewy

Vice President, Editorial Director: Jack W. Calhoun

Editor in Chief: Melissa Acuña

Senior Acquisitions Editor: Erin Joyner

Senior Developmental Editor: Mary Draper, Capstone Publishing Services

Editorial Assistant: Kayti Purkiss

Marketing Manager: Michelle Lockard

Associate Content Project Manager: Jana Lewis

Media Editor: John Rich

Frontlist Buyer, Manufacturing: Miranda Klapper

Marketing Communications Manager: Sarah Greber

Production Service: Cadmus Communications

Senior Art Director: Stacy Jenkins Shirley

Rights Acquisitions Specialist: Mardell Glinski-Schultz

Internal Designer: Lou Ann Thesing

Cover Designer: Lou Ann Thesing

Cover Image: ©Blend Images/Alamy

Library of Congress Control Number: 2010930837

Package ISBN-13: 978-0-538-46625-7

Package ISBN-10: 0-538-46625-1

Book-only ISBN 13: 978-0-538-46626-4

Book-only ISBN 10: 0-538-46626-X

South-Western Cengage Learning
5191 Natorp Boulevard
Mason, OH 45040
USA

Cengage Learning products are represented in Canada by Nelson Education, Ltd.

For your course and learning solutions, visit **www.cengage.com**
Purchase any of our products at your local college store or at our preferred online store **www.CengageBrain.com**

Printed in the United States of America
1 2 3 4 5 6 7 14 13 12 11 10

Dear Business Communication Instructors:

My coauthor Dr. Dana Loewy and I are proud to present to you the **Seventh Edition** of ***Business Communication: Process and Product.*** We know that it's a bit risky to make changes in the market-leading book. However, in an effort to bring you and your students the latest information and tools to succeed in today's increasingly interconnected workplace, we have made innumerable revisions and enhancements, a few of which are highlighted here:

- **Integrated, cutting-edge coverage of digital tools and social media.** The Seventh Edition prepares students to become accomplished communicators in today's digital workplace. A new Chapter 7, *Electronic Messages and Digital Media,* is solely dedicated to digital media. Every chapter has been thoroughly researched and updated to acquaint students with the latest trends in workplace communication technology.
- **New Chat About It questions!** Whether in class or in online chat rooms, students gain insight about workplace communication and polish their communication skills through these stimulating discussion questions related to chapter topics.
- **More figures and model documents.** The Seventh Edition has been enhanced with numerous new figures and model documents that show the use of Twitter, instant messages, podcasts, blogs, and wikis.
- **New workplace simulations!** Students gain real-world training through scenario-based case studies at the Premium Web site **(www.meguffey.com)**.
- **Stronger ethics coverage.** Chapter 1 sheds light on ethical lapses blamed by some for the recent economic downturn. Ethics Checks present brief scenarios to help students meet workplace dilemmas.
- **New *Technology in the Workplace* video.** Using humor to compare appropriate and inappropriate uses of digital media, this new video helps students distinguish between professional and social uses of digital media.
- **Expanded Premium Web site.** At **www.meguffey.com** we provide one convenient place for students to review concepts and practice their skills. They will find scenario-based case studies, two types of interactive chapter quizzes, downloadable documents to revise, PowerPoint slides, and unparalleled resources to achieve success in the course.
- **Independent Grammar Review.** Grammar/mechanics exercises in every chapter present a structured review to guide students through all of the rules.

We welcome your comments and suggestions as you use the No. 1 business communication book in this country and abroad.

Cordially,

Mary Ellen Guffey & Dana Loewy

Guffey ... *It's Just That Easy.*

The unrivaled market leader, ***Business Communication: Process and Product*** delivers the most current and authoritative communication technology and business communication concepts available. This renowned leader is hands down the most up-to-date and best researched text on the market, and the exciting Seventh Edition is bursting with new, interactive student resources and comprehensive coverage of workplace technology.

Innovative coverage enhances the hallmark features of this textbook: the 3-x-3 writing process, three-part case studies, abundant use of model documents, and comprehensive coverage in a 16-chapter textbook.

Zooming In — PART 1

Apple's Steve Jobs and His Keynotes

Come January, when CEO Steve Jobs launches yet another hot new Apple product during one of his famously simple, yet striking keynote presentations, the world listens. Weeks and months of feverish preparation and secrecy precede the "Stevenote" at the annual Macworld conference. Understandably, the tech world is abuzz on the Web. The pundits weigh in with their speculations about the latest unveiling, kept tightly under wraps until Jobs announces it. Sometimes not even the name of the newest gizmo is known, as was the case with the Apple iPad, a sleek tablet device promising to revolutionize computing. Until the last moment, the technorati were guessing at its specifications and names, ranging from iSlate, iBook, and iTablet to Canvas. A few hundred industry insiders, analysts, and members of the media gathered expectantly at the Yerba Buena Center in San Francisco.

During the launch of the iPad—a large iPhone or iPod Touch look-alike—some invited guests were covering the event live in their blogs and tweets. Bobbie Johnson, technology correspondent for the UK newspaper *The Guardian*, was one of them. His readers and Twitter followers all over the world were able to witness not only the actual keynote presentation, but rumors and speculation even before the event unfolded. Steve Jobs' impressive images, passionate delivery, and nearly messianic zeal are legendary. Johnson remarked later in his first hands-on review of the iPad: "Jobs trumpeted it as exactly that, a magical device that will change the way we use computers in our everyday lives. And while playing with the iPad was not exactly a religious experience, it's not hard to see that the gadget, or at least the ideas it contains, will be with us for a long time to come."[1]

The long buildup and the secrecy are calculated communication strategies. They work to stoke excitement and fascination, as one blogger put it: "The iPhone ... blew people away not only because of what it was capable of, but also because many of its features came as a complete surprise to even the most well-informed of Apple bloggers."[2] This expert also suggests that Jobs is hedging against the risk of hyping up products that are still under development. Instead of revealing unfinished devices too soon, Apple manages the public's expectations and prevents consumer disappointment. A master showman, Jobs calls himself "a big-bang guy,"[3] meaning that he likes flashy and fast launches. You will learn about the Apple executive's storied presentation techniques in Part 2 of this feature on page 467.

Critical Thinking

- What kinds of oral presentations might you have to make in your chosen career field?
- Why are most people fearful of making presentations?
- How do you think people become effective speakers?

http://www.apple.com/contact/

Preparing Effective Oral Presentations

LEARNING OBJECTIVE 1
Discuss two important first steps in preparing effective business presentations.

Like his archnemesis Bill Gates of Microsoft, Steve Jobs is a college dropout, but he is one who has elevated communication with the public to an art form. Few of us will ever talk to an audience of millions, whether face-to-face or mediated by technology, about a spectacular new product. At some point, however, all businesspeople have to inform others or sell an idea. Such information and persuasion are often conveyed in person and involve audiences of various sizes. If you are like most people, you have some apprehension when speaking in public. That's normal. Good speakers are made, not born. The good news is that you can conquer the fear of public speaking and hone your skills with instruction and practice.

Many future businesspeople fail to take advantage of opportunities in college to develop speaking skills. However, such skills often play an important role in a successful career. In fact, the No. 1 predictor of success and upward mobility, according to an AT&T and Stanford University study, is how much you enjoy public speaking and how effective you are at it.[4] Speaking skills are useful at every career stage. You might, for example, have to make a sales pitch before customers or speak to a professional gathering. You might need to describe your company's expansion plans to your banker, or you might need to persuade management to support your proposed marketing strategy. This chapter prepares you to use speaking skills in making oral presentations, whether alone or as part of a team.

For any presentation, you can reduce your fears and lay the foundation for a professional performance by focusing on five areas: preparation, organization, audience rapport, visual aids, and delivery.

Chapter 14: Business Presentations 457

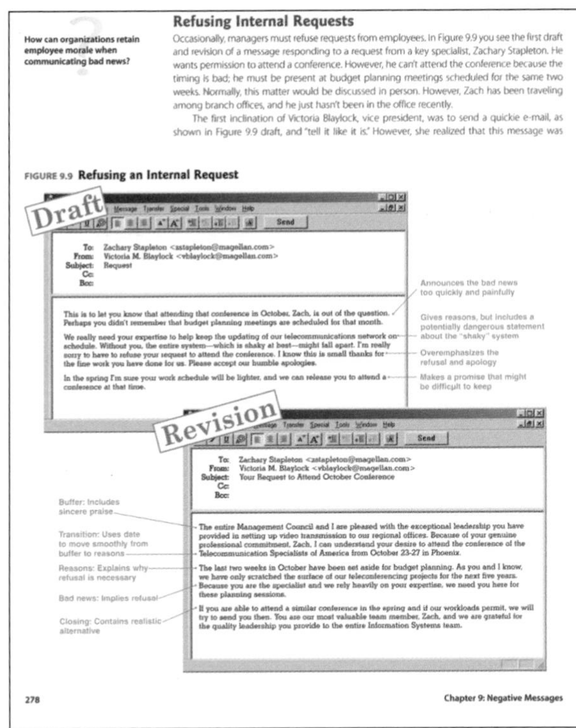

Refusing Internal Requests

How can organizations retain employee morale when communicating bad news?

Occasionally, managers must refuse requests from employees. In Figure 9.9 you see the first draft and revision of a message responding to a request from a key specialist, Zachary Stapleton. He wants permission to attend a conference. However, he can't attend the conference because the timing is bad; he must be present at budget planning meetings scheduled for the same two weeks. Normally, this matter would be discussed in person. However, Zach has been traveling among branch offices, and he just hasn't been in the office recently.

The first inclination of Victoria Blaylock, vice president, was to send a quickie e-mail, as shown in Figure 9.9 draft, and "tell it like it is." However, she realized that this message was

FIGURE 9.9 **Refusing an Internal Request**

278 **Chapter 9: Negative Messages**

Written by award-winning author Mary Ellen Guffey and new coauthor Dana Loewy, the Seventh Edition also retains unparalleled teaching resources to help you plan and manage your courses. The foremost authority on business communication, the new ***Business Communication: Process and Product, 7e,*** equips you and your students alike with all the tools you need to maximize course success.

Innovative Technology With Guffey… *It's Just That Easy*

Business Communication: Process and Product provides students and instructors with all the tools they need for effective and efficient communication. The Seventh Edition's preeminent technology coverage and groundbreaking technology resources are unrivaled. Authoritative and comprehensive, text content is thoroughly updated to reflect the latest trends and advances in our increasingly digital world.

WITH GUFFEY, IT'S JUST THAT EASY TO…

… ACCESS ONLINE RESOURCES

www.meguffey.com
Guffey's Premium Web Site.

Connecting you to a powerhouse of resources, **www.meguffey.com** gives you and your students one convenient place to find the support you need. You will find downloadable supplements such as the complete Instructor's Manual, PowerPoint® slides, transparency masters, certified test bank, and solutions to most activities.

By utilizing progressive resources at **www.meguffey.com**, students will polish their communication skills and build their knowledge through:

- New workplace simulations
- Two types of interactive chapter quizzes
- Downloadable documents to revise
- PowerPoint review slides

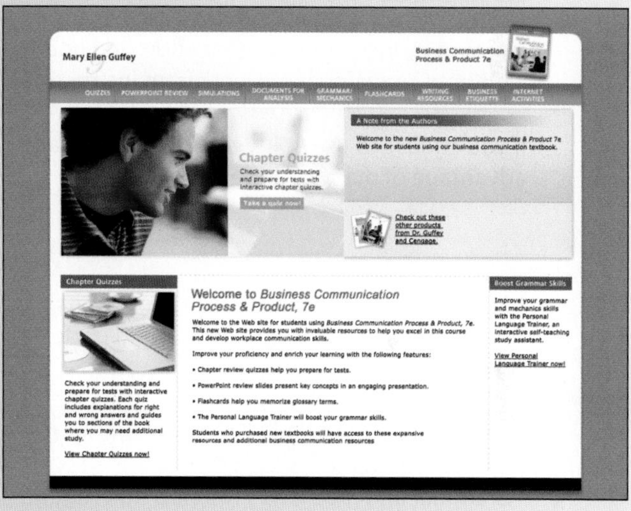

Innovative Technology With Guffey… *It's Just That Easy*

WITH GUFFEY, IT'S JUST THAT EASY TO…

… ENSURE STUDENTS ARE "GETTING IT"

Aplia™ for *Business Communication: Process and Product, 7e*

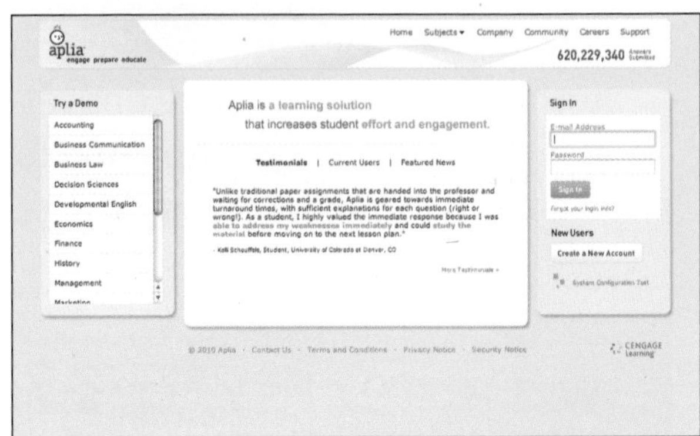

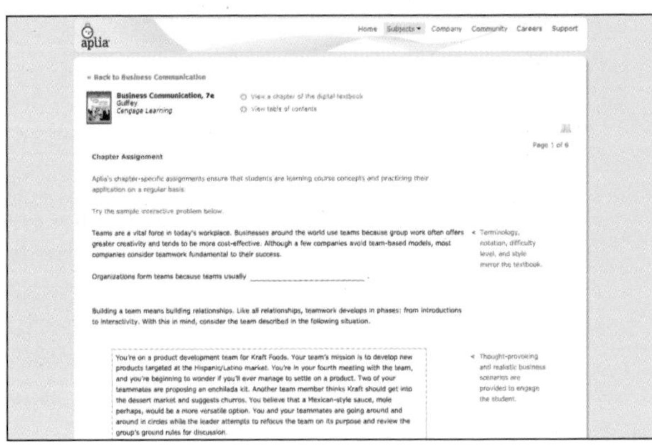

Through **Aplia's** unique online, interactive format, students review the basics of grammar and mechanics as well as important concepts throughout the text. Aplia improves learning by increasing student effort and engagement – without requiring more work from instructors.

If you choose to use Aplia, you'll be able to take advantage of many of these benefits:

- Auto-graded, chapter-specific assignments that hold students accountable for reading and understanding the text.
- Instant detailed feedback on every question.
- Grammar and mechanics tutorials that require students to brush up their key writing skills so that instructors spend less time reviewing and more time teaching advanced writing concepts.
- Access to a full ebook version of the text, which saves students money.

For more details on Aplia, visit www.aplia.com/cengage.

... GET STUDENTS WRITING MORE!

Write Experience for *Business Communication: Process and Product, 7e*

CENGAGE LEARNING'S
writexperience
POWERED BY MEASURED SUCCESS

Cengage Learning's *Write Experience* delivers. This breakthrough solution provides a new technology that scores select written work; assesses style, mechanics, and format of writing; and ensures originality of written work.

The assignments in *Write Experience* for *Business Communication* require students to demonstrate these skills in structured memos, customer service letters, complaint letters, media communication, and other messages.

Find out more at **www.cengage.com/writeexperience.**

... OFFER COST-SAVING PURCHASE OPTIONS

CENGAGEbrain.com

On CengageBrain.com students will be able to save up to 60 percent on their course materials through our full spectrum of options. Students will have the option to rent their text-books, purchase print textbooks, e-textbooks, or individual e-chapters and audio books all for substantial savings over average retail prices. CengageBrain.com also provides access to a broad range of homework and study tools, along with a selection of free content from Cengage Learning.

Find out more today at **www.CengageBrain.com**.

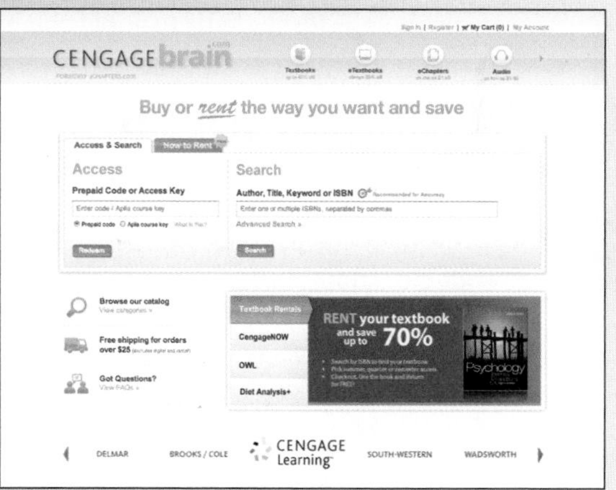

Innovative Features With Guffey...*It's Just That Easy.*

A premier business communication and workplace technology text, the Seventh Edition breaks new ground with a host of innovations to create the most complete business communication authority available. With its up-to-the-minute coverage, riveting examples, hands-on applications, and lively writing, ***Business Communication: Process and Product*** gives students a truly engaging text that equips them with the skills and technology prowess they need for effective communication throughout their careers.

WITH GUFFEY, IT'S JUST THAT EASY TO...

...IMPROVE CRITICAL THINKING

Workplace simulations at **www.meguffey.com** help students apply business communication principles to a variety of realistic communication situations. The purpose of the ***In the Loop*** simulation, for example, is for students to apply communication principles during a communication crisis.

...BRING SOCIAL MEDIA TO THE CLASSROOM

A new social media video, *Technology in the Workplace*, demonstrates the proper use of technology in today's media-rich workplace, including the use of social networking sites.

...STAY CURRENT ON THE LATEST WORKPLACE TECHNOLOGY

Expansive coverage of digital tools and media carefully explains and illustrates how to use these tools professionally in an increasingly connected workplace. For example, a new Chapter 7 is dedicated solely to digital media, acquainting students with the latest trends in workplace communication technology. In addition, all chapters have been enhanced to reflect the use of new digital tools.

PLUGGED IN

Managing Negative News on Facebook, Twitter, and Other Web Sites

Today's consumers eagerly embrace the idea of delivering their complaints to social networking sites rather than telling friends or calling customer service departments. Why rely on word of mouth or send a letter to a company about poor service or a defective product when you can shout your grievance to the entire world? Internet sites such as Complaints.com, Ripoff Report, and iRipoff.com encourage consumers to quickly share complaints about stores, products, and services that fall short of their standards. Twitter and Facebook are also favorite sites for consumers to make public their ire.

Why are online complaints so popular?
Complaint sites are gaining momentum for many reasons. Consumers may receive faster responses to tweets than to customer service calls. Airing gripes in public also helps other consumers avoid the same problems and may improve the complainer's leverage in solving a problem. In addition, sending a 140-word tweet is much easier and more satisfying than writing a complaint letter to a customer service department or navigating endless telephone menus to reach an agent.

How can business organizations manage negative news on social networking sites and blogs?

- **Recognize social networks as an emerging communication channel.** Instead of fearing social networks as a disruptive force, smart companies greet these channels as exciting opportunities to look into the true mind-set of customers.
- **Become proactive.** Company blogs and active Web sites with community forums help companies listen to their customers as well as to spread the word about their own good deeds. Home Depot's site describing its foundation, workshops, and careers now outranks Home DepotSucks.com, which used to rank No. 1 for searches on the keywords *home depot*.
- **Join the fun.** Wise companies have joined sites such as Twitter, Facebook, Flickr, YouTube, and LinkedIn so they can see how these sites function and benefit from site interaction.
- **Monitor comments.** Many companies employ tech-savvy staff members to monitor comments and respond immediately whenever possible. At Southwest Airlines, Paula Berg, manager of emerging media and affectionately called Blog Girl, manages a staff of seven who listen online to what people are saying about Southwest. Its policy is to engage the positive and address the negative.

Career Application
Visit Complaints.com, Ripoff Report, or another complaint site. Study ten or more complaints about products or companies (e.g., iPod, Starbucks, Delta Airline). Select one complaint and, as a company employee, respond to it employing some of the techniques presented in this chapter. Submit a copy of the complaint along with your response to your instructor.

...KEEP STUDENTS ENGAGED

New Chat About It questions in every chapter create opportunities for stimulating, healthy, in-class or online discussion of chapter topics.

Chat About It

In each chapter you will find five discussion questions related to the chapter material. Your instructor may assign these to
in class, in an online chat room, or on an online discussion board. Some of the discussion topics may require outside rese
asked to read and respond to postings made by your classmates.

Topic 1: Describe a time when a company delivered negative news to you effectively; that is, you understood and accept
why the company's strategy was effective.

Topic 2: Many people say they prefer the direct approach when receiving bad news. What situational factors might cause
approach with these people?

Topic 3: Create an effective buffer that you might use if you were a professor who had to tell a student expecting to earn
actually earned a C instead.

Topic 4: A flyer at a city bus stop announced a fare increase with the title *Rate Changes*. Was this title effective? If not, wha
worked better?

Topic 5: You are an executive at a company that suddenly has to lay off 400 employees within three days or risk financial
make the cuts quickly, but you don't want to be impersonal by announcing the cuts by e-mail. How would you anno

New margin notes bolster student retention of chapter concepts by adding questions in the margins that facilitate comprehension and generate classroom discussion.

ch as wikis and
ative software to
technology that
British Telecom,
campaigns, and
that's especially

What is a wiki, and how is it useful to businesses?

Numerous new figures and model documents illustrate the professional uses of the latest digital media at work, including the use of Twitter, instant messages, podcasts, blogs, and wikis.

FIGURE 9.7 **Blog Announcing Price Increase**

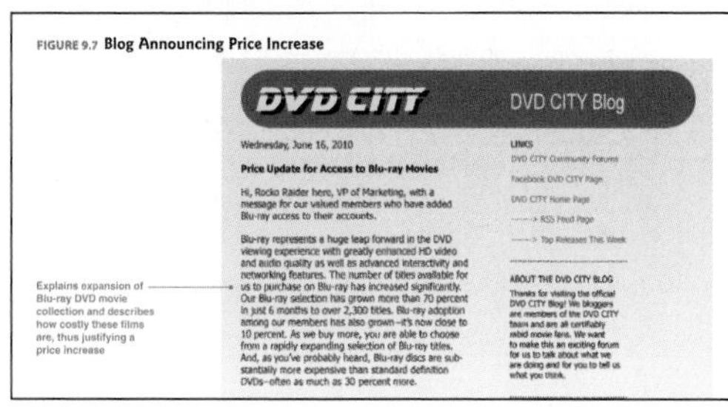

DVD CITY
DVD CITY Blog
Wednesday, June 16, 2010
Price Update for Access to Blu-ray Movies
Hi, Rocko Raider here, VP of Marketing, with a message for our valued members who have added Blu-ray access to their accounts.
Blu-ray represents a huge leap forward in the DVD viewing experience with greatly enhanced HD video and audio quality as well as advanced interactivity and networking features. The number of titles available for us to purchase on Blu-ray has increased significantly. Our Blu-ray selection has grown more than 70 percent in just 6 months to over 2,300 titles. Blu-ray adoption among our members has also grown—it's now close to 10 percent. As we buy more, you are able to choose from a rapidly expanding selection of Blu-ray titles. And, as you've probably heard, Blu-ray discs are substantially more expensive than standard definition DVDs—often as much as 30 percent more.
LINKS
DVD CITY Community Forums
Facebook DVD CITY Page
DVD CITY Home Page
RSS Feed Page
Top Releases This Week
ABOUT THE DVD CITY BLOG
Thanks for visiting the official DVD CITY Blog! We bloggers are members of the DVD CITY team and are all certifiably rabid movie fans. We want to make this an exciting forum for us to talk about what we are doing and for you to tell us what you think.
Explains expansion of Blu-ray DVD movie collection and describes how costly these films are, thus justifying a price increase

Nearly half of the **End-of-Chapter Activities and Cases are new** or have been refreshed to offer the most complete, descriptive, understandable, and relevant activities and cases on the market.

7.6 Twitter: Learning to Write Superefficient Tweets
(Objs. 1, 4, and 5)

Twitter forces its users to practice extreme conciseness. Some music reviewers have risen to the challenge and reviewed whole albums in no more than 140 characters. National Public Radio put Stephen Thompson, one of its music editors, to the test. "I approach Twitter as a science," Thompson says.[42] He sees well-designed tweets as online equivalents of haiku, a highly structured type of Japanese poetry. Thompson believes that tweets should be properly punctuated, be written in complete sentences, and of course, not exceed the 140-character limit. His rules also exclude abbreviations.

Innovative Features With Guffey...*It's Just That Easy.*

WITH GUFFEY, IT'S JUST THAT EASY TO...

...TEACH BUSINESS COMMUNICATION!

Expanded, certified test bank includes more questions in every chapter and a new question-selection matrix guide that allows you to easily design tests based on content, difficulty level, and question type.

Model Documents with callouts enable students to better understand strategies highlighted in the text. New intercultural communication model documents help students readily see differences in cultural adaptation.

FIGURE 3.5 **Ineffective Intercultural E-Mail Message**

To: Cheng Po <cheng.po@global.com>
From: Robert K. Crane <rcrane@organicproducts.com>
Subject: Awesome Herbs
Cc:
Bcc:

Dear Mr. Po:

While cruising the Web, I spotted your site and was totally blown away by your organic herbal products! Just what I'm looking for! If your herbs are half as good as they sound, and if they can get by U.S. customs, I am definitely interested.

People in this country are really into Chinese herbs. They're pounding down the doors to get some of the products you show on your Web site. Before I place an order and cash in on this craze, though, I need more information. For one thing, do your herbs and herbal products meet U.S. regulations? What I want to know is if they qualify as food supplements? Another important matter has to do with herbs as legal supplements. Are they? We also need a phytosanitary certificate to import bulk herbs into this country. Can you do that? One more thing. I don't want to put the horse before the cart, so maybe I should try out a small trial order to test the market in my country.

If you'll get back to me ASAP, preferably before 5/8, I might do an order. And if everything sounds on the up and up, I might even get over to see you in Shandong in the fall.

Ciao,

Bob

Robert K. Crane, Owner | rcrane@organicproducts.com
Organic Herbal Products | www.organicproducts.com
1540 N. Third Street | Coeur d'Alene, ID 83814 | 208.638.9842

Confuses first and last names; Chinese family names are listed before given names

Uses ambiguous expression (*really into*), idiom (*pounding down the doors*), figurative cliché (*cash in on craze*)

Fails to organize questions into clear format

Closes with *Ciao*, which is slang for "stinking" in Singapore

Begins informally with slang (*cruising, blown away*)

Uses overly casual tone throughout and may offend reader by suggesting that products are inferior

Includes unclear contraction (*you'll*), acronym (*ASAP*), and unclear date (*5/8*); uses imprecise expression (*might do an order*) and slang (*on the up and up*)

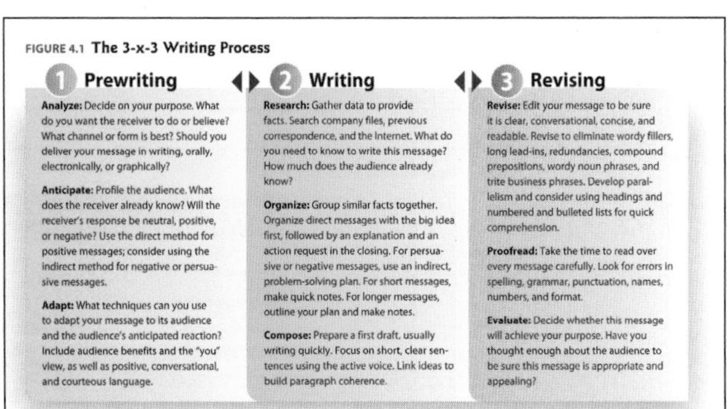

FIGURE 4.1 **The 3-x-3 Writing Process**

1 Prewriting

Analyze: Decide on your purpose. What do you want the receiver to do or believe? What channel or form is best? Should you deliver your message in writing, orally, electronically, or graphically?

Anticipate: Profile the audience. What does the receiver already know? Will the receiver's response be neutral, positive, or negative? Use the direct method for positive messages; consider using the indirect method for negative or persuasive messages.

Adapt: What techniques can you use to adapt your message to its audience and the audience's anticipated reaction? Include audience benefits and the "you" view, as well as positive, conversational, and courteous language.

2 Writing

Research: Gather data to provide facts. Search company files, previous correspondence, and the Internet. What do you need to know to write this message? How much does the audience already know?

Organize: Group similar facts together. Organize direct messages with the big idea first, followed by an explanation and an action request in the closing. For persuasive or negative messages, use an indirect, problem-solving plan. For short messages, make quick notes. For longer messages, outline your plan and make notes.

Compose: Prepare a first draft, usually writing quickly. Focus on short, clear sentences using the active voice. Link ideas to build paragraph coherence.

3 Revising

Revise: Edit your message to be sure it is clear, conversational, concise, and readable. Revise to eliminate wordy fillers, long lead-ins, redundancies, compound prepositions, wordy noun phrases, and trite business phrases. Develop parallelism and consider using headings and numbered and bulleted lists for quick comprehension.

Proofread: Take the time to read over every message carefully. Look for errors in spelling, grammar, punctuation, names, numbers, and format.

Evaluate: Decide whether this message will achieve your purpose. Have you thought enough about the audience to be sure this message is appropriate and appealing?

3-x-3 writing process provides students with a proven three-step strategy for developing effective communication.

Ethics questions, in the margin of the chapters, challenge students to formulate ethical responses to realistic business communication dilemmas — preparing them for the wide variety of ethical situations they may face in their own careers.

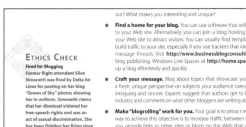

ETHICS CHECK

Fired for Blogging

Former flight attendant Ellen Simonetti was fired by Delta Air Lines for posting on her blog "Queen of Sky" photos showing her in uniform. Simonetti claims that her dismissal violated her free-speech rights and was an act of sexual discrimination. She has been fighting her firing since 2004, parlaying her fame into a book and even a few talk show appearances. Whose rights take precedence, the employee's or the employer's?

out? What makes you interesting and unique?

- **Find a home for your blog.** You can use software that will to your Web site. Alternatively, you can join a blog hosting your Web site to attract visitors. You can usually find templa build traffic to your site, especially if you use trackers that ide message threads. Visit **http://www.businessblogconsulti** blog publishing. Windows Live Spaces at **http://home.spa** up a blog effortlessly and quickly.
- **Craft your message.** Blog about topics that showcase you a fresh, unique perspective on subjects your audience cares intriguing and sincere. Experts suggest that authors get to k industry and comment on what other bloggers are writing ab
- **Make "blogrolling" work for you.** Your goal is to attract re way to achieve this objective is to increase traffic between b you provide links to other sites or blogs on the Web that y related to your business or industry. Respond to other blogg
- **Attract search engines by choosing the right keyw** emphasize potential search terms that may draw traffic to yo use a variety of synonyms to propel your blog to the top of se

...TEACH BUSINESS COMMUNICATION!

Numerous case studies, examples, and applications illustrate how business communication concepts are applied in the workplace, giving students a better understanding of today's digital work environment and business communication strategies. *Zooming In* case studies introduce students to businesses and their business communication challenges. Realistic homework activities add interest and relevance.

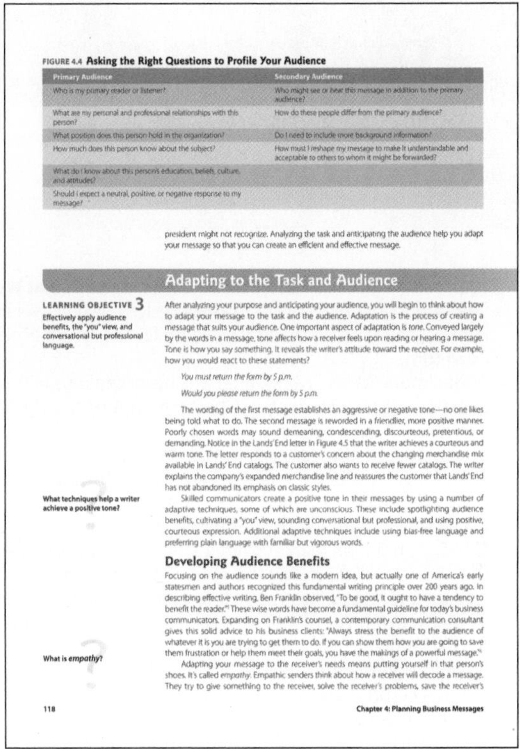

FIGURE 4.4 **Asking the Right Questions to Profile Your Audience**

Primary Audience	Secondary Audience
Who is my primary reader or listener?	Who might see or hear this message in addition to the primary audience?
What are my personal and professional relationships with this person?	How do these people differ from the primary audience?
What position does this person hold in the organization?	Do I need to include more background information?
How much does this person know about the subject?	How must I reshape my message to make it understandable and acceptable to others to whom it might be forwarded?
What do I know about this person's education, beliefs, culture, and attitudes?	
Should I expect a neutral, positive, or negative response to my message?	

president might not recognize. Analyzing the task and anticipating the audience help you adapt your message so that you can create an efficient and effective message.

Adapting to the Task and Audience

LEARNING OBJECTIVE 3
Effectively apply audience benefits, the "you" view, and conversational but professional language.

After analyzing your purpose and anticipating your audience, you will begin to think about how to adapt your message to the task and the audience. Adaptation is the process of creating a message that suits your audience. One important aspect of adaptation is *tone*. Conveyed largely by the words in a message, tone affects how a receiver feels upon reading or hearing a message. Tone is how you say something. It reveals the writer's attitude toward the receiver. For example, how you would react to these statements?

You must return the form by 5 p.m.

Would you please return the form by 5 p.m.

The wording of the first message establishes an aggressive or negative tone—no one likes being told what to do. The second message is reworded in a friendlier, more positive manner. Poorly chosen words may sound demeaning, condescending, discourteous, pretentious, or demanding. Notice in the Lands' End letter in Figure 4.5 that the writer achieves a courteous and warm tone. The letter responds to a customer's concern about the changing merchandise mix available in Lands' End catalogs. The customer also wants to receive fewer catalogs. The writer explains the company's expanded merchandise line and reassures the customer that Lands' End has not abandoned its emphasis on classic styles.

What techniques help a writer achieve a positive tone?

Skilled communicators create a positive tone in their messages by using a number of adaptive techniques, some of which are unconscious. These include spotlighting audience benefits, cultivating a "you" view, sounding conversational but professional, and using positive, courteous expression. Additional adaptive techniques include using bias-free language and preferring plain language with familiar but vigorous words.

Developing Audience Benefits

Focusing on the audience sounds like a modern idea, but actually one of America's early statesmen and authors recognized this fundamental writing principle over 200 years ago. In describing effective writing, Ben Franklin observed, "To be good, it ought to have a tendency to benefit the reader."[1] These wise words have become a fundamental guideline for today's business communicators. Expanding on Franklin's counsel, a contemporary communication consultant gives this solid advice to his business clients: "Always stress the benefit to the audience of whatever it is you are trying to get them to do. If you can show them how you are going to save them frustration or help them meet their goals, you have the makings of a powerful message."[2]

What is *empathy*?

Adapting your message to the receiver's needs means putting yourself in that person's shoes. It's called *empathy*. Empathic senders think about how a receiver will decode a message. They try to give something to the receiver, solve the receiver's problems, save the receiver's

118 Chapter 4: Planning Business Messages

Web-supported, integrated, teaching/learning systems make it easy to create and administer a Web-enhanced course. Together, the textbook and Web site give students a variety of alternatives for studying and reinforcing their understanding of chapter topics.

Grammar/mechanics exercises in every chapter present a structured review to guide students through all the rules.

Self-contained report projects in Chapter 12 allow students to forgo research and instead focus on the analysis of the information provided to them.

Prebuilt Course includes syllabus, class-by-class schedule, lecture plan, daily homework assignments, testing plan and exams, quiz schedule, student grade sheet, and assessment rubric. In short, the Prebuilt Course makes course planning a snap!

Unsurpassed Instructor Manual makes the course even easier to teach by providing chapter lectures, discussion points, enrichment lectures, classroom management tips, and solutions to nearly all textbook exercises and writing assignments.

Improvements: What's New in *Business Communication: Process And Product, 7e*

Chapter 1 — Effective and Ethical Communication at Work

- Strengthened ethics coverage as suggested by reviewers in light of ethical lapses blamed by some for the recent economic downturn.
- Added more Ethics Checks, brief business scenarios with moral questions, so that students are better equipped to meet ethical dilemmas in the workplace.
- Presented new chapter-opening case study featuring PepsiCo's Indra Nooyi, one of the country's most powerful businesswomen and a role model to many.
- Related the importance of communication skills to finding a job in today's tight job market so that students recognize the value of this course and improving their business communication skills.
- Added new figures illustrating information flow in organizations, as well as examples of messages flowing downward and upward, so that students better understand the functions and flow of organizational communication.
- Introduced practical guidance in how to respond to workplace gossip.
- Updated as well as added new end-of-chapter activities that provide engaging opportunities to apply chapter concepts.

Chapter 2 — Professionalism: Team, Meeting, Listening, Nonverbal, and Etiquette Skills

- Focused chapter on professional workplace skills to help students make a smooth transition from the classroom to the business world.
- Revised three-part opening case study to reflect the current economic downturn and importance of professional skills and teamwork.
- Distinguished between face-to-face and virtual meetings, emphasizing the latter because virtual meetings reduce travel costs, lessen employee fatigue, and connect remote workers.
- Added instructions and Web screenshot illustrating the use of digital calendars to schedule meetings so that students will know how to use this electronic tool.
- Added Web screenshot to illustrate e-mail meeting summary template so that students see how savvy companies are using digital tools to summarize key points and note action items to monitor.
- Provided many tips and specific ground rules on how to plan and interact professionally during virtual meetings.
- Emphasized the importance of soft skills and professionalism in regard to being hired and promoted.
- Changed nearly 40 percent of the end-of-chapter activities to offer instructors fresh, relevant, and practical exercises for students to apply chapter content.

Chapter 3 — Intercultural Communication

- Added several end-of-chapter social media assignments to ensure that students acquire business-relevant technology skills.
- Updated three-part Wal-Mart case study as well as created fresh critical thinking questions and assignments for each part to broaden students' perspective on intercultural issues.
- Designed a new figure showing how McDonald's is adjusting its menus around the world to suit local tastes reinforcing the concept of intercultural adaptability and localization.
- Prepared a new Tech Box displaying population figures in various countries around the world side by side with percentages of Internet access to help students broaden their own intercultural horizons.
- Included a provocative Ethical Insights feature to invite students to discuss a controversial case of stereotyping and prejudice toward Muslims in the United States.
- Provided two current Spotlights on Communicators shedding light on relevant chapter content.
- Created two new Ethics Checks and Ethical Issue for critical thinking and discussion, thus further strengthening the focus on ethics throughout the chapter and current edition.

Chapter 4 — Planning Business Messages

- Reorganized the chapter to introduce the writing process earlier so that students immediately grasp the three-phase process and its importance in planning business messages.
- Strengthened Figure 4.1 describing the writing process so that it is more specific and contains more details to enhance student comprehension.
- Expanded the discussion of channel selection by adding media richness theory.
- Added a new figure and discussion illustrating customer live chat so that students recognize the importance of communication skills in expanding technology applications in the workplace.
- Updated discussion of student collaboration tools including Google Docs and revised commands for Word 2007 Comment and Track Changes functions.
- Provided all new chapter review and writing improvement exercises so that instructors have a fresh set of these popular chapter reinforcement and application exercises.
- Added new Document for Analysis and new case study featuring Burger King regarding its channel selection for delivering news to its franchisees.

Chapter 5 — Organizing and Writing Business Messages

- Strengthened discussion of effective sentences by adding coverage of fragments, comma splices, and run-ons so that students will avoid this common set of writing faults.
- Expanded discussion of active voice and passive voice and added a figure illustrating the use of each to help business communicators better understand how to implement these tools effectively.
- Added Ethics Check feature about bloggers who use their writing skills to endorse products for pay.
- Streamlined coverage of techniques that build paragraph coherence.
- Revised 100 percent of the Chapter Review and Writing Improvement Exercises to give instructors and students fresh reinforcement material.
- Prepared new Document for Analysis to enable students to apply many writing techniques covered in the chapter.

Chapter 6 — Revising Business Messages

- Revamped opening Zooming In case study to update this feature, which leads to the popular revision exercise "Applying Your Skills at Taco Bell."
- Reorganized coverage of revision techniques to improve chapter flow and enhance coverage of revision techniques.
- Expanded coverage of document design so that students learn about white space, margins, typefaces, and fonts to prepare them for today's workplace where they will be expected to design effective, readable messages.
- Added Figure 6.1 showing students how to make revisions manually and digitally because writers today increasingly edit on screen.
- Added Figure 6.2 comparing typefaces so that students recognize font personalities and appropriate use.
- Added Figure 6.3 with before/after illustrations showing how the readability of an e-mail message can be greatly improved with document design.
- Added Figure 6.5 showing revisions on PDF files because many messages today are exchanged in this format and revisions must be done using markup software.
- Provided 100 percent new Writing Improvement Exercises offering fresh opportunities to apply and reinforce chapter content.

Chapter 7 — Electronic Messages and Digital Media

- Created a new chapter dedicated solely to digital media to acquaint students with the latest trends in workplace communication technology.
- Emphasized business uses of digital media so that readers will recognize their professional, rather than social, applications.
- Updated coverage of e-mail with special focus on format and message components to ensure that college graduates understand how business messages differ from personal e-mail messages.
- Introduced discussion of blogs, instant messaging, text messaging, podcasts, blogs, wikis, and social networking so that students see how these communication channels function in the workplace and comprehend the risks associated with their use.
- Covered RSS feeds and social bookmarking sites to help readers to share and manage information online efficiently.
- Inserted a new three-part case study about Twitter to pique interest, expose some of the risks of technology use, and relate the textbook to today's digital world.
- Provided a Plugged-In feature about cloud computing so that students glimpse future trends.
- Prepared three new Documents for Analysis, including one transcript of a live IM exchange for revision, to reflect the great variety of workplace digital communication today.
- Added two new Ethics Checks relevant to electronic communication to highlight moral quandaries presented by modern technology on the job.
- Included five Spotlights on Communicators, all of whom are commenting on cutting-edge technology in the workplace and provide up-to-date guidance to readers.
- Presented end-of-chapter activities for students that reinforce the use of new digital media.

Chapter 8 — Positive Messages

- Reorganized chapter to combine positive e-mails, interoffice memorandums, and business letters in one place so that students can recognize similarities in content and strategies regardless of channel choice.
- Explained the primary uses of interoffice memos and how they differ from e-mail messages so that students can make appropriate choices in selecting channels for these important workplace messages.
- Discussed the significance, primary functions, and value of business letters, regardless of the popularity of e-mail.
- Added discussion of how to write messages that describe instructions, a common workplace task.
- Illustrated the difference between indicative verbs and imperative (command) verbs to help readers prepare instructions.
- Prepared new case studies and exercises for two thirds of the end-of-chapter activities, thus providing fresh opportunities for students to apply their skills.

Chapter 9— Negative Messages

- Reorganized chapter to give more emphasis to the possible use of the direct strategy for delivering bad news so that students can use either direct or indirect strategy depending on the context.
- Revised opening three-part case study with current information about Southwest Airlines and its use of emerging channels such as blogs and social sites to communicate with customers.
- Streamlined the goals in communicating negative news to make them easier to comprehend and retain.
- Added specific real-world examples, including bad-news situations for Microsoft and Amazon.com, to illustrate how the writing process is applied to the delivery of negative news.
- Added coverage of managing negative news on Facebook, Twitter, and other Web sites to enable readers to be able to deal with unhappy customers in cyberspace.
- Added new section announcing rate increases and price hikes including a blog model document to show students that companies today are using new channels to deliver negative news.
- Streamlined the checklists for conveying negative news into one comprehensive list so that students have all the tips in one handy list.
- Changed 60 percent of the end-of-chapter activities so that students and instructors have new or fully revised activities to apply their skills in relation to new chapter content.

Chapter 10 — Persuasive and Sales Messages

- Streamlined chapter by combining related learning objectives and checklists to enhance readability and comprehension.
- Reorganized chapter to combine coverage of persuasive favor requests, claims, and complaints to simplify presentation and allow students to apply similar writing techniques.
- Moved coverage of internal communication (persuasive messages within organization) so that it follows the discussion of external communication (favor requests, claims, and complaints) for a more unified presentation.
- Added model document showing the use of a cover e-mail with an attached memo to help students see how businesspeople combine e-mail and attachments.
- Strengthened coverage of sales messages by adding e-marketing so that readers understand basic techniques for preparing successful e-mail sales messages.
- Illustrated press releases and effective writing techniques with a new model document featuring Sweet Earth Chocolates.
- Added a new Spotlight on Communicators highlighting Irene Rosenfeld, the persuasive and effective CEO of Kraft Foods.
- Created many new persuasive case studies or Documents for Analysis that engage students in interesting and relevant topics, such as wrapping bananas in plastic at 7-Eleven, adopting a four-day workweek, retaining free apples at an upscale hotel, and reducing health care costs.

Chapter 11— Report and Research Basics

- Created a new a real-world three-part business case study illustrating the need for research in business, particularly before launching a startup, to tie chapter concepts to business practice.
- Added new ethics checks highlighting dilemmas posed by research strategies and modern technology to reinforce a strong focus on business ethics.
- Introduced new communicators presented in the spotlight feature to offer students perspectives and comments by business practitioners.

- Expanded the discussion of scope and limitations to clarify for students how to establish the scale and extent of their research assignments.
- Added or changed at least 40 percent of the end-of-chapter activities to provide students and instructors with new and up-to-date examples demonstrating chapter content.
- Incorporated technology, for example by introducing SurveyMonkey and Zoomerang, wherever feasible to aid students in understanding how modern communication technology affects research and report writing.
- Created current end-of-chapter activities to which students can relate to help them stay engaged.

Chapter 12 — Informal Reports
- Updated Starbucks three-part business case study to provide students with an opportunity to analyze changing business problems.
- Added new ethics checks allowing students to confront the moral dilemmas facing executives, managers, and rank-and-file employees on the job.
- Introduced new Spotlight on Communicators feature to provide students with topical insights by business practitioners relevant to the material students are learning in the chapter.
- Replaced many end-of-chapter activities to present students with fresh activities, cases, and business scenarios.
- Added five new self-contained report tasks that enable instructors to assign business problems accompanied by data sets that require no outside research.
- Introduced a new figure showing a periodic (activity) report in bullet form sent by e-mail to reflect the latest technological trends in workplace communication.

Chapter 13 — Proposals, Business Plans, and Formal Business Reports
- Updated three-part case study Zooming In to reflect the most current practices in proposal writing.
- Added two new Spotlights highlighting business leaders sharing their insights into proposal and business plan writing.
- Created a photo essay featuring the NBC/Comcast merger to illustrate formal report writing.
- Added a photo essay about an alternative energy source, hydrokinetic power turbines, to demonstrate persuasion in formal proposals.
- Reorganized the content to make the chapter easier to grasp and easier to retain for students.
- Introduced new model documents that provide a glimpse of current business practices in proposal and report writing to readers.
- Added end-of-chapter activities to practice executive summaries as requested by reviewers to meet instructor and student needs.

Chapter 14 — Business Presentations
- Created new three-part Zooming In feature about Steve Jobs at Apple to provide students with a highly relevant, contemporary case study to stimulate analysis and critical thinking.
- Emphasized cutting-edge concepts in presentation software such as those introduced in Presentation Zen by Garr Reynolds to demonstrate to students the trend toward less text and more reliance on images.
- Added photo essay discussing the much-anticipated launch of Apple's iPad to illustrate its potential business uses including its benefits for oral presentations.
- Provided authentic coverage from business practitioners such as venture capitalist Guy Kawasaki to create interest and familiarize readers with current best practices in business slide presentations.
- Highlighted prominent communicators whose comments illustrate important chapter concepts.
- Added end-of-chapter activities to critique PowerPoint clips on YouTube and to evaluate or outline Apple Keynotes to help students understand what makes business presenters successful.
- Created two end-of-chapter activities to practice persuasive speaking skills.
- Devised a unique end-of-chapter activity to teach students how to text professionally.

Chapter 15 — The Job Search, Résumés, and Cover Letters
- Revised the Liz Ryan three-part business case study to include up-to-date information about networking and making oneself memorable during the job search.
- Updated section on today's workplace to provide information about cutting-edge employment trends.
- Added current statistics about the effectiveness of searching for a job online, and modified list of job boards to include those most widely used by today's job seekers.
- Expanded list of employment sites to include social media sites, which are widely used by both employers and job seekers today.
- Added a new section covering tips for conducting a safe and effective online job search, including strategies for avoiding identity theft.
- Expanded tips for using online networking to tap into the hidden job market by adding advice for using Twitter during the job search.
- Created a new photo essay that discusses the ethics of lying on a résumé using Notre Dame's George O'Leary as an example.
- Strengthened section about using technology to optimize one's résumé by including information on the latest trends.
- Organized résumé models into a new Résumé Gallery, and scrutinized every model to ensure each complies with the most up-to-date trends in résumé development.
- Included information about the ethics of using hidden keywords in online résumés.
- Added new end-of-chapter activities that cover using social media during the job search and e-portfolios.

Chapter 16 — Interviewing and Following Up
- Expanded section on screening interviews to include details about how companies are using virtual tools such as Second Life to conduct virtual job fairs and screening interviews.
- Added information about online interviews, which often take place using webcams.
- Created new photo essay that discusses how to succeed in interviews that take place over meals.
- Expanded the "Before the Interview" section to include tips for ensuring professional telephone techniques and for making the first telephone conversation with a prospective employer impressive.
- Updated company research section to include strategies for using Facebook, Twitter, and other social media sites to gather information about prospective employers.
- Enhanced section on digital dirt to provide specific examples of online information that could be looked at negatively by employers. Also added list of techniques for cleaning up one's online presence.
- Developed new photo essay that discusses tattoos and piercings and how to deal with them during the job search and on the job.
- Expanded the "During the Interview" section to include tips for traveling to and arriving at the job interview.
- Added a new Career Coach feature that provides techniques for fighting fear during the job interview.
- Added a new Ethics Check that looks at layoffs from the employer's perspective.
- Added new end-of-chapter activities that cover using social media sites (Facebook, Twitter, YouTube) for company research, appropriate interview attire, requesting a reference, and evaluating the course.

Brief Contents

Contents

WAL★MART

BEN & JERRY'S

SOUTHWEST
SOUTHWEST.COM
N260W

Chapter 10: Persuasive and Sales Messages 294

Unit 4: Reports, Proposals, and Presentations 335

Chapter 11: Report and Research Basics 336

STARBUCKS
COFFEE

Raytheon

Breakthrough deal with AT&T
$14.99 for up to 250 MB
$29.99 for unlimited data
Free use of AT&T WiFi hotspots
Activate on iPad
No contract – cancel anytime

Unit 5: Employment Communication 493

Appendixes

End Matter

Appreciation for Support

No successful textbook reaches a No. 1 position without a great deal of help. We are exceedingly grateful to the reviewers and other experts who contributed their pedagogic and academic expertise in shaping *Business Communication: Process and Product*.

We extend sincere thanks to many professionals at South-Western and Cengage, including Jack Calhoun, Vice President and Editorial Director; Melissa Acuña, editor in chief; Erin Joyner, senior acquisitions editor; Michelle Lockard, marketing manager; Stacy Shirley, art director; Jana Lewis, production editor; John Rich, media editor, and especially to Mary Draper, our exceptional and highly valued senior developmental editor.

Our heartfelt appreciation also goes to Carolyn Seefer, Diablo Valley College; John Donnellan, University of Texas, Austin; Amy Newman, Cornell University; and Jane Flesher and Catherine Peck, Chippewa Valley Technical College, for sharing their expertise in developing outstanding support materials.

Mary Ellen Guffey
Dana Loewy

Grateful Thanks to Previous Reviewers

Janet G. Adams, Minnesota State University, Mankato
Leslie Adams, Houston Baptist University
Kehinde A. Adesina, Contra Costa College
Asberine Parnell Alford, Suffolk Community College
Virginia Allen, Joliet Junior College
Cynthia Anderson, Youngstown State University
Linda Landis Andrews, University of Illinois, Chicago
Vanessa D. Arnold, University of Mississippi
Lois J. Bachman, Community College of Philadelphia
Rebecca Barksdale, University of Central Florida
Sandra Berill, Arkansas State University
Teresa L. Beyer, Sinclair Community College
Cathie Bishop, Parkland College
Randi Blank, Indiana University
Elizabeth Bowers, Orange Coast College and Golden West College
Martha E. Bradshaw, Southeastern Louisiana Univ.
Bernadine Branchaw, Western Michigan University
Maryanne Brandenburg, Indiana University of Pennsylvania
Charles P. Bretan, Northwood University
Paula E. Brown, Northern Illinois University
Vivian R. Brown, Loredo Community College
Domenic Bruni, University of Wisconsin Oshkosh
Phyllis C. Bunn, Delta State University
Mary Ann Burris, Pueblo Community College
Roosevelt D. Butler, College of New Jersey
Jane Campanizzi-Mook, Franklin University
James F. Carey, Onondaga Community College
Leila Chambers, Cuesta College
Patricia H. Chapman, University of South Carolina
Judie C. Cochran, Grand Canyon University
Randy E. Cone, University of New Orleans
James Conley, Eastern Michigan University
Billie Miller Cooper, Cosumnes River College
Linda W. Cooper, Macon State College
Jane G. Corbly, Sinclair Community College
Martha Cross, Delta State University
Linda Cunningham, Salt Lake Community College
Guy Devitt, Herkimer County Community College
Linda Di Desidero, University of Maryland University College
John Donnellan, University of Texas at Austin
J. Yellowless Douglas, University of Florida
Bertha Du-Babcock, City University of Hong Kong
Dorothy Drayton, Texas Southern University
Kay Durden, University of Tennessee
Anna Easton, Indiana University
Lorena B. Edwards, Belmont University
Donald E. English, Texas A&M University
Margaret Erthal, Southern Illinois University
Donna R. Everett, Morehead State University
Gwendolyn Bowie Ewing, Southwest Tennessee Community College
Peggy B. Fisher, Ball State University
Terry M. Frame, University of South Carolina
Gen Freese, Harrisburg Area Community College
Kerry J. Gambrill, Florida Community College

Judith L. Graham, Holyoke Community College
Carolyn G. Gray, The University of Texas, Austin
Diane Gruber, Arizona State University West
David Hamilton, Bemidji State University
Bill Hargrave, University of West Georgia
Paul Hegele, Elgin Community College
Susan A. Heller, Reading Area Community College
Virginia Hemby, Middle Tennessee State University
Rovena L. Hillsman, California State University, Sacramento
Kenneth Hoffman, Emporia State University
Shirley Houston, University of Nebraska
Warren B. Humphrey, University of Central Florida
Robert G. Insley, University of North Texas
Edna Jellesed, Lane Community College
Glen J. Jenewein, Portland Community College
Kathy Jesiolowski, Milwaukee Area Technical College
Carolyn Spillers Jewell, Pembroke State University
Pamela R. Johnson, California State University, Chico
Eric Johnstone, Montana State University
Cheryl L. Kane, University of North Carolina Charlotte
Diana K. Kanoy, Central Florida Community College
Tina S. Kazan, University of Illinois, Chicago
Carolyn E. Kerr, University of Pittsburgh
Sonia Khatchadourian, University of Wisconsin-Milwaukee
Margaret S. Kilcoyne, Northwestern State University
G. Scott King, Sinclair Community College
Suzanne P. Krissler, Orange County Com. College
Linda L. Labin, Husson College
Gary E. Lacefield, University of Texas at Arlington
Richard Lacy, California State University, Fresno
Suzanne Lambert, Broward Community College
Marilyn L. Lammers, California State University, Northridge
Lorita S. Langdon, Columbus State Community College
Joyce N. Larsen, Front Range Community College
Barbara Lea, West Valley College
Claire E. Legowski, North Dakota State University
Mary E. Leslie, Grossmont College
Kathy Lynn Lewis-Adler, University of North Alabama
Kristie J. Loescher, The University of Texas at Austin
Mary Jean Lush, Delta State University
Sonia Maasik, University of California, Los Angeles
Bruce MacBeth, Clarion University of Pennsylvania
Georgia E. Mackh, Cabrillo College
Andrew Madson, Milwaukee Area Technical College
Anna Maheshwari, Schoolcraft College
Maureen L. Margolies, University of Cincinnati
Leon Markowicz, Lebanon Valley College
Thomas A. Marshall II, Robert Morris College
Jeanette Martin, University of Mississippi
John F. Mastriani, El Paso Community College
Cynthia H. Mayfield, York Technical College
Susan Smith McClaren, Mt. Hood Community College
Beryl C. McEwen, North Carolina A&T State University
Marya McFadden, California State University Northridge
Nancy McGee, Davenport University
Diana McKowen, Indiana University
Mary C. Miller, Ashland University
Marci Mitchell, South Texas Community College
Nancy B. Moody, Sinclair Community College
Danne Moore, Shawnee State University
Wayne A. Moore, Indiana University of Pennsylvania
Paul W. Murphey, Southwest Wisconsin Technical College
Lin Nassar, Oakland Community College
Beverly H. Nelson, University of New Orleans
Matt Newby, Heald College
John P. Nightingale, Eastern Michigan University
Ed Nagelhout, University of Nevada
Jeanne E. Newhall, Middlesex Community College
Alexa B. North, State University of West Georgia
Rosemary Olds, Des Moines Area Community College
James S. O'Rourke IV, University of Notre Dame
Smita Jain Oxford, University of Mary Washington
Ed Peters, University of Texas at Arlington
Melinda Phillabaum, Indiana University
Betty Jane Robbins, University of Oklahoma
Janice Rowan, Rowan University
Calvin R. Parks, Northern Illinois University
Pamela A. Patey, Riverside Community College
Shara Toursh Pavlow, University of Miami
William Peirce, Prince George's Community College and University of Maryland University College
Joan Policano, Onondaga Community College
Paula J. Pomerenke, Illinois State University
Jean Anna Sellers, Fort Hays State University
Karen Sterkel Powell, Colorado State University
Gloria Power, Delgado Community College
Richard P. Profozich, Prince George's Community College
Carolyn Mae Rainey, Southeast Missouri State University
Richard David Ramsey, Southeastern Louisiana University
Richard G. Raspen, Wilkes University
Virginia L. Reynolds, Cleveland State University
Ruth D. Richardson, University of North Alabama
Joseph H. Roach, Middlesex County College
Terry D. Roach, Arkansas State University
Betty Jane Robbins, University of Oklahoma
Linda Sarlo, Rock Valley College
Christine A. Saxild, Mt. Senario College
Joseph Schaffner, State University of New York at Alfred
Annette Schley, North Seattle Community College
Betty L. Schroeder, Northern Illinois University
Carolyn M. Seefer, Diablo Valley Community College
Marilyn Simonson, Lakewood Community College
Sue C. Smith, Palm Beach Community Collage
Kathleen M. Sole, University of Phoenix
Charles L. Snowden, Sinclair Community College
Gayle A. Sobolik, California State University, Fresno
Jeanette Spender, Arkansas State University
Jan Starnes, The University of Texas at Austin
Judy Steiner-Williams, Indiana University
Ted D. Stoddard, Brigham Young University
Susan Switzer, Central Michigan University
Roni Szeliga, Gateway Technical College
Leslie S. Talley, University of Central Florida
Barbara P. Thompson, Columbus State Community College

Sally J. Tiffany, Milwaukee Area Technical College
Lori M. Townsend, Niagara County Community College
Mary L. Tucker, Ohio University
Richard F. Tyler, Anne Arundel Community College
Deborah Valentine, Emory University
Doris A. Van Horn Christopher, California State University, Los Angeles
David Victor, Eastern Michigan University
Deborah Von Spreecken, Anoka-Ramsey Community College
Lois Ann Wagner, Southwest Wisconsin Technical College
John L. Waltman, Eastern Michigan University
Marion Webb, Cleveland State University
Beverly A. Westbrook, Delta College
Carol Smith White, Georgia State University
Carol M. Williams, Pima County Community College
Debbie J. Williams, Abilene Christian University
Jane D. Williams, J. Sargeant Reynolds Community College
Rosemary B. Wilson, Washtenaw Community College
Beverly C. Wise, State University of New York, Morrisville
William E. Worth, Georgia State University
Myron D. Yeager, Chapman University
Karen Zempel, Bryant and Stratton College

About the Authors

Dr. Mary Ellen Guffey

A dedicated professional, Mary Ellen Guffey has taught business communication and business English topics for over thirty years. She received a bachelor's degree, *summa cum laude,* from Bowling Green State University; a master's degree from the University of Illinois, and a doctorate in business and economic education from the University of California, Los Angeles (UCLA). She has taught at the University of Illinois, Santa Monica College, and Los Angeles Pierce College.

Now recognized as the world's leading business communication author, Dr. Guffey corresponds with instructors around the globe who are using her books. She is the founding author of the award-winning *Business Communication: Process and Product,* the leading business communication textbook in this country and abroad. She also wrote *Business English,* which serves more students than any other book in its field; *Essentials of College English*; and *Essentials of Business Communication,* the leading text/workbook in its market. Dr. Guffey is active professionally, serving on the review board of the *Business Communication Quarterly* of the Association for Business Communication, participating in all national meetings, and sponsoring business communication awards.

Dr. Dana Loewy

Dana Loewy brings extensive international expertise, broad business communication teaching experience, and exceptional writing skills to this edition. Dana Loewy earned a magister artium (M.A.) degree in English, linguistics, and communication from Rheinische Friedrich-Wilhelms-Universität Bonn, Germany, where she also studied Slavic languages and literatures and took business administration courses. Before receiving a master's degree and PhD from the University of Southern California, Dr. Loewy expanded her teaching experience in freshman writing at USC. She also taught at Loyola Marymount College Palos Verdes and Glendale Community College. Since 1996 Dr. Loewy has taught both graduate and undergraduate business communication classes at Cal State Fullerton. As a guest lecturer, she regularly travels to Germany.

A longtime professional translator of film subtitles, writer, and brand-name consultant, Dr. Loewy has published several books, articles, and translations, both poetry and prose, most notably *The Early Poetry of Jaroslav Seifert* (1997) and On *the Waves of TSF* (2004). In addition to German, Dr. Loewy is fluent in her native tongue, Czech, and understands many Indo-European languages. To broaden her consulting and business expertise, Dr. Loewy has become a business etiquette consultant certified by The Protocol School of Washington.

UNIT 1

Communication Foundations

CHAPTER 1

Effective and Ethical Communication at Work

OBJECTIVES

After studying this chapter, you should be able to

1. Understand the importance of communication skills in relation to career success and explain the need for thinking critically and taking charge of your career.
2. Recognize significant trends in today's dynamic workplace and how these trends increase the need for excellent communication skills.
3. Analyze the process of communication and understand how to use it effectively.
4. Recognize barriers to interpersonal communication and examine specific strategies for overcoming those barriers.
5. Understand the internal and external functions of communication in organizations as well as compare and contrast the advantages and disadvantages of oral and written communication.
6. Examine critically the flow of communication in organizations, and understand how to overcome typical barriers and respond ethically to office gossip.
7. Analyze ethics in the workplace, understand the goals of ethical business communicators, recognize and avoid ethical traps, and apply tools for doing the right thing.

Want to do well on tests and excel in your course? Go to **www.meguffey.com** for helpful interactive resources.

- **Review the Chapter 1 PowerPoint slides to prepare for the first quiz.**

Zooming In PART 1

Led by Ambitious Indra Nooyi, PepsiCo Pushes Nutrition

© MANPREET ROMANA/AFP/Getty Images

An inside look at PepsiCo reveals a powerful CEO decidedly different from most leaders of Fortune 500 companies. Indra Nooyi is one of the few females in corporate America's highest echelons and probably the only Hindu. In her hometown of Chennai, India, she played in an all-girl rock band and majored in chemistry, physics, and math in college. After working in India, she was accepted into a graduate program at Yale University. She headed for the United States with meager financial support and warnings from her parents that such a move would dash all chances of marriage. Working as a dorm receptionist, she took the night shift to earn an extra 50 cents an hour. After completing a master's degree in management, Nooyi went to a job interview wearing an Indian sari because she couldn't afford an appropriate suit—and she got the job.

At Yale, Nooyi experienced a major turning point in her life. That education, she says, gave her the skills lacking in a newly arrived immigrant. She learned how to speak, how to communicate, and how to adapt to the environment. Recalling her program at Yale, she said that all first-year students were required to take—and pass—a course in effective communication. She confessed that this course was invaluable, especially for someone who came from a culture in which communication wasn't considered the most important aspect of business.

Gaining expertise as a business consultant and strategist, in 1994 Nooyi joined a struggling PepsiCo and became its chief strategist. Over the next decade and a half, she helped PepsiCo become a $43 billion food and beverage giant with 193,000 employees in nearly 200 countries. The giant conglomerate was recognized throughout the world for its Pepsi soft drink, Frito-Lay snack foods, and fast-food outlets including Taco Bell, Pizza Hut, and KFC. However, Nooyi's ambitious strategy for PepsiCo involved selling off its fast-food brands and moving into beverages and packaged food with a focus on nutrition. She engineered the acquisition of Tropicana, maker of orange juice products, and of Quaker Oats, maker of Gatorade.

Nooyi has pledged that by 2010 half of PepsiCo's U.S. revenue will come from healthful foods such as low-calorie Gatorade and whole-grain cereals. But observers wonder whether she can produce dependable profits as well as wholesome foods.

Many companies—even before the recent financial crisis and economic plunge—strove to improve their image by emphasizing ethics and social responsibility. In promoting baked whole-grain snacks and vitamin-enhanced beverages, PepsiCo could point the way to better nutrition for the entire industry. Nooyi is convinced that this initiative will benefit investors as well as consumers.[1] You will learn more about this case study on page 23.

Critical Thinking

- Indra Nooyi credited a college course in communication as an important step in her career. How do you think you could benefit from such a course?
- What skills do you think businesspeople need to succeed in today's workplace?
- How could an emphasis on ethics and social responsibility improve profits and benefit a business?

http://www.pepsico.com

Communication Skills and You

LEARNING OBJECTIVE 1
Understand the importance of communication skills in relation to career success and explain the need for thinking critically and taking charge of your career.

Communication skills played an important part in the success of Indra Nooyi, CEO of PepsiCo. Like you, she took a college course to improve her skills. Such skills are particularly significant at a time when jobs are scarce and competition is keen. During a recessionary period, many candidates vie for fewer job openings. Those candidates with exceptional communication skills will immediately have an edge over others. Whether you are already working or about to enter today's workplace, communication skills are critical to your career success. In this chapter you will learn about the importance of communication skills, the changing world of work, the process of communication and its barriers, and ethical goals and tools to help you do the right thing. Each section covers the latest information about relevant issues. Each section also provides tips and suggestions that will help you function effectively and ethically in today's fast-paced, information-laden workplace.

The Importance of Communication Skills to Your Career Success

Why are communication skills important for job applicants, even in technical fields?

Surveys of employers consistently show that communication skills are critical to effective job placement, performance, career advancement, and organizational success.[2] In making hiring decisions, employers often rank communication skills among the most requested competencies.[3]

Many job advertisements specifically ask for excellent oral and written communication skills. A poll of recruiters revealed oral and written communication skills were by a large margin the top skill set sought.[4] In another poll, executives were asked what they looked for in a job candidate. The top choices were teamwork skills, critical thinking, analytical reasoning skills, and oral and written communication skills.[5] When choosing managers, recruiters said that communication skills were the single most important factor in their decisions.[6]

One executive noted that it's tempting to scoff at advice telling you how important communication skills are, particularly in technical fields. "Tech people are becoming a dime a dozen, literally, so you need something more," said Bennett Ockrim, recruiting service specialist. "You need to prove to a potential employer that you can add value to the company beyond your technical qualifications."[7] This advice is important to all job candidates, especially in a gloomy economy in which hordes of job seekers vie for limited openings.

When we discuss communication skills, we generally mean reading, listening, nonverbal, speaking, and writing skills. In this book we focus on listening, nonverbal, speaking, and writing skills. Chapters are devoted to each of these skills. Special attention is given to writing skills because they are difficult to develop and increasingly significant.

Writing Skills Are More Important Than Ever

NOTE: Because this is a well-researched textbook, you will find small superscript numbers in the text. These announce information sources. Full citations begin on page N-1 near the end of the book. This edition uses a modified American Psychological Association (APA) format that provides superscripts leading to full citations in the Notes section.

Writing skills are especially important today. Technology enables us to transmit messages more rapidly, more often, and more widely than ever before. Writing skills take on a new importance because many people are not working together in one place. They stay connected through spoken and written messages. The ability to write well, which was always a career advantage, is now a necessity. Writing skills can be your ticket to work—or your ticket out the door, according to a business executive responding to a significant survey. This survey of 120 American corporations, by the National Commission on Writing, a panel established by the College Board, found that two thirds of salaried employees have some writing responsibility. However, about one third of them do not meet the writing requirements for their positions.[8]

"Businesses are crying out—they need to have people who write better," said Gaston Caperton, executive and College Board president. The ability to write opens doors to professional employment. People who cannot write and communicate clearly will not be hired. If already working, they are unlikely to last long enough to be considered for promotion. Writing is a marker of high-skill, high-wage, professional work, according to Bob Kerrey, university president and chair of the National Commission on Writing. If you can't express yourself clearly, he says, you limit your opportunities for many positions.[9]

How important is writing to your income? A *Fortune* magazine article reported this finding: "Among people with a two- or four-year college degree, those in the highest 20 percent in writing ability earn, on average, more than three times what those with the worst writing skills make."[10] One high-ranking executive explained that many people climbing the corporate ladder are good. When he faced a hard choice between candidates, he used writing ability as the deciding factor. He said that sometimes writing is the only skill that separates a candidate from the competition.

In a recent *New York Times* interview, Delta Air Lines CEO Richard Anderson echoed the importance of values and writing skills.[11] When looking for management talent, he said, "You're looking for a really strong set of values. Really good communication skills. More and more, the ability to speak well and write is important. You know, writing is not something that is taught as strongly as it should be in the educational curriculum." Like other business managers, he emphasizes the need for more instruction in writing skills, something you will find in this course.

Spotlight on Communicators

Aylwin Lewis, current CEO of Potbelly Sandwich Works and former CEO of Sears and Kmart chains, is recognized as one of the highest-ranking African-American executives in the U.S. retail and restaurant industries. He worked his way through the University of Houston, earning degrees in literature and business management. "I wanted to get a soft degree that I thought I would use," he explained. "But I wanted a hard degree to understand the world." His business degree honed his business skills, and his literature degree taught him how to research and write. Recognizing that soft skills can be learned, he said, "Leadership skills, communication skills, culture-building skills—those are all very transferable." Such skills are not only transferable but also critical to anyone entering today's constantly changing, information-driven workplace.

Communication Skills Must Be Learned

You are not born with the abilities to read, listen, speak, and write effectively. These skills must be learned. Thriving in the demanding work world depends on many factors, some of which you cannot

FIGURE 1.1 How This Book and Course Can Help You Build Communication Skills

This business communication book and this course will help you
• Apply a universal process to solve communication problems throughout your career.
• Learn writing techniques and organizational strategies to compose clear, concise, and purposeful business messages.
• Master effective presentation skills to get your ideas across to large and small groups.
• Learn to be a valuable team player.
• Work productively with the Internet and digital communication technologies.
• Value diversity so that you can function with sensitivity in intercultural work environments.
• Develop tools for meeting ethically challenging situations.
• Land the job of your dreams with invaluable job-search, résumé-writing, and interviewing tips.

control. However, one factor that you do control is how well you communicate. The goals of this book and this course are to teach you basic business communication skills, such as how to write an effective e-mail or a clear business letter and how to make a memorable presentation. You will also learn additional powerful communication skills, as summarized in Figure 1.1. This book and this course may well be the most important in your entire college curriculum because they will equip you with the skills most needed in today's dynamic, demanding workplace.

Thriving as a Knowledge Worker in the Information Age

Regardless of economic downturns and recoveries, we continue to live in an economy based on information and knowledge. The computer, the mobile phone, and the Internet are all instrumental in the continuing development of the Information Age. Previously, in the Industrial Age, raw materials and physical labor were the key ingredients in the creation of wealth. Today, however, wealth depends on the development and exchange of knowledge. Individuals in the workforce offer their knowledge, not their muscles. *Knowledge workers,* a term first coined by management guru Peter Drucker, get paid for their education and their ability to learn.[12] More recently, we are hearing the term *information worker (i-worker)* to describe those who work with informaton and technology.[13] Regardless of the terminology, knowledge and information workers engage in mind work. They deal with symbols: words, figures, and data. Estimates suggest that knowledge workers outnumber other workers in North America by at least a four-to-one margin.[14]

What is a knowledge worker, and do you expect to become one?

Some U.S. knowledge workers worry over the outsourcing of their jobs to skilled workers in India and China. Outsourcing overseas is a reality. Jobs that can be condensed to a set of rules are likely to go first—either to workers abroad or to computers. Although we cannot predict the kinds of future jobs that will be available, they will undoubtedly require brainpower and education. Existing jobs, in both good and bad times, give way to shifts in technology and competition. Recessions are followed by recoveries, and the economy adjusts, as it has always done in the past. In the current climate of outsourcing and changing job requirements, workers need to be flexible, to learn continually, and to have strong basic skills.

What Does This Mean for You?

As a knowledge and information worker, you can expect to be generating, processing, and exchanging information. Whether you work in *m-commerce* (mobile technology businesses), *e-commerce* (Internet-based businesses), or *bricks-and-mortar commerce*, nearly three out of four jobs will involve some form of mind work. Jobs that require thinking, brainpower, and decision-making skills are likely to remain plentiful. To be successful in these jobs, you will need to be able to think critically, make decisions, and communicate those decisions.

Learning to Think Critically

What does it mean to think critically?

Management and employees will be working together in such areas as product development, quality control, and customer satisfaction. All workers, from executives to subordinates, need to think creatively and critically. Even in factory production lines, workers are part of the knowledge

Spotlight on Communicators

"We are entering an age where intangible assets like expertise, intelligence, speed, agility, imagination, maneuverability, networks, passion, responsiveness and innovation—all facets of 'knowledge'—become more important than the tangibles of traditional balance-sheet perspectives," contends Oren Harari, management expert, futurist, and prolific author.

culture. One of the secrets of Toyota's success in the past, said Takis Athanasopoulos, chief executive of the Japanese carmaker's European operations, "is that the company encourages every worker, no matter how far down the production line, to consider himself a knowledge worker and to think creatively about improving his particular corner of the organization."[15]

Thinking creatively and critically means having opinions that are backed by reasons and evidence. When your boss or team leader says, "What do you think we ought to do?" you want to be able to supply good ideas. The accompanying Career Coach box provides a five-point critical-thinking plan to help you solve problems and make decisions. Having a plan, however, is not enough. You also need chances to try the plan out and get feedback from colleagues and your boss (your instructor, for the time being). At the end of each chapter, you will find activities and problems that will help you develop and apply your critical-thinking skills.

Taking Charge of Your Career

If you are already skilled in your specialty, why is it necessary to undergo continual retraining, learn cross-skills, or study new procedures?

In today's fast-paced, ever-changing world of work, you can look forward to constant training to acquire new skills that will help you keep up with evolving technologies and procedures. You can also expect to be exercising greater control over your career. Most workers today will not find nine-to-five jobs, predictable pay increases, lifetime security, and even conventional workplaces. Don't presume that companies will provide you with a clearly defined career path or planned developmental experiences. In the private sector you can expect to work for multiple

CAREER COACH

Sharpening Your Skills for Critical Thinking, Problem Solving, and Decision Making

Gone are the days when management expected workers to check their brains at the door and do only as told. As a knowledge worker, you will be expected to use your brains in thinking critically. You will be solving problems and making decisions. Much of this book is devoted to helping you learn to solve problems and communicate those decisions to management, fellow workers, clients, the government, and the public.

Faced with a problem or an issue, most of us do a lot of worrying before separating the issues or making a decision. All that worrying can become directed thinking by channeling it into the following procedure.

1. Identify and clarify the problem. Your first task is to recognize that a problem exists. Some problems are big and unmistakable, such as failure of an air-freight delivery service to get packages to customers on time. Other problems may be continuing annoyances, such as regularly running out of toner for an office copy machine. The first step in reaching a solution is pinpointing the problem area.

2. Gather information. Learn more about the problem situation. Look for possible causes and solutions. This step may mean checking files, calling suppliers, or brainstorming with fellow workers. The air-freight delivery service, for example, would investigate the tracking systems of the commercial airlines carrying its packages to determine what went wrong.

3. Evaluate the evidence. Where did the information come from? Does it represent various points of view? What biases could be expected from each source? How accurate is the information? Is it fact or opinion? For example, it is a fact that packages are missing; it is an opinion that they are merely lost and will turn up eventually.

4. Consider alternatives and implications. Draw conclusions from the gathered evidence and pose solutions. Then weigh the advantages and disadvantages of each alternative. What are the costs, benefits, and consequences? What are the obstacles, and how can they be handled? Most important, what solution best serves your goals and those of your organization? Here's where your creativity is especially important.

5. Choose the best alternative and test it. Select an alternative and try it out to see if it meets your expectations. If it does, implement your decision. If it doesn't, rethink your alternatives. The freight company decided to give its unhappy customers free delivery service to make up for the lost packages and downtime. Be sure to continue monitoring and adjusting the solution to ensure its effectiveness over time.

Career Application

EastCom Credit Union has a long-standing dress policy that even extends to casual Fridays with no jeans, sneakers, athletic wear, shorts, or halter tops permitted. It wants to encourage employees to dress properly and is willing to spend some money to help them do it. It has even considered modified uniforms for its conservative environment. Employee morale as well as looking professional is important. As a member of the management team, consider how the credit union can help its employees upgrade their wardrobes. How would the steps discussed here be helpful in approaching this situation?

employers, moving back and forth between work and education and between work and family responsibilities.[16] Whether you are currently employed or about to enter today's demanding workplace, you must be willing to continually learn new skills that supplement the strong foundation of basic skills you are acquiring in college.

Finding a Job in Today's Tight Job Market

In a tough employment market, you may understandably be concerned about finding a job. A recent study by the National Association of Colleges and Employers (NACE) focused on what makes the "perfect" job candidate in a gloomy economy. First, a prospective employee must meet the employer's fundamental criteria, including having the required major, course work, and GPA. By the way, nearly 70 percent of employers in the study reported that they screened candidates by grade point average, with 3.0 (a *B* average) considered the cutoff point. If a candidate passes these hurdles, then employers look for the following skills and attributes.

Ranking first were communication skills. Next came a strong work ethic, ability to work in a team, and initiative. Although these qualities are not new, "in times like these when job opportunities are tight," said Marilyn Mackes, NACE executive director, "it is perhaps even more important for job candidates to understand what employers want and find ways to demonstrate those qualities."[17]

Using This Course to Advance Your Career

This book and this course will help you develop and demonstrate the skills prospective employers want. The book is filled with model documents, practice exercises, procedures, tips, strategies, suggestions, summaries, and checklists—all meant to ensure that you develop the superior communication skills you need to locate a job and succeed as a businessperson today.

Remember, communication skills are not innate; they must be learned. Remember also to take advantage of the unique opportunity you now have. You have an expert who is willing to work with you to help improve your writing, speaking, and other communication skills. Many organizations pay thousands of dollars to communication coaches and trainers to teach employees the very skills you are learning in this course. Your instructor is your coach. Take advantage of this opportunity, and get your money's worth! With this book as your guide and your instructor as your coach, you will find that this course, as we mentioned earlier, could very well be the most important in your entire college curriculum.

Trends Affecting You in Today's Dynamic Workplace

LEARNING OBJECTIVE 2

Recognize significant trends in today's dynamic workplace and how these trends increase the need for excellent communication skills.

Today's workplace is undergoing profound and dynamic changes. As a businessperson and especially as a business communicator, you will undoubtedly be affected by many trends. Some of the most significant trends include global competition, flattened management hierarchies, and team-based projects. Other trends include constantly evolving technology; the "anytime, anywhere" office; a diverse workforce; and an emphasis on ethics. The following overview of trends reveals how communication skills are closely tied to your success in a demanding, dynamic workplace.

Heightened Global Competition

Small, medium, and large companies increasingly find themselves competing in global rather than local markets. Improved systems of telecommunication, advanced forms of transportation, and saturated local markets—all of these developments have encouraged companies to move beyond familiar territories to emerging markets around the world. Kraft Foods now drenches its familiar Oreo cookie in chocolate to sell well in China.[18] PepsiCo fights Coca-Cola for new customers in India, and McDonald's feeds hungry Russians at Pushkin Square, its busiest restaurant in the world.[19] Wal-Mart courts shoppers in China with exotic fruits and live seafood.[20] What is surprising is that many traditional U.S. companies now generate more profit abroad than at home.

How could dealing with people from different countries and cultures affect the process of communication?

Doing business in far-flung countries means dealing with people who may be very different from you. They may practice different religions, follow different customs, live different lifestyles, and rely on different approaches in business. Now add the complications of multiple time zones, vast distances between offices, and different languages. No wonder global communicators can blunder. Take, for example, the failure of Nike's "Just Do It" campaign in China. It emphasized individualistic youthful irreverence, which violates the culture of collectivist China. Nike replaced those ads with a 10-second spot featuring a school kid impressing classmates by spinning the globe on his finger. The ad expresses playfulness and daring without rebellion.[21]

Successful communication in these new markets requires developing new skills and attitudes. These include cultural knowledge and sensitivity, flexibility, and patience. Because these skills and attitudes may be difficult to achieve, you will receive special communication training to help you deal with intercultural business transactions.

Flattened Management Hierarchies

Why do flattened management hierarchies mean that workers must have better communication skills?

In response to intense global competition and other pressures, businesses have for years been cutting costs and flattening their management hierarchies. This flattening means that fewer layers of managers separate decision makers from line workers. In traditional companies, information flows through many levels of managers. In flat organizations, however, where the lines of communication are shorter, decision makers can react more quickly to market changes. Some time ago, toymaker Mattel transformed itself from an "out-of-control money loser" by tightening its organization and cutting six layers from its organizational hierarchy. As a result, when its Matchbox developers came up with a terrific idea for a toy firehouse that required no assembly, the idea could be rushed into production. It didn't languish in the pipeline, drowning in multiple layers of management. Like many restructured organizations, Mattel got rid of "silos" that slice the company up vertically into separate divisions for marketing, operations, production, and human resources. Restructured companies organize work with horizontal teams that allow various areas to interact more efficiently.

An important factor in the flattening of management hierarchies was movement away from mainframe computing. As recognized by Thomas Friedman in his smashingly successful book *The World Is Flat*, the combination of the personal computer, the microprocessor, the Internet, fiber optics, and, more recently, wireless networks "flipped the playing field." Management moved away from command and control to connecting and collaborating horizontally.[22] This means that work is organized to let people use their own talents more wisely.[23]

Today's flatter organizations, however, also pose greater communication challenges. In the past, authoritarian and hierarchical management structures did not require that every employee be a skilled communicator. Managers simply passed along messages to the next level. Today, however, frontline employees as well as managers participate in decision making. Nearly everyone is a writer and a communicator. Businesspeople prepare their own messages; secretaries no longer "clean up" their bosses' writing.

Expanded Team-Based Management

Along with flatter chains of command, companies are expanding team-based operations to empower employees and boost their involvement in decision making.

To generate new products, Johnson & Johnson started forming small teams and charged each with tackling a cosmetic problem. The acne team, composed of scientists along with marketing and production people, focused on finding ways to help teenagers zap zits. A pigmentation team struggled to create products that evened out skin tone.[24] At Cigna Corporation, a huge national insurance company, three organizational layers were flattened and teams were formed to reduce backups in processing customer claims. The formation of these teams forced technology specialists to communicate constantly with business specialists. Suddenly, computer programmers had to do more than code and debug; they had to listen, interpret, and explain. All members of the team had to analyze problems and negotiate solutions.

When companies form cross-functional teams, individuals must work together and share information. Working relationships can become strained when individuals don't share the same location, background, knowledge, or training. Some companies even hire communication coaches to help existing teams get along. They work to develop interpersonal, negotiation, and collaboration techniques. But companies would prefer to hire new workers who already possess these skills. That is why so many advertisements for new employees say "must possess good communication skills"—which you are learning in this book and this course.

Innovative Communication Technologies

New electronic technologies are dramatically affecting the way workers communicate. In our always-connected, everything-linked world, we exchange information and stay in touch by using e-mail, instant messaging, text messaging, PDAs, fax, voice mail, cell phones, powerful laptop computers, satellite communications, wireless networking, and even by "tweeting." Through teleconferencing and videoconferencing, we can conduct meetings with associates around the world. The rapid development of social software such as weblogs, wikis (multiuser weblogs), and peer-to-peer tools makes it easier for workers to communicate online and wirelessly almost instantaneously. One complaint about e-mail is that messages and documents with pertinent information are limited to senders and receivers.[25] The latest software, however, enables people in different offices to work on projects using a single Web calendar, a to-do list, and online discussion rooms. To share information graphically, presenters use sophisticated presentation software.

Ethics Check

Too Connected?

Office workers use smartphones, e-mail, voice mail, and text messaging. Many are literally always on call and feel overwhelmed. What are the limits of connectedness? Is it fair to dodge an unpleasant call by sending it to voice mail or to delay answering certain e-mail messages?

All businesspeople today rely heavily on the Internet and the Web to collect information, serve customers, and sell products and services. Figure 1.2 on pages 10 and 11 illustrates many new technologies you will meet in today's workplace.

To use these new resources most effectively, you, as a skilled business communicator, must develop a tool kit of new communication skills. You will want to know how to select the best communication channel, how to use each channel safely and effectively, and how to incorporate the latest technologies and search tools efficiently. All of these topics will be covered in coming chapters.

What are wikis and blogs, and how are they useful to business communicators?

"Anytime, Anywhere" and Nonterritorial Offices

Today's work environments are also changing profoundly. Thanks largely to advances in high-speed and wireless Internet access, millions of workers no longer report to nine-to-five jobs that confine them to offices. They have flexible working arrangements so that they can work at home or on the road. The "anytime, anywhere" office requires only a mobile phone and a wireless computer.[26] Telecommuting employees now represent 11 percent of the workforce, and this number increases annually.[27] To save on office real estate, a growing number of industries provide "nonterritorial" workspaces. Also known as "mobile platforms" and "hot desks," these unassigned workspaces are up for grabs. The first to arrive gets the best desk and the corner window.[28]

Now that Google is developing Web-based collaboration tools, e-mail is starting to look like the new rotary phone. By using the search giant's new messaging software called Google Wave, groups of professionals can share documents, work files, and videos. Wave's multiframe interface displays live team chats, and the recording feature warehouses real-time comment streams for ongoing collaboration and review. *Why are online communication tools more important than ever in today's business world?*[29]

FIGURE 1.2 Communication and Collaborative Technologies

◂ Communication Technologies Reshaping the World of Work
Today's workplace is changing dramatically as a result of innovative software, superfast wireless networks, and numerous technologies that allow workers to share information, work from remote locations, and be more productive in or away from the office. We're seeing a gradual progression from basic capabilities, such as e-mail and calendaring, to deeper functionality, such as remote database access, multifunctional devices, and Web-based collaborative applications.

Telephony: VoIP ▸
Savvy businesses are switching from traditional phone service to voice over Internet protocol (VoIP). This technology allows callers to communicate using a broadband Internet connection, thus eliminating long-distance and local telephone charges. Higher-end VoIP systems now support unified voice mail, e-mail, click-to-call capabilities, and softphones (phones using computer networking). Free or low-cost Internet telephony sites, such as the popular Skype, are also increasingly used by businesses.

Open Offices ▴
Widespread use of laptop computers, wireless technology, and VoIP have led to more fluid, flexible, and open workspaces. Smaller computers and flat-screen monitors enable designers to save space with boomerang-shaped workstations and cockpit-style work surfaces rather than space-hogging corner work areas. Smaller breakout areas for impromptu meetings are taking over some cubicle space, and digital databases are replacing file cabinets.

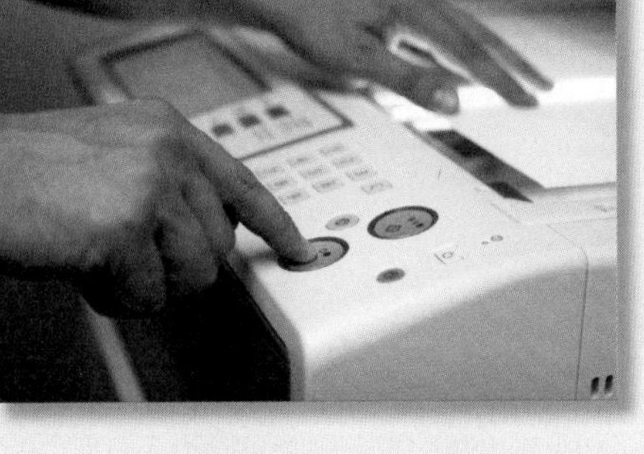

◂ Multifunctional Printers
Stand-alone copiers, fax machines, scanners, and printers have been replaced with multifunctional devices. Offices are transitioning from a "print and distribute" environment to a "distribute and print" environment. Security measures include pass codes and even biometric thumbprint scanning to make sure data streams are not captured, interrupted, or edited.

▸ Handheld Wireless Devices
A new generation of lightweight, handheld devices provide phone, e-mail, Web browsing, and calendar options anywhere there's a wireless network. Smartphones such as the BlackBerry, the Palm Treo, and the iPhone now allow you to tap into corporate databases and intranets from remote locations. You can check customers' files, complete orders, and send out receipts without returning

to the office. Increasingly businesses are issuing smartphones to their workforce, abandoning landlines completely.

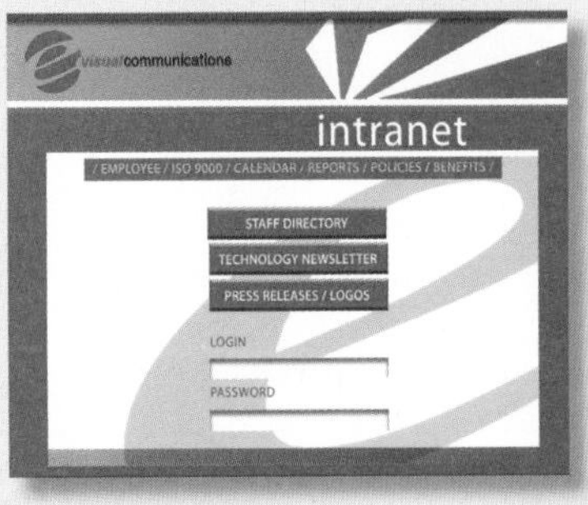

◂ Company Intranets
To share insider information, many companies provide their own protected Web sites called intranets. An intranet may handle company e-mail, announcements, an employee directory, a policy handbook, frequently asked questions, personnel forms and data, employee discussion forums, shared documents, and other employee information.

▾ Voice Recognition
Computers equipped with voice recognition software enable users to dictate up to 160 words a minute with accurate transcription. Voice recognition is particularly helpful to disabled workers and to professionals with heavy dictation loads, such as physicians and attorneys. Users can create documents, enter data, compose and send e-mails, browse the Web, and control the desktop—all by voice.

◂ Electronic Presentations
Business presentations in PowerPoint can be projected from a laptop or PDA or posted online. Sophisticated presentations may include animations, sound effects, digital photos, video clips, or hyperlinks to Internet sites. In some industries, PowerPoint slides ("decks") are replacing or supplementing traditional hard-copy reports.

Collaboration Technologies: Rethinking the Way We Work Together ▸

New tools make it possible to work together without being together. Your colleagues may be down the hall, across the country, or around the world. With today's tools, you can exchange ideas, solve problems, develop products, forecast future performance, and complete team projects any time of the day or night and anywhere in the world. Blogs and wikis, also part of the Web 2.0 era, are social tools that create multidirectional conversations among customers and employees. Web 2.0 moves Web applications from "read only" to "read-write," thus enabling greater participation and collaboration.

◂ Blogs, Podcasts, Wikis, and Tweets

A *blog* is a Web site with journal entries usually written by one person with comments added by others. Businesses use blogs to keep customers and employees informed and to receive feedback. Company developments can be posted, updated, and categorized for easy cross-referencing. When the writer adds audio, the blog becomes a *podcast*. A *wiki* is a Web site that allows multiple users to collaboratively create and edit pages. Information gets lost in e-mails, but blogs and wikis provide an easy way to communicate and keep track of what's said. Most companies are still trying to figure out how to harness Twitter for business. However, tech-savvy individuals already send *tweets*, short messages of up to 140 characters, to other users to issue up-to-date news about their products, to link to their blogs and Web sites, or to announce events and promotions.

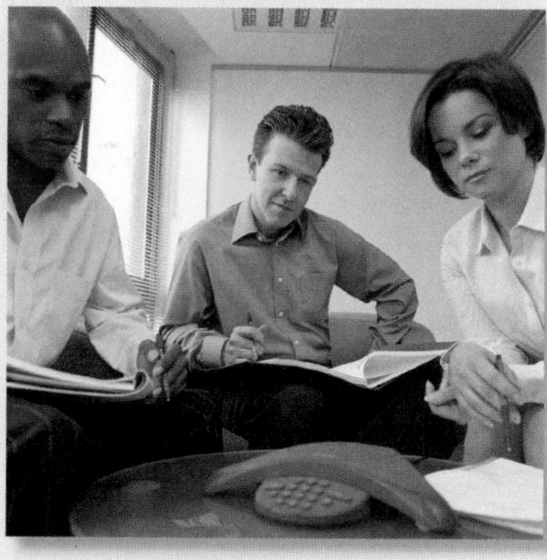

▴ Voice Conferencing

Telephone "bridges" allow two or more callers from any location to share the same call. *Voice conferencing* (also called *audioconferencing, teleconferencing*, or just plain *conference calling*) enables people to collaborate by telephone. Communicators at both ends use enhanced speakerphones to talk and be heard simultaneously.

Web Conferencing ▸

With services such as GoToMeeting, WebEx, and Microsoft LiveMeeting, all you need are a PC and an Internet connection to hold a meeting (*webinar*) with customers or colleagues in real time. Although the functions are constantly evolving, Web conferencing currently incorporates screen sharing, chats, slide presentations, text messaging, and application sharing.

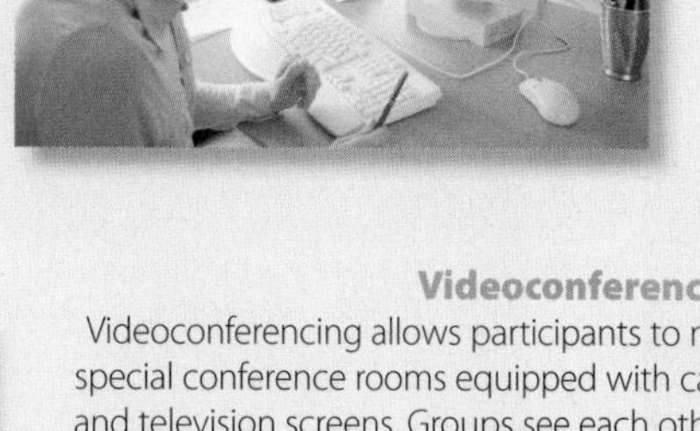

Videoconferencing ▸

Videoconferencing allows participants to meet in special conference rooms equipped with cameras and television screens. Groups see each other and interact in real time, although they may be far apart. Faster computers, rapid Internet connections, and better cameras now enable 2 to 200 participants to sit at their own PCs and share applications, spreadsheets, presentations, and photos.

▴ Video Phones

Using advanced video compression technology, video phones transmit real-time audio and video so that communicators can see each other as they collaborate. With a video phone, people can videoconference anywhere in the world over a broadband IP (Internet protocol) connection without a computer or a television screen.

◂ Presence Technology

Presence technology makes it possible to locate and identify a computing device as soon as users connect to the network. This technology is an integral part of communication devices including smartphones, laptop computers, PDAs, and GPS devices. Collaboration is possible wherever and whenever users are online.

How is the concept of a business office changing today?

Even in more traditional offices, employees work in open spaces with flexible workstations, shared conference rooms, and boomerang-shaped desks that save space. Moreover, many workers are part of virtual teams that complete projects without ever meeting each other. Tools such as e-mail, instant and text messaging, file sharing, conferencing software, and wireless networking make it easy for employees to collaborate or complete their work in the office, at home, or on the road.

As more and more employees work separately, communication skills become increasingly important. Staying connected involves sending messages, most of which are written. This means that your writing skills will constantly be on display. Those who can write clear and concise messages contribute to efficient operations and can expect to be rewarded.

Increasingly Diverse Workforce

Changes in today's work environments include more than innovative technology, team management, and different work environments. The U.S. workforce is becoming increasingly diverse. As shown in Figure 1.3, the white non-Hispanic population of the United States is expected to drop from 79 percent in 1980 to 64 percent in 2020. Hispanics will climb from 6 percent to 17 percent, African Americans will increase from 12 percent to 13 percent, and Asians and Pacific Islanders will rise from 2 percent to 6 percent.[30] In addition to increasing numbers of minorities, the workforce will see a big jump in older workers. By 2020, the number of workers aged 55 and older will grow to 20 percent.[31] As a result of these and other

FIGURE 1.3 Racial and Ethnic Makeup of U.S. Population, 1980 to 2020

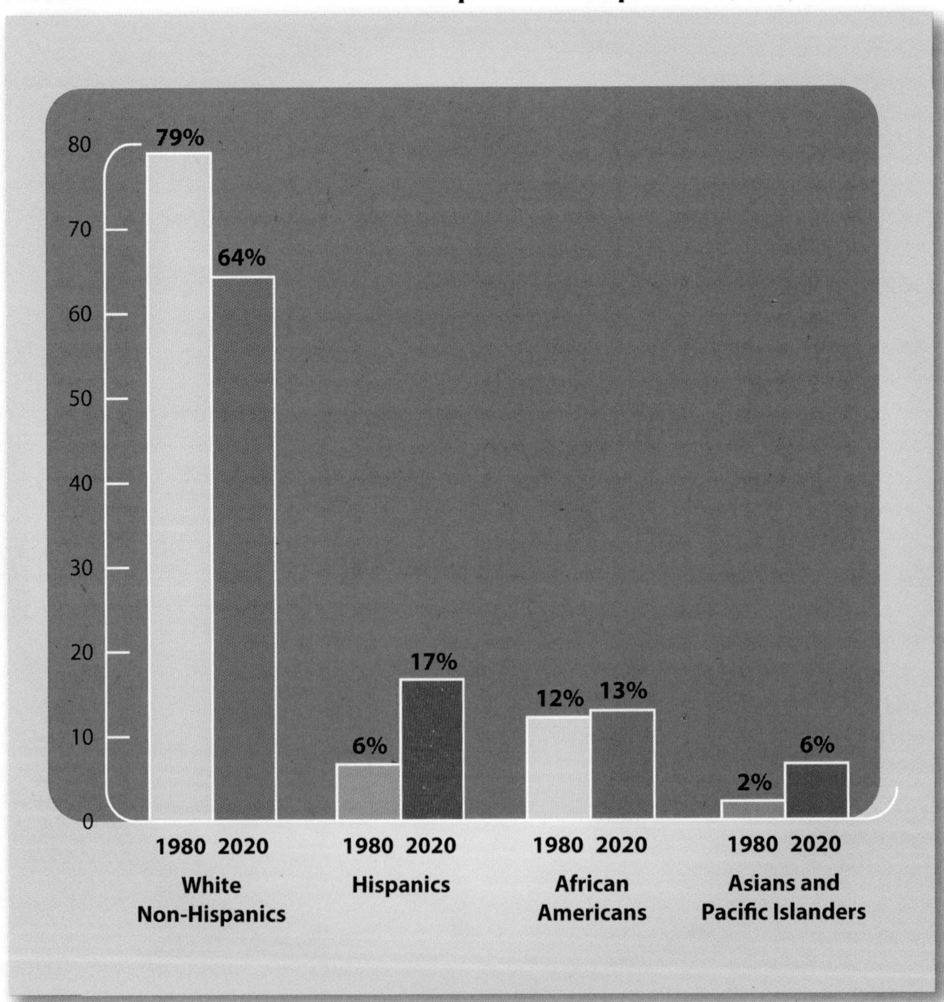

demographic trends, businesses must create work environments that value and support all people.

Communicating in this diverse work environment requires new attitudes and skills. Acquiring these new employment skills is certainly worth the effort because of the benefits diversity brings to consumers, work teams, and business organizations. A diverse staff is better able to read trends and respond to the increasingly diverse customer base in local and world markets. In the workplace, diversity also makes good business sense. Teams made up of people with various experiences are more likely to create the products that consumers demand. Customers also want to deal with companies that respect their values. They are more likely to say, "If you are a company whose ads do not include me, or whose workforce does not include me, I will not buy from you." Learning to cooperate and communicate successfully with diverse coworkers should be a major priority for all businesspeople.

Renewed Emphasis on Ethics

Ethics is once again a hot topic in business circles. Following the Enron and WorldCom scandals in the early 2000s, businesses responded with a flurry of programs emphasizing ethical awareness and training. Despite increased awareness, however, much training was haphazard[32] and characterized by lip service only. With the passage of the Sarbanes-Oxley Act, the government required greater accountability. Nevertheless, a calamitous recession followed, caused largely, some say, by greed and ethical lapses. As a result, businesses are now eager to regain public trust by building ethical environments. Many have written ethical mission statements, installed hotlines, and appointed compliance officers to ensure strict adherence to their high standards and the law.

How are businesses attempting to regain public trust?

In addition, individuals are more aware of their personal actions and accountability. After watching executive assistant Doug Faneuil, who was forced to testify against his boss and their biggest client, Martha Stewart, people realized that they cannot lie, even to protect their jobs or their bosses. It's unacceptable to excuse an action with "the company made me do it."

Ethics is indeed a hot topic and trend you will note in the workplace. But making ethical decisions is not always easy. Later in this chapter you will study the goals of business communicators and tools to help you do the right thing.

Understanding the Process of Communication

LEARNING OBJECTIVE 3
Analyze the process of communication and understand how to use it effectively.

Because communication is a central factor in the emerging knowledge economy and a major consideration for anyone entering today's workforce, we need to look more closely at the total process of communication. Just what is communication? For our purposes communication is the *transmission of information and meaning from one individual or group to another.* The crucial element in this definition is *meaning*. Communication has as its central objective the transmission of meaning. The process of communication is successful only when the receiver understands an idea as the sender intended it. Both parties must agree not only on the information transmitted but also on the meaning of that information. How does an idea travel from one person to another? Despite what you may have seen in futuristic science fiction movies, we can't just glance at another person and transfer meaning directly from mind to mind. We engage in a sensitive process of communication, discussed here and depicted in Figure 1.4.

Sender Has Idea

Why is the communication process so sensitive?

The process of communication begins when the person with whom the message originates—the *sender*—has an idea. The form of the idea will be influenced by complex factors surrounding the sender: mood, frame of reference, background, culture, and physical makeup, as well as the context of the situation and many other factors. The way you greet people on campus or on the job, for example, depends a lot on how you feel, whom you are addressing (a classmate, a professor, a colleague, or your boss), and what your culture has trained you to say (*Good morning, Hey, Hi, Howdy,* or *How ya doing?*).

The form of the idea, whether a simple greeting or a complex idea, is shaped by assumptions based on the sender's experiences. A manager sending an e-mail announcement to employees

FIGURE 1.4 The Communication Process

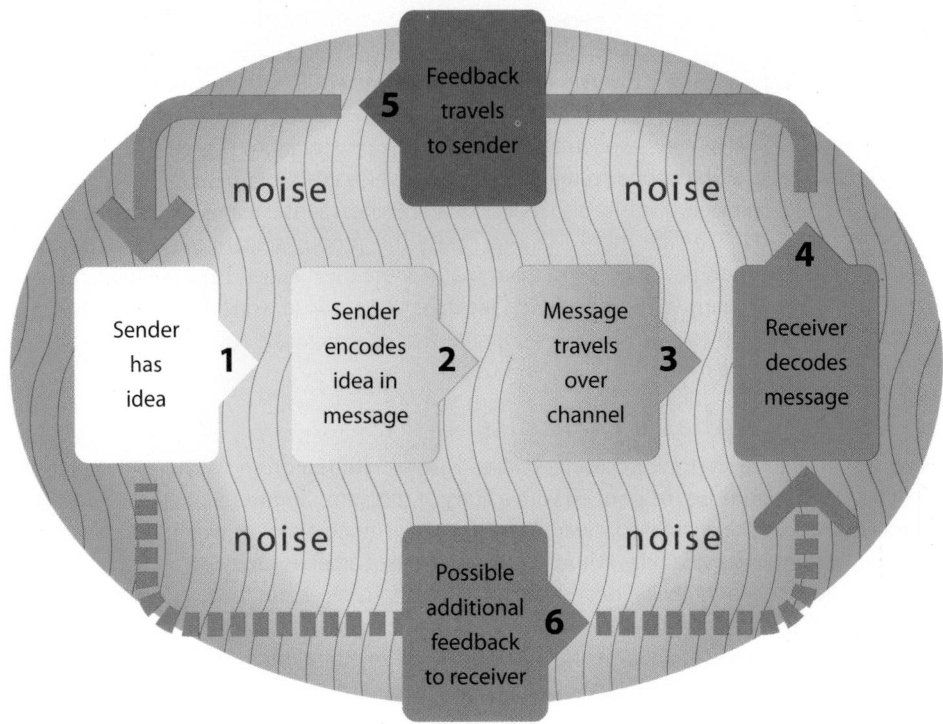

Note: A more comprehensive model of the communication process is available in the instructor's PowerPoint program.

assumes they will be receptive, whereas direct-mail advertisers assume that receivers will give only a quick glance to their message. The ability to accurately predict how a message will affect its receiver and skill in adapting that message to its receiver are key factors in successful communication.

Encoding involves converting an idea into words or gestures that convey meaning.

Sender Encodes Idea in Message

The next step in the communication process involves *encoding.* This means converting the idea into words or gestures that will convey meaning. A major problem in communicating any message verbally is that words have different meanings for different people. When misunderstandings result from missed meanings, it is called *bypassing*. Recognizing how easy it is to be misunderstood, skilled communicators choose familiar words with concrete meanings on which both senders and receivers agree. In selecting proper symbols, senders must be alert to the receiver's communication skills, attitudes, background, experiences, and culture: How will the selected words affect the receiver? In Great Britain, for example, a Dr. Pepper cola promotion failed miserably because American managers had not done their homework. They had to change their "I'm a Pepper" slogan after learning that *pepper* is British slang for *prostitute.*[33] Because the sender initiates a communication transaction, he or she has primary responsibility for its success or failure. Choosing appropriate words or symbols is critical to a successful message.

ETHICS CHECK

Bypassing or False Advertising?

J.C. Penney produced a T-shirt emblazoned with a ferocious red and blue eagle beneath the words "American Made." However, a small label inside revealed that the shirt was made in Mexico. In response to complaints that the slogan was deceptive, a Penney spokeswoman said that "American Made" referred to the actual person wearing the shirt, not to the manufacturer. Do you think this was a simple case of miscommunication?

Message Travels Over Channel

The medium over which the message is physically transmitted is the *channel.* Messages may be delivered by computer, telephone, cell phone, letter, memorandum, report, announcement, picture, spoken word, fax, Web page, or through some other channel. Because communication channels deliver both verbal and nonverbal messages, senders must choose the channel and shape the message carefully. A company may use its annual report, for example, as a channel to deliver many messages to stockholders. The verbal message lies in the report's financial and organizational news. Nonverbal messages, though, are conveyed by the report's appearance (showy versus bland), layout (ample white space versus tightly packed columns of print), and tone (conversational versus formal).

Anything that interrupts the transmission of a message in the communication process is called *noise*. Channel noise ranges from static that disrupts a telephone conversation to typographical and spelling errors in a letter or e-mail message. Such errors damage the credibility of the sender. Channel noise might even include the annoyance a receiver feels when the sender chooses an improper medium for sending a message, such as announcing a loan rejection via postcard or firing an employee by e-mail.

What is noise in the communication process, and how can it disrupt the process?

Receiver Decodes Message

The individual for whom the message is intended is the *receiver*. Translating the message from its symbol form into meaning involves *decoding*. Only when the receiver understands the meaning intended by the sender—that is, successfully decodes the message—does communication take place. Such success, however, is difficult to achieve because no two people share the same life experiences and because many barriers can disrupt the process.

Decoding involves translating the message from symbol form into meaning.

Decoding can be disrupted internally by the receiver's lack of attention to or bias against the sender. It can be disrupted externally by loud sounds or illegible words. Decoding can also be sidetracked by semantic obstacles, such as misunderstood words or emotional reactions to certain terms. A memo that refers to all the women in an office as "girls" or "chicks," for example, may disturb its receivers so much that they fail to comprehend the total message.

Feedback Travels to Sender

The verbal and nonverbal responses of the receiver create *feedback*, a vital part of the communication process. Feedback helps the sender know that the message was received and understood. If, as a receiver, you hear the message *How are you,* your feedback might consist of words (*I'm fine*) or body language (a smile or a wave of the hand). Although the receiver may respond with additional feedback to the sender (thus creating a new act of communication), we'll concentrate here on the initial message flowing to the receiver and the resulting feedback.

Senders can encourage feedback by asking questions such as, *Am I making myself clear?* and *Is there anything you don't understand?* Senders can further improve feedback by timing the delivery appropriately and by providing only as much information as the receiver can handle. Receivers can improve the process by paraphrasing the sender's message with comments, such as, *Let me try to explain that in my own words.* The best feedback is descriptive rather than evaluative. For example, here's a descriptive response: *I understand you want to launch a used golf ball business.* Here's an evaluative response: *Your business ideas are always goofy.* An evaluative response is judgmental and doesn't tell the sender whether the receiver actually understood the message.

How can you improve feedback in the communication process?

Overcoming Interpersonal Communication Barriers

LEARNING OBJECTIVE 4

Recognize barriers to interpersonal communication and examine specific strategies for overcoming those barriers.

The communication process is successful only when the receiver understands the message as intended by the sender. It sounds quite simple. Yet it is not. How many times have you thought that you delivered a clear message, only to learn later that your intentions were totally misunderstood? Most messages that we send reach their destination, but many are only partially understood.

Obstacles That Create Misunderstanding

You can improve your chances of communicating successfully by learning to recognize barriers that are known to disrupt the process. The most significant barriers for individuals are bypassing, differing frames of reference, lack of language skill, and distractions.

Bypassing. One of the biggest barriers to clear communication involves words. Each of us attaches a little bundle of meanings to every word, and these meanings are not always similar. Bypassing happens when people miss each other with their meanings.[34] Let's say your boss asks you to "help" with a large customer mailing. When you arrive to do your share, you learn that you are expected to do the whole mailing yourself. You and your boss attached different meanings to the word *help*. Bypassing can lead to major miscommunication because people assume that meanings are contained in words. Actually, meanings are in people. For communication to be

What is bypassing? Describe an example from your experience.

successful, the receiver and sender must attach the same symbolic meanings to their words. A recent study revealed a high likelihood of miscommunication when people use common but vague words such as *probably, always, never, usually, often, soon,* and *right away.* What do the words really mean?[35]

How is your frame of reference different from another business communicator's?

Differing Frames of Reference. Another barrier to clear communication is your *frame of reference.* Everything you see and feel in the world is translated through your individual frame of reference. Your unique frame is formed by a combination of your experiences, education, culture, expectations, personality, and other elements. As a result, you bring your own biases and expectations to any communication situation. Because your frame of reference is different from everyone else's, you will never see things exactly as others do. American managers eager to reach an agreement with a Chinese parts supplier, for example, were disappointed with the slow negotiations process. The Chinese managers, on the other hand, were pleased that so much time had been taken to build personal relationships with the American managers. Wise business communicators strive to prevent miscommunication by being alert to both their own frames of reference and those of others. You will learn more about communicating across cultures in Chapter 3.

Lack of Language Skill. No matter how extraordinary the idea, it won't be understood or fully appreciated unless the communicators involved have good language skills. Each individual needs an adequate vocabulary, a command of basic punctuation and grammar, and skill in written and oral expression. Moreover, poor listening skills can prevent us from hearing oral messages clearly and thus responding properly.

Distractions. Other barriers include emotional interference, physical distractions, and digital interruptions. Shaping an intelligent message is difficult when one is feeling joy, fear, resentment, hostility, sadness, or some other strong emotion. To reduce the influence of emotions on communication, both senders and receivers should focus on the content of the message and try to remain objective. Physical distractions such as faulty acoustics, noisy surroundings, or a poor cell phone connection can disrupt oral communication. Similarly, sloppy appearance, poor printing, careless formatting, and typographical or spelling errors can disrupt written messages. What's more, technology doesn't seem to be helping. Knowledge workers are increasingly distracted by multitasking, digital and information overload, conflicting demands, and being constantly available digitally. Clear communication requires focusing on what is important and shutting out interruptions.[36]

Overcoming Communication Obstacles

How can you overcome typical obstacles in the communication process?

Careful communicators can conquer barriers in a number of ways. Half the battle in communicating successfully is recognizing that the entire process is sensitive and susceptible to breakdown. Like a defensive driver anticipating problems on the road, a good communicator anticipates problems in encoding, transmitting, and decoding a message. Effective communicators also focus on the receiver's environment and frame of reference. They ask themselves questions such as, *How is that individual likely to react to my message?* or *Does the receiver know as much about the subject as I do?*

Misunderstandings are less likely if you arrange your ideas logically and use words precisely. Mark Twain was right when he said, "The difference between an almost-right word and the right word is like the difference between lightning and the lightning bug." But communicating is more than expressing yourself well. A large part of successful communication is listening. Management advisor Peter Drucker observed that "too many executives think they are wonderful with people because they talk well. They don't realize that being wonderful with people means listening well."[37]

Effective communicators create an environment for useful feedback. In oral communication this means asking questions such as, *Do you understand?* and *What questions do you have?* as well as encouraging listeners to repeat instructions or paraphrase ideas. As a listener it means providing feedback that describes rather than evaluates. In written communication it means asking questions and providing access: *Do you have my phone numbers in case you have questions?* or *Here's my e-mail address so that you can give me your response immediately.*

Communicating in Business Organizations

LEARNING OBJECTIVE 5
Understand the internal and external functions of communication in organizations as well as compare and contrast the advantages and disadvantages of oral and written communication.

Until now, you've probably been thinking about the communication you do personally. However, business communicators must also be concerned with the bigger picture, and that involves sharing information in organizations. On the job you will be sharing information by communicating internally and externally.

Understanding Internal and External Functions

Internal communication includes exchanging ideas and messages with superiors, coworkers, and subordinates. When those messages must be written, you will probably choose e-mail. Some of the functions of internal communication are to issue and clarify procedures and policies, inform management of progress, develop new products and services, persuade employees or management to make changes or improvements, coordinate activities, and evaluate and reward employees.

When you are communicating externally with customers, suppliers, the government, and the public, you may send letters on company stationery. External functions involve answering inquiries about products or services, persuading customers to buy products or services, clarifying supplier specifications, issuing credit, collecting bills, responding to government agencies, and promoting a positive image of the organization.

What are the three main functions of business communication?

Now look back over the preceding discussion of internal and external functions of communication in organizations. Although there appear to be a large number of diverse business communication functions, they can be summarized in three simple categories, as Figure 1.5 shows: (a) to inform, (b) to persuade, and/or (c) to promote goodwill.

Shifting to Interactive, Mobile, and Instant Communication

The flattening of organizations coupled with the development of sophisticated information technology has greatly changed the way we communicate internally and externally. One major shift is away from one-sided, slow forms of communication such as memos and letters to more interactive, fast-results communication. Speeding up the flow of communication are e-mail, instant messaging (IM), text messaging, smartphones, voice mail, cell phones, and wireless fidelity ("Wi-Fi") networks. Wi-Fi lets mobile workers connect to the Internet at ultrafast speeds without cables.

FIGURE 1.5 **Functions of Business Communication**

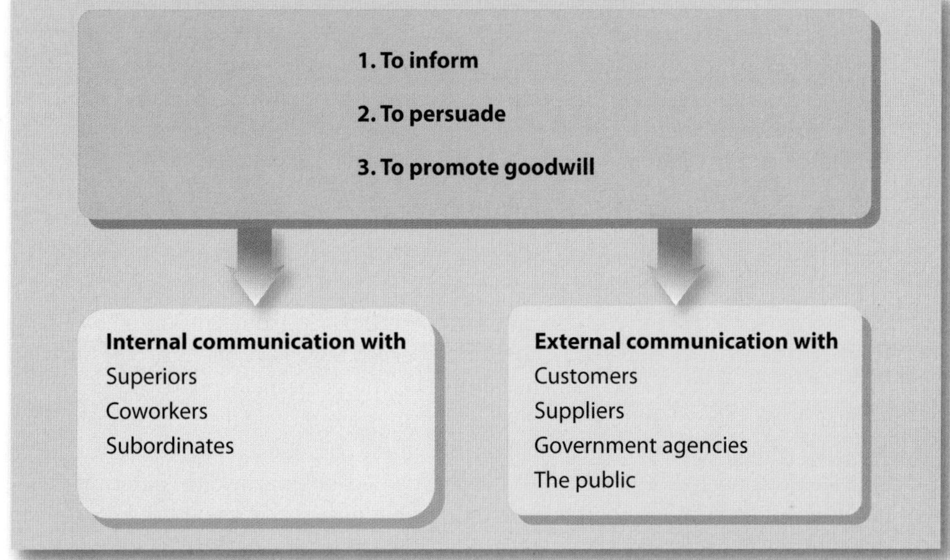

What communication technologies do you expect to use in your future workplace?

Many workers today can't imagine their lives without instant and text messaging. For example, Brad Weinstock, an insurance broker, uses IM to talk simultaneously with clients, colleagues, and friends. With IM, he can carry on many conversations at once, which helps him get his job done and serve clients better. *Instant messaging* is a type of communications service that allows you to create a private chat room to communicate in real time over the Internet. Typically, the instant messaging system alerts you when someone on your private list is online. *Text messaging* involves sending short text messages usually to a wireless device such as a cell phone or PDA. Many companies issue smartphones, notably the BlackBerry, to staff members who travel but must stay in connect with customers.

Other forms of interactive communication include intranets (company versions of the Internet), Web sites, video transmission, videoconferencing, and Web chats. The latter is rapidly becoming the preferred communication channel for online customer service. Consumers shopping online or inquiring about billing or technical support use the company Web site and "chat" with customer service representatives by typing their questions. Live service agents respond with a typed reply. You will be learning more about these and other forms of communication in coming chapters. Despite the range of interactive technologies, communicators are still working with two basic forms of communication: oral and written. Each has advantages and disadvantages.

Understanding the Advantages and Disadvantages of Oral Communication

Nearly everyone agrees that the best way to exchange information is orally in face-to-face conversations or meetings. Oral communication has many advantages. For one thing, it minimizes misunderstandings because communicators can immediately ask questions to clarify uncertainties. For another, it enables communicators to see each other's facial expressions and hear voice inflections, further improving the process. Oral communication is also an efficient way to develop consensus when many people must be consulted. Finally, most of us enjoy face-to-face interpersonal communication because it is easy, feels warm and natural, and promotes friendships.

The main disadvantages of oral communication are that it produces no written record, sometimes wastes time, and may be inconvenient. When individuals meet face-to-face or speak on the telephone, someone's work has to be interrupted. In addition, conversations take more time because we find it difficult to stick to business. Most of us consider it impolite to start a conversation without preliminaries such as *How are you?* Conversations may meander into chitchat, and some people do not know how to end a conversation. Nevertheless, oral communication has many advantages for communicators.

Understanding the Advantages and Disadvantages of Written Communication

Compare and contrast oral and written communication. Which is better?

Written communication is impersonal in the sense that two communicators cannot see or hear each other and cannot provide immediate feedback. Most forms of business communication—including e-mails, memos, letters, faxes, instructions, procedures, policies, proposals, manuals, newsletters, instant messages, Web sites, blogs, wikis, and résumés—fall into this category.

Organizations rely on written communication for many reasons. Written messages provide a permanent record, a necessity in these times of increasing litigation and extensive government regulation. Writing out ideas instead of delivering them orally enables communicators to develop organized, well-considered messages thus facilitating recall and comprehension for receivers. Written documents are also convenient. They can be composed and read when the schedules of both communicators permit, and they can be reviewed if necessary.

Written messages have drawbacks, of course. They require careful preparation. In addition, written messages can be dangerous. Words spoken in conversation may soon be forgotten, but words committed to hard or soft copy become a public record—and sometimes an embarrassing or risky one. E-mail and text-messaging records, even deleted ones, have often become "smoking guns" in court cases, revealing insider information that was never meant for public consumption.[38]

Another drawback to written messages is that they are more difficult to prepare. They demand good writing skills, and we are not born with these skills. But writing proficiency can be learned. Because as much as 90 percent of all business transactions may involve written messages and because writing skills are so important to your business success, you will be receiving special instruction in becoming a good writer. Compare the advantages and disadvantages of both oral and written communication in Figure 1.6.

FIGURE 1.6 Comparing Oral and Written Forms of Organizational Communication

	Forms	Advantages	Disadvantages
Oral Communication	Telephone call, conversation, interview, meeting, conference	Provides immediate feedback, can be adjusted to audience, can be delivered quickly, supplies nonverbal cues, may create warm feeling, can be forceful	Lacks permanent record, may contain careless or imprecise expression, may be inappropriate for formal or complex ideas, does not promote easy recall
Written Communication	E-mail, memo, letter, fax, instructions, procedures, policy, report, proposal, manual, newsletter, instant message, Web site, blog, wiki, résumé	Creates permanent record, is convenient to distribute, may be economical, promotes comprehension and recall, allows precise and uniform expression, gives audience flexibility in when and how to receive content	Leaves paper trail, requires skill and effort to produce, lacks verbal cues and warmth, cannot be immediately modified based on audience feedback, may seem impersonal

Improving the Flow of Information in Organizations

LEARNING OBJECTIVE 6

Examine critically the flow of communication in organizations, and understand how to overcome typical barriers and respond ethically to office gossip.

Information within organizations flows through formal and informal communication channels. A free exchange of information helps organizations respond rapidly to changing markets, boost efficiency and productivity, build employee morale, serve the public, and take full advantage of the ideas of today's knowledge workers. Barriers, however, can obstruct the flow of communication, as summarized in Figure 1.7.

Formal Communication Channels

Formal channels of communication generally follow an organization's chain of command. That is, a message originates with executives and flows down through managers to supervisors and finally to lower-level employees. Many organizations have formulated official communication policies that encourage regular open communication through newsletters, intranets, and official messages. Free-flowing, open communication invigorates organizations and makes them successful. Official information within an organization typically flows through formal channels in three directions: downward, upward, and horizontally, as shown in Figure 1.8.

FIGURE 1.7 Barriers Block the Flow of Communication in Organizations

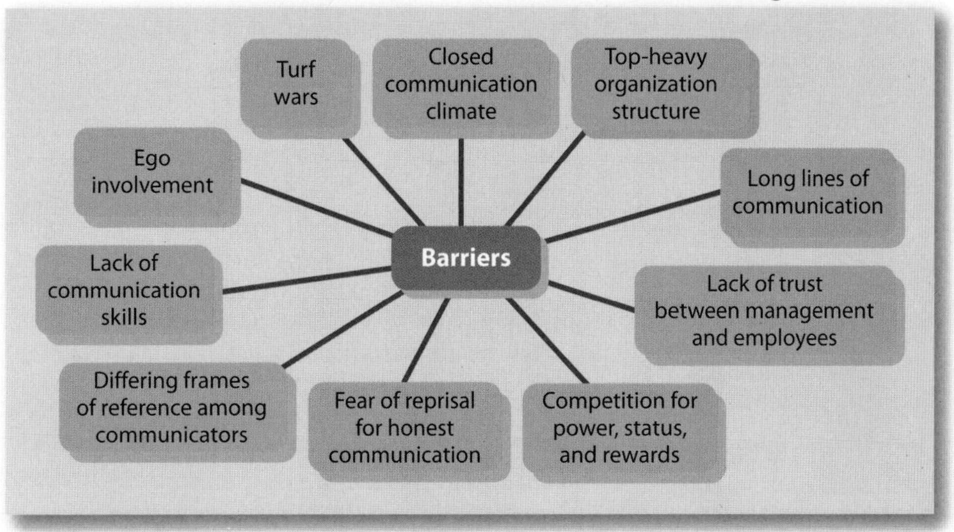

FIGURE 1.8 Information Flow in Organizations

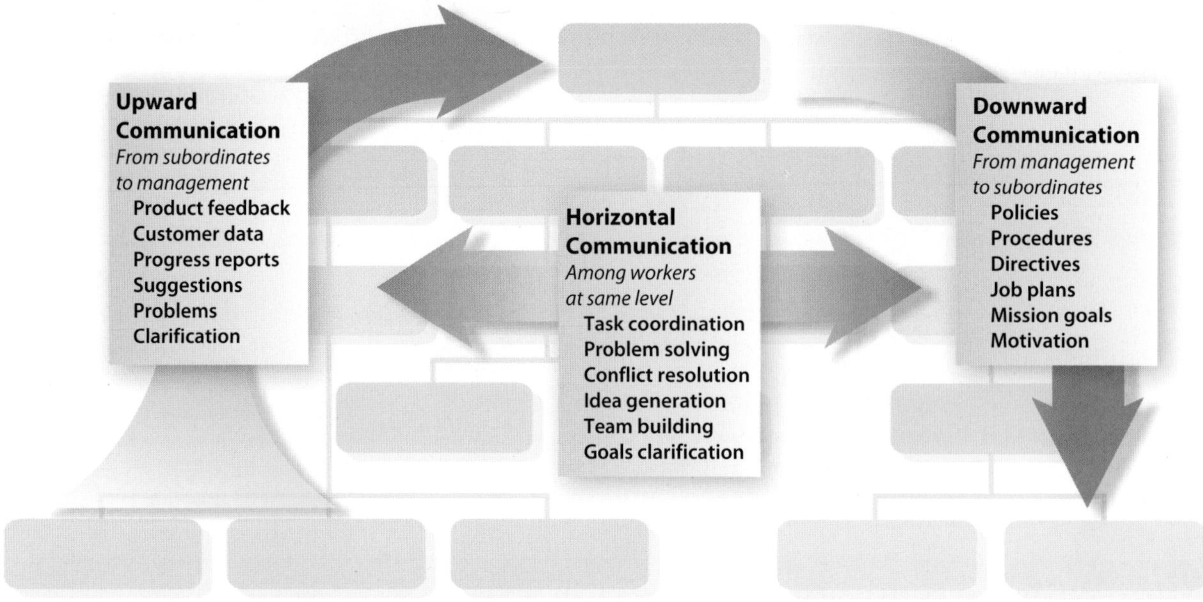

What types of messages typically flow downward in an organization?

Downward Flow. Information flowing downward moves from decision makers through the chain of command to subordinates. This information includes policies, procedures, directives, job plans, mission goals, and efforts to motivate staff members. Managers provide information about employee performance and instill a sense of mission in achieving the organization's goals. When a particularly important message such as a drug testing policy is announced, that message may flow downward directly from the CEO to employees, as shown in Figure 1.9.

Obstacles to Downward Information Flow. One obstacle that can impede the downward flow of information is distortion resulting from long lines of communication. Unlike the policy memo from the CEO shown in Figure 1.9, most messages regarding

FIGURE 1.9 Policy Message From Management Flowing Downward

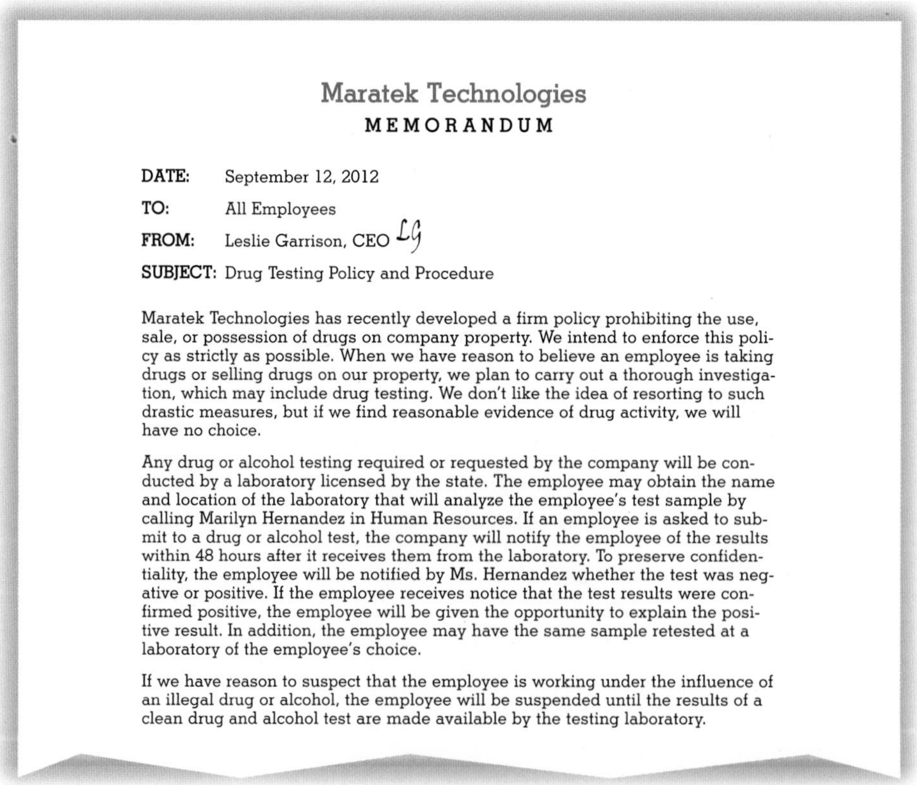

Maratek Technologies
MEMORANDUM

DATE: September 12, 2012
TO: All Employees
FROM: Leslie Garrison, CEO *LG*
SUBJECT: Drug Testing Policy and Procedure

Maratek Technologies has recently developed a firm policy prohibiting the use, sale, or possession of drugs on company property. We intend to enforce this policy as strictly as possible. When we have reason to believe an employee is taking drugs or selling drugs on our property, we plan to carry out a thorough investigation, which may include drug testing. We don't like the idea of resorting to such drastic measures, but if we find reasonable evidence of drug activity, we will have no choice.

Any drug or alcohol testing required or requested by the company will be conducted by a laboratory licensed by the state. The employee may obtain the name and location of the laboratory that will analyze the employee's test sample by calling Marilyn Hernandez in Human Resources. If an employee is asked to submit to a drug or alcohol test, the company will notify the employee of the results within 48 hours after it receives them from the laboratory. To preserve confidentiality, the employee will be notified by Ms. Hernandez whether the test was negative or positive. If the employee receives notice that the test results were confirmed positive, the employee will be given the opportunity to explain the positive result. In addition, the employee may have the same sample retested at a laboratory of the employee's choice.

If we have reason to suspect that the employee is working under the influence of an illegal drug or alcohol, the employee will be suspended until the results of a clean drug and alcohol test are made available by the testing laboratory.

procedures flow downward through a line of managers. If, for example, a CEO wants to change an accounting procedure, she or he would probably not send a memo directly to the staff accountants who would implement the change. Instead, the CEO would relay the idea through proper formal channels—from the vice president for finance, to the accounting manager, to the senior accountant, and so on—until the message reached the affected employees. Obviously, the longer the lines of communication, the greater the chance for message distortion.

Improving Downward Information Flow. To improve communication and to compete more effectively, many of today's companies have restructured and reengineered themselves into smaller operating units and work teams. Rather than being bogged down with long communication chains, management speaks directly to employees, as seen in Figure 1.9. This memo from the CEO describes the company's drug testing plan and illustrates direct downward communication.

In addition to shorter chains of communication, management can improve the downward flow of information through newsletters, announcements, meetings, videos, blogs, podcasts, and company intranets. Instead of hoarding information at the top, today's managers recognize the importance of letting workers know how well the company is doing and what new projects are planned.

Upward Flow. Information flowing upward provides feedback from nonmanagement employees to management. Subordinate employees describe progress in completing tasks, report roadblocks encountered, and suggest methods for improving efficiency. Channels for upward communication include phone messages, e-mails, memos, reports, departmental meetings, and suggestion systems. Ideally, the heaviest flow of information should be upward with information being fed steadily to decision makers. The e-mail message shown in Figure 1.10 is a response to a request from a manager to investigate focus group services.

Why should the flow of information in organizations be heavier upward than downward?

FIGURE 1.10 **Information From Employee Flowing Upward to Management**

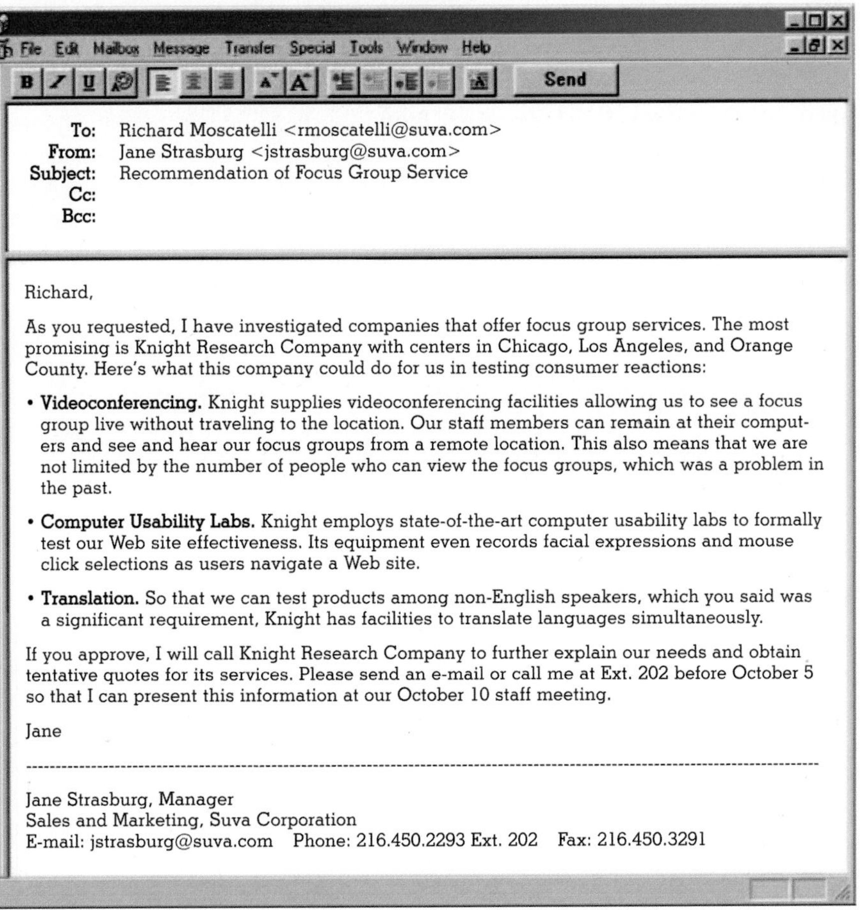

To: Richard Moscatelli <rmoscatelli@suva.com>
From: Jane Strasburg <jstrasburg@suva.com>
Subject: Recommendation of Focus Group Service
Cc:
Bcc:

Richard,

As you requested, I have investigated companies that offer focus group services. The most promising is Knight Research Company with centers in Chicago, Los Angeles, and Orange County. Here's what this company could do for us in testing consumer reactions:

- **Videoconferencing.** Knight supplies videoconferencing facilities allowing us to see a focus group live without traveling to the location. Our staff members can remain at their computers and see and hear our focus groups from a remote location. This also means that we are not limited by the number of people who can view the focus groups, which was a problem in the past.
- **Computer Usability Labs.** Knight employs state-of-the-art computer usability labs to formally test our Web site effectiveness. Its equipment even records facial expressions and mouse click selections as users navigate a Web site.
- **Translation.** So that we can test products among non-English speakers, which you said was a significant requirement, Knight has facilities to translate languages simultaneously.

If you approve, I will call Knight Research Company to further explain our needs and obtain tentative quotes for its services. Please send an e-mail or call me at Ext. 202 before October 5 so that I can present this information at our October 10 staff meeting.

Jane

Jane Strasburg, Manager
Sales and Marketing, Suva Corporation
E-mail: jstrasburg@suva.com Phone: 216.450.2293 Ext. 202 Fax: 216.450.3291

Obstacles to Upward Information Flow. A number of obstacles can interrupt the upward flow of communication. Employees who distrust their employers are less likely to communicate openly. Employees cease trusting managers if they feel they are being tricked, manipulated, criticized, or treated unfairly. Unfortunately, some employees today no longer have a strong trusting attitude toward employers. Downsizing, cost-cutting measures, the use of temporary workers, discrimination and harassment suits, outsourcing, outrageous compensation packages for chief executives, and many other factors have lessened the feelings of trust and pride that employees once felt toward their employers and their jobs. Other obstacles include fear of reprisal for honest communication, lack of adequate communication skills, and differing frames of reference. Imperfect communication results when individuals are not using words or symbols with similar meanings, when they cannot express their ideas clearly, or when they come from different backgrounds.

Improving Upward Information Flow. To improve the upward flow of communication, some companies are (a) hiring communication coaches to train employees, (b) asking employees to report customer complaints, (c) encouraging regular meetings with staff, (d) providing a trusting, nonthreatening environment in which employees can comfortably share their observations and ideas with management, and (e) offering incentive programs that encourage employees to collect and share valuable feedback. Companies are also building trust by setting up hotlines for anonymous feedback to management and by installing ombudsman programs. An *ombudsman* is a mediator who hears employee complaints, investigates, and seeks to resolve problems fairly.

What is horizontal information flow in organizations, and why is it important?

Horizontal Information Flow.

Lateral channels transmit information horizontally among workers at the same level. These channels enable individuals to coordinate tasks, share information, solve problems, and resolve conflicts. Horizontal communication takes place through personal contact, telephone, e-mail, memos, voice mail, and meetings. Most traditional organizations have few established regular channels for the horizontal exchange of information. Restructured companies with flattened hierarchies and team-based management, however, have discovered that when employees combine their knowledge with that of other employees, they can do their jobs better. Much information in these organizations travels horizontally among team members.[39]

Obstacles to Horizontal Information Flow. Obstacles to the horizontal flow of communication, as well as to upward and downward flow, include poor communication skills, prejudice, ego involvement, and turf wars. Some employees avoid sharing information if doing so might endanger their status or chances for promotion within the organization. Competition within units and an uneven reward system may also prevent workers from freely sharing information.

Improving Horizontal Information Flow. To improve horizontal communication, companies are (a) training employees in teamwork and communication techniques, (b) establishing reward systems based on team achievement rather than individual achievement, and (c) encouraging full participation in team functions. However, employees must also realize that they are personally responsible for making themselves heard, for really understanding what other people say, and for getting the information they need. Developing those business communication skills is exactly what this book and this course will do for you.

ETHICS CHECK

Office Grapevine

Like a game of "telephone," the grapevine can distort the original message because the news travels through many mouths and ears at the office. Knowing this, can you safely share with even a trusted colleague something that you would not comfortably discuss with everyone?

Informal Communication Channels

Most organizations today share company news through consistent, formal channels such as e-mail and staff meetings, a recent survey shows. However, as many as 20 percent do not provide consistent channels to share company news.[40] Even within organizations with consistent formal channels, people still gossip about company news. The *grapevine* is an informal channel of communication that carries organizationally relevant gossip. This powerful but informal channel functions through social relationships; people talk about work when they are lunching, working out, golfing, and carpooling, as well as in e-mails, texts, and blogs. At one time gossip took place around the water cooler. Today, however, a study of office workers reveals that gossip usually takes place in the office break room (36 percent), at a coworker's desk (33 percent), or in e-mails and instant messages (10 percent).[41]

Zooming In PART 2

PepsiCo

When Indra Nooyi joined PepsiCo as chief strategist, she convinced management to sell off its fast-food holdings in Taco Bell, Pizza Hut, and KFC. She was intent on moving the company "from snack food to health food, from caffeine colas to fruit juices, and from shareholder value to sustainable enterprise."[42] Her goal was to do good for business as well as doing good for people and the planet. PepsiCo, under her leadership, would favor wind and solar power, avoid fossil fuels, fight against obesity, and promote diversity.

To achieve these ambitious goals, Nooyi instituted "Performance With Purpose," a portion of which is explained in the following three components:

- Human sustainability refers to PepsiCo's efforts to nourish consumers with a range of products from treats to healthful eats.
- Environmental sustainability reinforces PepsiCo's commitment to work to protect natural resources and operate in a way that minimizes the company's environmental footprint.
- Talent sustainability focuses on developing the company's employees by creating a diverse and inclusive culture and making certain PepsiCo is an attractive destination for the world's best people.[43]

Convincing PepsiCo managers and employees to accept her "Performance With Purpose" plan was a monumental task that would involve significant changes in products and procedures within the enterprise. In any organization, change is accepted slowly and often reluctantly. Encouraging managers, employees, and investors to buy in to changes in company philosophy is often difficult.

© MANPREET ROMANA/AFP/Getty Images

Critical Thinking

- In communicating the changes in philosophy and practice within PepsiCo, should Indra Nooyi and her management team use formal or informal channels of communication? Give examples of each.
- In the midst of organizational changes at PepsiCo, what kinds of messages do you think will be traveling downward, upward, and horizontally?
- What kinds of barriers block the flow of communication in any organization undergoing change?

Using the Grapevine Productively. Researchers studying communication flow within organizations know that the grapevine can be a powerful, pervasive source of information. In some organizations it can account for as much as two thirds of an employee's information. Is this bad? Well, yes and no. The grapevine can be a fairly accurate and speedy source of organization information. Studies have demonstrated accuracy ratings of nearly 80 percent for many grapevine transmissions.[44] However, grapevine information is often incomplete because it travels in headlines: *Vice President Sacked* or *Jerk on the Fourth Floor Promoted.* When employees obtain most of their company news from the grapevine, management is not releasing sufficient information through formal channels.

Managers can use the grapevine productively by (a) respecting employees' desire to know, (b) increasing the amount of information delivered through formal channels, (c) sharing bad as well as good news, (d) monitoring the grapevine, and (e) acting promptly to correct misinformation.[45] The truth is that most employees want to know what's going on. In fact, one study found that regardless of how much information organization members reported receiving, they wanted more.[46] Many companies today have moved away from a rigid authoritarian management structure in which only managers were allowed to see vital information, such as product success and profit figures. Employees who know the latest buzz feel like important members of the team. Through formal and informal channels of communication, smart companies keep employees informed.

Responding Ethically to Office Gossip. To many of us, gossip is fun and even entertaining. It encourages social bonding and makes us feel close to others who share our trust. We feel a part of the group and that we can influence others when we share a significant tidbit. We might even argue that gossip is good because it can help people learn how to behave and how to respond to social miscues faster and less awkwardly than if they made the mistakes themselves. For example, you're not likely to wear that new revealing camisole after hearing

What can you do if you are a victim of malicious gossip?

the scathing remarks being circulated about a similar one worn by Lacy in the marketing department.

However, not all gossip is harmless. Someone known as an office gossip can be viewed as untrustworthy and unpromotable. Even more damaging, malicious gossip spread in e-mails or text messages can be used in defamation cases. It can also become evidence against employers in supporting charges of harassment or maintaining a hostile work environment. Unfounded gossip can ruin careers and harm companies. In addition, employers look upon gossip as a productivity drain. The time spent gossiping reduces the time spent working.

How can you respond ethically to gossip or reduce its occurrence? Workplace ethics expert Nan DeMars offers several helpful pointers, reproduced here from her Internet ethics site **(http:// www.office-ethics.com)**:

- **Run, don't walk, away from anyone who starts to gossip.** Even if you don't contribute to the conversation, just being present indicates consent.
- **End rumors about others.** If you overhear something that is untrue, step up and say so. People will respect your integrity.
- **Attack rumors about yourself.** Be aggressive and determine who originated the remark, if possible. Always follow with documentation explaining what really happened.
- **Keep confidences.** Become known as someone who is close-mouthed.
- **Limit the personal tidbits you share about yourself and keep them on the light side.** Too much information may be blown out of proportion and/or become tempting to someone else to expand. Trust only those who have demonstrated and earned your confidence.
- **Avoid any form of coworker belittlement.** Today's coworker may be tomorrow's senior vice president.
- **Build coworkers up; don't tear them down.** If you must use the grapevine, use it to praise coworkers. They will remember.[47]

Looking at Business and Ethics

LEARNING OBJECTIVE 7

Analyze ethics in the workplace, understand the goals of ethical business communicators, recognize and avoid ethical traps, and apply tools for doing the right thing.

The recent financial mess and economic tailspin forced many to wonder what caused the severe economic crisis. Who or what was to blame? Some observers claim that business organizations suffered from an ethics deficit; they were too intent on short-term profits and cared little about the dangerous risks they were taking. Executives and managers were so self-centered that they failed to see themselves as caretakers of their own institutions. Critics also extended their blame to business schools for not doing a better job of teaching ethics.[48] Still others complained that the financial debacle was caused by greedy individuals who were interested only in personal gain at all costs.

Although the financial mess was not directly created by any single factor, many believe that it would not have occurred if those involved had acted less selfishly and more ethically. The entire topic of ethics in business has captured the spotlight as a result of the financial crisis and economic downturn. The topic of ethics could fill entire books. However, we will examine aspects that specifically concern you as a business communicator in today's workplace.

What Is Ethics?

Ethics refers to conventional standards of right and wrong that prescribe what people should do. These standards usually consist of rights, obligations, and benefits to society. They also include virtues such as fairness, honesty, loyalty, and concern for others. Ethics is about having values and taking responsibility. Ethical individuals are expected to follow the law and refrain from theft, murder, assault, slander, and fraud.

In our discussion of ethics, we will first look at what business organizations and schools are doing to encourage an ethical culture. Then we will examine ethics in the workplace, study goals of ethical business communicators, and learn tools for doing the right thing.

What Are Business Organizations Doing to Encourage an Ethical Culture?

Why does being ethical make good business sense?

Businesses today are well aware of the criticism heaped on them following the financial meltdown, and many are striving to develop an ethical culture. Even before the recent economic downward spiral, they were trying to improve their poor public image and avoid government sanctions. The Sarbanes-Oxley Act required companies to adopt ethics programs, and many did so with workshops and Web-based training programs. Smart companies continue to incorporate ethics into their organizations and also to be more socially responsible. PepsiCo, for example, is striving to produce more healthful foods and beverages and also to reduce the company's impact on the environment through initiatives focused on water, energy, and packaging. Being ethical makes good business sense. Ethical companies endure less litigation, less resentment, and less government regulation.

Many business organizations are implementing policies and procedures to encourage an ethical culture. Companies are establishing codes of ethics, appointing ethics compliance officers, and instituting ethics training programs. Ethics codes typically cover five elements: responsibility, respect, fairness, honesty, and compassion. Companies are also developing Web-based programs and workshops that teach employees how to relate to each other, to the company, to customers, and to business partners. These trainings sometimes include ethical decision-making models and role-playing scenarios that help employees respond appropriately to dilemmas. Typical ethical topics include workplace romance, e-mail appropriateness, Internet use, integrity, confidentiality, security, and harassment.

If you join a large organization, you will probably be expected to sign a document assuring that you will comply with the company's code of ethics. In addition, you will be expected to comprehend the laws that apply to your job. Managers who conduct applicant interviews, for example, must know which questions are legal and which are not. Employees must understand what is allowed regarding vendor gifts. Should you accept those football game tickets or a free spa treatment from a vendor? What is the legal limit? You may also be encouraged to use an anonymous hotline to report suspected fraud or unethical actions.

What Are Schools Doing to Encourage an Ethical Culture?

Why were business schools criticized after the financial crisis and recent recession?

Although business organizations and their leaders took the brunt of the blame for the financial crisis, business schools were also singled out. Critics complained that emphasizing immediate gains encouraged graduates to make dangerous decisions. Instead of being taught to look at the bigger picture, students were given a narrow, profit-centered focus that encouraged them to behave in short-term, selfish ways in the workplace.[49]

To better encourage an ethical culture, concerned business schools are revamping their curricula to place more emphasis on values reflecting the greater good and less on short-term, immediate profits. Some ethics programs include coaching sessions and scripts for voicing responses to ethical dilemmas. For example, your boss may ask you to tell a visitor or caller that she is away from the office, when in fact she is sitting in a nearby office. Should you lie to please your boss? Rather than tell a lie, even a small one, you could reply, "No, I will never lie *for you*. But you should also know that I will never lie *to you* either."[50]

Schools are helping students recognize ethical dilemmas and giving them tools for responding effectively. You will be given such tools shortly, along with a list of the goals of ethical business communicators.

Examining Ethics in the Workplace

As a business communicator, you should understand basic ethical principles so that you can make logical decisions when faced with dilemmas in the workplace. Professionals in any field must deal with moral dilemmas on the job. However, just being a moral person and having sound personal ethics may not be sufficient to handle the ethical issues that you may face in the workplace. Consider the following ethical dilemmas:

E-mail message You accidentally receive a message outlining your company's restructuring plan. You see that your coworker's job will be eliminated. He and his wife are about to purchase a new home. Should you tell him that his job is in danger?

Customer letter You are writing a letter to a customer who is irate over a mistake you made. Should you blame it on a computer glitch, point the finger at another department, or take the blame and risk losing this customer's trust and possibly your job?

Progress report Should you write a report that ignores problems in a project, as your boss asks? Your boss controls your performance evaluation.

Sales report Should you inflate sales figures so that your team can meet its quarterly goal? Your team leader strongly urges you to do so, and you receive a healthy bonus if your team meets its goal.

Presentation You are rushing to prepare a presentation. On the Web you find perfect wording and great graphics. Should you lift the graphics and wording but change a few words? You figure that if it is on the Web, it must be in the public domain.

Proposal Your company urgently needs a revenue-producing project. Should you submit a proposal that unrealistically suggests a short completion schedule to ensure that you get the job?

Résumé Should you inflate your grade point average or give yourself more experience or a higher job title than your experience warrants to make your résumé more attractive? The job market is very competitive.

Is anything that is legal automatically ethical? Can you give an example?

On the job you will face many dilemmas, and you will want to react ethically. Determining the right thing to do, however, is not always an easy task. No solid rules guide us. For some people, following the law seems to be enough. They think that anything legal must also be ethical or moral. Most people, however, believe that ethical standards rise to a higher level. What are those standards? Although many ethical dilemmas have no "right" answer, one solution is often better than another. In deciding on that solution, keep in mind the goals of ethical business communicators.

Goals of Ethical Business Communicators

Taking ethics into consideration can be painful in the short term. In the long term, however, ethical behavior makes sense and pays off. Dealing honestly with colleagues and customers develops trust and builds stronger relationships. The following guidelines can help you set specific ethical goals. Although these goals hardly constitute a formal code of conduct, they will help you maintain a high ethical standard.

Abiding by the Law. Know the laws in your field and follow them. Particularly important for business communicators are issues of copyright law. Under the concept of fair use, individuals have limited rights to use copyrighted material without requiring permission. To be safe, you should assume that anything produced privately after 1989—including words, charts, graphs, photos, music—is copyrighted. By the way, don't assume that Internet items are in the public domain and free to be used or shared. Internet items are covered by copyright laws. A Swedish court recently convicted four men promoting Pirate Bay, an Internet file-sharing service.[51] If you are in accounting, financial management, investing, or corporate management, you should be aware of the restrictions set forth by the Sarbanes-Oxley Act. Whatever your field, become familiar with its regulations.

Ethics Check

Blurt Out the Truth?

While serving as an interviewer on behalf of your organization, you are expected to tell prospective employees that the firm is a great place to work. However, let's say you know that the work environment is bad, morale is low, and staff turnover is high. What should you do?

Telling the Truth. Ethical business communicators do not intentionally make statements that are untrue or deceptive. In recent corporate scandals some executives have landed in jail or lost their jobs for lying. Accused of selling stock based on insider information, Martha Stewart was actually jailed for lying about it. Hewlett-Packard CEO Patricia Dunn lost her job after authorizing "pretexting," which is pretending to be someone else, to investigate phone records. A high-profile football coach resigned after the discovery that he had lied about his academic and athletic background. These big-time lies made headlines, and you may see no correlation to your life. On a personal level, however, we all may lie and deceive in various ways. We say things that are not so. We may exaggerate to swell the importance of our assertions. We may minimize our responsibility when things go wrong. We may withhold information that leads to misunderstanding or fraud. All of these are examples of lying. Being truthful to yourself is a cornerstone of ethical behavior.

Labeling Opinions. Sensitive communicators know the difference between facts and opinions. Facts are verifiable and often are quantifiable; opinions are beliefs held with confidence but without substantiation. It is a fact, for example, that women are starting businesses at two times the rate of men.[52] It is an opinion, though, that the so-called "glass ceiling" has held women back, forcing them to start their own businesses. Such a cause-and-effect claim would be difficult to prove. It is a fact that many corporations are spending billions of dollars to be socially responsible, including using ethically made products and developing eco-friendly technology. It is an opinion that consumers are willing to pay more for a pound of coffee if they believe that the seller used ethical fair-trade production standards.[53] Assertions that cannot be proved are opinions, and stating opinions as if they were facts is unethical.

Why is it important ethically to distinguish between facts and opinions?

Being Objective. Ethical business communicators recognize their own biases and strive to keep them from distorting a message. Suppose you are asked to investigate laptop computers and write a report recommending a brand for your office. As you visit stores, you discover that an old high school friend is selling Brand X. Because you always liked this individual and have faith in his judgment, you may be inclined to tilt your recommendation in his direction. However, it is unethical to misrepresent the facts in your report or to put a spin on your arguments based on friendship. To be ethical, you could note in your report that you have known the person for ten years and that you respect his opinion. In this way, you have disclosed your relationship as well as the reasons for your decision. Honest reporting means presenting the whole picture and relating all facts fairly.

Communicating Clearly. Ethical business communicators feel an obligation to write clearly so that receivers understand easily and quickly. Some states have even passed "Plain English" (also called "Plain Language") laws that require businesses to write policies, warranties, and contracts in language comprehensible to average readers. Plain English means short sentences, simple words, and clear organization. Communicators who intentionally obscure the meaning with long sentences and difficult words are being unethical.

Why have some states passed Plain English laws?

Using Inclusive Language. Ethical business communicators use language that includes rather than excludes. They avoid expressions that discriminate against individuals or groups on the basis of their sex, ethnicity, disability, race, sexual orientation, or age. Language is discriminatory when it stereotypes, insults, or excludes people. You will learn more about how to use inclusive, bias-free language in Chapter 4.

Giving Credit. Ethical communicators give credit for ideas by (a) referring to originators' names within the text; (b) using quotation marks; and (c) documenting sources with endnotes, footnotes, or internal references. You will learn how to do this in Chapter 11 and Appendix C. Don't suggest that you did all the work on a project if you had help. In school or on the job, stealing ideas, words, graphics, or any other original material is unethical.

Members of the International Association of Business Communicators have developed a code of ethics with 12 guidelines (articles) that spell out criteria for determining what is right and wrong for members of its organization. You can see the IABC Code of Ethics for Professional Communicators at **http://www.iabc.com/about/code.htm**.

Obstacles to Ethical Decision Making

Even when business communicators are aware of their goals and want to do the right thing, a number of obstacles can prevent them from doing so. Businesses are downsizing staff and reducing resources. Employees may feel pressure to increase productivity by whatever means. Knowingly or not, managers under pressure to make profit quotas may send the message to workers that it's OK to lie, cheat, or steal to achieve company goals. These and other rationalizations can motivate unethical actions. In making ethical decisions, business communicators commonly face five traps that can make arriving at the right decision more difficult.

The False Necessity Trap. People act from the belief that they are doing what they must do. They convince themselves that they have no other choice, when in fact it's generally a matter of convenience or desire. Consider the Beech-Nut Corporation's actions when it discovered that its supplier was providing artificial apple juice. Beech-Nut canceled its contracts but continued to advertise and sell the adulterated "apple" juice as a 100 percent natural product in its baby food line. Falling into the false necessity trap, Beech-Nut felt it had no choice but to continue the deception. Similarly, a 23-year-old applicant was desperate for a retail job in a dwindling market. The retailer required a personality test. With a little digging on the Internet, he found an unauthorized answer key and scored well.[54] He apparently justified cheating on the test by telling himself that he really needed this job and the only way to score highly was to cheat.

The Doctrine-of-Relative-Filth Trap. Unethical actions sometimes look good when compared with worse behavior by others. What's a little fudging on an expense account compared with the pleasure cruise the boss took and charged as a business trip? How about using IM and Twitter at your desk to keep in touch with friends? Perhaps you will steal a little time at work to do some much-needed research on a hybrid car you are considering buying. After all, the guys in Engineering told you that they spend hours online checking sports scores, playing games, and conducting recreational Web surfing. While you are on the subject, how about Chelsea who spends hours playing Spider Solitaire but uses her "boss button" to temporarily hide the game when the manager is near? Your minor infractions seem insignificant compared with what others are doing.

What is rationalization? Can you give an example from your experience?

The Rationalization Trap. In falling into the rationalization trap, people try to explain away unethical actions by justifying them with excuses. Consider employees who "steal" time from their employers by taking long lunch and coffee breaks, claiming sick leave when not ill, and completing their own tasks on company time. It's easy to rationalize such actions: "I deserve an extra-long lunch break because I can't get all my shopping done on such a short lunch hour" or "I'll just write my class report at the office because the computer printer is much better than mine, and they aren't paying me what I'm worth anyway."

The Self-Deception Trap. Applicants for jobs often fall into the self-deception trap. They are all too willing to inflate grade point averages or exaggerate past accomplishments to impress prospective employers. One applicant, for example, claimed experience as a broker's assistant at a prestigious securities firm. A background check revealed that he had interviewed for the securities job but was never offered it. Another applicant claimed that he held a summer job in which he was "responsible for cross-corporate transferal of multidimensional client

© Hiroko Masuike/Getty Images

Bernie Madoff became the world's poster child of financial corruption when authorities discovered that the financier's asset management firm was a money racket—the biggest in Wall Street history. After defrauding a who's who of global investors and Hollywood stars including Steven Spielberg, Madoff confessed his Ponzi scheme to relatives and was later sentenced to 150 years in prison. Intended as a short-term ploy to manage a recessionary period, the multibillion dollar scam lasted decades. *What questions should professionals ask themselves to help avoid illegal or unethical behavior?*[55]

receivables." In other words, he moved boxes from sales to shipping. Self-deception can lead to unethical and possibly illegal behavior.

The Ends-Justify-the-Means Trap. Taking unethical actions to accomplish a desirable goal is a common trap. Consider a manager in a Medicare claims division of a large health insurance company who coerced clerical staff into working overtime without pay. The goal was to reduce a backlog of unprocessed claims. Despite the worthy goal, the means of reaching it was unethical.

Tools for Doing the Right Thing

It's easy to fall into ethical traps because of natural self-interests and the desire to succeed. In composing messages or engaging in other activities on the job, business communicators can't help being torn by conflicting loyalties. Do we tell the truth and risk our jobs? Do we show loyalty to friends even if it means bending the rules? Should we be tactful or totally honest? Is it our duty to make a profit or to be socially responsible?

Acting ethically means doing the right thing given the circumstances. Each set of circumstances requires analyzing issues, evaluating choices, and acting responsibly. Resolving ethical issues is never easy, but the task can be made less difficult if you know how to identify key issues. The following questions may be helpful.

- **Is the action you are considering legal?** No matter who asks you to do it or how important you feel the result will be, avoid anything that is prohibited by law. Giving a kickback to a buyer for a large order is illegal, even if you suspect that others in your field do it and you know that without the kickback you will lose the sale.
- **How would you see the problem if you were on the opposite side?** Looking at all sides of an issue helps you gain perspective. Consider the issue of mandatory drug testing among employees. From management's viewpoint, such testing could stop drug abuse, improve job performance, and lower health insurance premiums. From the employees' viewpoint, mandatory testing reflects a lack of trust of employees and constitutes an invasion of privacy. By weighing both sides of the issue, you can arrive at a more equitable solution.
- **What are alternate solutions?** Consider all dimensions of other options. Would the alternative be more ethical? Under the circumstances, is the alternative feasible? Can an alternate solution be implemented with a minimum of disruption and with a good possibility of success? Let's say you wrote a report about testing a new product, but your boss changed the report to distort the findings. Should you go to the head of the company and reveal that the report is inaccurate? A more tactful alternative would be to approach your boss and ask whether you misunderstood the report's findings or whether an error might have been made.
- **Can you discuss the problem with someone whose advice you trust?** Suppose you feel ethically bound to report accurate information to a client even though your manager has ordered you not to do so. Talking about your dilemma with a coworker or with a colleague in your field might give you helpful insights and lead to possible alternatives.

Why is it helpful to discuss a potential ethical problem with someone you trust?

- **How would you feel if your family, friends, employer, or coworkers learned of your action?** If the thought of revealing your action publicly produces cold sweats, your choice is probably unwise. Losing the faith of your friends or the confidence of your customers is not worth whatever short-term gains might be realized.

Perhaps the best advice in ethical matters is contained in the Golden Rule: Do unto others as you would have others do unto you. The ultimate solution to all ethics problems is treating others fairly and doing what is right to achieve what is good. In succeeding chapters you will find additional discussions of ethical questions as they relate to relevant topics.

Want to do well on tests and excel in your course?
Go to **www.meguffey.com** for helpful interactive resources.
- **Review the Chapter 1 PowerPoint slides to prepare for the first quiz.**

Zooming In YOUR TURN

Applying Your Skills at PepsiCo

Called the most powerful woman in corporate America, PepsiCo CEO Indra Nooyi is disarmingly frank about her success. She credits the achievements in her career in part to the United States, which she says is the largest meritocracy in existence. "If you saw me when I stepped off the boat in 1978, you would never imagine that I would get to this position," she says. She admits to not knowing how to dress and speaking so fast that no one could understand her. "I didn't know anything—zip!" she confesses.[56] In graduate school she learned how to speak properly and communicate effectively. On the job she focused on overdelivering whatever was assigned, staying out of office politics, and completing assigned tasks better than anyone expected. Having mentors and following their advice were also important. She claims that it does not matter if you are international, locally born, man, or woman. In the United States and at PepsiCo, merit will triumph. That is, effective leaders will rise to the top.

Your Task

Few have the opportunity to become the leader of a giant multinational company like Indra Nooyi at PepsiCo. But many of you will become leaders and managers in local and national organizations. As an intern at PepsiCo, assume you are part of a leadership training group. As part of your training program, your manager asks you and fellow interns to prepare a list of communication skills that you think are important to leadership success. What skills are important for initial hiring? How can these skills be identified among applicants? What skills are important for promotion? Are they the same? Why? Your intern manager wants to know whether you think communication and leadership skills can be taught on the job. In teams of three to five, discuss these questions. Summarize your conclusions and (a) appoint one team representative to report to the class or (b) write individual memos or e-mails describing your conclusions. (See Chapter 8 and Appendix B for tips on writing memos.)

© MANPREET ROMANA/AFP/Getty Images

Summary of Learning Objectives

1 Understand the importance of communication skills in relation to career success and explain the need for thinking critically and taking charge of your career. Communication skills are critical to job placement, performance, career advancement, and organizational success. Especially in a recessionary period, excellent communication skills can set you apart from other candidates. Communication skills include reading, listening, nonverbal, speaking, and writing skills. They are not inherent; they must be learned. Writing skills are particularly important because messages today travel more rapidly, more often, and to greater numbers of people than ever before. In today's demanding workplace you can expect to be a knowledge worker; that is, you will deal with words, figures, and data. You must learn to think critically and develop opinions backed by reasons and evidence. Because technologies and procedures are constantly evolving, you must be flexible and willing to engage in lifelong learning. You should expect to take charge of your career as you work for multiple employers. The most important foundation skill for knowledge workers is the ability to communicate. You can improve your skills by studying the principles, processes, and products of communication provided in this book and in this course.

2 Recognize significant trends in today's dynamic workplace and how these trends increase the need for excellent communication skills. The workplace is undergoing profound changes, such as the emergence of heightened global competition; flattened management hierarchies; expanded team-based management; innovative communication technologies; "anytime, anywhere" offices; an increasingly diverse workforce; and a renewed emphasis on ethics. Nearly all of these changes require that businesspeople have strong communication skills to be able to make decisions, exchange information, stay connected with remote colleagues, and meet ethics and accountability requirements.

Are you ready? Get more practice at **www.meguffey.com**

3 Analyze the process of communication and understand how to use it effectively. The sender encodes (selects) words or symbols to express an idea. The message is sent verbally over a channel (such as an e-mail, letter, or telephone call) or is expressed nonverbally, perhaps with gestures or body language. "Noise"—such as loud sounds, misspelled words, or other distractions—may interfere with the transmission. The receiver decodes (interprets) the message and attempts to make sense of it. The receiver responds with feedback, informing the sender of the effectiveness of the message. The objective of communication is the transmission of meaning so that a receiver understands a message as intended by the sender.

4 Recognize barriers to interpersonal communication and examine specific strategies for overcoming those barriers. *Bypassing* causes miscommunication because people have different meanings for the words they use. One's *frame of reference* creates a filter through which all ideas are screened, sometimes causing distortion and lack of objectivity. *Weak language skills* as well as *poor listening skills* impair communication efforts. *Emotional interference*—joy, fear, anger, and so forth—hampers the sending and receiving of messages. *Physical distractions*—noisy surroundings, faulty acoustics, and so forth—can disrupt oral communication. Multitasking, information overload, and being constantly available digitally also make it difficult to focus. You can reduce or overcome many interpersonal communication barriers if you (a) realize that the communication process is imperfect, (b) adapt your message to the receiver, (c) improve your language and listening skills, (d) question your preconceptions, (e) plan for feedback, (f) focus on what is important, and (g) shut out interruptions.

5 Understand the internal and external functions of communication in organizations as well as compare and contrast the advantages and disadvantages of oral and written communication. Internal functions of communication include issuing and clarifying procedures and policies, informing management of progress, persuading others to make changes or improvements, and interacting with employees. External functions of communication include answering inquiries about products or services, persuading customers to buy products or services, clarifying supplier specifications, and so forth. Oral communication provides immediate feedback, can be adjusted to receivers, can be delivered quickly, supplies nonverbal cues, may create a warm feeling, and can be forceful. Written communication creates a permanent record, is convenient to distribute, may be economical, promotes comprehension and recall, allows precise and uniform expression, and gives receivers flexibility in what and how to receive the content.

6 Examine critically the flow of communication in organizations, and understand how to overcome typical barriers and respond ethically to office gossip. Formal channels of communication follow an organization's hierarchy of command. Information flows downward from management to workers. Long lines of communication tend to distort information. Many organizations are improving the downward flow of communication through newsletters, announcements, meetings, videos, and company intranets. Information flows upward from employees to management, thus providing vital feedback for decision makers. Obstacles include mistrust, fear of reprisal for honest communication, lack of adequate communication skills, and differing frames of reference. To improve upward flow, companies are improving relations with staff, offering incentive programs that encourage employees to share valuable feedback, and investing in communication training programs. Horizontal communication occurs among workers at the same level. Obstacles include poor communication skills, prejudice, ego involvement, competition, and turf wars. Techniques for overcoming the obstacles include (a) training employees in communication and teamwork techniques, (b) establishing reward systems, and (c) encouraging full participation in team functions. Informal channels of communication, such as the grapevine, deliver unofficial news—both personal and organizational—among friends and coworkers. Smart communicators avoid office gossip.

7 Analyze ethics in the workplace, understand the goals of ethical business communicators, recognize and avoid ethical traps, and apply tools for doing the right thing. Because many blamed the recent economic recession on a lapse in ethics, business organizations and schools are increasing programs to encourage an ethical culture. The goals of ethical business communicators include abiding by the law, telling the truth, labeling opinions, being objective, communicating clearly, using inclusive language, and giving credit. Obstacles to ethical decision making include the false necessity trap, the doctrine-of-relative-filth trap, the rationalization trap, the self-deception trap, and the ends-justify-the means trap. When faced with a difficult decision, the following questions serve as valuable tools in guiding you to do the right thing: (a) Is the action you are considering legal? (b) How would you see the problem if you were on the opposite side? (c) What are alternate solutions? (d) Can you discuss the problem with someone whose advice you trust? (e) How would you feel if your family, friends, employer, or coworkers learned of your action?

Chapter Review

1. What does the expression *communication skills* include? (Obj. 1)
2. In today's workplace can you expect to be exercising more or less control of your career? Why? (Obj. 1)
3. Who are knowledge workers? Why are they hired? (Obj. 1)
4. Fewer layers of management mean greater communication challenges for frontline workers. Why? (Obj. 2)
5. What technologies enable workers to have "anytime, anywhere" offices? (Obj. 2)
6. What are the five steps in the communication process? (Obj. 3)
7. How can business communicators overcome some of the inevitable barriers in the communication process? (Obj. 4)
8. What are the three main functions of organizational communication? (Obj. 5)
9. Why is oral communication considered more effective than written communication? Why doesn't everyone use it exclusively? (Obj. 5)
10. Why is written communication important in business, and why doesn't everyone use it exclusively? (Obj. 5)
11. Compare formal and informal channels of communication within organizations. Which is more valuable to employees? (Obj. 6)
12. Who is generally involved and what information is typically carried in downward, upward, and horizontal communication channels? (Obj. 6)
13. How can you control or respond ethically to office gossip? (Obj. 7)
14. What are seven goals of ethical business communicators? (Obj. 7)
15. When you are faced with a difficult ethical decision, what questions should you ask yourself? (Obj. 7)

Critical Thinking

1. Communication skills are frequently listed among the desired qualifications for job candidates. What do these skills consist of? How would you rate your skills? (Obj. 1)
2. Recall a time when you experienced a problem as a result of poor communication. What were the causes of and possible remedies for the problem? (Objs. 3, 4)
3. Critics complain that e-mail is reducing the amount of face-to-face communication at work and that this is bad for business. Do you agree or disagree? (Objs. 3–5)
4. How are the rules of ethical behavior that govern businesses different from those that govern personal behavior? (Obj. 7)
5. **Ethical Issue:** Josh in the Accounting Department tells you that he heard from a reliable source that 15 percent of the staff will be released within 120 days. You would love to share this juicy news with other department members, for their own defense and planning. Should you? Why or why not?

Activities

1.1 Online Communication Skills Assessment: How Do You Rate? (Objs. 1–3)

Web

This course can help you dramatically improve your business communication skills. How much do you need to improve? This assessment exercise enables you to evaluate your skills with specific standards in four critical communication skill areas: writing, reading, speaking, and listening. How well you communicate will be an important factor in your future career—particularly if you are promoted into management, as many college graduates are.

Your Task. Either here or online at **www.meguffey.com**, select a number from 1 (indicating low ability) to 5 (indicating high ability) that best reflects your perception of yourself. Be honest in rating yourself. Think about how others would rate you. When you finish, see a rating of your skills. Complete this assessment online to see your results automatically!

Writing Skills	**Low High**
1. Possess basic spelling, grammar, and punctuation skills	1 2 3 4 5
2. Am familiar with proper e-mail, memo, letter, and report formats for business documents	1 2 3 4 5
3. Can analyze a writing problem and quickly outline a plan for solving the problem	1 2 3 4 5
4. Am able to organize data coherently and logically	1 2 3 4 5
5. Can evaluate a document to determine its probable success	1 2 3 4 5

Reading Skills	**Low High**
1. Am familiar with specialized vocabulary in my field as well as general vocabulary	1 2 3 4 5
2. Can concentrate despite distractions	1 2 3 4 5
3. Am willing to look up definitions whenever necessary	1 2 3 4 5

4. Am able to move from recreational to serious reading — 1 2 3 4 5
5. Can read and comprehend college-level material — 1 2 3 4 5

Speaking Skills	**Low High**
1. Feel at ease in speaking with friends	1 2 3 4 5
2. Feel at ease in speaking before a group of people	1 2 3 4 5
3. Can adapt my presentation to the audience	1 2 3 4 5
4. Am confident in pronouncing and using words correctly	1 2 3 4 5
5. Sense that I have credibility when I make a presentation	1 2 3 4 5

Listening Skills	**Low High**
1. Spend at least half the time listening during conversations	1 2 3 4 5
2. Am able to concentrate on a speaker's words despite distractions	1 2 3 4 5
3. Can summarize a speaker's ideas and anticipate what's coming during pauses	1 2 3 4 5
4. Provide proper feedback such as nodding, paraphrasing, and asking questions	1 2 3 4 5
5. Listen with the expectation of gaining new ideas and information	1 2 3 4 5

Total your score in each section. How do you rate?

22–24	Excellent! You have indicated that you have exceptional communication skills.
18–21	Your score is above average, but you could improve your skills.
14–17	Your score suggests that you have much room for improvement.
10–13	You recognize that you need serious study, practice, and follow-up reinforcement.

Where are you strongest and weakest? Are you satisfied with your present skills? The first step to improvement is recognition of a need. The second step is making a commitment to improve. The third step is following through, and this course will help you do that.

1.2 Collaborating on the Opening Case Study (Objs. 1–5)

Team | Web

Each chapter contains a three-part case study of a well-known company. To help you develop collaboration and speaking skills as well as to learn about the target company and apply the chapter concepts, your instructor may ask you to do the following.

Your Task. Individually or as part of a three-student team during your course, work on one of the 16 case studies in the textbook. Answer the questions posed in all parts of the case study, look for additional information in articles or on Web sites, complete the application assignment, and then make a five- to ten-minute presentation to the class with your findings and reactions.

1.3 Getting to Know You (Objs. 1, 2)

E-mail

Your instructor wants to know more about you, your motivation for taking this course, your career goals, and your writing skills.

Your Task. Send an e-mail or write a memo of introduction to your instructor. See Appendix B for memo formats and Chapters 7 and 8 for tips on preparing an e-mail message. In your message include the following:

a. Your reasons for taking this class
b. Your career goals (both temporary and long-term)
c. A brief description of your employment, if any, and your favorite activities
d. An assessment and discussion of your current communication skills, including your strengths and weaknesses

1.4 Small-Group Presentation: Getting to Know Each Other (Objs. 1, 2)

Team

Many business organizations today use teams to accomplish their goals. To help you develop speaking, listening, and teamwork skills, your instructor may assign team projects. One of the first jobs in any team is selecting members and becoming acquainted.

Your Task. Your instructor will divide your class into small groups or teams. At your instructor's direction, either (a) interview another group member and introduce that person to the group or (b) introduce yourself to the group. Think of this as an informal interview for a team assignment or for a job. You will want to make notes from which to speak. Your introduction should include information such as the following:

a. Where did you grow up?
b. What work and extracurricular activities have you engaged in?
c. What are your interests and talents? What are you good at doing?
d. What have you achieved?
e. How familiar are you with various computer technologies?
f. What are your professional and personal goals? Where do you expect to be five years from now?

To develop listening skills, team members should practice good listening techniques (see Chapter 2) and take notes. They should be prepared to discuss three important facts as well as remember details about each speaker.

1.5 Communication Skills: What Do Employers Want? (Obj. 1)

Team | Web

What do employers request when they list job openings in your field?

Your Task. Individually or in teams, check the listings at an online job board such as Monster, College Recruiter, Career Builder, or CollegeGrad. Use your favorite search engine to locate their sites. Follow the instructions to search job categories and locations. Also check college resources and local newspaper listings of job openings. Find five or more job listings in your field. If possible, print the results of your search. If you cannot print, make notes on what you find. Examine the skills requested. How often do the ads mention communication, teamwork, and computer skills? What tasks do the ads mention? Discuss your findings with your team members. Prepare a list of the most frequently requested skills. Your instructor may ask you to submit your findings and/or report to the class.

1.6 Language Skills: Who Me? I Won't Need to Write on the Job.

Some job candidates experience a disconnect between what they expect to be doing in their career fields and what they actually will do.

Your Task. In teams or in class, discuss the accuracy of the following statements. Are they myths or facts?

a. No one really writes anymore. They just text and send e-mails.
b. Because I'm in a technical field, I will work with numbers, not words.
c. Secretaries will clean up my writing problems.
d. Technical writers do most of the real writing on the job.
e. Today's sophisticated software programs can fix any of my writing mistakes.
f. I can use form letters for most messages.

1.7 Customer Service: Tech Skills Not Enough (Obj. 1–3)

Team

"One misspelled word and customers begin to doubt the validity of the information they are getting," warned Mary Jo Lichtenberg, former director of training, quality, and career development at CompUSA, in Plano, Texas. One of her big problems was training service agents with weak language skills. "Just because agents understand technically how to troubleshoot computers or pieces of software and can walk customers through solutions extremely well over the telephone doesn't mean they can do the same in writing," she complained. "The skill set for phone does not necessarily translate to the skill set needed for writing e-mail."[57] As more customers choose e-mail and Web chat sessions to obtain service and support, numerous service reps are finding it necessary to brush up their writing skills.

Your Task. In teams, discuss what communication skills are necessary for customer service agents troubleshooting computer and software problems as well as other companies offering chat and e-mail support. How are the skill sets different for answering phones and for writing e-mail responses? What suggestions could you make to a trainer preparing customer service reps for chat and e-mail responses?

1.8 Communication Process: Avoiding Misunderstandings (Objs. 3, 4)

Communication is not successful unless the receiver understands the message as the sender meant it.

Your Task. Analyze the following examples of communication failures. What went wrong?

a. David Brooks ran a family business selling T-shirts to young people at athletic events. To get permission to sell at an event in Louisiana, he spoke to a tournament committee member, who said the committee wasn't "concerned." Delighted, he began to make travel and staffing plans. In a follow-up call, however, he learned that "not concerned" to this committee member means "not enthusiastic."[58]

b. The editor of Salt Lake City's *Deseret News* told his staff to "change the picture" of film icon James Dean, who had a cigarette dangling from his lips. The staff thought that the editor wanted the cigarette digitally removed from the picture, which they did. When published, the altered picture drew considerable criticism. The editor later explained that he had expected the staff to find a new picture.

c. Team leader Tyson said to team member Alicia, "I could really use your help in answering these customer inquiries." Later Alicia was resentful when she found that he expected her to answer all the inquiries herself.

d. A supervisor issued the following announcement: "Effective immediately the charge for copying services in Repro will be raised 5 to 8 cents each." Receivers scratched their heads.

e. A China Airways flight, operating in zero visibility, crashed into the side of a mountain shortly after takeoff. The pilot's last words were "What does *pull up* mean?"

f. Skiers in an Austrian hotel saw the following sign in English: "Not to perambulate the corridors in the hours of repose in the boots of ascension."

g. The following statements actually appeared in letters of application for an advertised job opening. One applicant wrote, "Enclosed is my résumé in response to Sunday's New York Times." Another wrote, "Enclosed is my résumé in response to my search for an editorial/creative position." Still another wrote, "My experience in the production of newsletters, magazines, directories, and online data bases puts me head and shoulders above the crowd of applicants you have no doubtedly been inundated with."

1.9 Miscommunication in Organizations: Understanding the Boss (Objs. 3–6)

Team

Sales representative Tim Perez was underperforming. However, the vice president was unaware of this. At a busy sales reception where all of the sales reps were milling about, the CEO pulled the vice president aside and said, "Why is Perez still a sales rep?" The vice president assumed the CEO wanted Perez promoted. Unwilling to question the CEO, the vice president soon thereafter sent down orders to promote Perez. Later, when the CEO learned what had happened, he "came out of his chair like a Saturn rocket." He meant to say, "Why is that guy still on the payroll?"[59]

Your Task. In teams, discuss the factors contributing to this miscommunication. What went wrong in the process of communication? What role did feedback play?

1.10 Differing Frames of Reference: E-Mail Cross-Cultural Misunderstanding (Obj. 4)

Intercultural

A cultural misunderstanding nearly derailed an Indo-Japanese bridge-building project. An Indian firm sent a detailed list of technical questions to its Japanese counterpart. The Indian engineers panicked when they received no reply. They wondered what had happened. Was the deal off? A week later, the Japanese engineers responded. Unlike in India or in the United States, the Japanese encourage input from everyone involved in a project. The queries probably went to the heads of various departments so that a complete picture could be presented in the response. In the United States and in India, businesspeople expect an immediate response of some sort from e-mails.[60]

Your Task. Discuss how differing frames of reference affected this misunderstanding. How could such misunderstandings be averted?

1.11 Document for Analysis: Barriers to Communication (Objs. 3–5)

Note: All Documents for Analysis are provided at **www.meguffey.com** for you to download and revise.

The following memo is from an exasperated manager to her staff. Obviously, this manager has no secretary to clean up her writing.

Your Task. Comment on the memo's effectiveness, tone, and potential barriers to communication. Your instructor may ask you to revise the memo, improving its tone, grammar, and organization.

DATE: Current
TO: All Employees
FROM: Albertina Sindaha, Operations Manager
SUBJECT: Cleanup!

You were all suppose to clean up your work areas last Friday, but that didn't happen. A few people cleaned their desks, but no one pitched in to clean the common areas.

So we're going to try again. As you know, we don't have a big enough custodial budget anymore. Everyone must clean up himself. This Friday I want to see action in the copy machine area, things like emptying waste baskets and you should organize paper and toner supplies. The lunch room is a disaster area. You must do something about the counters, the refrigerator, the sinks, and the coffee machine. And any food left in the refrigerator on Friday afternoon should be thrown out because it stinks by Monday. Finally, the office supply shelves should be straightened.

If you can't do a better job this Friday, I will have to make a cleaning schedule. Which I don't want to do. But you may force me to.

Are you ready? Get more practice at **www.meguffey.com**

1.12 Oral or Written Communication: Which Channel Is Better? (Obj. 5)

Should the following messages be communicated orally or in writing? Explain the advantages and disadvantages of each.

a. At the request of the marketing manager, Roxanne has collected information about scheduling a promotional meeting for prospective customers at a hotel. How should she deliver her findings?
b. Richard, the information technology vice president, must tell employees about a new company blogging policy. He has two employees in mind who particularly need this information.
c. As soon as possible, you need to learn from Carolyn in Document Imaging whether she can make copies of a set of engineering blueprints. If she cannot, you need her advice on where you can get it done.
d. As a manager in human resources, you must terminate three employees in a company-wide initiative to reduce costs.
e. It wasn't your fault, but an order for printed checks for a longtime customer was mishandled. The checks are not ready, and the customer is mad.
f. As chairman of the employee benefits committee, you have worked with your committee for two months evaluating several health plan options. You are now ready to convey the recommendations of the committee to management.

1.13 Information Flow: What's Good and Bad About Gossip at Work? (Obj. 6)

Team

Jon Bender, a managing partner at PrincetonOne, an executive search firm, was surprised to receive a nasty, gossipy e-mail about himself. He was obviously not the intended receiver. Instead of shooting back an equally incendiary message, he decided to talk with the sender. He said, "You're upset. Let's talk about it, but it's not appropriate in an e-mail."[61]

Your Task. In groups, discuss Mr. Bender's response to gossip about himself. Did he do the right thing? How would you have reacted? Although gossip is generally considered unacceptable and a negative force, it can be a tool for managers and employees. Make a list of at least four benefits and four negative consequences of workplace gossip. Be prepared to explain and defend each item.

1.14 Workplace Ethics: Where Do You Stand? (Obj. 7)

Ethics

How do your ethics compare with those of workers across the country?

Your Task. Answer *yes* or *no* to each item in the following *The Wall Street Journal* workplace ethics quiz.[62] Be prepared to explain and defend your responses in class. At the end of this chapter you can see how others responded to this quiz.

1. Is it wrong to use company e-mail for personal reasons?
2. Is it wrong to use office equipment to help your children or spouse do schoolwork?
3. Is it wrong to play computer games on office equipment during the workday?
4. Is it wrong to use office equipment to do Internet shopping?
5. Is it unethical to blame an error you made on a technological glitch?
6. Is it unethical to visit pornographic Web sites using office equipment?
7. Is a $50 gift to a boss unacceptable?
8. Is a $50 gift FROM the boss unacceptable?
9. Is it OK to take a $200 pair of football tickets from a supplier?
10. Is it OK to accept a $75 prize won at a raffle at a supplier's conference?

1.15 Ethical Dilemmas: Applying Tools for Doing the Right Thing (Obj. 7)

Ethics

As a business communicator, you may face various ethical dilemmas in your career. Many factors can determine your choice of an action to take.

Your Task. Study the seven dilemmas appearing on pages 25–26 [e-mail, customer letter, progress report, etc.]. Select four of them and apply the tools for doing the right thing on page 29 in choosing an appropriate action. In a memo to your instructor or in a team discussion, explain the action you would take for each dilemma. Analyze your response to each question (Is the action you are considering legal? How would you see the problem if you were on the opposite side? And so forth).

1.16 Ethics: Rival Chicken Chains Tempt Ethics in Taste Test (Obj. 7)

Ethics

Kentucky Fried Chicken (KFC) is best known for its fried chicken. Right? Recently, however, it has become more health conscious and launched a new product—grilled chicken. In doing so, it ruffled the feathers of chicken rival, El Pollo Loco, a fast-food chain in Western states. For years El Pollo Loco has staked out the "healthful chicken" territory by claiming that its grilling technique offers a delicious and wholesome alternative to traditional fast food. "Marinated in a special blend of herbs, spices, and fruit juices and then flame-broiled over an open grill right before your eyes," El Pollo's chicken is both "healthful and great tasting."[63]

After KFC rolled out its Kentucky grilled chicken campaign, El Pollo Loco CEO Steve Carley challenged KFC to a taste test. Fast-food chicken lovers could call an 800 number to say whether they preferred the taste of KFC to El Pollo Loco grilled chicken. The 800-number taste test was sponsored by El Pollo Loco.[64]

Your Task. Assume you work for KFC, and you are convinced that your new grilled chicken tastes great. In fact, you think that its blend of secret spices makes it far superior to El Pollo Loco's citrus-marinated grilled chicken. One of your KFC coworkers feels the same way and urges you to join him and other KFC employees in calling the El Pollo 800 number to register your preference. You didn't hear about any restrictions regarding who could enter the taste test. Should you call? Apply the tools for doing the right thing that you studied in this chapter. Be prepared to defend your position in a team or class discussion.

Video Resources

Two exciting sets of videos accompany *Business Communication: Process and Product*, 7e. These short videos take you beyond the classroom to help build the communication skills you will need to succeed in today's rapidly changing workplace.

Video Library 1, *Building Workplace Skills,* presents eight videos that introduce and reinforce concepts in selected chapters. These tools ease the learning load by demonstrating chapter-specific material to strengthen your comprehension and retention of key ideas. Each video ends with critical thinking questions relating the video to chapter content.

Video Library 2, *Bridging the Gap,* presents six videos transporting you inside real companies such as Yahoo, ColdStone Creamery, and Hard Rock Café. These videos provide authentic contexts for you to apply new skills in structured situations aimed at bridging the gap between the classroom and the real world of work. Nearly all of these videos culminate in writing assignments.

The recommended video for this chapter is ***Communication Foundations*** from **Video Library 1**. This video provides an overview of the Chapter 1 concepts. Cliff, Jackie, Ramon, and others discuss the importance of communication skills at Integrity Investments. The film illustrates the changing workplace, flattened management hierarchies, the communication process, communication flow, ethics, listening, nonverbal communication, and other topics presented in Chapters 1–3. After you watch the video, be prepared to discuss these questions:

- How is the world of work changing?
- Why are communication skills increasingly important to your career success?
- What communication skills are most important for businesspeople today?
- What communication skills would you like to improve?

Responses to *The Wall Street Journal* Workplace Ethics Quiz in Activity 1.14.

1. Thirty-four percent said using company e-mail for personal reasons is wrong.
2. Thirty-seven percent said using office equipment to help your children or spouse do schoolwork is wrong.
3. Forty-nine percent said playing computer games at work is wrong.
4. Fifty-four percent said using office equipment to do Internet shopping is wrong.
5. Sixty-one percent said blaming your own error on faulty technology is unethical.
6. Eighty-seven percent said visiting pornographic Web sites using office equipment is unethical.
7. Thirty-five percent said making a $50 gift to a boss is unacceptable.
8. Thirty-five percent said accepting a $50 gift from the boss is unacceptable.
9. Seventy percent said accepting a $200 pair of football tickets from a supplier is unacceptable.
10. Forty percent said accepting a $75 prize won at a raffle at a supplier's conference is unacceptable.

Chat About It

In each chapter you will find five discussion questions related to the chapter material. Your instructor may assign these topics for you to discuss in class, in an online chat room, or on an online discussion board. Some of the discussion topics may require outside research. You may also be asked to read and respond to postings made by your classmates.

Topic 1: Which tips and suggestions in this chapter for functioning effectively and ethically in today's workplace do you think might be the most helpful to you in your current or future career?

Topic 2: In your chosen career, what sorts of continuing education do you think you might need to stay employed or to be promoted?

Topic 3: This chapter discusses how Nike had to replace ads in its "Just Do It" campaign because the ads violated the culture of collectivist China. Can you think of another popular ad that might not work in China as well as one that might work there?

Topic 4: With so many ways to stay connected (e-mail, voice mail, text messaging, and so on) and with many people feeling overwhelmed because of this high degree of connectedness, what are some ways to give yourself a break from always being on call while still being fair to people who need to contact you?

Topic 5: Some experts believe that although computer technology is improving our lives in many ways, it might be impairing our ability to think critically by putting answers at our fingertips. What do you think?

Grammar and Mechanics C.L.U.E. Review 1

Each chapter includes an exercise based on Appendix A, Grammar and Mechanics Guide: Competent Language Usage Essentials (C.L.U.E.). This appendix is a business communicator's condensed guide to language usage, covering 50 of the most used and abused language elements. It also includes a list of frequently misspelled words as well as a list of confusing words. In the first ten chapters, each exercise will focus on a specific set of grammar/mechanics guidelines. In the last six chapters, exercises will review all the guidelines plus spelling and confusing words.

Note: In addition to the C.L.U.E. exercises in the textbook, you will find similar C.L.U.E. exercises at **www.meguffey.com** under the *Grammar/Mechanics* tab. The interactive online exercises parallel these sentences and test the same principles. However, the online exercises provide feedback and explanations.

Sentence Structure

Study sentence structure in Guides 1–3 of Appendix A beginning on page A-2. Some of the following sentences have sentence faults. On a sheet of paper, write a correct version and identify the fault and also the relevant guide. If a sentence is correct, write *C*. Avoid adding new phrases or rewriting sentences in your own words. You may need to change or delete one or more words. However, your goal is to correct the sentence with as few marks as possible. When finished, compare your responses with the key beginning on page Key-1.

1. Whether you are already working or about to enter today's workplace. Communication skills are critical to your career success.
2. Surveys of employers consistently show that communication skills are important to job success, job advertisements often request excellent oral and written communication skills.
3. Technology enables us to transmit messages more rapidly, more often, and more widely than ever before.
4. We cannot predict future jobs, however they will undoubtedly require brainpower and education.
5. Face-to-face conversations have many advantages. Even though they produce no written record and sometimes waste time.
6. A vital part of the communication process is feedback, it helps the sender know that the message was received and understood.
7. Knowledge workers must be critical thinkers they must be able to make decisions and communicate those decisions.
8. Management uses many methods to distribute information downward. Such as newsletters, announcements, meetings, videos, and company intranets.
9. Ethical companies experience less litigation, and they also receive less resentment and less government regulation.
10. You may be expected to agree to a company's code of ethics, you will also be expected to know the laws applying to your job.

CHAPTER 2

Professionalism: Team, Meeting, Listening, Nonverbal, and Etiquette Skills

OBJECTIVES

After studying this chapter, you should be able to

1. Explain the importance of professionalism, soft skills, and teamwork in today's workplace.
2. Understand how you can contribute positively to team performance, including resolving workplace conflicts, avoiding groupthink, and reaching group decisions.
3. Discuss effective techniques for planning and participating in face-to-face workplace meetings.
4. Describe effective practices and technologies for planning and participating in virtual meetings.
5. Explain and implement active listening techniques.
6. Understand how the functions and forms of nonverbal communication can help you advance your career.
7. Enhance your competitive edge by developing professionalism and business etiquette skills.

Want to do well on tests and excel in your course? Go to **www.meguffey.com** for helpful interactive resources.

- **Review the Chapter 2 PowerPoint slides to prepare for the first quiz.**

Zooming In PART 1

Teams Help FedEx Office Deliver Solutions

When you think of FedEx, you probably picture FedEx trucks with orange and purple lettering delivering overnight mail. But the shipping giant also has 1,800 FedEx Office stores across the country with about 1,900 employees who work in the Dallas–Fort Worth area. FedEx Office provides document solutions and business services.

Like many national and international companies, FedEx Office uses teams to compete effectively in today's challenging economy. At its FedEx Office headquarters in Dallas, Daryl Thomas, senior manager of Sales Development and Education, says that teams work well within the FedEx business model. "We have a workforce distributed all over the country in many locations. Completing projects often requires drawing people with different areas of expertise from various locations to solve problems. I focus on training, but creating solutions often means involving people from sales, marketing, and products." Encouraging people from distinct "silos" within the company to share their expertise results in cross-functional teams that are better equipped than individuals to solve complex problems.

In developing teams, Thomas uses the forming-storming-norming-performing model and talks about what happens in each of these team-building stages and what roles team members play. Teams function best when members are willing to play the roles assigned to them. Thomas remembers hiring a person who was a good trainer. But his team already had a good trainer. He needed a product manager. To help the team, the new-hire learned to become a great product manager. Thomas compares this to a sports team. "You might have been a big scorer on a college basketball team. But when you got to the NBA, you were drafted by a team that already had a scoring superstar. To help the team and to gain floor time, you played the role needed by the team."

Workers in corporate American, similar to college students, sometimes resist becoming team members. They may think they can complete a task faster and better themselves. To that attitude, Thomas responds, "Get over it! In the workplace, it's not about you. It's about working together professionally to achieve long-term goals. In addition, if you do it all yourself, you may become the only person who can do it, and others check out and walk away. You have not helped others to grow."[1]

© AP Images/Jeff Chiu

Critical Thinking

- In what ways do employee work teams benefit organizations?
- Compare and contrast student and corporate work teams. In what ways are they similar and different?
- How could you make a positive contribution to a school or work team?

http://www.fedex.com

Becoming a Team Player in Professional Groups

LEARNING OBJECTIVE 1

Explain the importance of professionalism, soft skills, and teamwork in today's workplace.

FedEx Office is one of many companies with high expectations of employees. It expects employees to work in teams and interact professionally. Similarly, most businesses seek a workforce that gets along and delivers positive results that enhance profits and boost a company's image. As a budding business professional, you have a stake in acquiring skills that will make you a strong job applicant and a valuable employee.

What Do Employers Want?

What is the difference between hard and soft skills?

When you look for a job, employers typically want to know about four key areas: education, experience, hard skills, and soft skills. Hard skills refer to the technical skills in your field. Soft skills, however, are increasingly important in our knowledge-based economy. These include both oral and written communication skills, which you learned about in Chapter 1. Soft skills also include other competencies such as listening proficiency, nonverbal behavior, and proper business etiquette. Employers also want team players who can work together efficiently and productively. They want managers and employees who are comfortable with diverse coworkers, who can listen actively to customers and colleagues, who can make eye contact, who display good workplace manners, and who are able to work in teams. These skills are immensely important not only to be hired but also to be promoted.

Hiring managers naturally expect you to have technical expertise in your field. Such skills and a good résumé may get you in the door. However, your long-term success is most influenced by your ability to communicate with your boss, coworkers, and customers as well as your ability to work as an effective and contributing team member. Even in technical fields such as accounting and finance, employers are looking for soft skills. Based on a survey of international accounting executives, researchers concluded that "the future is bright for the next generation of accounting and finance professionals provided they are armed with such soft skills as the ability to communicate, deal with change, and work in a team setting."[2]

This chapter focuses on developing team, meeting, listening, nonverbal, and etiquette skills. These are some of the professional skills that employers seek in today's increasingly interconnected and competitive environments. You will learn many tips and techniques for becoming a productive team member as well as how to conduct meetings and enhance your listening, nonverbal, and etiquette skills.

Preparing to Work With Groups and Teams

As we discussed in Chapter 1, the workplace and economy are changing. In response to intense global competition, businesses are being forced to rethink and restructure their operations. They must find new and faster ways to develop advanced products and services and bring them to market efficiently and profitably.[3] Many are turning to teams to innovate, share knowledge, and solve problems. The reasoning behind this trend is that many heads are better than one.

As a result, today's workplace is teeming with teams. You might find yourself a part of a work team, project team, customer support team, supplier team, design team, planning team, functional team, or cross-functional team. You might be assigned to a committee, task force, steering group, quality control circle, flat team, hierarchical team, advisory team, action team, or some other group. All of these teams are formed to accomplish specific goals.

Why Form Groups and Teams?

Why do many organizations think that teams work better than individuals?

Businesses are constantly looking for ways to do jobs better at less cost. They are forming teams for the following reasons:

- **Better decisions.** Decisions are generally more accurate and effective because group members contribute different expertise and perspectives.

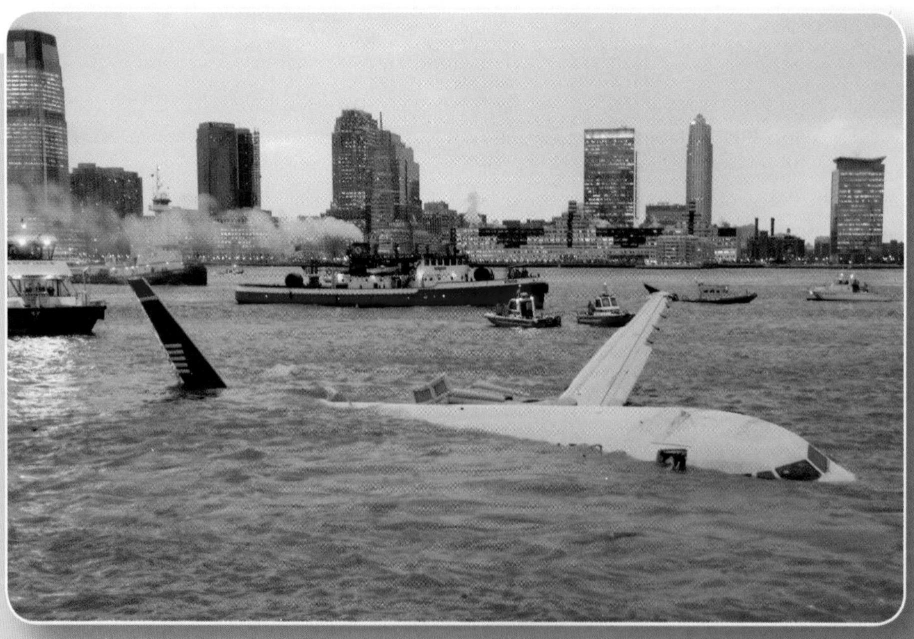

When US Airways Flight 1549 made an emergency landing in the Hudson River after a tangle with geese, rescue teams arrived in minutes to evacuate the aircraft's 155 passengers. Flight captain Chesley "Sully" Sullenberger became a national hero for skillfully ditching the Airbus A320. Crash survivors would have perished in the Hudson's frigid waters if not for the dramatic team effort of the highly trained New York City Fire Department, the NYPD, the Coast Guard, and numerous ferryboats. *What does 2009's "Miracle on the Hudson" illustrate about successful teamwork?*

- **Faster response.** When action is necessary to respond to competition or to solve a problem, small groups and teams can act rapidly.
- **Increased productivity.** Because they are often closer to the action and to the customer, team members can see opportunities for improving efficiency.
- **Greater buy-in.** Decisions arrived at jointly are usually better received because members are committed to the solution and are more willing to support it.
- **Less resistance to change.** People who have input into decisions are less hostile, aggressive, and resistant to change.
- **Improved employee morale.** Personal satisfaction and job morale increase when teams are successful.
- **Reduced risks.** Responsibility for a decision is diffused, thus carrying less risk for any individual.

Are teams always effective? What can go wrong?

Despite the current popularity of teams, however, they are not a panacea for all workplace problems. Some critics complain that they are just another management fad. Others charge that teams are a screen behind which management intensifies its control over labor.[4] Some time ago companies such as Ford, Levi-Strauss, Honda, and GM's Saturn plant retreated from teams, finding that they slowed decision making, shielded workers from responsibility, and created morale and productivity problems.[5] More recently Harvard professor and team expert J. Richard Hackman claims that research "consistently shows that teams underperform despite all their extra resources."[6] However, in most models of future organizations, teams—not individuals—function as the primary performance unit. In fact, many organizations evaluate managers on how well they develop teamwork among their employees. At Cisco Systems, the leading maker of computer networking equipment, managers who earn high marks for teamwork efforts can expect bonuses of as much as 20 percent annually.[7]

Examples of Effective Teams

Teams can be effective in solving problems and in developing new products. Take, for example, the creation of Red Baron's Stuffed Pizza Slices. Featuring a one-of-a-kind triangular, vented design, the product delivers taste, convenience, and style. But coming up with an innovative new hit required a cross-functional team with representatives from product development, packaging, purchasing, and operations. The entire team worked to shape an idea into a hit product using existing machinery.[8]

What is a virtual team, and how do members stay connected?

German auto manufacturer BMW likes to "throw together" designers, engineers, and marketing experts to work intensively on a team project. Ten team members, for example, working in an old bank building in London, collaborated on the redesign of the Rolls-Royce Phantom. The result was a best-selling superluxury automobile that remained true to the Rolls heritage. But the new model had twenty-first-century lines with BMW's technological muscle under the hood.[9]

The *Democrat*, the only newspaper in Tallahassee, Florida, found that its advertisements were riddled with errors. In one instance, a sloppy ad arrived by fax. It was unreadable, looking as if a rat had crossed the page. However, it found its way into print even after passing through the hands of seven employees. No one felt responsible for making it right. They just passed it along. The editor decided to appoint a special team of workers charged with eliminating all errors in advertisements. It took the name ELITE, standing for "ELIminate The Errors." A year later, under ELITE's leadership, advertising accuracy was greatly improved. It reached 99 percent and stayed there.[10]

Virtual Teams

The days when you could expect to work with a colleague who sat near you are long gone. Today you can look forward to collaborating with fellow workers in other cities and even in other countries.[11] Such collaborations are referred to as *virtual teams*. This is a group of people who work interdependently with a shared purpose across space, time, and organization boundaries using technology.[12] The lead author of this textbook, for example, works in her office in Santa Barbara, California. Her developmental editor is located in Kentucky, the copyeditor is in Vermont,

Spotlight on Communicators

© Daryl Thomas/FedEx Office

At FedEx Office, senior manager Daryl Thomas recognizes that lack of face time is a primary weakness of virtual teams. It's difficult to engage others personally when you can't shake hands, talk in the hallway, or share lunch. To overcome this obstacle, he recommends that virtual teams acknowledge their limitations and consciously strive to build relationships. If budget allows, he suggests that virtual teams begin a project with a kickoff meeting in person. If that's impossible, they can use Web conferencing software with cameras. In addition, team members can call or send e-mails asking how things are going.

the compositor is in Iowa, and the production editor and publisher are in Ohio. Important parts of the marketing team are in Singapore and Canada. Although they work in different time zones and rarely see each other, team members use e-mail and teleconferencing to exchange ideas, make decisions, and stay connected.

Virtual teams may be local or global. At Best Buy's corporate headquarters in Richfield, Minnesota, certain employees are allowed to work anywhere and anytime—as long as they successfully complete their assignments on time. They can decide how, when, and where they work.[13] Although few other organizations are engaging in such a radical restructuring of work, many workers today complete their tasks from remote locations, thus creating local virtual teams. Hyundai Motors exemplifies virtual teaming at the global level. For its vehicles, Hyundai completes engineering in Korea, research in Tokyo and Germany, styling in California, engine calibration and testing in Michigan, and heat testing in the California desert.[14] Members of its virtual teams coordinate their work and complete their tasks across time and geographic zones. As you can see, work is increasingly viewed as *what you do* rather than a place you go.

In some organizations remote coworkers may be permanent employees from the same office or may be specialists called together for temporary projects. Regardless of the assignment, virtual teams can benefit from shared views and skills. However, not all teams automatically work well together and are productive. The suggestions in the accompanying Plugged In box offer helpful strategies for avoiding pitfalls.

PLUGGED IN

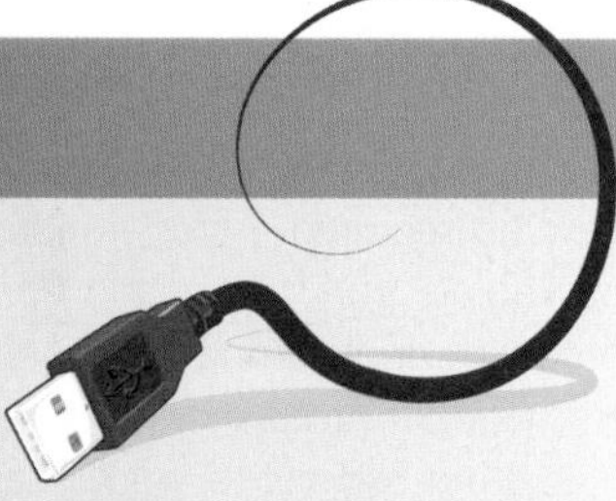

How to Form and Participate in Effective Virtual Teams

Virtual team members must overcome many obstacles not faced by groups that can meet in person. The following recommendations help members form virtual teams and interact effectively.

- **Select team members carefully.** Choose team members who are self-starters, good communicators, and experts in areas needed by the team.
- **Invest in beginnings.** If possible, meet face-to-face to work out procedures and to bond. Spending time together initially expedites reaching consensus about goals, tasks, and procedures.
- **Redefine "we."** Encourage behavior that reflects unity, such as including one another in decisions and sharing information. Consider having a team photograph taken and made into something used frequently such as a mouse pad or computer wallpaper.
- **Get the maximum benefit from technology.** Make use of speakerphones, collaborative software, e-mail, teleconferencing, videoconferencing, blogs, wikis, and instant messaging. But be sure that members are well trained in their professional use.
- **Concentrate on building credibility and trust.** Encourage team members to pay close attention to the way others perceive them. Acting consistently, fulfilling promises, considering other members' schedules, and responding promptly to e-mail and voice messages help build credibility and trust.
- **Establish responsibilities.** Identify expectations and responsibilities for each member. Make rules about e-mail response time and sharing information with all team members.
- **Keep track of information.** Capture information and decisions in a shared database, such as a wiki. Make sure all messages define expected actions, responsibilities, and time lines. Track to-do items and follow up as necessary. Expect messages to be more formal than in traditional same-time/same-place teams.
- **Avoid misinterpreting messages.** Because it is easy to misunderstand e-mail messages, be careful about responding quickly and negatively. Always take time to question your reactions.

Career Application

Why do you think increasing numbers of employees are joining virtual teams? What are the advantages and disadvantages for employees and for employers?

Four Phases of Team Development

Small groups and teams may be formed to complete single tasks or to function as permanent ongoing bodies. Regardless of their purpose, successful teams normally go through predictable phases as they develop. In this section we will discuss four phases of team development. You will learn how team members can perform positively or negatively in achieving the group's goals. You will also study the role of conflict and how to apply a six-step plan for resolving conflict.

Do teams go through the same development phases regardless of their size or purpose?

When groups are formed, they generally evolve through four phases, as identified by psychologist B. A. Tuckman: *forming, storming, norming,* and *performing.* Some groups get lucky and move quickly from forming to performing. But most struggle through disruptive, although ultimately constructive, team-building stages.

Forming. During the first stage, individuals get to know each other. They often are overly polite and feel a bit awkward. As they search for similarities and attempt to bond, they begin to develop trust in each other. Members discuss fundamental topics such as why the team is necessary, who "owns" the team, whether membership is mandatory, how large the team should be, and what talents members can contribute. A leader functions primarily as a traffic director. Groups and teams should resist the efforts of some members to dash through the first stages and race to the performing stage. Moving slowly through the stages is necessary to build a cohesive, productive unit.

Storming. During the second phase, members define their roles and responsibilities, decide how to reach their goals, and iron out the rules governing how they interact. Unfortunately, this stage often produces conflict, resulting in *storming*. A good leader, however, should step in to set limits, control the chaos, and offer suggestions. The leader will be most successful if she or he acts like a coach rather than a cop. Teams composed of dissimilar personality types may take longer to progress through the storming phase. Tempers may flare, sleep may be lost, leaders may be deposed. But most often the storm passes, and a cohesive group emerges.

Norming. Once the sun returns to the sky, teams and groups enter the *norming* stage. Tension subsides, roles are clarified, and information begins to flow among members. The group periodically checks its agenda to remind itself of its progress toward its goals. People are careful not to shake the hard-won camaraderie and formation of a single-minded purpose. Formal leadership is unnecessary because everyone takes on leadership functions. Important data are shared with the entire group, and mutual interdependence becomes typical. The group or team begins to move smoothly in one direction. Members make sure that procedures are in place to resolve future conflicts.

Performing. In Tuckman's team growth model, some groups never reach the final stage of *performing*. Problems that may cause them to fail are shown in Figure 2.1. For those that survive the first three phases, however, the final stage is gratifying. Group members have established routines and a shared language. They develop loyalty and a willingness to resolve all problems.

FIGURE 2.1 **Why Teams Fail: Typical Problems, Symptoms, and Solutions**

Problems	Symptoms	Solutions
Confused goals	People don't know what they're supposed to do.	Clarify team purpose and expected outcomes.
Mismatched needs	People with private agendas work at cross-purposes.	Get hidden agendas on the table by asking what people personally want from the team.
Unresolved roles	Team members are uncertain about what their jobs are.	Inform team members what is expected of them.
Senseless procedures	The team is at the mercy of an employee handbook from hell.	Throw away the book and develop procedures that make sense.
Bad leadership	Leader is tentative, inconsistent, or foolish.	The leader must learn to serve the team and keep its vision alive or give up the role.
Antiteam culture	The organization is not committed to the idea of teams.	Team for the right reasons or don't team at all; never force people onto a team.
Poor feedback	Performance is not being measured; team members are groping in the dark.	Create a system of free flow of useful information from all team members.

A "can-do" mentality pervades as they progress toward their goal. Fights are clean, and members continue working together without grudges. Best of all, information flows freely, deadlines are met, and production exceeds expectations.

Analyzing Positive and Negative Team Behavior

LEARNING OBJECTIVE 2

Understand how you can contribute positively to team performance, including resolving workplace conflicts, avoiding groupthink, and reaching group decisions.

Team members who are committed to achieving the group's purpose contribute by displaying positive behavior. How can you be a good team member? The most effective groups have members who are willing to establish rules and abide by them. Effective team members are able to analyze tasks and define problems so that they can work toward solutions. They offer information and try out their ideas on the group to stimulate discussion. They show interest in others' ideas by listening actively. Helpful team members also seek to involve silent members. They help to resolve differences, and they encourage a warm, supportive climate by praising and agreeing with others. When they sense that agreement is near, they review significant points and move the group toward its goal by synthesizing points of understanding.

What is negative team behavior, and have you ever experienced it on teams?

Not all groups, however, have members who contribute positively. Negative behavior is shown by those who constantly put down the ideas and suggestions of others. They insult, criticize, and aggress against others. They waste the group's time with unnecessary recounting of personal achievements or irrelevant topics. The team clown distracts the group with excessive joke-telling, inappropriate comments, and disruptive antics. Also disturbing are team members who withdraw and refuse to be drawn out. They have nothing to say, either for or against ideas being considered. To be a productive and welcome member of a group, be prepared to perform the positive tasks described in Figure 2.2 below. Avoid the negative behaviors.

Six-Step Procedure for Dealing With Conflict

How can conflict benefit teams?

Conflict is a normal part of every workplace and every team. Although the word alone is enough to make your heart begin to thump, conflict is not always negative. When managed properly, conflict can improve decision making, clarify values, increase group cohesiveness, stimulate creativity, decrease tensions, and undermine dissatisfaction. Unresolved conflict, however, can destroy productivity and seriously reduce morale. You will be better prepared to resolve workplace conflict if you are able to implement the following six-step procedure for dealing with conflict.[15]

1. **Listen.** To be sure you understand the problem, listen carefully. If the other person doesn't seem to be listening to you, you need to set the example and be the first to listen.
2. **Understand the other's point of view.** Once you listen, it is much easier to understand the other's position. Show your understanding by asking questions and paraphrasing. This will also verify what you think the other person means.
3. **Show a concern for the relationship.** By focusing on the problem, not the person, you can build, maintain, and even improve the relationship. Show an understanding of the other person's situation and needs. Show an overall willingness to come to an agreement.
4. **Look for common ground.** Identify your interests and help the other person identify his or her interests. Learn what you have in common, and look for a solution to which both of you can agree.

FIGURE 2.2 Positive and Negative Group Behaviors

Positive Team Behaviors	Negative Team Behaviors
Setting rules and abiding by them	Blocking the ideas and suggestions of others
Analyzing tasks and defining problems	Insulting and criticizing others
Contributing information and ideas	Wasting the group's time
Showing interest by listening actively	Making inappropriate jokes and comments
Encouraging members to participate	Failing to stay on task
Synthesizing points of agreement	Withdrawing, failing to participate

5. **Invent new problem-solving options.** Spend time identifying the interests of both sides. Then brainstorm to invent new ways to solve the problem. Be open to new options.

6. **Reach an agreement based on what is fair.** Seek to determine a standard of fairness that is acceptable to both sides. Then weigh the possible solutions, and choose the best option.

Avoiding Groupthink

Conflict is normal in team interactions, and successful teams are able to resolve it using the methods you just learned. But some teams avoid conflict. They smooth things over and in doing so may fall victim to *groupthink*. This is a term coined by theorist Irving Janis to describe faulty decision-making processes by team members who are overly eager to agree with one another. Several conditions can lead to groupthink: team members with similar backgrounds, a lack of systematic procedures, a demand for a quick decision, and a strong leader who favors a specific outcome. Symptoms of groupthink include pressure placed on any member who argues against the group's mutual beliefs, self-censorship of thoughts that stray from the group's agreement, collective efforts to rationalize, and an unquestioned belief in the group's moral authority. Teams suffering from groupthink fail to check alternatives, are biased in collecting and evaluating information, and ignore the risks of the preferred choice. They may also neglect to work out a contingency plan in case the preferred choice fails.[16]

Effective teams avoid groupthink by striving for team diversity—in age, gender, background, experience, and training. They encourage open discussion, search for relevant information, evaluate many alternatives, consider how a decision will be implemented, and plan for contingencies in case the decision doesn't work out.

Spotlight on Communicators

© Daniel Acker/Bloomberg via Getty Images

Groupthink can be a big problem or a big opportunity, says Steve Ballmer, Microsoft CEO. "If you really want to sail your ship [in] this direction, you want enough groupthink that people actually sail with you." You don't want to discourage innovative thinking or discussion of fundamental assumptions, he says. "But once you set course, you really don't want a cacophony that prevents progress."

How can teams fall into the groupthink trap?

What is the best method for reaching group decisions? Why?

Reaching Group Decisions

The way teams reach decisions greatly affects their morale and commitment, as well as the implementation of any team decision. In U.S. culture the majority usually rules, but other methods, five of which are discussed here, may be more effective. As you study these methods, think about which would be best for routine decisions and which would be best for dealing with emergencies.

- **Majority.** Group members vote and a majority wins. This method results in a quick decision but may leave an alienated minority uncommitted to implementation.
- **Consensus.** Discussion continues until all team members have aired their opinions and, ultimately, agree. This method is time-consuming; however, it produces creative, high-quality discussion and generally elicits commitment by all members to implement the decision.
- **Minority.** Typically, a subcommittee investigates and makes a recommendation for action. This method is useful when the full group cannot get together to make a decision or when time is short.
- **Averaging.** Members haggle, bargain, wheedle, and negotiate to reach a middle position, which often requires compromise. With this method, the opinions of the least knowledgeable members may cancel the opinions of the most knowledgeable.
- **Authority rule with discussion.** The leader, boss, or manager listens to team members' ideas, but the final decision is his or hers. This method encourages lively discussion and results in participatory decision making. However, team members must have good communication skills. This method also requires a leader who is willing to make decisions.

Ethics Check

Lazy Team Members, Anyone?

Teamwork is a staple in college classes today and usually works well for students and their instructors. However, occasionally a rogue member will take advantage of a group and barely collaborate. How do you deal with a student who does sloppy work, misses team meetings, and fails to respond to calls or e-mails?

Characteristics of Successful Teams

The use of teams has been called the solution to many ills in today's workplace.[17] Someone even observed that as an acronym TEAM means "Together, Everyone Achieves More."[18] Many teams, however, do not work well together. In fact, some teams can actually increase frustration,

Why are small, diverse teams likely to be more effective than large, homogeneous groups?

lower productivity, and create employee dissatisfaction. Experts who have studied team workings and decisions have discovered that effective teams share some or all of the following characteristics.

Small Size, Diverse Makeup. Teams may range from 2 to 25 members, although 4 or 5 is optimal for many projects. Larger groups have trouble interacting constructively, much less agreeing on actions.[19] For the most creative decisions, teams generally have male and female members who differ in age, ethnicity, social background, training, and experience. Members should bring complementary skills to a team. Paul Fireman, founder of sports shoe manufacturer Reebok, wisely remarked, "If you put five centers on the basketball court, you're going to lose the game. You need, we all need, people of different strengths and talents—and that means, among other things, people of different backgrounds."[20] The key business advantage of diversity is the ability to view a project and its context from multiple perspectives. Many of us tend to think that everyone in the world is like us because we know only our own experience. Teams with members from different ethnicities and cultures can look at projects beyond the limited view of one culture. Many organizations are finding that diverse teams can produce innovative solutions with broader applications than homogeneous teams can.

Agreement on Purpose. An effective team begins with a purpose. For example, when Magic Johnson Theatres developed its first movie theater, it hired a team whose sole purpose was to help the company move rapidly through the arduous state permit application process. Even the task of obtaining a license for the site's popcorn machine was surprisingly difficult.[21] Working from a general purpose to specific goals typically requires a huge investment of time and effort. Meaningful discussions, however, motivate team members to buy in to the project. When the Great Lakes Coast Guard faced the task of keeping commerce moving when the lakes and rivers froze, it brought all the stakeholders together to discuss the mission. The U.S. Coast Guard, the Canadian Coast Guard, and the maritime industry formed a partnership to clear and flush ice from the Great Lakes and connecting rivers during winter months. Agreeing on the purpose was the first step in developing a concerted team effort.

ETHICAL INSIGHT

Ethical Responsibilities of Group Members and Leaders

When people form a group or a team to achieve a purpose, they agree to give up some of their individual sovereignty for the good of the group. They become interdependent and commit to one another and to the group They become interdependent and assume responsibilities to one another and to the group. Here are important ethical responsibilities for members to follow:

- **Determine to do your best.** When you commit to the group process, you are obligated to offer your skills freely. Don't hold back, perhaps fearing that you will be repeatedly targeted because you have skills to offer. If the group project is worth doing, it is worth the best effort you can offer.
- **Decide to behave with the group's good in mind.** You may find it necessary to set aside your personal goals in favor of the group's goals. Decide to keep an open mind and to listen to evidence and arguments objectively. Strive to evaluate information carefully, even though it may contradict your own views or thwart your personal agendas.
- **Make a commitment to fair play.** Group problem solving is a cooperative, not a competitive, event. Decide that you cannot grind your private ax at the expense of the group project.
- **Expect to give and receive a fair hearing.** When you speak, others should give you a fair hearing. You have a right to expect them to listen carefully, provide you with candid feedback, strive to understand what you say, and treat your ideas seriously. Listeners do not have to agree with you, of course. However, all speakers have a right to a fair hearing.
- **Be willing to take on a participant/analyst role.** As a group member, it is your responsibility to pay attention, evaluate what is happening, analyze what you learn, and help make decisions.
- **As a leader, be ready to model appropriate team behavior.** It is a leader's responsibility to coach team members in skills and teamwork, to acknowledge achievement and effort, to share knowledge, and to periodically remind members of the team's missions and goals.

Career Application

Assume you are a member of a campus committee to organize a celebrity auction to raise funds for a local homeless shelter. Your friend Marika is committee chair, but she is carrying a heavy course load and is also working part time. As a result, she has taken no action. You call her, but she is evasive when you try to pin her down about committee plans. What should you do?

Preseason planning and daily phone conferences cemented the mission and gained buy-in from all stakeholders.[22]

Agreement on Procedures. The best teams develop procedures to guide them. They set up intermediate goals with deadlines. They assign roles and tasks, requiring all members to contribute equivalent amounts of real work. They decide how they will reach decisions using one of the strategies discussed earlier. Procedures are continually evaluated to ensure movement toward the attainment of the team's goals.

Ability to Confront Conflict. Poorly functioning teams avoid conflict, preferring sulking, gossiping, or bickering. A better plan is to acknowledge conflict and address the root of the problem openly using the six-step plan outlined earlier. Although it may feel emotionally risky, direct confrontation saves time and enhances team commitment in the long run. To be constructive, however, confrontation must be task oriented, not person oriented. An open airing of differences, in which all team members have a chance to speak their minds, should center on the strengths and weaknesses of the various positions and ideas—not on personalities. After hearing all sides, team members must negotiate a fair settlement, no matter how long it takes. Good decisions are based on consensus: all members agree.

Use of Good Communication Techniques. The best teams exchange information and contribute ideas freely in an informal environment. Team members speak clearly and concisely, avoiding generalities. They encourage feedback. Listeners become actively involved, read body language, and ask clarifying questions before responding. Tactful, constructive disagreement is encouraged. Although a team's task is taken seriously, successful teams are able to inject humor into their interactions.

Should teams behave formally and seriously to ensure maximum productivity?

Ability to Collaborate Rather Than Compete. Effective team members are genuinely interested in achieving team goals instead of receiving individual recognition. They contribute ideas and feedback unselfishly. They monitor team progress, including what's going right, what's going wrong, and what to do about it. They celebrate individual and team accomplishments.

Checklist

Developing Team Effectiveness

- **Establish small teams.** Smaller teams are thought to function more efficiently and more effectively than larger teams.
- **Encourage diversity.** Innovative teams typically include members who differ in age, gender, ethnicity, and background. Team members should possess technical expertise, problem-solving skills, and interpersonal skills.
- **Determine the purpose, procedures, and roles.** Members must understand the task at hand and what is expected of them. Teams function best when operating procedures are ironed out early and each member has a specific role.
- **Acknowledge and manage conflict.** Conflict is productive when it motivates a team to search for new ideas, increase participation, delay premature decisions, or discuss disagreements. Keep conflict centered on issues rather than on people.
- **Cultivate good communication skills.** Effective team members are willing and able to articulate ideas clearly and concisely, recognize nonverbal cues, and listen actively.
- **Advance an environment of open communication.** Teams are most productive when members trust each other and feel free to discuss all viewpoints openly in an informal atmosphere.
- **Encourage collaboration and discourage competition.** Sharing information in a cooperative effort to achieve the team purpose must be more important than competing with other members for individual achievement.
- **Share leadership.** Members with the most expertise should lead at various times during the project's evolution.
- **Create a sense of fairness in making decisions.** Effective teams resolve issues without forcing members into a win–lose situation.
- **Lighten up.** The most successful teams take their task seriously, but they are also able to laugh at themselves and interject humor to enliven team proceedings.
- **Continually assess performance.** Teams should establish checkpoints along the way to determine whether they are meeting their objectives and adjust procedures if progress is unsatisfactory.

Zooming In PART 2

Teams Help FedEx Office Deliver Solutions

Daryl Thomas, senior manager, FedEx Office Sales Development and Education, knows that meetings are most successful if they start with a purpose. Piling on two many goals for one meeting dilutes discussion and lengthens the gathering. Most important for successful meetings, says Thomas, is having a purpose and agenda that are in sync. If the topic is preparing customer training manuals that will help customers understand all the FedEx Office options, then don't also ask for an update from team members on their current projects. It's easy to wander off the meeting topic with digressions. Setting time frames on the agenda helps to structure meetings and ensure that the necessary topics are covered efficiently. Thomas cautions that each meeting should have its own goal and enough time set aside to reach that goal.

If Thomas has a project with a tight deadline and he needs an update, he pulls his team together for a 15-minute stand-up gathering. "Everyone stands and gives highlights in a round-robin approach: Here's where I am, here's what is happening, and here's what I need. It takes 15 minutes—done! We don't stop to explore specifics."

One way to reduce conflict at meetings is to be sure everyone agrees on ground rules, such as how to reach decisions. Are they made by the team leader, by majority, or when everyone agrees (consensus)? Most of us would rather not attend meetings. But they can be less tedious and more productive if they are treated professionally with an agenda and ground rules.

© AP Images/Jeff Chiu

Critical Thinking

- Why do you think workplace meetings are so disliked?
- Do you think 15-minute stand-up meetings could be effective? Why or why not?
- How can the attitude and behavior of attendees affect the success of a meeting?

Acceptance of Ethical Responsibilities. Teams as a whole have ethical responsibilities to their members, to their larger organizations, and to society. Members have a number of specific responsibilities to each other, as described in the accompanying Ethical Insights box. As a whole, teams have a responsibility to represent the organization's view and respect its privileged information. They should not discuss with outsiders any sensitive issues without permission. In addition, teams have a broader obligation to avoid advocating actions that would endanger members of society at large.

Shared Leadership. Effective teams often have no formal leader. Instead, leadership rotates to those with the appropriate expertise as the team evolves and moves from one phase to another. Many teams operate under a democratic approach. This approach can achieve buy-in to team decisions, boost morale, and create fewer hurt feelings and less resentment. In times of crisis, however, a strong team member may need to step up as leader. The checklist on page 47 summarizes effective techniques for developing successful teams.

Planning and Participating in Face-to-Face Workplace Meetings

LEARNING OBJECTIVE 3

Discuss effective techniques for planning and participating in face-to-face workplace meetings.

As you prepare to enter the workplace, you can expect to attend meetings—lots of them! Estimates suggest that workers spend from five to eight hours a week in meetings.[23] Managers spend even more time in meetings. A recent study of administrative professionals and managers in Europe and the United States revealed that managers devote nearly half of their workweeks to meetings, with the average meeting lasting nearly three hours.[24]

Meetings consist of three or more people who assemble to pool information, solicit feedback, clarify policy, seek consensus, and solve problems. However, as more and more people work separately, the character of meetings in today's workplace has changed. People are meeting regularly, but not always face-to-face. To be able to exchange information effectively and efficiently, you should know how to plan and participate in face-to-face as well as other kinds of meetings.

Making Face-to-Face Meetings More Productive

Despite their regular occurrence, meetings are almost universally disliked. Typical comments include, "We have too many of them," "They don't accomplish anything," and "What a waste of time!" One writer called them "the black holes of the workday."[25] In spite of their bad reputation, meetings are not going away. Our task, then, as business communicators is to learn how to make them more efficient, satisfying, and productive. The following suggestions will be especially helpful in face-to-face meeting, but the advice frequently applies to virtual meetings as well.

Although meetings are disliked, they serve an important purpose for you. They represent opportunities. Because meetings are a prime tool for developing staff, they are career-critical. "If you can't orchestrate a meeting, you're of little use to the corporation," said Morris Schechtman, head of a leadership training firm.[26] *The Wall Street Journal* concurred: "The inability to run effective meetings can torpedo a career."[27] Why are meetings so important to your career? At meetings, judgments are formed and careers are made. Therefore, instead of treating them as thieves of your valuable time, try to see them as golden opportunities to demonstrate your leadership, communication, and problem-solving skills. So that you can make the most of these opportunities, here are techniques for planning and conducting successful meetings.

Spotlight on Communicators

"As a general rule, meetings make individuals perform below their capacity and skill levels," asserts University of Chicago behavioral scientist Reid Hastie. In addition, he believes that every organization has too many meetings and too many poorly designed ones. The solution, he says, is to fix responsibility. Whoever calls a meeting should be explicit about its objectives and its time limit. Afterwards, participants assign credit or blame to the person in charge. If people repeatedly lead unproductive meetings, Hastie suggests replacing them with more effective leaders.

How can meetings be important to your career advancement?

Deciding Whether a Meeting Is Necessary. No meeting should be called unless the topic is important, can't wait, and requires an exchange of ideas. If the flow of information is strictly one way and no immediate feedback will result, then don't schedule a meeting. For example, if people are merely being advised or informed, send an e-mail, text message, memo, or letter. Leave a telephone or voice mail message, but don't call a costly meeting. Remember, the real expense of a meeting is the lost productivity of all the people attending. To decide whether the purpose of the meeting is valid, consult the key people who will be attending. Ask them what outcomes are desired and how to achieve those goals. This consultation also sets a collaborative tone and encourages full participation.

When should meetings be called?

Selecting Participants. The number of meeting participants is determined by the purpose of the meeting, as shown in Figure 2.3. If the meeting purpose is motivational, such as an awards ceremony for sales reps of cosmetics giant Avon, then the number of participants is unlimited. But to make decisions, according to studies at 3M Corporation, the best number is five or fewer participants.[28] Ideally, those attending should be people who will make the decision and people with information necessary to make the decision. Also attending should be people who will be responsible for implementing the decision and representatives of groups who will benefit from the decision. Let's say, for example, that the CEO of sportswear manufacturer Timberland is strongly committed to community service. He wants his company to participate more fully in community service. So he might meet with managers, employee representatives, and community leaders to decide how his employees could volunteer to refurbish a school, build affordable housing, or volunteer at a clinic.[29]

FIGURE 2.3 Meeting Purpose and Number of Participants

Purpose	Ideal Size
Intensive problem solving	5 or fewer
Problem identification	10 or fewer
Information reviews and presentations	30 or fewer
Motivational	Unlimited

What is a meeting agenda, and when should it be distributed?

Distributing Advance Information. At least two days in advance of a meeting, distribute an agenda of topics to be discussed. Also include any reports or materials that participants should read in advance. For continuing groups, you might also include a copy of the minutes of the previous meeting. To keep meetings productive, limit the number of agenda items. Remember, the narrower the focus, the greater the chances for success. A good agenda, as illustrated in Figure 2.4, covers the following information:

- Date and place of meeting
- Start time and end time
- Brief description of each topic, in order of priority, including the names of individuals who are responsible for performing some action
- Proposed allotment of time for each topic
- Any premeeting preparation expected of participants

FIGURE 2.4 **Typical Meeting Agenda**

AGENDA

Quantum Travel International
Staff Meeting
September 4, 2011
10 to 11 a.m.
Conference Room

I. Call to order; roll call

II. Approval of agenda

III. Approval of minutes from previous meeting

	Person	Proposed Time
IV. Committee reports		
A. Web site update	Jared	5 minutes
B. Tour packages	Lakisha	10 minutes
V. Old business		
A. Equipment maintenance	John	5 minutes
B. Client escrow accounts	Alicia	5 minutes
C. Internal newsletter	Adrienne	5 minutes
VI. New business		
A. New accounts	Garth	5 minutes
B. Pricing policy for Asian tours	Minh	15 minutes

VII. Announcements

VIII. Chair's summary, adjournment

Using Digital Calendars to Schedule Meetings. Finding a time when everyone can meet is often difficult. People have busy schedules, and ping-pong telephone conversations and e-mail messages sent back and forth to find an open time can be frustrating. Fortunately, digital calendars now make the task quicker and more efficient. Two of the most popular digital calendaring programs are Google Calendar and Yahoo Calendar. Microsoft Outlook also provides a calendar program, as shown in Figure 2.5. Online calendars enable you to make appointments, schedule meetings, and keep track of daily activities. To schedule meetings, you enter a new meeting request, add the names of attendees, and check the availability of each attendee on their calendars. You select a date when all are available, enter a start and end time, and list the meeting subject and location. Then the meeting request goes to each attendee. Later you check the attendee availability tab to see a list of all meeting attendees. As the meeting time approaches, the program automatically sends reminders to attendees.

What is a digital calendar, and how can it help you schedule meetings?

Getting the Meeting Started. To avoid wasting time and irritating attendees, always start meetings on time—even if some participants are missing. Waiting for latecomers causes resentment and sets a bad precedent. For the same reasons, don't give a quick recap to anyone who arrives late. At the appointed time, open the meeting with a three- to five-minute introduction that includes the following:

- Goal and length of the meeting
- Background of topics or problems
- Possible solutions and constraints
- Tentative agenda
- Ground rules to be followed

A typical set of ground rules might include arriving on time, communicating openly, being supportive, listening carefully, participating fully, confronting conflict frankly, and following the agenda. More formal groups follow parliamentary procedures based on Robert's Rules. After establishing basic ground rules, the leader should ask if participants agree thus far. The next step is to assign one attendee to take minutes and one to act as a recorder. The recorder uses a computer and projector or stands at a flipchart or whiteboard to list the main ideas being discussed and agreements reached.

FIGURE 2.5 Using Calendar Programs

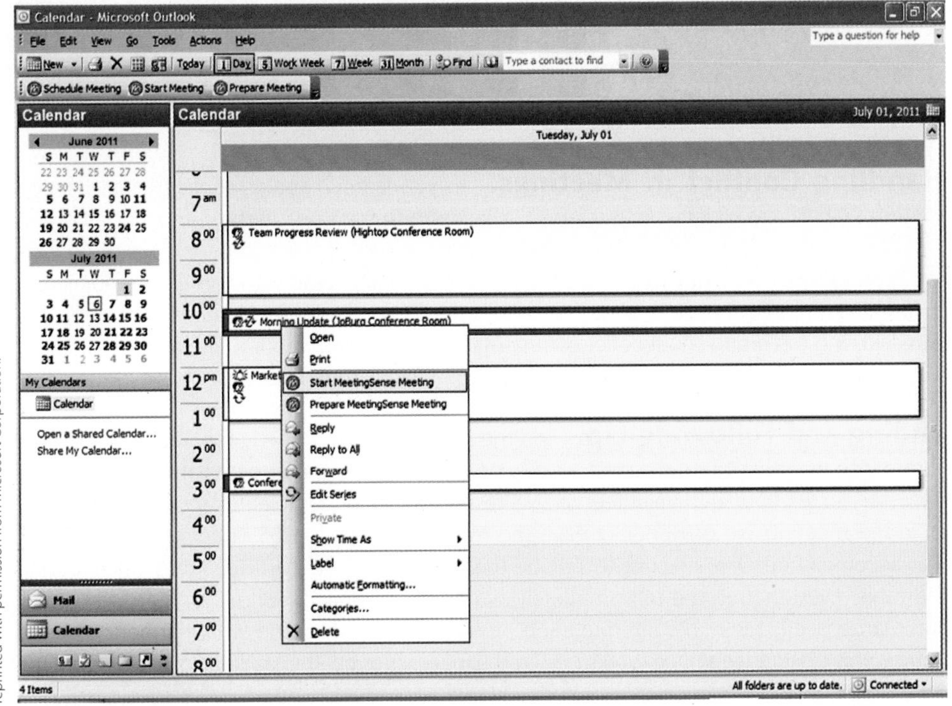

Calendar programs ease the frustration of scheduling meetings for busy people. The program allows you to check colleagues' calendars, locate a free time, schedule a meeting, send out an initial announcement, and follow up with reminders.

How can leaders prevent meetings from being sidetracked?

Moving the Meeting Along. After the preliminaries, the leader should say as little as possible. Like a talk show host, an effective leader makes "sure that each panel member gets some air time while no one member steals the show."[30] Remember that the purpose of a meeting is to exchange views, not to hear one person, even the leader, do all the talking. If the group has one member who monopolizes, the leader might say, "Thanks, Michelle, for that perspective, but please hold your next point while we hear how Ryan would respond to that." This technique also encourages quieter participants to speak up.

To avoid allowing digressions to sidetrack the group, try generating a "Parking Lot" list. This is a list of important but divergent issues that should be discussed later. Another way to handle digressions is to say, "Folks, we're drifting astray here. Please forgive me for pressing on, but let's return to the central issue of. . . ." It is important to adhere to the agenda and the time schedule. Equally important, when the group seems to have reached a consensus, is to summarize the group's position and check to see whether everyone agrees.

How can you as a participant get the most out of meetings?

Participating Actively and Productively. Meetings are an opportunity for you to showcase your abilities and boost your career. To get the most out of the meetings you attend, try these techniques:[31]

- **Arrive early.** You show respect and look well organized by arriving a little early.
- **Come prepared.** Bring the agenda and any distributed materials. Study the topics and be ready with questions, comments, and good ideas.
- **Have a positive attitude.** Use positive body language; speak energetically.
- **Contribute respectfully.** Wait your turn to speak; raise your hand to be recognized.
- **Wait for others to finish.** Show respect and good manners by not interrupting.
- **Keep your voice calm and pleasant, yet energetic.** Avoid showing anger as this focuses attention on your behavior rather than on your ideas.
- **Give credit to others.** Gain allies and enhance your credibility by recognizing others in front of peers and superiors.
- **Put the cell phone and laptop away.** Focus your attention on the meeting, not on answering e-mails or working on your computer.
- **Help summarize.** Assist the meeting leader by reviewing points you have noted.
- **Express your views IN the meeting.** Build trust by not holding postmeeting "sidebars" that involve criticism and judgments.
- **Follow up.** Send the signal that you are efficient and caring by completing the actions assigned to you.

Handling Conflict in Meetings. As you learned earlier, conflict is natural and even desirable. However, it can also cause awkwardness and uneasiness. In meetings, conflict typically develops when people feel unheard or misunderstood. If two people are in conflict, the best approach is to encourage each to make a complete case while group members give their full attention. Let each one question the other. Then, the leader should summarize what was said, and the group should offer comments. The group may modify a recommendation or suggest alternatives before reaching consensus on a direction to follow.

What tasks should be completed at the end of a meeting?

Ending and Following Up. End the meeting at the agreed time. The leader should summarize what has been decided, who is going to do what, and by what time. It may be necessary to ask people to volunteer to take responsibility for completing action items agreed to in the meeting. No one should leave the meeting without a full understanding of what was accomplished. One effective technique that encourages full participation is "once around the table." Even though the table is merely symbolic, the image works. Everyone is asked to summarize briefly his or her interpretation of what was decided and what happens next. Of course, this closure technique works best with smaller groups. The leader should conclude by

FIGURE 2.6 **E-Mail Meeting Minutes**

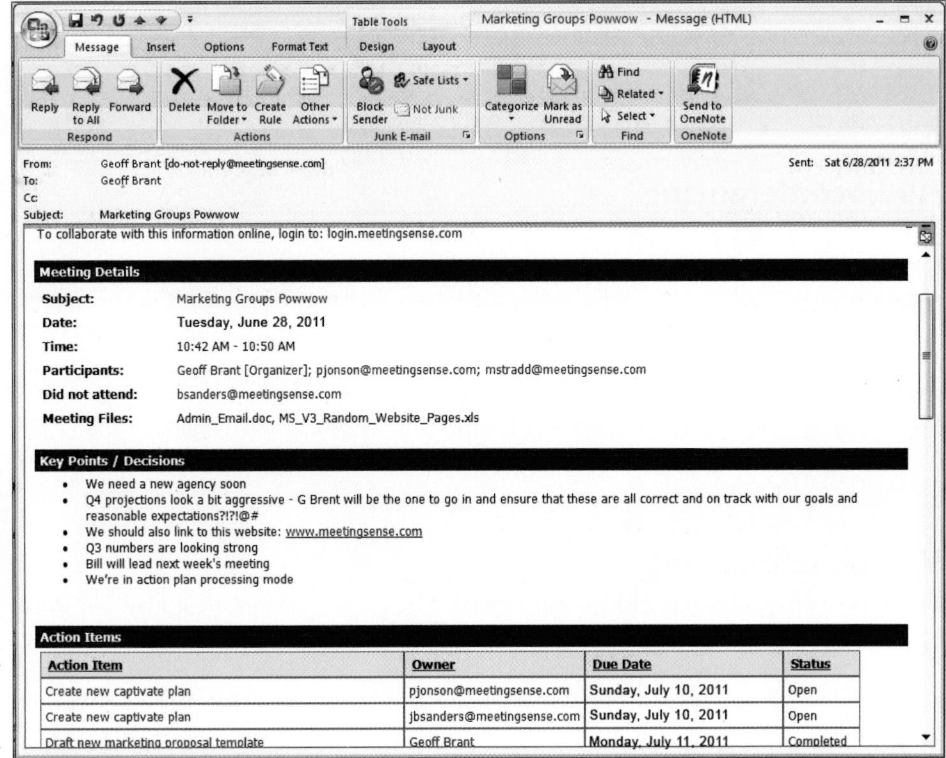

Marketing Groups Powwow - Message (HTML)

From: Geoff Brant [do-not-reply@meetingsense.com] Sent: Sat 6/28/2011 2:37 PM
To: Geoff Brant
Cc:
Subject: Marketing Groups Powwow

To collaborate with this information online, login to: login.meetingsense.com

Meeting Details

Subject: Marketing Groups Powwow
Date: Tuesday, June 28, 2011
Time: 10:42 AM - 10:50 AM
Participants: Geoff Brant [Organizer]; pjonson@meetingsense.com; mstradd@meetingsense.com
Did not attend: bsanders@meetingsense.com
Meeting Files: Admin_Email.doc, MS_V3_Random_Website_Pages.xls

Key Points / Decisions

- We need a new agency soon
- Q4 projections look a bit aggressive - G Brent will be the one to go in and ensure that these are all correct and on track with our goals and reasonable expectations?!?!@#
- We should also link to this website: www.meetingsense.com
- Q3 numbers are looking strong
- Bill will lead next week's meeting
- We're in action plan processing mode

Action Items

Action Item	Owner	Due Date	Status
Create new captivate plan	pjonson@meetingsense.com	Sunday, July 10, 2011	Open
Create new captivate plan	jbsanders@meetingsense.com	Sunday, July 10, 2011	Open
Draft new marketing proposal template	Geoff Brant	Monday, July 11, 2011	Completed

Meeting proceedings are efficiently recorded in a summary distribution template that provides subject, date, time, participant names, absentee names, meeting files, key points, decisions, and action items.

asking the group to set a time for the next meeting. He or she should assure the group that a report will follow. Finally, the leader should thank participants for attending.

If minutes were taken, they should be distributed within a couple of days after the meeting. Software programs, such as that shown in Figure 2.6, enable you to follow a structured template that includes brief meeting minutes, key points and decisions, and action items. It is up to the leader to see that what was decided at the meeting is accomplished. The leader may need to call people to remind them of their assignments and also to volunteer to help if necessary.

Using Effective Practices and Technologies in Virtual Meetings

LEARNING OBJECTIVE 4
Describe effective practices and technologies for planning and participating in virtual meetings.

One of the major trends in today's workplace is the rise of virtual meetings instead of face-to-face meetings. *Virtual meetings* are gatherings of participants who are connected technologically. As travel costs rise and companies slash budgets, many organizations are cutting back on meetings that require travel.[32] In addition, more and more people work together but are not located in the same spot. Instead of meeting face-to-face, people have found other ways to exchange ideas, brainstorm, build consensus, and develop personal relationships. They may meet in audioconferences using telephones or in videoconferences using the Internet. Steady improvement in telecommunications networks, software, and computer processing continues to fuel the shift to virtual meetings. These meetings have many purposes, including training employees, making sales presentations, coordinating team activities, and talking to customers.

Saving travel costs and reducing employee fatigue are significant reasons for the digital displacement of business travel. For example, when Hewlett-Packard moved its inkjet cartridge manufacturing line from Oregon to a plant in Singapore, it estimated that using videoconferences saved about six months in project time. Managers also avoided 45 trans-Pacific trips.[33] In another example of changing times, Darryl Draper, a Subaru customer service training manager, formerly traveled nine months of the year. Now she does nearly all of her training online. She estimates that when traveling she reached about 100 people every six months at a cost of $300 a person. Now she reaches 2,500 people every six months at a cost of 75 cents a person.[34]

Virtual meetings are possible through the use of a number of efficient tools including audioconferencing, videoconferencing, and Web conferencing.

Why are virtual meetings becoming increasingly popular?

Audioconferencing

Among the simplest collaboration tools is *audioconferencing* (also called *teleconferencing, conference calling,* or *phone conferencing*). One or more people in a work area use an enhanced speakerphone to confer with others by telephone. To make a call, a company engages a telecommunications carrier and participants dial a given number. They enter a pass code and are admitted to a conference bridge. This kind of audioconferencing enables people at both ends to speak and be heard simultaneously. Thanks to mobile phones, people can even participate in an audioconference from an airplane or the beach. Although audioconferencing is not as glitzy as other collaboration tools, it is a mainstay in the teleconferencing industry.

Videoconferencing

If meeting participants need to see each other or share documents, they may use *videoconferencing*. This tool combines video, audio, and communications networking technologies for real-time interaction.

At the high end of videoconferencing systems are *telepresence rooms*. These specially designed conference rooms are the next best thing to being there. Telepresence rooms typically are equipped with three huge curved screens, custom lighting, and advanced acoustics. Sharper than the best high-definition television sets, images may be magnified to scrutinize even the microcircuitry on new electronic products. Multiple high-definition monitors deliver life-size images so real that the next time you see a participant, you feel as if you've met that person before, says one proponent.[35] Although the price tag may reach $350,000 per room, companies such as Cisco Systems figure it saves $100 million in yearly travel costs. What's more, Cisco's reduced travel cuts greenhouse gas emissions from travel by 10 percent.[36]

More conventional videoconference rooms may cost $5,000 to $80,000 a room. Whether using high- or low-end conferencing tools, participants do not have to journey to distant meetings. Organizations reduce travel expenses, travel time, greenhouse gases, and employee fatigue.

FIGURE 2.7 Web conferencing

High-end enterprise-level telepresence systems employ extremely high definition, multiple-screen systems with such low latency (delay) that participants can carry on conversations and read the body language of participants half way around the world. At this conference Cisco Chairman and CEO John Chambers hosts a meeting of leading industry executives to introduce a new computing system.

FIGURE 2.8 **WebEx Conferencing on iPhone**

Simultaneous Web and audio-conferencing capabilities enable participants to attend meetings from remote locations using iPhones and other devices such as PDAs.

Web Conferencing

What are the advantages of Web conferencing?

Web conferencing is similar to videoconferencing but may work with or without the transmission of pictures of the participants. Attendees use their computers to access an online virtual meeting room where they can present PowerPoint slides or share spreadsheets or Word documents, just as they might do in a face-to-face meeting. Web conferencing is particularly useful for team meetings, training, and sales presentations. Participants can demonstrate products, make presentations, and interact with participants in real time.

Features of Web conferencing programs typically include slideshow presentations, live or streaming video, tours of Web sites in which users may participate, meeting recording, whiteboard with annotation capabilities, screen sharing, and text chat. GoToMeeting, a reasonably priced commercial conferencing tool, enables people to launch meetings by sending instant messages to attendees, who click on an embedded link to join the group. Participants are generally connected to a phone conference call. On their computers, attendees see the presenter's desktop and all the actions performed there—from viewing Web pages to advancing through a presentation. They participate with each other using instant messaging in a chat window. WebEx offers a richer Web conferencing tool, including whiteboarding and other advanced functions. It's even possible to participate in conferences using your iPhone or a smart phone while having breakfast on the way to work—or at the beach.

Skype, a virtually free conferencing tool popular with students and expatriates, is also used by businesspeople. It allows conferencing with or without a camera. All that is needed is a laptop or a smartphone, a headset with a microphone, and an optional Web camera. Constantly evolving, Web conferencing is changing the way businesspeople work together. Figure 2.9 shows how shoe manufacturer SideKick used Web conferencing to meet virtually and design a new athletic shoe.

Planning Virtual Meetings and Interacting Professionally

Because people are not physically together, virtual meetings and teleconferences require special awareness and planning. Although the same good meeting management techniques discussed for face-to-face meetings prevail, additional skills and practices are important. A major problem when people are not facing each other is that any small infraction or miscue can be blown out of proportion. Words and tone can be easily misinterpreted. In addition, bandwidth

FIGURE 2.9 Web Conferencing in Practice

Here's how SideKick Enterprises sets up a virtual meeting to design a new athletic shoe.

1. E-Mail Contact. Matt M., president of SideKick, a shoe company located in Los Angeles, sends an e-mail to Lisa G., chief designer at NYConcepts, located in New York, to discuss a new athletic shoe. The e-mail includes a date for the meeting and a link to launch the session.

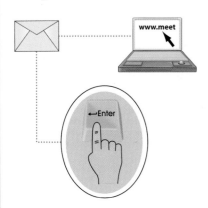

2. Virtual Meeting. When the Web conference begins, participants see live videos of each other's faces on their computer screens. They look at photos of athletic shoes, share ideas, sketch designs on a shared "virtual whiteboard," and review contract terms.

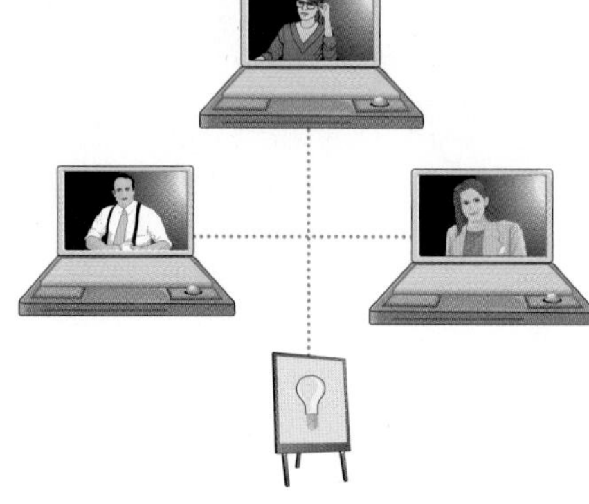

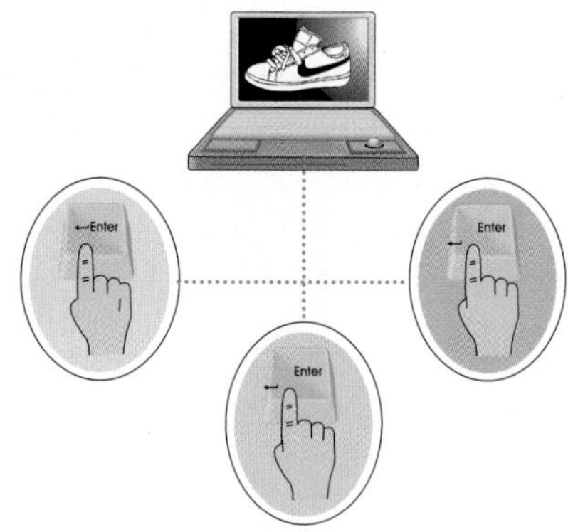

3. Design Collaboration. NYConcepts designers and SideKick managers use peer-to-peer software that allows them to share spaces on each other's computers. The software enables them to take turns modifying the designs, and it also tracks all the changes.

and technology issues can create chaos in virtual meetings. To help you plan and participate professionally in efficient virtual meetings, we present the following suggestions gathered from experienced meeting facilitators.[37]

What steps should be taken before a virtual meeting starts?

Premeeting Considerations.

A virtual meeting or teleconference will be more successful if you address a number of premeeting issues. Most important, decide what technology will be used. Check to be sure that everyone is able to participate fully using that technology. If someone can't see what is happening on screen, the entire meeting can be disrupted and delayed. A few participants may need coaching before the session begins so that they can interact comfortably. Set the time of the meeting, preferably using Coordinated Universal Time (UTC) so that participants in different time zones are not confused. Be particularly mindful of how the meeting schedule affects others. Avoid spanning a lunch hour, holding someone overtime, or making someone arrive extra early.

For global meetings decide what language will be used. If that language may be difficult for some participants, think about using simple expressions and repeating major ideas. Before the meeting distribute any materials that will be shared. If documents will be edited or marked during the meeting, be sure participants know how to use the online editing tools. Finally, to avoid panic at the last minute, encourage participants to log on 15 minutes early. Some programs require downloads and installations that can cause immense frustration if not done early.

What ground rules are important for virtual meetings?

Ground Rules for Virtual Meetings.

During virtual meetings, establishing a few ground rules achieves the best results. For one thing, explain how questions may be asked and answered. Many meeting programs allow participants to "raise their hand" with an icon on a side panel of the computer screen. Then they can type in their question for the leader and others to see. Unless the meeting involves people who know each other well, participants in audioconferences should always say their names before beginning to comment.

One of the biggest problems of virtual meetings is background noise from participants' offices or homes. You might hear dogs barking, telephones ringing, and toilets flushing. Meeting planners disagree on whether to require participants to put their phones on mute. Although the mute button reduces noise, it also prevents immediate participation and tends to deaden the conference. If you decide to ask participants to mute their phones, make it part of your ground rules and include a reminder at the beginning of the session. In addition, remind people to turn off cell phones and smartphones. As a personal ground rule, don't allow yourself to multitask—and that includes not checking your e-mail—during virtual meetings. Giving your full attention is critical if the meeting requires engagement and interaction.

Techniques for Collaborating Successfully in Virtual Meetings. Collaborating successfully in virtual meetings requires awareness of limitations and techniques for overcoming those limitations. For example, when individuals meet face-to-face, they usually can recognize blank looks when people do not understand something being discussed. But in virtual meetings participants and presenters cannot always see each other. "They [participants] will lose place, lose focus, and lose attention to the meeting," one meeting expert noted.[38] He also warned that participants won't tell you if they are lost. As a result, when presenting ideas at a virtual meeting, you should be as precise as possible. Give examples and use simple language. Recap and summarize often. Confirm your understanding of what is being discussed. If you are a presenter, project an upbeat, enthusiastic, and strong voice. Without eye contact and nonverbal cues, the best way to keep the attention of the audience is through a powerful voice.

What techniques can presenters use to prevent participants from getting lost during virtual meetings?

To encourage participation and avoid traffic jams with everyone talking at once, experts suggest a number of techniques. Participants soon lose interest if the leader is the only one talking. Therefore, encourage dialogue by asking questions of specific people. Often you will learn not only what the person is thinking but also what others feel but have not stated. Another technique that promotes discussion and gives everyone a chance to

Checklist

Planning and Participating in Productive Meetings

Before the Meeting

- **Consider alternatives.** Unless a topic is important and pressing, avoid calling a meeting. Perhaps an e-mail message, telephone call, or announcement would serve the purpose as well.
- **Invite the right people.** To make decisions, invite those people who have information and authority to make the decision and implement it.
- **Distribute an agenda.** Prepare and distribute an agenda that includes the date and place of the meeting, the starting and ending time, a brief description of each topic, the names of people responsible for any action, and a proposed time allotment for each topic.
- **Use a calendaring program.** If available, use calendaring software to set a meeting date, issue invitations, and send the agenda.
- **Train participants on technology.** Especially for virtual meetings, be sure participants are comfortable with the conferencing software.

During the Meeting

- **Start on time and introduce the agenda.** Discuss the goal and length of the meeting, provide background of topics for discussion, suggest possible solutions and constraints, propose a tentative agenda, and clarify the ground rules for the meeting.
- **Appoint a secretary and a recorder.** Ask one attendee to make a record of the proceedings, and ask another person to record discussion topics on a flipchart or whiteboard.
- **Encourage participation.** Strive to be sure that all participants' views are heard and that no one monopolizes the discussion. Avoid digressions by steering the group back to the topics on the agenda. In virtual meetings be sure participants identify themselves before speaking.
- **Confront conflict frankly.** Encourage people who disagree to explain their positions completely. Then restate each position and ask for group comments. The group may modify a recommendation or suggest alternatives before agreeing on a plan of action.
- **Summarize along the way.** When the group seems to reach a consensus, summarize and see whether everyone agrees.

Ending the Meeting and Following Up

- **Review meeting decisions.** At the end of the meeting, consider using "round the table" to be sure everyone understands what has been decided. Discuss action items, and establish a schedule for completion.
- **Distribute minutes of meeting.** A few days after the meeting, arrange to have the secretary distribute the minutes. Use an e-mail template, if available, to distribute meeting minutes.
- **Remind people of action items.** Follow up by calling people to see whether they are completing the actions recommended at the meeting.

speak is "round the table," which we mentioned earlier. Go through the list of participants inviting each to speak for 30 seconds without interruption. If individuals have nothing to say, they may pass when their names are called. A second "round the table" provides another opportunity to speak. Leaders should avoid asking leading questions such as, *Does everyone agree?* Remote attendees cannot answer easily without drowning out each other's responses.

One final suggestion involves building camaraderie and trust. For teams with distant members, it helps to leave time before or after the scheduled meeting for small talk. A few moments of chat builds personal bonds and establishes a warm environment. Even with larger, unfamiliar groups, you can build trust and interest by dialing in early and greeting others as they join the group.

Virtual meetings are the wave of the future. Learning to plan and participate in them professionally will enhance your career as a business communicator. The checklist on page 57 summarizes helpful techniques for both face-to-face and virtual meetings.

Listening in the Workplace

LEARNING OBJECTIVE 5

Explain and implement active listening techniques.

"No one ever listened himself out of a job," observed President Calvin Coolidge many years ago. His words are even more significant today as employers become increasingly aware that listening is a critical employee and management skill. Listening skills are part of the professional traits that employers seek when looking for well-rounded candidates who can be hired and promoted.

But, you may be thinking, everyone knows how to listen. Most of us believe that listening is an automatic response to noise. We do it without thinking. Perhaps that explains why so many of us are poor listeners. In this section we explore the importance of listening, the kinds of listening required in the workplace, and how to become a better listener. Although many of the tips for improving your listening skills will be effective in your personal life, our discussion centers primarily on workplace and employment needs.

As you learned earlier, workers are communicating more than ever before, largely because of the Internet, teamwork, global competition, and emphasis on customer service. A vital ingredient in every successful workplace is high-quality communication, and three quarters of high-quality communication involves listening.[39]

Listening skills are important for career success, organization effectiveness, and worker satisfaction. Numerous studies and experts report that good listeners make good managers and that good listeners advance more rapidly in their organizations.[40] Studies of Fortune 500 companies report that soft skills such as listening, writing, and speaking are most likely to determine hiring and career success.[41] Listening is especially important in the workplace because we spend so much time doing it. Although estimates vary, it is thought that most workers spend 30 to 45 percent of their communication time listening.[42] Executives spend 60 to 70 percent of their communication time listening.[43]

Poor Listening Habits

Why are most people poor listeners?

Although workplace executives and employees devote the bulk of their communication time to listening, research suggests that they're not very good at it. In fact, most of us are poor listeners. Some estimates indicate that only half of the oral messages heard in a day are completely understood.[44] Experts say that we listen at only 25 percent efficiency. In other words, we ignore, forget, distort, or misunderstand 75 percent of everything we hear.

Poor listening habits may result from several factors. Lack of training is one significant factor. Few schools give as much emphasis to listening as they do to the development of reading, speaking, and writing skills. In addition, our listening skills may be less than perfect because of the large number of competing sounds and stimuli in our lives that interfere with concentration. Finally, we are inefficient listeners because we are able to process speech much faster than others can speak. While most speakers talk at about 125 to 175 words per minute, listeners can listen at 450 words per minute.[45] The resulting lag time fosters daydreaming, which clearly reduces listening efficiency.

Types of Workplace Listening

What are three types of workplace listening? How do they differ?

On the job you can expect to be involved in many types of listening. These include listening to superiors, listening to fellow colleagues and team members, and listening to customers. If you are an entry-level employee, you will probably be most concerned with listening to superiors. But you also must develop skills for listening to colleagues and team members. As you advance in your career and enter the ranks of management, you will need skills for listening to subordinates. Finally, the entire organization must listen to customers to compete in today's service-oriented economy.

Listening to Superiors. On the job one of your most important tasks will be listening to instructions, assignments, and explanations about how to do your work. You will be listening to learn and to comprehend. To focus totally on the speaker, be sure you are not distracted by noisy surroundings or other tasks. Don't take phone calls, and don't try to complete another job while listening with one ear. Show your interest by leaning forward and striving for good eye contact.

Above all, take notes. Don't rely on your memory. Details are easy to forget. Taking selective notes also conveys to the speaker your seriousness about hearing accurately and completely. Don't interrupt. When the speaker finishes, paraphrase the instructions in your own words. Ask pertinent questions in a nonthreatening manner. Don't be afraid to ask "dumb" questions, if it means you won't have to do a job twice. Avoid criticizing or arguing when you are listening to a superior. Your goals should be to hear accurately and to convey an image of competence.

Listening to Colleagues and Teammates. Much of your listening will take place during interactions with fellow workers and teammates. In these exchanges two kinds of listening are important. *Critical listening* enables you to judge and evaluate what you are hearing. You will be listening to decide whether the speaker's message is fact, fiction, or opinion. You will also be listening to decide whether an argument is based on logic or emotion. Critical listening requires an effort on your part. You must remain objective, particularly when you disagree with what you are hearing. Control your tendency to prejudge. Let the speaker have a chance to complete the message before you evaluate it. *Discriminative listening* is necessary when you must understand and remember. It means you must identify main ideas, understand a logical argument, and recognize the purpose of the message.

Why is it important to listen to customers?

Listening to Customers. As the U.S. economy becomes increasingly service oriented, the new management mantra has become "customers rule." Many organizations know that listening to customers results in increased sales and profitability as well as improved customer acquisition and retention. The simple truth is that consumers feel better about companies that value their opinions. Listening is an acknowledgment of caring and is a potent retention tool. Customers want to be cared about. By doing so, companies fulfill a powerful human need.

How can organizations improve their customer listening techniques? Because employees are the eyes and ears of the organization, smart companies begin by hiring staff workers who genuinely care about customers. Listening organizations also train their employees to listen actively and to ask gentle, probing questions to ensure clear understanding. As you can see in Figure 2.10 on page 60, employees trained in listening techniques are far more likely to elicit customer feedback and promote goodwill than untrained employees are.

Improving Workplace Listening

Listening on the job is more difficult than listening in college classes where experienced professors present well-organized lectures and repeat important points. Workplace listening is more challenging because information is often exchanged casually. It may be disorganized, unclear, and cluttered with extraneous facts. Moreover, your fellow workers are usually friends. Because they are familiar with you, they may not be as polite and respectful as they are with strangers. Friends tend to interrupt, jump to conclusions, and take each other for granted.

Listening in groups or listening to nonnative speakers further complicates the listening process. In groups, more than one person talks at once, and topics change rapidly. Group

FIGURE 2.10 Listening to Customers: Comparing Trained and Untrained Listeners

Untrained Listeners	Trained Listeners
You tune out some of what the customer is saying because you know what the answer is.	You defer judgment. You listen for the customer's feelings and assess the situation.
You are quick to mentally criticize grammar, voice tone, and speaking style. You focus on style.	You pay most attention to content, not to appearances, form, or other surface issues.
You tend to listen mainly for facts and specific bits of information.	You listen completely, trying to really understand every nuance. This enthralls speakers.
You attempt to take in everything the customer is saying, including exaggerations and errors (referred to as "fogging") so that you can refute each comment.	You listen primarily for the main idea and avoid replying to everything, especially sidetracking issues.
You divide your attention among two or more tasks because listening is automatic.	You do one thing at a time, realizing that listening is a full-time job.
You tend to become distracted by emotional words and have difficulty controlling your angry responses.	You control your anger and refuse to fight fire with fire.
You interrupt the customer.	You are silent for a few seconds after a customer finishes to be sure the thought is completed.
You give few, if any, verbal responses.	You give affirming statements and invite additional comments.

© Viewstock/Inmagine

members are monitoring both verbal and nonverbal messages to learn what relates to their group roles. Listening to nonnative speakers often creates special challenges. The accompanying Career Coach box on page 61 offers suggestions for improving communication between native and nonnative speakers. Chapter 3 presents more suggestions for communicating across cultures.

Ten Keys to Building Powerful Listening Skills

Despite the complexities and challenges of workplace listening, good listeners on the job must remember that their goal is to listen carefully and to *understand* what is being said so that they can do their work well. The following recommendations can help you improve your workplace listening effectiveness.

Which of these ten keys to building listening skills is easiest to implement? Which is hardest?

1. **Control external and internal distractions.** Move to an area where you can hear without conflicting noises or conversations. Block out surrounding physical distractions. Internally, try to focus totally on the speaker. If other projects are on your mind, put them on the back burner temporarily. When you are emotionally charged, whether angry or extremely happy, it is a good idea to postpone any serious listening.

2. **Become actively involved.** Show that you are listening closely by leaning forward and maintaining eye contact with the speaker. Don't fidget or try to complete another task at the same time you are listening. Listen to more than the spoken words. How are they said? What implied meaning, reasoning, and feelings do you hear behind the spoken words? Does the speaker's body language (eye contact, posture, movements) support or contradict the main message?

3. **Separate facts from opinions.** Facts are truths known to exist; for example, *Microsoft is located in Redmond, Washington*. Opinions are statements of personal judgments or preferences; for example, *Microsoft stock is always a good investment.* Some opinions are easy to recognize because speakers preface them with statements such as, *I think, It seems to me,* and *As far as I'm concerned.*[46] Often, however, listeners must evaluate assertions to decide their validity. Good listeners consider whether speakers are credible

and speaking within their areas of competence. They do not automatically accept assertions as facts.

4. **Identify important facts.** Speakers on the job often intersperse critical information with casual conversation. Unrelated topics pop up—ball scores, a customer's weird request, a computer glitch, the boss's extravagant new SUV. Your task is to select what's important and register it mentally. What step is next in your project? Who does what? What is your role?

5. **Avoid interrupting.** While someone else has the floor, do not interrupt with a quick reply or opinion. And don't show nonverbal disagreement such as negative head shaking, rolling eyes, sarcastic snorting, or audible sighs. Good listeners let speakers have their say. Interruptions are not only impolite, but they also prevent you from hearing the speaker's complete thought. Listeners who interrupt with their opinions sidetrack discussions and cause hard feelings.

6. **Ask clarifying questions.** Good listeners wait for the proper moment and then ask questions that do not attack the speaker. Instead of saying, *But I don't understand how you can say that,* a good listener seeks clarification with statements such as, *Please help me understand by explaining more about. . . .* Because questions can put you in the driver's seat, think about them in advance. Use open questions (those without set answers) to draw out feelings, motivations, ideas, and suggestions. Use closed fact-finding questions to identify key factors in a discussion.[47] By the way, don't ask a question unless you are ready to be quiet and listen to the answer.

CAREER COACH

Listening to Nonnative Speakers in the Workplace

Many workplaces today involve interactions between native and nonnative English speakers. As immigration increases and as local businesses expand into global markets, the chances are good that you will at times be listening to speakers for whom English is a second or third language. Although many speakers have studied English and comprehend it, they may have difficulty speaking it. Why? Vowels and consonants are pronounced differently. Learning the inflection and sentence patterns of English is difficult when they conflict with the speaker's native tongue. Most "errors" in pronunciation occur in meaningful patterns traced to their home languages.

Moreover, nonnative speakers are intimidated by the fluency of native speakers; therefore, they don't try to become fluent. They worry about using incorrect verb forms and tenses. They may be trying to translate thoughts from their own language word for word into the foreign language. Often, they spend so long thinking about how to express a thought that the conversation moves on. Many worry about being judged negatively and losing face. What can native speakers do to become better listeners when nonnatives speak?

- **Avoid negative judgment of accented speech.** Many nonnative speakers of English speak an articulate, insightful, and complex variety of English. Their speech may retain remnants of their native language. Don't assume, however, that a nonnative speaker struggling with pronunciation is unintelligent. Instead, imagine how difficult it would be for you to learn that person's language.
- **Be patient.** Americans are notoriously poor listeners. Strive to overcome the need to hurry a conversation along. Give nonnative speakers time to express their thoughts.
- **Don't finish sentences.** Allow nonnative speakers to choose their words and complete their sentences without volunteering your help. You may find that they are saying something quite different from what you expected.
- **Don't correct grammar and pronunciation.** Although you may think you are helping nonnative speakers by correcting them, it is better to focus on what they are expressing and forget about teaching English. As one company caller said, "If I could speak better English, I would already be doing it."
- **Don't pretend to understand.** It is perfectly all right to tell a speaker that you are having a little difficulty understanding him or her.
- **Practice listening to many varieties of English.** Improving your skill at comprehending many accents as well as native dialects (for example, Southern, Western, and Northeastern) can be a valuable skill in today's diverse and intercultural workplace.

Career Application

In a class forum, discuss these questions: How do you think nonnative speakers feel when they must converse with native speakers in a work environment? For nonnative speakers, what is most frustrating in conversation? For native speakers, what is awkward or frustrating in talking with nonnative speakers? What embarrassing moments have you experienced as a result of mispronunciations or misunderstandings? What suggestions can native and nonnative speakers make for improving communication?

Spotlight on Communicators

© Tony Barson/WireImage/Getty Images

Celebrated talk show host Oprah Winfrey owes much of her success to the artful application of the simple process of listening and responding. "Communicating with people is how I always developed any kind of value about myself," said the most successful female entertainer in the world. On her show, she is able to block out external distractions, become actively involved, listen empathically without interrupting, paraphrase her guests' ideas, and ask clarifying questions to draw out deep meanings and issues that underlie their everyday lives.

7. **Paraphrase to increase understanding.** To make sure you understand a speaker, rephrase and summarize a message in your own words. Be objective and nonjudgmental. Remember, your goal is to understand what the speaker has said—not to show how mindless the speaker's words sound when parroted. Remember, too, that other workplace listeners will also benefit from a clear summary of what was said.

8. **Capitalize on lag time.** While you are waiting for a speaker's next idea, use the time to review what the speaker is saying. Separate the central idea, key points, and details. Sometimes you may have to supply the organization. Use lag time to silently rephrase and summarize the speaker's message. Another effective trick for keeping your mind from drifting is to try to guess what a speaker's next point will be. Most important, keep your mind focused on the speaker and his or her ideas—not on all the other work waiting for you.

9. **Take notes to ensure retention.** Do not trust your memory. A wise person once said that he would rather have a short pencil than a long memory. If you have a hallway conversation with a colleague and don't have a pencil handy, make a mental note of the important items. Then write them down as soon as possible. Even with seemingly easily remembered facts or instructions, jot them down to ease your mind and also to be sure you understand them correctly. Two weeks later you will be glad you did. Be sure you have a good place to store notes of various projects, such as file folders, notebooks, or computer files.

10. **Be aware of gender differences.** Men tend to listen for facts, whereas women tend to perceive listening as an opportunity to connect with the other person on a personal level.[48] Men tend to use interrupting behavior to control conversations, while women generally interrupt to communicate assent, to elaborate on an idea of another group member, or to participate in the topic of conversation. Women listeners tend to be attentive, provide steady eye contact, remain stationary, and nod their heads.[49] Male listeners are less attentive, provide sporadic eye contact, and move around. Being aware of these tendencies will make you a more sensitive and knowledgeable listener. To learn more about gender differences in communication, see the Career Coach box in Chapter 3.

Checklist

Improving Listening

- **Stop talking.** Accept the role of listener by concentrating on the speaker's words, not on what your response will be.
- **Work hard at listening**. Become actively involved; expect to learn something.
- **Block out competing thoughts**. Concentrate on the message. Don't allow yourself to daydream during lag time.
- **Control the listening environment**. Move to a quiet area where you won't be interrupted by telephone calls or visitors. Check to be certain that listeners can hear speakers.
- **Maintain an open mind.** Know your biases and try to correct for them. Be tolerant of less-abled and different-looking speakers. Provide verbal and nonverbal feedback. Encourage the speaker with comments such as, *Yes, I see, OK,* and *Uh huh.* Ask polite questions, and look alert by leaning forward.
- **Paraphrase the speaker's ideas**. Silently repeat the message in your own words, sort out the main points, and identify supporting details. In conversation sum up the main points to confirm what was said.
- **Listen between the lines.** Observe nonverbal cues and interpret the feelings of the speaker: What is really being said?
- **Distinguish between facts and opinions.** Know the difference between factual statements and opinions stated as assertions.
- **Capitalize on lag time.** Use spare moments to organize, review, anticipate, challenge, and weigh the evidence.
- **Use memory devices**. If the information is important, develop acronyms, links, or rhymes to help you remember.
- **Take selective notes**. If you are hearing instructions or important data, record the major points; then, revise your notes immediately or verify them with the speaker.

Communicating Through Nonverbal Messages

Understanding messages often involves more than merely listening to spoken words. Nonverbal cues also carry powerful meanings. Nonverbal communication includes all unwritten and unspoken messages, both intentional and unintentional. Eye contact, facial expression, body movements, space, time, distance, appearance—all of these nonverbal cues influence the way a message is interpreted, or decoded, by the receiver. Many of the nonverbal messages that we send are used intentionally to accompany spoken words. When Stacy slaps her monitor and shouts "This computer just crashed again!" we interpret the loudness of her voice and the act of slapping the machine as intentional emphasis of her words. But people can also communicate nonverbally even when they don't intend to. What's more, not all messages accompany words. When Jeff hangs on to the speaker's rostrum and barely looks at the audience during his presentation, he sends a nonverbal message of fear and lack of confidence.

LEARNING OBJECTIVE 6

Understand how the functions and forms of nonverbal communication can help you advance your career.

Because nonverbal communication is an important tool for you to use and control in the workplace, you need to learn more about its functions and forms.

Functions of Nonverbal Communication

Nonverbal communication helps to convey meaning in at least five ways. As you become more aware of the following functions of nonverbal communication, you will be better able to use these silent codes to your advantage in the workplace.

What important functions does nonverbal communication serve? Can you give original examples of each?

- **To complement and illustrate.** Nonverbal messages can amplify, modify, or provide details for a verbal message. For example, in describing the size of a cell phone, a speaker holds his fingers apart 5 inches. In pumping up sales reps, the manager jams his fist into the opposite hand to indicate the strong effort required.
- **To reinforce and accentuate.** Skilled speakers raise their voices to convey important ideas, but they whisper to suggest secrecy. A grimace forecasts painful news, whereas a big smile intensifies good news. A neat, well-equipped office reinforces a message of professionalism.
- **To replace and substitute.** Many gestures substitute for words: nodding your head for *yes*, giving a V for victory, making a thumbs-up sign for approval, and shrugging your shoulders for *I don't know* or *I don't care*. In fact, a complex set of gestures totally replaces spoken words in sign language.
- **To control and regulate.** Nonverbal messages are important regulators in conversation. Shifts in eye contact, slight head movements, changes in posture, raising of eyebrows, nodding of the head, and voice inflection—all of these cues tell speakers when to continue, to repeat, to elaborate, to hurry up, or to finish.
- **To contradict.** To be sarcastic, a speaker might hold his nose while stating that your new perfume is wonderful. During one election debate, a candidate was seriously attacking his opponent's "fuzzy" math. The other candidate smiled and winked at the audience. His body language contradicted the attack being made by his opponent. In the workplace, individuals may send contradictory messages with words or actions. The boss, for example, says he wants to promote Kevin, but he fails to submit the necessary recommendation.

In many situations people may not be aware that they are sending contradictory messages. Researchers have found that when verbal and nonverbal messages contradict each other, listeners tend to believe and act on the nonverbal message. How would you interpret the following?

If nonverbal cues contradict verbal messages, which do receivers tend to believe?

- Brenda assures her boss that she has enough time to complete her assigned research, but she misses two deadlines.
- Tyler protests that he's not really angry but slams the door when he leaves a group meeting.
- Kyoko claims she's not nervous about a team presentation, but her brow is furrowed and she perspires profusely.

The nonverbal messages in these situations speak louder than the words uttered. In one experiment speakers delivered a positive message but averted their eyes as they spoke. Listeners perceived the overall message to be negative. Moreover, listeners thought that gaze aversion suggested nonaffection, superficiality, lack of trust, and nonreceptivity.[50] The lesson to be learned here is that effective communicators must be certain that all their nonverbal messages reinforce their spoken words and their professional goals. To make sure that you're on the right track to nonverbal communication competency, let's look more carefully at the specific forms of nonverbal communication.

Forms of Nonverbal Communication

Instead of conveying meaning with words, nonverbal messages carry their meaning in a number of other forms ranging from facial expressions to body language and even clothes. Each of us sends and receives thousands of nonverbal messages daily in our business and personal lives. Although the following discussion covers all forms of nonverbal communication, we will be especially concerned with workplace applications. As you learn about the messages sent by eye contact, facial expressions, posture, gestures, as well as the use of time, space, territory, and appearance, think about how you can use these nonverbal cues positively in your career.

Why are the eyes thought to be the most accurate predictor of a speaker's true feelings?

Eye Contact. The eyes have been called the "windows to the soul." Even if communicators can't look directly into the soul, they consider the eyes to be the most accurate predictor of a speaker's true feelings and attitudes. Most of us cannot look another person straight in the eyes and lie. As a result, we tend to believe people who look directly at us. We have less confidence in and actually distrust those who cannot maintain eye contact. Sustained eye contact suggests trust and admiration; brief eye contact signifies fear or stress. Prolonged eye contact, however, can be intrusive and intimidating. One successful CEO says that he can tell from people's eyes whether they are focused, receptive, or distant. He also notes the frequency of eye blinks when judging a person's honesty.[51]

Good eye contact enables the message sender to determine whether a receiver is paying attention, showing respect, responding favorably, or feeling distress. From the receiver's perspective, good eye contact reveals the speaker's sincerity, confidence, and truthfulness. Because eye contact is a learned skill, however, you must be respectful of people who do not maintain it. You must also remember that nonverbal cues, including eye contact, have different meanings in various cultures. Chapter 3 presents more information about the cultural influence of nonverbal cues.

Facial Expression. The expression on a communicator's face can be almost as revealing of emotion as the eyes. Researchers estimate that the human face can display over 250,000 expressions.[52] Although a few people can control these expressions and maintain a "poker face" when they want to hide their feelings, most of us display our emotions openly. Raising or lowering the eyebrows, squinting the eyes, swallowing nervously, clenching the jaw, smiling broadly—these voluntary and involuntary facial expressions supplement or entirely replace verbal messages. In the workplace, maintaining a pleasant expression with frequent smiles promotes harmony.

Ethics Check

Impressing Your Instructor

Projecting a professional image begins in your business communication classroom and in other courses in which your instructors evaluate your work and your participation. Imagine how a professor perceives students who skip classes, arrive late, forget homework, yawn with their tonsils showing, chew gum or eat, and doodle during class. What message does such nonverbal behavior send?

Posture and Gestures. An individual's general posture can convey anything from high status and self-confidence to shyness and submissiveness. Leaning toward a speaker suggests attraction and interest; pulling away or shrinking back denotes fear, distrust, anxiety, or disgust. Similarly, gestures can communicate entire thoughts via simple movements. But remember that these nonverbal cues may have vastly different meanings in different cultures. An individual who signals success by forming the thumb and forefinger into a circle would be in deep trouble in Germany or parts of South America. The harmless OK sign is actually an obscene reference in those areas.[53]

In the workplace you can make a good impression by controlling your posture and gestures. When speaking, make sure your upper body is aligned with the person to whom you're talking. Erect posture sends a message of confidence, competence, diligence, and strength. During the Microsoft antitrust trial, CEO Bill Gates slouched in his chair and rocked back and forth as he pondered questions and responded. Body language experts thought his childlike, rhythmic rocking did not help his case.[54] Women are advised to avoid tilting their heads to the side when making an important point. This gesture diminishes the main thrust of the message.[55]

What nonverbal message does erect posture send?

Time. How we structure and use time tells observers about our personality and attitudes. For example, when Maritza Perez, a banking executive, gives a visitor a prolonged interview, she signals her respect for, interest in, and approval of the visitor or the topic being discussed. By sharing her valuable time, she sends a clear nonverbal message. Likewise, when David Ing twice arrives late for a meeting, it could mean that the meeting has low priority to David, that he is a self-centered person, or that he has little self-discipline. These are assumptions that typical Americans might make. In other cultures and regions, though, punctuality is viewed differently. In the workplace you can send positive nonverbal messages by being on time for meetings and appointments, staying on task during meetings, and giving ample time to appropriate projects and individuals.

What nonverbal message does being on time for an appointment send?

Space. How we arrange things in the space around us tells something about ourselves and our objectives. Whether the space is a dorm room, an office, or a department, people reveal themselves in the design and grouping of furniture within that space. Generally, the more formal the arrangement, the more formal and closed the communication environment. An executive who seats visitors in a row of chairs across from his desk sends a message of aloofness and desire for separation. A team leader who arranges chairs informally in a circle rather than in straight rows or a rectangular pattern conveys her desire for a more open, egalitarian exchange of ideas. A manager who creates an open office space with few partitions separating workers' desks seeks to encourage an unrestricted flow of communication and work among areas.

Territory. Each of us has certain areas that we feel are our own territory, whether it is a specific spot or just the space around us. Your father may have a favorite chair in which he is most comfortable, a cook might not tolerate intruders in her kitchen, and veteran employees may feel that certain work areas and tools belong to them. We all maintain zones of privacy in which we feel comfortable. Figure 2.11 categorizes the four zones of social interaction among Americans, as formulated by anthropologist Edward T. Hall. Notice that we North Americans are a bit standoffish; only intimate friends and family may stand closer than about 1½ feet. If someone violates that territory, we feel uncomfortable and defensive and may step back to reestablish our space. A classic episode in the Seinfeld TV program aptly described a close-talker as a "space invader." In the workplace be aware of the territorial needs of others and don't invade their space.

During conversation, how close do you allow people to stand to you?

Appearance of Business Documents. The way a letter, memo, or report looks can have either a positive or a negative effect on the receiver. Envelopes through their postage,

FIGURE 2.11 Four Space Zones for Social Interaction

© iStockphoto.com/morganl

Intimate Zone
(1 to 1½ feet)

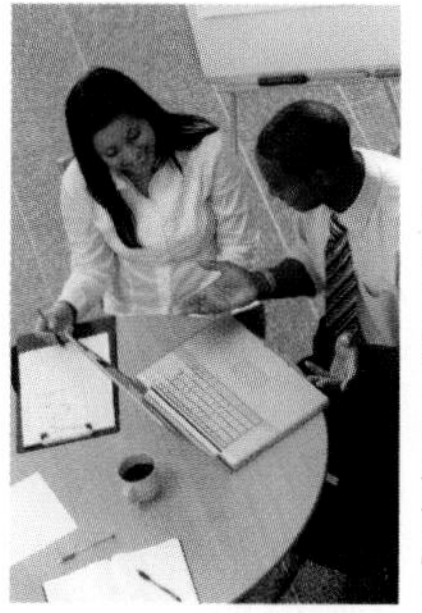
© iStockphoto.com/Dean Mitchell

Personal Zone
(1½ to 4 feet)

© iStockphoto.com/Catherine Yeulet

Social Zone
(4 to 12 feet)

© Kablonk Royalty-Free/ Inmagine

Public Zone
(12 or more feet)

CAREER COACH

Perils of Casual Apparel in the Workplace

Your choice of work clothes sends a strong nonverbal message about you. It also affects the way you work. Some surveys suggest that the pendulum is swinging back to more conservative attire in the workplace,[56] although employers and employees have mixed feelings about what to wear to work.

What Critics Are Saying

Some employers oppose casual dress because, in their opinion, too many workers push the boundaries of what is acceptable. They contend that absenteeism, tardiness, and flirtatious behavior have increased since dress-down policies began to be implemented. Relaxed dress codes also lead to reduced productivity and lax behavior. Image counselor Judith Rasband claimed that the general casualization of America has resulted in an overall decline in civility. "Manners break down, you begin to feel down, and you're not as effective," she said.[57] Others fear that the authority and credibility of casually attired executives, particularly females and minorities, are undermined.[58] Moreover, customers are often turned off by casually attired employees.[59]

What Supporters Are Saying

Supporters argue that comfortable clothes and relaxed working environments lift employee morale, increase employee creativity, and improve internal communication. Employees appreciate reduced clothing-related expenses, while employers use casual dress as a recruitment and retention tool. Because employees seem to love casual dress, nine out of ten employers have adopted casual-dress days for at least part of the workweek—even if it is just on Fridays during the summer.

What Employees Need to Know

The following suggestions, gleaned from surveys and articles about casual-dress trends in the workplace, can help future and current employees avoid casual-dress blunders.

- For job interviews, dress conservatively or call ahead to ask the interviewer or the receptionist what is appropriate.
- Find out what your company allows. Ask whether a dress-down policy is available. Observe what others are wearing on casual-dress days.
- If your company has no casual-dress policy, volunteer to work with management to develop relevant guidelines, including illustrations of suitable casual attire.
- Avoid wearing the following items: T-shirts, sandals, flip-flops, shoes without socks, backless dresses, tank tops, shorts, miniskirts, spandex, athletic shoes, hiking boots, baseball caps, and visors.[60]
- When meeting customers, dress as well as or better than they do.

Career Application

In small groups or in your full class, debate the following proposition: *Resolved: That business casual dress be made the dress standard throughout the United States.* Think of arguments beyond those presented here. Your instructor will provide details for arranging the debate.

stationery, and printing can suggest routine, important, or junk mail. Letters and reports can look neat, professional, well organized, and attractive—or just the opposite. Sloppy, hurriedly written documents convey negative nonverbal messages regarding both the content and the sender. Among the worst offenders are e-mail messages.

Although they seem like conversation, e-mails are business documents that create a permanent record and often a bad impression. Sending an e-mail message full of errors conveys a damaging nonverbal message. It says that the writer doesn't care enough about this message to take the time to make it read well or look good. The sender immediately doubts the credibility of the sender. How much faith can you put in someone who can't spell, capitalize, or punctuate and won't make the effort to communicate clearly?

In succeeding chapters you will learn how to create documents that send positive nonverbal messages through their appearance, format, organization, readability, and correctness.

What does a person's appearance communicate?

Appearance of People. The way you look—your clothing, grooming, and posture—telegraphs an instant nonverbal message about you. Based on what they see, viewers make quick judgments about your status, credibility, personality, and potential. Business communicators who look the part are more likely to be successful in working with superiors, colleagues, and customers. Because appearance is such a powerful force in business, some aspiring professionals are turning for help to image consultants (who charge up to $500 an hour!).

What do image consultants say? They suggest investing in appropriate, professional-looking clothing and accessories. Remember that quality is more important than quantity. Avoid flashy garments, clunky jewelry, garish makeup, and overpowering colognes. Pay attention to good

FIGURE 2.12 **Sending Positive Nonverbal Signals in the Workplace**

Eye contact	Maintain direct but not prolonged eye contact.
Facial expression	Express warmth with frequent smiles.
Posture	Convey self-confidence with erect stance.
Gestures	Suggest accessibility with open-palm gestures.
Time	Be on time; use time judiciously.
Space	Maintain neat, functional work areas.
Territory	Use closeness to show warmth and to reduce status differences.
Business documents	Produce careful, neat, professional, well-organized messages.
Appearance	Be well groomed, neat, and appropriately dressed.

grooming, including a neat hairstyle, body cleanliness, polished shoes, and clean nails. Project confidence in your posture, both standing and sitting.

One of the latest fashion rages is body art in the form of tattoos. Once seen primarily on bikers, prisoners, and sailors, inked images such as butterflies, bluebirds, spiders, and angels increasingly adorn the bodies of those who seek to be unique. Think twice, however, before displaying "tats" at work. Visible tattoos may make you feel distinctive and slightly daring, but they could derail a professional career.

A less risky trend is the movement toward one or more days per week of casual dress at work. Be aware, though, that casual clothes change the image you project and also may affect your work style. See the accompanying Career Coach box regarding the pros and cons of casual apparel.

In the preceding discussion of nonverbal communication, you have learned that each of us sends and responds to thousands of nonverbal messages daily in our personal and work lives. You can harness the power of silent messages by reviewing Figure 2.12 and by studying the tips in the following checklist.

Checklist

Techniques for Improving Nonverbal Communication Skills in the Workplace

- **Establish and maintain eye contact.** Remember that in the United States and Canada appropriate eye contact signals interest, attentiveness, strength, and credibility.
- **Use posture to show interest.** Encourage communication interaction by leaning forward, sitting or standing erect, and looking alert.
- **Reduce or eliminate physical barriers.** Move out from behind a desk or lectern; arrange meeting chairs in a circle.
- **Improve your decoding skills.** Watch facial expressions and body language to understand the complete verbal and nonverbal message being communicated.
- **Probe for more information.** When you perceive nonverbal cues that contradict verbal meanings, politely seek additional clues (*I'm not sure I understand, Please tell me more about…*, or *Do you mean that… ?*).
- **Avoid assigning nonverbal meanings out of context.** Make nonverbal assessments only when you understand a situation or a culture.
- **Associate with people from diverse cultures.** Learn about other cultures to widen your knowledge and tolerance of intercultural nonverbal messages.
- **Appreciate the power of appearance.** Keep in mind that the appearance of your business documents, your business space, and yourself send immediate positive or negative messages to others.
- **Observe yourself on video.** Ensure that your verbal and nonverbal messages are in sync by recording and evaluating yourself making a presentation.
- **Enlist friends and family.** Ask friends and family members to monitor your conscious and unconscious body movements and gestures to help you become a more effective communicator.

Developing a Competitive Edge With Professionalism and Business Etiquette Skills

LEARNING OBJECTIVE 7

Enhance your competitive edge by developing professionalism and business etiquette skills.

Good manners and a businesslike, professional demeanor are among the soft skills that employers seek in job candidates. Employers are far more likely to hire and promote someone who is courteous and professional than one who lacks these skills and traits. But can you really learn how to be courteous, civil, and professional? Of course! This section gives you a few pointers.

How can you develop a competitive edge with professionalism and business etiquette skills?

Professionalism Leads to Success

Not everyone who seeks a job is aware of the employer's expectations. Some new-hires have no idea that excessive absenteeism or tardiness is grounds for termination. Others are surprised to learn that they are expected to devote their full attention to their duties when on the job. One young man wanted to read *Harry Potter* novels when things got slow. Many employees don't realize that they are sabotaging their careers when they sprinkle their conversation with *like, you know,* and uptalk (making declarative statements sound like questions). Projecting and maintaining a professional image can make a real difference in helping you obtain the job of your dreams. Once you get that job, you are more likely to be taken seriously and much more likely to be promoted if you look and sound professional. Do not send the wrong message with unwitting or unprofessional behavior. Figure 2.13 reviews six areas you will want to check to be sure you are projecting professionalism.

FIGURE 2.13 Projecting Professionalism When You Communicate

	Unprofessional	Professional
Speech habits	Speaking in *uptalk*, a singsong speech pattern that has a rising inflection, making sentences sound like questions; using *like* to fill in mindless chatter; substituting *go* for *said;* relying on slang; or letting poor grammar and profanity slip into your conversation.	Recognizing that your credibility can be seriously damaged by sounding uneducated, crude, or adolescent.
E-mail	Writing messages with incomplete sentences, misspelled words, exclamation points, IM slang, and senseless chatting. Sloppy, careless messages send a nonverbal message that you don't care, don't know, or aren't smart enough to know what is correct.	Employers like to see subjects, verbs, and punctuation marks. They don't recognize IM abbreviations. Call it crazy, but they value conciseness and correct spelling, even in brief e-mail messages.
Internet	Using an e-mail address such as *hotbabe@hotmail.com, supasnugglykitty@yahoo.com,* or *buffedguy@aol.com.*	An e-mail address should include your name or a relevant, positive, businesslike expression. It should not sound cute or like a chat room nickname.
Voice mail	An outgoing message with strident background music, weird sounds, or a joke message.	An outgoing message that states your name or phone number and provides instructions for leaving a message.
Telephone	Soap operas, thunderous music, or a TV football game playing noisily in the background when you answer the phone.	A quiet background when you answer the telephone, especially if you are expecting a prospective employer's call.
Cell phones and smartphones	Taking or placing calls during business meetings or during conversations with fellow employees; raising your voice (cell yell) or engaging in cell calls when others must reluctantly overhear; using a PDA during meetings.	Turning off phone and message notification, both audible and vibrate, during meetings; using your cell only when conversations can be private.
Texting	Sending and receiving text messages during meetings, allowing texting to interrupt face-to-face conversations, or texting when driving.	Sending appropriate business text messages only when necessary (perhaps when a cell phone call would disturb others).

Gaining an Etiquette Edge

Etiquette, civility, and goodwill efforts may seem out of place in today's fast-paced, high-tech offices. However, an awareness of courtesy and etiquette can give you a competitive edge in the job market. When two candidates have equal qualifications, the one who appears to be more polished and professional is more likely to be hired and promoted.

Do good manners make any difference in today's workplace?

As workloads increase and face-to-face meetings decline, bad manners and incivility are becoming alarmingly common in the American workplace.[61] One survey showed that 71 percent of workers said they had been insulted, demeaned, ignored, or otherwise treated discourteously by their coworkers and superiors.[62] Employers, of course, suffer from the resulting drop in productivity and exodus of talent. Employees, too, suffer. They worry about incidents, think about changing jobs, and cut back their efforts on the job. It is not hard to understand why employers are looking for people who are courteous, polite, respectful, and well-mannered.

Good manners convey a positive image of an organization. People like to do business with those who show respect and treat others civilly. Most of us also like to work in a pleasant environment. Considering how much time is spent at work, you realize that it makes sense that people prefer an agreeable environment to one that is rude and uncivil.

Why is etiquette more about attitude than about formal rules of behavior?

Etiquette is more about attitude than about formal rules of behavior. Attitude is a desire to show others consideration and respect. It includes a desire to make others feel comfortable. You don't have to become an etiquette nut, but you might need to polish your social competencies a little to be an effective businessperson today. Here are a few simple pointers:

- **Use polite words.** Be generous with words and phrases such as *please, thank you*, and *you're welcome*.
- **Express sincere appreciation and praise.** Tell coworkers how much you appreciate their efforts. Remember that written thank-you notes are even better than saying thanks.
- **Be selective in sharing personal information.** Avoid talking about health concerns, personal relationships, or finances in the office.
- **Don't put people down.** If you have a reputation for criticizing people, your coworkers will begin to wonder what you are saying behind their backs.
- **Respect coworkers' space.** Turn down the ringer on your business phone, minimize the use of speakerphones, and turn your personal cell phone down or off during business hours. Avoid wearing heavy perfumes or bringing strong-smelling food.
- **Rise above others' rudeness.** Don't use profanity or participate in questionable joke telling.
- **Be considerate when sharing space and equipment with others.** Clean up after yourself.
- **Choose the high road in conflict.** Avoid letting discussions degenerate into shouting matches. Keep a calm voice tone and focus on the work rather than on personality differences.
- **Disagree agreeably.** You may not agree with everyone, but you should respect their opinions.
- To strengthen your etiquette skills, visit *Dr. Guffey's Guide to Business Etiquette and Workplace Manners* at **www.meguffey.com**. You will find the author's tips on topics such as networking manners, coping with cubicles, managers' manners, business gifts, dealing with angry customers, and gender-free etiquette. Your instructor may give you etiquette quizzes to test your skills from this online material.

Want to do well on tests and excel in your course? Go to **www.meguffey.com** for helpful interactive resources.

- **Review the Chapter 2 PowerPoint slides to prepare for the first quiz.**

Zooming In YOUR TURN

Teams Help FedEx Office Deliver Solutions

As an intern at FedEx Office, you have been given a task by senior manager Daryl Thomas. He wants to develop a concise guide with suggestions for engaging in virtual meetings. This guide would be helpful for interns as well as for new team members. He knows you have been studying team building and virtual meetings. He asks you to prepare a list that summarizes how to plan and interact professionally during virtual meetings.

© AP Images/Jeff Chiu

Your Task

Using what you learned in this chapter, prepare a list of suggestions for conducting virtual meetings (either video or audio). Work individually or as a team. In addition to the advice in this chapter, conduct Internet research and include at least two new ideas not covered here. Present your list to your team or discuss in class. Your instructor may ask you to prepare this information as a one-page single-spaced memo addressed to Daryl Thomas, Senior Manager, Sales Development and Education. See Chapter 8 for advice on preparing interoffice memos.

Summary of Learning Objectives

1 Explain the importance of professionalism, soft skills, and teamwork in today's workplace. Employers seek workers who have strong communication, team, listening, nonverbal, and etiquette skills. Team skills are especially important because many organizations are forming teams to compete in today's fast-paced, global economy. Virtual teams are groups of people who work independently with a shared purpose across space, time, and organization boundaries using technology. Teams typically go through four stages of development: forming, storming, norming, and performing. Some teams never reach the performing stage; however, when they do, information flows freely, deadlines are met, and production exceeds expectations.

2 Understand how you can contribute positively to team performance, including resolving workplace conflicts, avoiding groupthink, and reaching group decisions. You can contribute positively to team performance if you abide by team rules, analyze tasks in problem solving, offer ideas, stimulate discussion, listen actively, show interest in others' ideas, praise others, and move the group toward its goal. In resolving conflict, you should listen, understand the other's point of view, show a concern for the relationship, look for common ground, invent new problem-solving options, and reach an agreement that is fair. Open discussion of conflict prevents *groupthink*, a condition that leads to faulty decisions. Methods for reaching group decisions include majority, consensus, minority, averaging, and authority rule with discussion. Successful teams are small, diverse, and able to agree on their purpose, procedures, and method of conflict resolution. They use good communication techniques, collaborate rather than compete, accept ethical responsibilities, and share leadership.

3 Discuss effective techniques for planning and participating in face-to-face workplace meetings. Workplace meetings are called only when urgent two-way communication is necessary. Leaders should limit participation to those directly involved. Leaders should start the meeting on time and keep the discussion on track. Conflict should be confronted openly by letting each person present his or her views fully before having the group decide which direction to take. Leaders should summarize what was said, end the meeting on time, and distribute minutes afterwards. To participate actively, attendees should arrive early, come prepared, have a positive attitude, and contribute respectfully. They should wait for others to finish, use calm and pleasant voices, give credit to others, avoid using cell phones and laptops, help summarize the discussion, express views IN the meeting (not afterward), and follow up by completing assigned actions.

4 Describe effective practices and technologies for planning and participating in virtual meetings. Virtual meetings are gatherings that use technology to connect people who cannot be together physically. Such meetings are increasingly popular because they save travel time, trim costs, and reduce employee fatigue. *Audioconferencing* enables one or more people in a work area to use an enhanced speakerphone to confer with others by telephone. *Videoconferencing* combines video, audio, and communications networking technologies for real-time interaction in special telepresence rooms. *Web conferencing* enables participants to stay in their offices using their computers to present slides, share documents, and converse in real time. During virtual meetings, participants should control background noise, give full attention (avoiding cell phones or e-mail), mention their names before speaking, be precise, use simple language, and project a strong voice.

5 Explain and implement active listening techniques. Experts say that we listen at only 25 percent efficiency. While listening to superiors on the job, take selective notes, avoid interrupting, ask pertinent questions, and paraphrase what you hear. When listening to colleagues and teammates, listen critically to recognize facts and listen discriminately to identify main ideas and to understand logical arguments. When listening to customers, defer judgment, pay attention to content rather than form, listen completely, control emotions, give affirming statements, and invite additional comments. Keys to building powerful listening skills include controlling external and internal distractions, becoming actively involved, separating facts from opinions, identifying important facts, refraining from interrupting, asking clarifying questions, paraphrasing, taking advantage of lag time, taking notes to ensure retention, and being aware of gender differences.

6 Understand how the functions and forms of nonverbal communication can help you advance your career. Nonverbal communication includes all unwritten and unspoken messages, both intentional and unintentional. Nonverbal communication takes many forms including eye contact, facial expressions, posture, and gestures, as well as the use of time, space, and territory. To improve your nonverbal skills, establish and maintain eye contact, use posture to show interest, reduce or eliminate physical barriers, improve your decoding skills, probe for more information, avoid assigning nonverbal meanings out of context, associate with people from diverse cultures, appreciate the power of appearance, observe yourself on video, and enlist friends and family to monitor your conscious and unconscious body movements and gestures.

7 Enhance your competitive edge by developing professionalism and business etiquette skills. You are more likely to be hired and promoted if you project professionalism in the workplace. This includes avoiding speech habits that make you sound uneducated, crude, or adolescent. Professionalism also is reflected in writing carefully worded e-mails and other messages and having a businesslike e-mail address, as well as good voice mail, cell phone, and telephone manners. To gain a competitive etiquette edge, use polite words, express sincere appreciation and praise, be selective in sharing personal information with work colleagues, avoid criticizing people, respect coworkers' space, rise above others' rudeness, be considerate when sharing space, choose the high road in conflict, and disagree agreeably.

Chapter Review

1. List seven reasons that explain why organizations are forming groups and teams. (Obj. 1)
2. What are virtual teams, and how can misunderstandings among participants be reduced? (Obj. 1)
3. Compare and contrast positive and negative team behavior. (Obj. 2)
4. What is groupthink, and how can it be avoided? (Obj. 2)
5. Why are team decisions reached by consensus generally better than those reached by majority rule? (Obj. 2)
6. If you are considering organizing a meeting, what should you do before the meeting? (Obj. 3)
7. List five behaviors you consider most important to participate actively in workplace meetings. (Obj. 3)

Are you ready? Get more practice at **www.meguffey.com**

8. How is videoconferencing different from Web conferencing? (Obj. 4)
9. What techniques can make virtual meetings as effective as face-to-face meetings? (Obj. 4)
10. According to experts, we ignore, forget, distort, or misunderstand 75 percent of everything we hear. Why are we such poor listeners? (Obj. 5)
11. What are ten techniques for improving workplace listening? Be prepared to describe each. (Obj. 5)
12. List five functions of nonverbal communication. Provide an original example of each. (Obj. 6)
13. List ten techniques for improving nonverbal communication skills in the workplace. Be prepared to discuss each. (Obj. 6)
14. Compare and contrast examples of professional and unprofessional behavior in regard to workplace speech habits and e-mail. (Obj. 7)
15. What five specific behaviors do you think would be most important in giving you an etiquette edge in your business career? (Obj. 7)

Critical Thinking

1. Harvard professor and team expert J. Richard Hackman claims that research "consistently shows that teams underperform despite all their extra resources."[63] How would you, as a critical thinker, respond to this statement? (Obj. 1)
2. Evaluate the following statement: "Technical proficiency has never been enough for professionals to grow beyond the staff level."[64] Do you agree or disagree, and why? (Obj. 1)
3. Why do executives and managers spend more time listening than do workers? (Obj. 5)
4. What arguments could you give for or against the idea that body language is a science with principles that can be interpreted accurately by specialists? (Obj. 6)
5. **Ethical Issue:** Rochelle is a good member of your team. However, you are disturbed that she is constantly promoting her Arbonne beauty products to other members of the team. She shows catalogs and keeps a supply of samples ready to distribute during lunch or after hours. Her desk smells like a perfume counter. During team meetings, she puts an order form on the table. As a team member, what should you do? What if Rochelle were selling Girl Scout cookies?

Activities

2.1 Soft Skills: Identifying Personal Strengths (Obj. 1)

When hiring future workers, employers look for hard skills, which are those we learn such as mastery of software applications or accountancy procedures, and soft skills. Soft skills are personal characteristics, strengths, or other assets a person possesses. Studies have divided soft skills into four categories:

- Thinking/problem solving
- Oral/written communication
- Personal qualities/work ethic
- Interpersonal/teamwork

Your Task. Using the preceding categories to guide you, identify your own soft skills, paying attention to those attributes you think a potential employer would value. For each category prepare lists of at least four items. For example, as evidence of problem solving you might list a specific workplace or student problem you recognized and solved. You will want to weave these words and phrases into cover letters and résumés, which are covered in Chapter 15.

2.2 Team Effort: Denny's Hopes to Rock With All-Nighter Program (Obj. 1)

Team

Attempting to win back the late-night market from McDonald's and Wendy's, the venerable family dining chain, Denny's, is revamping its image and menu. From 10 p.m. to 5 a.m., selected restaurants offer rock music, and the wait staff wears jeans and T-shirts instead of black pants and collared shirts. To further appeal to a youth crowd, the menu features sharable items such as seasoned kettle chips, mini-burgers, and Sweet Ride Nachos (tortilla chips smothered in cinnamon sugar, fruit, hot fudge, and whipped cream). Alternative rock bands are paid to drop in and pump up the party scene.

Deciding on a makeover to grab late-night business was a no-brainer for Denny's. Nearly half of its late-night customers are under 24, and about two thirds are male. Most of these customers are not dropping by after work; they are coming from nightclubs or bowling alleys. A trip to Denny's prolongs the party.

Adding to the party scene, Denny's has coaxed several rock bands to help it concoct late-night snacks. One band dreamed up Bacon Cheeseburger Fries (fries topped with beef, cheese, bacon, and onions). In addition, a new Denny's Web site features a rock music blog, and the site encourages folks to vote for the rock band that the food chain should adopt by feeding it free while the band tours.[65]

Your Task. As a Denny's marketing director, you have been asked to investigate the success of Denny's All-Nighter program to see whether it should be expanded to the entire Southwest region. The vice president asks you to take on this task alone because it is more efficient and cost effective. Although you are flattered by the offer, you think the task should be tackled by a team of managers. What arguments could you bring to your boss to convince him that a team would be better for this task than a single individual? In teams or individually, prepare a list of points to convince the marketing vice president that a team should tackle this task.

2.3 Reaching Group Decisions: Majority, Consensus, or What? (Obj. 2)

Team

Your Task. In small groups decide which decision strategy is best for the following situations:

a. A team of nine employees must decide whether to choose Macs or PCs for their new equipment. They must all use the same computer system.
b. Company employees numbering 900 or more must decide whether to adopt a floating holiday plan proposed by management or stay with the current plan. An up-or-down vote is required.
c. The owner of your company is meeting with all managers to decide which departments will be allowed to move into a new facility.
d. Appointed by management, an employee team is charged with making recommendations regarding casual Fridays. Management feels that too many employees are abusing the privilege.
e. Members of a business club must decide which members will become officers.
f. A group of town officials and volunteers must decide how to organize a town Web site. Only a few members have technical expertise.
g. An employee committee of three members (two supervisors and the manager) must decide on promotions within a department.
h. A national professional organization with thousands of members must decide on the site for its next convention.

2.4 Resolving Workplace Conflicts: Apply a Plan (Obj. 2)

Team

Although conflict is a normal part of every workplace, if unresolved, it can create hard feelings and reduce productivity.

Your Task. Analyze the following scenarios. In teams, discuss each scenario and apply the six-step procedure for dealing with conflict described in this chapter. Choose two of the scenarios to role-play, with two of your team members taking roles.

a. Team member Ashton is angry. Once again he has been asked to represent the company at an evening charity event because he is not married, has no children, and therefore is available. Fellow team member Andrea declined saying that she has a family and children and must help them with their homework on school nights. Other team members keep ducking these invitations saying that they have families and cannot be expected to give up their evenings. Ashton has represented the company at three events in the past year, and he believes it is time for Andrea or the others to step up.
b. A company policy manual is posted and updated at the company intranet, an internal Web site. Employees must sign that they have read and understand the manual. A conflict arises when team member Brian insists that employees should sign electronically. Fellow team member Erika thinks that a paper form should be signed by employees so that better records may be kept.
c. Domino's Pizza is considering adopting new uniforms, called Domino's Gear. The new outfits include colorful polo shirts with side vents so that the shirts can be worn tucked in or out. Crewneck shirts, page-boy hats, and denim caps give employees a number of options. Considered a perk, the new uniforms are favored by most employees at the company-owned Domino's units. Employees of two franchised units, however, prefer the old uniforms with traditional polo shirts and khakis. What's more, the old uniforms require no new investment in clothing. The two sides must agree on new uniforms and who should wear them.
d. Two management team members disagree on a new company e-mail policy. One wants to ban personal e-mail totally. The other thinks that an outright ban is impossible to implement. He is more concerned with limiting Internet misuse, including visits to online game, pornography, and shopping sites. The management team members agree that they need an e-mail policy, but they disagree on what to allow and what to prohibit.
e. A manager and his assistant plan to attend a conference together at a resort location. Six weeks before the conference, the company announces a cutback and limits conference support to only one person. The assistant, who has developed a presentation specifically for the conference, feels that he should be the one to attend. Travel arrangements must be made immediately.
f. Customer service rep Jackie comes to work one morning and finds Alexa sitting at Workstation 2. Although the customer service reps have no special workstation assigned to them, Jackie has the longest seniority and has always assumed that Workstation 2 is hers. Other workstations were available, but the supervisor told Alexa to use Workstation 2 that morning because she didn't know that Jackie would be coming in. When Jackie arrives and sees her workstation occupied, she becomes angry and demands that Alexa vacate "her" station.

2.5 Groupthink: Fastest Decision May Not Be Best (Obj. 2)

You are a member of a team charged with recommending a vendor to perform an upgrade of your firm's computer systems. Greg, the group leader, suggests the company where his sister works, claiming it will give your firm a good price. Lucinda says she will go along with whatever the group decides. Estéban announces he has another meeting in five minutes. Paul says he would like to solicit bids from several companies before recommending any one firm, but Greg dismisses that idea saying, "The sooner we make a recommendation, the sooner we improve our computer systems. My sister's firm will make our job a top priority and besides, it's local. Let's support a company in our own community." The committee urges Paul to drop the idea of putting the job out to bid, and the group makes a unanimous decision to recommend the firm of Greg's sister.

Your Task. In class discussion answer the following questions:

a. What aspects of groupthink were at work in this committee?
b. What conditions contribute to groupthink?
c. What can groups do to avoid groupthink?

2.6 Lessons in Teamwork: What We Can Learn From Geese (Objs. 1, 2)

Team

When geese fly in formation, we can't help but look up and marvel at their beauty. But their behavior also represents successful teamwork patterns that have evolved over the ages.

Your Task. In small groups discuss what teamwork lesson might be learned from each of the following:

a. The V formation helps each follower goose derive energy from the flowfield generated by the goose immediately ahead. Every bird experiences lower drag and needs less energy to maintain its speed.
b. Whenever a goose gets out of formation, it tries to get back into formation.
c. When the lead goose gets tired, it rotates back into formation and another goose flies at the head.
d. The geese flying in the rear of the formation honk, apparently to encourage those up front to keep up their speed.
e. When a goose gets sick or wounded and falls, two geese fall out and stay with it until it revives or dies. Then they catch up or join another flock.[66]

2.7 Evaluating Meetings: Productive or Not? (Obj. 3)

A recent poll of senior executives revealed that 45 percent thought that employees could be more productive if meetings were banned one day a week.[67] Clearly, these executives would like to see their meetings improved. Now that you have studied how to plan and participate in productive meetings, you should be able to judge whether meetings are successful and why.

Your Task. Attend a structured meeting of a college, social, business, or other organization. Compare the way the meeting is conducted with the suggestions presented in this chapter. Why did the meeting succeed or fail? In class discussion or in a memo (see Chapter 8) to your instructor, discuss your analysis.

2.8 Virtual Meetings: Improving Distance Meeting Buy-In (Obj. 4)

Team

Marina Elliot works at the headquarters for a large HMO that contracts with physician groups in various locations across the nation. Her position requires her to impose organizational objectives and systems on smaller groups that often resist such interference. Marina recently needed to inform regional groups that the home office was instituting a systemwide change to hiring practices. To save costs, she set up a Web conference between her office in Charlotte and others in Chicago, Denver, and Seattle. Marina set the meeting for 10 a.m. Eastern Standard Time. At the designated date and hour, she found that the Seattle team was not logged on and she had to delay the session. When the Seattle team finally did log on, Marina launched into her presentation. She explained the reasons behind the change in a PowerPoint presentation that contained complex data she had not distributed prior to the conference. Marina heard cell phone ringtones and typing in the background as she spoke. Still, she pushed through her one-hour presentation without eliciting any feedback.

Your Task. In teams, discuss ways Marina might have improved the Web conference.

2.9 Web Conferencing: Take a Quick Tour (Obj. 4)

Web

Your office team finds it increasingly difficult to find times to meet. Tyler is frequently on assignment traveling across the country. Melissa wants to work from home since her baby arrived. Others are in and out of the office as their schedules demand. Team leader Susan asks you to check out WebEx and report how it works to the team.

Your Task. Visit the WebEx site and view its video called "Quick Tour" **(http://www.webex.com/how-it-works/index.html)**. If the URL fails, search for the WebEx Quick Tour using your favorite search engine. Watch the video tour. Take notes and report what you learn. Does it sound as if WebEx would work for your team? In class discussion or in a memo, describe how WebEx works.

2.10 Rating Your Listening Skills (Obj. 5)

Web

You can learn whether your listening skills are excellent or deficient by completing a brief quiz.

Your Task. Take *Dr. Guffey's Listening Quiz* at **www.meguffey.com**. What two listening behaviors do you think you need to work on the most?

2.11 Listening: Recognizing Good Habits (Obj. 5)

You have probably never paid much attention to listening. However, now that you have studied it, you have become more conscious of both good and bad listening behavior.

Your Task. For one week focus on the listening behavior of people around you—at work, at school, at home. Make a list of five good listening habits that you see and five bad habits. Identify the situation and participants for each item on your list. Who is the best listener you know? What makes that person a good listener? Be prepared to discuss your responses in class, with your team, or in a memo to your instructor.

2.12 Listening: Skills Required in Various Careers (Obj. 5)

Team

Do the listening skills and behaviors of individuals differ depending on their careers?

Your Task. Your instructor will divide you into teams and give each team a role to discuss, such as business executive, teacher, physician, police officer, attorney, accountant, administrative assistant, mentor, or team leader. Create a list of verbal and nonverbal cues that a member of this profession would display to indicate that he or she is listening. Would the cues and behavior change if the person were trying to listen discriminatively versus critically? How?

2.13 Nonverbal Communication: Recognizing Functions (Obj. 6)

Most of us use nonverbal cues and react to them unconsciously. We seldom think about the functions they serve.

Your Task. To become more aware of the functions of nonverbal communication, keep a log for one week. Observe how nonverbal communication is used by friends, family, instructors, coworkers, managers, politicians, newsmakers, businesses, and others. For each of the five functions of nonverbal communication identified in this chapter, list examples illustrating that function. For example, under *To reinforce and accentuate,* you might list a friend who whispers a message to you, thus suggesting that it is a secret. Under *To control and regulate,* you might list the steady gaze of your instructor who has targeted a student who is not paying attention. Train yourself to become more observant, and begin making notes in your log. How many examples can you name for each of the five functions? Be prepared to submit your list or discuss it in class.

2.14 Nonverbal Communication: How to Be More Influential (Obj. 6)

Assume you have just been hired into a prestigious job and you want to make a good impression. You also want very much to become influential in the organization.

Your Task. When you attend meetings, what nonverbal behaviors and signals can you send that will make a good impression as well as improve your influence? In interacting with colleagues, what nonverbal behavior will make you more impressive and influential?

2.15 Nonverbal Communication: Body Language (Obj. 6)

Your Task. What attitudes do the following body movements suggest to you? Do these movements always mean the same thing? What part does context play in your interpretations?

a. Whistling, wringing hands
b. Bowed posture, twiddling thumbs
c. Steepled hands, sprawling position
d. Rubbing hand through hair
e. Open hands, unbuttoned coat
f. Wringing hands, tugging ears

2.16 Nonverbal Communication: Universal Sign for *I Goofed* (Obj. 6)

Team

In an effort to promote tranquility on the highways and reduce road rage, motorists submitted the following suggestions. They were sent to a newspaper columnist who asked for a universal nonverbal signal admitting that a driver had "goofed."[68]

Your Task. In small groups consider the pros and cons of each of the following gestures intended as an apology when a driver makes a mistake. Why would some fail?

a. Lower your head slightly and bonk yourself on the forehead with the side of your closed fist. The message is clear: *I'm stupid. I shouldn't have done that.*
b. Make a temple with your hands, as if you were praying.
c. Move the index finger of your right hand back and forth across your neck—as if you were cutting your throat.
d. Flash the well-known peace sign. Hold up the index and middle fingers of one hand, making a V, as in victory.
e. Place the flat of your hands against your cheeks, as children do when they have made a mistake.
f. Clasp your hand over your mouth, raise your brows, and shrug your shoulders.
g. Use your knuckles to knock on the side of your head. Translation: *Oops! Engage brain.*
h. Place your right hand high on your chest and pat a few times, like a basketball player who drops a pass or a football player who makes a bad throw. This says, *I'll take the blame.*
i. Place your right fist over the middle of your chest and move it in a circular motion. This is universal sign language for *I'm sorry.*
j. Open your window and tap the top of your car roof with your hand.
k. Smile and raise both arms, palms outward, which is a universal gesture for surrender or forgiveness.
l. Use the military salute, which is simple and shows respect.
m. Flash your biggest smile, point at yourself with your right thumb and move your head from left to right, as if to say, *I can't believe I did that.*

2.17 Verbal Versus Nonverbal Signals (Obj. 6)

To show the power of nonverbal cues, the president of a large East Coast consulting company uses the following demonstration with new employees. Raising his right hand, he touches his pointer finger to his thumb to form a circle. Then he asks new employees in the session to do likewise. When everyone has a finger-thumb circle formed, the president tells each person to touch that circle to his or her chin. But as he says this, he touches his own finger-thumb circle to his cheek. What happens? You guessed it! About 80 percent of the group follow what they see the president do rather than following what they hear.[69]

Your Task. Try this same demonstration with several of your friends, family members, or work colleagues. Which is more effective—verbal or nonverbal signals? What conclusion could you draw from this demonstration? Do you think that nonverbal signals are always more meaningful than verbal ones? What other factors in the communication process might determine whether verbal or nonverbal signals were more important?

2.18 Nonverbal Communication: Signals Sent by Business Casual Dress (Obj. 6)

Team

Although many employers allow casual dress, not all employers and customers are happy with the results. To learn more about the implementation, acceptance, and effects of casual-dress programs, select one of the following activities, all of which involve some form of interviewing.

Your Task

a. In teams, gather information from human resources directors to determine which companies allow business casual dress, how often, and under what specific conditions. The information may be collected by personal interviews, by e-mail, or by telephone.
b. In teams, conduct inquiring-reporter interviews. Ask individuals in the community how they react to casual dress in the workplace. Develop a set of standard interview questions.
c. In teams, visit local businesses on both business casual days and on traditional business dress days. Compare and contrast the effects of business dress standards on such factors as the projected image of the company, the nature of the interactions with customers and with fellow employees, the morale of employees, and the productivity of employees. What generalizations can you draw from your findings?

2.19 Body Art: A Butterfly on Her Neck (Obj. 6)

Nearly 30 percent of American adults now display one or more tattoos, according to a report of the American Academy of Dermatology.[70] However, many people still consider body art edgy or rebellious.

© Cary Jobe/Aurora/Getty Images

Your Task. Your friend and fellow office worker Avalon proudly shows you a butterfly tattoo she just got on her neck. She wants to know whether you think she may display it at work. What advice would a career-conscious, ambitious person give to a friend?

2.20 Nonverbal Communication: Defining *Business Casual* (Obj. 6)

Although many business organizations are adopting business casual dress, most people cannot define the term. Your boss asks your internship team to use the Web to find out exactly what *business casual* means.

Your Task. Using a good search engine such as Google, explore the Web for *business casual dress code.* A few Web sites actually try to define the term and give examples of appropriate clothing. Visit many sites and decide whether they are reliable enough to use as sources of accurate information. Print several relevant pages. Get together with your team and compare notes. Then write a memo to your boss explaining what men and women should and shouldn't wear on business casual days.

2.21 Nonverbal Communication Around the World (Obj. 6)

Web

Gestures play an important role when people communicate. Because culture shapes the meaning of gestures, miscommunication and misunderstanding can easily result in international situations.

Your Task. Use the Web to research the meanings of selected gestures. Make a list of ten gestures (other than those discussed in the text) that have different meanings in different countries. Consider the fingertip kiss, nose thumb, eyelid pull, nose tap, head shake, and other gestures. How are the meanings different in other countries?

2.22 Guide to Business Etiquette and Workplace Manners: Sharpening Your Skills (Obj. 7)

Business communicators feel more confident and make better impressions when they are aware of current business etiquette and proper workplace manners. But how do you know what is the right thing to do? You can gauge your current level of knowledge and sharpen your etiquette skills with a little effort.

Your Task. At **www.meguffey.com** find *Dr. Guffey's Guide to Business Etiquette and Workplace Manners.* Take the preview test and then study the 17 business etiquette topics presented. Your instructor may give you one or more posttests to learn whether you fully understand the implications of the workplace manners discussed.

2.23 Business Etiquette: Mind Your Manners or Mind Your BlackBerry? (Obj. 7)

Businesspeople are increasingly caving in to the temptation to use their BlackBerrys and smartphones to check e-mail, Google, Facebook, and Twitter during meetings. Techies say that ignoring real-time text messages in today's hurry-up world risks danger. They are tuned in to what is happening and can respond immediately. Traditionalists say that checking messages and texting during meetings is tasteless and shows poor manners. But times are changing. A third of the workers recently polled by Yahoo HotJobs said they frequently checked e-mail during meetings. They also admitted, however, being castigated for poor manners in using wireless devices.

Many professionals insist that they use their wireless devices for legitimate purposes, such as surfing the Web for urgent information, meeting deadlines, taking notes, and responding to customers. Yet the practice annoys many observers. One college student sank his chances to land an internship with a hedge fund when he whipped out his BlackBerry during an interview to support an answer with an online fact. Unfortunately, he lingered to check an e-mail message from a friend, and watchful recruiters found this dalliance unprofessional. Among high-level professionals, the appearance of a BlackBerry is almost a boast. One consultant reported that it is "customary now for professionals to lay [their] BlackBerrys or iPhones on a conference table before a meeting—like gunfighters placing their Colt revolvers on the card tables in a saloon." These professionals seem to be announcing that they are connected, busy, and important, but they will give full attention. The implication, too, is that this meeting had better be essential and efficient because they have more important things to do.[71]

Your Task. Few organizations have established policies on smartphone use in meetings. Assume that your team has been asked to develop such a policy. Your boss can't decide whether to ask your team to develop a short policy or a more rigorous one. Unable to make a decision, he asks for two statements: (a) a short statement that treats employees as grownups who can exercise intelligent judgment, and (b) a more complete set of guidelines that spell out exactly what should and should not be done.

Video Resource

Video Library 2, Understanding Teamwork at Cold Stone Creamery

Inside Cold Stone Creamery, the fast-growing ice cream specialty chain, you see that teamwork permeates every facet of the corporate culture. After you watch the video, be prepared to discuss these questions:

- How is the term *team* defined in this video? Can you offer a more specific definition?
- What six kinds of teams were mentioned in the Cold Stone Creamery video? Can you provide examples of these kinds of teams in companies with which you are familiar?
- What characteristics make for effective teams? In your experience with teams, do you agree or disagree?

Chat About It

In each chapter you will find five discussion questions related to the chapter material. Your instructor may assign these topics for you to discuss in class, in an online chat room, or on an online discussion board. Some of the discussion topics may require outside research. You may also be asked to read and respond to postings made by your classmates.

Topic 1: Do you agree with the statement that it's harder to convince potential employers that you posses a soft skill than it is to convince potential employers that you possess a hard skill? How would you convincingly present your strongest soft skill on a résumé or in a job interview?

Topic 2: Think about an experience you had in working on a team project at work, in school or in some other setting. Without naming names, describe the characteristics of a valuable teammate. How would you modify your behavior in a team setting based on what you witnessed?

Topic 3: Suppose you are working in a team that has one or two dominant individuals who make most of the decisions and who sometimes don't consider your ideas. Instead of giving up and not participating, what could you do that would be more helpful to the team and to your career?

Topic 4: Because majority voting is faster than consensus for reaching decisions and because most people in the workplace are professionals, shouldn't employees who are in the minority on a vote simply "get over it" and support the decision? Why?

Topic 5: Which of the Ten Keys to Building Powerful Listening Skills would be most helpful to you? Why did you pick the one that you did, and how could you implement that suggestion?

Are you ready? Get more practice at **www.meguffey.com**

Grammar and Mechanics C.L.U.E. Review 2

Verbs

Review Guides 4–10 in Appendix A, Grammar and Mechanics Guide, beginning on page A-3. On a separate sheet, revise the following sentences to correct any errors in verbs. For each error that you locate, write the guide number that reflects this usage. If a sentence is correct, write *C*. When you finish, check your answers on page Key-1.

Note: Remember that you can complete a similar C.L.U.E. review exercise with feedback at **www.meguffey.com**.

Example: Her identity was **stole** when she charged a restaurant meal.
Revision: Her identity was **stolen** when she charged a restaurant meal. [Guide 4]

1. Our recruiter must chose from among four strong candidates.
2. The use of smartphones and laptops during meetings are prohibited.
3. If I was you, I would finish my degree program.
4. Considerable time and money was spent on communication training for employees.
5. Neither the president nor the operations manager have read the complete report.
6. Disagreement and dissension is normal and should be expected in team interactions.
7. Everything in the meeting minutes and company reports are open to public view.
8. A committee of three employees and two managers are working to establish office priorities.
9. Greg said that he seen the report before it was distributed to management.
10. Each of the office divisions are expected to work together to create common procedures.

CHAPTER 3

Intercultural Communication

OBJECTIVES

After studying this chapter, you should be able to

1. Understand how three significant trends have increased the importance of intercultural communication.
2. Define *culture,* describe five noteworthy cultural characteristics, and compare and contrast five key dimensions of culture including high and low context.
3. Explain the effects of ethnocentrism, and show how tolerance and patience help in achieving intercultural proficiency.
4. Apply techniques for improving nonverbal and oral communication in intercultural settings.
5. Identify techniques for improving written messages to intercultural audiences.
6. Discuss intercultural ethics, including business practices abroad, bribery, prevailing customs, and methods for coping.
7. Explain in what ways workforce diversity provides benefits and poses challenges, and how you can learn to be sensitive to racial and gender issues.

Want to do well on tests and excel in your course? Go to **www.meguffey.com** for helpful interactive resources.

- **Review the Chapter 3 PowerPoint slides to prepare for the first quiz.**

Zooming In PART 1

Costly Intercultural Lessons for World's Largest Retailer

"Why would you buy a box of shampoo bottles?" asked Lee Jin Sook, a Seoul housewife. Koreans favor smaller packages and walk or take the subway to shop daily at a variety of stores.[1] Consumers in this and other Asian countries don't buy in bulk. Moreover, Wal-Mart's no-frills warehouse stores and high racks frustrated diminutive shoppers who had to borrow ladders. Cultural differences and fierce local competition forced the world's largest retailer to leave Korea to stem heavy losses.

Shortly after its departure from Korea, the giant from Bentonville, Arkansas, also pulled out of its first European market, Germany, amid a loss of $1 billion. "The company's culture does not travel, and Wal-Mart does not understand the German customer," said the CEO of a large local competitor who predicted Wal-Mart's demise six years before the retail behemoth exited the German market.[2] *The New York Times* wrote that Wal-Mart's foray into its first European market had become "a template for how not to expand into a country."[3]

What went wrong in Germany? Aside from underestimating its discounter competitors and the legal environment, most of Wal-Mart's blunders seemed to be cultural. Top executives didn't speak German, and greeters with Midwestern folksiness were lost on German employees and local shoppers. The familiar morning chant was scrapped because staff members found it "strange."[4] A court overturned Wal-Mart's policy against dating coworkers, and Wal-Mart's antiunion stance fell flat in a country where unions and corporations collaborate closely.

Was Wal-Mart interculturally more proficient when it acquired the Japanese supermarket chain Seiyu several years ago? One marketer doesn't think so: "It's doomed. Japanese consumers are small-store-oriented and don't have the home storage for hypermarket buying.... It is similar to Germany as they [Wal-Mart] have not understood consumers."[5] Some analysts recommend that Wal-Mart leave Japan to prevent further losses.[6] Can Wal-Mart do better in its future international endeavors? You will learn more about this case on page 89.

© AP Images/Toby Talbot

Critical Thinking

- In its international expansion policy, Wal-Mart followed the advice of Harvard business professor Theodore Levitt, whose famous 1983 book *The Globalization of Markets* advocated standardization, not localization: "Gone are accustomed differences in national or regional preference." Whereas conventional multinational companies adapted to "superficial and even entrenched differences within and between nations," truly global firms sought to "force suitably standardized products and practices on the entire globe."[7] Should companies stick to a standardized approach or adapt to local markets?
- What domestic and global changes are taking place that encourage the international expansion of companies such as Wal-Mart?
- What other U.S. businesses can you name that have merged with foreign companies or expanded to become multinational in scope? Have you heard of any notable successes or failures?

http://www.walmart.com/

The Increasing Importance of Intercultural Communication

LEARNING OBJECTIVE 1
Understand how three significant trends have increased the importance of intercultural communication.

Domestic businesses today sell their products across borders and seek customers in diverse foreign markets. Especially in North America, this movement toward a global economy has swelled to a torrent. To be competitive, many organizations form multinational alliances, such as that between Wal-Mart, the U.S. super discounter, and Seiyu, Japan's fifth-largest food and retail chain. If you visit a European or Asian city, you will be likely to encounter familiar U.S. chains such as The Gap, Subway, Pizza Hut, and Timberland.

The "global village" predicted many years ago is emerging fast. To succeed in a global market, business communicators will need to become more aware of their own culture and how it differs from others. In this chapter you will learn basic characteristics and dimensions of culture, as well as how to achieve intercultural proficiency. We will focus on techniques for improving nonverbal, oral, and written messages to intercultural audiences. You will study intercultural ethics and techniques for capitalizing on workforce diversity at home.

Why is it helpful to learn how culture affects behavior?

But many expanding companies stumble when they are forced to confront obstacles never before encountered. Significant obstacles involve confusion and clashes resulting from intercultural differences. You may face such intercultural differences in your current or future jobs. Your employers, coworkers, or customers could very well be from other countries. You may travel abroad for your employer or on your own. Learning more about the powerful effect that culture has on behavior will help you reduce friction and misunderstanding in your dealings with people from other cultures. Before examining strategies for helping you overcome intercultural obstacles, let's take a closer look at three significant trends: (a) the globalization of markets, (b) technological advancements, and (c) an intercultural workforce.

Globalization of Markets

Which developments have helped businesses overcome national boundaries?

Doing business beyond borders is now commonplace. Frito-Lay pushes its potato chips in China.[8] Finnish cell phone maker Nokia promotes its mobile phones in the world's fastest-growing markets of India and China. Newell Rubbermaid offers stylish Pyrex cookware to European chefs, and McDonald's and Starbucks serve customers around the world.

Not only are market borders blurring, but acquisitions, mergers, alliances, and buyouts are obscuring the nationality of many companies. The quirky Vermont ice cream purveyor Ben & Jerry's is a division of Dutch multinational Unilever; Bridgestone Americas is owned by a Japanese conglomerate; the Arco gas station chain is a subsidiary of the third-largest energy company in the world, British Petroleum; and "Your Neighborhood Grocery Store," Trader Joe's, is owned by Germany's top discounter, Aldi. Two thirds of Colgate-Palmolive's employees work outside North America, and Nike is raking in more revenue overseas than in the United States. Procter & Gamble wants to more than double its sales over the next 15 years, primarily by expanding into developing markets.[9] What's more, 7-Eleven is the highest-grossing retailer in Japan and has nearly twice as many outlets there as it has in the United States.[10]

Why must American companies in global markets adapt to other cultures?

To be successful in this interdependent global village, American companies are increasingly finding it necessary to adapt to other cultures. In China, Frito-Lay had to accommodate yin and yang, the Chinese philosophy that nature and life must balance opposing elements. Chinese consider fried foods to be hot and avoid them in summer because two "hots" don't balance. They prefer "cool" snacks in summer; therefore, Frito-Lay created "cool lemon" potato chips dotted with lime specks and mint. The yellow, lemon-scented chips are delivered in a package with breezy-blue skies and rolling green grass.[11]

In promoting its shoes and apparel to kids from Rome to Rio de Janeiro, Nike features Brazilian soccer star Ronaldo, rather than a U.S. basketball star.[12] To sell its laundry products in Europe, Unilever learned that Germans demand a product that is gentle on lakes and rivers. Spaniards wanted cheaper products that get shirts white and soft, and Greeks preferred small packages that were cheap and easy to carry home.[13] To push ketchup in Japan, H. J. Heinz had to overcome a cultural resistance to sweet flavors. Thus, it offered Japanese homemakers cooking lessons instructing them how to use the sugary red sauce on omelets, sausages, and pasta.[14] Domino's Pizza catered to the Japanese by adding squid to its pizza toppings.[15]

When upscale sandwich chain New York NY Fresh Deli opened a franchise in Dubai, it had to replace all salad dressings that contained vinegar. Considered a spirit, vinegar and other alcoholic beverages can be served only in hotels and to non-Muslims.[16] In Taiwan, Dunkin' Donuts catered to local palates with flavors such as pineapple, sweet potato, and green apple.[17] As Figure 3.1 on page 81 shows, McDonald's is adjusting its menus to suit the dietary preferences of very diverse customers around the world.

How have favorable trade agreements, declining domestic markets, and middle-class growth changed business?

Why are U.S. businesses and those of other countries rushing to expand around the world? What is causing this dash toward globalization of markets and blurring of national identities? Many companies, such as Wal-Mart, are increasingly looking overseas as domestic markets mature. They can no longer expect double-digit sales growth at home. Another significant factor is the passage of favorable trade agreements. The General Agreement on Tariffs and Trade (GATT) promotes open trade globally, and the North American Free Trade Agreement (NAFTA) has expanded free trade among Canada, the United States, and Mexico. NAFTA has created the largest and richest free-trade region on earth. In addition, the opening of Eastern Europe and the shift away from communism in Russia further expanded world markets. In Asia, China's admission to the World Trade Organization unlocked its economy and suddenly provided access to a huge population.

Beyond favorable trade agreements, other changes fuel globalization. Parts of the world formerly considered underdeveloped now boast robust middle classes. These consumers crave everything from cola to smartphones and high-definition TVs. What's more, countries such as

FIGURE 3.1 Fries With Your Shrimp Burger?

In 2005 McDonald's was struggling. Its stock price plummeted. Changing customer preferences in the United States forced the fast-food giant to broaden its menu to include healthier fare such as salads, fruit, and low-fat offerings. Many restaurants now also remain open 24/7. The company has staged a remarkable turnaround.

The hamburger chain is expanding its presence in India and experiencing double-digit sales growth. Catering to a predominantly Hindu nation that reveres the cow, McDonald's doesn't serve beef. Instead, it dishes out vegetable patties, MacAloo Tikki, and Chicken Maharaja Mac. Chicken McNuggets have been so popular in India that some McDonald's restaurants occasionally run out.

In third place after the Czech Republic and Ireland in annual per capita consumption of the beverage, the Germans enjoy their beer. In a nod to local custom, McDonald's Germany serves brew on tap to guests 16 and over.

The McDonald's menu in Japan includes Ebi Filet-o (shrimp burgers), Koroke Burgers (a sandwich with mashed potato, cabbage, and a special sauce), and shrimp nuggets called Ebi-Chiki.

The Finns and Norwegians are known for their love of fish. Not surprisingly, McDonald's opted for menu items with salmon called McLaks and Laksewrap.

The two busiest McDonald's restaurants in the world are located on Pushkin Square in Moscow and Karlsplatz in Munich, Germany. The Russian location, with its 900 seats and free Internet access, serves about 30,000 customers each day. Cabbage pie, a local favorite, was added to the menu.

Last, France, a country known for its fine cuisine, is the second-biggest market after the United States in McDonald's global profits.

China and India have become less paranoid about foreign investment and free trade. Onerous rules and red tape previously prevented many companies from doing business at home, much less abroad. Of paramount importance in explaining the explosive growth of global markets is the development of new transportation and information technologies.

Technological Advancements

Which two advancements contribute to global interconnectivity?

Amazing new transportation and information technologies are major contributors to the development of our global interconnectivity. Supersonic planes now carry goods and passengers to other continents overnight. As a result, produce shoppers in Japan can choose from the finest artichokes, avocados, and apples only hours after they were picked in California. Americans enjoy bouquets of tulips, roses, and exotic lilies soon after harvesting in Holland and Colombia. In fact, 70 percent of the cut flowers in the United States now come from Colombia in South America. Many of us remember when asparagus and strawberries could be enjoyed only in early summer. Today we expect to see these items and other fruits and vegetables in our markets nearly year-round. Continent-hopping planes are so fast and reliable that most of the world is rapidly becoming an open market.

The Internet and the Web are changing the way we live, the way we do business, and the way we communicate. Advancements in communication and transportation have made markets and jobs more accessible. They've also made the world of business more efficient and more globally interdependent. High-speed, high-capacity, and relatively low-cost communications have opened new global opportunities and have made geographical location virtually irrelevant for many activities and services. Workers have access to company records, software programs, and colleagues whether they're working at home, in the office, or at the beach. As discussed in Chapters 1 and 2, technology is making a huge difference in the workplace. Wikis, blogs, wireless devices, teleconferencing, and intranets streamline business processes and improve access to critical company information.

The Internet permits instantaneous oral and written communication across time zones and continents. Managers in Miami or Milwaukee can use high-speed data systems to swap marketing plans instantly with their counterparts in Milan or Munich. IBM relies on 5,000 programmers in India to solve intricate computer problems and return the solutions overnight via digital transmission.[18] Employees at Procter & Gamble send their payroll questions to back-office service centers in England, Costa Rica, or Manila.[19] Fashion designers at Liz Claiborne can snap a digital photo of a garment and immediately transmit the image to manufacturers in Hong Kong and Djakarta, Indonesia.[20] They can even include a video clip to show a tricky alteration.

The changing landscape of business clearly demonstrates the need for technology savvy and connectedness around the world. Career success and personal wealth depend on the ability to use technology effectively. As the accompanying Plugged In feature indicates, countries with a high percentage of Internet users tend to have highly developed, thriving economies. You are in for a surprise if you believe that the United States is the only Internet powerhouse.

PLUGGED IN

Greenland and Iceland: The Most Connected Countries in the World?

The American Internet? Think again. Yes, the precursors of the Internet that emerged from the sciences and the military were U.S.-based. Early Web sites were almost always in English and meant for Americans.

Perhaps it's the cold climate, but Greenland—the least densely populated country in the world—is also the most connected one. The vast icy territory belonging to Denmark indeed boasts the most Internet users among its sparse population, closely followed by Iceland.

A look at per-capita use of the Internet reveals that Scandinavian countries—Iceland, Norway, Finland, Sweden, and Denmark—lead the world and rank up to 15 percentage points ahead of the United States.

Asia has the most Internet users in absolute numbers (658 million), followed by Europe (393 million) and North America (251 million). However, Internet users from Asia, the most populous continent, comprise a rather modest 17.4 percent. Europe shows a penetration of 48.9 and North America of 74.4 percent.

Career Application

Analyze the table and relate the percentage of Internet use to the country. For example, in China only 22.4 percent of the people have Internet access. Is this figure likely to increase in the future? How can you explain the low Internet penetration for Asia as a whole? Why do you think North European nations are so Internet friendly? What conclusions can you draw about Internet use worldwide?

Internet Use Around the World

Country	Current Population	Internet Users	Percent Population Penetration
Greenland	57,564	52,000	90.3
Iceland	304,367	273,930	90.0
Norway	4,644,457	3,993,400	86.0
Finland	5,244,749	4,353,142	83.0
The Netherlands	16,645,313	13,791,800	82.9
Sweden	9,045,389	7,295,200	80.7
Denmark	5,484,723	4,408,100	80.4
South Korea	48,379,392	36,794,800	76.1
United States	304,228,257	227,190,989	74.7
Japan	127,288,419	94,000,000	73.8
China	1,330,044,605	298,000,000	22.4
TOTAL WORLD	6,710,029,070	1,596,270,108	23.8

Source: Internet World Stats – www.internetworldstats.com, 2009.

Intercultural Workforce

As world commerce mingles more and more, another trend gives intercultural communication increasing importance: people are on the move. Lured by the prospects of peace, prosperity, education, or a fresh start, people from many cultures are moving to countries promising to fulfill their dreams. For generations the two most popular destinations have been the United States and Canada.

Why is learning to adapt to an intercultural workforce and multinational companies an important requirement for business communicators?

Because of increases in immigration, foreign-born persons comprise an ever-growing portion of the total U.S. population. Over the next 50 years, the population of the United States is expected to grow by nearly 50 percent, from about 275 million in the year 2000 to an estimated 394 million people in 2050. Two thirds of that increase will be the result of net immigration.[21] Estimates also suggest that immigrants will account for half of all new U.S. workers in the years ahead.[22]

This influx of immigrants is reshaping American and Canadian societies. Earlier immigrants were thought to be part of a "melting pot" of ethnic groups. Today, they are more like a "tossed salad" or "spicy stew," with each group contributing its own unique flavor. Instead of the exception, cultural diversity is increasingly the norm. As we seek to accommodate multiethnic neighborhoods, multinational companies, and an intercultural workforce, we can expect some changes to happen smoothly. Other changes will involve conflict and resentment, especially for people losing their positions of power and privilege. Learning to accommodate and manage intercultural change is an important part of the education of any business communicator.

Culture and Communication

LEARNING OBJECTIVE 2

Define *culture,* describe five noteworthy cultural characteristics, and compare and contrast five key dimensions of culture including high and low context.

Every country or region within a country has a unique common heritage, joint experience, or shared learning. This shared background produces the culture of a region, country, or society. For our purposes, *culture* may be defined as the complex system of values, traits, morals, and customs shared by a society. Culture teaches people how to behave, and it conditions their reactions. The important thing to remember is that culture is a powerful operating force that molds the way we think and behave. The purpose of this chapter is to broaden your view of culture and open your mind to flexible attitudes so that you can avoid frustration when cultural adjustment is necessary.

Characteristics of Culture

Culture is shaped by attitudes learned in childhood and later internalized in adulthood. As we enter this current period of globalization and interculturalism, we should expect to make

© Fotosearch/Photolibrary

Marketers of Crest toothpaste face numerous challenges in communicating the value of their brand across cultures—especially Chinese culture. China's citizens traditionally have ignored toothpaste products, choosing instead to freshen up the mouth with green tea. An estimated 57 percent of rural Chinese residents have never brushed their teeth. Though China is currently experiencing a beauty boom, decades ago the country frowned upon personal care products. *How might understanding the characteristics of culture help marketers sell toothpaste to China's over one billion people?*

adjustments and adopt new attitudes. Adjustment and accommodation will be easier if we understand some basic characteristics of culture.

Culture Is Learned. Rules, values, and attitudes of a culture are not inherent. They are learned and passed down from generation to generation. For example, in many Middle Eastern and some Asian cultures, same-sex people may walk hand-in-hand in the street, but opposite-sex people may not do so. In Arab cultures conversations are often held in close proximity, sometimes nose to nose. But in Western cultures if a person stands too close, one may react as if violated: *He was all over me like a rash.* Cultural rules of behavior learned from your family and society are conditioned from early childhood.

Cultures Are Inherently Logical. The rules in any culture originated to reinforce that culture's values and beliefs. They act as normative forces. For example, in Japan the original Barbie doll was a failure for many reasons, one of which was her toothy smile.[23] This is a country where women cover their mouths with their hands when they laugh so as not to expose their teeth. Exposing one's teeth is not only immodest but also aggressive. Although current cultural behavior may sometimes seem silly and illogical, nearly all serious rules and values originate in deep-seated beliefs. Rules about exposing teeth or how close to stand are linked to values about sexuality, aggression, modesty, and respect. Acknowledging the inherent logic of a culture is extremely important when learning to accept behavior that differs from one's own cultural behavior.

How does culture shape or determine us?

Culture Is the Basis of Self-Identity and Community. Culture is the basis for how we tell the world who we are and what we believe. People build their identities through cultural overlays to their primary culture. When North Americans make choices in education, career, place of employment, and life partner, they consider certain rules, manners, ceremonies, beliefs, languages, and values. These considerations add to their total cultural outlook and are major expressions of their self-identity.

Culture Combines the Visible and Invisible. To outsiders, the way we act—those things that we do in daily life and work—are the most visible parts of our culture. In Japan, for instance, harmony with the environment is important. Therefore, when attending a flower show, a woman would wear a dress with pastel rather than primary colors to avoid detracting from the beauty of the flowers. In India people avoid stepping on ants or insects because they believe in reincarnation and are careful about all forms of life. Such practices are outward symbols of deeper values that are invisible but that pervade everything we think and do.

Ethics Check

Cultural Change: From "Sexist" to Gender-Neutral Language

Just a generation ago, businesspeople were *businessmen*, letter carriers were *postmen*, and flight attendants were *stewardesses*. A sea change in language now dictates gender neutrality to avoid type casting. In business, the honorific *Ms.* is used for all women, regardless of their marital status. Does language reflect just the current culture, or does it have the power to effect change?

Culture Is Dynamic. Over time, cultures change. Changes are caused by advancements in technology and communication, as discussed earlier. Local differences are modified or slowly erased. Change is also caused by events such as migration, natural disasters, and wars. The American Civil War, for instance, produced far-reaching cultural changes for both the North and the South. Another major event in this country was the exodus of people from farms. When families moved to cities, major changes occurred in the way family members interacted. Attitudes, behaviors, and beliefs change in open societies more quickly than in closed societies.

Dimensions of Culture

The more you know about culture in general and your own culture in particular, the better able you will be to adopt an intercultural perspective. A typical North American has habits and beliefs similar to those of other members of Western, technologically advanced societies. In our limited space in this book, it is impossible to cover fully the infinite facets of culture. But we can outline some key dimensions of culture and look at them from a variety of viewpoints.

So that you will better understand your culture and how it contrasts with other cultures, we will describe five key dimensions of culture: context, individualism, formality, communication style, and time orientation.

Context. Context is probably the most important cultural dimension and also the most difficult to define. It is a concept developed by cultural anthropologist Edward T. Hall. In his model, context refers to the stimuli, environment, or ambience surrounding an event.

Communicators in low-context cultures (such as those in North America, Scandinavia, and Germany) depend little on the context of a situation to convey their meaning. They assume that listeners know very little and must be told practically everything. In high-context cultures (such as those in Japan, China, and Arab countries), the listener is already "contexted" and does not need to be given much background information.[24] To identify low- and high-context countries, Hall arranged them on a continuum, as shown in Figure 3.2.

What are typical characteristics of low-context cultures?

Low-context cultures tend to be logical, analytical, and action oriented. Business communicators stress clearly articulated messages that they consider to be objective, professional, and efficient. High-context cultures are more likely to be intuitive and contemplative. Communicators in high-context cultures pay attention to more than the words spoken. They emphasize interpersonal relationships, nonverbal expression, physical setting, and social setting. For example, a Japanese communicator might say *yes* when he really means *no*. From the context of the situation, the Japanese speaker would indicate whether *yes* really meant *yes* or whether it meant *no*. The context, tone, time taken to answer, facial expression, and body cues would convey the meaning of *yes*.[25] Thus, in high-context cultures, communication cues are transmitted by posture, voice inflection, gestures, and facial expression. Establishing relationships is an important part of communicating and interacting.

In terms of thinking patterns, low-context communicators tend to use *linear logic*. They proceed from Point A to Point B to Point C and finally arrive at a conclusion. High-context communicators, however, may use *spiral logic*, circling around a topic indirectly and looking at it from many tangential or divergent viewpoints. A conclusion may be implied but not argued directly. For a concise summary of important differences between low- and high-context cultures, see Figure 3.2.

What kind of values do members of many low-context cultures embrace?

Individualism. An attitude of independence and freedom from control characterizes individualism. Members of low-context cultures, particularly Americans, tend to value individualism. They believe that initiative and self-assertion result in personal achievement. They believe in individual action and personal responsibility, and they desire a large degree of freedom in their personal lives.

Members of high-context cultures are more collectivist. They emphasize membership in organizations, groups, and teams; they encourage acceptance of group values, duties, and decisions. They typically resist independence because it fosters competition and confrontation instead of consensus. In group-oriented cultures such as those in many Asian societies, for example, self-assertion and individual decision making are discouraged. "The nail that sticks up gets pounded down" is a common Japanese saying.[26] Business decisions are often made by all

FIGURE 3.2 Comparing Low- and High-Context Cultures

Low Context	High Context
Tend to prefer direct verbal interaction	Tend to prefer indirect verbal interaction
Tend to understand meaning at one level only	Tend to understand meanings embedded at many sociocultural levels
Are generally less proficient in reading nonverbal cues	Are generally more proficient in reading nonverbal cues
Value individualism	Value group membership
Rely more on logic	Rely more on context and feeling
Employ linear logic	Employ spiral logic
Say *no* directly	Talk around point; avoid saying *no*
Communicate in highly structured messages, provide details, stress literal meanings, give authority to written information	Communicate in simple, sometimes ambiguous, messages; understand visual messages readily

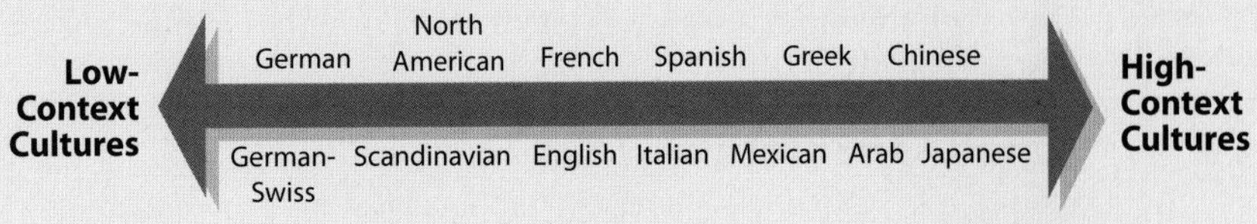

who have competence in the matter under discussion. Similarly, in China managers also focus on the group rather than on the individual, preferring a consultative management style over an autocratic style.[27]

Many cultures, of course, are quite complex and cannot be characterized as totally individualistic or group oriented. For example, European Americans are generally quite individualistic, whereas African Americans are less so, and Latin Americans are closer to the group-centered dimension.[28]

Are tradition, ceremony, and social rules equally important in all cultures?

Formality. People in some cultures place less emphasis on tradition, ceremony, and social rules than do members of other cultures. North Americans, for example, dress casually and are soon on a first-name basis with others. Their lack of formality is often characterized by directness. In business dealings North Americans come to the point immediately; indirectness, they feel, wastes time, a valuable commodity in American culture.

This informality and directness may be confusing abroad. In Mexico, for instance, a typical business meeting begins with handshakes, coffee, and an expansive conversation about the weather, sports, and other light topics. An invitation to "get down to business" might offend a Mexican executive.[29] In Japan signing documents and exchanging business cards are important rituals. In Europe first names are never used without invitation. In Arab, South American, and Asian cultures, a feeling of friendship and kinship must be established before business can be transacted.

In Western cultures people are more relaxed about social status and the appearance of power.[30] Deference is not generally paid to individuals merely because of their wealth, position, seniority, or age. In many Asian cultures, however, these characteristics are important and must be respected. Wal-Mart, facing many hurdles in breaking into the Japanese market, admits having difficulty training local employees to speak up to their bosses. In the Japanese culture lower-level employees do not question management. Deference and respect are paid to authority and power. Recognizing this cultural pattern, Marriott Hotel managers learned to avoid placing a lower-level Japanese employee on a floor above a higher-level executive from the same company.

In what ways does culture affect how words are used by people in low- and high-context cultures?

Communication Style. People in low- and high-context cultures tend to communicate differently with words. To Americans and Germans, words are very important, especially in contracts and negotiations. People in high-context cultures, on the other hand, place more emphasis on the surrounding context than on the words describing a negotiation. A Greek may see a contract as a formal statement announcing the intention to build a business for the future. The Japanese may treat contracts as statements of intention, and they assume changes will be made as a project develops. Mexicans may treat contracts as artistic exercises of what might be accomplished in an ideal world. They do not necessarily expect contracts to apply consistently in the real world. An Arab may be insulted by merely mentioning a contract; a person's word is more binding.[31]

North Americans tend to take words literally, whereas Latinos enjoy plays on words; and Arabs and South Americans sometimes speak with extravagant or poetic figures of speech that may be misinterpreted if taken literally. Nigerians prefer a quiet, clear form of expression; and Germans tend to be direct but understated.[32]

What communication style do North Americans value?

In communication style North Americans value straightforwardness, are suspicious of evasiveness, and distrust people who might have a "hidden agenda" or who "play their cards too close to the chest."[33] North Americans also tend to be uncomfortable with silence and impatient with delays. Some Asian businesspeople have learned that the longer they drag out negotiations, the more concessions impatient North Americans are likely to make.

Western cultures have developed languages that use letters describing the *sounds* of words. But Asian languages are based on pictographical characters representing the *meanings* of words. Asian language characters are much more complex than the Western alphabet; therefore, Asians are said to have a higher competence in the discrimination of visual patterns.

What is the attitude of North Americans toward time?

Time Orientation. North Americans consider time a precious commodity to be conserved. They correlate time with productivity, efficiency, and money. Keeping people waiting for business appointments wastes time and is also rude.

In other cultures time may be perceived as an unlimited and never-ending resource to be enjoyed. A North American businessperson, for example, was kept waiting two hours past a scheduled appointment time in South America. She wasn't offended, though, because she was familiar with South Americans' more relaxed concept of time.

How do Asians approach time?

Although Asians are punctual, their need for deliberation and contemplation sometimes clashes with an American's desire for speedy decisions. They do not like to be rushed. A Japanese businessperson considering the purchase of American appliances, for example, asked for five minutes to consider the seller's proposal. The potential buyer crossed his arms, sat back, and closed his eyes in concentration. A scant 18 seconds later, the American resumed his sales pitch to the obvious bewilderment of the Japanese buyer.[34]

As you can see, high-context cultures differ from low-context cultures in many dimensions. These differences can be significant for companies engaging in international business.

Stereotypes, Prototypes, Prejudices, and Generalizations

What is the difference between stereotypes and prototypes when applied to culture?

Most experts recognize that it is impossible to talk about cultures without using mental categories, representations, and generalizations to describe groups. These categories are sometimes considered *stereotypes*. Because the term *stereotype* has a negative meaning, intercultural authors Varner and Beamer suggested that we distinguish between *stereotype* and *prototype*.

A *stereotype* is an oversimplified behavioral pattern applied uncritically to groups. The term was used originally by printers to describe identical type set in two frames, hence *stereo type*. Stereotypes are fixed and rigid. Although they may be exaggerated and overgeneralized beliefs when applied to groups of people, stereotypes are not always entirely false.[35] Often they contain a grain of truth. When a stereotype develops into a rigid attitude and when it is based on erroneous beliefs or preconceptions, then it should be called a *prejudice*.

Varner and Beamer recommended using the term *prototype* to describe "mental representations based on general characteristics that are not fixed and rigid, but rather are open to new definitions."[36] Prototypes, then, are dynamic and change with fresh experience. Prototypes based on objective observations usually have a considerable amount of truth in them. That is why they can be helpful in studying culture. For example, South American businesspeople often talk about their families before getting down to business. This prototype is generally accurate, but it may not universally apply, and it may change over time.

Why is being able to draw valid generalizations necessary?

Some people object to making any generalizations about cultures whatever. It is wise to remember, however, that whenever we are confronted with something new and unfamiliar, we naturally strive to categorize the data to make sense out of them. In categorizing these new data, we are making generalizations. Significant intellectual discourse is impossible without generalizations. In fact, science itself would be impossible without generalizations, for what are scientific laws but valid generalizations? Much of what we teach in college courses could be called generalizations. Being able to draw generalizations from masses of data is a sign of intelligence and learning. Unfounded generalizations about people and cultures, of course, can lead to bias and prejudice. However, for our purposes, when we discuss cultures, it is important to be able to make generalizations and describe cultural prototypes.

The Benefits of Intercultural Proficiency

LEARNING OBJECTIVE 3
Explain the effects of ethnocentrism, and show how tolerance and patience help in achieving intercultural proficiency.

Being aware of your own culture and how it contrasts with others is an important first step in achieving intercultural proficiency. Another step involves recognizing barriers to intercultural accommodation and striving to overcome them. Some of these barriers occur quite naturally and require conscious effort to surmount. You might be thinking, why bother? Probably the most important reasons for becoming interculturally competent are that your personal life will be more satisfying and your work life will be more productive, gratifying, and effective.

Avoiding Ethnocentrism

The belief in the superiority of one's own race is known as *ethnocentrism*, a natural attitude inherent in all cultures. If you were raised in North America, many of the dimensions of culture described previously probably seem "right" to you. For example, it is only logical to think that time is money and you should not waste it. Everyone knows that, right? That is why an American businessperson in an Arab or Asian country might feel irritated at time spent over coffee or other social rituals before any "real" business is transacted. In these cultures, however, time is viewed differently. Moreover, personal relationships must be established and nurtured before credible negotiations may proceed.

Ethnocentrism causes us to judge others by our own values. We expect others to react as we would, and they expect us to behave as they would. Misunderstandings naturally result. A North American who wants to set a deadline for completion of negotiations is considered pushy by an Arab. That same Arab, who prefers a handshake to a written contract, is seen as naïve and possibly untrustworthy by a North American. These ethnocentric reactions can be reduced through knowledge of other cultures and the development of increased intercultural sensitivity.

Political conflict can reinforce ethnocentric gut-level reactions that are often fueled by ignorance and fear. Without a doubt, the fear of terrorism today is real and justified. Since the terror attacks on September 11, 2001, Americans feel threatened on their own soil. Radical Islam and the subsequent wars in Iraq and Afghanistan have fueled anti-Arab and anti-Muslim sentiments in general. Battling prejudice and even hate may be a tall order for diversity training in the workplace as the accompanying Ethical Insights box shows.

Bridging the Gap

Is the adage "You can't teach an old dog new tricks" true, or can we adopt new behaviors and attitudes toward culture?

Developing cultural competence often involves changing attitudes. Remember that culture is learned. Through exposure to other cultures and through training, such as you are receiving in this course, you can learn new attitudes and behaviors that help bridge gaps between cultures.

Tolerance. One desirable attitude in achieving intercultural proficiency is that of *tolerance*. Closed-minded people cannot look beyond their own ethnocentrism. But as global markets expand and as our own society becomes increasingly multiethnic, tolerance becomes especially significant. Some job descriptions now include statements such as, *Must be able to interact with ethnically diverse personnel.*

What is the meaning of *empathy*, and why is it important?

To improve tolerance, you will want to practice *empathy*. This means trying to see the world through another's eyes. It means being less judgmental and more eager to seek common

ETHICAL INSIGHT

Overcoming Prejudice: Negative Perceptions of Muslims in the United States

An assorted group of business professionals attending a diversity training class in Hartford, Connecticut, are asked for epithets they free-associate with the word *Muslim*. They call out: *poor, uneducated immigrant, Arab, foreigner,* and *terrorist.*

Goodwill Ambassadors. Aida Mansoor, wife of cardiologist Reza Mansoor, began teaching seminars explaining Islam immediately after September 11, 2001. Originally from Sri Lanka, the couple reluctantly embraced their role as ambassadors of their faith: "We were terrified, but we decided either we face this now or we pack up and leave," says Reza Mansoor. "If we were going to stay, we had to explain our faith. What was the other choice? To live in a country without self-respect or dignity?" Yet even in a diverse, tolerant city such as Hartford, Mansoor has fielded jokes about her hijab, the Islamic headscarf she wears, and endured hate mail sent to her mosque.

Reacting to Discrimination. To illustrate the daily reality of Muslims in America, Mansoor shows her classes an experiment staged by a TV station: A bagel shop employee ostensibly refuses to serve a Muslim woman wearing a hijab. The camera reveals the other customers' reactions. Three people thank the clerk for standing up to "un-American terrorists." However, several customers leave in protest, and one man tells the clerk with tears in his eyes: "Every person deserves to be treated with respect, dignity."

Reality Versus Prejudice. A recent survey shows that 46 percent of the Muslim population in the United States boast a college education, nearly 70 percent are younger than 40, and 12.4 percent are engineers. A majority of the world's Muslims are not Arabs; they live in India, many regions of Asia, Russia, and parts of Europe and Africa. Although the exact number is difficult to establish, experts generally agree that the United States is home to about 2 million Muslims, most of whom are U.S. citizens and oppose violence.

Career Application

Organize a debate or class discussion focused on these questions: How can we explain the different reactions of the bagel shop customers to the store clerk's refusal to serve the Muslim woman? What do they indicate? Why didn't Aida Mansoor and the woman in the TV scenario choose to be less conspicuous by shedding the hijab? What are the effects of prejudice, especially in the workplace?

ground. For example, one of the most ambitious intercultural business projects ever attempted joined Siemens AG, the giant German technology firm, with Toshiba Corporation of Japan and IBM. Scientists from each country worked at the IBM facility on the Hudson River in New York State to develop a revolutionary computer memory chip. All sides devoted extra effort to overcome communication and other problems.

The Siemens employees had been briefed on America's "hamburger style of management." When American managers must criticize subordinates, they generally start with small talk, such as *How's the family?* That, according to the Germans, is the bun on the top of the hamburger. Then they slip in the meat, which is the criticism. They end with encouraging words, which is the bun on the bottom. "With Germans," said a Siemens cross-cultural trainer, "all you get is the meat. And with the Japanese, it's all the soft stuff—you have to *smell* the meat."[37] Along the continuum of high-context, low-context cultures, you can see that the Germans are more direct, the Americans are less direct, and the Japanese are very subtle.

Recognizing these cultural differences enabled the scientists to work together with greater tolerance. They also sought common ground when trying to solve disagreements, such as one involving workspace. The Toshiba researchers were accustomed to working in big crowded areas like classrooms where constant supervision and interaction took place. But IBMers worked in small, isolated offices. The solution was to knock out some walls for cooperative work areas while also retaining smaller offices for those who wanted them. Instead of passing judgment and telling the Japanese that solitary workspaces are the best way for serious thinkers to concentrate, the Americans acknowledged the difference in work cultures and sought common ground. Accepting cultural differences and adapting to them with tolerance and empathy often results in a harmonious compromise.

Ethics Check

The World's Worst Tourists: Rude, Arrogant, Stingy, and Monolingual

You may have heard about the so-called "ugly American," the demanding, ethnocentric traveler who finds fault with all that is different abroad. But a recent survey among 4,500 hotel owners worldwide suggests that the least liked tourists come from France. The "best tourists" are the Japanese followed by the British and the Germans. What may account for such perceptions?

Saving Face. In business transactions North Americans often assume that economic factors are the primary motivators of people. It is wise to remember, though, that strong cultural influences are also at work. *Saving face*, for example, is important in many parts of the world. *Face* refers to the image a person holds in his or her social network. Positive comments raise a person's social standing, but negative comments lower it.

What does *saving face* mean, and how can it be accomplished?

Zooming In — PART 2

Wal-Mart in China

Despite setbacks in South Korea, Germany, and Japan, Wal-Mart International has successfully expanded to its neighboring countries, Canada and Mexico, and now enjoys solid growth in China. The retailer's concept of "always low prices" may work best in underserved foreign markets. In highly developed countries such as Japan, Wal-Mart often faces mistrust by its own employees and public resentment.[38]

So what's behind Wal-Mart's profitable expansion to China? The company apparently changed its strategy and was met halfway by customers eager to try the new one-stop-shopping experience. Wages in China are still low at $300 a month, and middle-class customers who make about $1,000 are still few. However, migrant workers and budding entrepreneurs in southern boomtowns such as Shenzhen frequent one of several Supercenters, some daily. They contribute to the 30 percent annual sales growth in China (as opposed to 2 percent in the United States). Customers praise the cleanliness and quality of the produce. Wal-Mart even introduced organic Chinese greens and organized tours to local organic farms.

But the secret of the retailer's success lies in the goods on the shelves. Accommodating the tiny size of Chinese homes, Wal-Mart offers compact, portable cots, closets, and folding chairs. Similarly, smaller packaging suits buyers with limited living space. Because Chinese customers prefer to purchase live fish, Wal-Mart's large seafood section features fish tanks and small nets to facilitate a dinner catch. Green tea tastings and Chinese sweets freshly baked in full view of the shoppers further bear witness to the Supercenters' attempt to cater to local tastes. The stores even ferry bicycle-riding customers and their purchases home by bus.[39]

© AP Images/Toby Talbot

Critical Thinking

- How do Chinese and Americans differ on key dimensions of culture as described in this chapter?
- In what ways does Wal-Mart's strategy in China compare to its misadventures in South Korea, Germany, and Japan?
- How can Wal-Mart and other multinational companies overcome the cultural barriers they face when expanding into other countries?

People in low-context cultures are less concerned with face. Germans and North Americans, for instance, value honesty and directness; they generally come right to the point and "tell it like it is." Mexicans, Asians, and members of other high-context cultures, on the other hand, are more concerned with preserving social harmony and saving face. They are indirect and go to great lengths to avoid giving offense by saying *no*. The Japanese, in fact, have 16 different ways to avoid an outright *no*. The empathic listener recognizes the language of refusal and pushes no further.

What is the value of tolerance, and what does it take to practice it?

Patience. Being tolerant also involves patience. If a foreigner is struggling to express an idea in English, Americans must avoid the temptation to finish the sentence and provide the word that they presume is wanted. When we put words into their mouths, our foreign friends often smile and agree out of politeness, but our words may in fact not express their thoughts. Remaining silent is another means of exhibiting tolerance. Instead of filling every lapse in conversation, North Americans, for example, should recognize that in Asian cultures people deliberately use periods of silence for reflection and contemplation.

Effective Communication in Intercultural Settings

LEARNING OBJECTIVE 4

Apply techniques for improving nonverbal and oral communication in intercultural settings.

Thus far we have discussed the increasing importance of intercultural proficiency as a result of globalization of markets, increasing migration, and technological advancements. We have described characteristics and dimensions of cultures, and we have talked about avoiding ethnocentrism. Our goal was to motivate you to unlock the opportunities offered by intercultural proficiency. Remember, the key to future business success may very well lie in finding ways to work harmoniously with people from different cultures at home and abroad.

Successful Nonverbal Communication in Intercultural Environments

Why is understanding nonverbal messages particularly difficult when cultures differ?

Verbal skills in another culture can generally be mastered if one studies hard enough. But nonverbal skills are much more difficult to learn. Nonverbal behavior includes the areas described in Chapter 2, such as eye contact, facial expression, posture, gestures, and the use of time, space, and territory. The messages sent by body language and the way we arrange time and space have always been open to interpretation. Does a raised eyebrow mean that your boss doubts your statement, or just that she is seriously considering it? Does that closed door to an office mean that your coworker is angry, or just that he is working on a project that requires concentration? Deciphering nonverbal communication is difficult for people who are culturally similar, and it is even more troublesome when cultures differ.

In Western cultures, for example, people perceive silence as negative. It suggests rejection, unhappiness, depression, regret, embarrassment, or ignorance. The English expression, "The silence was deafening," conveys its oppressiveness. However, the Japanese admire silence and consider it a key to success. A Japanese proverb says, "Those who know do not speak; those who speak do not know." Silence is equated with respect and wisdom.[40]

Are gestures universally understood, or do people in intercultural environments react differently to them?

Although nonverbal behavior is ambiguous within cultures and even more problematic between cultures, it nevertheless conveys meaning. If you've ever had to talk with someone who does not share your language, you probably learned quickly to use gestures to convey basic messages. Because gestures can create very different reactions in different cultures, one must be careful in using and interpreting them. In some societies it is extremely bad form to point one's finger, as in giving directions. Other hand gestures can also cause trouble. The thumbs-up symbol may be used to indicate approval in North America, but in Iran and Ghana it is a vulgar gesture.

As businesspeople increasingly interact with their counterparts from other cultures, they will become more aware of these differences. Some behaviors are easy to warn against, such as touching people from the Middle East with the left hand (because it is considered unclean and is used for personal hygiene). We are also warned not to touch anyone's head (including children) in Thailand, as the head is considered sacred. Numerous lists of cultural dos and don'ts have been compiled. However, learning all the nuances of nonverbal behavior in other cultures is impossible; such lists are merely the tip of the cultural iceberg.

Although we cannot ever hope to understand fully the nuances of meaning transmitted by nonverbal behavior in various cultures, we can grow more tolerant, more flexible, and eventually, more competent. An important part of achieving nonverbal competence is becoming more aware of our own nonverbal behaviors and their meanings. Much of our nonverbal behavior is learned in early childhood from our families and from society, and it is largely unconscious. Once we become more aware of the meaning of our own gestures, posture, eye gaze, and so on, we will become more alert and more sensitive to variations in other cultures. Striving to associate with people from different cultures can further broaden our intercultural competence.

Why is it important to become aware of our own use of nonverbal cues, and how can we benefit if we understand variations in other cultures?

Techniques for Achieving Intercultural Competence

In improving effectiveness and achieving intercultural competence, one expert, M. R. Hammer, suggested that three processes or attitudes are effective. *Descriptiveness* refers to the use of concrete and specific feedback. As you learned in Chapter 1 in regard to the process of communication, descriptive feedback is more effective than judgmental feedback. For example, using objective terms to describe the modest attire of Muslim women is more effective than describing it as unfeminine or motivated by oppressive and unequal treatment of females. A second attitude is what Hammer called *nonjudgmentalism*. This attitude goes a long way in preventing defensive reactions from communicators. Most important in achieving effective communication is *supportiveness*. This attitude requires us to support others positively with head nods, eye contact, facial expression, and physical proximity.[41]

Which three processes or attitudes will help you broaden your intercultural competence?

From a practical standpoint, when interacting with businesspeople in other cultures, it is always wise to follow their lead. If they avoid intense eye contact, don't stare. If no one is putting his or her elbows on a table, don't be the first to do so. Until you are knowledgeable about the meaning of gestures, it is probably a good idea to keep yours to a minimum. Learning the words for *please*, *yes*, and *thank you*, some of which are shown in Figure 3.3, is even better than relying on gestures.[42] Achieving intercultural competence in regard to nonverbal behavior may never be totally attained, but sensitivity, nonjudgmentalism, and tolerance go a long way toward improving interactions.

What kind of advice would you give someone wishing to master nonverbal behavior such as gestures in intercultural situations?

FIGURE 3.3 **Basic Expressions in Other Languages**

Language	Greeting (Hello)	Please	Thank you	Yes	No	Goodbye
Arabic	saBAH al-khayr	minFUDlak	shookRAAN	NAA-am	LAA	MAA-a salAAMuh
French	Bonjour [bohnzhoor]	S'il vous plait [see-voo-pleh]	Merci (beaucoup) [mare-see (bo-coo)]	Oui [weeh]	Non [nonh]	Au revoir [oh-vwar]
German	Guten Tag [Goo-ten taakh]	Bitte [bitteh]	Danke [dahn-keh]	Ja [yah]	Nein [nine]	Auf Wiedersehen [auwf vee-dur-zahn]
Italian	Buon giorno [bwon jorno]	Per favore/ per piacere	Grazie [gratsi-eh]	Si [see]	No [noh]	Arrividerla (Arrividerci, informal)
Japanese	Konnichiwa [con-ichi-vah]	oh-NEH-ga-ee she-mahss (requesting)	Arigato [ah-ree-GAH-tow (go-ZAI-mahss)]	Hai [high]	Ee-yeh	Sayonara
Norwegian	God dag [Goo dakh]	Vær så snill [var so snill]	Takk [tahk]	Ja [yah]	Nei [nay]	Ha det [haa dett]
Russian	Dobree-DYEN	Pa-JAA-oos-tah	Spa-SEE-bah	Dah	Nyet	Dasvi-DAnya
Spanish	Buenos días [BWEH-nos DEE-ahs]	Con permiso [con pair-ME-soh] Por favor [Pohr-fah-VOHR]	Gracias [GRAH-see-ahs]	Sí [seeh]	No [noh]	Adiós

Can we assume that speakers of English as a second language understand everything we say?

Successful Oral Communication in Intercultural Environments

Although it is best to speak a foreign language fluently, many of us lack that skill. Fortunately, global business transactions are increasingly conducted in English. English has become the language of technology, the language of Hollywood, and the language to know in global business even for traditionally non-English-speaking countries. English is so dominant in business that when Koreans go to China, English is the language they use to conduct business.[43] However, the level of proficiency may be limited among nonnative speakers of English. Americans abroad make a big mistake in thinking that people who speak English always understand what is being said. Comprehension can be fairly superficial. The following suggestions are helpful for situations in which one or both communicators may be using English as a second language.

- **Learn foreign phrases.** In conversations, even when English is used, foreign nationals appreciate it when you learn greetings and a few phrases in their language. See Figure 3.3 for a list of basic expressions in some of the world's major languages. Practice the phrases phonetically so that you will be understood.

How would you adjust your language to avoid misunderstandings and blunders when communicating with people for whom English is a second language?

- **Use simple English.** Speak in short sentences (under 20 words) with familiar short words. For example, use *old* rather than *obsolete* and *rich* rather than *luxurious* or *sumptuous*. Eliminate puns, sports and military references, slang, and jargon (special business terms). Be especially alert to idiomatic expressions that can't be translated, such as *burn the midnight oil* and *under the weather*.
- **Speak slowly and enunciate clearly.** Avoid fast speech, but don't raise your voice. Overpunctuate with pauses and full stops. Always write numbers for all to see.
- **Observe eye messages.** Be alert to a glazed expression or wandering eyes—these tell you the listener is lost.
- **Encourage accurate feedback.** Ask probing questions, and encourage the listener to paraphrase what you say. Do not assume that a *yes*, a nod, or a smile indicates comprehension.
- **Check frequently for comprehension.** Avoid waiting until you finish a long explanation to request feedback. Instead, make one point at a time, pausing to check for comprehension. Do not proceed to B until A has been grasped.
- **Accept blame.** If a misunderstanding results, graciously accept the blame for not making your meaning clear.
- **Listen without interrupting.** Curb your desire to finish sentences or to fill out ideas for the speaker. Keep in mind that North Americans abroad are often accused of listening too little and talking too much.
- **Smile when appropriate.** Roger Axtell, international behavior expert, calls the smile the single most understood and most useful form of communication in either personal or business transactions.[44] In some cultures, however, excessive smiling may seem insincere.[45]
- **Follow up in writing.** After conversations or oral negotiations, confirm the results and agreements with follow-up letters. For proposals and contracts, engage a translator to prepare copies in the local language.

LEARNING OBJECTIVE 5

Identify techniques for improving written messages to intercultural audiences.

Effective Written Messages to Intercultural Audiences

In sending letters, e-mails, and other documents to businesspeople in other cultures, try to adapt your writing style and tone appropriately. For example, in cultures where formality and tradition are important, be scrupulously polite. Don't even think of sharing the latest joke. Humor translates very poorly and can cause misunderstanding and negative reactions. Familiarize yourself with accepted channels of communication. Are letters, e-mails, and faxes common? Would a direct or indirect organizational pattern be more effective? What's more, forget about trying to cut through "red tape." In some cultures "red tape" is appreciated. The following suggestions, coupled with the earlier guidelines, can help you prepare successful written messages for intercultural audiences.

- **Consider local styles.** Learn how documents are formatted and addressed in the intended reader's country. Decide whether to use your organization's preferred format or adjust to local styles.
- **Observe titles and rank.** Use last names, titles, and other signals of rank and status. Send messages to higher-status people and avoid sending copies to lower-rank people.
- **Use short sentences and short paragraphs.** Sentences with fewer than 20 words and paragraphs with fewer than 8 lines are most readable.
- **Avoid ambiguous expressions.** Include relative pronouns (*that, which, who*) for clarity in introducing clauses. Stay away from contractions (especially ones like *Here's the problem*). Avoid idioms and figurative clichés (*once in a blue moon*), slang (*my presentation really bombed*), acronyms (*ASAP*, for *as soon as possible*), abbreviations (*DBA*, for *doing business as*), jargon (*input, bottom line*), and sports references (*play ball, slam dunk, ballpark figure*). Use action-specific verbs (*purchase a printer* rather than *get a printer*).

How would savvy business communicators adapt their written messages to communicate with people from other cultures?

- **Strive for clarity.** Avoid words that have many meanings (the word *light* has 18 different meanings!). If necessary, clarify words that may be confusing. Replace two-word verbs with clear single words (*return* instead of *bring back; delay* instead of *put off; maintain* instead of *keep up*).
- **Use correct grammar.** Be careful about misplaced modifiers, dangling participles, and sentence fragments. Use conventional punctuation.
- **Cite numbers carefully.** For international trade it is a good idea to learn and use the metric system. In citing numbers use figures (*12*) instead of spelling them out (*twelve*). Always convert dollar figures into local currency. Avoid using figures to express the month of the year. In North America, for example, June 12, 2011, might be written as 6/12/11, whereas in Europe the same date might appear as 12.6.11. See Figure 3.4 for additional guidelines on data formats.
- **Accommodate the reader in organization, tone, and style.** Organize your message to appeal to the reader. For example, use the indirect strategy for high-context audiences.

FIGURE 3.4 **Typical Data Formats**

	United States	United Kingdom	France	Germany	Portugal
Dates	June 12, 2011 6/12/11	12th June 2011 12/6/11	12 juin 2011 12.06.11	12. Juni 2011 12.06.11	12 de Junho de 2011 12/06/2011
Time	9:45 p.m.	9:45 pm	21.45 21 h 45	21:45 Uhr 21.45	21h45 21.45h
Currency	$123.45 USD 123.45	£123.45 GBP 123.45	123,45 € EUR 123,45	123,45 € EUR 123,45	€ 123,45 EUR 123,45
Large numbers	1,234,567.89	1,234,567.89	1.234.567,89	1.234.567,89	1.234.567,89
Phone numbers	(302) 567-1234 302.567.1234	020 7734 8624 +44 20 7734 8624	01 43 36 17 00 +33 1 43 36 1700	(030) 2261 1004 +49 30 2261 1004	21 315 02 12 +351 21 315 02 12

An Intercultural E-Mail Message That Misses the Mark

Figure 3.5 on page 94 illustrates an ineffective intercultural message. The writer uses a casual, breezy tone in a message to a Chinese company when a formal tone would be more appropriate. In addition, the e-mail includes slang and ambiguous expressions that would almost surely confuse readers for whom English is not a first language. Readers may misunderstand expressions such as *cruising the Web, totally blown away, pounding down the doors, cash in on this craze,* and *put the horse before the cart.*

Notice in the effective version of the e-mail in Figure 3.6 on page 95 that the writer starts off correctly by addressing the message to Mr. Cheng. It is often hard for Americans to know whether a Chinese name is the family or given name. In many parts of the world the family name is spoken and written first. Before writing, check to be sure you know the family name. In this e-mail, the given name is *Po* and the family name is *Cheng.*

FIGURE 3.5 Ineffective Intercultural E-Mail Message

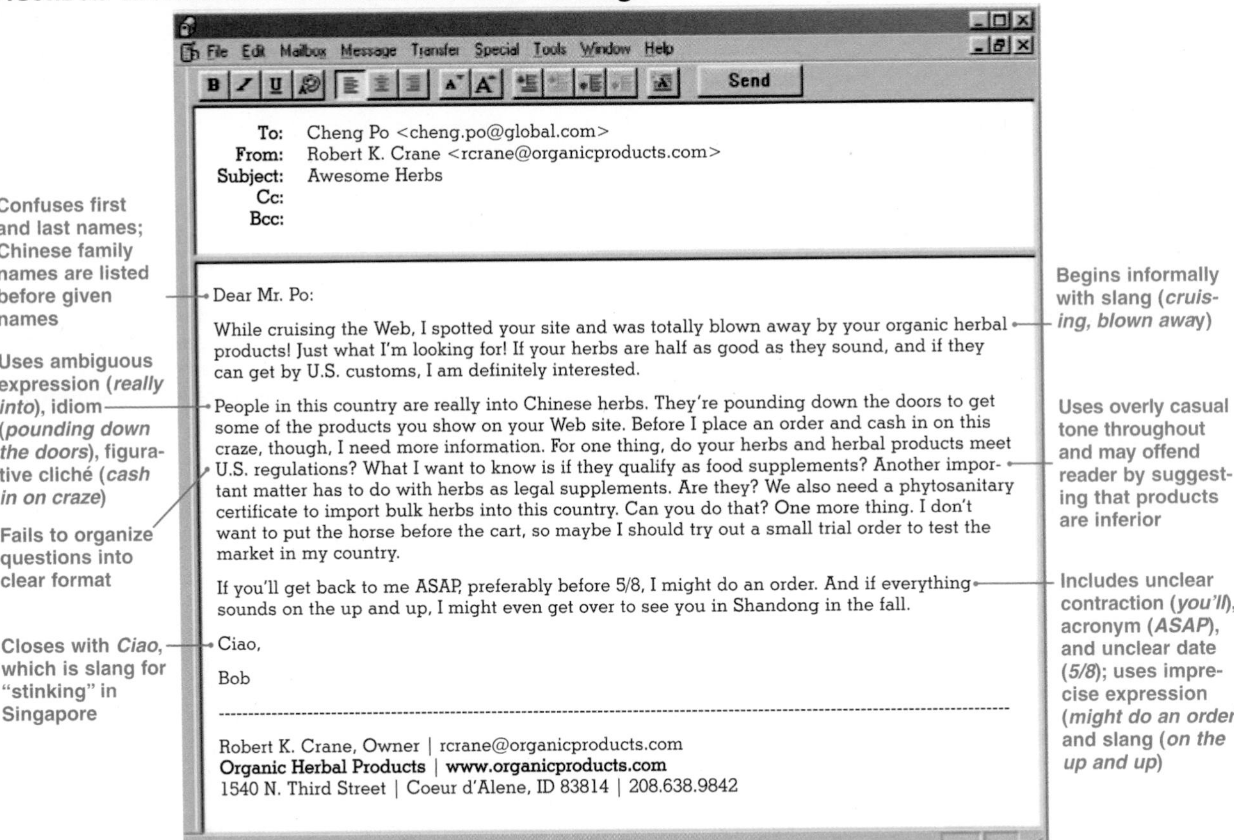

To: Cheng Po <cheng.po@global.com>
From: Robert K. Crane <rcrane@organicproducts.com>
Subject: Awesome Herbs
Cc:
Bcc:

Dear Mr. Po:

While cruising the Web, I spotted your site and was totally blown away by your organic herbal products! Just what I'm looking for! If your herbs are half as good as they sound, and if they can get by U.S. customs, I am definitely interested.

People in this country are really into Chinese herbs. They're pounding down the doors to get some of the products you show on your Web site. Before I place an order and cash in on this craze, though, I need more information. For one thing, do your herbs and herbal products meet U.S. regulations? What I want to know is if they qualify as food supplements? Another important matter has to do with herbs as legal supplements. Are they? We also need a phytosanitary certificate to import bulk herbs into this country. Can you do that? One more thing. I don't want to put the horse before the cart, so maybe I should try out a small trial order to test the market in my country.

If you'll get back to me ASAP, preferably before 5/8, I might do an order. And if everything sounds on the up and up, I might even get over to see you in Shandong in the fall.

Ciao,

Bob

Robert K. Crane, Owner | rcrane@organicproducts.com
Organic Herbal Products | **www.organicproducts.com**
1540 N. Third Street | Coeur d'Alene, ID 83814 | 208.638.9842

FIGURE 3.6 Effective Intercultural E-Mail Message

To: Cheng Po <cheng.po@global.com>
From: Robert K. Crane <rcrane@organicproducts.com>
Subject: Requesting Information Leading to Potential Business Partnership
Cc:
Bcc:

Dear Mr. Cheng:

Your excellent Web site describing organic Chinese herbs and herbal products has attracted my attention. Many people in our country are showing more interest in Chinese medicine. That is why I am interested in importing high-quality herbs.

Your Web site provides good information, but I still have a number of questions:

- Do your herbs and herbal products meet U.S. regulations as food supplements? As you know, our government regulates herbal imports closely.
- Can the products you list on your Web site legally be sold in the United States?
- Do you provide a phytosanitary certificate for bulk herbs that you sell?
- May I place a small wholesale trial order so that I can test the market in my country?

Because I am impressed with what I have learned about your company, I may visit Jinan to meet you and inspect your herbal products. I understand that Jinan is the capital of Shandong province and is close to famous and beautiful tourist sites.

Answers to my questions before May 8 would enable me to decide whether to place a trial order. I congratulate you on your successful business and look forward to a pleasant and profitable relationship with you as my supplier of high-quality Chinese herbs.

Sincerely yours,

Robert K. Crane

Robert K. Crane, Owner | rcrane@organicproducts.com
Organic Herbal Products | **www.organicproducts.com**
1540 N. Third Street | Coeur d'Alene, ID 83814 | 208.638.9842

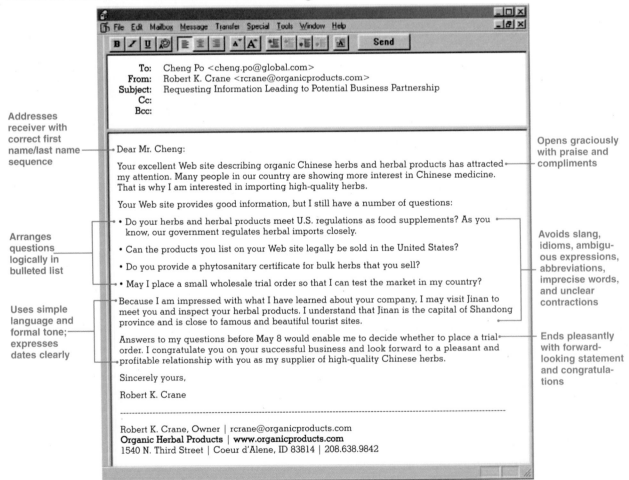

Addresses receiver with correct first name/last name sequence

Arranges questions logically in bulleted list

Uses simple language and formal tone; expresses dates clearly

Opens graciously with praise and compliments

Avoids slang, idioms, ambiguous expressions, abbreviations, imprecise words, and unclear contractions

Ends pleasantly with forward-looking statement and congratulations

Checklist

Improving Intercultural Proficiency and Communication

- **Study your own culture.** Learn about your customs, biases, and views and how they differ from those in other societies. This knowledge can help you better understand, appreciate, and accept the values and behavior of other cultures.
- **Learn about other cultures.** Education can help you alter cultural misconceptions, reduce fears, and minimize misunderstandings. Knowledge of other cultures opens your eyes and teaches you to expect differences. Such knowledge also enriches your life.
- **Curb ethnocentrism.** Avoid judging others by your personal views. Get over the view that the other cultures are incorrect, defective, or primitive. Try to develop an open mind-set.
- **Avoid judgmentalism.** Strive to accept other behavior as different, rather than as right or wrong. Try not to be defensive in justifying your culture. Strive for objectivity.
- **Seek common ground.** When cultures clash, look for solutions that respect both cultures. Be flexible in developing compromises.
- **Observe nonverbal cues in your culture.** Become more alert to the meanings of eye contact, facial expression, posture, gestures, and the use of time, space, and territory. How do they differ in other cultures?
- **Use plain English.** Speak and write in short sentences using simple words and standard English. Eliminate puns, slang, jargon, acronyms, abbreviations, and any words that cannot be easily translated.
- **Encourage accurate feedback.** In conversations ask probing questions and listen attentively without interrupting. Do not assume that a *yes* or a smile indicates agreement or comprehension.
- **Adapt to local preferences.** Shape your writing to reflect the document styles of the reader's culture, if appropriate. Express currency in local figures. Write out months of the year for clarity.

In the effective version on page 94, the writer adopts a formal but pleasant, polite tone, striving for complete sentences and correct grammar. The effective e-mail message avoids slang (*on the up and up*), idioms, imprecise words (*I might do an order*), unclear abbreviations (*ASAP*), and confusing dates (*5/8*). To further aid comprehension, the writer organizes the message into a bulleted list with clear questions. Notice, too, that the writer uses simple language throughout. The writer also ends with compliments and wishes for a profitable relationship. Businesspeople in high-context countries, such as China, place great importance on building relationships.

Can you name a few features of an effective intercultural message and especially its tone?

As the world economies continue to intermingle and globalization spreads, more businesspeople are adopting Western ways. Although Japanese writers may open letters with a seasonable greeting (*Cherry trees will soon be blooming*), it is unnecessary for a U.S. correspondent to do so.[46]

The accompanying checklist box summarizes suggestions for improving communication with intercultural audiences.

Ethics Across Cultures

LEARNING OBJECTIVE 6

Discuss intercultural ethics, including business practices abroad, bribery, prevailing customs, and methods for coping.

A perplexing problem faces conscientious organizations and individuals who do business around the world. Whose values, culture, and, ultimately, laws do you follow? Do you heed the customs of your country or those of the country where you are engaged in business? Some observers claim that when American businesspeople venture abroad, they're wandering into an ethical no-man's land, a murky world of payola where transactions often demand a gratuity to oil the wheels of business.[47]

What happens to our business ethics when we venture abroad and are confronted with different values?

Business Practices Abroad

As companies do more and more business around the globe, their assumptions about ethics are put to the test. Businesspeople may face simple questions regarding the appropriate amount of money to spend on a business gift or the legitimacy of payments to agents and distributors to "expedite" business. They may also encounter out-and-out bribery, child-labor abuse, environment mistreatment, and unscrupulous business practices. In the post-Enron era and in the wake of the banking crisis, the ethics of U.S. businesses are increasingly being scrutinized. Those who violate the law or company policy can land in big trouble. But what ethical standards do these companies follow when they do business abroad?

Today most companies that are active in global markets have ethical codes of conduct. These codes are public documents and can usually be found on company Web sites. They are an accepted part of governance. The growing sophistication of these codes results in ethics training programs that often include complicated hypothetical questions. Ethics trainers teach employees to solve problems by reconciling legal requirements, company policies, and conflicting cultural norms.[48]

Businesses in other countries are also adopting ethics codes and helping employees live up to the standards. Alan Boeckman, CEO of Fluor, the multinational construction firm, has worked very hard to rid his company of corruption. The battle against bribery in an industry where corruption is rampant hasn't been easy. Yet the company experienced success after installing a company lawyer as head of compliance.[49] In Mexico, where the World Bank estimates that corruption costs nearly 10 percent of the nation's gross domestic product, one food processing company cracked down on *mordidas* (bribes). The company adopted an ethics code forbidding drivers to pay bribes when their trucks were impounded—even though perishable food would go bad. Federal police officers eventually learned that they would receive no bribes, and they stopped impounding the company's trucks. Over time, the company saved more than $100 million because it was no longer paying off officials.[50]

According to the annual Corruption Perceptions Index, which four countries are the least corrupt?

Not all countries, of course, embrace honest dealings. Transparency International, a Berlin-based watchdog group, compiled a ranking of corruption in many countries. Based on polls and surveys of businesspeople and journalists, the index shown in Figure 3.7 presents a look at the perceptions of corruption. Gauging corruption precisely is impossible. But this graph reflects the feelings of individuals doing business in the countries shown. Of the countries selected for this graph, the least corrupt were Denmark, New Zealand, Sweden, and Singapore. The most corrupt were Russia, Bangladesh, Venezuela, Haiti, and Iraq. The United States ranked between Japan and France, in the upper half.

Spotlight on Communicators

"I would never have thought I'd go to jail for my company," Reinhard Siekaczek testified. The former mid-level Siemens accountant admitted that from 2002 to 2006 he managed an annual bribery budget of about $40 to $50 million at Siemens AG. The giant German engineering corporation used the slush fund to sway corrupt government officials worldwide. Convicted of breach of trust, Siekaczek tried to justify his actions by citing economic pressures: "We thought we had to do it," he said. "Otherwise, we'd ruin the company." Siekaczek was sentenced in Germany to two years' probation and a $150,000 fine. Siemens will pay more than $2.6 billion—$1.6 billion in fines and fees in Germany and the United States in addition to more than $1 billion for internal investigations and reforms. Does the fear of job losses and plunging profits justify bribery to gain a competitive advantage?

Laws Forbidding Bribery

The United States is not highest on the index of least corruptible countries. However, it has taken the global lead in fighting corruption. Over three decades ago, the U.S. government passed the Foreign Corrupt Practices Act of 1977. It prohibits payments to foreign officials for the purpose of obtaining or retaining business. But the law applied only to U.S. companies. Therefore, they were at a decided disadvantage when competing against less scrupulous companies from other nations. U.S. companies complained that they lost billions of dollars in contracts every year because they refused to bribe their way to success.

Most other industrialized countries looked the other way when their corporations used bribes. They considered the "greasing of palms" just a cost of doing business in certain cultures. Until 1999 German corporations were even allowed to deduct bribes as a business expense—as long as they got receipts. Recently, the engineering giant Siemens was slapped with billion-dollar fines in Germany and in the United States for systematically paying off foreign officials. In total, its corrupt practices cost the company $2.6 billion for fines and internal reforms.[51]

In the United States bribery is a criminal offense, and American corporate officials found guilty are fined and sent to jail. For example, Chiquita Brands has been the subject of lengthy litigation and

FIGURE 3.7 Corruption Perceptions Index

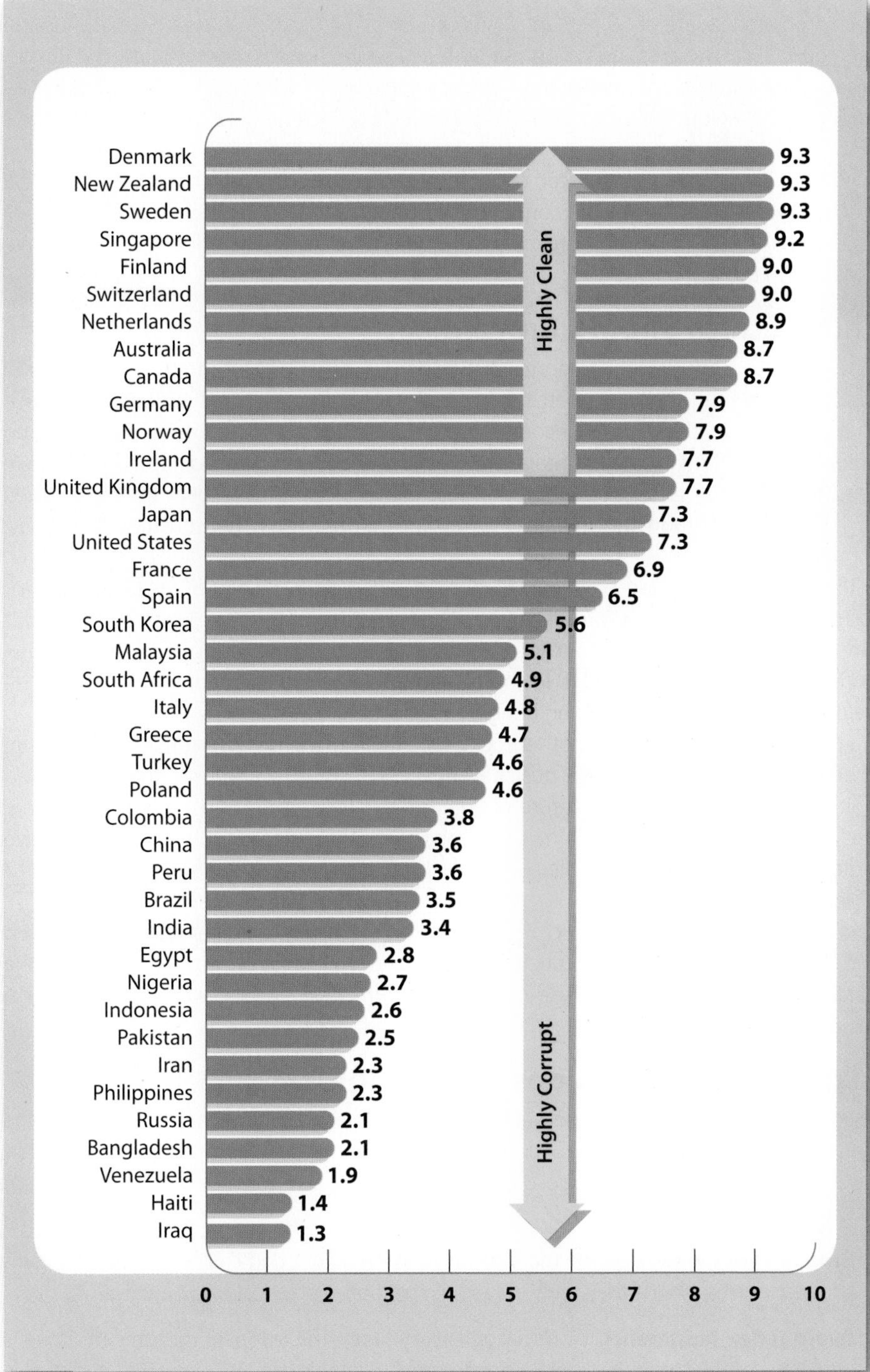

This index of selected countries represents a compilation of polls and surveys put together by Transparency International. The purpose of this Berlin-based watchdog organization is curbing the corruption that stunts the development of poor countries. The index relates to perceptions of corruption as seen by businesspeople, risk analysts, and the general public. It ranges between 10 (highly clean) and 0 (highly corrupt).

fines for its activities in Colombia. The company made "protection payments" to right-wing paramilitaries as well as a left-wing army, ostensibly to protect its employees.[52] Domestically, the Sarbanes-Oxley Act of 2002 is a new tool in the anticorruption battle. It forbids off-the-book bribes. However, American law does permit payments that may ease the way for routine government actions, such as expediting a visa request. Such payments are reportedly capped at about $500.[53]

More attention is now being paid to the problem of global corruption. With increased global interdependence, corruption is increasingly seen as costly as well as unethical. It has

The United States may not be among the top five of the least corrupt nations, but how would you characterize its efforts in the global fight against corruption?

been estimated that moving from a "clean" government like that of Singapore to one as corrupt as Mexico's would have the same effect on foreign direct investment as an increase in the corporate tax rate of 50 percent.[54] After investing $4 billion in Russia, Swedish furniture powerhouse, Ikea, is increasingly plagued by bureaucratic hurdles. For instance, the Russians demanded that an Ikea mall withstand hurricane-force winds when such severe weather was unknown in the region. Then they offered the Swedes "a quick remedy" to be provided by a local builder.[55]

Many of the world's industrialized countries formally agreed in 1999 to a new global treaty promoted by the Organization for Economic Cooperation and Development (OECD). This treaty bans the practice of bribery of foreign government officials. Today, bribery is illegal almost everywhere in the world.[56]

Whose Ethics Should Prevail?

Why is it difficult for world leaders to agree on ethical behavior although they share the view that bribery of officials is wrong?

Although world leaders seem to agree that bribery of officials is wrong, many other shady areas persist. Drawing the lines of ethical behavior here at home is hard enough. When faced with a cultural filter, the picture becomes even murkier. Most people agree that mistreating children is wrong. But in some countries, child labor is not only condoned, but also considered necessary for families to subsist. Although most countries want to respect the environment, they might also sanction the use of DDT because crops would be consumed by insects without it.

In some cultures "grease" payments to customs officials may be part of their earnings—not blackmail. In parts of Africa a "family" celebration at the conclusion of a business deal includes a party for which you are asked to pay. This payment is a sign of friendship and lasting business relationship, not a personal payoff. In some Third World countries, requests for assistance in developing technologies or reducing hunger may become part of a business package.[57]

What makes gifts ambivalent in intercultural business situations?

The exchanging of gifts is another tricky subject. In many non-Western cultures, the gift exchange tradition has become a business ritual. Gifts not only are a sign of gratitude and hospitality, but also generate a future obligation and trust. Americans, of course, become uneasy when gift giving seems to move beyond normal courtesy and friendliness. If it even remotely suggests influence peddling, they back off. Many companies suggest $50 as a top limit for gifts.

Can you describe practical solutions to ethical problems?

Whose ethics should prevail across borders? Unfortunately, no clear-cut answers can be found. Americans are sometimes criticized for being ethical "fanatics," wishing to impose their "moralistic" views on the world. Also criticized are ethical "relativists," who contend that no absolute values exist.[58]

Making Ethical Decisions Across Borders

Instead of trying to distinguish "good ethics" and "bad ethics," perhaps the best plan is to look for practical solutions to the cultural challenges of global business interaction. Following are suggestions that acknowledge different values but also respect the need for moral initiative.[59]

How can businesspeople abroad acknowledge different values but also respect the need for moral initiative?

- **Broaden your view.** Become more sensitive to the values and customs of other cultures. Look especially at what they consider moral, traditional, practical, and effective.
- **Avoid reflex judgments.** Don't automatically judge the business customs of others as immoral, corrupt, or unworkable. Assume they are legitimate and workable until proved otherwise.
- **Find alternatives.** Instead of caving in to government payoffs, perhaps offer nonmonetary public service benefits, technical expertise, or additional customer service.
- **Refuse business if options violate your basic values.** If an action seriously breaches your own code of ethics or that of your firm, give up the transaction.
- **Embrace transparency.** Conduct all relations and negotiations as openly as possible.
- **Don't rationalize shady decisions.** Avoid agreeing to actions that cause you to say, *This isn't really illegal or immoral, This is in the company's best interest,* or *No one will find out.*

- **Resist legalistic strategies.** Don't use tactics that are legally safe but ethically questionable. For example, don't call *agents* (who are accountable to employers) *distributors* (who are not).

When faced with an intercultural ethical dilemma, you can apply the same five-question test you learned in Chapter 1. Even in another culture, these questions can guide you to the best decision.

1. Is the action you are considering legal?
2. How would you see the problem if you were on the opposite side?
3. What are alternate solutions?
4. Can you discuss the problem with someone whose advice you trust?
5. How would you feel if your family, friends, employer, or coworkers learned of your action?

Advantages and Challenges of Workforce Diversity

LEARNING OBJECTIVE 7

Explain in what ways workforce diversity provides benefits and poses challenges, and how you can learn to be sensitive to racial and gender issues.

At the same time that North American businesspeople are interacting with people from around the world, the domestic workforce is becoming more diverse. This diversity has many dimensions—race, ethnicity, age, religion, gender, national origin, physical ability, and countless other qualities. No longer, say the experts, will the workplace be predominantly Anglo oriented or male. As discussed in Chapter 1, by 2020 many groups now considered minorities (African Americans, Hispanics, Asians, Native Americans) are projected to become 36 percent of the U.S. population. By 2050 these same groups are expected to surge to 47 percent of the U.S. population.[60] Women will become nearly 50 percent of the workforce. Moreover, it is estimated that the share of the population over 65 will jump dramatically from 13 percent now to 20 percent in 2050. Trends suggest that many of these older people will remain in the workforce. Because of technological advances, more physically challenged people are also joining the workforce.

Dividends of Diversity

Who benefits from a diverse workforce and why?

As society and the workforce become more diverse, successful interaction and communication among the various identity groups bring distinct challenges and dividends in three areas.

Consumers. A diverse staff is better able to read trends and respond to the increasingly diverse customer base in local and world markets. Diverse consumers now want specialized goods and services tailored to their needs. Teams made up of people with different experiences are better equipped to create products that these markets require. Consumers also want to deal with companies that respect their values and reflect themselves. "We find that more and more of our clients are demanding that our partners and staff—involved in securing new business as well as delivering the work—reflect diversity within their organizations," said Toni Riccardi. She represents PricewaterhouseCoopers, the world's largest accounting firm.[61] Sharing this view is Theo Fletcher, vice president of security, compliance, and diversity at IBM's Integrated Supply Chain Group. He said, "It is important that we have a supply base that looks like our employee base and that looks like the market we are trying to attract."[62]

Work Teams. As you learned in Chapter 2, employees today work in teams. Team members with different backgrounds may come up with more creative and effective problem-solving techniques than homogeneous teams. At Procter & Gamble a senior marketing executive hit the nail on the head when he said, "I don't know how

Spotlight on Communicators

© Norm Betts/Bloomberg via Getty Images

"I'm in this job because I believe I earned it through hard work and high performance," said Ursula M. Burns, the new CEO of Xerox. Known for her strong leadership, technical expertise, frankness, sense of humor, and willingness to embrace risk, Burns continued: "Did I get some opportunities early in my career because of my race and gender? Probably. I went to work for a company that was openly seeking to diversify its workforce. So, I imagine race and gender got the hiring guys' attention. And then the rest was really up to me."

you can effectively market to the melting pot that this country represents without a workforce and vendors who have a gut-level understanding of the needs and wants of all of these market segments. . . . When we started getting a more diverse workforce, we started getting richer [marketing] plans, because they came up with things that white males were simply not going to come up with on their own."[63] At PepsiCo, work teams created new products inspired by diversity efforts. Those products included guacamole-flavored Doritos chips and Gatorade Xtremo aimed at Hispanics, as well as Mountain Dew Code Red, which appeals to African Americans. One Pepsi executive said that companies that "figure out the diversity challenge first will clearly have a competitive advantage."[64]

Business Organizations. Companies that set aside time and resources to cultivate and capitalize on diversity will suffer fewer discrimination lawsuits, fewer union clashes, and less government regulatory action. Most important, though, is the growing realization among organizations that diversity is a critical bottom-line business strategy to improve employee relationships and to increase productivity. Developing a diverse staff that can work together cooperatively is one of the biggest challenges facing business organizations today.

Divisiveness of Diversity

Can you name and explain a few potentially negative aspects of diversity?

Diversity can be a positive force within organizations. But all too often it can also cause divisiveness, discontent, and clashes. Many of the identity groups, the so-called workforce "disenfranchised," have legitimate gripes.

What is the glass ceiling, and whom does it affect?

Women complain of the *glass ceiling*, that invisible barrier of attitudes, prejudices, and "old boy networks" blocking them from reaching important corporate positions. Some women feel that they are the victims of sexual harassment, unequal wages, sexism, and even their style of communication. See the Career Coach box on page 101 to learn more about gender talk and gender tension. On the other hand, men, too, have gender issues. One manager described gender discrimination in his office: "My boss was a woman and was very verbal about the opportunities for women to advance in my company. I have often felt she gave much more attention to the women in the office than the men."[65]

Older employees feel that the deck is stacked in favor of younger employees. Minorities complain that they are discriminated against in hiring, retention, wages, and promotions. Physically challenged individuals feel that their limitations should not hold them back, and they fear that their potential is often prejudged. People of different religions feel uncomfortable working alongside each other. A Jew, for example, may be stressed if he has to help train a Palestinian.

For a company like UPS, which delivers packages globally and employs workers in more than 200 countries, diversity comes naturally. UPS ranks among the 40 best companies for diversity according to *Black Enterprise* magazine, and the courier offers a Supplier Diversity Program to cultivate new business partnerships. At UPS, a "diverse supplier" is any minority-owned business, independent firm, or other special-interest company that is financially stable and capable of delivering quality products to its international offices. *How does UPS benefit from diversity?*

Similarly, a manager confessed, "I am half Jewish on my father's side. Very often someone will make a comment about Jews and I am always faced with the decision of speaking up or not."[66]

Tips for Improving Communication Among Diverse Workplace Audiences

Is a diverse workforce in itself productive, or would it benefit from training?

Integrating all this diversity into one seamless workforce is a formidable task and a vital one. Harnessed effectively, diversity can enhance productivity and propel a company to success well into the twenty-first century. Mismanaged, it can become a tremendous drain on a company's time and resources. How companies deal with diversity will make all the difference in how they compete in an increasingly global environment. This means that organizations must do more than just pay lip service to these issues. Harmony and acceptance do not happen automatically when people who are dissimilar work together. The following suggestions can help you and your organization find ways to improve communication and interaction.

- **Seek training.** Especially if an organization is experiencing diversity problems, awareness-raising sessions may be helpful. Spend time reading and learning about workforce diversity and how it can benefit organizations. Look upon diversity as an opportunity, not a threat. Intercultural communication, team building, and conflict resolution are skills that can be learned in diversity training programs.
- **Understand the value of differences.** Diversity makes an organization innovative and creative. Sameness fosters an absence of critical thinking called groupthink, which you learned about in Chapter 2. Case studies, for example, of the *Challenger* shuttle disaster suggest that groupthink prevented alternatives from being considered. Even smart people working collectively can make dumb decisions if they do not see the situation from different perspectives.[67] Diversity in problem-solving groups encourages independent and creative thinking.

Spotlight on Communicators

© LAURA CAVANAUGH/UPI/Landov

The longest-serving female CEO in the Fortune 500, Andrea Jung heads the world's largest direct sales cosmetics company, Avon Products. Jung has been successfully shepherding Avon's 50 businesses in 120 countries through the worst economic crisis in our lifetimes. Avon in part owes its success to steep growth in China, a market that until recently prohibited door-to-door sales, and to the CEO's inclusive management style. Asked whether women manage differently than men do, Jung emphasized similarities, not differences: "There are some gender traits. . . . Men can be more linear in decision-making, A to B, and there are a lot of times that I find women try and go from A to C to D to circle all options. One way is not better than another. What's important is to have both groups of thinking around the table."

CAREER COACH

He Said, She Said: Gender Talk and Gender Tension

Has the infiltration of gender rhetoric done great damage to the workplace? Are men and women throwing rotten tomatoes at each other as a result of misunderstandings caused by stereotypes of "masculine" and "feminine" attitudes? Deborah Tannen's book *You Just Don't Understand: Women and Men in Conversation,* as well as John Grey's *Men Are From Mars, Women Are From Venus,* caused an avalanche of discussion (and some hostility) by comparing the communication styles of men and women. Gender theorists suggest that one reason women can't climb above the glass ceiling is that their communication style is less authoritative than that of men. Compare the following observations (greatly simplified) from gender theorists:

	Women	Men
Object of talk	Establish rapport, make connections, negotiate inclusive relationships	Preserve independence, maintain status, exhibit skill and knowledge
Listening behavior	Attentive, steady eye contact; remain stationary; nod head	Less attentive, sporadic eye contact; move around
Pauses	Frequent pauses, giving chance for others to take turns	Infrequent pauses; interrupt each other to take turns
Small talk	Personal disclosure	Impersonal topics
Focus	Details first, pulled together at end	Big picture
Gestures	Small, confined	Expansive
Method	Questions, apologies; "we" statements; hesitant, indirect, soft speech	Assertions; "I" statements; clear, loud, take-charge speech

Career Application

In small groups or in a class discussion, consider these questions: Do men and women have different communication styles? Which style is more appropriate for today's team-based management? Do we need a kind of communicative affirmative action to give more recognition to women's ways of talking? Should training be given to men and women encouraging the interchangeable use of these styles depending on the situation?

Can we expect all workers to think or act alike?

- **Don't expect conformity.** Gone are the days when businesses could say, "This is our culture. Conform or leave."[68] Paul Fireman, former CEO of Reebok, stressed seeking people who have new and different stories to tell. "And then you have to make real room for them, you have to learn to listen, to listen closely, to their stories. It accomplishes next to nothing to employ those who are different from us if the condition of their employment is that they become the same as us. For it is their differences that enrich us, expand us, provide us the competitive edge."[69]

How can intercultural groups overcome differences and conflict?

- **Learn about your cultural self.** Begin to think of yourself as a product of your culture, and understand that your culture is just one among many. Try to stand outside and look at yourself. Do you see any reflex reactions and automatic thought patterns that are a result of your upbringing? These may be invisible to you until challenged by difference. Remember, your culture was designed to help you succeed and survive in a certain environment. Be sure to keep what works and yet be ready to adapt as environments change.
- **Make fewer assumptions.** Be careful of seemingly insignificant, innocent workplace assumptions. For example, don't assume that everyone wants to observe the holidays with a Christmas party and a decorated tree. Celebrating only Christian holidays in December and January excludes those who honor Hanukkah, Kwanzaa, and the Lunar New Year. Moreover, in workplace discussions don't assume anything about others' sexual orientation or attitude toward marriage. For invitations, avoid phrases such as *managers and their wives. Spouses* or *partners* is more inclusive. Valuing diversity means making fewer assumptions that everyone is like you or wants to be like you.
- **Build on similarities.** Look for areas in which you and others not like you can agree or at least share opinions. Be prepared to consider issues from many perspectives, all of which may be valid. Accept that there is room for different points of view to coexist peacefully. Although you can always find differences, it is much harder to find similarities. Look for common ground in shared experiences, mutual goals, and similar values.[70] Concentrate on your objective even when you may disagree on how to reach it.

Want to do well on tests and excel in your course? Go to **www.meguffey.com** for helpful interactive resources.

- **Review the Chapter 3 PowerPoint slides to prepare for the first quiz.**

Zooming In — YOUR TURN

Applying Your Skills at Wal-Mart

At the recent Wal-Mart Sustainability Summit in Sao Paolo, Brazil, the retailer announced plans to address some of the world's most pressing environmental problems. With its global clout, Wal-Mart Brazil will be able to rid its supply chain of slave labor, soybeans harvested in illegally deforested regions, and beef from newly cleared land in the Amazon. Deforestation emits more carbon than vehicles and is responsible for a fifth of the world's carbon emissions.

Wal-Mart also wants its suppliers to use less packaging, cut phosphates in detergent 70 percent by 2013, and reduce plastic bags 50 percent by 2013. Twenty major suppliers operating in Brazil—such as Johnson & Johnson, PepsiCo, Cargill, Sara Lee, and Unilever—signed these radical mandates.

This initiative is part of Wal-Mart's global sustainability effort to impose reduction targets on each of the 15 countries in which the company currently operates. In China, the Bentonville giant held an earlier summit with more than 1,000 suppliers to address social problems specific to that emerging economy. Businesses and the Chinese government agreed to (a) comply with environmental laws, (b) improve energy efficiency and use of natural resources, (c) increase quality standards, and (d) make manufacturing more transparent.[71]

© AP Images/Toby Talbot

Your Task

Andrew Winston, an expert on green business, wrote in his blog: "Wal-Mart is changing the world for the better and is setting the new pace in corporate sustainability. The rest of the business world—let alone the politicians still debating action on climate—can only try to keep up."[72] As a junior member of a joint task force at McKinsey & Co., a consulting firm advising Wal-Mart, you are working to improve the image of the global retailer. Despite several praiseworthy initiatives, Wal-Mart is still viewed by many with suspicion. As a team, discuss the global impact of Wal-Mart's sustainability effort. Create a communication strategy: How should Wal-Mart spread the news about its green policies to reach the broader public and young people in particular? Consider the use of social media, Facebook, Twitter, and so forth. Your team may be asked to explain its decision to the class or to write a summary of the pros and cons of each option. Be prepared to support your choice.

Summary of Learning Objectives

1 Understand how three significant trends have increased the importance of intercultural communication. Three trends are working together to crystallize the growing need for developing intercultural proficiencies and improved communication techniques. First, the globalization of markets means that you can expect to be doing business with people from around the world. Second, technological advancements in transportation and information are making the world smaller and more intertwined. Third, more and more immigrants from other cultures are settling in North America, thus changing the complexion of the workforce. Successful interaction requires awareness, tolerance, and accommodation.

2 Define *culture,* describe five noteworthy cultural characteristics, and compare and contrast five key dimensions of culture including high context and low context. *Culture* is the complex system of values, traits, morals, and customs shared by a society. Significant characteristics of culture include the following: (a) culture is learned, (b) cultures are inherently logical, (c) culture is the basis of self-identity and community, (d) culture combines the visible and invisible, and (e) culture is dynamic. Members of low-context cultures (such as those in North America, Scandinavia, and Germany) depend on words to express meaning, whereas members of high-context cultures (such as those in Japan, China, and Arab countries) rely more on context (social setting, a person's history, status, and position) to communicate meaning. Other key dimensions of culture include individualism, degree of formality, communication style, and time orientation.

3 Explain the effects of ethnocentrism, and show how tolerance and patience help in achieving intercultural proficiency. *Ethnocentrism* refers to the belief that one's own culture is superior to all others and holds all truths. To function effectively in a global economy, we must acquire knowledge of other cultures and be willing to change our attitudes. Developing tolerance often involves practicing *empathy*, which means trying to see the world through another's eyes. Saving face and promoting social harmony are important in many parts of the world. Moving beyond narrow ethnocentric views often requires tolerance and patience.

4 Apply techniques for improving nonverbal and oral communication in intercultural settings. We can minimize nonverbal miscommunication by recognizing that meanings conveyed by eye contact, posture, and gestures are largely culture dependent. Nonverbal messages are also sent by the use of time, space, and territory. Becoming aware of your own nonverbal behavior and what it conveys is the first step in broadening your intercultural competence. In improving oral messages, you can learn foreign phrases, use simple English, speak slowly and enunciate clearly, observe eye messages, encourage accurate feedback, check for comprehension, accept blame, listen without interrupting, smile, and follow up important conversations in writing.

5 Identify techniques for improving written messages to intercultural audiences. To improve written messages, adopt local formats, observe titles and rank, use short sentences and short paragraphs, avoid ambiguous expressions, strive for clarity, use correct grammar, and cite numbers carefully. Also try to accommodate the reader in organization, tone, and style.

6 Discuss intercultural ethics, including business practices abroad, bribery, prevailing customs, and methods for coping. In doing business abroad, businesspeople should expect to find differing views about ethical practices. Although deciding whose ethics should prevail is tricky, the following techniques are helpful. Broaden your understanding of values and customs in other cultures, and avoid reflex judgments regarding the morality or corruptness of actions. Look for alternative solutions, refuse business if the options violate your basic values, and conduct all relations as openly as possible. Don't rationalize shady decisions. Resist legalistic strategies, and apply a five-question ethics test when faced with a perplexing ethical dilemma.

7 Explain in what ways workforce diversity provides benefits and poses challenges, and how you can learn to be sensitive to racial and gender issues. Having a diverse workforce can benefit consumers, work teams, and business organizations. However, diversity

Are you ready? Get more practice at **www.meguffey.com**

can also cause divisiveness among identity groups. Business communicators should be aware of and sensitive to differences in the communication techniques of men and women. To promote harmony and communication in diverse workplaces, many organizations develop diversity training programs. You must understand and accept the value of differences. Don't expect conformity, and create zero tolerance for bias and prejudice. Learn about your cultural self, make fewer assumptions, and seek common ground when disagreements arise.

Chapter Review

1. Why is intercultural communication increasingly important, and what must business communicators do to succeed? (Obj. 1)
2. Why is geographical location virtually irrelevant for many activities and services today? (Obj. 1)
3. Describe five major characteristics of culture. (Obj. 2)
4. Briefly, contrast high- and low-context cultures. (Obj. 2)
5. How is a *stereotype* different from a *prototype*? (Obj. 3)
6. Name techniques for bridging the gap between cultures and achieving intercultural proficiency. (Obj. 3)
7. When interacting with people who do not use your language, why is it important to learn the words for *please, yes,* and *thank you* rather than relying on gestures? (Obj. 4)
8. What should you assume about the level of proficiency in non-native speakers of English? (Obj. 4)
9. Describe five specific ways you can improve oral communication with someone who speaks another language. (Obj. 4)
10. Describe at least five ways you can improve written communication with someone who speaks another language. (Obj. 5)
11. What categories of ambiguous expressions should be avoided because they could confuse readers for whom English is not a first language? (Obj. 5)
12. Are there laws forbidding bribery in the United States, and are they effective in stopping corruption? (Obj. 6)
13. List seven techniques for making ethical decisions across borders. (Obj. 6)
14. Name three groups that benefit from workforce diversity and explain why. (Obj. 7)
15. Describe six tips for improving communication among diverse workplace audiences. (Obj. 7)

Critical Thinking

1. Queen Elizabeth of England once said, "Stereotypes wither when human contacts flourish." What does this statement mean? Have you found this to be accurate in your own experience? (Objs. 1, 3)
2. English is becoming the world's business language because the United States is a dominant military and trading force. Why should Americans bother to learn about other cultures? (Objs. 1, 2, and 7)
3. Cultural expert John Engle complains that his American students resist references to cultural generalizations. He asserted, "Thoughtful generalizations are the heart of intercultural communication, allowing us to discuss meaningfully the complex web of forces acting upon individuals that we call culture." Do you agree or disagree? Why? (Objs. 2, 3)
4. We are told to overcome our natural tendency to show ethnocentrism, judging other cultures by our own values. Does this mean we should accept actions we find abhorrent in other world regions as a mere manifestation of the indigenous culture? Provide examples to support your answer. (Objs. 3, 6)
5. Some economists and management scholars argue that statements such as *diversity is an economic asset* or *diversity is a new strategic imperative* are unproved and perhaps unprovable assertions. Should social responsibility or market forces determine whether an organization strives to create a diverse workforce? Why? (Obj. 7)
6. **Ethical Issue:** You know that it's not acceptable to make ethnic jokes, least of all in the workplace, but a colleague of yours keeps invoking the worst ethnic and racial stereotypes. How do you respond? Do you remain silent and change the subject, or do you pipe up? What other options do you have in dealing with such a coworker? Consider whether your answer would change if the offender were your boss. (Objs. 6, 7)

Activities

3.1 Trouble on a Global Scale: Analyzing Intercultural Blunders (Objs. 1–3)

Intercultural

As business organizations become increasingly global in their structure and marketing, they face communication problems resulting from cultural misunderstandings.

Your Task. Based on what you have learned in this chapter, describe several broad principles that could be applied in helping the individuals involved understand what went wrong in the following events. What suggestions could you make for remedying the problems involved?

a. In Saudi Arabia an American businessman sat down and crossed his legs, so that the leather soles of his fine dress shoes were showing. He then refused an offer of a cup of coffee from his Saudi counterpart. A Southpaw, the visitor from the United States kept passing out handouts and his business card with his left hand. The business negotiations fizzled. Why?

b. An advertising agency manager, new to his post in Japan, gathered his team for an old-fashioned brainstorming session in the boardroom. A big presentation loomed, and he expected creative ideas from his staff. Instead, he was met with silence. What went wrong? How could he coax ideas from his staff?[73]

c. During a festive dinner for a delegation from Singapore visiting the government of the Czech Republic, the conversation turned to the tasty main course they were eating. One of the Czech hosts explained to the inquiring foreign guests that they were enjoying a Czech specialty, rabbit, known for its light white meat. The Singaporeans' faces mirrored shock, embarrassment, and irritation. As inconspicuously as possible they put down their silverware. Only later did the Czech delegation learn that rabbit is a pet in Singapore much like the house cat in European or North American households.[74]

d. The employees of a large U.S. pharmaceutical firm became angry over the e-mail messages they received from the firm's employees in Spain. The messages weren't offensive. Generally, these routine messages just explained ongoing projects. What riled the Americans was this: every Spanish message was copied to the hierarchy within its division. The Americans could not understand why e-mail messages had to be sent to people who had little or nothing to do with the issues being discussed. But this was accepted practice in Spain.[75]

e. As China moves from a planned to a market economy, professionals suffer the same signs of job stress experienced in Western countries. Multinational companies have long offered counseling to their expatriate managers. But locals frowned on any form of psychological therapy. Recently, China's largest bank hired Chestnut Global Partners to offer employee counseling services. Chestnut learned immediately that it could not talk about such issues as conflict management. Instead, Chestnut stressed workplace harmony. Chestnut also found that Chinese workers refused one-on-one counseling. They preferred group sessions or online counseling.[76] What cultural elements were at work here?

3.2 Mastering International Time (Objs. 1–5)

Web | Intercultural

Assume you are a virtual assistant working from your home. As part of your job, you schedule webcasts, online chats, and teleconference calls for businesspeople who are conducting business around the world.

Your Task. To broaden your knowledge of time zones, respond to the following:

a. What does the abbreviation UTC indicate? (Use Google and search for *UTC definition*.)

b. Internationally, time is shown with a 24-hour clock (sometimes called "military time"). What time does 13:00 indicate? (Use Google; search for *24-hour clock*.) How is a 12-hour clock different from a 24-hour clock? With which are you most familiar?

c. You must schedule an audioconference for a businessperson in Indianapolis, Indiana, who wants to talk with a person in Osaka, Japan. What are the best business hours (between 8 and 5) for them to talk? (Many Web sites provide time zone converters. For example, try **http://www.timeanddate.com**. Click **Meeting Planner.** Follow the instructions for selecting a day and locations.)

d. What are the best business hours for an online chat between an executive in Atlanta and a vendor in Singapore?

e. When is a businessperson in Arizona most likely to reach a contact in Belgium on Skype during office hours? Your instructor may select other cities for you to search.

3.3 The World Is Atwitter—Hot New Medium Opens up Countries and Cultures (Obj. 1)

Web

You may know the *share* feature in Facebook that lets you update your activities, favorite links, pictures, and whereabouts for your friends to see. Founded in 2006, Twitter started out as a toy for such updates and online banter in fewer than 140 characters.

Unlike Facebook, though, Twitter is a personal yet also very public broadcasting medium that lends itself to easy and speedy transmission. It is free and doubly mobile, running on the SMS network for cell phones and on the Internet as well.

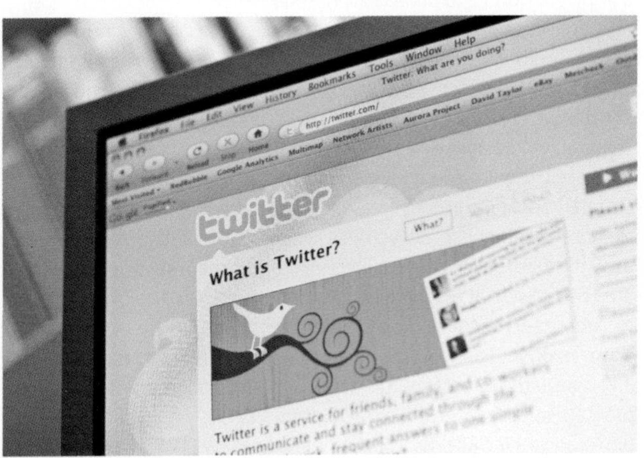

© David Taylor::Objects/Alamy

During Iranian protests following a suspect election, Twitter became what *Time* magazine called the "medium of the movement." It has been one of the fastest-growing phenomena on the Internet, in the words of *The New York Times*. Tweets from Iran emerged as free, unfiltered real-time news items from protesters and witnesses documenting government repression. Although officials could technically cut both Internet connections and the SMS network, never again will a dictator be able to impose a complete information monopoly. Even if some of the information may be unreliable and unverifiable, tweets are the latest means of instant cross-border, globe-spanning communication and a high-speed alternative to traditional mainstream media.[77]

Your Task. Go to **http://www.twitter.com.** You don't need to register to search for and view tweets in your Internet browser, but you should open a Twitter account to enjoy the full benefits of the free service. Signing up is quick and intuitive. Execute the onscreen directions and watch the brief instructional video clip, if you like. You will be able to follow not only friends and family, but also news, business updates, film reviews, and sports, or receive and share other up-to-the-minute messages.

Once you sign in, get started by viewing *trending topics*. Some may be business related. A few may be international in scope. Use the search box to type any current international or business event to see what "twitterers" are saying about it. For instance, check out the tweets of CNN's Anderson Cooper or those of another newscaster. In the classroom, discuss the usefulness of Twitter as you see it. Is the information you find interesting and trustworthy? You will learn more about Twitter and other highly portable new media in Chapter 7.

3.4 Global Economy (Obj. 1)

Intercultural

Fred Smith, CEO of FedEx, said, "It is an inescapable fact that the U.S. economy is becoming much more like the European and Asian economies, entirely tied to global trade."

Your Task. Read your local newspapers for a week and peruse national news periodicals (*Time, Newsweek, BusinessWeek, U.S. News, The Wall Street Journal,* and so forth) for articles that support this assertion. Your instructor may ask you to (a) report on many articles or (b) select one article to summarize. Report your findings orally or in a memo to your instructor. This topic could be expanded into a long report for Chapters 12 or 13.

3.5 Intercultural Gap at Resort Hotel in Thailand (Objs. 1–4)

Intercultural | Team

The Laguna Beach Resort Hotel in Phuket, Thailand, nestled between a tropical lagoon and the sparkling Andaman Sea, is one of the most beautiful resorts in the world. (You can take a virtual tour by using Google and searching for *Laguna Beach Resort Phuket.*) When Brett Peel arrived as the director of the hotel's kitchen, he thought he had landed in paradise. Only on the job six weeks, he began wondering why his Thai staff would answer *yes* even when they didn't understand what he had said. Other foreign managers discovered that junior staff managers rarely spoke up and never expressed an opinion that was contrary to those of senior executives. What's more, guests with a complaint thought that Thai employees were not taking them seriously because the Thais smiled at even the worst complaints. Thais also did not seem to understand deadlines or urgent requests.[78]

Your Task. In teams decide how you would respond to the following. If you were the director of this hotel, would you implement a training program for employees? If so, would you train only foreign managers, or would you include local Thai employees as well? What topics should a training program include? Would your goal be to introduce Western ways to the Thais? At least 90 percent of the hotel guests are non-Thai.

3.6 From Waterloo, Wisconsin, Trek Bicycles Goes Global (Objs. 1, 3, and 7)

Intercultural

In winning the Tour de France seven times and recently placing third in the world's most grueling bicycle race, Lance Armstrong brought international prestige to Waterloo, Wisconsin. That is the home of Trek Bicycle, manufacturer of the superlightweight carbon bikes Armstrong has ridden to victory over the years. The small town of Waterloo (population 2,888) is about the last place you would expect to find the world's largest specialty bicycle maker. Trek started its global business in a red barn smack in the middle of Wisconsin farm country. It employs 1,500 people in Waterloo and serves 2,000 stores in the United States alone and 4,000 dealers worldwide in 65 countries. Nearly 50 percent of the sales of the high-tech bicycles come from international markets. Future sales abroad look promising as Trek expands into Chinese and Indian markets. In Asia, bicycles are a major means of transportation. To accommodate domestic and international consumers, Trek maintains a busy Web site at **http://www.trekbikes.com.**

Like many companies, Trek encountered problems in conducting intercultural transactions. For example, in Mexico, cargo was often pilfered while awaiting customs clearance. In Singapore a buyer balked at a green bike helmet, explaining that when a man wears green on his head it means his wife is unfaithful. In Germany, Trek had to redesign its packaging to reduce waste and meet environmental requirements. Actually, the changes required in Germany helped to bolster the company's overall image of environmental sensitivity.

Your Task. Based on principles you studied in this chapter, name several lessons that other entrepreneurs can learn from Trek's international experiences.[79]

3.7 Interpreting Intercultural Proverbs (Objs. 2, 3)

Proverbs, which tell truths with metaphors and simplicity, often reveal fundamental values held by a culture.

Your Task. Discuss the following proverbs and explain how they relate to some of the cultural values you studied in this chapter. What additional proverbs can you cite, and what do they mean?

North American proverbs

An ounce of prevention is worth a pound of cure.
The squeaking wheel gets the grease.
A bird in the hand is worth two in the bush.
He who holds the gold makes the rules.

Japanese proverbs

A wise man hears one and understands ten.
The pheasant would have lived but for its cry.
The nail that sticks up gets pounded down.

German proverbs

What is bravely ventured is almost won.
He who wants to warm himself in old age must build a fireplace in his youth.
Charity sees the need, not the cause.

3.8 Negotiating Traps (Objs. 2–5)

Intercultural

Businesspeople often have difficulty reaching agreement on the terms of contracts, proposals, and anything that involves bargaining. They have even more difficulty when the negotiators are from different cultures.

Your Task. Discuss the causes and implications of the following common mistakes made by North Americans in their negotiations with foreigners.

a. Assuming that a final agreement is set in stone
b. Lacking patience and insisting that matters progress more quickly than the pace preferred by the locals
c. Thinking that an interpreter is always completely accurate
d. Believing that individuals who speak English understand every nuance of your meaning
e. Ignoring or misunderstanding the significance of rank

3.9 Learning About Other Countries (Objs. 4, 6)

Intercultural | Web

When meeting business people from other countries, you will feel more comfortable if you know the basics of business etiquette and intercultural communication, such as greetings, attire, or dos and don'ts. On the Web you will find many resources, some more reliable than others.

Your Task. Visit Executive Planet at **http://www.executiveplanet.com** and the International Business Center's site at **http://www.cyborlink.com.** (If the URL doesn't work, use Google to search for *International Business Etiquette.*) Click the region or the individual country link to obtain brief but useful information. For example, the International Business Center site is divided into some of the following aspects: *Fun facts, appearance, behavior, communication, resources,* and so forth. You can also ask questions and receive personalized feedback. This Web site provides analysis based on renowned Dutch psychologist Geert Hofstede's five dimensions of culture applied to each country. Peruse both Web sites and answer the following questions:

a. How do people greet each other in Australia, India, Japan, Korea, Netherlands, and Spain?
b. In what countries is it important to keep a certain distance from the person you are greeting?
c. In what countries is a kiss appropriate?

3.10 Calling iPhone or iPod Touch Owners: Pick up a Few Foreign Phrases (Objs. 3, 4)

Intercultural | Web

If you own an iPhone or an iPod Touch, you are familiar with the App Store. You can download thousands of low-cost or free applications for these devices. Try Oxford Translator for some of the world's most popular languages—Spanish, Chinese, French, Russian, German, and Portuguese. As opposed to the "pro" apps, the trial versions are free.
Your Task. After choosing a language and downloading its free Oxford Translator application to iTunes or directly to your Apple device, try out simple greetings and phrases. Repeat after the audio samples to perfect your pronunciation. After practicing, try to apply the expressions you learned in a brief exchange with a visitor or fellow student from your chosen country.

3.11 Tracking Facebook's Explosive International Growth (Objs. 1, 7)

Intercultural | Team | Web

With nearly 350 million global users, Facebook is currently the largest social networking site. It is growing exponentially, not so much in the United States but globally, mainly in Latin America and Europe. You may be surprised to hear that Chile contributed 2.3 million new users within a mere six months. Colombia's presence grew by 2 million, and Venezuelans made up 1 million new users. The growth is staggering: Chile showed a whopping 2,197 percent increase in 2008, when it was the fastest-growing country on Facebook.[80]
Your Task. As a team or alone, visit Inside Facebook, a platform for developers and marketers at **http://www.insidefacebook.com.** Study the tables listing the top 25 countries in various categories. Which country is currently the fastest-growing country in absolute numbers? Find out which country has the largest presence on Facebook outside the United States. To draw on a larger sample, write to *mail@insidefacebook.com* and request the source data for all 90 countries that Facebook is tracking.

Even if you don't speak another language, visit at last one non-English Facebook site and evaluate surface similarities and differences. Chances are that you will recognize some familiar features. Discuss similarities and differences in class. If you speak a foreign language, can you spot any customization that suggests adaptation to local preferences and customs?

As you will learn in Chapter 7 and in Chapter 15, Facebook is also playing an increasing role in recruiting and other business applications.

3.12 Examining Cultural Stereotypes (Objs. 1, 3)

As you have learned in this chapter, generalizations are necessary as we acquire and categorize new knowledge. As long as we remain open to new experiences, we won't be stymied by rigid, stereotypical perceptions of other cultures. Almost all of us are at some point in our lives subject to stereotyping by others, whether we are immigrants, minorities, women, members of certain professions, Americans abroad, and so forth. Generally speaking, negative stereotypes sting. However, even positive stereotypes can offend or embarrass because they fail to acknowledge the differences among individuals.
Your Task. Think about a nation or culture about which you have only a hazy idea. Jot down a few key traits that come to mind. For example, you may not know much about the Netherlands and the Dutch people. You can probably think of gouda cheese, wooden clogs, Heineken beer, tulips, and windmills. Anything else? Then consider a culture with which you are very familiar, whether it is yours or that of a country you visited or studied. In one column, write down a few stereotypical perceptions that are positive. Then, in another column, record negative stereotypes you associate with that culture. Share your notes with your team or the whole class, as the instructor may direct. How do you respond to others' descriptions of your culture? Which stereotypes irk you and why? For a quick fact check and overview at the end of this exercise, google the *CIA World Factbook* or *BBC News Country Profiles.*

3.13 Analyzing a Problem International Letter (Obj. 5)

Intercultural

American writers sometimes forget that people in other countries, even if they understand English, are not aware of the meanings of certain words and phrases.
Your Task. Study the following letter[81] to be sent by a U.S. firm to a potential supplier in another country. Identify specific weaknesses that may cause troubles for intercultural readers.

Dear Atsushi:

Because of the on-again/off-again haggling with one of our subcontractors, we have been putting off writing to you. We were royally turned off by their shoddy merchandise, the excuses they made up, and the way they put down some of our customers. Since we have our good name to keep up, we have decided to take the bull by the horns and see if you would be interested in bidding on the contract for spare parts.

By playing ball with us, your products are sure to score big. So please give it your best shot and fire off your price list ASAP. We will need it by 3/8 if you are to be in the running.

Yours,

3.14 Drop in Anytime: Ambiguous Expressions Invite New Friends (Obj. 5)

Intercultural

To end conversations, North Americans often issue casual invitations to new acquaintances and even virtual strangers, such as *Visit me when you come to New York,* or *Come on over anytime.* However, nonnative speakers and visitors may misinterpret such casual remarks. They may embarrass their hosts and suffer disappointment by taking the offhand invitation literally and acting on it. Psychologists Cushner and Brislin warn: "Those interacting across cultures would be wise to avoid using expressions that have multiple meanings."
Your Task. Assume you are a businessperson engaged in exporting and importing. As such, you are in constant communication with suppliers and customers around the world. In messages sent abroad or in situations with nonnative speakers of English at home, what kinds of ambiguous expressions should you avoid? In teams or individually, list three to five original examples of idioms, slang, acronyms, sports references, abbreviations, jargon, and two-word verbs. Which phrases or behavior could be taken literally by a person from a different culture?

3.15 *Baksheesh, Mordida,* and *Kumshah:* Making Grease Payments Abroad (Obj. 6)

Ethics | Intercultural

In the Middle East, bribes are called *baksheesh*. In Mexico, they are *mordida*; and in Southeast Asia, *kumshah*. Although it takes place in many parts of the world, bribery is not officially sanctioned by any country. In the United States the Foreign Corrupt Practices Act prohibits giving anything of value to a foreign official in an effort to win or retain business. However, this law does allow payments that may be necessary to expedite or secure "routine governmental action." For instance, a company could make small payments to obtain permits and licenses or to process visas or work orders. Also allowed are payments to secure telephone service and power and water supplies, as well as payments for the loading and unloading of cargo.

Your Task. In light of what you have learned in this chapter, how should you act in the following situations? Are the actions legal or illegal?[82]

a. Your company is moving toward final agreement on a contract in Pakistan to sell farm equipment. As the contract is prepared, officials ask that a large amount be included to enable the government to update its agriculture research. The extra amount is to be paid in cash to the three officials you have worked with. Should your company pay?
b. You have been negotiating with a government official in Niger regarding an airplane maintenance contract. The official asks to use your Diner's Club card to charge $2,028 in airplane tickets as a honeymoon present. Should you do it to win the contract?
c. You are trying to collect an overdue payment of $163,000 on a shipment of milk powder to the Dominican Republic. A senior government official asks for $20,000 as a collection service fee. Should you pay?
d. Your company is in the business of arranging hunting trips to East Africa. You are encouraged to give guns and travel allowances to officials in a wildlife agency that has authority to issue licenses to hunt big game. The officials have agreed to keep the gifts quiet. Should you make the gifts?
e. Your firm has just moved you to Malaysia, and your furniture is sitting on the dock. Cargo handlers won't unload it until you or your company pays off each local dock worker. Should you pay?
f. In Mexico your firm has been working hard to earn lucrative contracts with the national oil company, Pemex. One government official has hinted elaborately that his son would like to do marketing studies for your company. Should you hire the son?

3.16 Investigating Gifts, Gratuities, and Entertainment Limits (Obj. 6)

Ethics | Intercultural | Team | Web

You are one of a group of interns at a large company. As part of your training, your director asks your team to investigate the codes of conduct of other companies. In particular, the manager asks you to find comparison information on gifts, gratuities, and kickbacks.

Your Task. Search the Web for sections in codes of conduct that relate to gifts, gratuities, entertainment, and kickbacks. From three companies or organizations (such as BlueCross BlueShield, 3M Corporation, or a university), investigate specific restrictions. What do these organizations allow and restrict? Prepare a list summarizing your findings in your own words.

3.17 Investors Try to Push All-White Board to Diversify (Obj. 7)

Diversity sometimes comes at the price of conflict. A few years ago information-storage company EMC Corporation very publicly disagreed with Walden Asset Management. The money manager interested in socially responsible investing complained that EMC's ten-member board and most of its officers were white males. Walden filed several shareholder resolutions to effect change. However, EMC insisted that its board members were diverse enough, stating that they ranged in age from 43 to 71 and hailed from many different industries. Moreover, EMC claimed that by selecting "a less qualified female or minority candidate," the company would potentially miss out on an outstanding, experienced male candidate. In the years since, EMC's age "diversity" has shrunk somewhat to 50 to 71, and the board now includes a woman.[83]

Your Task. Assume you are a manager for EMC. You look around and notice that everyone looks alike. Pair off with a classmate to role-play a discussion in which you strive to convince another manager that your organization would be better if it were more diverse. The other manager (your classmate), however, is satisfied with the status quo. Suggest advantages for diversifying the staff. The opposing manager argues for homogeneity.

3.18 What Makes a "Best" Company for Minorities? (Obj. 7)

Web

In its ranking of the 50 Best Companies for Minorities, *Fortune* listed the following suggestions for fostering diversity:[84]

- Make an effort to hire, retain, and promote minorities.
- Interact with outside minority communities.
- Hold management accountable for diversity efforts.
- Create a culture where people of color and other minorities feel that they belong.
- Match a diverse workforce with diversity in an organization's management ranks and on its board.

Your Task. Assume you are the individual in **Activity 3.17** who believes your organization would be better if it were more diverse. Because of your interest in this area, your boss says he would like you to give a three- to five-minute informational presentation at the next board meeting. Your assignment is to present what the leading minority-friendly companies are doing. You decide to prepare your comments based on *Fortune* magazine's list of the 50 best companies for minorities, using as your outline the previous bulleted list. You plan to provide examples of each means of fostering diversity. Your instructor may ask you to give your presentation to the entire class or to small groups.

Video Resource

Video Library 1, Intercultural Communication at Work

This video transports viewers into the offices of Clifton-Harding Associates (CHA), a small New York advertising agency. The company was founded by Ella Clifton and her husband Rob Harding. In meeting with a prospective Japanese customer, Ella and Rob, together with their dippy receptionist Stephanie, illustrate numerous clashes between American and Asian cultures, expectations, and etiquette. After you watch the video, be prepared to discuss these questions:

- What cultural misunderstandings occurred during Ken'ichi Takahashi's meeting with Rob, Ella, and Stephanie?
- What suggestions would you offer Rob and Ella for improving their cultural competence?
- At the end of the meeting with Mr. Takahashi, Rob assumed that Clifton-Harding Associates would be hired to develop an advertising campaign. In fact, Rob asked that a contract be prepared outlining their agreement. Do you think Mr. Takahashi plans to hire Rob and Ella's firm? Why or why not?

Chat About It

In each chapter you will find five discussion questions related to the chapter material. Your instructor may assign these topics for you to discuss in class, in an online chat room, or on an online discussion board. Some of the discussion topics may require outside research. You may also be asked to read and respond to postings made by your classmates.

Topic 1: Find several examples of global interconnectivity in your home. For example, from what countries do your clothing, furniture, or appliances come? Were you surprised?

Topic 2: Describe a time when you experienced culture shock. *Merriam-Webster's Collegiate Dictionary* defines culture shock as a "sense of confusion and uncertainty sometimes with feelings of anxiety that may affect people exposed to an alien culture," such as one might experience when visiting a foreign country. What caused the culture shock you experienced? What did you do to adjust to the culture?

Topic 3: Name a time when you were aware of ethnocentrism in your own actions or those of friends, family members, or colleagues. In general terms, describe what happened. What made you think the experience was ethnocentric?

Topic 4: Do some research to determine why Transparency International ranked Denmark, New Zealand, Sweden, and Singapore as the least corrupt countries or why it ranked Russia, Bangladesh, Venezuela, Haiti, and Iraq as the most corrupt countries.

Topic 5: In your own experience, how accurate are characterizations that gender theorists make about differences between men and women? Support your views.

Grammar and Mechanics C.L.U.E. Review 3

Pronouns

Review Guides 11–18 about pronoun usage in Appendix A, Grammar and Mechanics Guide, beginning on page A-6. On a separate sheet, revise the following sentences to correct errors in pronouns. For each error that you locate, write the guide number that reflects this usage. Some sentences may have two errors. If the sentence is correct, write *C*. When you finish, check your answers on page Key-1.

Example: Me and her are the most senior sales reps in the Northeast Division.

Revision: She and I are the most senior sales reps in the Northeast Division. [Guide 12]

1. Direct the visitors to my boss and I; she and I will give them a tour of our facility.
2. Judging by you and I alone, this department will be the most productive one in the company.
3. The team knew that it's project was doomed once the funding was cut.
4. You and me did the work of three; she only did hers and poorly so.
5. The shift manager and I will work overtime tonight, so please direct all calls to him or myself.
6. Each new job candidate must be accompanied to their interview by a staff member.
7. Please deliver the printer supplies to whomever ordered them.
8. Most applications arrived on time, but your's and her's were not received.
9. As we were pulling out of the parking lot, one of our colleagues waved at Peter and me asking us to stop.
10. Whom did you say left messages for Connie and me?

UNIT 2

The Writing Process

CHAPTER 4

Planning Business Messages

Want to do well on tests and excel in your course? Go to **www.meguffey.com** for helpful interactive resources.

- **Review the Chapter 4 PowerPoint slides to prepare for the first quiz.**

OBJECTIVES

After studying this chapter, you should be able to

1. Identify four basic principles of business writing, summarize the 3-x-3 writing process, and explain how a writing process helps a writer.
2. Recognize the components of the first phase of the writing process (prewriting), including analyzing your purpose, anticipating the audience, selecting the best channel, and considering how to adapt your message to the audience.
3. Effectively apply audience benefits, the "you" view, and conversational but professional language.
4. Effectively employ positive and courteous tone, bias-free language, simple expression, and vigorous words.
5. Understand how teams approach collaborative writing projects and what collaboration tools support team writing.
6. Summarize the legal and ethical responsibilities of business communicators in the areas of investments, safety, marketing, human resources, and copyright law.

Zooming In PART 1

Suze Orman Preaches Financial Freedom in Simple Language

Personal finance guru Suze Orman has a mission. She wants to change the way people think, act, and talk about money. One of the most widely read financial authorities of our time, she has written seven best-selling financial guidance books. But she is probably best known for her television programs including specials for PBS, the syndicated *Financial Freedom Hour* on QVC network, and an advice show on CNBC. She is also a columnist for *O*, Oprah Winfrey's magazine, and for Yahoo's personal finance site.

Orman's advice is largely for people who are drowning in debt. "Sweetheart," she says to a caller, "burn those credit cards!" She delivers her gospel of financial freedom with an animated conviction and high-energy style that have become her hallmark.[1] In her books and magazine articles, she speaks with the same assurance. "Having talked to literally tens of thousands of people, I can say that what is good for America ... is not having credit card debt, not leasing a car, and not having mortgage debt. This is not good for a human being. It's just not!"[2]

Orman knows what it is like to be in debt. After graduating with a degree in sociology, she worked for seven years as a waitress at the Buttercup Bakery in Berkeley, California. With a $50,000 loan from her customers, she intended to finance her own restaurant. Because of bad advice from an investment firm, she lost her $50,000 within four months. However, "she made it all up and then some after the firm hired her as its only female broker."[3]

As a broker, she developed her financial planning skills and built a reputation for honesty and ethical advice. Her books and articles combine emotional and spiritual observations about money and how to avoid the financial problems that caused pain for her family as she was growing up. *The Money Book for the Young, Fabulous, & Broke* directs financial advice at young people early in their working lives.

She admits that her message is not new. "It's not the material that I know, but how I communicate the material I know that sets me apart."[4] Orman's advice is practical and cuts through much confusing, contradictory financial information. One of her greatest strengths is breaking complex ideas into easy-to-understand segments. Like many great communicators, she knows her audience, shapes her message accordingly, and uses simple language.

© Newscom

Critical Thinking

- Whether one is writing a book, making a speech, or composing a business letter, why is it important to anticipate the audience for the message?
- What does writing an effective financial help book have in common with writing an effective business message?
- Why is it important to follow a writing process?

http://www.suzeorman.com

Understanding the Writing Process for Business Messages

LEARNING OBJECTIVE 1

Identify four basic principles of business writing, summarize the 3-x-3 writing process, and explain how a writing process helps a writer.

The task of preparing a written business message or a presentation is easier and more efficient if you have a systematic process to follow. When financial expert Suze Orman starts a writing assignment, she focuses totally on the task at hand. She takes no phone calls, answers no e-mails, and allows no interruptions. In delivering a convincing message, she employs many of the writing techniques you are about to learn. This chapter presents a systematic writing process that you can use to approach all business communication problems, whether you are planning an e-mail message, a report, an oral presentation, or even an instant message. The 3-x-3 writing process guides you through three phases, making it easy for you to plan, organize, and complete any message. Following the 3-x-3 writing process takes the guesswork out of writing. It tells you what goes on in each phase and guides you to effective results.

Starting With the Basics

What distinguishes business writing from other kinds of writing?

The first thing you should recognize about business writing is that it differs from other writing you may have done. In preparing high school or college compositions and term papers, you probably focused on discussing your feelings or displaying your knowledge. Your instructors wanted to see your thought processes, and they wanted assurance that you had internalized the subject matter. You may have had to meet a minimum word count. Business writers, however, have different goals. For business messages and oral presentations, your writing should be:

- **Purposeful.** You will be writing to solve problems and convey information. You will have a definite purpose to fulfill in each message.
- **Persuasive.** You want your audience to believe and accept your message.
- **Economical.** You will try to present ideas clearly but concisely. Length is not rewarded.
- **Audience oriented.** You will concentrate on looking at a problem from the perspective of the audience instead of seeing it from your own.

These distinctions actually ease the writer's task. You will not be searching your imagination for creative topic ideas. You won't be stretching your ideas to make them appear longer. Writing consultants and businesspeople complain that many college graduates entering industry have at least an unconscious perception that quantity enhances quality. Wrong! Get over the notion that longer is better. Conciseness and clarity are prized in business.

The ability to prepare concise, audience-centered, persuasive, and purposeful messages does not come naturally. Very few people, especially beginners, can sit down and compose a terrific letter or report without training. However, following a systematic process, studying model messages, and practicing the craft can make nearly anyone a successful business writer or speaker.

Following the 3-x-3 Writing Process

What are the three phases of the writing process?

Whether you are preparing an e-mail message, memo, letter, or oral presentation, the process will be easier if you follow a systematic plan. The 3-x-3 writing process breaks the entire task into three phases: *prewriting, writing,* and *revising,* as shown in Figure 4.1.

To illustrate the writing process, let's say that you own a popular local McDonald's franchise. At rush times, you face a problem. Customers complain about the chaotic multiple waiting lines to approach the service counter. You once saw two customers nearly get into a fistfight over cutting into a line. What's more, customers often are so intent on looking for ways to improve their positions in line that they fail to examine the menu. Then they are

FIGURE 4.1 The 3-x-3 Writing Process

1 Prewriting

Analyze: Decide on your purpose. What do you want the receiver to do or believe? What channel or form is best? Should you deliver your message in writing, orally, electronically, or graphically?

Anticipate: Profile the audience. What does the receiver already know? Will the receiver's response be neutral, positive, or negative? Use the direct method for positive messages; consider using the indirect method for negative or persuasive messages.

Adapt: What techniques can you use to adapt your message to its audience and the audience's anticipated reaction? Include audience benefits and the "you" view, as well as positive, conversational, and courteous language.

2 Writing

Research: Gather data to provide facts. Search company files, previous correspondence, and the Internet. What do you need to know to write this message? How much does the audience already know?

Organize: Group similar facts together. Organize direct messages with the big idea first, followed by an explanation and an action request in the closing. For persuasive or negative messages, use an indirect, problem-solving plan. For short messages, make quick notes. For longer messages, outline your plan and make notes.

Compose: Prepare a first draft, usually writing quickly. Focus on short, clear sentences using the active voice. Link ideas to build paragraph coherence.

3 Revising

Revise: Edit your message to be sure it is clear, conversational, concise, and readable. Revise to eliminate wordy fillers, long lead-ins, redundancies, compound prepositions, wordy noun phrases, and trite business phrases. Develop parallelism and consider using headings and numbered and bulleted lists for quick comprehension.

Proofread: Take the time to read over every message carefully. Look for errors in spelling, grammar, punctuation, names, numbers, and format.

Evaluate: Decide whether this message will achieve your purpose. Have you thought enough about the audience to be sure this message is appropriate and appealing?

undecided when their turn arrives. You want to convince other franchise owners that a single-line (serpentine) system would work better. You could telephone the other owners. But you want to present a serious argument with good points that they will remember and be willing to act on when they gather for their next district meeting. You decide to write a letter that you hope will win their support.

What tasks are involved in the first phase of the writing process?

Prewriting. The first phase of the writing process prepares you to write. It involves *analyzing* the audience and your purpose for writing. The audience for your letter will be other franchise owners, some highly educated and others not. Your purpose in writing is to convince them that a change in policy would improve customer service. You are convinced that a single-line system, such as that used in banks, would reduce chaos and make customers happier because they would not have to worry about where they are in line.

Prewriting also involves *anticipating* how your audience will react to your message. You are sure that some of the other owners will agree with you, but others might fear that customers seeing a long single line might go elsewhere. In *adapting* your message to the audience, you try to think of the right words and the right tone that will win approval.

What tasks are involved in the second phase of the writing process?

Writing. The second phase involves researching, organizing, and then composing the message. In *researching* information for this letter, you would probably investigate other kinds of businesses that use single lines for customers. You might check out your competitors. What are Wendy's and Burger King doing? You might do some calling to see whether other franchise owners are concerned about chaotic lines. Before writing to the entire group, you might brainstorm with a few owners to see what ideas they have for solving the problem.

Once you have collected enough information, you would focus on *organizing* your letter. Should you start out by offering your solution? Or should you work up to it slowly, describing the problem, presenting your evidence, and then ending with the solution? The final step in the second phase of the writing process is actually *composing* the letter. Naturally, you will do it at your computer so that you can revise easily.

Revising. The third phase of the process involves revising, proofreading, and evaluating your letter. After writing the first draft, you will spend a lot of time *revising* the message for clarity, conciseness, tone, and readability. Could parts of it be rearranged to make your point more effectively? This is the time when you look for ways to improve the organization and tone of your message. Next, you will spend time *proofreading* carefully to ensure correct spelling, grammar, punctuation, and format. The final phase involves *evaluating* your message to decide whether it accomplishes your goal.

Scheduling the Writing Process

What percentage of your time should you spend on each phase of the writing process?

Although Figure 4.1 shows the three phases of the writing process equally, the time you spend on each varies depending on the complexity of the problem, the purpose, the audience, and your schedule. One expert gives these rough estimates for scheduling a project:

- Prewriting—25 percent (thinking and planning)
- Writing—25 percent (organizing and composing)
- Revising—50 percent (45 percent revising and 5 percent proofreading)

These are rough guides, yet you can see that good writers spend most of their time on the final phase of revising and proofreading. Much depends, of course, on your project, its importance, and your familiarity with it. What is critical to remember, though, is that revising is a major component of the writing process.

It may appear that you perform one step and progress to the next, always following the same order. Most business writing, however, is not that rigid. Although writers perform the tasks described, the steps may be rearranged, abbreviated, or repeated. Some writers revise every sentence and paragraph as they go. Many find that new ideas occur after they have begun to write, causing them to back up, alter the organization, and rethink their plan. Beginning business writers often follow the writing process closely. With experience, though, you will become like other good writers and presenters who alter, compress, and rearrange the steps as needed.

Ethics Check

Essays for Sale

Web sites with playful names such as Cramster, Course Hero, Koofers, and Spark Notes provide ready-made solutions and essays for students. Do such sites encourage cheating and undermine the mental sweat equity of day-to-day learning?

Analyzing Your Purpose and Selecting Your Channel

LEARNING OBJECTIVE 2

Recognize the components of the first phase of the writing process (prewriting), including analyzing your purpose, profiling the audience, and selecting the best channel.

We devote the remainder of this chapter to the first phase of the writing process. You will learn to analyze the purpose for writing, anticipate how your audience will react, and adapt your message to the audience. It's surprising how many people begin writing and discover only as they approach the end of a message what they are trying to accomplish. If you analyze your purpose before you begin, you can avoid backtracking and starting over.

Identifying Your Purpose

As you begin to compose a message, ask yourself two important questions: (a) Why am I sending this message? and (b) What do I hope to achieve? Your responses will determine how you organize and present your information.

What are the primary and secondary purposes of most business messages?

Your message may have primary and secondary purposes. For college work your primary purpose may be merely to complete the assignment; secondary purposes might be to make yourself look good and to earn an excellent grade. The primary purposes for sending business messages are typically to inform and to persuade. A secondary purpose is to promote goodwill. You and your organization want to look good in the eyes of your audience.

Most business messages do nothing more than *inform*. They explain procedures, announce meetings, answer questions, and transmit findings. Some business messages, however, are meant to *persuade*. These messages sell products, convince managers, motivate employees, and win over customers. Informative messages are developed differently from persuasive messages.

Selecting the Best Channel

After identifying the purpose of your message, you need to select the most appropriate communication channel. Some information is most efficiently and effectively delivered orally. Other messages should be written, and still others are best delivered electronically. Whether to set up a meeting, send a message by e-mail, or write a report depends on some of the following factors:

What factors influence your selection of the best delivery channel?

- Importance of the message
- Amount and speed of feedback and interactivity required
- Necessity of a permanent record
- Cost of the channel
- Degree of formality desired
- Confidentiality and sensitivity of the message

An interesting theory, called the media richness theory, describes the extent to which a channel or medium recreates or represents all the information available in the original message. A richer medium, such as face-to-face conversation, permits more interactivity and feedback. A leaner medium, such as a report or proposal, presents a flat, one-dimensional message. Richer media enable the sender to provide more verbal and visual cues, as well as allow the sender to tailor the message to the audience.

Many factors help you decide which of the channels shown in Figure 4.2 on page 116 is most appropriate for delivering a workplace message.

Switching to Faster Channels

Technology and competition continue to accelerate the pace of business today. As a result, communicators are switching to ever-faster means of exchanging information. In the past business messages within organizations were delivered largely by hard-copy memos. Responses would typically take a couple of days. However, that's too slow for today's communicators. They want answers and action now! Mobile phones, instant messaging, faxes, Web sites, and especially e-mail can deliver that information much faster than can traditional channels of communication.

FIGURE 4.2 Choosing Communication Channels

Channel	Best Use
Blog	When one person needs to present digital information easily so that it is available to others.
E-mail	When you need feedback but not immediately. Lack of security makes it problematic for personal, emotional, or private messages.
Face-to-face conversation	When you need a rich, interactive medium. Useful for persuasive, bad-news, and personal messages.
Face-to-face group meeting	When group decisions and consensus are important. Inefficient for merely distributing information.
Fax	When your message must cross time zones or international boundaries, when a written record is significant, or when speed is important.
Instant message	When you are online and need a quick response. Useful for learning whether someone is available for a phone conversation.
Letter	When a written record or formality is required, especially with customers, the government, suppliers, or others outside an organization.
Memo	When you want a written record to clearly explain policies, discuss procedures, or collect information within an organization.
Phone call	When you need to deliver or gather information quickly, when nonverbal cues are unimportant, and when you cannot meet in person.
Report or proposal	When you are delivering considerable data internally or externally.
Voice mail message	When you wish to leave important or routine information that the receiver can respond to when convenient.
Video- or audioconference	When group consensus and interaction are important, but members are geographically dispersed.
Wiki	When digital information must be made available to others. Useful for collaboration because participants can easily add, remove, and edit content.

Why is e-mail so popular for business messages?

Within many organizations, hard-copy memos are still written, especially for messages that require persuasion, permanence, or formality. They are also prepared as attachments to e-mail messages. Clearly, however, the channel of choice for corporate communicators today is e-mail. It's fast, inexpensive, and easy. Businesspeople are sending fewer hard-copy interoffice memos and fewer customer letters. Customer service functions can now be served through Web sites or by e-mail.

Many businesses now help customers with live chat, shown in Figure 4.3. Customers visit the company Web site and chat with representatives by keying their questions and answers back and forth. Customer representatives must have not only good keying skills but also an ability to write conversational and correct responses. One company found that it could not easily convert its telephone customer service people to chat representatives because many lacked the language skills necessary to write clear and correct messages. They were good at talking but not at writing, again making the point that the Internet has increased the need for good writing skills.

Whether your channel choice is live chat, e-mail, a hard-copy memo, or a report, you will be showcasing your communication skills and applying the writing process. The best writers spend sufficient time in the prewriting phase.

Anticipating the Audience

A good writer anticipates the audience for a message: What is the reader or listener like? How will that person react to the message? Although you can't always know exactly who the receiver is, you can imagine some of that person's characteristics. Even writers of direct-mail sales letters have a general idea of the audience they wish to target. Picturing a typical receiver is important in guiding what you write. One copywriter at Lands' End, the catalog company, pictures his sister-in-law whenever he writes product descriptions for the catalog. By profiling your audience and shaping a message to respond to that profile, you are more likely to achieve your communication goals.

FIGURE 4.3 **Live Chat Connects Service Reps and Customers**

John On www.FirstFederal.com - Customer Chat
General
Exit Chat
Exit Chat & Close
Transfer
Commands
Send Link
Canned Responses
Chat
Previous Chats
History
Block Visitor
Block
Lisa says:
Hi, my name is Lisa. Welcome to First Federal live chat. How can I help you?
John On www.FirstFederal.com says:
I would like to know whether my company can make deposits without coming in to the bank.
Lisa says:
Yes, we now offer Internet banking, and you can make deposits from your office or anywhere in the country.
John On www.FirstFederal.com says:
That's great! Do I need any special equipment?
Lisa says:
All you need is a personal computer, an Internet connection, and a scanner. If you have a high volume of checks, you might want to use a specialized scanner that we offer.
Send
John is typing a message.

Customer service reps in chat sessions require good writing skills to answer questions concisely, clearly, and conversationally. It takes special talent to be able to think and key immediate responses that are spelled correctly and are error-free.

Profiling the Audience

Visualizing your audience is a pivotal step in the writing process. The questions in Figure 4.4 will help you profile your audience. How much time you devote to answering these questions depends on your message and its context. An analytical report that you compose for management or an oral presentation before a big group would, of course, demand considerable audience anticipation. On the other hand, an e-mail message to a coworker or a letter to a familiar supplier might require only a few moments of planning. No matter how short your message, though, spend some time thinking about the audience so that you can tailor your words to your readers or listeners. Remember that most receivers will be thinking, *What's in it for me?* or, *What am I supposed to do with this information*?

Why is it important to profile the audience for a business message?

Responding to the Audience Profile

Profiling your audience helps you make decisions about shaping the message. You will discover what kind of language is appropriate, whether you are free to use specialized technical terms, whether you should explain everything, and so on. You will decide whether your tone should be formal or informal, and you will select the most desirable channel. Imagining whether the receiver is likely to be neutral, positive, or negative will help you determine how to organize your message.

Another advantage of profiling your audience is considering the possibility of a secondary audience. For example, let's say you start to write an e-mail message to your supervisor, Sheila, describing a problem you are having. Halfway through the message you realize that Sheila will probably forward this message to her boss, the vice president. Sheila will not want to summarize what you said; instead she will take the easy route and merely forward your e-mail. When you realize that the vice president will probably see this message, you decide to back up and use a more formal tone. You remove your inquiry about Sheila's family, you reduce your complaints, and you tone down your language about why things went wrong. Instead, you provide more background information, and you are more specific in identifying items the vice

Spotlight on Communicators

Warren Buffett, the second richest man in the United States and one of the most successful investors of all time, offers advice on how to improve your messages by profiling your audience and responding to that profile. When writing annual reports, he pretends that he's talking to his sisters. "I have no trouble picturing them. Though highly intelligent, they are not experts in accounting or finance. They will understand plain English but jargon may puzzle them. . . . No sisters to write to? Borrow mine. Just begin with 'Dear Doris and Bertie,'" he suggested.

FIGURE 4.4 Asking the Right Questions to Profile Your Audience

Primary Audience	Secondary Audience
Who is my primary reader or listener?	Who might see or hear this message in addition to the primary audience?
What are my personal and professional relationships with this person?	How do these people differ from the primary audience?
What position does this person hold in the organization?	Do I need to include more background information?
How much does this person know about the subject?	How must I reshape my message to make it understandable and acceptable to others to whom it might be forwarded?
What do I know about this person's education, beliefs, culture, and attitudes?	
Should I expect a neutral, positive, or negative response to my message?	

president might not recognize. Analyzing the task and anticipating the audience help you adapt your message so that you can create an efficient and effective message.

Adapting to the Task and Audience

LEARNING OBJECTIVE 3
Effectively apply audience benefits, the "you" view, and conversational but professional language.

After analyzing your purpose and anticipating your audience, you will begin to think about how to adapt your message to the task and the audience. Adaptation is the process of creating a message that suits your audience. One important aspect of adaptation is *tone*. Conveyed largely by the words in a message, tone affects how a receiver feels upon reading or hearing a message. Tone is how you say something. It reveals the writer's attitude toward the receiver. For example, how you would react to these statements?

You must return the form by 5 p.m.

Would you please return the form by 5 p.m.

The wording of the first message establishes an aggressive or negative tone—no one likes being told what to do. The second message is reworded in a friendlier, more positive manner. Poorly chosen words may sound demeaning, condescending, discourteous, pretentious, or demanding. Notice in the Lands' End letter in Figure 4.5 that the writer achieves a courteous and warm tone. The letter responds to a customer's concern about the changing merchandise mix available in Lands' End catalogs. The customer also wants to receive fewer catalogs. The writer explains the company's expanded merchandise line and reassures the customer that Lands' End has not abandoned its emphasis on classic styles.

What techniques help a writer achieve a positive tone?

Skilled communicators create a positive tone in their messages by using a number of adaptive techniques, some of which are unconscious. These include spotlighting audience benefits, cultivating a "you" view, sounding conversational but professional, and using positive, courteous expression. Additional adaptive techniques include using bias-free language and preferring plain language with familiar but vigorous words.

Developing Audience Benefits

Focusing on the audience sounds like a modern idea, but actually one of America's early statesmen and authors recognized this fundamental writing principle over 200 years ago. In describing effective writing, Ben Franklin observed, "To be good, it ought to have a tendency to benefit the reader."[5] These wise words have become a fundamental guideline for today's business communicators. Expanding on Franklin's counsel, a contemporary communication consultant gives this solid advice to his business clients: "Always stress the benefit to the audience of whatever it is you are trying to get them to do. If you can show them how you are going to save them frustration or help them meet their goals, you have the makings of a powerful message."[6]

What is *empathy*?

Adapting your message to the receiver's needs means putting yourself in that person's shoes. It's called *empathy*. Empathic senders think about how a receiver will decode a message. They try to give something to the receiver, solve the receiver's problems, save the receiver's

FIGURE 4.5 **Customer Response Letter**

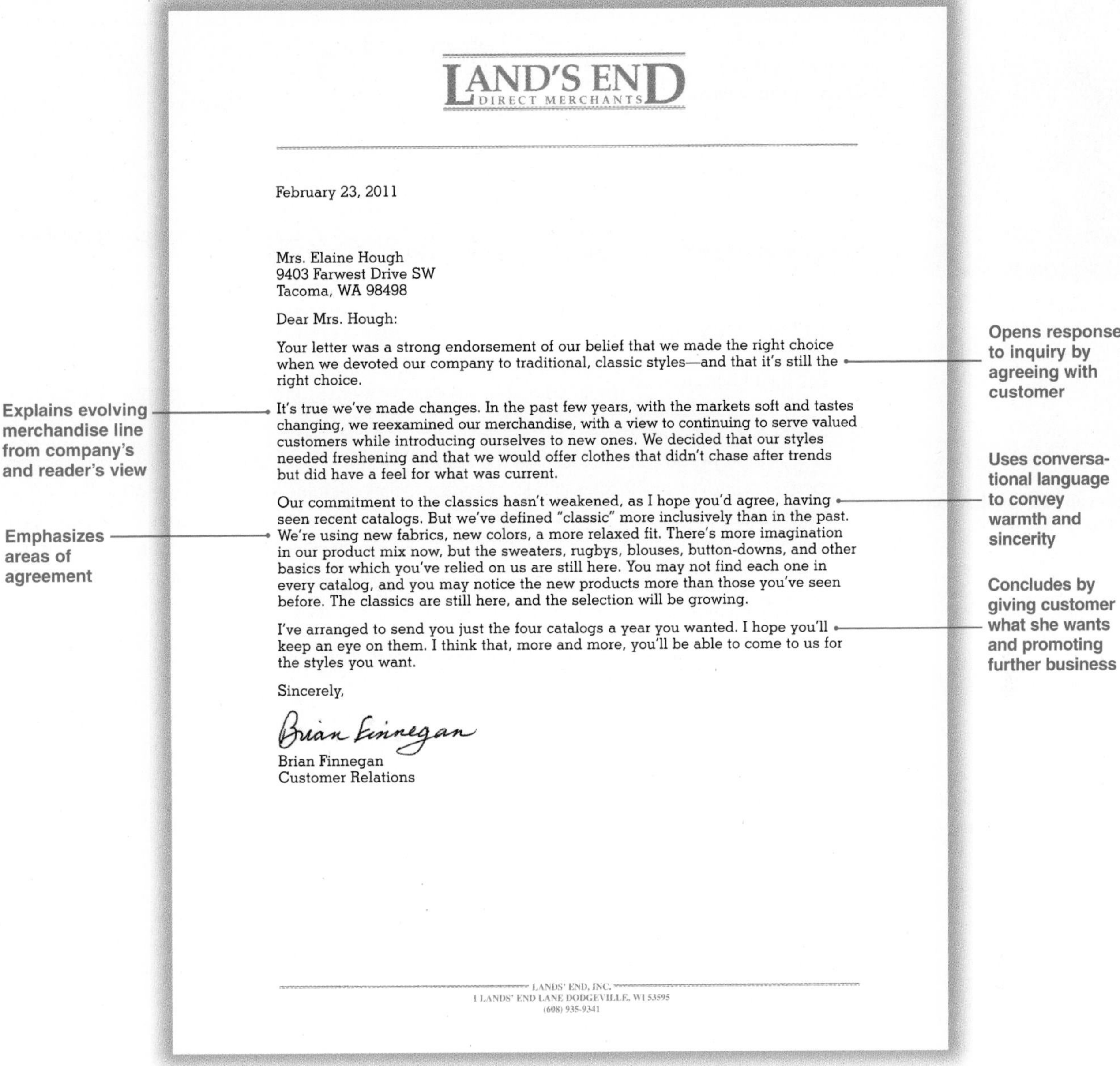

LAND'S END
DIRECT MERCHANTS

February 23, 2011

Mrs. Elaine Hough
9403 Farwest Drive SW
Tacoma, WA 98498

Dear Mrs. Hough:

Your letter was a strong endorsement of our belief that we made the right choice when we devoted our company to traditional, classic styles—and that it's still the right choice.

It's true we've made changes. In the past few years, with the markets soft and tastes changing, we reexamined our merchandise, with a view to continuing to serve valued customers while introducing ourselves to new ones. We decided that our styles needed freshening and that we would offer clothes that didn't chase after trends but did have a feel for what was current.

Our commitment to the classics hasn't weakened, as I hope you'd agree, having seen recent catalogs. But we've defined "classic" more inclusively than in the past. We're using new fabrics, new colors, a more relaxed fit. There's more imagination in our product mix now, but the sweaters, rugbys, blouses, button-downs, and other basics for which you've relied on us are still here. You may not find each one in every catalog, and you may notice the new products more than those you've seen before. The classics are still here, and the selection will be growing.

I've arranged to send you just the four catalogs a year you wanted. I hope you'll keep an eye on them. I think that, more and more, you'll be able to come to us for the styles you want.

Sincerely,

Brian Finnegan

Brian Finnegan
Customer Relations

LANDS' END, INC.
1 LANDS' END LANE DODGEVILLE, WI 53595
(608) 935-9341

Opens response to inquiry by agreeing with customer
Explains evolving merchandise line from company's and reader's view
Uses conversational language to convey warmth and sincerity
Emphasizes areas of agreement
Concludes by giving customer what she wants and promoting further business

money, or just understand the feelings and position of that person. Which version of the following messages is more appealing to the audience?

Sender Focus	**Audience Focus**
The Human Resources Department requires that the enclosed questionnaire be completed immediately so that we can allocate our training resource funds to employees.	By filling out the enclosed questionnaire, you can be one of the first employees to sign up for our training resource funds.
Our warranty becomes effective only when we receive an owner's registration.	Your warranty begins working for you as soon as you return your owner's registration.
We are proud to announce our new software virus checker that we think is the best on the market!	Now you can be sure that all your computers will be protected with our real-time virus scanning.

Cultivating the "You" View

Notice that many of the previous audience-focused messages included the word *you*. In concentrating on receiver benefits, skilled communicators naturally develop the "you" view. They

Spotlight on Communicators

© AP Images/David Kohl

Voted the greatest minority entrepreneur in American history, John H. Johnson was a master at profiling potential customers and cultivating the "you" view. He always focused on what they wanted rather than on what he wanted. His emphasis on the "you" view helped him build *Ebony* and *Jet* magazines, along with *Fashion Fair Cosmetics*, into multimillion-dollar businesses. In explaining his customer approach, he said, "I want to know where they came from, what are their interests, [and] what can I talk to them about." He worked to establish rapport with people by learning their interests.

emphasize second-person pronouns (*you, your*) instead of first-person pronouns (*I/we, us, our*). Whether your goal is to inform, persuade, or promote goodwill, the catchiest words you can use are *you* and *your*. Compare the following examples.

"I/We" View	"You" View
We are requiring all employees to respond to the attached survey about health benefits.	Because your ideas count, please complete the attached survey about health benefits.
I need your account number before I can do anything.	Would you mind giving me your account number so that I can locate your records and help you solve this problem?
We have shipped your order by UPS, and we are sure it will arrive in time for your sales promotion December 1.	Your order will be delivered by UPS in time for your sales promotion December 1.

How can you use the word *you* skillfully?

Although you want to focus on the reader or listener, don't overuse or misuse the second-person pronoun *you*. Readers and listeners appreciate genuine interest; on the other hand, they resent obvious attempts at manipulation. The authors of some sales messages, for example, are guilty of overkill when they include *you* dozens of times in a direct-mail promotion. Furthermore, the word can sometimes create the wrong impression. Consider this statement: *You cannot return merchandise until you receive written approval.* The word *you* appears twice, but the reader feels singled out for criticism. In the following version the message is less personal and more positive: *Customers may return merchandise with written approval.*

Another difficulty in emphasizing the "you" view and de-emphasizing *we/I* is that it may result in overuse of the passive voice. For example, to avoid *We will give you* (active voice), you might write *You will be given* (passive voice). The active voice in writing is generally preferred because it identifies who is doing the acting. You will learn more about active and passive voice in Chapter 5.

Should you remove all incidents of *I* and *we* in your messages?

In recognizing the value of the "you" attitude, writers do not have to sterilize their writing and totally avoid any first-person pronouns or words that show their feelings. Skilled communicators are able to convey sincerity, warmth, and enthusiasm by the words they choose. Don't be afraid to use phrases such as *I'm happy* or *We're delighted,* if you truly are.

When speaking face-to-face, communicators show sincerity and warmth with nonverbal cues such as a smile and a pleasant voice tone. In letters, memos, and e-mail messages, however, only expressive words and phrases can show these feelings. These phrases suggest hidden messages that say *You are important, I hear you,* and *I'm honestly trying to please you.* Mary Kay Ash, one of the most successful cosmetics entrepreneurs of all time, gave her salespeople wise advice. She had them imagine that any person they were addressing wore a sign saying, *Make me feel important.*

Being Conversational but Professional

How can a message be conversational and also professional?

Most instant messages, e-mail messages, business letters, memos, and reports replace conversation. Thus, they are most effective when they convey an informal, conversational tone instead of a formal, pretentious tone. Workplace messages should not, however, become so casual that they sound low level and unprofessional.

Instant messaging (IM) enables coworkers to have informal, spontaneous conversations. Some companies have accepted IM as a serious workplace tool. With the increasing use of instant messaging and e-mail, however, a major problem has developed. Sloppy, unprofessional expression appears in many workplace messages. You will learn more about the dangers of e-mail in Chapter 7. At this point, though, we focus on the tone of the language.

To project a professional image, you must sound educated and mature. Overuse of expressions such as *totally awesome, you know,* and *like,* as well as reliance on needless abbreviations (*BTW* for *by the way*), make a businessperson sound like a teenager. Professional messages do not include IM abbreviations, slang, sentence fragments, and chitchat. We urge you to strive for a warm, conversational tone that avoids low-level diction. Levels of diction, as shown in Figure 4.6, range from unprofessional to formal.

FIGURE 4.6 Levels of Diction

Unprofessional (Low-level diction)	Conversational (Middle-level diction)	Formal (High-level diction)
badmouth	criticize	denigrate
guts	nerve	courage
pecking order	line of command	dominance hierarchy
ticked off	upset	provoked
rat on	inform	betray
rip off	steal	expropriate
Sentence example: If we just hang in there, we can snag the contract.	**Sentence example:** If we don't get discouraged, we can win the contract.	**Sentence example:** If the principals persevere, they can secure the contract.

Your goal is a warm, friendly tone that sounds professional. Although some writers are too casual, others are overly formal. To impress readers and listeners, they use big words, long sentences, legal terminology, and third-person constructions. Stay away from expressions such as *the undersigned, the writer*, and *the affected party.* You will sound friendlier with familiar pronouns such as *I, we*, and *you.* Study the following examples to see how to achieve a professional, yet conversational tone:

Unprofessional	**Professional**
Hey, boss, Gr8 news! Firewall now installed!! BTW, check with me b4 announcing it.	Mr. Smith, our new firewall software is now installed. Please check with me before announcing it.
Look, dude, this report is totally bogus. And the figures don't look kosher. Show me some real stats. Got sources?	Because the figures in this report seem inaccurate, please submit the source statistics.

Zooming In PART 2

Suze Orman

America's most listened-to personal finance expert, Suze Orman, appears on TV, makes personal appearances, prepares magazine columns, and has written seven best-selling books. One might expect her to be a master multitasker, taking on many jobs at once and juggling all of them perfectly. Wrong, way wrong! When Orman starts a writing task, she focuses on that task only and allows no interruptions. "I came to this conclusion after watching the way racehorses win," she explained. "They come out of the gate with blinders on and go for the finish line." That's how she writes. "All I care about is what I do, and I do absolutely nothing else while I am doing it."[7] Trying to complete more than one task at the same time ends in the "absolute ruination" of any project, she contended. "When I'm writing, I don't answer phones. I don't care what else is going on."[8]

Her total focus enables her to target her advice to specific audiences. She seems to really care about people and is nonjudgmental toward those who have dug themselves into terrible financial trouble. Although much financial information is contradictory and confusing, she offers practical advice in simple, positive language. She explains the reasoning behind her advice and encourages others to learn to make their own financial decisions wisely.

Critical Thinking

- When writing, what are the advantages and disadvantages of multitasking?
- Suze Orman is known for using simple, familiar language to express complex ideas. Does a business writer lose credibility when using this kind of language?
- Why does it make sense for a business writer to express ideas positively instead of negatively?

© Newscom

Overly Formal	Conversational
All employees are herewith instructed to return the appropriately designated contracts to the undersigned.	Please return your contracts to me.
Pertaining to your order, we must verify the sizes that your organization requires prior to consignment of your order to our shipper.	We will send your order as soon as we confirm the sizes you need.

Expressing Yourself Positively

LEARNING OBJECTIVE 4

Effectively employ positive and courteous tone, bias-free language, simple expression, and vigorous words.

What are examples of loaded words that convey a negative tone?

You can improve the clarity, tone, and effectiveness of a message if you use positive rather than negative language. Positive language generally conveys more information than negative language does. Moreover, positive messages are uplifting and pleasant to read. Positive wording tells what *is* and what *can be done* rather than what *isn't* and what *can't be done*. For example, *Your order cannot be shipped by January 10* is not nearly as informative as *Your order will be shipped January 20*. An office supply store adjacent to an ice cream parlor in Portland, Maine, posted a sign on its door that reads: *Please enjoy your ice cream before you enjoy our store*. That sounds much more positive and inviting than *No food allowed!*[9]

Using positive language also involves avoiding negative words that create ill will. Some words appear to blame or accuse your audience. For example, opening a letter to a customer with *You claim that* suggests that you don't believe the customer. Other loaded words that can get you in trouble are *complaint, criticism, defective, failed, mistake*, and *neglected*. Often the writer is unconscious of the effect of these words. Notice in the following examples how you can revise the negative tone to create a more positive impression.

Negative	Positive
This plan definitely cannot succeed if we don't obtain management approval.	This plan definitely can succeed if we obtain management approval.
You failed to include your credit card number, so we can't mail your order.	We look forward to completing your order as soon as we receive your credit card number.
Your letter of May 2 claims that you returned a defective headset.	Your May 2 letter describes a headset you returned.
Employees cannot park in Lot H until April 1.	Employees may park in Lot H starting April 1.
You won't be sorry that....	You will be happy that....

Being Courteous

Why is it smart for a business communicator to remain cool and courteous even when angry?

Maintaining a courteous tone involves not just guarding against rudeness but also avoiding words that sound demanding or preachy. Expressions such as *you should, you must*, and *you have to* cause people to instinctively react with *Oh, yeah?* One remedy is to turn these demands into rhetorical questions that begin with *Will you please....* Giving reasons for a request also softens the tone.

Even when you feel justified in displaying anger, remember that losing your temper or being sarcastic will seldom accomplish your goals as a business communicator: to inform, to persuade, and to create goodwill. When you are irritated, frustrated, or infuriated, keep cool and try to defuse the situation. In dealing with customers in telephone conversations, use polite phrases such as *I would be happy to assist you with that, Thank you for being so patient*, and *It was a pleasure speaking with you.*

Less Courteous	More Courteous and Helpful
Can't you people get anything right? This is the second time I've written!	Please credit my account for $340. My latest statement shows that the error noted in my letter of May 15 has not yet been corrected.
Stewart, you must complete all performance reviews by Friday.	Stewart, will you please complete all performance reviews by Friday.

Less Courteous	More Courteous and Helpful
You should organize a car pool in this department.	Organizing a car pool will reduce your transportation costs and help preserve the environment.
Am I the only one who can read the operating manual?	Let's review the operating manual together so that you can get your documents to print correctly next time.

Choosing Bias-Free Language

In adapting a message to its audience, be sure your language is sensitive and bias-free. Few writers set out to be offensive. Sometimes, though, we all say things that we never thought might be hurtful. The real problem is that we don't think about the words that stereotype groups of people, such as *the boys in the mail room* or *the girls in the front office.* Be cautious about expressions that might be biased in terms of gender, race, ethnicity, age, and disability. Generally, you can avoid gender-biased language by leaving out the words *man* or *woman*, by using plural nouns and pronouns, or by changing to a gender-free word (*person* or *representative*). Avoid the *his or her* option whenever possible. It's wordy and conspicuous. With a little effort, you can usually find a construction that is graceful, grammatical, and unselfconscious.

What is biased language, and why should business communicators avoid it?

Specify age only if it is relevant, and avoid expressions that are demeaning or subjective (such as *spry old codger*). To avoid disability bias, do not refer to an individual's disability unless it is relevant. When necessary, use terms that do not stigmatize disabled individuals. The following examples give you a quick look at a few problem expressions and possible replacements. The real key to bias-free communication, though, lies in your awareness and commitment. Be on the lookout to be sure that your messages do not exclude, stereotype, or offend people.

Gender Biased	Improved
female doctor, woman attorney, cleaning woman	doctor, attorney, cleaner
waiter/waitress, authoress, stewardess	server, author, flight attendant
mankind, man-hour, man-made	humanity, working hours, artificial
office girls	office workers
the doctor ... he	doctors ... they
the teacher ... she	teachers ... they
executives and their wives	executives and their spouses
foreman, flagman, workman	lead worker, flagger, worker
businessman, salesman	businessperson, sales representative
Each employee had his picture taken.	Each employee had a picture taken. All employees had their pictures taken. Each employee had his or her picture taken.

Racially or Ethnically Biased	Improved
An Indian accountant was hired.	An accountant was hired.
James Lee, an African American, applied.	James Lee applied.

Age Biased	Improved
The law applied to old people.	The law applied to people over 65.
Sally Kay, 55, was transferred.	Sally Kay was transferred.
a spry old gentleman	a man
a little old lady	a woman

Disability Biased	Improved
afflicted with arthritis, suffering from ..., crippled by ...	has arthritis
confined to a wheelchair	uses a wheelchair

Why should business communicators strive to use familiar language?

Using Plain Language and Familiar Words

In adapting your message to your audience, use plain language and familiar words that you think audience members will recognize. Don't, however, avoid a big word that conveys your idea efficiently and is appropriate for the audience. Your goal is to shun pompous and pretentious language. Instead, use "GO" words. If you mean *begin,* don't say *commence* or *initiate.* If you mean *pay,* don't write *compensate.* By substituting everyday, familiar words for unfamiliar ones, as shown here, you help your audience comprehend your ideas quickly.

Unfamiliar	**Familiar**
commensurate	equal
interrogate	question
materialize	appear
obfuscate	confuse
remuneration	pay, salary
terminate	end

At the same time, be selective in your use of jargon. *Jargon* describes technical or specialized terms within a field. These terms enable insiders to communicate complex ideas briefly, but to outsiders they mean nothing. Human resources professionals, for example, know precisely what's meant by *cafeteria plan* (a benefits option program), but most of us would be thinking about lunch. Geologists refer to *plate tectonics,* and physicians discuss *metastatic carcinomas.* These terms mean little to most of us. Use specialized language only when the audience will understand it. In addition, don't forget to consider secondary audiences: Will those potential receivers understand any technical terms used?

How can you improve your vocabulary so that you can use precise, vigorous words?

Employing Precise, Vigorous Words

Strong verbs and concrete nouns give receivers more information and keep them interested. Don't overlook the thesaurus (or the thesaurus program on your computer) for expanding your word choices and vocabulary. Whenever possible, use specific words as shown here.

Imprecise, Dull	**More Precise**
a change in profits	a 25 percent hike in profits a 10 percent plunge in profits
to say	to promise, confess, understand to allege, assert, assume, judge
to think about	to identify, diagnose, analyze to probe, examine, inspect

The accompanying checklist feature on page 126 reviews important elements in the first phase of the 3-x-3 writing process. As you review these tips, remember the three basics of prewriting: analyzing, anticipating, and adapting. Figure 4.7 on page 125 illustrates a number of poor techniques that create a negative tone in an e-mail message. Notice what a difference revision makes. Many negative ideas could have been expressed positively. After revision, the message is shorter, is more conversational, and emphasizes audience benefits.

Writing in Teams

LEARNING OBJECTIVE 5

Understand how teams approach collaborative writing projects and what collaboration tools support team writing.

As you learned in Chapter 2, many of today's workers will work with teams to deliver services, develop products, and complete projects. It is almost assumed that today's progressive organizations will employ teams in some capacity to achieve their objectives. Because much of a team's work involves writing, you can expect to be putting your writing skills to work as part of a team.

FIGURE 4.7 **Improving the Tone in an E-Mail Message**

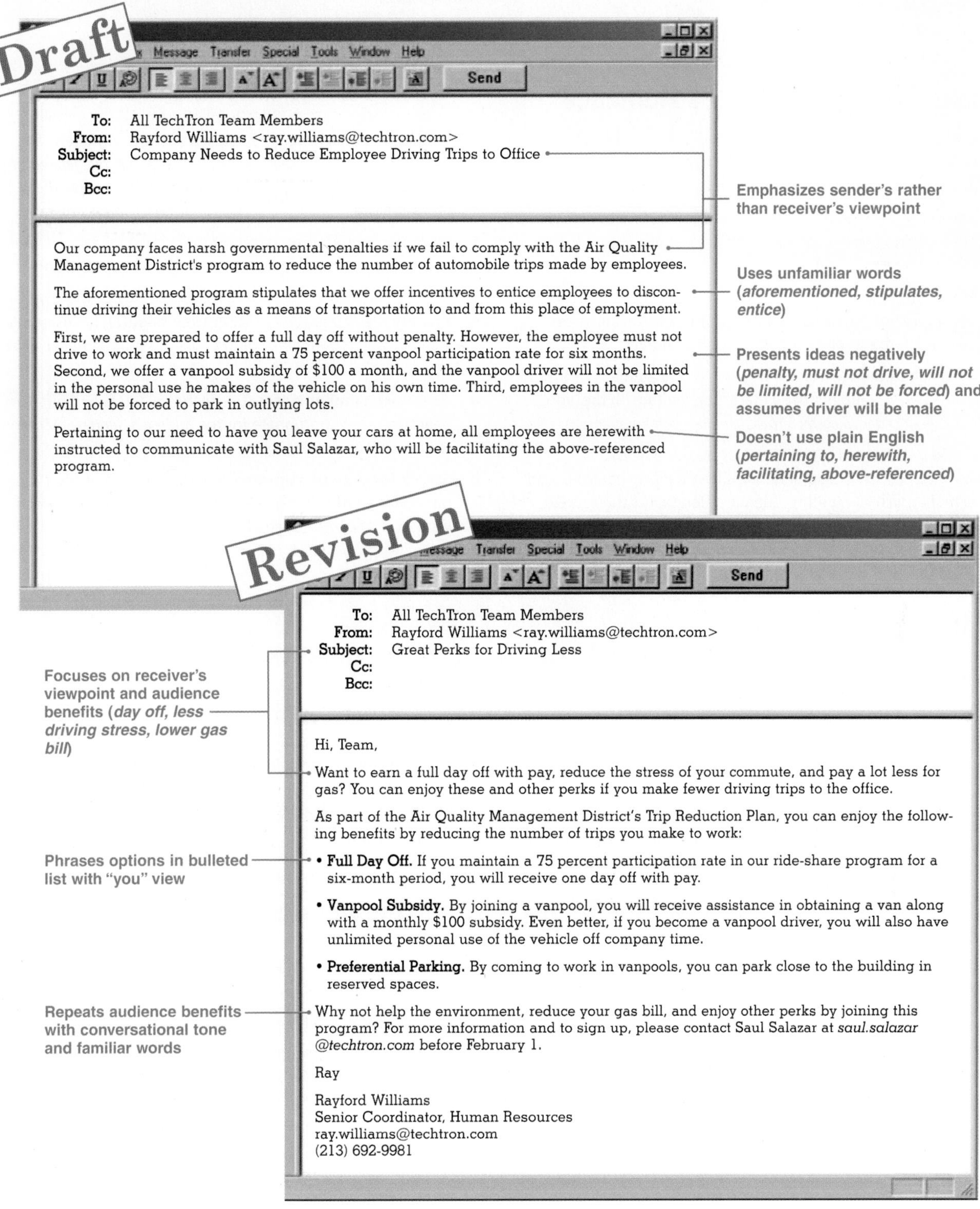

Draft
Send
To: All TechTron Team Members
From: Rayford Williams <ray.williams@techtron.com>
Subject: Company Needs to Reduce Employee Driving Trips to Office
Cc:
Bcc:
Our company faces harsh governmental penalties if we fail to comply with the Air Quality Management District's program to reduce the number of automobile trips made by employees.
The aforementioned program stipulates that we offer incentives to entice employees to discontinue driving their vehicles as a means of transportation to and from this place of employment.
First, we are prepared to offer a full day off without penalty. However, the employee must not drive to work and must maintain a 75 percent vanpool participation rate for six months. Second, we offer a vanpool subsidy of $100 a month, and the vanpool driver will not be limited in the personal use he makes of the vehicle on his own time. Third, employees in the vanpool will not be forced to park in outlying lots.
Pertaining to our need to have you leave your cars at home, all employees are herewith instructed to communicate with Saul Salazar, who will be facilitating the above-referenced program.
Emphasizes sender's rather than receiver's viewpoint
Uses unfamiliar words (aforementioned, stipulates, entice)
Presents ideas negatively (penalty, must not drive, will not be limited, will not be forced) and assumes driver will be male
Doesn't use plain English (pertaining to, herewith, facilitating, above-referenced)
Revision
Send
To: All TechTron Team Members
From: Rayford Williams <ray.williams@techtron.com>
Subject: Great Perks for Driving Less
Cc:
Bcc:
Hi, Team,
Want to earn a full day off with pay, reduce the stress of your commute, and pay a lot less for gas? You can enjoy these and other perks if you make fewer driving trips to the office.
As part of the Air Quality Management District's Trip Reduction Plan, you can enjoy the following benefits by reducing the number of trips you make to work:
• Full Day Off. If you maintain a 75 percent participation rate in our ride-share program for a six-month period, you will receive one day off with pay.
• Vanpool Subsidy. By joining a vanpool, you will receive assistance in obtaining a van along with a monthly $100 subsidy. Even better, if you become a vanpool driver, you will also have unlimited personal use of the vehicle off company time.
• Preferential Parking. By coming to work in vanpools, you can park close to the building in reserved spaces.
Why not help the environment, reduce your gas bill, and enjoy other perks by joining this program? For more information and to sign up, please contact Saul Salazar at saul.salazar@techtron.com before February 1.
Ray
Rayford Williams
Senior Coordinator, Human Resources
ray.williams@techtron.com
(213) 692-9981
Focuses on receiver's viewpoint and audience benefits (day off, less driving stress, lower gas bill)
Phrases options in bulleted list with "you" view
Repeats audience benefits with conversational tone and familiar words

When Are Team-Written Documents Necessary?

Collaboration on team-written documents is necessary for projects that (a) are big, (b) have short deadlines, and (c) require the expertise or consensus of many people. Businesspeople sometimes collaborate on short documents, such as memos, letters, information briefs, procedures, and policies. But more often, teams work together on big documents and presentations.

In what situations can you expect to share writing duties with a team?

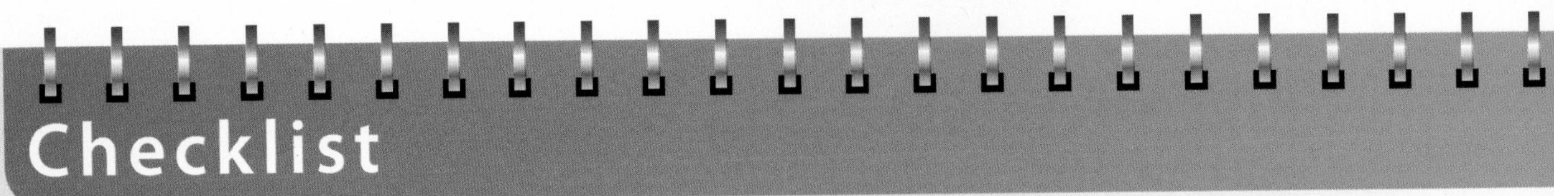

Checklist

Adapting a Message to Its Audience

- **Identify the message purpose.** Ask yourself why you are communicating and what you hope to achieve. Look for primary and secondary purposes.
- **Select the most appropriate form.** Determine whether you need a permanent record or whether the message is too sensitive to put in writing.
- **Profile the audience.** Identify your relationship with the reader and your knowledge about that individual or group. Assess how much the receiver knows about the subject.
- **Focus on audience benefits.** Phrase your statements from the readers' viewpoint, not the writer's. Concentrate on the "you" view (*Your order will arrive, You can enjoy, Your ideas count*).
- **Avoid gender and racial bias.** Use bias-free words (*businessperson* instead of *businessman; working hours* instead of *man-hours*). Omit ethnic identification unless the context demands it.
- **Avoid age and disability bias.** Include age only if relevant. Avoid potentially demeaning expressions (*spry old gentleman*), and use terms that do not stigmatize disabled people (*he is disabled* instead of *he is a cripple* or *he has a handicap*).
- **Be conversational but professional.** Strive for a warm, friendly tone that is not overly formal or familiar. Avoid slang and low-level diction.
- **Express ideas positively rather than negatively.** Instead of *Your order can't be shipped before June 1*, say *Your order can be shipped June 1*.
- **Use short, familiar words.** Use technical terms and big words only if they are appropriate for the audience (*end* not *terminate, required* not *mandatory*).
- **Search for precise, vigorous words.** Use a thesaurus if necessary to find strong verbs and concrete nouns (*announces* instead of *says, brokerage* instead of *business*).

Why Are Team-Written Documents Better?

Team-written documents and presentations are standard in most organizations because collaboration has many advantages. Most important, collaboration usually produces a better product because many heads are better than one. In addition, team members and organizations benefit from team processes. Working together helps socialize members. They learn more about the organization's values and procedures. They are able to break down functional barriers, and they improve both formal and informal chains of communication. Additionally, they buy in to a project when they are part of its development. Members of effective teams are eager to implement their recommendations.

How Are Team-Written Documents Divided?

In what phases of the writing process do team members work together and separately?

With big writing projects, teams may not actually function together for each phase of the writing process. Typically, team members gather at the beginning to brainstorm. They iron out answers to questions about the purpose, audience, content, organization, and design of their document or presentation. They develop procedures for team functioning, as you learned in Chapter 2. Then, they often assign segments of the project to individual members.

Teams work together closely in Phase 1 (prewriting) of the writing process. However, members generally work separately in Phase 2 (writing), when they conduct research, organize their findings, and compose a first draft. During Phase 3 (revising) teams may work together to synthesize their drafts and offer suggestions for revision. They might assign one person the task of preparing the final document, and another, the job of proofreading. The revision and evaluation phase might be repeated several times before the final product is ready for presentation.

What Online Collaboration Tools Support Team Writing?

One of the most frustrating tasks for teams is writing shared documents. Keeping the various versions straight and recognizing who made what comment can be difficult. Fortunately, online collaboration tools are constantly being developed and improved. They range from simple to complex, inexpensive to expensive, locally installed to remotely hosted, commercial to open source, and large to small. Online collaboration tools are especially necessary when team members are not physically in the same location. However, even when members are nearby, they may find it necessary to use online collaboration tools, such as the following:[10]

- **E-mail.** Despite its many drawbacks, e-mail remains a popular tool for online asynchronous (intermittent data transmission) collaboration. However, as projects grow more complex and involve more people who are not working nearby, e-mail becomes a clumsy, ineffective tool, especially for collaborative writing tasks.
- **Mailing lists.** With the right software, mailing lists can be archived online, providing a threaded listing of posts and full-text searching.
- **Discussion boards.** Participants can upload documents to the board instead of sending large files to everyone.
- **Instant messaging.** Because it ensures immediate availability, instant messaging is gaining acceptance. It allows members to clear up minor matters immediately, and it is helpful in initiating a quick group discussion.
- **Blogs and wikis.** A *blog* is a Web site with journal entries usually written by one person with comments added by others. A *wiki* is a Web site that allows multiple users to collaboratively create and edit pages. Wikis are good tools for building a knowledge repository that can be edited by participants. You will learn more about blogs and wikis in Chapter 7.
- **Groupware and portals.** Groupware and portals in the past involved expensive software featuring online discussion areas, document- and file-sharing areas, integrated calendaring, and collaborative authoring tools. More recently, less expensive tools including Basecamp, Box, Huddle, and Socialtext are available.

A team of investors and organic farmers in Bloomington, Indiana, began using Basecamp, an inexpensive Web-based collaboration program, to help the people in the field keep in touch with those in town. The 81-acre farm grows organic produce and sells it to Whole Foods Market, food co-ops, and farmers' markets. The farm's founders brought on four partners, but their jobs elsewhere prevented them from visiting the farm very often. One partner decided to install Basecamp on the farm house computer. For $24 a month this program offers to-do lists, a wiki, a chat room, 3 gigabytes of file storage, and a function that tracks due dates. Now the city folks can stay in the loop with the farmers and can share in decision making and farm progress.[11]

Collaboration software isn't just for multinational corporations. Stranger's Hill Organics, the oldest certified organics farm in Indiana, has joined the ranks of Adidas, Patagonia, Kellogg's and others in using Basecamp, a popular project-management tool that allows professionals to work together from different locations. The local grower, which serves markets and co-ops in Bloomington and Indianapolis, uses Basecamp to coordinate tasks, from crop maintenance and harvesting to tax planning. The results show in the farm's healthy squash, beans, cucumbers, and herbs. *How might farmers use online collaboration tools?*

PLUGGED IN

Using Technology to Edit and Revise Collaborative Documents

Collaborative writing and editing projects are challenging. Fortunately, Microsoft Word offers useful tools to help team members edit and share documents electronically. Two simple but useful editing tools are **Text Highlight Color** and **Font Color**. These tools, which are found on the **Home** tab in MS Office 2007, enable reviewers to point out errors and explain problematic passages through the use of contrast. However, some projects require more advanced editing tools such as **Track Changes** and **Comment**.

Track Changes. To suggest specific editing changes to other team members, **Track Changes** is handy. The revised wording is visible on screen, and deletions show up in callout balloons that appear in the right-hand margin (see Figure 4.2). Suggested revisions offered by various team members are identified and dated. The original writer may accept or reject these changes. In Office 2007 you will find **Track Changes** on the **Review** tab.

Comment. Probably the most useful editing tool is the **Comment** function, also shown in Figure 4.8. This tool allows users to point out problematic passages or errors, ask or answer questions, and share ideas without changing or adding text. When more than one person adds comments, the comments appear in different colors and are identified by the writer's name and a date/time stamp. To use this tool in Word 2007, click **New Comment** from the drop-down **Review** tab. Then type your comment, which can be seen in the Web or print layout view (click **View** and **Print Layout** or **Web Layout**).

Completing a Document. When a document is finished, be sure to accept or reject all changes on the **Review** tab, a step that removes the tracking information.

Career Application

Organize into groups of three. Using the latest version of Word, copy and respond to the Document for Analysis in 4.11. Set up a round-robin e-mail file exchange so that each member responds to the other group members' documents by using the **Comment** feature of Word to offer advice or suggestions for improvement. Submit a printout of the document with group comments, as well as a final edited document.

What Tools Work Well for Student Collaboration?

Student groups collaborating on assignments may find several helpful software tools. Google Docs is a free Web-based word processor, spreadsheet, presentation, and form application program that keeps documents current and lets team members update files from their own computers. A favorite feature of Google Docs is offline editing via Google Gears or the Chrome browser. In addition, Google Docs enables you to compose offline using your own word processor and upload into Docs to share and edit with teammates. Another free collaborative writing tool is Whiteboard. Check out either of these free tools by searching Google.

A number of tools accompanying Microsoft Word enable team writers to track changes and insert comments while editing one team document. The above Plugged In box discusses these tools, and Figure 4.8 illustrates how they work.

Adapting to Legal and Ethical Responsibilities

LEARNING OBJECTIVE 6

Summarize the legal and ethical responsibilities of business communicators in the areas of investments, safety, marketing, human resources, and copyright law.

One of your primary responsibilities in writing for an organization or for yourself is to avoid language that may land you in court. Another responsibility is to be ethical. Both of these concerns revolve around the use and abuse of language. You can protect yourself and avoid litigation by knowing what is legal and by adapting your language accordingly. Be especially careful when your messages address or include mentions of investments, safety, marketing, human resources, and copyright law.

Investment Information

Writers describing the sale of stocks or financial services must follow specific laws written to protect investors. Any messages—including e-mails, letters, newsletters, and pamphlets—must be free of misleading information, exaggerations, and half-truths. One company in Massachusetts inadvertently violated the law by declaring that it was "recession-proof." After going bankrupt, the company was sued by angry stockholders claiming that they had been

FIGURE 4.8 **Track Changes and Comment Features in Team Document**

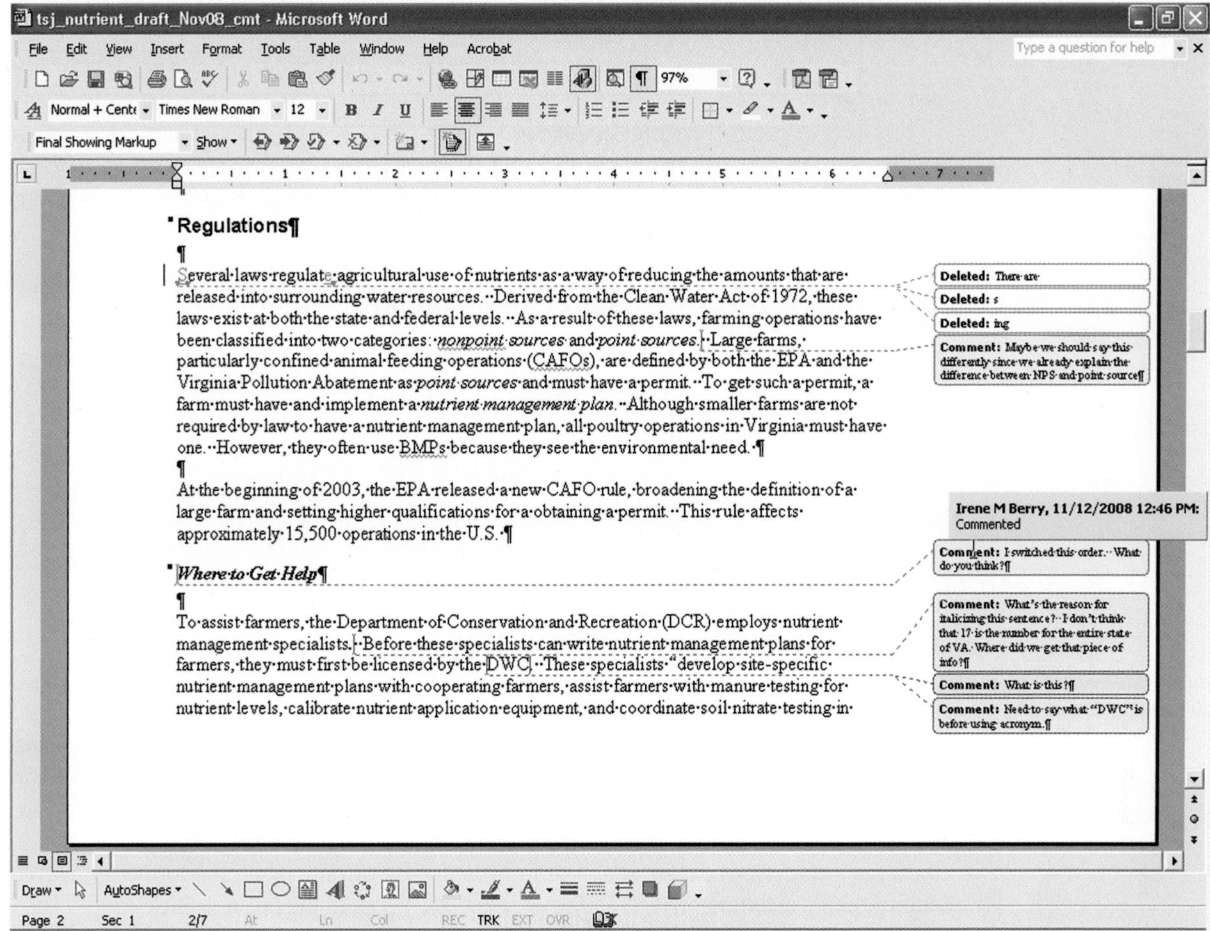

deceived. A software company caused a flurry of lawsuits by withholding information that revealed problems in a new version of one of its most popular programs. Stockholders sued, charging that managers had deliberately concealed the bad news, thus keeping stock prices artificially high. Experienced financial writers know that careless language and even poor timing may provoke litigation.

Safety Information

Why should warnings on dangerous products be written especially clearly?

Writers describing potentially dangerous products worry not only about protecting people from physical harm but also about being sued. During the past three decades, litigation arising from product liability has been one of the most active areas of tort law (*tort law* involves wrongful civil acts other than breach of contract). Manufacturers are obligated to warn consumers of any risks in their products. These warnings must do more than suggest danger; they must also clearly tell people how to use the product safely. In writing warnings, concentrate on major points. Omit anything that is not critical. In the work area describe a potential problem and tell how to solve it. For example, *Lead dust is harmful and gets on your clothes. Change your clothes before leaving work.*

Clearly written safety messages use easy-to-understand words, such as *doctor* instead of *physician*, *clean* instead of *sanitary*, and *burn* instead of *incinerate*. Technical terms are defined; for example, *Asbestos is a carcinogen (something that causes cancer)*. Effective safety messages also include highlighting techniques such as headings and bullets. In coming chapters you will learn more about these techniques for improving readability.

Marketing Information

Sales and marketing messages are illegal if they falsely advertise prices, performance capability, quality, or other product characteristics. Marketing messages must not deceive the buyer in any

What kinds of sales and marketing messages are illegal?

way. The marketers of CortiSlim and CortiStress paid huge fines and were forbidden to claim that their products caused rapid weight loss and reduced the risk of cancer, heart disease, and other ailments.[12]

Sellers of services must also be cautious about the language they use to describe what they will do. Letters, reports, and proposals that describe services to be performed are interpreted as contracts in court. Therefore, language must not promise more than intended. In Chapter 10 on page 315, you will learn more about what's legal and what's not in sales letters. Here are some dangerous words (and recommended alternatives) that have created misunderstandings leading to lawsuits.[13]

Dangerous Word	Court Interpretation	Recommended Alternative
inspect	to examine critically, to investigate and test officially, to scrutinize	to review, to study, to tour the facility
determine	to come to a decision, to decide, to resolve	to evaluate, to assess, to analyze
assure	to render safe, to make secure, to give confidence, to cause to feel certain	to facilitate, to provide further confidence, to enhance the reliability of

Human Resources Information

What kinds of statements should you avoid in evaluating employees in the workplace?

The vast number of lawsuits relating to human resources and employment makes this a treacherous area for business communicators. In evaluating employees in the workplace, avoid making unsubstantiated negative comments. It is also unwise to assess traits (*she is unreliable*) because doing so requires subjective judgment. Concentrate instead on specific incidents (*in the last month she missed four work days and was late three times*). Defamation lawsuits have become so common that some companies no longer provide letters of recommendation for former employees. To be safe, give recommendations only when the former employee authorizes the recommendation and when you can say something positive. Stick to job-related information.

Statements in employee handbooks also require careful wording, because a court might rule that such statements are "implied contracts." Consider the following handbook remark: "We at Hotstuff, Inc., show our appreciation for hard work and team spirit by rewarding everyone who performs well." This seemingly harmless statement could make it difficult to fire an employee because of the implied employment promise.[14] Companies are warned to avoid promissory phrases in writing job advertisements, application forms, and offer letters. Phrases that suggest permanent employment and guaranteed job security can be interpreted as contracts.[15]

In statements to existing and prospective employees, companies must recognize that oral comments may trigger lawsuits. A Minnesota television news anchor won damages when she gave up her job search because her station manager promised to extensively market her in a leading role. But he failed to follow through. A Vermont engineer won his case of negligent misrepresentation when he was not told that the defense project for which he was hired faced a potential cutback. Companies are warned to require employees to sign employment agreements indicating that all terms of employment orally agreed upon must be made in writing to be valid.[16]

In adapting messages to meet today's litigious business environment, be sensitive to the rights of others and to your own rights. The key elements in this adaptation process are awareness of laws, sensitivity to interpretations, and careful use of language.

Ethics Check

Barack Rip-Off

Poster artist Shepard Fairey created a popular "Hope" poster of Barack Obama from a striking photo he saw on the Internet. Freelance photographer Mannie Garcia cried foul and demanded licensing fees, which Fairey refused. Are items on the Internet free for the taking if they have been changed a little?

Copyright Information

What is *fair use* in relation to copyright law?

The Copyright Act of 1976 protects authors—literary, dramatic, and artistic—of published and unpublished works. The word *copyright* refers to "the right to copy," and a key provision is *fair use*. Under fair use, individuals have limited use of copyrighted material without requiring permission. These uses are for criticism, comment, news reporting, teaching, scholarship, and research. Unfortunately, the distinctions between fair use and infringement are not clearly defined.

Four-Factor Test to Assess Fair Use. What is fair use? Actually, it is a shadowy territory with vague and often disputed boundaries—now even more so with the addition of cyberspace. Courts use four factors as a test in deciding disputes over fair use:

- **Purpose and character of the use, particularly whether for profit.** Courts are more likely to allow fair use for nonprofit educational purposes than for commercial ventures.
- **Nature of the copyrighted work.** When information is necessary for public good—such as medical news—courts are more likely to support fair use.
- **Amount and substantiality of portion used.** Copying a 200-word passage from a 200,000-word book might be allowed but not 200 words from a 1,000-word article or a substantial part of a shorter work. A total of 300 words is mistakenly thought by many to be an acceptable limit for fair use, but courts have not upheld this figure. Don't rely on it.
- **Effect of the use on the potential market.** If use of the work may interfere with the author's potential profit from the original, fair use copying would not be allowed.

How to Avoid Copyright Infringement. Whenever you borrow words, charts, graphs, photos, music, or anything created privately, be sure you know what is legal and acceptable. The following guidelines will help:

Why should writers assume that everything is copyrighted?

- **Assume that everything is copyrighted.** Nearly everything created privately and originally after 1989 is copyrighted and protected whether or not it has a copyright notice.
- **Realize that Internet items are NOT in the public domain.** Nothing modern is in the public domain (free to be used by anyone) unless the owner explicitly says so.
- **Observe fair-use restrictions.** Be aware of the four-factor test. Avoid appropriating large amounts of outside material.
- **Ask for permission.** You are always safe if you obtain permission. Write to the source, identify the material you wish to include, and explain where it will be used. Expect to pay for permission.
- **Don't assume that a footnote is all that is needed.** Including a footnote to a source prevents plagiarism but not copyright infringement. Anything copied beyond the boundaries of fair use requires permission. You will learn more about citation methods and ways to avoid plagiarism in Chapter 12.

For more information about *copyright law, fair use, public domain,* and *work for hire,* you can search the Web with these keywords.

Want to do well on tests and excel in your course? Go to **www.meguffey.com** for helpful interactive resources.

- **Review the Chapter 4 PowerPoint slides to prepare for the first quiz.**

Zooming In — YOUR TURN

Applying Your Skills With Suze Orman

As an applicant for a research assistant at the Suze Orman Financial Group, you have been asked to submit a writing sample. Your assignment is to compose a one-page memo discussing why so many college students are in debt. All applicants are to provide tips to students who want to avoid getting into college-related debt. As a writing sample, your memo will be judged on its clear expression, simple language, and precise words.

© Newscom

Your Task

Address your memo to Melissa M., who is a recruiter hired by Suze Orman to screen applicants. See Chapter 8 for information about preparing memos.

Summary of Learning Objectives

1 Identify four basic principles of business writing, summarize the 3-x-3 writing process, and explain how a writing process helps a writer. Business writing differs from academic writing in that it strives to solve business problems. It is also economical, persuasive, and audience oriented. Phase 1 of the 3-x-3 writing process (prewriting) involves analyzing the message, anticipating the audience, and considering ways to adapt the message to the audience. Phase 2 (writing) involves researching the topic, organizing the material, and composing the message. Phase 3 (revising) includes proofreading and evaluating the message. A writing process helps a writer by providing a systematic plan describing what to do in creating messages.

2 Recognize the components of the first phase of the writing process (prewriting) including analyzing your purpose, profiling the audience, and selecting the best channel. Communicators must decide why they are delivering a message and what they hope to achieve. Although many messages only inform, some must also persuade. After identifying the purpose of a message, communicators must choose the most appropriate channel. That choice depends on the importance of the message, the amount and speed of feedback required, the need for a permanent record, the cost of the channel, and the degree of formality desired. Communicators should also anticipate the primary and secondary audiences in order to adapt the message appropriately.

3 Effectively apply audience benefits, the "you" view, and a conversational but professional tone. Skilled communicators strive to emphasize audience benefits in business messages. This involves looking for ways to give something to the receiver, solve the receiver's problems, save the receiver's money, or just understand the feelings and position of that person. Skilled communicators look at a message from the receiver's perspective applying the "you" view without attempting to manipulate. Effective business messages convey a warm, friendly tone but avoid expressions that may make the writer sound immature or unprofessional.

4 Effectively employ positive and courteous tone, bias-free language, simple expression, and vigorous words. Skilled communicators improve the clarity, tone, and effectiveness of messages by using positive language that tells what can be done rather than what can't be done (*The project will be successful with your support* rather than *The project won't be successful without your support*). A courteous tone means guarding against rudeness and avoiding sounding preachy or demanding. Messages should also avoid language that excludes, stereotypes, or offends people, such as *lady lawyer, spry old gentlemen,* and *confined to a wheelchair*). Messages are improved by strong verbs and concrete nouns rather than imprecise, dull expressions.

5 Understand how teams approach collaborative writing projects and what collaboration tools support team writing. Team writing, which is necessary for large projects or when wide expertise is necessary, alters the writing process. Teams often work together in brainstorming and working out their procedures and assignments. Then individual members write their portions of the report or presentation during Phase 2. During Phase 3 (revising) teams may work together to combine their drafts. Teams use online collaboration tools such as e-mail, mailing lists, discussion boards, instant messaging, blogs, wikis, groupware, and portals.

6 Summarize the legal and ethical responsibilities of business communicators in the areas of investments, safety, marketing, human resources, and copyright law. In writing about investments, communicators must avoid misleading information, exaggerations, and half-truths. Safety information, including warnings, must tell consumers clearly how to use a product safely and motivate them to do so. In addition to being honest, marketing information must not promise more than intended. Communicators in human resources must use careful wording (particularly in employment recommendations and employee handbooks) to avoid lawsuits. They must also avoid oral promises that can result in lawsuits. In publication, one must be mindful of copyright laws. Writers should assume that everything is copyrighted, even items borrowed from the Internet, and know the implications and limitations of *fair use*.

Are you ready? Get more practice at **www.meguffey.com**

Chapter Review

1. Why do you think business writing differs from school essay writing? (Obj. 1)
2. List the three phases of the writing process and summarize what happens in each phase. Which phase requires the most time? (Obj. 1)
3. What six factors are important in selecting an appropriate channel to deliver a message? What makes one channel richer than another? (Obj. 2)
4. How does profiling the audience help a business communicator prepare a message? (Obj. 2)
5. What is meant by "audience benefits"? (Obj. 3)
6. When is the "you" view appropriate, and when is it inappropriate? (Obj. 3)
7. Why is it OK to use instant messaging abbreviations (such as *BTW*) and happy faces in messages to friends but not OK in business messages? (Obj. 3)
8. What is wrong with using expressions such as *you claim, complaint, criticism, defective, failed, mistake,* and *neglected?* (Obj. 4)
9. What is wrong with the following statement? *Pertaining to the above-referenced infraction, all employees are herewith warned by the undersigned not to install private software on company computers.* (Obj. 4)
10. What is bias-free language? List original examples. (Obj. 4)
11. Why should business writers strive to use short, familiar, simple words? Does this "dumb down" business messages? (Obj. 4)
12. What is *jargon*, and when is it appropriate for business writing? (Obj. 4)
13. What are the advantages and disadvantages of team-written documents? (Obj. 5)
14. Under copyright law, what does *fair use* mean? (Obj. 6)
15. What kinds of works are protected by copyright laws? (Obj. 6)

Critical Thinking

1. Why do you think employers prefer messages that are not written like high school and college essays? (Obj. 1)
2. A wise observer once said that bad writing makes smart people look dumb. Do you agree or disagree, and why? (Objs. 1–4)
3. Discuss the following statement: "The English language is a land mine—it is filled with terms that are easily misinterpreted as derogatory and others that are blatantly insulting . . . . Being fair and objective is not enough; employers must also appear to be so."[17] (Obj. 4)
4. Why do you think that writing in a natural, conversational tone is difficult for many people? (Obj. 3)
5. **Ethical Issue:** Peter Whitney, an employee at Wells Fargo, launched an Internet blog to chat about his life, his friends, and his job. After criticizing some of his coworkers in his blog, he was fired from his job handling mail and the front desk. Whitney said, "There needs to be clearer guidelines. Some people go to a bar and complain about workers. I decided to do it online. Some people say I deserve what happened, but it was really harsh. It was unfair."[18] Do you agree or disagree, and why?

Writing Improvement Exercises

4.1 Audience Benefits and the "You" View (Obj. 3)

Your Task. Revise the following sentences to emphasize the perspective of the audience and the "you" view.

a. To avoid suffering the kinds of monetary losses we have experienced in the past, our credit union prohibits the cashing of third-party checks presented by our members.
b. To help us process your order with our new database software, we need you to go to this Web site and fill out the required customer information.
c. We regret to announce that our electronics center is able to honor iPhone discounts only for a limited initial offering during the next 30 days.
d. Under a new policy, reimbursement of travel expenses will be restricted to those related to work only.
e. We are pleased to announce that you have been approved to enroll in our management trainee program.
f. To allow us to continue our policy of selling name brands at discount prices, we can give store credit but we cannot give cash refunds on returned merchandise.

4.2 Conversational but Professional (Obj. 3)

Your Task. Revise the following to make the tone conversational yet professional.

a. Under separate cover the above-referenced items (printer toner and supplies) are being sent to your Oakdale office, as per your telephone conversation of April 1.
b. Kindly inform the undersigned whether or not your representative will be making a visitation in the near future.
c. It is recommended that you conceptualize and submit your departmental budget ASAP.
d. BTW, we've had some slippage in the schedule but don't have to scrap everything and start from ground zero.
e. To facilitate ratification of this agreement, your negotiators urge that the membership respond in the affirmative.
f. She didn't have the guts to badmouth him 2 hz face.

4.3 Positive and Courteous Expression (Obj. 4)

Your Task. Revise the following sentences to reflect positive and courteous expression.

a. Customers are ineligible for the 10 percent discount unless they show their membership cards.
b. Titan Insurance Company will not process any claim not accompanied by documented proof from a physician showing that the injuries were treated.
c. If you fail to follow each requirement, you will not receive your $50 rebate.
d. You have definitely not completed the job satisfactorily, and we will exercise our legal right to withhold payment until you do.
e. In the message you left at our Web site, you claim that you returned a defective headset.
f. We regret to announce that the special purchase netbook computers will be available only to the first 25 customers.

4.4 Bias-Free Language (Obj. 4)

Your Task. Revise the following sentences to reduce gender, racial, ethnic, age, and disability bias.

a. Any applicant for the position of fireman must submit a medical report signed by his physician.
b. Every employee is entitled to see his personnel file.
c. All waiters and waitresses are covered under our new benefits package.
d. A salesman would have to use all his skills to sell those condos.
e. Serving on the panel are a lady veterinarian, a female doctor, two businessmen, and an Indian CPA.
f. All conference participants and their wives are invited to the banquet.
g. How many man-hours are required to complete the project?

4.5 Plain Language and Familiar Words (Obj. 4)

Your Task. Revise the following sentences to use plain language and familiar words.

a. Please ascertain whether we must perpetuate our current contract despite perplexing profits.
b. He hypothesized that the vehicle was not operational because of a malfunctioning gasket.
c. Because we cannot monitor all cash payments, we must terminate the contract.
d. The contract stipulates that management must perpetuate the retirement plan.
e. I'll interface with Mark to access his people.
f. Unilateral nullification of the terms and conditions of the expiring agreement absent bona fide impasse is prohibited. (Legal talk!)

4.6 Precise, Vigorous Words (Obj. 4)

Your Task. From the choices in parentheses, select the most precise, vigorous words.

a. We plan to (*acknowledge, publicize, applaud*) the work of exemplary employees.
b. When replying to e-mail, (*bring in, include, put*) enough of the old message for (*someone, the person, the recipient*) to recognize the original note.
c. For a (*hard, long, complicated*) e-mail message, (*make, create, do*) the message in your word processing program.
d. If an e-mail (*thing, catch, glitch*) interferes while writing, you can easily (*get, have, retrieve*) your message.

For the following sentences provide more precise alternatives for the italicized words.

e. After (a) *going over* the proposal, I decided it was (b) *bad*.
f. In her e-mail message, she said that she would (a) *change* overtime hours in order to (b) *fix* the budget.
g. Our new manager (a) *said* that only (b) *the right kind of* applicants should apply.

4.7 Legal Language (Obj. 6)

Your Task. To avoid possible litigation, revise the italicized words in the following sentences taken from proposals.

a. We have *inspected* the environmental project and will send a complete report.
b. Our goal is to *assure* completion of the ecological program on schedule.
c. We will *determine* the amount of stress for each supporting column.

Activities

4.8 Document for Analysis: Improving the Tone of an E-Mail Message (Objs. 3–5)

Team

Your Task. Analyze the following demanding e-mail to be sent by the vice president to all employees. In teams or individually, discuss the tone and writing faults in this message. Your instructor may ask you to revise the message so that it reflects some of the writing techniques you learned in this chapter. How can you make this message more courteous, positive, and precise? Focus on conciseness, familiar words, and developing the "you" view. Consider revising this e-mail as a collaboration project using Word's **Comment** feature.

To: All Employees
From: B. A. Cartwright <bacartwright@integrity.com>
Subject: Your Excessive Use of E-Mail!
Cc:
Attached: E-Mail and Internet Policy

Once again I have the decidedly unpleasant task of reminding all employees that you may NOT utilize company computers or the Internet other than for work-related business and essential personal messages. Effective immediately a new policy will be implemented.

Our guys in IT tell me that our bandwidth is now seriously compromised by some of you boys and girls who are using company computers for gaming, blogging, shopping, chatting, and downloading streaming video. Yes, we have given you the right to use e-mail responsibly for essential personal messages. But that does not include checking your Facebook or MySpace accounts during work hours or downloading your favorite shows or sharing music.

We distributed an e-mail policy a little while ago. We have now found it necessary to amplify and extrapolate that policy to include use of the Internet. If our company does not control its e-mail and Internet use, you will continue to suffer slow downloads. You may also lose the right to use e-mail at all. In the past every employee has had the right to send a personal e-mail occasionally, but he must use that right carefully. We may have to prohibit the personal use of e-mail entirely. Don't make me do this!

You will be expected to study the attached E-Mail and Internet policy and return the signed form with your agreement to adhere to this policy. You must return this form by March 1. No exceptions!

4.9 Channel Selection: Burger King and the $1 Double Cheeseburger (Obj. 2)

To offer a budget sandwich during tough times, Burger King Holdings Inc. proposed a four-month promotion offering its double cheeseburger for $1 in the United States. But franchisees rejected the proposal because they thought it made no sense to sell the sandwich at a lower price than the cost of its ingredients. Burger King has 11,100 restaurants in more than 65 countries, and almost 90 percent of them are owned and operated by independent franchisees. Burger King management tried again by asking its U.S. franchisees to consider a six-week period for the $1 special, but operators voted against the modified plan as well. Results of the vote were delivered to franchisees in an audio recording.[19]

Your Task. Discuss the factors Burger King management may have considered before choosing a communication channel to deliver this important news. Was an audio recording (probably a recorded phone message) the best channel to deliver this news to thousands of franchisees in the United States?

4.10 Channel Selection: Various Business Scenarios (Obj. 2)

Your Task. Using Figure 4.2 on page 116, suggest the best communication channels for the following messages. Assume that all channels shown are available. Be prepared to explain your choices.

a. You need to know whether Crystal in Reprographics can produce a rush job for you in two days.
b. As part of a task force to investigate cell phone marketing, you need to establish a central location where each team member can see general information about the task as well as add comments for others to see. Task force members are located throughout the country.
c. You want to know what team members are available immediately for a quick teleconference meeting. They are all workaholics and glued to their computers.
d. As human resources manager during a company reorganization, you must tell six employees that they will lose their jobs.
e. A prospective client in Japan wants price quotes for a number of your products as soon as possible.
f. You must respond to a notice from the Internal Revenue Service insisting that you did not pay the correct amount for last quarter's employer's taxes.
g. As a member of the Information Technology Department, you must collect information about virus protection software for your office computers and make a recommendation to the hands-on company president.

4.11 Analyzing Audiences (Obj. 3)

Your Task. Using the questions in Figure 4.4 on page 118, write a brief analysis of the audience for each of the following communication tasks.

a. You are about to send an e-mail to your regional sales manager describing your visit to a new customer who is demanding special discounts.
b. You are preparing a cover letter for a job that you saw advertised in a local newspaper. You are confident that your qualifications match the job description.
c. As an administrator at the municipal water department, you must write a letter to water users explaining that the tap water may taste and smell bad; however, it poses no threats to health.
d. You are planning to write an e-mail to your boss to try to persuade her to allow you to attend a computer class that will require you to leave work early two days a week for ten weeks.
e. You are preparing an unsolicited sales letter to a targeted group of executives promoting part-time ownership in a corporate jet plane.

4.12 Copyright Confusion: Myths and Facts (Obj. 6)

Ethics

Your Task. You overheard the following statements as a group of college students discussed copyright issues.[20] Which of these statements do you think are true, and which are false?

a. If it doesn't have a copyright notice, it's not copyrighted.
b. If I don't charge for it, it's not a violation.
c. If it's posted to the Internet, it's in the public domain.
d. I can always argue that my posting was just fair use.
e. If you don't defend your copyright, you lose it.
f. If I make up my own stories, but base them on another work, my new work belongs to me.
g. They can't get me; defendants in court have powerful rights!
h. Copyright violation isn't a crime or anything, is it?
i. It doesn't hurt anybody. In fact, it's free advertising.
j. They e-mailed me a copy, so I can post it.

Video Resource

Video Library 1, Guffey's 3-x-3 Writing Process Develops Fluent Workplace Skills

This video combines narrative and role-playing to illustrate each phase of Guffey's 3-x-3 writing process. It shows three phases of the writing process including prewriting, writing, and revising. You will see how the writing process guides the development of a complete message. This video illustrates concepts in Chapters 4, 5, and 6. After viewing the film, be prepared to answer these questions:

- How can a writing process help a writer?
- Does the writing process always follow the same order?
- Why does revising take more time than any other part of the process?

Chat About It

In each chapter you will find five discussion questions related to the chapter material. Your instructor may assign these topics for you to discuss in class, in an online chat room, or on an online discussion board. Some of the discussion topics may require outside research. You may also be asked to read and respond to postings made by your classmates.

Topic 1: List and analyze the steps that you followed to write a document before you started this course. Based on what you are learning in this course, which steps were effective? Which were ineffective? How will you change your approach to writing?

Topic 2: After searching an alumni database, you decide to e-mail a professional who is working in the career you hope to enter. Your goal in writing this professional is to obtain firsthand information about this person's career and to receive career advice. However, you know nothing about this person. Why might this person help you? Why might this person refuse? Should you organize your message directly or indirectly?

Topic 3: Why should you avoid words such as *really, totally, very*, and *quite* in your business writing? Provide an example of a sentence with and without such words. How did the meaning of the sentence change?

Topic 4: Think back to the last time you were involved in a team project. What did the team do that resulted in an efficient working process and a successful product? What did the team do that resulted in an inefficient working process and an unsuccessful product?

Topic 5: Find a news article online that describes a company that used careless language in its communication with its customers, stockholders, or employees. Briefly explain what the company did and what it should have done instead.

Grammar and Mechanics C.L.U.E. Review 4

Adjectives and Adverbs

Review Guides 19–20 about adjectives and adverbs in Appendix A, Grammar and Mechanics Guide, beginning on page A-9. On a separate sheet, revise the following sentences to correct errors in adjectives and adverbs. For each error that you locate, write the guide number that reflects this usage. Some sentences may have two errors. If a sentence is correct, write *C*. When you finish, check your answers on page Key-1.

1. Business writers strive to use easy to understand language and familiar words.
2. Luis said he did good in his employment interview.
3. Having prepared for months, we won the contract easy.
4. Collaboration on team written documents is necessary for big projects.
5. Jenna felt badly when her team project was completed.
6. The 3-x-3 writing plan provides step by step instructions for writing messages.
7. Our recently-revised office handbook outlined all recommended document formats.
8. The project ran smooth after Maria organized the team.
9. Locally-installed online collaboration tools are easy-to-use and work well.
10. Well written safety messages include short, familiar words.

CHAPTER 5

Organizing and Writing Business Messages

Want to do well on tests and excel in your course? Go to **www.meguffey.com** for helpful interactive resources.

- **Review the Chapter 5 PowerPoint slides to prepare for the first quiz.**

OBJECTIVES

After studying this chapter, you should be able to

1. Apply Phase 2 of the 3-x-3 writing process, which begins with formal and informal methods for researching data and generating ideas.
2. Explain how to organize data into lists and alphanumeric or decimal outlines.
3. Compare direct and indirect patterns for organizing ideas.
4. Compose the first draft of a message, avoiding sentence fragments, run-on sentences, and comma splices as well as emphasizing important ideas, avoiding misplaced modifiers, and using active and passive voice effectively.
5. Compose effective paragraphs using three classic paragraph plans as well as applying techniques for achieving paragraph coherence.

Zooming In PART 1

Once the Height of Hip, Gap Struggles to Stop Sagging Sales

From humble beginnings in San Francisco, Gap Inc. grew to become the largest clothing chain in the United States. However, after spectacular growth, it fell from favor. Critics accused it of making every bad move a retailer could. Besides major misses in fashion, the company failed to differentiate among its three major brands—Banana Republic, Gap, and Old Navy—and it opened too many stores.

The company that had pioneered the casual cool look with fitted jeans, khakis, and simple T-shirts lost its fashion compass. "The Gap doesn't seem hip any longer," said one shopper. "They're too preppy and sterile."[1] Another young shopper said, "Gap seems to be stuck in the '90s. I always think of it as the clothes my parents wear."[2] Once the king of casual but classic clothing, Gap has been stung by retailing upstarts that woo young people with trendy fashions at affordable prices. Retailers such as Zara, Mango, Hot Topic, and Hollister are snagging customers with hip styles and competitive pricing.

At its zenith in 1994, Gap launched Old Navy as a fun fashion label with good prices and street-chic attitude. Emphasizing humor and mass appeal, Old Navy gave shoppers music and bright colors while promoting a quirky image. But like Gap, Old Navy lost its cult status and its aura of campy fashion. In attempting to right the sinking ship, Old Navy overcorrected and went overboard with inexpensive fashions.

Further compounding their woes, both Gap and Old Navy have saturated the market. Gap has 2,688 U.S. stores, and Old Navy has 1,066.[3] They are almost as ubiquitous as Starbucks. In the fashion business, bigness is not necessarily a plus. With stores in nearly every shopping center, Gap has overexposed the brand. Customers are staying away because its styles no longer seem unique or special.

Under new management, Gap Inc. is working to improve its merchandise mix, reduce inventories, halt capital spending, and enhance its online and global presence. Ultimately, though, Gap and Old Navy must find a way to lure their customers back.

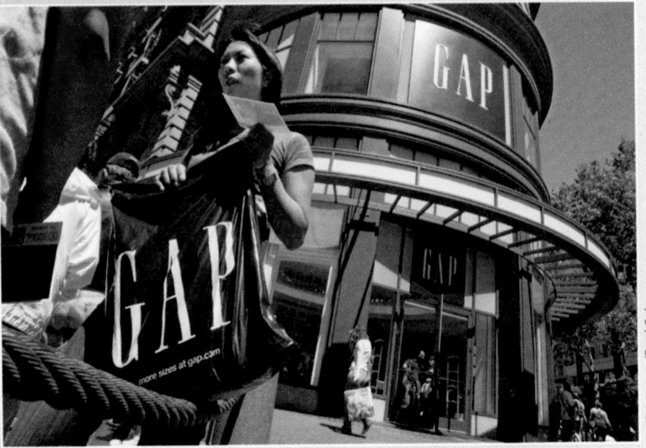

© AP Images/Paul Sakuma

Critical Thinking

- In what ways would research (gathering information) be important to Gap and Old Navy in getting their customers back?
- Why is it important for Gap managers, as well as other business communicators, to gather all necessary information before making management decisions?
- What techniques can business communicators at Gap Inc. and other companies use to generate ideas for new products as well as to improve business processes?

http://www.gap.com

Gathering Information Through Research

LEARNING OBJECTIVE 1

Apply Phase 2 of the 3-x-3 writing process, which begins with formal and informal methods for researching data and generating ideas.

Why is it necessary to gather information before beginning to write rather than gathering it as you write?

Business communicators at Gap and Old Navy face daily challenges that require data collection, idea generation, and concept organization. Before they can make decisions and convey those decisions in written messages or presentations, they must gather information and organize that information. These activities are part of the second phase of the 3-x-3 writing process. You will recall that the 3-x-3 writing process, as reviewed in Figure 5.1, involves three phases. This chapter focuses on the second phase of the process: researching, organizing, and writing.

No smart businessperson would begin writing a message before collecting all the needed information. We call this collection process *research*, a rather formal-sounding term. For simple documents, though, the process can be quite informal. Research is necessary before beginning to write because the information you collect helps shape the message. Discovering significant data after a message is half completed often means starting over and reorganizing. To avoid frustration and inaccurate messages, collect information that answers a primary question:

- What does the receiver need to know about this topic?

When the message involves action, search for answers to secondary questions:

- What is the receiver to do?
- How is the receiver to do it?

FIGURE 5.1 Guffey's 3-x-3 Writing Process

1 Prewriting	2 Writing	3 Revising
Analyze: Decide on the purpose of your message. What do you want the receiver to do or believe? What communication channel is best?	**Research:** Gather background data to provide facts. Search company files, previous correspondence, and the Internet. What do you need to know to write this message?	**Revise:** Edit your message to be sure it is clear, conversational, concise, and readable. Look for ways to highlight important information. Consider bullets, lists, and headings to help the reader understand related points.
Anticipate: Profile the audience. What does the receiver already know? Will the receiver's response be neutral, positive, or negative?	**Organize:** Group similar information together. Decide whether to organize your information directly or indirectly. Outline your plan and make notes.	**Proofread:** Read carefully to find and correct errors in spelling, grammar, punctuation, names, numbers, and format.
Adapt: What writing techniques and strategies can you use to adapt your message to its audience? How can you shape the message to achieve your purpose?	**Compose:** Prepare a first draft, usually writing quickly. Remember that you will be revising it to improve its readability and impact.	**Evaluate:** Will this message achieve your purpose? Have you thought enough about the audience to be sure this message is appropriate and appealing?

- When must the receiver do it?
- What will happen if the receiver doesn't do it?

Whenever your communication problem requires more information than you have in your head or at your fingertips, you must conduct research. This research may be formal or informal.

Formal Research Methods

How can you gather information formally?

Long reports and complex business problems generally require some use of formal research methods. Let's say you are part of the management team at Gap Inc. and you want to evaluate several locations for the placement of a new Old Navy store. Or, let's assume you must write a term paper for a college class. Both tasks require more data than you have in your head or at your fingertips. To conduct formal research, you could do the following:

- **Access electronically.** Much information is now available on the Internet, on CDs or DVDs, and in databases that can be accessed by computer. College and public libraries subscribe to retrieval services that permit you to access most periodic literature. You can

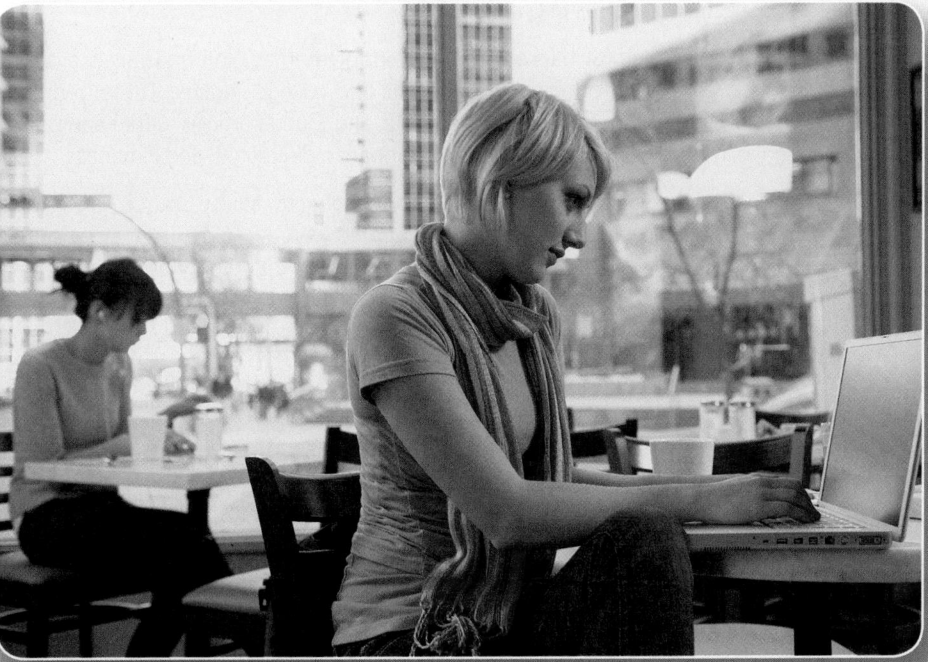

As consumers increasingly turn to the Internet to shop, recommend products, and rate businesses on their customer service, management teams are turning to a new kind of research to inform business decisions—online "buzz-tracking." Research firms such as Nielsen BuzzMetrics and Brandimensions traverse millions of fan sites, blogs, and chat rooms to analyze user feedback and spot consumer trends. *How can buzz-tracking research help communication professionals develop more effective written messages and presentations?*

FIGURE 5.2 Creating Cluster Diagram to Generate Ideas for an Old Navy/Gap Recruiting Brochure

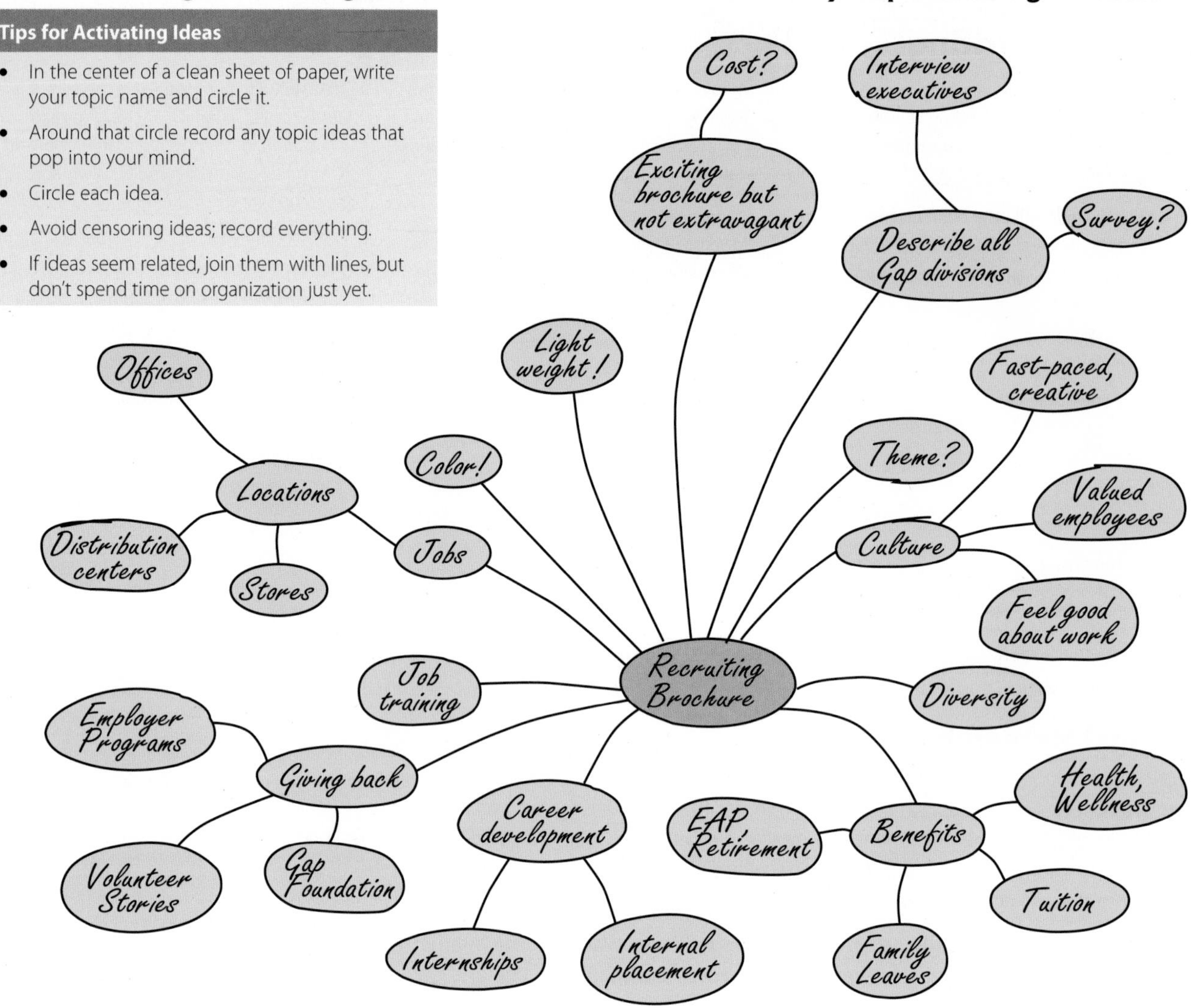

also find extraordinary amounts of information by searching the Web. You will learn more about using electronic sources in Chapter 11.

- **Search manually.** Helpful background and supplementary information is available through manual searching of resources in public and college libraries. These traditional sources include books and newspaper, magazine, and journal articles. Other sources are encyclopedias, reference books, handbooks, dictionaries, directories, and almanacs.
- **Go to the source.** For firsthand information, go directly to the source. If you were comparing the taste of Coca-Cola and Pepsi, for example, you could find out what consumers really think by conducting interviews or surveys, by putting together questionnaires, or by organizing focus groups. Formal research includes structured sampling and controls that enable investigators to make accurate judgments and valid predictions.
- **Investigate primary sources.** To develop firsthand, primary information for a project, go directly to the source. In searching for locations for Old Navy stores, you might travel to possible sites and check them out. If you need information about how many shoppers pass by a location or visit a shopping center, you might conduct a traffic count. To learn more about specific shoppers who might become Old Navy customers, you could use questionnaires, interviews, or focus groups. Formal research includes scientific sampling methods that enable investigators to make accurate judgments and valid predictions.
- **Conduct scientific experiments.** Another source of primary data is experimentation. Instead of merely asking for the target audience's opinion, scientific researchers present

FIGURE 5.3 Organizing Ideas From a Cluster Diagram Into Subclusters

Tips for Organizing Ideas

- Analyze the ideas generated in the original cluster diagram.
- Cross out ideas that are obviously irrelevant; simplify and clarify.
- Add new ideas that seem appropriate.
- Study the ideas for similarities.
- Group similar ideas into classifications (such as Content, Development, and Form).
- If the organization seems clear at this point, prepare an outline.
- For further visualization, make subcluster circles around each classification.

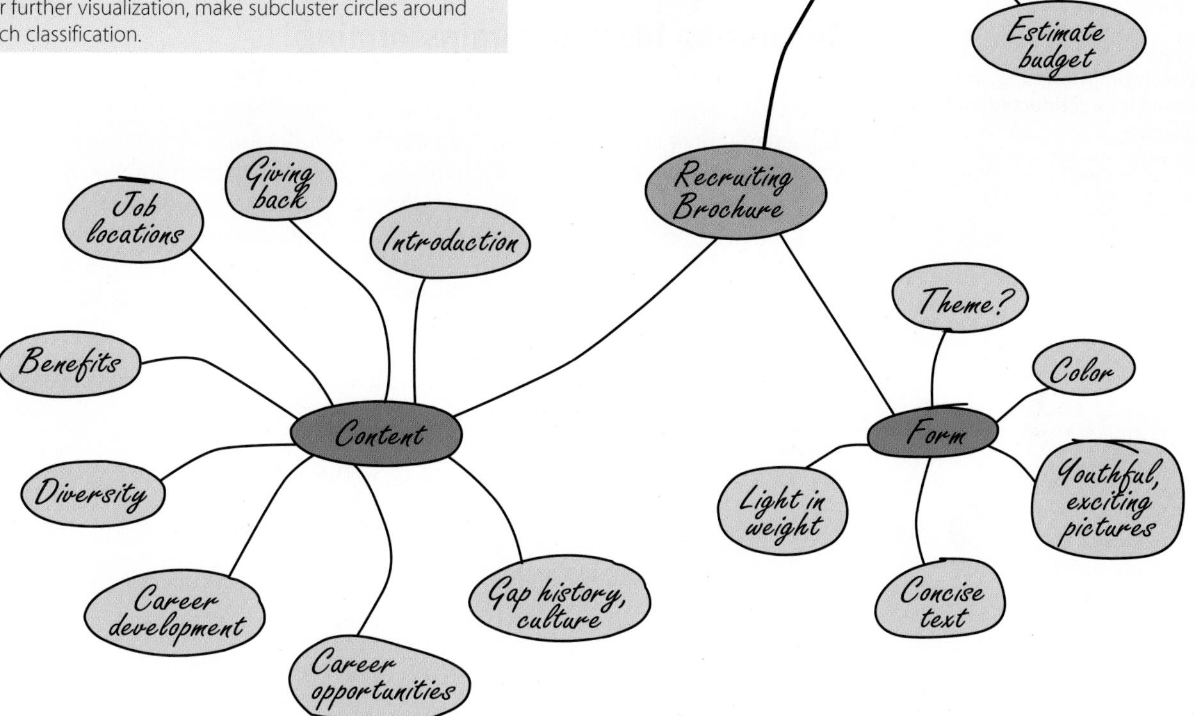

choices with controlled variables. Assume, for example, that the management team at Gap wants to know at what price and under what circumstances consumers would purchase jeans from the Gap instead of from Abercrombie & Fitch. Instead of jeans, let's say that management wants to study the time of year and type of weather conditions that motivate consumers to begin purchasing sweaters, jackets, and cold-weather gear. The results of such experimentation would provide valuable data for managerial decision making. Because formal research techniques are particularly necessary for reports, you will study resources and techniques more extensively in Unit 4.

Informal Research Methods

Most routine tasks—such as composing e-mails, memos, letters, informational reports, and oral presentations—require data that you can collect informally. For some projects, though, you rely more on your own ideas instead of—or in addition to—researching existing facts. Here are some techniques for collecting informal data and for generating ideas:

- **Look in the files.** If you are responding to an inquiry, you often can find the answer to the inquiry by investigating the company files or by consulting colleagues.

Spotlight on Communicators

Chris Heatherly and Len Mazzocco use systematic brainstorming to overhaul the Disney toy lineup every six months. A diverse group of designers, engineers, artists, animators, video game designers, marketers, and theme park employees gather 20 to 30 times a year for two- or three-day brainstorming sessions at hotels around the world. Three elements are crucial to their success: (a) icebreaker activities from 10 minutes to a half hour, (b) 45- to 60-minute brainstorming sessions in which teams list as many ideas as they can and then vote for their favorites, and (c) a product pitch including a storyboard record of the best toy ideas. When people have tried to ignore the icebreaker segment and cut to the chase, Chris says, "it just doesn't work. . . . You have to have some decompression time to be creative."

How can you gather information informally?

- **Talk with your boss.** Get information from the individual making the assignment. What does that person know about the topic? What slant should you take? What other sources would he or she suggest?
- **Interview the target audience.** Consider talking with individuals at whom the message is aimed. They can provide clarifying information that tells you what they want to know and how you should shape your remarks. Suggestions for conducting more formal interviews are presented in Chapter 11.
- **Conduct an informal survey.** Gather unscientific but helpful information through questionnaires, telephone surveys, or online surveys. In preparing a memo report predicting the success of a proposed company fitness center, for example, circulate a questionnaire asking for employee reactions.

What is brainstorming, and how should it be conducted for best results?

Generating Ideas by Brainstorming

One popular method for generating ideas is brainstorming. We should point out, however, that some critics argue that brainstorming groups "produce fewer and poorer quality ideas than the same number of individuals working alone." Even brainstorming proponents agree that, when done poorly, it can be a waste of time. But done properly, brainstorming is quite effective in unleashing ideas and creative energy.[4] One recent writer claims that groups can generate more and better ideas when "brainwriting"; that is, silently sharing written ideas in a structured group format.[5] Another group suggests using Twitter to exchange brainstorming ideas quickly.[6] Most business communicators, however, meet face to face to brainstorm, and they follow these suggestions to produce the best ideas:

- Define the problem and create an agenda that outlines the topics to be covered.
- Establish time limits, remembering that short sessions are best.
- Set a quota, such as a minimum of 100 ideas. The goal is quantity, not quality.
- Require every participant to contribute ideas, accept the ideas of others, or improve on ideas.
- Encourage wild, out-of-the-box thinking. Allow no one to criticize or evaluate ideas.
- Write ideas on flipcharts or on sheets of paper hung around the room.
- Organize and classify the ideas, retaining the best. Consider using cluster diagrams, discussed shortly.

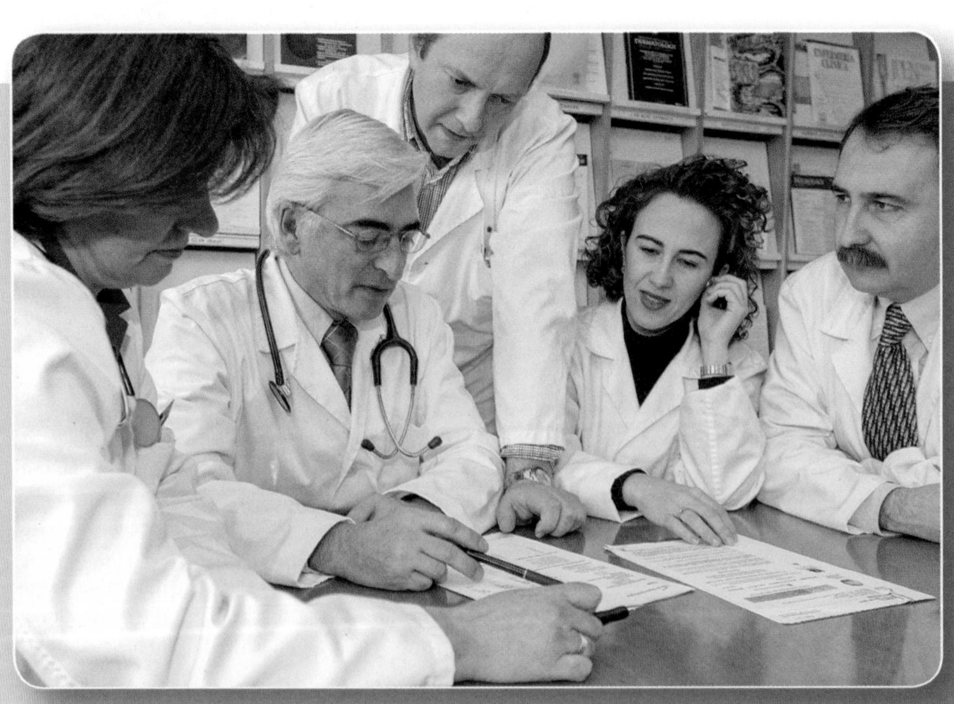

Thousands of hospital patients die every year after receiving the wrong medicine. To prevent this tragic loss and to improve overall hospital efficiency, one large managed care facility holds brainstorming sessions bringing together doctors, nurses, patients, and vendors. Their ground rules include focusing on quantity of ideas rather than quality, withholding criticism, welcoming unusual ideas, and combining and improving ideas. The facilitator begins with a clear problem statement. Participants write ideas on Post-It notes using Sharpie pens to prevent wordiness. *Why is it necessary for successful brainstorming to begin with a clear problem statement, and what is the benefit of conciseness?*

Collecting Information and Generating Ideas on the Job

Let's assume that you work in the corporate offices of Gap Inc. and that you have been given the task of developing a college recruiting brochure for all Gap stores. You think this is a great idea because Gap Inc. has thousands of stores, and many college students don't know about the exciting career opportunities and benefits it offers. You know right away that you want the brochure to be colorful, exciting, concise, youth oriented, lightweight (because it has to be carried to college campuses), and easily updated. Beyond that, you realize that you need ideas from others on how to develop this recruiting brochure.

To collect data for this project, you decide to use both formal and informal research methods. You study recruiting brochures from other companies. You talk with college students about information they would like to see in a brochure. You conduct more formal research among recently hired employees and among Gap division presidents and executives to learn what they think a recruiting brochure should include. Working with an outside consultant, you prepare a questionnaire to use in personal interviews with employees and executives. The interviews include some open-ended questions such as, *How did you start with the company?* The questionnaire also asks specific questions about career paths, degree requirements, personality traits desired, and so forth.

Next you ask five or six fellow employees and team members to help brainstorm ideas for the brochure. In a spirited session, your team comes up the cluster diagram shown in Figure 5.2. The ideas range from the cost of the brochure to career development programs and your company's appealing location in the San Francisco Bay area.

From the jumble of ideas in the initial cluster diagram, you see that you can organize most of the information into three main categories relating to the brochure—Development, Form, and Content. You eliminate, simplify, and consolidate some ideas and add other new ideas. Then you organize the ideas into subclusters, shown in Figure 5.3. This set of subclusters could form the basis for an outline, which we will talk about shortly. Or you could make another set of subclusters, further outlining the categories.

Organizing Ideas

LEARNING OBJECTIVE 2
Explain how to organize data into lists and alphanumeric or decimal outlines.

One of the most important tasks in preparing well-organized messages is grouping similar ideas together. These groups of ideas are then sequenced in a way that helps the reader understand relationships and accept the writer's views. Unorganized messages proceed free-form, jumping from one thought to another. They look like the jumbled ideas in our Figure 5.2 cluster diagram. Such messages fail to emphasize important points. Puzzled readers can't see how the pieces fit together, and they become frustrated and irritated. Many communication experts regard poor organization as the greatest failing of business writers. Two simple techniques can help you organize data: the scratch list and the outline.

Using Lists and Outlines

What are two techniques for organizing data?

In developing simple messages, some writers make a quick scratch list of the topics they wish to cover. Writers often jot this scratch list in the margin of the letter or memo to which they are responding (the majority of business messages are written in response to other documents). These writers then compose a message at their computers directly from the scratch list.

Most writers, though, need to organize their ideas—especially if the project is complex—into a hierarchy, such as an outline. The beauty of preparing an outline is that it gives you a chance to organize your thinking before you get bogged down in word choice and sentence structure. Figure 5.4 shows two outline formats: alphanumeric and decimal. The familiar alphanumeric format uses Roman numerals, letters, and numbers to show major and minor ideas. The decimal format, which takes a little getting used to, has the advantage of showing how every item at every level relates to the whole. Both outlining formats force you to focus on the topic, identify major ideas, and support those ideas with details, illustrations, or evidence.

Probably the hardest part of outlining is grouping ideas into components or categories—ideally three to five. These categories are very important because they will become the major headings in your report. If you have more than five components, look for ways to combine smaller segments into broader topics. The following example shows how a portion of the Gap recruiting brochure subclusters (Figure 5.3) can be organized into an alphanumeric outline.[7]

FIGURE 5.4 Two Outlining Formats

Format for Alphanumeric Outline	Format for Decimal Outline
Title: Major Idea, Purpose	Title: Major Idea, Purpose
I. First major component	1.0. First major component
A. First subpoint	1.1. First subpoint
1. Detail, illustration, evidence	1.1.1. Detail, illustration, evidence
2. Detail, illustration, evidence	1.1.2. Detail, illustration, evidence
B. Second subpoint	1.2. Second subpoint
1.	1.2.1.
2.	1.2.2.
II. Second major component	2.0. Second major component
A. First subpoint	2.1. First subpoint
1.	2.1.1.
2.	2.1.2.
B. Second subpoint	2.2. Second subpoint
1.	2.2.1.
2.	2.2.2.
III. Third major component	3.0. Third major component
A.	3.1.
1.	3.1.1.
2.	3.1.2.
B.	3.2.
1.	3.2.1.
2.	3.2.2.
(This method is simple and familiar.)	*(This method relates every item to the overall outline.)*

Tips for Making Outlines

- Define the main topic (purpose of message) in the title.
- Divide the main topic into major components or classifications (preferably three to five). If necessary, combine small components into one larger category.
- Break the components into subpoints.
- Don't put a single item under a major component; if you have only one subpoint, integrate it with the main item above it or reorganize.
- Strive to make each component exclusive (no overlapping).
- Use details, illustrations, and evidence to support subpoints.

How are alphanumeric and decimal outlines different, and how are they similar?

I. Introduction
  A. Brief history of Gap Inc.
    1. Founding
    2. Milestones
  B. Corporate culture
    1. Emphasize upbeat attitude
    2. Value diversity, employees
    3. Value social responsibility

II. Careers
  A. Opportunities
    1. Internships
    2. Management trainee programs
    3. MBA programs
  B. Development
    1. Internal promotion
    2. Job training

Notice that each major category is divided into at least two subcategories. These categories are then fleshed out with examples, details, statistics, case histories, and other data. In moving

FIGURE 5.5 **Typical Major Components in Business Outlines**

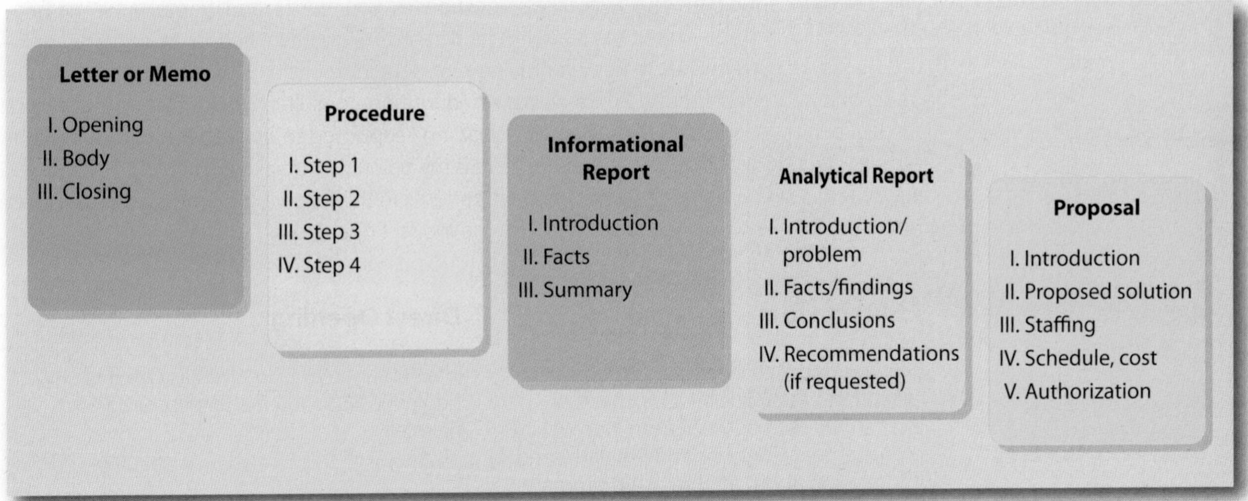

from major point to subpoint, you are progressing from large, abstract concepts to small, concrete ideas. Each subpoint could be further subdivided with more specific illustrations if you desired. You can determine the appropriate amount of detail by considering what your audience (primary and secondary) already knows about the topic and how much persuading you must do.

How you group ideas into components depends on your topic and your channel of communication. Business documents usually contain typical components arranged in traditional patterns, as shown in Figure 5.5.

Thus far, you've seen how to collect information, generate ideas, and prepare an outline. How you order the information in your outline, though, depends on the pattern or strategy you choose.

Organizing Ideas into Patterns

LEARNING OBJECTIVE 3
Compare direct and indirect patterns for organizing ideas.

Two organizational patterns provide plans of action for typical business messages: the direct pattern and the indirect pattern. The primary difference between the two patterns is where the main idea is placed. In the direct pattern, the main idea comes first, followed by details, explanation, or evidence. In the indirect pattern, the main idea follows the details, explanation, and evidence. The pattern you select is determined by how you expect the audience to react to the message, as shown in Figure 5.6.

FIGURE 5.6 **Audience Response Determines Pattern of Organization**

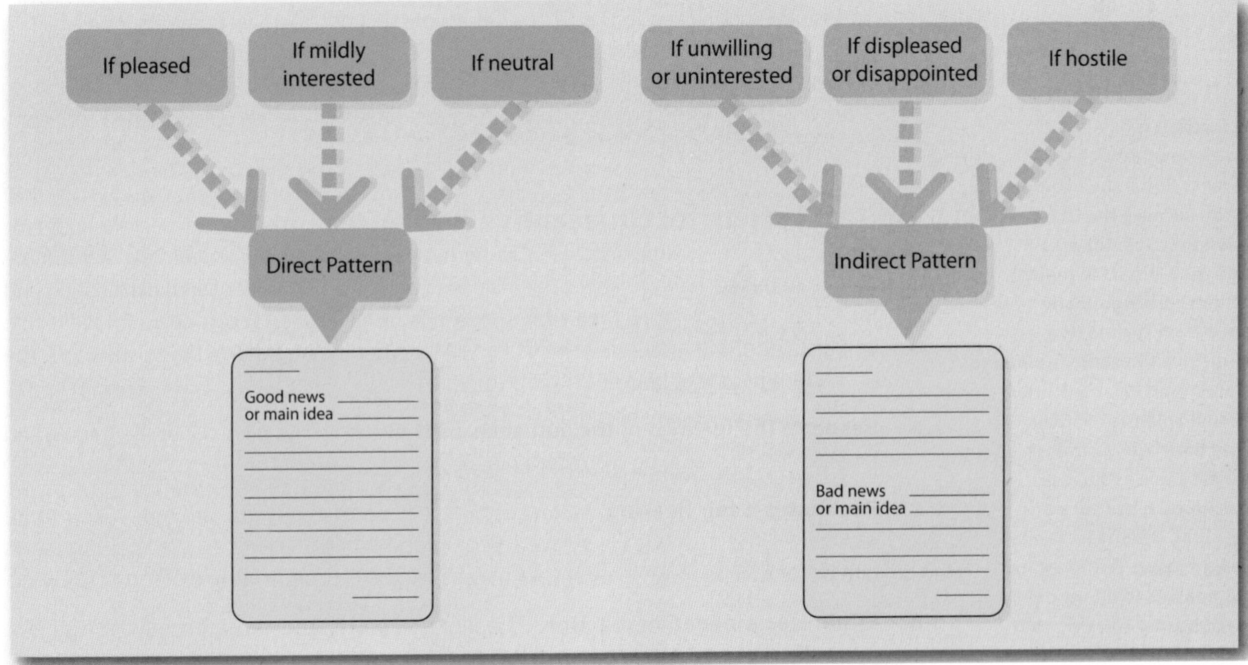

What pattern do business messages usually follow? Why?

Direct Pattern for Receptive Audiences. In preparing to write any message, you need to anticipate the audience's reaction to your ideas and frame your message accordingly. When you expect the reader to be pleased, mildly interested, or, at worst, neutral—use the direct pattern. That is, put your main point—the purpose of your message—in the first or second sentence. Dianna Booher, renowned writing consultant, pointed out that typical readers begin any message by saying, "So what am I supposed to do with this information?" In business writing you have to say, "Reader, here is my point!"[8] As quickly as possible, tell why you are writing. Compare the direct and indirect patterns in the following memo openings. Notice how long it takes to get to the main idea in the indirect opening.

Indirect Opening	Direct Opening
Our company has been concerned with attracting better-qualified prospective job candidates. For this reason, the Management Council has been gathering information about an internship program for college students. After considerable investigation, we have voted to begin a pilot program starting next fall.	The Management Council has voted to begin a college internship pilot program next fall.

What is frontloading, and how does it benefit receivers?

Explanations and details follow the direct opening. What's important is getting to the main idea quickly. This direct method, also called *frontloading*, has at least three advantages:

- **Saves the reader's time.** Many of today's businesspeople can devote only a few moments to each message. Messages that take too long to get to the point may lose their readers along the way.
- **Sets a proper frame of mind.** Learning the purpose up front helps the reader put the subsequent details and explanations in perspective. Without a clear opening, the reader may be thinking, "Why am I being told this?"
- **Reduces frustration.** Readers forced to struggle through excessive verbiage before reaching the main idea become frustrated. They resent the writer. Poorly organized messages create a negative impression of the writer.

This frontloading technique works best with audiences that are likely to be receptive to or at least not disagree with what you have to say. Typical business messages that follow the direct pattern include routine requests and responses, orders and acknowledgments, nonsensitive memos, e-mails, informational reports, and informational oral presentations. All these tasks have one element in common: none has a sensitive subject that will upset the reader. It should be noted, however, that some business communicators prefer to use the direct pattern for nearly all messages.

Ethics Check

How Sweet It Is

The makers of artificial sweetener Equal sued competitor Splenda because the latter claimed that Splenda was "made from sugar." In reality, Splenda's core ingredient is made from sucralose, a nonnutritive synthetic compound manufactured in laboratories. Although Splenda contains a sugar molecule, sucralose is not the same as sucrose, the technical name for pure table sugar, despite its similar-sounding name. Is it unethical for companies to intentionally advertise using wording that would confuse consumers?

Indirect Pattern for Unreceptive Audiences. When you expect the audience to be uninterested, unwilling, displeased, or perhaps even hostile, the indirect pattern is more appropriate. In this pattern you reveal the main idea only after you have offered explanation and evidence. This approach works well with three kinds of messages: (a) bad news, (b) ideas that require persuasion, and (c) sensitive news, especially when being transmitted to superiors. The indirect pattern has these benefits:

- **Respects the feelings of the audience.** Bad news is always painful, but the trauma can be lessened by preparing the receiver for it.
- **Facilitates a fair hearing.** Messages that may upset the reader are more likely to be read when the main idea is delayed. Beginning immediately with a piece of bad news or a persuasive request, for example, may cause the receiver to stop reading or listening.
- **Minimizes a negative reaction.** A reader's overall reaction to a negative message is generally improved if the news is delivered gently.

Zooming In

PART 2

Gap Inc.

Rebuilding its customer base and correcting its fashion missteps are major initiatives at Gap and its offspring, Old Navy. At the same time, the stores must be ever watchful that their garments are not made in sweatshops. Stiff competition and consumer demand for low prices have forced many U.S. apparel manufacturers to shift production offshore. Some of that production ends up in sweatshops, such as those found in Cambodia, Bangladesh, and Honduras. The worst sweatshops use child labor and demand 80-hour workweeks without overtime pay. Bosses routinely shout at workers and may send them home for talking on the job. Workers earn as little as 29 cents an hour.

Like other major apparel manufacturers, Gap Inc. strives to control working conditions with factory-monitoring and labor-standards programs. Around the world Gap Inc. has more than 90 employees whose sole focus is working to improve conditions in the factories that make its clothing. In one year these employees conducted 4,438 inspections at 2,118 garment factories around the world.[9] When a problem is found, Gap takes action. It works with contractors and factories to improve practices and conditions. If conditions don't improve, the retailer stops using errant contractors.[10] Enforcing its standards worldwide requires an ongoing effort.

When complaints from human rights activists and other watchdog groups arrive, Gap Inc. must investigate and respond to each inquiry.

Critical Thinking

- When a business communicator responds to an inquiry, such as a letter about human rights violations among contractors, is "research" necessary?
- What are the differences between formal and informal research?
- What are the advantages and disadvantages of brainstorming with groups?

Typical business messages that could be developed indirectly include letters, e-mails, and memos that refuse requests, deny claims, and disapprove credit. Persuasive requests, sales letters, sensitive messages, and some reports and oral presentations may also benefit from the indirect strategy. You will learn more about using the indirect pattern in Chapters 9 and 10.

In summary, business messages may be organized directly, with the main idea first, or indirectly, with the main idea delayed. Although these two patterns cover many communication problems, they should be considered neither universal nor inviolate. Every business transaction is distinct. Some messages are mixed: part good news, part bad; part goodwill, part persuasion. In upcoming chapters you will practice applying the direct and indirect patterns in typical situations. Then, you will have the skills and confidence to evaluate communication problems and vary these patterns depending on the goals you wish to achieve.

Composing the First Draft

LEARNING OBJECTIVE 4

Compose the first draft of a message, avoiding sentence fragments, run-on sentences, and comma splices as well as emphasizing important ideas, avoiding misplaced modifiers, and using active and passive voice effectively.

Once you have researched your topic, organized the data, and selected a pattern of organization, you are ready to begin composing. Most writers expect to use their computers for composition, but many are unaware of all the ways a computer can help create better written messages, oral presentations, and Web pages. See the accompanying Plugged In box to learn how you can take full advantage of your computer.

Even with a computer, some writers have trouble getting started, especially if they haven't completed the preparatory work. Organizing your ideas and working from an outline are very helpful in overcoming writer's block. Composition is also easier if you have a quiet environment in which to concentrate. Businesspeople with messages to compose set aside a given time and allow no calls, visitors, or other interruptions. This is a good technique for students as well.

What is freewriting, and how is it helpful?

As you begin composing, think about what style fits you best. Some experts suggest that you write quickly (*freewriting*). Get your thoughts down now and refine them in later versions. As you take up each idea, imagine that you are talking to the reader. Don't let yourself get bogged down. If you can't think of the right word, insert a substitute or type *find perfect word later.* Freewriting works well for some writers, but others prefer to move more slowly and think through their ideas more deliberately. Whether you are a speedy or a deliberate writer, keep in mind that you are writing the first draft. You will have time later to revise and polish your sentences.

PLUGGED IN

Seven Ways Computers Can Help You Create Better Written Messages, Oral Presentations, and Web Pages

Although computers can't actually do the writing for you, they provide powerful tools that make the composition process easier and the results more professional. Here are seven ways your computer can help you improve your written documents, oral presentations, and even Web pages.

1. **Fighting writer's block.** Because word processors enable ideas to flow almost effortlessly from your brain to a screen, you can expect fewer delays resulting from writer's block. You can compose rapidly, and you can experiment with structure and phrasing, later retaining and polishing your most promising thoughts.
2. **Collecting information electronically.** As a knowledge worker in an information economy, you must find information quickly. Much of the world's information is now accessible in databases or on the Web. You will learn more about these exciting electronic resources in Unit 4.
3. **Outlining and organizing ideas.** Most word processors include some form of "outliner," a feature that enables you to divide a topic into a hierarchical order with main points and subpoints. Your computer keeps track of the levels of ideas automatically so that you can easily add, cut, or rearrange points in the outline.
4. **Improving correctness and precision.** Nearly all word processing programs today provide features that catch and correct spelling and typographical errors. Grammar checkers detect many errors in capitalization, word use (such as *it's, its*), double negatives, verb use, subject–verb agreement, sentence structure, number agreement, number style, and other writing faults. But the errors are merely highlighted—not corrected. You have to do that.
5. **Adding graphics for emphasis.** Your letters, memos, and reports may be improved by the addition of graphs and artwork to clarify and illustrate data. You can import charts, diagrams, and illustrations created in database, spreadsheet, graphics, or draw-and-paint programs. Clip art is available to symbolize or illustrate ideas.
6. **Designing and producing professional-looking documents, presentations, and Web pages.** Most software now includes a large selection of scalable fonts (for a variety of character sizes and styles), italics, boldface, symbols, and styling techniques to help you format consistently and produce professional-looking results. Presentation software enables you to incorporate illustrative slide effects, color, sound, pictures, and video clips into your talks for management or customers. Web document builders also help you design and construct Web pages.
7. **Using collaborative software for team writing.** Special programs with commenting and revision features, described in Chapter 4, allow you to make changes and to identify each team member's editing.

Career Application

Individually or in teams, identify specific software programs that perform the tasks described here. Prepare a table naming each program, its major functions, and its advantages and disadvantages for business writers in your field.

Creating Effective Sentences

In creating your first draft, you will be working at the sentence level of composition. Although you have used sentences all your life, you may be unaware of how they can be shaped and arranged to express your ideas most effectively.

Recognizing Basic Sentence Elements

To avoid writing sentence fragments and making punctuation errors, let's review some basic sentence elements. Complete sentences have subjects and verbs and make sense.

What makes a sentence complete?

SUBJECT VERB

The manager of Information Technology sent an e-mail to all employees.

Clauses and phrases, the key building blocks of sentences, are related groups of words. Clauses have subjects and verbs; phrases do not.

PHRASE PHRASE

The manager of Information Technology sent an e-mail to all employees.

PHRASE PHRASE

By reading carefully, we learned about the latest computer viruses.

CLAUSE CLAUSE

Because he is experienced, Adam can repair most computer problems.

CLAUSE CLAUSE

When we have technology problems, we call a technician in our support group.

How are clauses different from phrases?

Clauses may be divided into two groups: independent and dependent. Independent clauses are grammatically complete. Dependent clauses depend for their meaning on independent clauses. In the two preceding examples the clauses beginning with *Because* and *When* are dependent. Dependent clauses are often introduced by words such as *if, when, because,* and *as.*

How are independent clauses different from dependent clauses?

INDEPENDENT CLAUSE

Adam solves our technology problems.

DEPENDENT CLAUSE INDEPENDENT CLAUSE

When employees need help, Adam solves our technology problems.

By learning to distinguish phrases, independent clauses, and dependent clauses, you will be able to punctuate sentences correctly and avoid three basic sentence faults: the fragment, the run-on sentence, and the comma splice.

Avoiding Three Common Sentence Faults

As you craft your sentences, beware of three common traps: fragments, run-on (fused) sentences, and comma-splice sentences. If any of these faults appears in a business message, the writer immediately loses credibility.

What are sentence fragments?

Fragments. One of the most serious errors a writer can make is punctuating a fragment as if it were a complete sentence. A fragment is usually a broken-off part of a complex sentence.

Fragment	Revision
Because most transactions require a permanent record. Good writing skills are critical.	Because most transactions require a permanent record, good writing skills are critical.
The recruiter requested a writing sample. Even though the candidate seemed to communicate well.	The recruiter requested a writing sample even though the candidate seemed to communicate well.

Fragments often can be identified by the words that introduce them—words such as *although, as, because, even, except, for example, if, instead of, since, such as, that, which,* and *when*. These words introduce dependent clauses. Make sure such clauses always connect to independent clauses.

What is a run-on (fused) sentence?

Run-On (Fused) Sentences. A sentence with two independent clauses must be joined by a coordinating conjunction (*and, or, nor, but*) or by a semicolon (;) or separated into two sentences. Without a conjunction or a semicolon, a run-on sentence results.

Run-On Sentence	Revision
Most job seekers present a printed résumé some are also using Web sites as electronic portfolios	Most job seekers present a printed résumé. Some are also using Web sites as electronic portfolios.
One candidate sent an e-mail résumé another sent a traditional résumé.	One candidate sent an e-mail résumé; another sent a traditional résumé.

What is a comma splice?

Comma-Splice Sentences. A comma splice results when a writer joins (splices together) two independent clauses with a comma. Independent clauses may be joined with a coordinating conjunction (*and, or, nor, but*) or a conjunctive adverb (*however, consequently, therefore,* and others). Notice that clauses joined by coordinating conjunctions require only a comma. Clauses joined by a coordinating adverb require a semicolon. On the following page are three possible revisions that rectify a comma splice.

Comma Splice	Possible Revisions
Some employees responded by e-mail, others picked up the telephone.	Some employees responded by e-mail, and others picked up the telephone.
	Some employees responded by e-mail; however, others picked up the telephone.
	Some employees responded by e-mail; others picked up the telephone.

Sentences should average how many words?

Preferring Short Sentences

Because your goal is to communicate clearly, you should strive for sentences that average 20 words. Some sentences will be shorter; some will be longer. The American Press Institute reports that reader comprehension drops off markedly as sentences become longer.[11] Therefore, in crafting your sentences, think about the relationship between sentence length and comprehension.

Sentence Length	Comprehension Rate
8 words	100%
15 words	90%
19 words	80%
28 words	50%

Instead of stringing together clauses with *and, but,* and *however*, break some of those complex sentences into separate segments. Business readers want to grasp ideas immediately. They can do that best when thoughts are separated into short sentences. On the other hand, too many monotonous short sentences will sound "grammar schoolish" and may bore or even annoy the reader. Strive for a balance between longer sentences and shorter ones. Your computer probably can point out long sentences and give you an average sentence length.

What techniques can be used to emphasize important ideas?

Emphasizing Important Ideas

You can stress prominent ideas mechanically by underscoring, italicizing, or boldfacing. You can also emphasize important ideas with five stylistic devices.

- **Use vivid words.** Vivid words are emphatic because the reader can picture ideas clearly.

General	Vivid
One business uses personal selling techniques.	Avon uses face-to-face selling techniques.

- **Label the main idea.** If an idea is significant, tell the reader as shown here.

Unlabeled	Labeled
Explore the possibility of leasing a site, but also hire a consultant.	Explore the possibility of leasing a site; but, *most important*, hire a consultant

- **Place the important idea first or last in the sentence.** Ideas have less competition from surrounding words when they appear first or last in a sentence. Observe how the date of the meeting can be emphasized.

Unemphatic	Emphatic
All production and administrative personnel will meet on May 23, at which time we will announce a new plan of salary incentives.	On May 23 all personnel will meet to learn about salary incentives.

- **Place the important idea in a simple sentence or in an independent clause.** Don't dilute the effect of the idea by making it share the spotlight with other words and clauses.

Unemphatic	Emphatic
Although you are the first trainee that we have hired for this program, we have interviewed many candidates and expect to expand the program in the future. (Main idea lost in introductory dependent clause.)	You are the first trainee that we have hired for this program. (Simple sentence contains main idea.)

- **Make sure the important idea is the sentence subject.** You will learn more about active and passive voice shortly, but at this point just focus on making the important idea the subject.

Unemphatic	Emphatic
The environmental report was written by Courtney. (De-emphasizes *Courtney*; emphasizes the report.)	Courtney wrote the environmental report. (Emphasizes *Courtney*.)

Managing Active and Passive Voice

How are active- and passive-voice sentences different?

In sentences with active-voice verbs, the subject is the doer of the action. In passive-voice sentences, the subject is acted upon.

Passive-Voice Verb	Active-Voice Verb
The tax return *was completed* before the April 15 deadline. (The subject, *tax return*, is acted upon.)	Marcelo *completed* his tax return before the April 15 deadline. (The subject, *Marcelo*, is the doer of the action.)

In the first sentence, the passive-voice verb emphasizes the tax return. In the second sentence, the active-voice verb emphasizes Marcelo. Active-voice sentences are more direct because they reveal the performer immediately. They are easier to understand and shorter. Most

FIGURE 5.7 Using Active and Passive Voice Effectively

Use active voice for directness, vigor, and clarity.

Direct and Clear in Active Voice	Indirect and Less Clear in Passive Voice
The manager completed performance reviews for all employees.	Performance reviews were completed for all employees by the manager.
Evelyn initiated a customer service blog last year.	A customer service blog was initiated last year.
IBM will accept applications after January 1.	Applications will be accepted after January 1 by IBM.
Coca-Cola created a Sprite page in Facebook to advertise its beverage.	A Sprite page was created in Facebook by Coca-Cola to advertise its beverage.

Use passive voice to be tactful or to emphasize the action rather than the doer.

Less Tactful or Effective in Active Voice	More Tactful or Effective in Passive Voice
We cannot grant you credit.	Credit cannot be granted.
The CEO made a huge error in projecting profits.	A huge error was made in projecting profits.
I launched a successful fitness program for our company last year.	A successful fitness program was launched for our company last year.
We are studying the effects of the Sarbanes-Oxley Act on our accounting procedures.	The effects of the Sarbanes-Oxley Act on our accounting procedures are being studied.

Spotlight on Communicators

"Wordiness and murkiness come from misuse of the passive voice," says writing coach Bob Knight. The passive voice also shields people from responsibility. For example, government officials often say, *Mistakes were made.* Passive voice abounds in corporate writing, he suspects, because writers are afraid to say things clearly or they don't want to stand out. He suggests, however, using passive voice for effect, especially when the subject is overwhelmingly important, as in, *A Rembrandt was stolen by two men in janitors' uniforms.* Passive voice is also helpful when you don't know who or what the subject would be in active voice, as in, *The cargo was damaged during an intercontinental flight.*

Courtesy of Bob Knight

business writing should be in the active voice. Nevertheless, passive voice is useful in certain instances such as the following:

- **To emphasize an action or the recipient of the action.** *An investigation was launched.*
- **To de-emphasize negative news.** *Cash refunds cannot be made.*
- **To conceal the doer of an action.** *An error was made in our sales figures.*

How can you tell whether a verb is active or passive? Identify the subject of the sentence and decide whether the subject is doing the acting or is being acted upon. For example, in the sentence *An appointment was made for January 1*, the subject is *appointment*. The subject is being acted upon; therefore, the verb (*was made*) is passive. Another clue in identifying passive-voice verbs is that they generally include a *to be* helping verb, such as *is, are, was, were, be, being,* or *been*. Figure 5.7 summarizes effective uses for active and passive voice.

What happens when modifiers are not close to the words they describe or limit?

Avoiding Dangling and Misplaced Modifiers

For clarity, modifiers must be close to the words they describe or limit. A dangling modifier describes or limits a word or words that are missing from the sentence. A misplaced modifier occurs when the word or phrase it describes is not close enough to be clear. To remedy a dangling modifier, supply the missing modifier. To remedy a misplaced modifier, move the modifier closer to the word(s) it describes or limits. Introductory verbal phrases are particularly dangerous; be sure to follow them immediately with the words they logically describe or modify.

Dangling Modifier	Improved
After working nine hours, the report was finally finished. *(Did the report work nine hours? The introductory verbal phrase must be followed by a logical subject.)*	After working nine hours, we finally finished the report.
Driving through Malibu Canyon, the ocean suddenly came into view. (*Is the ocean driving through Malibu Canyon?*)	As we drove through Malibu Canyon, the ocean suddenly came into view.
Speaking before the large audience, Luke's knees began to knock. (*Are Luke's knees making a speech?*)	Speaking before the large audience, Luke felt his knees begin to knock.

Try this trick for detecting and remedying these dangling modifiers. Ask the question *Who?* or *What?* after any introductory phrase. The words immediately following should tell the reader *who* or *what* is performing the action. Try the *who?* test on the previous danglers and on the following misplaced modifiers.

Misplaced Modifier	Improved
Seeing her error too late, the envelope was immediately resealed by Luna. (*Did the envelope see the error?*)	Seeing her error too late, Luna immediately resealed the envelope.
A wart appeared on my left hand that I want removed. (*Is the left hand to be removed?*)	A wart that I want removed appeared on my left hand.
The busy recruiter interviewed only candidates who had excellent computer skills in the morning. (*Were the candidates skilled only in the morning?*)	In the morning the busy recruiter interviewed only candidates who had excellent computer skills.

Drafting Powerful Paragraphs

LEARNING OBJECTIVE 5

Compose effective paragraphs using three classic paragraph plans as well as applying techniques for achieving paragraph coherence.

A paragraph is a group of sentences about one idea. To avoid muddled paragraphs, writers should be able to recognize basic paragraph elements, conventional sentence patterns, and ways to organize sentences using one of three classic paragraph plans. They must also be able to polish their paragraphs by building coherence and using transitional expressions.

Well-constructed paragraphs discuss only one topic. They reveal the primary idea in a topic sentence that usually, but not always, appears first. Paragraphs may be composed of three kinds of sentences:

How many topics should be covered in one paragraph?

Topic Sentence	Expresses the primary idea of the paragraph.
Supporting Sentences	Illustrates, explains, or strengthens the primary idea.
Limiting sentence	Opposes the primary idea by suggesting a negative or contrasting thought; may precede or follow the topic sentence.

These sentences may be arranged in three classic paragraph plans: direct, pivoting, and indirect.

Using the Direct Paragraph Plan to Define, Classify, Illustrate, or Describe

When should the direct paragraph plan be used?

Paragraphs arranged in the direct plan begin with the topic sentence, followed by supporting sentences. Most business messages use this paragraph plan because it clarifies the subject immediately. This plan is useful whenever you must define (a new product or procedure), classify (parts of a whole), illustrate (an idea), or describe (a process). Start with the topic sentence; then strengthen and amplify that idea with supporting ideas, as shown here:

Topic Sentence	A social audit is a report on the social performance of a company.
Supporting Sentences	Such an audit may be conducted by the company itself or by outsiders who evaluate the company's efforts to produce safe products, engage in socially responsible activities, and protect the environment. Many companies publish the results of their social audits in their annual reports. Ben & Jerry's Homemade, for example, devotes a major portion of its annual report to its social audit. The report discusses Ben & Jerry's efforts to support environmental restoration. Moreover, it describes workplace safety, employment equality, and peace programs.

You can alter the direct plan by adding a limiting sentence if necessary. Be sure, though, that you follow with sentences that return to the main idea and support it, as shown here:

Topic Sentence	Flexible work scheduling could immediately increase productivity and enhance employee satisfaction in our entire organization.
Limiting Sentence	Such scheduling, however, is impossible for all employees.
Supporting Sentences	Managers would be required to maintain their regular hours. For many other employees, though, flexible scheduling permits extra time to manage family responsibilities. Feeling less stress, employees are able to focus their attention better at work; hence they become more relaxed and more productive.

Using the Pivoting Paragraph Plan to Compare and Contrast

When is the pivoting paragraph plan appropriate?

Paragraphs using the pivoting plan start with a limiting sentence that offers a contrasting or negative idea before delivering the topic sentence. Notice in the following example how two limiting sentences about drawbacks to foreign service careers open the paragraph; only then do the topic and supporting sentences describing rewards in foreign service appear. The pivoting plan is especially useful for comparing and contrasting ideas. In using the pivoting plan, be sure you emphasize the turn in direction with an obvious *but* or *however*.

Limiting Sentences	Foreign service careers are certainly not for everyone. Many representatives are stationed in remote countries where harsh climates, health hazards, security risks, and other discomforts exist.
Topic Sentence	However, careers in the foreign service offer special rewards for the special people who qualify.
Supporting Sentences	Foreign service employees enjoy the pride and satisfaction of representing the United States abroad. They enjoy frequent travel, enriching cultural and social experiences in living abroad, and action-oriented work.

Using the Indirect Paragraph Plan to Explain and Persuade

When is the indirect paragraph plan appropriate?

Paragraphs using the indirect plan start with the supporting sentences and conclude with the topic sentence. This useful plan enables you to build a rationale, a foundation of reasons, before hitting the audience with a big idea—possibly one that is bad news. It enables you to explain your reasons and then in the final sentence draw a conclusion from them. In the following example, the vice president of a large accounting firm begins by describing the trend toward casual dress and concludes with a recommendation that his firm change its dress code. The indirect plan works well for describing causes followed by an effect.

Supporting Sentences	According to a recent poll, more than half of all white-collar workers are now dressing casually at work. Many high-tech engineers and professional specialists have given up suits and ties, favoring khakis and sweaters instead. In our own business, our consultants say they stand out like "sore thumbs" because they are attired in traditional buttoned-down styles, while the businesspeople they visit are usually wearing comfortable, casual clothing.
Topic Sentence	Therefore, I recommend that we establish an optional business casual policy allowing consultants to dress casually, if they wish, as they perform their duties both in and out of the office.

You will learn more techniques for implementing direct and indirect writing strategies when you prepare letters, memos, e-mails, reports, and oral presentations in subsequent chapters.

Building Paragraph Coherence

What is coherence, and what four techniques help build it in paragraphs?

Paragraphs are coherent when ideas cohere—that is, when the ideas stick together and when one idea logically leads to the next. Well-written paragraphs take the reader through a number of steps. When the author skips from Step 1 to Step 3 and forgets Step 2, the reader is lost. You can use several techniques to keep the reader in step with your ideas.

- **Sustaining the key idea.** Repeating a key expression or using a similar one throughout a paragraph helps sustain a key idea. In the following example, notice that the repetition of *guest* and *VIP* connects ideas.

  Our philosophy holds that every customer is really a ***guest****. All new employees to our theme parks are trained to treat* ***guests*** *as* ***VIPs****. We take great pride in respecting our guests. As* ***VIPs,*** *they are never told what they can or cannot do.*

- **Dovetailing sentences.** Sentences are "dovetailed" when an idea at the end of one connects with an idea at the beginning of the next. Dovetailing sentences is especially helpful with dense, difficult topics. It is also helpful with ordinary paragraphs, such as the following.

  New hosts and hostesses learn about the theme park and its ***facilities****. These* ***facilities*** *include telephones, food services, bathrooms, and attractions, as well as the location of* ***offices****. Knowledge of* ***offices*** *and the internal workings of the company is required of all staffers.*

- **Using pronouns.** Familiar pronouns, such as *we, they, he, she,* and *it,* help build continuity, as do demonstrative pronouns, such as *this, that, these,* and *those*. These words confirm that something under discussion is still being discussed. However, be careful with such

Ethics Check

Blogging for Pay

One single mother earned nearly $500 a month by putting her writing skills to use on "opps" (opportunities) at PayPerPost .com. This site pays consumers to write favorable comments in blogs about specific products. Is it ethical for bloggers to hide their motivation and affiliation when rating products?

pronouns. They often need a noun with them to make their meaning absolutely clear. In the following example, notice how confusing *this* would be if the word *training* were omitted.

All new park employees receive a two-week orientation. They learn that every staffer has a vital role in preparing for the show. This training includes how to maintain enthusiasm.

- **Including transitional expressions.** Transitional expressions are another excellent device for showing connections and achieving paragraph coherence. These words, some of which are shown in Figure 5.8 on page 156 act as verbal road signs to readers and listeners. Transitional expressions enable the receiver to anticipate what's coming, reduce uncertainty, and speed comprehension. They signal that a train of thought is moving forward, being developed, possibly detouring, or ending. As Figure 5.8 shows, transitions can add or strengthen a thought, show time or order, clarify ideas, show cause and effect, contradict thoughts, and contrast ideas. Look back at the examples of direct, pivoting, and indirect paragraphs to see how transitional expressions and other techniques build paragraph coherence. Remember that coherence in communication rarely happens spontaneously; it requires effort and skill.

Want to do well on tests and excel in your course? Go to **www.meguffey.com** for helpful interactive resources.
▸ **Review the Chapter 5 PowerPoint slides to prepare for the first quiz.**

Composing Short Paragraphs for Readability

Although no rule regulates the length of paragraphs, business writers recognize that short paragraphs are more attractive and readable than longer ones. Paragraphs with eight or fewer lines look inviting. Long, solid chunks of print appear formidable. If a topic can't be covered in eight or fewer printed lines (not sentences), consider breaking it up into smaller segments.

The accompanying Checklist summarizes the key points of composing a first draft.

To be inviting and readable, paragraphs should have no more than how many printed lines?

Checklist

Composing Sentences and Paragraphs

For Effective Sentences

- **Avoid common sentence faults.** To avoid un-on sentences, do not join two clauses without appropriate punctuation. To avoid comma splices, do not join two clauses with a comma. To avoid fragments, be sure to use periods only after complete sentences.
- **Control sentence length.** Use longer sentences occasionally, but rely primarily on short and medium-length sentences.
- **Emphasize important ideas.** Place main ideas at the beginning of short sentences for emphasis.
- **Apply active- and passive-voice verbs carefully.** Use active-voice verbs (*She sent the e-mail* instead of *The e-mail was sent by her*) most frequently; they immediately identify the doer. Use passive verbs to emphasize an action, to be tactful, or to conceal the performer.
- **Eliminate misplaced modifiers.** Be sure that introductory verbal phrases are followed by the words that can logically be modified. To check the placement of modifiers, ask *Who?* or *What?* after such phrases.

For Meaningful Paragraphs

- **Develop one idea.** Use topic, supporting, and limiting sentences to develop a single idea within each paragraph.
- **Use the direct plan.** Start most paragraphs with the topic sentence followed by supporting sentences. This direct plan is useful in defining, classifying, illustrating, and describing.
- **Use the pivoting plan.** To compare and contrast ideas, start with a limiting sentence; then, present the topic sentence followed by supporting sentences.
- **Use the indirect plan.** To explain reasons or causes first, start with supporting sentences. Build to the conclusion with the topic sentence at the end of the paragraph.
- **Build coherence with linking techniques.** Hold ideas together by repeating key words, dovetailing sentences (beginning one sentence with an idea from the end of the previous sentence), and using appropriate pronouns.
- **Provide road signs with transitional expressions.** Use verbal signals to help the audience know where the idea is going. Words and phrases such as *moreover, accordingly, as a result,* and *therefore* function as idea pointers.
- **Limit paragraph length.** Remember that paragraphs with eight or fewer printed lines look inviting. Consider breaking up longer paragraphs if necessary.

FIGURE 5.8 **Transitional Expressions That Build Coherence**

To Add or Strengthen	To Show Time or Order	To Clarify	To Show Cause and Effect	To Contradict	To Contrast
additionally	after	for example	accordingly	actually	as opposed to
accordingly	before	for instance	as a result	but	at the same time
again	earlier	I mean	consequently	however	by contrast
also	finally	in other words	for this reason	in fact	conversely
beside	first	put another way	hence	instead	on the contrary
indeed	meanwhile	that is	so	rather	on the other hand
likewise	next	this means	therefore	still	previously
moreover	now	thus	thus	yet	similarly

Zooming In — YOUR TURN

Applying Your Skills at Gap Inc.

The management team at Gap Inc. is struggling to regain its premier position in retailing. As part of a focus group, you and your team have been asked to brainstorm ideas that will help turn around its fortunes. Your team members are to visit a Gap or Old Navy store and take notes on store appearance, merchandise selection, and customer service. Team members should also look at the Gap Web site to learn about its commitment to social responsibility.

Your Task

Form teams of four or five people. Discuss your task and decide on a goal. Make assignments. Who will investigate Gap's Web site? Who will visit stores? Who will lead the brainstorming session? Hold a 10-minute brainstorming session following the suggestions in this chapter for generating ideas. What could be changed to attract more customers in your age group to Gap and Old Navy? Set a quota of at least 50 suggestions. Take notes on all suggestions. After 10 minutes, organize and classify the ideas, retaining the best. Prepare a cluster diagram. Organize the cluster diagram into an outline, and submit your cluster diagram and outline to your instructor. Your instructor may ask for individual or team submissions.

Summary of Learning Objectives

1 Apply Phase 2 of the 3-x-3 writing process, which begins with formal and informal methods for researching data and generating ideas. The second phase of the writing process includes researching, organizing, and writing. Researching means collecting information using formal or informal techniques. Formal research for long reports and complex problems may involve searching electronically or manually, as well as conducting interviews, surveys, focus groups, and experiments. Informal research for routine tasks may include looking in company files, talking with your boss, interviewing the target audience, conducting informal surveys, brainstorming for ideas, and creating cluster diagrams.

2 Explain how to organize data into lists and alphanumeric or decimal outlines. One method for organizing data in simple messages is to list the main topics to be discussed. Organizing more complex messages usually requires an outline. To prepare an outline, divide the main topic into three to five major components. Break the components into subpoints consisting of details, illustrations, and evidence. For an alphanumeric outline, arrange items using Roman numerals (I, II), capital letters (A, B), and numbers (1, 2). For a decimal outline, show the ordering of ideas with decimals (1., 1.1, 1.1.1).

Are you ready? Get more practice at **www.meguffey.com**

3 Compare direct and indirect patterns for organizing ideas. The direct pattern places the main idea first. This pattern is useful when audiences will be pleased, mildly interested, or neutral. It saves the reader's time, sets the proper frame of mind, and reduces reader frustration. The indirect pattern places the main idea after explanations. This pattern is useful for audiences that will be unwilling, displeased, or hostile. It respects the feelings of the audience, encourages a fair hearing, and minimizes negative reactions.

4 Compose the first draft of a message, avoiding sentence fragments, run-on sentences, and comma splices as well as emphasizing important ideas, avoiding misplaced modifiers, and using active and passive voice effectively. Compose the first draft of a message in a quiet environment where you won't be interrupted. Compose quickly but plan to revise. Avoid fragments (breaking off parts of sentences), comma splices (joining two clauses improperly), and run-on sentences (fusing two clauses improperly). Understand the difference between clauses and phrases so that you can write complete sentences. Remember that sentences are most effective when they are short (20 or fewer words). A main idea may be emphasized by making it the sentence subject, placing it first, and removing competing ideas. Effective sentences use active-voice verbs, although passive-voice verbs may be necessary for tact or de-emphasis. Effective sentences avoid dangling and misplaced modifiers.

5 Compose effective paragraphs using three classic paragraph plans as well as applying techniques for achieving paragraph coherence. Typical paragraphs follow one of three plans. Direct paragraphs (topic sentence followed by supporting sentences) are useful to define, classify, illustrate, and describe. Pivoting paragraphs (limiting sentence followed by topic sentence and supporting sentences) are useful to compare and contrast. Indirect paragraphs (supporting sentences followed by topic sentence) build a rationale and foundation of ideas before presenting the main idea. Paragraphs are more coherent when the writer links ideas by (a) sustaining a key thought, (b) dovetailing sentences, (c) using pronouns effectively and (d) employing transitional expressions.

Chapter Review

1. Compare the first phase of the writing process with the second phase. (Obj. 1)
2. For routine writing tasks, what are some techniques for collecting informal data and generating ideas? (Obj. 1)
3. Name seven specific techniques for a productive group brainstorming session. (Obj. 1)
4. What is the difference between a list and an outline? (Obj. 2)
5. What are the major components in a letter or memo? (Obj. 2)
6. What are the major components in an analytical report? (Obj. 2)
7. Why do many readers prefer the direct method for organizing messages? (Obj. 3)
8. When is the indirect pattern appropriate, and what are the benefits of using it? (Obj. 3)
9. What is the primary difference between the direct and indirect patterns of organization? (Obj. 3)
10. List four techniques for emphasizing important ideas in sentences. (Obj. 4)
11. When should business writers use active-voice sentences? When should they use passive-voice sentences? Give an original example of each. (Obj. 4)
12. What's wrong with this sentence? *After reading it carefully, the proposal doesn't interest us.* (Obj. 4)
13. What is a topic sentence, and where is it usually found? (Obj. 5)
14. Describe three paragraph plans. Identify the uses for each. (Obj. 5)
15. What is coherence, and how is it achieved? (Obj. 5)

Critical Thinking

1. Why is cluster diagramming considered an intuitive process whereas outlining is considered an analytical process? (Obj. 2)
2. Why is audience analysis so important in the selection of the direct or indirect pattern of organization for a business message? (Obj. 3)
3. How are speakers different from writers in the way they emphasize ideas? (Obj. 4)
4. Why are short sentences and short paragraphs appropriate for business communication? (Objs. 4, 5)
5. **Ethical Issue:** Discuss the ethics of the indirect pattern of organization. Is it manipulative to delay the presentation of the main idea in a message?

Are you ready? Get more practice at **www.meguffey.com**

Writing Improvement Exercises

5.1 Sentence Elements (Obj. 4)

Your Task. Identify the following groups of words using these abbreviations: independent clause (IC), dependent clause (DC), or phrase(s) (P). For clauses, circle the subject. Be prepared to explain your choices.

a. although you want to make a good impression during your interview
b. the interviewer will size you up in about seven seconds
c. during a study conducted by neuro-scientists from New York
d. when they examined brain activity
e. MRI results showed significant activity in two brain areas
f. as a matter of fact
g. because people make 11 decisions about you in the first seven seconds
h. in the areas of education, believability, trustworthiness, and economic level

5.2 Sentence Faults (Obj. 4)

In the following, identify the sentence fault (fragment, run-on, comma splice). Then revise to remedy the fault.

a. Because 90 percent of all business transactions involve written messages. Good writing skills are critical.
b. The recruiter requested a writing sample. Even though the candidate seemed to communicate well orally.
c. Major soft-drink companies considered a new pricing strategy, they tested vending machines that raise prices in hot weather.
d. Thirsty consumers may think that variable pricing is unfair they may also refuse to use the machine.
e. About half of Pizza Hut's 7,600 outlets make deliveries, the others concentrate on walk-in customers.
f. McDonald's sold its chain of Chipotle Mexican Grill restaurants the chain's share price doubled on the next day of trading.
g. Private equity players are betting they can breathe new life into old brands. Which explains why Golden Gate Partners paid millions for defunct retailer Eddie Bauer.

5.3 Emphasis (Obj. 4)

For each of the following sentences, circle (1) or (2). Be prepared to justify your choice.

a. Which is more emphatic?
   1. Our dress code is good.
   2. Our dress code reflects common sense and good taste.
b. Which is more emphatic?
   1. A budget increase would certainly improve hiring.
   2. A budget increase of $70,000 would enable us to hire two new people.
c. Which is more emphatic?
   1. The committee was powerless to act.
   2. The committee was unable to take action.
d. Which de-emphasizes the refusal?
   1. Although our resources are committed to other projects this year, we hope to be able to contribute to your worthy cause next year.
   2. We can't contribute to your charity this year.
e. Which sentence places more emphasis on the date?
   1. The deadline is November 30 for health benefit changes.
   2. November 30 is the deadline for health benefit changes.
f. Which sentence is *less* emphatic?
   1. One division's profits decreased last quarter.
   2. Profits in beauty care products dropped 15 percent last quarter.
g. Which sentence gives more emphasis to video game sales?
   1. Sales of video game consoles and software rose 40 percent in June.
   2. During the period ending June 30, sales of video game consoles and software rose significantly.
h. Which sentence gives more emphasis to leadership?
   1. Jason has many admirable qualities, but most important is his leadership skill.
   2. Jason has many admirable qualities, including leadership skill, good judgment, and patience.
i. Which sentence format is more emphatic?
   1. We notified three departments: (a) Marketing, (b) Accounting, and (c) Distribution.
   2. We notified three departments:
      (a) Marketing
      (b) Accounting
      (c) Distribution

5.4 Active Voice (Obj. 4)

Business writing is more forceful if it uses active-voice verbs.

Passive: Antivirus software was installed by Craig on his computer.
Active: Craig installed antivirus software on his computer.

Your Task. Revise the following sentences so that verbs are in the active voice. Put the emphasis on the doer of the action.

a. Employees were given their checks at 4 p.m. every Friday by the manager.
b. New spices and cooking techniques were tried by McDonald's to improve its hamburgers.
c. Our new company logo was designed by my boss.
d. The managers with the most productive departments were commended by the CEO.
e. All team members were asked by the leader to brainstorm for 10 minutes.

5.5 Passive Voice (Obj. 4)

Your Task. Revise the following sentences so that they are in the passive voice.

a. The auditor discovered a computational error in the company's tax figures.
b. We cannot ship your order for ten monitors until June 15.
c. Stacy did not submit the accounting statement on time.
d. The Federal Trade Commission targeted deceptive diet advertisements by weight-loss marketers.
e. Thieves are stealing corporate and financial information by using data-stealing malware on the Web.

5.6 Dangling and Misplaced Modifiers (Obj. 4)

Your Task. On a separate sheet, revise the following sentences to remedy dangling and misplaced modifiers. Add subjects as needed, but retain the introductory phrases. Mark *C* if correct.

a. By advertising extensively, all the open jobs were filled quickly.
b. To apply for early admission, submit your application by November 1. (Tricky!)
c. After leaving the midtown meeting, Angela's car would not start.
d. Walking up the driveway, the Hummer parked in the garage was immediately spotted by the detectives.
e. The manager's rules were to be observed by all staff members, no matter how silly they seemed.
f. To complete the project on time, a new deadline was established by the team.

g. Acting as manager, several new employees were hired by Mr. Lopez.
h. Michelle Mitchell presented a talk about workplace drug problems in our boardroom.

5.7 Paragraph Organization (Obj. 5)

In a memo to the college president, the athletic director is arguing for a new stadium scoreboard. One paragraph will describe the old scoreboard and why it needs to be replaced. Study the following list of ideas for that paragraph.

1. The old scoreboard is a tired warhorse that was originally constructed in the 1960s.
2. It's now hard to find replacement parts for it when something breaks.
3. The old scoreboard is not energy efficient.
4. Coca-Cola has offered to buy a new sports scoreboard in return for exclusive rights to sell soda on campus.
5. The old scoreboard should be replaced for many reasons.
6. It shows only scores for football games.
7. When we have soccer games or track meets, we are without a functioning scoreboard.

   a. Which sentence should be the topic sentence? ______
   b. Which sentence(s) should be developed in a different paragraph? ______
   c. Which supporting sentences should follow the topic sentence? ______
   d. Now write a well-organized paragraph using the preceding information. Strive to incorporate coherence techniques described in this chapter.

5.8 Paragraph Organization and Revision (Obj. 5)

Your Task. The following paragraphs are poorly organized and poorly expressed. Decide what the main idea is in each paragraph. Then revise each paragraph so that it has a topic sentence and is organized directly. Improve the sentence flow, structure, coherence, and correctness by using the techniques described in this chapter and the previous chapter.

a. We feel that the "extreme" strategy has not been developed fully in the fast-food market. Pizza Hut is considering launching a new product called The Extreme. We plan to price this new pizza at $19.99. It will be the largest pizza on the market. It will have double the cheese. It will also have double the toppings. The plan is to target the X and Y Generations. The same target audience that would respond to an extreme product also reacts to low prices. The X and Y Generations are the fastest-growing segments in the fast-food market. These population segments have responded well to other marketing plans using the extreme strategy.
b. You should always have your sound and video files ready for your PowerPoint presentation. When you move the presentation to a network folder or send it to someone else, the presentation has no sound. A common problem in PowerPoint involves lost sound and video files. Create a new folder for your presentation, and copy the sound and video files to that folder before you put them in your presentation. Then you will always have your sound files ready for use with your presentation.
c. Current employees may be interested in applying for new positions within the company. The Human Resources Department has a number of jobs available immediately. The positions are at a high level. Current employees may apply immediately for open positions in production, for some in marketing, and jobs in administrative support are also available. Interested people should come to the Human Resources Department. We have a list showing the open positions, what the qualifications are, and job descriptions are shown. Many of the jobs are now open, but application must be made immediately. That's why we are sending this now. To be hired, an interview must be scheduled within the next two weeks.

Activities

Note: All Documents for Analysis may be downloaded from **www.meguffey.com** so that you do not have to rekey the entire message.

5.9 Document for Analysis: Weak E-Mail Message (Objs. 3–5)

Team

Your Task. The following e-mail suffers from numerous writing faults such as dangling modifiers, overuse of passive voice, and fragments. Notice that small superscript numbers identify each sentence. Individually or in a group, analyze this message. For each sentence or group of words, identify the following faults: dangling modifier (DM), passive voice (PV), and fragment (FR). Your group should agree on its analysis. Your instructor may ask you to revise the message to remedy its faults.

To: Jeremy.Gibbons12@aol.com
From: Andrea Kelly <akelly@bodyfitness.com>
Subject: Improving Your Experience at Body Fitness Center
Cc:
Bcc:

Dear Mr. Gibbons,

[1]Body Fitness Center here in Scottsdale was probably chosen by you because it is one of the top-rated gyms in the Southwest. [2]Our principal goal has always been making your workouts enjoyable. [3]To continue to provide you with the best equipment and programs, your feedback is needed.

[4]An outstanding program with quality equipment and excellent training programs has been provided by Body Fitness. [5]However, more individual attention could be given by us to our customers if our peak usage time could be extended. [6]You have probably noticed that attendance at the gym increases from 4 p.m. to 8 p.m. [7]We wish it were possible to accommodate all our customers on their favorite equipment during those hours. [8]Although we can't stretch an hour. [9]We would like to make better use of the time between 8 p.m. and 11 p.m. [10]With more members coming later, we would have less crush from 4 p.m. to 8 p.m.

[11]To encourage you to stay later, security cameras for our parking area are being considered by my partner and me. [12]Cameras for some inside facilities may also be added. [13]This matter has been given a lot of thought. [14]Although Body Fitness has never previously had an incident that endangered a member.

[15]Please fill in the attached interactive questionnaire. [16]Which will give us instant feedback about scheduling your workouts. [17]By completing this questionnaire, your workouts and training sessions can be better planned so that you can enjoy exactly the equipment and trainers you prefer.

Cordially,

5.10 Collaborative Brainstorming (Obj. 1)

Team

Brainstorming can be a productive method for generating problem-solving ideas. You can improve your brainstorming skills through practice.

Your Task. In teams of four or five, analyze a problem on your campus such as the following: unavailable classes, unrealistic degree requirements, a lack of student intern programs, poor parking facilities, an inadequate registration process, a lack of diversity among students on campus, and so forth. Use brainstorming techniques to generate ideas that clarify the problem and explore its solutions. Each team member should prepare a cluster diagram to record the ideas generated. Either individually or as a team, organize the ideas into an outline with three to five main points and numerous subpoints. Assume that your ideas will become part of a letter to be sent to an appropriate campus official or to your campus newspaper discussing the problem and your solution. Remember, however, your role as a student. Be polite, positive, and constructive—not negative, hostile, or aggressive.

5.11 Individual Brainstorming (Objs. 1, 2)

E-mail

Brainstorming techniques can work for individuals as well as groups. Assume that your boss or department chair wants you to submit a short report analyzing a problem.

Your Task. Analyze a problem that exists where you work or go to school, such as long lines at the copy or fax machines, overuse of express mail services, understaffing during peak customer service hours, poor scheduling of employees, inappropriate cell phone use, an inferior or inflexible benefits package, outdated equipment, or one of the campus problems listed in **Activity 5.10.** Select a problem about which you have some knowledge. Prepare a cluster diagram to develop ideas. Then, organize the ideas into an outline with three to five main points and numerous subpoints. Be polite, positive, and constructive. E-mail the outline to your boss (your instructor). Include an introduction (such as, *Here is the outline you requested in regard to . . .*). Include a closing that offers to share your cluster diagram if your boss would like to see it.

5.12 Brainstorming Tips for Productive Sessions (Obj. 1)

Web

Casandra M., your supervisor at Gap Inc., has been asked to lead a brainstorming group in an effort to generate new ideas for the company's product line. Although Casandra knows a great deal about the company and its products, she doesn't know much about brainstorming. She asks you to research the topic quickly and give her a concise guide on how to brainstorm. One other thing—Casandra doesn't want to read a lot of articles. She wants you to outline tips for productive brainstorming.

Your Task. Conduct an Internet or database keyword search for brainstorming tips. Locate a number of articles with helpful tips. Prepare an outline that tells how to (a) prepare for a brainstorming session, (b) conduct the session, and (c) follow up after the meeting. Submit your outline in a memo or an e-mail to your supervisor (your instructor).

5.13 Collecting Primary Information: Research Interviewing (Obj. 1)

Team

In your follow-up meeting with Casandra M. from **Activity 5.12**, she asks you to complete one more task in preparation for the brainstorming session. She needs further insight in defining the problem and creating an agenda for the outline of topics to be covered in the brainstorming session. She asks you to conduct informal interviews of Gap and Old Navy shoppers.

Your Task. Form five-member class groups. Two members of each group, if possible, should be familiar with Gap and Old Navy. Decide who will role-play the interviewer and the two interviewees (those most familiar with Gap and Old Navy), and who will act as recorder and group spokesperson. If your group has fewer than five members, some will have to fill more than one role. The interviewer asks both interviewees the same three questions outlined below. The recorder takes notes, and the group spokesperson summarizes the group's research results during the class discussion. Use the following interview questions:

a. During your last two visits to Gap or Old Navy, were there any products you expected the two stores to carry but couldn't find?
b. Can you think of any seasonal products you would like Gap or Old Navy to carry? Specifically, identify products for winter, spring, summer, and fall.
c. If you were in charge of Gap or Old Navy's product lines, what three changes would you make to the existing product lines? What three totally new product lines would you want to create?

As a team or individually, prepare an outline that summarizes the information gathered from the in-class interviews.

5.14 Brainstorming: Are Ethics Programs Helpful? (Obj. 1)

Ethics | Team | Web

In the wake of the banking collapse and previous corporate scandals, more companies are hiring ethics officers—sometimes called "ethics cops." Companies are also investing in expensive interactive Web-based ethics training. You have been named to a team to discuss ethics compliance in your company, a large firm with thousands of employees. It has no current program. Other companies have ethics codes, conflicts-of-interest policies, ethics officers, training programs, and hotlines. Some authorities, however, say that ethics failures are usually not the result of ignorance of laws or regulations.[12] A variety of pressures may cause ethics lapses.

Your Task. Your boss, the Human Resources vice president, wants to learn more about employee feelings in regard to ethics programs. In teams, brainstorm to find reactions to these questions. What kinds of ethical dilemmas do typical entry-level and midlevel managerial employees face? Do you think ethics codes help employees be more ethical? What conditions might force employees to steal, lie, or break the rules? Can ethics be taught? What kind of workplace ethics program would you personally find helpful? Before your brainstorming session, you might want to investigate the topic of ethics programs on the Web. Record your ideas during the session. Then organize the best ones into an outline to be presented to Rita Romano, Human Resources Vice President.

5.15 Researching, Brainstorming, and Organizing: Student Loans (Objs. 1–3)

Team | Web

Sarah was all smiles when she graduated and got that degree in her hand. Soon, however, she began to worry about her student loans. Student debt has risen 58 percent in the last decade, according to the College Board, a New York–based college testing and information firm. One study showed that about one third of all recent graduates are unprepared to make their first student loan payment.[13] Another report stated that the average borrower leaves college owing more than $22,000.[14]

Your Task. In teams collect information about student debt. Who has it? How much debt does an average student carry? How do most students repay their loans? What strategies are proposed for helping students avoid, reduce, and repay educational loans? As a group, discuss your findings. Brainstorm for additional strategies. Then organize your findings into an outline with a title, an introduction, and recommendations for helping current students avoid, reduce, and repay their student loans. Submit your outline to your instructor.

Video Resource

Video Library 1, Guffey's 3-x-3 Writing Process Develops Fluent Workplace Skills

If you didn't see *Guffey's 3-x-3 Writing Process Develops Fluent Workplace Skills* when you studied a previous chapter, your instructor may show it with this chapter. It shows all three phases of the writing process so that you can see how it guides the development of a complete message. This video illustrates concepts in Chapters 4, 5, and 6.

Chat About It

In each chapter you will find five discussion questions related to the chapter material. Your instructor may assign these topics for you to discuss in class, in an online chat room, or on an online discussion board. Some of the discussion topics may require outside research. You may also be asked to read and respond to postings made by your classmates.

Topic 1: This chapter describes various techniques for generating ideas. Explore other methods by using Google to search for *generating writing ideas.* Select a method that appeals to you and explain why it would be effective.

Topic 2: In which phase of the 3-x-3 writing process do you suppose most beginners at business writing spend their time? In which phase have you been spending most of your time?

Topic 3: Some writers have trouble writing the opening sentence of a message. Occasionally, a quotation makes for an appropriate opening. Assume that you need to motivate an employee to achieve more at work. Find a famous quotation online about motivation that might be an appropriate opening for such a message. In addition, write a sentence that would effectively transition from this opening.

Topic 4: In your opinion, how many business managers know what a comma splice is? If some managers don't know what a comma splice is, then is it critical that you avoid comma splices in your writing?

Topic 5: Learn how to display the average sentence length in a document using Microsoft Office Word 2007. Not everyone using Word 2007 knows how to do that. Explain the process briefly.

Grammar and Mechanics C.L.U.E. Review 5

Commas

Review Guides 21–26 about commas in Appendix A, Grammar and Mechanics Guide, beginning on page A-10. On a separate sheet, revise the following sentences to correct errors in comma usage. For each error that you locate, write the guide number and abbreviation that reflects this usage. The more you recognize the reasons, the better you will learn these punctuation guidelines. If a sentence is correct, write *C.* When you finish, check your answers on page Key-1.

Guide 21, CmSer (Comma series)	Guide 24, CmDate (Comma, dates, addresses, geographical names, etc.)
Guide 22, CmIntr (Comma introductory)	Guide 25, CmIn (Comma, internal sentence interrupters)
Guide 23, CmConj (Comma conjunction)	

Example: Before beginning a message always collect the necessary information.

Revision: Before beginning a message, always collect the necessary information. [Guide 22, Cm Intr]

1. The 3-x-3 writing process includes prewriting, writing and revising.
2. Before asking others for information see what you can find yourself.
3. Formal research methods include accessing electronically, searching manually and investigating primary sources.
4. If a project is complex consider organizing it by outlining the major points.
5. Careful writers define the main topic and they divide it into three to five components.
6. We decided that Jill Hawkins who is the best writer on the team should prepare the final draft.
7. The company's executives expected new office construction to be finished by September 1, 2012 in Boulder Colorado.
8. Grammar checkers by the way often highlight passive voice as a grammar fault.
9. When you must be tactful and avoid naming the doer of an action the passive voice can be helpful.
10. The direct paragraph plan is useful when you want to define a process or when you must describe something such as a product.

CHAPTER 6

Revising Business Messages

OBJECTIVES

After studying this chapter, you should be able to

1. Complete business messages by revising for conciseness, which includes eliminating flabby expressions, long lead-ins, *there is/are* and *it is/was* fillers, redundancies, and empty words.
2. Improve clarity in business messages by keeping the ideas simple, dumping trite business phrases, dropping clichés and slang, unburying verbs, and controlling exuberance.
3. Enhance readability by understanding document design including the use of white space, margins, typefaces, fonts, numbered and bulleted lists, and headings.
4. Recognize proofreading problem areas and apply effective techniques to proofread both routine and complex documents.
5. Evaluate a message to judge its success.

Want to do well on tests and excel in your course? Go to **www.meguffey.com** for helpful interactive resources.

- **Review the Chapter 6 PowerPoint slides to prepare for the first quiz.**

Zooming In PART 1

Taco Bell Tweaks Menu to Rebuild Customer Base

After an outbreak of *E. coli* linked to its restaurants in five states followed by a highly publicized video of rats cavorting in one of its New York restaurants, Taco Bell struggled to regain its reputation. Eventually the restaurant chain overcame the bad publicity, and customers returned to its tacos, burritos, and tostadas. Taco Bell realized, however, that it had to keep rebuilding its customer base by improving its image and its menu.

© AP Images/Phil Coale

Yum Brands—owner of Taco Bell, Pizza Hut, and KFC—is the world's largest restaurant company, with more than 36,000 restaurants around the world.[1] Although Taco Bell is the most successful of Yum's fast-food chains, it must compete for customers with McDonald's, Burger King, and Wendy's as well as with trendy upstarts Baja Fresh, Chipotle, and Qdoba. Despite the competition, Taco Bell holds a commanding lead in the Mexican fast-food market.

In overcoming its bad image, Taco Bell plans to remodel or rebuild 375 locations. Major emphasis, however, goes to revamping its menu. One portion of the plan focuses on new breakfast products such as a sausage and bacon Grilled Stuft burrito; a Southwest sausage burrito; an egg, bacon, and cheese burrito; and cinnamon Toastadas.

Looking beyond breakfast fare, Emil Brolick, president of brand building at Yum, suggested that Taco Bell had higher aspirations. "[W]e believe we have a unique opportunity because while all the sandwich players are trying to one-up each other in the same game, we're going to play a different game."[2] His interest lies in unique flavors and better products. However, Taco Bell is also concerned with healthful food. Stinging from criticism that fast food contributes to the worldwide obesity epidemic, Taco Bell is looking for more nutritious menu choices.[3]

In the increasingly crowded fast-food market, customers are slowly but surely shifting away from the traditional burger and chicken fast foods. One food industry executive said, "Burgers are your dad's food, and Mexican is the choice of the new generation."[4] Poised to capitalize on this movement, Taco Bell remains keenly aware that (a) it sells a quasi-Mexican food, and (b) its customers are changing. Although its products cannot veer too far from what appeals to the masses, Taco Bell must also compete with new flavors, low-fat items, and fresh ingredients. A recently hired culinary product manager is charged with the task of coming up with menu suggestions and communicating them to management. You will learn more about this case on page 171.

Critical Thinking

- When new ideas must be generated and sold to management, what role does communication skill play in the process?
- Do you think the Taco Bell culinary product manager will be making an oral or a written presentation of new menu ideas?
- Why is a writing process helpful in developing a presentation of new ideas?

http://www.tacobell.com

Applying Phase 3 of the Writing Process

LEARNING OBJECTIVE 1

Complete business messages by revising for conciseness, which includes eliminating flabby expressions, long lead-ins, *there is/are* and *it is/was* fillers, redundancies, and empty words.

The final phase of the 3-x-3 writing process focuses on revising, proofreading, and evaluating. Revising means improving the content and sentence structure of your message. Proofreading involves correcting its grammar, spelling, punctuation, format, and mechanics. Evaluating is the process of analyzing whether your message achieves its purpose. One would not expect people in the restaurant business to require these kinds of skills. However, the new culinary product manager at Taco Bell—and many other similar businesspeople—realize that bright ideas are worth little unless they can be communicated effectively to fellow workers and to management. In the communication process, the techniques of revision can often mean the difference between the acceptance or rejection of ideas.

Although the composition process differs depending on the person and the situation, this final phase should occupy a significant share of the total time you spend on a message. As you learned earlier, some experts recommend devoting about half the total composition time to revising and proofreading.[5]

Why is the revision stage of the writing process so important?

Rarely is the first or even second version of a message satisfactory. Only amateurs expect writing perfection on the first try. The revision stage is your chance to make sure your message says what you mean. Many professional writers compose the first draft quickly without worrying about language, precision, or correctness. Then they revise and polish extensively. Other writers, however, prefer to revise as they go—particularly for shorter business documents.

Whether you revise immediately or after a break, you will want to examine your message critically. You should be especially concerned with ways to improve its conciseness, clarity, and readability.

Revising for Conciseness

In business, time is indeed money. Translated into writing, this means that concise messages save reading time and, thus, money. In addition, messages that are written directly and efficiently are easier to read and comprehend. In the revision process, look for shorter ways to say what you mean. Examine every sentence that you write. Could the thought be conveyed in fewer words? Your writing will be more concise if you eliminate flabby expressions, drop unnecessary introductory words, get rid of redundancies, and purge empty words.

Why is conciseness so important in business messages?

Eliminating Flabby Expressions

As you revise, focus on eliminating flabby expressions. This takes conscious effort. As one expert copyeditor observed, "Trim sentences, like trim bodies, usually require far more effort than flabby ones."[6] Turning out slim sentences and lean messages means that you will strive to "trim the fat." For example, notice the flabbiness in this sentence: *Due to the fact that sales are booming, profits are good.* It could be said more concisely: *Because sales are booming, profits are good.* Many flabby expressions can be shortened to one concise word as shown here and illustrated in Figure 6.1. Also notice in this figure that you may use different methods for revising printed documents and digital documents.

Flabby	Concise
as a general rule	generally
at a later date	later
at this point in time	now, presently
despite the fact that	although
due to the fact that, inasmuch as, in view of the fact that	because
feel free to	please
for the period of	for
in addition to the above	also
in all probability	probably
in the event that	if
in the near future	soon
in very few cases	seldom
until such time as	until

Why should you avoid long lead-ins in your messages?

Limiting Long Lead-Ins

Another way to create concise sentences is to delete unnecessary introductory words. Consider this sentence: *I am sending you this e-mail to announce that we have hired a new manager.* A more concise and more direct sentence deletes the long lead-in: *We have hired a*

FIGURE 6.1 Revising Manually and Digitally

Revising Digital Documents Using Strikethrough and Color

When revising digital documents, you can use simple word processing tools such as strikethrough and color. In this example, strikethroughs in red identify passages to be deleted. The strikethrough function is located on the **Font** tab. We used blue to show inserted words, but you may choose any color you prefer. If you need to add comments, use the MS Word **Comment** feature, shown in Chapter 4, Figure 4.8, on page 129.

~~This is a short note to let you know that, as~~ As you requested, I ~~made an investigation of~~ investigated several of our competitors' Web sites. Attached ~~hereto~~ is a summary of my findings. ~~of my investigation.~~ I was ~~really~~ most interested in ~~making a comparison of the employment of strategies for~~ comparing marketing strategies as well as ~~the use of~~ navigational graphics ~~used~~ to guide visitors through the sites. ~~In view of the fact that~~ Because we will be revising our own Web site ~~in the near future~~ soon, I was ~~extremely~~ intrigued by the organization, ~~kind of~~ marketing tactics, and navigation at ~~each and~~ every site I visited.

Revising Printed Documents Using Proofreading Symbols

When revising printed documents, use standard symbols to manually show your revisions.

~~This is a short note to let you know that,~~ as you requested, I ~~made an~~ investigat~~ion of~~ ed several of our competitors' Web sites. Attached ~~hereto~~ is a summary of my findings. ~~of my investigation.~~ I was ~~really~~ most interested in ~~making a comparison of the employment of~~ comparing marketing strategies ~~for marketing~~ as well as ~~the use of~~ navigational graphics ~~used~~ to guide visitors through the sites. ~~In view of the fact that~~ Because we will be revising our own Web site soon ~~in the near future,~~ I was ~~extremely~~ intrigued by the organization, ~~kind of~~ marketing tactics, and navigation at ~~each and~~ every site I visited.

Popular Proofreading Symbols

- Delete
- Capitalize
- Insert
- Insert comma
- Insert period
- Start paragraph

new manager. The meat of the sentence often follows the words *that* or *because*, as shown in the following:

Wordy	Concise
We are sending this announcement to let everyone know that new parking permits will be available January 1.	New parking permits will be available January 1.
This is to inform you that you may find lower airfares at our Web site.	You may find lower airfares at our Web site.
I am writing this letter because Professor John Donnellan suggested that your organization was hiring trainees.	Professor John Donnellan suggested that your organization was hiring trainees.

Dropping Unnecessary *there is/are* and *it is/was* Fillers

In many sentences the expressions *there is/are* and *it is/was* function as unnecessary fillers. In addition to taking up space, these fillers delay getting to the point of the sentence. Eliminate them by recasting the sentence. Many—but not all—sentences can be revised so that fillers are unnecessary.

Wordy	Concise
There are only two administrative assistants to serve five managers.	Only two administrative assistants serve five managers.
There was an unused computer in the back office.	An unused computer was in the back office.
It was our auditor who discovered the theft.	Our auditor discovered the theft.

What are redundancies?

Rejecting Redundancies

Expressions that repeat meaning or include unnecessary words are redundant. Saying *unexpected surprise* is like saying *surprise surprise* because *unexpected* carries the same meaning as *surprise*. Excessive adjectives, adverbs, and phrases often create redundancies and wordiness. Redundancies do not add emphasis, as some people think. Instead, they identify a writer as inexperienced. As you revise, look for redundant expressions such as the following:

Redundant	Concise
absolutely essential	essential
adequate enough	adequate
basic fundamentals	fundamentals *or* basics
big in size	big
combined together	combined
exactly identical	identical
each and every	each *or* every
necessary prerequisite	prerequisite
new beginning	beginning
refer back	refer
repeat again	repeat
true facts	facts

Purging Empty Words

Familiar phrases roll off the tongue easily, but many contain expendable parts. Be alert to these empty words and phrases: *case, degree, the fact that, factor, instance, nature,* and *quality*. Notice how much better the following sentences sound when we remove all the empty words:

> ~~*In the case of*~~ USA Today, ~~*the newspaper*~~ *improved its readability.*
>
> *Because of* ~~*the degree of*~~ *active participation by our sales reps, profits soared.*
>
> *We are aware* ~~*of the fact*~~ *that many managers need assistance.*
>
> *Except for* ~~*the instance of*~~ *Toyota, Japanese imports sagged.*
>
> *She chose a career in a field that was analytical* ~~*in nature*~~. [OR: *She chose a career in an analytical field.]*
>
> *Student writing in that class is excellent* ~~*in quality*~~.

Also avoid saying the obvious. In the following examples, notice how many unnecessary words we can omit through revision:

> ~~*When it arrived*~~, *I cashed your check immediately.* (Announcing the check's arrival is unnecessary. That fact is assumed in its cashing.)
>
> ~~*We need printer cartridges; therefore*~~, *please send me two dozen laser cartridges.* (The first clause is obvious.)

Finally, look carefully at clauses beginning with *that, which*, and *who*. They can often be shortened without loss of clarity. Search for phrases such as *it appears that*. These phrases often can be reduced to a single adjective or adverb, such as *apparently*.

> *successful*
> *Changing the name of a* ^ *company* ~~*that is successful*~~ *is always risky.*
>
> *All employees* ~~*who are among those*~~ *completing the course will be reimbursed.*
>
> *final*
> *Our* ^ *proposal,* ~~*which was*~~ *slightly altered* ~~*in its final form*~~, *won approval.*
>
> *weekly*
> *We plan to schedule* ^ *meetings* ~~*on a weekly basis*~~.

Revising for Clarity

LEARNING OBJECTIVE 2

Improve clarity in business messages by keeping the ideas simple, dumping trite business phrases, dropping clichés and slang, unburying verbs, and controlling exuberance.

A major revision task involves assessing the clarity of your message. A clear message is one that is immediately understood. Employees, customers, and investors increasingly want to be addressed in a clear and genuine way. Fuzzy and bombastic writing alienates these stakeholders.[7] Business writers appreciate clear messages that are immediately understandable. Techniques that improve clarity include applying the KISS formula (Keep It Short and Simple), dumping trite business phrases, and avoiding clichés and slang.

Keep It Short and Simple

What is the KISS formula, and how does it apply to business messages?

To achieve clarity, resist the urge to show off or be fancy. Remember that your goal is not to impress a reader. Instead, the goal of business writing is to *express*, not *impress*. One way to achieve clear writing is to apply the familiar KISS formula. Use active-voice sentences that avoid indirect, pompous language.

Wordy and Unclear	**Improved**
Employees have not been made sufficiently aware of the potentially adverse consequences regarding the use of these perilous chemicals.	Warn your employees about these dangerous chemicals.

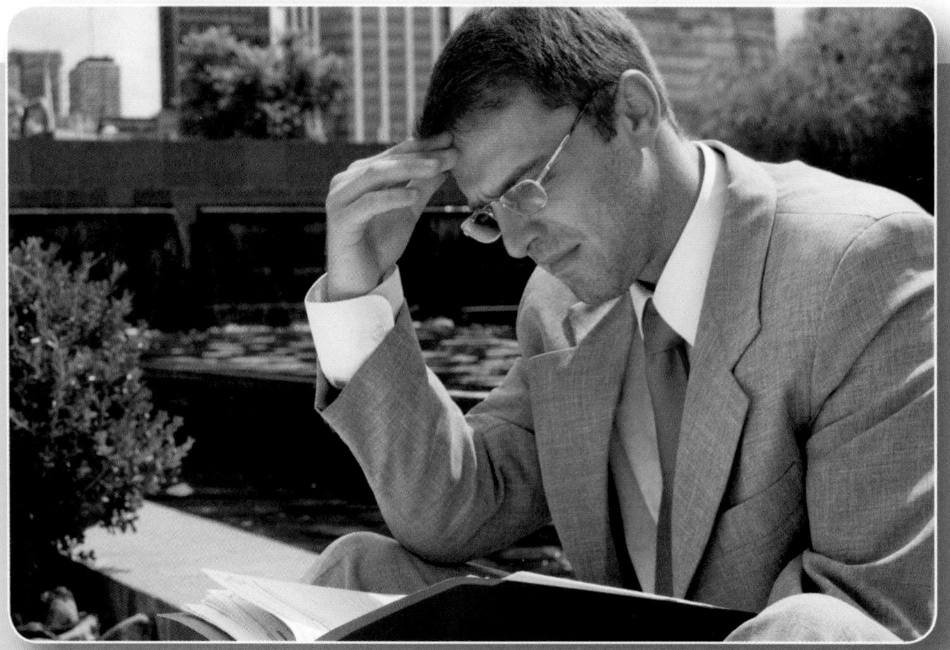

Communicating in clear, simple language is an uphill battle for some firms. That's why plain-language advocate Christopher Balmford founded Cleardocs.com, a document management company that helps law firms, accounting firms, and other highly technical businesses communicate clearly and effectively with clients. Cleardocs' online technology turns complex documents into market-focused plain language, transforming elaborate or technical letters and reports into easily understandable written communications. *What types of businesses have difficulty producing simple, conversational messages, and why?*

Wordy and Unclear	Improved
In regard to the matter of obtaining optimal results, it is essential that employees be given the implements that are necessary for jobs to be completed satisfactorily.	To get the best results, give employees the tools they need to do the job.

Dumping Trite Business Phrases

To sound "businesslike," many writers repeat the same stale expressions that other writers have used over the years. Your writing will sound fresher and more vigorous if you eliminate these trite phrases or find more original ways to convey the idea.

Trite Phrase	Improved
as per your request	as you request
pursuant to your request	at your request
enclosed please find	enclosed is
every effort will be made	we'll try
in accordance with your wishes	as you wish
in receipt of	have received
please do not hesitate to	please
thank you in advance	thank you
under separate cover	separately
with reference to	about

Dropping Clichés and Slang

Clichés are expressions that have become exhausted by overuse. Many cannot be explained, especially to those who are new to our culture. Clichés lack not only freshness but also clarity. Instead of repeating clichés such as the following, try to find another way to say what you mean.

below the belt	last but not least
better than new	make a bundle
beyond a shadow of a doubt	pass with flying colors
easier said than done	quick as a flash
exception to the rule	shoot from the hip
fill the bill	stand your ground
first and foremost	think outside the box
good to go	true to form

Spotlight on Communicators

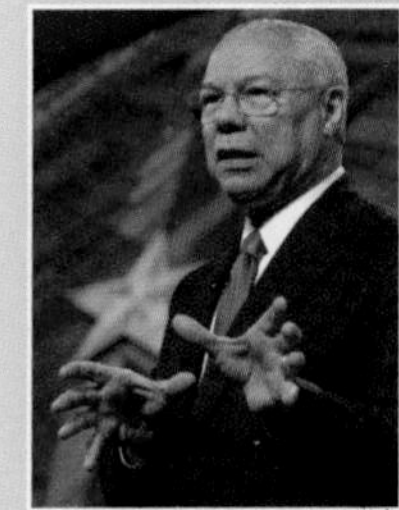

© AP Images/Jack Plunket

Former Secretary of State Colin Powell believes that effective leaders apply the KISS formula in keeping things simple. They articulate vivid, overarching goals and values. Their visions and priorities are lean and compelling, not cluttered and laden with buzzwords. One of Secretary Powell's favorite quotations illustrates his conviction: "Great leaders are almost always great simplifiers, who can cut through argument, debate and doubt, to offer a solution everybody can understand."

What is slang, and when is it appropriate in business messages?

Slang is composed of informal words with arbitrary and extravagantly changed meanings. Slang words quickly go out of fashion because they are no longer appealing when everyone begins to understand them. Consider the following statement of a government official who had been asked why his department was dropping a proposal to lease offshore oil lands: "The Administration has an awful lot of other things in the pipeline, and this has more wiggle room so they just moved it down the totem pole." He added, however, that the proposal might be offered again since "there is no pulling back because of hot-potato factors."

The meaning here, if the speaker really intended to impart any, is considerably obscured by the use of slang. If you want to sound professional, avoid expressions such as *snarky, lousy, blowing the budget, bombed,* and *getting burned.*

Unburying Verbs

What is a buried verb?

Buried verbs are those that are needlessly converted to wordy noun expressions. This happens when verbs such as *acquire, establish,* and *develop* are made into nouns such as *acquisition, establishment,* and *development.* Such nouns often end in *-tion, -ment,* and *-ance.* Using these nouns increases sentence length, drains verb strength, slows the reader, and muddies the thought. Notice how you can make your writing cleaner and more forceful by avoiding wordy verb/noun conversions:

Buried Verbs	Unburied Verbs
conduct a discussion of	discuss
create a reduction in	reduce
engage in the preparation of	prepare
give consideration to	consider
make an assumption of	assume
make a discovery of	discover
perform an analysis of	analyze
reach a conclusion that	conclude
take action on	act

Controlling Exuberance

Occasionally we show our exuberance with words such as *very, definitely, quite, completely, extremely, really, actually,* and *totally*. These intensifiers can emphasize and strengthen your meaning. Overuse, however, sounds unbusinesslike. Control your enthusiasm and guard against excessive use.

Excessive Exuberance	Businesslike
We *totally* agree that we *actually* did not *really* give his proposal a *very* fair trial.	We agree that we did not give his proposal a fair trial.
The manufacturer was *extremely* upset to learn that its printers were *definitely* being counterfeited.	The manufacturer was upset to learn that its printers were being counterfeited.

Designing Documents for Readability

LEARNING OBJECTIVE 3

Enhance readability by understanding document design including the use of white space, margins, typefaces, fonts, numbered and bulleted lists, and headings.

Well-designed documents improve your messages in two important ways. First, they enhance readability and comprehension. Second, they make readers think you are a well-organized and intelligent person. In the revision process, you have a chance to adjust formatting and make other changes so that readers grasp your main points quickly. Significant design techniques to improve readability include the appropriate use of white space, margins, typefaces, numbered and bulleted lists, and headings for visual impact.

Employing White Space

Empty space on a page is called *white space*. A page crammed full of text or graphics appears busy, cluttered, and unreadable. To increase white space, use headings, bulleted or numbered lists, and effective margins. As discussed earlier, short sentences (20 or fewer words) and short paragraphs (eight or fewer printed lines) improve readability and comprehension. As you revise, think about shortening long sentences. Consider breaking up long paragraphs into shorter chunks. Be sure, however, that each part of the divided paragraph has a topic sentence.

Understanding Margins and Text Alignment

What is a ragged-right margin?

Margins determine the white space on the left, right, top, and bottom of a block of type. They define the reading area and provide important visual relief. Business letters and memos usually have side margins of 1 to 1 ½ inches.

Your word processing program probably offers four forms of margin alignment: (a) lines align only at the left, (b) lines align only at the right, (c) lines align at both left and right (*justified*), and (d) lines are centered. Nearly all text in Western cultures is aligned at the left and reads from left to right. The right margin may be *justified* or *ragged right*. The text in books, magazines, and other long works is often justified on the left and right for a formal appearance.

However, justified text may require more attention to word spacing and hyphenation to avoid awkward empty spaces or "rivers" of spaces running through a document. When right margins are "ragged"—that is, without alignment or justification—they provide more white space and improve readability. Therefore, you are best served by using left-justified text and ragged-right margins without justification. Centered text is appropriate for headings but not for complete messages.

Choosing Appropriate Typefaces

What is the difference between serif and sans serif fonts?

Business writers today may choose from a number of typefaces on their word processors. A typeface defines the shape of text characters. As shown in Figure 6.2, a wide range of typefaces is available for various purposes. Some are decorative and useful for special purposes. For most business messages, however, you should choose from *serif* or *sans serif* categories.

Serif typefaces have small features at the ends of strokes. The most common serif typeface is Times New Roman. Other popular serif typefaces are Century, Georgia, and Palatino. Serif typefaces suggest tradition, maturity, and formality. They are frequently used for body text in

FIGURE 6.2 Typefaces With Different Personalities for Different Purposes

All-Purpose Sans Serif	Traditional Serif	Happy, Creative Script/Funny	Assertive, Bold Modern Display	Plain Monospaced
Arial	Century	Brush Script	Britannic Bold	Courier
Calibri	Garamond	Comic Sans	Broadway	Letter Gothic
Helvetica	Georgia	Gigi	Elephant	Monaco
Tahoma	Goudy	Jokerman	Impact	Prestige Elite
Univers	Palatino	Lucinda	Bauhaus 93	
Verdana	Times New Roman	Kristen	SHOWCARD	

business messages and longer documents. Because books, newspapers, and magazines favor serif typefaces, readers are familiar with them.

Sans serif typefaces include Arial, Calibri, Helvetica, Tahoma, Univers, and Verdana. These clean characters are widely used for headings, signs, and material that does not require continuous reading. Web designers often prefer sans serif typefaces for simple, pure pages. For longer documents, however, sans serif typefaces may seem colder and less accessible than familiar serif typefaces.

For less formal messages or special decorative effects, you might choose one of the happy fonts such as Comic Sans or a bold typeface such as Impact. You can simulate handwriting with a script typeface. Despite the wonderful possibilities available on your word processor, don't get carried away with fancy typefaces. All-purpose sans serif and traditional serif typefaces are most appropriate for your business messages. Generally, use no more than two typefaces within one document.

Capitalizing on Type Fonts and Sizes

Font refers to a specific style (such as *italic*) within a typeface family (such as Times New Roman). Most typeface families offer various fonts such as CAPITALIZATION, SMALL CAPS, **boldface**, *italic*, and underline, as well as fancier fonts such as outline and shadow.

How can font styles and typeface families be used to emphasize your words?

Font styles are a mechanical means of adding emphasis to your words. ALL CAPS, SMALL CAPS, and **bold** are useful for headings, subheadings, and single words or short phrases in the text. ALL CAPS, HOWEVER, SHOULD NEVER BE USED FOR LONG STRETCHES OF TEXT BECAUSE ALL THE LETTERS ARE THE SAME HEIGHT, MAKING IT DIFFICULT FOR READERS TO DIFFERENTIATE WORDS. In addition, excessive use of all caps feels like shouting and irritates readers. **Boldface,** *italics*, and underlining are effective for calling attention to important points and terms. Be cautious, however, when using fancy or an excessive number of font styles. Don't use them if they will confuse, annoy, or delay readers.

During the revision process, think about type size. Readers are generally most comfortable with 10- to 12-point type for body text. Smaller type enables you to fit more words into a space. Tiny type, however, makes text look dense and unappealing. Slightly larger type makes material more readable. Overly large type (14 points or more), however, looks amateurish and out of place for body text in business messages. Larger type, however, is appropriate for headings.

Numbering and Bulleting Lists for Quick Comprehension

What is "skim value," and how can it be enhanced in business messages?

One of the best ways to ensure rapid comprehension of ideas is through the use of numbered or bulleted lists. Lists provide high "skim value." This means that readers can browse quickly and grasp main ideas. By breaking up complex information into smaller chunks, lists improve readability, understanding, and retention. They also force the writer to organize ideas and write efficiently.

In the revision process, look for ideas that could be converted to lists and follow these techniques to make your lists look professional:

- **Numbered lists:** Use for items that represent a sequence or reflect a numbering system.
- **Bulleted lists:** Use to highlight items that don't necessarily show a chronology.

Spotlight on Communicators

© AP Images/Jennifer Szymaszek

Arthur Levitt, former chair of the U.S. Securities and Exchange Commission, is said to have been the most activist chair in the SEC's history. As a champion of "plain English," he was instrumental in requiring that disclosure documents written for investors be readable. To improve their readability, he advocated using the active voice, familiar words, and graphic techniques. He recommended emphasizing important ideas with boldface, graphics, headings, lists, and color. All of these techniques can vastly improve the readability of any business document.

- **Capitalization:** Capitalize the initial word of each line.
- **Punctuation:** Add end punctuation only if the listed items are complete sentences.
- **Parallelism:** Make all the lines consistent; for example, start each with a verb.

In the following examples, notice that the list on the left presents a sequence of steps with numbers. The bulleted list does not show a sequence of ideas; therefore, bullets are appropriate. Also notice the parallelism in each example. In the numbered list, each item begins with a verb. In the bulleted list, each item follows an adjective/noun sequence. Business readers appreciate lists because they focus attention. Be careful, however, not to use so many that your messages look like grocery lists.

What helps you decide whether to use a bulleted or a numbered list?

Numbered List

Our recruiters follow these steps when hiring applicants:

1. Examine the application.
2. Interview the applicant.
3. Check the applicant's references.

Bulleted List

To attract upscale customers, we feature the following:

- Quality fashions
- Personalized service
- A generous return policy

Should headings be used in business messages other than reports?

Adding Headings for Visual Impact

Headings are an effective tool for highlighting information and improving readability. They encourage the writer to group similar material together. Headings help the reader separate major ideas from details. They enable a busy reader to skim familiar or less important information. They also provide a quick preview or review. Headings appear most often in reports, which you will study in greater detail in Chapters 9 and 10. However, main headings, subheadings, and

Zooming In — PART 2

Taco Bell

The newly hired culinary product manager at Taco Bell has her job cut out for her. Management expects her to anticipate trends in Mexican foods and improve restaurant menus. Part of the challenge is recognizing trends that consumers haven't even picked up yet and then working these trends into restaurant products. In her words, "We want to kick it up a notch, but we still have to deliver to mainstream consumers." She needs to read the market and then create innovative menu ideas. The new chef is eager to incorporate some of the rich, complex flavors of authentic Mexican cuisine. But she must do it in ways that are acceptable to fast-food customers. Although she has excellent culinary references, the new chef has not been trained in communication. She has plenty of ideas to put into a memo or a presentation. Her job now depends on how well she can communicate these ideas to management.

© AP Images/Phil Coale

Critical Thinking

- Based on what you learned in this chapter, what specific advice can you give about keeping a message clear? Should a business message be conversational?
- Why is conciseness important, and what techniques can be used to achieve it?
- Would you advise the culinary chef to be direct with her ideas? What advice can you give for improving the directness and readability of a business message?

category headings can also improve readability in e-mails, memos, and letters. In the following example, they are used with bullets to summarize categories:

Category Headings

Our company focuses on the following areas in the employment process:

- **Attracting applicants.** We advertise for qualified applicants, and we also encourage current employees to recommend good people.
- **Interviewing applicants.** Our specialized interviews include simulated customer encounters as well as scrutiny by supervisors.
- **Checking references.** We investigate every applicant thoroughly. We contact former employers and all listed references.

In Figure 6.3 on page 174, the writer was able to convert a dense, unappealing e-mail message into an easier-to-read version by applying document design. Notice that the all-caps font in the first paragraph makes its meaning difficult to decipher. Justified margins and lack of white space further reduce readability. In the revised version, the writer changed the all-caps font to upper- and lowercase and also used ragged-right margins to enhance visual appeal. One of the best document design techniques in this message is the use of headings and bullets to help the reader see chunks of information in similar groups. All of these improvements are made in the revision process. You can make any message more readable by applying the document design techniques presented here.

ETHICS CHECK

Costly Writing

Bad writing can be expensive: A Philadelphia lawyer was charged with malpractice to the tune of $6.6 million for drafting a poor commercial lease. The judge in Los Angeles said the draft was "inartfully written and done so in a confusing fashion, which lends itself to ambiguities and disagreements." Can you think of other situations in which writing can be deliberately or accidentally misleading and cost money?

Proofreading

LEARNING OBJECTIVE 4

Recognize proofreading problem areas and apply effective techniques to proofread both routine and complex documents.

Once you have the message in its final form, it's time to proofread. Don't proofread earlier because you may waste time checking items that eventually are changed or omitted. Important messages—such as those you send to management or to customers or turn in to instructors for grades—deserve careful revision and proofreading. When you finish a first draft, plan for a cooling-off period. Put the document aside and return to it after a break, preferably after 24 hours or longer. Proofreading is especially difficult because most of us read what we thought we wrote. That's why it's important to look for specific problem areas.

What to Watch for in Proofreading

Careful proofreaders check for problems in the following areas.

- **Spelling.** Now is the time to consult the dictionary. Is *recommend* spelled with one or two *c*'s? Do you mean *affect* or *effect*? Use your computer spell checker, but don't rely on it totally.
- **Grammar.** Locate sentence subjects; do their verbs agree with them? Do pronouns agree with their antecedents? Review the grammar and mechanics principles in Appendix A if necessary. Use your computer's grammar checker, but be suspicious, as explained in the Plugged In box on page 175.
- **Punctuation.** Make sure that introductory clauses are followed by commas. In compound sentences put commas before coordinating conjunctions *(and, or, but, nor)*. Double-check your use of semicolons and colons.
- **Names and numbers.** Compare all names and numbers with their sources because inaccuracies are not always visible. Especially verify the spelling of the names of individuals receiving the message. Most of us immediately dislike someone who misspells our name.
- **Format.** Be sure that your document looks balanced on the page. Compare its parts and format with those of standard documents shown in Appendix B. If you indent paragraphs, be certain that all are indented.

Spotlight on Communicators

Courtesy of The Washington Post Writers Group - www.washpost.com

Pulitzer Prize–winning *Washington Post* columnist William Raspberry frequently promotes the value of language skills in relation to career success: "Misused words, haphazard sentences, failed subject–verb agreement can distract people from our ideas and get them concentrating on our inadequacies. Good English, carefully spoken and written, can open more doors than a college degree. Bad English can slam doors we don't even know about."

FIGURE 6.3 **Using Document Design to Improve E-Mail Readability**

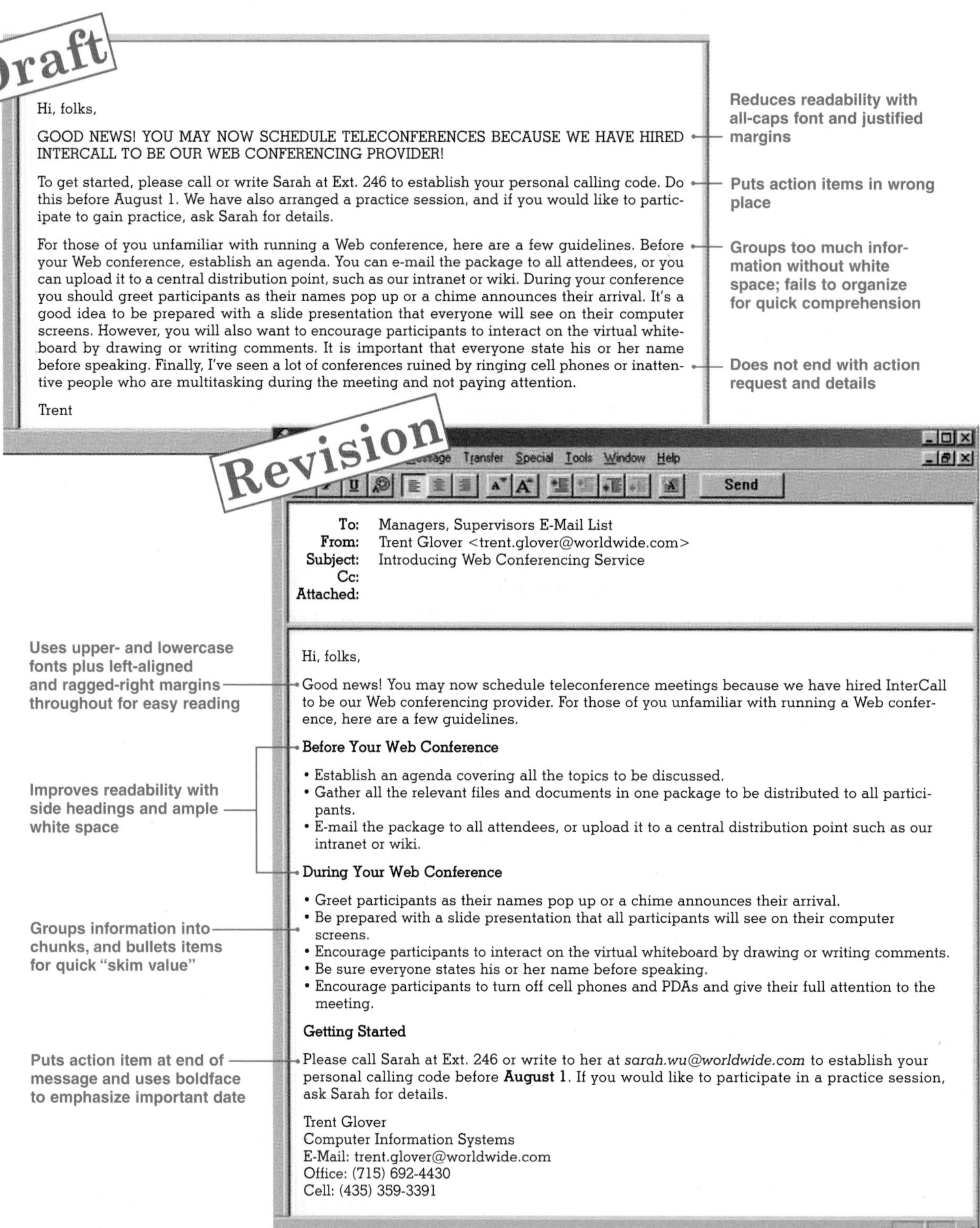

How does proofreading routine documents differ from proofreading complex documents?

How to Proofread Routine Documents

Most routine documents require a light proofreading. If you read on screen, use the down arrow to reveal one line at a time. This focuses your attention at the bottom of the screen. A safer proofreading method, however, is reading from a printed copy. Regardless of which method you use, look for typos and misspellings. Search for easily confused words, such as *to* for *too* and *then* for *than*. Read for missing words and inconsistencies. For handwritten or printed messages, use standard proofreading marks, shown in Figure 6.4, to indicate changes. For digital documents and collaborative projects, use the simple word processing tools shown in Figure 6.1 or use the **Comment** and **Track Changes** functions described in Figure 4.8 on page 129.

How to Proofread Complex Documents

Long, complex, or important documents demand more careful proofreading. Apply the previous suggestions but also add the following techniques:

- Print a copy, preferably double-spaced, and set it aside for at least a day. You will be more alert after a breather.
- Allow adequate time to proofread carefully. A common excuse for sloppy proofreading is lack of time.
- Be prepared to find errors. One student confessed, "I can find other people's errors, but I can't seem to locate my own." Psychologically, we don't expect to find errors, and we don't want to find them. You can overcome this obstacle by anticipating errors and congratulating, not criticizing, yourself each time you find one.
- Read the message at least twice—once for word meanings and once for grammar and mechanics. For very long documents (book chapters and long articles or reports), read a third time to verify consistency in formatting.
- Reduce your reading speed. Concentrate on individual words rather than ideas.
- For documents that must be perfect, enlist a proofreading buddy. Have someone read the message aloud. Spell names and difficult words, note capitalization, and read punctuation.
- Use standard proofreading marks shown in Figure 6.4 to indicate changes.

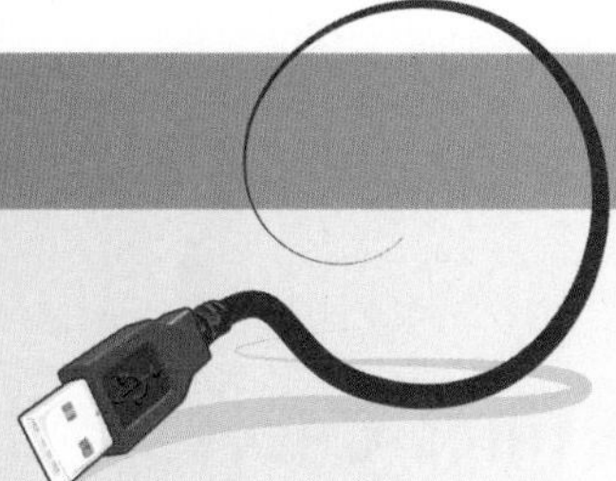

PLUGGED IN

Using Spell Checkers and Grammar/Style Checkers Wisely

Spell-checking and grammar-checking software are two useful tools that can save you from many embarrassing errors. They can also greatly enhance your revision techniques—if you know how to use them wisely.

Spell Checking

Although some writers dismiss spell checkers as an annoyance, most of us are only too happy to have our typos, repeated words, and misspelled words detected. If you are using Microsoft Word 2007, you need to set relevant options. (Click the **MS Office** button, choose **Word Options,** select **Proofing,** and check **Flag repeated words, Check spelling as you type,** and **Use contextual spelling**). When you see a wavy line under a word, you know that the highlighted word may be faulty. Right-click for a list of suggested replacements and other actions. Word 2007 can even detect the misuse of words in context. For example, it usually knows whether *they're, their,* and *there* are being used correctly and may automatically correct errors.

The latest spell checkers are indeed wonderful, but they are far from perfect. When you mistype a word, the spell checker may not be sure what you meant and the suggested replacements may be way off target. What's more, a spell checker cannot know when you type *form* that you meant *from.* Lesson: Don't rely totally on spell checkers to find all typos and spelling errors.

Grammar and Style Checking

Like spell checkers, today's grammar and style checkers are amazingly sophisticated. Microsoft Word marks faults in capitalization, possessives, plurals, punctuation, subject–verb agreement, and gender-specific words as well as misused words, double negatives, fragments, wordiness, and many other problems.

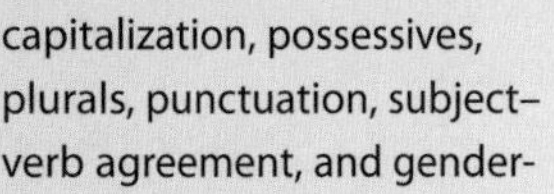

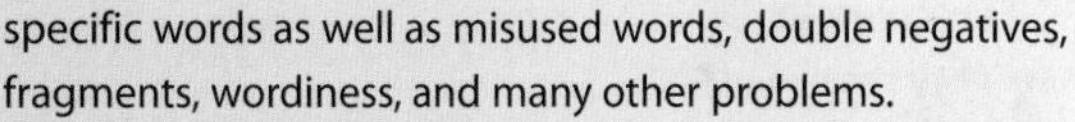

How does a grammar checker work? Say you typed the sentence, *The office and its equipment is for sale.* You would see a wavy line appear under *is.* If you right-click on it, a box identifies the subject–verb agreement error and suggests the verb *are* as a correction. When you click **Change**, the error is corrected. Be sure to set your grammar and style options (**MS Office** button **→ Word Options → Proofing → When correcting spelling and grammar in Word → Settings**). However, before you decide that a grammar checker will solve all your writing problems, think again. Even Word's highly developed software misses plenty of errors, and it also mismarks some correct expressions.

Career Application

Study the spelling and grammar/style settings on your computer. Decide which settings are most useful to you. As you prepare written messages for this class, analyze the suggestions made by your spell checker and grammar checker. For one or two documents, list the spelling, grammar, and style corrections suggested by Word. How many were valid?

FIGURE 6.4 Proofreading Marks

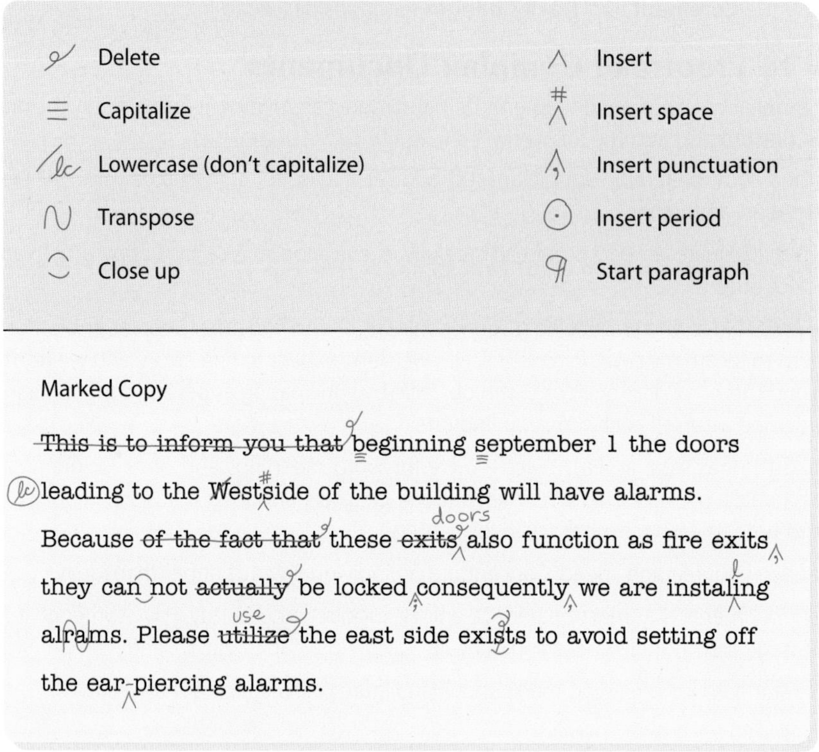

Mark	Meaning	Mark	Meaning
ɚ	Delete	^	Insert
≡	Capitalize	# ^	Insert space
/lc	Lowercase (don't capitalize)	^ with punctuation	Insert punctuation
∩∪	Transpose	⊙	Insert period
⌒ ⌣	Close up	¶	Start paragraph

Marked Copy

~~This is to inform you that~~ beginning september 1 the doors leading to the West side of the building will have alarms. Because ~~of the fact that~~ these ~~exits~~ doors also function as fire exits they can not ~~actually~~ be locked consequently we are instaling alrams. Please ~~utilize~~ use the east side exists to avoid setting off the ear piercing alarms.

Many of us struggle with proofreading our own writing because we are seeing the same information over and over. We tend to see what we expect to see as our eyes race over the words without looking at each one carefully. We tend to know what is coming next and glide over it. To change the appearance of what you are reading, you might print it on a different colored paper or change the font. If you are proofing on screen, enlarge the page view or change the background color of the screen.

ETHICS CHECK

Overly Helpful

Students may visit writing centers where they receive useful advice and help. However, some well-meaning tutors take over, revising documents until they don't resemble the original student work. Instructors worry that the resulting documents amount to cheating. Yet in the workplace today, writers must collaborate, and drafts go through multiple revisions. Individual authorship is often not relevant. How much revision is acceptable in a college setting? How much is acceptable in the workplace?

How to Proofread and Revise PDF Files

As documents are increasingly sent as PDF (portable document format) files, business writers are learning to proof without a pen. "Soft proofing" involves using Adobe Acrobat markup tools. The advantages of soft proofing include enabling collaborators in distant locales to proof each other's work electronically and saving days of time in sending hard-copy proofs back and forth. Corrections and edits can be transferred electronically among authors, editors, proofreaders, and typesetters—and then on to the printer without pen ever touching paper. The disadvantages of soft proofing include tired eyes, especially if you are working on long documents, and the fear of losing your work because of a computer crash.

Adobe Acrobat Pro and Standard provide a rich array of tools that can make markup and work flow fairly intuitive. You can insert, replace, highlight, delete, or underline material as well as add notes, all with an insertion point that looks like that used in traditional proofreading, as shown in Figure 6.5. Adobe Acrobat enables you to add comment easily, but the markup tools require practice to use effectively. You can even make your own proofreading marks using the **Create Custom Stamp** feature.

Evaluating

LEARNING OBJECTIVE 5

Evaluate a message to judge its success.

As part of applying finishing touches, take a moment to evaluate your writing. Remember that everything you write, whether for yourself for someone else, takes the place of a personal appearance. If you were meeting in person, you would be certain to dress appropriately and professionally. The same standard applies to your writing. Evaluate what

FIGURE 6.5 Proofreading and Marking PDF Files

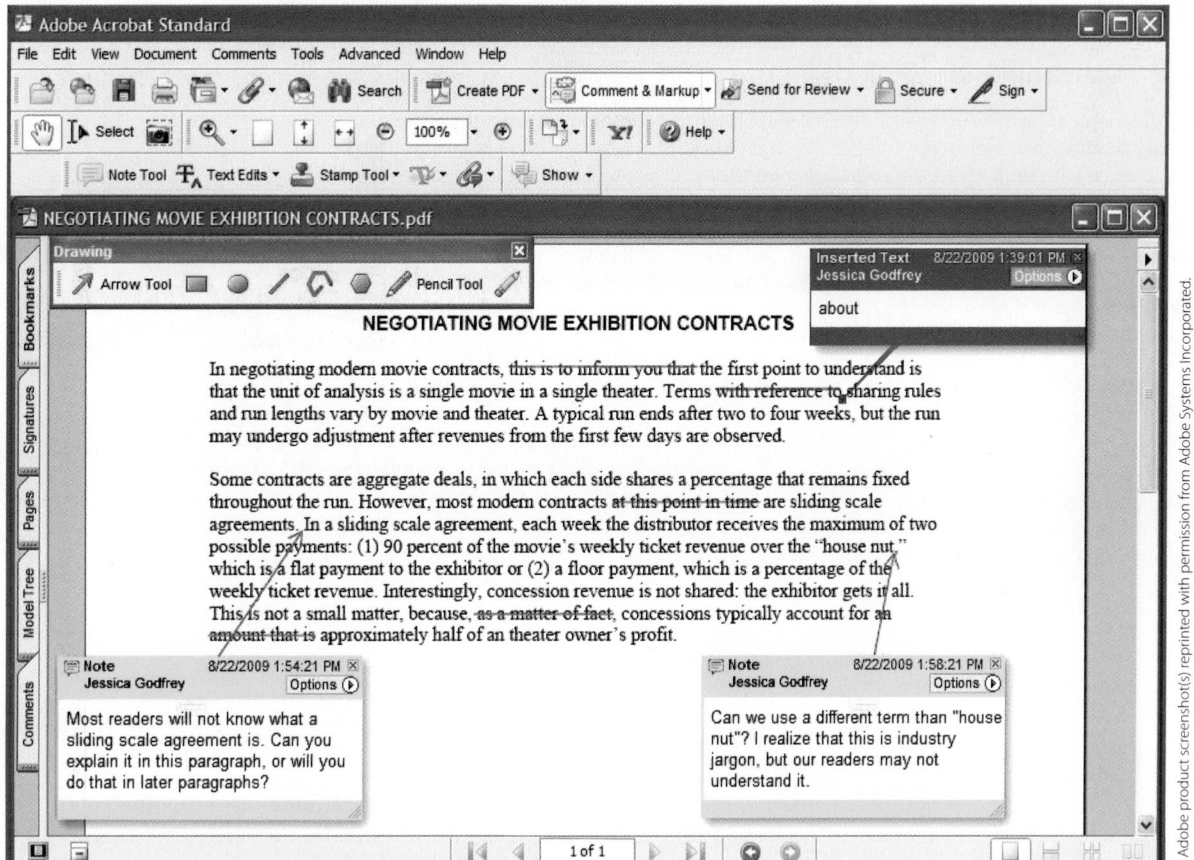

You may proofread and edit PDF files by using Adobe Acrobat software that allows you to insert, replace, highlight, delete, and underline material as well as add notes.

Checklist

Proofreading, Revising, and Evaluating

- **Eliminate flabby expressions.** Strive to reduce wordy phrases to single words (*as a general rule* becomes *generally*; *at this point in time* becomes *now*).
- **Avoid opening fillers and long lead-ins.** Revise sentences so that they don't start with fillers (*there is, there are, it is, it was*) and long lead-ins (*this is to inform you that*).
- **Shun redundancies.** Eliminate words that repeat meanings, such as *refer back.* Watch for repetitious adjectives, adverbs, and phrases.
- **Tighten your writing.** Check phrases that include *case, degree, the fact that, factor*, and other words and phrases that unnecessarily increase wordiness. Avoid saying the obvious.
- **Keep the message simple.** Express ideas directly. Don't show off or use fancy language.
- **Avoid trite business phrases.** Keep your writing fresh, direct, and contemporary by skipping such expressions as *enclosed please find* and *pursuant to your request*.
- **Don't use clichés or slang.** Avoid expressions that are overused and unclear (*below the belt, shoot from the hip*). Don't use slang, which is not only unprofessional but also often unclear to a wide audience.
- **Unbury verbs.** Keep your writing vigorous by not converting verbs to nouns ((*analyze* not *make an analysis of).*
- **Control exuberance.** Avoid overusing intensifiers such as *really, very, definitely, quite, completely, extremely, actually,* and *totally.*
- **Improve readability through document design.** Use bullets, lists, headings, capital letters, underlining, boldface, italics, and blank space to spotlight ideas and organization.
- **Proofread for correctness.** Check spelling, grammar, and punctuation. Compare names and numbers with their sources. Double-check the format to be sure you have been consistent.
- **Evaluate your final product.** Will your message achieve its purpose? Could it be improved? How will you know whether it is successful?

Zooming In — YOUR TURN

Applying Your Skills at Taco Bell

Upgrading the menu at Taco Bell is an exciting challenge for the new culinary product manager. In response to management's request, she comes up with terrific ideas for capitalizing on eating trends and converting them to mainstream tastes. She has been asked to submit a memo summarizing her longer report, which will be presented at a management meeting next week.

Although the new culinary product manager has exceptional talent in cuisine, she realizes that her writing skills are not as well developed as her cooking skills. She comes to the corporate communication department and shows your boss the first draft of her memo. Your boss is a nice guy; and, as a favor, he revises the first two paragraphs, as shown in Figure 6.6.

Your Task

Your boss, the head of corporate communication, has many important tasks to oversee. He hands the product manager's memo to you, his assistant, and tells you to finish cleaning it up. He adds, "Her ideas are right on target, but the main points are totally lost in wordy sentences and solid paragraphs. Revise this and concentrate on conciseness, clarity, and readability. Don't you think some bulleted lists would help this memo a lot?" Revise the remaining four paragraphs of the memo using the techniques you learned in this chapter. Prepare a copy of the complete memo to submit to your boss (your instructor).

you have written to be certain that it attracts the reader's attention. Is it polished and clear enough to convince the reader that you are worth listening to? How successful will this message be? Does it say what you want it to? Will it achieve your purpose? How will you know whether it succeeds?

How is feedback helpful in evaluating the effectiveness of a message?

As you learned in Chapter 1, the best way to judge the success of your communication is through feedback. For this reason you should encourage the receiver to respond to your message. This feedback will tell you how to modify future efforts to improve your communication technique.

Your instructor will also be evaluating some of your writing. Although any criticism is painful, try not to be defensive. Look on these comments as valuable advice tailored to your specific writing weaknesses—and strengths. Many businesses today spend thousands of dollars bringing in communication consultants to improve employee writing skills. You are getting the same training in this course. Take advantage of this chance—one of the few you may have—to improve your skills. The best way to improve your skills, of course, is through instruction, practice, and evaluation.

In this class you have all three elements: instruction in the writing process, practice materials, and someone to guide and evaluate your efforts. Those three elements are the reasons this book and this course may be the most valuable in your entire curriculum. Because it's almost impossible to improve your communication skills alone, take advantage of this opportunity.

The task of revising, proofreading, and evaluating, summarized in the checklist on the preceding page, is hard work. It demands objectivity and a willingness to cut, cut, cut. Though painful, the process is also gratifying. It's a great feeling when you realize your finished message is clear, concise, and effective.

Want to do well on tests and excel in your course? Go to **www.meguffey.com** for helpful interactive resources.

- **Review the Chapter 6 PowerPoint slides to prepare for the first quiz.**

FIGURE 6.6 Partially Revised First Draft

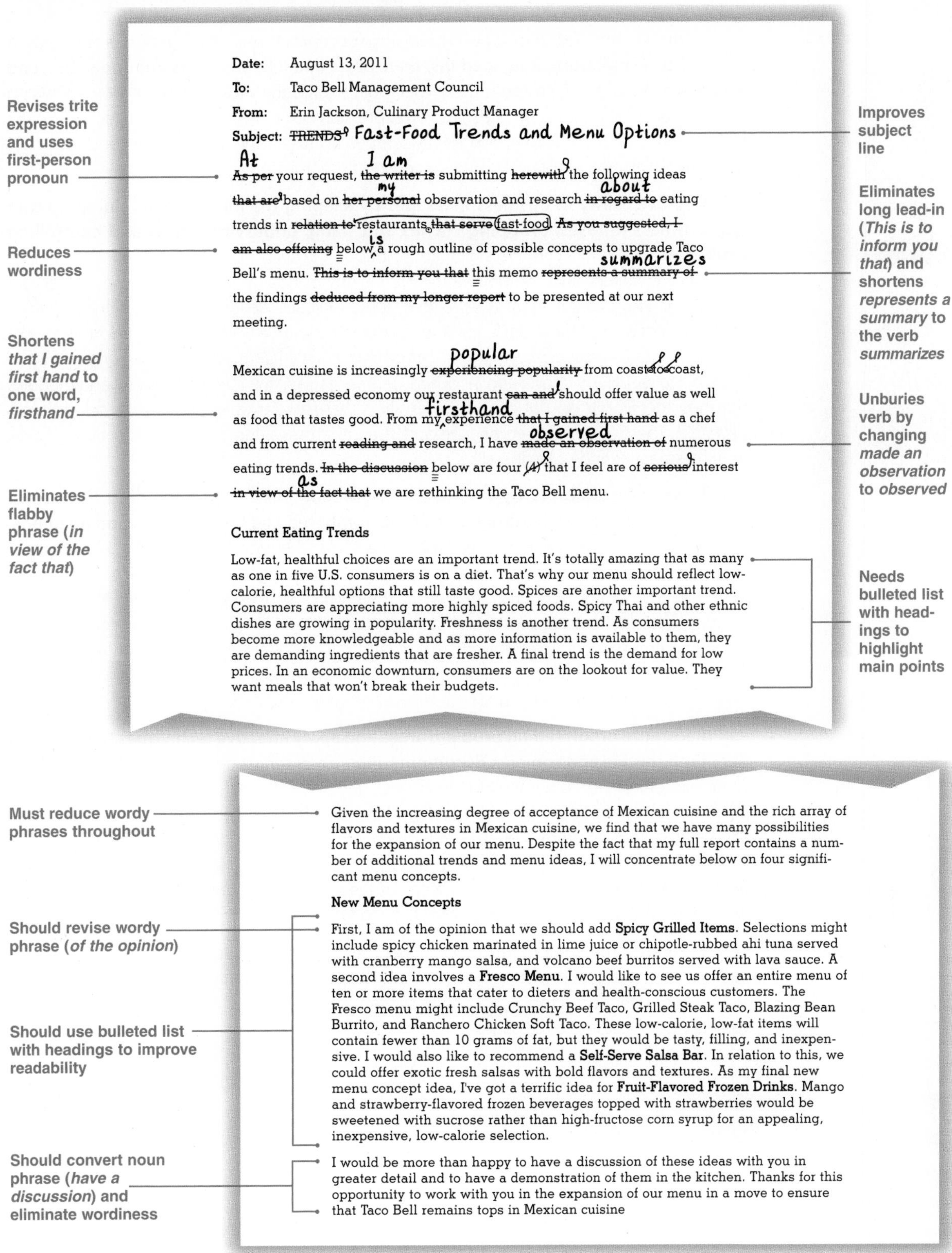

Date: August 13, 2011

To: Taco Bell Management Council

From: Erin Jackson, Culinary Product Manager

Subject: ~~TRENDS~~ Fast-Food Trends and Menu Options

~~As per~~ At your request, ~~the writer is~~ I am submitting ~~herewith~~ the following ideas ~~that are~~ based on ~~her personal~~ my observation and research ~~in regard to~~ about eating trends in ~~relation to~~ restaurants ~~that serve~~ fast-food. ~~As you suggested, I am also offering~~ below is a rough outline of possible concepts to upgrade Taco Bell's menu. ~~This is to inform you that~~ this memo ~~represents a summary of~~ summarizes the findings ~~deduced from my longer report~~ to be presented at our next meeting.

Mexican cuisine is increasingly ~~experiencing popularity~~ popular from coast ~~to~~ coast, and in a depressed economy our restaurant ~~can and~~ should offer value as well as food that tastes good. From my firsthand experience ~~that I gained first hand~~ as a chef and from current ~~reading and~~ research, I have ~~made an observation of~~ observed numerous eating trends. ~~In the discussion~~ below are four ~~(4)~~ that I feel are of ~~serious~~ interest ~~in view of the fact that~~ as we are rethinking the Taco Bell menu.

Current Eating Trends

Low-fat, healthful choices are an important trend. It's totally amazing that as many as one in five U.S. consumers is on a diet. That's why our menu should reflect low-calorie, healthful options that still taste good. Spices are another important trend. Consumers are appreciating more highly spiced foods. Spicy Thai and other ethnic dishes are growing in popularity. Freshness is another trend. As consumers become more knowledgeable and as more information is available to them, they are demanding ingredients that are fresher. A final trend is the demand for low prices. In an economic downturn, consumers are on the lookout for value. They want meals that won't break their budgets.

Given the increasing degree of acceptance of Mexican cuisine and the rich array of flavors and textures in Mexican cuisine, we find that we have many possibilities for the expansion of our menu. Despite the fact that my full report contains a number of additional trends and menu ideas, I will concentrate below on four significant menu concepts.

New Menu Concepts

First, I am of the opinion that we should add **Spicy Grilled Items**. Selections might include spicy chicken marinated in lime juice or chipotle-rubbed ahi tuna served with cranberry mango salsa, and volcano beef burritos served with lava sauce. A second idea involves a **Fresco Menu**. I would like to see us offer an entire menu of ten or more items that cater to dieters and health-conscious customers. The Fresco menu might include Crunchy Beef Taco, Grilled Steak Taco, Blazing Bean Burrito, and Ranchero Chicken Soft Taco. These low-calorie, low-fat items will contain fewer than 10 grams of fat, but they would be tasty, filling, and inexpensive. I would also like to recommend a **Self-Serve Salsa Bar**. In relation to this, we could offer exotic fresh salsas with bold flavors and textures. As my final new menu concept idea, I've got a terrific idea for **Fruit-Flavored Frozen Drinks**. Mango and strawberry-flavored frozen beverages topped with strawberries would be sweetened with sucrose rather than high-fructose corn syrup for an appealing, inexpensive, low-calorie selection.

I would be more than happy to have a discussion of these ideas with you in greater detail and to have a demonstration of them in the kitchen. Thanks for this opportunity to work with you in the expansion of our menu in a move to ensure that Taco Bell remains tops in Mexican cuisine

Revises trite expression and uses first-person pronoun
Reduces wordiness
Shortens *that I gained first hand* to one word, *firsthand*
Eliminates flabby phrase (*in view of the fact that*)
Improves subject line
Eliminates long lead-in (*This is to inform you that*) and shortens *represents a summary* to the verb *summarizes*
Unburies verb by changing *made an observation* to *observed*
Needs bulleted list with headings to highlight main points
Must reduce wordy phrases throughout
Should revise wordy phrase (*of the opinion*)
Should use bulleted list with headings to improve readability
Should convert noun phrase (*have a discussion*) and eliminate wordiness

Summary of Learning Objectives

1 Complete business messages by revising for conciseness, which includes eliminating flabby expressions, long lead-ins, *there is/are* and *it is/was* fillers, redundancies, and empty words. Concise messages make their points using the least number of words. Revising for conciseness involves eliminating flabby expressions (*as a general rule, at a later date, at this point in time*). Concise writing also excludes opening fillers *(there is, there are)*, redundancies *(basic essentials)*, and empty words (*in the case of, the fact that).*

2 Improve clarity in business messages by keeping the ideas simple, dumping trite business phrases, dropping clichés and slang, unburying verbs, and controlling exuberance. To be sure your messages are clear, apply the KISS formula: Keep It Short and Simple. Avoid foggy, indirect, and pompous language. Do not include trite business phrases (*as per your request, enclosed please fine, pursuant to your request*), clichés (*better than new, beyond a shadow of a doubt, easier said than done*), and slang (*snarky, lousy, bombed).* Also avoid transforming verbs into nouns (*to conduct an investigation* rather than *to investigate, to perform an analysis* rather than *to analyze*). Noun conversion lengthens sentences, saps the force of the verb, and muddies the message. Finally, do not overuse intensifiers that show exuberance (*totally, actually, very, definitely*). These words can emphasize and strengthen meaning, but overusing them makes your messages sound unbusinesslike.

3 Enhance readability by understanding document design including the use of white space, margins, typefaces, fonts, numbered and bulleted lists, and headings. Well-designed messages enhance readability and comprehension. The most readable messages have ample white space, appropriate side margins, and ragged-right (not justified) margins. Serif typefaces (fonts with small features at the ends of strokes, such as Times New Roman, Century, and Palatino) are most used for body text. Sans serif typefaces (clean fonts without small features, such as Arial, Helvetica, and Tahoma) are often used for headings and signs. Numbered and bulleted lists provide high "skim value" in messages. Headings add visual impact and aid readability in business messages as well as in reports.

4 Recognize proofreading problem areas and apply effective techniques to proofread both routine and complex documents. Proofreaders must be especially alert to spelling, grammar, punctuation, names, numbers, and document format. Routine documents may be proofread immediately after completion. They may be read line by line on the computer screen or, better yet, from a printed draft copy. More complex documents, however, should be proofread after a breather. To do a good job, you must read from a printed copy, allow adequate time, reduce your reading speed, and read the document at least three times—for word meanings, for grammar and mechanics, and for formatting.

5 Evaluate a message to judge its success. Encourage feedback from the receiver so that you can determine whether your communication achieved its goal. Try to welcome any advice from your instructor on how to improve your writing skills. Both techniques help you evaluate the success of a message.

Chapter Review

1. How is proofreading different from revising? (Objs. 1, 4)
2. Why should business writers strive for conciseness? (Obj. 1)
3. What's wrong with expressions such as *due to the fact that* and *in view of the fact that*? (Obj. 1)
4. What is a redundancy? Give an example. Why should writers avoid redundancies? (Obj. 1)
5. Why should a writer avoid the opening *I am sending this e-mail because we have just hired a new manager, and I would like to introduce her*? (Obj. 1)
6. Why should writers avoid opening a sentence with *There is* or *There are*? (Obj. 1)
7. What is a buried verb? Give an original example. Why should they be avoided? (Obj. 2)
8. Why would a good writer avoid this sentence? *When it arrived, I read your message and am now replying.* (Obj. 2)
9. What are five document design techniques that business writers can use to enhance readability? (Obj. 3)

Are you ready? Get more practice at **www.meguffey.com**

10. How can writers increase white space to improve readability? (Obj. 3)
11. What is the difference between serif and sans serif typefaces? What is the preferred use for each? (Obj. 3)
12. What are five specific items to check in proofreading? Be ready to discuss methods you find useful in spotting these errors. (Obj. 4)
13. In proofreading, why is it difficult to find your own errors? How can you overcome this barrier? (Obj. 4)
14. List four or more effective techniques for proofreading complex documents. (Obj. 4)
15. How can you overcome defensiveness when your writing is criticized constructively? (Obj. 5)

Critical Thinking

1. Is the revision and proofreading process different for short and long documents? Can you skip revising if your message is brief? (Objs. 1, 4)
2. Would you agree or disagree with the following statement by writing expert William Zinsser? "Plain talk will not be easily achieved in corporate America. Too much vanity is on the line." (Objs. 1–5)
3. Because business writing should have high "skim value," why not write everything in bulleted lists? (Obj. 3)
4. Conciseness is valued in business. However, can messages be too short? (Obj. 1)
5. **Ethical Issue:** What advice would you give in this ethical dilemma? Becky is serving as interim editor of the company newsletter. She receives an article written by the company president describing, in abstract and pompous language, the company's goals for the coming year. Becky thinks the article will need considerable revising to make it readable. Attached to the president's article are complimentary comments by two of the company vice presidents. What action should Becky take?

Writing Improvement Exercises

6.1 Flabby Expressions (Obj. 1)

Your Task. Revise the following sentences to eliminate flabby expressions.

a. Despite the fact that we lost the contract, we must at this time move forward.
b. Inasmuch as prices are falling, we will invest in the very near future.
c. We cannot fill the order until such time as payment is received for previous shipments.
d. As a general rule, we would not accept the return; however, we will in all probability make an exception in this case.

6.2 Long Lead-Ins (Obj. 1)

Your Task. Revise the following to eliminate long lead-ins.

a. This message is to let you know that I received your e-mail and its attachments.
b. This memo is to notify everyone that we will observe Monday as a holiday.
c. I am writing this letter to inform you that your homeowner's coverage expires soon.
d. This is to warn everyone that the loss of laptops endangers company security.

6.3 *There is/are* and *It is/was* Fillers (Obj. 1)

Your Task. Revise the following to avoid unnecessary *there is/are* and *it is/was* fillers.

a. There are many businesses that are implementing strict e-mail policies.
b. It is the CEO who must approve the plan.
c. There are several Web pages you must update.
d. The manager says that there are many employees who did not return the health surveys.

6.4 Redundancies (Obj. 1)

Your Task. Revise the following to avoid redundancies.

a. Because the proposals are exactly identical, we need not check each and every item.
b. All requests for iPods and BlackBerrys were combined together in our proposal.
c. The office walls were painted beige in color.
d. Our supervisor requested that team members return back to the office.

6.5 Empty Words (Obj. 1)

Your Task. Revise the following to eliminate empty words and saying the obvious.

a. He scheduled the meeting for 11 a.m. in the morning.
b. Because of the surprising degree of response, the company expanded its free gift program.
c. I have before me your proposal sent by FedEx, and I will distribute it immediately.
d. Are you aware of the fact that our budget has a deficit in the amount of approximately $100,000?

6.6 Trite Business Phrases (Obj. 2)

Your Task. Revise the following sentences to eliminate trite business phrases.

a. As per your request, we will no longer send you e-mail offers.
b. Thank you in advance for considering our plea for community support.
c. Pursuant to your request, we are sending the original copies under separate cover.
d. Enclosed please find a check in the amount of $700.

6.7 Clichés, Slang, and Wordiness (Obj. 2)

Your Task. Revise the following sentences to avoid confusing slang, clichés, and wordiness.

a. Although our last presentation bombed, we think that beyond the shadow of a doubt our new presentation will fly.
b. Our team must be willing to think outside the box in coming up with marketing ideas that pop.
c. True to form, our competitor has made a snarky claim that we think is way below the belt.

d. If you will refer back to the budget, you will see that there are provisions that prevent blowing the budget.

6.8 Buried Verbs (Obj. 2)

Your Task. Revise the following to unbury the verbs.

a. Ms. Nelson gave an appraisal of the home's value.
b. Web-based customer service causes a reduction in overall costs.
c. Management made a recommendation affirming abandonment of the pilot project.
d. The board of directors will give consideration to the contract at its next meeting.

6.9 Lists, Bullets, and Headings (Obj. 3)

a. Use the information in the following dense paragraph to compose a concise, easy-to-read bulleted vertical list with an introductory statement.

   Here at SecurityPlus we specialize in preemployment background reports, which we describe in the following. Among our preemployment background reports are ones that include professional reference interviews, criminal reports, driving records, employment verification, and credit information.

b. Create an introduction and a list from the following wordy paragraph.

   A high-powered MBA program costs hundreds of dollars an hour. Our program covers the same information. That information includes how to start a business. You will also learn information about writing a business plan and understanding taxes. In addition, our MBA program covers how to go about writing a marketing feasibility study. Another topic that students cover in our program is employment benefits plans and licensing requirements.

c. From the following wordy paragraph, create a concise bulleted list with category headings.

   This is to inform you that our on-site GuruGeek computer technicians can provide you with fast, affordable solutions to residential and also to small business clients. Our most popular offerings include antivirus security. This service involves having our GuruGeek protect your computer against viruses, worms, and spyware as well as help you avoid e-mail attacks, identity theft, and malicious hacker programs. Our wireless networking service enables you to share Internet access through a single wireless router so that many computer users use one network at the same time. They are all using the same network. Another popular service is data backup and recovery. Our technicians focus on helping small businesses and home users protect their data without making an investment of a lot of time and energy.

Activities

Note: All Documents for Analysis may be downloaded from **www.meguffey.com** so that you do not have to rekey the entire message.

6.10 Document for Analysis: Ineffective Customer Letter (Objs. 1–5)

Your Task. Study the following message. In teams or in class discussion, list at least five specific weaknesses. If your instructor directs, revise to remedy flabby expressions, long lead-ins, *there is/are* fillers, trite business expressions, clichés, slang, buried verbs, lack of parallelism, and general wordiness. Look for ways to improve readability with bulleted or numbered points.

Current date

Mr. Michael Chatham
329 Sycamore Street
Pikeville, KY 41605

Dear Mr. Chatham:

This is to inform you that we are changing your World Bank Credit Card Agreement. These changes will be effective for all billing periods that will be beginning on or after the date of February 3.

First, we want to tell you about the change in how the calculation of your APR is done. We are increasing your variable APR (annual percentage rate) for purchases. Your APR will be exactly identical to the U.S. prime rate plus 10.99 percent with a minimum APR of 16.99 percent.

Second, we must make an explanation of how the default APR will change. All of your APRs on all balances may automatically increase to the default APR in the event that you default under any card agreement you have with us because for either of the two following reasons: You do not make the minimum payment when due. You make a payment to us that is not honored.

The default APR takes effect as of the first day of the billing period in which you default. However, every effort will be made to lower the APR for new purchases or cash advances if you are able to meet the terms of all card agreements that you have with us for six billing periods.

To Opt Out
To opt out of these changes, call or write us by the date of March 31. It is absolutely essential for you to include your name, address, and account number in the letter that you write. Should you decide to opt out of these changes, you may use your account under the current terms until the ultimate end of your current membership year or the expiration date on your card. We will close your account at that point in time. You must then repay the balance under the current terms.

Please do not hesitate to take advantage of your World Card revolving line of credit and all the benefits and services we offer you.

Sincerely,

6.11 Document for Analysis: Poorly Written E-Mail Message (Objs. 1–5)

Your Task. Study the following message. In teams or in class discussion, list at least five specific weaknesses. If your instructor directs, revise to remedy flabby expressions, long lead-ins, *there is/are* fillers, trite business expressions, clichés, slang, buried verbs, lack of parallelism, and general wordiness. Look for ways to improve readability with bulleted or numbered points.

To: Marcy Love <marcy.love@sokia.com>
From: Shelton Matthews <shelton.matthews@sokia.com>
Subject: Improving Presentation Techniques
Cc:

Marcy,

I am writing this message because, pursuant to your request, I attended a seminar about the use of PowerPoint in business presentations. You suggested that there might be tips that I would learn that we could share with other staff members, many of whom make presentations that almost always include PowerPoint. The speaker, Gary Dixon, made some very good points on the subject of PowerPoint. There were several points of an important nature that are useful in avoiding what he called a "PowerPoint slumber party." Our staff members should give consideration to the following:

Create first the message, not the slide. Only after preparing the entire script should you think about how to make an illustration of it.

You should prepare slides with short lines. Your slides should have only four to six words per line. Short lines act as an encouragement to people to listen to you and not read the slide.

Don't put each and every thing on the slide. If you put too much on the slide, your audience will be reading Item C while you are still talking about Item A. As a last and final point, she suggested that presenters think in terms of headlines. What is the main point? What does it mean to the audience?

Please let me know whether you want me to elaborate and expand on these presentation techniques subsequent to the next staff meeting.

Shelton

6.12 Document for Analysis: Poorly Written Response Letter (Objs. 1–5)

Your Task. Study the following message. In teams or in class discussion, list at least five specific weaknesses. If your instructor directs, revise to remedy flabby expressions, long lead-ins, *there is/are* fillers, trite business expressions, clichés, slang, buried verbs, lack of parallelism, and general wordiness. Look for ways to improve readability with bulleted or numbered points.

Current date

Mr. DeJuan Wilson
Fairfield Associates, Inc.
4290 Park Avenue
Fairfield, CT 06435

Dear Mr. Wilson:

We have received your request for information. As per your request, the undersigned is transmitting to you the attached documents with regard to the improvement of security in your business. To ensure the improvement of your after-hours security, you should initially make a decision with regard to exactly what you contemplate must have protection. You are, in all probability, apprehensive not only about your electronic equipment and paraphernalia but also about your company records, information, and data.

Due to the fact that we feel you will want to obtain protection for both your equipment and data, we will make suggestions for taking a number of judicious steps to inhibit crime. First and foremost, we make a recommendation that you install defensive lighting. A consultant for lighting, currently on our staff, can design both outside and inside lighting, which brings me to my second point. Exhibit security signs, because of the fact that nonprofessional thieves are often as not deterred by posted signs on windows and doors.

As my last and final recommendation, you should install space alarms, which are sensors that look down over the areas that are to receive protection, and activate bells or additional lights, thus scaring off intruders.

After reading the materials that are attached, please call me to initiate a verbal discussion regarding protection of your business.

Sincerely,

6.13 Document for Analysis: Poorly Written Customer Letter (Objs. 1–5)

Your Task. Study the following message. In teams or in class discussion, list at least five specific weaknesses. If your instructor directs, revise to remedy flabby expressions, long lead-ins, *there is/are* fillers, trite business expressions, clichés, slang, buried verbs, lack of parallelism, and general wordiness. Look for ways to improve readability with bulleted or numbered points.

Current date

Ms. Monique Faria
Grey Wolf BioSolutions
4210 Geddes Road
Ann Arbor, MI 48105

Dear Ms. Faria:

This message is an opportunity to thank you for your interest in employee leasing through Enterprise Staffing Services. Small businesses like yours can, at this point in time, enjoy powerful personnel tools previously available only to firms that were larger.

The employee leasing concept allows you to outsource personnel duties so that you can focus on the basic fundamentals of running your business. There are many administrative burdens that you can reduce such as monthly payroll, quarterly taxes, and records related to personnel matters. There is also expert guidance available in the areas of human resources, compliance, and matters of a safety nature. In view of the fact that we have extensive experience, your employer liability can be reduced by a significant degree. You can be assured that the undersigned, as well as our entire staff, will assemble together a plan that will save you time and money as well as protect you from employee hassles and employer liability.

Whether or not you offer no benefits or a full benefits package, Enterprise Staffing Services can make an analysis of your needs and help you return back to the basics of running your business and improvement in profits. Please allow me to call you to arrange a time to meet and talk about your specific needs.

Cordially,

6.14 Learning About Writing Techniques in Your Field (Objs. 1–5)

How much writing is required by people working in your career area? The best way to learn about on-the-job writing is to talk with someone who has a job similar to the one you hope to have one day.

Your Task. Interview someone working in your field of study. Your instructor may ask you to present your findings orally or in a written report. Ask questions such as these: *What kind of writing do you do? What kind of planning do you do before writing? Where do you get information? Do you brainstorm? Make lists? Do you compose with pen and paper, a computer, or a dictating machine? How many e-mail messages do you typically write in a day? How long does it take you to compose a routine one- or two-page memo or letter? Do you revise? How often? Do you have a preferred method for proofreading? When you have questions about grammar and mechanics, what or whom do you consult? Does anyone read your drafts and make suggestions? Can you describe your entire composition process? Do you ever work with others to produce a document? How does this process work? What makes writing easier or harder for you? Have your writing methods and skills changed since you left school?*

6.15 Searching for Deadwood (Objs. 1, 2)

Team | Web

Many writers and speakers are unaware of "deadwood" phrases they use. Some of these are flabby expressions, redundancies, or trite business phrases.

Your Task. Using your favorite Web browser, locate two or three sites devoted to deadwood phrases. Your instructor may ask you to (a) submit a list of ten deadwood phrases (and their preferred substitutes) not mentioned in this textbook, or (b) work in teams to prepare a comprehensive "Dictionary of Deadwood Phrases," including as many as you can find. Be sure to include a preferred substitute.

6.16 Conciseness Is Hard Work (Objs. 1, 2)

Just as most people are unmotivated to read wordy documents, most are unmotivated to listen to wordy speakers. Effective communicators work to eliminate "rambling" in both their written and spoken words.

Abraham Lincoln expressed the relationship between conciseness and hard work with his reply to the question, "How long does it take you to prepare a speech?" "Two weeks for a 20-minute speech," he replied. "One week for a 40-minute speech; and I can give a rambling, two-hour talk right now." Rambling takes little thought and effort; conciseness takes a great deal of both.

Your Task. For a 24-hour period, think about conciseness violations in spoken words. Consider violations in five areas you studied in this chapter: (a) fillers, (b) long lead-ins, (c) redundancies, (d) buried verbs, and (e) empty words. Identify the source of the violation using descriptors such as *friend, family member, coworker, boss, instructor, actor in TV sitcom, interviewer or interviewee on a radio or TV talk show*, and so forth. Include the communication medium for each example (telephone, conversation, radio, television, etc.). Be prepared to share the results of this activity during a class discussion.

6.17 Communicating With a Nonnative English Speaker

Intercultural | Web

In the three chapters devoted to the writing process, most of the advice focuses on communicating clearly and concisely. As the world becomes more globally connected, businesspeople may be increasingly communicating with nonnative speakers and writers. Assume that you have been asked to present a talk to businesspeople in your area. What additional advice would you give to speakers and writers in communicating with nonnative English speakers?

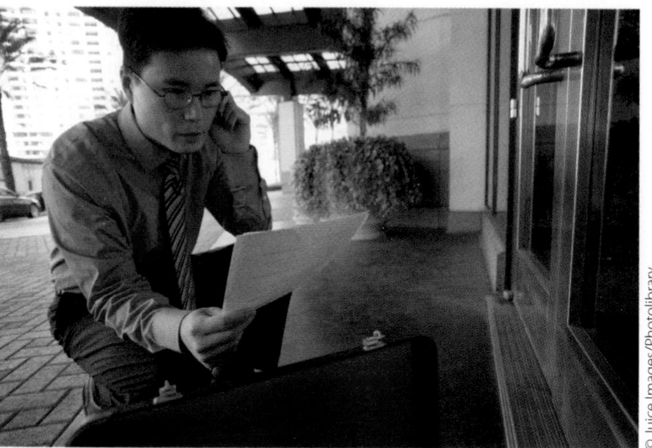

Your Task. Search the Web for advice in communicating with nonnative English speakers. Prepare a list of ten significant suggestions.

6.18 How Plain Is the English in Your Apartment Lease? (Objs. 1–3)

E-mail | Ethics | Team

Have you read your apartment lease carefully? Did you understand it? Many students—and their friends and family members—are intimidated, frustrated, or just plain lost when they try to comprehend an apartment lease.

Your Task. Locate an apartment lease—yours, a friend's, or a family member's. In teams, analyze its format and readability. What size is the paper? How large are the margins? Is the type large or small? How much white space appears on the page? Are paragraphs and sentences long or short? Does the lease contain legalese or obscure language? What makes it difficult to understand? In an e-mail message to your instructor, summarize your team's reaction to the lease. Your instructor may ask you to revise sections or the entire lease to make it more readable. In class, discuss how ethical it is for an apartment owner to expect a renter to read and comprehend a lease while sitting in the rental office.

Video Resource

Video Library 2, Writing Skills: The Little Guys

The Little Guys Home Electronics specializes in selling and installing home theater equipment. In just 12 years, it has grown from a start-up company to an established business with annual sales of more than $10 million. The owners—Dave and Evie Wexler and Paul Gerrity—describe their goals, motivations, and experiences in making their business successful. As you watch this video, look for (a) good business practices that helped the owners launch a successful business, (b) characteristics of successful entrepreneurs, and (c) reasons some small businesses remain successful whereas others fail.

Your Task. After watching the video, assume that you have been asked to summarize reasons for the success of The Little Guys. Building on what you have learned in this writing process chapter, compose a bulleted list with ten or more items. Use this opening sentence: *The Little Guys Home Electronics business succeeded because the owners did the following.*

Chat About It

In each chapter you will find five discussion questions related to the chapter material. Your instructor may assign these topics for you to discuss in class, in an online chat room, or on an online discussion board. Some of the discussion topics may require outside research. You may also be asked to read and respond to postings made by your classmates.

Topic 1: When you tackle a serious writing project, do you prefer freewriting, in which you rapidly record your thoughts, or do you prefer to polish and revise as you go? What are the advantages and disadvantages of each method for you? Do you use the same method for both short and long messages?

Topic 2: Think about your own speaking and writing. Do you recognize some favorite redundancies that you use in spoken or written messages? When did you realize that you could be more concise and precise by eliminating these expressions?

Topic 3: The default font in Microsoft Word used to be Times New Roman, a serif typeface. With Word 2007, the new default font is Calibri, a sans serif typeface. Why do you think Microsoft made the switch? In your opinion, is Calibri more readable than Times New Roman in printed documents, documents displayed on a computer screen, both, or neither?

Topic 4: What proofreading tasks can you safely ask a proofreading buddy to perform? What if that person is not a skilled writer?

Topic 5: Are you a good proofreader? Is it easier to find other people's errors than your own? Why? What are you good at finding? What do you frequently miss?

Grammar and Mechanics C.L.U.E. Review 6

Semicolons, Colons

Review Guides 27–30 about semicolons and colons in Appendix A, Grammar and Mechanics Guide, beginning on page A-12. On a separate sheet, revise the following sentences to correct errors in semicolon and colon usage. Do not start new sentences. For each error that you locate, write the guide number that reflects this usage. The more you recognize the reasons, the better you will learn these punctuation guidelines. If a sentence is correct, write *C*. When you finish, check your answers on page Key-1.

Example: Companies find it difficult to name new products consequently they often hire specialists.
Revision: Companies find it difficult to name new products; consequently, they often hire specialists. [Guide 27]

1. Successful product names may appear to have been named by magic, however the naming process is methodical and deliberate.
2. Choosing the right name and tagline is critical consequently companies are eager to hire specialists.
3. Naming is a costly endeavor, fees may range up to $70,000 for a global name.
4. Expanding markets are in Paris France Beijing China and Dubai City United Arab Emirates.
5. As she was about to name a fashion product, Rachel Hermes said "If I am launching a new fashion label, the task becomes very difficult. I have to find a name that communicates the creative style that the brand is to embody."
6. For a new unisex perfume, Hermes considered the following names Declaration, Serenity, and Earth.
7. Naming is not a problem for small companies however it is a big problem for global brands.
8. Hermes started with a thorough competitive analysis it included quantifying the tone and strength of competing names.
9. Attending the naming sessions were James Harper, marketing director, Reva Cruz, product manager, and Cheryl Chang, vice president.
10. Distribution of goods has become global therefore names have to be registered in many countries.

UNIT 3

Workplace Communication

© Ken Hurst/Shutterstock.com

CHAPTER 7

Electronic Messages and Digital Media

Want to do well on tests and excel in your course? Go to **www.meguffey.com** for helpful interactive resources.

- **Review the Chapter 7 PowerPoint slides to prepare for the first quiz.**

OBJECTIVES

After studying this chapter, you should be able to

1. Describe the role digital media play in the changing world of business in contrast to traditional paper-based messages.
2. Meet professional e-mail standards for usage, structure, and format; and follow the rules of netiquette and other best practices.
3. Explain how business professionals communicate by instant messaging and texting.
4. Identify professional uses of podcasts, blogs, and wikis; and describe prudent policies to protect authors of electronic content.
5. Understand business uses of social and professional networking sites as well as RSS feeds and social bookmarking.

Zooming In — PART 1

Twitter: From Obscure Tech Fad to Internet Sensation

Basketball giant Shaquille O'Neal has a Twitter account. Governor Arnold Schwarzenegger has one. Actor Ashton Kutcher was an early adopter. Paula Abdul announced her departure from *American Idol* on the popular microblogging service. During labor and childbirth, Sara Williams, wife of Twitter CEO Evan Williams, kept in touch by tweets (short public messages of up to 140 characters) with more than 16,000 followers.[1] Tweets also transmitted the first images of the US Airways jet that safely landed in the Hudson River in early 2009. Twitter allows users to share brief status updates about their lives and their whereabouts online.

What seemed like a novelty for tech heads when the service first emerged a few years ago has become an Internet phenomenon. The ranks of twitterers and users of other social sites have been swelling so explosively—currently to about 7 million on Twitter—that some investors see huge opportunities. They even speak of a new technological revolution, the "real-time Web."[2] High-speed Internet connections, smart mobile devices with Web browsers, and Internet messaging applications have enabled easy around-the-clock, real-time communication. Like other social sites, Twitter has yet to turn a profit. However, nearly 45 million visitors recently accessed its Web site. Roughly the same number used other sites and services to connect to it.[3]

That Twitter had come of age was evident when it became the target of hackers. Similarly, security breaches and other user missteps have highlighted the need for Twitter netiquette: Michigan Rep. Peter Hoekstra broke a national security embargo when he tweeted about his congressional trip to Baghdad, Iraq.[4]

First the tech companies, and now mainstream businesses, are looking for ways to make money using the service. For advice on what not to do on Twitter, see Part 2 of Zooming In later in this chapter. Your Turn on page 212 discusses how businesses are trying to harness the potential of Twitter and other social networks.

Critical Thinking

- In what ways have social media and the "real-time Web" changed how Internet users communicate? Have services such as Twitter improved the way we exchange information?
- What trends have facilitated the emergence of social media, specifically Twitter?
- What could be advantages and drawbacks of using Twitter for business?

http://twitter.com

How Organizations Exchange Messages and Information

LEARNING OBJECTIVE 1
Describe the role digital media play in the changing world of business in contrast to traditional paper-based messages.

Although today's workplaces are still far from paperless, increasingly information is exchanged electronically and on the go, as the preceding discussion of Twitter shows. Social media sites such as Twitter have highlighted the appetite of many people today for instant status updates and the immediate sharing of information. The Web itself has evolved from a mere repository of passively consumed information to Web 2.0—a dynamic, interactive environment. Users are empowered, active participants who create content, review products, and edit and share information.

Ever more data are stored on and accessed from remote networks, not individual computers. This storing and accessing of data along with software applications in remote network clusters, or "clouds," is called *cloud computing*. Mobile communication and cloud computing are the two prevailing technological trends today. In many businesses, desktop computers are fast becoming obsolete with the advent of ever smaller laptops, netbooks, smartphones, personal digital assistants (PDAs), and other compact mobile devices. Furthermore, virtual private networks (VPN) offer secure access to company information from any location in the world that provides an Internet connection.

Today's workforce must stay connected at all times. Knowledge and information workers are expected to remain tethered to their jobs wherever they are, even on the weekends or on vacation. The technological revolution of the last 25 years has resulted in amazing productivity gains. However, technological advances have also made 50-hour workweeks without overtime pay a reality for those "i-workers" lucky enough to snag or keep a promising position in a tough economy. Also, more employees than ever before are telecommuting.

Electronic communication is the lifeblood of a functioning organization today. Fewer layers of management after downsizing and the flattening of corporate hierarchies have meant that more rank-and-file staff members are now empowered to make decisions and tend to work in cross-functional teams. These significant changes would not be possible without a speedy yet accurate exchange of information. In this fast-paced workplace, you will be expected to collect, evaluate, and exchange information in clearly written messages, whether electronic or paper-based.

You may already be sharing digitally with your friends and family, but chances are that you need to understand how businesses transmit information electronically and how they use new technology. This chapter explores professional electronic communication, specifically e-mail, corporate blogs, instant messaging, and text messaging. Moreover, you will learn about business uses of podcasts, wikis, and social networking sites. You will read about best practices in composing e-mails and interacting through other electronic media. Knowing how to prepare an effective message and understanding business technology can save you time, reduce stress, and build your image as a professional.

Communicating With Paper-Based Messages

What role do paper-based messages play in organizations today?

Although the business world is quickly switching to electronic communication channels, paper-based documents still have definite functions.

Business letters. Writers prepare business letters on letterhead stationery. This is the best channel when a permanent record is necessary, when confidentiality is important, when sensitivity and formality are essential, and when you need to make a persuasive, well-considered presentation.

Interoffice memos. Paper-based interoffice memos were once the chief form of internal communication. Today, employees use memos primarily to convey confidential information, emphasize ideas, introduce lengthy documents, or lend importance to a message. Memos are especially appropriate for explaining organizational procedures or policies that become permanent guidelines. In Chapter 8 you will learn more about positive letters, memos, and e-mail messages that follow the direct pattern of organization.

Communicating With Electronic Messages

What role do electronic messages play in organizations today?

A number of electronic communication channels enable businesspeople to exchange information rapidly and efficiently. All of these new electronic channels showcase your writing skills.

Electronic mail. In most businesses today, e-mail is the communication channel of choice. It has been hailed as one of the greatest productivity tools of our time.[5] Users can send messages to single addressees or broadcast them to multiple recipients. When a message arrives in the inbox, the recipient may read, print, forward, store, or delete it. E-mail is most appropriate for short messages. It is inappropriate for sensitive, confidential, or lengthy documents. Increasingly, e-mail is written on laptops, netbooks, and smart devices such as the BlackBerry, Palm, and iPhone. The smaller screen poses its own challenges, yet even short mobile messages need to be correct and professional. You will learn more about safe e-mail practices later in the chapter.

Instant messaging. More interactive and immediate than e-mail, instant messaging (IM) involves the exchange of text messages in real time between two or more people logged into an IM service. IM creates a form of private chat room so that individuals can carry on conversations similar to telephone calls. IM is especially useful for back-and-forth online conversations, such as a customer communicating with a tech support person to solve a problem. Like e-mail, instant messaging creates a permanent text record and must be used carefully.

Text messaging. Sending really short messages (160 or fewer characters) from mobile phones and other wireless devices is called *text messaging* or *texting*. This method uses short message service (SMS) and is available on most mobile phones and personal digital assistants (PDAs). SMS gateways exist to connect mobile phones with instant message services, the Web, desktop computers, and even landline telephones. Busy communicators use text messaging for short person-to-person inquiries and responses that keep them in touch while away from the office.

Podcasts. A podcast is a digital media file that is distributed over the Internet and downloaded on portable media players and personal computers. Podcasts, also called *netcasts* or *webcasts*, are distinguished by their ability to be syndicated, subscribed to, or downloaded automatically when new content is added. In business, podcasts are useful for improving customer relations, marketing, training, product launches, and viral marketing (creating online buzz about new products).

Blogs. A blog is a Web site with journal entries (posts) usually written by one person with comments added by others. It may combine text, images, and links to other blogs or Web pages. Businesses use blogs to keep customers and employees informed and to receive feedback. Company news can be posted, updated, and categorized for easy cross-referencing. Blogs may be a useful tool for marketing and promotion as well as for showing a company's personal side. Twitter is often referred to as a microblogging site, but it also functions as a social networking site.

Wikis. A wiki is a public or private Web site that enables multiple users to collaboratively create, post, edit, and access information. A wiki serves as a central location where shared documents can be viewed and revised by a large or dispersed team. Unlike a standard Web site, a wiki is linked to a database that records all changes thus allowing the viewing of previous versions. The best-known wiki is the online encyclopedia Wikipedia, currently featuring 13 million articles in 262 languages.[6] Because a wiki can be used to manage and organize meeting notes, team agendas, and company calendars, it is a valuable project management tool.

Social networking. Over the past few years, social networking has grown to become one of the most popular uses of the Internet. Also called *social online communities,* social networking sites such as Facebook, MySpace, Classmates.com, and LinkedIn allow participants with various interests to connect and collaborate. Businesses have recognized e-commerce opportunities and use social media to reach out to customers and the public. Most of the sites are now targeting professionals who are welcome to establish business contacts, network, post their career credentials, apply for jobs, and seek advice.

Preparing and Composing Professional E-Mail Messages

LEARNING OBJECTIVE 2

Meet professional e-mail standards for usage, structure, and format; and follow the rules of netiquette and other best practices.

In what way has e-mail matured as a medium?

E-mail has replaced paper memos for many messages inside organizations and for some letters to external audiences. However, as Chapter 8 explains, paper-based documents still have their proper functions. Because they are committed to paper, hard-copy messages tend to carry more weight and are taken more seriously in certain situations. They are considered more formal than electronic communication. Moreover, even if e-mail writers have access to sophisticated HTML mail, the recipient may receive only plaintext messages. Poor layout and little eye appeal may result when elaborate formatting disappears on the receiver's end. The e-mail message may also be difficult to print. This is why business communicators often deliver electronic copies of memos or letters as attachments accompanied by a brief e-mail cover message. PDF documents in particular guarantee that the reader receives a message that looks exactly as the writer intended it.

Early e-mail users were encouraged to ignore stylistic and grammatical considerations. They thought that "words on the fly" required little editing or proofing. Correspondents used emoticons (such as sideways happy faces) to express their emotions. Some e-mail today is still quick and dirty. As this communication channel continues to mature, however, messages are becoming more proper and more professional.

Today it is estimated that more than 210 billion e-mails are sent each day worldwide.[7] E-mail is twice as likely as the telephone to be used to communicate at work.[8] E-mail growth has slowed recently, and rival services are booming. Twitter and Facebook, for example, offer faster, always-on connectedness. However, e-mail in the workplace is here to stay.

Because e-mail is a standard form of communication within organizations, it will likely be your most common business communication channel. E-mails perform critical tasks such as informing employees, giving directions, outlining procedures, requesting data, supplying responses, and confirming decisions.

Analyzing the Components of E-Mail Messages

Much like hard-copy memos, routine e-mails generally contain four parts: (a) an informative subject line that summarizes the message; (b) an opening that reveals the main idea immediately; (c) a body that explains and justifies the main idea; and (d) a closing that presents action information, summarizes the message, or offers a closing thought. Remember that routine messages deliver good news or standard information.

What is the purpose of a subject line?

Subject Line. In e-mail messages an informative subject line is essential. It summarizes the central idea, thus providing quick identification for reading and filing. Busy readers glance at a subject line and decide when and whether to read the message. Those without subject lines are often automatically deleted.

What does it take to get your message read? For one thing, stay away from meaningless or dangerous words. A sure way to get your message deleted or ignored is to use a one-word heading such as *Issue, Problem, Important,* or *Help*. Including a word such as *Free* is dangerous because it may trigger spam filters. Try to make your subject line "talk" by including a verb. Explain the purpose of the message and how it relates to the reader (*Need You to Showcase Two Items at Our Next Trade Show* rather than *Trade Show*). Finally, update your subject line to reflect the current message (*Staff Meeting Rescheduled for May 12* rather than *Re: Re: Staff Meeting*). Remember that a subject line is usually written in an abbreviated style, often without articles *(a, an, the)*. It need not be a complete sentence, and it does not end with a period.

How do most routine e-mails open?

Opening. Most e-mails cover nonsensitive information that can be handled in a straightforward manner. Begin by frontloading; that is, reveal the main idea immediately. Even though the purpose of the e-mail is summarized in the subject line, that purpose should be restated—and amplified—in the first sentence. As you learned in Chapters 5 and 6, busy readers want to know immediately why they are reading a message. Notice how the following indirect opener can be improved by frontloading.

© Doug Kanter/Bloomberg via Getty Images

Has Starbucks lost its soul? That's the claim made by Starbucks founder Howard Schultz in an e-mail to top management. According to Schultz, the coffee company's chain-oriented growth has watered down the Starbucks experience, turned the brand into a commodity, and created a "sterile cookie-cutter" atmosphere in the stores. After lamenting numerous changes, including the disappearance of Starbucks' traditional Italian espresso makers, Shultz's memo closes: "Let's get back to the core...and do the things necessary to once again differentiate Starbucks from all others." *What makes this an effective closing?*

Indirect Opening	**Direct Opening**
For the past six months, the Human Resources Development Department has been considering changes to our employees' benefits plan.	Please review the following proposal regarding employees' benefits, and let me know by May 20 if you approve these changes.

What type of information is covered in the body?

Body. The body provides more information about the reason for writing. It explains and discusses the subject logically. Good e-mails generally discuss only one topic. Limiting the topic helps the receiver act on the subject and file it appropriately. A writer who describes a computer printer problem and also requests permission to attend a conference runs a 50 percent failure risk. The reader may respond to the printer problem but delay or forget about the conference request.

Design your data for easy comprehension by using numbered lists, headings, tables, and other document design techniques introduced in Chapter 6. Compare the following versions of the same message. Notice how the graphic devices of bullets, columns, headings, and white space make the main points easier to comprehend.

Hard-to-Read Paragraph Version

Effective immediately are the following air travel guidelines. Between now and December 31, only account executives may take company-approved trips. These individuals will be allowed to take a maximum of two trips, and they are to travel economy or budget class only.

Improved Version

Effective immediately are the following air travel guidelines:

- Who may travel: Account executives only
- How many trips: A maximum of two trips
- By when: Between now and December 31
- Air class: Economy or budget class only

Which three features typically appear in the closing of a message?

Which components are generally used to format e-mail messages?

Closing. Generally conclude an e-mail with (a) action information, dates, or deadlines; (b) a summary of the message; or (c) a closing thought. Here again the value of thinking through the message before actually writing it becomes apparent. The closing is where readers look for deadlines and action language. An effective e-mail closing might be, *Please submit your report by June 15 so that we can have your data before our July planning session.*

In more detailed messages, a summary of main points may be an appropriate closing. If no action request is made and a closing summary is unnecessary, you might end with a simple concluding thought *(I'm glad to answer your questions* or *This sounds like a useful project).* You needn't close messages to coworkers with goodwill statements such as those found in letters to customers or clients. However, some closing thought is often necessary to prevent a feeling of abruptness. Closings can show gratitude or encourage feedback with remarks such as *I sincerely appreciate your help* or *What are your ideas on this proposal?* Other closings look forward to what's next, such as *How would you like to proceed?* Avoid closing with overused expressions such as *Please let me know if I may be of further assistance.* This ending sounds mechanical and insincere.

Ethics Check

Hiding Blind Copies

Some workers use *Bcc* (*blind carbon copy*) to copy their friends and colleagues on e-mails when they do not want the recipient to know that a third party will also read the message. Do you believe that hiding copies from the recipient is harmless and acceptable? Or is secretly distributing messages wrong because it means "going behind someone's back"?

Applying E-Mail Formats

Although e-mail is still a fairly new communication channel, people are beginning to agree on specific formatting and usage conventions. The following suggestions identify current formatting standards. Always check with your organization, however, to observe its practices.

Guide Words. Following the guide word *To*, some writers insert just the recipient's electronic address, such as *william.harding@schilling-voigt.com*. Other writers prefer to include the receiver's full name plus the electronic address, as shown in Figure 7.1. By including full names in the *To* and *From* slots, both receivers and senders are better able to identify the message. By the way, the order of *Date, To, From, Subject*, and other guide words varies depending on your e-mail program and whether you are sending or receiving the message.

Most e-mail programs automatically add the current date after *Date*. On the *Cc* line (which stands for *carbon copy* or *courtesy copy*), you can type the address of anyone who is to receive a copy of the message. Remember, though, to send copies only to those people directly involved with the message. Most e-mail programs also include a line for *Bcc (blind carbon copy)*. This sends a copy without the addressee's knowledge. Many savvy writers today use *Bcc* for the names and addresses of a list of receivers, a technique that avoids revealing the addresses to the entire group. On the subject line, identify the subject of the message. Be sure to include enough information to be clear and compelling.

Greeting. Begin your message with a friendly greeting such as the following:

Hi, Rudy,	Thank you, Haley,
Greetings, Amy,	Dear Mr. Cotter:
Mike,	Dear Leslie:

In addition to being friendly, a greeting provides a visual cue marking the beginning of the message. Many messages are transmitted or forwarded with such long headers that finding the beginning of the message can be difficult. A greeting helps, as shown in Figure 7.1 on page 194.

What purpose do greetings serve?

Where do you include the e-mail writer's contact information, and why is it helpful?

In what contexts may e-mail messages be dangerous?

Body. When typing the body of an e-mail message, use standard caps and lowercase characters—never all uppercase or all lowercase characters. Cover just one topic, and try to keep the total message under three screens in length. To assist you, many e-mail programs have basic text-editing features, such as cut, copy, paste, and word-wrap.

Complimentary Closing and Signature Block. In closing your message, you may elect to sign off with a complimentary closing such as *Cheers, All the best*, or *Many thanks*. Such a closing is optional. However, providing your name is mandatory. It is also smart to include full contact information as part of your signature block. Some writers prepare a number of "signatures" in their e-mail programs, depending on what information they want to reveal. They can choose a complete signature with all their contact information, or they can use a brief version. See Figure 7.1 for an example of a complete signature.

Composing Professional E-Mail Messages

Wise business communicators are aware of the importance as well as the dangers of e-mail as a communication channel. They know that their messages can travel, intentionally or unintentionally, long distances. A quickly drafted e-mail may end up in the boss's inbox or be forwarded to an enemy. Making matters worse, computers—like elephants and spurned lovers—never forget. Even erased messages can remain on multiple servers that are backed up by companies or Internet service providers. Increasingly, e-mail has turned into the "smoking gun" uncovered by prosecutors to prove indelicate or even illegal intentions.

E-mail has become the digital equivalent of DNA evidence. A workplace study found that 21 percent of companies have been ordered by courts to surrender employee e-mail, and 13 percent of companies have battled discrimination claims stemming from e-mail or Internet abuse.[9] "E-mail has become the place where everybody loves to look," according

Spotlight on Communicators

© Courtesy of NetworkWorld.com and Gaskin.com

Network consultant and author James E. Gaskin recommends writing e-mails backward: "Common e-mail composition problems include forgetting the attachment, too much information in the body of the message, a poor subject, and sending the message to the wrong people. So write your e-mails in that order: attachment, message body, subject, addressees.

When you attach your files first, you won't forget them (if you have a file attachment, of course). When you write your message text, focus on the single bit of information you are providing or the request you are making of the recipient. If you're attaching a file, the message text should address the recipient's responsibility for the attached file or files. Edit and return? Agree or not? Forward to the boss? Explain exactly why you're sending the person a file, and what you want them to do with that file."

Despite its dangers and limitations, e-mail has become a mainstream channel of communication. That's why it's important to take the time to organize your thoughts, compose carefully, and be concerned with correct grammar and punctuation. Understanding netiquette and proper tone is also important if you wish to be perceived as a professional. The pointers in Figure 7.2 will help you get off to a good start in using e-mail smartly and safely.

FIGURE 7.1 Formatting an E-Mail Message

1 Prewriting

Analyze: The purpose of this e-mail is to solicit feedback regarding a casual-dress policy.

Anticipate: The message is going to a subordinate who is busy but probably eager to be consulted in this policy matter.

Adapt: Use a direct approach beginning with the most important question. Strive for a positive, professional tone rather than an autocratic, authoritative tone.

2 Writing

Research: Collect secondary information about dress-down days in other organizations. Collect primary information by talking with company managers.

Organize: Begin with the main idea followed by a brief explanation and questions. Conclude with an end date and a reason.

Compose: Prepare the first draft remembering that the receiver is busy and appreciates brevity.

3 Revising

Revise: Rewrite questions to ensure that they are parallel and readable.

Proofread: Decide whether to hyphenate *casual-dress policy* and *dress-down days*. Be sure commas follow introductory clauses. Check question marks.

Evaluate: Does this memo encourage participatory management? Will the receiver be able to answer the questions and respond easily?

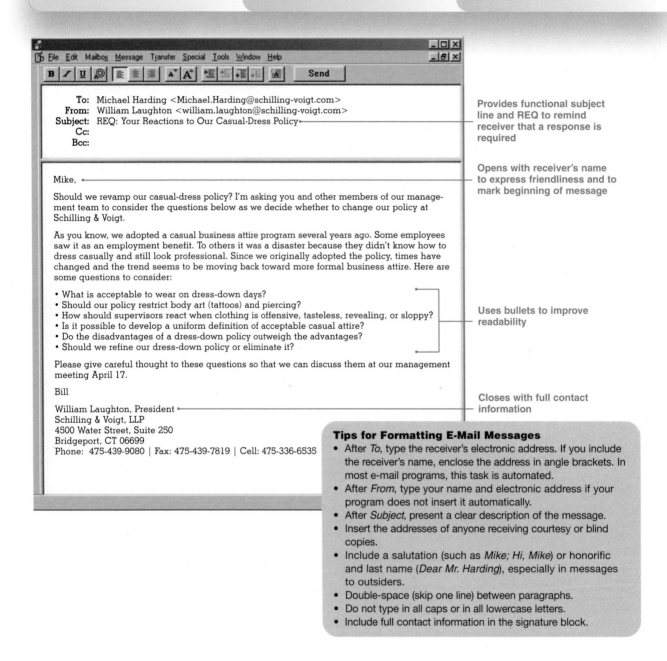

File Edit Mailbox Message Transfer Special Tools Window Help

Send

To: Michael Harding <Michael.Harding@schilling-voigt.com>
From: William Laughton <william.laughton@schilling-voigt.com>
Subject: REQ: Your Reactions to Our Casual-Dress Policy
Cc:
Bcc:

Provides functional subject line and REQ to remind receiver that a response is required

Mike,

Opens with receiver's name to express friendliness and to mark beginning of message

Should we revamp our casual-dress policy? I'm asking you and other members of our management team to consider the questions below as we decide whether to change our policy at Schilling & Voigt.

As you know, we adopted a casual business attire program several years ago. Some employees saw it as an employment benefit. To others it was a disaster because they didn't know how to dress casually and still look professional. Since we originally adopted the policy, times have changed and the trend seems to be moving back toward more formal business attire. Here are some questions to consider:

- What is acceptable to wear on dress-down days?
- Should our policy restrict body art (tattoos) and piercing?
- How should supervisors react when clothing is offensive, tasteless, revealing, or sloppy?
- Is it possible to develop a uniform definition of acceptable casual attire?
- Do the disadvantages of a dress-down policy outweigh the advantages?
- Should we refine our dress-down policy or eliminate it?

Uses bullets to improve readability

Please give careful thought to these questions so that we can discuss them at our management meeting April 17.

Bill

William Laughton, President
Schilling & Voigt, LLP
4500 Water Street, Suite 250
Bridgeport, CT 06699
Phone: 475-439-9080 | Fax: 475-439-7819 | Cell: 475-336-6535

Closes with full contact information

Tips for Formatting E-Mail Messages

- After *To*, type the receiver's electronic address. If you include the receiver's name, enclose the address in angle brackets. In most e-mail programs, this task is automated.
- After *From*, type your name and electronic address if your program does not insert it automatically.
- After *Subject*, present a clear description of the message.
- Insert the addresses of anyone receiving courtesy or blind copies.
- Include a salutation (such as *Mike; Hi, Mike*) or honorific and last name (*Dear Mr. Harding*), especially in messages to outsiders.
- Double-space (skip one line) between paragraphs.
- Do not type in all caps or in all lowercase letters.
- Include full contact information in the signature block.

Checklist

Professional E-Mail

Subject Line

- **Summarize the central idea.** Express concisely what the message is about and how it relates to the reader.
- **Include labels if appropriate.** Labels such as *FYI* (for your information) and *REQ* (required) help receivers recognize how to respond.
- **Avoid empty or dangerous words.** Don't write one-word subject lines such as *Help, Problem*, or *Free*.

Opening

- **State the purpose for writing.** Include the same information that is in the subject line, but expand it.
- **Highlight questions.** If you are requesting information, begin with the most important question, use a polite command *(Please answer the following questions about ...)*, or introduce your request courteously.
- **Supply information directly.** If responding to a request, give the reader the requested information immediately in the opening. Explain later.

Body

- **Explain details.** Arrange information logically. For detailed topics develop separate coherent paragraphs.
- **Enhance readability.** Use short sentences, short paragraphs, and parallel construction for similar ideas.
- **Apply document design.** If appropriate, provide bulleted or numbered lists, columns, tables, or other graphic devices to improve readability and comprehension.
- **Be cautious.** Remember that e-mail messages often travel far beyond their intended audiences.

Closing

- **Request action.** If appropriate, state specifically what you want the reader to do. Include a deadline, with reasons, if possible.
- **Provide a goodwill statement or a closing thought.** When communicating outside of the company or with management, include a positive goodwill statement such as *Our team enjoyed working on the feasibility report, and we look forward to your feedback*. If no action request is necessary, end with a closing thought.
- **Avoid cliché endings.** Use fresh remarks rather than overused expressions such as *If you have additional questions, please do not hesitate to call* or *Thank you for your cooperation.*

to Irwin Schwartz, president of the National Association of Criminal Defense Lawyers.[10] Recently, hundreds of e-mail messages and files were hacked from accounts owned by acclaimed British and American climate scientists, encouraging climate-change skeptics to believe that the scientists conspired to overstate the case for a human contribution to global warming. In one exchange a scientist was discussing a statistical "trick" in illustrating a sharp warming trend. Another scientist referred to climate skeptics as "idiots."[11]

Writers simply forget that their e-mail messages are permanent and searchable and can be forwarded as easily to a thousand people as to just one.[12] Another observer noted that e-mail is like an electronic truth serum.[13] Writers blurt out thoughts without thinking. For these reasons, e-mail and other electronic communication channels pose a number of dangers, to both employees and employers. Best practices for using electronic media in general are discussed at the end of the chapter.

Sometimes taken lightly, e-mail messages, like other business documents, should be written carefully. Once they leave the author's hands, they are essentially published. They can't be retrieved, corrected, or revised. Review the accompanying Checklist and Figure 7.2 for tips for writing typical e-mail messages that will accomplish what you intend.

Using Instant Messaging and Texting Professionally

LEARNING OBJECTIVE 3

Explain how business professionals communicate by instant messaging and texting.

Making their way from teen bedrooms to office boardrooms, instant messaging (IM) and text messaging have become permanent and powerful communication tools. IM enables you to use the Internet to communicate in real time in a private chat room with one or more individuals. It is like live e-mail or a text telephone call. More and more workers are using it as a speedy communication channel to exchange short messages.

FIGURE 7.2 Using E-Mail Safely and Smartly

Tips	E-Mail Best Practices Explained
Try composing offline.	Especially for important messages, use your word processing program to write offline. Then upload your message to your e-mail. This avoids "self-destructing" (losing all your writing through some glitch or pressing the wrong key) when working online.
Get the address right.	If you omit one character or misread the character *l* for the number 1, your message bounces. Solution: Use your electronic address book for people you write to frequently. Double-check every address that you key in manually. Don't accidentally reply to a group of receivers when you intend to answer only one.
Avoid misleading subject lines.	Make sure your subject line is relevant and helpful. Generic tags such as *Hi!* and *Important!* may cause your message to be deleted before it is opened.
Apply the top-of-screen test.	When readers open your message and look at the first screen, will they see what is most significant? Your subject line and first paragraph should convey your purpose. Frontload the message.
Be concise.	Omit unnecessary information. Remember that monitors are small and typefaces are often difficult to read. Organize your ideas tightly.
Don't send anything you wouldn't want published.	E-mail creates a permanent record that does not go away even when deleted. Every message is a corporate communication that can be used against you or your employer. Don't write anything that you wouldn't want your boss, your family, or a judge to read.
Don't use e-mail to avoid contact.	E-mail is inappropriate for breaking bad news or for resolving arguments. For example, it's improper to fire a person by e-mail. It is also a poor channel for clashing with supervisors, subordinates, or others. Before risking hurt feelings, call or pay the person a visit.
Care about correctness.	People are still judged by their writing, whether electronic or paper based. Sloppy e-mail messages (with missing apostrophes, haphazard spelling, and jumbled writing) make readers work too hard. They resent not only the message but also the writer.
Care about tone.	Your words and writing style affect the reader. Avoid sounding curt, negative, or domineering.
Resist humor and sarcasm.	Without the nonverbal cues conveyed by your face and your voice, humor and sarcasm can easily be misunderstood.
Limit any tendency to send blanket copies.	Send copies only to people who really need to see a message. Don't document every business decision and action with an electronic paper trail.
Never send "spam."	Sending unsolicited advertisements ("spam") either by fax or e-mail is illegal in the United States.
Use capital letters only for emphasis.	Avoid writing entire messages in all caps, which is like SHOUTING.
Don't forward without permission, and beware of long threads.	Obtain approval before forwarding a message. Beware of forwarding e-mail consisting of a long thread (string) of messages. Some content at the beginning of the thread may be inappropriate for the third receiver. Leaving sensitive information in the thread can lead to serious trouble.
Use attachments sparingly.	Because attachments may carry viruses, some receivers won't open them. Consider including short attachments within an e-mail message. If you must send a longer attachment, announce it.
Scan all messages in your inbox before replying to each individually.	Because subsequent messages often affect the way you respond, skim all messages first (especially all those from the same individual). Respond immediately to messages that can be answered in two minutes or less.
Print only when necessary.	Read and answer most messages online without saving or printing. Use folders to archive messages on special topics. Print only those messages that are complex, controversial, or involve significant decisions and follow-up.
Acknowledge receipt.	If you can't reply immediately, tell when you can (*Will respond Friday*).
Don't automatically return the sender's message.	When replying, cut and paste the relevant parts. Avoid irritating your recipients by returning the entire thread (sequence of messages) on a topic.
Revise the subject line if the topic changes.	When replying or continuing an e-mail exchange, revise the subject line as the topic changes.
Provide a clear, complete first sentence.	Avoid fuzzy replies such as *That's fine with me* or *Sounds good!* Busy respondents forget what was said in earlier messages, so be sure to fill in the context and your perspective when responding.
Never respond when you are angry.	Calm down before shooting off a response to an upsetting message. You will come up with different and better options after thinking about what was said. If possible, iron out differences in person.

(continued)

FIGURE 7.2 (Continued)

Tips	E-Mail Best Practices Explained
Don't use company computers for personal matters.	Unless your company specifically allows it, never use your employer's computers for personal messages, personal shopping, or entertainment.
Assume that all e-mail is monitored.	Employers legally have the right to monitor e-mail, and about 75 percent of them do.
Design your messages effectively.	When a message requires several screens, help the reader with headings, bulleted lists, side headings, and perhaps an introductory summary that describes what will follow. Although these techniques lengthen a message, they shorten reading time.
Consider cultural differences.	Be clear and precise in your language. Remember that figurative clichés (*pull up stakes, playing second fiddle,*) sports references (*hit a home run, play by the rules*), and slang (*cool, stoked*) may confuse nonnative speakers of English.
Double-check before hitting the Send button.	Avoid the necessity of sending a second message, which makes you look careless. Use spell check and reread for fluency before sending. Verify important facts and the spelling of names.

Text messaging, or texting, is another popular means for exchanging brief messages in real time. Usually delivered by smartphone, texting requires a short message service (SMS) supplied by a cell phone service provider. Increasingly, both IM and text messages are sent by computer or handheld device.

How do instant messaging and text messaging work?

How Instant Messaging and Texting Work

To send an instant message, you might use a public IM service, called a client, such as AOL's Instant Messenger, Yahoo Messenger, Google Talk, Jabber, or Microsoft's Windows Live Messenger. These are public IM services. Once the client is installed, you enter your name and password to log on. The software checks whether any of the users in your contact list are currently logged on. If the server finds any of your contacts, it sends a message to your computer. If the person you wish to contact is online, you can click that person's name and a window opens that you can enter text into. You enter a message such as that shown in Figure 7.3 and click **Send**. Because your client has the Internet address and port number for the computer of the person you addressed, your message is sent directly to the client on that person's computer.

Typically, IM communication is exchanged between two computers that are linked by servers. However, new applications allow people to use IM not only on their computers but also on their handheld devices such as the popular iPhone shown in Figure 7.4. Many smartphones work on a 3G cell phone network where they consume minutes, but they may also allow generally "free" Wi-Fi access where available.

Texting, on the other hand, usually requires a smartphone or PDA, and users are charged for the service, often by choosing a flat rate for a certain number of text or media messages per month. Lately, voice over Internet providers such as Skype offer texting. For a small fee, Skype subscribers can send text messages to SMS-enabled cell phones in the United States and IM messages both domestically and internationally. Again, Skype and other formerly computer-based applications are simultaneously available on mobile devices and are making communication on the go more convenient than ever before.

Pros and Cons of Instant Messaging and Texting

What are the pros and cons of instant messaging and text messaging?

In today's fast-paced world, instant messaging (IM) offers numerous benefits. Its major attraction is real-time communication with colleagues anywhere in the world—so long as a cell phone signal or a Wi-Fi connection is available. IM is a convenient alternative to the telephone and may eventually even replace e-mail. Because IM allows people to share information immediately and make decisions quickly, its impact on business communication has been dramatic. Group online chat capabilities allow coworkers on far-flung project teams to communicate instantly. The popular Skype, the voice over Internet protocol powerhouse, is but one of many providers.

Texting by SMS is rapidly spreading around the world within individual markets and regions, but incompatible wireless standards have prevented the reach of SMS across continents. Like IM, texting can be a low-cost substitute for voice calls, delivering a message

FIGURE 7.3 Instant Message for Brief, Fast Communication

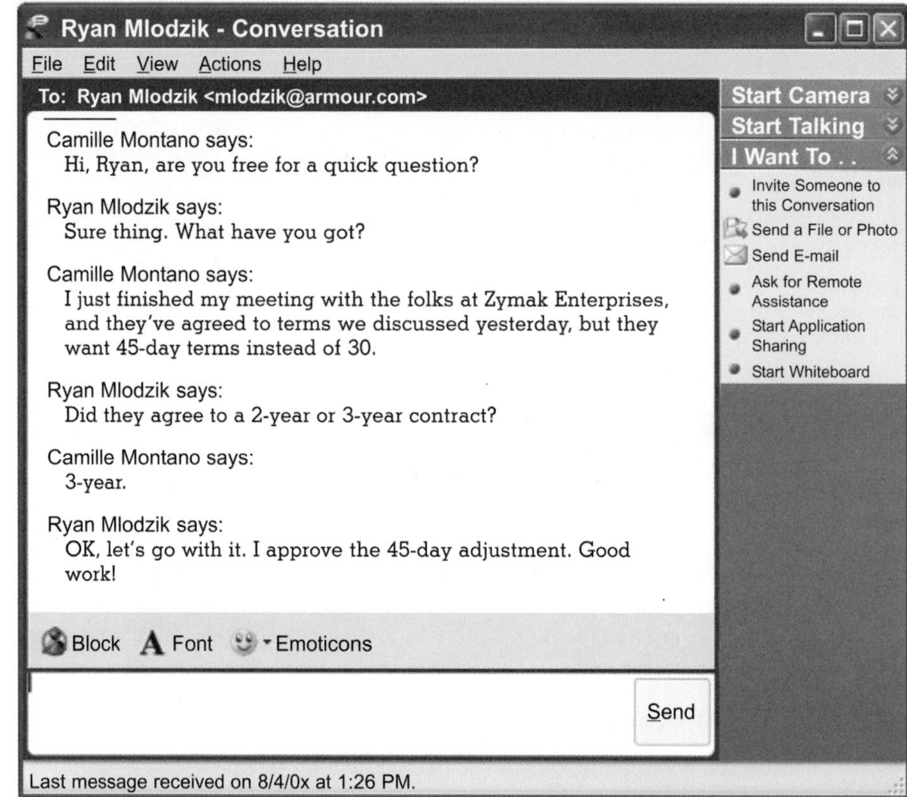

Figure 7.3 shows a brief IM exchange between a supervisor and a subordinate. Both are using a computer-based IM program. Texting is a convenient tool that enables team members to locate quick information and answers in solving immediate problems even when they are apart.

between private mobile phone users quietly and discreetly. SMS is particularly popular in Europe, New Zealand, Australia, and Asia.[14] In bulk text messages, companies around the world provide news alerts, financial information, and advertising to customers. Texts have been used in game shows for TV voting, in the United States most notably to select contestants on *American Idol*.

FIGURE 7.4 Texting and Instant Messaging with the iPhone

Despite Apple's exclusive distribution agreement with AT&T, the iPhone is one of the most popular handheld devices in the United States. Users like the touch-screen interface and access to countless smart applications ("apps"), many of which are free.

The immediacy of instant and text messaging has created many fans. A user knows right away whether a message was delivered. Messaging avoids phone tag and eliminates the downtime associated with personal telephone conversations. Another benefit includes "presence functionality." Coworkers can locate each other online, thus avoiding wild goose chases hunting someone who is out of the office. Many people consider instant messaging and texting productivity boosters because they enable users to get answers quickly and allow multitasking.

Despite its popularity among workers, some organizations forbid employees to use instant and text messaging for a number of reasons. Employers consider instant messaging yet another distraction in addition to the telephone, e-mail, and the Web. Organizations also fear that privileged information and company records will be revealed through public instant messaging systems, which hackers can easily penetrate. The First National Bank of Bosque County in Valley Mills, Texas, banned IM because of the risk of information leaving the institution without approval.

Companies also worry about *phishing* (fraudulent) schemes, viruses, malware (malicious software programs), and *spim* (IM spam). Like e-mail, instant and text messages are subject to discovery (disclosure); that is, they can become evidence in lawsuits. Moreover, companies fear instant messaging and texting because the services necessitate that businesses track and store messaging conversations to comply with legal requirements. This task may be overwhelming. Finally, IM and texting have been implicated in traffic accidents and inappropriate uses such as the notorious *sexting*.

Best Practices for Instant Messaging and Texting

What are some useful guidelines for writers of instant messages and text messages?

Instant messaging and texting can definitely save time and simplify communication with coworkers and customers. Before using IM or text messaging on the job, however, be sure you have permission. Do not use public systems without checking with your supervisor. If your organization does allow IM or texting, you can use it efficiently and professionally by following these best practice guidelines:

- Learn about your organization's IM policies. Are you allowed to use instant and text messaging? With whom may you exchange messages?
- Don't text or IM while driving a car. Pull over if you must read or send a message.
- Make yourself unavailable when you need to complete a project or meet a deadline.
- Organize your contact lists to separate business contacts from family and friends.
- Keep your messages simple and to the point. Avoid unnecessary chitchat, and know when to say goodbye.
- Don't use IM or text messages to send confidential or sensitive information.
- Be aware that instant or text messages can be saved. As with e-mail, don't say anything that would damage your reputation or that of your organization.
- If personal messaging is allowed, keep it to a minimum. Your organization may prefer that personal chats be done during breaks or the lunch hour.
- Show patience by not blasting multiple messages to coworkers if a response is not immediate.
- Keep your presence status up-to-date so that people trying to reach you don't waste their time.
- Beware of jargon, slang, and abbreviations, which, although they may reduce keystrokes, may be confusing and appear unprofessional.
- Respect your receivers by using good grammar and proper spelling and by proofreading carefully.

Spotlight on Communicators

© Jill & Rose Bennett Photography

Nancy Flynn, founder and executive director of the ePolicy Institute, says it's important that employers create a clear online policy and then explain it. She offers advice to companies that wish to lower their Internet risk and enhance electronic communication. Flynn believes not enough employers have instituted formal training on confidentiality and online liability. She warns any employee: "Don't start blogging. Don't start tweeting. Don't even start e-mailing until you read the company policy."

Zooming In — PART 2

Got Something to Tweet About at Work? Think Again.

The modern workplace is a potential digital minefield. The imprudent use of practically any online tool—whether e-mail, IM, texting, tweeting, blogging, or posting to Facebook—can land workers in hot water and even lead to dismissal. Here are five ways Twitter can get you canned for showing poor judgment:

1. **Sending hate tweets about the boss.** Example: *My retard boss said he put in for raises. I think he lies. He is known for that. His daddy owns the company.*

   The difference between venting around the water cooler or over lunch to a close friend and trumpeting to the world one's dislike for the superior could not be more obvious. Twitter messages can be forwarded (retweeted) and find their way to unintended recipients.

2. **Lying to the boss and bragging about it.** Example: *I so lied to my boss ... I was late but I said I forgot my badge and got away with it.*

   Although lying to the boss may be woefully common, broadcasting it to one's followers on Twitter is risky. The Web and Twitter make it easy to track people, and lies have a way of emerging most unexpectedly.

3. **Romancing the boss (kissing and telling).** Example: *I give the boss what he wants, and the fringe benefits are amazing.*

   Again, even if the indiscreet twitterer had a private profile, a contact could easily retweet the message and make it retrievable. Besides, amorous relationships between superiors and subordinates are frowned on in many companies because they could open firms up to sexual harassment lawsuits. Also, the boss could be tracking the tattletale on Twitter and would probably not appreciate the leaking of the affair.

4. **Announcing the desire to quit.** Example: *So close to quitting my job right now. Sometimes I can't [expletive] stand this place [expletive] moron assistant plant manager I'm about to deck him.*

   © JOHN MACDOUGALL/AFP/Getty Images

   The wish to quit may come true, but prematurely so and not according to plan. If you hate your job, complain to your pet or vent with your friends over dinner, but don't shout it out on Twitter. Smart workers leave a workplace on good terms knowing that they may need references. They do not burn bridges, much less publicly.

5. **Blocking your boss.** Example: *i kept my promise ... my boss thought she was gonna follow me on here ... i BLOCKED her* [expletive] *ASAP.*

   Preventing the boss from seeing your profile is no guarantee that he or she won't receive your hateful missives through another source. As Mark, an expert blogger, advises: "The golden rule of not getting yourself fired over 'tweets' is simple—just don't vent your work and boss frustrations publicly."[15]

Critical Thinking

- How do you explain the amazing lapses of judgment apparent in the tweets above?
- How widespread is the use of Twitter among your friends, and how do they benefit from the service?
- What are the most effective ways to warn young people about the dangers to their careers that lurk online?

Using Podcasts or Webcasts, Blogs, and Wikis for Business

LEARNING OBJECTIVE 4

Identify professional uses of podcasts, blogs, and wikis; and describe prudent policies to protect authors of electronic content.

What is Web 2.0, and what are its characteristics?

What purposes do business podcasts serve?

Like Twitter, podcasts, blogs, and wikis are part of the new user-centered virtual environment called Web 2.0. Far from being passive consumers, today's Internet users have the power to create Web content; interact with businesses and each other; review products, self-publish, or blog; contribute to wikis; or tag and share images and other files. Individuals wield enormous power because they can potentially reach huge audiences. Businesses often rightly fear the wrath of disgruntled employees and customers, or they curry favor with influential plugged-in opinion leaders.

The democratization of the Web means that in the online world, Internet users can bypass gatekeepers who filter content in the traditional print and visual media. Hence, even extreme views often reach audiences of thousands or even millions. The dangers are obvious. Fact checking often falls by the wayside, buzz may become more important than truth, and a single keystroke can make or destroy a reputation. This section addresses prudent business uses of podcasts, blogs, and wikis because you are likely to encounter these and other electronic communication tools on the job.

Business Podcasts or Webcasts

Although the terms *podcast* and *podcasting* have caught on, they are somewhat misleading. The words *broadcasting* and *iPod* combined to create the word *podcast*; however, audio and video files can be played on any number of devices, not just Apple's iPod. *Webcasting* for audio and *vcasting* for video content would be more accurate, but most people simply refer to them as podcasting. Podcasts can extend from short clips of a few minutes to 30-minute or longer digital files. Naturally, large video files gobble up a lot of memory, so they tend to be streamed on a Web site rather than downloaded.

Spotlight on Communicators

© Terri Miller/E-Visual Communications, Inc.

Donagh Herlihy, chief information officer of Avon Products, says "The big vision: We're finally getting there. Today, wherever you are, you can connect to all the information you need." Avon's 150,000 sales leaders are now equipped with a cloud-based computer system that they can tap into with smartphones and PCs anywhere in the world. No longer is information stored on individual machines; rather, it is combined into a digital "cloud," or remote computer networks, accessible from various smart devices.

How Organizations Use Podcasts. Like blogging, podcasting has experienced large growth and has spread among various user groups online. Major news organizations and media outlets podcast radio shows (e.g., National Public Radio) and TV shows, from ABC to Fox. Podcasts are also used in education. Students can access instructors' lectures, interviews, sporting events, and other content. Apple's iTunes U is perhaps the best-known example of free educational podcasts from Berkeley, Stanford, and other universities. Unlike streaming video that users can view only with an active Internet connection, podcasts encoded as MP3 files can be downloaded to a computer, a smartphone, or an MP3 player to be enjoyed on the go, often without subsequent Web access.

Delivering and Accessing Podcasts. Businesses have embraced podcasting for sending audio and video messages that do not require a live presence yet offer a friendly human face. Because they can broadcast repetitive information that does not require interaction, podcasts can replace costlier live teleconferences. IBM is training its sales force with podcasts that are available anytime. Real estate agents create podcasts to enable buyers to take virtual walking tours of available properties at their leisure. HR policies can also be presented in the

PLUGGED IN

Cloud Computing

© iStockphoto.com/Alex Slobodkin

For businesses, cloud computing might as well mean "cloud nine." Companies are increasingly relying on "cloud-based" computer systems that can be accessed by mobile phones and PCs anytime and anywhere. Google is spearheading efforts to enable future consumers to use inexpensive gadgets to manage their files and media in huge data centers on the Internet. If you use Flickr, Gmail, or Facebook, to name a few, you are already participating in cloud computing. Your photos and other data are stored in a remote location, and you can access them by using your PC, laptop, netbook, smartphone, or PDA.

The Lure and Lucre of the Cloud. Companies are lured to cloud computing by the promise of greater efficiency and higher profits. Avon hopes that its move to manage a sales force of 6 million reps worldwide with cloud computing will lead to greater effectiveness and higher sales. Blue Cross of Pennsylvania has enabled its 300,000 members to access medical histories and claims information with their smartphones. Like other tech companies, Serena Software has fully embraced the cloud, even using Facebook as the primary source of internal communication. Coca-Cola Enterprises has provided 40,000 sales reps, truck drivers, and other workers in the field with portable devices to connect with the home office instantly to respond to changing customer needs and problems on the road.

Vast Opportunities and Risks. The shift from storing information on isolated machines to information sharing in digital and social networks is seen by some as the largest growth opportunity since the Internet boom. The market for cloud products and services will likely soar. However, skeptics warn that caution about the risks of convenience is in order. For one thing, once the information leaves our computing device for the cloud, we don't know who may intercept it. In addition to data security, networks must be reliable, so that users can access them anytime. Google's recent software glitch allowed unauthorized access to a certain percentage of user files and left some Gmail customers unable to use their online applications.

Career Application

Which cloud services or applications are you already using? What are their advantages and disadvantages? Can you identify security risks that our desire for convenience may invite? Is convenience worth the risk? Should sensitive data and potentially revealing information be entrusted to the cloud?

form of podcasts for unlimited viewing on demand or as convenient. Marketing pitches also lend themselves to podcasting.

Podcasts are featured on media Web sites and company portals or shared on social networking sites and blogs. They can usually be streamed or downloaded as media files. As we will see, really simple syndication (RSS) allows the distribution of current information published in podcasts, blogs, video files, and news items. Users can select RSS feeds from various sources and personalize the information they wish to receive. GreenTalk Radio, shown in Figure 7.5, is just one example of a Web site that provides podcasts on many topics, such as green living and environmental stewardship. Frequently, business podcasts include short commercial segments. Nonprofit organizations may play public-service announcements to raise money. Interestingly, this ease of access has not produced multitudes of independent podcasters; the medium is still dominated by professional news organizations such as National Public Radio. Moreover, despite its growth in the last three years, podcasting is far from being a huge Internet phenomenon: fewer than 20 percent of Internet users have listened to a podcast this year.[16]

How is a simple podcast created?

Creating a Podcast. Producing a simple podcast does not require sophisticated equipment. With inexpensive recording, editing, and publishing software such as the popular Propaganda, ePodcast Creator, Audacity, or Gabcast, users can inform customers, mix their own music, or host interviews. In fact, any digital recorder can be used to create a quality primitive podcast, especially if the material is scripted and well rehearsed. If you are considering creating your own podcast, here are a few tips:

- **Decide whether to record one podcast or a series.** You can create a one-time podcast for a specific purpose or a series of podcasts on a related subject. Make sure you have enough material to sustain a steady flow of information.
- **Download software.** The program Audacity is available for free; other popular recording and editing software programs are relatively inexpensive.

FIGURE 7.5 GreenTalk Radio Podcasts

In his audio podcasts, host Sean Daily examines eco-friendly lifestyles and dispenses tips on becoming more "green." Although he maintains a Web site shown here, Daily connects more personally with viewers and listeners through his podcasts.

- **Obtain hardware.** Depending on the sound quality you desire, you may need a sophisticated microphone and other audio equipment. The recording room must be properly shielded against noise, echo, and other interference. Many universities and some libraries provide language labs that feature recording booths.
- **Organize the message.** Make sure your broadcast has a beginning, middle, and end. Build in some redundancy. Tell the listeners what you will tell them, then tell them, and finally, tell them what you've told them. This principle, known to effective PowerPoint users, also applies to podcasting. Previews, summaries, and transitions are important to help your audience follow the message.
- **Choose an extemporaneous or scripted delivery.** Think about how you will deliver the information, whether speaking freely or using a manuscript. Extemporaneous delivery means that you prepare, but you use only brief notes. It usually sounds more spontaneous and natural than reading from a script, but it can also lead to redundancy, repetition, and flubbed lines. Reading from a script, if done skillfully, can sound natural and warm. However, in the wrong hands, reading can come across as mechanical and amateurish.
- **Prepare and practice.** Before recording, do a few practice runs. Editing audio or video is difficult and time-consuming. Try to get your recording right, so that you won't have to edit much.
- **Publish and distribute your message.** If you post the podcast to a blog, you can introduce it and solicit your audience's feedback. Consider distributing your podcast by an RSS feed.

Professional Blogs

How do companies use blogs?

A blog is a Web site with journal entries on any imaginable topic usually written by one person, although some blogs feature multiple commentators. Typically, readers leave feedback. Businesses use blogs to keep customers and employees informed and to interact with them. The biggest advantage of business blogs is that they potentially reach a far-flung, vast audience. Marketing firms and their clients are looking closely at blogs because blogs can produce unbiased consumer feedback faster and more cheaply than such staples of consumer research as focus groups and surveys. Employees and executives at companies such as Google, Sun Microsystems, IBM, and Hewlett-Packard maintain blogs. They use blogs to communicate internally with employees and externally with clients. Currently, 78 (15.6 percent) of Fortune 500 companies are blogging.[17]

As an online diary or journal, a blog allows visitors to leave public comments. At this time, writers have posted 70 million blogs, up nearly 30 percent in one year.[18] However, only about half of these blogs are active, meaning that posts were published within three months. A recent Forrester Research study suggests that 25 percent of the U.S. population read a blog once a month.[19] Although blogs may still be underused, they do represent an amazing new information stream if used wisely.

How Companies Use Blogs

The potential applications of blogs in business are vast. Like other Web 2.0 phenomena, corporate blogs usually invite feedback and help build communities. Specifically, companies use blogs for public relations, customer relations, crisis communication, market research, viral marketing, internal communication, and recruiting.

Public Relations, Customer Relations, and Crisis Communication.

One of the prominent uses of blogs is to provide up-to-date company information to the press and the public. Blogs can be written by executives or by rank-and-file employees. Jonathan Schwartz, president and CEO of Sun Microsystems, is an occasional blogger. General Electric's Global research blog addresses industry insiders and the interested public. Ask a Blueshirt, a site authored by Best Buy employees, offers tips and other types of customer support.

A company blog is a natural forum for late-breaking news, especially when disaster strikes. Business bloggers can address rumors and combat misinformation. Although a blog cannot replace other communication channels in an emergency, it should be part of the overall effort to soothe the public's emotional reaction with a human voice of reason.

Market Research and Viral Marketing. Because most blogs invite feedback, they can be invaluable sources of opinion from customers and industry experts. In addition to monitoring visitor comments on their corporate blogs, many companies now have appointed employees who scrutinize the blogosphere for buzz and positive or negative postings about their organization and products.

The term *viral marketing* refers to the rapid spread of messages online, much like infectious diseases that pass from person to person. Marketers realize the potential of getting the word out about their products and services in the blogosphere, where their messages are often cross-referenced and linked by interested bloggers. Viral messages must be unexpected and elicit an emotional response, much like BMW's hip series of short films by popular directors starring Clive Owen.

Online Communities. Like Twitter, which has a loyal core following, company blogs can attract a devoted community of participants who want to keep informed about company events, product updates, and other news. In turn, those enthusiasts can contribute new ideas. Similar to Dell's Ideastorm, Starbucks' blog Ideas In Action solicits product and service ideas from customers.

Internal Communication and Recruiting. Blogs can be used to keep virtual teams on track and share updates on the road. Members in remote locations can stay in touch by smartphone and other devices, exchanging text, images, sound, and video clips. In many companies, blogs have replaced hard-copy publications in offering late-breaking news or tidbits of interest to employees. They may feature profiles of high-performing workers, information about benefits, and so forth.

Blogs mirror the company culture and present an invaluable opportunity for job candidates to size up a potential employer and the people working there.

What are some tips for crafting effective professional blogs?

Tips for Creating a Professional Blog

Blogging has grown up as a commercial activity and now offers sound business opportunities. Some bloggers make a living, although most remain unknowns in the boundless thickets of information on the Internet. To even have a shot at competing with established blog sites, consider the following guidelines if you would like to start a successful business blog:

- **Identify your audience.** As with any type of communication, you must know your audience to decide what to write to get people to read your blog. Does your blog stand out? What makes you interesting and unique?
- **Find a home for your blog.** You can use software that will let you attach a blog function to your Web site. Alternatively, you can join a blog hosting site that will provide a link on your Web site to attract visitors. You can usually find templates and other options to help build traffic to your site, especially if you use trackers that identify recent posts and popular message threads. Visit **http://www.businessblogconsulting.com** to learn more about blog publishing. Windows Live Spaces at **http://home.spaces.live.com** will help you set up a blog effortlessly and quickly.
- **Craft your message.** Blog about topics that showcase your expertise and insights. Offer a fresh, unique perspective on subjects your audience cares about. Your writing should be intriguing and sincere. Experts suggest that authors get to know the blogosphere in their industry and comment on what other bloggers are writing about. Stick with what you know.
- **Make "blogrolling" work for you.** Your goal is to attract repeat visitors to your blog. One way to achieve this objective is to increase traffic between blogs. "Blogrolling" means that you provide links to other sites or blogs on the Web that you find valuable and that are related to your business or industry. Respond to other bloggers' postings and link to them.
- **Attract search engines by choosing the right keywords.** In headlines and text, emphasize potential search terms that may draw traffic to your site. Focus on one topic and use a variety of synonyms to propel your blog to the top of search engine listings. An import

Ethics Check

Fired for Blogging

Former flight attendant Ellen Simonetti was fired by Delta Air Lines for posting on her blog "Queen of Sky" photos showing her in uniform. Simonetti claims that her dismissal violated her free-speech rights and was an act of sexual discrimination. She has been fighting her firing since 2004, parlaying her fame into a book and even a few talk show appearances. Whose rights take precedence, the employee's or the employer's?

company doing business with China would want to stress the keywords *import* and *China* as well as *trade, Asia,* and so forth, in addition to more industry-specific terms, such as *toys.*

- **Blog often.** Provide fresh content regularly. Stay current. Stale information puts off visitors. Post short, concise messages, but do so often.
- **Monitor the traffic to your site.** If necessary, vary your subjects to attract interest. If traffic slows down, experiment with new themes while staying with your core business and expertise. Also, evaluate the effectiveness of your publishing platform. Some blog publishing sites are more valuable than others in increasing your blog's visibility to search engines.
- **Seek permission.** If you are employed, explore your company's blogging policy. Even if neither a policy nor a prohibition against blogging exists, avoid writing about your employer, coworkers, customers, and events at the office, however veiled your references may be. The Internet is abuzz with stories about bloggers who got fired for online indiscretions.
- **Stay away from inappropriate topics.** Whether you are a rank-and-file employee or a freelance blogger, remember not to write anything you wouldn't want your family, friends, and the public at large to read. Blogs are not private journal entries; therefore, don't entrust to them any risqué, politically extreme, or private information.

Wikis and Collaboration

What is a wiki, and how is it useful to businesses?

At least as important to business as blogs are new communication tools such as wikis and social networking sites. A wiki is a Web site that employs easy-to-use collaborative software to allow users to create documents that can be edited by tapping into the same technology that runs the well-known online encyclopedia Wikipedia. Large companies, such as British Telecom, encourage their employees to team up to author software, launch branding campaigns, and map cell phone stations. Most projects are facilitated with the help of wikis, a tool that's especially valuable across vast geographic distances and multiple time zones.[20]

How Businesses Use Wikis. Far from being just a tool for geeks, wikis are used beyond information technology departments. The five main uses range from providing a shared internal knowledge base to storing templates for business documents:

- **The global wiki.** For companies with a global reach, a wiki is an ideal tool for information sharing between headquarters and satellite offices. Team members can easily edit their work and provide input to the home office and each other.
- **The wiki knowledge base.** Teams or departments use wikis to collect and disseminate information to large audiences creating a database for knowledge management. For example, an IT department may compile frequently asked questions that help users resolve the most common problems themselves. Human resources managers may update employee policies, make announcements, and convey information about benefits.
- **Wikis for meetings.** Wikis can facilitate feedback before and after meetings or serve as repositories of meeting minutes. In fact, wikis may replace some meetings, yet still keep a project on track. An often-cited example of a huge global wiki meeting is IBM's famous massive online discussion and brainstorming session that involved more than 100,000 participants from more than 160 countries.
- **Project management with wikis.** Wikis offer a highly interactive environment ideal for projects by enabling information to be centralized for easy access and user input. All participants have the same information available and can share ideas freely, more freely than in traditional face-to-face meetings. Instead of a top-down information flow, wikis empower employees and foster a team environment in which ideas can thrive.
- **Documentation and wikis.** Wikis can help to document projects large and small as well as technical and nontechnical. Wikis may also provide templates for reports.

FIGURE 7.6 **Creating a Wiki With Google Sites and Google Docs**

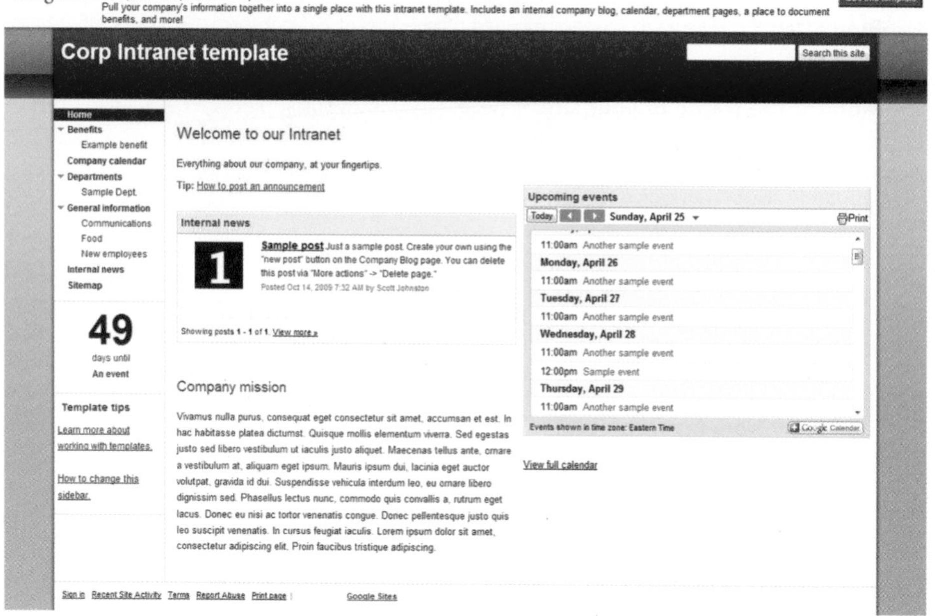

© Courtesy of Google, Inc.

This screen shot of Organic City's intranet shows a template created in Google Sites, a simple, template-driven wiki and document editor. Google Sites and the user-friendly document editing and revision tool Google Docs allow users to create, edit, share, and manage documents online in real time. Unlike in typical wikis, here multiple editors can modify files simultaneously.

What are a few helpful guidelines for wiki contributors?

How to Be a Valuable Wiki Contributor. Whether you wish to contribute to a wiki on the Web or at work, try to be an effective participant. As with most electronic communication, abide by the conventions of polite society, and follow the commonsense rules explained here.

First, show respect and watch out for improper or ambiguous language. Don't attack or otherwise severely criticize another contributor. Don't be a "troll," an annoying individual who posts irrelevant, controversial, or provocative comments online that may anger fellow users and disrupt a discussion. Because expression online allows for little subtlety, give some thought to how your words could be interpreted. Members of online communities can form deep bonds and strongly dislike contributors they consider vicious or mean.

Pay attention to correct grammar and spelling, and verify your facts. Every comment you contribute is essentially published on the Web and available to any reader. If the content appears on the company intranet, it is for the whole company to see. Don't be sloppy; it could cause you to suffer embarrassment or worse. Wikipedia, a wiki that is trying to marry credibility with its desire for openness, recently tightened the rules for its editors after Internet vandals prematurely announced Senator Edward Kennedy's death and pronounced his colleague, Senator Robert Byrd, dead as well. Errors introduced by cyber attacks and innocent errors alike are often perpetuated by people who blindly trust wiki content.

Follow the guidelines for contributors, and give credit where credit is due. Read the rules to make sure your work fits into the group effort in style, content, and format. As a newbie, ask for help if necessary. Leave your ego behind. Contributors to a wiki are part of a team, not individual authors who can reasonably expect recognition or maintain control over their writing. When borrowing, be sure to cite your sources to avoid plagiarism.

Negotiating Social and Professional Networking Sites

LEARNING OBJECTIVE 5

Understand business uses of social and professional networking sites as well as RSS feeds and social bookmarking.

Far from being only entertaining leisure sites, social networking sites such as Facebook, MySpace, and Twitter are used by businesses for similar reasons and in much the same way as podcasts, blogs, and wikis. Social networking sites enable businesses to connect with customers and employees, share company news, and exchange ideas. Social online communities for professional audiences (e.g., LinkedIn) help recruiters find talent and encounter potential employees before hiring them.

Tapping Into Social Networks

How are businesses using social networking sites?

Business interest in social networking sites is not surprising if we consider that 73 percent of millennials, also called Generation Y, regularly socialize and chat online. An average of 55 percent of all consumers between 14 and 75 regularly visit social online communities. All groups spend between 11 and 19 hours a week on the Internet solely for entertainment.[21] Not surprisingly, then, businesses are trying to catch on and tap the vast potential of social networking.

How Businesses Use Social Networks. Some firms use social online communities for brainstorming and teamwork. They provide the collaboration tools and watch what happens. British Telecom (BT) has about 11,000 employees on Facebook in addition to offering its own internal social network. A British Telecom IT executive says that his company can observe online relationships to see how information travels and decision making occurs. The company is able to identify teams that form spontaneously and naturally and then assigns targeted projects to them. Idea generators are easy to spot. The BT executive considers these contributors invaluable, suggesting that "a new class of supercommunicators has emerged."[22] The key to all the new media is that they thrive in a highly mobile and interactive Web 2.0 environment.

Other companies harness the power of online communities to boost their brand image or to provide a forum for collaboration. McDonald's has a strong presence on Facebook boasting nearly 1.5 million "fans." The fast-food chain also maintains a private networking site, StationM, for its 650,000 hourly employees in 15,000 locations across the United States and Canada.[23]

McDonald's and British Telecom are not the only companies running their own social networks. Insurer MetLife has launched connect.MetLife, an online social network collaboration tool. Resembling Facebook, this internal networking tool sits safely behind the corporate firewall.[24] Best Buy has created its own social network, Blue Shirt Nation, with currently more than 20,000 participants, most of them sales associates. IBM's in-house social network, Beehive, has 30,000 employees on it. Managers notice avid networkers who create buzz and promote the brand. The drawback is that quieter employees may be overlooked.[25]

What dangers does social networking pose for businesses?

Potential Risks of Social Networks for Businesses. Online social networks hold great promise for businesses while also presenting some risk. Most managers want plugged-in employees with strong tech skills. They like to imagine their workers as brand

FIGURE 7.7 **Big Companies Rule on Facebook: Netflix**

Facebook recently reached 350 million users. The site allows registered users to create individual home pages and to choose from more than 200 groups based on their interests. Large corporations seem to thrive on Facebook. *Slate* magazine ranked Coca-Cola "first among companies with the best Facebook presences." Newer companies such as online film rental service Netflix may draw 100,000 fans, as opposed to Coca-Cola's whopping 5,300,000 fans.

ambassadors. They fantasize about their products becoming overnight sensations thanks to viral marketing. However, they also fret about incurring productivity losses, compromising trade secrets, attracting the wrath of huge Internet audiences, and facing embarrassment over inappropriate and damaging employee posts.[26]

Businesses take different approaches to the "dark side" of social networking. Some, such as Zappos.com, take a hands-off approach to employee online activity. Others, such as IBM, have drafted detailed policies to cover all forms of self-expression online. Some of IBM's guidelines include being honest about one's identity, accepting personal responsibility for published posts, and hitting **Send** only after careful thought. The technology giant asks its workers to avoid any controversies outside their professional role. The company wants workers to "add value" as they are building their social reputations, not dwell on trivia.[27] Finally, Enterprise Rent-A-Car and other organizations block some or all social sites.

ETHICS CHECK

Social Media Help Spread Errors Like Wildfire

Electronics retailer Best Buy recently offered a 52-inch flat-screen TV worth $1,799.99 for $9.99 on its Web site. Within hours bloggers and Twitter users posted jokes about this "steal," and some insisted that Best Buy honor the advertised price. The company quickly corrected the online pricing error and would not accept orders at the incorrect price. Was Best Buy obligated to honor the offer?

Younger workers in particular are often stunned when their employers block access to Facebook, Gmail, and other popular Web destinations. One 27-year-old Chicago resident complained about his former employer: "It was a constant battle between the people that saw technology as an advantage, and those that saw it as a hindrance."[28] The key is to strike a balance between allowing employees access to the Web and protecting security and ensuring productivity. Consultant Gary Rudman sees parallels to old-fashioned chatting around the water cooler or making personal phone calls, grudgingly accepted as they were by managers: "These two worlds will continue to collide until there's a mutual understanding that performance, not Internet usage, is what really matters."[29]

Personal mobile devices make monitoring during work time tougher, and some companies are beginning to open access. Kraft Foods allows "reasonable" personal use as long as it does not interfere with job duties. Because the lines between work time and personal time are increasingly blurry, many companies hesitate to ban the Internet outright on the job. Some allow partial access by limiting what employees can do online. They may disable file sharing to protect sensitive information.

Tips for Using Social Networking Sites and Keeping Your Job. Experts agree that, as with any public online activity, users of social networking sites would do well to exercise caution. Privacy is a myth, and sensitive information should not be shared lightly, least of all risqué photographs. Furthermore, refusing "friend" requests or "unfriending" individuals could jeopardize professional relationships. Consider the following tip by career counselor Julie Powell[30] if you like to visit social networking sites and want to keep your job: Establish boundaries. Don't share information online that you would not be comfortable sharing openly in the office.

The advice to think twice before posting online applies to most communication channels used on the job. Facebook expert and blogger Nick O'Neill cautions account holders never to assume that the content they post on a social networking site is protected unless they have activated the privacy option. Many users leave their pages open and risk trouble with their employers by assuming that online comments are hidden from view.[31] Even privacy settings, however, do not guarantee complete protection from prying eyes.

Among the many risks in the cyber world are inappropriate photographs and making "friends" online. Tags make pictures searchable so that an embarrassing college incident may resurface years later. Another potential minefield, says consultant Rachel Weingarten, is rejecting friend requests from some colleagues while accepting such offers from others.[32] The snubbed coworker may harbor ill feelings as a result. Blocking a user for no apparent reason could also be interpreted as a rude rejection.

Harnessing the Potential of Professional Networking Sites

What are the potential rewards of using professional networking sites such as LinkedIn?

Experts agree that connecting online offers professional opportunities by expanding the traditional Rolodex. They see social networking online as a natural extension of work.[33] Small businesses may view such sites as forums for sharing slideshow presentations and other office documents. Artists may feature their work. Medical doctors can discuss surgical techniques with peers.

As we have seen, the lines between social and professional networking are increasingly blurry. However, among business-oriented Web sites where users can post job openings, résumés, and career profiles, LinkedIn is the most popular networking tool, at least in the United States. Xing is attracting large professional audiences in Europe. A great value of such business networking sites is that they can serve as a source for referrals and recommendations. Job seekers can also browse jobs posted by a company with a LinkedIn presence, such as Adobe Systems shown in Figure 7.8.

FIGURE 7.8 **Adobe Systems Jobs on LinkedIn**

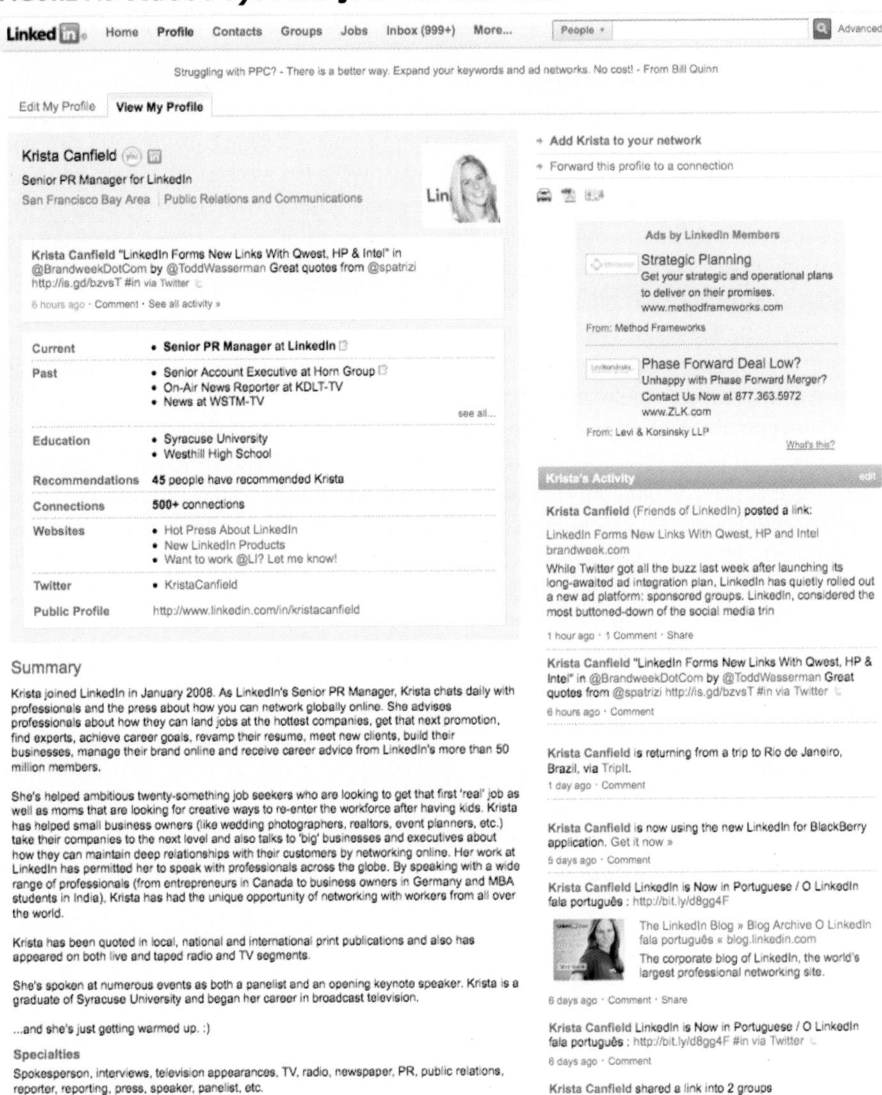

Multimedia and creativity software company Adobe Systems uses the professional networking site LinkedIn to post job openings in its global branch offices.

Hiring experts agree that about three quarters of U.S. companies view social media—mostly LinkedIn—as indispensable outlets for recruiting.[34] They recommend that job seekers keep their profiles "clean"—that is, free of risqué photos, profanity, and negative comments. Instead, job candidates are encouraged to highlight awards, professional goals, and accomplishments. Although professional networking sites cannot replace face-to-face interviews, they allow hiring managers to form first impressions before inviting job hunters, or to vet interviewees being considered for an open position.

The advantages that social and professional networking sites offer recruiters and applicants are plain. In the right hands, the sites are inexpensive, simple, and fast ways to advertise current business opportunities and to connect. However, as innovative as this new type of job search seems to be, the basics remain the same. Candidates need to craft their profiles with the same care they use when putting together their traditional résumés and cover letters. The job hunter's public appearance online must always be professional, and the profile should be up-to-date. You will learn more about job searching online in Chapter 15.

Sharing Information Through RSS Feeds and Social Bookmarking

What is really simple syndication (RSS), and how is it used?

You may wonder how businesspeople navigate the vast resources available on the Internet. Seeking information on the Web that is relevant to you and your business can be time-consuming and sometimes tedious, especially if it means browsing many Web sites for updates. Really simple syndication, RSS for short, is a time-saver, allowing users to monitor many news sources in one convenient spot. Likewise, social bookmarking helps busy professionals stay informed about topics of interest and negotiate the vast information jungle of the Web.

Really Simple Syndication. RSS, a fast and easy way to search and manage information, is a data file format capable of transmitting changing Web content. News organizations, bloggers, and other online information providers syndicate (i.e., publish and distribute) their content to subscribers. RSS documents are called feeds or channels, and they can be read most efficiently with a Web-based feed reader (also known as an aggregator), an easy-to-use software application. Feeds help alert subscribers to up-to-the-minute blog entries, news items, videos, and podcasts from various sources.

How does RSS work? Each time a syndicated Web site is updated, a summary of the new information travels by RSS feed to the site's subscribers. Users can read RSS feeds within their Internet browsers and in e-mail programs such as MS Outlook, but local files are likely to become very large. This is why many subscribers prefer stand-alone "cloud" reader programs online that automatically receive updates from the subscribers' favorite Web sites. Some of the popular news aggregators are Google Reader, Bloglines, SharpReader, NetNewsWire, and Straw. Web-based feed readers also work well with mobile devices, helping busy executives keep up with customized news feeds on the go.

Content providers have a vital interest in providing RSS feeds. For one thing, feeds increase traffic to syndicated Web sites because they can be indexed in search engines and tagged to appear in feed lists, making them easier to find. This helps content providers stay ahead of the vast competition in cyberspace. A number of software applications automatically create RSS feeds—Mambo or Drupal are just two among many free, open-source programs available. Forward-looking companies such as retailer Target, online travel sites such as Travelocity, and many airlines have been using RSS feeds to alert customers to weekly sales and special offers.

In what ways is social bookmarking helpful to business users?

Social Bookmarking. In the battle for "eyeballs" on the Internet, social bookmarking is another critical component. Business Web sites, blogs, and other online content gain an edge if readers link to them and, thus, share content with other online users. Digg, Del.icio.us, Reddit, StumbleUpon, and Squidoo are just a few of the many fast-growing social bookmarking and content aggregator (collector) Web sites. Social bookmarking helps users search, organize, manage, and store bookmarks on the Web with the help of metadata—that is, information tags or keywords.

Many Web sites, blogs, and other content providers on the Internet offer various widgets or icons of social bookmarking sites to enable content sharing. Web publishers hope readers will link their information to social bookmarking sites and alert others to the information. Figure 7.9 shows

Bloggers and other online content providers don't need to list dozens of buttons so that users can spread content on the Internet. Just one *Share* widget allows visitors to choose which social service they want to use for sharing or bookmarking.

FIGURE 7.9 **Social Bookmarking Sites**

common configurations of bookmarking icons that Web designers insert into Web pages to allow visitors to share content.

Typical search engines favor Web resources generating the most traffic. High-traffic Web sites are those that rack up the most hits and are indexed and bookmarked the most. As a result, they receive a high ranking and pop up topmost in keyword searches. Social bookmarking sites are aggregators, which means that they compile and list current, popular news items that will most likely appeal to their readers.

Perhaps you can see now how RSS feeds and social bookmarking sites could help you stay abreast of breaking news from many sources and save you valuable time. Whether you wish to grab a broadcast from CNN.com or check the most recent sports scores, look for the square orange RSS feed icon on your favorite Web sites or a rectangular button with the letters RSS or XML. On most high-traffic Web sites, you will also see *Share* links, or widgets, that will take you to social bookmarking sites.

Spotlight on Communicators

© Scott Townsend

Scott Townsend, marketing director for United Linen & Uniform Services in Oklahoma, uses Twitter along with a corporate blog to share information with customers and to listen to them: "Businesses need to be careful when using social media outlets such as Twitter because they tend to want to start selling.... But Twitter is more about creating and furthering a relationship with a customer, becoming a resource to them and yourself [to be] available to provide solutions."

Checklist

Using Electronic Media Professionally: Dos and Don'ts

Dos: Know Workplace Policies and Avoid Private Use of Media at Work

- **Learn your company's rules.** One employee knew that her employer restricted personal use of work computers, but she believed it focused on Web surfing, not e-mail. She was stunned when her agency fired her after finding 418 personal e-mail messages on her PC.[37] Companies have been slow to adapt Internet policies to advances such as IM, texting, and tweeting. Being informed is your best protection.
- **Avoid or minimize sending personal e-mail, IM messages, or texts from work.** Even if your company allows personal use during lunch or after hours, keep it to a minimum. Better yet, wait to use your home computer to access your personal e-mail and social networking sites.
- **Separate work and personal data.** Keep information that could embarrass you or expose you to legal liability on your personal storage devices or hard drives, never on your office computer.

Dos: Treat All Online Speech as Public and Protect Your Computer

- **Be careful when blogging, tweeting, or posting on social networking sites.** A Canadian blogger lost his job for an entry that read, "Getting to blog for three hours while being paid: priceless."[38]
- **Keep your virus and malicious software protection current.** Always download the newest definitions and updates to your operating system, browser, antivirus program, and antispyware.
- **Pick strong passwords and vary them.** Use a combination of letters, numbers, and symbols. Select a different password for each Web service, and never use your Web passwords as PIN codes on credit or debit cards. Change your passwords every few months.
- **Keep sensitive information private.** Monitor the privacy settings on social networking sites, but don't trust the "private" areas on Facebook, Flickr, and other services that provide public access to most material they store.

Don'ts: Avoid Questionable Content, Personal Documents, and File Sharing

- **Don't send, download, print, or exhibit pornography, sexually explicit jokes, or inappropriate screen savers.** Anything that might "poison" the work environment is prohibited.
- **Don't open attachments sent by e-mail.** Attachments with executable files or video files may carry viruses, spyware, or other malware (malicious programs).
- **Don't download free software and utilities to company machines.** Employees can unwittingly introduce viruses, phishing schemes, and other cyber "bugs."
- **Don't store your music library and photos on a company machine (or server), and don't watch streaming videos.** Capturing precious company bandwidth for personal use is a sure way to be shown the door.
- **Don't share files and avoid file-sharing services.** At work, clarify whether you may use Google Docs and other services that offer optional file sharing. As with any free cloud-based application, exercise caution. Security breaches are always possible. Stay away from LimeWire, and other distributors of pirated files. File-sharing services and downloads can subject you to breaches by third parties.

Best Practices for Using Electronic Media Smartly, Safely, and Professionally

What are some guidelines for the effective and professional use of electronic media?

As advances in computer technology continue to change the way we work and play, Internet use on and off the job has become a danger zone for employees and employers. Misuse costs employers millions of dollars in lost productivity and litigation, and it can cost employees their jobs. A survey by the American Management Association revealed that 26 percent of employers fired employees for e-mail misuse. In addition, 2 percent terminated employees for using instant messaging, and another 2 percent for posting offensive blog content from a company or even a home computer.[35] Companies struggle with fair Internet use policies knowing that over half of their employees with Web access shop online from the office.[36]

Recreational activities, as well as unintentional but careless miscues, can gobble up precious network resources and waste valuable work time. Even more important is concern over lawsuits and network security. Companies must maintain a workplace free of harassment. If employees download pornography, transmit sexually explicit jokes, or use inappropriate screen savers, the work environment can become "poisoned" and employers may be sued. Furthermore, security problems arise when employees open phishing e-mail or fall for malware when browsing the Web.

The accompanying Checklist feature highlights some employee dos and don'ts that you should abide by to keep out of trouble on the job.

Want to do well on tests and excel in your course? Go to **www.meguffey.com** for helpful interactive resources.

- **Review the Chapter 7 PowerPoint slides to prepare for the first quiz.**

Zooming In — YOUR TURN

Twitter

Most mainstream businesses are waiting on the sidelines to see how Twitter will evolve. However, in some industries companies are already using Twitter and other social media to monitor what is being said about them, to engage with customers, and to market to other businesses. Take the airlines: JetBlue's Cheeps and United's Twares offer special deals on domestic and international flights in 140-character tweets. JetBlue and Southwest appointed "tweet watchers" who troubleshoot air travelers' problems. American, Alaska, Air New Zealand, and the Virgin group also tweet actively.[39]

IT firms were not the only early adopters of Twitter. Many large companies have discovered Twitter as a tool to avert public-relations disasters. Eastman Kodak seeks customers' conversations by searching Twitter and creates marketing campaigns focused on Twitter. Ford teaches employees to represent the company and communicate with customers on Twitter. Coca-Cola and PepsiCo are both quick to apologize to irate customers and to correct problems that they discover on Twitter or other social media network sites. Southwest Airlines employs a six-member "emerging-media team." Coke even appointed its first head of social media, Adam Brown, who says: "We're getting to a point if you're not responding, you're not being seen as an authentic type of brand."[40]

Your Task

You are one of three staffers working for Adam Brown at Coca-Cola. Your job is to comb through tweets to find those that are both positive about and critical of your company and to inform your boss about any that could potentially end up hurting Coke's image. Deciding which post could cause trouble is difficult, given that even with tracking software you may need to scan hundreds of posts every day. You know that if many users "retweet," or redistribute the news, the problem may get out of hand. Create a Twitter account at **http://twitter.com** and search for posts about Coca-Cola or any other company your instructor may assign. Search long enough until you have a good sense of what posters are saying. If you identify a trend, make a note of it and report it either in class or in writing as directed by your instructor.

Summary of Learning Objectives

1 Describe the role digital media play in the changing world of business in contrast to traditional paper-based messages. The exchange of information in organizations today is increasingly electronic and mobile, although office workers still send paper-based messages when they need a permanent record; wish to maintain confidentiality; and need to convey formal, long, and important messages. E-mail is still the lifeblood of businesses today, but instant messaging is gaining popularity. Likewise, phone-based SMS services enable cellular customers to send each other short text messages, images, and videos. Businesses have embraced podcasts, blogs, wikis, and social networking to help them communicate with employees, customers, and clients. The use of all digital media requires professionalism and caution because they create permanent records.

2 Meet professional e-mail standards for usage, structure, and format; and follow the rules of netiquette and other best practices. Direct (nonsensitive) e-mails begin with a subject line that summarizes the central idea. The opening repeats that idea and amplifies it. The body explains and provides more information. The closing includes (a) action information, dates, and deadlines; (b) a summary; and/or (c) a closing thought. E-mail messages should be formatted with a meaningful subject line, a greeting, a single-spaced body that is typed with a combination of upper- and lowercase letters, and a closing "signature" that includes contact information. Careful e-mail users write concisely and don't send anything they wouldn't want published. They care about correctness, resist humor, never send spam, use identifying labels when appropriate, and use attachments sparingly. They don't access company computers for personal use unless specifically allowed to do so, and they realize that e-mail may be monitored. They strive to improve readability through design and consider cultural differences.

3 Explain how business professionals communicate by instant messaging and texting. Both instant messaging (IM) and text messaging have become increasingly relevant for business in communicating with customers, employees, and suppliers. IM participants must share the same software to conduct private chats in real time. Texting generally requires a smartphone-delivered SMS service from a wireless company. Text and IM messages can be delivered by a computer or a handheld device. To keep IM and texts professional, know your company's policies, separate personal from business contacts, stay away from personal messaging at work, make yourself unavailable when you need to concentrate, wait until receiving a reply before shooting off multiple messages, avoid sending confidential information, and use correct grammar and spelling.

4 Identify professional uses of podcasts, blogs, and wikis; and describe prudent policies to protect authors of electronic content. Business podcasts are digital audio or video files ranging from short clips to long media files. Any applications that do not require a human presence (e.g., certain training videos) lend themselves to podcast recordings that users can stream or download on demand. Creating simple podcasts requires only inexpensive or free recording software and low-cost equipment. Blogs help businesses to keep customers, employees, and suppliers informed and receive feedback. Online communities can form around a blog. Companies employ blogs for public relations and crisis communication, market research and viral marketing, internal communication, and recruiting. Before blogging, seek permission and know company policies. Avoid sensitive or inappropriate topics. Wikis enable far-flung team members to share information and build a knowledge base, and can be used to replace meetings, manage projects, and document projects large and small. When contributing to a wiki, don't post irrelevant or annoying content, check your facts and your grammar, follow guidelines for contributors, and give credit where appropriate.

5 Understand business uses of social and professional networking sites as well as RSS feeds and social bookmarking. Facebook, MySpace, and Twitter allow firms to share company news; exchange ideas; and connect with customers, employees, other stakeholders, and the public at large. Tech companies in particular harness the power of social networking for teamwork and brainstorming. Other companies boost their brand recognition and provide a forum for collaboration by participating in established social networks or by creating their own in-house communities. The downsides of social media participation are productivity losses, fallout from inappropriate employee posts, leaking of trade secrets, and angry Internet users. Keep safe by sharing only information that you would openly discuss in the office. Be sure to activate your privacy options. Don't post questionable photographs. Professional networking sites such as LinkedIn help companies and job seekers to connect. The virtual network is a logical extension of face-to-face networking, and members need to conduct themselves professionally in both. Really simple syndication and social bookmarking allow users to navigate the huge resources on the Internet. RSS feeds are time-savers because they allow businesspeople to monitor many news sources in one convenient online location. Social bookmarking sites such as Digg, Del.icious, and Reddit can help you search, organize, share, and store bookmarks on the Web.

Chapter Review

1. What is Web 2.0, and how has it changed the way users engage with information? (Obj. 1)
2. Name and describe the two prevailing technological trends today. (Obj. 1)
3. List and concisely describe at least six electronic communication channels used most commonly by businesspeople today. (Obj. 1)
4. List and briefly describe the four parts of typical e-mails. (Obj. 2)
5. Suggest at least ten pointers that you could give to a first-time e-mail user. (Obj. 2)
6. How can you use instant messaging and texting safely on the job? (Obj. 3)
7. Name at least five reasons some organizations forbid employees to use instant and text messaging. (Obj. 3)
8. How can you show professionalism and respect for your receivers in writing business IM messages and texts? (Obj. 3)
9. Describe the process of creating a simple podcast. (Obj. 4)
10. Explain why companies use blogs. (Obj. 4)
11. What is a wiki, and what are its advantages to businesses? (Obj. 4)
12. Name a few of the potential risks that social networking sites may pose to business. (Obj. 5)
13. What do employment and hiring experts recommend to young job seekers who wish to connect with companies on LinkedIn and other professional networking sites? (Obj. 5)
14. What is really simple syndication (RSS), and why is it helpful? (Obj. 5)
15. Explain the role of social bookmarking sites such as Digg, Del.icio.us, Reddit, StumbleUpon, and Squidoo. (Obj. 5)

Critical Thinking

1. How could IM be useful in your career field? Does IM produce a permanent record? Do you think that common abbreviations such as *lol* and *imho* and all-lowercase writing are acceptable in text messages for business? Will the use of shorthand abbreviations as well as creative spelling negatively affect writing skills? (Obj. 3)
2. Tweeting, texting, and quickie e-mailing all may foster sloppy messages. Author Mark Garvey argued, "In business, in education, in the arts, in any writing that takes place outside the linguistic cul-de-sac of our close friends and relatives, writers are expected to reach for certain standards of clarity, concision and care."[41] What did Garvey mean? Do you agree? (Objs. 2, 3)
3. Why are lawyers and technology experts warning companies to store, organize, and manage computer data, including e-mails and instant messages, with sharper diligence? (Obj. 2)
4. Discuss the ramifications of the following statement: *Once an e-mail, instant message, text, or any other document leaves your hands, you have essentially published it.* (Obj. 2)
5. **Ethical Issue:** What Internet behavior could get employees fired? Do employees deserve broad Internet access on the job—if they are responsible? Should employers block access to Web sites? If so, what kind? (Objs. 2, 3, 4, and 5)

Activities

Note: All Documents for Analysis are provided at **www.meguffey.com** for you to revise online.

7.1 Document for Analysis: Jumbled E-Mail Message
(Obj. 2)

Your Task. Analyze the following poorly written e-mail. List its weaknesses. Consider redundancies, wordiness, poor organization, weak subject line, and lack of contact information. If your instructor directs, revise it.

To: Greta Targa <greta.targa@gamma.com>
From: Jim Morales <jim.morales@gamma.com>
Subject: HELP!
Cc:
Bcc:

As you already know, we have been working hard to plan the Gamma Fall Training Conference. It will be held in Miami. Here are the speakers I have lined up for training sessions. I'm thinking that on Tuesday, November 12, we will have Nicole Gold. Her scheduled topic is "Using E-Mail and IM Effectively." Anthony Mills said he could speak to our group on November 13 (Wednesday). "Leading Groups and Teams" is the topic for Mills. Here are their e-mail addresses: tony.mills@sunbelt.net. and n.gold@etc.com.

You can help us make this one of the best training sessions ever. I need you to send each of these people an e-mail and confirm the dates and topics. Due to the fact that we must print the program soon (by September 1), I will need this done as soon as possible. Don't hesitate to call if you have any questions.

Jim

7.2 Document for Analysis: Poorly Organized E-Mail (Obj. 2)

Your Task. Analyze the following poorly written and poorly organized e-mail. List its specific weaknesses. Would bulleted headings improve readability? If your instructor directs, revise it.

To: Mitchell Moraga <mitchell.moraga@media.com>
From: Eleanor Hutchinson <ehutchinson@media.com>
Subject: My Report
Cc:
Bcc:

Mitchell,

This is in response to your request that I attend the Workplace Issues and tell you about it. As you know, I attended the Workplace Issues conference on November 3, as you suggested. The topic was how to prevent workplace violence, and I found it very fascinating. Although we have been fortunate to avoid serious incidents at our company, it's better to be safe than sorry. Because I was the representative from our company and you asked for a report, here it is. Kit Adkins was the presenter, and she made suggestions in three categories, which I will summarize here.

Ms. Atkins cautioned organizations to prescreen job applicants. As a matter of fact, wise companies do not offer employment until after a candidate's background has been checked. Just the mention of a background check is enough to make some candidates withdraw. These candidates, of course, are the ones with something to hide.

A second suggestion was that companies should prepare a good employee handbook that outlines what employees should do when they suspect potential workplace violence. This handbook should include a way for informers to be anonymous.

A third recommendation had to do with recognizing red-flag behavior. This involves having companies train managers to recognize signs of potential workplace violence. What are some of the red flags? One sign is an increasing number of arguments (most of them petty) with coworkers. Another sign is extreme changes in behavior or statements indicating depression over family or financial problems. Another sign is bullying or harassing behavior. Bringing a firearm to work or displaying an extreme fascination with firearms is another sign.

I think that the best recommendation is prescreening job candidates. This is because it is most feasible. If you want me to do more research on prescreening techniques, do not hesitate to let me know. Let me know by November 18 if you want me to make a report at our management meeting, which is scheduled for December 3.

Ellie

7.3 Document for Analysis: Instant Messaging at Local Auto Dealer (Obj. 3)

Read the following log of a live IM chat between a customer service representative and a visitor to a Glendora car dealership's Web site.
Your Task. In class discuss how Alex could have made this interaction with a customer more effective. Is his IM chat with Mr. Rhee professional, polite, and respectful? If your instructor directs, rewrite Alex's responses to Mr. Rhee's queries.

Service rep: Hey, I'm Alex. How's it goin? Welcome to Harkin BMW of Glendora!

Customer: ??

Service rep: Im supposed to provid live assistance. What can I do you for?

Customer: I want buy car.

Service rep: May I have your name fist?

Customer: Jin Bae Rhee

Service rep: Whoa! Is that a dude's name? Okay. What kind? New inventory or preowned?

Customer: BMW. 2011 model. for family, for business.

Service rep: New, then, huh? Where are you from?

Customer: What car you have?

Service rep: We got some that will knock your socks off.

Customer: I want green car, low mileage, less gasoline burn.

Service rep: My man, if you can't afford the gas on these puppies, you shouldn't buy a Beemer, you know what I mean? Or ya want green color?

Customer: ?

Service rep: Okeydoke, we got a full lineup. Which series, 3, 5, 6, or 7? Or an X3 or X5? A Z4 convertible?

Customer: 760 sedan?

Service rep: Nope. We got just two 550i, one for $68,695 and one for 71,020

Customer: Eureopean delivery?

Service rep: Oh, I know zip about that. Let me find someone who does. Can I have your phone number and e-mail?

Customer: i prefer not get a phone call yet … but 299-484-9807 is phone numer and jrhee@techtrade.com email

Service rep: Awsome. Well give you a jingle back or shoot you an email pronto! Bye.

7.4 Choosing a Holiday Plan (Obj. 2)

E-mail

In the past your company offered all employees 11 holidays, starting with New Year's Day in January and proceeding through Christmas Day the following December. Other companies offer similar holiday schedules. In addition, your company has given all employees one floating holiday. That day was determined by a company-wide vote. As a result, all employees had the same day off. Now, however, management is considering a new plan that involves a floating holiday that each employee may choose. Selections, however, would be subject to staffing needs within individual departments. If two people wanted the same day, the employee with the most seniority would have the day off.

Your Task. As a member of the Human Resources staff, write an e-mail to employees asking them to choose between continuing the current company-wide uniform floating holiday or instituting a new plan for an individual floating holiday. Be sure to establish an end date.

7.5 Reaching Consensus About Business Attire (Obj. 2)

E-mail Team

Casual dress in professional offices has been coming under attack. Your boss, Michael Harding, received the e-mail shown in Figure 7.1. He thinks it would be a good assignment for his group of management trainees to help him respond to that message. He asks your team to research answers to the first five questions in CEO William Laughton's message. He doesn't expect you to answer the final question, but any information you can supply to the first questions would help him shape a response.

Schilling & Voigt is a public CPA firm with a staff of 120 CPAs, bookkeepers, managers, and support personnel. Located in downtown Bridgeport, Connecticut, the plush offices on Water Street overlook Waterfront Park and the Long Island Sound. The firm performs general accounting and audit services as well as tax planning and preparation. Accountants visit clients in the field and also entertain them in the downtown office.

Your Task. Decide whether the entire team will research each question in Figure 7.1 or whether team members will be assigned certain questions. Collect information, discuss it, and reach consensus on what you will report to Mr. Harding. As a team write a concise one-page response. Your goal is to inform, not persuade. Remember that you represent management, not students or employees.

7.6 Twitter: Learning to Write Superefficient Tweets (Objs. 1, 4, and 5)

Twitter forces its users to practice extreme conciseness. Some music reviewers have risen to the challenge and reviewed whole albums in no more than 140 characters. National Public Radio put Stephen Thompson, one of its music editors, to the test. "I approach Twitter as a science," Thompson says.[42] He sees well-designed tweets as online equivalents of haiku, a highly structured type of Japanese poetry. Thompson believes that tweets should be properly punctuated, be written in complete sentences, and of course, not exceed the 140-character limit. His rules also exclude abbreviations.

Here are two samples of Thompson's mini reviews: "Mos Def is a hip-hop renaissance man on smart songs that look to the whole world and its conflicts. Slick Rick's guest spot is a nice touch." The second one reads: "The Phenomenal Handclap Band: Chugging, timeless, jammy throwback from eight shaggy Brooklyn hipsters. Starts slowly, gets hypnotically fun."[43]

Your Task. As an intern in Stephen Thompson's office, review your favorite album in 140 characters or fewer, following your boss's rules. After you have warmed up, your instructor may direct you to other concise writing tasks. Send a tweet to your instructor, if appropriate, or practice writing Twitter posts in MS Word. The best tweets could be shared with the class.

7.7 Instant Messaging: Practicing Your Professional IM Skills (Obj. 3)

Web Team

Your instructor will direct this role-playing group activity. Using instant messaging, you will simulate one of several typical business scenarios—for example, responding to a product inquiry, training a new-hire, troubleshooting with a customer, or making an appointment. For each scenario, two or more students will chat professionally with only a minimal script to practice on-the-spot yet courteous professional interaction by IM. Your instructor will determine which software you will need and provide brief instructions to prepare you for your role in this exercise.

If you don't have instant messaging software on your computer or smart device yet, download the application first—for example, AOL's Instant Messenger, Yahoo Messenger, Microsoft's Windows Live Messenger, or Skype. Yahoo Messenger, for instance, allows you to IM your friends on Yahoo Messenger but also on Windows Live Messenger. You control who sees you online; if you don't wish to be interrupted, you can use stealth settings. All IM software enables users to share photos and large media files (up to 2 gigabytes on Yahoo). You can make voice calls and use webcam video as well. These advanced features turn IM software into a simple conferencing tool and video phone. You can connect with users who have the same software all around the world. Contrary to calling landlines or cell phones, peer-to-peer voice calls are free. Most IM clients also have mobile applications for your smartphone, so that you can IM or call other users while you are away from a computer.

Your Task. Log on to the IM program your instructor chooses. Follow your instructor's directions closely as you role-play the business situation you were assigned with your partner or team. The scenario will involve two or more people who will communicate by instant messaging in real time.

7.8 Podcast, Twitter, Texting: Analyzing a Podcast (Obj. 4)

E-mail

Browsing the podcasts at iTunes, you stumble across the Quick and Dirty Tips series, specifically Money Girl, who dispenses financial advice. You sign up for the free podcasts that cover a variety of business topics. You also visit the Web site at **http://www.quickanddirtytips.com/**.

Your Task. Pick a QDNow.com podcast that interests you. Listen to it or obtain a transcript on the Web site and study it for its structure. Is it direct or indirect? Informative or persuasive? At your instructor's request, write an e-mail that discusses the podcast you analyzed. Alternatively, if your instructor allows, you could also send a very concise summary of the podcast by text message from your cell phone or an ultrashort tweet (140 characters or fewer) to your instructor.

7.9 Podcast: Turning Text to Video in a Jiffy (Obj. 4)

Web

Have you ever wondered how software converts text to video in a matter of minutes? Article Video Robot (AVR) is an application that automates the process of animating your text. You can create something resembling a simple podcast by inputting your text and letting the application do the rest. The AVR Web site provides an entertaining video with step-by-step instructions. To get a taste of creating an animated video from a text you prepare, use the free trial version. When you finish your trial video, you will see that the software makes distribution to about 17 Web sites very easy. Of course, this service may require a fee. Even though the voices sound a bit tinny and robotic, you will have created a rudimentary video in no time.

Your Task. Write a page-long text that delivers information, provides instructions, or conveys a sales pitch. Go to **http://www.articlevideorobot.com/** and view the introduction video. After that, you can register for the free trial. You can use the application only once at no cost, so prepare your text ahead of time. This video tool is suitable for informational, instructional, and persuasive messages.

7.10 Blog: Analyzing the Nuts About Southwest Blog (Obj. 4)

Web

When you browse the Southwest Airlines blog, you will find the following terms of use:

> *We want to build a personal relationship between our Team and you, and we need your participation. Everyone is encouraged to*

join in, and you don't need to register to read, watch, or comment. However, if you would like to share photos or videos or rate a post, among other things, you will need to complete a profile. . . .

This is the point where we insert the "fine print" and discuss the guidelines for posting. Nuts About Southwest is a moderated site because we want to ensure that everyone stays on topic—or at least pretty close to it. We would LUV for you to post your thoughts, comments, suggestions, and questions, but when you post, make sure that they are of general interest to most readers. Of course, profanity, racial and ethnic slurs, and rude behavior like disparaging personal remarks won't be tolerated nor published.

Even though Nuts About Southwest is moderated, we pledge to present opposing viewpoints as we have done since our blog first went "live" several years ago, and we will strive to keep posts interesting, diverse, and multi-sided. Our Team wants to engage in a conversation with you, but not every post will receive a response from us. . . .

Your Task. Visit the Southwest.com blog at **www.blogsouthwest.com/about**. Click About and read the entire User Guide. In class, discuss the tone of the guidelines. How are they presented? Who is authoring the blog, and what is its purpose? What assumptions can you make about the company culture when you read the guidelines and the blog entries? If your instructor directs, write a clear, direct memo or an e-mail message reporting your observations.

7.11 Blog and Wiki: Reviewing Fortune 500 Business Blogging Wiki (Obj. 4)

Web

Here is your opportunity to view and evaluate a corporate blog. The site Socialtext.net is a wiki listing the 78 Fortune 500 companies that have a business blog at this time, defined as "active public blogs by company employees about the company and/or its products." You will find a range of large business organizations such as Amazon.com, Disney, Motorola, Safeway, and Toys"R"Us. Socialtext.net is hosting a wiki of reviews that critique Fortune 500 business blogs. The reviews are posted on a variety of blogs authored by various writers and hyperlinked to the Socialtext.net wiki.

Your Task. Browse the Fortune 500 Business Blogging Wiki at **http://www.socialtext.net/bizblogs/index.cgi**. Follow the links provided there to view some of the corporate blogs on the site. Select a company blog you find interesting, browse the pages, and read some of the contents. Pick a corporate blog that has already been reviewed by an independent blogger. Read the blogger's review. Consider the style and length of the review. If your instructor directs, write a brief informational memo or e-mail describing the business blog as well as its review, the style of the blogger's critique, the review's accuracy, and so forth.

Alternatively, your instructor may ask you to write an original review of a Fortune 500 company blog that has not yet been evaluated. You may be called on to write your own blog entry discussing an unreviewed company blog of your choice. You could compose the blog response in MS Word or e-mail it to your instructor as appropriate.

7.12 Creating a Twitter Group (Obj. 4)

Web

Tweetworks.com is designed to make microblogging useful for private individuals and businesses. The site is based on the premise that people like to talk with other like-minded people. Users come together in communities around specific topics (politics, sports, art, business, and so on). Tweetworks invites members to talk about the big news stories of the day, bounce ideas off other participants online, or just join the conversation—all in fewer than 140 characters. Your instructor may choose to create a public or private group for the class. Within this Tweetworks group for your course, you may be asked to complete short assignments in the form of tweets. Posts in a private group are not shared with other general users, yet they should be relevant to the class content and professional.

Your Task. Use your Twitter username and password to log on at **www.tweetworks.com/groups**. Sign into and follow the group designated by your instructor. Your instructor may ask you to comment on a topic he or she assigns or may encourage you to enter into a freewheeling discussion with other members of your class online. Your instructor may act as a group moderator evaluating the frequency and quality of your contributions.

7.13 Social Networking: Building an Online Community on Facebook (Obj. 5)

Web Team

Chances are you already have a Facebook profile and communicate with friends and family. You may be a fan of a celebrity or a business. Now you can also become a fan of your business communication class if your instructor decides to create a course page on Facebook. The main purpose of such a social networking site for a class is to exchange links and interesting stories relevant to the material being learned. Intriguing tidbits and business news might also be posted on the "wall" to be shared by all signed-up fans. Everybody, even students who are quiet in class, could contribute. However, before you can become a fan of your business communication class, it needs to be created online.

Your Task. If you posted a profile on Facebook, all you need to do is search for the title of the newly created business communication Facebook page and become a fan. If you don't have an account yet, begin by signing up at **www.facebook.com**. On-screen prompts will make it easy for you to build a profile.

7.14 Social Networking: Preparing a Professional LinkedIn Profile (Obj. 5)

Team

Virtual networking on a professional networking site such as LinkedIn is an extension of seeking face-to-face contacts—the most effective way to find a job to date. Consider creating a credible, appealing presence on LinkedIn to make yourself attractive to potential business connections and hiring managers. Your LinkedIn site should serve purely to build your career and professional reputation.

Your Task. Go to **www.linkedin.com** and sign up for a free account. Follow the on-screen directions to create a profile, add a professional-looking photograph, and upload a polished résumé. You will be prompted to invite contacts from your e-mail address books. If your instructor directs, form teams and critique each other's profiles. Link to those profiles of your peers that have been prepared most diligently and strike you as having the best eye appeal.

7.15 E-Mail Simulation: Writeaway Hotels (Obj. 2)

At **www.meguffey.com**, you can build your e-mail skills in our Writeaway Hotels simulation. You will be reading, writing, and responding to messages in an exciting game that helps you make appropriate decisions about whether to respond to e-mail messages and how to write clear, concise messages under pressure. The game can be played in a computer lab, in a classroom, or even on your own computer and on your own time.

Your Task. Check out the Writeaway Hotels simulation at your student site. If your instructor directs, follow the instructions to participate.

Video Resource

Video Library 1, Technology in the Workplace

What is the proper use of technology in today's workplace? This video takes you to H. B. Jones, a small landscape design and supply firm. You will meet Elliott, the owner and founder; Helena, a competent office worker; James, East Coast manager; and Ian, an inept employee. This fast-paced video gives you a glimpse of appropriate and inappropriate uses of workplace technology. It moves so quickly that you may want to watch it twice to be able to answer these questions:

- Do you see significant differences between Helena's and Ian's use of social networking sites? Are their visits to Facespace legitimate?
- What efficiencies and inefficiencies do you detect in how each character uses his or her smartphone?
- Is the featured company a technologically functional workplace, or can it be called dysfunctional? Which remedies would you propose if you identify any shortcomings?
- How would you describe Ian's and Helena's behavior upon entering the office in the morning?

Chat About It

In each chapter you will find five discussion questions related to the chapter material. Your instructor may assign these topics for you to discuss in class, in an online chat room, or on an online discussion board. Some of the discussion topics may require outside research. You may also be asked to read and respond to postings made by your classmates.

Topic 1: How could dashing off quick e-mails, tweets, or instant messages with incorrect style, grammar, or mechanics hurt one's ability to write longer, more formal messages correctly?

Topic 2: Describe a time when you should have had a face-to-face meeting instead of sending an electronic message. Why would the face-to-face meeting have been better?

Topic 3: Find an example of an e-mail that caused a problem for the sender because the message found its way to an unintended recipient. What problem did the situation cause?

Topic 4: What is your strategy to avoid sending an IM, tweet, or text message that you might regret later?

Topic 5: Why do businesses host public blogs with negative postings of their products or services?

Grammar and Mechanics C.L.U.E. Review 7

Apostrophes and Other Punctuation

Review Guides 31–38 about apostrophes and other punctuation in Appendix A, Grammar and Mechanics Guide, beginning on page A-14. On a separate sheet or on your computer, revise the following sentences to correct errors in the use of apostrophes and other punctuation. For each error that you locate, write the guide number that reflects this usage. The more you recognize the reasons, the better you will learn these punctuation guidelines. If a sentence is correct, write *C*. When you finish, check your answers on page Key-1.

Example: We needed the boss signature before we could mail the report.
Revision: We needed the **boss's** signature before we could mail the report. [Guide 32]

1. Facebook users accounts will be suspended if the members don't abide by the sites policies.
2. James performance review was outstanding again.
3. Would you please give me directions to your downtown headquarters
4. The shipping supervisor resented Barbara being late almost every morning.
5. Is it true that the CEO decided to write a weekly blog
6. You must replace the ink cartridge see page 8 in the manual, before printing.
7. Justin wondered whether all sales managers databases needed to be updated.
8. (Direct quotation) Health care costs said the CEO will increase substantially this year.
9. In just two months time, we expect to interview five candidates for the opening.
10. The meeting starts at 10 a.m. sharp, doesn't it

CHAPTER 8

Positive Messages

Want to do well on tests and excel in your course? Go to **www.meguffey.com** for helpful interactive resources.

- **Review the Chapter 8 PowerPoint slides to prepare for the first quiz.**

OBJECTIVES

After studying this chapter, you should be able to

1. Apply the 3-x-3 writing process to creating successful positive messages, including e-mails, interoffice memos, and business letters.
2. Understand the appropriate use of e-mails, interoffice memos, and business letters.
3. Compose direct messages that make requests and respond to inquiries.
4. Write messages that clearly explain step-by-step instructions.
5. Prepare messages that make direct claims.
6. Create adjustment messages that regain the confidence of customers and promote further business.
7. Write special messages that convey kindness and goodwill.
8. Modify international messages to accommodate readers from other cultures.

Zooming In PART 1

Ben & Jerry's Uses Positive Messages to Sweeten Relations With Customers

America's love affair with numbingly rich ice cream may have finally plateaued. Health and weight worries have apparently cut the breakneck growth of superpremium ice creams. However, Ben & Jerry's Homemade, premier purveyor of the superpremiums, remains one of the country's most visible ice cream companies.

In growing from a 12-flavor miniparlor in Burlington, Vermont, into a Fortune 500 company called a "national treasure," Ben & Jerry's has been showered with publicity. The flood of press notices flowed partly from its rapid ascent and its funky flavor hits such as Chubby Hubby, Half Baked Carb Karma, New York Super Fudge Chunk, and Phish Food. During the 2008 presidential campaign, it introduced Yes Pecan (a variation of Barack Obama's campaign mantra, "Yes we can"), made of "amber waves of buttery ice cream with roasted non-partisan pecans." Of even greater media interest was the New Age business philosophy of founders Ben Cohen and Jerry Greenfield. Unlike most entrepreneurs, their aim was to build a successful business but, at the same time, have fun and be a force for social change.

Some time ago Ben and Jerry resigned their symbolic positions as brand icons after the company was purchased by the Anglo-Dutch megaconglomerate Unilever. Despite the change in ownership, Ben & Jerry's continues its efforts to improve local and global quality of life. The company promotes a progressive, nonpartisan social mission to balance economic, product, and social goals on the way to a sustainable business.

Although no longer locally owned, Ben & Jerry's is a visible company with a popular national product and a strong social image. It naturally generates a good deal of correspondence. Customer messages typically fall into three categories: (a) fan mail, (b) information requests, and (c) claims. Fan mail contains praise and testimonials: "Tried the new Cherry Garcia Frozen Yogurt and . . . I want to go to Vermont and shake your sticky hands." Information requests may involve questions about ingredients or food processing. Some messages inquire about Ben & Jerry's position on milk from cloned cows or eggs from caged chickens. Claim requests generally present a problem and require immediate response. Responding to customer messages in all three categories is a critical element in maintaining customer goodwill and market position for Ben & Jerry's.[1] You will learn more about this case on page 239.

© Andre Jenny/Alamy

Critical Thinking

- Have you ever written a letter or sent an e-mail to a company? What might motivate you to do so? Would you expect a response?
- If a company such as Ben & Jerry's receives a fan letter complimenting products or service, is it necessary to respond?
- Why is it important for companies to answer claim messages immediately?

http://www.benjerry.com

Successful Positive Messages Start With the Writing Process

LEARNING OBJECTIVE 1

Apply the 3-x-3 writing process to creating successful positive messages, including e-mails, interoffice memos, and business letters.

Business and professional organizations thrive on information that is exchanged externally and internally. At Ben & Jerry's external messages go to customers, vendors, other businesses, and the government. Internal messages travel upward to superiors, downward to employees, and horizontally among workers. Most of those messages are positive, straightforward communications that conduct everyday business and convey goodwill.

In this book we divide business messages into three content areas: (a) **positive** messages communicating straightforward requests, replies, and goodwill, covered in this chapter; (b) **negative** messages delivering refusals and bad news, covered in Chapter 9; and (c) **persuasive** messages, including sales pitches, covered in Chapter 10. Most of these business messages are exchanged in the form of e-mails, memos, or letters. As you study how to prepare positive, negative, and persuasive messages, you will also be learning which channel is appropriate for the message and situation you face. Should you send an e-mail or a memo? If the message is going outside the organization, should it be a letter?

This chapter focuses on routine, positive messages. These will make up the bulk of your messages. Although such messages may be short and straightforward, they benefit from attention to the composition process. "At the heart of effective writing is the ability to organize a series of thoughts," says writing expert and executive Max Messmer. Taking the time to think through what you want to achieve and how the audience will react makes writing much easier.[2] Here is a quick review of the 3-x-3 writing process to help you think through its application to positive messages.

Phase 1: Analysis, Anticipation, and Adaptation

What questions should you ask yourself before you begin a message?

In Phase 1, prewriting, you will need to spend some time analyzing your task. It is amazing how many of us are ready to put our pens or computers into gear before engaging our minds. Too often, writers start a message without enough preparation. Alice Blachly, a veteran writer from Ben & Jerry's, realized the problem. She said, "If I'm having trouble with a letter and it's not coming out right, it's almost always because I haven't thought through exactly what I want to say."[3] In the Ben & Jerry's letter shown in Figure 8.1, Blachly responds to a request from a young Ben & Jerry's customer. Before writing the letter, she thought about the receiver and tried to find a way to personalize what could have been a form letter.

As you prepare a message, ask yourself these important questions:

- **Do I really need to write this e-mail, memo, or letter?** A phone call or a quick visit to a nearby coworker might solve the problem—and save the time and expense of a written message. On the other hand, some written messages are needed to provide a permanent record or to show a well-conceived plan.
- **Why am I writing?** Know why you are writing and what you hope to achieve. This will help you recognize what the important points are and where to place them.
- **How will the reader react?** Visualize the reader and the effect your message will have. In preparing written messages, imagine that you are sitting and talking with your reader. Avoid speaking bluntly, failing to explain, or ignoring your reader's needs. Consider ways to shape the message to benefit the reader. Also remember that with e-mails, your message may very well be forwarded to someone else.
- **What channel should I use?** It's tempting to use e-mail for much of your correspondence. However, a phone call or face-to-face visit is a better channel choice if you need to (a) convey enthusiasm, warmth, or another emotion; (b) supply a context; or (c) smooth over disagreements. A business letter is better when the matter requires (a) a permanent record, (b) confidentiality, or (c) formality.
- **How can I save my reader's time?** Think of ways that you can make your message easier to comprehend at a glance. Use bullets, asterisks, lists, headings, and white space to improve readability. Notice in the Ben & Jerry's letter in Figure 8.1 that Alice Blachly used bullets to highlight the enclosures.

Phase 2: Research, Organization, and Composition

What steps should you take in Phase 2 of the writing process?

In Phase 2, writing, you will first want to check the files, gather documentation, and prepare your message. Make an outline of the points you wish to cover. For short messages jot down notes on the document you are answering or make a scratch list at your computer. In Alice Blachly's letter shown in Figure 8.1, she made a scratch outline of the points she wanted to cover before writing.

For longer documents that require formal research, use a cluster diagram or the outlining techniques discussed in Chapter 5. As you compose your message, avoid amassing huge blocks of text. No one wants to read endless lines of type. Instead, group related information into paragraphs, preferably short ones. Paragraphs separated by white space look inviting. Be sure that each paragraph includes a topic sentence backed up by details and evidence. If you bury your main point in the middle of a paragraph, the reader may miss it. Also plan for revision, because excellence is rarely achieved on the first effort.

Phase 3: Revision, Proofreading, and Evaluation

What questions should you ask yourself in Phase 3 of the writing process?

Phase 3, revising, involves putting the final touches on your message. Careful and caring writers ask themselves the following questions:

FIGURE 8.1 **Analyzing Ben & Jerry's Customer Response**

Prewriting

Analyze: The purpose of this letter is to build goodwill and promote Ben & Jerry's products.

Anticipate: The reader is young, enthusiastic, and eager to hear from Ben & Jerry's. She will appreciate personalized comments.

Adapt: Use short sentences, cheerful thoughts, and plenty of references to the reader, her club, her school, and her request.

2 Writing

Research: Reread the customer's letter. Decide on items to enclose and locate them.

Organize: Open directly with a positive response. Explain the enclosed items. Find ways to make the reader feel a special connection with Ben & Jerry's.

Compose: Write the first draft quickly. Realize that revision will improve it.

3 Revising

Revise: Revise the message striving for a warm tone. Use the receiver's name. Edit long paragraphs and add bulleted items.

Proofread: Check the address of the receiver. Decide whether to hyphenate *cofounder* and how to punctuate quotations.

Evaluate: Consider how you would feel if you received this letter.

BEN & JERRY'S®
VERMONT'S FINEST • ICE CREAM & FROZEN YOGURT™

January 18, 2012

Ms. Jennifer Ball
1401 Churchville Lane
Bel Air, MD 21014

Dear Jennifer:

We're delighted to hear of your Ben & Jerry's Club at Franklin Middle School and to send the items you requested.

[Opens directly with response to customer's request]

Your club sounds as though it resembles its parent in many ways. We, too, can't seem to control our growth; and we, too, get a little out of control on Friday afternoons. Moreover, the simplicity of your club rules mirrors the philosophy of our cofounder, who says, "If it's not fun, why do it?"

[Personalizes reply and builds goodwill with reference to writer's letter]

Enclosed are the following items:

- A list of all flavors available in pints. If you can't find these flavors at your grocer's, I'm sending you some "ballots" for your club's use in encouraging your grocer to stock your favorites.
- The latest issue of Ben & Jerry's "Chunk Mail." We're also putting you on our mailing list so that your club will receive our Chunk Mail newsletter regularly.

[Itemizes and explains enclosures requested by customer]

We hope, Jennifer, that you'll soon tour our plant here in Vermont. Then, you can be on an equal footing with your prez and sport one of our tour buttons. This seems only appropriate for the consensus-building, decision-making model you are pioneering in your Ben & Jerry's Club!

[Uses receiver's name to make letter sound conversational and personal]

[Ties in cordial closing with more references to customer's letter]

Sincerely,

Alice

Alice Blanchly
Consumer Affairs

Enc: Flavor list, ballots, Chunk Mail

P.O. BOX 240, WATERBURY, VERMONT 05676 (802)244-6957 FAX (802)244-5944
100% Post-Consumer Recycle Paper

- **Is the message clear?** Viewed from the receiver's perspective, are the ideas clear? Did you use plain English? If the message is passed on to others, will they need further explanation? Consider having a colleague critique your message if it is an important one.
- **Is the message correct?** Are the sentences complete and punctuated properly? Did you overlook any typos or misspelled words? Remember to use your spell checker and grammar checker to proofread your message before sending it.
- **Did I plan for feedback?** How will you know whether this message is successful? You can improve feedback by asking questions (such as *Are you comfortable with these suggestions?* or *What do you think?*). Remember to make it easy for the receiver to respond.
- **Will this message achieve its purpose?** The last step in the 3-x-3 writing process is evaluating the product. Before any message left her desk at Ben & Jerry's, Alice Blachly always reread it and put herself in the shoes of the reader: "How would I feel if I were receiving it?"

Spotlight on Communicators

© Courtesy of Peggy Foran

Peggy Foran, who has served as executive vice president at Sara Lee Corporation and senior executive with Pfizer Pharmaceutical, was known for "pushing the envelope" in practicing good communication with investors. In correspondence, news releases, and proxy statements, Foran insisted on clear, basic English. Although accustomed to dense legal language, she admitted to confusion. "I do this for a living, and I can't understand a lot of [corporate material] on the first read." She demands clear expression in all messages. "Transparency is part of our culture. We believe in plain English." To be sure their communication is clear, company writers are encouraged to put themselves in the shoes of readers, which is good advice for all business communicators.

Watching the Writing Process in Action

To see how the writing process can improve an internal message, look at Figure 8.2. It shows the first draft and revision of an e-mail that Madeleine Espinoza, senior marketing manager, wrote to her boss, Keith Milton. Although it contained solid information, the first draft was so wordy and dense that the main points were lost.

In the revision stage, Madeleine realized that she needed to reorganize her message into an opening, body, and closing. She desperately needed to improve the readability. In studying what she had written, she recognized that she was talking about two main problems. She discovered that she could present a three-part solution. These ideas didn't occur to her until she had written the first draft. Only in the revision stage was she able to see that she was talking about two separate problems as well as a three-part solution. The revision process can help you think through a problem and clarify a solution.

As she revised, Madeleine was more aware of the subject line, opening, body, and closing. She used an informative subject line and opened directly by explaining why she was writing. Her opening outlined the two main problems so that her reader understood the background of the following recommendations. In the body of the message, Madeleine identified three corrective actions, and she highlighted them for improved readability. Notice that she listed her three recommendations using numbers with boldface headings, and she started each item with an action verb. Madeleine closed her message with a deadline and a reference to the next action to be taken.

Positive Messages: E-Mails, Memos, and Letters

LEARNING OBJECTIVE 2
Understand the appropriate use of e-mails, interoffice memos, and business letters.

In the workplace positive messages may take the form of e-mails, memos, and letters. When you need information from a team member in another office, you might send an e-mail. If you must explain to employees a new procedure for ordering supplies, you would probably write an interoffice memo. When you respond to a customer asking about your products, you would most likely prepare a letter.

Comparing E-Mails and Memos

What kinds of messages are most appropriate for workplace e-mails?

Most internal messages will be exchanged as e-mails or interoffice memos. E-mail is most appropriate for short messages, such as sharing "need to know" facts, setting up appointments, distributing documents, giving updates, requesting information, getting answers to specific questions, and documenting conversations when a paper trail is needed. You probably have already written many e-mails to your friends. However, professional e-mails sent on the job are

FIGURE 8.2 **Applying the Writing Process to an E-Mail**

Prewriting

Analyze: The purpose of this memo is to describe database problems and recommend solutions.

Anticipate: The audience is the writer's boss, who is familiar with the topic and who appreciates brevity.

Adapt: Because the reader requested this message, the direct strategy is most appropriate.

Writing

Research: Gather data documenting the customer database and how to use Access software.

Organize: Announce recommendations and summarize problems. In the body, use action verbs to list the three actions for solving the problem. In the closing, describe reader benefits, provide a deadline, and specify the next action.

Compose: Prepare the first draft.

Revising

Revise: Highlight the two main problems and the three recommendations. Use bullets, caps, and headings to improve readability. Make the bulleted ideas parallel.

Proofread: Double-check to see whether *database* is one word or two. Use spell checker.

Evaluate: Does this e-mail supply concise information the boss wants in an easy-to-read format?

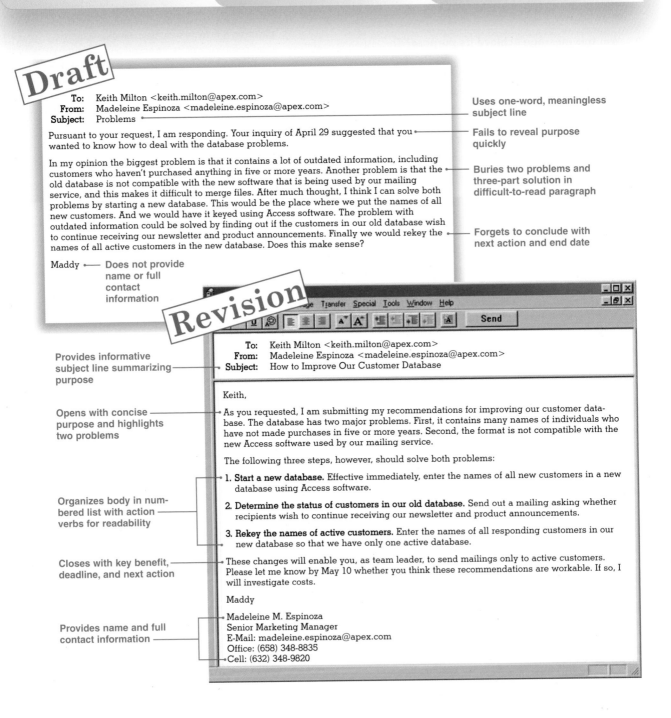

Draft

To: Keith Milton <keith.milton@apex.com>
From: Madeleine Espinoza <madeleine.espinoza@apex.com>
Subject: Problems — *Uses one-word, meaningless subject line*

Pursuant to your request, I am responding. Your inquiry of April 29 suggested that you wanted to know how to deal with the database problems. — *Fails to reveal purpose quickly*

In my opinion the biggest problem is that it contains a lot of outdated information, including customers who haven't purchased anything in five or more years. Another problem is that the old database is not compatible with the new software that is being used by our mailing service, and this makes it difficult to merge files. After much thought, I think I can solve both problems by starting a new database. This would be the place where we put the names of all new customers. And we would have it keyed using Access software. The problem with outdated information could be solved by finding out if the customers in our old database wish to continue receiving our newsletter and product announcements. Finally we would rekey the names of all active customers in the new database. Does this make sense? — *Buries two problems and three-part solution in difficult-to-read paragraph* — *Forgets to conclude with next action and end date*

Maddy — *Does not provide name or full contact information*

Revision

To: Keith Milton <keith.milton@apex.com>
From: Madeleine Espinoza <madeleine.espinoza@apex.com>
Subject: How to Improve Our Customer Database — *Provides informative subject line summarizing purpose*

Keith,

As you requested, I am submitting my recommendations for improving our customer database. The database has two major problems. First, it contains many names of individuals who have not made purchases in five or more years. Second, the format is not compatible with the new Access software used by our mailing service. — *Opens with concise purpose and highlights two problems*

The following three steps, however, should solve both problems:

1. **Start a new database.** Effective immediately, enter the names of all new customers in a new database using Access software.
2. **Determine the status of customers in our old database.** Send out a mailing asking whether recipients wish to continue receiving our newsletter and product announcements.
3. **Rekey the names of active customers.** Enter the names of all responding customers in our new database so that we have only one active database.

Organizes body in numbered list with action verbs for readability

These changes will enable you, as team leader, to send mailings only to active customers. Please let me know by May 10 whether you think these recommendations are workable. If so, I will investigate costs. — *Closes with key benefit, deadline, and next action*

Maddy

Madeleine M. Espinoza
Senior Marketing Manager
E-Mail: madeleine.espinoza@apex.com
Office: (658) 348-8835
Cell: (632) 348-9820

Provides name and full contact information

quite different from notes to friends. The purpose of business e-mails is to get work done rather than interact socially with people.[4] In Chapter 7 you learned about formatting of e-mail, and you studied best practices for using e-mail effectively and safely in the workplace. In this chapter we discuss composing e-mails, interoffice memos, and business letters. You may be thinking, *What are memos? Haven't memos been eclipsed by e-mail?*

The truth is that, although e-mail is very popular, printed hard-copy memos still serve vital functions in the workplace. They remain useful for important internal messages that require a permanent record or formality. For example, organizations use memos to deliver instructions, official policies, short reports, long internal documents, and important announcements. The formatting of memos makes them easy to read and understand, especially when compared with e-mails that have long threads of comments by many receivers. The sender and receiver of memos are always recognizable. The guide words in memos immediately tell you what you want to know—who wrote the message, who was the intended receiver, the date it was sent, and what it is about.

ETHICS CHECK

Surprising the Boss

Kyra M. uses e-mail for nearly all messages. She is ecstatic over a new job offer and quickly sends an e-mail to her manager announcing that she is leaving. He did not know she was looking for a new position. Is this an appropriate use of e-mail?

Preparing Interoffice Memos

The formatting of interoffice memos has much in common with e-mails, which you studied in Chapter 7. Like e-mails, interoffice memos begin with guide words such as *Date, To, From,* and *Subject.* Some organizations have preprinted memo letterhead paper with the name of the organization at the top. In addition to guide words, these forms may include other identifying headings, such as *File Number*, *Floor*, *Extension*, *Location*, and *Distribution*. Because of the difficulty of aligning computer printers with preprinted forms, business writers may use default templates available on their word processors (sometimes called *wizards).* Writers can customize these templates with their organization's name.

How do you format an interoffice memo prepared on plain paper?

If you are preparing a memo on plain paper, set 1-inch top and bottom margins and left and right margins of 1.25 inches. Provide a heading that includes the name of the company plus the word *Memo* or *Memorandum.* Begin the guide words a triple space (two blank lines) below the last line of the heading. Key in bold the guide words: **Date:, To:, From:,** and **Subject:** at the left margin. The guide words may appear in all caps or with only the initial letter capitalized. Triple-space (two blank lines) after the last line of the heading. Do not justify the right margins. As discussed in the document design section of Chapter 6, ragged-right margins in printed messages make them easier to read. Single-space the message, and double-space between paragraphs, as shown in Figure 8.3.

Preparing Memos as E-Mail Attachments

E-mail has become increasingly important for exchanging internal messages. However, it is inappropriate for long documents or for items that require formality or permanence. For such messages, writers may prepare the information in standard memo format and send it as an attachment to a cover e-mail.

In preparing e-mail attachments, be sure to include identifying information. Because the cover e-mail may become separated from the attachment, the attachment must be fully identified. Preparing the e-mail attachment as a memo provides a handy format that identifies the date, sender, receiver, and subject.

Understanding Business Letters

Thus far we have discussed positive messages that circulate inside an organization. Now let's talk about positive messages that are delivered outside an organization. One important channel for external communication is business letters. Even with the new media available today, a business letter remains one of the most powerful and effective ways to get your message across.

Knowing When to Send a Letter

You will know when to send a business letter by the situation and by the preference of your organization. Although you may be tempted to dash off an e-mail, think twice before descending into digital mode. This section discusses reasons business letters are still indispensable.

When should you send a business letter rather than an e-mail?

Business letters are necessary when the situation calls for a permanent record. For example, when a company enters into an agreement with another company, business letters introduce the agreement and record decisions and points of understanding. Although telephone

FIGURE 8.3 Interoffice Memo That Responds to a Request

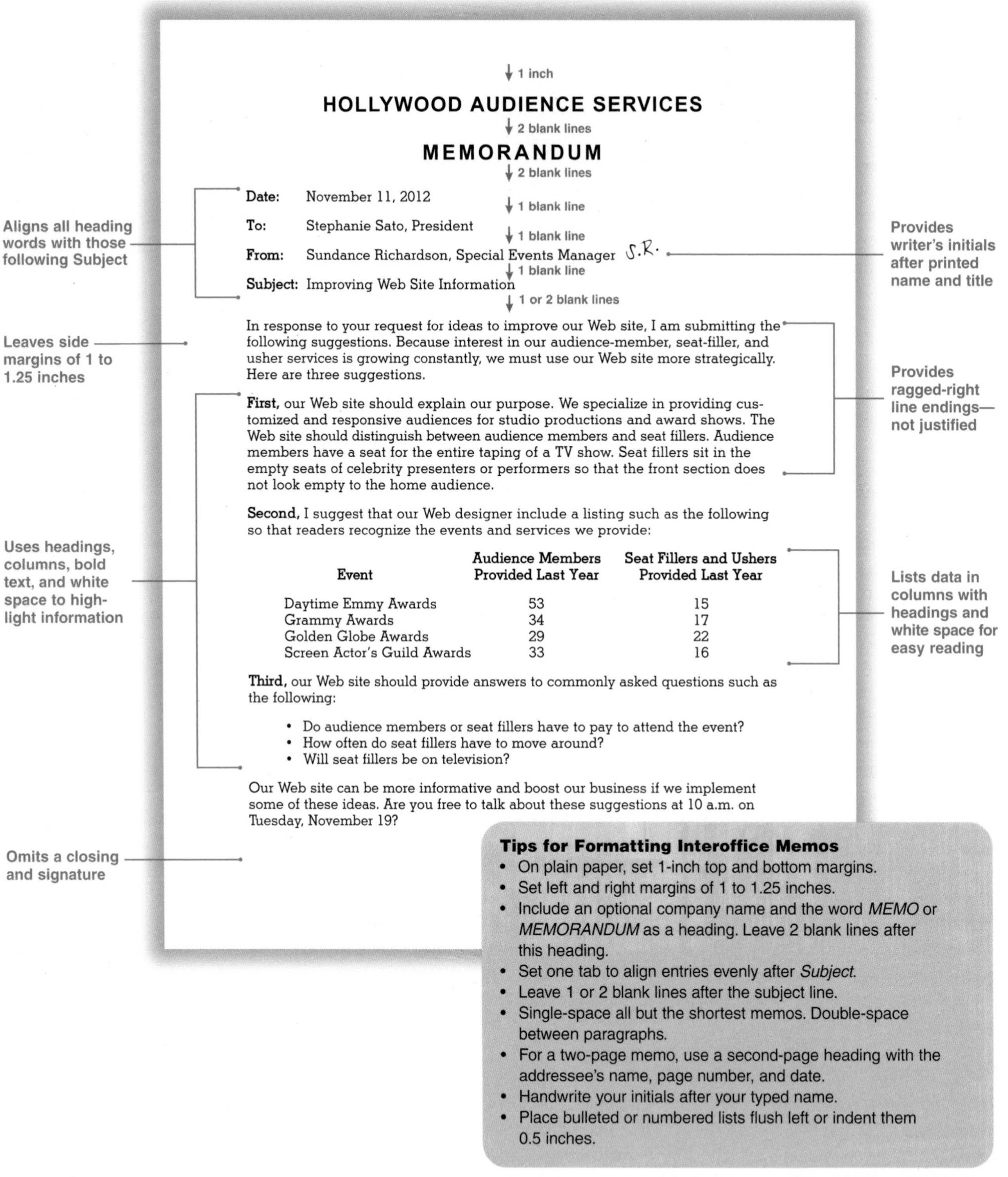

↓ 1 inch

HOLLYWOOD AUDIENCE SERVICES

↓ 2 blank lines

MEMORANDUM

↓ 2 blank lines

Date: November 11, 2012 ↓ 1 blank line

To: Stephanie Sato, President ↓ 1 blank line

From: Sundance Richardson, Special Events Manager S.R. ↓ 1 blank line

Subject: Improving Web Site Information

↓ 1 or 2 blank lines

In response to your request for ideas to improve our Web site, I am submitting the following suggestions. Because interest in our audience-member, seat-filler, and usher services is growing constantly, we must use our Web site more strategically. Here are three suggestions.

First, our Web site should explain our purpose. We specialize in providing customized and responsive audiences for studio productions and award shows. The Web site should distinguish between audience members and seat fillers. Audience members have a seat for the entire taping of a TV show. Seat fillers sit in the empty seats of celebrity presenters or performers so that the front section does not look empty to the home audience.

Second, I suggest that our Web designer include a listing such as the following so that readers recognize the events and services we provide:

Event	Audience Members Provided Last Year	Seat Fillers and Ushers Provided Last Year
Daytime Emmy Awards	53	15
Grammy Awards	34	17
Golden Globe Awards	29	22
Screen Actor's Guild Awards	33	16

Third, our Web site should provide answers to commonly asked questions such as the following:

- Do audience members or seat fillers have to pay to attend the event?
- How often do seat fillers have to move around?
- Will seat fillers be on television?

Our Web site can be more informative and boost our business if we implement some of these ideas. Are you free to talk about these suggestions at 10 a.m. on Tuesday, November 19?

Aligns all heading words with those following Subject
Provides writer's initials after printed name and title
Leaves side margins of 1 to 1.25 inches
Provides ragged-right line endings—not justified
Uses headings, columns, bold text, and white space to highlight information
Lists data in columns with headings and white space for easy reading
Omits a closing and signature

Tips for Formatting Interoffice Memos

- On plain paper, set 1-inch top and bottom margins.
- Set left and right margins of 1 to 1.25 inches.
- Include an optional company name and the word *MEMO* or *MEMORANDUM* as a heading. Leave 2 blank lines after this heading.
- Set one tab to align entries evenly after *Subject*.
- Leave 1 or 2 blank lines after the subject line.
- Single-space all but the shortest memos. Double-space between paragraphs.
- For a two-page memo, use a second-page heading with the addressee's name, page number, and date.
- Handwrite your initials after your typed name.
- Place bulleted or numbered lists flush left or indent them 0.5 inches.

conversations and e-mails may be exchanged, important details are generally recorded in business letters that are kept in company files. Business letters deliver contracts, explain terms, exchange ideas, negotiate agreements, answer vendor questions, and maintain customer relations.

Business letters are confidential. Carefree use of e-mail was once a sign of sophistication. Today, however, communicators know how dangerous it is to entrust confidential and sensitive information to digital channels. A writer in *The New York Times* explained, "Despite the sneering term *snail mail*, plain old letters are the form of long-distance communication least likely to be intercepted, misdirected, forwarded, retrieved, or otherwise inspected by someone you didn't have in mind."[5]

Business letters presented on company stationery carry a sense of formality and importance not possible with e-mail. They look important. They carry a nonverbal message that the writer considered the message so significant and the receiver so prestigious that the writer cared enough to write a real message. Business letters deliver more information than e-mail because they are written on stationery that usually is printed with company information such as logos, addresses, titles, and contact details.

Finally, business letters deliver persuasive, well-considered messages. When a business communicator must be persuasive and can't do it in person, a business letter is more effective than other communication channels. Letters can persuade people to change their actions, adopt new beliefs, make donations, contribute their time, and try new products. Direct-mail letters remain a powerful tool to promote services and products, boost online and retail traffic, and solicit contributions. Business letters represent deliberate communication. They give you a chance to think through what you want to say, organize your thoughts, and write a well-considered argument. You will learn more about writing persuasive and sales messages in Chapter 10.

Using Correct Form in Business Letters

What are justified margins, and should business letters have them?

A business letter conveys silent messages beyond those contained in its printed words. The letter's appearance and format reflect the writer's carefulness and experience. A short letter bunched at the top of a sheet of paper, for example, looks as though it were prepared in a hurry or by an amateur.

For your letters to make a good impression, you need to select an appropriate format. The block style shown in Figure 8.4 is a popular format. In this style the parts of a letter—dateline, inside address, body, and so on—are set flush left on the page. The letter is arranged on the page so that it is centered and framed by white space. Most letters have margins of 1 to 1.5 inches.

In preparing business letters, be sure to use ragged-right margins; that is, don't allow your computer to justify the right margin and make all lines end evenly. Unjustified margins improve readability, say experts, by providing visual stops and by making it easier to tell where the next line begins. Although book publishers use justified right margins, as you see on this page, your letters should use ragged-right margins. Study Figure 8.4 for more tips on making your letters look professional. Appendix B provides more information about letter forms and formats.

Routine Request and Response Messages

LEARNING OBJECTIVE 3
Compose direct messages that make requests and respond to inquiries.

The majority of your business messages will involve routine requests and responses to requests, which are organized directly. Requests and replies may take the form of e-mails, memos, or letters. You might, for example, need to request information from a hotel as you plan a company conference. You might be answering an inquiry from a customer about your services or products. These kinds of routine requests and replies follow a similar pattern.

Creating Request Messages

When you write messages that request information or action and you think your request will be received positively, start with the main idea first. The most emphatic positions in a message are the opening and closing. Readers tend to look at them first. You should capitalize on this tendency by putting the most significant statement first. The first sentence of an information request is usually a question or a polite command. It should not be an explanation or justification, unless resistance to the request is expected. When the information or action requested is likely to be forthcoming, immediately tell the reader what you want.

A letter inquiring about hotel accommodations, shown in Figure 8.4, begins immediately with the most important idea: Can the hotel provide meeting rooms and accommodations for 250 people? Instead of opening with an explanation of who the writer is or why the writer happens to be writing this message, the letter begins directly.

FIGURE 8.4 Formatting a Direct Request Business Letter in Block Style

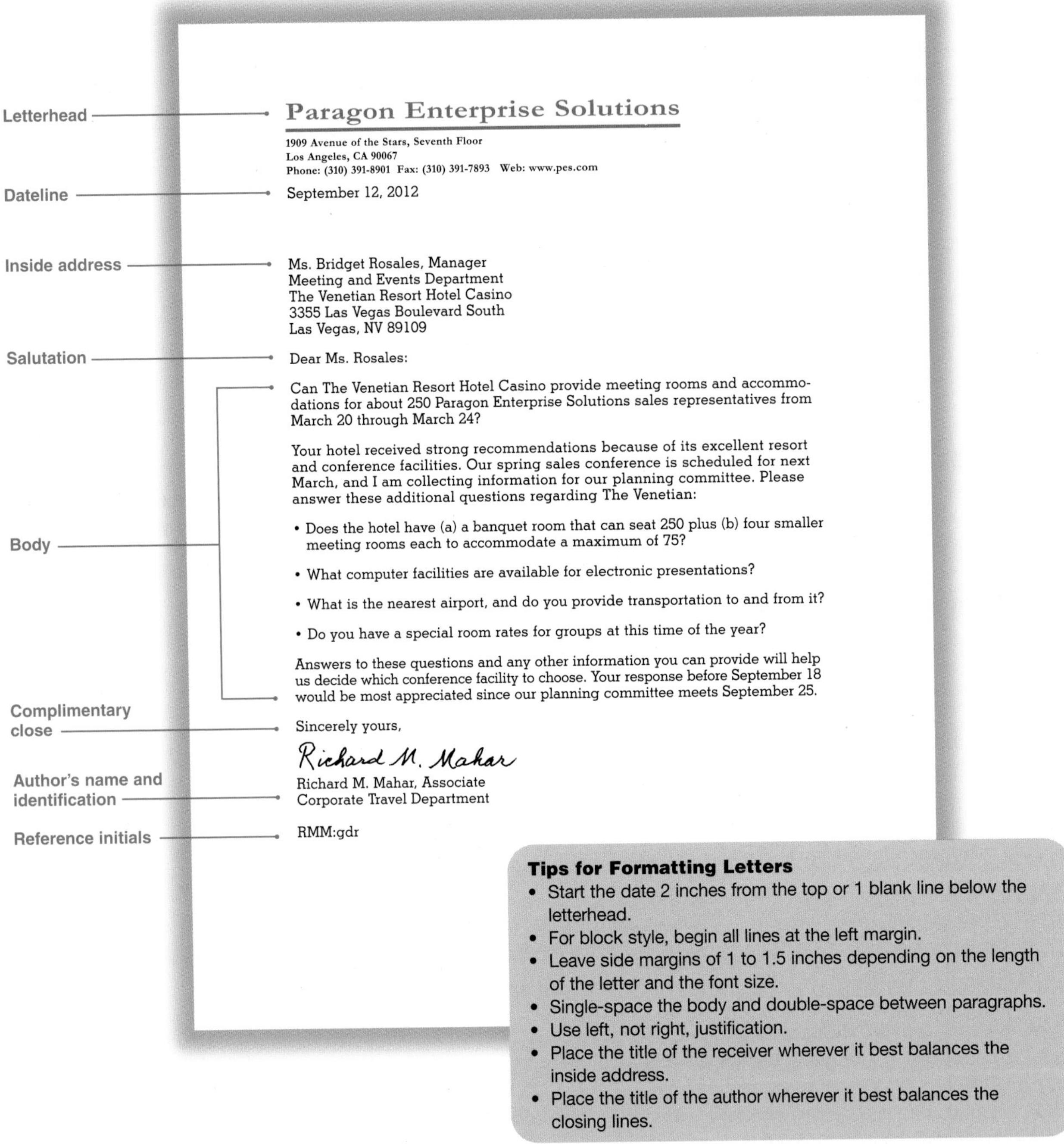

Paragon Enterprise Solutions

1909 Avenue of the Stars, Seventh Floor
Los Angeles, CA 90067
Phone: (310) 391-8901 Fax: (310) 391-7893 Web: www.pes.com

September 12, 2012

Ms. Bridget Rosales, Manager
Meeting and Events Department
The Venetian Resort Hotel Casino
3355 Las Vegas Boulevard South
Las Vegas, NV 89109

Dear Ms. Rosales:

Can The Venetian Resort Hotel Casino provide meeting rooms and accommodations for about 250 Paragon Enterprise Solutions sales representatives from March 20 through March 24?

Your hotel received strong recommendations because of its excellent resort and conference facilities. Our spring sales conference is scheduled for next March, and I am collecting information for our planning committee. Please answer these additional questions regarding The Venetian:

- Does the hotel have (a) a banquet room that can seat 250 plus (b) four smaller meeting rooms each to accommodate a maximum of 75?
- What computer facilities are available for electronic presentations?
- What is the nearest airport, and do you provide transportation to and from it?
- Do you have a special room rates for groups at this time of the year?

Answers to these questions and any other information you can provide will help us decide which conference facility to choose. Your response before September 18 would be most appreciated since our planning committee meets September 25.

Sincerely yours,

Richard M. Mahar

Richard M. Mahar, Associate
Corporate Travel Department

RMM:gdr

Tips for Formatting Letters

- Start the date 2 inches from the top or 1 blank line below the letterhead.
- For block style, begin all lines at the left margin.
- Leave side margins of 1 to 1.5 inches depending on the length of the letter and the font size.
- Single-space the body and double-space between paragraphs.
- Use left, not right, justification.
- Place the title of the receiver wherever it best balances the inside address.
- Place the title of the author wherever it best balances the closing lines.

If several questions must be asked, you have two choices. You can ask the most important question first, as shown in Figure 8.4, or you can begin with a summary statement, such as *Please answer the following questions about providing meeting rooms and accommodations for 250 people from March 20 through March 24.* Avoid beginning with *Will you please. . . .* Although such a statement sounds like a question, it is actually a disguised command. Because you expect an action rather than a reply, you should punctuate this polite command with a period instead of a question mark. To avoid having to choose between a period and a question mark, just omit *Will you* and start with *Please answer.*

How do you make a group of questions parallel in construction?

Providing Details. The body of a message that requests information or action provides necessary details. Remember that the quality of the information obtained from a request depends on the clarity of the inquiry. If you analyze your needs, organize your ideas, and frame your request logically, you are likely to receive a meaningful answer that doesn't require a follow-up message. Whenever possible, focus on benefits to the reader (*To ensure that you receive the exact sweater you want, send us your color choice*). To improve readability, itemize appropriate information in bulleted or numbered lists. Notice that the questions in Figure 8.4 are bulleted, and they are parallel. That is, they use the same balanced construction.

Closing With Appreciation and an Action Request. In the closing tell the reader courteously what is to be done. If a date is important, set an end date to take action and explain why. Some careless writers end request messages simply with *Thank you*, forcing the reader to review the contents to determine what is expected and when. You can save the reader time by spelling out the action to be taken. Avoid other overused endings such as *Thank you for your cooperation* (trite), *Thank you in advance for* ... (trite and presumptuous), and *If you have any questions, do not hesitate to call me* (suggests that you didn't make yourself clear).

Showing appreciation is always appropriate, but try to do so in a fresh and efficient manner. For example, you could hook your thanks to the end date *(Thanks for returning the questionnaire before May 5, when we will begin tabulation)*. You might connect your appreciation to a statement developing reader benefits *(We are grateful for the information you will provide because it will help us serve you better)*. You could briefly describe how the information will help you *(I appreciate this information, which will enable me to ...)*. When possible, make it easy for the reader to comply with your request *(Note your answers on this sheet and return it in the postage-paid envelope* or *Here is my e-mail address so that you can reach me quickly)*.

ETHICS CHECK

Stretching the Truth

A magazine publisher sends you a letter saying that you should renew your subscription immediately to ensure continued delivery. Your subscription is paid for at least a year in advance, but nowhere in the letter or magazine label does your subscription end date appear. How far can a writer go in stretching the truth to achieve a purpose?

Responding to Requests

Often, your messages will respond directly and favorably to requests for information or action. A customer wants information about a product, a supplier asks to arrange a meeting, an employee inquires about a procedure, or a manager requests your input on a marketing campaign. In complying with such requests, you will want to apply the same direct strategy you used in making requests.

Why might a business letter include a subject line?

The opening of a customer response letter might contain an optional subject line, as shown in Figure 8.5. A subject line helps the reader recognize the topic immediately. Usually appearing two lines below the salutation, the subject line refers in abbreviated form to previous correspondence and/or summarizes the message *(Subject: Your July 12 Inquiry About WorkZone Software)*. Knowledgeable business communicators use a subject line to refer to earlier correspondence so that in the first sentence, the most emphatic spot in a letter, they are free to emphasize the main idea.

In the first sentence of a direct response letter, deliver the information the reader wants. Avoid wordy, drawn-out openings such as *I have before me your letter of August 5, in which you request information about....* More forceful and more efficient is an opener that answers the inquiry *(Here is the information you wanted about ...)*. When agreeing to a request for action, announce the good news promptly *(Yes, I will be happy to speak to your business communication class on the topic of ...)*.

In the body of your response, supply explanations and additional information. Because a letter written on company stationery is considered a legally binding contract, be sure to check facts and figures carefully. If a policy or procedure needs authorization, seek approval from a supervisor or executive before writing the letter.

Should a customer response message include more than the information requested?

When customers or prospective customers inquire about products or services, your response should do more than merely supply answers. Try to promote your organization and products. Be sure to present the promotional material with attention to the "you" view and to reader benefits *(You can use our standardized tests to free you from time-consuming employment screening)*.

In concluding a response message, refer to the information provided or to its use. *(The enclosed list summarizes our recommendations. We wish you all the best in redesigning your Web site.)* If further action is required, describe the procedure and help the reader with specifics *(The Small Business Administration publishes a number of helpful booklets. Its Web address is ...)*. Avoid signing off with clichés *(If I may be of further assistance, don't hesitate to ...)*.

The checklist on page 231 reviews the direct strategy for information or action requests and replies to such messages.

FIGURE 8.5 **Customer Response Letter**

1 Prewriting

Analyze: The purpose of this letter is to provide helpful information and to promote company products.

Anticipate: The reader is the intelligent owner of a small business who needs help with personnel administration.

Adapt: Because the reader requested this data, he will be receptive to the letter. Use the direct strategy.

2 Writing

Research: Gather facts to answer the business owner's questions. Consult brochures and pamphlets.

Organize: Prepare a scratch outline. Plan for a fast, direct opening. Use numbered answers to the business owner's three questions.

Compose: Write the first draft on a computer. Strive for short sentences and paragraphs.

3 Revising

Revise: Eliminate jargon and wordiness. Look for ways to explain how the product fits the reader's needs. Revise for the "you" view.

Proofread: Double-check the form of numbers *(July 12, page 6, 8 to 5 PST).*

Evaluate: Does this letter answer the customer's questions and encourage an order?

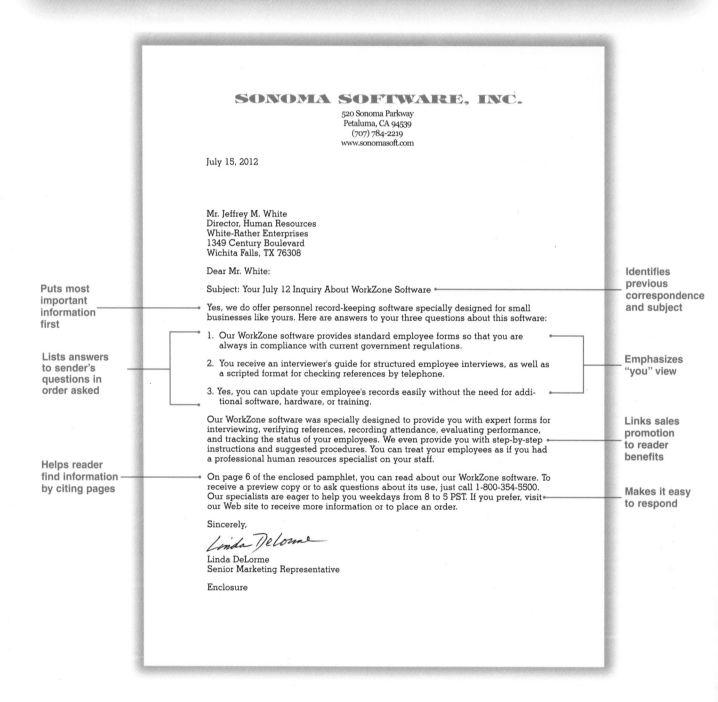

SONOMA SOFTWARE, INC.
520 Sonoma Parkway
Petaluma, CA 94539
(707) 784-2219
www.sonomasoft.com

July 15, 2012

Mr. Jeffrey M. White
Director, Human Resources
White-Rather Enterprises
1349 Century Boulevard
Wichita Falls, TX 76308

Dear Mr. White:

Subject: Your July 12 Inquiry About WorkZone Software — *Identifies previous correspondence and subject*

Puts most important information first — Yes, we do offer personnel record-keeping software specially designed for small businesses like yours. Here are answers to your three questions about this software:

Lists answers to sender's questions in order asked / *Emphasizes "you" view*

1. Our WorkZone software provides standard employee forms so that you are always in compliance with current government regulations.

2. You receive an interviewer's guide for structured employee interviews, as well as a scripted format for checking references by telephone.

3. Yes, you can update your employee's records easily without the need for additional software, hardware, or training.

Our WorkZone software was specially designed to provide you with expert forms for interviewing, verifying references, recording attendance, evaluating performance, and tracking the status of your employees. We even provide you with step-by-step instructions and suggested procedures. You can treat your employees as if you had a professional human resources specialist on your staff. — *Links sales promotion to reader benefits*

Helps reader find information by citing pages — On page 6 of the enclosed pamphlet, you can read about our WorkZone software. To receive a preview copy or to ask questions about its use, just call 1-800-354-5500. Our specialists are eager to help you weekdays from 8 to 5 PST. If you prefer, visit our Web site to receive more information or to place an order. — *Makes it easy to respond*

Sincerely,

Linda DeLorme

Linda DeLorme
Senior Marketing Representative

Enclosure

Checklist

Writing Direct Requests and Reponses

Requesting Information or Action

- **Open by stating the main idea.** To elicit information, ask a question or issue a polite command *(Please answer the following questions ...)*.
- **Explain and justify the request.** In the body arrange questions or information logically in parallel, balanced form. Clarify and substantiate your request.
- **Request action in the closing.** Close a request by summarizing exactly what is to be done, including dates or deadlines. Express appreciation. Avoid clichés *(Thank you for your cooperation, Thanking you in advance)*.

Responding to Requests

- **Open directly.** Immediately deliver the information the receiver wants. Avoid wordy, drawn-out openings (*I have before me your request of August 5*). When agreeing to a request, announce the good news immediately.
- **Supply additional information.** In the body provide explanations and expand initial statements. For customer letters, promote products and the organization.
- **Conclude with a cordial statement.** Refer to the information provided or its use. If further action is required, describe the procedures and give specifics. Avoid clichés (*If you have questions, please do not hesitate to let me know)*.

Instruction Messages

LEARNING OBJECTIVE 4
Write messages that clearly explain step-by-step instructions.

Instruction messages describe how to complete a task. You may be asked to write instructions about how to repair a paper jam in the photocopier, order supplies, file a grievance, or hire new employees. Instructions are different from policies and official procedures, which establish rules of conduct to be followed within an organization. We are most concerned with creating messages that clearly explain how to complete a task.

Like requests and responses, instruction messages follow a straightforward, direct approach. Before writing instructions for a process, be sure you understand the process completely. Practice doing it yourself. A message that delivers instructions should open with an explanation of why the procedure or set of instructions is necessary.

Dividing Instructions Into Steps

Why should instructions be written in steps using the imperative mood?

The body of an instruction message should use plain English and familiar words to describe the process. Your messages explaining instructions will be most readable if you follow these guidelines:

- Divide the instructions into steps.
- List the steps in the order in which they are to be carried out.
- Arrange the items vertically with numbers.
- Begin each step with an action verb using the imperative (command) mood rather than the indicative mood.

Indicative Mood	**Imperative (Command) Mood**
The contract should be sent immediately.	Send the contract immediately.
The first step involves loading the software.	Load the software first.
A survey of employees is necessary to learn what options they prefer.	Survey employees to learn the options they prefer.

In the closing of a message issuing instructions, consider connecting following the instructions with benefits to the organization or individual.

If you are asked to prepare a list of instructions that is not part of a message, include a title such as *How to Clear Paper Jams.* Include an opening paragraph explaining why the instructions are needed.

Revising a Message Delivering Instructions

Figure 8.6 shows the first draft of an interoffice memo written by Troy Bell. His memo was meant to announce a new method for employees to follow in advertising open positions. However, the tone was negative, the explanation of the problem rambled, and the new method was

FIGURE 8.6 Interoffice Memo Delivering Instructions

Draft

Date: January 5, 2012
To: Ruth DiSilvestro, Manager
From: Troy Bell, Human Resources
Subject: Job Advertisement Misunderstanding

We had no idea last month when we implemented a new hiring process that major problems would result. Due to the fact that every department is now placing Internet advertisements for new-hires individually, the difficulties occurred. This cannot continue. Perhaps we did not make it clear at the time, but all newly hired employees who are hired for a position should be requested through this office.

Do not submit your advertisements for new employees directly to an Internet job bank or a newspaper. After you write them, they should be brought to Human Resources, where they will be centralized. You should discuss each ad with one of our counselors. Then we will place the ad at an appropriate Internet site or other publication. If you do not follow these guidelines, chaos will result. You may pick up applicant folders from us the day after the closing date in an ad.

Uses vague, negative subject line

Fails to pinpoint main idea in opening

New process is hard to follow

Uses threats instead of showing benefits to reader

Revision

MEMORANDUM

Date: January 5, 2012

To: Ruth DiSilvestro, Manager

From: Troy Bell, Human Resources TB

Subject: Please Follow New Job Advertisement Process

To find the right candidates for your open positions as fast as possible, we are implementing a new routine. Effective today, all advertisements for departmental job openings should be routed through the Human Resources Department.

A major problem resulted from the change in hiring procedures implemented last month. Each department is placing job advertisements for new-hires individually, when all such requests should be centralized in this office. To process applications more efficiently, please follow these steps:

1. Write an advertisement for a position in your department.
2. Bring the ad to Human Resources and discuss it with one of our counselors.
3. Let Human Resources place the ad at an appropriate Internet job bank or submit it to a newspaper.
4. Pick up applicant folders from Human Resources the day following the closing date provided in the ad.

Following these guidelines will save you work and will also enable Human Resources to help you fill your openings more quickly. Call Ann Edmonds at Ext. 2505 if you have questions about this process.

Employs informative, courteous, upbeat subject line

Combines "you" view with main idea in opening

Explains why change in procedures is necessary

Lists easy-to-follow steps and starts each step with a verb

Closes by reinforcing benefits to reader

Tips for Writing Instructions

- Arrange each step in the order it should be completed.
- Start each instruction with an action verb in the imperative (command) mood.
- Be careful of tone when writing messages that give orders.
- Show reader benefits if you are encouraging use of the process.

unclear. Notice, too, that Troy's first draft told readers what they *shouldn't* do (*Do not submit advertisements for new employees directly to an Internet job bank or a newspaper*). It is more helpful to tell readers what they *should* do. Finally, Troy's first memo closed with a threat instead of showing readers how this new practice will help them.

In the revision Troy improved the tone considerably. The subject line contains a *please*, which is always pleasant to see even if one is giving an order. The subject line also includes a verb and specifies the purpose of the memo. Instead of expressing his ideas with negative words and threats, Troy revised his message to explain objectively and concisely what went wrong.

Troy realized that his original explanation of the new procedure was vague and unclear. To clarify the instructions, he itemized and numbered the steps. Each step begins with an action verb in the imperative (command) mood (*Write, Bring, Let,* and *Pick up*). It is sometimes difficult to force all the steps in a list into this kind of command language. Troy struggled, but by trying different wording, he finally found verbs that worked.

Why do numbered steps and action verbs improve the clarity of instructions?

Why should you go to so much trouble to make lists and achieve parallelism? Because readers can comprehend what you have said much more quickly. Parallel language also makes you look professional and efficient.

In writing messages that deliver instructions, be careful of tone. Today's managers and team leaders seek employee participation and cooperation. These goals can't be achieved, though, if the writer sounds like a dictator or an autocrat. Avoid making accusations and fixing blame. Rather, explain changes, give reasons, and suggest benefits to the reader. Assume that employees want to contribute to the success of the organization and to their own achievement. Notice in the Figure 8.6 revision that Troy tells readers that they will save time and have their open positions filled more quickly if they follow the new method.

Learning More About Writing Instructions

The writing of instructions is so important that we have developed a special bonus online supplement called *How to Write Instructions.* It provides more examples and information. This online supplement at **www.meguffey.com** extends your textbook with in-depth material including links to real businesses showing you examples of well-written instructions.

Where can you go to learn more about how to write instructions?

Direct Claims

LEARNING OBJECTIVE 5
Prepare messages that make direct claims.

In business, things can and do go wrong—promised shipments are late, warrantied goods fail, or service is disappointing. When you as a customer must write to identify or correct a wrong, the letter is called a *claim*. Straightforward claims are those to which you expect the receiver to agree readily. Even these claims, however, often require a letter. Your first action may be a telephone call or an e-mail to submit your claim, but you may not be satisfied with the result. Claims written as letters are taken more seriously than telephone calls or e-mails, and letters also establish a record of what happened. Straightforward claims use a direct approach. Claims that require a persuasive response are presented in Chapter 10.

Opening a Claim With a Clear Statement

When you, as a customer, have a legitimate claim, you can expect a positive response from a company. Smart businesses want to hear from their customers. They know that retaining a customer is far less costly than recruiting a new customer.

Why is a letter better than a telephone call or e-mail when making a claim?

Open your claim with a compliment, point of agreement, statement of the problem, brief review of action you have taken to resolve the problem, or a clear statement of the action you want. You might expect a replacement, a refund, a new product, credit to your account, correction of a billing error, free repairs, free inspection, or cancellation of an order. When the remedy is obvious, state it immediately (*Please send us 25 Sanyo digital travel alarm clocks to replace the Sanyo analog travel alarm clocks sent in error with our order shipped January 4*). When the remedy is less obvious, you might ask for a change in policy or procedure or simply for an explanation (*Because three of our employees with confirmed reservations were refused rooms September 16 in your hotel, would you please clarify your policy regarding reservations and late arrivals*).

ETHICS CHECK

Renting or Buying?

Lucky U.S. consumers enjoy some of the world's most generous merchandise return policies. It is no wonder, perhaps, that some customers presumably buy video cameras or dresses for special events and return them afterward, no questions asked. Is this so-called renting, or wardrobing, wrong? Do retailers invite such behavior with their liberal policies?

Explaining and Justifying a Claim

In the body of a claim letter, explain the problem and justify your request. Provide the necessary details so that the difficulty can be corrected without further correspondence. Avoid becoming angry or trying to fix blame. Although you may be upset, bear in mind that the person reading your letter is seldom responsible for the problem. Instead, state the facts logically, objectively, and unemotionally; let the reader decide on the causes. Include copies of all pertinent documents such as invoices, sales slips, catalog descriptions, and repair records. By the way, be sure to send copies and NOT your originals, which could be lost. When service is involved, cite the names of individuals you spoke to and the dates of the calls. Assume that a company honestly wants to satisfy its customers—because most do. When an alternative remedy exists, spell it out *(If you are unable to send 25 Sanyo digital travel alarm clocks immediately, please credit our account now and notify us when they become available).*

Concluding a Claim With an Action Request

End a claim with a courteous statement that promotes goodwill and summarizes your action request. If appropriate, include an end date *(We realize that mistakes in ordering and shipping sometimes occur. Because we've enjoyed your prompt service in the past, we hope that you will be able to send us the Sanyo digital travel alarm clocks by January 15).* Finally, in making claims, act promptly. Delaying claims makes them appear less important. Delayed claims are also more difficult to verify. By taking the time to put your claim in writing, you indicate your seriousness. A written claim starts a record of the problem, should later action be necessary. Be sure to keep a copy of your message.

Why do you think claims submitted promptly are taken more seriously than delayed ones?

When Keith Krahnke received a statement showing a charge for a three-year service warranty that he did not purchase, he was furious. He called the store but failed to get satisfaction. Then he decided to write. You can see the first draft of his direct claim letter in Figure 8.7. This draft gave him a chance to vent his anger, but it accomplished little else. The tone was belligerent, and it assumed that the company intentionally mischarged him. Furthermore, it failed to tell the reader how to remedy the problem. The revision, also shown in Figure 8.7, tempered the tone, described the problem objectively, and provided facts and figures. Most important, it specified exactly what Keith wanted to be done.

Notice in Figure 8.7 that Keith used the personal business letter style, which is appropriate for you to use in writing personal messages. Your return address, but not your name, appears above the date.

Royal Caribbean International's service reputation ran aground temporarily when a scheduling error sank one couple's plans for a romantic honeymoon cruise. The vacation company's alternate arrangements also went adrift when representatives failed to notify the newlyweds about their rescheduled trip. Although the newlyweds eventually received a $1,700 voucher from Royal Caribbean for a future cruise, the couple was disappointed that Royal Caribbean's initial apology letter wasn't accompanied by a full refund. *What are the key elements of an effective adjustment letter?*

FIGURE 8.7 Direct Claim Letter

Dear Good Vibes:

You call yourselves Good Vibes, but all I'm getting from your service is bad vibes! I'm furious that you have your salespeople slip in unwanted service warranties to boost your sales.

Sounds angry; jumps to conclusions

When I bought my Panatronic DVR from Good Vibes, Inc., in August, I specifically told the salesperson that I did NOT want a three-year service warranty. But there it is on my Visa statement this month! You people have obviously billed me for a service I did not authorize. I refuse to pay this charge.

Forgets that mistakes happen

How can you hope to stay in business with such fraudulent practices? I was expecting to return this month and look at HDTVs, but you can be sure I'll find an honest dealer this time.

Fails to suggest solution

Angrily,

Personal business letter style

1201 Lantana Court
Lake Worth, FL 33461
September 3, 2012

Ms. Ernestine Sanborn
Manager, Customer Satisfaction
Good Vibes, Inc.
2003 53rd Street
West Palm Beach, FL 33407

Dear Ms. Sanborn:

States simply and clearly what to do

Please credit my Visa account, No. 0000-0046-2198-9421, to correct an erroneous charge of $299.

Doesn't blame or accuse; uses friendly tone · *Explains objectively what went wrong* · *Documents facts*

On August 1, I purchased a Panatronic DVR from Good Vibes, Inc. Although the salesperson discussed a three-year extended warranty with me, I decided against purchasing that service for $299. However, when my credit card statement arrived this month, I noticed an extra $299 charge from Good Vibes, Inc. I suspect that this charge represents the warranty I declined. Enclosed is a copy of my sales invoice along with my Visa statement on which I circled the charge.

Summarizes request and courteously suggests continued business once problem is resolved

Please authorize a credit immediately and send a copy of the transaction to me at the above address. I'm enjoying all the features of my Panatronic DVR and would like to be shopping at Good Vibes for an HDTV shortly.

Sincerely,

Keith Krahnke

Keith Krahnke

Enclosure

Tips for Submitting Claims

- Begin with a compliment, point of agreement, statement of the problem, brief review of action you have taken to resolve the problem, or clear statement of the action you want taken.
- Prove that your claim is valid; explain why the receiver is responsible.
- Enclose document copies supporting your claim.
- Appeal to the reader's fairness, ethics, legal responsibilities, or desire for return business.
- Avoid sounding angry, emotional, or irrational.
- Close by restating what you want done and looking forward to future business.

Adjustments

LEARNING OBJECTIVE 6

Create adjustment messages that regain the confidence of customers and promote further business.

Even the best-run and best-loved businesses occasionally receive claims from consumers. When a company receives a claim and decides to respond favorably, the message is called an *adjustment.* Most businesses make adjustments promptly: they replace merchandise, refund money, extend discounts, send coupons, and repair goods. Businesses make favorable adjustments to legitimate claims for two reasons. First, consumers are protected by contractual and tort law for recovery of damages. If, for example, you find an insect in a package of frozen peas, the food processor of that package is bound by contractual law to replace it. If you suffer injury, the processor may be liable for damages. Second, and more obviously, most organizations genuinely want to satisfy their customers and retain their business.

What is an adjustment message?

In responding to customer claims, you must first decide whether to grant the claim. Unless the claim is obviously fraudulent or excessive, you will probably grant it. When you say yes, your adjustment message will be good news to the reader. Deliver that good news by using the direct strategy. When your response is no, the indirect strategy might be more appropriate. Chapter 9 discusses the indirect strategy for conveying negative news. You have three goals in adjustment letters:

- Rectifying the wrong, if one exists
- Regaining the confidence of the customer
- Promoting further business

Revealing Good News Up Front in an Adjustment Message

Why should adjustment messages begin with the good news?

Instead of beginning with a review of what went wrong, present the good news immediately. When Kimberly Patel responded to the claim of customer Yonkers Digital & Wireless about a missing shipment, her first draft, shown at the top of Figure 8.8, was angry. No wonder. Yonkers Digital had apparently provided the wrong shipping address, and the goods were returned. Once Kimberly and her company decided to send a second shipment and comply with the customer's claim, however, she had to give up the anger. Her goal was to regain the goodwill and the business of this customer. The improved version of her letter announces that a new shipment will arrive shortly.

If you decide to comply with a customer's claim, let the receiver know immediately. Don't begin your letter with a negative statement (*We are very sorry to hear that you are having trouble with your dishwasher*). This approach reminds the reader of the problem and may rekindle the heated emotions or unhappy feelings experienced when the claim was written. Instead, focus on the good news. The following openings for various letters illustrate how to begin a message with good news:

> *You're right! We agree that the warranty on your American Standard Model UC600 dishwasher should be extended for six months.*
>
> *You will be receiving shortly a new slim Nokia cell phone to replace the one that shattered when dropped recently.*
>
> *Please take your portable Admiral microwave oven to A-1 Appliance Service, 200 Orange Street, Pasadena, where it will be repaired at no cost to you.*
>
> *The enclosed check for $325 demonstrates our desire to satisfy our customers and earn their confidence.*

In announcing that you will make an adjustment, be sure to do so without a grudging tone—even if you have reservations about whether the claim is legitimate. Once you decide to comply with the customer's request, do so happily. Avoid halfhearted or reluctant responses (*Although the American Standard dishwasher works well when used properly, we have decided to allow you to take yours to A-1 Appliance Service for repair at our expense*).

Explaining Compliance in the Body of an Adjustment Message

Why do most businesses comply with claims?

In responding to claims, most organizations sincerely want to correct a wrong. They want to do more than just make the customer happy. They want to stand behind their products and services; they want to do what is right.

FIGURE 8.8 Customer Adjustment Letter

Draft

Dear Sir:

I have before me your recent complaint about a missing shipment. First, let me say that it's very difficult to deliver merchandise when we have been given the wrong address.

Blames customer and fails to reveal good news immediately

After receiving your complaint, our investigators looked into your problem shipment and determined that it was sent immediately after we received the order. According to the shipper's records, it was delivered to the warehouse address given on your stationery: 451 Main Street, Yonkers, NY 10708. Unfortunately, no one at that address would accept delivery, so the shipment was returned to us. I see from your current stationery that your company has a new address. With the proper address, we probably could have delivered this shipment.

Creates ugly tone with negative words and sarcasm

Although we feel that it is entirely appropriate to charge you shipping and restocking fees, as is our standard practice on returned goods, in this instance we will waive those fees. We hope this second shipment finally catches up with you at your current address.

Sounds grudging and reluctant in granting claim

Sincerely,

Revision

DD

DIGITAL DEPOT
1405 Chambersburg Road
Trenton, NJ 08619-3590

Phone: (619) 839-2202
Fax: (619) 839-3320
Web: www.ddepot.com

April 24, 2012

Mr. Christopher Durante
Yonkers Digital & Wireless
359 South Broadway Avenue
Yonkers, NY 10705

Uses customer's name in salutation

Dear Mr. Durante:

Subject: Your April 19 Letter About Your Purchase Order

Announces good news immediately

You should receive by April 26 a second shipment of the speakers, VCRs, headphones, and other digital equipment that you ordered April 2.

Regains confidence of customer by explaining what happened and by suggesting plans for improvement

The first shipment of this order was delivered April 10 to 451 Main Street, Yonkers, NY. When no one at that address would accept the shipment, it was returned to us. Now that I have your letter, I see that the order should have been sent to 359 South Broadway Avenue, Yonkers, NY 10705. When an order is undeliverable, we usually try to verify the shipping address by telephoning the customer. Somehow the return of this shipment was not caught by our normally painstaking shipping clerks. You can be sure that I will investigate shipping and return procedures with our clerks immediately to see if we can improve existing methods.

Closes confidently with genuine appeal for customer's respect

Your respect is important to us, Mr. Durante. Although our rock-bottom discount prices have enabled us to build a volume business, we don't want to be so large that we lose touch with valued customers like you. Over the years our customers' respect has made us successful, and we hope that the prompt delivery of this shipment will retain yours.

Sincerely,

Kimberly Patel

Kimberly Patel
Distribution Manager

c Emanuel Chavez
Shipping Department

In the body of the letter, explain how you are complying with the claim. In all but the most routine claims, you should seek to regain the confidence of the customer. You might reasonably expect that a customer who has experienced difficulty with a product, with delivery, with billing, or with service has lost faith in your organization. Rebuilding that faith is important for future business.

How to rebuild lost confidence depends on the situation and the claim. If procedures need to be revised, explain what changes will be made. If a product has defective parts, tell how the product is being improved. If service is faulty, describe genuine efforts to improve it. Notice in Figure 8.8 that the writer promises to investigate shipping procedures to see whether improvements might prevent future mishaps.

Sometimes the problem is not with the product but with the way it is being used. In other instances customers misunderstand warranties or inadvertently cause delivery and billing mix-ups by supplying incorrect information. Remember that rational and sincere explanations will do much to regain the confidence of unhappy customers.

In your explanation avoid emphasizing negative words such as *trouble, regret, misunderstanding, fault, defective, error, inconvenience,* and *unfortunately*. Keep your message positive and upbeat.

Deciding Whether to Apologize

What are the arguments for and against apologies in adjustment messages?

Whether to apologize is a debatable issue. Attorneys generally discourage apologies fearing that they admit responsibility and will trigger lawsuits. However, both judges and juries tend to look on apologies favorably. More than 20 U.S. states have passed some form of an "apology law" that allows an expression of regret without fear that those statements would be used as a basis for liability in court.[6] Some business writing experts advise against apologies, contending that they are counterproductive and merely remind the customer of the unpleasantness related to the claim. If, however, apologizing seems natural, do so.

People like to hear apologies. It raises their self-esteem, shows the humility of the writer, and acts as a form of "psychological compensation."[7] Don't, however, fall back on the familiar phrase, *I'm sorry for any inconvenience we may have caused*. It sounds mechanical and insincere. Instead, try something like this: *We understand the frustration our delay has caused you, We're sorry you didn't receive better service,* or *You're right to be disappointed.* If you feel that an apology is appropriate, do it early and briefly. You will learn more about delivering effective apologies in Chapter 9 when we discuss negative messages.

The primary focus of an adjustment message is on how you are complying with the request, how the problem occurred, and how you are working to prevent its recurrence.

Using Sensitive Language in Adjustment Messages

What are examples of words that create negative reactions?

The language of adjustment messages must be particularly sensitive, because customers are already upset. Here are some don'ts:

- Don't use negative words *(trouble, regret, misunderstanding, fault, error, inconvenience, you claim).*
- Don't blame customers—even when they may be at fault.
- Don't blame individuals or departments within your organization; it's unprofessional.
- Don't make unrealistic promises; you can't guarantee that the situation will never recur.

To regain the confidence of your reader, consider including resale information. Describe a product's features and any special applications that might appeal to the reader. Promote a new product if it seems appropriate.

Showing Confidence in the Closing

How should you close an adjustment message?

End positively by expressing confidence that the problem has been resolved and that continued business relations will result. You might mention the product in a favorable light, suggest a new product, express your appreciation for the customer's business, or anticipate future business. It's often appropriate to refer to the desire to be of service and to satisfy customers. Notice how the following closings illustrate a positive, confident tone:

> *You were most helpful in informing us of this situation and permitting us to correct it. We appreciate your thoughtfulness in writing to us.*

Checklist

Direct Claim and Adjustment Messages

Messages That Make Claims

- **Begin directly with the purpose.** Present a clear statement of the problem or the action requested such as a refund, a replacement, credit, an explanation, or the correction of an error. Consider adding a compliment if you have been pleased in other respects.
- **Explain objectively.** In the body tell the specifics of the claim. Consider reminding the receiver of ethical and legal responsibilities, fairness, and a desire for return business. Provide copies of necessary documents.
- **Conclude by requesting action.** Include an end date, if important. Add a pleasant, forward-looking statement. Keep a copy of the letter.

Messages That Make Adjustments

- **Open with approval.** Comply with the customer's claim immediately. Avoid sounding grudging or reluctant.
- **In the body win back the customer's confidence.** Explain the cause of the problem, or describe your ongoing efforts to avoid such difficulties. Focus on your efforts to satisfy customers. Apologize if you feel that you should, but do so early and quickly. Avoid negative words, accusations, and unrealistic promises. Consider including resale and sales promotion information.
- **Close positively.** Express appreciation to the customer for writing, extend thanks for past business, anticipate continued patronage, refer to your desire to be of service, and/or mention a new product if it seems appropriate.

Thanks for writing. Your satisfaction is important to us. We hope that this refund check convinces you that service to our customers is our No. 1 priority. Our goals are to earn your confidence and continue to justify that confidence with quality products and excellent service.

For your patience and patronage, we are truly grateful.

Zooming In PART 2

Ben & Jerry's

Customer letters arriving at Ben & Jerry's received special attention from Alice Blachly, a former consumer affairs coordinator. In responding to fan letters, Blachly prepared handwritten cards or printed letters that promoted good feelings and cemented a long-lasting bond between Ben & Jerry's and its satisfied consumers. To letters with questions, Blachly located the information and responded. For example, a consumer worried that cottonseed oil, formerly contained in the one of the nut-butter portions of an exotic ice cream, might be contaminated by pesticides. Blachly checked with company quality assurance experts and also investigated articles about cottonseed oil before responding. Other consumers wondered about Ben & Jerry's position on using milk from cloned cows and eggs from cage-free egg growers.

However, letters with consumer grumbles, such as *My pint didn't have quite enough cookie dough*, always received top priority. "We have trained our consumers to expect the best," said Blachly, "so they are disappointed when something goes wrong. And we are disappointed, too. We refund the purchase price, and we explain what caused the problem, if we know."

Critical Thinking

- When customers write to Ben & Jerry's for information and the response must contain both positive and negative news, what strategy should the respondent follow?
- If a customer writes to complain about something for which Ben & Jerry's is not responsible (such as ice in frozen yogurt), should the response letter contain an apology? Why or why not?
- Why is responding to customer inquiries an important function for a company such as Ben & Jerry's?

Your Asus Netbook will come in handy whether you are connecting with friends, surfing the net, listening to music, watching movies, or playing games. What's more, you can add an HDTV tuner and built-in GPS for a little more. Take a look at the enclosed booklet detailing the big savings for essential technology on a budget. We value your business and look forward to your future orders.

Although the direct strategy works for many requests and replies, it obviously won't work for every situation. With more practice and experience, you will be able to alter the pattern and apply the writing process to other communication problems. See the checklist on page 239 for a summary of what to do when you must write claim and adjustment messages.

Goodwill Messages

LEARNING OBJECTIVE 7

Write special messages that convey kindness and goodwill.

Many communicators are intimidated when they must write goodwill messages expressing thanks, recognition, and sympathy. Finding the right words to express feelings is often more difficult than writing ordinary business documents. That is why writers tend to procrastinate when it comes to goodwill messages. Sending a ready-made card or picking up the telephone is easier than writing a message. Remember, though, that the personal sentiments of the sender are always more expressive and more meaningful to readers than are printed cards or oral messages. Taking the time to write gives more importance to our well-wishing. Personal notes also provide a record that can be reread, savored, and treasured.

Why are personal goodwill messages more meaningful than ready-made cards?

In expressing thanks, recognition, or sympathy, you should always do so promptly. These messages are easier to write when the situation is fresh in your mind. They also mean more to the recipient. Don't forget that a prompt thank-you note carries the hidden message that you care and that you consider the event to be important. The best goodwill messages—whether thanks, congratulations, praise, or sympathy—concentrate on the five Ss. Goodwill messages should be

- **Selfless.** Be sure to focus the message solely on the receiver, not the sender. Don't talk about yourself; avoid such comments as *I remember when I. . . .*
- **Specific.** Personalize the message by mentioning specific incidents or characteristics of the receiver. Telling a colleague *Great speech* is much less effective than *Great story about McDonald's marketing in Moscow.* Take care to verify names and other facts.
- **Sincere.** Let your words show genuine feelings. Rehearse in your mind how you would express the message to the receiver orally. Then transform that conversational language to your written message. Avoid pretentious, formal, or flowery language *(It gives me great pleasure to extend felicitations on the occasion of your firm's twentieth anniversary).*
- **Spontaneous.** Keep the message fresh and enthusiastic. Avoid canned phrases *(Congratulations on your promotion, Good luck in the future).* Strive for directness and naturalness, not creative brilliance.
- **Short.** Although goodwill messages can be as long as needed, try to accomplish your purpose in only a few sentences. What is most important is remembering an individual. Such caring does not require documentation or wordiness. Individuals and business organizations often use special note cards or stationery for brief messages.

Spotlight on Communicators

Courtesy of Intel Corporation

Andrew S. Grove, cofounder and former chairman of Intel, the nation's principal computer chip maker, is best known as an Information Age leader and a technology visionary. But he also recognized the value of promoting personal relationships through goodwill messages. A mere thank-you followed by general comments is rather hollow, he said. Instead, when sending thanks or good wishes, Grove suggested making the thanks match the deed. Ask yourself what was special, unusual, extraordinary, or over and above the call of duty—and then describe it. Being specific, warm, and sincere is as important as the difference between a personal note and a computerized form letter.

Expressing Thanks

When someone has done you a favor or when an action merits praise, you need to extend thanks or show appreciation. Letters of appreciation may be written to customers for their orders, to hosts and hostesses for their hospitality, to individuals for kindnesses performed, and especially to customers who complain. After all, complainers are actually providing you with "free consulting reports from the field." Complainers who feel that their complaints were heard often become the greatest promoters of an organization.[8]

Written notes that show appreciation and express thanks are significant to their receivers. In expressing thanks, you generally write a short note on special notepaper or heavy card stock. The following messages provide models for expressing thanks for a gift, for a favor, and for hospitality.

To Express Thanks for a Gift. When expressing thanks, tell what the gift means to you. Use sincere, simple statements.

> *Thanks, Laura, to you and the other members of the department for honoring me with the elegant Waterford crystal vase at the party celebrating my twentieth anniversary with the company. The height and shape of the vase are perfect to hold roses and other bouquets from my garden. Each time I fill it, I'll remember your thoughtfulness in choosing this lovely gift for me.*

To Send Thanks for a Favor. In showing appreciation for a favor, explain the importance of the gesture to you.

> *I sincerely appreciate your filling in for me last week when I was too ill to attend the planning committee meeting for the spring exhibition. Without your participation, much of my preparatory work would have been lost. Knowing that competent and generous individuals like you are part of our team, Mark, is a great comfort. Moreover, counting you as a friend is my very good fortune. I'm grateful to you.*

To Extend Thanks for Hospitality. When you have been a guest, send a note that compliments the fine food, charming surroundings, warm hospitality, excellent host and hostess, and good company.

> *Jeffrey and I want you to know how much we enjoyed the dinner party for our department that you hosted Saturday evening. Your charming home and warm hospitality, along with the lovely dinner and sinfully delicious chocolate dessert, combined to create a truly memorable evening. Most of all, though, we appreciate your kindness in cultivating togetherness in our department. Thanks, Jennifer, for being such a special person.*

Responding to Goodwill Messages

Why should you respond to goodwill messages?

Should you respond when you receive a congratulatory note or a written pat on the back? By all means! These messages are attempts to connect personally; they are efforts to reach out, to form professional and/or personal bonds. Failing to respond to notes of congratulations and most other goodwill messages is like failing to say *You're welcome* when someone says *Thank you.* Responding to such messages is simply the right thing to do. Do avoid, though, minimizing your achievements with comments that suggest you don't really deserve the praise or that the sender is exaggerating your good qualities.

To Answer a Congratulatory Note. In responding to congratulations, keep it short and simple.

> *Thanks for your kind words regarding my award, and thanks, too, for sending me the newspaper clipping. I truly appreciate your thoughtfulness and warm wishes.*

To Respond to a Pat on the Back. When acknowledging a pat-on-the-back note, use simple words in conveying your appreciation.

> *Your note about my work made me feel good. I'm grateful for your thoughtfulness.*

Conveying Sympathy

What should go into a message of sympathy?

Most of us can bear misfortune and grief more easily when we know that others care. Notes expressing sympathy, though, are probably more difficult to write than any other kind of message. Commercial "In sympathy" cards make the task easier—but they are far less meaningful. Grieving friends want to know what you think—not what Hallmark's card writers think. To help you get started, you can always glance through cards expressing sympathy. They will supply ideas about

Checklist

Goodwill Messages

General Guidelines: The Five Ss

- **Be selfless.** Discuss the receiver, not the sender.
- **Be specific.** Instead of generic statements *(You did a good job)*, include special details *(Your marketing strategy to target key customers proved to be outstanding)*.
- **Be sincere.** Show your honest feelings with conversational, unpretentious language *(We are all very proud of your award)*.
- **Be spontaneous.** Strive to make the message natural, fresh, and direct. Avoid canned phrases *(If I may be of service, please do not hesitate ...)*.
- **Keep the message short.** Remember that, although they may be as long as needed, most goodwill messages are fairly short.

Giving Thanks

- **Cover three points in gift thank-yous.** (a) Identify the gift, (b) tell why you appreciate it, and (c) explain how you will use it.
- **Be sincere in sending thanks for a favor.** Tell what the favor means to you. Avoid superlatives and gushiness. Maintain credibility with sincere, simple statements.
- **Offer praise in expressing thanks for hospitality.** Compliment, as appropriate, the (a) fine food, (b) charming surroundings, (c) warm hospitality, (d) excellent host and hostess, and (e) good company.

Responding to Goodwill Messages

- **Respond to congratulations.** Send a brief note expressing your appreciation. Tell how good the message made you feel.
- **Accept praise gracefully.** Don't make belittling comments *(I'm not really all that good!)* to reduce awkwardness or embarrassment.

Extending Sympathy

- **Refer to the loss or tragedy directly but sensitively.** In the first sentence, mention the loss and your personal reaction.
- **For deaths, praise the deceased.** Describe positive personal characteristics *(Howard was a forceful but caring leader)*.
- **Offer assistance.** Suggest your availability, especially if you can do something specific.
- **End on a reassuring, positive note.** Perhaps refer to the strength the receiver finds in friends, family, colleagues, or religion.

the kinds of thoughts you might wish to convey in your own words. In writing a sympathy note, (a) refer to the death or misfortune sensitively, using words that show you understand what a crushing blow it is; (b) in the case of a death, praise the deceased in a personal way; (c) offer assistance without going into excessive detail; and (d) end on a reassuring, forward-looking note. Sympathy messages may be typed, although handwriting seems more personal. In either case, use notepaper or personal stationery.

© iStockphoto.com/netrun78

Businesses express condolences to bereaved employees in many ways. Flowers, cards, "comfort baskets," and pictures are popular corporate sympathy gifts that allow coworkers to grieve their loss with caring support from the company. Though such gift ideas are appropriate, a note of personal sympathy from a boss or colleague can be a more meaningful way to console an individual who is coping with misfortune and loss. *What important guidelines should be followed when extending sympathy in a personal message?*

To Express Condolences. Mention the loss tactfully, recognize good qualities of the deceased, assure the receiver of your concern, offer assistance, and conclude on a reassuring note.

> *We are deeply saddened, Gayle, to learn of the death of your husband. Warren's kind nature and friendly spirit endeared him to all who knew him. He will be missed.*
>
> *Although words seem empty in expressing our grief, we want you to know that your friends at QuadCom extend their profound sympathy to you. If we may help you or lighten your load in any way, you have but to call.*
>
> *We know that the treasured memories of your many happy years together, along with the support of your family and many friends, will provide strength and comfort in the months ahead.*

International Messages

LEARNING OBJECTIVE 8

Modify international messages to accommodate readers from other cultures.

The writing suggestions you have just studied work well for correspondence in this country. You may need, however, to modify the organization, format, and tone of messages going abroad.

American businesspeople appreciate efficiency, straightforwardness, and conciseness in messages. American business letters, for example, tend to be informal and conversational. Foreign correspondents, however, may look upon such directness and informality as inappropriate, insensitive, and abrasive.[9] Letters in Japan may begin with deference, humility, and references to nature:

> *The season for cherry blossoms is here with us and everybody is beginning to feel refreshed. We sincerely congratulate you on becoming more prosperous in your business.*[10]

How do Chinese sales letters differ from American sales letters?

The writers of Chinese letters strive to build relationships. A sales letter might begin with the salutation *Honored Company*, indicating a high level of respect. Figure 10.8 in Chapter 10 illustrates a Chinese persuasive letter, which contains a low-key sales approach. Although American business writers might use high-pressure tactics and direct requests, Chinese writers are more tentative. For example, a Chinese sales letter might say, *I hope you will take a moment to complete and mail the enclosed application.* The verb *hope* reduces the imposition of a direct request. Avoiding pressure tactics results from the cultural need to show respect and preserve harmony. Demonstrating humility, Chinese writers may refer to their own supposedly meager skills.[11] A typical closing in Chinese letters, *wishing good health*, emphasizes the importance of showing respect and developing reciprocal relationships.

Business letters in Germany tend to be informal. Business correspondents, however, generally address each other with honorifics and last names (Sehr geehrter Herr Woerner = Dr. Mr. Woerner), even if they have known each other for years. Letter introductions may refer to past encounters, meetings, or subjects previously discussed.[12] Italian business letters may refer to the receiver's family and children.

French correspondents would consider it rude to begin a letter with a request before it is explained. French letters typically include an ending with this phrase (or a variation of it): *I wish to assure you* [insert reader's most formal title] *of my most respectful wishes* [followed by the writer's title and signature].[13] Foreign letters are also more likely to include passive-voice constructions *(your letter has been received)*, exaggerated courtesy *(great pleasure, esteemed favor)*, and obvious flattery *(your distinguished firm)*.

Foreign letters may use different formatting techniques than American letters. Whereas American business letters are typewritten and single-spaced, in other countries they may be handwritten and single- or double-spaced. Address arrangements vary as well, as shown in the following:

German	**Japanese**
Herr [title, Mr., on first line]	Ms. Atsuko Takagi [title, name]
Dieter Woerner [name]	5-12 Koyo-cho 4 chome [street, house number]
Fritz-Kalle-Straße 4 [street, house number]	Higashinada-ku [city]
6200 Wiesbaden [postal district, city]	Tokyo 194 [prefecture, postal district]
Germany [country]	Japan [country]

Zooming In — YOUR TURN

Applying Your Skills at Ben & Jerry's

Alice Blachly, former customer affairs coordinator at Ben & Jerry's, is overloaded with work. She asks you, her assistant, to help as she hands you a stack of letters. The top one is from a customer who complains that she didn't get quite enough cookie and chocolate chunks in her last pint. The customer also wants to know why Ben & Jerry's has strayed from its Vermont roots and rural values by setting up dairy operations in Nevada. However, she agrees with Ben & Jerry's strong stand against using milk from cloned cows.

Blachly tells you to explain that, although we work hard and long at it, the chunking equipment for nuts, chocolate, and cookies is as not always as consistent as B & J would like and that you will report the problem of cookie and chocolate chunks to production. She tells you to refund the estimated purchase price for one pint of ice cream. As she walks away, she says that B & J went to Nevada to supply its product to ice cream eaters on the West Coast. "Saves energy costs," she said. "We don't truck milk across the country."

© Andre Jenny/Alamy

Your Task

Respond to all three of the comments in the letter of Cora Nicol, 246 Falls Overlook Drive, Niagara Falls, NY 14109. Although her complaint was gentle, it is, nevertheless, a complaint that warrants an adjustment. In your response strive to maintain her goodwill and favorable opinion of Ben & Jerry's.

Dates and numbers can be particularly confusing, as shown here:

United States	Some European Countries
June 3, 2012	3rd of June 2012
6/3/12	3.6.12
$5,320.00	US $5.320,00

Want to do well on tests and excel in your course? Go to **www.meguffey.com** for helpful interactive resources.

- **Review the Chapter 8 PowerPoint slides to prepare for the first quiz.**

To be safe, spell out the names of months instead of using figures. Verify sums of money and identify the currency unit.

Because the placement and arrangement of letter addresses and closing lines vary greatly, you should always research local preferences before writing. For important letters going abroad, have someone familiar with local customs read and revise the message. An American graduate student learned this lesson when she wrote a letter, in French, to a Paris museum asking for permission to do research. She received no response. Before writing a second time, she took the letter to her French tutor, who said: "No, no, mademoiselle! It will never do! It must be more respectful. You must be very careful of individuals' titles. Let me show you!" The second letter won the desired permission.

Summary of Learning Objectives

1 Apply the 3-x-3 writing process to creating successful positive messages, including e-mails, interoffice memos, and business letters. Positive messages—whether e-mails, interoffice memos, or business letters—can be straightforward and direct because they carry nonsensitive, routine information. In applying Phase 1 of the writing process for positive messages, you should determine your purpose, visualize the audience, and anticipate the reaction of the reader to your message. In Phase 2 you should collect information, make an outline of the points to cover, and write the first draft. In Phase 3 you should revise for clarity, proofread for correctness, and look for ways to promote "skim value." Finally, you should decide whether the message accomplishes its goal.

2 **Understand the appropriate use of e-mails, interoffice memos, and business letters.** E-mail is appropriate for short, informal messages. Interoffice memos are appropriate for internal messages that are important, lengthy, or formal. Like e-mails, interoffice memos follow a standard form with guide words *Date, To, From,* and *Subject*. Memos that serve as attachments to e-mails must be properly identified. Business letters are necessary when a permanent record is required; when confidentiality is critical; when formality and sensitivity are essential; and when a persuasive, well-considered presentation is important. Business letters written on company stationery often use block style with all lines starting at the left margin.

3 **Compose direct messages that make requests and respond to inquiries.** In direct messages requesting information or action, the opening immediately states the purpose of the message, perhaps asking a question. The body explains and justifies the request. If many questions are asked, they should be expressed in parallel form and balanced grammatically. The closing tells the reader courteously what to do and shows appreciation. In a message that replies directly and complies with a request, a subject line may identify previous correspondence, and the opening immediately delivers the good news. The body explains and provides additional information. The closing is cordial and personalized. If action is necessary, the ending tells the reader how to proceed and gives helpful details.

4 **Write messages that clearly explain step-by-step instructions.** When writing messages that explain instructions, you should (a) divide the instructions into steps, (b) list each step in the order in which it is to be carried out, (c) arrange the items vertically with bullets or numbers, and (d) begin each step with an action verb using the imperative (command) mood rather than the indicative mood (e.g., *Open the paper drawer, load the paper, and push the Start button)*. Messages that give instructions should not sound dictatorial. When changing existing procedures, avoid making accusations and fixing blame. Explain changes, give reasons, and suggest benefits to the reader.

5 **Prepare messages that make direct claims.** When a customer writes to identify a wrong and request a correction, the message is called a *claim*. A direct claim is one to which the receiver is expected to readily agree. A well-written claim begins by describing the problem clearly or telling what action is to be taken. The body of the claim explains and justifies the request without anger or emotion. The closing summarizes the request or action to be taken. It includes an end date, if appropriate, and courteously looks forward to continued business if the problem is resolved. Copies of relevant documents should be enclosed.

6 **Create adjustment messages that regain the confidence of customers and promote further business.** When a company grants a customer's claim, it is called an *adjustment*. An adjustment message has three goals: (a) rectifying the wrong, if one exists; (b) regaining the confidence of the customer; and (c) promoting further business. The opening immediately grants the claim without sounding grudging. To regain the confidence of the customer, the body may explain what went wrong and how the problem will be rectified. However, the writer may strive to avoid accepting responsibility for any problems. The closing expresses appreciation, extends thanks for past business, refers to a desire to be of service, and may mention a new product. If an apology is offered, it should be presented early and briefly.

7 **Write special messages that convey kindness and goodwill.** Messages that deliver thanks, praise, or sympathy should be selfless, specific, sincere, spontaneous, and short. Gift thank-yous should identify the gift, tell why you appreciate it, and explain how you will use it. Favor thank-yous should tell, without gushing, what the favor means to you. Expressions of sympathy should mention the loss tactfully; recognize good qualities in the deceased (in the case of a death); offer assistance; and conclude on a positive, reassuring note.

8 **Modify international messages to accommodate readers from other cultures.** Messages going to individuals in some areas, such as South Asia and Europe, should probably use a less direct organizational strategy and be more formal in tone. Because the placement and arrangement of business letter addresses and closing lines vary greatly, always research local preferences before writing business letters. For important messages going abroad, have someone familiar with local customs read and revise the message.

Are you ready? Get more practice at **www.meguffey.com**

Chapter Review

1. Into what three content categories can most business messages be organized? What group will make up the bulk of your messages? (Obj. 1)
2. How can you save the reader's time and make your business message easy to comprehend at a glance? (Obj. 1)
3. What kinds of messages are sent as are interoffice memos? (Obj. 2)
4. When is it important to send a business letter rather than an e-mail? (Obj. 2)
5. What are the most emphatic positions in a message, and what goes there? (Obj. 3)
6. What should you include in the closing of a request message? (Obj. 3)
7. How should instructions be written? Give a brief original example. (Obj. 4)
8. What is the imperative mood, and why is it important to use it in writing instructions? (Obj. 4)
9. What is a claim? When should it be straightforward? (Obj. 5)
10. Why should a direct claim be made by letter rather than by e-mail or a telephone call? (Obj. 5)
11. What is an adjustment message? (Obj. 6)
12. What are a writer's three goals in composing adjustment messages? (Obj. 6)
13. What are five characteristics of goodwill messages? (Obj. 7)
14. What are four groups of people to whom business communicators might write letters of appreciation? (Obj. 7)
15. What are three elements of business letters going abroad that might be modified to accommodate readers from other cultures? (Obj. 8)

Critical Thinking

1. Are the writing skills that are required for sending business e-mails and text messages different from those required for writing interoffice memos and business letters? Explain. (Objs. 1, 2)
2. In promoting the value of letter writing, a well-known columnist recently wrote, "To trust confidential information to e-mail is to be a rube."[14] What did he mean? Do you agree? (Obj. 2)
3. Why is it important to regain the confidence of a customer in an adjustment message? How can it be done? (Obj. 6)
4. How are American business letters different from those written in other countries? Why do you suppose this is so? (Obj. 8)
5. **Ethical Issue:** Assume that you have drafted a letter to a customer in which you apologize for the way the customer's account was fouled up by the Accounting Department. You show the letter to your boss, and she instructs you to remove the apology. It admits responsibility, she says, and the company cannot allow itself to be held liable. You are not an attorney, but you can't see the harm in a simple apology. What should you do? Refer to the section "Tools for Doing the Right Thing" in Chapter 1 to review the five questions you might ask yourself in trying to do the right thing.

Writing Improvement Exercises

8.1 Direct Openings (Objs. 1–7)

Revise the following openings so that they are more direct. Add information if necessary.

a. Despite the economy, Liberty Bank has been investigating the possibility of initiating an internship program within our Financial Services Department. I have been appointed as the point person to conduct research regarding our proposed program. We are fully aware of the benefits of a strong internship program, and our management team is eager to take advantage of some of these benefits. We would be deeply appreciative if you would be kind enough to help us out with answers to a number of specific questions.

b. My name is Kimberly Sanchez, and I am assistant to the manager of Information Services & Technology at Onyz, Inc. We are interested in your voice recognition software that we understand allows you to dictate and copy text without touching a keyboard. We are interested in answers to a number of questions, such as the cost for a single-user license and perhaps the availability of a free trial version. Will you please answer the following questions.

c. Your letter of March 4 has been referred to me. Pursuant to your inquiry, I have researched your question in regard to whether or not we offer our European-style patio umbrella in colors. This unique umbrella is one of our most popular items. Its 10-foot canopy protects you when the sun is directly overhead, but it also swivels and tilts to virtually any angle for continuous sun protection all day long. It comes in two colors: cream and forest green.

d. I am pleased to receive your inquiry regarding the possibility of my acting as a speaker at the final semester meeting of your business management club on May 2. The topic of online résumés interests me and is one on which I think I could impart helpful information to your members. Therefore, I am responding in the affirmative to your kind invitation.

8.2 Writing Instructions (Obj. 4)

Revise each of the following wordy, dense paragraphs into a set of concise instructions. Include an introductory statement.

a. Orders may be placed at our Web site by following certain steps. Here they are. As a visitor to our site, you should first look over everything and find the items you want from our catalog. Then your shopping cart is important. You will add items to your shopping cart. When you are finished adding things to your shopping cart, the next step is to proceed to checkout. But wait! Have you created a new account? After creating a new account, we next need to know what shipping address to ship your items to. We will also need to have you choose a shipping method. Then you will be expected to provide payment information. Finally, you are nearly done! Payment information must be provided, and then you are ready to review your order and submit it.

b. If you want to make a YouTube video, here are some important tips for those who have not done it before. First, you will need to obtain a video recording device such as a cell phone, webcam, or camcorder. Another thing you will have to do is make a decision on whether or not to make a video blog, comedy skit, how-to video, or a video that is about travel. Remember that your video must be 10 minutes or less for traditional YouTube membership accounts. You will want to create a video with good light quality, and that usually means daytime recording. Finally, be sure to use computer editing software to change or delete anything.

c. A number of employees have asked about how to make two-sided copies. Here's what to do. The copy for Side 1 of the original goes facedown on the document glass. Then the document cover should be closed. Next you should select the quantity that you require. To copy Side 1, you should then press Start. Now you remove the first original and place the second original facedown on the document glass. The document cover should be closed. Now you remove Side 1 copy from the output tray. It should be inserted facedown into the paper bypass tray. Then select the alternate paper tray and press Start.

Activities

Note: All Documents for Analysis are provided at **www.meguffey.com** for you to download and revise.

8.3. Document for Analysis: Direct Request (Obj. 3)

Your Task. Analyze the following poorly written message. List at least five weaknesses. If your instructor directs, revise the message using the suggestions you learned in this and previous chapters.

To: Amsoft Manager List
From: Stella Soto <stella.soto@amsoft.com>
Subject: E-Mail Problems
Cc:
Bcc:

Dear Managers,

As Amsoft vice president, I am troubled by a big problem. I am writing this note to ask for your help and advice to address an urgent problem—the problem of excessive e-mail. If you will do me the favor of answering the questions below, I'm sure your ideas will assist us in the development of a plan that should benefit your staff, yourself, and our organization will be improved. Your replies in writing to these questions (preferably by May 5) will help me prepare for our supervisory committee meeting on May 10.

Although e-mail is a great productivity tool, I'm afraid that its use is becoming extremely excessive. For our organization it is actually cutting into work time. Did you know that one study found that the average office worker is spending 3 hours a day on e-mail? In our organization we may be spending even more than this. It's exceedingly difficult to get any work done because of writing and answering an extraordinary number of e-mails coming in each and every day. Excessive e-mail is sapping the organization's strength and productivity. I would like to have your answers to some questions before the above referenced dates to help us focus on the problem.

Can you give a ballpark figure for how many e-mails you receive and answer on a personal basis each day? Think about how many hours the staff members in your department spend on e-mail each day. Approximately how many hours would you estimate? Do you have any ideas about how we can make a reduction in the volume of e-mails being sent and received within our own organization? Do you think that e-mail is being used by our employees in an excessive manner?

I'm wondering what you think about an e-mail-free day once a week. How about Fridays? I appreciate your suggestions and advice in developing a solution to the problem of controlling e-mail and making an improvement in productivity.

Stella Soto
Vice President, Operations

8.4 Document for Analysis: Direct Response (Obj. 3)

Your Task. Analyze the following poorly written interoffice memo that reports information from a symposium. List at least five weaknesses. If your instructor directs, revise the message.

Date: March 4, 2012
To: Trevor Kurtz, CEO
From: Emily Lopez-Rush
Subject: Instant Messaging

Thanks for asking me to attend the Instant Messaging Symposium. It was sponsored by Pixel Link and took place March 2. Do you think you will want me to expand on what I learned at the next management council meeting? I believe that meeting is March 25.

Anyway, here's my report. Jason Howard, the symposium leader told us that over 80 million workers are already using instant messaging and that it was definitely here to stay. But do the risks outweigh the advantages? He talked about benefits, providers, costs involved, and risks. The top advantages of IM are speed, documentation, and it saves costs. The major problems are spam, security, control, and disruptive. He said that the principal IM providers for consumers were AOL Instant Messenger, Windows Live Messenger, and Yahoo Messenger.

Misuse of IM can result in reductions in productivity. However, positive results can be achieved with appropriate use. Although some employees are using consumer IM services, for maximum security many organizations are investing in enterprise-level IM systems, and they are adopting guidelines for employees. These enterprise-level IM systems range in cost from $30 to $100 per user license. The cost depends on the amount of functionality.

This is just a summary of what I learned. If you want to hear more, please do not hesitate to call.

8.5 Document for Analysis: Direct Claim (Obj. 5)

Your Task. Analyze the following poorly written claim letter. List at least five weaknesses. If your instructor directs, revise it using the suggestions you learned in this chapter.

Current date

Ms. Melanie Cholston, Manager
Nationwide Car Rentals
1325 Commerce Street
Dallas, TX 75202

Dear Melanie Cholston:

I am writing this letter to inform you that you can't have it both ways. Either you provide customers with cars with full gas tanks or you don't. And if you don't, you shouldn't charge them when they return with empty tanks!

In view of the fact that I picked up a car at the Dallas-Ft. Worth International Airport on June 23 with an empty tank, I had to fill it immediately. Then I drove it until June 26. When I returned the car to Houston, as previously planned, I naturally let the tank go nearly empty, since that is the way I received the car in Dallas-Ft. Worth.

But your attendant in Houston charged me to fill the tank—$49.43 (premium gasoline at premium prices)! Although I explained to her that I had received it with an empty tank, she kept telling me that company policy required that she charge for a fill-up. My total bill came to $426.50, which, you must agree, is a lot of money for a rental period of only three days. I have the signed rental agreement and a receipt showing that I paid the full amount and that it included $49.43 for a gas fill-up when I returned the car. Any correspondence should be directed to the undersigned at Criterion Enterprises, 402 North Griffin Street, Dallas, TX 74105.

Inasmuch as my company is a new customer and inasmuch as we had hoped to use your agency for our future car rentals because of your competitive rates, I trust that you will give this matter your prompt attention.

Your unhappy customer,

8.6 Document for Analysis: Instructions (Obj. 4)

Your Task. This e-mail message is addressed to one employee, but it will also be sent to others. List at least five weaknesses. If your instructor directs, revise the message.

To: Sam Oliver <sam.oliver@stcc.edu>
From: Alexandra Tutson <alex.tutson@stcc.edu>
Cc:
Subject: Repairs

This message is to let you know that we have recently instituted a new process for all equipment repairs. Effective immediately, we are no longer using the "Equipment Repair Form" that we formerly used. We want to move everyone to an online database system. This new process will help us repair your equipment faster and keep track of it better. You will find the new procedure at http://www.BigWebDesk.net. That's where you log in. You should indicate the kind of repair you need. It may be for AudioVisual, Mac, PC, or Printer. Then you should begin the process of data entry for your specific problem by selecting **Create New Ticket**. The new ticket should be printed and attached securely to the equipment. Should you have questions or trouble, just call Sylvia at Extension 255. You can also write to her at *sylvia.freeman@stcc.edu.* The warehouse truck driver will pick up and deliver your equipment as we have always done in the past.

Alexandra Tutson, Manager
Operations and Facilities
alex.tutson@stcc.edu
(813) 355-3200, Ext. 230

8.7 Direct Request: Seeking a New Look for the Company Web Site (Obj. 3)

E-mail

You are part of the newly formed Committee on Web Site Redesign. Its function is to look into the possible redesign of your company Web site. Some managers think that the site is looking a bit dated. The committee delegates you to ask Cole Prewarski, Web master and manager, some questions. The committee wonders whether he has done any usability tests on the current site. The committee wants to know how much a total Web redesign might cost.

It also would like to know about the cost of a partial redesign. Someone wanted to know whether animation, sound, or video could be added and wondered if Cole would recommend doing so. Someone else thought that the timing of a redesign might be important. The committee asks you to add other questions to your memo. Invite Cole to a meeting April 6. Assume that he knows about the committee.

Your Task. Write an e-mail to Cole Prewarski (*cprewarski@global.net*) requesting answers to several questions and inviting him to a meeting.

8.8 Direct Request: Heading to Las Vegas (Obj. 3)

Web

Your company, Software.com, wants to hold its next company-wide meeting in a resort location. The CEO has asked you, as marketing manager, to find a conference location for your 85 engineers, product managers, and marketing staff. He wants the company to host a four-day combination sales conference/vacation/retreat at some spectacular spot. He suggests that you start by inquiring at the amazing Caesars Palace Las Vegas. You check its Web site and discover interesting information. However, you decide to write a letter so that you can have a permanent, formal record of all the resorts you investigate.

You estimate that your company will require about 80 rooms. You will also need three conference rooms (to accommodate 25 or more) for one and a half days. You want to know room rates, conference facilities, and entertainment options for families. You have two periods that would be possible: April 20-24 or July 10-14. You know that one of these is at an off-peak time, and you wonder whether you can get a good room rate. You are interested in entertainment at Caesars during these times. One evening the CEO will want to host a banquet for about 125 people.

Your Task. Write a well-organized letter to Ms. Isabella Cervantes, Manager, Convention Services, Caesars Palace, 257 Palace Drive, Las Vegas, NV 87551. Before writing, you might like to look at the Caesars Web site for information.

8.9 Direct Response: Restaurants Join Obesity Fight (Obj. 3)

As consumers become increasingly concerned about obesity and the health risks associated with nutrition, many seek more information about restaurant foods. American families are estimated to spend as much as half of their food dollars at restaurants and to consume about one third of their calories outside the home.

One U.S. senator is pushing a bill to require chain restaurants to list nutritional information for all menu items. Although this law has not been passed, your city would like to encourage restaurants to offer more nutritious menu choices.

Assume that you work for Partners for a Healthier Community (PHC), which is part of the City Health and Human Services Department. PHC has been working on a program called Healthy Dining. Its goal is to offer food establishments the opportunity to be recognized as Healthy Dining restaurants. In order to be listed, owners must meet certain criteria.

A PHC team devoted to the Healthy Dining program discussed a number of requirements. The team thought that restaurants ought to offer at least two choices of fruits or vegetables. They wanted choices other than potato dishes. The team was much opposed to french fries. What could be substituted for them? Perhaps salads? In regard to the menu, the team thought that Healthy Dining restaurants should have some low-fat and low-calorie menu items, and when they are offered, customers should know what they are. However, no minimum on the number of such items would be required. The team also thought that Healthy Dining restaurants should try to provide at least some dishes in smaller portion sizes or perhaps half portions. Milk was discussed, and team members suggested that restaurants move away from offering whole milk. Team members preferred 1 percent or skim milk when milk was offered as a beverage.

The team gave you the task of drafting a letter to restaurant owners who inquired about the Health Dining rating.

Your Task. Prepare a response letter to be sent to owners who want to know how to earn the Healthy Dining rating for their restaurants. Explain the goal of the Healthy Dining program, and show the requirements in a bulleted list. Address the first letter as a response to Mr. Adrian Hammersmith, Adrian's Steak House, 974 South Cobb Drive, Marietta, GA 30060. Explain that an application form and additional information are available at http://www.healthydining.com.

8.10 Direct Response Memo: Luxury Hotels Embrace Signature Scents (Obj. 3)

Web

Hotel chains are constantly seeking new ways to make guests want to return. Comfy beds and smiling clerks are not enough. Many hotels are now developing signature scents to waft through lobbies, restaurants, meeting rooms, and pool areas.

As an assistant to Michelle Long, CEO of a small hotel chain, you received an interesting assignment. Ms. Long recently visited the Park Hyatt in Washington, DC, and was impressed not only with its $24 million makeover and chic guest rooms but also with its custom fragrance. She asks you to conduct research online to discover what hotels are using fragrances and what scents are associated with each property. Her goal is to decide whether this trend is something her small hotel chain might follow.

In your research you discovered that Omni Hotels engage hidden machines to spray a lemongrass and green tea scent into the lobby. Omni also uses a coconut fragrance, for a tropical effect, near the pool. Apparently finding that scents are appealing, Omni plans to extend its fragrances to its meeting spaces. It is considering citrus, which is supposed to enhance energy.

You discovered that Westin Hotels & Resorts favors a white tea aroma. In Paris the fashionable Hotel Costes treats guests to an exclusive custom scent with notes of lavender, bay tree, coriander, white pepper, rose, incense, woods, and musk. Luxury properties are embracing signature fragrances to create an emotional connection to their hotels.

Your research also reveals a Web site complaining that hotels are contributing to the "sick building syndrome" by masking chemical smells with fragrances. Proponents of fragrance-free hotels recommend striving for fresh, not perfumed, air.

Your Task. Conduct additional Web research so that you can report on at least five hotels and their signature scents. Address a concise interoffice memo (or an e-mail if your instructor directs) to CEO Michelle Long. Decide whether to mention the argument for fragrance-free hotels. In addition, think about how you can make your findings most readable.

8.11 Direct Response Memo: Arranging Interviews for Environmental Architect/Designer (Obj. 3)

James F. Becker, founder and CEO of Becker & Associate Architects, is a busy architect. As he expands his business, he is looking for ecologically conscious designers who can develop sustainable architecture that minimizes the negative environmental impact of buildings. His company has an open position for an environmental architect/designer. Three candidates were scheduled to be interviewed on March 14. However, Mr. Becker now finds he must be in Dallas during that week to consult with the builders of a 112-unit planned golf course community. He asks you, his office manager, to call the candidates, reschedule for March 28 or March 29, and prepare a memo with the new times as well as a brief summary of the candidates' backgrounds.

Fortunately, you were able to reschedule all three candidates. Scott Hogarth will come on March 29 at 11 a.m. Mr. Hogarth specializes in passive solar energy and has two years of experience with SolarPlus, Inc. He has a bachelor's degree from the University of Southern California. Amanda Froescher has a master's degree from Boise State University and worked for five years as an architect planner for Boise Builders, with expertise in sustainable building materials. She will come on March 28 at 2 p.m. Without a degree but with ten years of building experience, Raul Ramirez is scheduled for March 28 at 10 a.m. He is the owner of Green Building Consulting and has experience with energy efficiency, sustainable materials, domes, and earth-friendly design. You are wondering whether Mr. Becker forgot to include Stanley Grafsky, his partner, who usually helps make personnel selections.

Your Task. Prepare a memo (or e-mail if your instructor directs) to Mr. Becker with all the information he needs in the most readable format. Consider using a three-column table format for the candidate information.

8.12 Instruction E-Mail or Memo: New Process for Purchase Requests (Obj. 4)

E-mail

Along with your parents, brothers, and sisters, you own a share of a growing family business with 55 employees. As the head of the Purchasing Department, you realize that the business must keep better track of purchases. Some employees use the company purchasing order forms, but others submit sloppy e-mails or handwritten notes that are barely legible. What's worse, you are not sure whether the requested purchase has been authorized by the budget manager. You talk to the family management council, and they urge you to establish a standard procedure for submitting purchase requests.

Because the business has a good Web site, you decide that purchase requests must now be downloaded from the company intranet (http://www.lynch.com/intranet). To provide the fastest service, employees should fill out the new purchase request form. This may be done manually or digitally. Employees must include complete information for each requested purchase: date, quantities, catalog numbers, complete descriptions, complete vendor mailing address and contact information, delivery requirements, and shipping methods (usually f.o.b.). The Purchasing Department should be sent the original, and a copy should be kept by the requesting employee. An important step in the new procedure is approval by the budget manager on the request form. That is, employees should talk to the budget manager and get her approval before submitting the purchase request. You think this new procedure will solve many problems for you and for employees.

Your Task. As Purchasing Department manager, write an e-mail or a hard-copy memo (as your instructor directs) to all employees informing them of the new procedure.

8.13 Instruction E-Mail or Memo: Cell Phone Use and Texting While Driving (Obj. 4)

E-mail Team Web

As one of the managers of Capri, a hair care and skin products company, you are alarmed at a newspaper article you just saw. A stockbroker for Morgan Stanley Smith Barney was making cold calls on his personal cell phone while driving. His car hit and killed a motorcyclist. The brokerage firm was sued and accused of contributing to an accident by encouraging employees to use cell phones while driving. To avoid the risk of paying huge damages awarded by an emotional jury, the brokerage firm offered the victim's family a $500,000 settlement.

You begin to worry, knowing that your company has provided its 75 sales representatives with cell phones to help them keep in touch with the home base while they are in the field. You are also worried about texting while driving. At the next management meeting, other members agree that you should draft a message detailing some cell phone safety rules for your sales reps. On the Web you learn several tips: Anyone with a cell phone should get to know its features, including speed dial, automatic memory, and redial. Another suggestion involves using a hands-free device. (Management members decide to purchase these for every sales rep and have the devices available within one month.)You also learn that cell phones in cars should be within easy reach so drivers can grab them without removing their eyes from the road. If they get an incoming call at an inconvenient time, they should allow their voice mail to pick up the call. They should never talk, of course, during hazardous driving conditions, such as rain, sleet, snow, and ice.

Texting while driving is totally out of the question! In addition, taking notes or looking up phone numbers is also dangerous. The more you think about it, the more you think that sales reps should not use their cell phones while the car is moving. They really should pull over. But you know that would be hard to enforce.

Your Task. Individually or in teams, write a memo or e-mail to Capri sales reps outlining company suggestions (or should they be rules?) for the safe use of wireless devices in cars. You may wish to check the Web for additional safety ideas. Try to suggest reader benefits in this message. How is safety beneficial to the sales reps? The message is from you acting as operations manager.

8.14 Instruction E-Mail or Memo: Describing a Workplace Procedure (Obj. 4)

E-mail

At your job or organization, assume that a new employee has joined the staff and the boss has asked you to write out a set of instructions for some task. It could be sending faxes, printing copies, answering the phone, setting up appointments, scheduling conferences, training employees, greeting customers, closing a cash register, opening the office, closing the office, or any other task that has at least five steps.

Your Task. Prepare an e-mail or memo to your manager, Josh Washington, in response to his request for a set of instructions for the task.

8.15 Instruction E-Mail or Memo: How to be Safe at Work (Obj. 4)

E-mail Web

After a recent frightening experience, your boss, Kathryn Gossoni, realized that she must draft a memo about office security. Here's why she's concerned. A senior associate, Barbara Williams, was working overtime cleaning up overdue reports. At about 9 p.m. she heard the office door open, but the intruder quickly left when it was clear that someone was in the office. Your boss hurriedly put together the following memo to be distributed to office managers in five branch offices. But she was on her way out of town, and she asked you to revise her draft and have it ready for her approval when she returns. One other thing—she wondered whether you would do online research to find other helpful suggestions. Your boss trusts you to totally revise, if necessary.

Your Task. Conduct a database or Web search to look for reasonable office security suggestions. Study the following memo. Then improve its organization, clarity, conciseness, correctness, and readability. Don't be afraid to do a total overhaul. Bulleted points are a must, and check the correctness, too. Your boss is no Ms. Grammar! Be sure to add an appropriate closing. This may be either a memo or an e-mail, as your instructor directs.

Date: Current
To: Branch Managers
From: Kathryn Gossoni, Vice President
Subject: Staying Safe in the Office

Office security is a topic we have not talked enough about. I was terrified recently when a senior associate, who was working late, told me she heard the front door of the branch office open and she thought she heard a person enter. When she called out, the person apparently left. This frightening experience reminded me there are several things that each branch can do to improve it's office security. The following are a few simple things, but we will talk more about this at our next quarterly meeting (June 8?). Please come with additional ideas.

If an office worker is here early or late, then it is your responsibility to talk with them about before and after hours security. When someone comes in early it is not smart to open the doors until most of the rest of the staff arrive. Needless to say, employees working overtime should make sure the door is locked and they should not open there office doors after hours to people they don't know, especially if you are in the office alone. Dark offices are especially attractive to thieves with valuable equipment.

Many branches are turning off lights at points of entry and parking areas to conserve energy. Consider changing this policy or installing lights connected to motion detectors, which is an inexpensive (and easy!) way to discourage burglars and intruders. I also think that "cash-free" decals are a good idea because they make thieves realize that not much is in this office to take. These signs may discourage breaking and entering. On the topic of lighting, we want to be sure that doors and windows that are secluded and not visible to neighbors or passersby is illuminated.

We should also beware of displaying any valuable equipment or other things. When people walk by, they should not be able to look in and see expensive equipment. Notebook computers and small portable equipment is particularly vulnerable at night. It should be locked up. In spite of the fact that most of our branches are guarded by Broadview Security, I'm not sure all branches are displaying the decals prominently—especially on windows and doors. We want people to know that our premises are electronically protected.

8.16 Writing Clear Instructions (Obj. 4)

At **www.meguffey.com**, you will find a supplement devoted to writing instructions. It includes colorful examples and links to Web sites with relevant examples of real sets of instructions from business Web sites.

Your Task. Locate "How to Write Instructions" and study all of its sections. Then choose one of the following application activities:

A-5, "Revising the Instructions for an Imported Fax Machine," or A-6, "Evaluation: Instructions for Dealing With Car Emergencies." Complete the assignment and submit it to your instructor.

8.17 Direct Claim: Protesting Unexpected Charges (Obj. 5)

As vice president of Rochester Preferred Travel, you are upset with Premier Promos. Premier is a catalog company that provides imprinted promotional products for companies. Your travel service was looking for something special to offer in promoting its cruise ship travel packages. Premier offered free samples of its promotional merchandise, under its "No Surprise" policy.

You thought, *What can we lose?* So on January 11, you placed a telephone order for a number of samples. These included an insulated lunch sack, a portable power strip in a zippered case, a square-ended barrel bag with fanny pack, as well as a deluxe canvas attaché case and two colors of garment-dyed sweatshirts. All items were supposed to be free. You did think it odd that you were asked for your company's MasterCard number, but Premier promised to bill you only if you kept the samples.

When the items arrived, you were not pleased, and you returned them all on January 21 (you have a postal receipt showing the return). But your February credit card statement showed a charge of $258.20 for the sample items. You called Premier in February and spoke to Virginia, who assured you that a credit would be made on your next statement. However, your March statement showed no credit. You called again and received a similar promise. It's now April and no credit has been made. You realize that this situation is now too complicated for another telephone call, and you decide to write and demand action.

Your Task. Write a claim letter that documents the problem and states the action that you want taken. Add any information you feel is necessary. Address your letter to Ms. Arletta Sandusky, Customer Services, Premier Promos, 2445 Bermiss Road, Valdosta, GA 31602.

8.18 Direct Claim: Short Door for Tall Player (Obj. 5)

As the owner of Contempo Interiors, you recently worked on the custom Indiana home of an NBA basketball player. He requested an oversized 12-foot mahogany entry door. You ordered by telephone the solid mahogany door ("Provence") from American Custom Wood on May 17. When it arrived on June 28, your carpenter gave you the bad news. Magnificent as it was, the huge door was cut too small. Instead of measuring a total of 12 feet 2 inches, the door measured 11 feet 10 inches. In your carpenter's words, "No way can I stretch that door to fit this opening!" You waited four weeks for this handcrafted custom door, and your client wanted it installed immediately. Your carpenter said, "I can rebuild this opening for you, but I'm going to have to charge you for my time." His extra charge came to $940.50.

You feel that the people at American Custom Wood should reimburse you for this amount since it was their error. In fact, you actually saved them a bundle of money by not returning the door. You decide to write to American Custom Wood and enclose a copy of your carpenter's bill. You wonder whether you should also include a copy of the invoice, even though it does not show the exact door measurements. You are a good customer of American Custom Wood, having used its quality doors and windows on many other jobs. You are confident that it will grant this claim.

Your Task. Write a claim letter to Michael Medina, Operations Manager, American Custom Wood, 140 NE 136 Avenue, Vancouver, WA 98654.

8.19 Direct Claim: The Real Thing (Obj. 5)

Like most consumers, you have probably occasionally been unhappy with service or with products you have used.

Your Task. Select a product or service that has disappointed you. Write a claim letter requesting a refund, replacement, explanation, or whatever seems reasonable. Generally, such letters are addressed to customer service departments. For claims about food products, be sure to include bar-code identification from the package, if possible. Your instructor may ask you to actually mail this letter. Remember that smart companies want to know what their customers think, especially if a product could be improved. Give your ideas for improvement. When you receive a response, share it with your class.

8.20 Direct Claim: Barking Mad With Happpypets.com (Obj. 5)

E-mail

As the owner/operator of Posh Paws, a mobile dog grooming service, you recently purchased several items from Happypets.com. You encountered the Web site when surfing the Internet and were impressed with the variety and prices of its products. Because Happypets.com offered free shipping on orders over $100, you decided to take a chance on a company you had never heard of and place an order.

Using the online shopping cart, you ordered two bottles each of Top Performance UltraCoat Hot Oil Treatment and UltraCoat A-1 Hot Oil Shampoo. To qualify for the free shipping, you added one Very Berry Bow Canister. The holidays are approaching, and customers like bows on their freshly groomed pets. As you entered your credit card and delivery information, you had to check a box and agree to no exchanges because the items were on sale. You had previously used the hot oil products, so you figured you had nothing to lose and completed the $107.93 transaction. To be safe, you printed a copy of your order (number 0095644-1) for your records.

When the package arrived, you were barking mad. Although the packing slip accurately listed the items you requested, Happypets.com must have shipped you someone else's order: six bottles each of Pet Effects Watermelon and Pear Shampoo and Top Performance Soothing Suds Shampoo. Because the holiday season is fast approaching, you must purchase your supplies locally.

Your Task. Write an e-mail that documents the problem and states the action you want taken. Add any information you feel is necessary. Send the e-mail to *Customer Services@Happypets.com.*

8.21 Direct Claim: But It Doesn't Work! (Obj. 5)

E-mail

After you receive an unexpected bonus, you decide to indulge and buy a new HDTV. You conduct research to compare prices and decide on a Panasonic 42-inch Plasma HDTV Model TC-P42X1. You find a great deal at Digital Depot for $599.95 plus tax. Although the closest store is a 45-minute drive, the price is so good you decide it's worth the trip. You sell your old TV to make room for the Panasonic and spend several hours installing the new set. It works perfectly, but the next day when you go to turn it on, nothing happens. You check everything, but no matter what you do, you can't get a picture. You're irritated! You are without a TV and have wasted hours hooking up the Panasonic. Assuming it's just a faulty set, you pack up the TV and drive back to Digital Depot. You have no trouble returning the item and come home with a second Panasonic.

Again you install the TV, and again you enjoy your new purchase. But the next day, you have no picture for a second time. Now you are fuming! Not looking forward to your third trip to Digital Depot, you repack the Panasonic and return it. The customer service representative tries to offer you another Panasonic, but you decline. You point out all the trouble you have been through and say you would prefer a more reliable TV from a different manufacturer that is the same size and in the same price range as the Panasonic. Digital Depot carries a Samsung (Model PN42B450B1D) that fits your criteria, but at $729.00, it is more than you had budgeted. You feel that after all the problems you have endured, Digital Depot should sell you the Samsung at the same price. However, when you called to discuss the matter, you were told to submit a written request.

Your Task. Write a direct claim letter to Dennis Garcia, Manager, Digital Depot, 2300 Austin Street, Houston, TX 77074, asking him to sell you the TV for less than the advertised price.

8.22 Adjustment: Responding to Short Door for Tall Player (Obj. 6)

As Michael Medina, operations manager, American Custom Wood, you have a problem. Your firm manufactures quality precut and custom-built doors and frames. You have received a letter from Erica Adams (described in **Activity 8.18**), an interior designer. Her letter explained that the custom mahogany door ("Provence") she received was cut to the wrong dimensions. She ordered an oversized door measuring 12 feet 2 inches. The door that arrived was 11 feet 10 inches.

Ms. Adams kept the door because her client, an NBA basketball player, insisted that the front of the house be closed up. Therefore, she had her carpenter resize the opening. He charged $940.50 for this corrective work. She claims that you should reimburse her for this amount, since your company was responsible for the error. You check her May 17 order and find that the order was filled correctly. In a telephone order, Ms. Adams requested the Provence double-entry door measuring 11 feet 10 inches, and that is what you sent. Now she says that the doors should have been 12 feet 2 inches.

Your policy forbids refunds or returns on custom orders. Yet, you remember that around May 15 you had two new people working the phones taking orders. It is possible that they did not hear or record the measurements correctly. You don't know whether to grant this claim or refuse it. But you do know that you must look into the training of telephone order takers and be sure that they verify all custom order measurements. It might also be a good idea to have your craftspeople call a second time to confirm custom measurements.

Ms. Adams is a successful interior designer who has provided American Custom Wood with a number of orders. You value her business but aren't sure how to respond. You would like to remind her that American Custom Wood has earned a reputation as a premier manufacturer of wood doors and frames. Your doors feature prime woods, meticulous craftsmanship, and award-winning designs. What's more, the engineering is ingenious. You also have a wide range of classic designs.

Your Task. After much deliberation, you decide to grant this claim. Respond to Erica Adams, Contempo Interiors, 2304 River Ridge Road, Indianapolis, IN 46031. You might mention that you have a new line of greenhouse windows that are available in three sizes. Include a brochure describing these windows.

8.23 Adjustment: We Can Restretch But Not Replace (Obj. 6)

E-mail

Your company, ArtWorkOnline, sells paintings through its Web site and catalogs. It specializes in workplace art intended for offices, executive suites, conference rooms, and common areas. To make shopping for office art easy, your art consultants preselect art, making sure that the finished product is framed and delivered in perfect shape. You are proud that ArtWorkOnline can offer fine works of original art at incredibly low prices.

© dbimages/Alamy

Recently you received an e-mail from Huntzinger Construction claiming that a large canvas of an oil painting that your company sent had arrived in damaged condition. The e-mail said, "This painting sags, and we can't possibly hang it in our executive offices." You were surprised at this message because the customer had signed for delivery and not mentioned any damage. The e-mail went on to demand a replacement.

You find it difficult to believe that the painting is damaged because you are so careful about shipping. You give explicit instructions to shippers that large paintings must be shipped standing up, not lying down. You also make sure that every painting is wrapped in two layers of convoluted foam and one layer of Perf-Pack foam, which should be sufficient to withstand any bumps and scrapes that negligent shipping may cause. On the other hand, you will immediately review your packing requirements with your shippers.

It's against your company policy to give refunds or replace paintings that the receiver found acceptable when delivered. However, you could offer Huntzinger Construction the opportunity to take the painting to a local framing shop for restretching at your expense. The company could send the restretching bill to ArtWorkOnline at 438 West 84th Street, New York, NY 10024.

Your Task. Compose an e-mail adjustment message that regains the customer's confidence. Send it to Charles M. Huntzinger at *cmhuntzinger@huntzconstruction.com*.

8.24 Adjustment: Pigeon Problems (Obj. 6)

You didn't want to do it. But guests were complaining about the pigeons that roost on the Scottsdale Hilton's upper floors and tower. Pigeon droppings splattered sidewalks, furniture, and people. As the hotel manager, you had to take action. You called an exterminator, who recommended Avitrol. This drug, he promised, would disorient the birds, preventing them from finding their way back to the Hilton. The drugging, however, produced a result you didn't expect: pigeons began dying.

After a story hit the local newspapers, you began to receive complaints. The most vocal came from the Avian Affairs Coalition, a local bird-advocacy group. It said that the pigeons are really Mediterranean rock doves, the original "dove of peace" in European history and the same species the Bible said Noah originally released from his ark during the great flood. Activists claimed that Avitrol is a lethal drug causing birds, animals, and even people who ingest as little as 1/600th of a teaspoon to convulse and die lingering deaths of up to two hours.

Repulsed at the pigeon deaths and the bad publicity, you stopped the use of Avitrol immediately. You are now considering installing wires that offer a mild, nonlethal electrical shock. These wires, installed at the Maricopa County Jail in downtown Phoenix for $50,000, keep thousands of pigeons from alighting and could save $1 million in extermination and cleanup costs over the life of the building. You are also considering installing netting that forms a transparent barrier, sealing areas against entry by birds.

Your Task. Respond to Mrs. Tia Walsh, 24 Canyon Lake Shore Drive, Spring Branch, TX 52319, a recent Scottsdale Hilton guest. She sent a letter condemning the pigeon poisoning and threatening to never return to the hotel unless it changed its policy. Try to regain the confidence of Mrs. Walsh and promote further business.[15]

8.25 Adjustment: Backing Up "No Surprise" Offer (Obj. 6)

Premier Promos prides itself on its "No Surprise" offer. This means that anything ordered from its catalog of promotional products may be returned for a full refund within two weeks of purchase. The claim from Rochester Preferred Travel (see **Activity 8.17**) describes an order placed January 11 and returned January 21. As assistant to the Customer Services manager, you check the return files and see that items were received January 25. You speak with service agent Virginia, who agrees with you—the credit of $258.20 should have been granted to Rochester Preferred Travel. She reminds you that a new system for handling returns was implemented in February. Perhaps the Rochester return slipped through the cracks. Regardless of the reason, you decide to tell accounting to issue the credit immediately.

Your Task. In an adjustment letter, try to regain the confidence and the business of Rochester Preferred Travel, 245 East Avenue, Rochester, NY 14604. Include a sample imprinted travel mug in a gift box and a Coleman 8-quart jug cooler. You know that you are the most reliable source for the lowest-priced imprinted promotional products in the field, and this travel agency should be able to find something suitable in your catalog. Address your letter to Leticia Vascellaro, and sign it with your name.

8.26 Thanks for a Favor: Got the Job! (Obj. 7)

Congratulations! You completed your degree and got a terrific job in your field. One of your instructors was especially helpful to you when you were a student. This instructor also wrote an effective letter of recommendation that was instrumental in helping you obtain your job.

Your Task. Write a letter thanking your instructor.

8.27 Thanks for the Hospitality: Holiday Entertaining (Obj. 7)

You and other members of your staff or organization were entertained at an elegant dinner during the winter holiday season.

Your Task. Write a thank-you letter to your boss (supervisor, manager, vice president, president, or chief executive officer) or to the head of an organization to which you belong. Include specific details that will make your letter personal and sincere.

8.28 Sending Good Wishes: Personalizing Group Greeting Cards (Obj. 7)

Team | Web

When a work colleague has a birthday, gets promoted, or retires, someone generally circulates a group greeting card. In the past it wasn't a big deal. Office colleagues just signed their names and passed the store-bought card along to others. But the current trend is toward personalization with witty, oh-so-clever quips. And that presents a problem. What should you say—or not say?

You know that people value special handwritten quips, but you realize that you are not particularly original and you don't have a store of *bon mots* (clever sayings, witticisms). You are tired of the old standbys, such as *This place won't be the same without you* and *You are only as old as you feel.*

Your Task. To be prepared for the next greeting card that lands on your desk at work, you decide to work with some friends to make a list of remarks appropriate for business occasions. Use the Web to research witty sayings appropriate for promotions, birthdays, births, weddings, illnesses, or personal losses. Use a search term such as *birthday sayings, retirement quotes,* or *cool sayings.* You may decide to assign each category (birthday, retirement, promotion, and so forth) to a separate team. Submit the best sayings in a memo to your instructor.

8.29 Responding to Good Wishes: Saying Thank You (Obj. 7)

Your Task. Write a short note thanking a friend who sent you good wishes when you recently completed your degree.

8.30 Extending Sympathy: To a Spouse (Obj. 7)

Your Task. Imagine that the spouse of a coworker recently died of cancer. Write the coworker a letter of sympathy.

8.31 International Message: Negotiating a Cool Deal With a Chinese Supplier (Obj. 8)

E-mail | Intercultural

Your company, Pioneer Cable, seeks a cable assembly supplier in China. A few representatives of Pioneer just had a videoconference with AmRep China, a company specializing in finding Chinese manufacturers for American companies. Terrance Shaw, CEO and son of the owner, has been corresponding with Michael Zhu, who represents AmRep. The videoconference went well, but Mr. Shaw, the owner, wants Terrance to confirm in writing what was discussed. Terrance, better known as Terry around the office, is an upbeat, gadget-loving young executive who would rather be using IM than writing e-mail. He manages to put together a rough draft, but he asks you to help him improve it.

Your Task. Revise the following e-mail to make it more formal, readable, and interculturally acceptable.

To: Michael Zhu <Michael.zhu@AmRep.com>
From: Terrance Shaw <tshaw@pioneercable.com>
Subject: Videoconference Info
Cc:

Hey, Michael, it was great seeing and talking with you and your crew in the September 14 videoconference. Everyone here at Pioneer Cable is totally stoked about having AmRep China hook us up with a Chinese cable assembly supplier. We're sure you'll turn over every stone to find us a terrific supplier!

Because of all the heavy accents, it was a little hard to understand some speakers in our videoconference, so let me go over some things we agreed on. AmRep China is going to look for a cable assembly supplier for Pioneer. Right? You'll make no bones about getting us the best price/quality ratio you can possibly manage. This is obviously easier for you to do than for us because you'll be communicating in Chinese.

Unless I misunderstood, I heard one of your staff say that there would be continuous data feedback on quality control and that your company would provide technical conformance to the specifications that we submit. Is that right? There was also quite a discussion on ISO 9001:2000 standards and procedures, and you said that AmRep would definitely find a supplier that adheres to those standards. This is super important to us. I believe I also heard that AmRep would help us manage production and delivery schedules with our Chinese supplier.

The owner says that we must have confirmation of these points before we can continue our negotiations. Hope to hear from you soon!

Terry
CEO, Pioneer Cable
E-Mail: tshaw@pioneercable.com
Phone: (814) 739-2901
FAX: (814) 739-3445

Video Resource

Video Library 2, Adjustment Letter: Ben & Jerry's

In this video you see Ben & Jerry's managers discussing six factors that determine its continuing success. Toward the end of the video, you hear staffers discuss a new packaging material made with unbleached paper. As a socially responsible company, Ben & Jerry's wanted to move away from ice cream packages made from bleached papers. Bleaching requires chlorine, a substance that contains dioxin, which is known to cause cancer, genetic and reproductive defects, and learning disabilities. In producing paper, pulp mills using chlorine are also adding to dioxin contamination of waterways. After much research, Ben & Jerry's found a chlorine-free, unbleached paperboard for its packages. That was the good news. The bad news is that the inside of the package is now brown.

Assume you have been hired at Ben & Jerry's to help answer incoming letters. Although you are fairly new, your boss gives you a letter from an unhappy customer. This customer opened a pint of Ben & Jerry's World's Best Vanilla and then threw it out. After seeing the brown inner lid, he decided that his pint must have been used for chocolate before it was used for vanilla. Or, he said, "the entire pint has gone bad and somehow turned the sides brown." Whatever the reason, he wasn't taking any chances. He wants his money back.

Your Task. Write a letter that explains the brown carton, justifies the reason for using it, and retains the customer's business. Address the letter to Mr. Daniel Gilstrap, 17263 Blackhawk Avenue, Friendswood, TX 77546.

Chat About It

In each chapter you will find five discussion questions related to the chapter material. Your instructor may assign these topics for you to discuss in class, in an online chat room, or on an online discussion board. Some of the discussion topics may require outside research. You may also be asked to read and respond to postings made by your classmates.

Topic 1: In preparing to write a message, you learned that you should ask yourself (a) whether a written message is necessary, (b) what your goal is in writing, (c) how the reader might react, (d) what the best channel is, and (e) how you can write the message in a way that saves the reader time. Which of these questions do you feel is most important, and why?

Topic 2: Describe a time when you or someone you know wrote a letter that was successful in its purpose, such as gaining a refund, changing a decision, or achieving something that the reader might have opposed. Was another form of communication, such as a phone call, tried first? Why do think the letter was successful?

Topic 3: When responding favorably to a request that you are not thrilled to grant, why is it important in business to nevertheless sound gracious or even agreeable?

Topic 4: Conduct research regarding costly mistakes that resulted from unclear instructions. What is the most costly mistake you discovered?

Topic 5: Describe an occasion when you should have written a goodwill message but failed to do so. Why was it difficult to write that message? What would make it easier for you to do so?

Grammar and Mechanics C.L.U.E. Review 8

Capitalization

Review Guides 39–46 about capitalization in Appendix A, Grammar and Mechanics Guide, beginning on page A-16. On a separate sheet, revise the following sentences to correct capitalization errors. For each error that you locate, write the guide number that reflects this usage. Sentences may have more than one error. If a sentence is correct, write C. When you finish, check your answers on page Key-1.

Example: Neither the President nor the Operations Manager would comment on the Company rumor that it would close its midwest factory.

Revision: Neither the **president** nor the **operations manager** would comment on the **company** rumor that it would close its **Midwest** factory. [Guides 41, 43]

1. Once the Management Team and the Union members finally agreed, mayor knox signed the Agreement.
2. All delta airlines passengers must exit the Plane at gate 14 when they reach los angeles international airport.
3. The vice president of the united states urged members of the european union to continue to seek peace in the middle east.
4. My Uncle, who lives in the south, has Skippy Peanut Butter and coca-cola for Breakfast.
5. Our Marketing Manager and Director of Sales thought that the Company should purchase BlackBerry Smartphones for all Sales Reps.
6. Personal Tax Rates for japanese citizens are low by International standards, according to professor yamaguchi at osaka university.
7. Jinhee Kim, who heads our customer communication division, has a Master's Degree in social psychology from the university of new mexico.
8. Please consult figure 4.5 in chapter 4 to obtain U.S. census bureau population figures for the pacific northwest.
9. Last Fall did you see the article titled "The global consequences of using crops for fuel"?
10. Toby plans to take courses in Marketing, Business Law, and English in the Spring.

CHAPTER 9

Negative Messages

OBJECTIVES

After studying this chapter, you should be able to

1. Describe the goals and strategies of business communicators in conveying negative news effectively, including applying the writing process and avoiding legal liability.
2. Decide whether to use the direct or indirect strategy in conveying negative news.
3. Analyze the components of effective negative messages, including opening with a buffer, apologizing, conveying empathy, presenting the reasons, cushioning the bad news, and closing pleasantly.
4. Describe and apply effective techniques for refusing typical requests.
5. Explain and apply effective techniques for handling bad news with customers.
6. Understand and apply effective techniques for delivering bad news within organizations.
7. Compare strategies for revealing bad news in other cultures.

Want to do well on tests and excel in your course? Go to **www.meguffey.com** for helpful interactive resources.

- **Review the Chapter 9 PowerPoint slides to prepare for the first quiz.**

© George Doyle & Ciaran Griffin/Stockbyte/Getty Images

Zooming In

PART 1

Being Proactive Lessens Bad-News Nightmares at Southwest Airlines

Delayed flights, mishandled baggage, and passengers stranded on tarmacs are among the many nightmares of today's flyers. One carrier, however, leads the industry with the fewest consumer complaints. Southwest Airlines takes a proactive approach, giving its customers timely and regular updates—even when the news is bad. An ice storm caused a several-hour delay on a flight leaving St. Louis. Southwest flight attendants and pilots walked through the plane regularly, answering passengers' questions and providing information on connecting flights. Passengers on that flight were pleasantly surprised when vouchers for free round-trip flights arrived a few days later. The vouchers were accompanied by a letter from the airline apologizing for the inconvenience.

Such practices are the norm for Southwest. The Dallas-based discount airline—known for its low fares, lack of frills, and efficient service—has become a powerful brand in a competitive industry since its humble beginnings in 1971. Founders Rollin King and Herb Kelleher had a unique vision for their new company: Get passengers where they want to go, on time, at the lowest price—and make flying fun for both employees and passengers.

Their formula worked. Today, Southwest is the largest carrier in the United States based on domestic departures. It currently operates more than 3,100 flights a day and has nearly 35,000 employees.[1] Whereas other airlines are struggling and adding baggage and fuel fees, Southwest remains profitable and prides itself on its theme of "Fees Don't Fly With Us."[2]

High satisfaction ratings have won Southwest a spot on *BusinessWeek's* ranking of the country's 25 best customer service providers. Like its peers, however, Southwest has its share of problems. Irate customers complain about lost baggage, weather delays, and canceled flights. The difference is its response strategy. Fred Taylor, senior manager of proactive customer communications, tracks operating disruptions across the organization. He meets daily with department representatives to discuss possible problems and develop strategies to minimize difficulties before they happen. Capitalizing on social media, Southwest uses Twitter to send tweets with chatty trivia as well as travel updates and official announcements.[3]

Regardless of his proactive efforts to minimize customer complaints, Taylor still must respond occasionally to disappointed customers.[4] Delivering bad news and responding to customer complaints are major responsibilities of his job. You will learn more about this case on page 277.

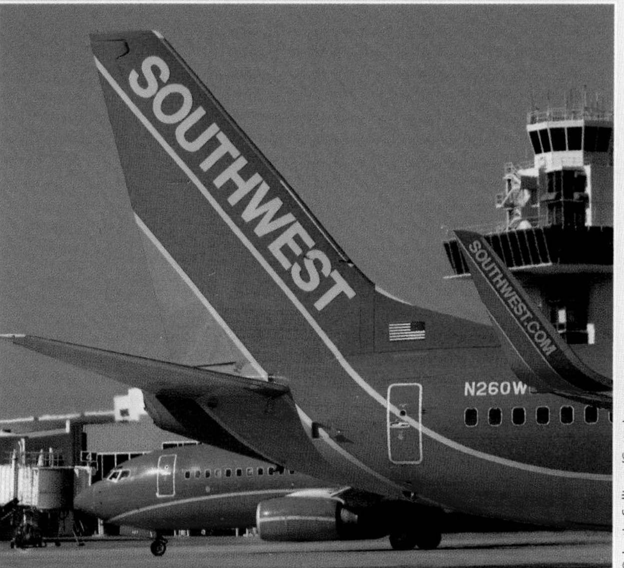

© Justin Sullivan/Getty Images

Critical Thinking

- Suppose you applied for a job that you really wanted, but the company hired someone else. To notify you of the bad news, the company sends a letter. Should the letter blurt out the bad news immediately or soften the blow somewhat?
- What are some techniques you could use if you have to deliver bad news in business messages?
- What goals should you try to achieve when you have to give disappointing news to customers, employees, suppliers, or others on behalf of your organization?

http://www.southwest.com

Conveying Negative News Effectively

LEARNING OBJECTIVE 1

Describe the goals and strategies of business communicators in conveying negative news effectively, including applying the writing process and avoiding legal liability.

Bad things happen in all businesses. At Southwest Airlines, storms cancel or delay flights, baggage is misplaced, and air traffic interrupts schedules. In other businesses, goods are not delivered, products fail to perform as expected, service is poor, billing gets fouled up, or customers are misunderstood. You may have to write messages ending business relationships, declining proposals, announcing price increases, refusing requests for donations, terminating employees, turning down invitations, or responding to unhappy customers. You might have to apologize for mistakes in orders, errors in pricing, the rudeness of employees, overlooked appointments, substandard service, pricing errors, faulty accounting, defective products, or jumbled instructions. As a company employee, you may even have to respond to complaints voiced to the world on Twitter, Facebook, or complaint Web sites.

The sad truth is that everyone occasionally must deliver bad news in business. Because bad news disappoints, irritates, and sometimes angers the receiver, such messages must be written carefully. The bad feelings associated with disappointing news can generally be reduced if the receiver (a) knows the reasons for the rejection, (b) feels that the news was revealed sensitively, and (c) believes the matter was treated seriously and fairly.

In this chapter you will learn when to use the direct strategy and when to use the indirect strategy to deliver bad news. You will study the goals of business communicators in working with bad news and learn techniques for achieving those goals.

Establishing Goals in Communicating Negative News

What can the writer of a bad-news message strive to achieve in minimizing bad feelings?

Delivering negative news is not the happiest communication task you may have, but it can be gratifying if you do it effectively. As a business communicator working with bad news, you will have many goals, the most important of which are these:

- **Explaining clearly and completely.** Your message should be so clear that the receiver understands and, we hope, accepts the bad news. The receiver should not have to call or write to clarify the message.
- **Projecting a professional image.** You will strive to project a professional and positive image of you and your organization. Even when irate customers use a threatening tone or overstate their claims, you must use polite language, control your emotions, and respond with clear explanations of why a negative message was necessary.
- **Conveying empathy and sensitivity.** Bad news is better accepted if it is delivered sensitively. Use language that respects the receiver and attempts to reduce bad feelings. Accepting blame, when appropriate, and apologizing goes far in smoothing over negative messages. But avoid creating legal liability or responsibility for you or your organization.
- **Being fair.** Show that the situation or decision was fair, impartial, and rational. Receivers are far more likely to accept negative news if they feel they were treated fairly.
- **Maintaining friendly relations.** Make an effort to include statements that show your desire to continue pleasant relations with the receiver. As you learned in Chapter 8 in writing adjustment messages, one of your goals is to regain the confidence of customers.

These are ambitious goals, and we are not always successful in achieving them all. However, many senders have found the strategies and techniques you are about to learn helpful in conveying disappointing news sensitively and safely. With experience, you will be able to vary these strategies and adapt them to your organization's specific communication tasks.

Applying the 3-x-3 Writing Process

Why is the 3-x-3 writing process especially helpful in crafting bad-news messages?

Thinking through the entire writing process is especially important in bad-news messages because the way bad news is revealed often determines how it is accepted. You have probably heard people say, "I didn't mind the news so much, but I resented the way I was told!" Certain techniques can help you deliver bad news sensitively, beginning with the familiar 3-x-3 writing process.

Analysis, Anticipation, and Adaptation. In Phase 1 (prewriting), you need to analyze the bad news and anticipate its effect on the receiver. When Microsoft launched its first widescale layoff, an administrative glitch caused it to pay more severance than intended to some laid-off employees. After the mistake was discovered, Microsoft sent a bad-news letter bluntly asking the ex-workers to return the money. Employees not only suffered the loss of their jobs, but, adding insult to injury, Microsoft then demanded the return of $4,000 to $5,000 in severance pay. Some employees had already spent the money, and others were planning their futures with it. Obviously, the sender of the bad-news message had not considered the effect it would have on its readers. After the letters seeking repayment began to surface on the Web, Microsoft reversed course and allowed the workers to keep the overpayment.[5] However, the entire situation might have been handled better if Microsoft had given more thought to analyzing the situation and anticipating its effect.

When you have bad news to convey, one of your first considerations is how that message will affect its receiver. If the disappointment will be mild, announce it directly. For example, a small rate increase in a newspaper or Web subscription can be announced directly. If the bad news is serious or personal, consider techniques to reduce the pain. In the Microsoft situation, the bad-news letter should have prepared the reader, given reasons for the payback request, possibly offered alternatives, and sought the goodwill of the receiver.

Choose words that show you respect the reader as a responsible, valuable person. Select the best channel to deliver the bad news. In many negative situations, you will be dealing with a customer. If your goal is retaining the goodwill of a customer, a letter on company stationery will be more impressive than an e-mail.

Research, Organization, and Composition. In Phase 2 (writing), you will gather information and brainstorm for ideas. Jot down all the reasons you have that explain the bad news. If four or five reasons prompted your negative decision, concentrate on the strongest and safest ones. Avoid presenting any weak reasons; readers may seize on them to reject the entire message. Include ample explanation of the negative situation, and avoid fixing blame.

When the U.S. Post Office has to deliver damaged mail, it includes an explanation, such as the following: "Because the Post Office handles millions of pieces of mail daily, we must use mechanical methods to ensure prompt delivery. Damage can occur if mail is insecurely enveloped or bulky contents are enclosed. When this occurs and the machinery jams, it often causes damage to other mail that was properly prepared." Notice that the Post Office message offers the strongest reason for the problem, although other reasons may have been possible. Notice, too, that the explanation tactfully skirts the issue of who caused the problem.

In composing any negative message, conduct research if necessary to help you explain what went wrong and why a decision or action is necessary.

Revision, Proofreading, and Evaluation. In Phase 3 (revising), you will read over your message carefully to ensure that it says what you intend. Check your wording to be sure you are concise without being brusque. If you find that you have overused certain words, click on your word processing thesaurus to find synonyms. Read your sentences to see if they sound like conversation and flow smoothly. This is the time to edit and improve coherence and tone. In bad-news messages, the tone is especially important. Readers are more likely to accept negative messages if the tone is friendly and respectful. Even when the bad news can't be changed, its effect can be reduced somewhat by the way it is presented.

In the last phase of the writing process, proofread to make sure your verbs agree with their subjects, your sentences are properly punctuated, and all words are spelled correctly. Pay attention to common mistakes (*its/it's; than/then; their/there*). If your word processing program checks grammar, be sure to investigate those squiggly underscores. Finally, evaluate your message. Is it too blunt? Too subtle? Have you delivered the bad news clearly but professionally?

Avoiding Legal Liability in Conveying Negative News

Before we examine the components of a negative message, let's look more closely at how you can avoid exposing yourself and your employer to legal liability in writing negative messages. Although we can't always anticipate the consequences of our words, we should be alert to three causes of legal difficulties: (a) abusive language, (b) careless language, and (c) the good-guy syndrome.

When does language become legally actionable?

Abusive Language. Calling people names (such as *deadbeat, crook,* or *quack*) can get you into trouble. *Defamation* is the legal term for any false statement that harms an individual's reputation. When the abusive language is written, it is called *libel*; when spoken, it is *slander*.

To be actionable (likely to result in a lawsuit), abusive language must be (a) false, (b) damaging to one's good name, and (c) "published"—that is, written or spoken within the presence of others. Therefore, if you were alone with Jane Doe and accused her of accepting bribes and selling company secrets to competitors, she couldn't sue because the defamation wasn't published. Her reputation was not damaged. However, if anyone heard the words or if they were written, you might be legally liable.

In a new wrinkle, you may now be prosecuted if you transmit a harassing or libelous message by e-mail or post it on social networking sites such as Facebook and Twitter.[6] Such electronic transmissions are considered to be published. Moreover, a company may incur liability for messages sent through its computer system by employees. That's why many companies

When accelerator defects threatened Toyota's quality reputation and defied easy diagnosis in Lexus and other models, management took to the Internet to communicate directly with customers. President Akio Toyoda led the public relations blitz with an 800-word letter published at online news outlets, and Internet teams posted recall videos and information for more than 100,000 followers at Toyota's Twitter, Facebook, and YouTube accounts. *Is the Internet an appropriate channel for addressing customers negatively affected by product recalls?*

are increasing their monitoring of both outgoing and internal messages. "Off-the-cuff, casual e-mail conversations among employees are exactly the type of messages that tend to trigger lawsuits and arm litigators with damaging evidence," says e-mail guru Nancy Flynn.[7] Instant messaging adds another danger for companies. Whether your message is in print or electronic, avoid making unproven charges or letting your emotions prompt abusive language.

What does careless language include, and why is it dangerous?

Careless Language. As the marketplace becomes increasingly litigious, we must be certain that our words communicate only what we intend. Take the case of a factory worker injured on the job. His attorney subpoenaed company documents and discovered a seemingly harmless letter sent to a group regarding a plant tour. These words appeared in the letter: "Although we are honored at your interest in our company, we cannot give your group a tour of the plant operations as it would be too noisy and dangerous." The court found in favor of the worker, inferring from the letter that working conditions were indeed hazardous.[8] The letter writer did not intend to convey the impression of dangerous working conditions, but the court accepted that interpretation.

What is meant by the good-guy syndrome?

The Good-Guy Syndrome. Most of us hate to have to reveal bad news—that is, to be the bad guy. To make ourselves look better, to make the receiver feel better, and to maintain good relations, we are tempted to make statements that are legally dangerous. Consider the case of a law firm interviewing job candidates. One of the firm's partners was asked to inform a candidate that she was not selected. The partner's letter said, "Although you were by far the most qualified candidate we interviewed, unfortunately, we have decided we do not have a position for a person of your talents at this time." To show that he personally had no reservations about this candidate and to bolster the candidate, the partner offered his own opinion. However, he differed from the majority of the recruiting committee. When the rejected interviewee learned later that the law firm had hired two male attorneys, she sued, charging sexual discrimination. The court found in favor of the rejected candidate. It agreed that a reasonable inference could be made from the partner's letter that she was the "most qualified candidate."[9]

Two important lessons emerge. First, business communicators act as agents of their organizations. Their words, decisions, and opinions are assumed to represent those of the organization. If you want to communicate your personal feelings or opinions, use your home computer or write on plain paper (rather than company letterhead) and sign your name without title or affiliation. Second, volunteering extra information can lead to trouble. Therefore, avoid supplying data that could be misused, and avoid making promises that can't be fulfilled. Don't admit or imply responsibility for conditions that caused damage or injury. Even apologies *(We're sorry that a faulty bottle cap caused damage to your carpet)* may suggest liability.

Examining Negative News Strategies

LEARNING OBJECTIVE 2
Decide whether to use the direct or indirect strategy in conveying negative news.

You have at your disposal two basic strategies for delivering negative news: direct and indirect. Which approach is best suited for your particular message? One of the first steps you will take before delivering negative news is analyzing how your receiver will react to this news. In earlier chapters we discussed applying the direct strategy to positive messages. We suggested using the indirect strategy when the audience might be unwilling, uninterested, displeased, disappointed, or hostile. In this chapter we expand on that advice and suggest additional considerations that help you decide which strategy to use.

When to Use the Direct Strategy

Many actual bad-news messages are organized indirectly, beginning with a buffer and reasons. However, the direct strategy, with the bad news first, may be more effective in situations such as the following:

- **When the bad news is not damaging.** If the bad news is insignificant (such as a small increase in cost) and doesn't personally affect the receiver, then the direct strategy certainly makes sense.
- **When the receiver may overlook the bad news.** Changes in service, new policy requirements, legal announcements—these critical messages may require boldness to ensure attention.
- **When the organization or receiver prefers directness.** Some companies and individuals expect all internal messages and announcements—even bad news—to be straightforward and presented without frills.
- **When firmness is necessary.** Messages that must demonstrate determination and strength should not use delaying techniques. For example, the last in a series of collection letters that seek payment of overdue accounts may require a direct opener.

Notice in Figure 9.1 that a small rate increase for a newspaper subscription is announced directly because it is unlikely to upset or irritate the receiver. However, many companies prefer to announce even small rate increases more indirectly. They usually want to explain why the increase is necessary before announcing it. Let's now explore when and how to use the indirect strategy in delivering negative news.

When to Use the Indirect Strategy

What guides you in deciding whether to announce bad news directly or indirectly?

Many communicators prefer to use the indirect strategy to present negative news. Whereas good news can be revealed quickly, bad news may be easier to accept when broken gradually. Here are instances when the indirect strategy works well:

- **When the bad news is personally upsetting.** If the negative news involves the receiver personally, such as a layoff notice, the indirect strategy makes sense. Telling an employee that he or she no longer has a job is probably best done in person and by starting indirectly and giving reasons first. When a company has made a mistake that inconveniences or disadvantages a customer, the indirect strategy makes sense.
- **When the bad news will provoke a hostile reaction.** When your message will irritate or infuriate the recipient, the indirect method may be best. It begins with a buffer and reasons, thus encouraging the reader to finish reading or hearing the message. A blunt announcement may make the receiver stop reading.

FIGURE 9.1 Announcing Bad News Directly

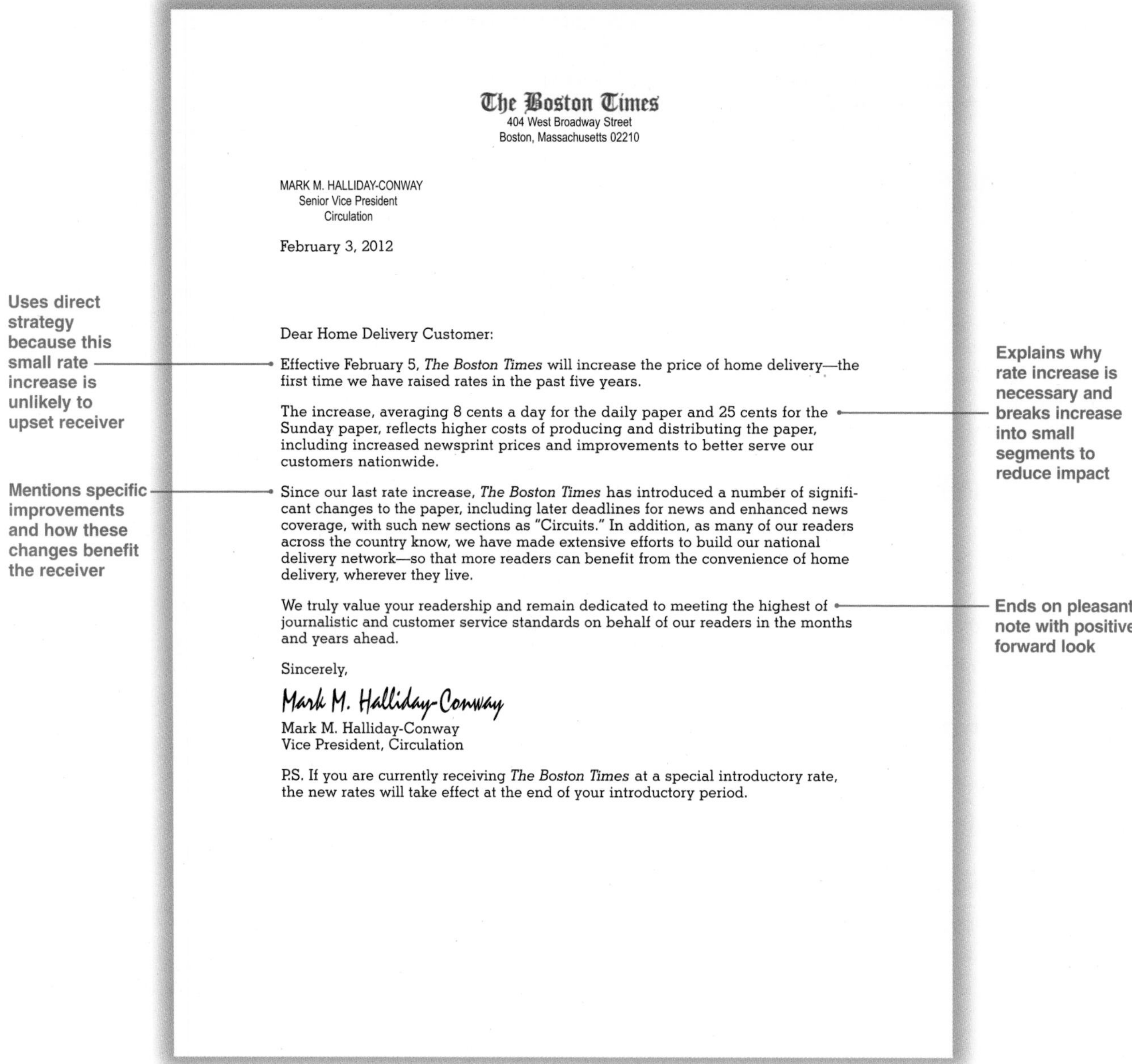

The Boston Times
404 West Broadway Street
Boston, Massachusetts 02210

MARK M. HALLIDAY-CONWAY
Senior Vice President
Circulation

February 3, 2012

Dear Home Delivery Customer:

Effective February 5, *The Boston Times* will increase the price of home delivery—the first time we have raised rates in the past five years.

The increase, averaging 8 cents a day for the daily paper and 25 cents for the Sunday paper, reflects higher costs of producing and distributing the paper, including increased newsprint prices and improvements to better serve our customers nationwide.

Since our last rate increase, *The Boston Times* has introduced a number of significant changes to the paper, including later deadlines for news and enhanced news coverage, with such new sections as "Circuits." In addition, as many of our readers across the country know, we have made extensive efforts to build our national delivery network—so that more readers can benefit from the convenience of home delivery, wherever they live.

We truly value your readership and remain dedicated to meeting the highest of journalistic and customer service standards on behalf of our readers in the months and years ahead.

Sincerely,

Mark M. Halliday-Conway

Mark M. Halliday-Conway
Vice President, Circulation

P.S. If you are currently receiving *The Boston Times* at a special introductory rate, the new rates will take effect at the end of your introductory period.

Uses direct strategy because this small rate increase is unlikely to upset receiver
Mentions specific improvements and how these changes benefit the receiver
Explains why rate increase is necessary and breaks increase into small segments to reduce impact
Ends on pleasant note with positive forward look

- **When the bad news threatens the customer relationship.** If the negative message may damage a customer relationship, the indirect strategy may help salvage the customer bond. Beginning slowly and presenting reasons that explain what happened can be more helpful than directly announcing bad news or failing to adequately explain the reasons.
- **When the bad news is unexpected.** Readers who are totally surprised by bad news tend to have a more negative reaction than those who expected the bad news. If a company suddenly closes an office or a plant and employees had no inkling of the closure, that bad news would be better received if it were revealed cautiously with reasons first.

Whether to use the direct or indirect strategy depends largely on the situation, the reaction you expect from the audience, and your goals. The direct method saves time and is preferred by some who consider it to be more professional and even more ethical than the indirect method. Others think that revealing bad news slowly and indirectly shows sensitivity to the receiver. By preparing the receiver, you tend to soften the impact. As you can see in Figure 9.2, the major

FIGURE 9.2 Comparing the Direct and Indirect Strategies for Negative Messages

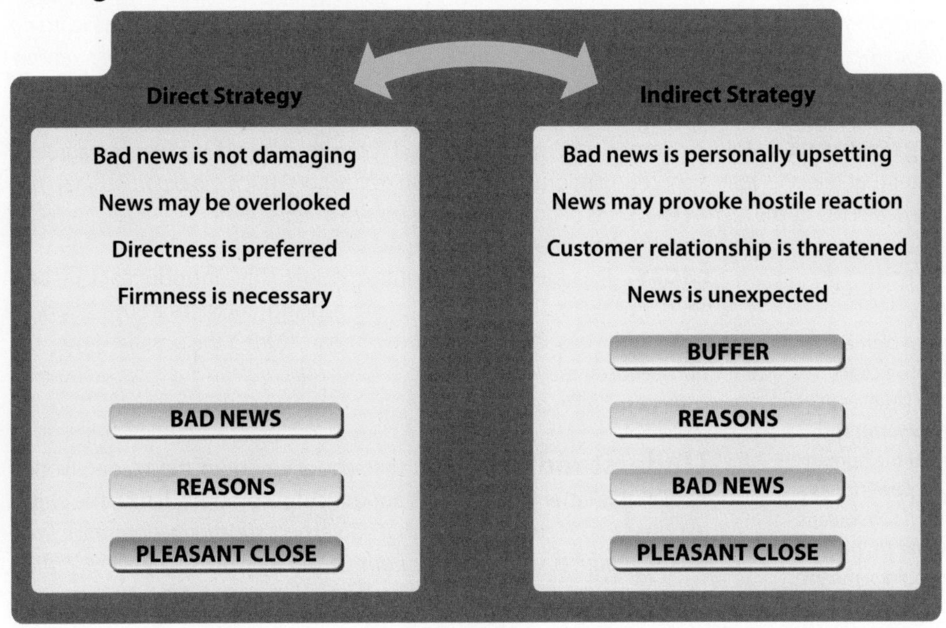

differences between the two strategies depend on whether you start with a buffer and how early you explain the reasons for the negative news.

Direct Strategy
Indirect Strategy
Bad news is not damaging
News may be overlooked
Directness is preferred
Firmness is necessary
BAD NEWS
REASONS
PLEASANT CLOSE
Bad news is personally upsetting
News may provoke hostile reaction
Customer relationship is threatened
News is unexpected
BUFFER
REASONS
BAD NEWS
PLEASANT CLOSE

Analyzing the Components of Effective Negative Messages

LEARNING OBJECTIVE 3
Analyze the components of effective negative messages, including opening with a buffer, apologizing, conveying empathy, presenting the reasons, cushioning the bad news, and closing pleasantly.

Even though it may be impossible to make the receiver happy when delivering negative news, you can reduce bad feelings and resentment by structuring your message sensitively. Most negative messages contain some or all of these parts: buffer, reasons, bad news, and closing. This section also discusses apologies and how to convey empathy in delivering bad news.

Buffer to Open Indirect Messages

If you decide to use the indirect strategy, your message might begin with a buffer. A buffer is a device to reduce shock or pain. To buffer the pain of bad news, begin with a neutral but meaningful statement that makes the reader continue reading. The buffer should be relevant and concise and provide a natural transition to the explanation that follows. The individual situation, of course, will help determine what you should put in the buffer. Avoid trite buffers such as *Thank you for your letter.*

It should be noted that not all business communication authors agree that buffers actually increase the effectiveness of negative messages. However, in many cultures softening bad news is appreciated. Following are various buffer possibilities.

Best News. Start with the part of the message that represents the best news. For example, a message to workers announced new health plan rules limiting prescriptions to a 34-day supply and increasing co-payments. With home delivery, however, employees could save up to $24 on each prescription. To emphasize the good news, you might write, *You can now achieve significant savings and avoid trips to the drugstore by having your prescription drugs delivered to your home.*[10]

How can you buffer the opening of a bad-news message?

Compliment. Praise the receiver's accomplishments, organization, or efforts, but do so with honesty and sincerity. For instance, in a letter declining an invitation to speak, you could write, *The Thalians have my sincere admiration for their fund-raising projects on behalf of hungry children. I am honored that you asked me to speak Friday, November 5.*

Appreciation. Convey thanks for doing business, for sending something, for showing confidence in your organization, for expressing feelings, or simply for providing feedback. Suppose you had to draft a letter that refuses employment. You could say, *I appreciated learning about the hospitality management program at Cornell and about your qualifications in our interview last Friday.* Avoid thanking the reader, however, for something you are about to refuse.

Agreement. Make a relevant statement with which both reader and receiver can agree. A letter that rejects a loan application might read, *We both realize how much the export business has been affected by the relative weakness of the dollar in the past two years.*

Spotlight on Communicators

Courtesy of Marshall Goldsmith

When leaders accept blame or apologize, executive coach Marshall Goldsmith believes, it is "one of the most powerful and resonant gestures in the human arsenal—almost as powerful as a declaration of love. If love means, 'I care about you, and I'm happy about it,' then an apology means, 'I hurt you, and I'm sorry about it.'" Named one of the 50 greatest thinkers and business management leaders, Goldsmith explains that the best thing about apologizing is that it forces everyone to let go of the past. In effect, an apology says, *I screwed up, I'm sorry, I'll do better.* "That's tough for even the most cold-hearted to resist," says Goldsmith.

Facts. Provide objective information that introduces the bad news. For example, in a memo announcing cutbacks in the hours of the employees' cafeteria, you might say, *During the past five years, the number of employees eating breakfast in our cafeteria has dropped from 32 percent to 12 percent.*

Understanding. Show that you care about the reader. Notice how in this letter to customers announcing a product defect, the writer expresses concern: *We know that you expect superior performance from all the products you purchase from OfficeCity. That's why we're writing personally about the Omega printer cartridges you recently ordered.*

Apologizing

You learned about making apologies in adjustment messages discussed in Chapter 8. We expand that discussion here because apologies are often part of negative-news messages. The truth is that sincere apologies work. Peter Post, great-grandson of famed etiquette expert Emily Post and director of the Emily Post Institute, said that Americans love apologies. They will forgive almost anything if presented with a sincere apology.[11] An apology is defined as an "admission of blameworthiness and regret for an undesirable event."[12] Apologies to customers are especially important if you or your company erred. They cost nothing, and they go a long way in soothing hard feelings. Here are some tips on how to apologize effectively in business messages:

- **Apologize sincerely.** People dislike apologies that sound hollow (*We regret that you were inconvenienced* or *We regret that you are disturbed*). Focusing on your regret does not convey sincerity. Explaining what you will do to prevent recurrence of the problem projects sincerity in an apology.
- **Accept responsibility.** One CEO was criticized for the following weak apology: *I want our customers to know how much I personally regret any difficulties you may experience as a result of the unauthorized intrusion into our computer systems.* Apology experts faulted this apology because it did not acknowledge responsibility.[13]
- **Use good judgment.** Don't admit blame if it might prompt a lawsuit.

Ethics Check

Apology or Excuse?

District Attorney Mike Nifong apologized to three Duke University lacrosse players that he had indicted on charges of attacking an exotic dancer. How ethical and effective is his apology? "To the extent that I made judgments that ultimately proved to be incorrect, I apologize to the three students that were wrongly accused."

Consider these poor and improved apologies:

Poor apology: *We regret that you are unhappy with the price of ice cream purchased at one of our scoop shops.*
Improved apology: *We are genuinely sorry that you were disappointed in the price of ice cream recently purchased at one of our scoop shops. Your opinion is important to us, and we appreciate your giving us the opportunity to look into the problem you describe.*

Poor apology: *We apologize if anyone was affected.*
Improved apology: *I apologize for the frustration our delay caused you. As soon as I received your message, I began looking into the cause of the delay and realized that our delivery tracking system must be improved.*

Poor apology: *We are sorry that mistakes were made in filling your order.*
Improved apology: *You are right to be concerned. We sincerely apologize for the mistakes we made in filling your order. To prevent recurrence of this problem, we are . . . .*

Conveying Empathy

One of the hardest things to do in negative messages is to conveying sympathy and empathy. As discussed in Chapter 3, *empathy* is the ability to understand and enter into the feelings of another. When ice storms trapped JetBlue Airways passengers on hot planes for hours, CEO Neeleman wrote a letter of apology that sounded as if it came from his heart. He said, "Dear JetBlue Customers: We are sorry and embarrassed. But most of all, we are deeply sorry." Later in his letter he said, "Words cannot express how truly sorry we are for the anxiety, frustration, and inconvenience that you, your family, friends, and colleagues experienced."[14] Neeleman put himself into the shoes of his customers and tried to experience their pain.

What is empathy, and how can it be conveyed?

Here are other examples of ways to express empathy in written messages:

- In writing to an unhappy customer: *We did not intentionally delay the shipment, and we sincerely regret the disappointment and frustration you must have suffered.*
- In laying off employees: *It is with great regret that we must take this step. Rest assured that I will be more than happy to write letters of recommendation for anyone who asks.*
- In responding to a complaint: *I am deeply saddened that our service failure disrupted your sale, and we will do everything in our power to. . . .*
- In showing genuine feelings: *You have every right to be disappointed. I am truly sorry that. . . .*

Presenting the Reasons

The most important part of a negative message is the section devoted to reasons. Without sound reasons for denying a request, refusing a claim, or revealing other bad news, a message will fail, no matter how cleverly it is organized or written. For example, if you must deny a customer's request, as part of your planning before writing, you analyzed the request and decided to refuse it for specific reasons. Where do you place your reasons? In the indirect strategy, explain your reasons before disclosing the bad news. In the direct strategy, the reasons appear immediately after the disclosure of the bad news. Providing an explanation reduces feelings of ill will and improves the chances that readers will accept the bad news.

What is the most important part of a bad-news message? Why?

Spotlight on Communicators

© Yvonne Hemsey/Contributor/Getty Images

Millionaire publisher Malcolm Forbes recognized that being agreeable while disagreeing is truly an art. He advised being positive and "nice." Contrary to the cliché, genuinely nice people most often finish first or very near it. He suggested using the acid test, particularly for a bad-news message. After you finish, read it out loud. You will know whether it sounds natural, positive, and respectful.

Explaining Clearly. If the reasons are not confidential and if they will not create legal liability, you can be specific: *Growers supplied us with a limited number of patio roses, and our demand this year was twice that of last year.* In responding to a billing error, explain what happened: *After you informed us of an error on your January bill, we investigated the matter and admit the mistake was ours. Until our new automated system is fully online, we are still subject to the frailties of human error. Rest assured that your account has been credited as you will see on your next bill.* In refusing a speaking engagement, tell why the date is impossible: *On January 17 we have a board of directors meeting that I must attend.* Don't, however, make unrealistic or dangerous statements in an effort to be the "good guy."

Citing Reader or Other Benefits, if Plausible. Readers are more open to bad news if in some way, even indirectly, it may help them. In refusing a customer's request for free hemming of skirts and slacks, Lands' End wrote: "We tested our ability to hem skirts a few months ago. This process proved to be very time-consuming. We have decided not to offer this service because the additional cost would have increased the selling price of our skirts substantially, and we did not want to impose that cost on all our customers."[15] Readers also accept bad news more readily if they recognize that someone or something else benefits, such as other workers or the environment: *Although we would like to consider your application, we prefer to fill managerial positions from within.* Avoid trying to show reader benefits, though, if they appear insincere: *To improve our service to you, we are increasing our brokerage fees.*

Explaining Company Policy. Readers resent blanket policy statements prohibiting something: *Company policy prevents us from making cash refunds* or *Contract bids may be accepted from local companies only* or *Company policy requires us to promote from within.* Instead of hiding

How can you reduce the resentment that people feel when told that company policy prohibits what they want?

behind company policy, gently explain why the policy makes sense: *We prefer to promote from within because it rewards the loyalty of our employees. In addition, we have found that people familiar with our organization make the quickest contribution to our team effort.* By offering explanations, you demonstrate that you care about readers and are treating them as important individuals.

Choosing Positive Words. Because the words you use can affect a reader's response, choose carefully. Remember that the objective of the indirect strategy is holding the reader's attention until you have had a chance to explain the reasons justifying the bad news. To keep the reader in a receptive mood, avoid expressions with punitive, demoralizing, or otherwise negative connotations. Stay away from such words as *cannot, claim, denied, error, failure, fault, impossible, mistaken, misunderstand, never, regret, rejected, unable, unwilling, unfortunately,* and *violate.*

Showing That the Matter Was Treated Seriously and Fairly. In explaining reasons, demonstrate to the reader that you take the matter seriously, have investigated carefully, and are making an unbiased decision. Receivers are more accepting of disappointing news when they feel that their requests have been heard and that they have been treated fairly. In canceling funding for a program, board members provided this explanation: *As you know, the publication of* Urban Artist *was funded by a renewable annual grant from the National Endowment for the Arts. Recent cutbacks in federally sponsored city arts programs have left us with few funds. Because our grant has been discontinued, we have no alternative but to cease publication of* Urban Artist. *You have my assurance that the board has searched long and hard for some other viable funding, but every avenue of recourse has been closed before us. Accordingly, June's issue will be our last.*

Cushioning the Bad News

What writing techniques can be used to cushion bad news?

Although you can't prevent the disappointment that bad news brings, you can reduce the pain somewhat by breaking the news sensitively. Be especially considerate when the reader will suffer personally from the bad news. A number of thoughtful techniques can cushion the blow.

Positioning the Bad News Strategically. Instead of spotlighting it, sandwich the bad news between other sentences, perhaps among your reasons. Don't let the refusal begin or end a paragraph; the reader's eye will linger on these high-visibility spots. Another technique that reduces shock is putting a painful idea in a subordinate clause: *Although another candidate was hired, we appreciate your interest in our organization and wish you every success in your job search.* Subordinate clauses often begin with words such as *although, as, because, if,* and *since.*

Using the Passive Voice. Passive-voice verbs enable you to depersonalize an action. Whereas the active voice focuses attention on a person *(We don't give cash refunds),* the passive voice highlights the action *(Cash refunds are not given because . . .).* Use the passive voice for the bad news. In some instances you can combine passive-voice verbs and a subordinate clause: *Although franchise scoop shop owners cannot be required to lower their ice cream prices, we are happy to pass along your comments for their consideration.*

Accentuating the Positive. As you learned earlier, messages are far more effective when you describe what you can do instead of what you can't do. Rather than *We will no longer allow credit card purchases,* try a more positive appeal: *We are now selling gasoline at discount cash prices.*

Implying the Refusal. It is sometimes possible to avoid a direct statement of refusal. Often, your reasons and explanations leave no doubt that a request has been denied. Explicit refusals may be unnecessary and at times cruel. In this refusal to contribute to a charity, for example, the writer never actually says *no*: *Because we will soon be moving into new offices in Glendale, all our funds are earmarked for relocation costs. We hope that next year we will be able to support your worthwhile charity.* The danger of an implied refusal, of course, is that it is so subtle that the reader misses it. Be certain that you make the bad news clear, thus preventing the need for further correspondence.

Suggesting a Compromise or an Alternative. A refusal is not so depressing—for the sender or the receiver—if a suitable compromise, substitute, or alternative is available. In denying permission to a group of students to visit a historical private residence, for instance, this writer softens the bad news by proposing an alternative: *Although private tours of the grounds are not given, we do open the house and its gardens for one charitable event in the fall.* You can further reduce the impact of the bad news by refusing to dwell on it. Present it briefly (or imply it), and move on to your closing.

Closing Pleasantly

How can you close a negative message pleasantly?

After explaining the bad news sensitively, close the message with a pleasant statement that promotes goodwill. The closing should be personalized and may include a forward look, an alternative, good wishes, freebies, an off-the-subject remark, or resale information. *Resale* refers to mentioning a product or service favorably to reinforce the customer's choice. For example, *you chose our best-selling model.*

Forward Look. Anticipate future relations or business. A letter that refuses a contract proposal might read: *Thanks for your bid. We look forward to working with your talented staff when future projects demand your special expertise.*

Alternative Follow-Up. If an alternative exists, end your letter with follow-through advice. For example, in a letter rejecting a customer's demand for replacement of landscaping plants, you might say: *I will be happy to give you a free inspection and consultation. Please call 746-8112 to arrange a date for my visit.* In a message to a prospective homebuyer: *Although the lot you saw last week is now sold, we do have two excellent view lots available at a slightly higher price.* In reacting to an Internet misprint: *Please note that our Web site contained an unfortunate misprint offering $850-per-night Bora Bora bungalows at $85. Although we cannot honor that rate, we are offering a special half-price rate of $425 to those who responded.*

Good Wishes. A letter rejecting a job candidate might read: *We appreciate your interest in our company, and we extend to you our best wishes in your search to find the perfect match between your skills and job requirements.*

Freebies. When customers complain—primarily about food products or small consumer items—companies often send coupons, samples, or gifts to restore confidence and to promote future business. In response to a customer's complaint about a frozen dinner, you could write: *Your loyalty and your concern about our frozen entrées are genuinely appreciated. Because we want you to continue enjoying our healthful and convenient dinners, we are enclosing a coupon that you can take to your local market to select your next Green Valley entrée.*

Resale or Sales Promotion. When the bad news is not devastating or personal, references to resale information or promotion may be appropriate: *The computer workstations*

FIGURE 9.3 **Delivering Bad News Sensitively**

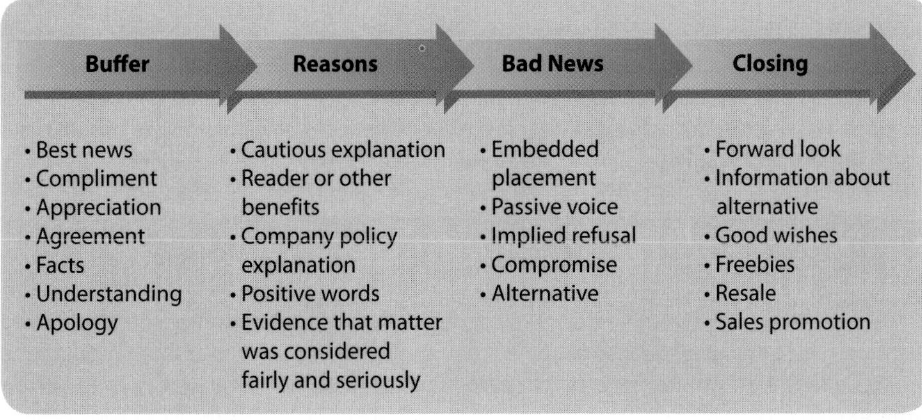

you ordered are unusually popular because of their stain-, heat-, and scratch-resistant finishes. To help you locate hard-to-find accessories for these workstations, we invite you to visit our Web site where our online catalog provides a huge selection of surge suppressors, multiple outlet strips, security devices, and PC tool kits.

Avoid endings that sound canned, insincere, inappropriate, or self-serving. Don't invite further correspondence *(If you have any questions, do not hesitate . . .)*, and don't refer to the bad news. Figure 9.3 reviews suggestions for delivering bad news sensitively.

Refusing Typical Requests

LEARNING OBJECTIVE 4
Describe and apply effective techniques for refusing typical requests.

As you move forward in your career and become a professional or a representative of an organization, you may receive requests for favors or contributions. You may also be invited to speak or give presentations. When you must refuse typical requests, you will first think about how the receiver will react to your refusal and decide whether to use the direct or the indirect strategy. If you have any doubt, use the indirect strategy.

Rejecting Requests for Favors, Money, Information, and Action

Why does the reasons-before-refusal plan work well when turning down requests for favors, money, information, and action?

Requests for favors, money, information, and action may come from charities, friends, or business partners. Many are from people representing commendable causes, and you may wish you could comply. However, resources are usually limited. In a letter from First Franklin Securities, shown in Figure 9.4, the company must refuse a request for a donation to a charity. Following the indirect strategy, the letter begins with a buffer acknowledging the request. It also praises the good works of the charity and uses those words as a transition to the second paragraph. In the second paragraph, the writer explains why the company cannot donate. Notice that the writer reveals the refusal without actually stating it (*Because of sales declines and organizational downsizing, we are forced to take a much harder look at funding requests that we receive this year*). This gentle refusal makes it unnecessary to be more blunt in stating the denial.

In some donation refusal letters, the reasons may not be fully explained: *Although we can't provide financial support at this time, we all unanimously agree that the Make-A-Wish Foundation contributes a valuable service to sick children.* The emphasis is on the foundation's good deeds rather than on an explanation for the refusal. In the letter shown in Figure 9.4, the writer felt a connection to the charity. Thus, he wanted to give a fuller explanation. If you were required to write frequent refusals, you might prepare a form letter, changing a few variables as needed.

Declining Invitations

What techniques can be used to decline an invitation?

When you must decline an invitation to speak or make a presentation, you generally try to provide a response that says more than *I can't* or *I don't want to*. Unless the reasons are confidential or business secrets, try to explain them. Because responses to invitations are often taken personally, make a special effort to soften the refusal. In the letter shown in Figure 9.5, an accountant must say no to the invitation from a friend's son to speak before the young man's college business club. This refusal starts with conviviality and compliments.

The writer then explains why she cannot accept. The refusal is embedded in a long paragraph and de-emphasized in a subordinate clause (*Although your invitation must be declined*). The reader naturally concentrates on the main clause that follows (*I would like to recommend . . .*). If no alternative is available, focus on something positive about the situation (*Although I'm not an expert, I commend your organization for selecting this topic*). Overall, the tone of this refusal is warm, upbeat, and positive.

Handling Bad News With Customers

LEARNING OBJECTIVE 5
Explain and apply effective techniques for handling bad news with customers.

Businesses must occasionally respond to disappointed customers. In some instances disappointed customers are turning to the Internet to air their grievances. Complaints about products and services now appear on sites such as Complaints.com and iRipoff.com, as well as on Facebook,

FIGURE 9.4 Refusing Donation Request

Prewriting

Analyze: The purpose of this letter is to reject the request for a monetary donation without causing bad will.

Anticipate: The reader is proud of her organization and the good work it pursues.

Adapt: The writer should strive to cushion the bad news and explain why it is necessary.

2 Writing

Research: Collect information about the receiver's organization as well as reasons for the refusal.

Organize: Use the indirect strategy. Begin with complimentary comments, present reasons, reveal the bad news gently, and close pleasantly.

Compose: Write message and consider keeping copy to serve as form letter.

3 Revising

Revise: Be sure that the tone of the message is positive and that it suggests that the matter was taken seriously.

Proofread: Check the receiver's name and address to be sure they are accurate. Check the letter's format.

Evaluate: Will this message retain the goodwill of the receiver despite its bad news?

First Franklin Securities

5820 Macon Cove Avenue
Memphis, TN 38135
800.640.2305
www.firstfranklinsecurities.com

May 18, 2012

Ms. Sierra Robinson
Executive Director
Outreach Children's Charity
3501 Beale Street
Memphis, TN 36110

Dear Ms. Robinson:

Opens with praise and compliments

We appreciate your letter describing the care and support the Outreach Children's Charity gives to disadvantaged, physically challenged, sick, and needy children around the world. Your organization is to be commended for its significant achievements and outstanding projects such as the Sunshine Coach program, which provides passenger vans to worthy children's organizations around the globe.

Doesn't say *yes* or *no*

Transitions with repetition of key ideas (*good work and worthwhile projects*)

Supporting the good work and worthwhile projects of your organization and others, although unrelated to our business, is a luxury we have enjoyed in past years. Because of sales declines and organizational downsizing, we are forced to take a much harder look at funding requests that we receive this year. We feel that we must focus our charitable contributions on areas that relate directly to our business.

Explains sales decline and cutback in gifts, thus revealing refusal without actually stating it

Closes graciously with forward look

We are hopeful that the worst days are behind us and that we will be able to renew our support for good work and worthwhile projects like yours next year.

Sincerely,

Andrew Hollingsworth

Andrew Hollingsworth
Vice President

FIGURE 9.5 **Declining an Invitation**

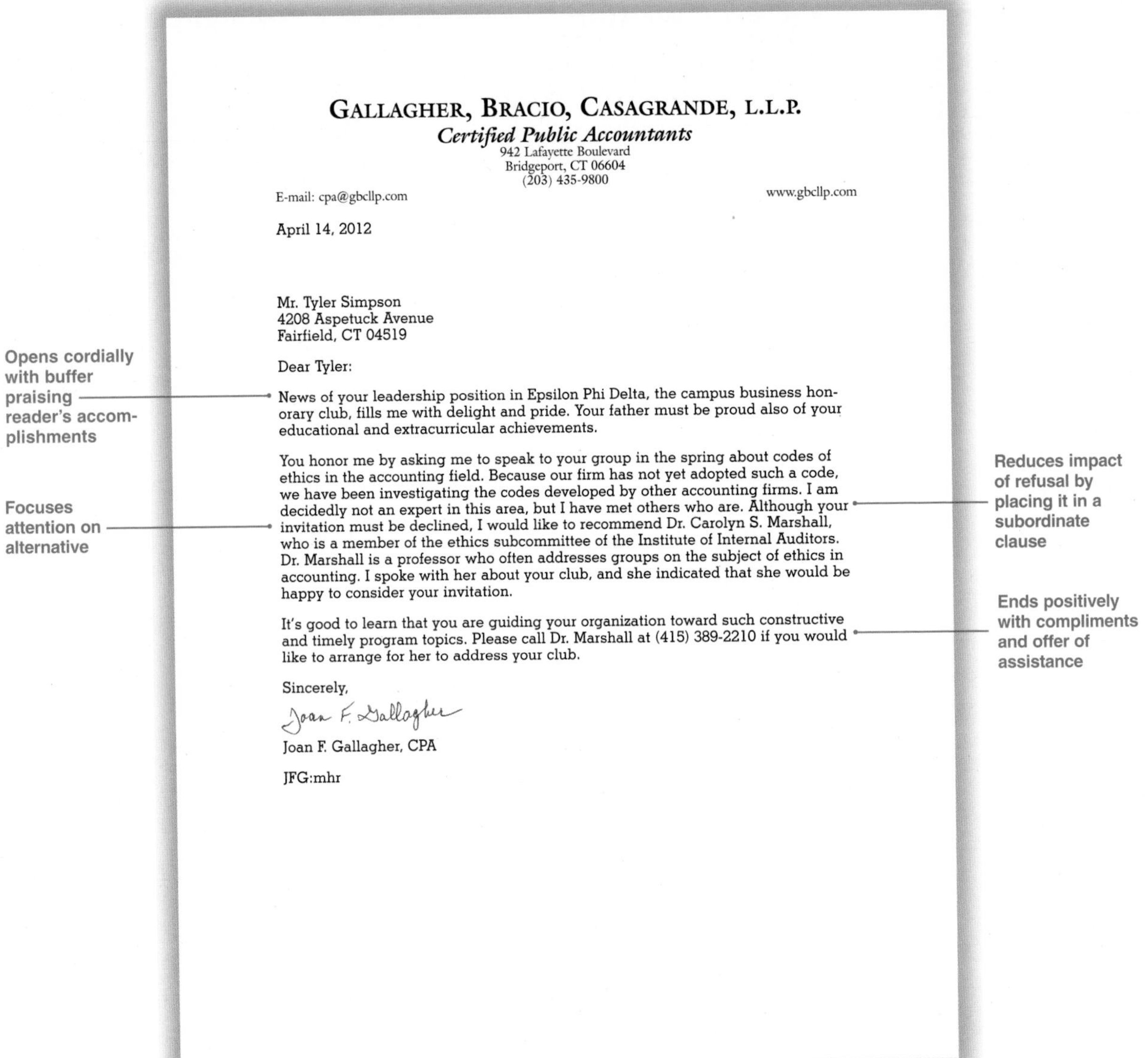

GALLAGHER, BRACIO, CASAGRANDE, L.L.P.
Certified Public Accountants
942 Lafayette Boulevard
Bridgeport, CT 06604
(203) 435-9800

E-mail: cpa@gbcllp.com www.gbcllp.com

April 14, 2012

Mr. Tyler Simpson
4208 Aspetuck Avenue
Fairfield, CT 04519

Dear Tyler:

News of your leadership position in Epsilon Phi Delta, the campus business honorary club, fills me with delight and pride. Your father must be proud also of your educational and extracurricular achievements.

You honor me by asking me to speak to your group in the spring about codes of ethics in the accounting field. Because our firm has not yet adopted such a code, we have been investigating the codes developed by other accounting firms. I am decidedly not an expert in this area, but I have met others who are. Although your invitation must be declined, I would like to recommend Dr. Carolyn S. Marshall, who is a member of the ethics subcommittee of the Institute of Internal Auditors. Dr. Marshall is a professor who often addresses groups on the subject of ethics in accounting. I spoke with her about your club, and she indicated that she would be happy to consider your invitation.

It's good to learn that you are guiding your organization toward such constructive and timely program topics. Please call Dr. Marshall at (415) 389-2210 if you would like to arrange for her to address your club.

Sincerely,

Joan F. Gallagher

Joan F. Gallagher, CPA

JFG:mhr

Opens cordially with buffer praising reader's accomplishments
Focuses attention on alternative
Reduces impact of refusal by placing it in a subordinate clause
Ends positively with compliments and offer of assistance

Twitter, and MySpace. See the accompanying Plugged In box for tips on how companies are responding to negative messages appearing in these emerging communication channels.

Whether companies deal with unhappy customers in cyberspace or up close and personal, they face the same challenges. Maintaining market share and preserving goodwill require sensitive and skillful communication. In Chapter 8 you learned to use the direct strategy in granting claims and making adjustments—because these were essentially good-news messages. But in some situations, you have little good news to share. Sometimes your company is at fault, in which case an apology is generally in order. Other times the problem is with orders you can't fill, claims you must refuse, or credit you must deny. Messages with bad news for customers generally follow the same pattern as other negative messages. Customer messages, though, differ in one major way: they usually include resale information or sales promotions.

Damage Control: Dealing With Disappointed Customers

When a customer problem arises and your company is at fault, how should you react?

All companies occasionally disappoint their customers. Merchandise is not delivered on time, a product fails to perform as expected, service is deficient, charges are erroneous, or customers are misunderstood. All businesses offering products or services must sometimes deal with troublesome situations that cause unhappiness to customers. Whenever possible, these problems should be dealt with immediately and personally. Most business professionals strive to control the damage and resolve such problems in the following manner:[16]

© AP Images/Paul Sakuma

As the global recession deepens and budget shortfalls spread to all sectors of the economy, city managers are struggling to deliver negative news to workers. Faced with a $522 million annual deficit, San Francisco Mayor Gavin Newsom delivered pink slips to more than 15,000 city workers as part of a plan for "saving people's jobs and city services." In response to criticism over his characterization of the situation, Mayor Newsom replied that he was "lawyered up." *How can employers avoid legal liability in conveying bad news?*

- Call the individual involved.
- Describe the problem and apologize.
- Explain why the problem occurred, what you are doing to resolve it, and how you will prevent it from happening again.
- Follow up with a message that documents the phone call and promotes goodwill.

Dealing with problems immediately is very important in resolving conflict and retaining goodwill. Written correspondence is generally too slow for problems that demand immediate attention. But written messages are important (a) when personal contact is impossible, (b) to establish a record of the incident, (c) to formally confirm follow-up procedures, and (d) to promote good relations.

Why are follow-up messages important in the damage-control process?

A bad-news follow-up letter is shown in Figure 9.6. Consultant Catherine Martinez found herself in the embarrassing position of explaining why she had given out the name of her client to a salesperson. The client, Alliance Resource International, had hired her firm, Cartus Consulting Associates, to help find an appropriate service for outsourcing its payroll functions. Without realizing it, Catherine had mentioned to a potential vendor (Payroll Services, Inc.) that her client was considering hiring an outside service to handle its payroll. An overeager salesperson from Payroll Services immediately called on Alliance, thus angering the client. The client had hired the consultant to avoid this very kind of intrusion. Alliance did not want to be hounded by vendors selling their payroll services.

When she learned of the problem, the first thing consultant Catherine Martinez did was call her client to explain and apologize. She was careful to control her voice and rate of speaking. A low-pitched, deliberate pace gives the impression that you are thinking clearly, logically, and reasonably—not emotionally and certainly not irrationally. However, she also followed up with the letter shown in Figure 9.6. The letter not only confirms the telephone conversation but also adds the right touch of formality. It sends the nonverbal message that the writer takes the matter seriously and that it is important enough to warrant a written letter.

Many consumer problems are handled with letters, either written by consumers as complaints or by companies in response. However, the social networking sites on the Internet are an emerging channel for delivering complaints and negative messages.

Spotlight on Communicators

© AFP PHOTO/Emmanuel Dunand/Newscom

When Amazon discovered that it lacked permission to offer two classic books, *1984* and *Animal Farm*, on its Kindle e-reader, it removed them—without warning and without explanation. Zap—the titles just disappeared! The ensuing firestorm of protest forced founder and CEO Jeff Bezos to control the damage by admitting the company's error and promising not to repeat its mistake. He said, "Our 'solution' to the problem was stupid, self-inflicted, and we deserve the criticism we've received. We will use the scar tissue from this painful mistake to help make better decisions going forward, ones that match our mission."

FIGURE 9.6 Bad-News Follow-Up Message

CARTUS CONSULTING ASSOCIATES

4350 Camelback Blvd.
Scottsdale, AZ 85255

Voice: (480) 259-0971
Web: www.cartusassociates.com

May 7, 2012

Mr. Eric Nasserizad
Director, Administrative Operations
Alliance Resource International
538 Maricopa Plaza, Suite 1210
Phoenix, AZ 85001

Dear Mr. Nasserizad:

Opens with agreement and apology

You have every right to expect complete confidentiality in your transactions with an independent consultant. As I explained in yesterday's telephone call, I am very distressed that you were called by a salesperson from Payroll Services, Inc. This should not have happened, and I apologize to you again for inadvertently mentioning your company's name in a conversation with a potential vendor, Payroll Services, Inc.

Explains what caused the problem and how it was resolved

Takes responsibility and promises to prevent recurrence

All clients of Cartus Consulting are assured that their dealings with our firm are held in the strictest confidence. Because your company's payroll needs are so individual and because you have so many contract workers, I was forced to explain how your employees differed from those of other companies. Revealing your company name was my error, and I take full responsibility for the lapse. I can assure you that it will not happen again. I have informed Payroll Services that it had no authorization to call you directly and its actions have forced me to reconsider using its services for my future clients.

Closes with forward look

A number of other payroll services offer outstanding programs. I'm sure we can find the perfect partner to enable you to outsource your payroll responsibilities, thus allowing your company to focus its financial and human resources on its core business. I look forward to our next appointment when you may choose from a number of excellent payroll outsourcing firms.

Sincerely,

Catherine Martinez

Catherine Martinez
Partner

Tips for Resolving Problems and Following Up

- Whenever possible, call or see the individual linvolved.
- Describe the problem and apologize.
- Explain why the problem occurred.
- Take responsibility, if appropriate.
- Explain what you are doing to resolve it.
- Explain what you are doing to prevent recurrence.
- Follow up with a message that documents the personal contact.
- Look forward to positive future relations.

Handling Problems With Orders

What strategy should you follow when your company can't fill an order?

Not all customer orders can be filled as received. Suppliers may be able to send only part of an order or none at all. Substitutions may be necessary, or the delivery date may be delayed. Suppliers may suspect that all or part of the order is a mistake; the customer may actually want something else. In writing to customers about problem orders, it is generally wise to use the direct strategy if the message has some good-news elements. However, when the message is disappointing, the indirect strategy may be more appropriate.

Let's say you represent Live and Learn Toys, a large West Coast toy manufacturer, and you are scrambling for business in a slow year. A big customer, Child Land, calls in August and asks you to hold a block of your best-selling toy, the Space Station. Like most vendors, you require a deposit on large orders. September rolls around, and you still haven't received any money from Child Land. You must now write a tactful letter asking for the deposit—or else

PLUGGED IN

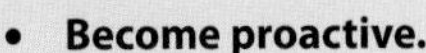

Managing Negative News on Facebook, Twitter, and Other Web Sites

Today's consumers eagerly embrace the idea of delivering their complaints to social networking sites rather than telling friends or calling customer service departments. Why rely on word of mouth or send a letter to a company about poor service or a defective product when you can shout your grievance to the entire world? Internet sites such as Complaints.com, Ripoff Report, and iRipoff .com encourage consumers to quickly share complaints about stores, products, and services that fall short of their standards. Twitter and Facebook are also favorite sites for consumers to make public their ire.

Why are online complaints so popular?
Complaint sites are gaining momentum for many reasons. Consumers may receive faster responses to tweets than to customer service calls. Airing gripes in public also helps other consumers avoid the same problems and may improve the complainer's leverage in solving a problem. In addition, sending a 140-word tweet is much easier and more satisfying than writing a complaint letter to a customer service department or navigating endless telephone menus to reach an agent.

How can business organizations manage negative news on social networking sites and blogs?

- **Recognize social networks as an emerging communication channel.** Instead of fearing social networks as a disruptive force, smart companies greet these channels as exciting opportunities to look into the true mind-set of customers.
- **Become proactive.** Company blogs and active Web sites with community forums help companies listen to their customers as well as to spread the word about their own good deeds. Home Depot's site describing its foundation, workshops, and careers now outranks Home DepotSucks.com, which used to rank No. 1 for searches on the keywords *home depot*.
- **Join the fun.** Wise companies have joined sites such as Twitter, Facebook, Flickr, YouTube, and LinkedIn so they can see how these sites function and benefit from site interaction.
- **Monitor comments.** Many companies employ tech-savvy staff members to monitor comments and respond immediately whenever possible. At Southwest Airlines, Paula Berg, manager of emerging media and affectionately called Blog Girl, manages a staff of seven who listen online to what people are saying about Southwest. Its policy is to engage the positive and address the negative.

Career Application
Visit Complaints.com, Ripoff Report, or another complaint site. Study ten or more complaints about products or companies (e.g., iPod, Starbucks, Delta Airline). Select one complaint and, as a company employee, respond to it employing some of the techniques presented in this chapter. Submit a copy of the complaint along with your response to your instructor.

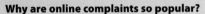

you will release the toy to other buyers. The problem, of course, is delivering the bad news without losing the customer's order and goodwill. Another challenge is making sure the reader understands the bad news. An effective letter might begin with a positive statement that also reveals the facts:

> *You were smart to reserve a block of 500 Space Stations, which we have been holding for you since August. As the holidays approach, the demand for all our learning toys, including the Space Station, is rapidly increasing.*

Next, the letter should explain why the payment is needed and what will happen if it is not received:

> *Toy stores from Florida to California are asking us to ship these Space Stations. One reason the Space Station is moving out of our warehouses so quickly is its assortment of gizmos that children love, including a land rover vehicle, a shuttle craft, a hover craft, astronauts, and even a robotic arm. As soon as we receive your deposit of $4,000, we will have this popular item on its way to your stores. Without a deposit by September 20, though, we must release this block to other retailers.*

The closing makes it easy to respond and motivates action:

> *Use the enclosed envelope to send us your check immediately. You can begin showing this fascinating Live and Learn toy in your stores by November 1.*

Announcing Rate Increases and Price Hikes

How can you introduce the concept of audience benefits into messages announcing rate increases and price hikes?

Informing customers and clients of rate increases or price hikes can be like handling a live grenade. These messages necessarily cause consumers to recoil. With skill, however, you can help your customers understand why the rate or price increase is necessary.

The important steps in these negative messages are explaining the reasons and hooking the increase to benefits. For example, a price increase might be necessitated by higher material costs, rising taxes, escalating insurance, driver pay increase—all reasons you cannot control. You might cite changing industry trends or technology innovations as causes of increased costs.

In developing audience benefits and building goodwill, think about how the increase will add new value or better features, make use more efficient, or make customers' lives easier. Whenever possible, give advance warning of rate increases—for example: *Because you are an important customer to us, I wanted to inform you about this right away. Our energy costs have almost doubled over the last year, forcing us to put through a 10 percent price increase effective July 1. You order these items regularly, so I thought I'd better check with you to see if it would make sense to reorder now to save you money and prevent last-minute surprises.*

In today's digital environment, rate and price increases may be announced online, as shown in Figure 9.7. DVD City had to increase the charge for access to Blu-ray movies. In its blog it explained how Blu-ray discs are not only superior to DVDs but also more expensive. To provide its customers with a comprehensive library of Blu-ray movies, DVD City has to raise its rates. Notice that the rate increase is tied to benefits to customers.

FIGURE 9.7 Blog Announcing Price Increase

DVD CITY

DVD CITY Blog

Wednesday, June 16, 2010

Price Update for Access to Blu-ray Movies

Hi, Rocko Raider here, VP of Marketing, with a message for our valued members who have added Blu-ray access to their accounts.

Blu-ray represents a huge leap forward in the DVD viewing experience with greatly enhanced HD video and audio quality as well as advanced interactivity and networking features. The number of titles available for us to purchase on Blu-ray has increased significantly. Our Blu-ray selection has grown more than 70 percent in just 6 months to over 2,300 titles. Blu-ray adoption among our members has also grown–it's now close to 10 percent. As we buy more, you are able to choose from a rapidly expanding selection of Blu-ray titles. And, as you've probably heard, Blu-ray discs are substantially more expensive than standard definition DVDs–often as much as 30 percent more.

Explains expansion of Blu-ray DVD movie collection and describes how costly these films are, thus justifying a price increase

Because DVD CITY is committed to providing an extensive library of high quality Blu-ray films for our members who choose to add Blu-ray access, we need to adjust Blu-ray pricing. As a result, the monthly charge for Blu-ray access is increasing for most plans and will now vary by plan.

Connects increase in cost to bigger library and wider choice of best movies for customers

This change will take effect on your next billing date. You will receive an e-mail from us letting you know the monthly charge for your plan. For more information, call Betsy at 1-800-556-2002.

Provides name and number for more information

LINKS

DVD CITY Community Forums

Facebook DVD CITY Page

DVD CITY Home Page

-------> RSS Feed Page

-------> Top Releases This Week

ABOUT THE DVD CITY BLOG

Thanks for visiting the official DVD CITY Blog! We bloggers are members of the DVD CITY team and are all certifiably rabid movie fans. We want to make this an exciting forum for us to talk about what we are doing and for you to tell us what you think.

Courtesy of M.E. Guffey

Denying Claims

Customers occasionally want something they are not entitled to or that you can't grant. They may misunderstand warranties or make unreasonable demands. Because these customers are often unhappy with a product or service, they are emotionally involved. Letters that say no to emotionally involved receivers will probably be your most challenging communication task. As publisher Malcolm Forbes observed, "To be agreeable while disagreeing—that's an art."[17]

Should the direct or indirect strategy be used in denying customer claims?

Fortunately, the reasons-before-refusal plan helps you be empathic and artful in breaking bad news. Obviously, in denial letters you will need to adopt the proper tone. Don't blame customers, even if they are at fault. Avoid *you* statements that sound preachy *(You would have known that cash refunds are impossible if you had read your contract)*. Use neutral, objective language to explain why the claim must be refused. Consider offering resale information to rebuild the customer's confidence in your products or organization. In Figure 9.8 the writer denies a customer's claim for the difference between the price the customer paid for speakers and the price he saw advertised locally (which would have

FIGURE 9.8 Denying a Claim

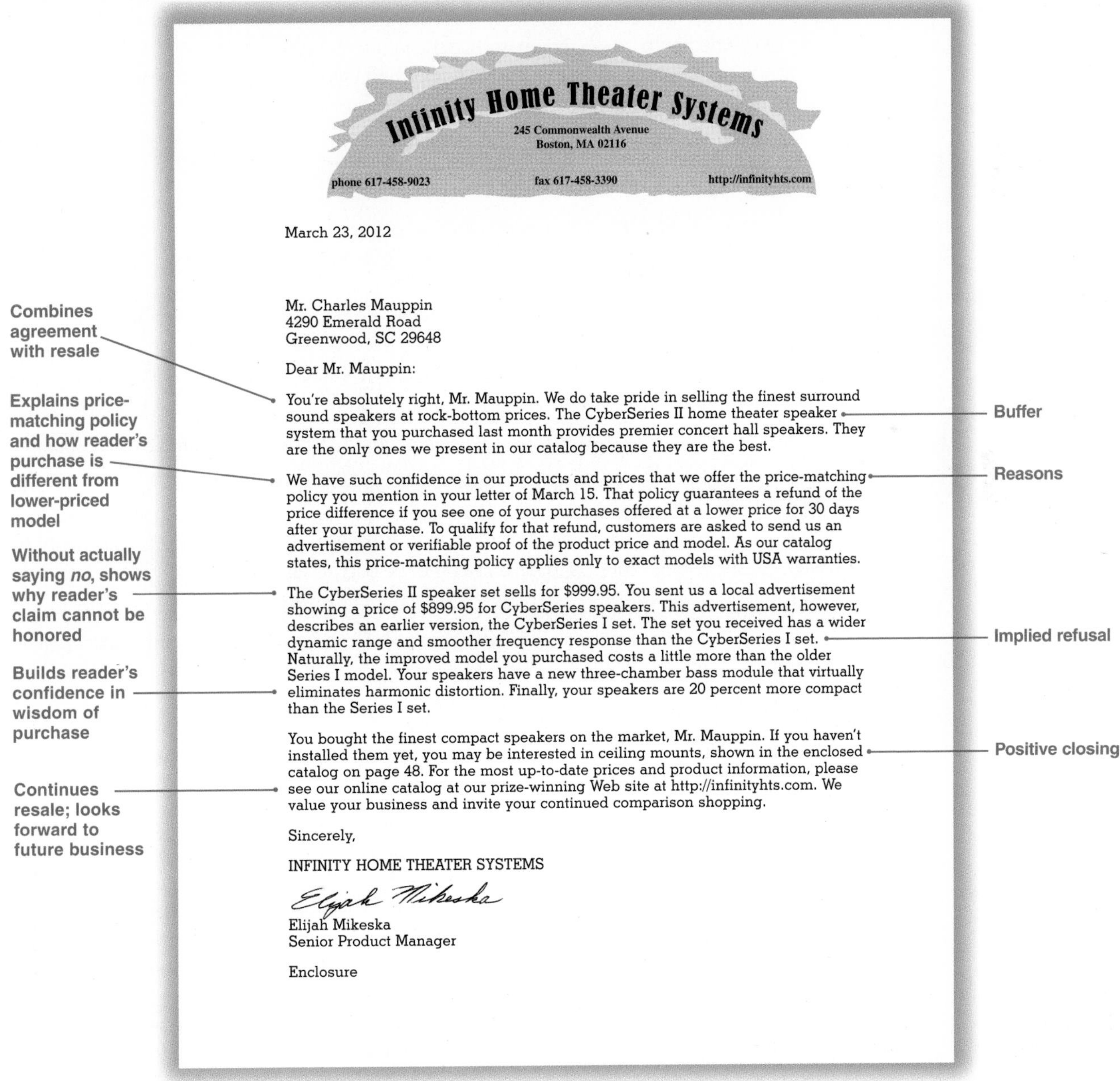

Infinity Home Theater Systems
245 Commonwealth Avenue
Boston, MA 02116
phone 617-458-9023 fax 617-458-3390 http://infinityhts.com

March 23, 2012

Mr. Charles Mauppin
4290 Emerald Road
Greenwood, SC 29648

Dear Mr. Mauppin:

You're absolutely right, Mr. Mauppin. We do take pride in selling the finest surround sound speakers at rock-bottom prices. The CyberSeries II home theater speaker system that you purchased last month provides premier concert hall speakers. They are the only ones we present in our catalog because they are the best.

We have such confidence in our products and prices that we offer the price-matching policy you mention in your letter of March 15. That policy guarantees a refund of the price difference if you see one of your purchases offered at a lower price for 30 days after your purchase. To qualify for that refund, customers are asked to send us an advertisement or verifiable proof of the product price and model. As our catalog states, this price-matching policy applies only to exact models with USA warranties.

The CyberSeries II speaker set sells for $999.95. You sent us a local advertisement showing a price of $899.95 for CyberSeries speakers. This advertisement, however, describes an earlier version, the CyberSeries I set. The set you received has a wider dynamic range and smoother frequency response than the CyberSeries I set. Naturally, the improved model you purchased costs a little more than the older Series I model. Your speakers have a new three-chamber bass module that virtually eliminates harmonic distortion. Finally, your speakers are 20 percent more compact than the Series I set.

You bought the finest compact speakers on the market, Mr. Mauppin. If you haven't installed them yet, you may be interested in ceiling mounts, shown in the enclosed catalog on page 48. For the most up-to-date prices and product information, please see our online catalog at our prize-winning Web site at http://infinityhts.com. We value your business and invite your continued comparison shopping.

Sincerely,

INFINITY HOME THEATER SYSTEMS

Elijah Mikeska

Elijah Mikeska
Senior Product Manager

Enclosure

Combines agreement with resale
Explains price-matching policy and how reader's purchase is different from lower-priced model
Without actually saying *no*, shows why reader's claim cannot be honored
Builds reader's confidence in wisdom of purchase
Continues resale; looks forward to future business
Buffer
Reasons
Implied refusal
Positive closing

resulted in a cash refund of $100). Although the catalog service does match any advertised lower price, the price-matching policy applies *only* to exact models. This claim must be rejected because the advertisement the customer submitted showed a different, older speaker model.

The letter to Charles Mauppin opens with a buffer that agrees with a statement in the customer's letter. It repeats the key idea of product confidence as a transition to the second paragraph. Next comes an explanation of the price-matching policy. The writer does not assume that the customer is trying to pull a fast one. Nor does he suggest that the customer is a dummy who didn't read or understand the price-matching policy. The safest path is a neutral explanation of the policy along with precise distinctions between the customer's speakers and the older ones. The writer also gets a chance to resell the customer's speakers and demonstrate what a quality product they are. By the end of the third paragraph, it is evident to the reader that his claim is unjustified.

Refusing Credit

What are the writer's goals when refusing credit to a customer?

When customers apply for credit, they must be notified if that application is rejected. The Fair Credit Reporting Act and Equal Credit Opportunity Act state that consumers who are denied loans must receive a notice of "adverse action" explaining the decision.[18] This notification may come directly from the credit reporting agency, such as Experian, Equifax, or TransUnion. More often, however, the credit agency reports its findings to the business. The business then makes a decision whether to grant credit based on the information supplied.

If you must write a letter to a customer denying credit, you have four goals in conveying the refusal:

- Avoiding language that causes hard feelings
- Retaining the customer on a cash basis
- Preparing for possible future credit without raising false expectations
- Avoiding disclosures that could cause a lawsuit

Because credit applicants are likely to continue to do business with an organization even if they are denied credit, you will want to do everything possible to encourage that patronage. Thus, keep the refusal respectful, sensitive, and upbeat. A letter to a customer denying her credit application might begin as follows:

> *We genuinely appreciate your application of January 12 for a Fashion Express credit account.*

To avoid possible litigation, many companies offer no explanation of the reasons for a credit refusal. Instead, they provide the name of the credit reporting agency and suggest that inquiries be directed to it. In the following example, notice the use of passive voice (*credit cannot be extended)* and a long sentence to de-emphasize the bad news:

> *After we received a report of your current credit record from Experian, it is apparent that credit cannot be extended at this time. To learn more about your record, you may call an Experian credit counselor at (212) 356-0922.*

The cordial closing looks forward to the possibility of a future reapplication:

> *Thanks, Ms. Love, for the confidence you have shown in Fashion Express. We invite you to continue shopping at our stores, and we look forward to your reapplication in the future.*

Some businesses do provide reasons explaining credit denials *(Credit cannot be granted because your firm's current and long-term credit obligations are nearly twice as great as your firm's total assets).* They may also provide alternatives, such as deferred billing or cash discounts. When the letter denies a credit application that accompanies an order, the message may contain resale information. The writer tries to convert the order from credit to cash. For example, if a big order cannot be filled on a credit basis, perhaps part of the order could be filled on a cash basis.

Whatever form the bad-news message takes, it is a good idea to have the message reviewed by legal counsel because of the litigation land mines awaiting unwary communicators in this area.

Zooming In PART 2

Southwest Airlines

For Fred Taylor, Southwest's senior manager of proactive customer communications, delivering bad news and apologizing to customers is all in a day's work. He is the point person when it comes to informing employees of problem situations and providing them with appropriate responses. When Southwest falls short of satisfying its customers, he prepares personal apology letters to passengers—about 20,000 in an average year, covering more than 180 flight disruptions. The letters have his direct phone number, and many include a free flight voucher. As he explained to customers on a recent flight from Phoenix to Albuquerque, the strange odor in the plane was from a defective valve but not dangerous. "Erring on the side of caution, our captain decided to return to Phoenix rather than second-guess the smell that was in the cabin," he wrote. Southwest's apologies even cover circumstances beyond Southwest's control, such as an ice storm that delayed a St. Louis flight. "It's not something we had to do," he says. "It's just something we feel our customers deserve."[19]

Critical Thinking

- What are the advantages to Southwest of its proactive approach to passenger problems?
- How might Fred Taylor use the writing plan suggested in this chapter to compose his apology letters to passengers?
- Contrast the strategies Taylor would develop to deliver bad news to Southwest's employees and to its passengers.

© Justin Sullivan/Getty Images

Delivering Bad News Within Organizations

LEARNING OBJECTIVE 6
Understand and apply effective techniques for delivering bad news within organizations.

A tactful tone and a reasons-first approach help preserve friendly relations with customers. These same techniques are useful when delivering bad news within organizations. Interpersonal bad news might involve telling the boss that something went wrong or confronting an employee about poor performance. Organizational bad news might involve declining profits, lost contracts, harmful lawsuits, public relations controversies, and changes in policy. Whether you use a direct or an indirect strategy in delivering that news depends primarily on the anticipated reaction of the audience. Generally, bad news is better received when reasons are given first. Within organizations, you may find yourself giving bad news in person or in writing.

Giving Bad News Personally

Whether you are an employee or a supervisor, you may have the unhappy responsibility of delivering bad news. First, decide whether the negative information is newsworthy. For example, trivial, noncriminal mistakes or one-time bad behaviors are best left alone. However, fraudulent travel claims, consistent hostile behavior, or failing projects must be reported.[20] For example, you might have to tell the boss that the team's computer crashed losing all its important files. As a team leader or supervisor, you might be required to confront an underperforming employee. If you know that the news will upset the receiver, the reasons-first strategy is most effective. When the bad news involves one person or a small group nearby, you should generally deliver that news in person. Here are pointers on how to do so tactfully, professionally, and safely:[21]

When delivering bad news in person, how can you do it tactfully, professionally, and safely?

- **Gather all the information.** Cool down and have all the facts before marching in on the boss or confronting someone. Remember that every story has two sides.
- **Prepare and rehearse.** Outline what you plan to say so that you are confident, coherent, and dispassionate.
- **Explain: past, present, future.** If you are telling the boss about a problem such as the computer crash, explain what caused the crash, the current situation, and how and when you plan to fix it.
- **Consider taking a partner.** If you fear a "shoot the messenger" reaction, especially from your boss, bring a colleague with you. Each person should have a consistent and credible

part in the presentation. If possible, take advantage of your organization's internal resources. To lend credibility to your view, call on auditors, inspectors, or human resources experts.

- **Think about timing.** Don't deliver bad news when someone is already stressed or grumpy. Experts also advise against giving bad news on Friday afternoon when people have the weekend to dwell on it.
- **Be patient with the reaction.** Give the receiver time to vent, think, recover, and act wisely.

Refusing Internal Requests

How can organizations retain employee morale when communicating bad news?

Occasionally, managers must refuse requests from employees. In Figure 9.9 you see the first draft and revision of a message responding to a request from a key specialist, Zachary Stapleton. He wants permission to attend a conference. However, he can't attend the conference because the timing is bad; he must be present at budget planning meetings scheduled for the same two weeks. Normally, this matter would be discussed in person. However, Zach has been traveling among branch offices, and he just hasn't been in the office recently.

The first inclination of Victoria Blaylock, vice president, was to send a quickie e-mail, as shown in Figure 9.9 draft, and "tell it like it is." However, she realized that this message was

FIGURE 9.9 Refusing an Internal Request

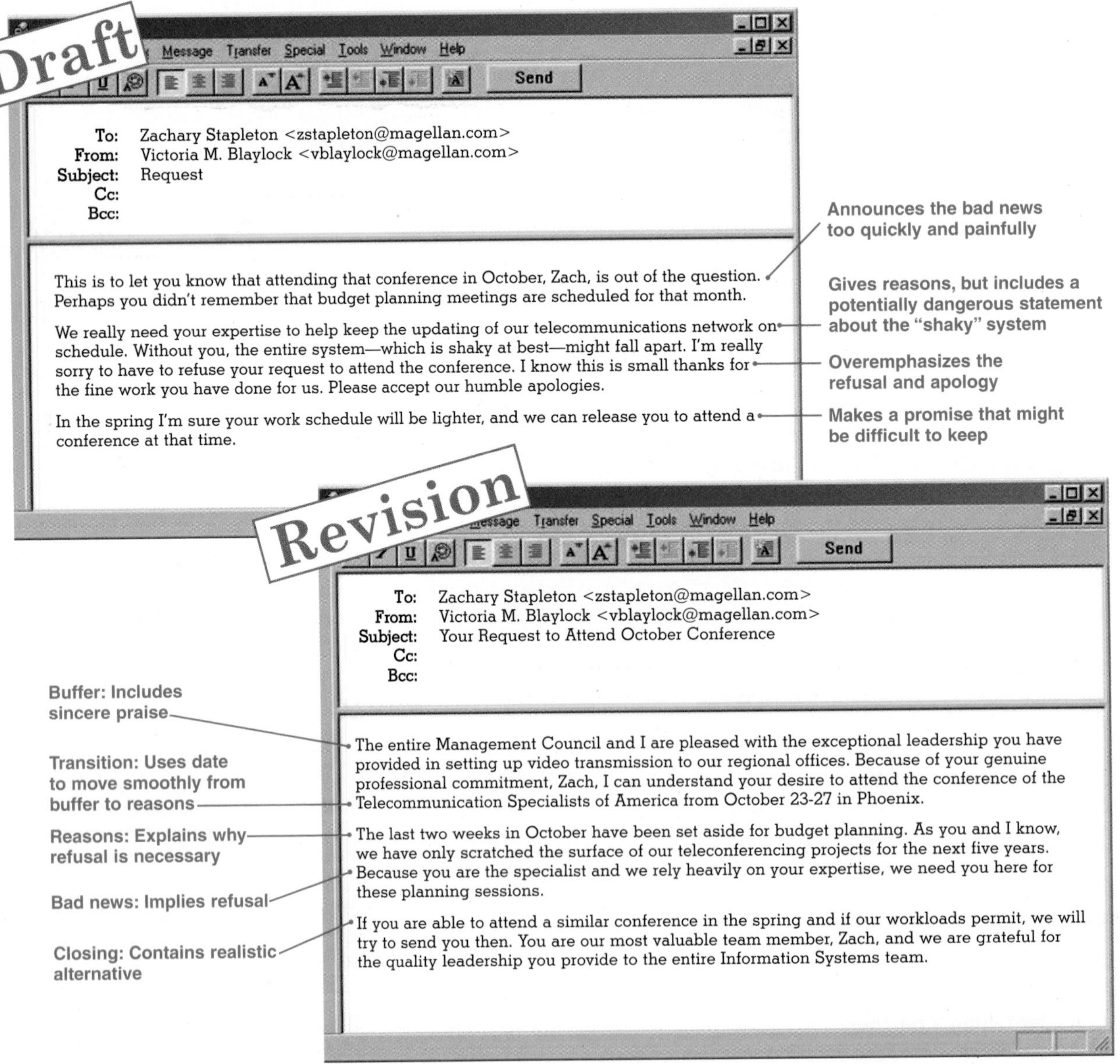
Draft

To: Zachary Stapleton <zstapleton@magellan.com>
From: Victoria M. Blaylock <vblaylock@magellan.com>
Subject: Request
Cc:
Bcc:

This is to let you know that attending that conference in October, Zach, is out of the question. Perhaps you didn't remember that budget planning meetings are scheduled for that month.

We really need your expertise to help keep the updating of our telecommunications network on schedule. Without you, the entire system—which is shaky at best—might fall apart. I'm really sorry to have to refuse your request to attend the conference. I know this is small thanks for the fine work you have done for us. Please accept our humble apologies.

In the spring I'm sure your work schedule will be lighter, and we can release you to attend a conference at that time.

Revision

To: Zachary Stapleton <zstapleton@magellan.com>
From: Victoria M. Blaylock <vblaylock@magellan.com>
Subject: Your Request to Attend October Conference
Cc:
Bcc:

The entire Management Council and I are pleased with the exceptional leadership you have provided in setting up video transmission to our regional offices. Because of your genuine professional commitment, Zach, I can understand your desire to attend the conference of the Telecommunication Specialists of America from October 23-27 in Phoenix.

The last two weeks in October have been set aside for budget planning. As you and I know, we have only scratched the surface of our teleconferencing projects for the next five years. Because you are the specialist and we rely heavily on your expertise, we need you here for these planning sessions.

If you are able to attend a similar conference in the spring and if our workloads permit, we will try to send you then. You are our most valuable team member, Zach, and we are grateful for the quality leadership you provide to the entire Information Systems team.

going to hurt and that it had possible danger areas. Moreover, the message misses a chance to give Zach positive feedback. An improved version of the e-mail starts with a buffer that delivers honest praise (*pleased with the exceptional leadership you have provided* and *your genuine professional commitment*). By the way, don't be stingy with compliments; they cost you nothing. As a philosopher once observed: "We don't live by bread alone. We need buttering up once in a while." The buffer also includes the date of the meeting, used strategically to connect the reasons that follow. You will recall from Chapter 5 that repetition of a key idea is an effective transitional device to provide smooth flow between components of a message.

The middle paragraph provides reasons for the refusal. Notice that they focus on positive elements: Zach is the specialist; the company relies on his expertise; and everyone will benefit if he passes up the conference. In this section it becomes obvious that the request will be refused. The writer is not forced to say, *No, you may not attend.* Although the refusal is implied, the reader gets the message.

The closing suggests a qualified alternative (*if our workloads permit, we will try to send you then*). It also ends positively with gratitude for Zach's contributions to the organization and with another compliment (*you're a valuable player*). The improved version focuses on explanations and praise rather than on refusals and apologies. The success of this message depends on attention to the entire writing process, not just on using a buffer or scattering a few compliments throughout.

Delivering Bad News to Groups

Should bad news to groups of employees be delivered personally or in writing?

Many of the same techniques used to deliver bad news personally are useful when organizations face a crisis or must deliver bad news to groups. Smart organizations involved in a crisis prefer to communicate the news openly to employees and stockholders. A crisis might involve serious performance problems, a major relocation, massive layoffs, a management shakeup, or public controversy. Instead of letting rumors distort the truth, managers explain the organization's side of the story honestly and early. Morale can be destroyed when employees learn of major events affecting their jobs through the grapevine or from news accounts—rather than from management.

When bad news must be delivered to employees, management may want to deliver the news personally. With large groups, however, this is generally impossible. Instead, organizations deliver bad news through hard-copy memos, which are formal and create a permanent record. Today's organizations are also experimenting with other delivery channels such as e-mail, videos, webcasts, and voice mail.

The draft of the memo shown in Figure 9.10 announces a substantial increase in the cost of employee health care benefits. However, the memo suffers from many problems. It announces jolting news bluntly in the first sentence. Worse, it offers little or no explanation for the steep increase in costs. It also sounds insincere (*We did everything possible . . .*) and arbitrary. In a final miscue, the writer fails to give credit to the company for absorbing previous health cost increases.

Ethics Check

Canned by E-Mail

When downsizing, RadioShack used e-mail to fire about 400 employees at its Fort Worth headquarters. The messages said, "The work force reduction notification is currently in progress. Unfortunately, your position is one that has been eliminated." Is it ethical to send such bad news by e-mail, and how do you feel about the tone of the message?

The revision of this bad-news memo uses the indirect strategy and improves the tone considerably. Notice that it opens with a relevant, upbeat buffer regarding health care—but says nothing about increasing costs. For a smooth transition, the second paragraph begins with a key idea from the opening (*comprehensive package*). The reasons section discusses rising costs with explanations and figures. The bad news (*you will be paying $119 a month*) is clearly presented but embedded within the paragraph. Throughout, the writer strives to show the fairness of the company's position. The ending, which does not refer to the bad news, emphasizes how much the company is paying and what a wise investment it is.

Notice that the entire memo demonstrates a kinder, gentler approach than that shown in the first draft. Of prime importance in breaking bad news to employees is providing clear, convincing reasons that explain the decision. This message could have been sent by e-mail, but a memo is more formal, more permanent, and more appropriate for bad news. This channel choice, however, may change as e-mail increasingly gains acceptance.

Saying No to Job Applicants

Should you include specifics in messages that refuse job candidates?

Being refused a job is one of life's major rejections. Tactless letters intensify the blow (*Unfortunately, you were not among the candidates selected for . . .*).

FIGURE 9.10 Announcing Bad News to Employees

Prewriting

Analyze: The purpose of this memo is to tell employees that they must share with the company the cost of increasing health care costs.

Anticipate: The audience will be employees who are unaware of specific health care costs and, most likely, reluctant to pay more.

Adapt: Because the readers will be unhappy, use the indirect strategy. Choose to send an interoffice memo, which is more permanent and more formal than e-mail.

2 Writing

Research: Collect facts and statistics that document health care costs.

Organize: Begin with a buffer describing the company's commitment to health benefits. Provide an explanation of health care costs. Announce the bad news. In the closing, focus on the company's major share of the cost.

Compose: Draft the first version with the expectation to revise.

3 Revising

Revise: Remove negativity (*unfortunately, we can't, the company was forced, inadvisable*). Explain the increase with specific figures.

Proofread: Use quotation marks around *defensive* to show its special sense. Spell out *percent* after *300*.

Evaluate: Is there any other way to help readers accept this bad news?

Draft

Beginning January 1 your monthly payment for health care benefits will be increased $119 a month for a total payment of $639 for each employee. — Hits readers with bad news without any preparation

Every year health care costs go up. Although we considered dropping other benefits, Northern decided that the best plan was to keep the present comprehensive package. Unfortunately, we can't do that unless we pass along some of the extra cost to you. Last year the company was forced to absorb the total increase in health care premiums. However, such a plan this year is inadvisable. — Offers no explanation for increase; Sounds defensive and arbitrary

We did everything possible to avoid the sharp increase in costs to you this year. A rate schedule describing the increases in payments for your family and dependents is enclosed. — Fails to take credit for absorbing previous increases

Revision

NORTHERN INDUSTRIES, INC.
MEMORANDUM

Date: October 2, 2012
To: Fellow Employees
From: Victor Q. Markelson, President VQM
Subject: Maintaining Quality Health Care

Begins with positive buffer — Health care programs have always been an important part of our commitment to employees at Northern Industries, Inc. We are proud that our total benefits package continues to rank among the best in the country.

Offers reason explaining why costs are rising — Such a comprehensive package does not come cheaply. In the last decade, health care costs alone have risen over 300 percent. We are told that several factors fuel the cost spiral: aging population, technology improvements, increased cost of patient services, and "defensive" medicine practiced by doctors to prevent lawsuits.

Reveals bad news clearly but embeds it in paragraph — Just two years ago our monthly health care cost for each employee was $515. It rose to $569 last year. We were able to absorb that jump without increasing your contribution. But this year's hike to $639 forces us to ask you to share the increase. To maintain your current health care benefits, you will be paying $119 a month. The enclosed rate schedule describes the costs for families and dependents.

Ends positively by stressing the company's major share of the costs — Northern continues to pay the major portion of your health care program ($520 each month). We think it's a wise investment.

Enclosure

FIGURE 9.11 **Saying No to Job Candidate**

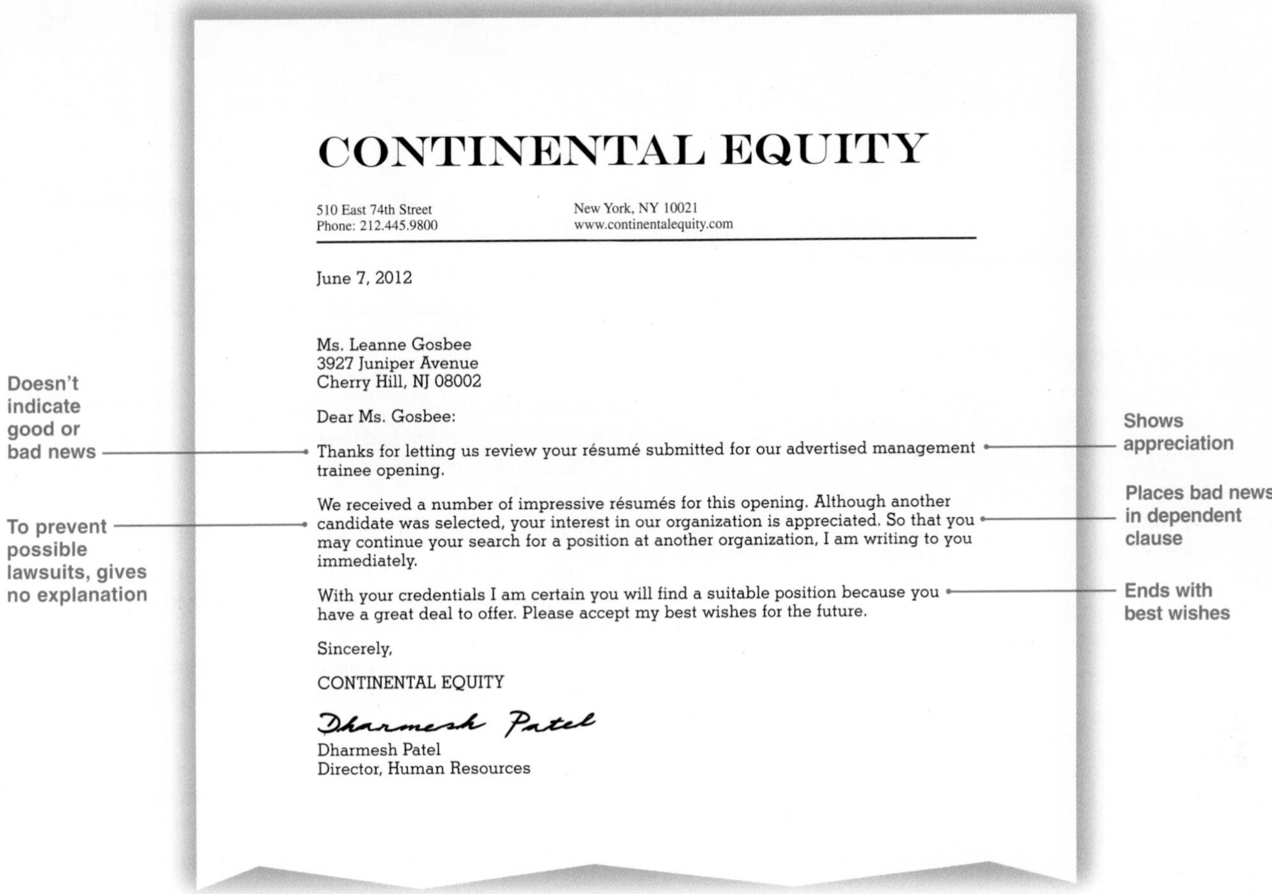

CONTINENTAL EQUITY

510 East 74th Street
Phone: 212.445.9800

New York, NY 10021
www.continentalequity.com

June 7, 2012

Ms. Leanne Gosbee
3927 Juniper Avenue
Cherry Hill, NJ 08002

Dear Ms. Gosbee:

Thanks for letting us review your résumé submitted for our advertised management trainee opening.

We received a number of impressive résumés for this opening. Although another candidate was selected, your interest in our organization is appreciated. So that you may continue your search for a position at another organization, I am writing to you immediately.

With your credentials I am certain you will find a suitable position because you have a great deal to offer. Please accept my best wishes for the future.

Sincerely,

CONTINENTAL EQUITY

Dharmesh Patel

Dharmesh Patel
Director, Human Resources

Doesn't indicate good or bad news
To prevent possible lawsuits, gives no explanation
Shows appreciation
Places bad news in dependent clause
Ends with best wishes

You can reduce the receiver's disappointment somewhat by using the indirect strategy—with one important variation. In the reasons section, it is wise to be vague in explaining why the candidate was not selected. First, giving concrete reasons may be painful to the receiver *(Your grade point average of 2.7 was low compared with the GPAs of other candidates)*. Second, and more important, providing extra information may prove fatal in a lawsuit. Hiring and firing decisions generate considerable litigation today. To avoid charges of discrimination or wrongful actions, legal advisors warn organizations to keep employment rejection letters general, simple, and short.

The job refusal letter shown in Figure 9.11 is tactful but intentionally vague. It implies that the applicant's qualifications don't match those needed for the position, but the letter doesn't reveal anything specific. The writer could have included this alternate closing: *We wish you every success in finding a position that exactly fits your qualifications.*

The checklist on page 282 summarizes tips on how to communicate negative news inside and outside your organization.

Presenting Bad News in Other Cultures

LEARNING OBJECTIVE 7
Compare strategies for revealing bad news in other cultures.

To minimize disappointment, Americans generally prefer to present negative messages indirectly. Communicators in other cultures may treat bad news differently.

In Germany, for example, business communicators occasionally use buffers but tend to present bad news directly. British writers also tend to be straightforward with bad news, seeing no reason to soften its announcement. In Latin countries the question is not how to organize negative messages but whether to present them at all. It is considered disrespectful and impolite to report bad news to superiors. Thus, reluctant employees may fail to report accurately any negative situations to their bosses.

Checklist

Conveying Negative News

Prewrite

- Decide whether to use the direct or indirect strategy. If the bad news is minor and will not upset the receiver, open directly. If the message is personally damaging and will upset the receiver, consider techniques to reduce its pain.
- Think through the reasons for the bad news.
- Remember that your primary goal is to make the receiver understand and accept the bad news as well as maintain a positive image of you and your organization.

Plan the Opening

- In the indirect strategy, start with a buffer. Pay a compliment to the reader, show appreciation for something done, or mention some mutual understanding. Avoid raising false hopes or thanking the reader for something you will refuse.
- In the direct strategy, begin with a straightforward statement of the bad news.

Provide Reasons in the Body

- Except in credit and job refusals, explain the reasons for the negative message.
- In customer mishaps, clarify what went wrong, what you are doing to resolve the problem, and how you will prevent it from happening again.
- Use objective, nonjudgmental, and nondiscriminatory language.
- Avoid negativity (e.g., words such as *unfortunately, unwilling,* and *impossible)* and potentially damaging statements.
- Show how your decision is fair and perhaps benefits the reader or others, if possible.

Soften the Bad News

- Reduce the impact of bad news by using (a) a subordinate clause, (b) the passive voice, (c) a long sentence, or (d) a long paragraph.
- Consider implying the refusal, but be certain it is clear.
- Suggest an alternative, such as a lower price, a different product, a longer payment period, or a substitute. Provide help in implementing an alternative.
- Offset disappointment by offering gifts, a reduced price, benefits, tokens of appreciation, or something appropriate.

Close Pleasantly

- Supply more information about an alternative, look forward to future relations, or offer good wishes and compliments.
- Maintain a bright, personal tone. Avoid referring to the refusal.

Why might it be necessary to use a different strategy when communicating bad news in other cultures?

In Asian cultures, harmony and peace are sought in all relationships. Disrupting the harmony with bad news is avoided. To prevent discord, Japanese communicators use a number of techniques to indicate *no*—without being forced to say it. In conversation they may respond with silence or with a counter question, such as *Why do you ask?* They may change the subject or tell a white lie to save face for themselves and for the questioner. Sometimes the answer sounds like a qualified yes: *I will do my best, but if I cannot, I hope you will understand.* If the response is *Yes, but ...*, or *Yes* followed by an apology, beware. All of these responses should be recognized as meaning *no.*

In China, Westerners often have difficulty understanding the hints given by communicators.

> *I agree* might mean *I agree with 15 percent of what you say.*
> *We might be able to* could mean *Not a chance.*
> *We will consider* could mean *WE will, but the real decision maker will not.*
> *That is a little too much* might equate to *That is outrageous.*[22]

Why might low-context, literal-minded communicators misunderstand subtle messages from some Asians?

In Thailand the negativism represented by a refusal is completely alien; the word *no* does not exist. In many cultures negative news is offered with such subtlety or in such a positive light that it may be overlooked or misunderstood by literal-minded Americans.

In many high-context cultures, saving face is important. A refusal is a potential loss of face for both parties. To save face, a person who must refuse an invitation to dine out with a business associate might say, *You must be very tired and want to have a quiet evening.*[23] This subtle refusal avoids putting it in words. To understand the meaning of what's really being communicated, we must look beyond an individual's actual words and consider the communication style, the culture, and especially the context.

Zooming In — YOUR TURN

Applying Your Skills at Southwest Airlines

Southwest Airlines, whose motto is "Share the Spirit," is actively involved in the communities it serves. Its high level of participation has earned the company a place on the 100 Best Corporate Citizens list. Employees volunteer in dozens of local events. On a national level, it partners with a wide range of charities, including the Hispanic Association of Colleges and Universities' national educational travel award program, the Ronald McDonald House, Junior Achievement, Read Across America, and Parkland Burn Camp. Through its award-winning Adopt-a-Pilot program, a fifth-grade classroom is paired with a pilot mentor for four weeks. Students correspond with their pilots and track their travels, engaging in aviation-themed science, math, research, writing, history, geography, and career-planning lessons and activities.

With such a high public profile, the airline receives many requests for donations, from monetary contributions and event sponsorships to numerous appeals for free flight tickets from charities holding fund-raising events. Its detailed guidelines for groups seeking donations, published on its Web site, state, "A standard donation is two round-trip passes good for transportation between any two cities Southwest Airlines serves within the continental U.S." Charities must mail their requests for free tickets to the Charitable Giving Department at Southwest's Dallas headquarters, which then determines the recipients.

Your Task

© Justin Sullivan/Getty Images

Assume that you are an intern in the Southwest Airlines Charitable Giving Department. Your manager hands you a letter from Elizabeth Dunbar, Director, Animal Rescue League of Iowa, 5452 Northeast 22nd Street, Des Moines, IA 50313. This organization never turns away an animal in need, but it has run out of space and desperately needs a new shelter. To build a $6.5 million state-of-the-art facility, it is sponsoring a local raffle. One prize would be ten round-trip tickets anywhere in the United States, and it asks Southwest to provide those tickets. The problem is that the request arrived 30 days before the event and is nonstandard. Deny the request, but offer an alternative. You like animals, too!

A recent study showed that business letters conveying bad news in Latin America were quite short and did not employ buffers. This may be a result of the desire to avoid negative news completely, feeling it is discourteous to bring bad news.[24]

Conveying bad news in any culture is tricky and requires sensitivity to and awareness of cultural practices.

Want to do well on tests and excel in your course?
Go to **www.meguffey.com** for helpful interactive resources.

- **Review the Chapter 9 PowerPoint slides to prepare for the first quiz.**

Summary of Learning Objectives

1 Describe the goals and strategies of business communicators in conveying negative news effectively, including applying the writing process and avoiding legal liability. All businesses occasionally deal with problems. Good communicators have many goals in delivering bad news: explaining clearly and completely, projecting a professional image, conveying empathy and sensitivity, being fair, and maintaining friendly relations. Applying the 3-x-3 writing process helps you prepare, compose, and revise your message so that it accomplishes your purpose. Careful communicators avoid careless and abusive language, which is actionable when it is false, damages a person's reputation, and is "published" (spoken within the presence of others or written). Messages written on company stationery represent that company and can be legally binding.

2 Decide whether to use the direct or indirect strategy in conveying negative news. The indirect strategy involves beginning with a buffer and delaying the bad news until reasons have been presented. The direct strategy reveals the main idea immediately. The direct strategy is preferable when the bad news is not damaging, when the receiver may overlook the bad news, when the organization policy suggests directness, when the receiver prefers directness, and when firmness is necessary. The indirect strategy works well when the bad news is personally upsetting, provokes a hostile reaction, threatens the customer relationship, and is unexpected.

3 Analyze the components of effective negative messages, including opening with a buffer, apologizing, conveying empathy, presenting the reasons, cushioning the bad news, and closing pleasantly. If you use the indirect strategy for a negative message, begin with a buffer, such as a compliment, appreciation, a point of agreement, objective information, understanding, or some part of the message that represents good news. Then explain the reasons that necessitate the bad news, trying to cite benefits to the reader or others. If you use the direct strategy, begin directly with the bad news followed by the reasons. When apologizing, do so sincerely, accept responsibility, and use good judgment. Throughout a negative message, strive to cushion the bad news by positioning it strategically, using the passive voice, accentuating the positive, choosing positive words, and suggesting a compromise or alternative. Close pleasantly with a forward-looking goodwill statement.

4 Describe and apply effective techniques for refusing typical requests. Typical requests ask for favors, money, information, action, and other items. When the answer will be disappointing, use the reasons-before-refusal pattern. Open with a buffer; provide reasons; announce the refusal sensitively; suggest possible alternatives; and end with a positive, forward-looking comment.

5 Explain and apply effective techniques for handling bad news with customers. When a company disappoints its customers, most organizations (a) call the individual involved, (b) describe the problem and apologize (when the company is to blame), (c) explain why the problem occurred and what is being done to prevent its recurrence, and (d) follow up with a message that documents the phone call and promotes goodwill. Some organizations also offer gifts or benefits to offset customers' disappointment and to reestablish the business relationship. In announcing rate increases and price hikes, tie the increase to customer benefits. In denying claims, begin indirectly, provide reasons for the refusal, and close pleasantly, looking forward to future business. When appropriate, resell a product or service. When refusing credit, avoid language that causes hard feelings, strive to retain the customer on a cash basis, prepare for possible future credit, and avoid disclosures that could cause a lawsuit.

6 Understand and apply effective techniques for delivering bad news within organizations. When delivering bad news personally to a superior, gather all the information, prepare and rehearse, explain what happened and how the problem will be repaired, consider taking a colleague with you, think about timing, and be patient with the reaction. In delivering bad news to groups of employees, use the indirect strategy but be sure to provide clear, convincing reasons that explain the decision. In refusing job applicants, however, keep letters short, general, and tactful.

7 Compare strategies for revealing bad news in other cultures. American communicators often prefer to break bad news slowly and indirectly. In other low-context cultures, such as Germany and Britain, however, bad news is revealed directly. In most high-context cultures, such as China and Japan, straightforwardness is avoided. In Latin cultures bad news may be totally suppressed. In Asian cultures negativism is avoided and hints may suggest bad news. Subtle meanings must be interpreted carefully.

Chapter Review

1. When delivering bad news, how can a communicator reduce the bad feelings of the receiver? (Obj. 1)
2. What is the most important part of Phase 1 of the writing process for negative messages? (Obj. 1)
3. When should you use the direct strategy in delivering bad news? (Obj. 2)
4. When should you use the indirect strategy in delivering bad news? (Obj. 2)
5. What are the major differences between the direct and indirect strategies in delivering bad news? (Obj. 2)
6. What is a buffer? Name five or more techniques to buffer the opening of a bad-news message. (Obj. 3)
7. What is an apology? When should an apology be offered to customers? (Obj. 3)
8. Name four or more techniques that cushion the delivery of bad news. (Obj. 3)
9. What are some typical requests that big and small businesses must refuse? (Obj. 4)
10. Identify a process used by a majority of business professionals in resolving problems with disappointed customers. (Obj. 5)
11. If you must deny the claim of a customer who is clearly at fault, should you respond by putting the blame squarely on the customer? (Obj. 5)
12. What is an effective technique in announcing rate increases and price hikes? (Obj. 5)
13. How can a subordinate tactfully, professionally, and safely deliver upsetting news personally to a superior? (Obj. 6)
14. What are some channels that large organizations may use when delivering bad news to employees? (Obj. 6)
15. In Latin countries why may employees sometimes fail to report accurately any negative situations to management? (Obj. 7)

Critical Thinking

1. Communication author Dana Bristol-Smith likens delivering bad news to removing a Band-Aid—you can do it slowly or quickly. She thinks that quickly is better, particularly when companies must give bad news to employees.[25] Do you agree or disagree? (Objs. 1–6)
2. Respected industry analyst Gartner Research issued a report naming social networking as one of the top ten disruptive influences shaping information technology in the next five years.[26] Should organizations fear Web sites where consumers post negative messages about products and services? What actions can companies take in response to this disruptive influence? (Objs. 1–5)
3. Consider times when you have been aware that others were using the indirect strategy in writing or speaking to you. How did you react? (Obj. 2)
4. When Boeing Aircraft reported that a laptop containing the names, salary information, and social security numbers of 382,000 employees had been stolen from an employee's car, CEO Jim McNerney wrote this e-mail to employees: "I've received many e-mails over the past 24 hours from employees expressing disappointment, frustration, and downright anger about yesterday's announcement of personal information belonging to thousands of employees and retirees being on a stolen computer. I'm just as disappointed as you are about it. I know that many of us feel that this data loss amounts to a betrayal of the trust we place in the company to safeguard our personal information. I certainly do." Critics have faulted this apology for its timing and content. Do you agree?
5. **Ethical Issue:** You work for a large corporation with headquarters in a small town. Recently you received shoddy repair work and a huge bill from a local garage. Your car's transmission has the same problems that it did before you took it in for repair. You know that a complaint letter written on your corporation's stationery would be much more authoritative than one written on plain stationery. Should you use corporation stationery? (Obj. 1)

Writing Improvement Exercises

9.1 Organizational Strategies (Objs. 1–5)

Your Task. Identify which organizational strategy you would use for the following messages: direct or indirect.

a. A letter from a credit card company announcing a small increase in rates.
b. A letter from a theme park refusing the request of a visitor who wants free tickets. The visitor was unhappy that he had to wait in line a very long time to ride a new thrill roller coaster.
c. An e-mail from a manager refusing an employee's request for funds and time off to attend a professional seminar.
d. A letter refusing a request by a charitable organization to use your office equipment on the weekend.
e. A memo from the manager denying an employee's request for special parking privileges. The employee works closely with the manager on many projects.
f. An announcement to employees that a financial specialist has canceled a scheduled lunchtime talk and cannot reschedule.
g. A letter to bank customers revealing that its central computer system had been hacked revealing customer addresses, dates of birth, account numbers, and the value of investments.
h. A form letter from an insurance company announcing new policy requirements that many policyholders may resent. If policyholders do not indicate the plan they prefer, they may lose their insurance coverage.

i. A memo from an executive refusing a manager's proposal to economize by purchasing reconditioned computers. The executive and the manager both appreciate efficient, straightforward messages.
j. A letter informing a company that the majority of the company's equipment order will not be available for six weeks.

9.2 Employing Passive-Voice Verbs (Obj. 3)

Your Task. Revise the following sentences to present the bad news with passive-voice verbs.

a. We cannot offer free shipping after January 1.
b. Our retail stores will no longer be accepting credit cards for purchases under $5.
c. Because management now requires more stringent security, we are postponing indefinitely requests for company tours.
d. We do not examine patients until we have verified their insurance coverage.
e. Your car rental insurance coverage does not cover large SUVs.
f. Company policy prevents us from offering health and dental benefits until employees have been on the job for 12 months.

9.3 Subordinating Bad News (Obj. 3)

Your Task. Revise the following sentences to position the bad news in a subordinate clause. (**Hint:** Consider beginning the clause with *Although*.) Use passive-voice verbs for the bad news.

a. We regret that we cannot replace the cabinet hinge you need. The manufacturer no longer offers it. A new hinge should work for you, and we are sending it to you.
b. State law does not allow smoking within 5 feet of a state building. But the college has set aside 16 outdoor smoking areas.
c. We now offer all of our catalog choices at our Web site, which is always current. Unfortunately, we no longer print or mail a complete catalog.
d. We are sorry to report that we are unable to ship your complete order at this point in time. However, we are able to send two corner workstations now, and you should receive them within five days.
e. We appreciate your interest in our organization, but we are unable to extend an employment offer to you at this time.

9.4 Implying Bad News (Obj. 3)

Your Task. Revise the following statements to *imply* the bad news. If possible, use passive-voice verbs and subordinate clauses to further de-emphasize the bad news.

a. Unfortunately, we find it impossible to contribute to your excellent and worthwhile fund-raising campaign this year. At present all the funds of my organization are needed to lease equipment and offices for our new branch in Hartford. We hope to be able to support this commendable endeavor in the future.
b. We cannot ship our fresh fruit baskets c.o.d. Your order was not accompanied by payment, so we are not shipping it. We have it ready, though, and will rush it to its destination as soon as you call us with your credit card number.
c. Because of the holiday period, all our billboard space was used this month. Therefore, we are sorry to say that we could not give your charitable group free display space. However, next month, after the holidays, we hope to display your message as we promised.

Activities

Note: All Documents for Analysis are provided at **www.meguffey.com** for you to download and revise.

9.5 Document for Analysis: Wedding Request Refusal (Objs. 1–4)

Your Task. Analyze the following poorly written request refusal. List its weaknesses. If your instructor directs, revise it using the suggestions you learned in this chapter.

Current date

Ms. Sonya Capretta
2459 Sierra Avenue
Fresno, CA 93710

Dear Ms. Capretta:

We regret to inform you that the wedding date you request in your letter of February 2 at the Napa Valley Inn is unavailable. Unfortunately, we are fully booked for all of the Saturdays in June, as you probably already suspected.

June is our busiest month, and smart brides make their reservations many months—even years—in advance. That's because the Napa Valley Inn is the ideal romantic getaway for weddings. With unparalleled cuisine and service, along with panoramic Napa Valley and vineyard views, our Inn offers unique, intimate ambiance in a breathtaking location for your special event.

We apologize if we have caused you any inconvenience. However, if you could change your wedding date to the middle of the week, we would try to accommodate your party. We do have a few midweek spots open in June, but even those dates are rapidly filling up. With 45 Mediterranean-style rooms and suites, each with its own sunny private terrace, the Napa Valley Inn is the perfect location for you and your partner to begin your married lives. Afternoon ceremonies typically begin at 11 a.m., while golden sunsets at the Napa Valley Inn offer a romantic prelude of the evening to come. Evening ceremonies usually begin at 6 p.m. I'm available if you want to arrange something.

Sincerely,

9.6 Document for Analysis: Copier Request Refusal (Objs. 1–4)

Your Task. Analyze the following letter. List its weaknesses. If your instructor directs, revise it using the suggestions you learned in this chapter. Add any needed information.

Current date

Mr. Tyler Venable
Great Atlantic Financial Services
105 Washington Avenue
Glassboro, NJ 08071

Dear Mr. Venable:

We find it impossible to convert the payments you have been making on your Sharp CopyCenter C20 to the purchase of a new copier. This request has been forwarded to me, and I see that you have been making regular payments for the past 11 months.

Some time ago we instituted a company policy prohibiting such conversion of leasing monies. Perhaps you have noticed that we offer extremely low leasing and purchase prices. Obviously, these low prices would never be possible if we agreed to many proposals such as yours. Because we are striving to stay in business, we must deny your request asking us to convert all 11 months of rental payments toward the purchase of our popular new equipment.

It is our understanding, Mr. Venable, that you have been using the Sharp CopyCenter C20 color copier for 11 months, and you claim that it has been reliable and versatile. We would like to tell you about another Sharp model—one that is perhaps closer to your limited budget.

Sincerely,

9.7 Document for Analysis: Refusing Internal Request for Time Off (Objs. 1–4, 6)

Your Task. Analyze the following poorly written e-mail, and list its weaknesses. If your instructor directs, revise it using the suggestions you learned in this and previous chapters.

To: Sylvia Greene (sgreene@financialsolutions.com)
From: Chester Goings (cgoings@financialsolutions.com)
Subject: No Go on Baby Charity Thing
Cc:
Bcc:

Hey, Syl, you're one in a million. But we can't give you time off to work on that charity fashion show/luncheon thingy you want to coordinate. And Financial Solutions can't make a big contribution as we've done in previous years. It's no, no, no, all the way around.

Look, we admire the work you have done for the Newborn Hope Foundation. It has raised millions of dollars to make differences in the lives of babies, particularly premature ones. But we need you here!

With the upcoming release of our Planning Guide 5.0, we need you to interview clients. We need you to make video testimonials, and you are the one to search for stories about customer successes. Plus a zillion other tasks! Our new Web site will launch in just six short weeks, and all that content stuff must be in final form. With the economy in the tank and our bare-bones staff, you certainly must realize that each and every team member must be here and making a difference. If our Planning Guide 5.0 doesn't make a big splash, we'll all have a lot of time off.

Due to the fact that we're the worldwide leader in on-demand financial planning and reporting software, and in view of the fact that we are about to launch our most important new product ever, you must understand our position. When things get better, we might be able to return back to our past practices. But not now!

Chet

9.8 Document for Analysis: Refusing a Job Applicant (Objs. 1, 2, and 6)

Your Task. Analyze the following letter. List its weaknesses. If your instructor directs, revise it.

Current date

Mr. Kent W. Bradshaw
2140 Azalea Avenue
Louisville, KY 40216

Dear Mr. Bradshaw:

Mrs. Lujan and I wish to thank you for the pleasure of allowing us to interview you last Thursday. We were totally delighted to learn about your superb academic record, and we also appreciated your attentiveness in listening to our description of the operations of Appalachian Technologies.

Unfortunately, we had many well-qualified applicants who were interested in the advertised position of human resources assistant. As you may have guessed, we were particularly eager to find a minority individual who could help us fill our diversity goals. Although you did not fit one of our goal areas, we enjoyed talking with you. We hired a female graduate from the University of Kentucky who had most of the qualities we sought.

We realize that the job market is difficult at this time, and you have our heartfelt wishes for good luck in finding precisely what you are looking for.

Sincerely,

9.9 Request Refusal: Helping Abused Children (Objs. 1–4)

As a vice president of a financial services company, you serve many clients and they sometimes ask your company to contribute to their favorite charities. You recently received a letter from Olivia Hernandez asking for a substantial contribution to the National Court Appointed Special Advocate (CASA) Association. On visits to your office, she has told you about its programs to recruit, train, and support volunteers in their work with abused children. She herself is active in your town as a CASA volunteer, helping neglected children find safe, permanent homes. She told you that children with CASA volunteers are more likely to be adopted and are less likely to reenter the child welfare system. You have a soft spot in your heart for children and especially for those who are mistreated. You sincerely want to support CASA and its good work. But times are tough, and you can't be as generous as you have been in the past. Ms. Hernandez wrote a special letter to you asking you to become a Key contributor, with a pledge of $1,000.

Your Task. Write a refusal letter that maintains good relations with your client. Address it to Ms. Olivia Hernandez, 3592 Marine Creek Parkway, Fort Worth, TX 76179.

9.10 Request Refusal: Jamba Asks for Juicy Favor (Objs. 1–4)

In an aggressive expansion effort, Jamba Juice became a good customer of your software company. You have enjoyed the business it brought, and you are also quite fond of its products—especially Banana Berry and Mega Mango smoothies. Jamba Inc. is in the midst of expanding its menu with the goal of becoming the Starbucks of the smoothie. "Just as Starbucks defined the category of coffee, Jamba has the opportunity to define the category of the healthy snack," said analyst Brian Moore. One goal of Jamba is to boost the frequency of customer visits by offering some products that are more filling. Then it could attract hungry customers as well as thirsty ones. It was experimenting with adding grains such as oatmeal or nuts such as almonds so that a smoothie packs more substance and could substitute for a meal.

You receive a letter from Joe Wong, your business friend and contact at Jamba Juice. He asks you to do him and Jamba Juice a favor. He wants to set up a juice tasting bar in your company cafeteria to test his new experimental drinks. All the drinks would be free, of course, but employees would have to fill out forms to evaluate each recipe. The details could be worked out later.

You definitely support healthy snacks, but you think this idea is terrible. First of all, your company doesn't even have a cafeteria. It has a small lunchroom, and employees bring their own food. Secondly, you would be embarrassed to ask your boss to do this favor for Jamba Juice, despite the business it has brought your company.

Your Task. Write a letter that retains good customer relations with Jamba Juice but refuses this request. What reasons can you give, and what alternatives are available? Address your message to Joe Wong, Vice President, Product Development, Jamba Inc., 450 Golden Gate Avenue, San Francisco, CA 94102.[27]

9.11 Request Refusal: Greening the Office (Objs. 1–4)

Hines, an international real estate firm, has developed a green office program designed to enhance the sustainable features and operation of its 230 offices on four continents. Its program, called HinesGO (short for Hines Green Office), helps identify and implement no-cost and low-cost green alternatives for standard indoor office environments. What's outstanding about the HinesGo program is its emphasis on improvements that can be achieved at minimal cost. For example, installation of occupancy light sensors can save enough money to offset the up-front investment.

Scored on a scale of 100, offices are evaluated in seven categories: energy efficiency; people and atmosphere; travel and commuting; reduce, reuse, and recycle; cleaning and pest control; remodeling and construction; and LEED and/or ENERGY STAR. (LEED is an internationally recognized green building certification system.) When a specific strategy has been implemented in the HinesGo program, participants earn Leaf Credits.[28]

Although its HinesGO program was initially intended for Hines offices only, the program generated so much attention that other businesses now want to duplicate its success. As a manager at Hines in charge of communication for HinesGo, you receive numerous invitations to speak to groups interested in creating greener workplace choices. However, you can't always accept. The most recent invitation came from Florida, where a group of realtors wants you to tell them about the HinesGO program. You were invited to speak October 12, but you are booked up. You don't see an opening until sometime in late January.

Your Task. Prepare a letter that refuses the invitation but suggests an alternative and promotes the HinesGO program. Send your letter to Donna Payne, Society of Commercial Realtors of Greater Fort Lauderdale, 1765 NE 26th Street, Fort Lauderdale, FL 33305.

9.12 Request Refusal: Rejecting Agent's Appeal for Wireless Device (Objs. 1–4)

Warren R. Sims, founder of Sims South Florida Realty, runs a successful real estate brokerage with 22 agents in three offices. Jon Tabaldo, an eager, new, tech-savvy agent, has discovered a handheld device that he thinks is the perfect tool to continuously access and monitor multiple listing service (MLS) data. This wireless device provides fast, complete Web access, enabling real estate professionals to increase productivity. They spend less time in the office and more time with their customers. The device also increases customer satisfaction because agents can respond quickly with data and full graphics for any-where-anytime service. Jon sent a persuasive e-mail to his boss asking that the realty company provide these handheld devices for all agents.

Mr. Sims uses e-mail, but he is not keen on employing technology to sell real estate. Regardless, he gave considerable thought to Jon's message recommending the devices. Mr. Sims did the math and figures it would cost him close to $8,000 for the initial investment plus $5,000 per year/per office for updates. He thinks this is a lot of money for technology he's not convinced is needed or that may not be used. He also worries about ownership responsibility.

He could pick up the phone and talk to Jon personally. But Mr. Sims wants to respond in an interoffice memo because he can control exactly what he says. He also thinks that a written response is more forceful and that it provides a permanent record of this decision in case agents make similar requests in the future. The more he ponders the request, the more Mr. Sims thinks that this kind of investment in software and hardware should be made by agents themselves—not by the agency. Don't they already purchase their own laptops?

Your Task. Put yourself in the place of Mr. Sims and prepare an interoffice memo that refuses the request but retains the goodwill of the agent. What reasons can you give for the refusal?

9.13 Request Refusal: Fun Ship Slams Door on Under-21 Crowd (Objs. 1–4)

The world's largest cruise line finds itself in a difficult position. Carnival climbed to the No. 1 spot by promoting fun at sea and pitching its appeal to younger customers who were drawn to on-board discos, swim-up bars, and hassle-free partying. But apparently the partying of high school and college students went too far. Roving bands of teens had virtually taken over some cruises in recent years. Travel agents complained of "drunken, loud behavior," as reported by Mike Driscoll, editor of *Cruise Week*.

To crack down, Carnival raised the drinking age from 18 to 21 and required more chaperoning of school groups. But young individual travelers were still unruly and disruptive. Therefore, Carnival instituted a new policy, effective immediately. No one under 21 may travel unless accompanied by an adult over 25. Vicki Freed, Carnival's vice president for marketing, said, "We will turn them back at the docks, and they will not get refunds." As Demetrice Hawkins, a Carnival marketing manager, you must respond to the inquiry of Elizabeth Neil, of Leisure World Travel, a Chicago travel agency that features special spring- and summer-break packages for college and high school students.

Leisure World Travel has been one of Carnival's best customers. However, Carnival no longer wants to encourage unaccompanied young people. You must refuse the request of Ms. Neil to help set up student tour packages. Carnival discourages even chaperoned tours. Its target market is now families. You must write to Leisure World Travel and break the bad news. Try to promote fun-filled, carefree cruises destined for sunny, exotic ports of call that remove guests from the stresses of everyday life. By the way, Carnival attracts more passengers than any other cruise line—over a million people a year from all over the world. Over 98 percent of Carnival's guests say that they were well satisfied.

Your Task. Write your letter to Elizabeth Neil, Leisure World Travel Agency, 636 South Michigan Avenue, Chicago, IL 60605. Send her a schedule for spring and summer Caribbean cruises. Tell her you will call during the week of January 15 to help her plan special family tour packages.[29]

9.14 Request Refusal: Can't Evict Noisy Tenant (Objs. 1-4)

Web

As the owner of Peachtree Business Plaza, you must respond to the request of Michael Vazquez, one of the tenants in your three-story office building. Mr. Vazquez, a CPA, demands that you immediately evict a neighboring tenant who plays loud music throughout the day, interfering with Mr. Vazquez' conversations with clients and with his concentration. The noisy tenant, Anthony Chomko, seems to operate an entertainment booking agency and spends long hours in his office. You know you can't evict Mr. Chomko because, as a legal commercial tenant, he is entitled to conduct his business. However, you might consider adding soundproofing, an expense that you would prefer to share with Mr. Chomko and Mr. Vazquez. You might also discuss limiting the time of day that Mr. Chomko could make noise.

Your Task. Before responding to Mr. Vazquez, you decide to find out more about commercial tenancy. Use the Web to search the keywords *commercial eviction*. Then develop a course of action. In a letter to Mr. Vazquez, deny his request but retain his goodwill. Tell him how you plan to resolve the problem. Write to Michael Vazquez, CPA, Suite 230, Peachtree Business Plaza, 116 Krog Street, Atlanta, GA 30307. Your instructor may also ask you to write an appropriate message to Mr. Anthony Chomko, Suite 225.

9.15 Claim Denial: Refusing Refund for Japandroids and Bugskull Concert (Objs. 1–4)

As manager of Promotions and Advertising at Adventureland Park, you must respond to a recent letter. Avianna Jones complained that she was "taken" by Adventureland when the park had to substitute performers for the Japandroids and Bugskull Summertime Slam performance Sunday, July 4. Explain to her that the concert was planned by an independent promoter. Your only obligation was to provide the venue and advertising. Three days before the event, the promoter left town, taking with him all advance payments from financial backers. As it turned out, many of the artists he had promised to deliver were not even planning to attend.

Left with a messy situation, you decided on Thursday to go ahead with a modified version of the event because you had been advertising it and many would come expecting some kind of talent. At that time you changed your radio advertising to say that for reasons beyond your control, the Japandroids and Bugskull bands would not be appearing. You described the new talent and posted signs at the entrance and in the parking lot announcing the change. Contrary to Ms. Jones's claim, no newspaper advertising featuring Japandroids or Bugskull appeared on the day of the concert (at least you did not pay for any to appear that day). Somehow she must have missed your corrective radio advertising and signs at the entrance. You feel you made a genuine effort to communicate the changed program. In your opinion, most people who attended the concert thought that Adventureland had done everything possible to salvage a rather unfortunate situation.

Ms. Jones wants a cash refund of $160 (two tickets at $80 each). Adventureland has a no-money-back policy on concerts after the event takes place. If Ms. Jones had come to the box office before the event started, you could have returned her money. But she stayed to see the concert. She claims that she didn't know anything about the talent change until after the event was well underway. This sounds unlikely, but you don't quarrel with customers. Nevertheless, you can't give her cash back. You already took a loss on this event. But you can give two complimentary passes to Adventureland Park.

Your Task. Write a refusal letter to Ms. Avianna Jones, 2045 Live Oak Drive, Sacramento, CA 95841. Invite her and a friend to return as guests under happier circumstances.

9.16 Claim Denial: She Wants Reimbursement for Her Eyeglasses (Objs. 1–4)

American Southern Airline (ASA) had an unhappy customer. Annette Boyer-Parker flew from New York to Los Angeles. The flight stopped briefly at Chicago O'Hare, where she got off the plane for half an hour. When she returned to her seat, her $400 prescription reading glasses were gone. She asked the flight attendant where the glasses were, and the attendant said they probably were thrown away since the cleaning crew had come in with big bags and tossed everything in them. Ms. Tomlinson tried to locate the glasses through the airline's lost-and-found service, but she failed.

Then she wrote a strong letter to the airline demanding reimbursement for the loss. She felt that it was obvious that she was returning to her seat. The airline, however, knows that an overwhelming number of passengers arriving at hubs switch planes for their connecting flights. The airline does not know who is returning. What's more, flight attendants usually announce that the plane is continuing to another city and that passengers who are returning should take their belongings. Cabin cleaning crews speed through planes removing newspapers, magazines, leftover foods, and trash. Airlines feel no responsibility for personal items left in cabins.[30]

Your Task. As a staff member of the customer relations department of American Southern Airline, deny the customer's claim but retain her goodwill using techniques learned in this chapter. The airline never refunds cash, but it might consider travel vouchers for the value of the glasses. Remember that apologies cost nothing. Write a claim denial to Mrs. Annette Boyer-Parker, 3560 Veteran Avenue, Santa Monica, CA 90401.

9.17 Claim Denial: Sorry—Smokers Must Pay (Objs. 1–4)

Recently the Century Park Hotel embarked on a two-year plan to provide enhanced value and improved product quality to its guests. It always strives to exceed guest expectations. As part of this effort, Century Park has been refurbishing many rooms with updated finishes. The new carpet, paint, upholstery, and draperies, however, absorb the heavy odor of cigarette smoke. In order to protect the hotel's investment, Century Park enforces a strict nonsmoking policy for its nonsmoking rooms.

Century Park makes sure that guests know about its policy regarding smoking in nonsmoking rooms. It posts a notice in each nonsmoking room, and it gives guests a handout from the manager detailing its policy and the consequences for smoking in nonsmoking rooms. The handout clearly says, "Should a guest opt to disregard our nonsmoking policy, we will process a fee of $150 to the guest's account." For those guests who prefer to smoke, a smoking accommodation can be provided.

On May 10 Wilson M. Weber was a guest in the hotel. He stayed in a room clearly marked "Nonsmoking." After he left, the room cleaners reported that the room smelled of smoke. According to hotel policy, a charge of $150 was processed to Mr. Weber's credit card. Mr. Weber has written to demand that the $150 charge be removed. He doesn't deny that he smoked in the room. He just thinks that he should not have to pay.

Your Task. As hotel manager, deny Mr. Weber's claim. You would certainly like to see Mr. Weber return as a Century Park guest, but you cannot budge on your smoking policy. Address your response to Mr. Wilson M. Weber, 634 Wetmore Avenue, Everett, WA 98201.

9.18 Bad News to Customers: The StairClimber or the LifeStep? (Objs. 1–3, 5)

You are delighted to receive a large order from Greg Waller at New Bodies Gym. This order includes two Lifecycle Trainers (at $1,295 each), four Pro Abdominal Boards (at $295 each), three Tunturi Muscle Trainers (at $749 each), and three Dual-Action StairClimbers (at $1,545 each).

You could ship immediately except for one problem. The Dual-Action StairClimber is intended for home use, not for gym or club use. Customers like it because they say it is more like scaling a mountain than climbing a flight of stairs. With each step, users exercise their arms to pull or push themselves up. Its special cylinders absorb shock so that no harmful running impact results. However, this model is not what you would recommend for gym use. You feel Mr. Waller should order your premier stair climber, the LifeStep (at $2,395 each) This unit has sturdier construction and is meant for heavy use. Its sophisticated electronics provide a selection of customer-pleasing programs that challenge muscles progressively with a choice of workouts. It also quickly multiplies workout gains with computer-controlled interval training. Electronic monitors inform users of step height, calories burned, elapsed time, upcoming levels, and adherence to fitness goals. For gym use the LifeStep is clearly better than the StairClimber. The bad news is that the LifeStep is considerably more expensive.

You get no response when you try to telephone Mr. Waller to discuss the problem. Should you ship what you can, or hold the entire order until you learn whether he wants the StairClimber or the LifeStep? Or perhaps you should substitute the LifeStep and send only two of them.

Your Task. Decide what to do and write a letter to Greg Waller, New Bodies Gym, 3402 Copeland Drive, Athens, OH 45701.

9.19 Bad News to Customers: University Admission Message Erroneously Welcomes All Who Applied (Objs. 1–3, 5)

E-mail

The University of California, San Diego, recently made a big mistake. It inadvertently invited all applicants to the LaJolla campus to an orientation—even those who had been rejected. The message said, "We're thrilled that you've been admitted to UC San Diego, and we're showcasing our beautiful campus on Admit Day." That message was intended to be sent to about 18,000 students who had been accepted. Instead, it went to all 47,000 students who applied. Admissions Director Mae Brown quickly realized the mistake. "The minute the e-mails were sent out, we noted that it was sent to a much larger pool than was admitted. We immediately recognized the error," she said.

What could the university do to correct this massive slip-up? One applicant, who had already received a rejection from UCSD, said she was confused. Her mother said, "It is adding insult to injury for kids who have already been through the wringer." When asked if anyone had been disciplined for the mistake, Brown said that the university was undertaking a complete review of the process.[31]

Your Task. For Admissions Director Mae Brown, write an appropriate bad-news message to the students who received the message in error. Many applicants will be wondering what their real admission status is.

9.20 Bad News to Customers: Rate Increase of Your Choice (Objs. 1–3, 5)

Select a product or service that you now use. It could be your newspaper, Internet service provider, local water or electricity company, propane or natural gas supplier, cell or landline provider, car insurance company, or some other product or service you regularly use. Assume that the provider must raise its rates, and you are the employee who must notify customers. Should you use a letter, e-mail, company Web site, or blog? Decide whether you should use the direct or indirect strategy. Gather as much information as you can about the product or service. What, if anything, justifies the increase? What benefits can be cited?

Your Task. Prepare a rate increase announcement. Submit it along with a memo explaining your rationale for the strategy you chose.

9.21 Bad News to Customers: Your Credit Card Is Refused (Objs. 1–3, 5)

Travel writer Arlene Getz was mystified when the sales clerk at a Paris department store refused her credit card. "Sorry," the clerk said, "your credit card is not being accepted. I don't know why." Getz found out soon enough. Her bank had frozen her account because of an "unusual" spending pattern. The problem? "We've never had a charge from you in France before," a bank official told her. The bank didn't seem to remember that Getz had repeatedly used that card in cities ranging from Boston to Tokyo to Cape Town over the past six years, each time without incident.

Getz was a victim of neural-network technology, a tool that is intended to protect credit cardholders from thieves who steal cards and immediately run up huge purchases. This technology tracks spending patterns. If it detects anything unusual—such as a sudden splurge on easy-to-fence items like jewelry—it sets off an alarm. Robert Boxberger, senior vice president of fraud management at Fleet Credit Card Services, says that the system is "geared toward not declining any travel and entertainment expenses, like hotels, restaurants, or car rentals." But somehow it goofed and did not recognize that Arlene Getz was traveling, although she had used her card earlier to rent a car in Paris, a sure sign that she was traveling.

Getz was what the credit card industry calls a false positive—a legitimate cardholder inconvenienced by the hunt for fraudsters. What particularly riled her was finding out that 75 percent of the transactions caught in the neural network turn out to be legitimate. Yet the technology has been immensely successful for credit card companies. Since Visa started using the program, its fraud rate dropped from 15 cents to 6 cents per $100. To avoid inconveniencing cardholders, the company doesn't automatically suspend a card when it suspects fraud. Instead, it telephones the cardholder to verify purchases. Of course, cardholders who are traveling are impossible to reach.

Angry at the inconvenience and embarrassment she experienced, Getz sent a letter to Visa demanding an explanation in writing.

Your Task. As an assistant to the vice president in charge of fraud detection at Visa, you have been asked to draft a letter that can be used to respond to Arlene Getz as well as to other unhappy customers whose cards were wrongly refused by your software. You know that the program has been an overwhelming success. It can, however, inconvenience people, especially when they are traveling. You have heard your boss tell travelers that it is a good idea to touch base with the bank before leaving and take along the card's customer service number (1-800-553-0321). Write a letter that explains what happened, retains the goodwill of the customer, and suggests reader benefits. Address your letter to Ms. Arlene Getz, 68 Riverside Drive, Apt. 35, New York, NY 10025.

9.22 Damage Control for Disappointed Customers: J. Crew Goofs on Cashmere Turtleneck (Objs. 1–3, 5)

E-mail

Who wouldn't want a cashmere zip turtleneck sweater for $18? At the J. Crew Web site, many delighted shoppers scrambled to order the bargain cashmere. Unfortunately, the price should have been $218! Before

J. Crew officials could correct the mistake, several hundred e-shoppers had bagged the bargain sweater for their digital shopping carts.

When the mistake was discovered, J. Crew immediately sent an e-mail to the soon-to-be disappointed shoppers. The subject line shouted "Big Mistake!" Emily Woods, chairwoman of J. Crew, began her message with this statement: "I wish we could sell such an amazing sweater for only $18. Our price mistake on your new cashmere zip turtleneck probably went right by you, but rather than charge you such a large difference, I'm writing to alert you that this item has been removed from your recent order."

As an assistant in the communication department at J. Crew, you saw the e-mail that was sent to customers and you tactfully suggested that the bad news might have been broken differently. Your boss says, "OK, hot stuff. Give it your best shot."

Your Task. Although you have only a portion of the message, analyze the customer bad-news message sent by J. Crew. Using the principles suggested in this chapter, write an improved e-mail. In the end, J. Crew decided to allow customers who ordered the sweater at $18 to reorder it for $118.80 to $130.80, depending on the size. Customers were given a special Web site to go to, to reorder (make up an address). Remember that J. Crew customers are youthful and hip. Keep your message upbeat.[32]

9.23 Damage Control for Disappointed Customers: No Payroll Checks (Objs. 1–3, 5)

Team

Trenton Hughes, a printing company sales manager, must tell one of his clients that the payroll checks his company ordered are not going to be ready by the date Hughes had promised. The printing company's job scheduler overlooked the job and didn't get the checks into production in time to meet the deadline. As a result, Hughes' client, a major insurance company, is going to miss its pay run.

Hughes meets with internal department heads. They decide on the following plan to remedy the situation: (a) move the check order to the front of the production line; (b) make up for the late production date by shipping some of the checks—enough to meet their client's immediate payroll needs—by air freight; (c) deliver the remaining checks by truck.[33]

Your Task. Form groups of three to four students. Discuss the following issues about how to present the bad news to Jessica Dyhala, Hughes' contact person at the insurance company.

a. Should Hughes call Dyhala directly or delegate the task to his assistant?
b. When should Dyhala be informed of the problem?
c. What is the best procedure for delivering the bad news?
d. What follow-up would you recommend to Hughes?

Be prepared to share your group's responses during a class discussion. Your instructor may ask two students to role-play the presentation of the bad news.

9.24 Damage Control for Disappointed Customers: Worms in Her PowerBars! (Objs. 1–3, 5)

Web

In a recent trip to her local grocery store, Kelly Keeler decided for the first time to stock up on PowerBars. These are low-fat, high-carbohydrate energy bars that are touted as a highly nutritious snack food specially formulated to deliver long-lasting energy. Since 1986, PowerBar (**http://www.powerbar.com**) has been dedicated to helping athletes and active people achieve peak performance. It claims to be "the fuel of choice" for top athletes around the world. Kelly is a serious runner and participates in many track meets every year.

On her way to a recent meet, Kelly grabbed a PowerBar and unwrapped it while driving. As she started to take her first bite, she noticed something white and shiny in the corner of the wrapping. An unexpected protein source wriggled out of her energy bar—a worm! Kelly's first inclination was to toss it out the window and never buy another PowerBar. On second thought, though, she decided to tell the company. When she called the toll-free number on the wrapper, Sophie, who answered the phone, was incredibly nice, extremely apologetic, and very informative about what happened. "I'm very sorry you experienced an infested product," said Sophie.

She explained that the infamous Indian meal moth is a pantry pest that causes millions of dollars in damage worldwide. It feeds on grains or grain-based products, such as cereal, flour, dry pasta, crackers, dried fruits, nuts, spices, and pet food. The tiny moth eggs lie dormant for some time or hatch quickly into tiny larvae (worms) that penetrate food wrappers and enter products.

At its manufacturing facilities, PowerBar takes stringent measures to protect against infestation. It inspects incoming grains, supplies proper ventilation, and shields all grain-storage areas with screens to prevent insects from entering. It also uses light traps and electrocuters; these devices eradicate moths with the least environmental impact.

PowerBar President Brian Maxwell makes sure every complaint is followed up immediately with a personal letter. His letters generally tell customers that it is rare for infestations like this to occur. Entomologists say that the worms are not toxic and will not harm humans. Nevertheless, as President Maxwell says, "it is extremely disgusting to find these worms in food."

Your Task. For the signature of Brian Maxwell, PowerBar president, write a bad-news follow-up letter to Kelly Keeler, 932 Opperman Drive, Eagan, MN 55123. Keep the letter informal and personal. Explain how pests get into grain-based products and what you are doing to prevent infestation. You can learn more about the Indian meal moth by searching the Web. In your letter include a brochure titled "Notes About the Indian Meal Moth," along with a kit for Kelly to mail the culprit PowerBar to the company for analysis in Boise, Idaho. Also send a check reimbursing Kelly $26.85 for her purchase.[34]

9.25 Damage Control for Disappointed Customers: Costly SUV Upgrade to a Ford Excursion (Obj. 4)

Steven Chan, a consultant from Oakland, California, was surprised when he picked up his rental car from Budget in Seattle over Easter weekend. He had reserved a full-size car, but the rental agent told him he could upgrade to a Ford Excursion for an additional $25 a day. "She told me it was easy to drive," Mr. Chan reported. "But when I saw it, I realized it was huge—like a tank. You could fit a full-size bed inside."

On his trip Mr. Chan managed to scratch the paint and damage the rear-door step. He didn't worry, though, because he thought the damage would be covered since he had charged the rental on his American Express card. He knew that the company offered backup car rental insurance coverage. To his dismay, he discovered that its car rental coverage excluded large SUVs. "I just assumed they'd cover it," he confessed. He wrote to Budget to complain about not being warned that certain credit cards may not cover damage to large SUVs or luxury cars.

Budget agents always encourage renters to sign up for Budget's own "risk product." But they don't feel that it is their responsibility to study the policies of customers' insurance carriers and explain what may or may not be covered. Moreover, they try to move customers into their rental cars as quickly as possible and avoid lengthy discussions of insurance coverage. Customers who do not purchase insurance are at risk. Mr. Chan does not make any claim against Budget, but he is upset about being "pitched" to upgrade to the larger SUV, which he didn't really want.[35]

Your Task. As a member of the communication staff at Budget, respond to Mr. Chan's complaint. Budget obviously is not going to pay for the SUV repairs, but it does want to salvage his goodwill and future business. Offer him a coupon worth two days' free rental of any full-size sedan. Write to Steven Chan, 5300 Park Ridge, Apt. 4A, Oakland, CA 93578.

9.26 Credit Refusal: Paying Cash at Atlanta Athletic Club (Objs. 1–4)

As manager of the Atlanta Athletic Club, you must refuse the application of Cherie Liotta for an Extended Membership. This is strictly a business decision. You liked Cherie very much when she applied, and she seems genuinely interested in fitness and a healthful lifestyle. However, your Extended Membership plan qualifies the member for all your testing, exercise, recreation, yoga, and aerobics programs. This multiservice program is expensive for the club to maintain because of the large staff required. Applicants must have a solid credit rating to join. To your disappointment, you learned that Cherie's credit rating is decidedly negative. Her credit report indicates that she is delinquent in payments to four businesses, including Total Body Fitness Center, your principal competitor.

You do have other programs, including your Drop In and Work Out plan, which offers use of available facilities on a cash basis. This plan enables a member to reserve space on the racquetball and handball courts. The member can also sign up for yoga and exercise classes, space permitting. Since Cherie is far in debt, you would feel guilty allowing her to plunge in any more deeply.

Your Task. Refuse Cherie Liotta's credit application, but encourage her cash business. Suggest that she make an inquiry to the credit reporting company Experian to learn about her credit report. She is eligible to receive a free credit report if she mentions this application. Write to Cherie Liotta, 2015 Springdale Hills, Apt. 15, Sandy Springs, GA 30328.

9.27 Credit Refusal: Camcorders for Rudy's Camera Shop (Objs. 1–3, 5)

As a Uniworld Electronics sales manager, you are delighted to land a sizable order for your new Canon Vixia camcorder. This hot new camcorder features sleek lightweight design, brilliant optical quality, vibrant images, and outstanding image capture in low light conditions.

The purchase order comes from Rudy's Camera Shop, a retail distributor in Beaumont, Texas. You send the order on to Pamela Kahn, your credit manager, for approval of the credit application attached. To your disappointment, Pam tells you that Rudy's Camera doesn't qualify for credit. Experian Credit Services reports that extending credit to Rudy's would be risky for Uniworld.

Because you think you can be more effective in writing than on the telephone, you decide to write to Rudy's Camera with the bad news and offer an alternative. Suggest that Rudy's order a smaller number of the Canon camcorders. If it pays cash, it can receive a 2 percent discount. After Rudy's has sold these fast-moving camcorders, it can place another cash order through your toll-free order number. With your fast delivery system, its inventory will never be depleted. Rudy's can get the camcorders it wants now and can replace its inventory almost overnight. Credit Manager Kahn tells you that your company generally reveals to credit applicants the name of the credit reporting service it used and encourages them to investigate their credit record.

Your Task. Write a credit refusal to Ron Kasbekar, Rudy's Camera Shop, 3016 East Lucas Drive, Beaumont, TX 77657. Add any information needed.

9.28 Bad News to Employees: Company Games Are Not Date Nights (Objs. 1–3, 6)

E-mail

As director of Human Resources at Weyerman Paper Company, you received an unusual request. Several employees asked that their spouses or friends be allowed to participate in Weyerman intramural sports teams. Although the teams play only once a week during the season, these employees claim that they can't afford more time away from friends and family. Over 100 employees currently participate in the eight coed volleyball, softball, and tennis teams, which are open to company employees only. The teams were designed to improve employee friendships and to give employees a regular occasion to have fun together.

If nonemployees were to participate, you fear that employee interaction would be limited. Although some team members might have fun if spouses or friends were included, you are not so sure all employees would enjoy it. You are not interested in turning intramural sports into "date night." Furthermore, the company would have to create additional teams if many nonemployees joined, and you don't want the administrative or equipment costs of more teams. Adding teams also would require changes to team rosters and game schedules. This could create a problem for some employees. You do understand the need for social time with friends and families, but guests are welcome as spectators at all intramural games. Also, the company already sponsors a family holiday party and an annual company picnic.

Your Task. Write an e-mail or hard-copy memo to the staff denying the request of several employees to include nonemployees on Weyerman's intramural sports teams.

9.29 Bad News to Employees: We Can't Pay Your Tuition (Objs. 1–3, 6)

Team

Yasmin Qajar, a hardworking bank teller, has sent a request asking that the company create a program to reimburse the tuition and book expenses for employees taking college courses. Although some companies have such a program, Middleton Bank has not felt that it could indulge in such an expensive employee perk. Moreover, the CEO is not convinced that companies see any direct benefit from such programs. Employees improve their educational credentials and skills, but what is to keep them from moving that education and those skill sets to other employers? Middleton Bank has over 200 employees. If even a fraction of them started classes, the company could see a huge bill for the cost of tuition and books. Because the bank is facing stiff competition and its profits are sinking, the expense of such a program is out of the question. In addition, it would involve administration—applications, monitoring, and record keeping. It is just too much of a hassle. When employees were hard to hire and retain, companies had to offer employment perks. But with a soft economy, such inducements are unnecessary.

Your Task. As director of Human Resources, send an individual response to Yasmin Qajar. The answer is a definite no, but you want to soften the blow and retain the loyalty of this conscientious employee.

9.30 Negative News in Other Cultures (Obj. 7)

Your Task. Interview fellow students or work colleagues who are from other cultures. How is negative news handled in their cultures? How would typical individuals refuse a request for a favor, for example? How would a business refuse credit to customers? How would an individual be turned down for a job? Is directness practiced? Report your findings to the class.

Video Resource

Video Library 2, Bad News: BuyCostumes

This video features BuyCostumes, the world's largest online costume and accessories retailer. After watching the video, play the part of a customer service representative.

BuyCostumes is proud of its extensive stock of costumes, its liberal return policy, and its many satisfied customers. But one day a letter arrived with a request that went beyond the company's ability to deliver. The customer said that he had ordered the Gorilla Blinky Eye With Chest costume. This popular gorilla costume comes with a unique gorilla mask, attractive suit with rubber chest, foot covers, and hands. The customer complained that the gorilla costume did not arrive until two days after his Halloween party. He planned an elaborate party with a gorilla theme, and he was extremely unhappy that he did not have his costume. He asks BuyCostumes to reimburse $300 that he spent on theme-related decorations, which he says were useless when he failed to receive his costume.

As a customer service representative, you checked his order and found that it was not received until five days before Halloween, the busiest time of the year for your company. The order was filled the next day, but standard shipping requires three to six business days for delivery. The customer did not order express or premium delivery; his shipping option was marked "Standard."

You showed the letter to the owner, Mr. Getz, who said that this request was ludicrous. However, he wanted to retain the customer's goodwill. Obviously, BuyCostumes was not going to shell out $300 for late delivery of a costume. But Mr. Getz suggested that the company would allow the customer to return the costume (in its original packaging). In addition, BuyCostumes would send a coupon for $20 off on the next costume purchase.

Your Task. Mr. Getz asks you to write a letter that retains the goodwill of this customer. Address your bad-news letter to Mr. Christopher King, 3579 Elm Street, Buffalo, NY 14202. Check the company Web site (**http://www.buycostumes.com**) for more information.

Chat About It

In each chapter you will find five discussion questions related to the chapter material. Your instructor may assign these topics for you to discuss in class, in an online chat room, or on an online discussion board. Some of the discussion topics may require outside research. You may also be asked to read and respond to postings made by your classmates.

Topic 1: Describe a time when a company delivered negative news to you effectively; that is, you understood and accepted the news. Explain why the company's strategy was effective.

Topic 2: Many people say they prefer the direct approach when receiving bad news. What situational factors might cause you to use the indirect approach with these people?

Topic 3: Create an effective buffer that you might use if you were a professor who had to tell a student expecting to earn an A that the student actually earned a C instead.

Topic 4: A flyer at a city bus stop announced a fare increase with the title *Rate Changes*. Was this title effective? If not, what title might have worked better?

Topic 5: You are an executive at a company that suddenly has to lay off 400 employees within three days or risk financial disaster. You have to make the cuts quickly, but you don't want to be impersonal by announcing the cuts by e-mail. How would you announce the bad news?

Grammar and Mechanics C.L.U.E. Review 9

Confusing Words and Frequently Misspelled Words

Review the lists of confusing words and frequently misspelled words in Appendix A, Grammar and Mechanics Guide, beginning on page A-1. On a separate sheet, revise the following sentences to correct word usage errors. Sentences may have more than one error. If a sentence is correct, write *C*. When you finish, check your answers on page Key-1.

Example: Have you allready sent the reccomendation?
Revision: Have you **already** sent the **recommendation?**

1. Included in her bad-news message was a complement and valuable advise.
2. His principle reason for declining the invitation was his busy calander.
3. In her damage-control message, the manager made a conscience effort to regain the customer's confidence.
4. In your every day business affairs, you must show patients even when irritated.
5. Before you procede with the report, please check those embarassing statistics.
6. Although we will look into this matter farther, I am not suprised at your report.
7. The judge declared that the comments of there attorneys were irrevelant to the case at hand.
8. Because the property was to difficult to apprise, its value was unrecorded.
9. Meredith hoped to illicit advice from her counselor, but she was disapointed.
10. The manager reccommended that we switch to an annual maintinance schedule.

Are you ready? Get more practice at **www.meguffey.com**

CHAPTER 10

Persuasive and Sales Messages

OBJECTIVES

After studying this chapter, you should be able to

1. Define the concept of persuasion, identify effective and ineffective persuasive techniques, and apply the 3-x-3 writing process to persuasive messages.
2. Explain the four major elements in successful persuasive messages and how to blend those elements into effective and ethical business messages.
3. Write persuasive messages that request favors and actions, make claims, and deliver complaints.
4. Write persuasive messages within organizations.
5. Write effective and ethical direct-mail and e-mail sales messages.
6. Compare effective persuasion techniques in high- and low-context cultures.
7. Understand basic patterns and techniques in developing persuasive press releases.

Want to do well on tests and excel in your course?
Go to **www.meguffey.com** for helpful interactive resources.

- **Review the Chapter 10 PowerPoint slides to prepare for the first quiz.**

Zooming In

PART 1

Hands on Miami

"We make a living by what we get, but we make a life by what we give," said Winston Churchill. To the people at Hands on Miami, this is a creed to live by.

"For me, it is about trying to make a difference in my community," said Pat Morris, former CEO of Hands on Miami, a volunteer organization dedicated to making Miami a better place to live. "Giving to others," said Morris, "often comes back to you many, many times."[1]

Morris helped found Hands on Miami (HOM) to create a user-friendly approach to community service. HOM's new method involves making it easy for volunteers to participate regardless of their hectic schedules. Projects take place outside traditional work hours, and flexible time commitments permit volunteers to serve once a week, once a month, or whenever they can.

Hands on Miami partners with schools, social service organizations, and environmental organizations to offer more than 80 service opportunities each month. This gives thousands of Miamians the chance to make a difference in their community. Volunteers can spend a morning delivering care packages to AIDS patients in a local hospital, an afternoon planting native vegetation to restore natural beauty and ecosystems, or an evening reading bedtime stories to children at an emergency shelter. What's distinctive about HOM's program is that it makes community service accessible to anyone regardless of schedule. Because volunteerism is essential to enriching a community's well-being, most HOM projects are team based and take place in the evenings and on weekends, making it easy for busy people to give back to the community. HOM's hallmark flexible volunteering program has been a resounding success.

In addition to organizing volunteers, HOM acts as a consultant on a fee-for-service basis to design volunteer opportunities to meet a company's particular needs. Carnival Cruise Lines and other local companies often use the expertise of HOM in planning their own volunteer programs. Corporate donors provide further assistance by sponsoring big events such as Hands on Miami Day.

As CEO, Pat Morris used persuasion to keep his staff energized, motivated, and organized. He had to be persuasive in reaching out to corporate donors to persuade them to send volunteers to participate in Hands on Miami programs. He also had to sway corporations to sponsor events with cash contributions. Persuasion is a large part of the leadership role at Hands on Miami, as well as in every organization.[2] You will learn more about Hands on Miami on page 303.

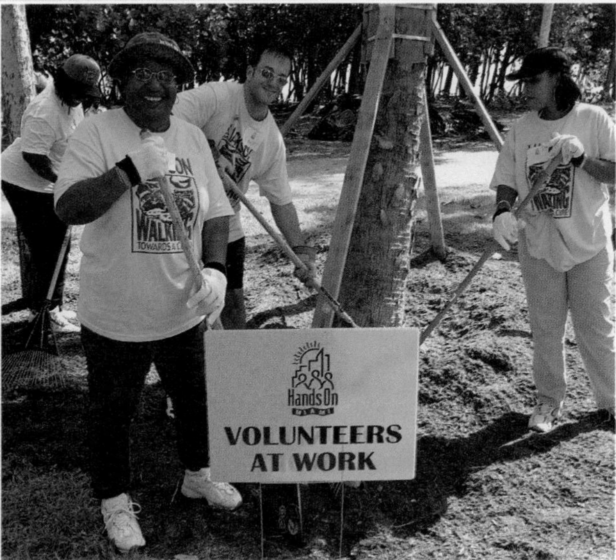

© Jeff Greenberg/PhotoEdit

Critical Thinking

- Persuasion is vital to the CEO at Hands on Miami. Who must the CEO effectively persuade to ensure the success of the organization?
- In your own career, when might you find it necessary to be persuasive?
- From your experience, what techniques are effective or ineffective in persuading others to accept your views?

http://www.handsonmiami.org

Understanding Persuasion and How to Use It Effectively and Ethically

LEARNING OBJECTIVE 1

Define the concept of persuasion, identify effective and ineffective persuasive techniques, and apply the 3-x-3 writing process to persuasive messages.

Convincing others that your point of view is the right one is a critical business communication skill. At Hands on Miami, CEO Pat Morris had to be persuasive in all aspects of his job—in convincing his staff about the importance of their tasks, in winning over corporate sponsors, and in swaying volunteers to support community projects. For all businesspeople, persuasion is a critical skill. However, many of us do it poorly or unconsciously.[3] You have already studied techniques for writing routine request messages that required subtle forms of persuasion. This chapter focuses on messages that require deliberate and skilled persuasion. You will learn what persuasion is and how to apply it effectively when you write requests for favors and actions, make claims, and prepare sales messages. This is one of the most important chapters in the book because much of your success in business depends on how skilled you are at persuading people to believe, accept, and act on what you are saying.

What Is Persuasion?

Persuasion is defined as the ability to use argument or discussion to influence an individual's beliefs or actions. Parents use persuasion to cajole their kids into doing their homework. A team member uses persuasion to convince her technology-averse manager that instant messaging is an excellent tool to keep all team members informed about a project. You might want to persuade your boss to allow you to work at home part of the time. In Figure 10.1 Charmaine Williams, general manager of Oak Park Town Center, uses persuasion in a memo to the mall owner and president. She wants to convince him to restrict the access of unchaperoned teenagers on weekends and evenings.

Some people think that persuasion involves coercion or trickery. They think that you can achieve what you seek only if you twist an arm or deceive someone. Such negative tactics are ineffective and unethical. What's more, these tactics don't truly represent persuasion. To persuade is to present information enabling others to see the benefits of what you are offering, without browbeating or tricking them into agreement.

Successful persuasion depends largely on the reasonableness of your request, your credibility, and your ability to make the request attractive to the receiver. Many techniques can help you be effective in getting your ideas accepted by your fellow workers, superiors, and clients.

What techniques can make your persuasive arguments more effective?

Effective Persuasion Techniques

When you want your ideas to prevail, spend some time thinking about how to present them. Listeners and readers will be more inclined to accept what you are offering if you focus on the following important strategies, which are outlined here and further discussed with illustrations throughout the chapter.

- **Establish credibility.** To be persuasive, you must engender trust. People must believe that you are telling the truth, are experienced, and know what you are talking about. Most of us would not be swayed if a soccer or film star told us how to ease world tensions. If you lack credentials or experience, use testimonials, expert opinion, and research to support your position.

- **Make a reasonable, precise request.** Persuasion is most effective if your request is realistic, doable, and attainable. Don't ask for $100,000 worth of equipment when your department's budget is $5,000. Also, be clear about your objective. In one research study, students posed as beggars and asked for money. If they asked for an unspecified amount, they received money 44 percent of the time. If they asked for a precise sum (say, $1), they received money 64 percent of the time.[4] Precise requests are more effective than vague ones.

In one of the most unusual marketing campaigns of recent memory, Domino's Pizza sided with critics who said that its pies were little more than cardboard and ketchup. A pizza franchising wonder during the 1980s, Domino's has lost market share to rival chains and become the target of bad-food jokes, especially for ranking alongside Chuck E. Cheese in taste surveys. Instead of hiding the pizza's reputation for blandness, marketers endorsed the company's harshest consumer feedback and commissioned expert chefs to perform a complete makeover the product. *What makes the Domino's "pizza turnaround" campaign persuasive?*

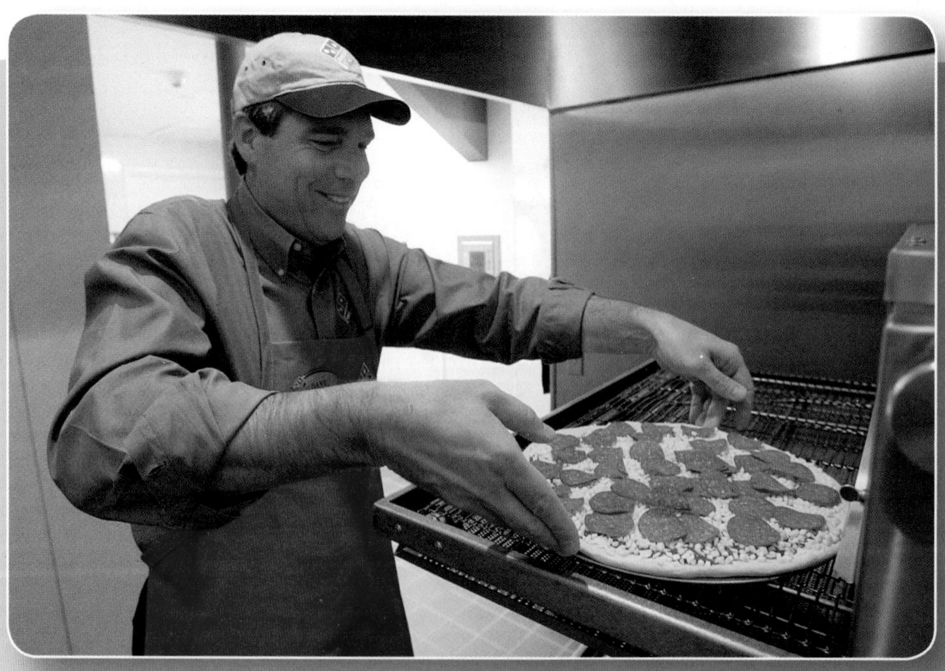

- **Tie facts to benefits.** Line up solid information to support your view. Use statistics, printed resources, examples, and analogies to help people understand. Remember, however, that information alone rarely changes attitudes. Marketers have pumped huge sums into failed advertising and public relations campaigns that provided facts alone. More important is converting those facts into benefits for the audience, as Charmaine did in Figure 10.1.
- **Recognize the power of loss.** Describing the benefits of your proposal is a powerful motivator. Another powerful motivator is the thought of what the other person will lose if he or she doesn't agree. The threat of losing something one already possesses—such as time, money, competitive advantage, profits, reputation—seems to be more likely to motivate people than the idea of gaining that very same thing.[5]
- **Expect and overcome resistance.** When proposing ideas, be prepared for resistance. This may arise in the form of conflicting beliefs, negative attitudes, apathy, skepticism, and opposing loyalties. Recognize any weakness in your proposal and be prepared to counter with well-reasoned arguments and facts. In Figure 10.1 Charmaine realized that

FIGURE 10.1 **Persuasive Action Request**

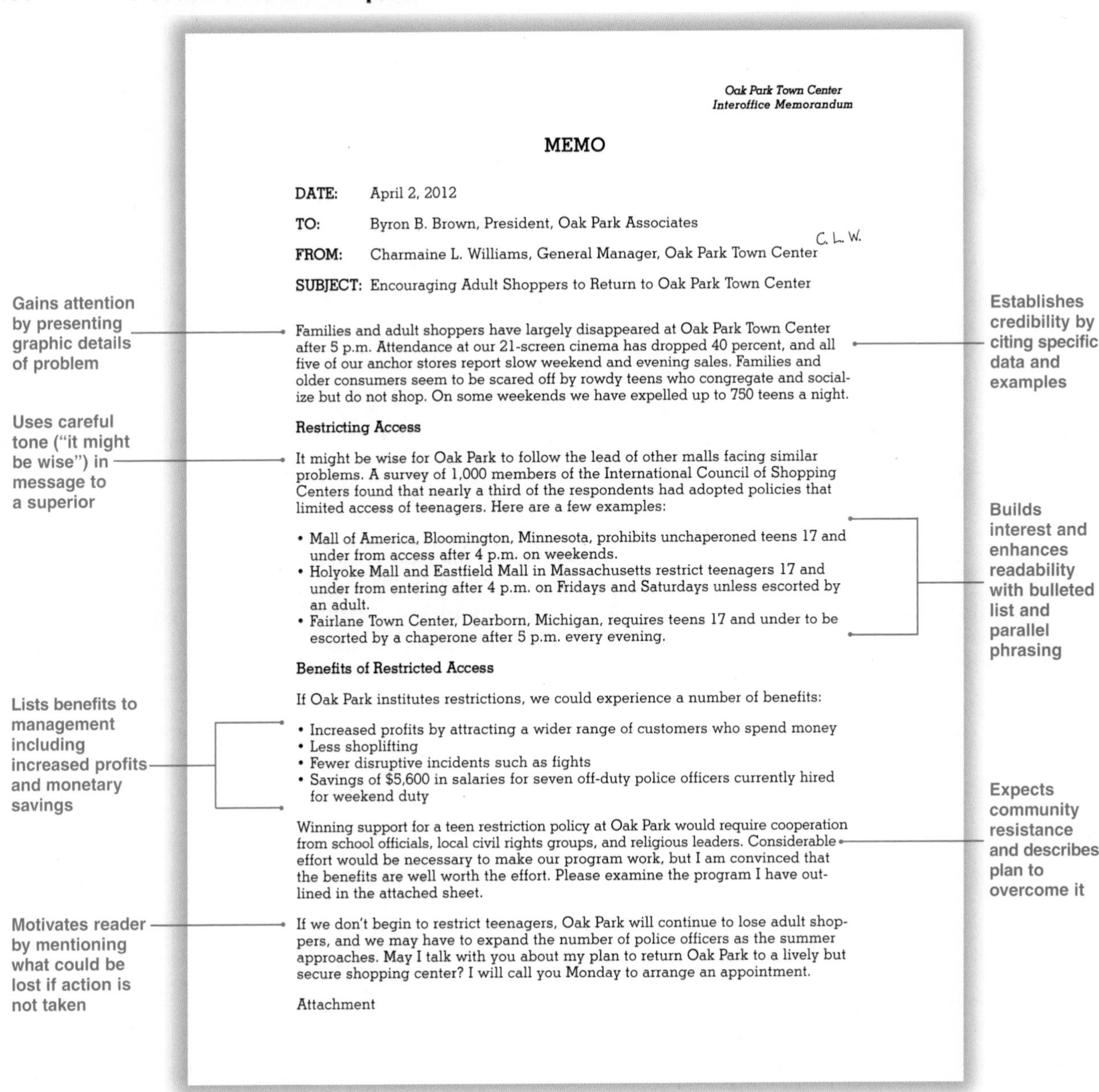
Oak Park Town Center
Interoffice Memorandum

MEMO

DATE: April 2, 2012

TO: Byron B. Brown, President, Oak Park Associates

FROM: Charmaine L. Williams, General Manager, Oak Park Town Center C. L. W.

SUBJECT: Encouraging Adult Shoppers to Return to Oak Park Town Center

Families and adult shoppers have largely disappeared at Oak Park Town Center after 5 p.m. Attendance at our 21-screen cinema has dropped 40 percent, and all five of our anchor stores report slow weekend and evening sales. Families and older consumers seem to be scared off by rowdy teens who congregate and socialize but do not shop. On some weekends we have expelled up to 750 teens a night.

Restricting Access

It might be wise for Oak Park to follow the lead of other malls facing similar problems. A survey of 1,000 members of the International Council of Shopping Centers found that nearly a third of the respondents had adopted policies that limited access of teenagers. Here are a few examples:

- Mall of America, Bloomington, Minnesota, prohibits unchaperoned teens 17 and under from access after 4 p.m. on weekends.
- Holyoke Mall and Eastfield Mall in Massachusetts restrict teenagers 17 and under from entering after 4 p.m. on Fridays and Saturdays unless escorted by an adult.
- Fairlane Town Center, Dearborn, Michigan, requires teens 17 and under to be escorted by a chaperone after 5 p.m. every evening.

Benefits of Restricted Access

If Oak Park institutes restrictions, we could experience a number of benefits:

- Increased profits by attracting a wider range of customers who spend money
- Less shoplifting
- Fewer disruptive incidents such as fights
- Savings of $5,600 in salaries for seven off-duty police officers currently hired for weekend duty

Winning support for a teen restriction policy at Oak Park would require cooperation from school officials, local civil rights groups, and religious leaders. Considerable effort would be necessary to make our program work, but I am convinced that the benefits are well worth the effort. Please examine the program I have outlined in the attached sheet.

If we don't begin to restrict teenagers, Oak Park will continue to lose adult shoppers, and we may have to expand the number of police officers as the summer approaches. May I talk with you about my plan to return Oak Park to a lively but secure shopping center? I will call you Monday to arrange an appointment.

Attachment

Gains attention by presenting graphic details of problem
Establishes credibility by citing specific data and examples
Uses careful tone ("it might be wise") in message to a superior
Builds interest and enhances readability with bulleted list and parallel phrasing
Lists benefits to management including increased profits and monetary savings
Expects community resistance and describes plan to overcome it
Motivates reader by mentioning what could be lost if action is not taken

her proposal to restrict the access of unchaperoned teenagers would require acceptance and cooperation from community groups.

- **Share solutions and compromise.** The process of persuasion may involve being flexible and working out a solution that is acceptable to all concerned. Sharing a solution requires listening to people and developing a new position that incorporates their input. When others' views become part of a solution, they gain a sense of ownership; they buy in and are more eager to implement the solution.

The Importance of Tone

How can the tone of a persuasive argument be improved?

Tone is particularly important in persuasion today because the workplace has changed. Gone are the days when managers could simply demand compliance. Today's managers and team leaders strive to generate cooperation and buy-in instead of using intimidation, threats, and punishment to gain compliance.[6] Team members no longer accept command-and-control, top-down, unquestioned authority.[7] How can persuaders improve the tone of their requests?

- **Avoid sounding preachy or parental.** People don't want to be lectured or instructed in a demeaning manner. No one likes to be treated like a child.
- **Don't pull rank.** Effective persuasion doesn't result from status or authority. People want to be recognized as individuals of worth. Pulling rank may secure compliance but not buy-in.
- **Avoid making threats.** People may comply when threatened, but their compliance may disappear over time. For example, many drivers follow the speed limit only when a patrol car is near. Threats also may result in retaliation, reduced productivity, and low morale.
- **Soften your words when persuading upward.** When you must persuade someone who has more clout than you, use words such as *suggest* and *recommend*. Craft sentences that begin with *It might be a good idea to*. . . . Make suggestions without threatening authority.
- **Be enthusiastic, positive, and likable.** Convey your passion for an idea through your body language, voice, and words. When you enthusiastically request something to be done, people feel more confident that they can do it. Use sincere compliments and praise. Describe what a positive impact others have had. Offer to reciprocate, if you are asking a favor.

Applying the 3-x-3 Writing Process to Persuasive Messages

Persuasion means changing people's views, and that's often a difficult task. Pulling it off demands planning and perception. The 3-x-3 writing process provides you with a helpful structure for laying a foundation for persuasion. Of particular importance here are (a) analyzing the purpose, (b) adapting to the audience, (c) collecting information, and (d) organizing the message.

Why is it important to analyze your purpose before preparing a persuasive message?

Analyzing the Purpose: Knowing What You Want to Achieve. The purpose of a persuasive message is to convert the receiver to your ideas or to motivate action. A message without a clear purpose is doomed. Not only must you know what your purpose is and what response you want, but you must know these things when you start writing your message or planning a presentation. Too often, inexperienced writers reach the end of the first draft of a message before discovering exactly what they want the receiver to do. Then they must start over, giving the request a different spin or emphasis. Because your purpose establishes the strategy of the message, determine it first.

Let's say you must convince Rachel, your department manager, that you could be more productive if you could work from home. Before approaching Rachel, know exactly what you want. How much time do you want to work at home? Full time? Part time? On special projects? Do you want Rachel to merely talk about it with you? Do you want her to set a time when you could start? Should you suggest a trial period? By identifying your purpose up front, you can shape the message to point toward it. This planning effort saves considerable rewriting time and produces the most successful persuasive messages.

Adapting to the Audience by Finding Ways to Make Your Message Heard. While you are considering the purpose of a persuasive message, you also need to concentrate on the receiver. How can you adapt your request to that individual so that your message is heard? Zorba the Greek wisely observed, "You can knock forever on a deaf man's door." A persuasive message is equally futile unless it meets the needs of its audience. In a broad sense, you will be seeking to show how your request helps the receiver achieve some of life's major goals or fulfills key needs: money, power, comfort, confidence, importance, friends, peace of mind, and recognition, to name a few.

On a more practical level, you want to show how your request solves a problem, achieves a personal or work objective, or just makes life easier for your audience. In your request for a flexible work schedule, you could appeal to Rachel's expressed concern for increasing productivity. Your goal is to make the boss look good by granting your request. To adapt your request to the receiver, consider these questions that receivers will very likely be asking themselves:

Why should I?
What's in it for me?
What's in it for you?
Who cares?

Spotlight on Communicators

Kraft Foods CEO Irene Rosenfeld can be very persuasive. Early in her career with Kraft, she convinced her bosses that Kool-Aid should be marketed at kids (not mothers) and that Jell-O could be modernized with new flavors. In Canada she was persuasive in turning around Kraft's troubled business. "When she is trying to persuade you of something, she will be relentless in coming back with facts and showing you she has the support of other people," said a former Kraft executive. With a PhD in marketing and statistics, Rosenfeld conducts meticulous research. In building interest and reducing resistance, "she will be totally emotionally and intellectually committed to her idea."

Adapting to your audience means being ready to answer these questions. It means learning about audience members and analyzing why they might resist your proposal. It means searching for ways to connect your purpose with their needs. If completed before you begin writing, such analysis goes a long way toward overcoming resistance and achieving your goal.

Researching and Organizing Persuasive Data. Once you have analyzed the audience and considered how to adapt your message to its needs, you are ready to collect data and organize it. You might brainstorm and prepare cluster diagrams to provide a rough outline of ideas. For your request for a flexible work schedule, you might gather information describing how other comparable companies have developed telecommuting programs and how effective they are. You could work out a possible schedule outlining when you would be working at home and when you would be in the office for meetings and face-to-face discussions. You are certain you could complete more work at home, but how can you prove it in your request? To overcome resistance, you might describe your work-at-home office, equipment, and procedures. You could also explain your plan for staying in touch with and being responsive to inquiries and requests.

The next step in a persuasive message is organizing your data into a logical sequence. If you are asking for something that you know will be approved, little persuasion is required. Thus, you would make a direct request, as you studied in Chapter 8. But when you expect resistance or when you need to educate the receiver, the indirect strategy often works better. The following four-part indirect strategy works well for many persuasive requests:

1. Gain attention
2. Build interest
3. Reduce resistance
4. Motivate action

Blending Four Major Elements in Successful Persuasive Messages

LEARNING OBJECTIVE 2
Explain the four major elements in successful persuasive messages and how to blend those elements into effective and ethical business messages.

Although the indirect strategy appears to contain separate steps, successful persuasive messages actually blend the four steps into a seamless whole. Also, the sequence of the elements may change depending on the situation and the emphasis. Regardless of where they are placed, the key elements in persuasive requests are (a) gaining your audience's attention, (b) building interest by convincing your audience that your proposal is worthy, (c) reducing resistance, and (d) motivating action.

How can you gain attention in a persuasive message?

Gaining Attention in Persuasive Messages

To grab attention, the opening statement in a persuasive request should be brief, relevant, and engaging. When only mild persuasion is necessary, the opener can be low-key and factual. If, however, your request is substantial and you anticipate strong resistance, provide a thoughtful, provocative opening. Following are some examples.

- **Problem description.** In a recommendation to hire temporary employees: *Last month legal division staff members were forced to work 120 overtime hours, costing us $6,000 and causing considerable employee unhappiness.* With this opener you have presented a capsule of the problem your proposal will help solve.
- **Unexpected statement.** In a memo to encourage employees to attend an optional sensitivity seminar: *Men and women draw the line at decidedly different places in identifying what behavior constitutes sexual harassment.* Note how this opener gets readers thinking immediately.
- **Reader benefit.** In a letter promoting Clear Card, a service that helps employees make credit card purchases without paying interest: *The average employee carries nearly $13,000 in revolving debt and pays $2,800 in interest and late fees. The Clear Card charges zero percent interest. You can't beat it!* Employers immediately see this offer as a benefit it can offer employees.
- **Compliment.** In a letter inviting a business executive to speak: *Because our members admire your success and value your managerial expertise, they want you to be our speaker.* In offering praise or compliments, however, be careful to avoid obvious flattery.
- **Related facts.** In a message to company executives who are considering restricting cell phone use by employee drivers: *A recent study revealed that employers pay an average of $16,500 each time an employee is in a traffic accident.* This relevant fact sets the scene for the interest-building section that follows.
- **Stimulating question.** In a plea for funds to support environmental causes: *What do golden tortoise beetles, bark spiders, flounders, and Arctic foxes have in common?* Readers will be curious to find the answer to this intriguing question. [They all change color depending on their surroundings.]

What techniques help you build interest in a persuasive message?

Building Interest in Persuasive Messages

After capturing attention, a persuasive request must retain that attention and convince the audience that the request is reasonable. To justify your request, be prepared to invest in a few paragraphs of explanation. Persuasive requests are likely to be longer than direct requests because the audience must be convinced rather than simply instructed. You can build interest and conviction through the use of the following:

- Facts, statistics
- Expert opinion
- Direct benefits
- Examples
- Specific details
- Indirect benefits

Showing how your request can benefit the audience directly or indirectly is a key factor in persuasion. If you were asking alumni to contribute money to a college foundation, for example, you might promote *direct benefits* such as listing the donor's name in the college magazine or sending a sweatshirt with the college logo. Another direct benefit is a tax write-off for the contribution. An *indirect benefit* might be feeling good about helping the college and knowing that students will benefit from the gift. Nearly all charities rely in large part on indirect benefits to promote their causes.

How can you reduce resistance in persuasive requests?

Reducing Resistance in Persuasive Requests

One of the biggest mistakes in persuasive requests is the failure to anticipate and offset audience resistance. How will the receiver object to your request? In brainstorming for clues, try *What if?* scenarios. Let's say you are trying to convince management that the employees' cafeteria should switch from paper and plastic plates and cups to ceramic. What if managers say the change is too expensive? What if they argue that they are careful recyclers of paper and plastic? What if they contend that ceramic dishes would increase cafeteria labor and energy costs tremendously? What if they protest that ceramic is less hygienic? For each of these *What if?* scenarios, you need a counterargument.

Unless you anticipate resistance, you give the receiver an easy opportunity to dismiss your request. Countering this resistance is important, but you must do it with finesse *(Although ceramic dishes cost more at first, they actually save money over time)*. You can minimize objections by presenting your counterarguments in sentences that emphasize benefits: *Ceramic dishes may require a little more effort in cleaning, but they bring warmth and graciousness to meals. Most important, they help save the environment by requiring fewer resources and eliminating waste.* However, don't spend too much time on counterarguments, thus making them overly important. Finally, avoid bringing up objections that may never have occurred to the receiver in the first place.

Another factor that reduces resistance is credibility. Receivers are less resistant if your request is reasonable and if you are believable. When the receiver does not know you, you may have to establish your expertise, refer to your credentials, or demonstrate your competence. Even when you are known, you may have to establish your knowledge in a given area. If you are asking your manager for a new laptop computer, you might have to establish your credibility by showing your manager articles about the latest laptops. You could point out that a laptop would enable you to work away from the office while staying in touch by e-mail. Some charities establish their credibility by displaying on their stationery the names of famous people who serve on their boards. The credibility of speakers making presentations is usually outlined by someone who introduces them.

Motivating Action in Persuasive Messages

How can you motivate action in the closing of a persuasive message?

After gaining attention, building interest, and reducing resistance, you will want to inspire the receiver to act. This is where your planning pays dividends. Knowing exactly what action you favor before you start to write enables you to point your arguments toward this important final paragraph. Here you will make your recommendation as specifically and confidently as possible—without seeming pushy. A proposal from one manager to another might conclude with, *So that we can begin using the employment assessment tests by May 1, please send a return e-mail immediately.* In making a request, don't sound apologetic *(I'm sorry to have to ask you this, but . . .)*, and don't supply excuses *(If you can spare the time, . . .)*. Compare the following closings for a persuasive memo recommending training seminars in communication skills.

Too General

We are certain we can develop a series of training sessions that will improve the communication skills of your employees.

Too Timid

If you agree that our training proposal has merit, perhaps we could begin the series in June.

Too Pushy

Because we are convinced that you will want to begin improving the skills of your employees immediately, we have scheduled your series to begin in June.

Effective

You will see decided improvement in the communication skills of your employees. Please call me at 439-2201 by May 1 to give your approval so that training sessions may start in June, as we discussed.

Note how the last opening suggests a specific and easy-to-follow action. It also provides a deadline and a reason for that date. Figure 10.2 summarizes a four-part plan for overcoming resistance and crafting successful persuasive messages.

Being Persuasive and Ethical

What techniques do unethical persuaders use?

Business communicators may be tempted to make their persuasion even more forceful by fudging on the facts, exaggerating a point, omitting something crucial, or providing deceptive emphasis. Consider the case of a manager who sought to persuade employees to accept a

FIGURE 10.2 **Four-Part Plan for Persuasive Messages**

Gaining Attention	Building Interest	Reducing Resistance	Motivating Action
Summary of problem	Facts, figures	Anticipate objections	Describe specific request
Unexpected statement	Expert opinion	Offer counterarguments	Sound confident
Reader benefit	Examples	Employ *What if?* scenarios	Make action easy to take
Compliment	Specific details	Establish credibility	Offer incentive
Related fact	Direct benefits	Demonstrate competence	Don't provide excuses
Stimulating question	Indirect benefits	Show value of proposal	Repeat main benefit

change in insurance benefits. His memo emphasized a small perk (easier handling of claims) but de-emphasized a major reduction in total coverage. Some readers missed the main point—as the manager intended. Others recognized the deception, however, and before long the manager's credibility was lost. A persuader is effective only when he or she is believable. If receivers suspect that they are being manipulated or misled or if they find any part of the argument untruthful, the total argument fails. Persuaders can also fall into traps of logic without even being aware of it. Take a look at the accompanying Ethical Insights box to learn about common logical fallacies that you will want to avoid.

Persuasion becomes unethical when facts are distorted, overlooked, or manipulated with an intent to deceive. Of course, persuaders naturally want to put forth their strongest case. But that argument must be based on truth, objectivity, and fairness.

In prompting ethical and truthful persuasion, two factors act as powerful motivators. The first is the desire to preserve your reputation and credibility. Once lost, a good name or reputation is difficult to regain. An equally important force prompting ethical behavior, though, is your opinion of yourself. Glen Senk, president of the retailer Anthropologie, tells a story of a supersaleswoman at his store. She vastly outsold her colleagues on virtually every shift she worked. Senk went to her store one day to watch and realized that the saleswoman would push anything on customers. It didn't matter whether items matched or the clothes looked good. She was fired. "Our customers are our friends," explained Senk. "It's never about the quick sale."[8] Senk was more concerned with preserving the store's reputation and his own self-image than making money.

ETHICAL INSIGHT

What's Fair in Persuasion? Avoiding Common Logical Fallacies

While being persuasive, we must be careful to remain ethical. In our eagerness to win others over to our views, we may inadvertently overstep the bounds of fair play. Philosophers through the years have pinpointed a number of logical fallacies. Here are three you will want to avoid in your persuasive messages.

- **Circular reasoning.** When the support given for a contention merely restates the contention, the reasoning is circular. For example, *Investing in the stock market is dangerous for short-term investors because it is unsafe.* The evidence (*because it is unsafe*) offers no proof. It merely circles back to the original contention. Revision: *Investing in the stock market is dangerous for short-term investors because stock prices fluctuate widely.*
- **Begging the question.** A statement such as *That dishonest CEO should be replaced* begs the question. Merely asserting that the CEO is dishonest is not enough. Be sure to supply solid evidence for such assertions. Revision: *That CEO is dishonest because he awards contracts only to his friends. A good manager would require open bidding.*
- **Post hoc (*after, thus, because*).** Although two events may have happened in immediate sequence, the first did not necessarily cause the second. For example, *The company switched to team-based management, and its stock price rose immediately afterward.* Switching to teams probably had no effect on the stock price. Revision: *At about the same time the company switched to team-based management, its stock price began to rise, although the two events are probably unrelated.*

Career Application

In teams or in a class discussion, cite examples of how these fallacies could be used in persuasive messages or sales letters. Provide a logical, ethical revision for each.

Zooming In PART 2

Hands on Miami

Being good corporate citizens ranks high with many businesses today, and Hands on Miami helps them do just that. Its Corporate Services Program assists businesses in developing community service projects. More and more business organizations today realize that their commitment to social responsibility provides many advantages. In a Points of Light Foundation poll, 90 percent of companies surveyed believed their employer-sponsored community service programs enhanced their public image, boosted employee morale and job satisfaction, helped recruit and retain quality employees, and built better work teams.

Volunteerism gives corporations an edge. Many corporations, however, do not have the staff resources or expertise to develop and manage corporate volunteer efforts. That's where Hands on Miami's Corporate Services program comes in. Its fee-based consulting services can survey employees about their volunteer interests, develop employee volunteer programs, and design and lead corporate volunteer days. It can also facilitate long-term employee volunteering, train and educate employee volunteers, and track employee volunteer hours.

Hands on Miami helped organize and now serves as advisor to Carnival Cruise Lines' employee volunteer program, the F.U.N. Team (Friends Uniting Neighbors). Their ongoing volunteer activities not only support the community but also improve company pride, teamwork, and leadership skills.

Hands on Miami knows that its Corporate Services program can help organizations develop successful employee volunteer initiatives that fit their business climate, employees' interests, and community goals. The problem is persuading more corporations to do it.

© Jeff Greenberg/PhotoEdit

Critical Thinking

- Do you agree that corporations derive benefits from sponsoring volunteer programs and encouraging employees to participate?
- The CEO of Hands on Miami must write a letter persuading Miami corporations to use its fee-based Corporate Services program. What direct benefits could be cited?
- What indirect benefits could the CEO cite in a persuasive letter?

Requesting Favors and Actions, Making Claims, and Delivering Complaints

LEARNING OBJECTIVE 3
Write persuasive messages that request favors and actions, make claims, and deliver complaints.

Many of your persuasive messages will be requests for favors or actions. For example, you may ask a businessperson to make a presentation to your club. You might ask a company to encourage its employees to participate in a charity drive. Another form of persuasion involves claims or complaints. All of these messages require skill in persuasion. Convincing someone to change a belief or to perform an action when that person is reluctant requires planning and skill—and sometimes a little luck. A written, rather than face-to-face, request may require more preparation but can be more effective. Persuasion is often more precise and controlled when you can think through your purpose and prepare a thoughtful message in writing. The indirect strategy gives you an effective structure.

Preparing Persuasive Requests for Favors and Actions

Why are individuals and companies willing to grant requests for time, money, information, cooperation, and special privileges?

Persuading someone to do something that largely benefits you may not be the easiest task. Fortunately, many individuals and companies are willing to grant requests for time, money, information, cooperation, and special privileges. They grant these favors for a variety of reasons. They may just happen to be interested in your project, or they may see goodwill potential for themselves. Professionals sometimes feel obligated to contribute their time or expertise to "pay their dues." Often, though, businesses and individuals comply because they see that others will benefit from the request.

Figure 10.3 shows a persuasive favor request from Michelle Moreno. Her research firm seeks to persuade other companies to complete a questionnaire revealing salary data. To most organizations, salary information is strictly confidential. What can she do to convince strangers to part with such private information?

FIGURE 10.3 Persuasive Favor Request

1 Prewriting

Analyze: The purpose of this letter is to persuade the reader to complete and return a questionnaire.

Anticipate: Although the reader is busy, he may respond to appeals to his professionalism and to his need for salary data in his own business.

Adapt: Because the reader may be uninterested at first and require persuasion, use the indirect strategy.

2 Writing

Research: Study the receiver's business and find ways to relate this request to company success.

Organize: Gain attention by opening with relevant questions. Build interest by showing how the reader's compliance will help his company and others. Reduce resistance by promising confidentiality and offering free data.

Compose: Prepare a first draft with the intention to revise.

3 Revising

Revise: Revise to show direct and indirect benefits more clearly. Make sure the message is as concise as possible.

Proofread: In the first sentence, spell out *percent* rather than using the symbol. Check the use of all question marks. Start all lines at the left for a block-style letter.

Evaluate: Will this letter convince the reader to complete and return the questionnaire?

ITHACA RESEARCH INSTITUTE
430 Seneca Street, Ithaca, NY 14850 www.ithacaresearch.com
PH 570.888.2300
FAX 570.888.4359

May 17, 2012

Mr. Trevor M. Mansker
All-Star Financial Advisors
240 Lomb Memorial Drive
Rochester, NY 14623

Dear Mr. Mansker:

Have you ever added a unique job title but had no idea what compensation the position demanded? Has your company ever lost a valued employee to another organization that offered 20 percent more in salary for the same position?

To remain competitive in hiring and to retain qualified workers, companies rely on survey data showing current salaries. Ithaca Research Institute has been collecting business data for a quarter century and has been honored by the American Management Association for its accurate data. We need your help in collecting salary data for today's workers. Information from the enclosed questionnaire will supply companies like yours with such data.

Your information, of course, will be treated confidentially. The questionnaire takes but a few moments to complete, and it can provide substantial dividends for professional organizations that need comparative salary data.

To show our gratitude for your participation, we will send you comprehensive salary surveys for your industry and your metropolitan area. Not only will you find basic salaries, but you will also learn about bonus and incentive plans, special pay differentials, expense reimbursements, and perquisites such as a company car and credit card.

Comparative salary data are impossible to provide without the support of professionals like you. Please complete the questionnaire and return it in the prepaid envelope before June 1, our spring deadline. Participating in this survey means that you will no longer be in the dark about how much your employees earn compared with others in your industry.

Sincerely yours,

ITHACA RESEARCH INSTITUTE

Michelle Moreno

Michelle Moreno
Director, Survey Research

Enclosures

Margin annotations:

- Poses two short questions related to the reader — Gains attention
- Presents reader benefit tied to request explanation; establishes credibility — Builds interest
- Anticipates and counters resistance to confidentiality and time/effort objections — Reduces resistance
- Offers free salary data as a direct benefit
- Appeals to professionalism, an indirect benefit
- Provides deadline and a final benefit to prompt action — Motivates action

To gain attention, she begins her persuasive favor request by posing two short questions that spotlight the need for salary information. To build interest and establish trust, she mentions that Ithaca Research Institute has been collecting business data for a quarter century and has received awards from the American Management Association. Developing credibility is especially important when persuading strangers to do something. Making a reasonable request tied to benefits is also important. Michelle does this by emphasizing the need for current salary information.

To reduce resistance, Michelle promises confidentiality and explains that the questionnaire takes but a few moments to complete. She offers free salary data as a direct benefit. This data may help the receiver learn how its salary scale compares with others in its industry. But Michelle doesn't count on this offer as the only motivator. As an indirect benefit, she appeals to the professionalism of the receiver. She's hoping that the receiver will recognize the value of providing salary data to the entire profession. To motivate action, Michelle closes with a deadline and reminds the reader that her company need not be in the dark about comparative salaries within its industry.

This favor request incorporates many of the techniques that are effective in persuasion: establishing credibility, making a reasonable and precise request, tying facts to benefits, and overcoming resistance.

Writing Persuasive Claims

Persuasive claims typically involve damaged products, mistaken billing, inaccurate shipments, warranty problems, limited return policies, insurance snafus, faulty merchandise, and so on. Generally, the direct strategy is best for requesting straightforward adjustments (see Chapter 8). When you feel your request is justified and will be granted, the direct strategy is most efficient. But if a past request has been refused or ignored or if you anticipate reluctance, then the indirect strategy is appropriate.

When making a claim or delivering a complaint, when is the direct strategy appropriate? When is the indirect strategy appropriate?

Developing a Logical Persuasive Argument. Strive for logical development in a claim letter. You might open with sincere praise, an objective statement of the problem, a point of agreement, or a quick review of what you have done to resolve the problem. Then you can explain precisely what happened or why your claim is legitimate. Don't provide a blow-by-blow chronology of details; just hit the highlights. Be sure to enclose copies of relevant invoices, shipping orders, warranties, and payments. Close with a clear statement of what you want done: a refund, replacement, credit to your account, or other action. Be sure to think through the possibilities and make your request reasonable.

Using a Moderate Tone. The tone of your message is important. Don't suggest that the receiver intentionally deceived you or intentionally created the problem. Rather, appeal to the receiver's sense of responsibility and pride in the company's good name. Calmly express your disappointment in view of your high expectations of the product and of the company. Communicating your feelings without rancor is often your strongest appeal.

Ethics Check

Complaint Bullying

As any salesperson will tell you, some customers seem to believe that if they vent their anger and make a scene at the store, bullying and intimidating a fearful sales representative, they are more likely to get their way. Indeed, some sales staff may cave in, wishing to defuse the ruckus. Is it fair to resort to such tactics to get what one wants? Does the end justify the means?

Composing Effective Complaints

As their name suggests, complaints deliver bad news. Some complaint messages just vent anger. However, if the goal is to change something (and why bother to write except to motivate change?), then persuasion is necessary. Effective claim messages make a reasonable and valid request, present a logical case with clear facts, and adopt a moderate tone. Anger and emotion are not effective persuaders.

Martine Romaniack's letter, shown in Figure 10.4, follows the persuasive pattern as she seeks credit for two VoIP (voice over Internet protocol) systems. Actually, she was quite upset because her company was counting on these new Internet systems to reduce its phone bills. Instead, the handsets produced so much static that incoming and outgoing calls were all but impossible to hear. What's more, she was frustrated that the Return Merchandise Authorization form she filled out at the company's Web site seemed to sink into a dark hole in cyberspace. She had reason to be angry! But she resolved to use a moderate tone in writing her complaint letter.

Why are anger and emotion poor persuaders?

Notice that her tone is objective, rational, and unemotional. She begins with a compliment and explains why her company needs a VoIP system. She provides identifying data and justifies her claim by explaining that installation instructions were carefully followed. Claim messages are particularly effective when writers express their personal disappointment and feelings. Martine explains her strong disappointment in view of the promotional statement assuring a clear signal. She would like to have been more forceful, but she knew that a calm, unemotional tone would be more effective. She wondered whether she should say that she was really ticked off that she had spent hours researching the product. The new system took additional hours to install and troubleshoot. After all that work, she couldn't use it because of the static. Nevertheless, she stuck to the plan of using a positive opening, a well-documented claim, and a request for specific action in the closing.

FIGURE 10.4 Claim (Complaint) Letter

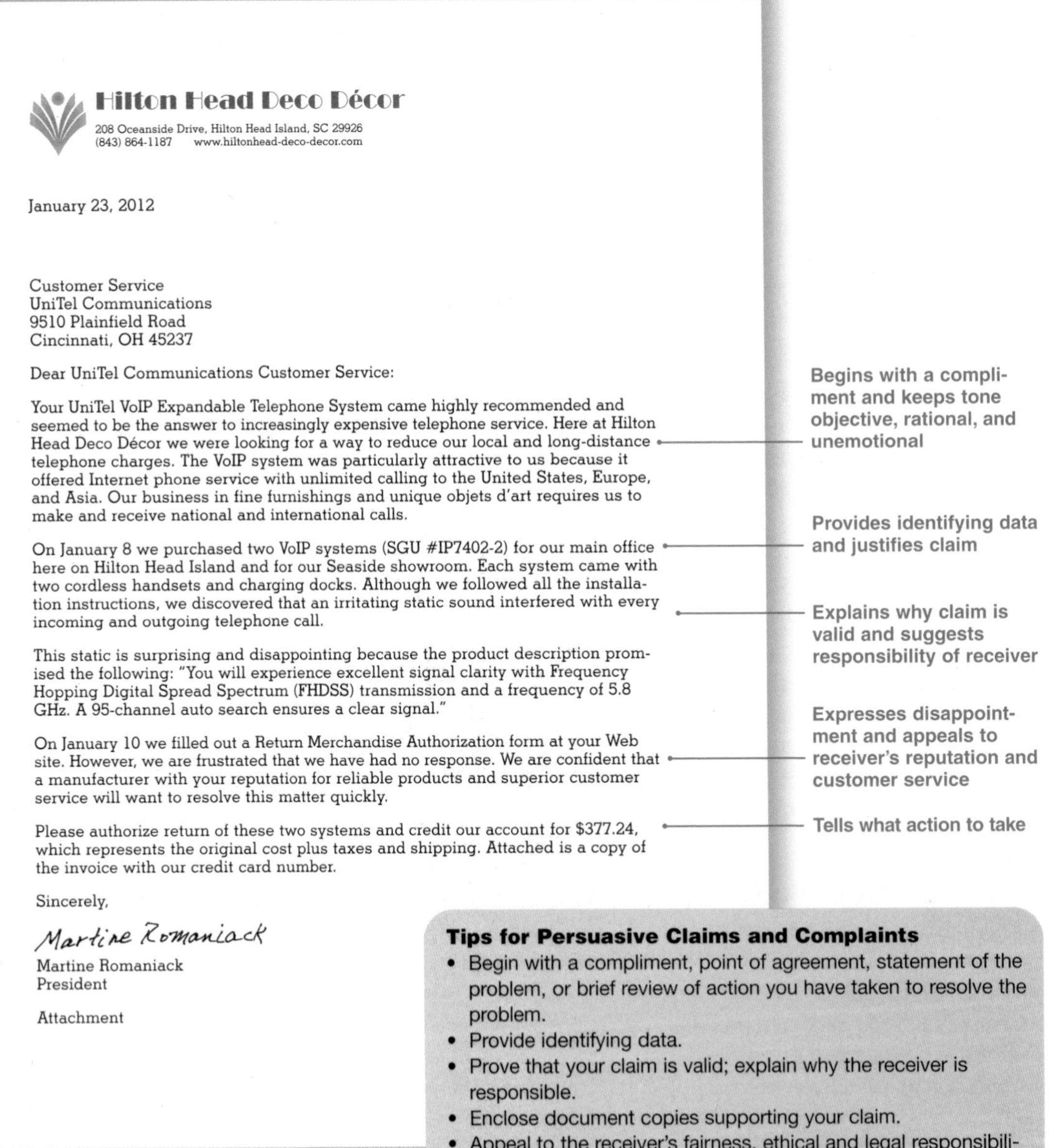

Hilton Head Deco Décor
208 Oceanside Drive, Hilton Head Island, SC 29926
(843) 864-1187 www.hiltonhead-deco-decor.com

January 23, 2012

Customer Service
UniTel Communications
9510 Plainfield Road
Cincinnati, OH 45237

Dear UniTel Communications Customer Service:

Your UniTel VoIP Expandable Telephone System came highly recommended and seemed to be the answer to increasingly expensive telephone service. Here at Hilton Head Deco Décor we were looking for a way to reduce our local and long-distance telephone charges. The VoIP system was particularly attractive to us because it offered Internet phone service with unlimited calling to the United States, Europe, and Asia. Our business in fine furnishings and unique objets d'art requires us to make and receive national and international calls.

On January 8 we purchased two VoIP systems (SGU #IP7402-2) for our main office here on Hilton Head Island and for our Seaside showroom. Each system came with two cordless handsets and charging docks. Although we followed all the installation instructions, we discovered that an irritating static sound interfered with every incoming and outgoing telephone call.

This static is surprising and disappointing because the product description promised the following: "You will experience excellent signal clarity with Frequency Hopping Digital Spread Spectrum (FHDSS) transmission and a frequency of 5.8 GHz. A 95-channel auto search ensures a clear signal."

On January 10 we filled out a Return Merchandise Authorization form at your Web site. However, we are frustrated that we have had no response. We are confident that a manufacturer with your reputation for reliable products and superior customer service will want to resolve this matter quickly.

Please authorize return of these two systems and credit our account for $377.24, which represents the original cost plus taxes and shipping. Attached is a copy of the invoice with our credit card number.

Sincerely,

Martine Romaniack

Martine Romaniack
President

Attachment

Begins with a compliment and keeps tone objective, rational, and unemotional
Provides identifying data and justifies claim
Explains why claim is valid and suggests responsibility of receiver
Expresses disappointment and appeals to receiver's reputation and customer service
Tells what action to take

Tips for Persuasive Claims and Complaints

- Begin with a compliment, point of agreement, statement of the problem, or brief review of action you have taken to resolve the problem.
- Provide identifying data.
- Prove that your claim is valid; explain why the receiver is responsible.
- Enclose document copies supporting your claim.
- Appeal to the receiver's fairness, ethical and legal responsibilities, and desire for customer satisfaction.
- Describe your feelings and disappointment.
- Avoid sounding angry, emotional, or irrational.
- Close by telling exactly what you want done.

Checklist

Requesting Favors and Actions, Making Claims, Delivering Complaints

Prewrite

- Determine your purpose. Know exactly what you are requesting.
- Anticipate the reaction of your audience. Remember that the receiver is thinking *Why should I? What's in it for me? What's in it for you? Who cares?*

Gain Attention

- Use the indirect strategy rather than blurting out the request immediately.
- Begin with a problem description, unexpected statement, compliment, praise, related facts, stimulating question, or reader benefit to grab attention.

Build Interest

- Develop interest by using facts, statistics, examples, testimonials, and specific details.
- Establish your credibility, if necessary, by explaining your background and expertise. Use testimonials, expert opinion, or research if necessary.
- Support your request by tying facts to direct benefits (increased profits, more efficient operations, better customer relations, saving money, a returned favor) or indirect benefits (improving the community, giving back to the profession, helping the environment).
- In claims and complaints, be objective but prove the validity of your request.

Reduce Resistance

- Anticipate objections to your request and provide counterarguments.
- Suggest what might be lost if the request is not granted, but don't make it sound like a threat.
- In claims and complaints, use a moderate, unemotional tone.

Motivate Action

- Make a precise request that spells out exactly what you want done. Add a deadline date if necessary.
- Repeat a benefit, provide additional details, or offer an incentive. Express appreciation.

Writing Persuasive Messages Within Organizations

LEARNING OBJECTIVE 4
Write persuasive messages within organizations.

As discussed in Chapter 1, messages within organizations move in one of three ways: downward, upward, or horizontally. The strategies and tone employed in these messages depend on the organizational position of the sender and that of the receiver. Let's say you want to persuade your boss to handle orders differently on the company's Web site. Your message would follow the indirect strategy. But the tone and content of your message would be different from that of the boss sending a similar persuasive message on the same topic. In this section we focus on messages flowing downward and upward within organizations. Horizontal messages traveling between coworkers are similar to those discussed earlier in requesting favors and actions.

Persuading Employees: Messages Flowing Downward

Why do messages flowing downward require attention to tone?

Instructions or directives moving downward from superiors to subordinates usually require little persuasion. Employees expect to be directed in how to perform their jobs. These messages (such as information about procedures, equipment, or customer service) use the direct strategy, with the purpose immediately stated. However, employees are sometimes asked to volunteer for projects. For example, some organizations ask employees to join programs to stop smoking, lose weight, or start exercising. Organizations may ask employees to participate in capacities outside their work roles—such as spending their free time volunteering for charity projects. In such cases, the four-part indirect strategy provides a helpful structure.

Messages flowing downward require attention to tone. Warm words and a conversational tone convey a caring attitude. Persuasive requests coming from a trusted superior are more likely to be accepted than requests from a dictatorial executive who relies on threats and punishments to secure compliance. As mentioned earlier, the proverbial carrot has always been more persuasive than the stick. Managers should avoid sounding preachy or parental.

Employees don't want to be treated as children. Because the words *should* and *must* sometimes convey a negative tone, be careful in using them.

Figure 10.5 shows a memo from Jessica Jeffers, director of Human Resources at a large bank. Her goal is to persuade employees to participate in Hands on Miami Day, a fund-raising and community service event that her bank sponsors. In addition to volunteering their services for a day, employees also have to pay $20 to register! You can see that this will be no small persuasion task for Jessica.

Jessica decides to follow the four-part indirect strategy beginning with gaining attention. Notice that she strives to capture attention by describing specific benefits of volunteering in Miami. She explains ways that volunteers make Miami a better place to live and work. Feeding the homeless, providing companionship to the elderly, building low-income housing, restoring the natural environment—all these examples of selfless giving not only gain attention but also suggest indirect benefits to the reader.

The second paragraph of this persuasive message builds interest by listing examples of what volunteers have accomplished during previous Hands on Miami events. Volunteers can

FIGURE 10.5 Persuasive Organizational Message Flowing Downward

MEMO

DATE: June 10, 2012

TO: All First Federal Staff Members

FROM: Jessica M. Jeffers, Human Resources J.M.J.

SUBJECT: Serving Our Community and Having Fun at Hands on Miami Day, November 5

Every day in Miami volunteers make our community a better place to live and work. They feed the homeless, provide companionship to the elderly, build low-income housing, restore the natural environment, tutor at-risk children, read to children in shelters, participate in hurricane recovery efforts, and even care for homeless pets! These and other volunteer opportunities will be available during Hands on Miami Day, a fund-raising event that we at First Federal endorse with immense pride.

Captures attention by describing indirect benefits of volunteering in Miami

Gains attention

In partnership with United Way of Miami-Dade County and with Carnival Cruise Lines, we at First Federal are joining in this day of change for our community. You can be part of the change as 6,000 hands come together to paint, plant, create murals, and clean neighborhoods and beaches. Last year a First Federal team landscaped and repainted the Miami Beach boardwalk during Hands on Miami Day. Afterwards, a survey showed that 86 percent of the volunteers thought the experience was worthwhile and that their efforts made a difference.

Develops interest with examples and survey results

Builds interest

To participate, each volunteer pays a registration fee of $20. You may wonder why you should pay to volunteer. Hands on Miami Day is the agency's only fund-raising event, and it supports year-round free services and programs for the entire Miami-Dade community. For your $20, you receive breakfast and an event T-shirt. Best of all, you share in making your community a better place to live and work.

Reduces resistance by emphasizing both direct and indirect benefits

Reduces resistance

To provide the best registration process possible, we are excited to work with TeamFootWorks, which has extensive experience managing registration for large-scale community events. Just go to http://www.TeamFootWorks.com and request a registration form before October 20.

Makes it easy to comply with request

You can make a huge difference to your community by volunteering for Hands on Miami Day, November 5. Join the fun and your First Federal colleagues in showing Miami that we value volunteerism that achieves community goals. For every employee who volunteers before October 20, First Federal will contribute $20 to United Way. Sign up now and name the team members you will work with.

Prompts action by providing deadline and incentive

Motivates action

expect to join 6,000 other "hands" who paint, plant, create murals, and clean neighborhoods and beaches. To build further interest, the letter includes the results of a survey showing that a vast majority of volunteers thought the experience was worthwhile and that their efforts made a difference. People are more inclined to agree to do something if they know that others have done it in the past and found it beneficial.

To reduce resistance, the third paragraph explains why the $20 fee makes sense. Jessica skillfully combines both direct benefits (free breakfast and an event T-shirt) with indirect benefits (sharing in making the community a better place to live and work).

Why are audience benefits important in persuasive messages?

Good persuasive requests close by making it easy to comply and by finding some way to motivate action. In complying with the request in this message, all the reader has to do is go to a Web site and request a registration form. To motivate action in the closing, Jessica saved a strong indirect benefit. The bank will chip in $20 for every employee who volunteers before the deadline. Readers can see that their participation reaches beyond their individual contribution. Although readers don't benefit directly from the company's contribution to United Way, they can see that others will benefit. This significant indirect benefit along with the direct benefits of having fun and joining colleagues in a community activity combine for a strong persuasive message.

Persuading the Boss: Messages Flowing Upward

Why is saving money important in selling ideas to management?

Another form of persuasion within organizations centers on suggestions made by subordinates. Convincing management to adopt a procedure or invest in a product or new equipment requires skillful communication. Managers are just as resistant to change as others are. Providing evidence is critical when subordinates submit recommendations to their bosses. Be ready to back up your request with facts, figures, and evidence. When selling an idea to management, strive to make a strong dollars-and-cents case.[9] A request that emphasizes how the proposal saves money or benefits the business is more persuasive than one that simply announces a good deal or tells how a plan works.

In describing an idea to your boss, state it confidently and fairly. Don't undermine your suggestions with statements such as *This may sound crazy* or *I know we tried this once before but*. . . . Show that you have thought through the suggestion by describing the risks involved as well as the potential benefits. You may wonder whether you should even mention the downside of a suggestion. Most bosses will be relieved and impressed to know that you have considered the risks as well as the benefits to a proposal.[10] Two-sided arguments are generally more persuasive because they make you sound credible and fair. Presenting only one side of a proposal reduces its effectiveness because such a proposal seems biased, subjective, and flawed. You can make a stronger argument by acknowledging and neutralizing opposing points of view.

Persuasive messages traveling upward require a special sensitivity to tone. When asking superiors to change views or take action, use words such as *suggest* and *recommend* rather than *you must* and *we should*. Avoid sounding pushy or argumentative. Strive for a conversational, yet professional, tone that conveys warmth, competence, and confidence.

When Marketing Manager Monique Hartung wanted her boss to authorize the purchase of a multifunction color laser copier, she knew she had to be persuasive. Her memo, shown in Figure 10.6, illustrates an effective approach. First, she researched prices, features, and the maintenance of color laser copiers. These machines often serve as copiers, faxes, scanners, and printers and can cost several thousand dollars. Monique found an outstanding deal offered by a local office supplier. Because she knew that her boss, Samuel Neesen, favored "cold, hard facts," she listed current monthly costs for copying at Copy Quick to increase her chances of gaining approval. Finally, she calculated the amortization of the purchase price and monthly costs of running the new color copier.

Are persuasive messages that are developed indirectly longer or shorter than those developed directly? Why?

Notice that Monique's memo isn't short. A successful persuasive message will typically take more space than a direct message because proving a case requires evidence. In the end, Monique chose to send her memo as an e-mail attachment accompanied by a polite short e-mail because she wanted to keep the document format in MS Word intact. She also felt that the message was too long to paste into her e-mail program. Monique's persuasive memo and her e-mail include subject lines that announce the purpose of the message without disclosing the actual request. By delaying the request until she has had a chance to describe the problem and discuss a solution, Monique prevented the reader's premature rejection.

FIGURE 10.6 Persuasive E-Mail and Memo Flowing Upward

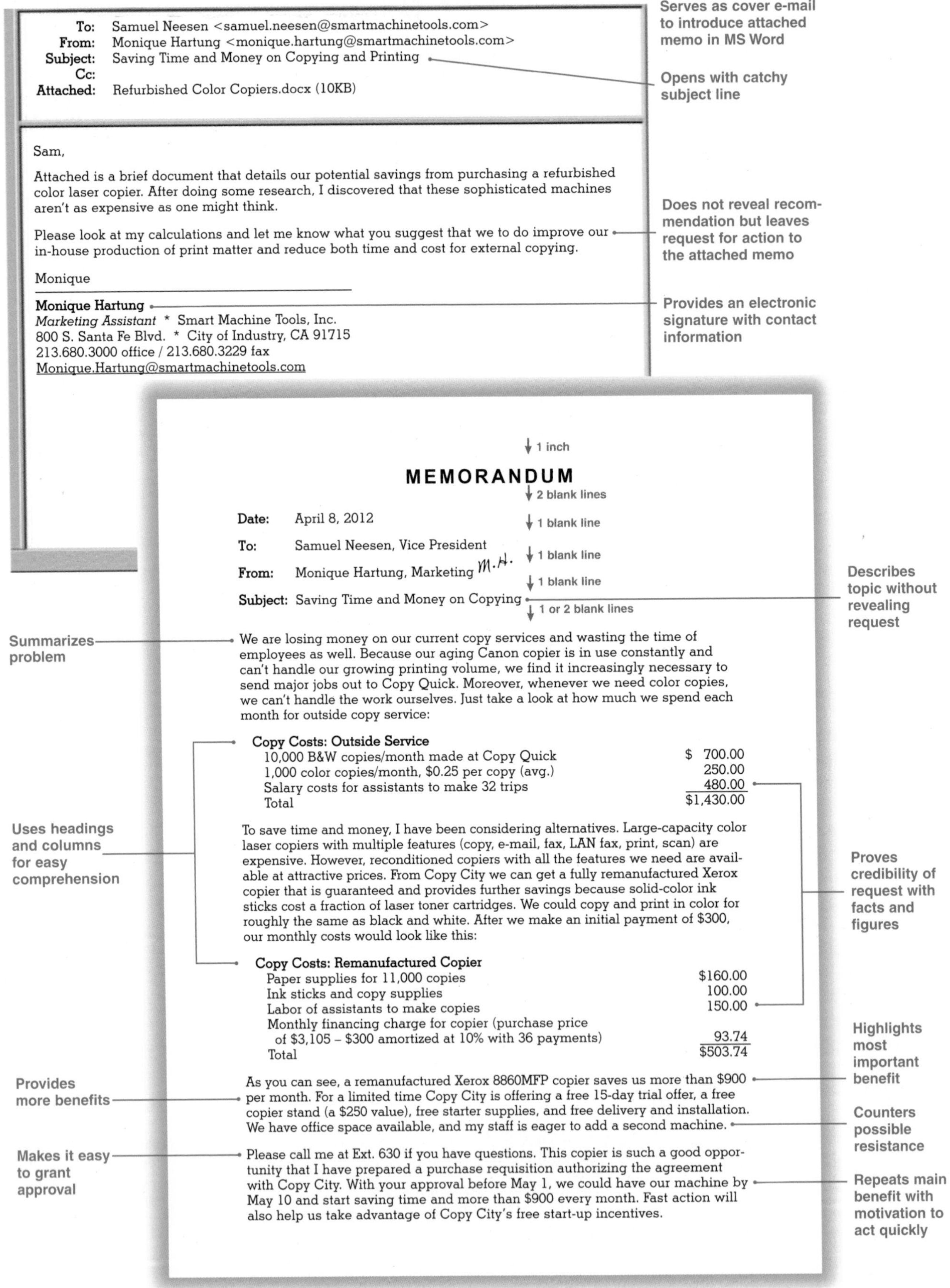
To: Samuel Neesen <samuel.neesen@smartmachinetools.com>
From: Monique Hartung <monique.hartung@smartmachinetools.com>
Subject: Saving Time and Money on Copying and Printing
Cc:
Attached: Refurbished Color Copiers.docx (10KB)

Sam,

Attached is a brief document that details our potential savings from purchasing a refurbished color laser copier. After doing some research, I discovered that these sophisticated machines aren't as expensive as one might think.

Please look at my calculations and let me know what you suggest that we to do improve our in-house production of print matter and reduce both time and cost for external copying.

Monique

Monique Hartung
Marketing Assistant * Smart Machine Tools, Inc.
800 S. Santa Fe Blvd. * City of Industry, CA 91715
213.680.3000 office / 213.680.3229 fax
Monique.Hartung@smartmachinetools.com

MEMORANDUM

Date: April 8, 2012

To: Samuel Neesen, Vice President

From: Monique Hartung, Marketing M.H.

Subject: Saving Time and Money on Copying

We are losing money on our current copy services and wasting the time of employees as well. Because our aging Canon copier is in use constantly and can't handle our growing printing volume, we find it increasingly necessary to send major jobs out to Copy Quick. Moreover, whenever we need color copies, we can't handle the work ourselves. Just take a look at how much we spend each month for outside copy service:

Copy Costs: Outside Service	
10,000 B&W copies/month made at Copy Quick	$ 700.00
1,000 color copies/month, $0.25 per copy (avg.)	250.00
Salary costs for assistants to make 32 trips	480.00
Total	$1,430.00

To save time and money, I have been considering alternatives. Large-capacity color laser copiers with multiple features (copy, e-mail, fax, LAN fax, print, scan) are expensive. However, reconditioned copiers with all the features we need are available at attractive prices. From Copy City we can get a fully remanufactured Xerox copier that is guaranteed and provides further savings because solid-color ink sticks cost a fraction of laser toner cartridges. We could copy and print in color for roughly the same as black and white. After we make an initial payment of $300, our monthly costs would look like this:

Copy Costs: Remanufactured Copier	
Paper supplies for 11,000 copies	$160.00
Ink sticks and copy supplies	100.00
Labor of assistants to make copies	150.00
Monthly financing charge for copier (purchase price of $3,105 – $300 amortized at 10% with 36 payments)	93.74
Total	$503.74

As you can see, a remanufactured Xerox 8860MFP copier saves us more than $900 per month. For a limited time Copy City is offering a free 15-day trial offer, a free copier stand (a $250 value), free starter supplies, and free delivery and installation. We have office space available, and my staff is eager to add a second machine.

Please call me at Ext. 630 if you have questions. This copier is such a good opportunity that I have prepared a purchase requisition authorizing the agreement with Copy City. With your approval before May 1, we could have our machine by May 10 and start saving time and more than $900 every month. Fast action will also help us take advantage of Copy City's free start-up incentives.

Serves as cover e-mail to introduce attached memo in MS Word
Opens with catchy subject line
Does not reveal recommendation but leaves request for action to the attached memo
Provides an electronic signature with contact information
1 inch
2 blank lines
1 blank line
1 blank line
1 blank line
1 or 2 blank lines
Describes topic without revealing request
Summarizes problem
Uses headings and columns for easy comprehension
Proves credibility of request with facts and figures
Highlights most important benefit
Provides more benefits
Counters possible resistance
Makes it easy to grant approval
Repeats main benefit with motivation to act quickly

Checklist

Writing Persuasive Messages Within Organizations

Prewrite

- Know your purpose and be able to state it precisely and concisely. What do you want the receiver to do? Make sure your request is doable and attainable.
- Profile the audience. Play *What if?* scenarios to anticipate how the receiver will react to your request. What direct or indirect benefits can you cite?

Gain Attention

- Make the reader aware of a problem, use a startling statement, provide a significant fact related to the request, describe possible benefits, ask a stimulating question, or offer compliments and praise.
- Establish your credibility, but don't pull rank.

Build Interest

- Use facts, statistics, examples, and specific details to build a solid foundation for your request.
- Strive for a personal but professional tone. Be enthusiastic and positive.
- Soften your words when persuading upward. Suggest benefits to the reader.

Reduce Resistance

- Recognize any weakness in your proposal and suggest well-reasoned counterarguments and facts.
- In requests flowing upward, consider making a strong dollars-and-cents appeal for requests involving budgets.
- In requests flowing downward, avoid sounding preachy, parental, or overly authoritarian.

Motivate Action

- State a specific request including a deadline if appropriate. Suggest ways to make it effortless and painless for the receiver to respond.
- Repeat a major benefit that appeals to the reader.
- Include an incentive or reason to act, and express appreciation if appropriate.

The strength of this persuasive document, though, is in the clear presentation of comparison figures showing how much money the company can save by purchasing a remanufactured copier. Buying a copier that uses low-cost solid ink instead of expensive laser cartridges is another argument in this machine's favor. Although the organization pattern is not obvious, the memo begins with an attention-getter (a frank description of the problem), builds interest (with easy-to-read facts and figures), provides benefits, and reduces resistance. Notice that the conclusion tells what action is to be taken, makes it easy to respond, and repeats the main benefit to motivate action.

Planning and Composing Effective Direct-Mail and E-Mail Sales Messages

Sales messages use persuasion to promote specific products and services. In our coverage we are most concerned with sales messages delivered by mail or by e-mail. Many of the concepts you will learn about sales persuasion, however, can be applied to online, wireless, TV, print, radio, and other media. The best sales messages, whether delivered by direct mail or by e-mail, have much in common. In this section we look at how to apply the 3-x-3 writing process to sales messages. We also present techniques developed by experts to draft effective sales messages, both in print and online.

LEARNING OBJECTIVE 5

Write effective and ethical direct-mail and e-mail sales messages.

Applying the 3-x-3 Writing Process to Sales Messages

Marketing professionals analyze and perfect every aspect of a sales message to encourage consumers to read and act on the message. Like the experts, you will want to pay close attention to the preparatory steps of analysis and adaptation before writing the actual message.

What aspects of a product should you study before writing a sales message promoting it?

Analyzing the Product and Purpose for Writing. Prior to sitting down to write a sales message promoting a product, you must study the item carefully. What can you learn about its design, construction, raw materials, and manufacturing process? What can you learn about its ease of use, efficiency, durability, and applications? Be sure to consider warranties, service, price, premiums, exclusivity, and special appeals. At the same time, evaluate the competition so that you can compare your product's strengths against the competitor's weaknesses.

Now you are ready to identify your central selling points. At Lands' End a central selling point for one marketing campaign was economical custom clothing. The company used a testimonial from a real customer who said that the $49 Lands' End custom dress shirts he bought were better than the $120 shirts he previously purchased from custom shops.[11] Analyzing your product and studying the competition help you determine what to emphasize in your sales letter.

Equally important is determining the specific purpose of your letter. Do you want the reader to call for a free video and brochure? Listen to a podcast at your Web site? Fill out an order form? Send a credit card authorization? Before you write the first word of your message, know what response you want and what central selling points you will emphasize to achieve that purpose.

How do the senders of direct-mail messages target audiences?

Adapting a Sales Message to Its Audience. Blanket mailings sent "cold" to occupants generally produce low responses—typically less than 2 percent. That means that 98 percent of the receivers usually toss direct-mail sales letters right into the trash. But the response rate can be increased dramatically by targeting the audience through selected database mailing lists. These lists can be purchased or compiled. By directing your message to a selected group, you can make certain assumptions about the receivers. Let's say you are selling fitness equipment. A good mailing list might come from subscribers to fitness or exercise magazines. You would expect similar interests, needs, and demographics (age, income, and other characteristics). With this knowledge you can adapt the sales letter to a specific audience.

Crafting Direct-Mail Sales Letters

What advantages do direct-mail messages enjoy?

Sales letters are usually part of direct-mail marketing campaigns. These letters are a powerful means to make sales, generate leads, boost retail traffic, solicit donations, and direct consumers to Web sites. Direct mail allows a personalized, tangible, three-dimensional message that is less invasive than telephone solicitations and less reviled than unsolicited e-mail.

Professionals who specialize in traditional direct-mail services have made it a science. They analyze a market, develop an effective mailing list, study the product, prepare a sophisticated campaign aimed at a target audience, and motivate the reader to act. You have probably received many direct-mail packages, often called junk mail. These packages typically contain a sales letter, a brochure, a price list, illustrations of the product, testimonials, and other persuasive appeals.

What is a primary goal of a sales message?

We are most concerned here with the sales letter: its strategy, organization, and evidence. Because sales letters are generally written by specialists, you may never write one on the job. Why, then, learn how to write a sales letter? In many ways, every letter we create is a form of sales letter. We sell our ideas, our organizations, and ourselves. Learning the techniques of sales writing will help you be more successful in any communication that requires persuasion and promotion. What's more, you will recognize sales strategies that enable you to become a more perceptive consumer of ideas, products, and services.

Your primary goal in writing a sales message is to get someone to devote a few moments of attention to it. You may be promoting a product, a service, an idea, or yourself. In each case the most effective messages will (a) gain attention, (b) build interest, (c) reduce resistance, and (d) motivate action. This is the same recipe we studied earlier, but the ingredients are different.

Spotlight on Communicators

© Jon Frellich/Bloomberg via Getty Images

In writing winning sales messages, beware of impossible promises, warns Herb Kelleher, cofounder of Southwest Airlines. He believes his company has the quickest baggage delivery in the industry—only eight minutes from Jetway to pickup. But when his marketing staff proposed making such a promise in the Southwest baggage promotions, Kelleher balked. On rare occasions Southwest wouldn't be able to deliver, he reasoned, and broken promises are not easily forgotten.

Gaining Attention in Sales Messages. One of the most critical elements of a sales message is its opening paragraph. This opener should be short (one to five lines), honest, relevant, and stimulating. Marketing pros have found that eye-catching typographical arrangements or provocative messages, such as the following, can hook a reader's attention:

What sales message openers are effective in gaining attention?

- **Offer:** *A free trip to Hawaii is just the beginning!*
- **Promise:** *Now you can raise your sales income by 50 percent or even more with the proven techniques found in . . . .*
- **Question:** *Do you yearn for an honest, fulfilling relationship?*
- **Quotation or proverb:** *Necessity is the mother of invention.*
- **Fact:** *The Greenland Eskimos ate more fat than anyone in the world. And yet . . . they had virtually no heart disease.*
- **Product feature:** *Volvo's snazzy new convertible ensures your safety with a roll bar that pops out when the car tips 40 degrees to the side.*
- **Testimonial:** *My name is Sheldon Schulman. I am a practicing medical doctor. I am also a multimillionaire. I didn't make my millions by practicing medicine, though. I made them by investing in my spare time.*
- **Startling statement:** *Let the poor and hungry feed themselves! For just $100 they can.*
- **Personalized action setting:** *It's 4:30 p.m. and you've got to make a decision. You need everybody's opinion, no matter where they are. Before you pick up your phone to call them one at a time, pick up this card: WebEx Teleconference Services.*

Other openings calculated to capture attention might include a solution to a problem, an anecdote, a personalized statement using the receiver's name, or a relevant current event.

Building Interest With Rational and Emotional Appeals. In this phase of your sales message, you should describe clearly the product or service. In simple language emphasize the central selling points that you identified during your prewriting analysis. Those selling points can be developed using rational or emotional appeals.

Rational appeals are associated with reason and intellect. They translate selling points into references to making or saving money, increasing efficiency, or making the best use of resources. In general, rational appeals are appropriate when a product is expensive, long-lasting, or important to health, security, and financial success. Emotional appeals relate to status, ego, and sensual feelings. Appealing to the emotions is sometimes effective when a product

With motorists at risk from texting while driving, highway safety groups are sending the message that texting kills. One police department in the United Kingdom sparked controversy by creating a Hollywood-styled PSA so disturbing that viewers complained it should not air on television. The graphic video, which follows three teenage girls as they text-and-drive their way into a head-on collision with another vehicle, left international viewers shocked and in tears. But one tracking firm found that 80 percent of viewers planned to quit texting while on the road. *Are safety messages delivered best using emotional appeals?*

How are rational appeals different from emotional appeals?

is inexpensive, short-lived, or nonessential. Many clever sales messages, however, combine emotional and rational strategies for a dual appeal. Consider these examples:

Rational Appeal

You can buy the things you need and want, pay household bills, and pay off higher-cost loans and credit cards—as soon as you are approved and your Credit-Line account is opened.

Emotional Appeal

Leave the urban bustle behind and escape to sun-soaked Bermuda! To recharge your batteries with an injection of sun and surf, all you need are your bathing suit, a little suntan lotion, and your Credit-Line card.

Dual Appeal

New Credit-Line cardholders are immediately eligible for a $200 travel certificate and additional discounts at fun-filled resorts. Save up to 40 percent while lying on a beach in picturesque, sun-soaked Bermuda, the year-round resort island.

ETHICS CHECK

Scare Tactics

Direct marketers sometimes resort to scare tactics—for example, to make us purchase alarm systems or subscribe to monitoring services. They may also appeal to our compassion and guilt before the holidays in soliciting money for the less fortunate. Are such emotional appeals ethical?

A physical description of your product is not enough, however. Zig Ziglar, thought by some to be America's greatest salesperson, pointed out that no matter how well you know your product, no one is persuaded by cold, hard facts alone. In the end, people buy because of product benefits.[12] Your job is to translate those cold facts into warm feelings and reader benefits. Let's say a sales message promotes a hand cream made with aloe and cocoa butter extracts, along with vitamin A. Those facts become, *Nature's hand helpers—including soothing aloe and cocoa extracts, along with firming vitamin A—form invisible gloves that protect your sensitive skin against the hardships of work, harsh detergents, and constant environmental assaults.*

Why is it important to turn facts into warm feelings and benefits?

Reducing Resistance and Building Desire. Marketing specialists use a number of techniques to overcome resistance and build desire. When price is an obstacle, consider these suggestions:

- Delay mentioning price until after you've created a desire for the product.
- Show the price in small units, such as the price per issue of a magazine.
- Demonstrate how the reader saves money—for instance, by subscribing for two or three years.
- Compare your prices with those of a competitor.

In addition, you need to anticipate other objections and questions the receiver may have. When possible, translate these objections into selling points *(If you are worried about training your staff members on the new software, remember that our offer includes $1,000 worth of on-site one-on-one instruction)*. Other techniques to overcome resistance and prove the credibility of the product include the following:

What techniques are effective in reducing resistance?

- **Testimonials:** *"I never stopped eating, yet I lost 107 pounds." — Tina Rivers, Greenwood, South Carolina*
- **Names of satisfied users** (with permission, of course): *Enclosed is a partial list of private pilots who enthusiastically subscribe to our service.*
- **Money-back guarantee or warranty:** *We offer the longest warranties in the business—all parts and service on-site for five years!*
- **Free trial or sample:** *We are so confident that you will like our new accounting program that we want you to try it absolutely free.*
- **Performance tests, polls, or awards:** *Our TP-3000 was named Best Web Phone, and* Etown.com *voted it Smartphone of the Year.*

How can you motivate action in a sales message?

Motivating Action at the Conclusion of a Sales Message. All the effort put into a sales message goes to waste if the reader fails to act. To make it easy for readers to act, you can provide a reply card, a stamped and preaddressed envelope, a toll-free telephone number, an easy-to-scan Web site, or a promise of a follow-up call. Because readers often need an extra push, consider including additional motivators, such as the following:

- **Offer a gift:** *You will receive a free cell phone with the purchase of any new car.*
- **Promise an incentive:** *With every new, paid subscription, we will plant a tree in one of America's Heritage Forests.*
- **Limit the offer:** *Only the first 100 customers receive free travel mugs.*
- **Set a deadline:** *You must act before June 1 to get these low prices.*
- **Guarantee satisfaction:** *We will return your full payment if you are not entirely satisfied—no questions asked.*

The final paragraph of the sales letter carries the punch line. This is where you tell readers what you want them to do and give them reasons for doing it. Most sales letters also include postscripts because they make irresistible reading. Even readers who might skim over or bypass paragraphs are drawn to a P.S. Therefore, use a postscript to reveal your strongest motivator, to add a special inducement for a quick response, or to reemphasize a central selling point.

Although you want to be persuasive in sales letters, you must guard against overstepping legal and ethical boundaries. Information contained in sales letters has landed some writers in hot water. See the accompanying Ethical Insights box to learn how to stay out of trouble.

ETHICAL INSIGHT

What's Legal and What's Not in Sales Messages

In promoting products and writing sales message, be careful about the words you use and the claims you make. How far can you go in praising and selling your product?

- **Puffery.** In a sales message, you can write, *Hey, we've got something fantastic! It's the very best product on the market!* Called "puffery," such promotional claims are not taken literally by reasonable consumers.
- **Proving your claims.** If you write that *three out of four dentists recommend* your toothpaste, you had better have competent and reliable scientific evidence to support the claim. Such a claim goes beyond puffery and requires proof. Vital Basics paid a $1 million settlement for claiming that its Focus Factor helped improve memory, a claim unsubstantiated by proof, said the Federal Trade Commission.[13] As part of a crackdown on deceptive drug advertising, the Food and Drug Administration forced Bayer to run new ads correcting its previous marketing overstating the ability of its birth control pill Yaz to improve women's moods and clear up acne.[14] Similarly, UPS had to stop running ads saying it was the "most reliable" shipping company after FedEx sued.[15]
- **Celebrities.** The unauthorized use of a celebrity's name, likeness, or nickname is not permitted in sales messages. For example, late-night talk show host Johnny Carson won a case against a portable toilet firm that promoted a "Here's Johnny" toilet. Similarly, film star Dustin Hoffman won millions of dollars for the unauthorized use of a digitally altered photo showing him in an evening gown and Ralph Lauren heels. Even a commercial showing the image of a celebrity such as Beyonce on a camera phone is risky.
- **Misleading statements.** You cannot tell people that they are winners or finalists in a sweepstake unless they actually are. American Family Publishers was found guilty of sending letters tricking people into buying magazine subscription in the belief that they had won $1.1 million. Similarly, the Damart clothing company was reprimanded for sending a mailing with *final reminder* printed in bold, red lettering on the envelope. Instead of referring to an overdue bill, it merely referred to a final reminder about a Damart offer, clearly a deceptive message.[16] Companies also may not misrepresent the nature, characteristics, qualities, or geographic origin of goods or services they are promoting.
- **Unwanted merchandise.** If you enclose unsolicited merchandise with a letter, don't expect the receiver to be required to pay for it or return it. Express Publishing, for example, sent a copy of its *Food & Wine Magazine's Cookbook with a letter* inviting recipients to preview the book. It read: "If you don't want to preview the book, simply return the advance notice card within 14 days." Courts, however, have ruled that recipients are allowed to retain, use, or discard any unsolicited merchandise without paying for it or returning it.

Career Application

Bring to class at least three sales letters or advertisements that may represent issues described here. What examples of puffery can you identify? Are claims substantiated by reliable evidence? What proof is offered? Do any of your examples include names, images, or nicknames of celebrities? How likely is it that the celebrity authorized this use? Have you ever received unwanted merchandise as part of a sales campaign? What were you to do with it?

Putting Together All the Parts of a Sales Message. Sales letters are a preferred marketing medium because they can be personalized, directed to target audiences, and filled with a more complete message than other advertising media. But direct mail is expensive. That's why crafting and assembling all the parts of a sales message are so critical.

Figure 10.7 shows a sales letter addressed to a target group of small business owners. To sell the new magazine *Small Business Monthly*, the letter incorporates all four components of an effective persuasive message. Notice that the personalized action-setting opener places the reader in a familiar situation (getting into an elevator) and draws an analogy between failing to reach the top floor and failing to achieve a business goal. The writer develops a rational central selling point (a magazine that provides valuable information for a growing small business) and repeats this selling point in all the components of the letter. Notice, too, how a testimonial from a small business executive lends support to the sales message and how the closing pushes for action. Because the price of the magazine is not a selling feature, price is mentioned only on the reply card. This sales letter saves its strongest motivator—a free booklet—for the high-impact P.S. line.

Writing Successful E-Mail Sales Messages

How are direct-mail and e-marketing similar, and how are they different?

To make the best use of limited advertising dollars while reaching a great number of potential customers, many businesses are turning to the Internet and to e-mail marketing campaigns in particular. E-mails cost about $7 per consumer response versus about $48 per response for traditional direct mail.[17] Much like traditional direct mail, e-mail marketing can attract new customers, keep existing ones, encourage future sales, cross-sell, and cut costs. However, e-marketers can create and send a promotion in half the time it takes to print and distribute a traditional message. As consumers feel more comfortable and secure with online purchases, e-marketing has become more popular.

Selling by E-Mail. If you will be writing online sales messages for your organization, try using the following techniques gleaned from the best-performing e-mails. Although much e-marketing dazzles receivers with colorful graphics, we focus on the words involved in persuasive sales messages.

What is the first rule of e-marketing?

The first rule of e-marketing is to communicate only with those who have given permission. By sending messages only to "opt-in" folks, you greatly increase your "open rate"—those e-mails that will be opened. E-mail users detest spam. However, receivers are surprisingly receptive to offers tailored specifically for them. Remember that today's customer is somebody—not just anybody. Here are a few guidelines that will help you create effective e-mail sales messages:

- **Craft a catchy subject line.** Offer discounts or premiums: *Spring Sale: Buy now and save 20 percent!* Promise solutions to everyday work-related problems. Highlight hot new industry topics. Invite readers to scan a top-ten list of items such as issues, trends, or people.
- **Keep the main information "above the fold."** E-mails should be top heavy. Primary points should appear early in the message so that they capture the reader's attention.
- **Make the message short, conversational, and focused.** Because on-screen text is taxing to read, be brief. Focus on one or two central selling points only.
- **Convey urgency.** Top-performing e-mails state an offer deadline or demonstrate why the state of the industry demands action on the reader's part. Good messages also tie the product to relevant current events.
- **Sprinkle testimonials throughout the copy.** Consumers' own words are the best sales copy. These comments can serve as callouts or be integrated into the copy.
- **Provide a means for opting out.** It's polite and a good business tactic to include a statement that tells receivers how to be removed from the sender's mailing database.

Whether you actually write sales message on the job or merely receive them, you will better understand their organization and appeals by reviewing this chapter and the tips in the checklist on page 318.

FIGURE 10.7 Sales Letter

Prewriting

Analyze: The purpose of this letter is to persuade the reader to return the reply card and subscribe to *Small Business Monthly.*

Anticipate: The targeted audience consists of small-business owners. The central selling point is providing practical business data that will help their business grow.

Adapt: Because readers will be reluctant, use the indirect pattern.

Writing

Research: Gather facts to promote your product, including testimonials.

Organize: Gain attention by opening with a personalized action picture. Build interest with an analogy and a description of magazine features. Use a testimonial to reduce resistance. Motivate action with a free booklet and an easy-reply card.

Compose: Prepare first draft for pilot study.

3 Revising

Revise: Use short paragraphs and short sentences. Replace *malfunction* with *glitch.*

Proofread: Indent long quotations on the left and right sides. Italicize or underscore titles of publications. Hyphenate *hard-headed* and *first-of-its-kind.*

Evaluate: Monitor the response rate to this letter to assess its effectiveness.

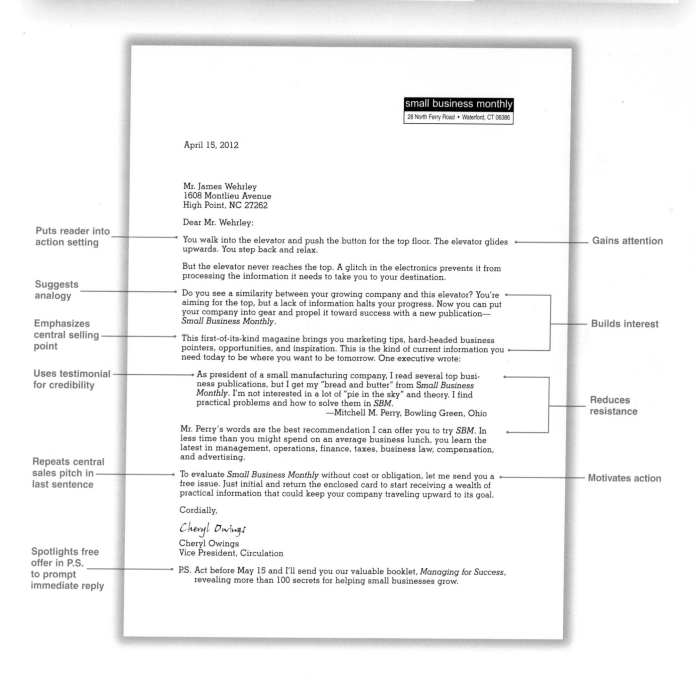

small business monthly
28 North Ferry Road • Waterford, CT 06386

April 15, 2012

Mr. James Wehrley
1608 Montlieu Avenue
High Point, NC 27262

Dear Mr. Wehrley:

Puts reader into action setting

Gains attention

You walk into the elevator and push the button for the top floor. The elevator glides upwards. You step back and relax.

But the elevator never reaches the top. A glitch in the electronics prevents it from processing the information it needs to take you to your destination.

Suggests analogy

Builds interest

Do you see a similarity between your growing company and this elevator? You're aiming for the top, but a lack of information halts your progress. Now you can put your company into gear and propel it toward success with a new publication—*Small Business Monthly*.

Emphasizes central selling point

This first-of-its-kind magazine brings you marketing tips, hard-headed business pointers, opportunities, and inspiration. This is the kind of current information you need today to be where you want to be tomorrow. One executive wrote:

Uses testimonial for credibility

Reduces resistance

> As president of a small manufacturing company, I read several top business publications, but I get my "bread and butter" from *Small Business Monthly*. I'm not interested in a lot of "pie in the sky" and theory. I find practical problems and how to solve them in *SBM*.
>
> —Mitchell M. Perry, Bowling Green, Ohio

Mr. Perry's words are the best recommendation I can offer you to try *SBM*. In less time than you might spend on an average business lunch, you learn the latest in management, operations, finance, taxes, business law, compensation, and advertising.

Repeats central sales pitch in last sentence

Motivates action

To evaluate *Small Business Monthly* without cost or obligation, let me send you a free issue. Just initial and return the enclosed card to start receiving a wealth of practical information that could keep your company traveling upward to its goal.

Cordially,

Cheryl Owings

Cheryl Owings
Vice President, Circulation

Spotlights free offer in P.S. to prompt immediate reply

P.S. Act before May 15 and I'll send you our valuable booklet, *Managing for Success*, revealing more than 100 secrets for helping small businesses grow.

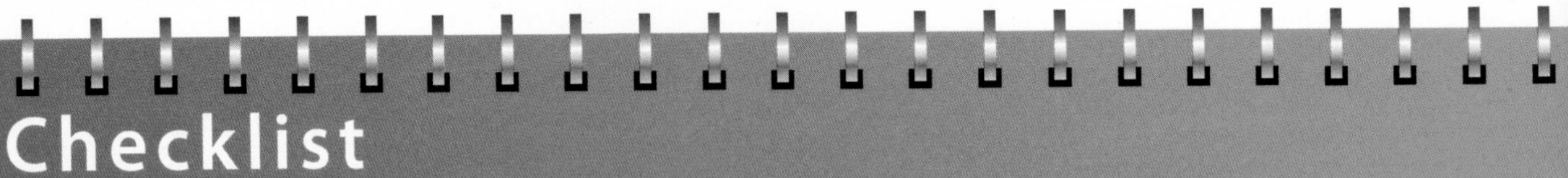

Checklist

Preparing Persuasive Direct-Mail and E-Mail Sales Messages

Prewrite

- Analyze your product or service. What makes it special? What central selling points should you emphasize? How does it compare with the competition?
- Profile your audience. How will this product or service benefit this audience?
- Decide what you want the audience to do at the end of your message.
- For e-mails, send only to those who have opted in.

Gain Attention

- Describe a product feature, present a testimonial, make a startling statement, or show the reader in an action setting.
- Offer something valuable, promise the reader a result, or pose a stimulating question.
- Suggest a solution to a problem, offer a relevant anecdote, use the receiver's name, or mention a meaningful current event.

Build Interest

- Describe the product or service in terms of what it does for the reader. Connect cold facts with warm feelings and needs.
- Use rational appeals if the product or service is expensive, long-lasting, or important to health, security, and financial success. Use emotional appeals to suggest status, ego, or sensual feelings.
- Explain how the product or service can save or make money, reduce effort, improve health, produce pleasure, or boost status.

Reduce Resistance

- Counter anticipated reluctance with testimonials, money-back guarantees, attractive warranties, trial offers, or free samples.
- Build credibility with results of performance tests, polls, or awards.
- If price is not a selling feature, describe it in small units *(only 99 cents an issue)*, show it as savings, or tell how it compares favorably with that of the competition.

Motivate Action

- Close by repeating a central selling point and describing an easy-to-take action.
- Prompt the reader to act immediately with a gift, incentive, limited offer, deadline, or guarantee of satisfaction.
- Put the strongest motivator in a postscript.
- In e-mails include an opportunity to opt out.

Comparing Persuasion in High- and Low-Context Cultures

LEARNING OBJECTIVE 6

Compare effective persuasion techniques in high- and low-context cultures.

The explosion of global communication, transportation, and marketing, along with the continuing migration of people, has moved all of us closer to a global society. As a business communicator, you can expect to interact with people from different cultures both at home and abroad. To be effective, as discussed in Chapter 3, you must be aware of your own culture. In addition, you should learn about other cultures to better understand how to be effective and to avoid confusion and miscommunication. What works in a low-context culture such as the United States may not be as effective in a high-context culture such as China.

Being Persuasive in High-Context Cultures

Countries in Asia, Africa, South America, and much of the Middle East are considered *high context*. As you learned in Chapter 3, high-context cultures generally value group sense rather than individualism. In such cultures, much information is not explicit; that is, it is not transmitted as words in a message. Meaning may be conveyed by clues in the situational context. Advertisements in high-context cultures are often indirect, polite, modest, and ambiguous. Even business messages can be so subtle that the meaning is unclear. Advertisements tend to emphasize harmony and beauty. For example, pictures of butterflies, flowers, nature scenes, and cultural artifacts are often seen on Japanese Web sites. Because of the respect for harmony and politeness, direct comparisons in persuasive messages are considered in bad taste. Nike advertisements in Japan would not mention its superior styling compared to Reebok or another named brand.

In high-context cultures, advertisements, Web sites, and sales letters such as that shown in Figure 10.8 may be characterized by the following:

How are persuasive efforts in high-context cultures characterized?

- **Indirectness.** Use of indirect expressions (such as *perhaps, probably, somewhat*). Preference for softened words (*would appreciate* rather than *must* or *expect*). Aversion to blunt hard-sell tactics and long, verbose messages.
- **Politeness.** Expressions of politeness, use of honorifics *(Esteemed* and *Revered Customer),* flowery language, wishful requests (*we hope)*, and overall humility.
- **Soft-sell approach.** Use of simple facts without embellishment or superlatives. Web sites may feature an entertainment theme to promote products. Emphasis on harmony.
- **Relationship appeal.** Attempts to establish a long-term relationship.
- **Collectivist view.** Emphasis on *we* and *our* rather than on *I* or the "you" view.

FIGURE 10.8 Sales Message From High-Context Culture (English translation)

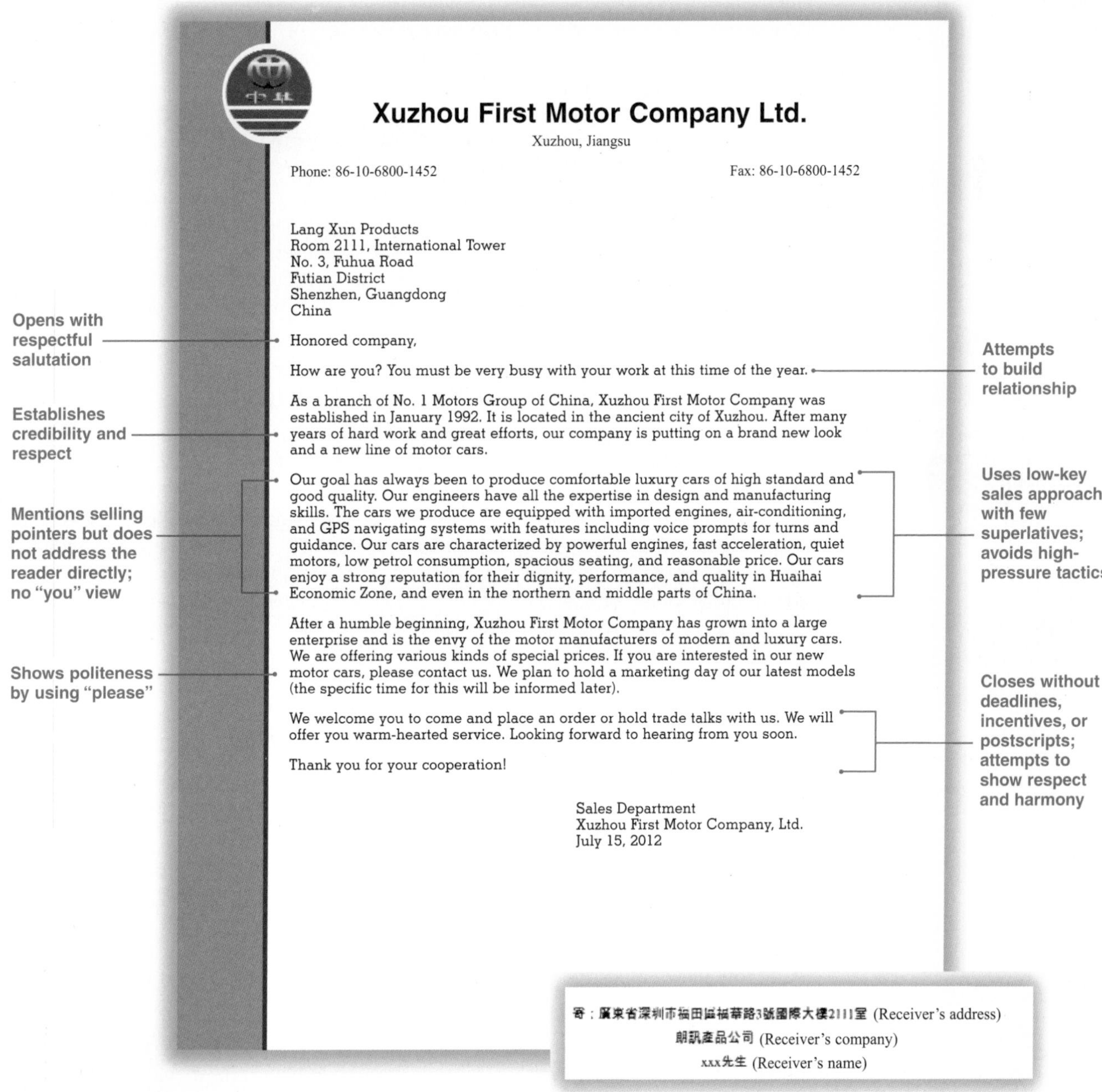

Xuzhou First Motor Company Ltd.
Xuzhou, Jiangsu

Phone: 86-10-6800-1452 Fax: 86-10-6800-1452

Lang Xun Products
Room 2111, International Tower
No. 3, Fuhua Road
Futian District
Shenzhen, Guangdong
China

Honored company,

How are you? You must be very busy with your work at this time of the year.

As a branch of No. 1 Motors Group of China, Xuzhou First Motor Company was established in January 1992. It is located in the ancient city of Xuzhou. After many years of hard work and great efforts, our company is putting on a brand new look and a new line of motor cars.

Our goal has always been to produce comfortable luxury cars of high standard and good quality. Our engineers have all the expertise in design and manufacturing skills. The cars we produce are equipped with imported engines, air-conditioning, and GPS navigating systems with features including voice prompts for turns and guidance. Our cars are characterized by powerful engines, fast acceleration, quiet motors, low petrol consumption, spacious seating, and reasonable price. Our cars enjoy a strong reputation for their dignity, performance, and quality in Huaihai Economic Zone, and even in the northern and middle parts of China.

After a humble beginning, Xuzhou First Motor Company has grown into a large enterprise and is the envy of the motor manufacturers of modern and luxury cars. We are offering various kinds of special prices. If you are interested in our new motor cars, please contact us. We plan to hold a marketing day of our latest models (the specific time for this will be informed later).

We welcome you to come and place an order or hold trade talks with us. We will offer you warm-hearted service. Looking forward to hearing from you soon.

Thank you for your cooperation!

Sales Department
Xuzhou First Motor Company, Ltd.
July 15, 2012

寄：廣東省深圳市福田區福華路3號國際大樓2111室 (Receiver's address)
朗訊產品公司 (Receiver's company)
xxx先生 (Receiver's name)

Opens with respectful salutation
Establishes credibility and respect
Mentions selling pointers but does not address the reader directly; no "you" view
Shows politeness by using "please"
Attempts to build relationship
Uses low-key sales approach with few superlatives; avoids high-pressure tactics
Closes without deadlines, incentives, or postscripts; attempts to show respect and harmony

Analyzing a High-Context Sales Letter. Sales letters in high-context cultures definitely aim to be persuasive, but the tone and strategy are different from the techniques discussed thus far in this chapter. The letter from the Xuzhou First Motor Company in China, shown in Figure 10.8, promotes its renovated facilities and new line of motor cars. The formal salutation (*Honored company*) reflects respect for the addressee. The first sentences in the letter (*How are you? You must be very busy with your work at this time of the year*) are quite different from typical U.S. sales letters. These leisurely opening sentences attempt to build a relationship. They signal that the company is interested in more than a quick sale. Although such an opening might be considered naïve in this country, it is seen differently in China. The motor company wants to appear friendly and recognizes that all business dealings proceed more smoothly when the goal is a long-term relationship.

To establish its credibility, the company points out that it is part of a large national motor car manufacturer. This ensures that readers will respect the company because it is not a small-time facility, lacking the skills, expertise, and automobile models of a big company. To build interest, the letter uses facts and details about its cars (*imported engines, air-conditioning, GPS navigation systems*). The letter touts the cars' features (*powerful engines, fast acceleration, quiet motors, low petrol consumption, spacious seating, reasonable price*). Notice, however, that the letter neither uses superlatives (*the biggest and best GPS system in today's cars!*), nor attempts to focus on benefits to the reader. No effort is made to develop a "you" view; benefits are described in general terms. The entire approach is low-key, rather than focusing on appeals to the reader. Notice, too, that most references are to *our* and *we*, which are appropriate in a collectivist culture.

In reducing resistance, the letter again refers to the motor company's size (*a large enterprise*) and its reputation (*the envy of motor manufacturers*). However, the statements are all fairly formal, dignified, polite, and bland. One clear contrast with sales letters in this country and in other low-context cultures is the lack of high pressure. Notice that the closing is genteel and friendly (*we welcome you to come and place an order*). Again, it attempts to build a relationship, assuring *warm-hearted service*. This sales letter lacks high-pressure incentives, deadlines, and P.S. statements hammering home important reader benefits. The letter is also fairly short, contrasting with longer sales letters in this country. In low-context cultures, writers tend to use more words to ensure that they can be precise in explaining and persuading.

Being Persuasive in Low-Context Cultures

How are persuasive efforts in low-context cultures characterized?

Countries in Northern Europe, North America, Scandinavia, and Australia are classified as *low context*. As discussed in Chapter 3, low-context cultures tend to be logical, linear, and action oriented. Information is explicit and formalized in written documents. People in low-context cultures use words precisely and expect them to be understood literally. They rely less on the unspoken context and nonverbal clues to convey important messages. They are comfortable with direct, explicit, and confrontational appeals in advertising and persuasion. Sales letters, advertisements, Web sites, and other persuasive efforts within low-context cultures may be characterized by the following:

- **Directness.** Expression of requests may be made directly without attempts to use soft wording. Precision in expression is preferred.
- **Superlatives.** Use of superlatives such as *The lowest price, highest quality, and best customer service on the planet!* Little hesitation to "toot one's own horn." General acceptance of puffery. No expectation of humility or modesty in advertising or sales.
- **Hard-sell approach.** Aggressive promotions, incentives, testimonials, deadlines, and an emphasis on product advantages using explicit comparisons with competitors.
- **Short-term goal.** Little attempt to establish long-term relationships. Tendency to develop transitory personal relationships.
- **"You" view.** Emphasis on projecting benefits to an individual, instead of focusing on group perspectives.

As globalization expands and the huge markets of China and India open up, Western business practices may become more dominant even in high-context cultures. We may see more evidence of low-context strategies in sales messages in high-context cultures. Underlying cultural differences, however, will continue to exert considerable influence. Savvy business communicators who understand the powerful influence of high- and low-context cultures will always have a distinct advantage.

Developing Persuasive Press Releases

LEARNING OBJECTIVE 7
Understand basic patterns and techniques in developing persuasive press releases.

Press (news) releases announce information about your company to the media: new products, new managers, new location, sponsorships, participation in community projects, awards given or received, joint ventures, donations, or seminars and demonstrations. Naturally, you hope that this news will be published and provide good publicity for your company. But this kind of largely

FIGURE 10.9 Press Release Announces Chocolate Shop

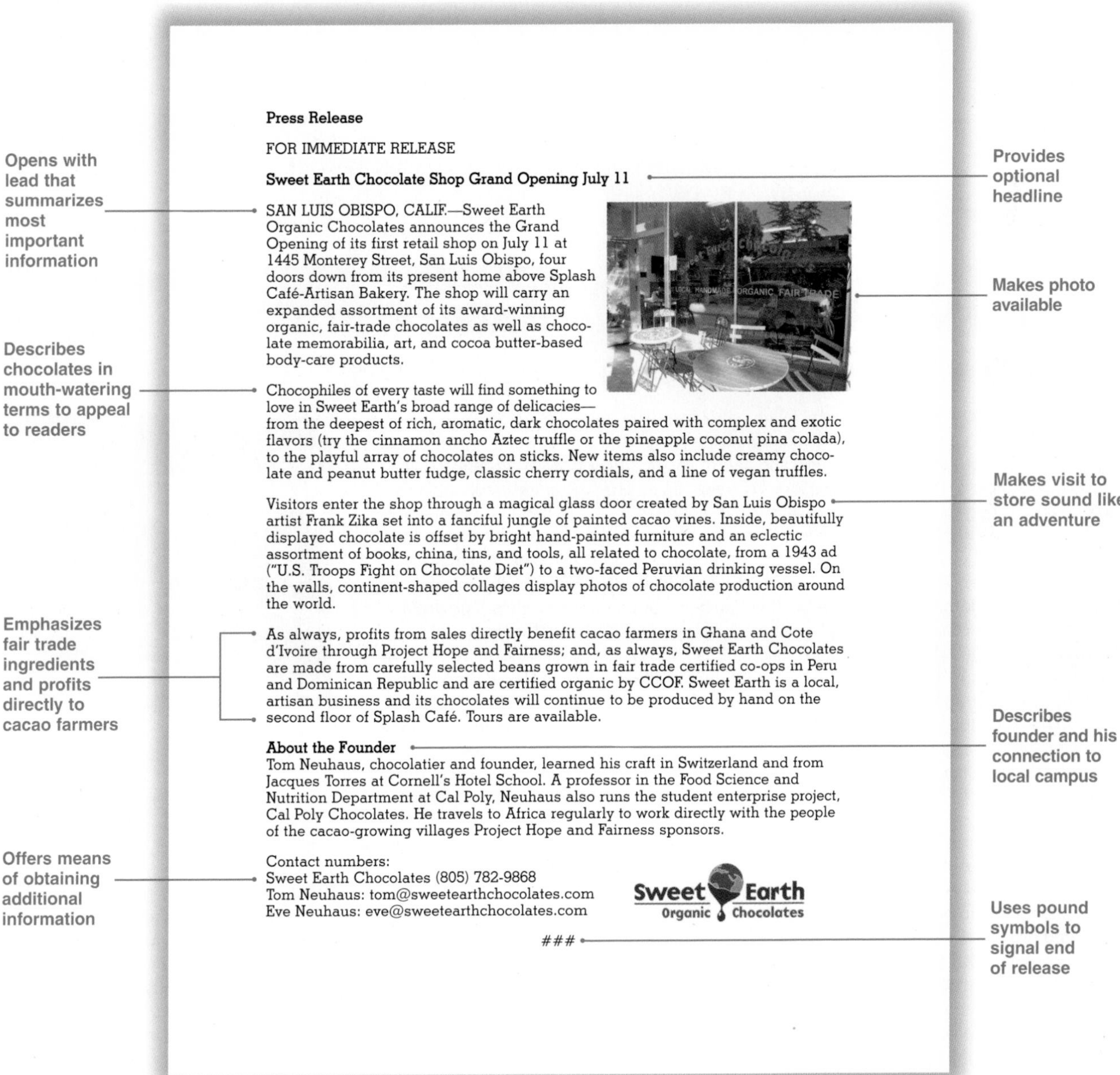

Press Release

FOR IMMEDIATE RELEASE

Sweet Earth Chocolate Shop Grand Opening July 11

SAN LUIS OBISPO, CALIF.—Sweet Earth Organic Chocolates announces the Grand Opening of its first retail shop on July 11 at 1445 Monterey Street, San Luis Obispo, four doors down from its present home above Splash Café-Artisan Bakery. The shop will carry an expanded assortment of its award-winning organic, fair-trade chocolates as well as chocolate memorabilia, art, and cocoa butter-based body-care products.

Chocophiles of every taste will find something to love in Sweet Earth's broad range of delicacies—from the deepest of rich, aromatic, dark chocolates paired with complex and exotic flavors (try the cinnamon ancho Aztec truffle or the pineapple coconut pina colada), to the playful array of chocolates on sticks. New items also include creamy chocolate and peanut butter fudge, classic cherry cordials, and a line of vegan truffles.

Visitors enter the shop through a magical glass door created by San Luis Obispo artist Frank Zika set into a fanciful jungle of painted cacao vines. Inside, beautifully displayed chocolate is offset by bright hand-painted furniture and an eclectic assortment of books, china, tins, and tools, all related to chocolate, from a 1943 ad ("U.S. Troops Fight on Chocolate Diet") to a two-faced Peruvian drinking vessel. On the walls, continent-shaped collages display photos of chocolate production around the world.

As always, profits from sales directly benefit cacao farmers in Ghana and Cote d'Ivoire through Project Hope and Fairness; and, as always, Sweet Earth Chocolates are made from carefully selected beans grown in fair trade certified co-ops in Peru and Dominican Republic and are certified organic by CCOF. Sweet Earth is a local, artisan business and its chocolates will continue to be produced by hand on the second floor of Splash Café. Tours are available.

About the Founder
Tom Neuhaus, chocolatier and founder, learned his craft in Switzerland and from Jacques Torres at Cornell's Hotel School. A professor in the Food Science and Nutrition Department at Cal Poly, Neuhaus also runs the student enterprise project, Cal Poly Chocolates. He travels to Africa regularly to work directly with the people of the cacao-growing villages Project Hope and Fairness sponsors.

Contact numbers:
Sweet Earth Chocolates (805) 782-9868
Tom Neuhaus: tom@sweetearthchocolates.com
Eve Neuhaus: eve@sweetearthchocolates.com

Sweet Earth Organic Chocolates

###

Opens with lead that summarizes most important information
Describes chocolates in mouth-watering terms to appeal to readers
Emphasizes fair trade ingredients and profits directly to cacao farmers
Offers means of obtaining additional information
Provides optional headline
Makes photo available
Makes visit to store sound like an adventure
Describes founder and his connection to local campus
Uses pound symbols to signal end of release

Courtesy of Sweet Earth Chocolate Shop

What are press releases, and how are they usually organized?

self-serving information is not always appealing to magazine and newspaper editors or to TV producers. To get them to read beyond the first sentence, try these suggestions:

- Open with an attention-getting lead or a summary of the important facts.
- Include answers to the five *W*s and one *H* (*who, what, when, where, why*, and *how*) in the article—but not all in the first sentence!
- Appeal to the audience of the target media. Emphasize reader benefits written in the style of the focus publication or newscast.
- Present the most important information early, followed by supporting information. Don't put your best ideas last because they may be chopped off or ignored.
- Make the release visually appealing. Limit the text to one or two double-spaced pages with attractive formatting.
- Look and sound credible—no typos, no imaginative spelling or punctuation, no factual errors.

The most important ingredient of a press release, of course, is *news*. Articles that merely plug products end up in the circular file. The press release in Figure 10.9 announced the grand opening of Sweet Earth Chocolate Shop in the college town of San Luis Obispo, California. Sweet Earth features hand-made organic, fair-trade chocolates as well as chocolate memorabilia, art, and cocoa butter-based body care products.

Zooming In — YOUR TURN

Applying Your Skills at Hands on Miami

As a communication intern at Hands on Miami, you have been learning the ropes about publicizing and organizing programs. One day your boss sees a newspaper article and says to you, "Listen to this! Did you know that service organizations can earn up to $10 for used print cartridges and up to $20 for recycled cell phones? This sounds like a terrific idea for raising funds for our Community Bridges program. Why don't you do some research and find out more about this. Then I'd like you to draft a message that we could send to Miami businesses letting them know how they can help our programs. This is a good chance for you to try out your persuasion skills!"

In your research you discover that 300 million ink cartridges are discarded every year. You are horrified to learn that the industrial plastics in these cartridges take a thousand years to decompose. You find out that 40,000 tons of plastic could be diverted from landfills every year if ink cartridges were recycled. Your research also reveals that hundreds of thousands of cell phones are no longer being used as new models flood the market. Where do all of those unused cell phones go?

In doing your research, you discover that cartridges and cell phones may be dropped off at recycling centers. They can also be mailed in, or they can even be picked up. The best way for businesses to learn how to do this is to visit **http://www.miamidaderecycling.org** or call 1-800-534-9989 for details.

Your boss has asked you to focus on raising funds for Community Bridges, one of the flexible calendar programs at Hands on Miami. Volunteers like this program because it allows them to choose their hours and be personally involved. Some volunteers provide food service at the Miami Rescue Mission. Some are part of work crews to restore mangroves to wetlands, and those with carpentry skills enjoy working with Habitat for Humanity. Some volunteers help maintain the Miami Beach Botanical Gardens. One group of business professionals reads bedtime stories at the Salvation Army. Other volunteers care for animals at the humane society. These are just a few of the many volunteer services that make Miami a better place to live and work.

© Jeff Greenberg/PhotoEdit

Your Task

In teams or individually, draft a persuasive letter to be sent to 50 or more Miami area businesses. Ask the businesses to save used ink cartridges and old cell phones for Hands on Miami. As you compose your letter, follow the plan described in this chapter. You know the benefits that Hands on Miami will enjoy, but what benefits can you cite for the receiver? What incentive or final idea can you use to motivate action? Use your imagination, but stay within reason.

Figure 10.9 illustrates many good techniques for creating effective press releases. The announcement provides a headline, interesting photo, and descriptions of the shop's chocolate delicacies ranging from cinnamon Aztec truffles to pineapple-coconut pina coladas and vegan truffles. The best press releases focus on information that appeals to a targeted audience. To attract college students and educated townspeople, this press release describes the shop's use of fair trade ingredients with profits from sales directly benefitting cacao farmers in Ghana and Cote d'Ivorie. The press release also makes a visit to Sweet Earth Chocolates sound like an adventure by featuring a magical glass door, local art works, and chocolate memorabilia.

Newspapers and magazines are more likely to publish a press release that is informative, interesting, and helpful. The Web sites of many companies today provide readily available press information including releases and photos.

Summary of Learning Objectives

1 **Define the concept of persuasion, identify effective and ineffective persuasive techniques, and apply the 3-x-3 writing process to persuasive messages.** Persuasion may be defined as the ability to use argument or discussion to influence an individual's beliefs or actions. Effective persuasive techniques include establishing credibility, making a reasonable and precise request, tying facts to benefits, recognizing the power of loss, expecting and overcoming resistance, sharing solutions, and compromising. Persuasion is more effective if one avoids sounding preachy or parental, doesn't pull rank, softens the tone when persuading upward, sounds enthusiastic, and presents a positive and likeable image. The first step in the writing process for a persuasive message is deciding what you want the receiver to do or think. The second step involves thinking of ways to adapt the message to the audience. The writer must collect information and organize it into an appropriate strategy. An indirect strategy is best if the audience might resist the request.

2 **Explain the four major elements in successful persuasive messages and how to blend those elements into effective and ethical business messages.** The most effective persuasive messages include four major elements: gaining attention, building interest, reducing resistance, and motivating action. Writers gain attention by opening with a problem, unexpected statement, reader benefit, compliment, related fact, stimulating question, or similar device. They build interest with facts, expert opinions, examples, details, and direct and indirect reader benefits. They reduce resistance by anticipating objections and presenting counterarguments. They conclude by motivating a specific action and making it easy for the reader to respond. Skilled communicators avoid distortion, exaggeration, and deception when making persuasive arguments.

3 **Write persuasive messages that request favors and actions, make claims, and deliver complaints.** In asking for favors and actions, writers must know exactly what they are requesting and anticipate the receiver's reaction. The opening may begin indirectly with a problem description, an unexpected statement, a compliment, praise, related facts, a stimulating question, or a reader benefit. Interest is built with facts, statistics, examples, testimonials, and details. Claims and complaints require an objective, unemotional tone and proof of the validity of the request. Resistance can be reduced by anticipating objections and providing counterarguments. Action is motivated by stating exactly what is to be done and by when. Add a deadline date if necessary and express appreciation.

4 **Write persuasive messages within organizations.** Before writing a persuasive business message, writers should profile the audience, know exactly what the receiver is to do or believe, and anticipate resistance. To gain attention, the writer might make the receiver aware of a problem, use a startling statement, provide a significant fact related to the request, describe possible benefits, ask a stimulating question, or offer compliments and praise. Facts, statistics, examples, and specific details build a foundation for the request. Receivers are interested in direct benefits such as how agreeing to the request will help them solve problems or improve

their work and career. Recognizing weaknesses in the proposal and offering well-reasoned counterarguments are effective ways to reduce resistance. In messages flowing downward, avoid sounding preachy or overly authoritarian. In messages flowing upward, consider making a strong dollars-and-cents appeal for requests involving budgets. Persuasive messages should end with a specific request and a deadline if appropriate.

5 **Write effective and ethical print and e-mail sales messages.** Careful analysis of the product or service is necessary before one composes a sales message. Effective sales messages usually begin with an attention-getting statement that is short, honest, relevant, and stimulating. Simple language describing appropriate appeals builds interest. Testimonials, a money-back guarantee, a free trial, or some other device can reduce resistance. A gift, incentive, deadline, or other device can motivate action. E-marketing messages should be sent only to opt-in receivers. Writers of effective e-mails begin with a catchy subject line, keep the main information "above the fold," make the message short and focused, convey urgency, sprinkle testimonials throughout, and provide a means for opting out.

6 **Compare effective persuasion techniques in high- and low-context cultures.** Sales letters, advertisements, Web sites, and other persuasive efforts aimed at high-context cultures often exhibit politeness, indirectness, a soft-sell approach, and attempts to establish a long-term client relationship. Persuasive messages in low-context cultures, on the other hand, may be characterized by directness, superlatives, and a hard-sell approach.

7 **Understand basic patterns and techniques in developing persuasive press releases.** Press releases usually open with an attention-getting lead or summary of the important facts. They attempt to answer the questions *who, what, when, where, why*, and *how*. They are written carefully to appeal to the audience of the target media. The best press releases present the most important information early, are visually appealing, and look and sound credible.

Chapter Review

1. What is persuasion? (Obj. 1)
2. What four questions are receivers of persuasive messages likely to be asking themselves? (Obj. 2)
3. What are the four parts of successful persuasive messages? (Obj. 2)
4. List six ways to gain attention in a persuasive message. (Obj. 2)
5. Why is a written favor request or action request often more effective than a face-to-face request? (Obj.3)
6. Name five of more examples of typical situations requiring persuasive claim messages. (Obj. 3)
7. How can you reduce resistance in requesting favors, making claims, and delivering complaints? (Obj. 3)
8. When is persuasion necessary in business messages flowing downward in an organization? (Obj. 4)
9. When might persuasion be necessary in messages flowing upward? (Obj. 4)
10. Before composing a letter to sell a product, what should the writer do? (Obj. 5)
11. Name eight or more ways to attract attention in the opening of a sales message. (Obj. 5)
12. How can a writer motivate action in a sales letter? (Obj. 5)
13. Name four areas of the world where the culture is generally considered to be high context. Name four areas of the world where the culture is generally considered to be low context. (Obj. 6)
14. How do persuasive messages in high- and low-context cultures differ? (Obj. 6)
15. List five or more topics that an organization might feature in a press release. (Obj. 7)

Critical Thinking

1. The word *persuasion* turns some people off. What negative connotations can it have? (Obj. 1)
2. What are some of the underlying motivations that prompt individuals to agree to requests that do not directly benefit themselves or their organizations? (Obj. 2)
3. Why is it important to know your needs and have documentation when you make requests of superiors? (Obj. 4)
4. How are direct-mail sales messages and e-mail sales messages similar, and how are they different? (Obj. 5)
5. **Ethical Issue:** What is puffery, and how can it be justified in marketing messages? Consider the following: Dr. Phil calls himself "America's most trusted relationship counselor." Rush Limbaugh claims to be "America's anchorman." Sony's Cyber-Shot camera advertisement says "Make time stand still."

Activities

Note: All Documents for Analysis are provided at **www.meguffey.com** for you to download and revise.

10.1 Document for Analysis: Going Bananas at 7-Eleven (Objs. 1–3)

Your Task. Analyze the following poorly written persuasive e-mail request. List its weaknesses. If your instructor directs, revise it using the suggestions you learned in this chapter.

To: Members of the 7-Eleven Franchise Owners Association of Chicagoland
From: Nicholas Barajas <nicholas.barajas@hotmail.com>
Subject: Can You Believe Plastic-Wrapped Bananas?
Cc:
Bcc:

Hey, have you heard about this new thing coming at us? As a 7-Eleven franchise owner and member of the 7-Eleven Franchise Owners Association of Chicagoland, I am seriously put off about this move to wrap our bananas in plastic. Sure, it would extend their shelf life to five days. And I know that our customers want yellow–not brown—bananas. But wrapping them in plastic?? I mentioned this at home, and my teen-age daughter immediately turned up her nose and said, "A banana wrapped in plastic? Eeeyooo! Do we really need more plastic clogging up the environment?" She's been studying sustainability and said that more plastic packaging is not a sustainable solution to our problem.

I realize that we 7-Eleven franchisees are increasingly dependent on fresh food sales as cigarette sales tank. But plastic-wrapped bananas is going too far, even if the wrapping slows ripening. As members of the 7-Eleven Franchise Owners Association, we have to do something. I think we could insist that our supplier Fresh Del Monte come up with a wrapper that's biodegradable. On the other hand, extending the shelf life of bananas cuts the carbon footprint by cutting down all those deliveries to our stores.

We have a meeting of franchisees coming up on January 20. Let's resist this banana thing!

Nick

10.2 Document for Analysis: Weak Favor Request (Obj. 3)

Your Task. Analyze the following poorly written invitation. List its weaknesses. If your instructor directs, revise the letter. Add appropriate information if needed.

Current date

Ms. Danielle Watkins
The Beverly Hills Hotel
9641 Sunset Boulevard
Beverly Hills, CA 90210

Dear Ms. Watkins:

We know you are a very busy hospitality professional as chef at the Beverly Hills Hotel, but we would like you to make a presentation to the San Francisco chapter of the National Restaurant Association. I was asked to write you since I am program chair.

I heard that you made a good presentation at your local chapter in Los Angeles recently. I think you gave a talk called "Avoiding the Seven Cardinal Sins in Food Service" or something like that. Whatever it was, I'm sure we would like to hear the same or a similar presentation. All restaurant operators are interested in doing what we can to avoid potential problems involving discrimination, safety at work, how we hire people, etc. As you well know, operating a fast-paced restaurant is frustrating—even on a good day. We are all in a gigantic rush from opening the door early in the morning to shutting it again after the last customer has gone. It's a rat race and easy to fall into the trap with food service faults that push a big operation into trouble.

Enclosed please find a list of questions that our members listed. We would like you to talk in the neighborhood of 45 minutes. Our June 10 meeting will be in the Oak Room of the Westin St. Francis Hotel in San Francisco and dinner begins at 7 p.m.

How can we get you to come to San Francisco? We can only offer you an honorarium of $200, but we would pay for any travel expenses. You can expect a large crowd of restaurateurs who are known for hooting and hollering when they hear good stuff! As you can see, we are a rather informal group. Hope you can join us!

Sincerely,

10.3 Document for Analysis: Weak Persuasive Memo Flowing Upward (Obj. 4)

Your Task. Analyze the following memo, which suffers from many writing faults. List its weaknesses. If your instructor directs, revise the letter.

DATE: Current
TO: Bryanna Mazzetta, Vice President, Marketing
FROM: Luke Downey, Exhibit Manager
SUBJECT: Possible Change for Saving Money

We always try our best to meet customers and sell Worldclass Trainer equipment at numerous trade shows. But instead of expanding our visits to these trade shows, the company continues to cut back the number that we attend. And we have fewer staff members attending. I know that you have been asking us to find ways to reduce costs, but I don't think we are going about it right.

With increased airfares and hotel charges, my staff has tried to find ways to live within our very tight budget. Yet, we are being asked to find other ways to reduce our costs. I'm currently thinking ahead to the big Las Vegas trade show coming up in September.

One area where we could make a change is in the gift that we give away. In the past we have presented booth visitors with a nine-color T-shirt that is silk-screened and gorgeous. But it comes at a cost of $23 for each and every one of these beauties from a top-name designer. To save money, I suggest that we try a $6 T-shirt made in China, which is reasonably presentable. It's got our name on it, and, after all, folks just use these shirts for workouts. Who cares if it is a fancy silk-screened T-shirt or a functional Chinese one that has "Worldclass Trainer" plastered on the chest? Because we give away 2,000 T-shirts at our largest show, we could save big bucks by dumping the designer shirt. But we have to act quickly. I've enclosed a cheap one for you to see.

Let me know what you think.

10.4 Document for Analysis: Poor Claim Letter (Obj. 3)

Your Task. Analyze the following poorly written claim letter. List its weaknesses. If your instructor directs, revise it.

Current date

Mr. Jason M. Amato
TEK Copier Solutions
13429 North 59th Avenue
Glendale, AZ 85307

Dear Sir:

I hate to write to you with a complaint, but my company purchased four of your Multifunction SX500 photocopiers, and we've had nothing but trouble ever since.

Your salesperson, Gary Kazan, assured us that the Multifunction SX500 could easily handle our volume of 3,000 copies a day. This seemed strange since the sales brochure said that the Multifunction SX500 was meant for 500 copies a day. But we put our faith in Mr. Kazan. What a mistake! Our four SX copiers are down constantly, and we can't go on like this. Because they are still under warranty, they eventually get repaired. But we are losing considerable business in downtime.

Because your Mr. Kazan has been less than helpful, I telephoned the district manager, Victor Martineau. I suggested that we trade in our Multifunction SX500 copiers (which we got for $2,500 each) on two Multifunction XX800 models (at $13,500 each). However, Mr. Martineau said he would have to charge 50 percent depreciation on our SX500 copiers. What a rip-off! I think that 20 percent depreciation is more reasonable since we've had the machines only three months. Mr. Martineau said he would get back to me, and I haven't heard from him since.

Now I'm forced to write to your headquarters because I have no faith in either Ms. Kazan or Mr. Martineau, and I need to see some action on these machines. If you understood anything about business, you would see what a sweet deal I'm offering you. I'm willing to stick with your company and purchase your most expensive model—but I can't take such a steep loss on the SX500 copiers. These copiers are relatively new; you should be able to sell them with no trouble. And think of all the money you will save by not having your repair technicians making constant trips to service our underpowered Multifunction SX500 copiers! Please let me hear from you immediately.

Sincerely yours,

10.5 Persuasive Favor/Action Request: Inviting an Alumna to Speak (Obj. 3)

E-mail

As public relations director for the Business and Accounting Association on your campus, you have been asked to find a keynote speaker for the first meeting of the school year. The owner of a successful local firm, TempHelp4You, is an alumna of your university. You think not only that many students would enjoy learning about how she started her business, but also that some might like to sign up with her temporary help agency. She would need to prepare a 30-minute speech and take questions after the talk. The event will be held from noon until 1:30 p.m. on a date of your choosing in Branford Hall. You can offer her lunch at the event and provide her with a parking permit that she can pick up at the information kiosk at the main entrance to your campus. You need to have her response by a deadline you set.

Your Task. Write a direct approach e-mail to Marion Minter in which you ask her to speak at your club's meeting. Send it to *mminter@temphelp4you.com*.

10.6 Persuasive Favor/Action Request: Asking Beijing to Use Excel (Objs. 3, 6)

Intercultural

Mario Franchini, regional sales manager for a multinational manufacturer, is always in a hurry and doesn't take the time to write careful messages. As his assistant, you sometimes revise messages for him. Today he asks you to look over his message to Zhu Chen, regional sales manager for the company's prosperous branch in Beijing. On his way out the door, Mario says to you, "Please fix up the following memo. Make it sound better!"

> Hi there, Zhu! I know you haven't heard from me 4 a while, so don't hit the panic button! I need you to do me a big favor. I'm going to skip the bull and drive right to the point. I need your sales figures to be submitted in Excel spreadsheets. You could hit a home run by zeroing in on the sales for your region and zapping them to us in a better format. We just can't use the ledger account forms you usually send. They may work for your office in Beijing, but they won't fly here in Seattle. I'm counting on you to come through for me by using Excel in submitting your future sales figures. You already have the software available through our home office intranet. Just download it. You will see it's easy as pie to learn. When you send your next quarterly figures at the end of September, I expect to see them in Excel. Chow!

Your Task. You know that messages to your office from Beijing are usually more formal and often begin with a friendly greeting. You decide to try out your intercultural skills in writing a better favor request. For your boss's signature, revise this message using memo format. After approval, the memo will be faxed.

10.7 Persuasive Favor/Action Request: Borrowing Suits for Interviews (Obj. 3)

You saw an interesting article describing a Suitable Suits program at Barnard College. Its College of Career Development kept a closet filled with 21 crisp black suits that students could borrow for job interviews. Students made an appointment with the office and agreed to dry clean the suits before returning them. At Barnard the program was paid for with a grant from a prominent financial firm.[18] You think that a Suitable Suits program is worth exploring with your dean.

Your Task. Write a persuasive letter requesting an appointment with your dean to discuss a Suitable Suits program at your school. You don't have all the answers and you are not sure how such a program would operate, but you think the idea is worth discussing. Can you convince the dean to see you?

10.8 Persuasive Favor/Action Request: A Helping Hand for College Expenses (Obj. 3)

Team

After working a few years, you would like to extend your college education on a part-time basis. You know that your education can benefit your employer, but you can't really afford the fees for tuition and books. You have heard that many companies offer reimbursement for fees and books when employees complete approved courses with a grade of C or higher.

Your Task. In teams discuss the best way to approach an employer whom you wish to persuade to start a tuition/books reimbursement program. How could such a program help the employer? Remember that the most successful requests help receivers see what's in it for them. What objections might your employer raise? How can you counter them? After discussing strategies in teams, write a team memo or individual memos to your boss (for a company where you now work or one with which you are familiar). Persuade her or him to act on your action request.

10.9 Persuasive Favor/Action Request: Dear Senator or Representative (Obj. 3)

Web

Assume you are upset about an issue, and you want your representative or senator to know your position. Choose a national issue about which you feel strongly: student loans, social security depletion, human rights in other countries, the federal deficit, federal safety regulations for employees, environmental protection, gun control, taxation of married couples, finding a cure for obesity, or some other area regulated by Congress.

How does one write to a congressional representative? For the best results, consider these tips:

a. Use the proper form of address (*The Honorable John Smith, Dear Senator Smith* or *The Honorable Joan Doe, Dear Representative Doe*).
b. Identify yourself as a member of his or her state or district.
c. Immediately state your position (*I urge you to support/oppose . . . because . . .*).
d. Present facts and illustrations and explain how they affect you personally. If legislation were enacted, how would you or your organization be better or worse off? Avoid generalities.
e. Offer to provide further information.
f. Keep the message polite, constructive, and brief (one page, tops).

Your Task. Search the Web to obtain your congressional representative's address. Try the search term *contacting Congress.* You should be able to find e-mail and land addresses, along with fax and telephone numbers. Remember that although e-mail and fax messages are fast, they don't carry as much influence as personal letters. Moreover, congressional representatives are having trouble responding to the overload of e-mails they receive. Decide whether it would be better to send an e-mail or a letter.

10.10 Persuasive Favor/Action Request: School Vending Machines Become Weighty Problem (Obj. 3)

Team Web

© Glow Images/Photolibrary

"If I start to get huge, then, yeah, I'll cut out the chips and Coke," says 17-year-old Nicole O'Neill, as she munches sour-cream-and-onion potato chips and downs a cold can of soda fresh from the snack machine. Most days her lunch comes from a vending machine. The trim high school junior, however, isn't too concerned about how junk food affects her weight or overall health. Although she admits she would prefer a granola bar or fruit, few healthful selections are available from school vending machines.

Vending machines loaded with soft drinks and snacks are increasingly under attack in schools and lunchrooms. Some school boards, however, see them as cash cows. In Gresham, Oregon, the school district is considering a lucrative soft drink contract. If it signs an exclusive 12-year agreement with Coca-Cola to allow vending machines at Gresham High School, the school district will receive $75,000 up front. Then it will receive an additional $75,000 three years later. Commission sales on the 75-cent drinks will bring in an additional $322,000 over the 12-year contract, provided the school sells 67,000 cans and bottles every year. In the past the vending machine payments supported student body activities such as sending students to choir concerts and paying athletic participation fees. Vending machine funds also paid for an electronic reader board in front of the school and a sound system for the gym. The latest contract would bring in $150,000, which is already earmarked for new artificial turf on the school athletic field.

Coca-Cola's vending machines would dispense soft drinks, Fruitopia, Minute Maid juices, Powerade, and Dasani water. The hands-down student favorite, of course, is calorie-laden Coke. Because increasing childhood and adolescent obesity across the nation is a major health concern, the Gresham Parent Teacher Association (PTA) decided to oppose the contract. The PTA realizes that the school board is heavily influenced by the income generated from the Coca-Cola contract. It wonders what other school districts are doing about their vending machine contracts.

Your Task. As part of a PTA committee, you have been given the task of researching and composing a persuasive but concise (no more than one page) letter addressed to the school board. Use the Web or databases to locate articles that might help you develop arguments, alternatives, and counterarguments. Meet with your team to discuss your findings. Then, individually or as a group, write a letter to the Board of Directors, Gresham-Barlow School District, P.O. Box 310, Gresham, OR 97033.

10.11 Persuasive Claim: Overcharged and Unhappy (Obj. 3)

As regional manager for an electronics parts manufacturer, you and two other employees attended a conference in Nashville. You stayed at the Country Inn because your company recommends that employees use this hotel chain. Generally, your employees have liked their accommodations, and the rates have been within your company's budget.

Now, however, you are unhappy with the charges you see on your company's credit statement from Country Inn. When your department's administrative assistant made the reservations, she was assured that you would receive the weekend rates and that a hot breakfast—in the hotel restaurant, the Atrium—would be included in the rate. You hate those cold sweet rolls and instant coffee "continental" breakfasts, especially when you have to leave early and won't get another meal until afternoon. So you and the other two employees went to the restaurant and ordered a hot meal from the menu.

When you received the credit statement, though, you see a charge for $114 for three champagne buffet breakfasts in the Atrium. You hit the ceiling! For one thing, you didn't have a buffet breakfast and certainly no champagne. The three of you got there so early that no buffet had been set up. You ordered pancakes and sausage, and for this you were billed $35 each. You are outraged! What's worse, your company may charge you personally for exceeding the expected rates.

In looking back at this event, you remembered that other guests on your floor were having a "continental" breakfast in a lounge on your floor. Perhaps that's where the hotel expected all guests on the weekend rate to eat. However, your administrative assistant had specifically asked about this matter when she made the reservations, and she was told that you could order breakfast from the menu at the hotel's restaurant.

Your Task. You want to straighten out this matter, and you can't do it by telephone because you suspect that you will need a written record of this entire mess. Write a claim request to Customer Service, Country Inn, Inc., 428 Church Street, Nashville, TN 37219. Should you include a copy of the credit statement showing the charge?

10.12 Persuasive Claim: Legal Costs for Sharing a Slice of Heaven (Obj. 3)

Originally a shipbuilding village, the town of Mystic, Connecticut, captures the spirit of the nineteenth-century seafaring era. But it is best known for Mystic Pizza, a bustling local pizzeria featured in a movie that launched the film career of Julia Roberts. Today, customers line the sidewalk waiting to taste its pizza, called by some "a slice of Heaven."

Assume that you are the business manager for Mystic Pizza's owners. They were approached by an independent vendor who wants to use the Mystic Pizza name and secret recipes to distribute frozen pizza through grocery and convenience stores. As business manager, you worked with a law firm, Giordano, Murphy, and Associates. This firm was to draw up contracts regarding the use of Mystic Pizza's name and quality standards for the product. When you received the bill from Henry Giordano, you were flabbergasted. It itemized 38 hours of attorney preparation, at $400 per hour, and 55 hours of paralegal assistance, at $100 per hour. The bill also showed $415 for telephone calls, which might be accurate because Mr. Giordano had to talk with the owners, who were vacationing in Italy at the time. You seriously doubt, however, that an experienced attorney would require 38 hours to draw up the contracts in question. When you began checking, you discovered that excellent legal advice could be obtained for $200 an hour.

Your Task. Decide what you want to request, and then write a persuasive request to Henry Giordano, Attorney at Law, Giordano, Murphy, and Associates, 254 Sherborn Street, Boston, MA 02215. Include an end date and a reason for it.

10.13 Persuasive Claim: Botched Print Job (Obj. 3)

As president of Holiday Travel, you brought a very complex print job to the Jiffy Printers in Brighton, New York. It took almost 15 minutes to explain the particulars of this job to the printer. When you left, you wondered whether all of the instructions would be followed precisely. You even brought in your own special paper, which added to the cost of printing.

When you got the job back (a total of 1,500 sheets of paper) and returned to your office, you discovered a host of problems. One of the pages had 300 copies made on cheap 20-pound paper. This means that the printer must have run out of your special paper and substituted something else for one of the runs. The printer also made copies of your original photos and graphics, so that all the final prints were run from second-generation prints, which reduced the quality of the graphics enormously. What's more, many of the sheets were poorly or improperly cut. In short, the job was unacceptable.

Because you were desperate to complete the job, you allowed the print shop to repeat the job using its paper supply. When you inquired about the cost, the counter person Don was noncommittal. He said you would have to talk to the owner, who worked in the Rochester shop. The repeat print job turned out fairly well, and you paid the full price of $782. But you are unhappy, and Don sensed that Jiffy Printers would not see Holiday Travel again as a customer. He encouraged you to write to the owner and ask for an adjustment.

Your Task. Write a claim letter to Mr. Howard Moscatelli, Jiffy Printers, 3402 South Main Street, Rochester, NY 14634. What is a reasonable claim to make? Do you simply want to register your unhappiness, or do you want a refund? Supply any needed information.

10.14 Persuasive Claim: Honolulu Country Club Gets Scammed on Phony Toner Phoner (Obj. 3)

Heather W. was new to her job as administrative assistant at the Waialae Country Club in Honolulu. Alone in the office one morning, she answered a phone call from Rick, who said he was the country club's copier contractor. "Hey, look, Babydoll," Rick purred, "the price on the toner you use is about to go way up. I can offer you a great price on this toner if you order right now." Heather knew that the copy machine regularly needed toner, and she thought she should probably go ahead and place the order to save the country club some money. Ten days later two bottles of toner arrived, and Heather was pleased at the perfect timing. The copy machine needed it right away. Three weeks later Maureen, the bookkeeper, called to report a bill from Copy Machine Specialists for $960.43 for two bottles of toner. "What's going on here?" said Maureen. "We don't purchase supplies from this company, and this price is totally off the charts!"[19]

Heather spoke to the manager, Steven Tanaka, who immediately knew what had happened. He blamed himself for not training Heather. "Never, never order anything from a telephone solicitor, no matter how fast-talking or smooth he sounds," warned Steven. He outlined an office policy for future supplies purchases. Only certain people can authorize or finalize a purchase, and purchases require a confirmed price including shipping costs settled in advance. But what to do about this $960.43 bill? The country club had already begun to use the toner, although the current copies were looking faint and streaked.

Your Task. As Steven Tanaka, decide how to respond to this obvious scam. Should you pay the bill? Should you return the unused bottle? Write a persuasive claim to Copy Machine Specialists, 4320 Admiralty Way, Honolulu, HI 96643. Supply any details necessary.

10.15 Persuasive Organizational Message Flowing Upward: How About a Four-Day Week? (Obj. 4)

Team | Web

Gas prices are skyrocketing, and many companies and municipalities are switching to a four-day workweek to reduce gas consumption and air pollution. Compressing the workweek into four 10-hour days sounds pretty good to you. You would much prefer having Friday free to schedule medical appointments and take care of family business, in addition to leisurely three-day weekends.

As a manager at Skin Essentials, a mineral-based skin care products and natural cosmetics company, you are convinced that the company's 400 employees could switch to a four-day workweek with many resulting benefits. For one thing, they would save on gasoline and commute time. You know that many cities and companies have already implemented a four-day workweek with considerable success. You took a quick poll of immediate employees and managers and found that 80 percent thought that a four-day workweek was a good idea. One said, "This would be great! Think of what I could save on babysitting and lunches!"

Your Task. With a group of other managers, conduct research on the Web and discuss your findings. What are the advantages of a four-day workweek? What organizations have already tried it? What appeals could be used to persuade management to adopt a four-day workweek? What arguments could be expected, and how would you counter them? Individually or as a group, prepare a one-page persuasive memo addressed to Skin Essentials Management Council. Decide on a goal. Do you want to suggest a pilot study? Meet with management to present your ideas? Start a four-day workweek immediately?

10.16 Persuasive Organizational Message Flowing Upward: Providing Handheld GPS Devices to Hotel Guests (Obj. 4)

Always seeking to solve problems, you have a great idea for an amenity at the hotel where you work. Hotel guests often ask for directions to local restaurants or special local sights. But they sometimes get lost or exasperated when they can't find what they seek. Guests also go walking, jogging, or sightseeing and can't find their way back to the hotel.

As the assistant manager at an upscale hotel in your town or area, you saw a newspaper article about the five-star Rosewood hotel chain. It offers use of handheld GPS navigators free at select properties. You have a GPS device in your car, and you know how amazing it is when it can talk you right to your destination. Clearly, your hotel could distinguish itself competitively and be among the first to offer this new perk to guests. Rosewood hotels offering this service include The Carlyle (Manhattan), The Mansion on Turtle Creek (Dallas), and Hotel Crescent Court (Dallas).[20] La Jolla Shores, near San Diego, also offers this amenity.

You would like to convince your manager to offer this service. On the Web you discover that a Garmin nüvi 260 is just the right size. If a hotel guest is out jogging or sightseeing and loses the way, the guest can hit "home" and the GPS tells the direction back to the hotel from anywhere. The Garmin costs $250, which you think is not excessive. Although your manager is cost-conscious, he loves gadgets. You think that if the GPS device could attract just two guests per month, it would probably be worth it. You like the fact that when hotel guests at Rosewood hotels ask for directions, a concierge can plug in the desired location, hit "go," and the GPS will talk guests through the drive or walk until they arrive.

Your Task. Write a convincing message to Manager Martin Zatari. Before writing, decide what you want to ask. Should you ask for a meeting to discuss the proposal? Should you request a trial period in which you try out one or two GPS navigators? You haven't worked out all of the details of a GPS program, but you think the idea is worth talking about. You will need to gather information about a GPS device that might work for your purpose. Name specific restaurants or local attractions in your memo. What benefits can you suggest for your manager and for the hotel?

10.17 Persuasive Organizational Message Flowing Upward: An Apple a Day (Obj. 4)

During the recent economic downturn, Omni Hotels looked for ways to slice expenses. Omni operates 43 luxury hotels and resorts in leading business gateways and leisure destinations across North America. From exceptional golf and spa retreats to dynamic business settings, each Omni showcases the local flavor of the destination while featuring four-diamond services.

Omni Hotels ranks in the top three in "Highest in Guest Satisfaction Among Upscale Hotel Chains," according to J. D. Power. One signature amenity it has offered for years is a bowl of free apples in its lobbies. However, the practice of providing apples costs hundreds of thousands of dollars a year. They have to cut costs somewhere, and executives are debating whether to cut out apples as a way to save money with minimum impact on guests.

Omni Hotels prides itself on providing guests with superior service through The Power of One, a service program that provides associates the training and authority to make decisions that exceed the expectations of guests. The entire culture of the hotel provides a positive, supportive environment that rewards associates through the Omni Service Champions program. As an Omni associate, you are disturbed that the hotel is considering giving up its free apples. You hope that executives will find other ways to cut expenses, such as purchasing food in smaller amounts or reducing the hours of its lobby cafes.[21]

Your Task. In the true sense of The Power of One, you decide to express your views to management. Write a persuasive message to Richard Johnson, (*rjohnson@omni.com*), Vice President, Operations, Omni Hotels, 420 Decker Drive, Irving, TX 75062. Should you write a letter or an e-mail? In a separate note to your instructor, explain your rationale for your channel choice and your message strategy.

10.18 Persuasive Organizational Message Flowing Upward: Keeping Track of Office Projects (Obj. 4)

E-mail

© iStockphoto.com/Justin Horrocks

As the supervisor of administrative support at an architectural engineering firm, you serve five project managers. You find it difficult to keep track of what everybody is doing and where they are working. Mike is in New Orleans, Jason just left for Kansas City, Brian is working on a project in St. Louis, and Andrea is completing a job in Houston. With so many people working on projects in various places, it is hard to know where people are and what they are doing. Assigning administrative assistants and tracking their work is difficult. Although digital tools would be ideal, this office has shown no interest in wikis or similar collaborative tools. You decide that you and your managers need a dry erase board in the office to record projects and their status. Plain dry erase boards are not expensive at Wal-Mart. But can you persuade the managers to accept this new tool? They are largely independent engineers who are not attuned to following office procedures. Moreover, who will keep the board current?

Your Task. Write a convincing e-mail that persuades managers that your office needs a dry erase board to record weekly projects. Outline the benefits. How can you make it easy for them to buy in to using this new tool? Fill in any details from your imagination, but keep the message fairly simple. Address the first e-mail to *Mike.Kuryia@walters_inc.com*.

10.19 Persuasive Organizational Message Flowing Upward: Training Telecommuters (Obj. 4)

E-mail Team Web

James Lush arose from bed in his Connecticut home and looked outside to see a heavy snowstorm creating a fairyland of white. But he felt none of the giddiness that usually accompanies a potential snow day. Such days were a gift from heaven when schools closed, businesses shut down, and the world ground to a halt. As an on-and-off telecommuter for many years, he knew that snow days were a thing of the past. These days, work for James Lush and 23.5 million other American employees is no farther than their home office.[22]

More and more employees are becoming telecommuters. They want to work at home, where they feel they can be more productive and avoid the hassle of driving to work. Some need to telecommute only temporarily, while they take care of family obligations, births, illnesses, or personal problems. Others are highly skilled individuals who can do their work at home as easily as in the office. Businesses definitely see advantages to telecommuting. They don't have to supply office space for workers. What's more, as businesses continue to flatten management structures, bosses no longer have time to micromanage employees. Increasingly, they are leaving workers to their own devices.

But the results have not been totally satisfactory. For one thing, in-house workers resent those who work at home. More important are problems of structure and feedback. Telecommuters don't always have the best work habits, and lack of communication is a major issue. Unless the telecommuter is expert at coordinating projects and leaving instructions, productivity can fizzle. Appreciating the freedom but recognizing that they need guidance, employees are saying, "Push me, but don't leave me out there all alone!"

As human resources manager at your company, you already have 83 employees who are either full- or part-time telecommuters. With increasing numbers asking to work in remote locations, you decide that workers and their managers must receive training on how to do it effectively. You are considering hiring a consultant to train your prospective telecommuters and their managers. Another possibility is developing an in-house training program.

Your Task. As human resources manager, you must convince Victor Vasquez, vice president, that your company needs a training program for all workers who are currently telecommuting or who plan to do so. Their managers should also receive training. You decide to ask your staff of four to help you gather information. Using the Web, you and your team read several articles on what such training should include. Now you must decide what action you want the vice president to take. Meet with you to discuss a training program? Commit to a budget item for future training? Hire a consultant or agency to come in and conduct training programs? Individually or as a team, write a convincing e-mail to *victor.vasquet@beta.com* that describes the problem, suggests what the training should include, and asks for action by a specific date. Add any reasonable details necessary to build your case.

10.20 Persuasive Organizational Message Flowing Upward: Dear Boss (Obj. 4)

E-mail

In your own work or organization experience, identify a problem for which you have a solution. Should a procedure be altered to improve performance? Would a new or different piece of equipment help you perform your work better? Could some tasks be scheduled more efficiently? Are employees being used most effectively? Could customers be better served by changing something? Do you want to work other hours or perform other tasks? Do you deserve a promotion? Do you have a suggestion to improve profitability?

Your Task. Once you have identified a situation requiring persuasion, write a memo or an e-mail to your boss or organization head. Use actual names and facts. Employ the concepts and techniques in this chapter to help you convince your boss that your idea should prevail. Include concrete examples, anticipate objections, emphasize reader benefits, and end with a specific action to be taken.

10.21 Persuasive Organizational Message Flowing Upward: Demanding Mandatory Tipping (Obj. 4)

Team

Centered in the heart of a 2,400-acre Florida paradise, the Bayside Inn Golf and Beach Resort offers gracious hospitality and beautiful accommodations. Its restaurant, Dolphin Watch, overlooks the scenic Choctawhatchee Bay, a perfect place to spy dolphins. As a server in the Dolphin Watch, you enjoy working in this resort setting—except for one thing. You have occasionally been "stiffed" by a patron who left no tip. You know your service is excellent, but some customers just don't get it. They seem to think that tips are optional, a sign of appreciation. For servers, however, tips are 80 percent of their income.

In a recent *New York Times* article, you learned that some restaurants—such as the famous Coach House Restaurant in New York—automatically add a 15 percent tip to the bill. In Santa Monica the Lula restaurant prints "gratuity guidelines" on checks, showing customers what a 15 or 20 percent tip would be. You also know that American Express recently developed a gratuity calculation feature on its terminals. This means that diners don't even have to do the math!

Your Task. Because they know you are studying business communication, your fellow servers have asked you to write a serious letter to Nicholas Ruiz, General Manager, Bayside Inn Golf and Beach Resort, 9300 Emerald Coast Parkway West, Sandestin, FL 32550-7268. Persuade him to adopt mandatory tipping guidelines in the restaurant. Talk with fellow servers (your classmates) to develop logical persuasive arguments.

10.22 Persuasive Organizational Message Flowing Downward: Reducing Your Health Insurance Costs (Obj. 4)

As part of the management team at Bank of Westfield, you want to help your employees improve their health and reduce their health costs at the same time. Because the Bank of Westfield is a small company, its risk is greater than those of larger firms. Individuals with health problems have always paid more for health insurance. However, federal law requires that all employees who are covered by employer insurance programs must pay the same premium. That means that those with poor health cannot be charged more for insurance than those with good health. Recent legislation now allows some exceptions if employers offer wellness programs.

Working with its insurance carrier, the Bank of Westfield developed a plan that would enable employees to reduce their deductible $500 for each health benchmark the employee reached. For example, a nonsmoker receives a $500 deduction in the overall deductible of $2,500. Other benchmark categories are cholesterol, body mass index, and blood pressure. If the Bank of Westfield can persuade employees to meet benchmarks in these areas, employees can reduce their deductibles by $500 for each benchmark. This should help quiet the grumbling that resulted last year when the insurance deductible jumped from $500 to $2,500.

All of the benchmarks are explained in the "Road to Health" brochure provided by the insurance carrier. To get employees started, the Bank of Westfield wants them to fill out an application (before January 15) to see a fitness counselor who will develop a customized fitness plan for each employee who signs up. The company will provide literature, fitness programs, and counseling to help employees meet their benchmarks.

Your Task. As Melissa Mendoza, Human Resources, prepare a persuasive action request memo to send to Bank of Westfield staff members. Promote both direct and indirect benefits. Anticipate obstacles and address them. Close with an action request. Your message should tell exactly what you want the receiver to do and provide an extension number for anyone who has questions. Send a memo rather than an e-mail because you want to enclose the "Road to Health" brochure and application.

10.23 Persuasive Organizational Messages Flowing Downward: And Now We Want Your Blood! (Obj. 4)

Team

Companies are increasingly asking employees to take on-site blood tests. Because forcing employees to do so would invade their privacy, companies must persuade them to volunteer. Why should companies bother?

Blood tests are part of health risk assessment. Such assessments are considered the first step toward controlling chronic and expensive health problems such as diabetes, obesity, and tobacco addiction. According to American Healthways, employers using blood tests have seen between a $300 and $1,440 decrease in health care costs per participant, depending on what kind of incentive they offer to participants.

Snap-on, a well-known manufacturer of power and hand tools, began offering blood tests as part of a health assessment program a year ago. Although the first-year sign-up was slow, Snap-on saw a 50 percent increase in sign-ups the following year as employees became familiar with the plan. Employees filled out health risk questionnaires. Then they received the results of their questionnaires so that they could see how their blood work compared with their own assessments. Snap-on assured employees that the company would never see the results. The blood tests, conducted by American Healthways, screened for cholesterol, diabetes, hypertension, body fat, liver function, and nicotine. Employers receive only combined data about their employees.

Even though employees were the benefactors of these blood tests, Snap-on had to offer an incentive to urge them to participate. Employees received a $20 monthly discount on health care premiums for agreeing to the full assessment process, including the blood test.

However, another company found that the penalty approach was more effective in encouraging employee participation. Westell Technologies, which makes broadband communication equipment, charged employees 10 percent higher health care premiums if they refused to take the blood tests. This penalty program resulted in 80 percent participation. Regardless of the method used to encourage participation, any on-site blood testing must be voluntary.[23]

Assume you are part of a group of interns at manufacturer Colman International, which employs 900 people. The director of interns, Christine Davis, is also vice president of Human Resources. One day she calls your group together and says, "Listen up! Colman needs employees to take these blood tests and fill out health risk assessment forms. We know this is a hard sell, but we think it is the right thing to do—not only for employees but also for the company because it will lower our skyrocketing health care costs. So here's what I want you interns to do as a training exercise. Get together and decide what you think is the best way for us to persuade employees to participate. Should we offer incentives or threaten penalties?"

Seeing the blank expressions on your faces, she said, "Oh, you can assume that the company will back whatever decision you make—so long as it's not out of line with what other companies are doing. Once you decide what to do, I want you to prepare a message to employees. Medical staff from American Healthways will be in the human resources training room to conduct the blood tests on Monday, November 17, through Friday, November 21. Appointments are available between 7:30 a.m. and 5:30 p.m. Employees may sign up for appointments by e-mailing me before November 10 at *cdavis@colman.com* and requesting an appointment time. They will receive a confirmation e-mail stating the date and appointment time."

Your Task. Individually or as a group, prepare two messages. Address one to Christine Davis. Explain what your group decided and justify the rationale for your decisions. Address the second message to Colman employees for the signature of Ms. Davis. Persuade employees to participate in the program. Remember to anticipate objections to your request. How can these objections be overcome? Should you emphasize benefits to the reader or to the company? What direct and indirect benefits can you name? What is the best communication channel for this message? How can you make it easy for receivers to respond?

10.24 Persuasive Organizational Message Flowing Downward: Cutting Overnight Shipping Costs (Obj. 4)

As office manager of an East Coast software company, write a memo persuading your technicians, engineers, programmers, and other employees to reduce the number of overnight or second-day mail shipments. Your FedEx and other shipping bills have been sky high, and you feel that staff members are overusing these services.

You think employees should send messages by e-mail or fax. Sending a zipped file or PDF file as an e-mail attachment costs very little. What's more, a fax costs only about 35 cents a page to most long-distance areas and nothing to local areas. Compare this with $15 to $20 for FedEx service! Whenever possible, staff members should obtain the FedEx account number of the recipient and use it for charging the shipment. If staff members plan ahead and allow enough time, they can use UPS or FedEx ground service, which takes three to five days and is much cheaper. You wonder whether staff members consider whether the recipient is really going to use the message as soon as it arrives. Does it justify an overnight shipment? You would like to reduce overnight delivery services voluntarily by 50 percent over the next two months. Unless a sizable reduction occurs, the CEO threatens severe restrictions in the future.

Your Task. Address your memo to all staff members. What other ways could employees reduce shipping costs?

10.25 Persuasive Organizational Message Flowing Downward: Supporting Project H.E.L.P. (Obj. 4)

E-mail

As employee relations manager of The Prudential Insurance Company, one of your tasks is to promote Project H.E.L.P. (Higher Education Learning Program), an on-the-job learning opportunity. Project H.E.L.P. is a combined effort of major corporations and the Newark Unified School District. You must recruit 12 employees who will volunteer as instructors for 50 or more students. The students will spend four hours a week at the Prudential Newark facility earning an average of five units of credit a semester.

This semester the students will be serving in the Claims, Word Processing, Corporate Media Services, Marketing, Communications, Library, and Administrative Support departments. Your task is to convince employees in these departments to volunteer. They will be expected to supervise and instruct the students. In return, employees will receive two hours of release time per week to work with the students. The program has been very successful thus far. School officials, students, and employees alike express satisfaction with the experience and the outcomes.

Your Task. Write a persuasive memo or e-mail with convincing appeals that will bring you 12 volunteers to work with Project H.E.L.P.

10.26 Persuasive Organizational Message Flowing Downward: Revising Miserable Memo (Obj. 4)

The following memo (with names changed) was actually sent.

Your Task. Based on what you have learned in this chapter, improve the memo. Expect the staff to be somewhat resistant because they have never before had meeting restrictions.

TO: All Managers and Employees
FROM: Rita Nelson, CEO
SUBJECT: Scheduling Meetings

Please be reminded that travel in the greater Los Angeles area is time consuming. In the future we are asking that you set up meetings that

1. Are of critical importance
2. Consider travel time for the participants
3. Consider phone conferences (or video or e-mail) in lieu of face-to-face meetings
4. Meetings should be at the location where most of the participants work and at the most opportune travel times
5. Traveling together is another way to save time and resources.

We all have our traffic horror stories. A recent one is that a certain manager was asked to attend a one-hour meeting in Burbank. This required one hour travel in advance of the meeting, one hour for the meeting, and two and a half hours of travel through Los Angeles afterward. This meeting was scheduled for 4 p.m. Total time consumed by the manager for the one-hour meeting was four and a half hours.

Thank you for your consideration.

10.27 Persuasive Organizational Message Flowing Downward: Curbing Profanity on the Job (Obj. 4)

E-mail Web

As sales manager for a large irrigation parts manufacturer, you are concerned about the use of profanity by your sales associates. Some defend profanity, claiming that it helps them fit in. Your female sales reps have said that it helps relax listeners, drives home a point, and makes them "one of the boys." You have done some research, however, and learned that courts have ruled that profanity can constitute sexual harassment—whether in person or in print. In addition to causing legal problems, profanity on the job projects a negative image of the individual and of the company. Although foul language is heard increasingly on TV and in the movies, you think it is a bad habit and you want to see it curbed on the job.

Your Task. Use the Web or databases to locate articles related to the use of profanity and strategies employed by organizations for dealing with it. One good resource is **http://www.cusscontrol.com**. In small groups or in class, discuss the place of formal and informal language in communication. Prepare a list of reasons people curse and reasons not to do so. Your instructor may ask you to interview employers to learn their reactions to the issue of workplace profanity. As sales manager at Rain City, compose a persuasive e-mail or memo to your sales staff that will encourage them to curb their use of profanity.[24]

10.28 Sales Letter Analysis (Obj. 5)

Your Task. Select a one- or two-page sales letter received by you or a friend. Study the letter and then answer these questions:

a. What techniques capture the reader's attention?
b. Is the opening effective? Explain.
c. What are the central selling points?
d. Does the letter use rational, emotional, or a combination of appeals? Explain.
e. What reader benefits are suggested?
f. How does the letter build interest in the product or service?
g. How is price handled?
h. How does the letter anticipate reader resistance and offer counter-arguments?
i. What action is the reader to take? How is the action made easy?
j. What motivators spur the reader to act quickly?

10.29 Sales Letter: Weighing In at Work (Obj. 5)

Web

Nearly 68 percent of adults in America are overweight, and 34 percent are obese.[25] In addition to the risks to individuals, obesity costs American companies billions in lost productivity caused by disability, illness, and death.[26] Companies from Wall Street to the Rust Belt are launching or improving programs to help employees lose weight. Union Pacific Railroad is considering giving out pedometers to track workers around the office, as well as dispensing weight loss drugs. Merrill Lynch sponsors Weight Watchers meetings. Caterpillar instituted the Healthy Balance program. It promotes long-term behavioral change and healthier lifestyles for Caterpillar workers. Estimates suggest that employers and employees could save a total of $1,200 a year for each person's medical costs if overweight employees shed their excess pounds.

As a sales representative for Fitness for Life, one of the country's leading fitness operators, you are convinced that your fitness equipment and programs are instrumental in helping people lose weight. With regular exercise at an on-site fitness center, employees lose weight and improve overall health. As employee health improves, absenteeism is reduced and overall productivity increases. What's more, employees love working out before or after work. They make the routine part of their workday, and they often have work buddies who share their fitness regimens.

Although many companies resist spending money to save money, fitness centers need not be large or expensive to be effective. Studies show that moderately sized centers coupled with motivational and training programs yield the greatest success. For just $30,000, Fitness for Life will provide exercise equipment including treadmills, elliptical trainers, exercise bikes, multigyms, and weight machines. Their fitness experts will design a fitness room, set up the equipment, and create appropriate programs. Best of all, the one-time cost is usually offset by cost savings within one year of center installation. For additional fees Fitness for Life can provide fitness consultants for employee fitness assessments. Fitness for Life specialists will also train employees on the proper use of the equipment and clean and manage the facility—for an extra charge, of course.

Your Task. Use the Web to update your obesity statistics. Then prepare a sales letter addressed to Carol Wong, Director, Human Resources, Prophecy Financial Services, 790 Lafayette Boulevard, Bridgeport, CT 06604. Ask for an appointment to meet with her. Send a brochure detailing the products and services that Fitness for Life provides. As an incentive, offer a free fitness assessment for all employees if Prophecy Financial Services installs a fitness facility by December 1.

10.30 Sales Message: Adapting From Low Context to High Context (Obj. 6)

Intercultural Team

The following letter, adapted from an Australian sales message, is intended for a low-context culture.[27]

Your Task. In teams, study the following letter. List at least six factors and techniques used in this letter that typify low-context persuasive sales messages. Then discuss how the letter could be changed to appeal to high-context cultures. Your instructor may ask your team to compose a high-context version of the letter.

Dear Mr. Smith,

Since you are one of our important customers who appreciate convenience and value, I am writing to share an opportunity to enjoy both!

For example, would you like to choose $60 worth of Innovations merchandise—absolutely FREE? And could you benefit from a very convenient credit card—one that offers you a free Rewards program, unsurpassed card protection, free PhotoCard, free Purchase Cover, exceptional personal customer service—and is accepted at over 400,000 locations in Australia, more than 14 million establishments worldwide, and gives you cash access at over 341,000 ATMs?

Realistically, how could you pass up these attractive opportunities? They each represent the very practical (and innovative!) reasons for you to apply for a Citibank Visa or MasterCard. Because I feel so confident that you will truly appreciate a Citibank Credit Card, I would like you to have two $30 vouchers for anything in our Innovations catalogue. Use them separately or together. They are valid until 28 February on your choice of items. But you must reply to this very special offer before 28 November.

= = = = = = = = = [More incentives detailed here]

I hope you will take a moment to complete and mail (or fax) the enclosed application for your Citibank Credit Card today. I'm certain you will enjoy its many benefits—as well as $60 of vouchers for Innovations merchandise with our compliments. Happy shopping!

Yours sincerely,

Judy Powell, Managing Director

P.S. We can only reserve this exclusive offer until 28 November. So apply for your Citibank Visa or MasterCard today. Once you are approved, you will receive $60 of Innovations vouchers shortly after your new card. And for Double Rewards points, use your card on any Innovations purchase until 28 February of next year!

10.31 Sales Letter: Promoting Your Product or Service (Obj. 5)

Identify a situation in your current job or a previous one in which a sales letter is or was needed. Using suggestions from this chapter, write an appropriate sales letter that promotes a product or service. Use actual names, information, and examples. If you have no work experience, imagine a business you would like to start: word processing, pet grooming, car detailing, tutoring, specialty knitting, balloon decorating, delivery service, child care, gardening, lawn care, or something else. Write a letter selling your product or service to be distributed to your prospective customers. Be sure to tell them how to respond.

10.32 Press Release: Preparing News for Your Local Newspaper (Obj. 7)

Web

You have been interviewed for a terrific job in corporate communications at an exciting organization. To test your writing skills, the organization asks you to rewrite one of its press releases for possible submission to your local newspaper. This means revising the information you find into a new press release that your local newspaper would be interested in publishing.

Your Task. Select an organization and study its press releases. For example, search the Web for *FBI press release, Ben & Jerry's press release, Mars candy press release, World Honda news release, Screen Actors Guild press release*, or an organization of your choice. Study its current press releases. Select one event or product that you think would interest your local newspaper. Although you can use the information from current press releases, don't copy the exact wording because the interviewer wants to see how you would present that information. Use the organization's format and submit the press release to your instructor with a cover note identifying the newspaper or other publication where you would like to see your press release published.

10.33 Press Release: This Is New! (Obj. 7)

Your Task. For a company where you now work or an organization you belong to, identify a product or service that could be publicized. Consider writing a press release announcing a new course at your college, a new president, new equipment, or a campaign to raise funds. The press release is intended for your local newspaper.

Video Resources

Video Library 2, Hard Rock Café

This video takes you inside the Hard Rock Café where you learn about changes it has undergone in surviving over 30 years in the rough-and-tumble world of hospitality. One problem involves difficulty in maintaining its well-known logo around the world. As you watch the video, look for references to the changes taking place and the discussion of brand control.

Your Task. As an assistant in the Hard Rock Corporate Identity Division, you have been asked to draft a persuasive message to be sent to the Edinburgh Festival Fringe. In doing research, you learned that this festival is the largest arts festival in the world, bringing thousands of performances to Scotland's capital city. An annual event, the Edinburgh Festival takes over the city in August with stand-up comedy, cabaret, theater, street performance, film, television, radio, and visual arts programs. Some of the programs raise funds for charity.

The problem is that the festival is staging some of its events at the Hard Rock Café, and the festival is using outdated Hard Rock logos at its Web site and in print announcements. Your task is to persuade the Edinburgh Festival Fringe organizers to stop using the old logos. Explain why it is necessary to use the official Hard Rock logo. Make it easy for them to obtain the official logo at **http://hardrock.com/corporate/logos/logos.asp**. Organizers must also sign the logo usage agreement. Organizers may be resistant because they have invested in announcements and Web designs with the old logo. If they don't comply by June 1, Hard Rock attorneys may begin legal actions. However, you need to present this date without making it sound like a threat. Your boss wants this message to develop goodwill, not motivate antagonism.

Write a persuasive e-mail to Edinburgh Festival Fringe organizer Barry Cook at *bcook@edinburghfestival.com*. Add any reasonable details.

Video Library 2, Innovation, Learning, and Communication: A Study of Yahoo

This video familiarizes you with managers and inside operating strategies at the Internet company Yahoo. After watching the film, assume the role of assistant to John Briggs, senior producer, who appeared in the video. John has just received a letter asking for permission from another film company to use Yahoo offices and personnel in an educational video, similar to the one you just saw.

Briggs wants you to draft a message for him to send to the operations manager, Ceci Lang, asking for permission for VX Studios to film. VX says it needs about 15 hours of filming time and would like to interview four or five managers as well as founders David Filo and Jerry Yang. VX would need to set up its mobile studio van in the parking lot and would need permission to use advertising film clips. Although VX hopes to film in May, it is flexible about the date. John Briggs reminds you that Yahoo has participated in a number of films in the past two years, and some managers are complaining that they can't get their work done.

Your Task. After watching the video, write a persuasive memo or e-mail to Ceci Lang, operations manager, asking her to allow VX Studios to film at Yahoo. Your message should probably emphasize the value of these projects in enhancing Yahoo's image among future users. Provide any other details you think are necessary to create a convincing request message that will win authorization from Ceci Lang to schedule this filming.

Chat About It

In each chapter you will find five discussion questions related to the chapter material. Your instructor may assign these topics for you to discuss in class, in an online chat room, or on an online discussion board. Some of the discussion topics may require outside research. You may also be asked to read and respond to postings made by your classmates.

Topic 1: When you think about persuasion, does the term suggest deception or dishonesty? Compare negative and positive aspects of persuasion. Share descriptions of when you have experienced both kinds of persuasion.

Topic 2: In your own experience, when have you had to persuade someone (boss, parent, instructor, friend, colleague) to do something or to change a belief? What strategies did you use? Were they successful? How could you improve your technique?

Topic 3: When have you had to complain to a company, organization, or person about something that went wrong or that offended you? Share your experience. What channel did you use for your complaint? How effective was your channel choice and strategy? What would you change in your method for future complaints?

Topic 4: Think of a product you have used and like. If you were trying to sell that product, what rational appeals would you use? What emotional appeals would you use? Try to sell that product to your classmates.

Grammar and Mechanics C.L.U.E. Review 10

Number Use

Review Guides 47–50 about number usage in Appendix A, Grammar and Mechanics Guide, beginning on page xxx. On a separate sheet, revise the following sentences to correct number usage errors. For each error that you locate, write the guide number that reflects this usage. Sentences may have more than one error. If a sentence is correct, write C. When you finish, check your answers on page Key-1.

Example: 13 candidates submitted applications for the position.
Revision: Thirteen candidates submitted applications for the position. [Guide 47]

1. Susan showed me 5 different customer messages with the same 2 complaints.
2. 28 employees indicated they would change their health benefits.
3. Did Mike request three hundred dollars to attend the 1-day seminar?
4. Most deliveries arrive before 10:00 o'clock a.m.
5. Personal income tax returns must be mailed by April 15th.
6. We earned 2.5% dividends on our three thousand dollar investment.
7. Our company applied for a one hundred thousand dollar loan at six%.
8. Average attendance at Major League Baseball games totaled 80,000,000 in the United States and Canada.
9. I bought the item on eBay for one dollar and fifty cents and sold it for fifteen dollars.
10. That store offers a thirty-day customer satisfaction return policy.

Reports, Proposals, and Presentations

CHAPTER 11

Report and Research Basics

OBJECTIVES

After studying this chapter, you should be able to

1. Describe basic features of business reports, including functions, strategies (indirect or direct), writing style, and formats.
2. Apply the 3-x-3 writing process to business reports to create well-organized documents that show a firm grasp of audience and purpose.
3. Find, evaluate, and use print and electronic secondary sources.
4. Understand how to generate and use primary data while avoiding researcher bias.
5. Comprehend fast-changing communication technology: the Web, electronic databases, and other resources for business writers and researchers.
6. Recognize the purposes and techniques of documentation in business reports, and avoid plagiarism.
7. Create meaningful and interesting graphics; display numeric information in the appropriate graphic form; and skillfully generate, use, and convert data to visual aids.

Want to do well on tests and excel in your course? Go to **www.meguffey.com** for helpful interactive resources.

- **Review the Chapter 11 PowerPoint slides to prepare for the first quiz.**

Zooming In PART 1

"Pawsengers" Enjoy Creature Comforts With Pet Airways

Zoe, a Jack Russell terrier, may have inspired a nifty business idea and helped Dan Wiesel and Alysa Binder launch a successful enterprise, Pet Airways. The unique start-up is the first pet-only carrier, transporting cats and dogs (more animals are to follow) between regional airports in nine major U.S. cities. The company's three Beech 1900 aircraft, reliable 19-passenger turboprop planes, were modified to accommodate up to 50 four-legged travelers. One-way fares start as low as $150 and average about $250. Most customers of Pet Airways are pet owners going on vacation or relocating; others include rescue and adoption missions and organizers of animal shows. Typically, business owners preface the big step of starting a company with research. In most cases they must then raise capital. To accomplish this difficult task, they need to persuade potential investors and banks that their proposed venture, usually presented in a business plan, is worthy of support and economically viable. Like many pet owners, Dan and Alysa were unhappy with commercial airlines' treating their precious dog like baggage or, recently reclassified, as cargo on commercial flights. If Fido or Fluffy doesn't fit into a pet crate stowed under a passenger seat in the main cabin, the critter is banned to the cargo section, a potentially terrifying, uncomfortable, even deadly place for a pet. Each year animals freeze to death, are lost, or die from a lack of cabin pressure en route. Only since 2005 are airlines required to report injuries, losses, and deaths of companion animals.[1] At the same time, commercial and private transport of live animals is a multimillion-dollar business for the major airlines.

This is how the husband-and-wife team describes the origins of their pet enterprise: "Of course, there's one thing Zoe is certainly not, and that's cargo. As we're fond of telling our neighbor Janet, her boxer Samson isn't Samsonite, and she agreed. In fact, we met lots of neighbors, friends, and even complete strangers who felt exactly the same way." The couple relied on their consulting and business experience and wondered: "Instead of trying to convince the human airlines to treat pets better, why not start up an airline just for pets?" The response, so far, has been overwhelming. The secret? Dan and Alysa write on the company Web site: "You see, on Pet Airways, your pets aren't packages; they're 'pawsengers.' And every step of the journey, we'll take care of them as if they were our own. Because that's exactly the way we'd want Zoe to be treated."

Although quizzing friends and neighbors does not qualify as a representative sample in empirical research, it could lead in the right direction and accurately reflect what a greater sample of the population may want or believe. Observation has many limitations; nevertheless, it can be applied effectively in primary research, as this chapter shows.

© Benassi/Splash News/Newscom

Hatching a brilliant business idea is only the start. To make generalizations and predictions and to secure funds, entrepreneurs need solid data. You will learn more about business plans and other formal reports and proposals in Chapter 13. We will revisit Pet Airways on page 347.

Critical Thinking

- Why might a U.S. airline dedicated strictly to traveling pets be an easy sell to the public? Why might it not be?[2]
- Today's entrepreneurs have many technological resources at their disposal to do research and spread the news when launching a new business. What channels may Dan Wiesel and Alysa Binder have used to explore their business idea and to find potential customers?
- To hear Dan Wiesel and Alysa Binder tell it on their Web site, before launching Pet Airways, they apparently relied a great deal on anecdotal evidence, a very limited empirical research method. Do you think an entrepreneur's hunch is enough on which to start a business?

http://petairways.com/

Understanding Report Essentials

LEARNING OBJECTIVE 1

Describe basic features of business reports, including functions, strategies (indirect or direct), writing style, and formats.

Reports are indispensable in business. The larger an organization, the more vital the exchange and flow of information becomes. Employees report their activities vertically to supervisors. At the same time, the various divisions of a business communicate horizontally with each other through reports. Occasionally, reports are generated for outside organizations or government agencies. In North America, a low-context culture, our values and attitudes seem to prompt us to write reports. We analyze problems, gather and study the facts, and then assess the alternatives. We pride ourselves on being practical and logical as we apply scientific procedures. When we wish to persuade financiers that our business merits a capital investment, as Dan Wiesel and Alysa Binder have, we generally write a business plan or a report outlining our case.

Management decisions in many organizations are based on information submitted in the form of reports. Routine reports keep managers informed about completed tasks, projects, and work in progress. Reports help us understand and study systematically the challenges we encounter in business before we can outline the steps toward solving them. Historian and author David McCullough said it best: "Trying to plan for the future without a sense of the past is like trying to plant cut flowers."[2] Business solutions are unthinkable without a thorough examination of the problems that prompted them.

This chapter examines the functions, strategies, writing style, and formats of typical business reports. It also introduces the report-writing process and discusses methods of collecting, documenting, and illustrating data.

What are the purposes of effective business reports?

Business reports range from informal bulleted lists and half-page trip reports to formal 200-page financial forecasts. Reports may be presented orally in front of a group or electronically on a computer screen. In many organizations, reports still take the form of paper documents such as traditional memos and letters. Other reports present primarily numerical data, such as tax reports and profit-and-loss statements. Increasingly, reports are delivered and presented digitally—for instance, as e-mail messages, PDF (portable document format) files, or electronic "slide decks." These files can then be e-mailed, distributed on the company intranet, or posted on the Internet. Hyperlinks tie together content within the document, between associated files, and with Web sources. Such linking adds depth and flexibility to traditional linear texts.

Some reports provide information only; others analyze and make recommendations. Although reports vary greatly in length, content, form, and formality level, they all have one or more of the following purposes: *to convey information, answer questions, and solve problems.*

Report Functions and Types

In terms of what they do, most reports fit into two broad categories: informational reports and analytical reports.

What is the difference between informational and analytical reports?

Informational Reports. Reports that present data without analysis or recommendations are primarily informational. For such reports, writers collect and organize facts, but they do not analyze the facts for readers. A trip report describing an employee's visit to a trade show, for example, presents information. Weekly bulleted status reports distributed by e-mail to a team record the activities of each group member and are shared with supervisors. Other reports that present information without analysis involve routine operations, compliance with regulations, and company policies and procedures.

Analytical Reports. Reports that provide data or findings, analyses, and conclusions are analytical. If requested, writers also supply recommendations. Analytical reports may intend to persuade readers to act or change their beliefs. For example, if you were writing a yardstick report that compares several potential manufacturing locations for a new automobile plant, you might conclude by recommending one site after discussing several criteria. Alternatively, let's say you work for a company that is considering a specific building for a women-only gym, and you are asked to study the location's suitability. You may have to write a feasibility report, an analysis of alternatives and a recommendation, that attempts to persuade readers to accept that site.

To distinguish among findings, conclusions, and recommendations, consider the example of an audit report. The auditor compiles facts and figures—the findings of the report—to meet the purpose or objective of the audit. Drawing inferences from the findings, the auditor arrives at conclusions. With the audit objectives in mind, the auditor may then propose corrective steps or actions, the recommendations.

Organizational Strategies

Like other business messages, reports may be organized directly or indirectly. The reader's expectations and the content of a report determine its development strategy, as illustrated in Figure 11.1. In long reports, such as corporate annual reports, some parts may be developed directly whereas other parts are arranged indirectly.

Where do the conclusions and recommendations appear in an analytical report written using the direct strategy, and why?

Direct Strategy. When the purpose for writing is presented close to the beginning of a report, the organizational strategy is direct. Informational reports, such as the letter report

FIGURE 11.1 **Audience Analysis and Report Organization**

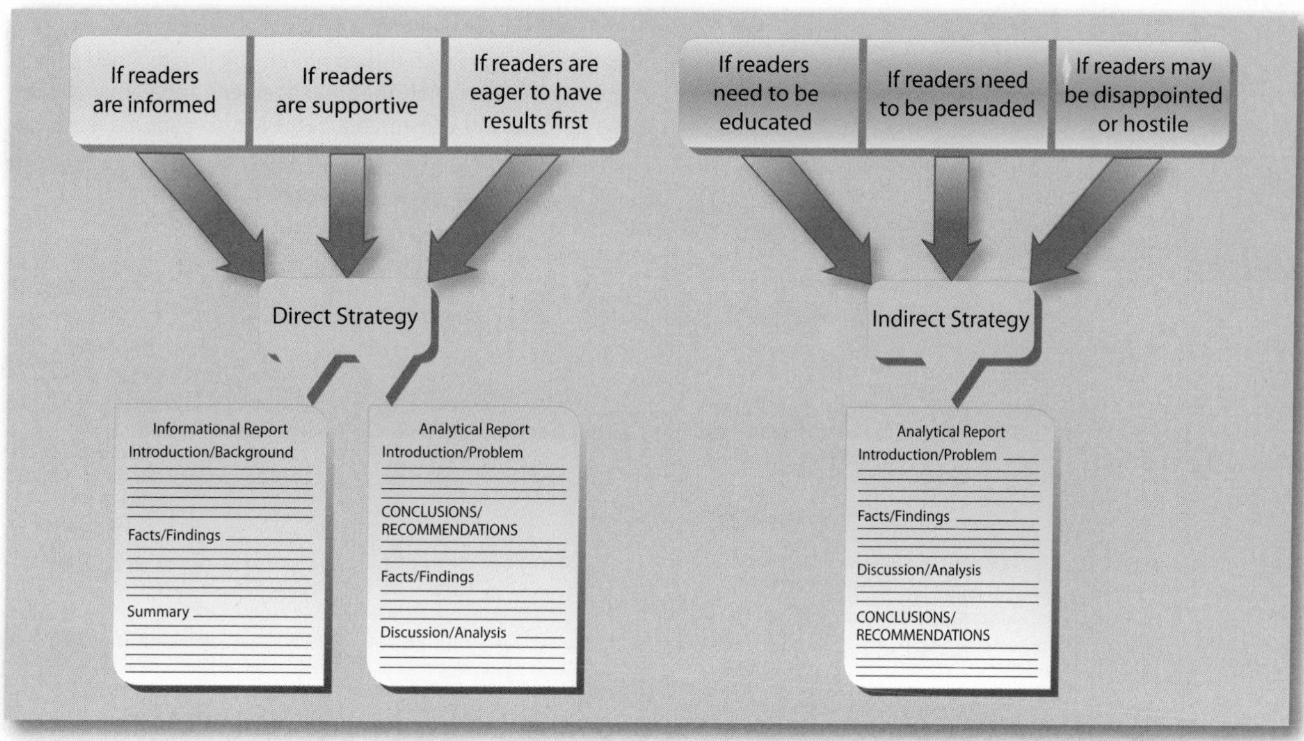

shown in Figure 11.2, are usually arranged directly. They open with an introduction, which is followed by the facts and a summary. In Figure 11.2 the writer explains a legal services plan using a letter report. The report begins with an introduction. The facts, divided into three subtopics and identified by descriptive headings, follow. The report ends with a summary and a complimentary close.

Analytical reports may also be organized directly, especially when readers are supportive of or familiar with the topic. Many busy executives prefer this strategy because it gives them the results of the report immediately. They don't have to spend time wading through the facts, findings, discussion, and analyses to get to the two items they are most interested in—the conclusions and recommendations. Figure 11.3 illustrates such an arrangement. This analytical memo report describes environmental hazards of a property that a realtor has just listed. The realtor is familiar with the investigation and eager to find out the recommendations. Therefore, the memo is organized directly. You should be aware, though, that unless readers are familiar with the topic, they may find the direct strategy confusing. Many readers prefer the indirect strategy because it seems logical and mirrors the way they solve problems.

When is the indirect strategy the best choice for analytical reports?

Indirect Strategy. The organizational strategy is indirect when the conclusions and recommendations, if requested, appear at the end of the report. Such reports usually begin with an introduction or description of the problem, followed by facts and interpretations from the writer. They end with conclusions and recommendations. This pattern is helpful when readers are unfamiliar with the problem. This pattern is also useful when readers must be persuaded or when they may be disappointed in or hostile toward the report's findings. The writer is more likely to retain the reader's interest by first explaining, justifying, and analyzing the facts and then making recommendations. This strategy also seems most rational to readers because it follows the normal thought process: problem, alternatives (facts), solution.

Writing Style

When should you use a formal report-writing style, and when should you use an informal style?

Like other business messages, reports can range from informal to formal, depending on their purpose, audience, and setting. Research reports from consultants to their clients tend to be rather formal. Such reports must project objectivity, authority, and impartiality. However, depending on the industry, a report to your boss describing a trip to a conference would probably be informal.

An office worker once called a grammar hotline service with this problem: "We've just sent a report to our headquarters, and it was returned with this comment, 'Put it in the third person.' What do they mean?" The hotline experts explained that management apparently wanted a more formal writing style, using third-person constructions *(the company* or *the researcher* instead of *we* and *I*). Figure 11.4, which compares the characteristics of formal and informal

FIGURE 11.2 Informational Report—Letter Format

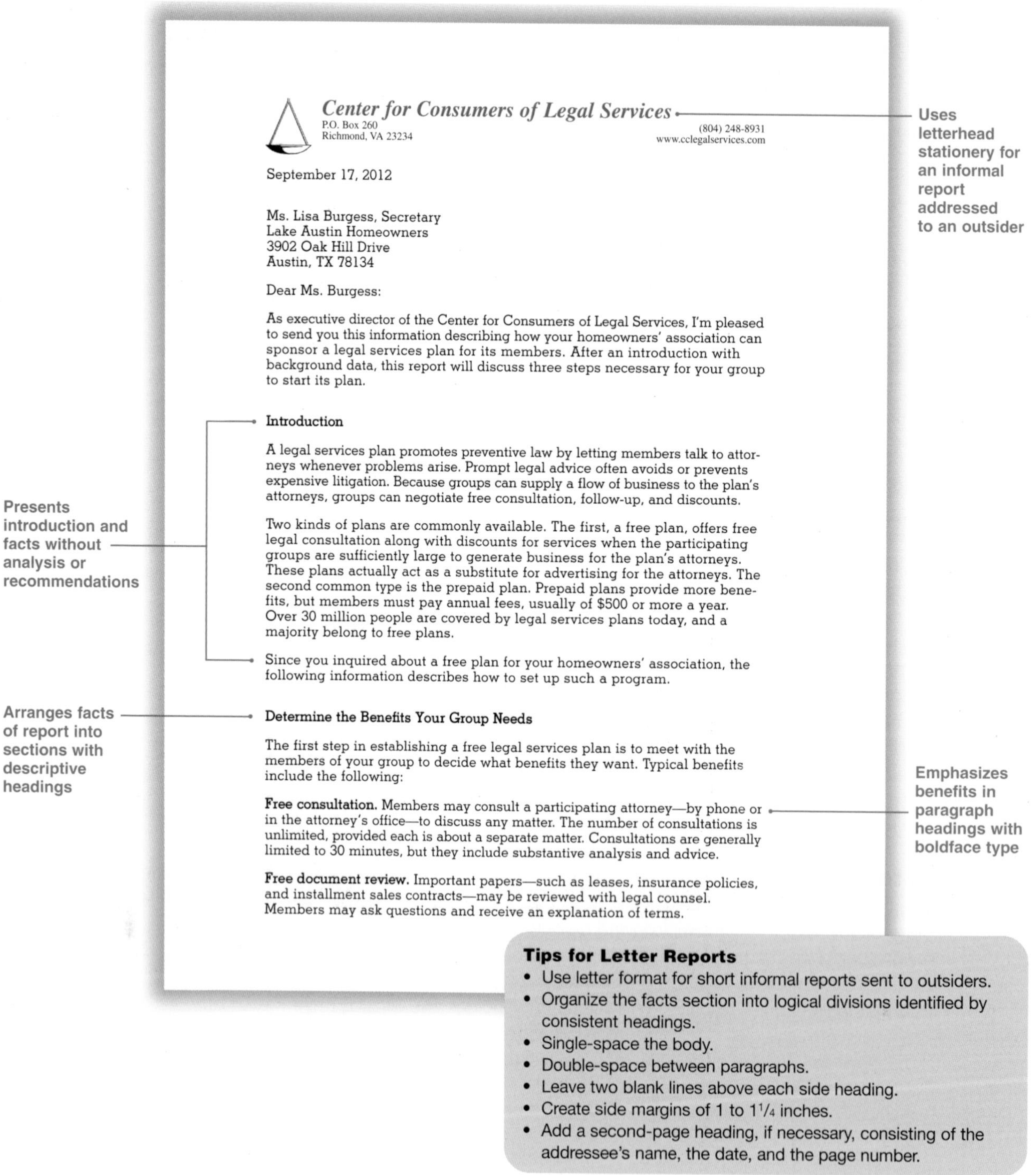

Center for Consumers of Legal Services
P.O. Box 260
Richmond, VA 23234
(804) 248-8931
www.cclegalservices.com

September 17, 2012

Ms. Lisa Burgess, Secretary
Lake Austin Homeowners
3902 Oak Hill Drive
Austin, TX 78134

Dear Ms. Burgess:

As executive director of the Center for Consumers of Legal Services, I'm pleased to send you this information describing how your homeowners' association can sponsor a legal services plan for its members. After an introduction with background data, this report will discuss three steps necessary for your group to start its plan.

Introduction

A legal services plan promotes preventive law by letting members talk to attorneys whenever problems arise. Prompt legal advice often avoids or prevents expensive litigation. Because groups can supply a flow of business to the plan's attorneys, groups can negotiate free consultation, follow-up, and discounts.

Two kinds of plans are commonly available. The first, a free plan, offers free legal consultation along with discounts for services when the participating groups are sufficiently large to generate business for the plan's attorneys. These plans actually act as a substitute for advertising for the attorneys. The second common type is the prepaid plan. Prepaid plans provide more benefits, but members must pay annual fees, usually of $500 or more a year. Over 30 million people are covered by legal services plans today, and a majority belong to free plans.

Since you inquired about a free plan for your homeowners' association, the following information describes how to set up such a program.

Determine the Benefits Your Group Needs

The first step in establishing a free legal services plan is to meet with the members of your group to decide what benefits they want. Typical benefits include the following:

Free consultation. Members may consult a participating attorney—by phone or in the attorney's office—to discuss any matter. The number of consultations is unlimited, provided each is about a separate matter. Consultations are generally limited to 30 minutes, but they include substantive analysis and advice.

Free document review. Important papers—such as leases, insurance policies, and installment sales contracts—may be reviewed with legal counsel. Members may ask questions and receive an explanation of terms.

Uses letterhead stationery for an informal report addressed to an outsider
Presents introduction and facts without analysis or recommendations
Arranges facts of report into sections with descriptive headings
Emphasizes benefits in paragraph headings with boldface type

Tips for Letter Reports

- Use letter format for short informal reports sent to outsiders.
- Organize the facts section into logical divisions identified by consistent headings.
- Single-space the body.
- Double-space between paragraphs.
- Leave two blank lines above each side heading.
- Create side margins of 1 to 1¼ inches.
- Add a second-page heading, if necessary, consisting of the addressee's name, the date, and the page number.

FIGURE 11.2 **(Continued)**

Ms. Lisa Burgess Page 2 September 17, 2012

Identifies second and succeeding pages with headings

Discount on additional services. For more complex matters, participating attorneys will charge members 75 percent of the attorney's normal fee. However, some organizations choose to charge a flat fee for commonly needed services.

Select the Attorneys for Your Plan

Groups with geographically concentrated memberships have an advantage in forming legal plans. These groups can limit the number of participating attorneys and yet provide adequate service. Generally, smaller panels of attorneys are advantageous.

Assemble a list of candidates, inviting them to apply. The best way to compare prices is to have candidates submit their fees. Your group can then compare fee schedules and select the lowest bidder, if price is important. Arrange to interview attorneys in their offices.

Uses parallel side headings for consistency and readability

After selecting an attorney or a panel, sign a contract. The contract should include the reason for the plan, what the attorney agrees to do, what the group agrees to do, how each side can end the contract, and the signature of both parties. You may also wish to include references to malpractice insurance, assurance that the group will not interfere with the attorney–client relationship, an evaluation form, a grievance procedure, and responsibility for government filings.

Publicize the Plan to Your Members

Members won't use a plan if they don't know about it, and a plan will not be successful if it is unused. Publicity must be vocal and ongoing. Announce it in newsletters, meetings, bulletin boards, and flyers.

Persistence is the key. All too frequently, leaders of an organization assume that a single announcement is all that is needed. They expect members to see the value of the plan and remember that it is available. Most organization members, though, are not as involved as the leadership. Therefore, it takes more publicity than the leadership usually expects in order to reach and maintain the desired level of awareness.

Summary

A successful free legal services plan involves designing a program, choosing the attorneys, and publicizing the plan. To learn more about these steps or to order a $35 how-to manual, call me at (804) 355-9901.

Sincerely,

Richard M. Ramos, Esq.

Includes complimentary close and signature

Richard M. Ramos, Esq.
Executive Director

pas

report-writing styles, can help you decide which style is appropriate for your reports. Note that, increasingly, formal reports are written with contractions and in the active voice. Today, report writers try to avoid awkward third-person references to themselves as *the researchers* or *the authors* because it sounds stilted and outdated.

Report Formats

The format of a report depends on its length, topic, audience, and purpose. After considering these elements, you will probably choose from among the following formats.

What criteria determine a report's format?

Letter Format. Use letter format for short informal reports (usually eight or fewer pages) addressed outside an organization. Prepared on office stationery, a letter report contains a date, inside address, salutation, and complimentary close, as shown in Figure 11.2. Although they may carry information similar to that found in correspondence, letter reports usually are longer and show more careful organization than most letters. They also include headings.

FIGURE 11.3 Analytical Report—Memo Format

Applies memo format for short, informal internal report

Presents recommendations first (direct pattern) because reader is supportive and familiar with topic

Combines findings and analyses in short report

Uses first paragraph as introduction

Atlantic Environmental, Inc.
Interoffice Memo

DATE: March 7, 2012

TO: Kermit Fox, President

FROM: Cynthia M. Rashid, Environmental Engineer CMR

SUBJECT: Investigation of Mountain Park Commercial Site

For Allegheny Realty, Inc., I've completed a preliminary investigation of its Mountain Park property listing. The following recommendations are based on my physical inspection of the site, official records, and interviews with officials and persons knowledgeable about the site.

Recommendations

To reduce its potential environmental liability, Allegheny Realty should take the following steps in regard to its Mountain Park listing:

- Conduct an immediate asbestos survey at the site, including inspection of ceiling insulation material, floor tiles, and insulation around a gas-fired heater vent pipe at 2539 Mountain View Drive.
- Prepare an environmental audit of the generators of hazardous waste currently operating at the site, including Mountain Technology.
- Obtain lids for the dumpsters situated in the parking areas and ensure that the lids are kept closed.

Findings and Analyses

My preliminary assessment of the site and its immediate vicinity revealed rooms with damaged floor tiles on the first and second floors of 2539 Mountain View Drive. Apparently, in recent remodeling efforts, these tiles had been cracked and broken. Examination of the ceiling and attic revealed further possible contamination from asbestos. The insulation for the hot-water tank was in poor condition.

Located on the property is Mountain Technology, a possible hazardous waste generator. Although I could not examine its interior, this company has the potential for producing hazardous material contamination.

In the parking area, large dumpsters collect trash and debris from several businesses. These dumpsters were uncovered, thus posing a risk to the general public.

In view of the construction date of the structures on this property, asbestos-containing building materials might be present. Moreover, this property is located in an industrial part of the city, further prompting my recommendation for a thorough investigation. Allegheny Realty can act immediately to eliminate one environmental concern: covering the dumpsters in the parking area.

Tips for Memo Reports

- Use memo format for short (ten or fewer pages) informal reports within an organization.
- Leave side margins of 1 to 1¼ inches.
- Sign your initials on the *From* line.
- Use an informal, conversational style.
- For direct analytical reports, put recommendations first.
- For indirect analytical reports, put recommendations last.

Memo and E-Mail Formats. For short informal reports that stay within organizations, the memo format is appropriate. Memo reports begin with essential background information, using standard headings: *Date, To, From,* and *Subject*, as shown in Figure 11.3. Like letter reports, memo reports differ from regular memos in length, use of headings, and deliberate organization. Today, memo reports are rarely distributed in hard copy; rather, they are attached to e-mails or, if short, contained in the body of e-mails.

FIGURE 11.4 Report-Writing Styles

	Formal Writing Style	Informal Writing Style
Use	Theses Research studies Controversial or complex reports (especially to outsiders)	Short, routine reports Reports for familiar audiences Noncontroversial reports Most reports for company insiders
Effect	Impression of objectivity, accuracy, professionalism, fairness Distance created between writer and reader	Feeling of warmth, personal involvement, closeness
Characteristics	Traditionally, no first-person pronouns; use of third person *(the researcher, the writer)*; increasingly, however, first-person pronouns and contractions are beginning to gain acceptance. Absence of contractions *(can't, don't)* Use of passive-voice verbs *(the study was conducted)* Complex sentences; long words Absence of humor and figures of speech Reduced use of colorful adjectives and adverbs Elimination of "editorializing" (author's opinions, perceptions)	Use of first-person pronouns *(I, we, me, my, us, our)* Use of contractions Emphasis on active-voice verbs *(I conducted the study)* Shorter sentences; familiar words Occasional use of humor, metaphors Occasional use of colorful speech Acceptance of author's opinions and ideas

Manuscript Format. For longer, more formal reports, use the manuscript format. These reports are usually printed on plain paper instead of letterhead stationery or memo forms. They begin with a title followed by systematically displayed headings and subheadings. You will see examples of proposals and formal reports using the manuscript format in Chapter 13.

Preprinted Forms. Preprinted forms are often used for repetitive data, such as monthly sales reports, performance appraisals, merchandise inventories, and personnel and financial reports. Standardized headings on these forms save time for the writer. Preprinted forms also make similar information easy to locate and ensure that all necessary information is provided.

Digital Format. Digital media allow writers to produce and distribute reports in electronic form, not in hard copy. With Adobe Acrobat any report can be converted into a PDF document that retains its format and generally cannot be changed. In addition, today's communicators can use programs such as Microsoft's PowerPoint or Apple's Keynote to create electronic presentations in the form of slides. Because the purpose of such presentations is to concisely display the contents of reports, they are often not intended for verbal delivery. Rather, these text-heavy slides are often posted online or e-mailed. When printed out, the stacks of hard-copy slides resemble decks of playing cards, which is why they are called slide decks. Digital delivery has also changed Microsoft Word documents. This popular program lets users hyperlink multimedia content within the document or with associated text or media files. Thus, such digital documents create a nonlinear reading experience similar to that of browsing Web pages.

Applying the 3-x-3 Writing Process to Reports

LEARNING OBJECTIVE 2
Apply the 3-x-3 writing process to business reports to create well-organized documents that show a firm grasp of audience and purpose.

Because business reports are systematic attempts to compile often complex information, answer questions, and solve problems, the best reports are developed methodically. In earlier chapters the 3-x-3 writing process was helpful in guiding short projects such as e-mails, memos, and letters. That same process is even more necessary when preparing longer projects such as reports and proposals. After all, an extensive project poses a greater organizational challenge than a short one and, therefore, requires a rigorous structure to help readers grasp the message. Let's channel the writing process into seven specific steps:

What are the seven steps of the report-writing process?

Step 1: Analyze the problem and purpose.

Step 2: Anticipate the audience and issues.

Step 3: Prepare a work plan.

Step 4: Conduct research.

Step 5: Organize, analyze, interpret, and illustrate the data.

Step 6: Compose the first draft.

Step 7: Revise, proofread, and evaluate.

How much time you spend on each step depends on your report task. A short informational report on a familiar topic might require a brief work plan, little research, and no data analysis. A complex analytical report, on the other hand, might demand a comprehensive work plan, extensive research, and careful data analysis. In this section we consider the first three steps in the process—analyzing the problem and purpose, anticipating the audience and issues, and preparing a work plan.

To illustrate the planning stages of a report, we will watch Diane Camas develop a report she's preparing for her boss, Mike Rivers, at Mycon Pharmaceutical Laboratories. Mike asked Diane to investigate the problem of transportation for sales representatives. Currently, some Mycon reps visit customers (mostly doctors and hospitals) using company-leased cars. A few reps drive their own cars, receiving reimbursements for use. In three months Mycon's leasing agreement for 14 cars expires, and Mike is considering a major change. Diane's task is to investigate the choices and report her findings to Mike.

Analyzing the Problem and Purpose

What is a problem statement, and why should you prepare one as you begin work on a report?

The first step in writing a report is understanding the problem or assignment clearly. For complex reports, prepare a written problem statement to clarify the task. In analyzing her report task, Diane had many questions: Is the problem that Mycon is spending too much money on leased cars? Does Mycon wish to invest in owning a fleet of cars? Is Mike unhappy with the paperwork involved in reimbursing sales reps when they use their own cars? Does he suspect that reps are submitting inflated mileage figures? Before starting research for the report, Diane talked with Mike to define the problem. She learned several dimensions of the situation and wrote the following statement to clarify the problem—both for herself and for Mike.

Problem statement: *The leases on all company cars will be expiring in three months. Mycon must decide whether to renew them or develop a new policy regarding transportation for sales reps. Expenses and paperwork for employee-owned cars seem excessive.*

Diane further defined the problem by writing a specific question that she would try to answer in her report:

Problem question: *What plan should Mycon follow in providing transportation for its sales reps?*

Now Diane was ready to concentrate on the purpose of the report. Again, she had questions: Exactly what did Mike expect? Did he want a comparison of costs for buying and leasing cars? Should she conduct research to pinpoint exact reimbursement costs when employees drive their own cars? Did he want her to do all the legwork, present her findings in a report, and let him make a decision? Or did he want her to evaluate the choices and recommend a course of action? After talking with Mike, Diane was ready to write a simple purpose statement for this assignment.

What function does a simple purpose statement serve?

Simple statement of purpose: *To recommend a plan that provides sales reps with cars to be used in their calls.*

Preparing a written purpose statement is a good idea because it defines the focus of a report and provides a standard that keeps the project on target. In writing useful purpose statements, choose action verbs telling what you intend to do: *analyze, choose, investigate, compare, justify, evaluate, explain, establish, determine,* and so on. Notice that Diane's statement begins with the action verb *recommend.*

Some reports require only a simple statement of purpose: *to investigate expanded teller hours, to select a manager from among four candidates, to describe the position of accounts supervisor.* Many assignments, though, demand additional focus to guide the project. An expanded statement of purpose considers three additional factors: scope, limitations, and significance.

Scope and Limitations. What issues or elements will be investigated? The scope statement prepares the audience by clearly defining which problem or problems will be analyzed and solved. To determine the scope, Diane brainstormed with Mike and others to pin down her task. She learned that Mycon currently had enough capital to consider purchasing a fleet of cars outright. Mike also told her that employee satisfaction was almost as important as cost-effectiveness. Moreover, he disclosed his suspicion that employee-owned cars were costing Mycon more than leased cars. Diane had many issues to sort out in setting the boundaries of her report.

What is the value of setting boundaries to determine the scope of a report?

What conditions affect the generalizability and utility of a report's findings? As part of the scope statement, the limitations further narrow the subject by focusing on constraints or exclusions. For this report Diane realized that her conclusions and recommendations might apply only to reps in her Kansas City sales district. Her findings would probably not be reliable for reps in Seattle, Phoenix, or Atlanta. Another limitation for Diane was time. She had to complete the report in four weeks, thus restricting the thoroughness of her research.

Significance. Why is the topic worth investigating at this time? Some topics, after initial examination, turn out to be less important than originally thought. Others involve problems that cannot be solved, making a study useless. For Diane and Mike the problem had significance because Mycon's leasing agreement would expire shortly and decisions had to be made about a new policy for transportation of sales reps.

Diane decided to expand her statement of purpose to define the scope, describe the limitations of the report, and explain the significance of the problem.

> ***Expanded statement of purpose:*** *The purpose of this report is to recommend a plan that provides sales reps with cars to be used in their calls. The report will compare costs for three plans: outright ownership, leasing, and compensation for employee-owned cars. It will also measure employee reactions to each plan. The report is significant because Mycon's current leasing agreement expires April 1 and an improved plan could reduce costs and paperwork. The study is limited to costs for sales reps in the Kansas City district.*

What are the components of an expanded purpose statement?

After expanding her statement of purpose, Diane checked it with Mike Rivers to be sure she was on target.

© Chris Chambers/Getty Images

Sports fans aren't the only ones who follow March Madness. Each year, interactive marketing firm Unicast issues its NCAA Basketball Tournament Fever Report to identify where hoops watchers get their daily fix of scores, highlights, bracket updates, and pool information. The agency's 2010 report found that 44% of March Madness fans tracked the tournament online, and 10% followed along using mobile devices. Not surprisingly, favorite online destinations included ESPN.com and Yahoo Sports—familiar brands that own the loyalty of sports enthusiasts online. *Who are the primary and secondary readers of this report?*

Anticipating the Audience and Issues

After defining the purpose of a report, a writer must think carefully about who will read it. Concentrating solely on a primary reader is a major mistake. Although one individual may have solicited the report, others within the organization may eventually read it, including upper management and people in other departments. A report to an outside client may first be read by someone who is familiar with the problem and then be distributed to others less familiar with the topic. Moreover, candid statements to one audience may be offensive to another audience. Diane could make a major blunder, for instance, if she mentioned Mike's suspicion that sales reps were padding their mileage statements. If the report were made public—as it probably would be to explain a new policy—the sales reps could feel insulted that their integrity was questioned.

How can you take into account both primary and secondary readers?

As Diane considered her primary and secondary readers, she asked herself these questions:

- *What do my readers need to know about this topic?*
- *What do they already know?*
- *What is their educational level?*
- *How will they react to this information?*
- *Which sources will they trust?*
- *How can I make this information readable, believable, and memorable?*

Answers to these questions help writers determine how much background material to include, how much detail to add, whether to include jargon, what method of organization and presentation to follow, and what tone to use.

Why should major report problems be broken down into subproblems, and what is this process called?

In the planning stages, a report writer must also break the major investigative problem into subproblems. This process, sometimes called factoring, identifies issues to be investigated or possible solutions to the main problem. In this case Mycon must figure out the best way to transport sales reps. Each possible solution or issue that Diane considers becomes a factor or subproblem to be investigated. Diane came up with three tentative solutions to provide transportation to sales reps: (a) purchase cars outright, (b) lease cars, or (c) compensate employees for using their own cars. These three factors form the outline of Diane's study.

Diane continued to factor these main points into the following subproblems for investigation:

What plan should Mycon use to transport its sales reps?

I. Should Mycon purchase cars outright?
   A. How much capital would be required?
   B. How much would it cost to insure, operate, and maintain company-owned cars?
   C. Do employees prefer using company-owned cars?

II. Should Mycon lease cars?
   A. What is the best lease price available?
   B. How much would it cost to insure, operate, and maintain leased cars?
   C. Do employees prefer using leased cars?

III. Should Mycon compensate employees for using their own cars?
   A. How much has it cost in the past to compensate employees who used their own cars?
   B. How much paperwork is involved in reporting expenses?
   C. Do employees prefer being compensated for using their own cars?

Each subproblem would probably be further factored into additional subproblems. These issues may be phrased as questions, as Diane's are, or as statements. In factoring a complex problem, prepare an outline showing the initial problem and its breakdown into subproblems. Make sure your divisions are consistent (don't mix issues), exclusive (don't overlap categories), and complete (don't skip significant issues).

Preparing a Work Plan

After analyzing the problem, anticipating the audience, and factoring the problem, you are ready to prepare a work plan. A good work plan includes the following:

What role does a work plan play in the completion of a report?

- Statement of the problem (based on key background/contextual information)
- Statement of the purpose including scope with limitations and significance
- Research strategy including a description of potential sources and methods of collecting data
- Tentative outline that factors the problem into manageable chunks
- Work schedule

Preparing a plan encourages you to evaluate your resources, set priorities, outline a course of action, and establish a schedule. Having a plan keeps you on track and provides management a means of measuring your progress.

A work plan gives a complete picture of a project. Because the usefulness and quality of any report rest primarily on its data, you will want to develop a clear research strategy, which includes allocating plenty of time to locate sources of information. For firsthand information you might interview people, prepare a survey, or even conduct a scientific experiment. For secondary information you will probably search electronic materials on the Internet and printed materials such as books and magazines. Your work plan describes how you expect to generate or collect data. Because data collection is a major part of report writing, the next section of this chapter treats the topic more fully.

Figure 11.5 shows a complete work plan for a proposal pitched by BzzAgent's advertising executive Dave Balter to his client Lee Jeans. A work plan is useful because it outlines the issues to be investigated. Notice that considerable thought and discussion and even some preliminary research are necessary to be able to develop a useful work plan.

Zooming In — PART 2

"Bone Voyage" on Pet Airways

As cute as ferrying animals in style across the United States may sound, it is not easy to turn an appealing idea into a profitable business. Nor is it easy to secure financing for a fledgling pet airline, least of all during severe economic turbulences. To obtain funding, most would-be entrepreneurs must write a business plan, as you will see in Chapter 13. You can assume that Dan and Alysa worked hard to chart the potential market, their competition, and the road to success.

The odds of start-up success vary greatly, depending on the source. Some claim that first-time entrepreneurs and those who have previously failed in a business venture face a 20 percent chance of succeeding. The U.S. Census Bureau pegs the success rate much higher, suggesting that 65 percent of new businesses still operate four years after launching. Dan and Alysa took the plunge after researching opportunities and potential threats. They had to figure out what makes their business special, what, in advertising terms, its unique selling point is. Other relocation specialists offer to move animals, not only domestically but also globally. Pet Airways, however, is the first pet-only carrier offering pet-friendly "Travel For Your Best Friend" (company motto), not in cargo but in a climate-controlled main cabin.

Pet Airways hopes to differentiate itself from the competition by providing a comfortable and safe travel experience for its four-legged "pawsengers." Cat and dog owners drop off their darlings at the airline's Pet Lounge located at the airport. The animals get potty breaks less than two hours before the flight and also along the way. They board the plane escorted by "pet attendants," and their pet carriers are securely stowed. When airborne, the animals are monitored every 15 minutes and given a last potty break after disembarking at their destination. They are then ready for pickup at the Pet Lounge.

© Benassi/Splash News/Newscom

Critical Thinking

- When writing their funding proposal or business plan, do you think Dan and Alysa chose an informational or analytical approach? Why?
- Do you think Dan's and Alysa's proposal was developed directly or indirectly? Why? Should it have been written formally or informally?
- What are some of the questions Dan and Alysa should have asked themselves about their audience before pitching their business idea or writing their proposal?

FIGURE 11.5 Work Plan for a Formal Report

Statement of Problem

Many women between the ages of 18 and 34 have trouble finding jeans that fit. Lee Jeans hopes to remedy that situation with its One True Fit line. We want to demonstrate to Lee that we can create a word-of-mouth campaign that will help it reach its target audience.

Statement of Purpose

Defines purpose, scope, limits, and significance of report

The purpose of this report is to secure an advertising contract from Lee Jeans. We will examine published accounts about the jeans industry and Lee Jeans in particular. In addition, we will examine published results of Lee's current marketing strategy. We will conduct focus groups of women in our company to generate campaign strategies for our pilot study of 100 BzzAgents. The report will persuade Lee Jeans that word-of-mouth advertising is an effective strategy to reach women in this demographic group and that Bzz Agent is the right company to hire. The report is significant because an advertising contract with Lee Jeans would help our company grow significantly in size and stature.

Research Strategy (Sources and Methods of Data Collection)

Describes primary and secondary data

We will gather information about Lee Jeans and the product line by examining published marketing data and conducting focus group surveys of our employees. In addition, we will gather data about the added value of word-of-mouth advertising by examining published accounts and interpreting data from previous marketing campaigns, particularly those with similar age groups. Finally, we will conduct a pilot study of 100 BzzAgents in the target demographic.

Tentative Outline

Factors problem into manageable chunks

I. How effectively has Lee Jeans marketed to the target population (women, ages 22–35)?
   A. Historically, who has typically bought Lee Jeans products? How often? Where?
   B. How effective are the current marketing strategies for the One True Fit line?
II. Is this product a good fit for our marketing strategy and our company?
   A. What do our staff members and our sample survey of BzzAgents say about this product?
   B. How well does our pool of BzzAgents correspond to the target demography in terms of age and geographic distribution?
III. Why should Lee Jeans engage BzzAgent to advertise its One True Fit line?
   A. What are the benefits of word of mouth in general and for this demographic in particular?
   B. What previous campaigns have we engaged in that demonstrate our company's credibility?
   C. What are our marketing strategies, and how well did they work in the pilot study?

Work Schedule

Estimates time needed to complete report tasks

Task	Dates
Investigate Lee Jeans and the One True Fit line's current marketing strategy	July 15–25
Test product using focus groups	July 15–22
Create campaign materials for BzzAgents	July 18–31
Run a pilot test with a selected pool of 100 BzzAgents	August 1–21
Evaluate and interpret findings	August 22–25
Compose draft of report	August 26–28
Revise draft	August 28–30
Submit final report	September 1

Tips for Preparing a Work Plan

- Start early; allow plenty of time for brainstorming and preliminary research.
- Describe the problem motivating the report.
- Write a purpose statement that includes the report's scope, significance, and limitations.
- Describe the strategy including data collection sources and methods.
- Divide the major problem into subproblems stated as questions to be answered.
- Develop a realistic work schedule citing dates for completion of major tasks.
- Review the work plan with whoever authorized the report.

Although this tentative outline guides the investigation, it does not determine the content or order of the final report. You may, for example, study five possible solutions to a problem. If two prove to be useless, your report may discuss only the three winners. Moreover, you will organize the report to accomplish your goal and satisfy the audience. Remember that a busy executive who is familiar with a topic may prefer to read the conclusions and recommendations before a discussion of the findings. If someone authorizes the report, be sure to review the work plan with that person (your manager, client, or professor, for example) before proceeding with the project.

Gathering Information From Secondary Sources

LEARNING OBJECTIVE 3

Find, evaluate, and use print and electronic secondary sources.

One of the most important steps in the process of writing a report is that of gathering information (research). As the philosopher Goethe once said: "The greater part of all mischief in the world arises from the fact that men do not sufficiently understand their own aims. They have undertaken to build a tower, and spend no more labor on the foundation than would be necessary to erect a hut." Think of your report as a tower. Because a report is only as good as its foundation—the questions you ask and the data you gather to answer those questions—the remainder of this chapter describes the fundamental work of finding, documenting, and illustrating data.

Why are data important in report writing?

As you analyze a report's purpose and audience and prepare your research strategy, you will identify and assess the data you need to support your argument or explain your topic. As you do, you will answer questions about your objectives and audience: Will the audience need a lot of background or contextual information? Will your readers value or trust statistics, case studies, or expert opinions? Will they want to see data from interviews or surveys? Will summaries of focus groups be useful? Should you rely on organizational data? Figure 11.6 lists five forms of data and provides questions to guide you in making your research accurate and productive.

What are the main differences between primary data and secondary data?

Data fall into two broad categories: primary and secondary. Primary data result from firsthand experience and observation. Secondary data come from reading what others have experienced or observed and written down. Coca-Cola and Pepsi-Cola, for example, produce primary data when they stage taste tests and record the reactions of consumers. These same sets

FIGURE 11.6 Gathering and Selecting Report Data

Form of Data	Questions to Ask
Background or historical	How much do my readers know about the problem? Has this topic/issue been investigated before? Are those sources current, relevant, and/or credible? Will I need to add to the available data?
Statistical	What or who is the source? How recent are the data? How were the figures derived? Will this data be useful in this form?
Expert opinion	Who are the experts? What are their biases? Are their opinions in print? Are they available for interviewing? Do we have in-house experts?
Individual or group opinion	Whose opinion(s) would the readers value? Have surveys or interviews been conducted on this topic? If not, do questionnaires or surveys exist that I can modify and/or use? Would focus groups provide useful information?
Organizational	What are the proper channels for obtaining in-house data? Are permissions required? How can I learn about public and private companies?

of data become secondary after they have been published and, let's say, a newspaper reporter uses them in an article about soft drinks. Secondary data are easier and cheaper to gather than primary data, which might involve interviewing large groups or sending out questionnaires.

We discuss secondary data first because that is where nearly every research project should begin. Often, something has already been written about your topic. Reviewing secondary sources can save time and effort and prevent you from reinventing the wheel. Most secondary material is available either in print or electronically.

Print Resources

Are print sources and libraries irrelevant today?

Although we are seeing a steady movement away from print data and toward electronic data, print sources are still the most visible part of most libraries. Much information is available only in print.

By the way, if you are an infrequent library user, begin your research by talking with a reference librarian about your project. Librarians won't do your research for you, but they will steer you in the right direction. Moreover, they are very accommodating. Several years ago a *Wall Street Journal* poll revealed that librarians are perceived as among the friendliest, most approachable people in the working world. Many librarians help you understand their computer, cataloging, and retrieval systems by providing advice, brochures, handouts, and workshops.

Books. Although quickly outdated, books provide excellent historical, in-depth data. Books can be located through print or online listings.

- **Card catalogs.** A few small public or high school libraries still maintain card catalogs with all books indexed on 3-by-5 cards alphabetized by author, title, and subject.
- **Online catalogs.** Most libraries today have computerized their card catalogs. Some systems are fully automated, thus allowing users to learn not only whether a book is located in the library but also whether it is currently available. Moreover, online catalogs can help you trace and retrieve items from other area libraries if your college doesn't own them.

Periodicals. Magazines, pamphlets, and journals are called *periodicals* because of their recurrent, or periodic, publication. Journals are compilations of scholarly articles. Articles in journals and other periodicals are extremely useful because they are concise, limited in scope, and current and can supplement information in books.

What is the main difference between books and periodicals, and when would you want to use each?

- **Print indexes.** Most university libraries now offer online access to *The Readers' Guide to Periodical Literature*. You may still find print copies of this valuable index of general-interest magazine article titles in small libraries. It includes such magazines as *Time, Newsweek, The New Yorker,* and *U.S. News & World Report*. However, business writers today rely almost totally on electronic indexes and databases.
- **Electronic indexes.** Online indexes are stored in digital databases. Most libraries now provide such databases to help you locate references, abstracts, and full-text articles from magazines, journals, and newspapers, such as *The New York Times*. When using Web-based online indexes, follow the on-screen instructions or ask for assistance from a librarian. Beginning with a subject search such as *manufacturers' recalls* is helpful because it generally turns up more relevant citations than keyword searches—especially when searching for names of people (*Akio Toyoda*) or companies (*Toyota*). Once you locate usable references, print a copy of your findings, save them to a portable flash memory device, or send them to your e-mail address.

Electronic Databases

As a writer of business reports today, you will probably begin your secondary research with electronic resources. Online databases have become the staple of secondary research. Most writers turn to them first because they are fast and easy to use. You can conduct detailed searches without ever leaving your office, home, or dorm room.

Where do most researchers begin to look?

A database is a collection of information stored electronically so that it is accessible by computer and digitally searchable. Databases provide bibliographic information (titles of documents and brief abstracts) and full-text documents. Most researchers prefer full-text

FIGURE 11.7 ABI/INFORM (ProQuest) Search Result

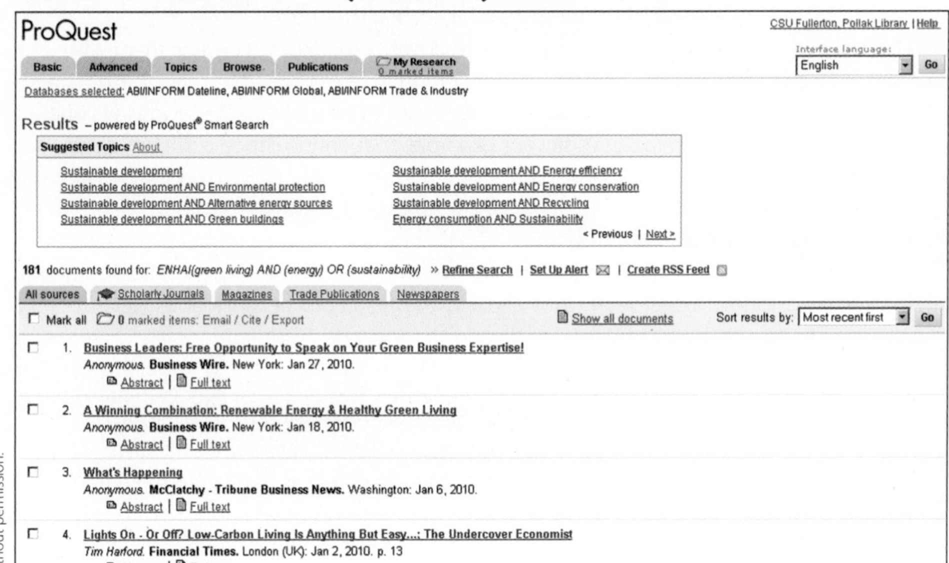

ABI/INFORM indexes over 4,000 journals and features 3,000 full-text documents about business topics. Users can access newspapers, magazines, reports, dissertations, book reviews, scholarly journals, and trade publications. Figure 11.7 shows that the search terms *green living* and energy or *sustainability* brought up 181 full-text search results.

documents because they are convenient. Various databases contain a rich array of magazine, newspaper, and journal articles, as well as newsletters, business reports, company profiles, government data, reviews, and directories. The four databases most useful to business writers for general searches are ABI/INFORM (ProQuest), Factiva (Dow Jones), LexisNexis Academic, and Academic Search Elite (EBSCO). Your college library and many businesses probably subscribe to these expensive resources and perhaps to other, more specialized commercial databases. Figure 11.7 shows the ABI/INFORM search menu.

What kind of information can be found in commercial databases?

Developing a search strategy and narrowing your search can save time. Think about the time frame for your search, the language of publication, and the types of materials you will need. Most databases enable you to focus a search easily. For example, if you were researching the banking crisis that occurred recently and wanted to look at articles published in a specific year, most search tools would enable you to limit your search to that period. All databases and search engines allow you to refine your search and increase the precision of your hits. In addition, for research in international business, don't limit yourself to English-language articles only; some Web sites, most notably AltaVista's Babel Fish, offer rough but free translations. What's more, many organizations overseas present their Web content in multiple languages.

Electronic resources may take time to master. Therefore, before wasting time and retrieving lots of useless material, talk to a university librarian. College and public libraries as well as some employers offer free access to several commercial databases, sparing you the high cost of individual subscriptions.

Gathering Information From Primary Sources

LEARNING OBJECTIVE 4

Understand how to generate and use primary data while avoiding researcher bias.

Up to this point, we have been talking about secondary data. You should begin nearly every business report assignment by evaluating the available secondary data. However, you will probably need primary data to give a complete picture. Business reports that solve specific current problems typically rely on primary, firsthand data. If, for example, management wants to discover the cause of increased employee turnover in its Seattle office, it must investigate conditions in Seattle by collecting recent information. Providing answers to business problems often means generating primary data through surveys, interviews, observation, or experimentation.

What are primary data, and when would you want to use them?

Surveys

Surveys collect data from groups of people. Before developing new products, for example, companies often survey consumers to learn their needs. The advantages of surveys are that they gather data economically and efficiently. Snail-mailed or e-mailed surveys reach big groups

What are the advantages and disadvantages of surveys and mailed questionnaires?

nearby or at great distances. Moreover, people responding to mailed or e-mailed surveys have time to consider their answers, thus improving the accuracy of the data.

Mailed or e-mailed surveys, of course, have disadvantages. Most of us rank them with junk mail or spam, so response rates may be no higher than 5 percent. Furthermore, those who do respond may not represent an accurate sample of the overall population, thus invalidating generalizations from the group. Let's say, for example, that an insurance company sends out a questionnaire asking about provisions in a new policy. If only older people respond, the questionnaire data cannot be used to generalize what people in other age groups might think. If a survey is only e-mailed, it may miss audiences that do not use the Internet.

A final problem with surveys has to do with truthfulness. Some respondents exaggerate their incomes or distort other facts, thus causing the results to be unreliable. Nevertheless, surveys may be the best way to generate data for business and student reports. In preparing print or electronic surveys, consider these pointers:

- **Select the survey population carefully.** Many surveys question a small group of people (a sample) and project the findings to a larger population. Let's say that a survey of your class reveals that the majority prefer *phở*, the Vietnamese beef and rice noodle soup. Can you then say with confidence that all students on your campus (or in the nation) prefer pho? To be able to generalize from a survey, you need to make the sample as large as possible. In addition, you need to determine whether the sample represents the larger population. For important surveys you will want to consult books on or experts in sampling techniques. As for pho, in a recent Sodexo survey, the soup ranked among the top three comfort foods favored by American college students.[3]

What are the characteristics of effective surveys?

- **Explain why the survey is necessary.** In a cover letter or an opening paragraph, describe the need for the survey. Suggest how someone or something other than you will benefit. If appropriate, offer to send recipients a copy of the findings.
- **Consider incentives.** If the survey is long, persuasive techniques may be necessary. Response rates can be increased by offering money (such as a $1 bill), coupons, gift certificates, free books, or other gifts.
- **Limit the number of questions.** Resist the temptation to ask for too much. Request only information you will use. Don't, for example, include demographic questions (income, gender, age, and so forth) unless the information is necessary to evaluate responses.
- **Use questions that produce quantifiable answers.** Check-off, multiple-choice, yes–no, and scale (or rank-order) questions, illustrated in Figure 11.8, provide quantifiable data that are easily tabulated. Responses to open-ended questions (*What should the bookstore do about plastic bags?*) reveal interesting, but difficult-to-quantify perceptions.[4] To obtain workable data, give interviewees a list of possible responses, as shown in items 5 through 8 of Figure 11.8. For scale and multiple-choice questions, try to present all the possible answer choices. To be safe, add an *Other* or *Don't know* category in case the choices seem insufficient to the respondent. Many surveys use scale questions because they capture degrees of feelings. Typical scale headings are *Agree strongly, Agree somewhat, Neutral, Disagree somewhat,* and *Disagree strongly.*

Why is it important to craft survey questions carefully?

- **Avoid leading or ambiguous questions.** The wording of a question can dramatically affect responses to it.[5] When respondents were asked, "Are we spending too much, too little, or about the right amount on *assistance to the poor?"* [emphasis added], 13 percent responded *Too much.* When the same respondents were asked, "Are we spending too much, too little, or about the right amount on *welfare?"*[emphasis added], 44 percent responded *Too much.* Because words have different meanings for different people, you must strive to use objective language and pilot test your questions with typical respondents. Stay away from questions that suggest an answer (*Don't you agree that the salaries of CEOs are obscenely high?*). Instead, ask neutral questions (*Do CEOs earn too much, too little, or about the right amount?*). Also, avoid queries that really ask two or more things (*Should the salaries of CEOs be reduced or regulated by government legislation?*). Instead, break them into separate questions (*Should the salaries of CEOs be reduced by government legislation? Should the salaries of CEOs be regulated by government legislation?*).

FIGURE 11.8 **Preparing a Survey**

Prewriting

Analyze: The purpose is to help the bookstore decide if it should replace plastic bags with cloth bags for customer purchases.

Anticipate: The audience will be busy students who will be initially uninterested.

Adapt: Because students will be unwilling to participate, the survey must be short and simple. Its purpose must be significant and clear.

Writing

Research: Ask students how they would react to cloth bags. Use their answers to form question response choices.

Organize: Open by explaining the survey's purpose and importance. In the body ask clear questions that produce quantifiable answers. Conclude with appreciation and instructions.

Compose: Write the first draft of the questionnaire.

Revising

Revise: Try out the questionnaire with a small representative group. Revise unclear questions.

Proofread: Read for correctness. Be sure that answer choices do not overlap and that they are complete. Provide an *Other* category if appropriate (as in No. 9).

Evaluate: Is the survey clear, attractive, and easy to complete?

North Shore College Bookstore
STUDENT SURVEY

The North Shore College Bookstore wants to do its part in protecting the environment. Each year we give away 45,000 plastic bags for students to carry off their purchases. We are considering changing from plastic to cloth bags or some other alternative, but we need your views.

Explains need for survey (use cover letter for longer surveys)

Please place checks below to indicate your responses.

1. How many units are you presently carrying?
   ___ 15 or more units
   ___ 9 to 14 units
   ___ 8 or fewer units

___ Male
___ Female

Uses groupings that do not overlap (not *9 to 15* and *15 or more*)

2. How many times have you visited the bookstore this semester?
   ___ 0 times ___ 1 time ___ 2 times ___ 3 times ___ 4 or more times
3. Indicate your concern for the environment.
   ___ Very concerned ___ Concerned ___ Unconcerned
4. To protect the environment, would you be willing to change to another type of bag when buying books?
   ___ Yes
   ___ No

Indicate your feeling about the following alternatives.

For major purchases the bookstore should	Agree	Undecided	Disagree
5. Continue to provide plastic bags.	___	___	___
6. Provide no bags; encourage students to bring their own bags.	___	___	___
7. Provide no bags; offer cloth bags at reduced price (about $3).	___	___	___
8. Give a cloth bag with each major purchase, the cost to be included in registration fees.	___	___	___
9. Consider another alternative, such as			

____

Uses scale questions to channel responses into quantifiable alternatives, as opposed to open-ended questions

Allows respondent to add an answer in case choices provided seem insufficient

Please return the completed survey form to your instructor or to the survey box at the North Shore College Bookstore exit. Your opinion counts.

Tells how to return survey form

Thanks for your help!

- **Make it easy for respondents to return the survey.** Researchers often provide prepaid self-addressed envelopes or business-reply envelopes. Low-cost Web survey software such as SurveyMonkey and Zoomerang help users develop simple, template-driven questions and allow survey takers conveniently to follow a link to take the survey.
- **Conduct a pilot study.** Try the questionnaire with a small group so that you can remedy any problems. For example, the survey shown in Figure 11.8 revealed that female students generally favored cloth bags and were willing to pay for them. Male students opposed purchasing cloth bags. By adding a gender category, researchers could verify this finding. The pilot study also revealed the need to ensure an appropriate representation of male and female students in the survey.

Interviews

When are interviews with experts appropriate?

Some of the best report information, particularly on topics about which little has been written, comes from individuals. These individuals are usually experts or veterans in their fields. Consider both in-house and outside experts for business reports. Tapping these sources will call for in-person, telephone, or online interviews. To elicit the most useful data, try these techniques:

- **Locate an expert.** Ask managers and individuals who are considered to be most knowledgeable in their areas. Check membership lists of professional organizations, and consult articles about the topic or related topics. Most people enjoy being experts or at least recommending them. You could also post an inquiry to an Internet newsgroup. An easy way to search newsgroups in a topic area is through the **Browse all groups** category indexed by the popular search tool Google.
- **Prepare for the interview.** Learn about the individual you are interviewing, and make sure you can pronounce the interviewee's name. Research the background and terminology of the topic. Let's say you are interviewing a corporate communication expert about producing an in-house newsletter. You ought to be familiar with terms such as *font* and software such as QuarkXPress and Adobe InDesign. In addition, be prepared by making a list of questions that pinpoint your focus on the topic. Ask the interviewee if you may record the talk. Practice using the recording device so that you are familiar with it by the time of the interview.
- **Maintain a professional attitude**. Call before the interview to confirm the arrangements, and then arrive on time. Be prepared to take notes if your recorder fails (and remember to ask permission beforehand if you want to record). Use your body language to convey respect.
- **Make your questions objective and friendly.** Adopt a courteous and respectful attitude. Don't get into a debating match with the interviewee, and don't interrupt. Remember that you are there to listen, not to talk! Use open-ended rather than yes-or-no questions to draw experts out.
- **Watch the time.** Tell interviewees in advance how much time you expect to need for the interview. Don't overstay your appointment. If your subject rambles, gently try to draw him or her back to the topic; otherwise, you may run out of time before asking all your questions.
- **End graciously.** Conclude the interview with a general question, such as *Is there anything you would like to add?* Express your appreciation, and ask permission to telephone later if you need to verify points.

Spotlight on Communicators

© AP Images/Toby Talbot

Premier management consultant and best-selling author Tom Peters recognizes the value of ongoing primary and secondary research. He recommends collecting data not only about the performance of your own company but also about that of the competition. To stay abreast of rivals and their techniques, businesses must (a) collect data, (b) update them regularly, and (c) share them widely within the firm.

Observation and Experimentation

When do firsthand observation and investigation provide useful report data?

Some kinds of primary data can be obtained only through firsthand observation and investigation. If you determine that the questions you have require observational data, then you need to plan the observations carefully. Most important is deciding what or whom you are observing and how often those observations are necessary to provide reliable data. For example, if you want to learn more about an organization's telephone customer service, you probably need to conduct an observation (along with interviews and perhaps even surveys). You will want to answer questions such as *How long does a typical caller wait before a customer service rep answers the call?* and *Is the service consistent?* Recording observations for 60-minute periods at various times throughout a week will give you a better picture than just observing for an hour on a Friday before a holiday.

When you observe, plan ahead. Arrive early enough to introduce yourself and set up whatever equipment you think is necessary. Make sure you have received permissions beforehand, particularly if you are recording. In addition, take notes, not only of the events or actions but also of the settings. Changes in environment often have an effect on actions. Famous for his out-of-the box thinking, Howard Schultz, the CEO of Starbucks, is known to hate research, advertising, and customer surveys. Instead of relying on sophisticated marketing research, Schultz visits 25 Starbucks locations a week to learn about his customers.[6]

Experimentation produces data suggesting causes and effects. Informal experimentation might be as simple as a pretest and posttest in a college course. Did students expand their knowledge as a result of the course? More formal experimentation is undertaken by scientists and professional researchers, who control variables to test their effects. Assume, for example, that Hershey's wants to test the hypothesis (which is a tentative assumption) that chocolate lifts people out of the doldrums. An experiment testing the hypothesis would separate depressed people into two groups: those who ate chocolate (the experimental group) and those who did not (the control group). What effect did chocolate have? Such experiments are not done haphazardly, however. Valid experiments require sophisticated research designs and careful attention to matching the experimental and control groups.

ETHICS CHECK

Cribbing From References?

Doing last-minute research for a class or work project, you are in a hurry; therefore, you decide to copy some sources from the list of references that you found in an article on your topic to boost your number of works cited. Is it unethical to list sources you have not actually read?

The World Wide Web

LEARNING OBJECTIVE 5

Comprehend fast-changing communication technology: the Web, electronic databases, and other resources for business writers and researchers.

If you are like most adults today, you probably use the Web for entertainment and work every day. You stay in touch with your friends by instant messaging and e-mail, not to mention text and picture messages you exchange between increasingly more capable smartphones. Chances are you have a personal page on a social networking site such as Facebook or MySpace, and perhaps you play one of the countless free online games. You have probably looked up directions on Google Maps and may have bid on or sold items on eBay. You are likely to download ringtones for your cell phone, and perhaps you obtain your favorite music from iTunes, not some illegal file-sharing site. Your generation is much more likely to follow the news online than in the daily paper or even on TV. In short, you rely on the Internet daily for information and entertainment. You are part of a vast virtual community that, in turn, consists of many smaller communities all over the world. The Web and the Internet as a whole are referred to as a global village for a reason.

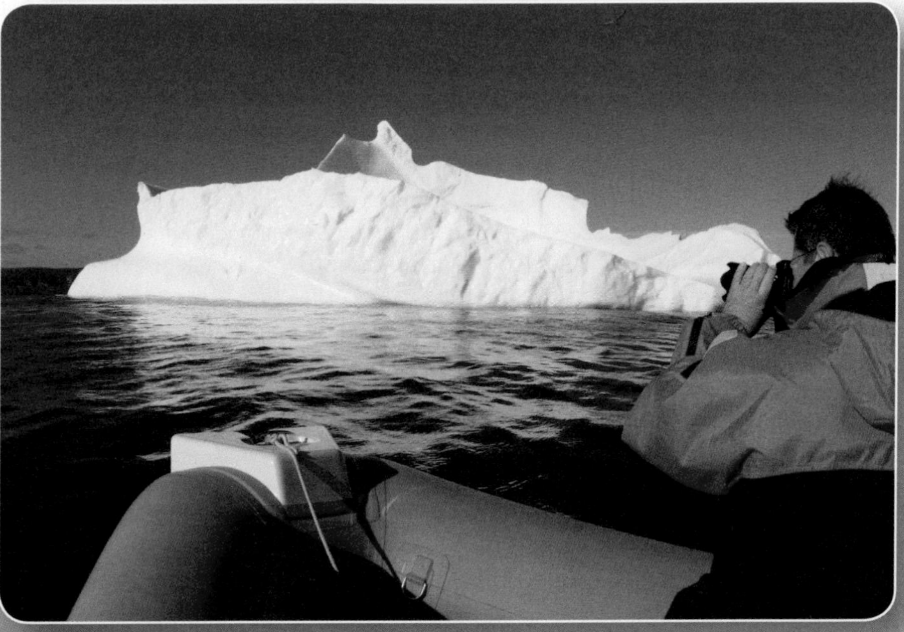

© Darryl Leniuk/Stone/ Getty Images

It's back to basics for scientists at the Intergovernmental Panel on Climate Change (IPCC) after the group's world-renowned Assessment Report had its most sensational claims rescinded due to invalid data. Among the claims lacking scientific backing were the assertion that the Himalayan glaciers would melt away by 2035 and that nearly half of the Amazon rainforest would disappear. The IPCC said it hoped to restore public confidence by submitting to an independent scientific review board and by adopting quality standards for future reports. *How do researchers produce valid primary data?*

Spotlight on Communicators

© Courtesy of Eric Dezenhall

One of America's top crisis management gurus explains the unbridled power of the Web: "The CEOs of the largest 50 companies in the world are practically hiding under their desks in terror about Internet rumors." Eric Dezenhall, author of *Damage Control,* adds that "[m]illions of dollars of labor are being spent discussing whether or not you should respond to the Web."

Understanding the Dynamic Complexity of the Web. The Web is an amazing resource. It started as a fast, but exclusive network linking scientists, academics, military people, and other "tech heads." In the beginning information traveled purely in text form. Today the Web is interactive, mobile, and user-friendly with multimedia content ranging from digital sound files to vivid images and video files. Most important for report writers, the Web is considered an ever-expanding democratic medium where anyone can be a publisher and consume most of its boundless content free of charge. Armed with camera phones, average citizens post their videos on the hugely popular site YouTube and act as virtual reporters. Interest groups of all stripes gather in Usenet communities or newsgroups (digital bulletin boards and discussion forums). They exchange news, opinions, and other information.

- **Virtual communities.** The so-called Web 2.0 has fostered interactive environments that have resulted in the emergence of virtual communities that encourage teamwork among strangers all over the United States and the world. One such democratic, free-access tool is wiki. This group communication software enables users to create and change Web pages. The best known perhaps is Wikipedia, a free online reference that can be edited even by a layperson. Behind company firewalls many wikis help technical experts and other specialists collaborate.
- **Information mobility.** Digital content on the Web has also become more mobile in recent years. Thanks to browser-enabled smartphones and wireless personal digital assistants (PDAs), businesspeople can surf Web pages and retrieve text messages, instant messages, and e-mails on the go with devices that fit into their pockets. Similarly, users can listen to podcasts (digital recordings of radio or TV programs) and other media files on demand. Podcasts are distributed for downloading to a computer, a smartphone such as the iPhone or BlackBerry, or an MP3 audio player such as the iPod.

Ethics Check

Legitimate Gripe or Character Assassination?

Few would deny that customers should have an outlet for reasonable complaints against companies that slighted them. However, today, increasingly anonymous cyber threats against companies often erupt suddenly and turn nasty, leaving firms unsure about how to deal with them, whether to respond, and if so, how. In this light, can we trust the information on the Web?

How has the Web changed how we access information, and what types of information are available?

As we have seen in Chapter 7, the fastest-growing sector of the Internet is social networking sites. Social networking is a boon, but it also presents risks. On the one hand, online social media and a growing variety of prominent blogs, sometimes labeled the blogosphere, have empowered citizens to get their voices heard and to voice discontent. Online social media such as Twitter and blogs allow users to comment on any imaginable topic or event and post their views instantly. Companies have recognized the potential of the new media to reach vast audiences. Corporate blogs and social networks are growing as companies begin to understand their marketing potential.

However, the dark side of the power in the hands of "netizens" is that rumors and savage, no-holds-barred attacks can go "viral," which means they travel around the globe overnight, ruining reputations and tarnishing carefully honed brands. Therefore, more and more businesses engage in damage control after online threats surface. In short, the Web is an invaluable resource, but report writers must approach it with caution and sound judgment.

With nearly 80 percent of Americans online[7] and literally trillions of pages of information available on the World Wide Web, odds are that if you have a question, an answer exists online. To a business researcher, the Web offers a wide range of organizational and commercial information. You can expect to find such items as product and service facts, public relations material, mission statements, staff directories, press releases, current company news, government information, selected article reprints, collaborative scientific project reports, and employment information.

Why is it important to learn to navigate the depths of the Web?

Although a wealth of information is available, finding exactly what you need can be frustrating and time-consuming. The constantly changing contents of the Web and its lack of organization make it more problematic for research than searching commercial databases, such as LexisNexis. Moreover, Web content is uneven, and often the quality is questionable. The problem of gathering information is complicated by the fact that the total number of Web sites recently surpassed 200 million, growing at the rate of about 4 million new domain addresses each month.[8]

To succeed in your search for information and answers, you need to understand the search tools available to you. You also need to understand how to evaluate the information you find.

Identifying Search Tools. Finding what you are looking for on the Web is hopeless without powerful, specialized search tools, such as Google, Bing, Yahoo Search, AOL, and Ask.com. These search tools can be divided into two types: subject (or Web) directories and search engines. In addition, some search engines specialize in "metasearching." This means they combine several powerful search engines into one (e.g., Dogpile). See Figure 11.9 for an overview of useful Web search tools. Large search sites such as Yahoo and Google Directory are actually search engines and subject directories combined. Subject directories fall into two categories—commercial (e.g., Yahoo, About.com, and others) and academic (e.g., InfoMine).

What can Google, Bing, and Yahoo do for a researcher?

FIGURE 11.9 Web Search Tools for Business Writers

Business Databases (Subscription based, commercial)	**Features**
ABI/INFORM Complete (ProQuest)	Best database for reliable, scholarly sources; recommended first stop for business students
LexisNexis Academic	Database of over 5,000 newspapers, magazines, etc.; very current; forces users to limit their search to fewer than 1,000 hits
Factiva	Stores over 5,000 periodicals; very current; best with a narrow search subject or to add results to other searches (unlimited results)
JSTOR	Scholarly articles; best for historical, not current, information
Search Engines (open-access business information)	
Business.com http://www.business.com	Search engine and subject directory/portal in one; features all business-related subjects
CEO Express http://www.ceoexpress.com	Human-selected directories of subjects relevant to business executives and researchers
Google Scholar http://scholar.google.com	Scholarly articles in various disciplines, including business, administration, finance, and economics
Search Engines (general)	
Google http://www.google.com	Relevance ranking; most popular search site or portal (65 percent of Web searches); advanced search options and subject directories
Yahoo http://www.yahoo.com	Search engine and directory; popular free e-mail site; relevance ranking; ranks second after Google with 16 percent of Web searches
Bing http://www.bing.com/	Microsoft's latest search engine indexing 200 million Web sites; MSN/Bing is in third place with nearly 11 percent of Web searches
All the Web http://www.alltheweb.com	Advanced search option; searches for audio and video files
Ask http://www.ask.com	Plain English (natural language) questions
Metasearch Engines (results from several search sites)	
Vivísimo/Clusty http://vivisimo.com http://clusty.com	Metasearch function clusters results into categories; offers advanced search options and help
InfoSpace http://search.infospace.com http://www.dogpile.com	Metasearch technology; searches Google, Yahoo, Bing, Ask, and more; owns other metasearch engines (e.g., Dogpile, WebCrawler, MetaCrawler)
Search http://www.search.com	Searches Google, Ask, LookSmart, and dozens of other leading search engines
Subject Directories or Portals	
About http://www.about.com	Directory that organizes content from over 2 million sites with commentary from 750 "guides" (chosen experts on 70,000+ topics)
Ipl2 http://www.ipl.org/	Award-winning public service organization and learning/teaching environment maintained by librarians of several universities

FIGURE 11.10 **Business.com**

Courtesy of Business.com

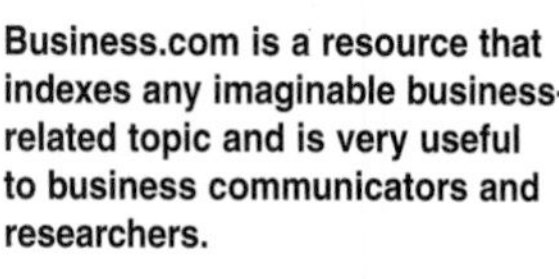
Business.com is a resource that indexes any imaginable business-related topic and is very useful to business communicators and researchers.

Can any single search engine or directory index all Web pages?

Organized into subject categories, these human-compiled directories contain a collection of links to Internet resources submitted by site creators or evaluators.

Search engines differ in the way they trawl the vast amount of data on the Web. Google uses automated software "spiders" that crawl through the Web at regular intervals to collect and index the information from each location visited. Clusty by Vivísimo not only examines several search engines, but also groups results into topics called clusters. Some search tools (e.g., Ask.com) use natural-language-processing technology to enable you to ask questions to gather information. Both search engines and subject directories will help you find specific information. Figure 11.10 shows Business.com, a search engine and subject directory in one.

Search engines such as Google used to boast about the numbers of items they had indexed, but they stopped after hitting the 1 trillion milestone of unique links, recognizing that the number of individual Web pages is potentially infinite.[9] No single search engine or directory can come close to indexing all pages on the Internet. However, if you try a multiple-search site such as Dogpile, you can save much time because its metasearch technology compares the results of at least seven major search engines, eliminates duplicates, and then ranks the best hits for you.[10] To search for data effectively, consider using the search tools listed in Figure 11.9.

Applying Internet Search Strategies and Techniques. To conduct a thorough search for the information you need, build a (re)search strategy by understanding the tools available.

How can you make Web research less time-consuming and frustrating?

- **Use two or three search tools.** Begin by conducting a topic search. Use a subject directory such as Yahoo, About.com, or Open Directory Project (dmoz.org). Once you have narrowed your topic, switch to a search engine or metasearch engine.
- **Know your search tool.** When connecting to a search site for the first time, always read the description of its service, including its FAQs (frequently asked questions), Help, and How to Search sections. Often there are special features (e.g., the News, Images, Video, Books, and other categories on Google) that can speed up the search process.
- **Understand case sensitivity.** Generally use lowercase for your searches, unless you are looking for a term that is usually written in upper- and lowercase, such as a person's name.
- **Use nouns as search words and up to eight words in a query.** The right keywords—and more of them—can narrow the search effectively.

- **Combine keywords into phrases.** Phrases, marked by the use of quotation marks (e.g., "business ethics"), will limit results to specific matches.
- **Omit articles and prepositions.** Known as stop words, articles and prepositions do not add value to a search. Instead of *request for proposal*, use *proposal request*.
- **Use wild cards.** Most search engines support wildcards, such as asterisks. For example, the search term *cent** will retrieve *cents*, while *cent*** will retrieve both *center* and *centre*.
- **Learn basic Boolean search strategies.** You can save yourself a lot of time and frustration by narrowing your search with the following Boolean operators:

AND	Identifies only documents containing all of the specified words: **employee AND productivity AND morale**
OR	Identifies documents containing at least one of the specified words: **employee OR productivity OR morale**
NOT	Excludes documents containing the specified word: **employee productivity NOT morale**
NEAR	Finds documents containing target words or phrases within a specified distance, for instance, within ten words: **employee NEAR productivity**.

- **Bookmark the best.** To keep track of your favorite Internet sites, save them as bookmarks or favorites.
- **Keep trying.** If a search produces no results, check your spelling. If you are using Boolean operators, check the syntax of your queries. Try synonyms and variations on words. Try to be less specific in your search term. If your search produces too many hits, try to be more specific. Use the Advanced feature of your search engine to narrow your search. Think of words that uniquely identify what you are looking for. Use as many relevant keywords as possible.

How do search engines vary in their ability to retrieve data, and why should you learn about their advanced features?

- **Repeat your search a week later.** For the best results, return to your search a couple of days or a week later. The same keywords will probably produce additional results. That's because millions of new pages are being added to the Web every day. The ranking of hits can also change depending on how often a link is accessed by Internet users.

Remember, subject directories and search engines vary in their contents, features, selectivity, accuracy, and retrieval technologies. Only through clever cyber searching can you uncover the jewels hidden in the Internet.

Which four criteria should you consider when judging the value of a Web site?

Evaluating Web Sources. Most of us using the Web have a tendency to assume that any information turned up by a search engine has somehow been evaluated as part of a valid selection process. Wrong! The truth is that the Internet is rampant with unreliable sites that reside side by side with reputable ones. Anyone with a computer and an Internet connection can publish anything on the Web. Unlike library-based research, information at many sites has not undergone the editing or scrutiny of scholarly publication procedures. The information we read in journals and most reputable magazines is reviewed, authenticated, and evaluated. That's why we have learned to trust these sources as valid and authoritative.

Information on the Web is much less reliable than data from traditional sources. Wikis, blogs, and discussion forum entries are a case in point. Although they turn up in many Internet searches, they are mostly useless because they are short-lived. They change constantly and may disappear fast, so that your source can't be verified. Many don't provide any references or reveal sources that are either obscure or suspect. Academic researchers prefer lasting, scholarly sources. Many professors will not allow you to cite from Wikipedia, for example, because this collaborative tool and online reference can be edited by almost any contributor and is considered to be unreliable. Moreover, citing from an encyclopedia shows poor research skills. Some Web sites exist to propagandize; others want to sell you something. To use the Web meaningfully, you must scrutinize what you find and check who authored and published it. Here are specific criteria to consider as you examine a site:

- **Currency.** What is the date of the Web page? When was it last updated? Is some of the information obviously out-of-date? If the information is time sensitive and the site has not been updated recently, the site is probably not reliable.
- **Authority.** Who publishes or sponsors this Web page? What makes the presenter an authority? Is information about the author or creator available? Is a contact address available for the presenter? Learn to be skeptical about data and assertions from individuals and organizations whose credentials are not verifiable.
- **Content.** Is the purpose of the page to entertain, inform, convince, or sell? How would you classify this page (e.g., news, personal, advocacy, reference)? Who is the intended audience, based on content, tone, and style? Can you judge the overall value of the content compared with the other resources on this topic? Web presenters with a slanted point of view cannot be counted on for objective data. Be particularly cautious with blogs. They often abound with grandstanding and ranting but lack factual information. Read them side by side with reputable news sources.
- **Accuracy.** Do the facts that are presented seem reliable to you? Do you find errors in spelling, grammar, or usage? Do you see any evidence of bias? Are footnotes provided? If you find numerous errors and if facts are not referenced, you should be alert that the data may be questionable.

PLUGGED IN

Staying on Top of Research Data

In collecting electronic search results, you can easily lose track of Web sites and articles you quoted. To document Web data that may change, as well as to manage all your electronic sources, you need a specific plan for saving the information. At the very least, you will want to create a *working bibliography* or list of *references* in which you record the URL of each electronic source and its access date. Here are techniques that can help you build your list of references and stay in control of your electronic data:

- **Saving sources to disk or portable flash memory device** has advantages, including being able to open the document in a browser even if you don't have access to the Internet. More important, saving sources to disk or memory stick ensures that you will have access to information that may or may not be available later. Using either the **File** and **Save As** or the **File** and **Save Page As** menu command in your browser, you will be able to store the information permanently. Saving images and other kinds of media can be accomplished with your mouse by either right-clicking or command clicking on the item, followed by a command such as **Save Picture As** or **Save Image As** from a pop-up window.
- **Copying and pasting** information you find on the Web into word processing documents is an easy way to save and store it. Remember to copy and paste the URL into the file as well, and record the URL in your working bibliography. If you invest in Adobe's PDF Converter, you can save a Web page or an MS Word document in the portable document format simply by choosing the **Print** command and selecting Adobe PDF in the **Printer** window of the **Print** menu. The URL, access date, and time stamp will be automatically saved on the document. You can keep your PDF documents as electronic files or print out paper copies later.
- **Printing** pages is a handy way to gather and store information. Doing so enables you to have copies of important data that you can annotate or highlight. Make sure the URL prints with the document (usually on the bottom of the page). If not, write it on the page.
- **Bookmarking favorites** is an option within browsers to enable you to record and store the URLs for important sources. The key to using this option is creating folders with names that are relevant and using names for bookmarks that make sense and are not redundant. Pay attention or the browser will provide the information for you, relying on the name the Web page creator gave it. If no name is provided, the browser will default to the URL.
- **E-mailing** documents, URLs, or messages to yourself is another useful strategy. Many databases and online magazines permit you to e-mail information and sometimes the entire article to your account. If you combine the copy-and-paste function with e-mail, you can send yourself nearly any information you find on the Web.

Career Application

Use Google or another search engine that supports Boolean searches to investigate a topic such as carbon footprint or sustainability. Explore the same topic using (a) keywords and (b) Boolean operators. Which method produces more relevant hits? Save two relevant sources from each search using two or more of the strategies presented here. Remember to include the URL for each article. In a memo to your instructor, list the bibliographic information from all four sources and explain briefly which method was more productive.

Documenting Information

LEARNING OBJECTIVE 6

Recognize the purposes and techniques of documentation in business reports, and avoid plagiarism.

In writing business and other reports, you will often build on the ideas and words of others. In Western culture, whenever you "borrow" the ideas of others, you must give credit to your information sources. This is called *documentation*.

Recognizing the Purposes of Documentation

Why is it necessary to document data you use to write reports?

As a careful writer, you should take pains to document report data properly for the following reasons:

- **To strengthen your argument.** Including good data from reputable sources will convince readers of your credibility and the logic of your reasoning.
- **To protect yourself against charges of plagiarism.** Acknowledging your sources keeps you honest. Plagiarism, which is unethical and in some cases illegal, is the act of using others' ideas without proper documentation.
- **To instruct the reader.** Citing references enables readers to pursue a topic further and make use of the information themselves.

Distinguishing Between Academic Documentation and Business Practices

In the academic world, documentation is critical. Especially in the humanities and sciences, students are taught to cite sources by using quotation marks, parenthetical citations, footnotes, and bibliographies. College term papers require full documentation to demonstrate that a student has become familiar with respected sources and can cite them properly in developing an argument. Giving credit to the author is extremely important. Students who plagiarize risk a failing grade in a class and even expulsion from school.

Do business writers follow the same strict documentation standards as academic writers do?

In the business world, however, documentation and authorship are sometimes viewed differently. Business communicators on the job may find that much of what is written does not follow the standards they learned in school. In many instances, individual authorship is unimportant. For example, employees may write for the signature of their bosses. The writer receives no credit. Similarly, teams turn out documents for which none of the team members receive individual credit. Internal business reports, which often include chunks of information from previous reports, also fail to acknowledge sources or give credit. Even information from outside sources may lack proper documentation. However, if facts are questioned, business writers must be able to produce their source materials.

Although both internal and external business reports are not as heavily documented as school assignments or term papers, business communication students are well advised to learn proper documentation methods. In the workplace, stealing the ideas of others and passing them off as one's own can be corrosive to the business because it leads to resentment and worse. One writer suggests that the wronged employee may quit and speak about the unethical behavior, destroying the integrity of the business.[11]

Plagiarism of words or ideas is a serious charge and can lead to loss of a job. Famous historians, several high-level journalists, and even college professors[12] suffered serious consequences for copying from unnamed sources. Your instructor may use a commercial plagiarism detection service such as Turnitin.com, which can cross-reference much of the information on the Web, looking for documents with similar phrasing. The result, an "originality report," provides the instructor with a clear idea of whether you have been accurate and honest. You can avoid charges of plagiarism as well as add clarity to your work by knowing what to document and by developing good research habits.

Spotlight on Communicators

In academic circles, plagiarism remains a serious offense. But many see the Internet as a free-for-all. A Pew Research study found that nearly half of all bloggers have admitted to having appropriated text, images, and other media without attributing them to their original sources. "People are incredibly sloppy," says CRMMastery.com blog author Jim Berkowitz, who insists that he clearly identifies content that he borrows from others. "It's like the Wild West out there," Berkowitz claims.

When do you have to give credit?

Learning What to Document

When you write reports, especially in college, you are continually dealing with other people's ideas. You are expected to conduct research, synthesize ideas, and build on the work of others. But you are also expected to give proper credit for borrowed material. To avoid plagiarism, you must give credit whenever you use the following:[13]

- Another person's ideas, opinions, examples, or theory
- Any facts, statistics, graphs, and drawings that are not common knowledge
- Quotations of another person's actual spoken or written words
- Paraphrases of another person's spoken or written words

Information that is common knowledge requires no documentation. For example, the statement *The Wall Street Journal is a popular business newspaper* would require no citation. Statements that are not common knowledge, however, must be documented. For example, *Eight of the nation's top-ten fastest-growing large cities (100,000 or more population) since Census 2000 lie in the Western states of Arizona, Nevada, and California* would require a citation because most people do not know this fact. Cite sources for proprietary information such as statistics organized and reported by a newspaper or magazine. You probably know to use citations to document direct quotations, but you must also cite ideas that you summarize in your own words.

Developing Good Research Habits

Report writers who are gathering information have two methods available for recording the information they find. The time-honored manual method of notetaking works well because information is recorded on separate cards, which can then be arranged in the order needed to develop a thesis or argument. Today, however, writers rely heavily on electronic researching. Traditional notetaking methods may seem antiquated and laborious in comparison. Let's explore both methods.

What are the advantages of handwritten note cards?

Manual Notetaking. To make sure you know whose ideas you are using, train yourself to take excellent notes. If possible, know what you intend to find before you begin your research so that you won't waste time on unnecessary notes. Here are some pointers on taking good notes:

- Record all major ideas from various sources on separate note cards.
- Include all publication information (author, date, title, and so forth) along with precise quotations.
- Consider using one card color for direct quotes and a different color for your paraphrases and summaries.
- Put the original source material aside when you are summarizing or paraphrasing.

How can you stay safe from charges of plagiarism when taking notes electronically?

Electronic Notetaking. Instead of recording facts on note cards, savvy researchers today take advantage of electronic tools, as noted in the earlier Plugged In box. Beware, however, of the risk of cutting and pasting your way into plagiarism. Here are some pointers on taking good electronic notes:

- Begin your research by setting up a folder on your hard drive. On the go, you can use a storage device such as a USB flash drive (memory stick) or a rewritable disk (CD-RW) to carry your data.
- Create subfolders for major sections, such as introduction, body, and closing.
- When you find facts on the Web or in electronic databases, highlight the material you want to record, copy it, and paste it into a document in an appropriate folder.
- Be sure to include all publication data.
- As discussed in the section on managing research data, consider archiving on a memory stick or external USB drive those Web pages or articles used in your research in case the data must be verified.

Practicing the Fine Art of Paraphrasing

In writing reports and using the ideas of others, you will probably rely heavily on *paraphrasing*, which means restating an original passage in your own words and in your own style. To do a good job of paraphrasing, follow these steps:

What is paraphrasing, and how can you do it correctly?

1. Read the original material intently to comprehend its full meaning.
2. Write your own version without looking at the original.
3. Avoid repeating the grammatical structure of the original and merely replacing words with synonyms.
4. Reread the original to be sure you covered the main points but did not borrow specific language.

To better understand the difference between plagiarizing and paraphrasing, study the following passages. Notice that the writer of the plagiarized version uses the same grammatical construction as the source and often merely replaces words with synonyms. Even the acceptable version, however, requires a reference to the source author.

Source

While the BlackBerry has become standard armor for executives, a few maverick leaders are taking action to reduce e-mail use. . . . The concern, say academics and management thinkers, is misinterpreted messages, as well as the degree to which e-mail has become a substitute for the nuanced conversations that are critical in the workplace.[14]

Plagiarized version

What exactly is wrong with the plagiarized version, and what makes the acceptable paraphrase correct and ethical?

Although smartphones are standard among business executives, some pioneering bosses are acting to lower e-mail usage. Business professors and management experts are concerned that messages are misinterpreted and e-mail substitutes for nuances in conversations that are crucial on the job (Brady, 2006).

Acceptable paraphrase

E-mail on the go may be the rage in business. However, some executives are rethinking its use, as communication experts warn that e-mail triggers misunderstandings. These specialists believe that e-mail should not replace the more subtle face-to-face interactions needed on the job (Brady, 2006).

Knowing When and How to Quote

On occasion, you will want to use the exact words of a source. But beware of overusing quotations. Documents that contain pages of spliced-together quotations suggest that writers have few ideas of their own. Wise writers and speakers use direct quotations for three purposes only:

What are appropriate uses of direct quotations?

- To provide objective background data and establish the severity of a problem as seen by experts
- To repeat identical phrasing because of its precision, clarity, or aptness
- To duplicate exact wording before criticizing

When you must use a long quotation, try to summarize and introduce it in your own words. Readers want to know the gist of a quotation before they tackle it. For example, to introduce a quotation discussing the shrinking staffs of large companies, you could precede it with your words: *In predicting employment trends, Charles Waller believes the corporation of the future will depend on a small core of full-time employees.* To introduce quotations or paraphrases, use wording such as the following:

According to Waller, ...

Waller argues that . . . .

In his recent study, Waller reported . . . .

Use quotation marks to enclose exact quotations, as shown in the following: "*The current image,*" *says Charles Waller,* "*of a big glass-and-steel corporate headquarters on landscaped grounds directing a worldwide army of tens of thousands of employees may soon be a thing of the past*" (2006, p. 51).

Using Citation Formats

You can direct readers to your sources with parenthetical notes inserted into the text and with bibliographies. The most common citation formats are those presented by the Modern Language Association (MLA) and the American Psychological Association (APA). Learn more about how to use these formats in Appendix C.

Creating Effective Visual Aids

LEARNING OBJECTIVE 7

Create meaningful and interesting graphics; display numeric information in the appropriate graphic form; and skillfully generate, use, and convert data to visual aids.

After collecting and interpreting information, you need to consider how best to present it. If your report contains complex data and numbers, you may want to consider graphics such as tables and charts. These graphics clarify data, create visual interest, and make numerical data meaningful. By simplifying complex ideas and emphasizing key data, well-constructed graphics make key information easier to remember. However, the same data can be shown in many forms; for example, in a chart, table, or graph. That's why you need to know how to match the appropriate graphic with your objective and how to incorporate it into your report.

Matching Graphics and Objectives

What purpose should graphics serve to be effective?

In developing the best graphics, you must decide what data you want to highlight and which graphics are most appropriate to your objectives. Tables? Bar charts? Pie charts? Line charts? Surface charts? Flowcharts? Organization charts? Pictures? Figure 11.11 summarizes appropriate uses for each type of graphic. The following sections discuss each type in more detail.

Tables. Probably the most frequently used graphic in reports is the table. Because a table presents quantitative or verbal information in systematic columns and rows, it can clarify large quantities of data in small spaces. The disadvantage is that tables do not readily display

FIGURE 11.11 Matching Graphics to Objectives

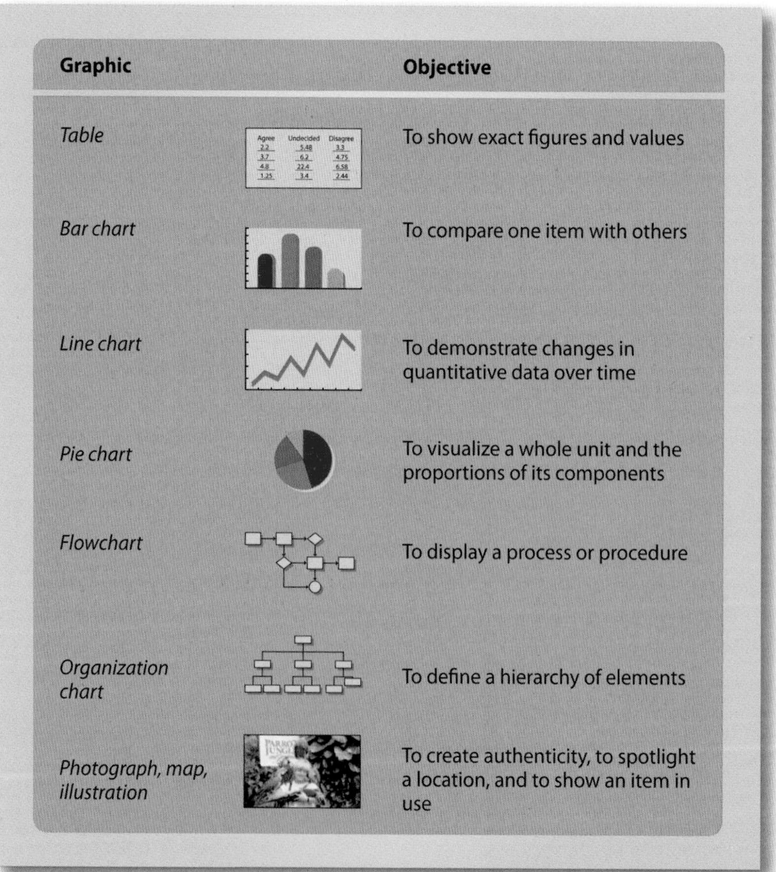

Graphic	Objective
Table	To show exact figures and values
Bar chart	To compare one item with others
Line chart	To demonstrate changes in quantitative data over time
Pie chart	To visualize a whole unit and the proportions of its components
Flowchart	To display a process or procedure
Organization chart	To define a hierarchy of elements
Photograph, map, illustration	To create authenticity, to spotlight a location, and to show an item in use

FIGURE 11.12 Table Summarizing Precise Data

Figure 1 MPM ENTERTAINMENT COMPANY Income by Division (in millions of dollars)				
	Theme Parks	Motion Pictures	DVDs & Videos	Total
2008	$15.8	$39.3	$11.2	$66.3
2009	18.1	17.5	15.3	50.9
2010	23.8	21.1	22.7	67.6
2011	32.2	22.0	24.3	78.5
2012 (projected)	35.1	21.0	26.1	82.2

Source: *Industry Profiles* (New York: DataPro, 2011) 225.

trends. You may have made rough tables to help you organize the raw data collected from questionnaires or interviews. In preparing tables for your readers or listeners, however, you need to pay more attention to clarity and emphasis. Here are tips for making good tables, one of which is provided in Figure 11.12:

What are the relative advantages of tables as opposed to charts and graphs, and when would tables be used?

- Place titles and labels at the top of the table.
- Arrange items in a logical order (alphabetical, chronological, geographical, highest to lowest), depending on what you need to emphasize.
- Provide clear headings for the rows and columns.
- Identify the units in which figures are given (percentages, dollars, units per worker hour) in the table title, in the column or row heading, with the first item in a column, or in a note at the bottom.
- Use *N/A* (*not available*) for missing data.
- Make long tables easier to read by shading alternate lines or by leaving a blank line after groups of five.
- Place tables as close as possible to the place where they are mentioned in the text.

How do we determine which graphic is appropriate?

Figure 11.11 shows the purposes of various graphics. Tables, as illustrated in Figure 11.12, are especially suitable for illustrating exact figures in systematic rows and columns. The table in our figure is particularly useful because it presents data about the MPM Entertainment Company over several years, making it easy to compare several divisions. Figures 11.13 through 11.16 highlight some of the data shown in the MPM Entertainment Company table, illustrating vertical, horizontal, grouped, and segmented 100 percent bar charts, each of which creates a unique effect.

Bar Charts. Although they lack the precision of tables, bar charts enable you to make emphatic visual comparisons by using horizontal or vertical bars of varying lengths. Bar charts are useful for comparing related items, illustrating changes in data over time, and showing segments as a part of the whole. Note how the varied bar charts present information in differing ways.

Many techniques for constructing tables also hold true for bar charts. Here are a few additional tips:

- Keep the length and width of each bar and segment proportional.
- Include a total figure in the middle of the bar or at its end if the figure helps the reader and does not clutter the chart.
- Start dollar or percentage amounts at zero.
- Place the first bar at some distance (usually half the amount of space between bars) from the *y* axis.
- Avoid showing too much information, thus avoiding clutter and confusion.
- Place each bar chart as close as possible to the place where it is mentioned in the text.

FIGURE 11.13 Vertical Bar Chart

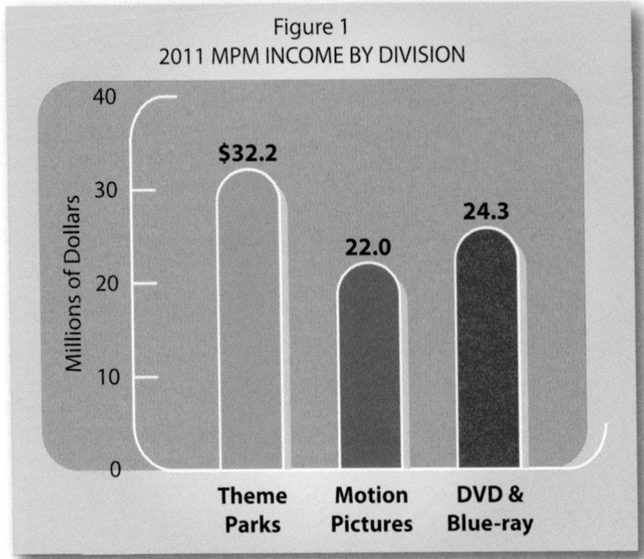

Source: *Industry Profiles*(New York: DataPro, 2011), 225.

FIGURE 11.14 Horizontal Bar Chart

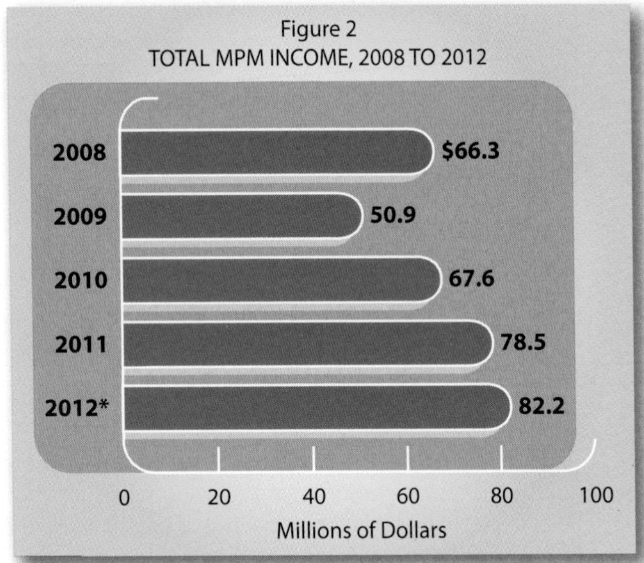

*Projected
Source: *Industry Profiles*(New York: DataPro, 2011), 225.

FIGURE 11.15 Grouped Bar Chart

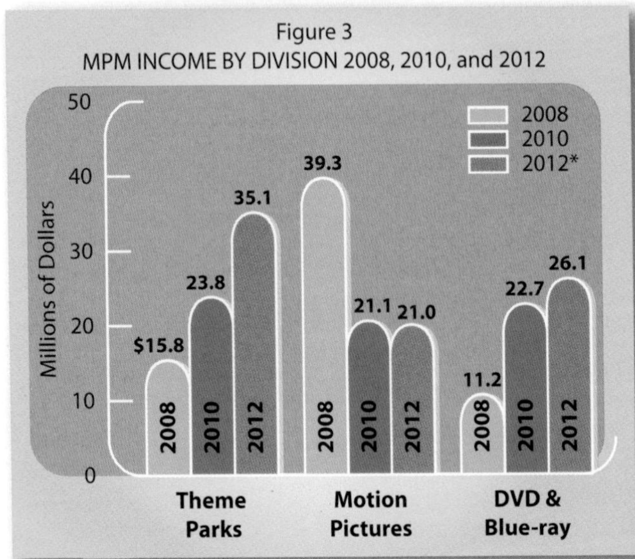

*Projected
Source: *Industry Profiles*

FIGURE 11.16 Segmented 100 Percent Bar Chart

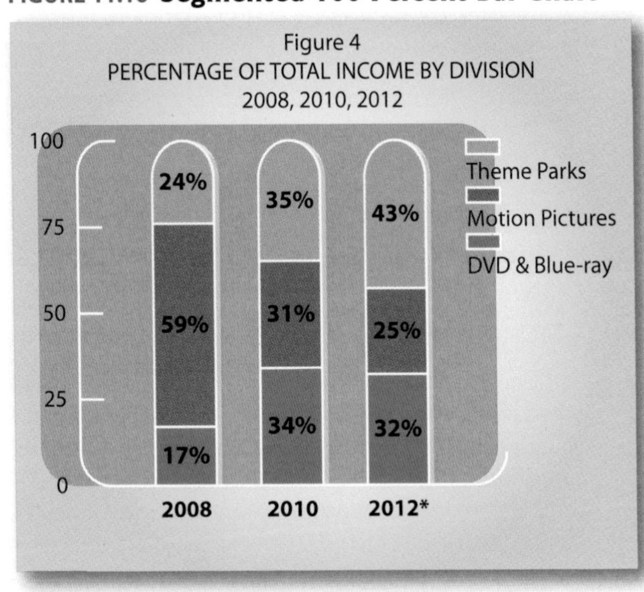

*Projected
Source: *Industry Profiles*

What is the purpose of line charts?

Line Charts. The major advantage of line charts is that they show changes over time, thus indicating trends. The vertical axis is typically the dependent variable; and the horizontal axis, the independent one. Simple line charts (Figure 11.17) show just one variable. Multiple line charts compare items, such as two or more data sets, using the same variable (Figure 11.18). Segmented line charts (Figure 11.19), also called surface charts, illustrate how the components of a whole change over time. To prepare a line chart, remember these tips:

- Begin with a grid divided into squares.
- Arrange the time component (usually years) horizontally across the bottom; arrange values for the other variable vertically.
- Draw small dots at the intersections to indicate each value at a given year.
- Connect the dots and add color if desired.

FIGURE 11.17 Simple Line Chart

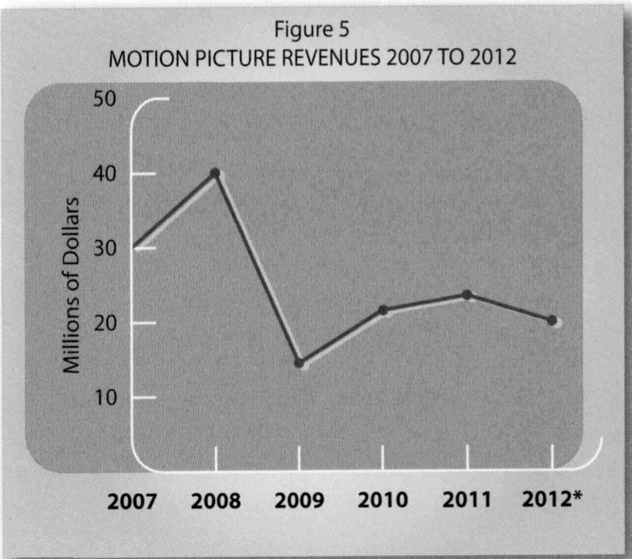

*Projected
Source: *Industry Profiles*

FIGURE 11.18 Multiple Line Chart

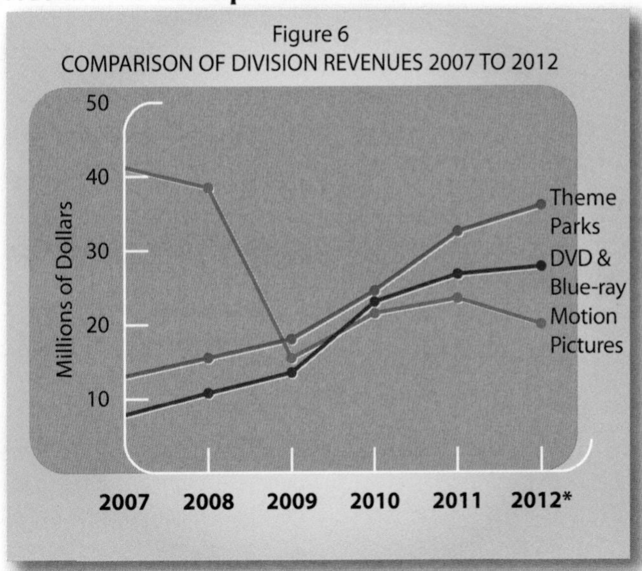

*Projected
Source: *Industry Profiles*

FIGURE 11.19 Segmented Line (Area) Chart

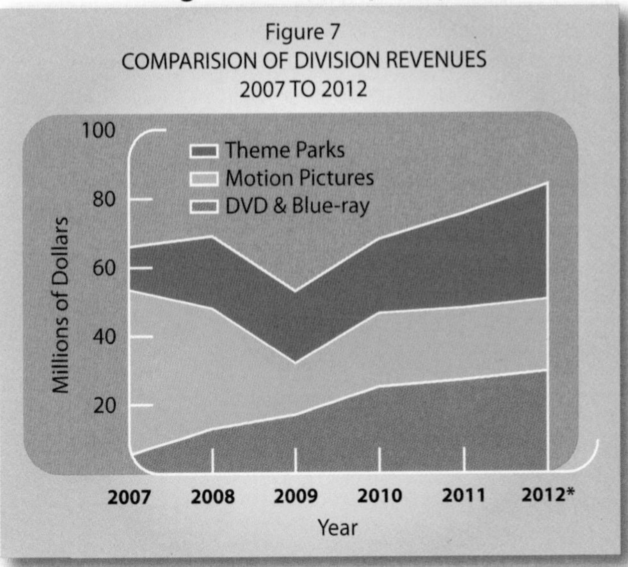

*Projected
Source: *Industry Profiles*

FIGURE 11.20 Pie Chart

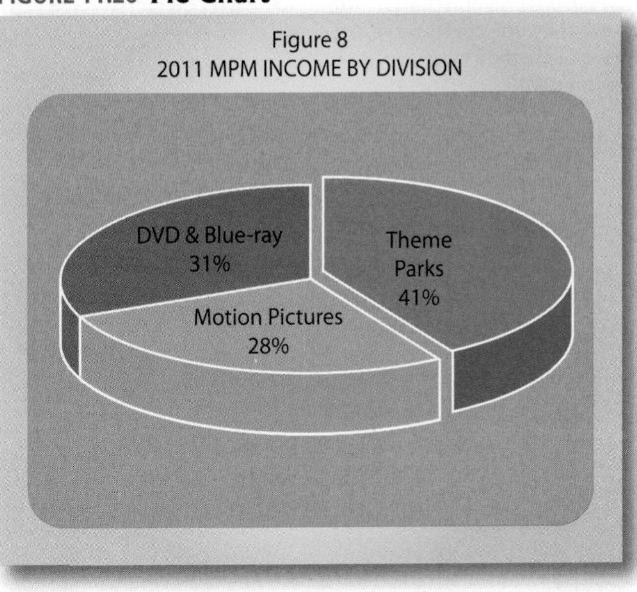

Source: *Industry Profiles*

- To prepare a segmented (surface) chart, plot the first value (say, DVD and Blu-ray disc income) across the bottom; add the next item (say, motion picture income) to the first figures for every increment; for the third item (say, theme park income), add its value to the total for the first two items. The top line indicates the total of the three values.

When are pie charts most suitable and useful?

Pie Charts. Pie charts, or circle graphs, enable readers to see a whole and the proportion of its components, or wedges. Although less flexible than bar or line charts, pie charts are useful for showing percentages, as Figure 11.20 illustrates. They are very effective for lay, or nonexpert, audiences. Notice that a wedge can be "exploded," or popped out, for special emphasis, as seen in Figure 11.20. MS Excel and other spreadsheet programs provide a selection of three-dimensional pie charts. For the most effective pie charts, follow these suggestions:

- Make the biggest wedge appear first. Computer spreadsheet programs correctly assign the biggest wedge first (beginning at the 12 o'clock position) and arrange the others in order of decreasing size as long as you list the data representing each wedge on the spreadsheet in descending order.
- Include, if possible, the actual percentage or absolute value for each wedge.
- Use four to six segments for best results; if necessary, group small portions into a wedge called *Other.*
- Draw radii from the center.
- Distinguish wedges with color, shading, or cross-hatching.
- Keep all the labels horizontal.

Flowcharts. Procedures are simplified and clarified by diagramming them in a flowchart, as shown in Figure 11.21. Whether you need to describe the procedure for handling a customer's purchase, highlight steps in solving a problem, or display a problem with a process, flowcharts help the reader visualize the process. Traditional flowcharts use the following symbols:

- Ovals to designate the beginning and end of a process
- Diamonds to designate decision points
- Rectangles to represent major activities or steps

What purpose do flowcharts and organization charts serve, and when are they most appropriate?

Organization Charts. Many large organizations are so complex that they need charts to show the chain of command, from the boss down to the line managers and employees. Organization charts provide such information as who reports to whom, how many subordinates work for each manager (the span of control), and what channels of official communication

FIGURE 11.21 Flowchart

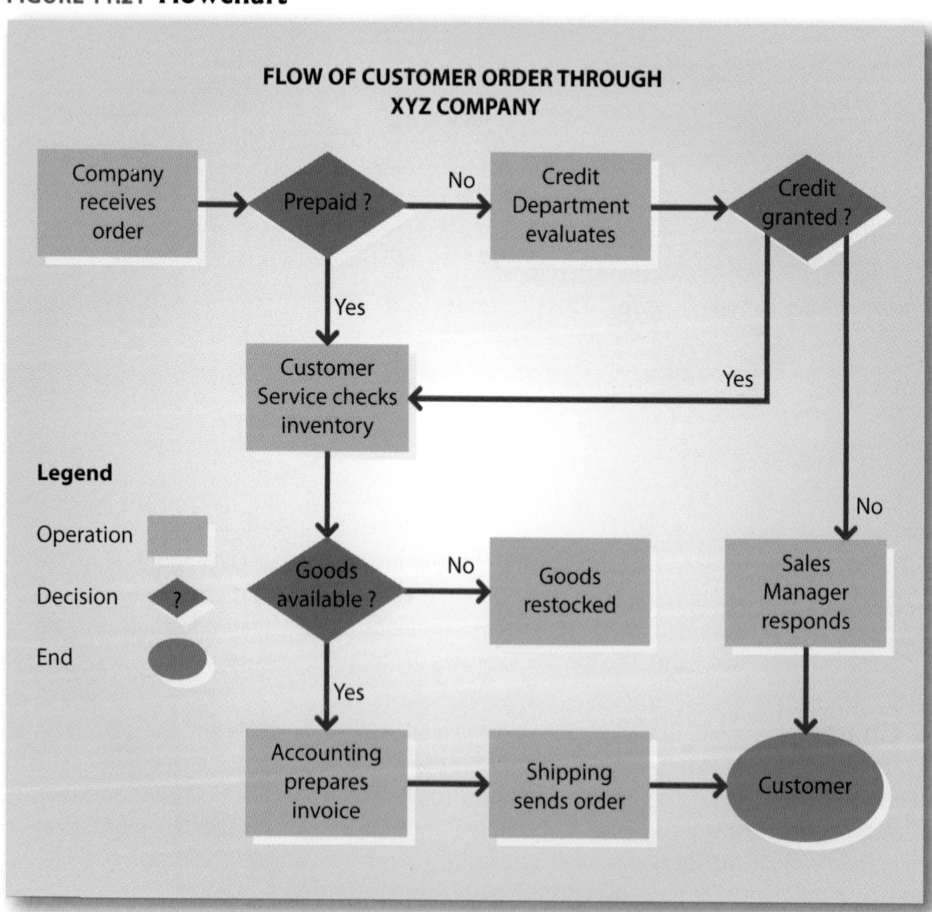

exist. These charts may illustrate a company's structure—for example, by function, customer, or product. They may also be organized by the work being performed in each job or by the hierarchy of decision making.

Photographs, Maps, and Illustrations. Some business reports include photographs, maps, and illustrations to serve specific purposes. Photos, for example, add authenticity and provide a visual record. An environmental engineer may use photos to document hazardous waste sites. Maps enable report writers to depict activities or concentrations geographically, such as dots indicating sales reps in states across the country. Illustrations and diagrams are useful in indicating how an object looks or operates. A drawing showing the parts of a printer with labels describing their functions, for example, is more instructive than a photograph or verbal description. With today's computer technology, photographs, maps, and illustrations can be scanned directly into business reports, or accessed through hyperlinks within electronically delivered documents.

When are photographs, maps, and illustrations suitable enhancements for reports?

Incorporating Graphics in Reports

Used appropriately, graphics make reports more interesting and easier to understand. In putting graphics into your reports, follow these suggestions for best effects:

How can you ensure that you use graphics accurately and ethically?

- **Evaluate the audience.** Consider the reader, the content, your schedule, and your budget. Graphics take time and can be costly to print in color, so think carefully before deciding

ETHICAL INSIGHT

Making Ethical Charts and Graphics

Business communicators must present graphical data in the same ethical, honest manner required for all other messages. Remember that the information shown in your charts and graphics will be used to inform others or help them make decisions. If this information is not represented accurately, the reader will be incorrectly informed; any decisions based on the data are likely to be faulty. And mistakes in interpreting such information may have serious and long-lasting consequences.

Chart data can be distorted in many ways. Figure 1 shows advertising expenses displayed on an appropriate scale. Figure 2 shows the same information, but the horizontal scale, from 2007 to 2012, has been lengthened. Notice that the data have not changed, but the increases and decreases are smoothed out, so changes in expenses appear to be slight. In Figure 3 the vertical scale is taller and the horizontal scale is shortened, resulting in what appear to be sharp increases and decreases in expenses.

To avoid misrepresenting data, keep the following pointers in mind when designing your graphics:

- Use an appropriate type of chart or graphic for the message you wish to convey.
- Design the chart so that it focuses on the appropriate information.
- Include all relevant or important data; don't arbitrarily leave out necessary information.
- Don't hide critical information by including too much data in one graphic.
- Use appropriate scales with equal intervals for the data you present.

Career Application

Locate one or two graphics in a newspaper, magazine article, or annual report. Analyze the strengths and weaknesses of each graphic. Is the information presented accurately? Select a bar or line chart. Sketch the same chart but change the vertical or horizontal scales on the graphic. How does the message of the chart change?

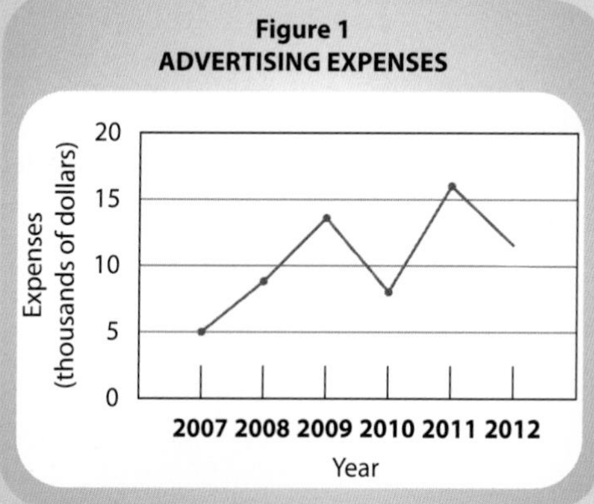

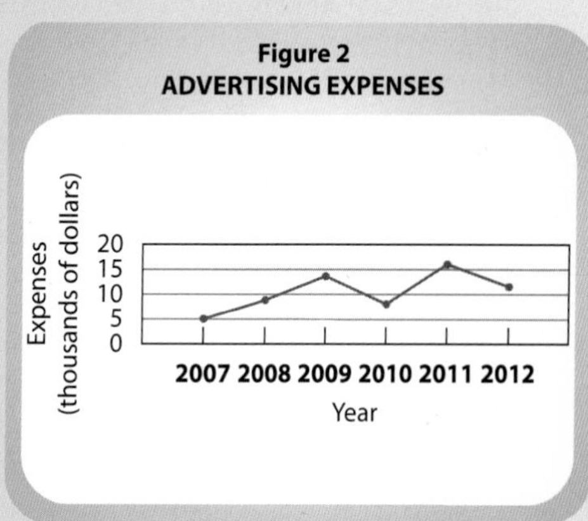

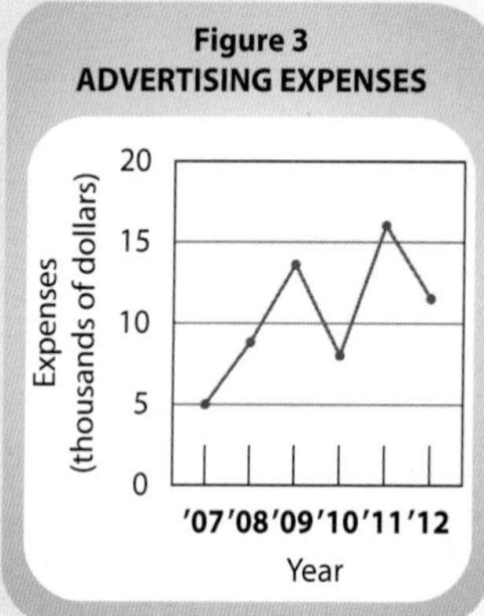

Zooming In — YOUR TURN

Applying Your Skills at Pet Airways

Although Pet Airways is a start-up and the carrier's long-term survival will depend on the viability of its business model, its current prospects seem bright. With average one-way ticket prices at $250, the pet airline is booked two months in advance. Serving nine cities today, the company is planning to expand in the next two years to new routes carrying its furry pawsengers between as many as 25 U.S. cities. In the future Pet Airways is also planning to accommodate creatures other than cats and dogs—for example, birds and reptiles.

To do good and create media buzz, Pet Airways works with pet rescue organizations to save animals from euthanasia. The airline occasionally flies discarded animals to new homes. Recently, the carrier took 35 saved pets from Kern County, California, and 29 tiny pooches from Los Angeles to Colorado, where they were greeted by their new owners. This Los Angeles Chihuahua rescue drew the attention of the George Lopez show, whose host is a dog lover.

Your Task

As writing and research consultants, you and several of your colleagues have been asked by Dan and Alysa to help with a persuasive proposal that outlines the strategies and predicts the success of the pending expansion to new cities and, potentially, to other types of pets. You have been assigned the task of researching the prospects of Pet Airways and gathering general market information about pet relocation. Using both electronic databases and the Web, put together a short report that lists articles that will be useful for the report writers. Add a short summary of your findings as an introduction. Submit your results in a memo or e-mail message to your instructor.

Want to do well on tests and excel in your course? Go to **www.meguffey.com** for helpful interactive resources.

- **Review the Chapter 11 PowerPoint slides to prepare for the first quiz.**

how many graphics to use. Six charts in an internal report to an executive may seem like overkill; however, in a long technical report to outsiders, six may be too few.

- **Use restraint.** Don't overuse color or decorations. Although color can effectively distinguish bars or segments in charts, too much color can be distracting and confusing. Remember, too, that colors themselves sometimes convey meaning: reds suggest deficits or negative values; blues suggest calmness and authority; and yellow may suggest warning.
- **Be accurate and ethical.** Double-check all graphics for accuracy of figures and calculations. Be certain that your visuals aren't misleading—either accidentally or intentionally. Manipulation of a chart scale can make trends look steeper and more dramatic than they really are. Moreover, be sure to cite sources when you use someone else's facts. The accompanying Ethical Insights box discusses in more detail how to make ethical charts and graphs.

Why should graphics be accompanied by introductory statements or captions?

- **Introduce a graph meaningfully.** Refer to every graphic in the text, and place the graphic close to the point where it is mentioned. Most important, though, help the reader understand the significance of the graphic. You can do this by telling your audience what to look for or by summarizing the main point of the graphic. Don't assume the reader will automatically draw the same conclusions you reached from a set of data. Instead of saying, *The findings are shown in Figure 3,* tell the reader what to look for: *Two thirds of the responding employees, as shown in Figure 3, favor a flextime schedule.* The best introductions for graphics interpret them for readers.
- **Choose an appropriate caption or title style.** Like reports, graphics may use "talking" titles or generic, descriptive titles. Talking titles are more persuasive; they tell the reader what to think. Descriptive titles describe the facts more objectively.

Talking Title	Descriptive Title
Rising Workplace Drug Testing Unfair and Inaccurate	Workplace Drug Testing Up 277 Percent
Rising Random Drug Testing Unfair and Often Inaccurate	Workplace Drug Testing up 277 Percent Since 1987

Summary of Learning Objectives

1 Describe basic features of business reports, including functions, strategies (indirect or direct), writing style, and formats. Business reports generally function either as informational reports (without analysis or recommendations) or as analytical reports (with analysis, conclusions, and possibly recommendations). Reports organized directly present the purpose and conclusions immediately. This strategy is appropriate when the audience is supportive and familiar with the topic. Reports organized indirectly provide the conclusions and recommendations last. This strategy is helpful when the audience is unfamiliar with the problem or may be disappointed or hostile. Reports written in a formal style use third-person constructions (*the researcher* instead of *I*), avoid contractions (*do not* instead of *don't*), and may include passive-voice verbs (*the findings were analyzed*). Reports written informally use first-person constructions, contractions, shorter sentences, familiar words, and active-voice verbs. Reports may be formatted as letters, memos, e-mails, manuscripts, prepared forms, or electronic slides.

2 Apply the 3-x-3 writing process to business reports to create well-organized documents that show a firm grasp of audience and purpose. Report writers begin by analyzing a problem and writing a problem statement, which may include the scope, significance, and limitations of the project. Writers then analyze the audience and define major issues. They prepare a work plan, including a tentative outline and work schedule. They collect, organize, interpret, and illustrate their data. Then they compose the first draft. Finally, they revise (often many times), proofread, and evaluate.

3 Find, evaluate, and use print and electronic secondary sources. Secondary data may be located by searching for books, periodicals, and newspapers through print or electronic indexes. Writers can look for information using electronic databases such as ABI/INFORM and LexisNexis. They may also find information on the Internet, but searching for it requires a knowledge of search tools and techniques. Popular search tools include Google, Yahoo, and Bing. Once found, however, information obtained on the Internet should be scrutinized for currency, authority, content, and accuracy.

4 Understand how to generate and use primary data while avoiding researcher bias. Researchers generate firsthand, primary data through surveys (in-person, print, and online), interviews, observation, and experimentation. Surveys are most economical and efficient for gathering information from large groups of people. Interviews are useful when working with experts in a field. Firsthand observation can produce rich data, but they must be objective. Experimentation produces data suggesting causes and effects. Valid experiments require sophisticated research designs and careful attention to matching the experimental and control groups.

5 Comprehend fast-changing communication technology: the Web, electronic databases, and other resources for business writers and researchers. The World Wide Web is used every day by individuals and organizations for business and pleasure. A vast resource, the Web offers a wealth of varied and often uneven secondary data. It is a complex network of information from private citizens, businesses, and other institutions that form a global virtual community. At the same time, these users also announce and advertise their local presence. Business communicators must be aware that information online changes rapidly and is not considered as lasting as scholarly sources. Making the most of Web sites means being a critical consumer of the information retrieved and understanding the function of Web search tools. Honest researchers keep track of the retrieved data and incorporate them ethically into their documents.

6 Recognize the purposes and techniques of documentation in business reports, and avoid plagiarism. Documentation means giving credit to information sources. Careful writers document data to strengthen an argument, protect against charges of plagiarism, and instruct readers. Although documentation is less strict in business reports than in academic reports, business writers should learn proper techniques to be able to verify their sources and to avoid charges of plagiarism. Report writers should document others' ideas, facts that are not common knowledge, quotations, and paraphrases. Good notetaking, either manual or electronic, enables writers to give accurate credit to sources. Paraphrasing involves putting another's ideas into one's own words. Quotations may be used to provide objective background data, to repeat memorable phrasing, and to duplicate exact wording before criticizing.

7 **Create meaningful and interesting graphics; display numeric information in the appropriate graphic form; and skillfully generate, use, and convert data to visual aids.** Good graphics improve reports by clarifying, simplifying, and emphasizing data. Tables organize precise data into rows and columns. Bar and line charts enable data to be compared visually. Line charts are especially helpful in showing changes over time. Pie charts show a whole and the proportion of its components. Organization charts, pictures, maps, and illustrations serve specific purposes. In choosing or crafting graphics, effective communicators evaluate their audience, purpose, topic, and budget to determine the number and kind of graphics. They write "talking" titles (telling readers what to think about the graphic) or descriptive titles (summarizing the topic objectively). Finally, they work carefully to avoid distorting visual aids.

Chapter Review

1. What are the main purposes of business reports? (Obj. 1)
2. Describe the writing style of typical business reports. (Obj. 1)
3. Name five common report formats. (Obj. 1)
4. List the seven steps in the report-writing process. (Obj. 2)
5. What is a statement of purpose, and what function does it serve? (Obj. 2)
6. Compare primary data and secondary data. Give an original example of each. (Objs. 3, 4)
7. Name at least two of the top four business databases and identify their chief strengths. (Objs. 3, 5)
8. List four major sources of primary information. (Obj. 4)
9. How can you ensure that your survey will be effective and appeal to as many respondents as possible? (Obj. 4)
10. Why are your professors likely to discourage your use of Wikipedia, blogs, and many other sources found on the Web as sources in your reports? (Obj. 5)
11. Can any single search engine index all Web pages? How can you optimize your search of Web sources? (Obj. 5)
12. Describe what documentation is and why it is necessary in reports. (Obj. 6)
13. In what way is documentation of sources different in colleges and universities than in business? (Obj. 6)
14. Briefly compare the advantages and disadvantages of illustrating data with charts (bar and line) versus tables. (Obj. 7)
15. Name five techniques you can use to ensure that visual aids do not distort graphic information. (Obj. 7)

Critical Thinking

1. Howard Schultz, Starbucks president and CEO, has been described as a "classic entrepreneur: optimistic, relentless, mercurial, and eager to prove people wrong." Before Starbucks' latest stumbles, Schultz successfully followed his gut instinct, not established management practices. Unlike other executives, until recently he was not interested in cost control, advertising, and customer research. "I despise research," he said. "I think it's a crutch. But people smarter than me pushed me in this direction, and I've gone along." Starbucks continues to be the most followed company on Facebook. It made $300 million in profit last year.[15] What do you think Howard Schultz meant when he called consumer research a "crutch"? Can you explain why the corporate maverick hates it so much? (Obj. 4)
2. Why must report writers anticipate their audiences and issues? (Obj. 2)
3. Is information obtained on the Web as reliable as information obtained from journals, newspapers, and magazines? (Obj. 5)
4. Some people say that business reports never contain footnotes. If you were writing your first report for a business and you did considerable research, what would you do about documenting your sources? (Obj. 6)
5. **Ethical Issue:** You are conducting one-hour-long interviews with high-level banking executives using a questionnaire featuring open-ended questions (qualitative survey) for a market research firm. You receive $75 per completed interview when you deliver legible notes. You tape the talks for accuracy, but then you transcribe the conversations, and you are not required to hand in the tapes. Busy executives are reluctant to sit down with you; you struggle to find the ten top bankers you were contracted to interview. The other interviewer hired for this study tells you that she invented at least two interviews and suggests you do the same. Should you follow her example? Should you not follow her example but stay silent, or should you tell the supervisor that your colleague has been falsifying survey results? (Obj. 4)

Activities

11.1 Report Functions, Strategies, and Formats (Obj. 1)

Your Task. For the following reports, (1) name the report's primary function (informational or analytical), (2) recommend a direct or indirect strategy of development, and (3) select a report format (memo or e-mail, letter, or manuscript).

a. A proposal from a group of citizens to their county government asking for funds to silence the train whistles and create a "quiet zone" around private residences near above-ground railroad tracks.
b. A yardstick report in the leisure industry put together by consultants who compare the potential of a future theme park at three different sites.
c. A report submitted by a sales rep to her manager describing her attendance at a marathon pre-race exhibition, including the reactions of runners to a new low-carbohydrate energy drink.
d. A feasibility report from an administrative assistant to his boss exploring the savings from buying aftermarket ink-jet cartridges as opposed to the original refills recommended by the manufacturer.
e. A progress report from a location manager to a Hollywood production company describing safety, fire, and environmental precautions taken for the shooting of a stunt involving blowing up a power boat in the Downtown Long Beach marina.
f. A report from a national shipping company telling state authorities how it has improved its safety program so that its trucks now comply with state regulations. The report describes but doesn't interpret the program.
g. A report prepared by an outside consultant examining whether a sports franchise should refurbish its stadium or look to relocate to another city.

11.2 Collaborative Project: Report Portfolio (Obj. 1)

Team

Your Task. In teams of three or four, collect several corporate annual reports. For each report identify and discuss the following characteristics:

a. Function (informational or analytical)
b. Strategy (primarily direct or indirect)
c. Writing style (formal or informal)
d. Format (memo or e-mail, letter, manuscript, preprinted form, digital)
e. Effectiveness (clarity, accuracy, expression)

In an informational memo report to your instructor, describe your findings.

11.3 Data Forms and Questions (Obj. 3)

Your Task. In conducting research for the following reports, name at least one form of data you will need and questions you should ask to determine whether that set of data is appropriate (see Figure 11.6).

a. A report about the suitability of a university campus–adjacent location for a low-cost health food store and snack bar.
b. A report on business attire in banking that you must submit to your company's executives, who want to issue a formal professional dress code on the job.
c. A report by the Center for Science in the Public Interest investigating the nutritional value of products advertised during afternoon and Saturday kids' television shows[16]
d. A report by the Agricultural Research Service of the U.S. Department of Agriculture on the nutritional value of oats.
e. A report examining the effectiveness of ethics codes in American businesses.

11.4 Problem, Purpose, and Scope Statements (Obj. 2)

Your Task. The following situations require reports. For each situation write (1) a concise problem question, (2) a simple statement of purpose, and (3) a scope statement with limitations if appropriate.

a. The use of handheld cell phones while driving has been banned in many U.S. states and in a number of countries around the world. The penalties vary in severity and enforcement. Most jurisdictions allow hands-free units, although recent studies have cast suspicion on the effectiveness of hands-free kits in preventing accidents. It seems that drivers are distracted when making emotional phone calls regardless of the device used. A Minnesota state government task force is exploring the connection between cell phone use and accident rates.
b. Car buyers regularly complain in postpurchase surveys about the persuasive tactics of the so-called closers (salespeople trained to finalize the deal). Your car dealership wishes to improve customer satisfaction in the stressful price negotiation process.
c. Last winter a severe ice storm damaged well over 50 percent of the pecan trees lining the main street in the small town of Ardmore. The local university's experts believe that well over 70 percent of the damaged trees will die in the next two years and that this variety is not the best one for providing shade (one of the major goals behind planting them ten years ago).
d. New York enacted strict regulations banning trans fats in restaurant fare. Food processors nationwide are wondering if they need to make changes before being forced to switch to nonhydrogenated fats by law. Food and Drug Administration regulations have already changed the definitions of common terms such as *fresh, fat free, low in cholesterol,* and *light.* The Thin Crust Bakery worries that it may have to change its production process and rewrite all its package labels. Thin Crust doesn't know whether to hire a laboratory or a consultant for this project.
e. Customers placing telephone orders for outdoor gear with REI typically order only one or two items. The company wonders whether it can train telephone service reps to motivate customers to increase the number of items ordered per call.

11.5 Problem and Purpose Statements (Obj. 2)

Your Task. Identify a problem in your current job or a previous job, such as inadequate use of technology, inefficient procedures, spotty customer service, poor product quality, low morale, or a personnel problem. Assume your boss agrees with your criticism and asks you to prepare a report. Write (a) a two- or three-sentence statement describing the problem, (b) a problem question, and (c) a simple statement of purpose for your report.

11.6 Plagiarism, Paraphrasing, and Citing Sources (Obj. 6)

One of the biggest problems of student writers is paraphrasing secondary sources correctly to avoid plagiarism.

Your Task. For each of the following, read the original passage. Analyze the paraphrased version. List the weaknesses in relation to what you have learned about plagiarism and the use of references. Then write an improved version.

a. **Original Passage**
Developing casual online game titles can be much less risky than trying to create a game that runs on a console such as an Xbox.

Casual games typically cost less than $200,000 to produce, and production cycles are only six months to a year. There's no shelf space, packaging, or CD production to pay for. Best of all, there's more room for innovation.[17]

Paraphrased Passage

The development of casual online games offers less risk than creating games running on Xbox and other consoles. Usually, casual games are cheaper, costing under $200,000 to create and six to twelve months to produce. Developers save on shelf space, packaging, and CD production too. Moreover, they have more freedom to innovate.

b. **Original Passage**

The collapse in the cost of computing has made cellular communication economically viable. Worldwide, one in two new phone subscriptions is cellular. The digital revolution in telephony is most advanced in poorer countries because they have been able to skip the outdated technological step of relying on landlines.

Paraphrased Passage

The drop in computing costs now makes cellular communication affordable around the world. In fact, one out of every two new phones is cellular. The digital revolution in cellular telephones is developing faster in poorer countries because they could skip the outdated technological process of using landlines (Henderson 44).

c. **Original Passage**

Search site Yahoo kept world news prominent on its front page because users feel secure knowing that it is easily accessible, even if they don't often click it. Conspicuous placement also went to entertainment, which draws heavy traffic from people seeking a diversion at work. By contrast, seemingly work-related content such as finance gets ample use in the evening when people pay bills and manage personal portfolios.[18]

Paraphrased Passage

Search giant Yahoo kept news prominent on its portal since its customers feel good knowing it is there, even though they don't read it much. Such noticeable placement was also used for entertainment news that attracts heavy traffic from users searching for a distraction at work. As opposed to that, what may seem work related, such as finance, is much visited at night when people pay their bills and manage their portfolios.

d. **Original Passage**

The bid to offer more fashionable apparel was a bid for Target's business. With designer names and fashion flair, Target has made customers comfortable buying dental floss and flirty dresses under one giant, uber-hip roof. . . . Wal-Mart found out that though its edgier Metro7 line for women sold well in several hundred stores, the line's skinny jeans and other higher-style fashions bombed when the company expanded it to 3,000 stores.[19]

Paraphrased Passage

By offering more fashionable clothes, Wal-Mart was bidding for Target's business. With fashion flair and designer names, Target had attracted customers who would buy dental floss and sexy dresses under one roof. Wal-Mart learned that its hip Metro7 line for women sold well in hundreds of stores, but the skinny jeans and higher-style clothes misfired when the retailer took them to 3,000 of its stores.

11.7 Factoring and Outlining a Problem (Obj. 2)

Virgin America has asked your company, Connections International, to prepare a proposal for a training school for tour operators. Virgin America wants to know whether Burbank would be a good spot for its school. Burbank interests Virgin America, but only if nearby entertainment facilities can be used for tour training. The airline also needs an advisory committee consisting, if possible, of representatives of the travel community and perhaps executives of other major airlines. The real problem is how to motivate these people to cooperate with Virgin America.

You have heard that NBC Studios in Burbank offers training seminars, guest speakers, and other resources for tour operators. You wonder whether Magic Mountain in Valencia would also be willing to cooperate with the proposed school. Moreover, you remember that Griffith Park is nearby and might make a good tour training spot. Before Virgin America will settle on Burbank as its choice, it wants to know if access to air travel is adequate. Virgin America's management team is also concerned about available school building space. Moreover, the carrier wants to know whether city officials in Burbank would be receptive to this tour training school proposal.

Your Task. To guide your thinking and research, factor this problem into an outline with several areas to investigate. Further divide the problem into subproblems, phrasing each entry as a question. For example, *Should the Virgin America tour training program be located in Burbank?* (See the work plan model in Figure 11.5.)

11.8 Developing a Work Plan (Obj. 2)

Any long report project requires a structured work plan.

Your Task. Select a report topic from those listed at the ends of Chapters 12 and 13 and at **www.meguffey.com**. For that report prepare a work plan that includes the following:

a. Statement of the problem
b. Expanded statement of purpose (including scope, limitations, and significance)
c. Research strategy to answer the questions
d. Tentative outline of key questions to answer
e. Work schedule (with projected completion dates)

11.9 Using Secondary Sources (Obj. 3)

Web

Secondary sources can provide quite different information depending on your mode of inquiry.

Your Task. Pick a business-related subject you want to know more about, and run it through a search engine such as Google. Compare your results with Dogpile, a metasearch site. Write a short memo or e-mail message to your instructor explaining the differences in the search results. In your message describe what you have learned about the advantages and disadvantages of each search tool.

11.10 Creating an Online Survey With SurveyMonkey or Zoomerang (Obj. 4)

Team Web

Your University Business Club (UBC) is abuzz about a Sodexo study that surveyed American college students about their favorite comfort foods. Food service provider Sodexo tracks flavor trends, holds taste test focus groups with students, and consults with top-notch chefs to identify students' favorite college foods. The current top three items are apricot-glazed turkey, meatloaf with frizzle-dried onions, and pho, a wholesome Vietnamese beef and rice noodle soup. You read the Sodexo press release and decide to use this quotation in your report:

> "Comfort food is trendy for students because familiar favorites can alleviate stress linked to studying and being away from

home," said Tom Post, Sodexo president of campus services. "The biggest change we're seeing is that students are expanding the category of feel-good foods to include comfort world cuisine, such as a Mexican stew or a Vietnamese noodle soup and they are more open to vegetarian dishes with a flair."[20]

UBC wants to advocate for a new small student-run restaurant in the campus food court. Your club colleagues have chosen you to create an online survey to poll fellow students, staff, and faculty about their preferences. You hope to generate data that will support the feasibility of the eatery.

The two main providers of online survey software, SurveyMonkey and Zoomerang, make creating questionnaires fast, fun, and easy. Depending on their research needs and the survey features they desire, businesses subscribe to the two survey creation services for fees ranging from \$17 to \$20 (SurveyMonkey) or \$20 to \$150 (Zoomerang) per month. As long as you sign up for the free no-frills basic plans, you can create brief online questionnaires and e-mail the links to your targeted respondents. The programs analyze and display the results for you—at no charge.

Your Task. In pairs or teams of three, design a questionnaire to survey students on your campus about comfort food options in the campus cafeteria. Visit **http://www.surveymonkey.com** or **http://www.zoomerang.com**, and sign up for the basic plan. You may also want to view the Sodexo Web site at **http://www.sodexousa.com**. After creating the online survey, e-mail the survey link to as many members of the campus community as possible. Interpret the results. As a team, write a memo to the campus food services advocating for the top-scoring national or regional comfort food type.

Your instructor may ask you to complete this activity as a report or proposal assignment after you study Chapter 12. If so, write a feasibility report or proposal for the campus food services and support your advocacy with the survey results.

11.11 Researching Secondary Sources: Debunking Myths About Young People (Obj. 3)

E-mail | Web

Are you tired of hearing that you are spending too much time online? The perception that teens and college students are the biggest consumers of Internet content is intractable—a largely unexamined assumption based on little more than anecdotal evidence. To learn more about teens' true media usage, you could turn to Nielsen Company research.

Your boss, Akiko Kimura, doesn't believe in stereotyping. She encourages her market researchers to be wary of all data. She asked you to explore so-called niche marketing opportunities in targeting teens, a notoriously fickle consumer group. Primarily, Ms. Kimura wants to know how teenagers spend their free time, and, more specifically, how they use media. Understanding teen behavior is invaluable for the success of any promotional or ad campaign.

A casual glance at the latest Nielsen numbers reveals surprising key findings: Teens watch more TV than ever and spend much less time browsing the Internet than adults 25 to 34 years of age do (11 hours versus the average of 29 hours, 15 minutes for adults). They also spend 35 percent less time watching online videos than adults do. In their preferences for TV shows, top Web sites, and across media, they mirror the tastes of their parents. They also read newspapers, listen to the radio, and like advertising more than most. In short, "teens are actually pretty normal in their usage and more attentive than most give them credit for," said Nic Covey, director of insights for The Nielsen Company.[21]

Your Task. Ms. Kimura requested a brief informational e-mail report summarizing the main Nielsen findings. Paraphrase correctly and don't just copy from the online report. Ms. Kimura may ask you later to analyze more comprehensive data in an analytical report and create a media use profile of U.S. teens. You have already identified additional teenager-related Nielsen studies titled "Special Report: What Do Teens Want?," "Breaking Teen Myths," and "Teens Don't Tweet; Twitter's Growth Not Fueled by Youth."

11.12 Finding Secondary Data: The Future of Tech (Objs. 3, 5, and 6)

Team | Web | E-mail

Are you a member of the "thumb generation"? Can you work the keyboard of your cell phone or personal digital assistant faster than most people can speak? The term *thumb generation* was coined in South Korea and Japan and is applied to people under 25 who furiously finger their handheld devices to text, e-mail, and complete other electronic functions at lightning speeds.

More technological innovations are coming that are likely to transform our lives. WiMAX is a new wireless supertechnology that will cover entire cities at cable speeds. Near-field communication (NFC) takes the Bluetooth technology a step further to connect cell phones and other devices. NFC is touted for its boundless commercial applications enabling Americans soon to complete many sales transactions by cell phone, as is already customary in Korea, Japan, and Finland. These and other trends were described in a *BusinessWeek* article titled "The Future of Tech,"[22] which your boss pulled out of his files to show you. However, you know that you can find more current discussions of future trends on MIT's Technology Review Web site at **http://www.technologyreview.com**.

Your Task. You are one of several marketing interns at MarketNet Global, a worldwide e-commerce specialist. Your busy boss, Jack Holden, wants to be up to speed on cutting-edge tech and communication trends, especially those that could be successfully used in selling and marketing. Individually or as a team, research one or several high-tech concepts. On the MIT Technology Review Web site, focus on the tabs **Business, Computing, Web**, and **Communications**. Chances are you will not find scholarly articles on these subjects because peer-reviewed publications take years to complete. Instead, you must rely on the Web and on electronic databases to find up-to-date information. If you use search engines, you will retrieve many forum and discussion board contributions as well. Examine them critically for authority and validity. In teams or individually, write an e-mail or informational memo to Jack Holden, complete with a short list of references in MLA or APA documentation style. Explain what each new trend is. Your instructor may ask you to complete this activity as a report assignment after you study Chapter 12. You could use your research to write a short informational memo report describing to Jack Holden what your sources suggest the new trends may mean for the future of business, specifically e-commerce and online marketing.

11.13 Researching and Evaluating Data: How Wired Is the World? (Objs. 3, 5)

Team | Web | E-mail

Out of more than 1.7 billion global Internet users, North America is in third place behind Asia and Europe as the continent with the most people online, according to Internet World Stats.[23] Data analyzing which nations have the most connected populations suggest that Scandinavians rank high; the tiny country of Iceland is often cited as the top Internet presence per resident. On the opposite side of the spectrum, Internet access is very low in Africa, where less than 1 percent of the population is online. This is why chip maker AMD and scientists at MIT have independently announced plans to build and distribute low-cost computers to poor children in developing countries.

As an entry-level employee at AMD, you are part of a young team entrusted with the task of researching global Internet use and market saturation with computers. In other words, you are to examine access to computers and the Internet in a given population or geographic region. Find Internet World Stats or comScore's World Metrix data and examine how they were collected. Are they credible? Do other reputable sources reference this survey? Retrieve other statistical information from the Internet or electronic databases that discuss online access and Internet use in relation to population size. How does a focus on absolute numbers as opposed to percentages of the population skew the outcome? What conclusions can you draw from such information?

Your Task. As a team, write an e-mail or a memo to the head of the task force at AMD, Patricia Charbonneau, about the challenges of interpreting such numeric data. In addition, Ms. Charbonneau is looking for volunteers to research attempts by competitors and independent organizations (e.g., the United Nations, other corporations, and universities) to provide basic computing devices to developing countries. Write an informational e-mail or memo to Ms. Charbonneau listing your findings without comments or recommendations. Your instructor may ask you to complete this activity as an analytical report after you study Chapters 12 and 13.

11.14 Researching Data: Target Aims at Charitable Giving (Objs. 3, 6, and 7)

Team Web

Lauren Bacall and Robert Redford have both promoted it. And Oprah Winfrey thinks it is so chic that she pronounces its name in mock French (*Tar-jay*). Unlike its big-box competitors, Target is an American discount retailer that appeals to many female shoppers with trendy and edgy but affordable fashions. However, Target is also proud of its positive corporate image. The company has been praised for giving back to the community with higher-than-usual charitable contributions. At 5 percent of pretax earnings, Target's annual donations are more than double the national average among big corporations (in absolute dollars recently as high as $101 million a year). The company gives 5 percent of pretax profits consistently, in fat and in lean times.

This tradition was established six decades ago by Target's founder, George Dayton. Such generosity is more than a public relations move because Target polls its core group of shoppers, 35- to 45-year-old mothers, about their favorite causes. Then it distributes funds to those community charities. The company even managed to regain the goodwill of the Salvation Army after driving out its bell ringers citing no-solicitation rules.[24]

Your Task. Select one of the following tasks.

a. As a summer intern at Wal-Mart, you are asked to prepare an informational memo to your boss, Salvador Ramirez, about Target's charitable practices. Wal-Mart is seeking greater community involvement to boost its public image. What types of projects does the Target Corporation fund? What other policies set this company apart from its competitors when it comes to giving back to the community? Write an individual informational e-mail or memo or one collaborative e-mail or memo as a team of summer interns. Alternatively, Salvador Ramirez could ask you to write an e-mail or memo describing how Target handled the Salvation Army controversy and what its actions say about the company's management and its philosophy.

b. As a team of summer interns for Wal-Mart, research charitable giving of Target and other major corporations. Prepare an informational memo comparing and contrasting corporate practices. Target ranks fourth behind Wal-Mart, Home Depot, and Lowe's in size. How much of their pretax earnings are these and other big chain stores spending on philanthropy? What types of causes do they embrace, and why? Do their policies seem consistent and purposeful over the long term? How do they justify charitable giving to their shareholders?

In each case, compile a bibliography of sources you used. Whenever appropriate, display numbers visually by creating charts, graphs, and tables.

You may want to start by viewing company mission statements and annual reports for discussions of corporate social responsibility, charitable giving, and worthy causes companies support. Then, go to independent sources for a more detached, objective perspective.

11.15 Gathering Data: Fortune 100 Best Companies to Work For (Objs. 3, 4)

Web

Even in these tough economic times, some companies continue to spend lavishly on unusual employee perks such as massages and sauna visits, hold on to generous compensation and benefits, and don't lay off workers as a matter of principle. At the same time, they remain profitable. Chances are that you haven't heard of the newest top three among *Fortune*'s 100 Best Companies to Work For—tech giant SAS, investment advisor Edward Jones, and New York–based Wegmans Food Markets. The perennial favorite, Google, slipped to fourth place. Fourteenth-ranked outdoor powerhouse REI attracts active types who may bring their dogs to work, go on a midday bike ride, and test the products they sell. Sound nice? Just as companies have their distinctive corporate cultures, they also differ in why they are perceived as ideal employers.

Your Task. Visit the *Fortune* magazine Web site at **http://www.fortune.com/bestcompanies** for the most current 100 Best Companies to Work For. Examine the information about the top 20 or 25 highest-ranked companies. Watch the short video clips profiling each business. After studying the information, identify factors that attract and please workers. Take note of features shared across the board, but don't overlook quirky, unusual benefits. Summarize these trends in an informational memo report. Alternatively, prepare an analytical report investigating employee satisfaction gleaned from the secondary data obtained on the *Fortune* site.

11.16 Selecting Graphics (Obj. 7)

Your Task. Identify the best graphics form to illustrate the following data.

a. Properties listed for sale in a beach community
b. Month-to-month unemployment figures by the Bureau of Labor Statistics
c. Government unemployment data by industry and sector in percent
d. Figures showing the distribution of the H1N1 virus in humans by state
e. Figures showing the process of delivering electricity to a metropolitan area
f. Areas in the United States most likely to have earthquakes
g. Figures showing what proportion of every state tax dollar is spent on education, social services, transportation, debt, and other expenses

h. Academic, administrative, and operation divisions of a college, from the president to department chairs and division managers
i. Figures comparing the sales of smartphones, netbooks, and laptop computers over the past five years

11.17 Evaluating Graphics (Obj. 7)

Your Task. Select four graphics from newspapers or magazines, in hard copy or online. Look in *The Wall Street Journal, USA Today, BusinessWeek, U.S. News & World Report, Fortune,* or other business news publications. In an e-mail or memo to your instructor, critique each graphic based on what you have learned in this chapter. What is correctly shown? What is incorrectly shown? How could the graphic be improved?

11.18 Creating a Bar Chart (Obj. 7)

Your Task. Prepare a bar chart comparing the tax rates in eight industrial countries: Canada, 33 percent; France, 45 percent; Germany, 41 percent; Japan, 28 percent; Netherlands, 38 percent; Sweden, 49 percent; United Kingdom, 38 percent; United States, 28 percent. These figures represent a percentage of the gross domestic product for each country. The sources of the figures are the rankings of "fiscal freedom" established by the Heritage Foundation. Arrange the entries logically. Write two titles: a talking title and a descriptive title. What should you emphasize in the chart and title?

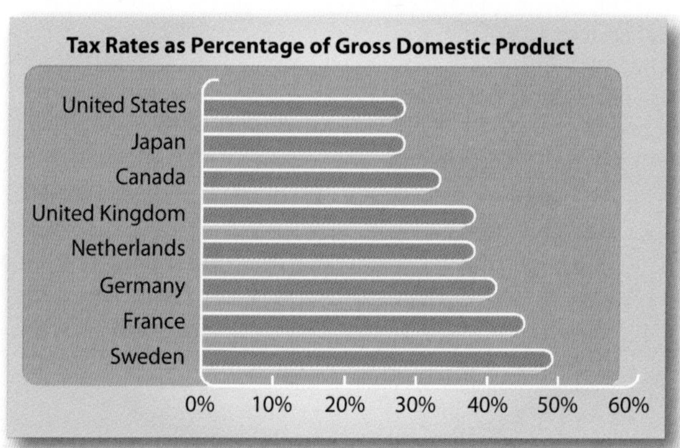

11.19 Creating a Line Chart (Obj. 7)

Your Task. Prepare a line chart showing the sales of Sidekick Athletic Shoes, Inc., for these years: 2011, $6.7 million; 2010, $5.4 million; 2009, $3.2 million; 2008, $2.1 million; 2007, $2.6 million; 2006, $3.6 million. In the chart title, highlight the trend you see in the data.

11.20 Studying Graphics in Annual Reports(Obj. 7)

Your Task. In an e-mail or memo to your instructor, evaluate the use and effectiveness of graphics in three to five corporation annual reports. Critique their readability, clarity, and effectiveness in visualizing data. How were they introduced in the text? What suggestions would you make to improve them?

11.21 Avoiding Huge Credit Card Debt for College Students (Objs. 3, 5, and 6)

Web

College students represent a new push for credit card companies. An amazing 84 percent of students carried at least one credit card in the most recent study of undergraduate card use, and half of college students had four or more cards.[25] Credit cards are a contributing factor when students graduate with an average of $20,000 debt. Because they can't buy cars, rent homes, or purchase insurance, graduates with big credit debt see a bleak future for themselves.

A local newspaper plans to run a self-help story about college credit cards. The editor asks you, a young part-time reporter, to prepare a memo with information that could be turned into an article. The article would focus on parents of students who are about to leave for college. What can parents do to help students avoid sinking deeply into credit card debt?

Your Task. Using ABI/INFORM, Factiva, or LexisNexis and the Web, locate basic information about student credit card options. In an e-mail or memo discuss shared credit cards and other options. Your goal is to be informative, not to reach conclusions or make recommendations. Use one or more of the techniques discussed in this chapter to track your sources. Address your memo to Janice Arrington, editor.

11.22 Netflix & Co.: Movies After DVD and Blu-Ray (Objs. 3, 5, and 6)

Web E-mail

The competition for consumer film rental dollars is fierce. A 400-employee company, Netflix offers online flat rates for DVD and Blu-ray disc rentals by mail. Users can also stream certain movie titles on the Web and view them on their computers. Netflix has joined the race against Blockbuster, Amazon, Apple, and the cable companies all jostling to become the leading provider of online films. Netflix is waging a battle on two fronts, against Blockbuster for online DVD rentals and with Apple for leadership in digital streaming services. Experts predict that DVDs and Blu-ray discs will go the way of such dinosaurs as VHS tapes and, eventually, music CDs. Apple's release of the iPad only intensifies the rivalry among the competing streaming services. Netflix CEO Reed Hastings has no plans to stream films to the Apple device.

Your Task. Using ABI/INFORM, Factiva, or LexisNexis and the Web, find information about the movie rental market today. Research the latest trends in the use of DVD/Blu-ray discs and Web streaming. In a memo or e-mail report, discuss the future of this important entertainment sector. Based on your research, expert opinion, and other resources, reach conclusions about the current state and future prospects of the movie rental business. If possible, make recommendations detailing how the business model could be modified to help Netflix survive the cutthroat competition. Use one or more of the techniques discussed in this chapter to track your sources. Address your memo or e-mail to Netflix CEO Reed Hastings.

Chat About It

In each chapter you will find five discussion questions related to the chapter material. Your instructor may assign these topics for you to discuss in class, in an online chat room, or on an online discussion board. Some of the discussion topics may require outside research. You may also be asked to read and respond to postings made by your classmates.

Topic 1: What is your biggest concern about writing a long report? How might you overcome this concern?
Topic 2: Why do you suppose reports created using Microsoft PowerPoint are becoming popular?

Are you ready? Get more practice at **www.meguffey.com**

Topic 3: What questions would you create to factor the problem for a report about improving the course registration process at your college or university?
Topic 4: Why is it important for a non-expert on a topic to use professional journals as report sources?
Topic 5: Is plagiarism worth the risk of being caught? Why or why not?

Grammar/Mechanics C.L.U.E. Review 11

Total Review

The first ten chapters reviewed specific guides from Appendix A: Grammar and Mechanics Guide. The exercises in this and the remaining chapters are total reviews, covering all of the grammar and mechanics guides plus confusing words and frequently misspelled words.

Each of the following sentences has **three** errors in grammar, punctuation, capitalization, usage, or spelling. On a separate sheet, write a correct version. Avoid adding new phrases, starting new sentences, or rewriting in your own words. When finished, compare your responses with the key beginning on page Key-1.

Example: To succede as a knowledge worker in todays digital workplace you need highly developed communication skills.
Revision: To **succeed** as a knowledge worker in **today's** digital **workplace**, you need highly developed communication skills.

1. The recruiter cited studys showing that mangers leave, when they lose autonomy.
2. As they work more than forty hours a week without overtime pay, most proffesionals today are wondering whether there jobs can survive the recession.
3. One organization paid three thousand dollars each for twelve employees to attend a one week workshop in communication training.
4. My company spend five hundred dollars on ink cartridges every month, but the cost doesn't worry my partner and I because our printed materials look sharp and professional.
5. If you find a open document on a colleague's computer screen its inappropriate to peek.
6. Todays workers should brush up their marketable skills otherwise they may not find another job after being laid off.
7. On June 1st our company President revealed a four million dollar drop in profits, which was bad news for everyone.
8. Most of us prefer to be let down gently, when we are being refused something, that is why the reasons before refusal pattern is effective.
9. Between you and I, if we where to share a ride each morning we would save a lot of money.
10. Despite the recent economic downturn our President and CEO gave an optimistic assessment of the companys outlook.

CHAPTER 12

Informal Business Reports

Want to do well on tests and excel in your course?
Go to **www.meguffey.com** for helpful interactive resources.

▸ **Review the Chapter 12 PowerPoint slides to prepare for the first quiz.**

OBJECTIVES

After studying this chapter, you should be able to

1. Tabulate information, use statistical techniques, and create decision matrices to sort and interpret business report data skillfully and accurately.
2. Draw meaningful conclusions and make practical report recommendations after sound and valid analysis.
3. Organize report data logically and provide cues to aid comprehension.
4. Write short informational reports that describe routine tasks.
5. Compose short analytical reports that solve business problems.

Zooming In

PART 1

Starbucks Perks Up: Recapturing the Soul of the Coffeehouse

As Starbucks customers face shrinking disposable incomes, the purveyor of premium exotic drinks such as Iced Caramel Macchiato and Espresso Frappuccino has introduced lower-cost alternatives. Simple drip coffee, Pike Place Roast, and most notably, Via Ready Brew, Starbucks' line of instant coffee, signal attempts by chairman and CEO Howard Schultz to lead his company back to recovery in recessionary times. A costly indulgence, the $4 latte is now competing with Starbucks' own coffee drinks priced $3 on average; the chain has also introduced $3.95 breakfast meals. Howard Schultz returned to the helm of his company after an eight-year absence determined to restore Starbucks to its former glory by taking it back to its roots.

Despite setbacks, Starbucks continues to reign as the world's largest coffee shop chain, with some 16,000 retail locations in North America, Latin America, Europe, the Middle East, and the Pacific Rim—50 countries in all. Before the recession hit, the company served more than 50 million customers weekly and generated $10 billion in annual sales. Adding to its accolades, Starbucks has until recently ranked among the top ten in the *Fortune* magazine list of America's Most Admired Companies. Moreover, the retailer was repeatedly named among *Fortune's* 100 Best Companies to Work For, even after being forced to close 800 U.S. stores and cutting 30,000 employees worldwide. (As a result, Starbucks slid from position 24 to 93.) However, last year alone more than 150,000 applicants vied for jobs with the company.

Before the economy turned sour, Starbucks bucked traditional retail wisdom. As it grew explosively, the company regularly broke the retail rule about locating stores so closely that they cannibalize each other's sales. In metropolitan areas such as London and New York City, you may find as many as 170 Starbucks outlets within a five-mile radius. This "being everywhere" approach created several distinct advantages. Its numerous locations meant that Starbucks intercepted consumers on their way to work, home, or anywhere in between. Moreover, ubiquity builds brand awareness.

However, explosive growth may have led to complacency: "We got swept up," says Schultz. "We stopped asking: How can we do better? We had a sense of entitlement."[1] Fearing for his company's "soul," Schultz revamped Starbucks, at one point closing 7,100 stores for three hours to retrain employees on the Starbucks experience. He also abandoned flavor-locked packaging and introduced improved espresso machines. You will learn more about this case on page 401.

© AP Images/Seth Perlman

Critical Thinking

- What kind of information should Starbucks gather to help it decide how closely to locate its stores?
- How could Howard Schultz test his impression that the intimate communal coffee-drinking experience is fading at Starbucks?
- How can collected information be transmitted to Starbucks' decision makers?

http://www.starbucks.com

Interpreting Data

LEARNING OBJECTIVE 1

Tabulate information, use statistical techniques, and create decision matrices to sort and interpret business report data skillfully and accurately.

How can you extract meaningful information from data?

To respond nimbly to changing economic times, Starbucks and other businesses need information to stay abreast of what is happening inside and outside of their firms. Much of the information that allows decision makers to run their organizations efficiently comes to them in the form of reports. This chapter focuses on interpreting and organizing data, drawing conclusions, providing reader cues, and writing informal business reports.

Collecting information is effortless today, given the easy access to electronic databases, the Web, and other sources of digitized information. However, making sense of the massive amounts of data you may collect is much harder. You may feel overwhelmed as you look at a jumble of digital files, printouts, note cards, copies of articles, interview notes, questionnaire results, and statistics. It is a little like being a contractor who allowed suppliers to dump all the building materials for a new house in a monstrous pile. Like the contractor, you must sort the jumble of raw material into meaningful, usable groups. Unprocessed data become meaningful information through skillful and accurate sorting, analysis, combination, and recombination. You will be examining each item to see what it means by itself and what it means when connected with other data. You are looking for meanings, relationships, and answers to the research questions posed in your work plan.

Tabulating and Analyzing Responses

If you have collected considerable numerical and other information, you must tabulate and analyze it. Fortunately, several tabulating and statistical techniques can help you create order from the chaos. These techniques are used to simplify, summarize, and classify large amounts of data into meaningful terms. From the condensed data, you are more likely to be able to draw valid conclusions and make reasoned recommendations. The most helpful summarizing techniques include tables, statistical concepts (mean, median, and mode), correlations, grids, and decision matrices.

Ethics Check

Starbucks CEO Howard Schultz explains his company's Shared Planet initiative: "We feel now is the time to invest—truly and authentically—in ways to help create a better future for the world we share." Starbucks also teamed up with (Product) RED, the global anti-AIDS project spearheaded by U2's Bono. The coffee chain wishes to pursue its vision of community involvement, commitment to the environment, and ethical sourcing of coffee. Do you view favorably companies that are "green" and wish to appear ethical? Do such considerations influence your buying decisions?

Tables. Numerical data from questionnaires or interviews are usually summarized and simplified in tables. Using systematic columns and rows, tables make quantitative information easier to comprehend. After assembling your data, you will want to prepare preliminary tables to enable you to see what the information means. Here is a table summarizing the response to one question from a campus survey about student parking:

Question: Should student fees be increased to build parking lots?

	Number	Percent	
Strongly agree	76	11.5	To simplify the table, combine these items.
Agree	255	38.5	
No opinion	22	3.3	
Disagree	107	16.1	To simplify the table, combine these items.
Strongly disagree	203	30.6	
Total	**663**	**100.0**	

What are some techniques to bring order to raw numerical data?

Notice that this preliminary table includes a total number of responses and a percentage for each response. (To calculate a percentage, divide the figure for each response by the total number of responses times 100.) To simplify the data and provide a broad overview, you can join categories. For example, combining *Strongly agree* (11.5 percent) and *Agree* (38.5 percent) reveals that 50 percent of the respondents supported the proposal to finance new parking lots with increased student fees.

Sometimes data become more meaningful when cross-tabulated. This process allows analysis of two or more variables together. By breaking down our student survey data into male and female responses, shown in the following table, we make an interesting discovery.

Question: Should student fees be increased to build parking lots?

	Total		Male		Female	
	Number	**Percent**	**Number**	**Percent**	**Number**	**Percent**
Strongly agree	76	11.5	8	2.2	68	22.0
Agree	255	38.5	54	15.3	201	65.0
No opinion	22	3.3	12	3.4	10	3.2
Disagree	107	16.1	89	25.1	18	5.8
Strongly disagree	203	30.6	191	54.0	12	4.0
Total	**663**	**100.0**	**354**	**100.0**	**309**	**100.0**

Although 50 percent of all student respondents supported the proposal, among females the approval rating was much stronger. Notice that 87 percent of female respondents (combining 22 percent *Strongly agree* and 65 percent *Agree*) endorsed the proposal to increase fees for new parking lots. However, among male students, only 17 percent agreed with the proposal. You naturally wonder why such a disparity exists. Are female students unhappier than male students with the current parking situation? If so, why? Is safety a reason? Are male students more concerned with increased fees than female students are?

By cross-tabulating the findings, you sometimes uncover data that may help answer your problem question or that may prompt you to explore other possibilities. Do not, however, undertake cross-tabulation unless it serves more than merely satisfying your curiosity. Tables also help you compare multiple data collected from questionnaires and surveys. Figure 12.1 shows, in raw form, responses to several survey items. To convert these data into a more usable form, you need to calculate percentages for each item. Then you can arrange the responses in some rational sequence, such as largest percentage to smallest.

Once the data are displayed in a table, you can more easily draw conclusions. As Figure 12.1 shows, South Bay College students apparently are not interested in public transportation or shuttle buses from satellite lots. They want to park on campus, with restricted visitor parking; and only half are willing to pay for new parking lots.

FIGURE 12.1 Converting Survey Data into Finished Tables

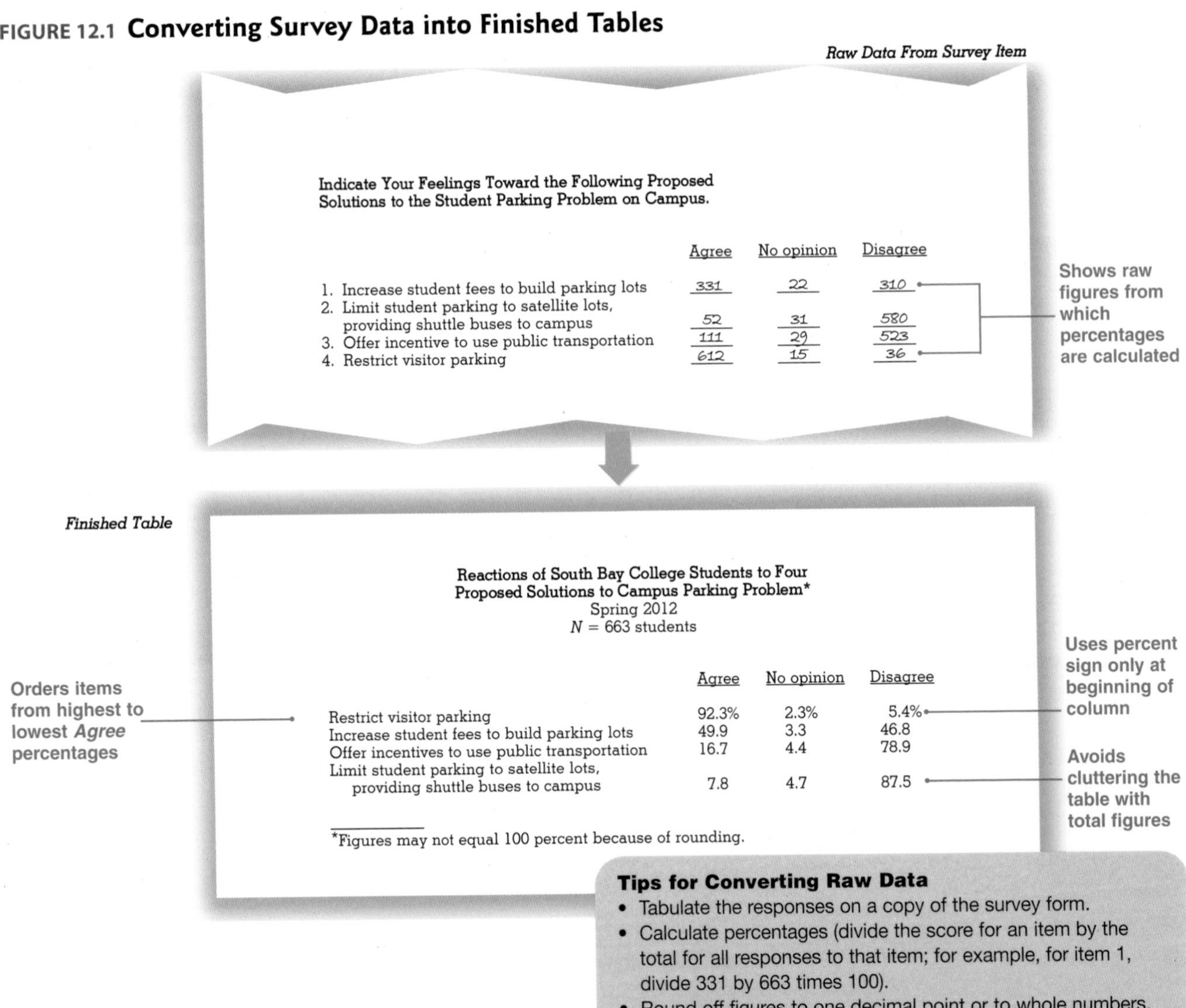

Raw Data From Survey Item

Indicate Your Feelings Toward the Following Proposed Solutions to the Student Parking Problem on Campus.

	Agree	No opinion	Disagree
1. Increase student fees to build parking lots	331	22	310
2. Limit student parking to satellite lots, providing shuttle buses to campus	52	31	580
3. Offer incentive to use public transportation	111	29	523
4. Restrict visitor parking	612	15	36

Shows raw figures from which percentages are calculated

Finished Table

Reactions of South Bay College Students to Four Proposed Solutions to Campus Parking Problem*
Spring 2012
N = 663 students

	Agree	No opinion	Disagree
Restrict visitor parking	92.3%	2.3%	5.4%
Increase student fees to build parking lots	49.9	3.3	46.8
Offer incentives to use public transportation	16.7	4.4	78.9
Limit student parking to satellite lots, providing shuttle buses to campus	7.8	4.7	87.5

*Figures may not equal 100 percent because of rounding.

Orders items from highest to lowest *Agree* percentages
Uses percent sign only at beginning of column
Avoids cluttering the table with total figures

Tips for Converting Raw Data
- Tabulate the responses on a copy of the survey form.
- Calculate percentages (divide the score for an item by the total for all responses to that item; for example, for item 1, divide 331 by 663 times 100).
- Round off figures to one decimal point or to whole numbers.
- Arrange items in a logical order, such as largest to smallest percentage.
- Prepare a table with a title that tells such things as who, what, when, where, and why.
- Include the total number of respondents.

The Three Ms: Mean, Median, Mode. Tables help you organize data, and the three Ms help you describe it. These statistical terms—mean, median, and mode—are all occasionally used loosely to mean "average." To be safe, though, you should learn to apply these statistical terms precisely.

What are three statistical concepts that help you describe data and make them meaningful?

When people say *average*, they usually intend to indicate the *mean*, or arithmetic average. Let's say that you are studying the estimated starting salaries of graduates from various disciplines, ranging from education to medicine:

Education	$41,000	*Mode (figure occurring most frequently)*
Sociology	41,000	
Humanities	41,000	
Biology	45,000	
Health sciences	50,000	*Median (middle point in continuum)*
Business	56,000	*Mean (arithmetic average)*
Engineering	60,000	
Law	65,000	
Medicine	105,000	

To find the mean, you simply add up all the salaries and divide by the total number of items ($504,000 ÷ 9 = $56,000). Therefore, the mean salary is $56,000. Means are very useful to indicate central tendencies of figures, but they have one major flaw: extremes at either end cause distortion. Notice that the $105,000 figure makes the mean salary of $56,000 deceptively high. It does not represent a valid average for the group. Because means can be misleading, you should use them only when extreme figures do not distort the result.

What are the differences among the mean, the median, and the mode?

The *median* represents the midpoint in a group of figures arranged from lowest to highest (or vice versa). In our list of salaries, the median is $50,000 (health sciences). In other words, half the salaries are above this point and half are below it. The median is useful when extreme figures may warp the mean. Although salaries for medicine distort the mean, the median, at $50,000, is still a representative figure.

The *mode* is simply the value that occurs most frequently. In our list $41,000 (for education, sociology, and the humanities) represents the mode because it occurs three times. The mode has the advantage of being easily determined—just a quick glance at a list of arranged values reveals it. Although researchers use mode infrequently, knowing the mode is useful in some situations. Assume that 7-Eleven sampled its customers to determine what Big Gulp fountain drink size they preferred: 20-ounce, 32-ounce, or Super Big Gulp 44-ounce. Finding the mode—the most frequently named figure—makes more sense than calculating the median, which might yield a size that 7-Eleven does not even offer. (To remember the meaning of *mode*, think about fashion: the most frequent response, the mode, is the most fashionable.)

Mean, median, and mode figures are especially helpful when the range of values is also known. Range represents the span between the highest and lowest values. To calculate the range, you simply subtract the lowest figure from the highest. In starting salaries for graduates, the range is $64,000 (105,000 – 41,000). Knowing the range enables readers to put mean and median figures into perspective. This knowledge also prompts researchers to wonder why such a range exists, thus stimulating hunches and further investigation to solve problems.

Correlations. In tabulating and analyzing data, you may see relationships among two or more variables that help explain the findings. If your data for graduates' starting salaries also included years of education, you would doubtless notice that graduates with more years of education received higher salaries. For example, beginning teachers, with four years of schooling, earn less than beginning physicians, who have completed nine or more years of education. Therefore, a correlation may exist between years of education and starting salary.

What are correlations among variables?

Intuition suggests correlations that may or may not prove to be accurate. Is there a relationship between studying and good grades? Between new office computers and increased productivity? Between the rise and fall of hemlines and the rise and fall of the stock market (as some newspaper writers have suggested)? If a correlation seems to exist, can we say that one event caused the other? Does studying cause good grades? Does more schooling guarantee increased salary? Although one event may not be said to cause another, the business researcher who sees a correlation begins to ask why and how the two variables are related. In this way, apparent correlations stimulate investigation and present possible solutions to be explored.

In reporting correlations, you should avoid suggesting that a cause-and-effect relationship exists when none can be proved. Only sophisticated research methods can statistically prove correlations. Instead, present a correlation as a possible relationship (*The data suggest that beginning salaries are related to years of education*). Cautious statements followed by explanations gain you credibility and allow readers to make their own decisions.

How can grids help you analyze raw verbal data?

Grids. Another technique for analyzing raw data—especially verbal data—is the grid. Let's say you have been asked by the CEO to collect opinions from all vice presidents about the CEO's four-point plan to build cash reserves. The grid shown in Figure 12.2 enables you to summarize the vice presidents' reactions to each point. Notice how this complex verbal information is transformed into concise, manageable data; readers can see immediately which points are supported and which are opposed. Imagine how long you could have struggled to comprehend the meaning of this verbal information without a grid.

Arranging data in a grid also works for projects such as feasibility studies and yardstick reports that compare many variables. Assume you must recommend a new printer to your manager. To see how four models compare, you could lay out a grid with the names of printer models across the top. Down the left side, you would list such significant variables as price, warranty, service, capacity, compatibility, and specifications. As you fill in the variables for each model, you can see quickly which model has the lowest price, longest warranty, and so forth. *Consumer Reports* often uses grids to show information.

In addition, grids help classify employment data. For example, suppose your boss asks you to recommend one individual from among many job candidates. You could arrange a grid with names across the top and distinguishing characteristics—experience, skills, education, and other employment interests—down the left side. Summarizing each candidate's points offers a helpful tool for drawing conclusions and writing a report.

Decision Matrices. A decision matrix is a special grid that helps managers make the best choice among complex options. Designed to eliminate bias and poor judgment, decision matrices are helpful in many fields. Assume you need to choose the most appropriate laptop computer for your sales representatives. You are most interested in weight, battery life, price, and hard drive size. You want to compare these features in four laptop models. Figure 12.3 shows a simple decision matrix to help you make the choice. In this case, the most important criteria were weight, battery, price, and hard drive. In Table 1, you evaluate each of these features on a scale of 1 to 5. Because the Dell Inspiron has a spacious hard drive, you give it a score of 5. However, its battery life is less desirable, and you give it a score of 2.

FIGURE 12.2 **Grid to Analyze Complex Verbal Data About Building Cash Reserves**

	Point 1	Point 2	Point 3	Point 4	Overall Reaction
Vice President 1	Disapproves. "Too little, too late."	Strong support. "Best of all points."	Mixed opinion. "Must wait and see market."	Indifferent.	Optimistic, but "hates to delay expansion for six months."
Vice President 2	Disapproves. "Creates credit trap."	Approves.	Strong disapproval.	Approves. "Must improve receivable collections."	Mixed support. "Good self–defense plan."
Vice President 3	Strong disapproval.	Approves. "Key to entire plan."	Indifferent.	Approves, but with "caveats."	"Will work only with sale of unproductive fixed assets."
Vice President 4	Disapproves. "Too risky now."	Strong support. "Start immediately."	Approves, "but may damage image."	Approves. "Benefits far outweigh costs."	Supports plan. Suggests focus on Pacific Rim markets.

FIGURE 12.3 Decision Matrix Used to Choose a Laptop for Sales Reps

Unweighted Decision Matrix—Table 1

Features	Weight	Battery Life	Price	Hard Drive	Total
Laptop Options					
Dell Inspiron i1464-4382OBK: 2.13 GHz, Intel Core i3 330M, 4.8 lbs, 3:20 hrs, $699, 500 GB	3	2	5	5	
Apple MacBook Pro: 2.26 GHz, Intel Core 2 Duo P7550, 4.5 lbs, 4:44 hrs, $1,200, 160 GB	4	3	1	1	
Acer Aspire Timeline AS4810TZ-4120: 1.3 GHz, Intel Dual-Core SU4100, 5.1 lbs, 9:10 hrs, $830, 320 GB	2	5	2	3	
HP Pavilion dv4-2153cl: 2.13 GHz, Intel Core i3 330M, 5.2 lbs, 3:13 hrs, $780, 320 GB	2	2	3	3	

Weighted Decision Matrix—Table 2

Features	Weight	Battery LIfe	Price	Hard Drive	Total
Laptop Options **Weights:**	**5**	**10**	**5**	**7**	
Dell Inspiron i1464-4382OBK: 2.13 GHz, Intel Core i3 330M, 4.8 lbs, 3:20 hrs, $699, 500 GB	15	20	25	35	95
Apple MacBook Pro: 2.26 GHz, Intel Core 2 Duo P7550, 4.5 lbs, 4:44 hrs, $1,200, 160 GB	20	30	5	7	62
Acer Aspire Timeline AS4810TZ-4120: 1.3 GHz, Intel Dual-Core SU4100, 5.1 lbs, 9:10 hrs, $830, 320 GB	10	50	10	21	91
HP Pavilion dv4-2153cl: 2.13 GHz, Intel Core i3 330M, 5.2 lbs, 3:13 hrs, $780, 320 GB	10	20	15	21	66

Tips for Creating a Decision Matrix

- **Select the most important criteria.** For a laptop computer, the criteria were weight, battery life, price, and size of hard drive.
- **Create a matrix.** List each laptop model (Dell, Apple, and others) down the left side. Place the features across the top of the columns.
- **Evaluate the criteria.** Use a scale of 1 (lowest) to 5 (highest). Rate each feature for each option, as shown in Table 1.
- **Assign relative weights.** Decide how important each feature is and give it a weight.
- **Multiply the scores.** For each feature in Table 1, multiply by the weights in Table 2 and write the score in the box.
- **Total the scores.** The total reveals the best choice.

After you have evaluated all of the laptop models in Table 1, you assign relative weights to each feature. You decide to assign a factor of 5 to weight as well as to unit price because these two aspects are of average importance. However, your field sales reps want laptops with batteries that last. Therefore, battery life is twice as important; you assign it a factor of 10. You assign a factor of 7 to the size of the hard drive because this option is slightly more important than price, but somewhat less important than battery life. Then you multiply the scores in Table 1 with the weights and total them, as shown in Table 2. According to the weighted matrix and the rating system used, the Dell Inspiron should be purchased for the sales reps because it received the highest score of 95 points, closely followed by the Acer Aspire with 91 points.

Drawing Conclusions and Making Recommendations

LEARNING OBJECTIVE 2

Draw meaningful conclusions and make practical report recommendations after sound and valid analysis.

The most widely read portions of a report are the sections devoted to conclusions and recommendations. Knowledgeable readers go straight to the conclusions to see what the report writer thinks the data mean. Because conclusions summarize and explain the findings, they represent the heart of a report.

Your value in an organization rises considerably if you can draw conclusions that analyze information logically and show how the data answer questions and solve problems. To tap into a potential $1 billion market for cellular phones in developing countries, Finnish mobile phone manufacturer Nokia researched the needs of its customers. It created handsets that can withstand the tough living conditions and harsh weather in India and Africa. To reach customers, the company sent vans into rural India. Kai Oistamo, executive vice president and general manager for mobile phones, said: "You have to understand where people live, what the shopping patterns are. You have to work with local means to reach people—even bicycles or rickshaws."[2] Doing research and drawing logical conclusions from data are crucial to business success.

Analyzing Data to Arrive at Conclusions

What kind of information is included in conclusions?

Any set of data can produce a variety of meaningful conclusions. Always bear in mind, though, that the audience for a report wants to know how these data relate to the problem being studied. What do the findings mean in terms of solving the original report problem?

For example, the Marriott Corporation recognized a serious problem among its employees. Conflicting home and work requirements seemed to be causing excessive employee turnover and decreased productivity. To learn the extent of the problem and to consider solutions, Marriott surveyed its staff. It learned, among other things, that nearly 35 percent of its employees had children under age twelve, and 15 percent had children under age five. Other findings, shown in Figure 12.4, indicated that one third of its staff with young children took time off because of child care difficulties. Moreover, many current employees left previous jobs because of work and family conflicts. The survey also showed that managers did not consider child care or family problems to be appropriate topics for discussion at work.

A sample of possible conclusions that could be drawn from these findings is shown in Figure 12.4. Notice that each conclusion relates to the initial report problem. Although only a few possible findings and conclusions are shown here, you can see that the conclusions try to explain the causes for the home/work conflict among employees. Many report writers would expand the conclusion section by explaining each item and citing supporting evidence. Even for simplified conclusions, such as those shown in Figure 12.4, you will want to itemize each item separately and use parallel construction (balanced sentence structure).

How can you ensure that your conclusions are effective?

Although your goal is to remain objective, drawing conclusions naturally involves a degree of subjectivity. Your goals, background, and frame of reference all color the inferences you make. When the Big Three automakers posted staggering losses just before the federal rescue plan kicked in, a public debate raged over whether to give loan guarantees to the companies or let them go bankrupt. The facts could not be disputed. But what conclusions could be drawn? The CEOs of GM, Ford, and Chrysler went to Washington to ask for loans because they wanted to buy time until they retooled their operations and before they ran out of cash. The workers and the government concluded that the potential for up to 3 million job losses was reason enough to bail out the Detroit companies. The taxpayers, still reeling from a $700 billion bank bailout, viewed even the relatively small rescue package with suspicion. Moreover, consumers kept fleeing big gas guzzlers in favor of smaller, more efficient imports. All writers interpret findings from their own perspectives, but they should not manipulate them to achieve a preconceived purpose.

You can make your report conclusions more objective by using consistent evaluation criteria. Let's say you are comparing computers for an office equipment purchase. If you evaluate each by the same criteria (such as price, specifications, service, and warranty), your conclusions are more likely to be bias-free.

You also need to avoid the temptation to sensationalize or exaggerate your findings or conclusions. Be careful of words such as *many, most,* and *all.* Instead of *many of the respondents felt...,* you might more accurately write *some of the respondents felt....* Examine your motives before drawing conclusions. Do not let preconceptions or wishful thinking color your reasoning.

Preparing Report Recommendations

Conclusions explain what the problem is, whereas recommendations tell how to solve it. Typically, readers prefer specific, practical recommendations. They want to know exactly how to implement the suggestions. The specificity of your recommendations depends on your authorization. What are you commissioned to do, and what does the reader expect? In the

What is the difference between conclusions and recommendations?

FIGURE 12.4 Report Conclusions and Recommendations

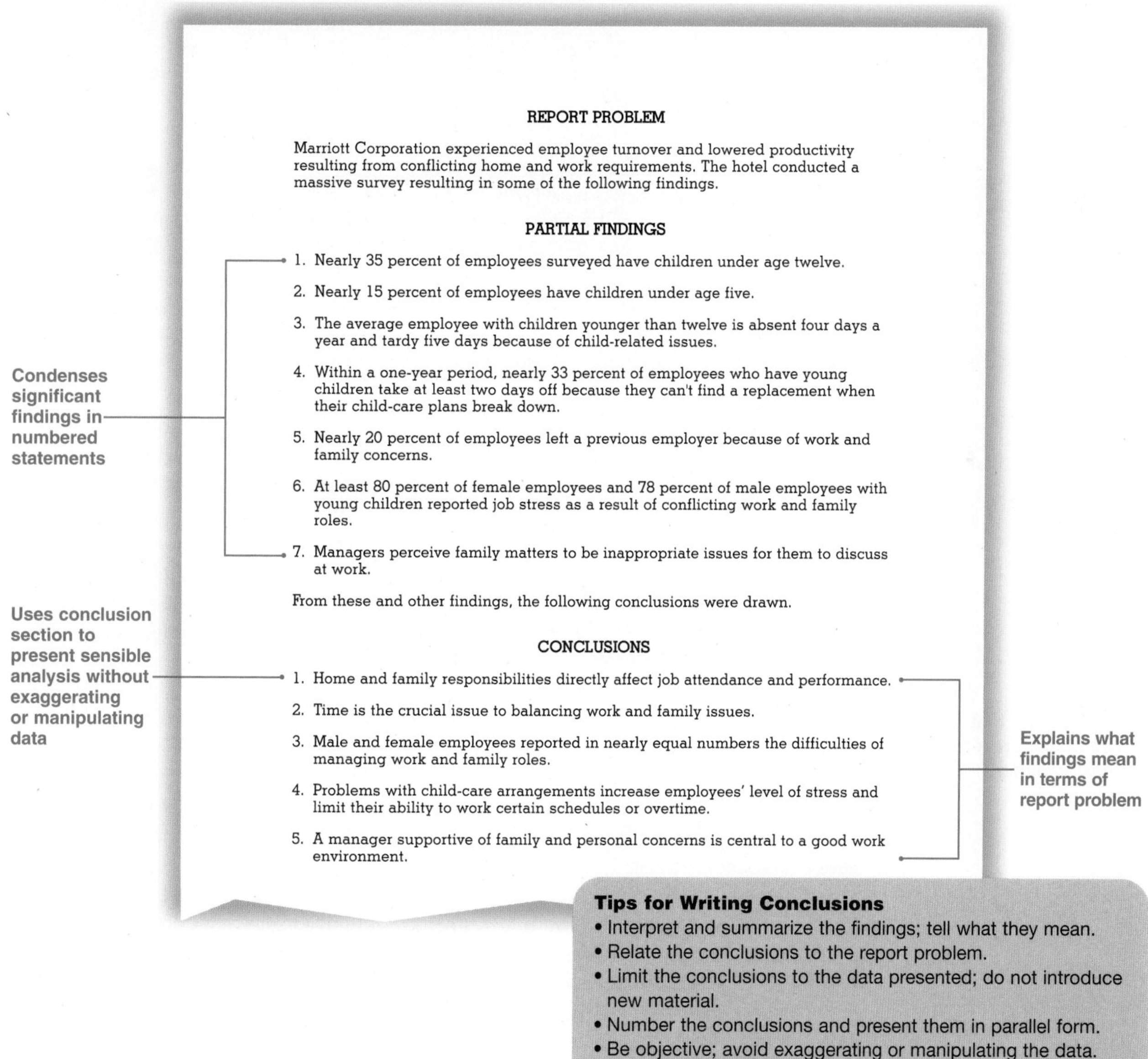
REPORT PROBLEM

Marriott Corporation experienced employee turnover and lowered productivity resulting from conflicting home and work requirements. The hotel conducted a massive survey resulting in some of the following findings.

PARTIAL FINDINGS

1. Nearly 35 percent of employees surveyed have children under age twelve.
2. Nearly 15 percent of employees have children under age five.
3. The average employee with children younger than twelve is absent four days a year and tardy five days because of child-related issues.
4. Within a one-year period, nearly 33 percent of employees who have young children take at least two days off because they can't find a replacement when their child-care plans break down.
5. Nearly 20 percent of employees left a previous employer because of work and family concerns.
6. At least 80 percent of female employees and 78 percent of male employees with young children reported job stress as a result of conflicting work and family roles.
7. Managers perceive family matters to be inappropriate issues for them to discuss at work.

From these and other findings, the following conclusions were drawn.

CONCLUSIONS

1. Home and family responsibilities directly affect job attendance and performance.
2. Time is the crucial issue to balancing work and family issues.
3. Male and female employees reported in nearly equal numbers the difficulties of managing work and family roles.
4. Problems with child-care arrangements increase employees' level of stress and limit their ability to work certain schedules or overtime.
5. A manager supportive of family and personal concerns is central to a good work environment.

Condenses significant findings in numbered statements
Uses conclusion section to present sensible analysis without exaggerating or manipulating data
Explains what findings mean in terms of report problem
Tips for Writing Conclusions
• Interpret and summarize the findings; tell what they mean.
• Relate the conclusions to the report problem.
• Limit the conclusions to the data presented; do not introduce new material.
• Number the conclusions and present them in parallel form.
• Be objective; avoid exaggerating or manipulating the data.
• Use consistent criteria in evaluating options.

FIGURE 12.4 **(Continued)**

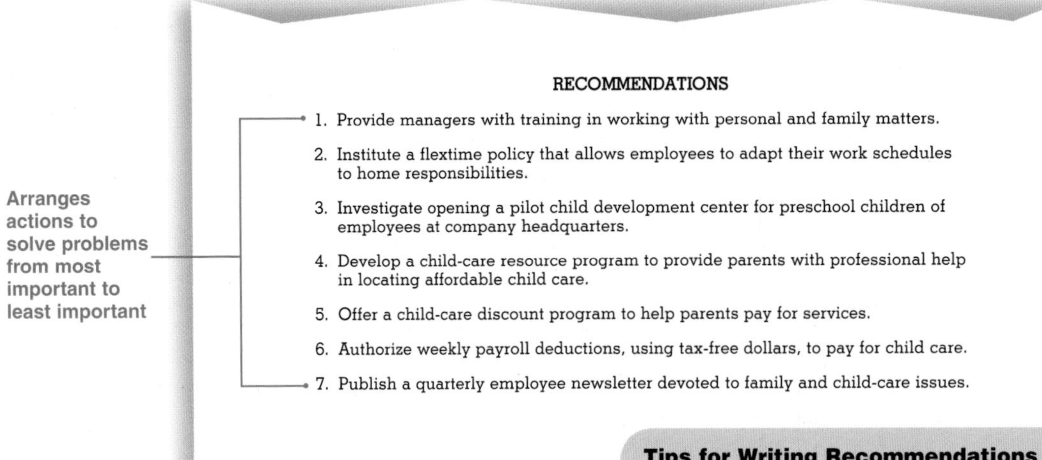

RECOMMENDATIONS

1. Provide managers with training in working with personal and family matters.
2. Institute a flextime policy that allows employees to adapt their work schedules to home responsibilities.
3. Investigate opening a pilot child development center for preschool children of employees at company headquarters.
4. Develop a child-care resource program to provide parents with professional help in locating affordable child care.
5. Offer a child-care discount program to help parents pay for services.
6. Authorize weekly payroll deductions, using tax-free dollars, to pay for child care.
7. Publish a quarterly employee newsletter devoted to family and child-care issues.

Arranges actions to solve problems from most important to least important

Tips for Writing Recommendations

- Make specific suggestions for actions to solve the report problem.
- Prepare practical recommendations that will be agreeable to the audience.
- Avoid conditional words such as *maybe* and *perhaps.*
- Present each suggestion separately as a command beginning with a verb.
- Number the recommendations for improved readability.
- If requested, describe how the recommendations may be implemented.
- When possible, arrange the recommendations in an announced order, such as most important to least important.

planning stages of your report project, you anticipate what the reader wants in the report. Your intuition and your knowledge of the audience indicate how far your recommendations should be developed.

In the recommendations section of the Marriott employee survey, shown in Figure 12.4, many of the recommendations are summarized. In the actual report, each recommendation could have been backed up with specifics and ideas for implementing them. For example, the child care resource recommendation would be explained: it provides parents with names of agencies and professionals who specialize in locating child care across the country.

How can you ensure that your recommendations are received well by your audience?

A good report provides practical recommendations that are agreeable to the audience. In the Marriott survey, for example, report researchers knew that the company wanted to help employees cope with conflicts between family and work obligations. As a result, the report's conclusions and recommendations focused on ways to resolve the conflict. If Marriott's goal had been merely to save money by reducing employee absenteeism, the recommendations would have been quite different.

If possible, make each recommendation a command. Note in Figure 12.4 that each recommendation begins with a verb. This structure sounds forceful and confident and helps the reader comprehend the information quickly. Avoid words such as *maybe* and *perhaps*; they suggest conditional statements that reduce the strength of recommendations.

Experienced writers may combine recommendations and conclusions. In short reports writers may omit conclusions and move straight to recommendations. An important point about recommendations is that they include practical suggestions for solving the report problem. Furthermore, they are always the result of prior logical analysis.

Moving From Findings to Recommendations

Recommendations evolve from the interpretation of the findings and conclusions. Consider the following examples from the Marriott survey:

Finding

Managers perceive family matters to be inappropriate issues to discuss at work.

Conclusion

Managers are neither willing nor trained to discuss family matters that may cause employees to miss work.

Recommendation

Provide managers with training in recognizing and working with personal and family matters that affect work.

Finding

Within a one-year period, nearly 33 percent of employees who have young children take at least two days off because they can't find a replacement when their child care plans break down.

Conclusion

Problems with child care arrangements increase employees' level of stress and limit their ability to work certain schedules or overtime.

Recommendation

Develop a child care resource program to provide parents with professional help in locating affordable child care.

Organizing Data

LEARNING OBJECTIVE 3
Organize report data logically and provide cues to aid comprehension.

When would you choose the direct strategy to organize data, and when would the indirect strategy be more appropriate?

After collecting sets of data, interpreting them, drawing conclusions, and thinking about the recommendations, you are ready to organize the parts of the report into a logical framework. Poorly organized reports lead to frustration. Readers will not understand, remember, or be persuaded. Wise writers know that reports rarely "just organize themselves." Instead, organization must be imposed on the data, and cues must be provided so the reader can follow the logic of the writer.

Informational reports, as you learned in Chapter 11, generally present data without interpretation. As shown in Figure 12.5, informational reports typically consist of three parts: (a) introduction/background, (b) facts/findings, and (c) summary/concluding remarks. Analytical reports, which generally analyze data and draw conclusions, typically contain four parts: (a) introduction/problem, (b) facts/findings, (c) discussion/analysis, and (d) conclusions/recommendations. However, the parts in analytical reports do not always follow this sequence. For readers who know about the project, are supportive, or are eager to learn the results quickly, the direct strategy is appropriate. Conclusions and recommendations, if requested,

FIGURE 12.5 Organizational Patterns for Informational and Analytical Reports

	Analytical Reports	
Informational Reports	**Direct Pattern**	**Indirect Pattern**
I. Introduction/background	I. Introduction/problem	I. Introduction/problem
II. Facts/findings	II. Conclusions/recommendations	II. Facts/findings
III. Summary/conclusion	III. Facts/findings	III. Discussion/analysis
	IV. Discussion/analysis	IV. Conclusions/recommendations

appear up front. For readers who must be educated or persuaded, the indirect strategy works better. Conclusions/recommendations appear last, after the findings have been presented and analyzed.

Although every report is unique, the overall organizational patterns described here typically hold true. The real challenge, though, lies in (a) organizing the facts/findings and discussion/analysis sections and (b) providing reader cues.

Ordering Information Logically

What are some organizational patterns that help readers comprehend data?

Whether you are writing informational or analytical reports, the data you have collected must be structured coherently. Five common organizational methods are by time, component, importance, criteria, or convention. Regardless of the method you choose, be sure that it helps the reader understand the data. Reader comprehension, not writer convenience, should govern organization. For additional examples of organizational principles, please go to page 460 in Chapter 14.

Time. Ordering data by time means establishing a chronology of events. Agendas, minutes of meetings, progress reports, and procedures are usually organized by time. For example, a report describing an eight-week training program would most likely be organized by weeks. A plan for step-by-step improvement of customer service would be organized by steps. A monthly trip report submitted by a sales rep might describe customers visited Week 1, Week 2, and so on. Beware of overusing chronologies (time) as an organizing method for reports, however. Although this method is easy and often mirrors the way data are collected, chronologies—like the sales rep's trip report—tend to be boring, repetitious, and lacking in emphasis. Readers cannot always pick out what is important.

Component. Especially for informational reports, data may be organized by components such as location, geography, division, product, or part. For instance, a report detailing company expansion might divide the plan into West Coast, East Coast, and Midwest expansion. The report could also be organized by divisions: personal products, consumer electronics, and household goods. A report comparing profits among makers of athletic shoes might group the data by company: Nike, Reebok, Adidas, and so forth. Organization by components works best when the classifications already exist.

What are the advantages of organizing data by level of importance?

Importance. Organization by importance involves beginning with the most important item and proceeding to the least important—or vice versa. For example, a report discussing the reasons for declining product sales would present the most important reason first followed by less important ones. The Marriott report describing work/family conflicts might begin by discussing child care, if the writer considered it the most important issue. Using importance to structure findings involves a value judgment. The writer must decide what is most important, always keeping in mind the readers' priorities and expectations. Busy readers appreciate seeing important points first; they may skim or skip other points. On the other hand, building to a climax by moving from least important to most important enables the writer to focus attention at the end. Thus, the reader is more likely to remember the most important item. Of course, the writer also risks losing the reader's attention along the way.

Criteria. Establishing criteria by which to judge helps writers to treat topics consistently. Let's say your report compares health plans A, B, and C. For each plan you examine the same standards: Criterion 1, cost per employee; Criterion 2, amount of deductible; and Criterion 3, patient benefits. The resulting data could then be organized either by plans or by criteria:

How can you make sure that you evaluate choices or plans fairly?

By Plan	**By Criteria**
Plan A	Criterion 1
Criterion 1	Plan A
Criterion 2	Plan B
Criterion 3	Plan C

By Plan	By Criteria
Plan B	Criterion 2
Criterion 1	Plan A
Criterion 2	Plan B
Criterion 3	Plan C
Plan C	Criterion 3
Criterion 1	Plan A
Criterion 2	Plan B
Criterion 3	Plan C

Although you might favor organizing the data by plans (because that is the way you collected the data), the better way is by criteria. When you discuss patient benefits, for example, you would examine all three plans' benefits together. Organizing a report around criteria helps readers make comparisons, instead of forcing them to search through the report for similar data.

Convention. Many operational and recurring reports are structured according to convention. That is, they follow a prescribed plan that everyone understands. For example, an automotive parts manufacturer might ask all sales reps to prepare a weekly report with these headings: *Competitive observations* (competitors' price changes, discounts, new products, product problems, distributor changes, product promotions), *Product problems* (quality, performance, needs), and *Customer service problems* (delivery, mailings, correspondence). Management gets exactly the information it needs in an easy-to-read form.

What are the advantages of organizing by convention?

Like operating reports, proposals are often organized conventionally. They might use such groupings as background, problem, proposed solution, staffing, schedule, costs, and authorization. As you might expect, reports following these conventional, prescribed structures greatly simplify the task of organization. Proposals and long reports are presented in Chapter 13.

Providing Reader Cues

When you finish organizing a report, you probably see a neat outline in your mind: major points, supported by subpoints and details. Readers, however, do not know the material as well as you do; they cannot see your outline. To guide them through the data, you need to provide the equivalent of a map and road signs. For both formal and informal reports, devices such as introductions, transitions, and headings prevent readers from getting lost.

Introduction. One of the best ways to point a reader in the right direction is to provide a report introduction that does three things:

What purpose does a good opener serve?

- Tells the purpose of the report
- Describes the significance of the topic
- Previews the main points and the order in which they will be developed

The following paragraph includes all three elements in introducing a report on computer security:

This report examines the security of our current computer operations and presents suggestions for improving security. Lax computer security could mean loss of information, loss of business, and damage to our equipment and systems. Because many former employees released during recent downsizing efforts know our systems, major changes must be made. To improve security, I will present three recommendations: (a) begin using smart cards that limit access to our computer system, (b) alter sign-on and log-off procedures, (c) move central computer operations to a more secure area.

This opener tells the purpose (examining computer security), describes its significance (loss of information and business, damage to equipment and systems), and outlines how the report is organized (three recommendations). Good openers in effect set up a contract with the reader. The writer promises to cover certain topics in a specified order. Readers expect the writer to fulfill the contract. They want the topics to be developed as promised—using the same wording and presented in the order mentioned. For example, if in your introduction you state that you will discuss the use of *smart cards*, do not change the heading for that section to *access cards*. Remember that the introduction provides a map to a report; switching the names on the map will ensure that readers get lost. To maintain consistency, delay writing the introduction until after you have completed the report. Long, complex reports may require introductions, brief internal summaries, and previews for each section.

What are the benefits of transitional expressions?

Transitions. Expressions such as *on the contrary, at the same time*, and *however* show relationships and help reveal the logical flow of ideas in a report. These transitional expressions enable writers to tell readers where ideas are headed and how they relate. Notice how abrupt the following two sentences sound without a transition: *The Microsoft Zune player offers several technological advances that exceed the capabilities of Apple's iPod devices. The Zune [however] is locked into a clunky online music store that isn't likely to win many fans.*

The following transitional expressions (see Chapter 5, Figure 5.8 for a complete list) enable you to show readers how you are developing your ideas.

To present additional thoughts: *additionally, again, also, moreover, furthermore*

To suggest cause and effect: *accordingly, as a result, consequently, therefore*

To contrast ideas: *at the same time, but, however, on the contrary, though, yet*

To show time and order: *after, before, first, finally, now, previously, then, to conclude*

To clarify points: *for example, for instance, in other words, that is, thus*

In using these expressions, recognize that they do not have to sit at the head of a sentence. Listen to the rhythm of the sentence, and place the expression where a natural pause occurs. If you are unsure about the placement of a transitional expression, position it at the beginning of the sentence. Used appropriately, transitional expressions serve readers as guides; misused or overused, they can be as distracting and frustrating as too many road signs on a highway.

What makes for good headings, and why are they important?

Headings. Good headings are another structural cue that assists readers in comprehending the organization of a report. They highlight major ideas, allowing busy readers to see the big picture at a glance. Moreover, headings provide resting points for the mind and for the eye, breaking up large chunks of text into manageable and inviting segments.

Report writers may use functional or talking headings. Functional headings (for example, *Background, Findings, Personnel*, and *Production Costs*) describe functions or general topics. They show the outline of a report but provide little insight for readers. Functional headings are useful for routine reports. They are also appropriate for sensitive topics that might provoke emotional reactions. By keeping the headings general, experienced writers hope to minimize reader opposition or response to controversial subjects. Talking headings (for example, *Lack of Space and Cost Compound Campus Parking Problem* or *Survey Shows Support for Parking Fees*) provide more information and spark interest. Unless carefully written, however, talking headings can fail to reveal the organization of a report. With some planning, though, headings can be both functional and talking, such as *Parking Recommendations: Shuttle and New Structures*.

The best strategy to help you create helpful talking headings is to write a few paragraphs first and then generate talking headings that sum up the major point of each paragraph. To create the most effective headings, follow a few basic guidelines:

- **Use appropriate heading levels.** The position and format of a heading indicate its level of importance and relationship to other points. Figure 12.6 illustrates and discusses a commonly used heading format for business reports. For an overview of alphanumeric and decimal outlines, please see page 144.

- **Capitalize and emphasize carefully.** Most writers use all capital letters (without underlines) for main titles, such as the report, chapter, and unit titles. For first- and second-level headings, they capitalize only the first letter of main words such as nouns, verbs, adjectives, adverbs, names, and so on. Articles (*a, an, the*), conjunctions (*and, but, or, nor*), and prepositions with three or fewer letters (*in, to, by, for*) are not capitalized unless they appear at the beginning or ending of the heading. For additional emphasis, most writers use a bold font, as shown in Figure 12.6.

- **Try to balance headings within levels.** Although it may not be always possible, attempt to create headings that are grammatically similar at a given level. For example, *Developing Product Teams* and *Presenting Plan to Management* are balanced, but *Development of Product Teams* and *Presenting Plan to Management* are not.

- **For short reports use first-level or first- and second-level headings.** Many business reports contain only one or two levels of headings. For such reports use first-level headings (centered, bolded) and, if needed, second-level headings (flush left, bolded). See Figure 12.6.

- **Include at least one heading per report page, but don't end the page with a heading.** Headings increase the readability and attractiveness of report pages. Use at least one per page to break up blocks of text. Move a heading that is separated from the text that follows from the bottom of the page to the top of the following page.

FIGURE 12.6 **Levels of Headings in Reports**

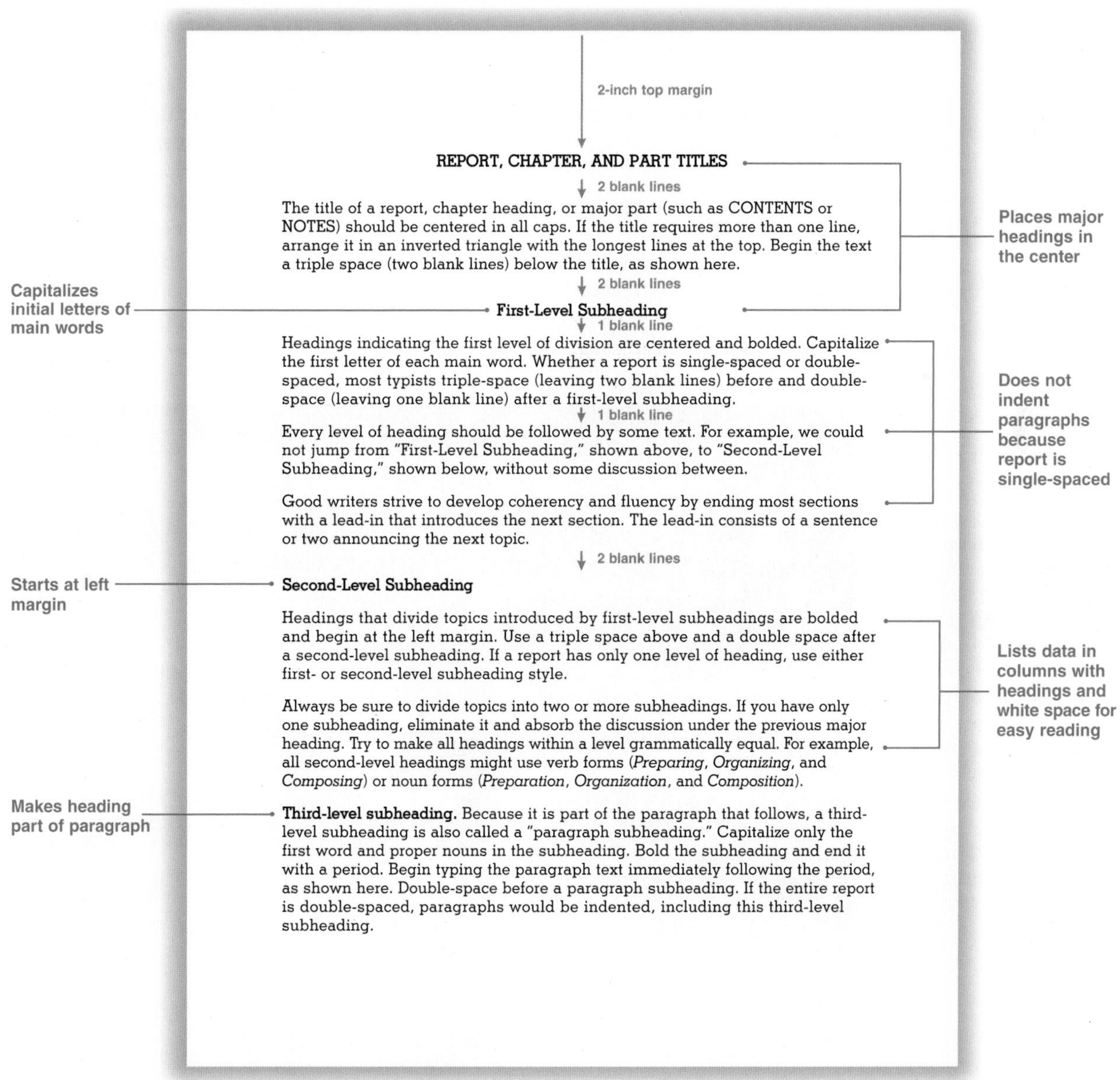

- **Apply punctuation correctly.** Omit end punctuation in first- and second-level headings. End punctuation is required in third-level headings because they are capitalized and punctuated like sentences. Proper nouns (names) are capitalized in third-level headings as they would be in a sentence.
- **Keep headings short but clear.** One-word headings are emphatic but not always clear. For example, the heading *Budget* does not adequately describe figures for a summer project involving student interns for an oil company in Texas. Try to keep your headings brief (no more than eight words), but make sure they are understandable. Experiment with headings that concisely tell who, what, when, where, and why.

Writing Short Informational Reports

LEARNING OBJECTIVE 4
Prepare short informational reports that describe routine tasks.

What is the purpose of informational reports?

Now that we have covered the basics of gathering, interpreting, and organizing data, we are ready to put it all together into short informational or analytical reports. Informational reports often describe periodic, recurring activities (such as monthly sales or weekly customer calls) as well as situational, nonrecurring events (such as trips, conferences, and progress on special projects). Short informational reports may also include summaries of longer publications. What all these reports have in common is delivering information to readers who do not have to be persuaded. Informational report readers usually are neutral or receptive.

You can expect to write many informational reports as an entry-level or middle-management employee. Because these reports generally deliver nonsensitive data and, therefore, will not upset the reader, they are organized directly. Often they need little background material or introductory comments because readers are familiar with the topics. Although they are generally conversational and informal, informational reports should not be so casual that the reader struggles to find the important points. Main points must be immediately visible. Headings, lists, bulleted items, and other graphic design elements, as well as clear organization, enable readers to grasp major ideas immediately. The lessons that you have learned about conciseness, clarity, courtesy, and effective writing in general throughout earlier chapters apply to report writing as well. After all, competent reports can boost your visibility in the company and promote your advancement. The accompanying Career Coach box provides additional pointers on design features and techniques that can improve your reports.

Film production crews have tight deadlines, and unforeseen studio mishaps can throw a multi-million dollar blockbuster off schedule. Producers at England's Leavesden Film Studios struggled to keep *Harry Potter* and the *Deathly Hallows* on track following the injury of Harry's stunt double and a pyrotechnics fire at Hogwart's Castle. Despite setbacks, executives announced that the studio would deliver the boy wizard's big screen adventure on time. *How do informational reports help managers keep projects on schedule?*

Summaries

A summary compresses the main points from a book, report, article, Web site, meeting, or convention. A summary saves time because it can reduce a report or article 85 to 95 percent. Employees are sometimes asked to write summaries that condense technical reports, periodical articles, or books so that their staffs or superiors may grasp the main ideas quickly. Students may be asked to write summaries of articles, chapters, or books to sharpen their writing skills and to confirm their knowledge of reading assignments. In writing a summary, you will follow these general guidelines:

- Present the goal or purpose of the document being summarized. Why was it written?
- Highlight the research methods (if appropriate), findings, conclusions, and recommendations.
- Omit illustrations, examples, and references.
- Organize for readability by including headings and bulleted or enumerated lists.
- Include your reactions or an overall evaluation of the document if asked to do so.

Spotlight on Communicators

© Courtesy of Relmond P. Van Daniker, DBA, CPA

"We believe that the traditional methods of communicating government financial information—through reams of audited financial statements that have little relevance to the taxpayer—must be supplemented by government financial reporting that expresses complex financial details in an understandable form," said Relmond Van Daniker, executive director of the Association of Government Accountants (AGA). The association he heads recommends that government financial information be clear and understandable, updated regularly, delivered to all, easy to locate, and honest in breadth yet technically accurate in detail. A recent AGA survey revealed that the public overwhelmingly believes government has the obligation to report and explain how it generates and spends its money, but is failing to meet expectations.

An *executive summary* summarizes a long report, proposal, or business plan. It concentrates on what management needs to know from a longer report. How to prepare an executive summary is covered in Chapter 13 on page 430.

What do summaries cover and what are their advantages?

Periodic (Activity) Reports

Most businesses—especially larger ones—require periodic reports (sometimes called *activity reports)* to keep management informed of operations. These recurring reports are written at regular intervals—weekly, monthly, yearly—so that management can monitor business strategies and, if necessary, remedy any problems. Some periodic reports simply contain figures, such as sales volume, number and kind of customer service calls, shipments delivered, accounts payable, and personnel data. More challenging periodic reports require descriptions and discussions of activities. In preparing a narrative description of their activities, employees writing periodic reports usually do the following:

Why are periodic reports written?

- Summarize regular activities and events performed during the reporting period
- Describe irregular events deserving the attention of management
- Highlight special needs and problems

Managers naturally want to know that routine activities are progressing normally. Employees today enjoy a great deal of independence and shoulder much responsibility due to flattened hierarchies on the job. They often work flexible hours in far-flung locations. Keeping track of their activities and the tasks they were assigned is crucial in such an environment. Increasingly, routine reports are sent by e-mail and take the form of efficient bulleted lists without commentary.

Figure 12.7 shows a weekly activity report prepared by Siddharth Singh, a senior Web producer at the information technology firm Sygnal Macro in Silicon Valley. Sid is responsible for his firm's Web presence in Asian countries or territories, mainly Japan, China, Hong Kong, and Vietnam. In his weekly reports to his supervisor, Tomas Esposito, Sid neatly divides his projects into *completed*, *in progress*, and *ongoing*. Tomas, the manager, then combines the activity reports from all his subordinates into a separate periodic report detailing the department's activities to his superiors.

Sid justifies the use of jargon, missing salutation and complimentary close, and ultrashort bulleted items as follows: "We e-mail our reports internally, so some IT jargon can be expected. The readers will understand it. Tomas and upper management all want reporting to be brief and to the point. Bullets fit us just fine." Periodic reports ensure that information within the company flows steadily and that supervisors know the status of current and pending projects. This efficient information flow is all the more important because Sid works at home two days a week to spend time with his young children. Several of his coworkers also telecommute.

What is the purpose of trip and conference reports, and what information do they convey?

Trip, Convention, and Conference Reports

Employees sent on business trips or to conventions and conferences typically must submit reports when they return. Organizations want to know that their money was well spent in funding the travel. These reports inform management about new procedures, equipment, and laws as well as supply information affecting products, operations, and service.

The hardest parts of writing these reports are selecting the most relevant material and organizing it coherently. Generally, it is best not to use chronological sequencing (*in the morning we did X, at lunch we heard Y, and in the afternoon we did Z*). Instead, you should focus on three to five topics in which your reader will be interested. These items become the body of the report.

CAREER COACH

The Top Ten Tips for Designing Better Documents

Desktop publishing packages, high-level word processing programs, and advanced printers now make it possible for you to turn out professional-looking documents and promotional materials. Resist the temptation, however, to overdo it by incorporating too many features in one document. Here are the top ten design tips for applying good sense and solid design principles in "publishing" your documents.

1. Analyze your audience. Sales brochures and promotional letters can be flashy—with color print, oversized type, and fancy borders—to attract attention. However, such effects are out of place for most traditional business documents. Also, will your readers be reading painstakingly or merely browsing? Lists and headings help those readers who are in a hurry.

2. Avoid amateurish effects. Strive for simple, clean, and forceful effects. Many beginning writers, eager to display every graphic device a program offers, produce busy, cluttered documents. Too many typefaces, ruled lines, oversized headlines, and images will overwhelm readers.

3. Choose an appropriate type size. For most business memos, letters, and reports, the body text should be 11 to 12 points tall (a point is 1/72 of an inch). Larger type looks amateurish, and smaller type is hard to read and faxes poorly.

4. Use a consistent type font. Although your software may provide a variety of fonts, stay with a single family of type within one document—at least until you become more expert. The most popular fonts are Times New Roman and Arial. In Word 2007, Cambria and Calibri are the two default fonts and, as a result, may become more popular. For emphasis and contrast, you can vary the font size and weight with **bold**, *italic*, ***bold italic,*** and other selections.

5. Do not justify right margins. Textbooks, novels, newspapers, magazines, and other long works are usually set with justified (even) right margins. However, for shorter works ragged-right margins are recommended because such margins add white space and help readers locate the beginnings of new lines. Slower readers find ragged-right copy more legible.

6. Separate paragraphs and sentences appropriately. In single-spaced business documents, the first line of a paragraph is preceded by a blank line, and the line begins flush left. In double-spaced documents, the first line is indented five spaces from the left margin, and no space. To separate sentences, typists have traditionally left two spaces after the period. This spacing is still acceptable, and proponents argue that this practice enhances readability, but most writers now follow printers' standards and leave only one space. Whichever standard you adopt, maintain it consistently.

7. Design readable headings. Presenting headings in all caps is generally discouraged because solid blocks of capital letters interfere with the recognition of word patterns. To further improve readability, select a sans serif typeface (one without cross strokes or embellishment), such as Arial or Calibri.

8. Strive for an attractive page layout. In designing title pages or graphics, provide a balance between print and white space. Also consider placing the focal point (something that draws the reader's eye) at the optical center of a page—about three lines above the actual center. Moreover, remember that the average reader scans a page from left to right and top to bottom in a *Z* pattern. Plan your graphics accordingly.

9. Use graphics and clip art with restraint. You can import, copy, or scan charts, original drawings, photographs, and clip art into documents. Use such images, however, only when they are well drawn, relevant, purposeful, and appropriately sized.

10. Develop expertise. Learn to use the desktop publishing features of your current word processing software, or investigate one of the special programs, such as QuarkXPress, Adobe's InDesign, and Corel's Ventura. Although the learning curve for many of these programs is steep, such effort is well spent if you will be producing newsletters, brochures, announcements, visual aids, and promotional literature.

Career Application

Buy or borrow a book or two on designing documents, and select ten tips that you could share with the class. In teams of three or four, analyze the design and layout of three or four annual reports. Evaluate the appropriateness of typeface and type size, white space, headings, and graphics.

FIGURE 12.7 Periodic (Activity) Report—E-Mail Format

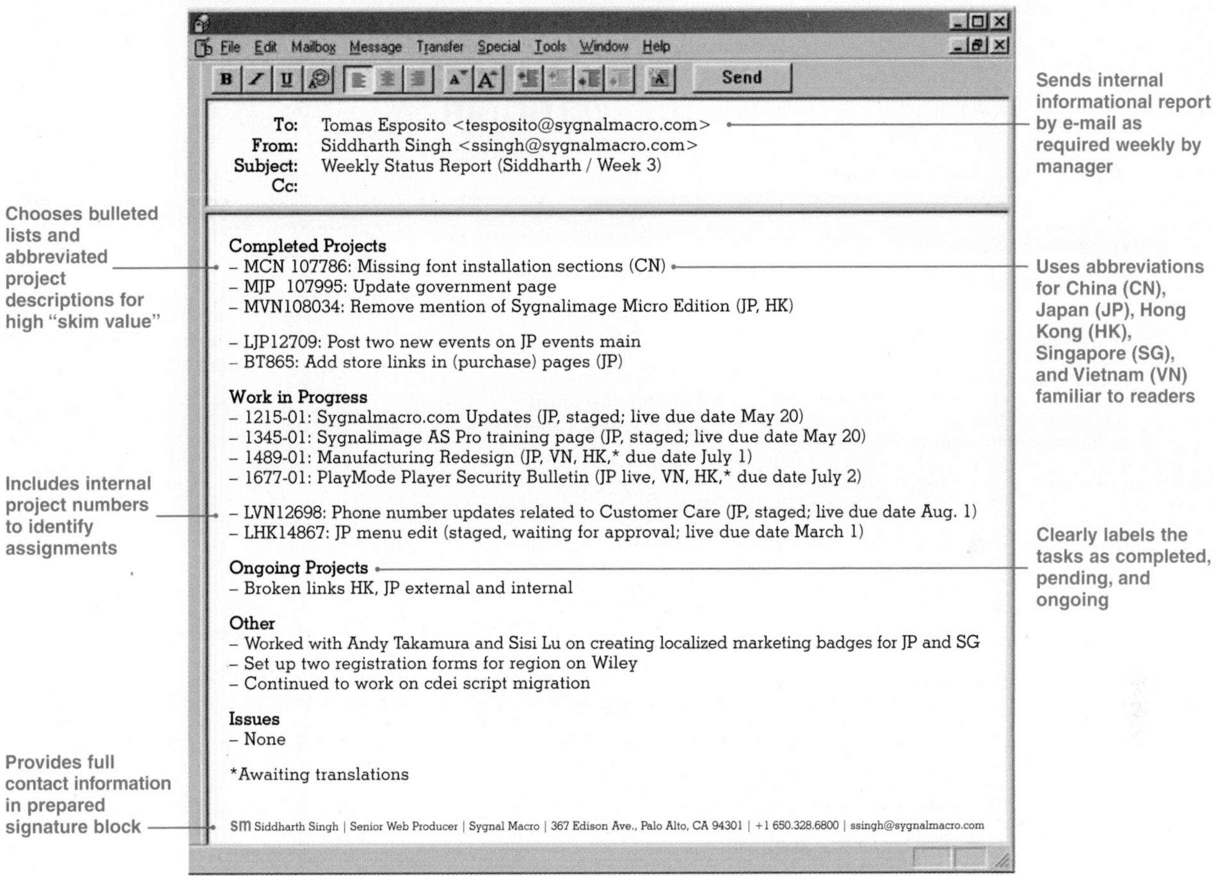

To: Tomas Esposito <tesposito@sygnalmacro.com>
From: Siddharth Singh <ssingh@sygnalmacro.com>
Subject: Weekly Status Report (Siddharth / Week 3)
Cc:

Completed Projects
- MCN 107786: Missing font installation sections (CN)
- MJP 107995: Update government page
- MVN108034: Remove mention of Sygnalimage Micro Edition (JP, HK)

- LJP12709: Post two new events on JP events main
- BT865: Add store links in (purchase) pages (JP)

Work in Progress
- 1215-01: Sygnalmacro.com Updates (JP, staged; live due date May 20)
- 1345-01: Sygnalimage AS Pro training page (JP, staged; live due date May 20)
- 1489-01: Manufacturing Redesign (JP, VN, HK,* due date July 1)
- 1677-01: PlayMode Player Security Bulletin (JP live, VN, HK,* due date July 2)

- LVN12698: Phone number updates related to Customer Care (JP, staged; live due date Aug. 1)
- LHK14867: JP menu edit (staged, waiting for approval; live due date March 1)

Ongoing Projects
- Broken links HK, JP external and internal

Other
- Worked with Andy Takamura and Sisi Lu on creating localized marketing badges for JP and SG
- Set up two registration forms for region on Wiley
- Continued to work on cdei script migration

Issues
- None

*Awaiting translations

SM Siddharth Singh | Senior Web Producer | Sygnal Macro | 367 Edison Ave., Palo Alto, CA 94301 | +1 650.328.6800 | ssingh@sygnalmacro.com

File Edit Mailbox Message Transfer Special Tools Window Help
Send
Sends internal informational report by e-mail as required weekly by manager
Chooses bulleted lists and abbreviated project descriptions for high "skim value"
Uses abbreviations for China (CN), Japan (JP), Hong Kong (HK), Singapore (SG), and Vietnam (VN) familiar to readers
Includes internal project numbers to identify assignments
Clearly labels the tasks as completed, pending, and ongoing
Provides full contact information in prepared signature block

Then simply add an introduction and closing, and your report is organized. Here is a general outline for trip, conference, and convention reports:

- Begin by identifying the event (exact date, name, and location) and previewing the topics to be discussed.
- Summarize in the body three to five main points that might benefit the reader.
- Itemize your expenses, if requested, on a separate sheet.
- Close by expressing appreciation, suggesting action to be taken, or synthesizing the value of the trip or event.

Jack Horn was recently named employment coordinator in the Human Resources Department of an electronics appliance manufacturer headquartered in central Ohio. Recognizing his lack of experience in interviewing job applicants, he asked permission to attend a one-day conference on the topic. His boss, Elizabeth Greene, encouraged Jack to attend, saying, "We all need to brush up on our interviewing techniques. Come back and tell us what you learned." When he returned, Jack wrote the conference report shown in Figure 12.8. Here is how he described its preparation: "I know my boss values brevity, so I worked hard to make my report no more than a page and a quarter. The conference saturated me with great ideas, far too many to cover in one brief report. So, I decided to discuss three topics that would be most useful to our staff. Although I had to be brief, I nonetheless wanted to provide as many details—especially about common interviewing mistakes—as possible. By the third draft, I had compressed my ideas into a manageable size without sacrificing any of the meaning."

FIGURE 12.8 Conference Report—Memo Format

//TriCom
Total HR Services
Interoffice Memo

DATE: April 22, 2011

TO: Elizabeth Greene

FROM: Jack Horn *JH*

SUBJECT: Conference on Employment Interviews

I enjoyed attending the "Interviewing People" training conference sponsored by the National Business Foundation. This one-day meeting, held in Columbus on April 19, provided excellent advice that will help us strengthen our interviewing techniques. Although the conference covered many topics, this report concentrates on three areas: structuring the interview, avoiding common mistakes, and responding to new legislation.

Identifies topic and previews how the report is organized

Structuring the Interview

Job interviews usually have three parts. The opening establishes a friendly rapport with introductions, a few polite questions, and an explanation of the purpose for the interview. The body of the interview consists of questions controlled by the interviewer. The interviewer has three goals: (a) educating the applicant about the job, (b) eliciting information about the applicant's suitability for the job, and (c) promoting goodwill about the organization. In closing, the interviewer should encourage the applicant to ask questions, summarize main points, and indicate what actions will follow.

Sets off major topics with centered headings

Avoiding Common Mistakes

Probably the most interesting and practical part of the conference centered on common mistakes made by interviewers, some of which I summarize here:

1. Not taking notes at each interview. Recording important facts enables you to remember the first candidate as easily as you remember the last—and all those in between.
2. Not testing the candidate's communication skills. To be able to evaluate a candidate's ability to express ideas, ask the individual to explain some technical jargon from his or her current position.
3. Having departing employees conduct the interviews for their replacements. Departing employees may be unreliable as interviewers because they tend to hire candidates not quite as strong as they are.
4. Failing to check references. As many as 45 percent of all résumés may contain falsified data. The best way to check references is to network: ask the person whose name has been given to suggest the name of another person.

Covers facts that will most interest and help reader

Elizabeth Greene Page 2 April 22, 2011

Responding to New Legislation

Current federal provisions of the Americans With Disabilities Act prohibit interviewers from asking candidates—or even their references—about candidates' disabilities. A question we frequently asked ("Do you have any physical limitations which would prevent you from performing the job for which you are applying?") would now break the law. Interviewers must also avoid asking about medical history; prescription drug use; prior workers' compensation claims; work absenteeism due to illness; and past treatment for alcoholism, drug use, or mental illness.

Concludes with offer to share information

Sharing This Information

This conference provided me with valuable training that I would like to share with other department members at a future staff meeting. Let me know when it can be scheduled.

Progress and Interim Reports

Continuing projects often require progress or interim reports to describe their status. These reports may be external (advising customers regarding the headway of their projects) or internal (informing management of the status of activities). Progress reports typically follow this pattern of development:

What type of information do progress and interim reports describe, and which audiences do they address?

- Specify in the opening the purpose and nature of the project.
- Provide background information if the audience requires filling in.
- Describe the work completed.
- Explain the work currently in progress, including personnel, activities, methods, and locations.
- Describe current problems and anticipate future problems and possible remedies.
- Discuss future activities and provide the expected completion date.

As a location manager for Eagle Video Productions, Gina Genova frequently writes progress reports, such as the one shown in Figure 12.9. Producers want to know what she is doing, and a phone call does not provide a permanent record. Here is how she described the reasoning behind her progress report: "I usually include background information in my reports because a director does not always know or remember exactly what specifications I was given for a location search. Then I try to hit the high points of what I have completed and what I plan to do next, without getting bogged down in tiny details. Although it would be easier to skip them, I have learned to be up front with any problems that I anticipate. I do not tell how to solve the problems, but I feel duty-bound to at least mention them."

Investigative Reports

Investigative reports deliver data for a specific situation—without offering interpretation or recommendations. These nonrecurring reports are generally arranged using the direct strategy with three segments: introduction, body, and summary. The body—which includes the facts, findings, or discussion—may be organized by time, component, importance, criteria, or convention. What is important is dividing the topic into logical segments—say, three to five areas that are roughly equal and do not overlap.

What are the main characteristics of investigative reports?

Writing Informational Reports

Introduction

- **Begin directly.** Identify the report and its purpose.
- **Provide a preview.** If the report is over a page long, give the reader a brief overview of its organization.
- **Supply background data selectively.** When readers are unfamiliar with the topic, briefly fill in the necessary details.
- **Divide the topic.** Strive to group the facts or findings into three to five roughly equal segments that do not overlap.

Body

- **Arrange the subtopics logically.** Consider organizing by time, component, importance, criteria, or convention.
- **Use clear headings.** Supply functional or talking headings (at least one per page) that describe each important section.
- **Determine degree of formality.** Use an informal, conversational writing style unless the audience expects a more formal tone.
- **Enhance readability with graphic highlighting.** Make liberal use of bullets, numbered and lettered lists, headings, underlined items, and white space.

Summary/Concluding Remarks

- **When necessary, summarize the report.** Briefly review the main points and discuss what action will follow.
- **Offer a concluding thought.** If relevant, express appreciation or describe your willingness to provide further information.

FIGURE 12.9 Progress Report

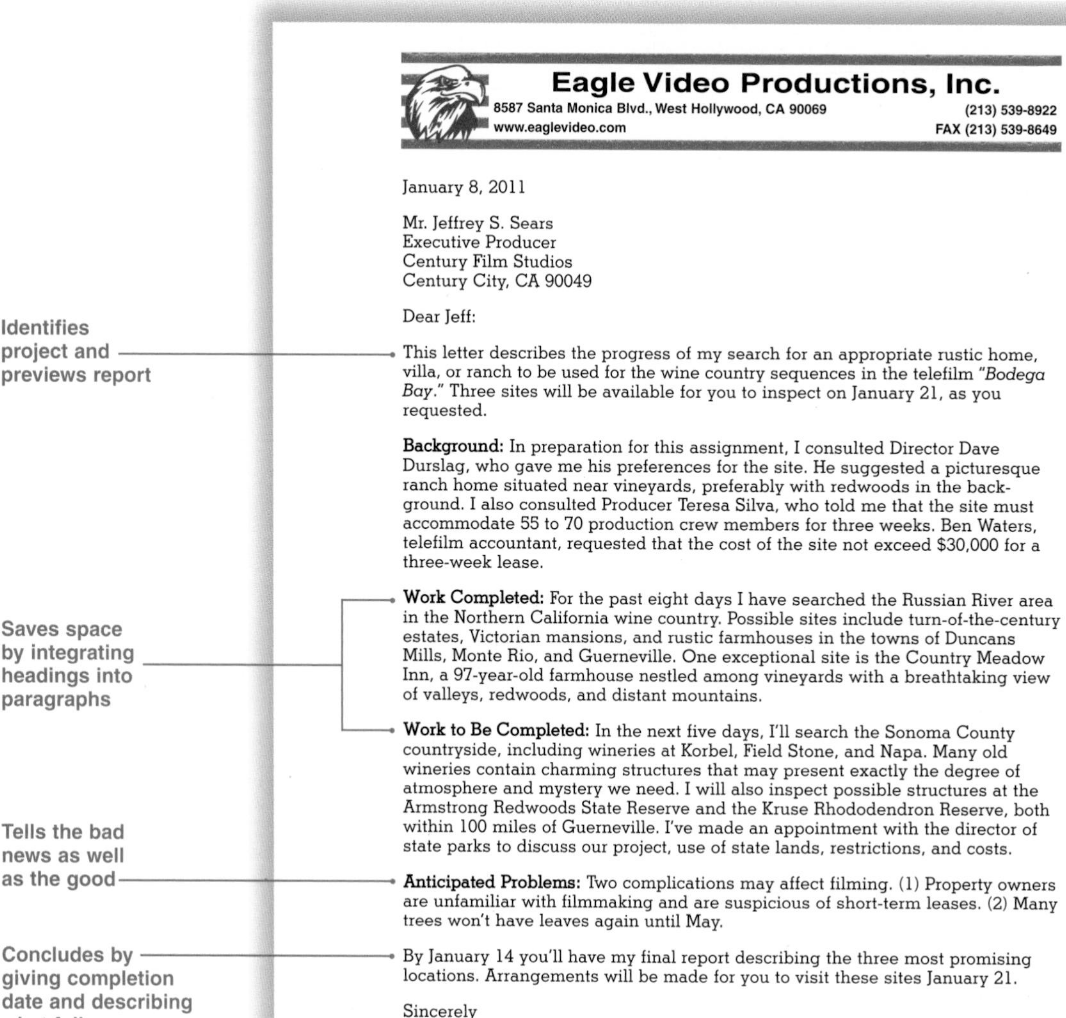

Eagle Video Productions, Inc.

8587 Santa Monica Blvd., West Hollywood, CA 90069 (213) 539-8922
www.eaglevideo.com FAX (213) 539-8649

January 8, 2011

Mr. Jeffrey S. Sears
Executive Producer
Century Film Studios
Century City, CA 90049

Dear Jeff:

This letter describes the progress of my search for an appropriate rustic home, villa, or ranch to be used for the wine country sequences in the telefilm *"Bodega Bay."* Three sites will be available for you to inspect on January 21, as you requested.

Background: In preparation for this assignment, I consulted Director Dave Durslag, who gave me his preferences for the site. He suggested a picturesque ranch home situated near vineyards, preferably with redwoods in the background. I also consulted Producer Teresa Silva, who told me that the site must accommodate 55 to 70 production crew members for three weeks. Ben Waters, telefilm accountant, requested that the cost of the site not exceed $30,000 for a three-week lease.

Work Completed: For the past eight days I have searched the Russian River area in the Northern California wine country. Possible sites include turn-of-the-century estates, Victorian mansions, and rustic farmhouses in the towns of Duncans Mills, Monte Rio, and Guerneville. One exceptional site is the Country Meadow Inn, a 97-year-old farmhouse nestled among vineyards with a breathtaking view of valleys, redwoods, and distant mountains.

Work to Be Completed: In the next five days, I'll search the Sonoma County countryside, including wineries at Korbel, Field Stone, and Napa. Many old wineries contain charming structures that may present exactly the degree of atmosphere and mystery we need. I will also inspect possible structures at the Armstrong Redwoods State Reserve and the Kruse Rhododendron Reserve, both within 100 miles of Guerneville. I've made an appointment with the director of state parks to discuss our project, use of state lands, restrictions, and costs.

Anticipated Problems: Two complications may affect filming. (1) Property owners are unfamiliar with filmmaking and are suspicious of short-term leases. (2) Many trees won't have leaves again until May.

By January 14 you'll have my final report describing the three most promising locations. Arrangements will be made for you to visit these sites January 21.

Sincerely

Gina

Gina Genova
Production Scout

Identifies project and previews report

Saves space by integrating headings into paragraphs

Tells the bad news as well as the good

Concludes by giving completion date and describing what follows

Tips for Writing Progress Reports

- Identify the purpose and the nature of the project immediately.
- Supply background information only if the reader must be educated.
- Describe the work completed.
- Discuss the work in progress, including personnel, activities, methods, and locations.
- Identify problems and possible remedies.
- Consider future activities.
- Close by telling the expected date of completion.

Zooming In — PART 2

Starbucks Perks Up: Recapturing the Soul of the Coffeehouse

Under the leadership of chairman, president, and CEO Howard Schultz, Starbucks shelved plans to expand the number of stores and to pursue other avenues of growth beyond its coffeehouse business. The recession required a new approach, "to transform Starbucks and return the company to sustainable, profitable growth while at the same time [remaining] true to our core values and guiding principles" in the words of Howard Schultz.[3]

An entrepreneur who thinks outside the box, Schultz grudgingly introduced new efficiencies to reinvigorate Starbucks. Instead of relying on his instincts and free-flowing growth, he has agreed to do advertising and follows store sales data to understand customer preferences for drinking coffee in the morning (out of necessity) as opposed to in the afternoon (when it becomes a treat). Schultz also started to pay attention to controlling costs and simplifying operations. He reluctantly standardized how baristas prepare coffee, from "anything goes" to a consistent six-step process.

Pursuing the right business strategy is difficult, and Starbucks has experienced flops. The chain scaled back its music business by handing over Hear Music, its short-lived label, to Concord Music Group. Starbucks also abandoned plans to allow customers to customize CDs in its stores and got burned by promoting at least one film that became a box office dud. The poor economy forced the company to rethink its strategy. CEO Schultz said: "We are committed to examining all aspects of our business that are not directly related to our core."[4]

As for competition, Starbucks still remains the front-runner. Specialty retailers such as Caribou Coffee—the second-largest nonfranchised coffee chain in the United States—The Coffee Bean & Tea Leaf, and Peet's Coffee & Tea are all much smaller than the market leader. However, Starbucks knows that competitors never sleep. In a lagging economy, its biggest rivals are the low-end, low-cost coffee powerhouses Dunkin' Donuts and McDonald's. Ironically, Starbucks has led the coffee revolution of the last 20 years and forced its competitors to improve their coffee quality and selection. The question now is whether the in-store experience at Starbucks is so unique that customers will pay higher prices for it. Both McDonald's and Dunkin' Donuts have taken direct potshots at Starbucks' premium prices and attitude in their advertising, eager to draw away Starbucks' customers. You will learn more about this case on page 412.

© AP Images/Seth Perlman

Critical Thinking

- How important to Starbucks are the collection, organization, and distribution of up-to-date information regarding food and beverage trends, competition, and product development?
- In what ways could Starbucks use the Internet to monitor its main competitors, Caribou Coffee, McDonald's McCafé, and Dunkin' Donuts?
- What kind of reports might employees assigned the task of monitoring Starbucks' competition write to management?

The subject matter of the report usually suggests the best way to divide or organize it. Beth Givens, an information specialist for a Minneapolis health care consulting firm, was given the task of researching and writing an investigative report for St. John's Hospital. Her assignment: study the award-winning patient service program at Good Samaritan Hospital and report how it improved its patient satisfaction rating from 6.2 to 7.8 in just one year. Beth collected data and then organized her findings into four parts: management training, employee training, patient services, and follow-up program. Although we do not show Beth's complete report here, you can see a similar informational report in Chapter 11, Figure 11.2.

Whether you are writing a periodic, trip, conference, progress, or investigative report, you will want to review the suggestions found in the accompanying checklist.

Preparing Short Analytical Reports

LEARNING OBJECTIVE 5
Compose short analytical reports that solve business problems.

Analytical reports differ significantly from informational reports. Although both seek to collect and present data clearly, analytical reports also analyze the data and typically try to persuade the reader to accept the conclusions and act on the recommendations. Informational reports emphasize facts; analytical reports emphasize reasoning and conclusions.

What purpose do analytical reports serve, and how do they present information?

For some readers you may organize analytical reports directly with the conclusions and recommendations near the beginning. Directness is appropriate when the reader has confidence in the writer, based on either experience or credentials. Frontloading the recommendations also works when the topic is routine or familiar and the reader is supportive.

Directness can backfire, though. If you announce the recommendations too quickly, the reader may immediately object to a single idea. You may have had no suspicion that this idea would trigger a negative reaction. Once the reader is opposed, changing an unfavorable mind-set may be difficult or impossible. A reader may also think you have oversimplified or overlooked something significant if you lay out all the recommendations before explaining how you arrived at them. When you must lead the reader through the process of discovering the solution or recommendation, use the indirect strategy: present conclusions and recommendations last.

Most analytical reports answer questions about specific problems and aid in decision making. How can we use a Web site most effectively? Should we close the El Paso plant? Should we buy or lease company cars? How can we improve customer service? Three typical analytical reports answer business questions: justification/recommendation reports, feasibility reports, and yardstick reports. Because these reports all solve problems, the categories are not mutually exclusive. What distinguishes them are their goals and organization.

Ethics Check

Is This $100 Bill Yours?

Purchasing managers at Frito-Lay, Safeway, and B&G Foods have pleaded guilty to taking bribes that led to tainted foods purchased at inflated prices. Company officials relied on false reports and documentation supplied by their managers. How did food suppliers know whom to bribe? New Jersey businessman and food broker Randall Rahal said he could guess who would be susceptible to bribery by dropping a $100 bill on the floor, then picking it up and saying, "You must have dropped this. Is it yours?" Is this a good test?

Justification/Recommendation Reports

Both managers and employees must occasionally write reports that justify or recommend something, such as buying equipment, changing a procedure, hiring an employee, consolidating departments, or investing funds. These reports may also be called *internal proposals* because their persuasive nature is similar to that of external proposals (presented in Chapter 13). Large organizations sometimes prescribe how these reports should be organized; they use forms with conventional headings. When you are free to select an organizational plan yourself, however, let your audience and topic determine your choice of the direct or indirect strategy.

When would you follow the direct strategy in a justification/recommendation report, and when would you choose the indirect strategy?

Direct Strategy. For nonsensitive topics and recommendations that will be agreeable to readers, you can organize directly according to the following sequence:

- Identify the problem or need briefly.
- Announce the recommendation, solution, or action concisely and with action verbs.

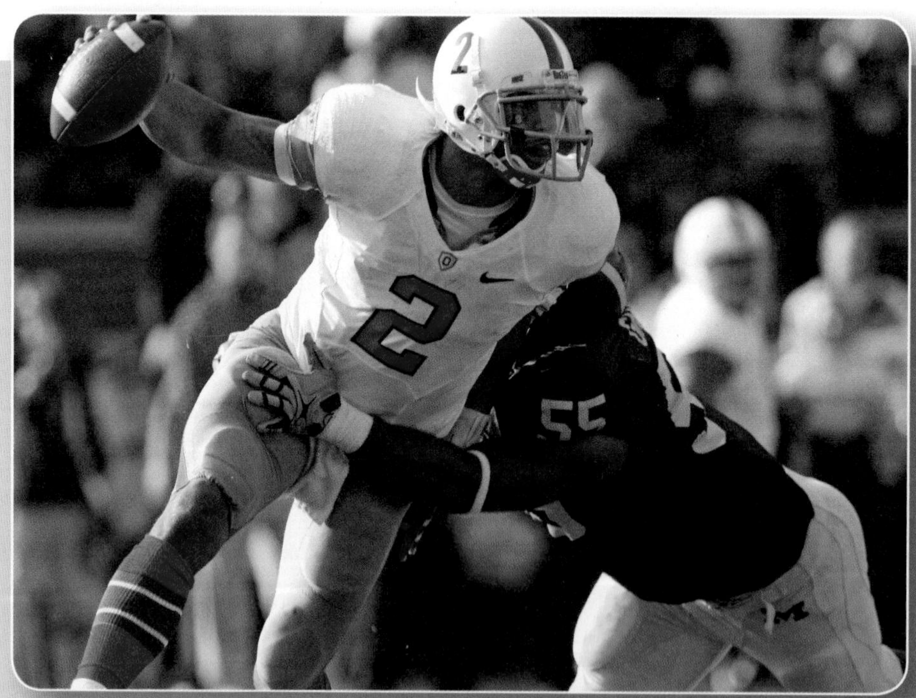

© AP Images/Tony Ding

The Big Ten Conference may soon grow to twelve or more teams, if officials adopt a recent recommendation report by investment firm William Blair & Company. In examining whether league expansion would be profitable, the report concluded that adding teams like Rutgers, Syracuse, or Notre Dame would boost the $22 million in annual revenue that universities receive from league play. Notably, the recommended expansion would include a Big Ten title game to generate $15 million in the postseason. *What are the key elements of a persuasive justification report?*

- Explain more fully the benefits of the recommendation or steps necessary to solve the problem.
- Include a discussion of pros, cons, and costs.
- Conclude with a summary specifying the recommendation and necessary action.

Here is how Cory Black applied the process in justifying a purchase. Cory is operations manager in charge of a fleet of trucks for a large parcel delivery company in Atlanta. When he heard about a new Goodyear smart tire with an electronic chip, Cory thought his company should give the new tire a try. Because new tires would represent an irregular purchase and because they would require a pilot test, he wrote the justification/recommendation report shown in Figure 12.10 to his boss. Cory described his report in this way: "As more and more parcel delivery companies crop up, we have to find ways to cut costs so that we can remain competitive. Although more expensive initially, smart tires may solve many of our problems and save us money in the long run. I knew Jim Jordan, operations vice president, would be interested in them, especially in view of a recent Toyo truck tire recall and the huge Firestone tire fiasco that is still a vivid memory.[5] Because Jim would be most interested in what the smart tires could do for us, I concentrated on benefits. In my first draft, the benefits were lost in a couple of long paragraphs. Only after I read what I had written did I see that I was really talking about four separate benefits. Then I looked for words to summarize each one as a heading. So that Jim would know exactly what he should do, I concluded with specifics. All he had to do was say 'Go.'"

Indirect Strategy. When a reader may oppose a recommendation or when circumstances suggest caution, do not rush to reveal your recommendation. Consider using the following sequence for an indirect approach to your recommendations:

- Refer to the problem in general terms, not to your recommendation, in the subject line.
- Describe the problem or need your recommendation addresses. Use specific examples, supporting statistics, and authoritative quotes to lend credibility to the seriousness of the problem.
- Discuss alternative solutions, beginning with the least likely to succeed.
- Present the most promising alternative (your recommendation) last.
- Show how the advantages of your recommendation outweigh its disadvantages.
- Summarize your recommendation. If appropriate, specify the action it requires.
- Ask for authorization to proceed if necessary.

Why is it important to footnote or otherwise document sources in justification/recommendation reports?

Lara Brown, an executive assistant at a large petroleum and mining company in Grand Prairie, Texas, received a challenging research assignment. Her boss, the director of Human Resources, asked her to investigate ways to persuade employees to quit smoking. Here is how she described her task: "We banned smoking many years ago inside our buildings, but we never tried very hard to get smokers to actually kick their habits. My job was to gather information about the problem and learn how other companies have helped workers stop smoking. The report would go to my boss, but I knew he would pass it along to the management council for approval. If the report were just for my boss, I would put my recommendation right up front, because I'm sure he would support it. But the management council is another story. They need persuasion because of the costs involved—and because some of them are smokers. Therefore, I put the alternative I favored last. To gain credibility, I footnoted my sources. I had enough material for a ten-page report, but I kept it to two pages in keeping with our company report policy."

Lara single-spaced her report, shown in Figure 12.11, because her company prefers this style. Some companies prefer the readability of double spacing. Be sure to check with your organization for its preference before printing your reports.

Feasibility Reports

What is the purpose of feasibility reports?

Feasibility reports examine the practicality and advisability of following a course of action. They answer this question: Will this plan or proposal work? Feasibility reports typically are internal reports written to advise on matters such as consolidating departments, offering a wellness

FIGURE 12.10 Justification/Recommendation Report—Memo Format

Prewriting

Analyze: The purpose of this report is to persuade the manager to authorize the purchase and pilot testing of smart tires.

Anticipate: The audience is a manager who is familiar with operations but not with this product. He will probably be receptive to the recommendation.

Adapt: Present the report data in a direct, straightforward manner.

Writing

Research: Collect data on how smart tires could benefit operations.

Organize: Discuss the problem briefly. Introduce and justify the recommendation by noting its cost-effectiveness and paperwork benefits. Explain the benefits of smart tires. Describe the action to be taken.

Compose: Write and print first draft.

Revising

Revise: Revise to break up long paragraphs about benefits. Isolate each benefit in an enumerated list with headings.

Proofread: Double-check all figures. Be sure all headings are parallel.

Evaluate: Does this report make its request concisely but emphatically? Will the reader see immediately what action is required?

DATE: July 19, 2011

TO: Jim Jordan

FROM: Cory Black, Operations Manager *CB*

SUBJECT: Goodyear Smart Tires—Pilot Test

Next to fuel, truck tires are our biggest operating cost. Last year we spent $236,000 replacing and retreading tires for 495 trucks. This year the costs will be greater because prices have jumped at least 12 percent and because we have increased our fleet to 550 trucks. Truck tires are an additional burden because they require labor-intensive paperwork to track their warranties, wear, and retread histories. To reduce our long-term costs and to improve our tire tracking system, I recommend that we do the following:

Introduces problem briefly

- Purchase 24 Goodyear smart tires.
- Begin a one-year pilot test on six trucks.

Presents recommendations immediately

How Smart Tires Work

Smart tires have an embedded computer chip that monitors wear, performance, and durability. The chip also creates an electronic fingerprint for positive identification of a tire. By passing a handheld sensor next to the tire, we can learn where and when a tire was made (for warranty and other identification), how much tread it had originally, and its serial number.

How Smart Tires Could Benefit Us

Although smart tires are initially more expensive than other tires, they could help us improve our operations and save us money in four ways:

Justifies recommendation by explaining product and benefits

1. **Retreads.** Goodyear believes that the wear data is so accurate that we should be able to retread every tire three times, instead of our current two times. If that's true, in one year we could save at least $27,000 in new tire costs.
2. **Safety.** Accurate and accessible wear data should reduce the danger of blowouts and flat tires. Last year, drivers reported six blowouts.
3. **Record keeping and maintenance.** Smart tires could reduce our maintenance costs considerably. Currently, we use an electric branding iron to mark serial numbers on new tires. Our biggest headache is manually reading those serial numbers, decoding them, and maintaining records to meet safety regulations. Reading such data electronically could save us thousands of dollars in labor.
4. **Theft protection.** The chip can be used to monitor each tire as it leaves or enters the warehouse or yard, thus discouraging theft.

Enumerates items for maximum impact and readability

Summary and Action

Specifically, I recommend that you do the following:

- Authorize the special purchase of 24 Goodyear smart tires at $500 each, plus one electronic sensor at $1,500.
- Approve a one-year pilot test in our Atlanta territory that equips six trucks with smart tires and tracks their performance.

Explains recommendation in more detail

Specifies action to be taken

FIGURE 12.11 Justification/Recommendation Report, MLA Style

DATE: October 11, 2011

TO: Gordon McClure, Director, Human Resources

FROM: Lara Brown, Executive Assistant *LB*

SUBJECT: Smoking Cessation Programs for Employees

At your request, I have examined measures that encourage employees to quit smoking. As company records show, approximately 23 percent of our employees still smoke, despite the antismoking and clean-air policies we adopted in 2009. To collect data for this report, I studied professional and government publications; I also inquired at companies and clinics about stop-smoking programs.

Introduces purpose of report, tells method of data collection, and previews organization

Avoids revealing recommendation immediately

This report presents data describing the significance of the problem, three alternative solutions, and a recommendation based on my investigation.

Uses headings that combine function and description

Significance of Problem: Health Care and Productivity Losses

Employees who smoke are costly to any organization. The following statistics show the effects of smoking for workers and for organizations:

- Absenteeism is 40 to 50 percent greater among smoking employees.
- Accidents are two to three times greater among smokers.
- Bronchitis, lung and heart disease, cancer, and early death are more frequent among smokers (Arhelger 4).

Documents data sources for credibility, uses MLA style citing author and page number in the text

Although our clean-air policy prohibits smoking in the building, shop, and office, we have done little to encourage employees to stop smoking. Many workers still go outside to smoke at lunch and breaks. Other companies have been far more proactive in their attempts to stop employee smoking. Many companies have found that persuading employees to stop smoking was a decisive factor in reducing their health insurance premiums. Below is a discussion of three common stop-smoking measures tried by other companies, along with a projected cost factor for each (Rindfleisch 4).

Discuss least effective alternative first

Alternative 1: Literature and Events

The least expensive and easiest stop-smoking measure involves the distribution of literature, such as "The Ten-Step Plan" from Smokefree Enterprises and government pamphlets citing smoking dangers. Some companies have also sponsored events such as the Great American Smoke-Out, a one-day occasion intended to develop group spirit in spurring smokers to quit. "Studies show, however," says one expert, "that literature and company-sponsored events have little permanent effect in helping smokers quit" (Mendel 108).

Cost: Negligible

program to employees, or hiring an outside firm to handle a company's accounting or computing operations. These reports may also be written by consultants called in to investigate a problem. The focus in these reports is on the decision: rejecting or proceeding with the proposed option. Because your role is not to persuade the reader to accept the decision, you will want to present the decision immediately. In writing feasibility reports, consider these suggestions:

- Announce your decision immediately.
- Provide a description of the background and problem necessitating the proposal.
- Discuss the benefits of the proposal.
- Describe the problems that may result.
- Calculate the costs associated with the proposal, if appropriate.
- Show the time frame necessary for implementing the proposal.

FIGURE 12.11 **(Continued)**

Gordon McClure October 11, 2011 Page 2

Alternative 2: Stop-Smoking Programs Outside the Workplace

Local clinics provide treatment programs in classes at their centers. Here in Houston we have the Smokers' Treatment Center, ACC Motivation Center, and New-Choice Program for Stopping Smoking. These behavior-modification stop-smoking programs are acknowledged to be more effective than literature distribution or incentive programs. However, studies of companies using off-workplace programs show that many employees fail to attend regularly and do not complete the programs.

Cost: $1,200 per employee, three-month individual program (New-Choice Program)
$900 per employee, three-month group session

Highlights costs for easy comparison

Alternative 3: Stop-Smoking Programs at the Workplace

Many clinics offer workplace programs with counselors meeting employees in company conference rooms. These programs have the advantage of keeping a firm's employees together so that they develop a group spirit and exert pressure on each other to succeed. The most successful programs are on company premises and also on company time. Employees participating in such programs had a 72 percent greater success record than employees attending the same stop-smoking program at an outside clinic (Honda 35). A disadvantage of this arrangement, of course, is lost work time—amounting to about two hours a week for three months.

Arranges alternatives so that most effective is last

Cost: $900 per employee, three-month program for two hours per week release time for three months

Conclusions and Recommendation

Summarizes findings and ends with specific recommendation

Smokers require discipline, counseling, and professional assistance in kicking the nicotine habit, as explained at the University of Michigan Health System Web site (Guide to Quitting Smoking). Workplace stop-smoking programs on company time are more effective than literature, incentives, and off-workplace programs. If our goal is to reduce health care costs and lead our employees to healthful lives, we should invest in a workplace stop-smoking program with release time for smokers. Although the program temporarily reduces productivity, we can expect to recapture that loss in lower health care premiums and healthier employees.

Therefore, I recommend that we begin a stop-smoking treatment program on company premises with two hours per week of release time for participants for three months.

Reveals recommendation only after discussing all alternatives

Lists all references in MLA Style

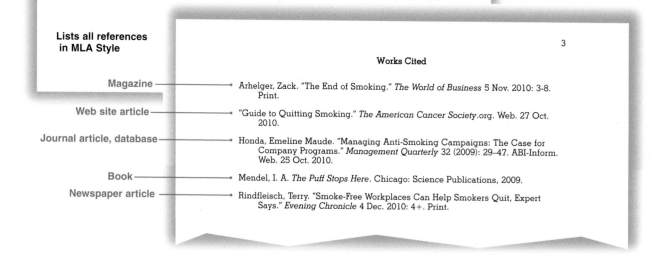

3

Works Cited

Magazine — Arhelger, Zack. "The End of Smoking." *The World of Business* 5 Nov. 2010: 3-8. Print.

Web site article — "Guide to Quitting Smoking." *The American Cancer Society*.org. Web. 27 Oct. 2010.

Journal article, database — Honda, Emeline Maude. "Managing Anti-Smoking Campaigns: The Case for Company Programs." *Management Quarterly* 32 (2009): 29–47. ABI-Inform. Web. 25 Oct. 2010.

Book — Mendel, I. A. *The Puff Stops Here*. Chicago: Science Publications, 2009.

Newspaper article — Rindfleisch, Terry. "Smoke-Free Workplaces Can Help Smokers Quit, Expert Says." *Evening Chronicle* 4 Dec. 2010: 4+. Print.

Ashley Denton-Tait, human resources manager for a large public accounting firm in San Antonio, Texas, wrote the feasibility report shown in Figure 12.12. Because she discovered that the company was losing time and money as a result of personal e-mail and Internet use by employees, she talked with the vice president, Eileen Heffernan, about the problem. Eileen didn't want Ashley to take time away from her job to investigate what other companies were doing to prevent this type of problem. Instead, she suggested that they hire a consultant to investigate what other companies were doing to prevent or limit personal e-mail and Internet use. The vice president then wanted to know whether the consultant's plan was feasible. Although Ashley's report is only one page long, it provides all the necessary information: background, benefits, employee acceptance, costs, and time frame.

What are the components of a typical feasibility report?

Yardstick Reports

What is a yardstick report, and what purpose does it serve?

Yardstick reports examine problems with two or more solutions. To determine the best solution, the writer establishes criteria by which to compare the alternatives. The criteria then act as a yardstick against which all the alternatives are measured. The yardstick approach is effective

FIGURE 12.12 Feasibility Report—Memo Format

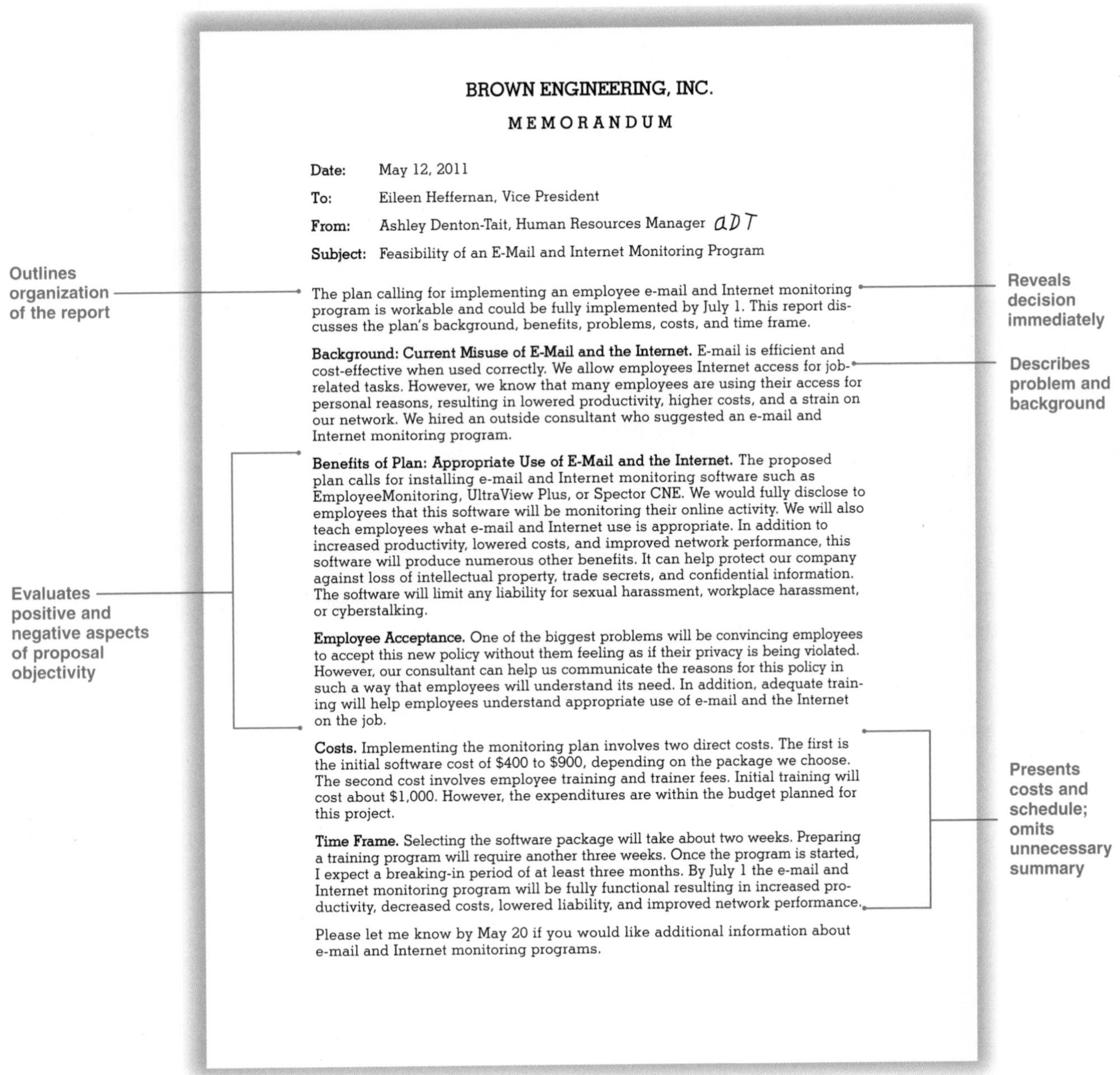
BROWN ENGINEERING, INC.

MEMORANDUM

Date: May 12, 2011

To: Eileen Heffernan, Vice President

From: Ashley Denton-Tait, Human Resources Manager *ADT*

Subject: Feasibility of an E-Mail and Internet Monitoring Program

The plan calling for implementing an employee e-mail and Internet monitoring program is workable and could be fully implemented by July 1. This report discusses the plan's background, benefits, problems, costs, and time frame.

Background: Current Misuse of E-Mail and the Internet. E-mail is efficient and cost-effective when used correctly. We allow employees Internet access for job-related tasks. However, we know that many employees are using their access for personal reasons, resulting in lowered productivity, higher costs, and a strain on our network. We hired an outside consultant who suggested an e-mail and Internet monitoring program.

Benefits of Plan: Appropriate Use of E-Mail and the Internet. The proposed plan calls for installing e-mail and Internet monitoring software such as EmployeeMonitoring, UltraView Plus, or Spector CNE. We would fully disclose to employees that this software will be monitoring their online activity. We will also teach employees what e-mail and Internet use is appropriate. In addition to increased productivity, lowered costs, and improved network performance, this software will produce numerous other benefits. It can help protect our company against loss of intellectual property, trade secrets, and confidential information. The software will limit any liability for sexual harassment, workplace harassment, or cyberstalking.

Employee Acceptance. One of the biggest problems will be convincing employees to accept this new policy without them feeling as if their privacy is being violated. However, our consultant can help us communicate the reasons for this policy in such a way that employees will understand its need. In addition, adequate training will help employees understand appropriate use of e-mail and the Internet on the job.

Costs. Implementing the monitoring plan involves two direct costs. The first is the initial software cost of $400 to $900, depending on the package we choose. The second cost involves employee training and trainer fees. Initial training will cost about $1,000. However, the expenditures are within the budget planned for this project.

Time Frame. Selecting the software package will take about two weeks. Preparing a training program will require another three weeks. Once the program is started, I expect a breaking-in period of at least three months. By July 1 the e-mail and Internet monitoring program will be fully functional resulting in increased productivity, decreased costs, lowered liability, and improved network performance.

Please let me know by May 20 if you would like additional information about e-mail and Internet monitoring programs.

Outlines organization of the report
Reveals decision immediately
Describes problem and background
Evaluates positive and negative aspects of proposal objectivity
Presents costs and schedule; omits unnecessary summary

for companies that must establish specifications for equipment purchases and then compare each manufacturer's product with the established specs. The yardstick approach is also effective when exact specifications cannot be established.

For example, before Nissan Motor Company decided to move its U.S. headquarters from Los Angeles to Franklin, Tennessee, the No. 8 global carmaker evaluated several sites, including Dallas, Texas, and multiple locations in the Nashville, Tennessee, region. For each site, Nissan compared tax incentives, real estate and utility costs, workforce education levels, proximity to its existing plant in Smyrna (Tennessee), and other criteria that would allow the company to save money.[6]

The real advantage to yardstick reports is that alternatives can be measured consistently using the same criteria. Writers using a yardstick approach typically do the following:

- Begin by describing the problem or need.
- Explain possible solutions and alternatives.
- Establish criteria for comparing the alternatives; tell how the criteria were selected or developed.
- Discuss and evaluate each alternative in terms of the criteria.
- Draw conclusions and make recommendations.

Jenny Gomez, benefits administrator for computer manufacturer CompuTech, was called on to write a report comparing outplacement agencies. These agencies counsel discharged employees and help them find new positions; fees are paid by the former employer. Jenny knew that times were bad for CompuTech and that extensive downsizing would take place in the next two years. Her task was to compare outplacement agencies and recommend one to CompuTech.

After collecting information, Jenny found that her biggest problem was organizing the data and developing a system for making comparisons. All the outplacement agencies she investigated seemed to offer the same basic package of services. Here is how she described her report, shown in Figure 12.13:

How can grids help you when you are writing a yardstick report?

> *"With the information I gathered about three outplacement agencies, I made a big grid listing the names of the agencies across the top. Down the side I listed general categories—such as services, costs, and reputation. Then I filled in the information for each agency. This grid, which began to look like a table, helped me organize all the bits and pieces of information. After studying the grid, I saw that all the information could be grouped into four categories: counseling services, administrative and research assistance, reputation, and costs. I made these the criteria I would use to compare agencies. Next, I divided my grid into two parts, which became Table 1 and Table 2. In writing the report, I could have made each agency a separate heading, followed by a discussion of how it measured up to the criteria. Immediately, though, I saw how repetitious that would become. So I used the criteria as headings and discussed how each agency met each criterion—or failed to meet it. Making a recommendation was easy once I had made the tables and could see how the agencies compared."*

Want to do well on tests and excel in your course? Go to **www.meguffey.com** for helpful interactive resources.

- **Review the Chapter 12 PowerPoint slides to prepare for the first quiz.**

FIGURE 12.13 Yardstick Report

DATE: April 28, 2011

TO: Graham T. Burnett, Vice President

FROM: Jenny Gomez, Benefits Administrator JG

SUBJECT: Selecting Outplacement Services

Introduces purpose and gives overview of report organization

Here is the report you requested April 1 investigating the possibility of CompuTech's use of outplacement services. It discusses the problem of counseling services for discharged staff and establishes criteria for selecting an outplacement agency. It then evaluates three prospective agencies and presents a recommendation based on that evaluation.

Problem: Counseling Discharged Staff

Discusses background briefly because readers already know the problem

In an effort to reduce costs and increase competitiveness, CompuTech will begin a program of staff reduction that will involve releasing up to 20 percent of our workforce over the next 12 to 24 months. Many of these employees have been with us for ten or more years, and they are not being released for performance faults. These employees deserve a severance package that includes counseling and assistance in finding new careers.

Uses dual headings, giving function and description

Solution and Alternatives: Outplacement Agencies

Announces solution and the alternatives it presents

Numerous outplacement agencies offer discharged employees counseling and assistance in locating new careers. This assistance minimizes not only the negative feelings related to job loss but also the very real possibility of litigation. Potentially expensive lawsuits have been lodged against some companies by unhappy employees who felt they were unfairly released.

In seeking an outplacement agency, we should find one that offers advice to the sponsoring company as well as to dischargees. Frankly, many of our managers need help in conducting termination sessions. The law now requires certain procedures, especially in releasing employees over forty. CompuTech could unwittingly become liable to lawsuits because our managers are uninformed of these procedures. Here in the metropolitan area, I have located three potential outplacement agencies appropriate to serve our needs: Gray & Associates, Right Access, and Careers Plus.

Establishing Criteria for Selecting Agency

Tells how criteria were selected

In order to choose among the three agencies, I established criteria based on professional articles, discussions with officials at other companies using outplacement agencies, and interviews with agencies. Here are the four groups of criteria I used in evaluating the three agencies:

Creates four criteria for use as yardstick in evaluating alternatives

1. Counseling services—including job search advice, résumé help, crisis management, corporate counseling, and availability of full-time counselors
2. Administrative and research assistance—including availability of administrative staff, librarian, and personal computers
3. Reputation—based on a telephone survey of former clients and listing with a professional association
4. Costs—for both group programs and executive services

FIGURE 12.13 (Continued)

Vice President Burnett   Page 2   April 28, 2011

Discussion: Evaluating Agencies by Criteria

Each agency was evaluated using the four criteria just described. Data comparing the first three criteria are summarized in Table 1.

Table 1

A COMPARISON OF SERVICES AND REPUTATIONS FOR THREE LOCAL OUTPLACEMENT AGENCIES

	Gray & Associates	Right Access	Careers Plus
Counseling services			
Résumé advice	Yes	Yes	Yes
Crisis management	Yes	No	Yes
Corporate counseling	Yes	No	No
Full-time counselors	Yes	No	Yes
Administrative, research assistance			
Administrative staff	Yes	Yes	Yes
Librarian, research library	Yes	No	Yes
Personal computers	Yes	No	Yes
Listed by National Association of Career Consultants	Yes	No	Yes
Reputation (telephone survey of former clients)	Excellent	Good	Excellent

Counseling Services

All three agencies offered similar basic counseling services with job-search and résumé advice. They differed, however, in three significant areas.

Right Access does not offer crisis management, a service that puts the discharged employee in contact with a counselor the same day the employee is released. Experts in the field consider this service especially important to help the dischargee begin "bonding" with the counselor immediately. Immediate counseling also helps the dischargee through the most traumatic moments of one of life's great disappointments and helps him or her learn how to break the news to family members. Crisis management can be instrumental in reducing lawsuits because dischargees immediately begin to focus on career planning instead of concentrating on their pain and need for revenge. Moreover, Right Access does not employ full-time counselors; it hires part-timers according to demand. Industry authorities advise against using agencies whose staff members are inexperienced and employed on an "as-needed" basis.

In addition, neither Right Access nor Careers Plus offers regular corporate counseling, which I feel is critical in training our managers to conduct terminal interviews. Careers Plus, however, suggested that it could schedule special workshops if desired.

Administrative and Research Assistance

Both Gray & Associates and Careers Plus offer complete administrative services and personal computers. Dischargees have access to staff and equipment to assist them in their job searches. These agencies also provide research libraries, librarians, and databases of company information to help in securing interviews.

Places table close to spot where it is first mentioned

Summarizes complex data in table for easy reading and reference

Highlights the similarities and differences among the alternatives

Does not repeat obvious data from table

FIGURE 12.13 (Continued)

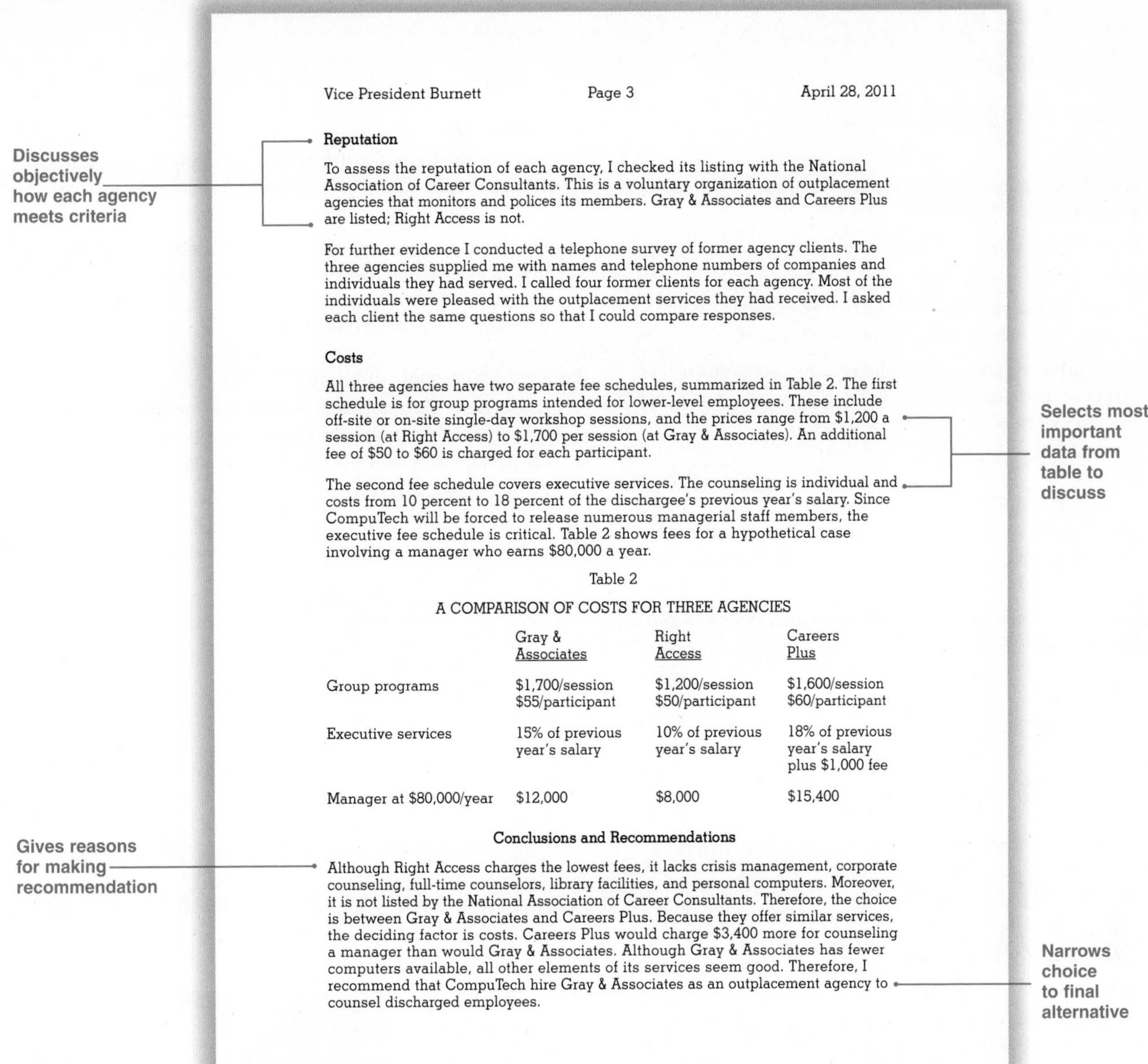

Discusses objectively how each agency meets criteria
Selects most important data from table to discuss
Gives reasons for making recommendation
Narrows choice to final alternative

Vice President Burnett Page 3 April 28, 2011

Reputation

To assess the reputation of each agency, I checked its listing with the National Association of Career Consultants. This is a voluntary organization of outplacement agencies that monitors and polices its members. Gray & Associates and Careers Plus are listed; Right Access is not.

For further evidence I conducted a telephone survey of former agency clients. The three agencies supplied me with names and telephone numbers of companies and individuals they had served. I called four former clients for each agency. Most of the individuals were pleased with the outplacement services they had received. I asked each client the same questions so that I could compare responses.

Costs

All three agencies have two separate fee schedules, summarized in Table 2. The first schedule is for group programs intended for lower-level employees. These include off-site or on-site single-day workshop sessions, and the prices range from $1,200 a session (at Right Access) to $1,700 per session (at Gray & Associates). An additional fee of $50 to $60 is charged for each participant.

The second fee schedule covers executive services. The counseling is individual and costs from 10 percent to 18 percent of the dischargee's previous year's salary. Since CompuTech will be forced to release numerous managerial staff members, the executive fee schedule is critical. Table 2 shows fees for a hypothetical case involving a manager who earns $80,000 a year.

Table 2

A COMPARISON OF COSTS FOR THREE AGENCIES

	Gray & Associates	Right Access	Careers Plus
Group programs	$1,700/session $55/participant	$1,200/session $50/participant	$1,600/session $60/participant
Executive services	15% of previous year's salary	10% of previous year's salary	18% of previous year's salary plus $1,000 fee
Manager at $80,000/year	$12,000	$8,000	$15,400

Conclusions and Recommendations

Although Right Access charges the lowest fees, it lacks crisis management, corporate counseling, full-time counselors, library facilities, and personal computers. Moreover, it is not listed by the National Association of Career Consultants. Therefore, the choice is between Gray & Associates and Careers Plus. Because they offer similar services, the deciding factor is costs. Careers Plus would charge $3,400 more for counseling a manager than would Gray & Associates. Although Gray & Associates has fewer computers available, all other elements of its services seem good. Therefore, I recommend that CompuTech hire Gray & Associates as an outplacement agency to counsel discharged employees.

Checklist

Writing Analytical Reports

Introduction

- **Identify the purpose of the report.** Explain why the report is being written.
- **Describe the significance of the topic.** Explain why the report is important.
- **Preview the organization of the report.** Especially for long reports, explain how the report will be organized.
- **Summarize the conclusions and recommendations for receptive audiences.** Use the direct strategy only if you have the confidence of the reader.

Findings

- **Discuss pros and cons.** In recommendation/justification reports, evaluate the advantages and disadvantages of each alternative. For unreceptive audiences consider placing the recommended alternative last.
- **Establish criteria to evaluate alternatives.** In yardstick reports, create criteria to use in measuring each alternative consistently.
- **Support the findings with evidence.** Supply facts, statistics, expert opinion, survey data, and other proof from which you can draw logical conclusions.
- **Organize the findings for logic and readability.** Arrange the findings around the alternatives or the reasons leading to the conclusion. Use headings, enumerations, lists, tables, and graphics to focus emphasis.

Conclusions/Recommendations

- **Draw reasonable conclusions from the findings.** Develop conclusions that answer the research question. Justify the conclusions with highlights from the findings.
- **Make recommendations, if asked.** For multiple recommendations prepare a list. Use action verbs. Explain fully the benefits of the recommendation or steps necessary to solve the problem or answer the question.

Zooming In

YOUR TURN

Applying Your Skills at Starbucks

In an attempt to infuse his company with fresh ideas and reinvigorate the Starbucks experience, CEO Howard Schultz went back to basics—to the coffee chain's heady beginnings. He turned to current Starbucks employees and asked them to reinvent a new, improved coffeehouse. The result was the opening of several concept stores in Seattle under different names, not under the famous Starbucks banner, one of the most recognized brands in the world.

Schultz had asked a handpicked group of employees: If you were going to open a store to compete with Starbucks, how would you do it? The team received a moderate budget and was free to improvise. The concept of 15th Ave. Coffee & Tea was born. This new Seattle coffeehouse features reused, recycled, and locally sourced design elements and furnishings. It was inspired by Starbucks and even sells Starbucks brand products, but the materials are raw and repurposed to create the vibe of a neighborhood store. Gone are the automated espresso machines that Schultz has always scorned. The food is baked locally. The same philosophy was brought to bear on Seattle's Roy Street Coffee & Tea, another highly customized take on the original Starbucks concept. Schultz is proud of the Starbucks partners' creativity: "It reminds me of the early days, when we were fighting for survival, for respect. To me this hearkens back to when we were at our best."[7]

Both new creations are in line with Schultz's latest "green" initiative. The Starbucks CEO is pursuing the ambitious goal to have all new company-owned stores worldwide LEED-certified beginning in late 2010. LEED, short for Leadership in Energy and Environmental Design, was established by the U.S. Green Building Council and applied originally to energy-efficient office buildings. Starbucks seems bent on leading the field in environmental stewardship.

© AP Images/Seth Perlman

Your Task

As assistant to Howard Schultz, you are asked to form two research teams. One is to study the feasibility of creating additional environmentally sound, locally sourced concept stores. The Starbucks CEO is considering this back-to-basics approach for cities other than Seattle. The other team must decide whether to recommend phasing out Starbucks Entertainment, the label under which the coffee chain is offering music, books, and films to its customers.

http://www.starbucks.com

Summary of Learning Objectives

1 Tabulate information, use statistical techniques, and create decision matrices to sort and interpret business report data skillfully and accurately. Report data are more meaningful when sorted into tables or when analyzed by mean (the arithmetic average), median (the midpoint in a group of figures), and mode (the most frequent response). Range represents a span between the highest and lowest figures. Grids help organize complex data into rows and columns. Decision matrices employ a special grid with weights to help decision makers choose objectively among complex options. Accuracy in applying statistical techniques is crucial to gain and maintain credibility with the reader.

2 Draw meaningful conclusions and make practical report recommendations after sound and valid analysis. Conclusions tell what the survey data mean—especially in relation to the original report problem. They interpret key findings and may attempt to explain what caused the report problem. They are usually enumerated. In reports that call for recommendations, writers make specific suggestions for actions that can solve the report problem. Recommendations should be feasible, practical, and potentially agreeable to the audience. They should all relate to the initial problem. Recommendations may be combined with conclusions.

3 Organize report data logically and provide cues to aid comprehension. Reports may be organized in many ways, including by (a) time (establishing a chronology or history of events), (b) component (discussing a problem by geography, division, or product), (c) importance (arranging data from most important to least important, or vice versa), (d) criteria (comparing items by standards), or (e) convention (using an already established grouping). To help guide the reader through the text, introductions, transitions, and headings serve as cues.

4 Write short informational reports that describe routine tasks. Periodic, trip, convention, progress, and investigative reports are examples of typical informational reports. Such reports include an introduction that may preview the report purpose and supply background data if necessary. The body of the report is generally divided into three to five segments that may be organized by time, component, importance, criteria, or convention. The body should include clear headings and may use an informal, conversational style unless the audience expects a more formal tone. The summary or conclusion reviews the main points and discusses the action that will follow. The conclusion may offer a final thought, express appreciation, or signal a willingness to provide further information. Like all professional business documents, a clear, concise, well-written report cements the writer's credibility with the audience. Because they are so important, reports require writers to apply all the writing techniques addressed in Chapters 4, 5, and 6.

5 Compose short analytical reports that solve business problems. Typical analytical reports include justification/recommendation reports, feasibility reports, and yardstick reports. Justification/recommendation reports organized directly identify a problem, immediately announce a recommendation or solution, explain and discuss its merits, and summarize the action to be taken. Justification/recommendation reports organized indirectly describe a problem, discuss alternative solutions, prove the superiority of one solution, and ask for authorization to proceed with that solution. Feasibility reports study the advisability of following a course of action. They generally announce the author's proposal immediately. Then they describe the background of, advantages and disadvantages of, costs of, and time frame for implementing the proposal. Yardstick reports compare two or more solutions to a problem by measuring each against a set of established criteria. They usually describe a problem, explain possible solutions, establish criteria for comparing alternatives, evaluate each alternative in terms of the criteria, draw conclusions, and make recommendations. The advantage to yardstick reports is consistency in comparing alternatives. Most reports serve as a basis for decision making in business.

Are you ready? Get more practice at **www.meguffey.com**

Chapter Review

1. What is cross-tabulation, and when is it useful? (Obj. 1)
2. Calculate the mean, median, and mode for these figures: 5, 15, 15, 15, 30. (Obj. 1)
3. What are correlations? (Obj. 1)
4. Why is a decision matrix a valuable managerial tool? (Obj. 1)
5. Why is the ability to do research and draw conclusions likely to increase your value to your employer? (Obj. 2)
6. How can you make your report conclusions as objective and bias-free as possible? (Obj. 2)
7. Name five methods for organizing report data. Be prepared to discuss each. (Obj. 3)
8. What three devices can report writers use to prevent readers from getting lost in the text? (Obj. 3)
9. Name at least four guidelines for creating effective headings, and be prepared to explain them (Obj. 3)
10. How do business writers organize most informational reports, and what can writers assume about the audience? (Obj. 4)
11. Describe periodic reports and what they generally contain. (Obj. 4)
12. What should progress reports include? (Obj. 4)
13. When is the indirect strategy appropriate for justification/recommendation reports? (Obj. 5)
14. What is a feasibility report? Are such reports generally intended for internal or external audiences? (Obj. 5)
15. What is a yardstick report? (Obj. 5)

Critical Thinking

1. When tabulating and analyzing data, you may discover relationships among two or more variables that help explain the findings. Can you trust these correlations and assume that their relationship is one of cause and effect? (Obj. 1)
2. Researchers can draw various conclusions from a set of data. How do you know how to shape conclusions and recommendations? (Obj. 2)
3. How can you increase your chances that your report recommendations will be implemented? (Obj. 2)
4. Should all reports be organized so that they follow the sequence of investigation—that is, a description of the initial problem, an analysis of the issues, data collection, data analysis, and conclusions? Why or why not? (Obj. 3)
5. What are the major differences between informational and analytical reports? (Objs. 4, 5)
6. **Ethical Issue:** You have learned that drawing conclusions involves subjectivity, although your goal is to remain objective. Even the most even-handed researchers bring their goals, background, and frame of reference to bear on the inferences they make. Consider the contentious issue of climate change. Most mainstream scientists now believe climate change to be real and induced by human activity. However, some scientists cast doubt on the extent to which global warming is human-made and constitutes an imminent threat. How can something objectively measurable be so contentious? (Obj. 2)

Activities

12.1 Tabulation and Interpretation of Survey Results (Obj. 1)

Team

Your business communication class at South Bay College was asked by the college bookstore manager, Harry Locke, to conduct a survey. Concerned about the environment, Locke wants to learn students' reactions to eliminating plastic bags, of which 45,000 are given away annually by the bookstore. Students answered questions about a number of proposals, resulting in the following raw data:

For major purchases the bookstore should:

	Agree	Undecided	Disagree
1. Continue to provide plastic bags	132	17	411
2. Provide no bags; encourage students to bring their own bags	414	25	121
3. Provide no bags; offer cloth bags at a reduced price (about $3)	357	19	184
4. Give a cloth bag with each major purchase, the cost to be included in registration fees	63	15	482

Your Task. In groups of four or five, do the following:

a. Convert the data into a table (see Figure 12.1) with a descriptive title. Arrange the items in a logical sequence.
b. How could these survey data be cross-tabulated? Would cross-tabulation serve any purpose?
c. Given the conditions of this survey, name at least three conclusions that could be drawn from the data.
d. Prepare three to five recommendations to be submitted to Mr. Locke. How could they be implemented?
e. Role-play a meeting in which the recommendations and implementation plan are presented to Mr. Locke. One student plays the role of Mr. Locke; the remaining students play the role of the presenters.

12.2 Evaluating Conclusions (Obj. 2)

E-mail

Your Task. Read an in-depth article (800 or more words) in *BusinessWeek, Fortune, Forbes*, or *The Wall Street Journal*. What conclusions does the author draw? Are the conclusions valid, based on the evidence presented? In an e-mail message to your instructor, summarize the main points in the article and analyze the conclusions. What conclusions would you have drawn from the data?

12.3 Distinguishing Between Conclusions and Recommendations (Obj. 2)

A study of red light traffic violations produced the following findings: Red light traffic violations were responsible for more than 25,000 crashes in one state. Crashes from running red lights decreased by 10 percent in areas using camera programs to cite offenders. Two out of seven local governments studied showed a profit from the programs; the others lost money.[8]

Your Task. Based on the preceding facts, indicate whether the following statements are conclusions or recommendations:

a. Red light violations are dangerous offenses.
b. Red light cameras are an effective traffic safety tool.
c. Local governments should be allowed to implement red light camera programs.
d. Although red light camera programs are expensive, they prevent crashes and are, therefore, worthwhile.
e. The city of Centerville should not implement a red light program because of the program's cost.
f. Red light programs are not necessarily profitable for local governments.

12.4 Using Decision Matrices (Objs. 1, 2)

You want to buy a low-cost laptop for your college work and consider price the most important feature.

Your Task. Study Figure 12.3 on page 385 and change the weights in Table 2 to reflect your emphasis on low price, to which you will assign a factor of 10 because it is twice as important to you as unit weight, which receives a factor of 5. The hard drive is likewise secondary to you, so you give it a 5 also. Last, you change battery life to a factor of 7 from 10 because it is less important than price, but more important than unit weight and hard drive size. Calculate the new scores. Which low-budget computer wins this time?

12.5 Buying a Car: Create a Decision Matrix (Objs. 1, 2)

David, an outrigger canoe racer, needs to buy a new car. He wants a vehicle that will carry his disassembled boat and outrigger. At the same time he will need to travel long distances on business. His passion is soft-top sports cars, but he is also concerned about gas mileage. These four criteria are impossible to find in one vehicle.

David has the following choices:

- Station wagon
- SUV with or without a sun roof
- Four-door sedan, a high-miles-per-gallon "family car"
- Sports car, convertible

He wants to consider the following criteria:

- Price
- Ability to carry cargo such as a canoe
- Fuel efficiency
- Comfort over long distances
- Good looks and fun
- Quality build/manufacturer's reputation

Your Task. Follow the steps outlined in Figure 12.3 to determine an assessment scale and to assign a score to each feature. Then, consider which weights are probably most important to David, given his needs. Calculate the totals to find the vehicle that's most suitable for David.

Table 1: Unweighted Matrix (scale from 1 to 5, from worst to best)

Features:	Price	Cargo	Fuel	Comfort	Look	Quality	Total
Weights:							
Station wagon	3	4	3	4	1	2	
4-door sedan	4	2	5	3	1	4	
SUV	1	5	1	4	3	2	
Sports car	1	1	1	1	5	4	

Table 2: Weighted Matrix (factors range from 1 to 5)

Features:	Price	Cargo	Fuel	Comfort	Look	Quality	Total
Weights:	**4**	**5**	**3**	**2**	**4**	**3**	
Station wagon	12	20	9	8	4	6	59
4-door sedan	16	10	15	6	4	12	63
SUV	4	25	3	8	12	6	58
Sports car	4	5	3	2	20	12	46

12.6 Organizing Data (Obj. 3)

Your Task. In groups of three to five, discuss how the findings in the following reports could be best organized. Consider these methods: time, component, importance, criteria, and convention.

a. A weekly bulleted activity report sent by e-mail to the supervisor.
b. An agenda previewing a week-long management retreat and training program.
c. A report comparing the benefits of buying or leasing a fleet of hybrid vehicles. The report presents data on depreciation, upfront cost, maintenance, emissions, fuel consumption, and other factors.
d. A report describing the history of the development of dwarf and spur apple trees, starting with the first genetic dwarfs discovered about 100 years ago and progressing to today's grafted varieties on dwarfing rootstocks.
e. A report comparing the sales volume among the largest fast-food outlets in the United States.
f. A recommendation report to be submitted to management presenting four building plans to improve access to your building, in compliance with federal regulations. The plans range considerably in feasibility and cost.
g. An informational report describing a company's expansion plans in South America, Europe, Australia, and Southeast Asia.
h. An employee performance appraisal submitted annually.

12.7 Evaluating Headings and Titles (Obj. 3)

Your Task. Identify the following report headings and titles as *functional, talking,* or *combination.* Discuss the usefulness and effectiveness of each.

a. Disadvantages
b. Why Fast Food Has Slowed Down
c. Discussion
d. Balancing Worker Productivity and Social Media Use
e. Case History: Glatfelter's Direct-Mail Campaign Heralds Sustainability
f. Recommendations: Solving Our Applicant-Tracking Problem
g. Comparing Costs of Hiring Exempt and Nonexempt Employees
h. Equipment

12.8 Writing a Survey: Studying Employee Use of Instant Messaging (Obj. 1)

Web

Instant messaging (IM) is a popular way to exchange messages in real time. It offers the convenience of telephone conversations and e-mail. Best of all, it allows employees to contact anyone in the world while retaining a written copy of the conversation—without a whopping telephone bill! But instant messaging is risky for companies. They may lose trade secrets or confidential information over insecure lines. They also may be liable if inappropriate material is exchanged. Moreover, IM opens the door to viruses that can infect a company's entire computer system.

Your boss just read an article stating that 40 percent of companies now use IM for business and up to 90 percent of employees use instant messaging WITHOUT their manager's knowledge or authorization. She asks you to prepare a survey of your 48-member staff to learn how many are using IM. She wants to know what type of IM software they have downloaded, how many hours a day they spend on IM, what the advantages of IM are, and so forth. The goal is not to identify those using or abusing IM. Instead, the goal is to learn when, how, and why employees use instant messaging so that appropriate policies can be designed.

Your Task. Use the Web or an electronic database to learn more about instant messaging. Then prepare a short employee survey (see Figure 11.8). Include an appropriate introduction that explains the survey and encourages a response. Should you ask for names on the survey? How can you encourage employees to return the forms? Your instructor may wish to expand this survey into a report by having you produce fictitious survey results, analyze the findings, draw conclusions, and make recommendations.

12.9 Executive Summary: Condensing the Facts for Your Boss (Obj. 4)

Web

Like many executives, your boss is too rushed to read long journal articles. But she is eager to keep up with developments in her field. Assume she has asked you to help her stay abreast of research in her field. She asks you to submit to her one summary every month on an article of interest.

Your Task. In your field of study, select a professional journal, such as the *Journal of Management*. Using an electronic database search or a Web search, look for articles in your target journal. Select an article that is at least five pages long and is interesting to you. Write an executive summary in memo format. Include an introduction that might begin with *As you requested, I am submitting this executive summary of. . . .* Identify the author, article name, journal, and date of publication. Explain what the author intended to do in the study or article. Summarize three or four of the most important findings of the study or article. Use descriptive rather than functional headings. Summarize any recommendations you make. Your boss would also like a concluding statement indicating your reaction to the article. Address your memo to Susan Wright.

12.10 Periodic Report: Filling in the Boss (Obj. 4)

E-mail

You work hard at your job, but you rarely see your boss. He or she has asked to be informed of your activities and accomplishments and any problems you are encountering.

Your Task. For a job that you currently hold or a previous one, describe your regular activities, discuss irregular events that management should be aware of, and highlight any special needs or problems you are having. If you don't have a job, communicate to your instructor your weekly or monthly activities as they are tied to your classes, homework, and writing assignments. Establish components or criteria such as those in the bulleted e-mail in Figure 12.7. Use the memo format or write an e-mail report in bullet form as shown in Figure 12.7. Address the memo or the e-mail report to your boss or, alternatively, to your instructor.

12.11 Progress Report: Checking In (Obj. 4)

E-mail

Students writing a long report either for another course or for the long report assignment described in Chapter 13 will want to keep their instructors informed of their progress.

Your Task. Write a progress report informing your instructor of your work. Briefly describe the project (its purpose, scope, limitations, and methodology), work completed, work yet to be completed, problems encountered, future activities, and expected completion date. Address the e-mail report to your instructor. If your instructor allows, try your hand at the bulleted e-mail report introduced in Figure 12.7.

12.12 Investigative Report: Ensuring Fair Employment Practices Abroad (Obj. 4)

Intercultural Web

Nike's image took a big hit in the late 1990s when the company became associated with sweatshop conditions in Asian factories that supplied its shoes and apparel. Other sports and garment companies also became targets of criticism and campus boycotts in the United States for their ties to sweatshop labor. Since then, American companies have tried to investigate and end the abuses.

However, oversight is difficult, and Chinese factories dodge the labor auditors sponsored by American retail chains and manufacturers. To complicate matters, China is the largest supplier of American imports, to the tune of $280 billion annually. U.S. consumers have come to expect inexpensive goods—athletic shoes, clothing, and electronic gadgets. The pressure to keep prices down may be prompting the Chinese suppliers to cut corners and ignore the fair labor regulations of American companies. According to *BusinessWeek*, U.S. corporations are struggling with imposing "Western labor standards on a nation that lacks real labor unions and a meaningful rule of law."[9]

Your Task. Investigate the efforts of the Fair Labor Association, a coalition of 20 retailers and apparel manufacturers, such as Nike, Adidas, Nordstrom, and Eddie Bauer. The problem is not confined to the garment industry; violations also occur in offshore suppliers producing household appliances, computers, and electronics. Explore the types of abuses and the obstacles to reform. Then recommend actions that could make offshore factories play by the rules. Start by visiting the Fair Labor Association's Web site: **http://www.fairlabor.org.**

12.13 Investigative Report: Exploring a Possible Place to Work (Obj. 4)

Web

You are thinking about taking a job with a Fortune 500 company, and you want to learn as much as possible about the company.

Your Task. Select a Fortune 500 company, and collect information about it on the Web. Visit **http://www.hoovers.com** for basic facts. Then take a look at the company's Web site; check its background, news releases, and annual report. Learn about its major product, service, or emphasis. Find its Fortune 500 ranking, its current stock price (if listed), and its high and low range for the year. Look up its profit-to-earnings ratio. Track its latest marketing plan, promotion, or product. Identify its home office, major officers, and number of employees. In a memo report to your instructor, summarize your research findings.

Explain why this company would be a good or bad employment choice.

12.14 Investigative Report: Marketing Abroad (Obj. 4)

Intercultural | Web

You have been asked to prepare a training program for U.S. companies doing business outside the country.

Your Task. Select a country to investigate. Check to see whether your school or library subscribes to CultureGrams, an online resource with rich data about the daily lives and cultures of the world's peoples. Collect data from CultureGrams files, the CountryWatch Web site, or from the country's embassy in Washington. Interview on-campus international students. Use the Web to discover data about the country. See Activity 13.7 and Figure 13.5 in Chapter 13 for additional ideas on gathering information on intercultural communication. Collect information about formats for written communication, observance of holidays, customary greetings, business ethics, and other topics of interest to businesspeople. Remember that your report should promote business, not tourism. Prepare a memo report addressed to Kelly Johnson, editor for the training program materials.

12.15 Investigative Report: Expanding Operations Abroad (Obj. 4)

Intercultural | Team | Web

You have been asked to brief your boss, Dori Lundy, about the status of women in business, customs, and general business etiquette in a country that may not be friendly to Western businesswomen. Ms. Lundy is planning an international trip to expand her high-tech company.

Your Task. Select a country to investigate that has a culture markedly different from our own—for example, Saudi Arabia, Egypt, Iran, Japan, or South Korea, but don't forget Italy, Spain, Germany, or the Scandinavian countries. Collect data from CultureGrams, to which many libraries subscribe; search CountryWatch and other Web sites. Interview international students on campus. See Activity 13.7 and Figure 13.5 in Chapter 13 for additional ideas on gathering information on intercultural communication. Collect information about customary greetings, business ethics, dress codes, and other topics of interest to a traveling businesswoman. The purpose of your report is to promote business, not tourism, and to help your boss avoid embarrassment or worse. Prepare a memo report addressed to Dori Lundy, president of Paradigm CompuTech.

12.16 Progress Report: Heading Toward That Degree (Obj. 4)

You have made an agreement with your parents (or spouse, relative, or significant friend) that you would submit a progress report at this time.

Your Task. Prepare a progress report in letter format. Describe your headway toward your educational goal (such as employment, degree, or certificate). List your specific achievements, and outline what you have left to complete.

12.17 Conference or Trip Report: In Your Dreams (Obj. 4)

You have been sent to a meeting, conference, or seminar in an exotic spot at company expense.

Your Task. From a business periodical, select an article describing a conference or meeting connected with your major area of study. The article must be at least 500 words long. Assume you attended the meeting. Prepare a memo report to your supervisor.

12.18 Justification/Recommendation Report: Searching for the Best Philanthropic Project (Obj. 5)

Web

Great news! MegaTech, the start-up company where you work, has become enormously successful. Now the owner wants to support some kind of philanthropic program. He does not have time to check out the possibilities, so he asks you, his assistant, to conduct research and report to him and the board of directors.

Your Task. He wants you to investigate the philanthropic projects at 20 high-profile companies of your choice. Visit their Web sites and study programs such as volunteerism, cause-related marketing, matching funds, charitable donations, and so forth. In a recommendation report, discuss five of the best programs and recommend one that can serve as a philanthropic project model for your company.

12.19 Justification/Recommendation Report: Solving a Campus Problem (Obj. 5)

Team

Your Task. In groups of three to five, investigate a problem on your campus, such as inadequate parking, slow registration, limited dining options, poor class schedules, inefficient bookstore, weak job placement program, unrealistic degree requirements, or lack of internship programs. Within your group develop a solution to the problem. If possible, consult the officials involved to ask for their input in arriving at a feasible solution. Do not attack existing programs; strive for constructive discussion and harmonious improvements. After reviewing the persuasive techniques discussed in Chapter 10, write a group or individual justification/recommendation report. Address your report to the vice president of student affairs or the college president. Copy your instructor.

12.20 Justification/Recommendation Report: Developing an Organizational Media Use Policy (Obj. 5)

Team | Web

As a manager in a midsized engineering firm, you are aware that members of your department frequently use e-mail, social networking sites, instant messaging, and texting for private messages, shopping, and games. In addition to the strain on computer facilities, you worry about declining productivity as well as security problems. When you walked by one worker's computer and saw what looked like pornography on the screen, you knew you had to do something. Although workplace privacy is a hot-button issue for unions and employee rights groups, employers have legitimate reasons for wanting to know what is happening on their computers or during the time they are paying their employees to work. A high percentage of lawsuits involve the use and abuse of e-mail and increasingly more often other media as well. You think that the executive council should establish some kind of e-mail policy. The council is generally receptive to sound suggestions, especially if they are inexpensive. At present no explicit media use policy exists, and you fear that the executive council is not fully aware of the dangers. You decide to talk with other managers about the problem and write a justification/recommendation report.

Your Task. In teams discuss the need for a comprehensive media use policy. Using the Web and electronic databases, find information about other firms' adoption of such policies. Look for examples of companies struggling with lawsuits over abuse of technology on the job. In your report, should you describe suitable policies? Should you recommend computer monitoring and surveillance software? Should the policy cover instant messaging, social networking sites, blogging, and smartphone use? Each member of the team should present and support his or her ideas regarding what should be included in the report. Individually or as a team, write a convincing justification/recommendation report to the executive council based on the conclusions you draw from your research and discussion. Decide whether you should be direct or indirect.

12.21 Feasibility Report: International Organization (Obj. 5)

Intercultural

To fulfill a senior project in your department, you have been asked to submit a letter report to the dean evaluating the feasibility of starting an organization of international students on campus.

© Image Source/Photolibrary

Your Task. Find out how many international students are on your campus, what nations they represent, how one goes about starting an organization, and whether a faculty sponsor is needed. Assume that you conducted an informal survey of international students. Of the 39 who filled out the survey, 31 said they would be interested in joining.

12.22 Feasibility Report: Improving Employee Fitness (Obj. 5)

Your company is considering ways to promote employee fitness and morale.

Your Task. Select a fitness program that seems reasonable for your company. Consider a softball league, bowling teams, a basketball league, lunchtime walks, lunchtime fitness speakers and demos, company-sponsored health club memberships, a workout room, a fitness center, a fitness director, and so on. Assume that your boss has tentatively agreed to the programs you select and has asked you to write a memo report investigating its feasibility.

12.23 Yardstick Report: Evaluating Equipment (Obj. 5)

You recently complained to your boss that you were unhappy with a piece of equipment that you use (printer, computer, copier, fax, or the like). After some thought, the boss decided that your complaint was valid and told you to go shopping.

Your Task. Compare at least three manufacturers' models and recommend one. Because the company will be purchasing ten or more units and because several managers must approve the purchase, write a careful report documenting your findings. Establish at least five criteria for comparing the models. Submit a memo report to your boss.

12.24 Yardstick Report: Measuring the Alternatives (Obj. 5)

Your Task. Identify a problem or procedure that must be changed at your work or in an organization you know. Consider challenges such as poor scheduling of employees, outdated equipment, slow order processing, failure to encourage employees to participate fully, restrictive rules, inadequate training, or disappointed customers. Consider several solutions or courses of action (retaining the present status could be one alternative). Develop criteria that you could use to evaluate each alternative. Write a report measuring each alternative by the yardstick you have created. Recommend a course of action to your boss or to the organization head.

Self-Contained Report Activities

No Additional Research Required

12.25 Justification/Recommendation Report: Faster Service at Seguiti Family Pizza's Service* (Obj. 5)

You work for Paul Seguiti, the owner of Seguiti Family Pizza, a small, casual pizza shop he founded 30 years ago. Its signature items are eight-inch-diameter individual pizzas. The no-frills eatery also serves fries, onion rings, and assorted beverages.

The pizza shop is located in the warehouse district of Chicago, where it originally served truckers who delivered their meat, fruits, and vegetables in the middle of the night and then whisked off to the next city. Just for the truckers, Seguiti designed a pizza that was large enough to be satisfying, yet small enough for a driver to fold in half and eat with one hand while driving with the other hand. Later the pizza shop caught on with the nightclub crowd and with students who studied late. The shop opens at 11 p.m. and closes at 6 a.m.

The concept was a hit. However, success brings competition. Three imitators opened their pizza shops within a five-mile radius of Seguiti Family Pizza. You know that the family has been using the same system of delivering orders to customers that it has for years, and you know service could be faster.

The current system at Seguiti's works as follows. A counter clerk records the customer's order and table number on a ticket. The customer pays, and the counter person gives the order to the pizza makers. The pizza makers remove the dough from the refrigerator, shape it, add the sauce and other ingredients, put the pie in the oven, and remove it from the oven when baked. The counter clerk takes the order to the customer's table. Seguiti Family Pizza has three counter clerks, two pizza makers, and one cash register that is shared by the counter clerks. It takes two minutes to prep a pizza before it can go in the oven. The pizza shop uses an old-fashioned Bartho Model A pizza deck oven, which cooks a pizza in eight minutes.

You think the entire system is inefficient, and when you discuss the problem with Mr. Seguiti, he says, "Although the old ways are comfortable for me, I see that change is needed."

You suggest observing the three competitors' methods of serving customers to understand why their service is faster. Currently, the average time it takes a customer to receive an order at Seguiti Family Pizza is 18 minutes. The following are notes from your observations of the competitors.

* Instructors: See the Instructor's Manual for additional report-writing resources.

Crunchy Crust Pizza

- Similar menu
- Orders are taken using an electronic system that includes the customer's number
- Customers pay immediately
- Customers pick up their orders after their numbers have been called
- One counter employee at one register; two pizza makers
- Preprepared dough; prep time: one minute
- One state-of-the art TurboCrust Model 100 convection oven—six minutes to cook a pizza
- Average time a customer waits to receive an order: 11 minutes

Tomasia's

- Similar menu
- Order takers call out the menu item as the order is taken
- Customers pay immediately
- Customers wait at the counter to pick up their orders
- Four counter employees at four registers; two pizza makers
- Preprepared dough; prep time: one minute
- One state-of-the art TurboCrust Model 100 convection oven—six minutes to cook a pizza
- Average time a customer waits to receive an order: nine minutes

Velluti's Pizza

- Similar menu
- Tickets are used to record the customers' orders
- Customers pay immediately
- Counter staff take the order to customers' tables
- Three counter staff, two pizza makers, and one cash register
- Pizza prep the same as Seguiti Family Pizza: two minutes
- One Baker's Friend Model AC3 pizza deck oven—seven minutes to cook a pizza
- Average time a customer waits to receive an order: 17 minutes

Your Task. Now it is up to you to analyze the data you have collected. In a short memo report to Paul Seguiti, present your findings, discuss your conclusions, and make recommendations. You may want to present the data using visual aids, but you also realize you must emphasize the important findings by presenting them in an easy-to-read list.

12.26 Justification/Recommendation Report: Analyzing Service at Sporting World (Obj. 5)

Sporting World is one of the largest sporting goods retail chains in the United States, operating 102 stores across the Midwest. Paula Taylor opened the first Sporting World Store in Beckland, Missouri, in 1953 and sold military surplus supplies. Over the years, Sporting World evolved into one of the premier sporting goods chains, offering golf equipment and apparel; footwear; camping, hunting, and fishing gear; and general outdoor apparel. It has established a reputation for outstanding customer service, a great selection, and discount prices.

As an in-house consultant who reports to the vice president of operations, you have been assigned the task of analyzing checkout and customer service lanes to ensure efficient service. Employees have already been cross-trained to work in multiple departments, and all employees already know how to operate the cash registers. Remote cash registers are located in several departments to reduce customer flow at the registers nearest the exit. To improve communication among employees, Sporting World recently started to equip employees in some of its stores with headsets.

Despite these efforts, things can go wrong, and this usually happens during holidays such as Christmas, Memorial Day, Fourth of July, and Labor Day. With the Labor Day weekend only one month away, you want to help avoid the occasional gridlock encountered last Labor Day at one of the chain's busiest stores.

Sporting World's goal is to achieve at least a 35 percent *Excellent* response rating from customers. Often, ratings of *Good* are acceptable to businesses, but not to Sporting World and certainly not to its founder, Paula Taylor, who accepts nothing less than *Excellent* ratings.

Customer Survey Data

To gather information from customers, you decide to tabulate responses to questions from surveys the store received last month. You are particularly interested in the time customers spent in the checkout lines. Here are the results of 442 customer surveys:

	Responses/Score (5 = Excellent, 4 = Very good, 3 = Good, 2 = Fair, 1 = Poor)				
Customer Survey Questions	**5**	**4**	**3**	**2**	**1**
1. Based on your shopping experience, how would you rate this Sporting World store?	155	141	87	40	19
2. Based on your shopping experience, how would you rate the likelihood that you will return to this Sporting World store?	233	134	61	11	3
3. How would you rate the likelihood that you would recommend this Sporting World store to a friend?	163	122	105	32	20
4. How would you rate the efficiency of checkout at the register?	70	111	199	44	18
5. How would you rate the efficiency of service at the customer service counter?	26	52	177	133	54
6. How would you rate the service staff's handling of problems?	36	133	75	177	21

Staff Survey

To gather additional information, you conduct a survey of 33 staff members, including cashiers, customer service representatives, and salespeople. Here are the results of your survey:

Which of the following has caused a delay at a register?

Soft tag (security tag) removal	64
Approval or override	86
Register malfunction	3
Price check	7
Purchase of hunting and fishing licenses	23
Employee error	6

Figures do not total 100 percent because of multiple answers.

Your Observations

Finally, you selected nine registers at random (five near the front entrance, two in customer service, and one each in the fishing and footwear departments) and observed them for five minutes, as you took notes. You chose Saturday for these observations because of the typically higher volume of business. Following is a summary of your observations:

- During all five of your visits to registers near the front entrance, you noticed that most of the delays were caused when a manager was needed for a check approval or override. You also observed five instances in which an employee needed to go to another cash register to remove security tags because the employee's security tag remover wasn't working. Finally, you noticed six customers in the line for fishing rods and fishing reels and overheard that they really wanted to buy fishing licenses.
- In both of your visits to the service counter, only one employee was operating one of two available registers. For this reason, three customers were left waiting in line for service. During one visit, you observed that when a product needed to be opened to make sure all parts were included before it could be exchanged, the employee had to walk to the technical department to locate a technician, causing further delay.
- During your visits to the fishing and footwear departments, the two highest-volume departments in the store, you saw that floor personnel were overwhelmed with customers asking questions about the goods. In other words, no one seemed to be available to handle transactions at the open registers. You then walked to the camping department (the department with the lowest sales in the store), where you saw three customers and four employees in the area.

Your Task. After carefully comparing customer and employee perceptions, present your findings in a memo report to Red Armbruster, vice president of operations, Sporting World. In your report, include as much information from the tables as possible, but present it in an easy-to-understand way. What conclusions can you draw from your findings? What recommendations will you make to Mr. Armbruster to ensure a successful Labor Day weekend?

12.27 Yardstick Report: Comparing Textbook Options

(Obj. 5)

Assume you are the finance committee chairperson for Lambda Gamma Phi, a business association at your college or university. After some members bought textbooks at the campus bookstore recently, they complained about how expensive the textbooks were and how their costs were steadily rising. Some members said that because of the expense, they didn't buy some of their textbooks last semester, which hurt their grades. Lower grades could lead to the loss of scholarships and reduced job opportunities.

The executive committee of Lambda Gamma Phi asks you to identify alternatives to buying full-priced hard-copy books at the campus bookstore. What factors are most important? The committee is most interested in the best price (including shipping charges) and availability. Even a good price is useless if the book is not readily available. Another big concern is readability.

One option for students, of course, is to continue buying books at the campus bookstore. Some instructors and students, however, are buying books for the Fleetfoot Reader. This is a proprietary hardware/software device for reading e-books, but books play only on this device. Some publishers and bookstores are now renting books, which is a distinct possibility. Students can also buy books online, or they can download e-books as PDF files. All of these options seem like reasonable alternatives to buying full-priced hard-copy books at the campus bookstore.

For the study, you choose a representative sample of four textbooks: *Calculus Classics*, *The Basics of College Writing*, *Art History: The Impressionists and Beyond*, and *Physics Is Fun*. You check the prices and availability of the books at the campus bookstore, on Web sites that specialize in renting textbooks, on Web sites that sell hard-copy books, and on Web sites that sell e-books. You check the price of the Fleetfoot Reader as well as the prices and availability of books that play on this device. You evaluate readability by seeing how easy a textbook is to read (only a concern with e-books and the Fleetfoot Reader). Delivery times for books purchased online are immaterial because most online vendors deliver books in two business days.

Price is easily the most important criterion, so you assign it a weight of 5. You assign availability a weight of 3 and readability a weight of 1.

Average Price

At the campus bookstore, the average price of each book is $170 and the average buyback price is $40, making the average net price $130. The better the condition of the book is when you return it, the more the campus bookstore pays. The lowest price on the Fleetfoot Reader is $259 at handheldgadgets.com, and the average price of books is $10, making the average price of a book $259 / 4 + $10 = $74.75. The average price to rent the four books for one semester is $38 per book. The average price is $65 per book to buy the four books online. None of the online booksellers has a buyback option. The average price of the four books as e-books is $80 per book. The following chart shows those data.

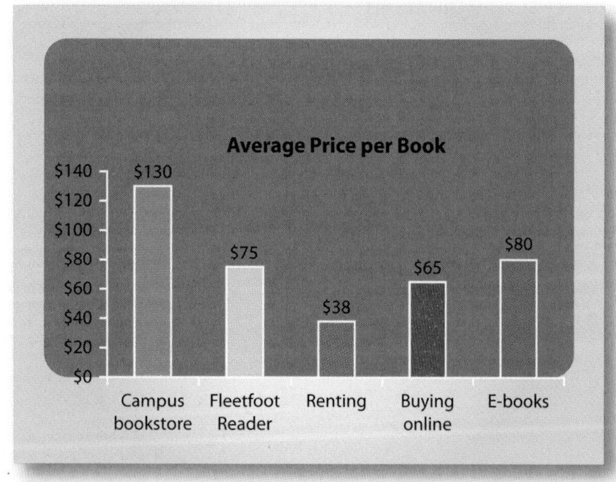

Availability

The campus bookstore has all four of the books in stock. Only one of the four books is available for the Fleetfoot Reader. A much wider selection of books for the Fleetfoot Reader is available for the mass market than for the college market. Bookrentingsite.com says it has over 2.1 million textbooks for rent and offers prepaid return shipping. Three of the four books are available on this site, which consistently offered the lowest prices on book rentals. Two online booksellers excelled in availability—reallycheap.com and savvybuyer.com. Each had three of the four books. Smartclass.com had two of the four books as e-books. No other e-bookseller came close to its selection.

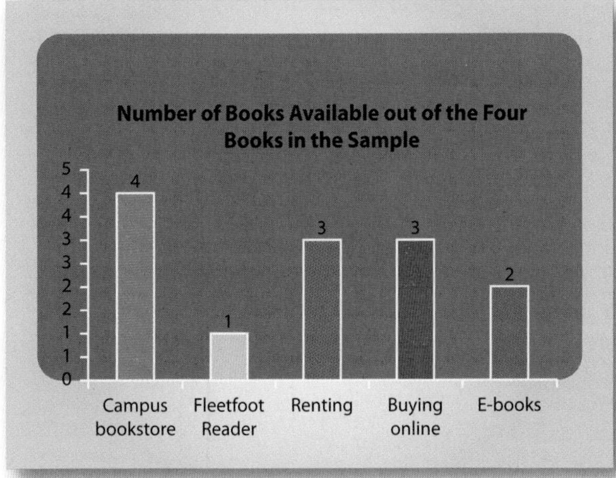

Readability

You judge all hard-copy books most readable. Formatting issues and small print on small screens, especially on iPods, make e-books the least readable. Although books on the Fleetfoot Reader are easier to read than e-books, the device is hard to use.

Your Task. Write a memo report of five or fewer pages and address it to the organization's members. Include conclusions and recommendations, a bar chart showing the availability of books, and a decision matrix.

12.28 Feasibility Report: Can Rainbow Precision Instruments Afford a Children's Center? (Obj. 5)

Rainbow Precision Instruments (RPI) is a $60 million manufacturer of specialty gauges for the aerospace industry, mainly flight deck or cockpit instruments, located in a small town in the Pacific Northwest. To accommodate its workforce of approximately 55 percent female employees, the company has been operating a state-of-the art Children's Center. More than a child care center, the facility is an award-winning and well-equipped learning center that covers two shifts, from 7:00 a.m. until 10:30 p.m.

Such innovation and extensive coverage are not cheap. A recent overhaul of the facility cost $150,000, and the annual budget to instruct and care for 145 children reached $300,000. The Children's Center provides a state-certified curriculum taught by professional preschool faculty. The children also receive their meals at the facility. At its inception, the costly investment seemed fully justified. However, the number of employee children started slowly dropping until fewer than 10 percent of enrollees were children of RPI workers. The company responded by opening the Center to surrounding communities, where quality day care is scarce.

YEAR	2003	2008	2010
Percent of employee children at the Center	55 percent	25 percent	10 percent

Instead of raising the tuition to market levels to recoup some of its investment, RPI continues to subsidize the Center annually with approximately $200,000, not differentiating between Rainbow employees and parents from the local area. The annual tuition is $696 per child.

To make matters worse, RPI has suffered financial setbacks and is currently losing about $2.5 million annually. Finding alternatives for looking after the few remaining company children would seem less expensive than keeping the Center open. RPI has unsuccessfully pursued other options, such as selling the Children's Center or finding an independent operator to run it.

Your Task. From the available evidence, decide whether it is advisable for the company to close the Children's Center or keep it open. If you choose to keep it open, you will need to argue for some substantial changes in company operations. In your memo report, announce the decision, describe the problem, and discuss both the advantages and disadvantages of your proposal. Last, focus on costs and the time frame needed to implement your decision.

12.29 Feasibility Report: Should We Continue to Outsource Personal Computer Manufacturing Jobs to India? (Obj. 5)

You are a senior analyst for the prestigious Cyberdynamic Systems Corporation (CSC), a multinational computer company. Its core products are servers and workstations, but it also manufactures personal computers (PCs). During the past three years, as the economy has slumped, overall CSC profits have slipped by 44 percent. When the economy slumps, companies outsource more activities and jobs to cut costs.

Two years ago, CSC started outsourcing PC manufacturing to India, an initiative the company calls Project India. The problem is that laying off employees and outsourcing their jobs to foreign countries is unpopular with the public. It also slightly lowers the morale of the remaining employees. In a recent Gallup survey, 74 percent of the American public had a negative opinion of outsourcing, 19 percent had a positive opinion, and 7 percent were neutral.

Your boss asks you to recommend whether CSC should continue to outsource PC manufacturing to India. As part of the study, your boss also wants you to evaluate alternatives to outsourcing and potential savings in operating costs that the company is trying or considering. You decide to interview employees to learn their views about Project India, research the pros and cons of outsourcing, and analyze the effectiveness of the alternatives to outsourcing the company is trying or considering.

Benefits of Outsourcing PC Manufacturing

From your research, you discover four main benefits to outsourcing PC manufacturing. First, outsourcing noncore operations such as PC manufacturing enables CSC to focus on its core products—servers and workstations. Second, outsourcing lowers labor costs. CSC pays an Indian employee $22 per hour to make a PC, while it pays a U.S. employee $98 per hour to make the same PC.

Third, product quality reports suggest that Indian-made PCs have a 0.14 percent defect rate, the same as domestically made PCs. Fourth, profits and market share increase because of outsourcing. Last year, CSC profits after outsourcing PC manufacturing were $1.65 billion, while profits were only $900 million before outsourcing (roughly half). Market share after outsourcing of PC manufacturing increased from 34 percent to 45 percent.

Equal Job Program

You learn that, as an alternative to layoffs, CSC created Equal Job, a program designed to deflect criticism from its outsourcing actions. Equal Job offers affected employees the option of keeping their jobs by relocating to the country to which their jobs will be outsourced. Employees who choose relocation remain employed by CSC but work for lower, local wages. Although some outsiders think the approach is creative, 88 percent of employees surveyed about the program are against it and in fact were shocked and angry at the program's announcement. Only 8 percent of the employees who were offered the relocation accepted it.

Operation Web Office

As another alternative to layoffs, you discover that CSC launched an experimental program called Operation Web Office. Still under development, the program involves creating a virtual online workplace in which each employee sits at his or her own computer at home and is connected to other employees by the Internet through an application on each employee's computer. The projected savings from Operation Web Office are about $23 million per year in reduced costs for office space. Eighty-three percent of the test group of 218 employees like the program. However, development efforts have been plagued by server crashes, software malfunctions, and computer viruses. Worse, the company has to date been unable to uncover the sources of these problems.

Onshoring

You also investigate the possibility of "onshoring"—relocating workers to areas in the United States with lower costs of living and paying them less. Based on your interviews, only 17 percent of the employees surveyed said they would consider relocation accepted it. In addition, 56 percent of the American public had a negative opinion of onshoring.

Your Task. Write a memo report of three or fewer pages addressed to your boss. Include conclusions, recommendations, and a pie chart illustrating public opinion of outsourcing. Should Cyberdynamic Systems Corporation continue to outsource its PC manufacturing?

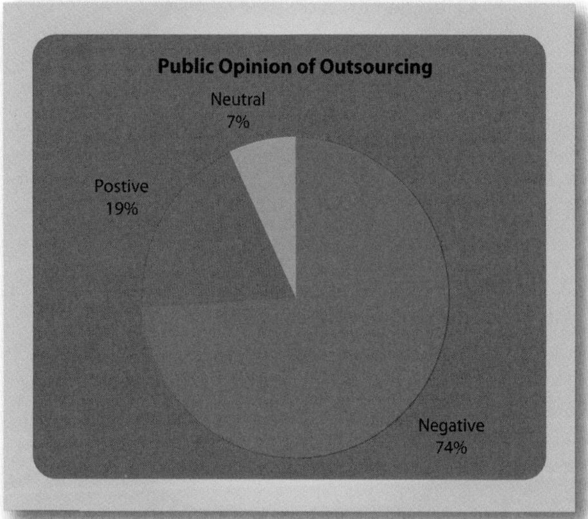

12.30 Yardstick Report: Parking Problem at Caputi's Italian Restaurant (Obj. 5)

You have always enjoyed the great food at Caputi's Italian Restaurant, owned by your Uncle Guido. Caputi's is a formal, upscale dining Italian food restaurant in downtown Tempe, Arizona, near the campus of a major university where you are a student. Because of its steadily increasing business, Caputi's has outgrown its small parking lot, which has only 20 parking spaces.

Frustrated over their inability to park in the restaurant's lot, some potential customers give up and go elsewhere to eat. Some of the regulars have also disappeared. Caputi's cannot add parking spaces because adjacent land is unavailable. However, according to Guido, "The problem is not a lack of parking spaces; it's a lack of willingness on the part of customers to walk from where they parked to the restaurant." To pay its debts, the restaurant needs to continue to grow. Uncle Guido says, "Relocation is out of the question—this spot is too good!"

Guido wants you to evaluate options to ease the parking problem, using criteria that he and you develop. The options are to (a) use a valet service, attendants who park and later retrieve cars for patrons, (b) run a free shuttle service between the restaurant and a nearby parking garage, and (c) advertise the availability of nearby parking garages and bus routes on the restaurant's Web site and in the restaurant. The criteria are (a) the cost to the restaurant to implement the solution, (b) the cost to the customer to use the solution, (c) the ease of implementation for the restaurant, and (d) convenience to the customer.

Besides talking to Guido, you interview a valet parking company about its services and fees, and you interview the managers of the nearby parking garages about availability and prices. You survey 40 of the restaurant's customers about their willingness to use a valet service and the price they would be willing to pay for the service.

Decision Matrix

You explain what a decision matrix is to Guido, and together you decide on the weights of the criteria. The net profit (or loss) to the restaurant to implement the solution receives a weight of 10. The cost to the customer to use the solution receives a weight of 6. The ease of implementation for the restaurant receives a weight of 4. The convenience to the customer receives a weight of 8.

Cost to the Restaurant to Implement a Solution

The least expensive valet service in town sent you a quotation that pegs a patron's charge at $7 per car, an amount that includes a $2 flat fee for parking at a nearby parking garage. The valet parking company has offered its service free of charge to the restaurant.

The major costs of operating a shuttle service are about $1,500 to buy a van and $200 per week to pay an employee to drive the van between the garage and the restaurant during dinner hours. Costs to advertise available parking options on the restaurant's Web site and at the restaurant are about $200.

Cost to the Customer

The per-vehicle charge of $7 plus a customer tips for valet service of about $3 makes the valet service the costliest option. The shuttle service is free to customers. Similarly, learning about the availability of nearby parking garages and bus routes on the restaurant's Web site and at the restaurant is free to customers.

Ease of Implementation

Advertising parking options is the most convenient option for the restaurant because it takes the least amount of time and effort. Offering a valet service is the second most convenient option for the restaurant. Although the valet service does most of the work, this option requires more weekly administrative work for the restaurant than advertising requires. Caputi's may also need to provide food and beverages for valets. Operating a shuttle service is the least convenient option for the restaurant because it requires the restaurant to buy a van; pay a driver; and provide fuel, maintenance, and insurance.

Convenience to the Customer

A valet service is the most convenient option for customers because this option results in the fastest entry into the restaurant. Your survey shows that 90 percent of the customers are willing to use the service. A shuttle service is the second most convenient option for customers. It is not as convenient as driving to the restaurant entrance and leaving a car with a valet. Advertising offers information to customers but not any significant convenience, making it the least convenient option.

Your Task. Uncle Guido is relying on you to analyze the data and help him make a decision. Write a memo report of three or fewer pages to him. Prepare a decision matrix with the weights provided. For each criterion in the decision matrix, give the option that ranks highest a ranking of 3, the option that ranks second highest a ranking of 2, and the option that ranks lowest a ranking of 1. Multiply each weight by the ranking, repeat for the other criteria, and then sum up the results to compute a total. From your decision matrix, draw conclusions and then make recommendations. Overall, which option is best? Should you still recommend advertising the parking options?

Chat About It

In each chapter you will find five discussion questions related to the chapter material. Your instructor may assign these topics for you to discuss in class, in an online chat room, or on an online discussion board. Some of the discussion topics may require outside research. You may also be asked to read and respond to postings made by your classmates.

Topic 1: If you were asked to study the relationship between traffic speeds and traffic accidents, what statistic might be most useful: the mean, median, or mode? Why?

Topic 2: What criteria would you use to determine whether required courses for a given academic major are necessary?

Topic 3: Provide a simple example that illustrates the differences between findings, conclusions, and recommendations.

Topic 4: What do you think might be a good rule of thumb regarding the number of graphics (charts, tables, and so on) to put in a report and the size of the graphics? Why?

Topic 5: If your boss asked you to write a report that is formatted differently or with ideas sequenced differently than how you're learning in this course, what would you do? Would you ask your boss if you could instead write the report the way you learned to write reports? Would you identify the differences to your boss?

Grammar/Mechanics C.L.U.E. Review 12

Total Review

The first ten chapters reviewed specific guides from Appendix A, Grammar and Mechanics Guide. The exercises in this and the remaining chapters are total reviews, covering all of the grammar and mechanics guides plus confusing words and frequently misspelled words.

Each of the following sentences has a total of **three** errors in grammar, punctuation, capitalization, usage, or spelling. On a separate sheet, write a correct version. Avoid adding new phrases, starting new sentences, or rewriting in your own words. When finished, compare your responses with the key beginning on page Key-1.

Example: After our supervisor and her returned from their meeting at 2:00 p.m. we were able to sort the customers names more quickly.

Revision: After our supervisor and **she** returned from their meeting at **2 p.m.**, we were able to sort the **customers'** names more quickly.

1. Toyota, the best-selling japanese carmaker, had enjoyed a strong favorable perception of high quality therefore it long remained unharmed by a string of much-publicized recalls.
2. The auditors report, which my boss and me read very closely, featured the following three main flaws, factual inaccuracies, omissions, and incomprehensible language.
3. 8 of the 20 workers in my department were fired, as a result, we had to work much harder to acheive our objectives.
4. As a matter of principal, we offer some form of financial support to more than sixty percent of our current MBA candidates. Which proves our commitment to executive education.
5. To post easily to your blog on the Web you could use Mozilla's web browser firefox and an add-on called ScribeFire.
6. Peters presentation to a nonprofit group on advanced Internet marketing netted him only two hundred dollars, a fifth of his usual honorarium but he believes in pro bono work.
7. The old company manual covers the basics of: searching, selecting interpreting and organizing data.
8. Our latest press release which was written in our Corporate Communication Department announces the opening of 3 Canadian offices.
9. Letter reports usualy has side margins of one and one quarter inches.
10. The CEO and Manager, who had went to a meeting in the West, delivered a report to Jeff and I when they returned.

CHAPTER 13

Proposals, Business Plans, and Formal Business Reports

OBJECTIVES

After studying this chapter, you should be able to

1. Discuss the general uses and basic components of informal proposals, and grasp their audience and purpose.
2. Discuss formal proposals and their specific components.
3. Identify the components of typical business plans, and ethically create buy-in for your business ideas.
4. Describe the components of the front matter in formal business reports, and show how they further the purpose of your report.
5. Describe the body and back matter of formal business reports and how they serve the purpose of your report.
6. Specify tips that aid writers of formal business reports.

Want to do well on tests and excel in your course?
Go to **www.meguffey.com** for helpful interactive resources.

▸ **Review the Chapter 13 PowerPoint slides to prepare for the first quiz.**

Zooming In PART 1

Writing Winning Proposals at Raytheon

It was a sunny November morning in Southern California. The director of operations at Raytheon Company's Santa Barbara business unit stood in front of an audience of about 20 engineers and managers—the individuals selected by management to write a proposal for the Aerosol Polarimetry Sensor on the National Polar-Orbiting Operational Environmental Satellite System. He began by telling them, "The request for proposal (RFP) has finally arrived. I know that many of you have been thinking about how to win this contract for more than a year. Now it's time to turn that thinking into words—time to write the proposal!"[1]

He then introduced the proposal volume managers. They would be directing most of the team's writing efforts. Finally, he identified the proposal team's newest member, Dr. Mark Grinyer, a Raytheon proposal specialist who had been asked to write the vitally important executive summary volume. He closed with a final comment: "Remember, everyone, we're on the clock now. We've got less than 60 days to build a winning proposal for almost $100 million in new business."

As Dr. Grinyer listened, he thought, "It'll be a busy holiday season." Such schedules, however, are typical for aerospace industry proposals. Several companies were competing for this contract, and only one proposal would win.

A leading aerospace company, Raytheon is a Fortune 500 giant with about 75,000 employees worldwide. Most are technicians, engineers, scientists, and managers involved in high-technology military and government programs. Raytheon's Remote Sensing business unit in Santa Barbara specializes in high-quality electro-optical sensor systems for weather satellites and other space-based vehicles. The company's sensors on weather satellites provide images seen on TV every day and enable quality weather predictions around the world.

Like most aerospace companies, Raytheon's success depends on its ability to produce winning proposals selling complex systems that involve many disciplines. High-tech companies use a structured proposal development process. This process enables teams of employees who are neither professional writers nor proposal experts to work together, often under pressing time constraints. Their goal is to develop winning proposals against tough competition.

©PAT GREENHOUSE/Boston Globe /Landov

Critical Thinking

- Why are proposals vitally important to a company like Raytheon?
- How are proposals written at Raytheon similar to and different from proposals or long reports written by students?
- How can team members maintain consistency and meet deadlines when writing important, time-constrained, multivolume documents such as this proposal?

http://www.raytheon.com

Preparing Informal Proposals

LEARNING OBJECTIVE 1

Discuss the general uses and basic components of informal proposals, and grasp their audience and purpose.

Proposals are written offers to solve problems, provide services, or sell equipment. Some proposals are internal, often taking the form of justification and recommendation reports. You learned about these persuasive reports in Chapter 12. Most proposals, however, are external, such as those written at Raytheon. They are a critical means of selling equipment and services that generate income for the giant aerospace company.

Why do government agencies and many companies use requests for proposals (RFPs)?

Proposals may be divided into two categories: solicited and unsolicited. When government organizations or firms know exactly what they want, they prepare a request for proposal (RFP), specifying their requirements. Government agencies as well as private businesses use RFPs to solicit competitive bids from vendors. Most proposals are solicited, such as that presented by the city of Las Vegas, Nevada. Its 30-page RFP was seeking bids for a parking initiative from public and private funding sources.[2] Enterprising companies looking for work or a special challenge might submit unsolicited proposals—for example, the world-renowned architect who designed the Louvre Museum pyramid in Paris, among other landmarks. I. M. Pei was so intrigued by the mission of the Buck Institute for Age Research that he submitted an unsolicited proposal to design the biomedical research facility in Novato, California.[3]

While many companies tout the benefits of wind and solar energy, the Free Flow Power Corporation (FFP) has a different idea for renewable energy: water power. The Massachusetts-based firm recently drafted a proposal to submerge dozens of hydroelectric turbines along the Mississippi River. If the Federal Energy Regulatory Commission approves the proposal, the turbines could transform natural river currents into electricity for thousands of homes, delivering hundreds of times more energy than wind or solar installations. *What persuasive "hooks" might FFP include in the introduction of its proposals?*

Courtesy of Free Flow Power Corporation

Components of Informal Proposals

Informal proposals may be presented in short (two- to four-page) letters. Sometimes called *letter proposals*, they may contain six principal components: introduction, background, proposal, staffing, budget, and authorization request. As you can see in Figure 13.1, both informal and formal proposals contain these six basic parts. Figure 13.2, an informal letter proposal to a Boston dentist to improve patient satisfaction, illustrates the six parts of letter proposals.

FIGURE 13.1 Components of Formal and Informal Proposals

Appendix
Authorization
Budget
Staffing
Proposal, plan, schedule
Background, problem, purpose
Introduction
List of figures
Table of contents
Title page
Abstract or summary
Letter of transmittal
Copy of RFP (optional)

Generally appear in both formal and informal proposals:

Optional in informal proposals:

FIGURE 13.2 **Informal Proposal**

Prewriting

Analyze: The purpose is to persuade the reader to accept this proposal.

Anticipate: The reader must be convinced that this survey project is worth its hefty price.

Adapt: Because the reader will be resistant at first, use a persuasive approach that emphasizes benefits.

Writing

Research: Collect data about the reader's practice and other surveys of patient satisfaction.

Organize: Identify four specific purposes (benefits) of this proposal. Specify the survey plan. Promote the staff, itemize the budget, and ask for approval.

Compose: Prepare for revision by composing at a word processor.

Revising

Revise: Revise to emphasize benefits. Improve readability with functional headings and lists. Remove jargon and wordiness.

Proofread: Check spelling of client's name. Verify dates and calculation of budget figures. Recheck all punctuation.

Evaluate: Is this proposal convincing enough to sell the client?

---

approach market research
research | PR | consulting

205 Carlton Place | Watertown, MA 02478
phone 617.900.2005 | fax 617.900.2020
e-mail: info@approach.com

June 2, 2012

Diane Corbett, DDS
1600 Beacon Street, Suite 105
Boston, MA 02215

Dear Dr. Corbett:

Understanding the views of your patients is the key to meeting their needs. Approach Market Research is pleased to propose a plan to help you become even more successful by learning what patients expect of your practice, so that you can improve your services.

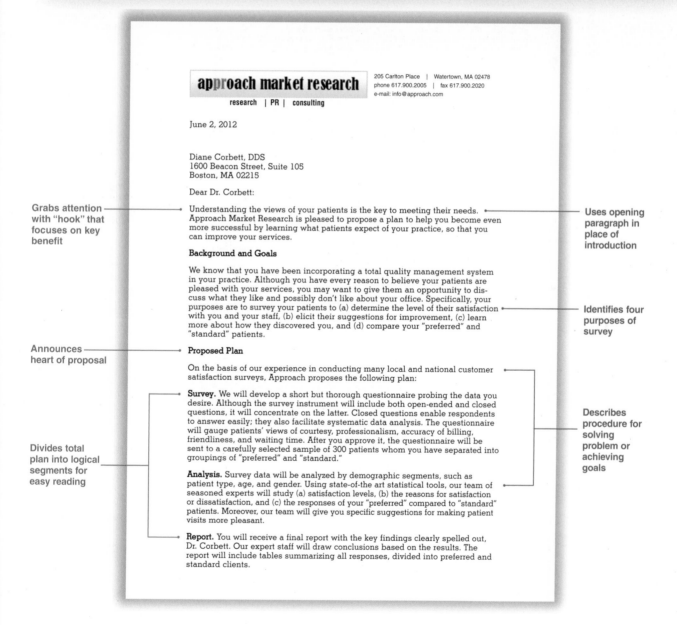

Grabs attention with "hook" that focuses on key benefit

Uses opening paragraph in place of introduction

Background and Goals

We know that you have been incorporating a total quality management system in your practice. Although you have every reason to believe your patients are pleased with your services, you may want to give them an opportunity to discuss what they like and possibly don't like about your office. Specifically, your purposes are to survey your patients to (a) determine the level of their satisfaction with you and your staff, (b) elicit their suggestions for improvement, (c) learn more about how they discovered you, and (d) compare your "preferred" and "standard" patients.

Identifies four purposes of survey

Proposed Plan

Announces heart of proposal

On the basis of our experience in conducting many local and national customer satisfaction surveys, Approach proposes the following plan:

Describes procedure for solving problem or achieving goals

Divides total plan into logical segments for easy reading

Survey. We will develop a short but thorough questionnaire probing the data you desire. Although the survey instrument will include both open-ended and closed questions, it will concentrate on the latter. Closed questions enable respondents to answer easily; they also facilitate systematic data analysis. The questionnaire will gauge patients' views of courtesy, professionalism, accuracy of billing, friendliness, and waiting time. After you approve it, the questionnaire will be sent to a carefully selected sample of 300 patients whom you have separated into groupings of "preferred" and "standard."

Analysis. Survey data will be analyzed by demographic segments, such as patient type, age, and gender. Using state-of-the art statistical tools, our team of seasoned experts will study (a) satisfaction levels, (b) the reasons for satisfaction or dissatisfaction, and (c) the responses of your "preferred" compared to "standard" patients. Moreover, our team will give you specific suggestions for making patient visits more pleasant.

Report. You will receive a final report with the key findings clearly spelled out, Dr. Corbett. Our expert staff will draw conclusions based on the results. The report will include tables summarizing all responses, divided into preferred and standard clients.

FIGURE 13.2 (Continued)

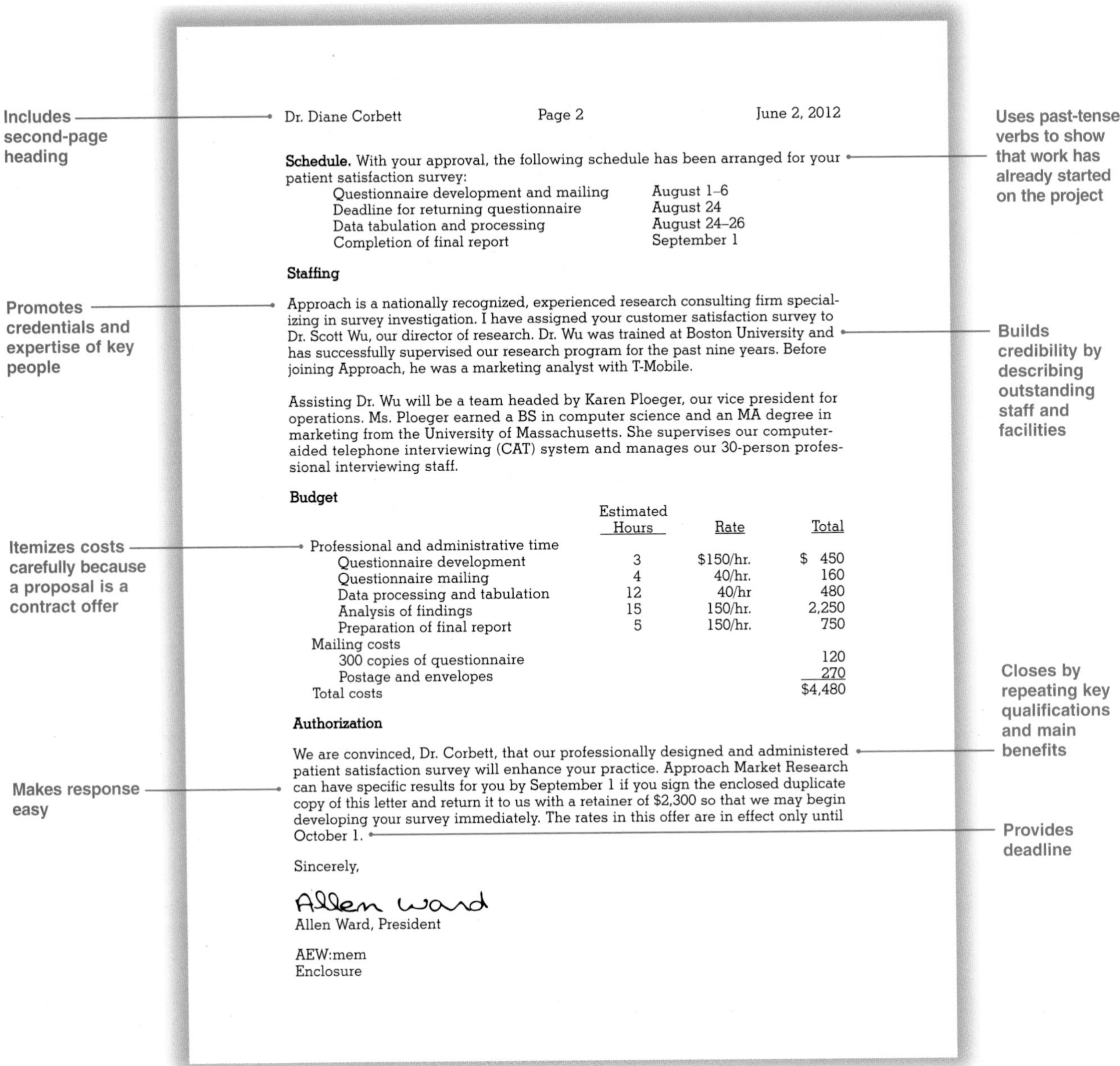

Dr. Diane Corbett — Page 2 — June 2, 2012

Schedule. With your approval, the following schedule has been arranged for your patient satisfaction survey:

Questionnaire development and mailing	August 1–6
Deadline for returning questionnaire	August 24
Data tabulation and processing	August 24–26
Completion of final report	September 1

Staffing

Approach is a nationally recognized, experienced research consulting firm specializing in survey investigation. I have assigned your customer satisfaction survey to Dr. Scott Wu, our director of research. Dr. Wu was trained at Boston University and has successfully supervised our research program for the past nine years. Before joining Approach, he was a marketing analyst with T-Mobile.

Assisting Dr. Wu will be a team headed by Karen Ploeger, our vice president for operations. Ms. Ploeger earned a BS in computer science and an MA degree in marketing from the University of Massachusetts. She supervises our computer-aided telephone interviewing (CAT) system and manages our 30-person professional interviewing staff.

Budget

	Estimated Hours	Rate	Total
Professional and administrative time			
Questionnaire development	3	$150/hr.	$ 450
Questionnaire mailing	4	40/hr.	160
Data processing and tabulation	12	40/hr	480
Analysis of findings	15	150/hr.	2,250
Preparation of final report	5	150/hr.	750
Mailing costs			
300 copies of questionnaire			120
Postage and envelopes			270
Total costs			$4,480

Authorization

We are convinced, Dr. Corbett, that our professionally designed and administered patient satisfaction survey will enhance your practice. Approach Market Research can have specific results for you by September 1 if you sign the enclosed duplicate copy of this letter and return it to us with a retainer of $2,300 so that we may begin developing your survey immediately. The rates in this offer are in effect only until October 1.

Sincerely,

Allen Ward

Allen Ward, President

AEW:mem
Enclosure

Includes second-page heading
Promotes credentials and expertise of key people
Itemizes costs carefully because a proposal is a contract offer
Makes response easy
Uses past-tense verbs to show that work has already started on the project
Builds credibility by describing outstanding staff and facilities
Closes by repeating key qualifications and main benefits
Provides deadline

What are the six main components of informal proposals?

Introduction. Most proposals begin by briefly explaining the reasons for the proposal and highlighting the writer's qualifications. To make your introduction more persuasive, you need to provide a "hook," such as the following:

- Hint at extraordinary results with details to be revealed shortly.
- Promise low costs or speedy results.
- Mention a remarkable resource (well-known authority, new computer program, well-trained staff) available exclusively to you.
- Identify a serious problem (worry item) and promise a solution, to be explained later.
- Specify a key issue or benefit that you feel is the heart of the proposal.

Although writers may know what goes into the proposal introduction, many face writer's block before they can get started. Proposal expert Tom Sant recommends a method he calls *cognitive webbing* to overcome the paralyzing effects of writer's block and arrive at a proposal writing plan. Dr. Sant advises that proposal writers (a) identify the outcome the client seeks, (b) brainstorm by writing down every idea and detail that will help the client achieve that objective, and (c) prioritize by again focusing on the client's most pressing needs.[4] You may have brainstormed using a very similar technique, mind mapping, by creating cluster diagrams to generate ideas for your papers.

In the proposal introduction shown in Figure 13.2, Allen Ward focused on what the customer was looking for. He analyzed the request of the Boston dentist, Dr. Diane Corbett, and decided that she was most interested in specific recommendations for improving service to her patients. However, Ward did not hit on this hook until he had written a first draft and had come back to it later. Indeed, it is often a good idea to put off writing the proposal introduction until after you have completed other parts. In longer proposals the introduction also describes the scope and limitations of the project, as well as outlining the organization of the material to come.

Where do you discuss the problem and goals of the project?

Background, Problem, and Purpose. The background section identifies the problem and discusses the goals or purposes of the project. In an unsolicited proposal, your goal is to convince the reader that a problem exists. Therefore, you must present the problem in detail, discussing such factors as monetary losses, failure to comply with government regulations, or loss of customers. In a solicited proposal, your aim is to persuade the reader that you understand the problem completely. Therefore, if you are responding to an RFP, this means repeating its language. For example, if the RFP asks for the *design of a maintenance program for wireless communication equipment*, you would use the same language in explaining the purpose of your proposal. This section might include segments titled *Basic Requirements, Most Critical Tasks*, or *Most Important Secondary Problems*.

What role does the actual proposal section play, and how much detail must it provide?

Proposal, Plan, and Schedule. In the proposal section itself, you should discuss your plan for solving the problem. In some proposals this is tricky because you want to disclose enough of your plan to secure the contract without giving away so much information that your services aren't needed. Without specifics, though, your proposal has little chance, so you must decide how much to reveal. Tell what you propose to do and how it will benefit the reader. Remember, too, that a proposal is a sales presentation. Sell your methods, product, and "deliverables" (items that will be left with the client). In this section some writers specify how the project will be managed and how its progress will be audited. Most writers also include a schedule of activities or timetable showing when events will take place.

What is the purpose of the staffing section?

Staffing. The staffing section of a proposal describes the credentials and expertise of the project leaders. It may also identify the size and qualifications of the support staff, along with other resources such as computer facilities and special programs for analyzing statistics. The staffing section is a good place to endorse and promote your staff and to demonstrate to the client that your company can do the job. Some firms, like Raytheon, follow industry standards and include staff qualifications in an appendix. Raytheon features the résumés of the major project participants, such as the program manager, the technical director, and team leaders. If key contributors must be replaced in the course of the project, Raytheon commits to providing only individuals with equivalent qualifications. The first rule is to give clients exactly what they asked for regarding staff qualifications, the number of project participants, and proposal details.

Why must you carefully research the proposal budget?

Budget. A central item in most proposals is the budget, a list of proposed project costs. You need to prepare this section carefully because it represents a contract; you cannot raise the price later—even if your costs increase. You can—and should—protect yourself from rising costs with a deadline for acceptance. In the budget section, some writers itemize hours and costs; others present a total sum only. A proposal to install a complex computer system might, for example, contain a detailed line-by-line budget. Similarly, Allen Ward felt that he needed to justify the budget for his firm's patient satisfaction survey, so he itemized the costs, as shown in Figure 13.2. However, the budget included for a proposal to conduct a one-day seminar to improve employee communication skills might be a lump sum only. Your analysis of the project will help you decide what kind of budget to prepare.

Authorization Request. Informal proposals often close with a request for approval or authorization. In addition, the closing should remind the reader of key benefits and motivate action. It might also include a deadline beyond which the offer is invalid. At Raytheon authorization information can be as simple as naming in the letter of transmittal the company official who would approve the contract resulting from the proposal. However, in most cases, a *model contract* is sent along that responds to the requirements specified by the RFP. This model contract almost always results in negotiations before the final project contract is awarded.

Preparing Formal Proposals

LEARNING OBJECTIVE 2
Discuss formal proposals and their specific components.

Proposals became a staple in the aerospace industry in the 1950s to streamline the bidding for government defense projects. Because proposals are vital to their success, high-tech companies and defense contractors maintain specialists, like Dr. Mark Grinyer at Raytheon, who do nothing but write proposals. Such proposals typically tell how a problem can be solved, what procedure will be followed, who will do it, how long it will take, and how much it will cost. When receiving bids, companies today want to be able to "compare apples with apples." They also want the protection offered by proposals, which are legal contracts. As you can imagine, writing a formal proposal to bid on a multimillion-dollar contract requires careful preparation, expertise, and countless staff hours.

Special Components of Formal Proposals

Formal proposals differ from informal proposals not in style but in size and format. Formal proposals respond to big projects and may range from 5 to 200 or more pages. To facilitate comprehension and reference, they are organized into many parts, as shown in Figure 13.1. In addition to the six basic components described for informal proposals, formal proposals may contain some or all of the following front matter and back matter components.

Which additional components might formal proposals contain that are usually missing in informal proposals?

Copy of the RFP. A copy of the request for proposal may be included in the front matter of a formal proposal. Large organizations may have more than one RFP circulating, and identification is necessary.

Letter of Transmittal. A letter of transmittal, usually bound inside formal proposals, addresses the person who is designated to receive the proposal or who will make the final decision. The letter describes how you learned about the problem or confirms that the proposal responds to the enclosed RFP. This persuasive letter briefly presents the major features and benefits of your proposal. Here, you should assure the reader that you are authorized to make the bid and mention the time limit for which the bid stands. You may also offer to provide additional information and ask for action, if appropriate.

What are the main differences between an abstract and an executive summary in proposals?

Abstract or Executive Summary. An abstract is a brief summary (typically one page) of a proposal's highlights intended for specialists or technical readers. An executive summary also reviews the proposal's highlights, but it is written for managers and should be less technically oriented. An executive summary tends to be longer than an abstract, up to 10 percent of the original text. In reports and proposals, the executive summary typically represents a nutshell version of the entire document and addresses all its sections or chapters. Formal proposals may contain either an abstract or an executive summary or both. For more information about writing executive summaries and abstracts, use a search engine such as Google.

Title Page. The title page includes the following items, generally in this order: title of proposal, name of client organization, RFP number or other announcement, date of submission, authors' names, and/or the name of their organization.

Table of Contents. Because most proposals do not contain an index, the table of contents becomes quite important. A table of contents should include all headings and their beginning page numbers. Items that appear before the contents (copy of RFP, letter of transmittal, abstract, and title page) typically are not listed in the contents. However, any appendixes should be listed.

Spotlight on Communicators

© Michael Asner

Author, coach, and proposal-writing expert Michael Asner considers a successful bid as nothing short of a work of art: "Given the complexity of meeting the demands stipulated in government documents—being able to satisfy them and compose a successful bid takes a tremendous amount of knowledge and discipline and it's really an art form." Asner is offering the first online library and how-to guide to composing proposals for government contracts on the Internet.

Checklist

Writing Proposals

Introduction

- **Indicate the purpose.** Specify why you are making the proposal.
- **Develop a persuasive "hook."** Suggest excellent results, low costs, or exclusive resources. Identify a serious problem or name a key issue or benefit.

Background, Problem, Purpose

- **Provide necessary background.** Discuss the significance of the proposal and the goals or purposes that matter to the client.
- **Introduce the problem.** For unsolicited proposals convince the reader that a problem exists. For solicited proposals show that you fully understand the customer's problem and its ramifications.

Proposal, Plan, Schedule

- **Explain the proposal.** Present your plan for solving the problem or meeting the need.
- **Discuss plan management and evaluation.** If appropriate, tell how the plan will be implemented and evaluated.
- **Outline a timetable.** Furnish a schedule showing what will be done and when.

Staffing

- **Promote the qualifications of your staff.** Explain the specific credentials and expertise of the key personnel for the project.
- **Mention special resources and equipment.** Show how your support staff and resources are superior to those of the competition.

Budget

- **Show project costs.** For most projects itemize costs. Remember, however, that proposals are contracts.
- **Include a deadline.** Here or in the conclusion, present a date beyond which the bid figures are no longer valid.

Authorization

- **Ask for approval.** Make it easy for the reader to authorize the project (for example, *Sign and return the duplicate copy*).

List of Illustrations. Proposals with many tables and figures often contain a list of illustrations. This list includes each figure or table title and its page number. If you have just a few figures or tables, however, you may omit this list.

Appendix. Ancillary material of interest to only some readers goes in appendixes. Appendix A might include résumés of the principal investigators or testimonial letters. Appendix B

Zooming In — PART 2

Writing Winning Proposals at Raytheon

Raytheon's proposal process involves adapting the writing process to a team-writing environment. Dr. Mark Grinyer, who was assigned the task of writing the important executive summary, described how he used this process to complete his portion of Raytheon's Aerosol Polarimetry Sensor proposal.

First, he studied the customer's RFP looking for what the client really cared about. Then he talked to proposal team members and read descriptions of the company's offering. He turned this information into persuasive themes, outlines, and visuals, which he organized into ten storyboards (graphic organizers), one for each section of the summary. Proposal team members and a "Pink Team" of company executives reviewed these storyboards and made suggestions for improvement. "They focused on content quality, organization, and accuracy," Dr. Grinyer said.

Using the storyboards, Dr. Grinyer quickly wrote the first draft working section by section. He and his teammates revised the draft until all contributors were satisfied that it effectively addressed the interests of its audience of decision makers. A formal "Red Team" of company executives confirmed this assessment. The proposal was then ready for final corrections, formatting, proofreading, printing, and submission to the customer. "Overall," Dr. Grinyer explained, "the guidance provided by my teammates and reviewers kept me on target throughout the proposal effort."

©PAT GREENHOUSE/Boston Globe /Landov

Critical Thinking

- What aspects of Raytheon's proposal writing process can you apply to your own work?
- How do you think the various reviewers and their reviews help ensure the success of a proposal effort?
- Why do you think Raytheon puts so much effort into proposal executive summaries?

might include examples or a listing of previous projects. Other appendixes could include audit procedures, technical graphics, or professional papers cited in the body of the proposal.

Proposals in the past were always paper-based and delivered by mail or special messenger. Today, however, companies increasingly prefer *online proposals*. Receiving companies may transmit the electronic proposal to all levels of management without ever printing a page; this appeals to many environmentally conscious organizations.

Well-written proposals win contracts and business for companies and individuals. Many companies depend entirely on proposals to generate their income, so proposal writing is extremely important. The accompanying checklist summarizes key elements to remember in writing proposals.

Creating Effective Business Plans

LEARNING OBJECTIVE 3

Identify the components of typical business plans, and ethically create buy-in for your business ideas.

Another form of proposal is a business plan. Let's say you want to start your own business. Unless you can count on the Bank of Mom and Dad, you will need financial backing such as a bank loan, seed money from an individual angel investor, or funds supplied by venture capitalists. A business plan is critical for securing financial support of any kind. Such a plan also ensures that you have done your homework and know what you are doing in launching your business. It provides you with a detailed road map to chart a course to success.

According to the Small Business Administration, most entrepreneurs spend about 400 hours writing a good business plan. The average consultant can do it in about 40 hours.[5] Nevertheless, many budding entrepreneurs prefer to save the cash and do it themselves. Increasingly sophisticated software such as Business Plan Pro, PlanWrite, and PlanMagic is available for those who have done their research, assembled the relevant data, and just want formatting help. Free shareware can also be found on the Internet.[6]

Components of Typical Business Plans

If you are serious about starting a business, the importance of a comprehensive, thoughtful business plan cannot be overemphasized, says the Small Business Administration. Your business plan is more likely to secure the funds you need if it is carefully written and includes the following elements:

Letter of Transmittal and/or Executive Summary With Mission Statement. Explain your reason for writing. Provide your name, address, and telephone number, along with contact information for all principals. Include a concise mission statement for your business. Describe your business explaining the reasons it will succeed. Because potential investors will be looking for this mission statement, consider highlighting it with a paragraph heading (*Mission Statement*) or use bolding or italics. Some consultants say that you should be able to write your mission statement on the back of a business card. Others think that one or two short paragraphs might be more realistic. To give it special treatment, you could make the mission statement a section of its own following the table of contents. Your executive summary is a business plan in miniature and should not exceed two pages. It should conclude by introducing the parts of the following plan and asking for financial backing.

Table of Contents. List the page numbers and topics included in your plan. Free sample business plans featuring typical components and headings are available on the Internet from the U.S. Small Business Administration or private outfits such as Bplans.com.

Company Description. Identify the form of your business (proprietorship, partnership, or corporation) and its type (merchandising, manufacturing, or service). For existing companies, describe the company's founding, growth, sales, and profit.

Product or Service Description. In jargon-free language, explain what you are providing, how it will benefit customers, and why

Spotlight on Communicators

Courtesy of Tim Berry

President of Palo Alto Software and *Entrepreneur* magazine columnist Tim Berry advises would-be business owners not to delay writing their business plans: "Don't wait to write your plan until you think you'll have enough time. 'I can't plan. I'm too busy getting things done,' business people say." Berry suggests dropping the excuses: "The busier you are, the more you need to plan. If you are always putting out fires, you should build firebreaks or a sprinkler system. You can lose the whole forest for paying too much attention to the individual burning trees."

it is better than existing products or services. For start-ups, explain why the business will be profitable. Investors aren't always looking for a unique product or service. Instead, they are searching for a concept whose growth potential distinguishes it from others competing for funds.

Market Analysis. Discuss market characteristics, trends, projected growth, customer behavior, complementary products and services, and barriers to entry. Identify your customers and how you will attract, hold, and increase your market share. Discuss the strengths and weaknesses of your direct and indirect competitors.

Operations and Management. Explain specifically how you will run your business, including location, equipment, personnel, and management. Highlight experienced and well-trained members of the management team and your advisors. Many investors consider this the most important factor in assessing business potential. Can your management team implement this business plan?

Financial Analysis. Outline a realistic start-up budget that includes fees for legal and professional services, occupancy, licenses and permits, equipment, insurance, supplies, advertising and promotions, salaries and wages, accounting, income, and utilities. Also present an operating budget that projects costs for personnel, insurance, rent, depreciation, loan payments, salaries, taxes, repairs, and so on. Explain how much money you have, how much you will need to start up, and how much you will need to stay in business.

Appendixes. Provide necessary extras such as managers' résumés, promotional materials, and product photos. Most appendixes contain tables that exhibit the sales forecast, a personnel plan, anticipated cash flow, profit and loss, and a balance sheet.

ETHICS CHECK

Honesty Is Key

A business plan's purpose is to help manage a company and raise capital; hence, it is a persuasive document that must be accurate and honest. Whether the goal is to persuade a lender or investors or whether it is the blueprint for running operations, the business plan must be realistic. What are the risks of "fudging" numbers or sugarcoating potential challenges?

Seeing Sample Business Plans on the Web

Writing a business plan is easier if you can see examples and learn from experts' suggestions. On the Web you will find many sites devoted to business plans. Some sites want to sell you something; others offer free advice. One of the best sites **(http://www.bplans.com)** does try to sell business plans and software. However, in addition to useful advice and blogs from experts, the site also provides over 100 free samples of business plans ranging from aircraft rental to wedding consultant businesses. These simple but helpful plans, provided by Palo Alto Software, Inc., illustrate diverse business start-ups.

At the Small Business Administration (SBA) Web site **(http://www.sba.gov/smallbusinessplanner/)**, you will find more business plan advice. In addition to suggestions for writing and using a business plan, the SBA site provides helpful business start-up information about financing, marketing, employees, taxes, and legal matters. The SBA site also provides local resources and tools for the budding entrepreneur.

Writing Formal Business Reports

LEARNING OBJECTIVE 4

Describe the components of the front matter in formal business reports, and show how they further the purpose of your report.

Formal business reports are similar to formal proposals in length, organization, and serious tone. Instead of making an offer, however, formal reports represent the end product of thorough investigation and analysis. They present ordered information to decision makers in business, industry, government, and education. In many ways formal business reports are extended versions of the analytical business reports presented in Chapter 12. Figure 13.3 shows the components of typical formal reports, their normal sequence, and parts that might be omitted in informal reports.

Front Matter Components of Formal Business Reports

What is the purpose of formal business reports?

A number of front matter and back matter items lengthen formal reports but enhance their professional tone and serve their multiple audiences. Formal reports may be read by many levels of managers, along with technical specialists and financial consultants. Therefore, breaking a long, formal report into small segments makes its information more accessible and easier to understand

FIGURE 13.3 **Components of Formal and Informal Reports**

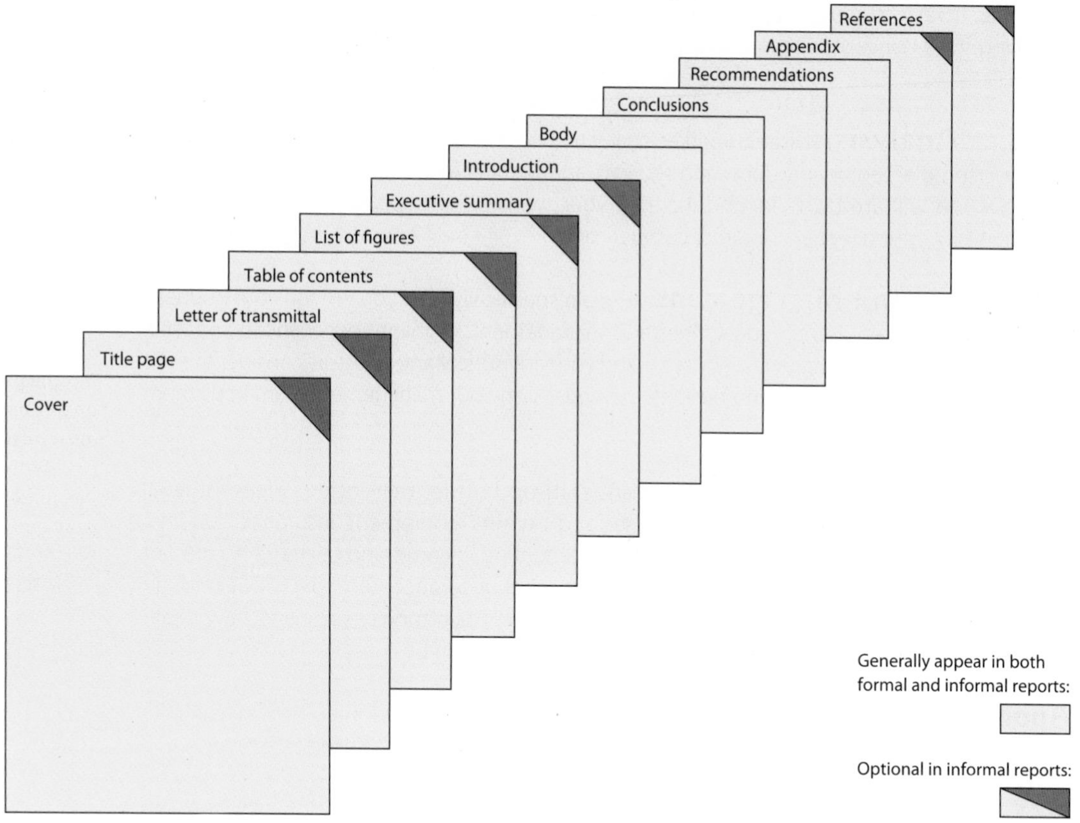

for all readers. The segments in the front of the report, called front matter or preliminaries, are discussed in this section. They are also illustrated in the model report shown later in the chapter (Figure 13.4). This analytical report studies the economic impact of an industrial park on Flagstaff, Arizona, and makes recommendations for increasing the city's future revenues.

Why are formal reports divided into many segments?

Cover. Formal reports are usually enclosed in vinyl or heavy paper binders to protect the pages and to give a professional, finished appearance. Some companies have binders imprinted with their name and logo. The title of the report may appear through a cut-out window or may be applied with an adhesive label. Good stationery and office supply stores usually stock an assortment of report binders and labels.

Title Page. A report title page, as illustrated in the Figure 13.4 model report, begins with the name of the report typed in uppercase letters (no underscore and no quotation marks). Next comes *Prepared for* (or *Submitted to*) and the name, title, and organization of the individual receiving the report. Lower on the page is *Prepared by* (or *Submitted by*) and the author's name plus any necessary identification. The last item on the title page is the date of submission. All items after the title are typed in a combination of upper- and lowercase letters.

What is the purpose of a letter or memo of transmittal?

Letter or Memo of Transmittal. Generally written on organization stationery, a letter or memorandum of transmittal introduces a formal report. You will recall that letters are sent to outsiders and memos to insiders. A transmittal letter or memo uses the direct strategy and is usually less formal than the report itself (for example, the letter or memo may use contractions and the first-person pronouns *I* and *we*). The transmittal letter or memo typically (a) announces the topic of the report and tells how it was authorized; (b) briefly describes the project; (c) highlights the report's findings, conclusions, and recommendations, if the reader is expected to be supportive; and (d) closes with appreciation for the assignment, instruction for the reader's follow-up actions, acknowledgement of help from others, or offers of assistance in answering questions. If a report is going to various readers, a special transmittal letter or memo should be prepared for each, anticipating how each reader will use the report.

© AP Images/Mark Lennihan

When Comcast and NBC announced plans to combine their businesses in a $28.2 billion joint venture, the move launched a lengthy merger process governed by the FCC and other regulators. Opponents claimed that merging NBC with the top U.S. cable provider would increase prices and drive out independent media. Proponents argued that integrating cable with NBC would give consumers unprecedented access to popular programming on mobile phones and computers. *In what section of a formal report do businesses generally deliver a full written justification of their proposed actions?*

Table of Contents. The table of contents shows the headings in the report and their page numbers. It gives an overview of the report topics and helps readers locate them. You should wait to prepare the table of contents until after you have completed the report. For short reports you should include all headings. For longer reports you might want to list only first- and second-level headings. Leaders (spaced or unspaced dots) help guide the eye from the heading to the page number. Items may be indented in outline form or typed flush with the left margin.

List of Illustrations. For reports with several figures or tables, you may wish to include a list to help readers locate them. This list may appear on the same page as the table of contents, space permitting. For each figure or table, include a title and page number. Some writers distinguish between tables and all other illustrations, which they call figures. If you make the distinction, you should prepare separate lists of tables and figures. Because the model report in Figure 13.4 has few illustrations, the writer labeled them all "figures," a method that simplifies numbering.

What purpose does an executive summary serve in a long formal report?

Executive Summary. The purpose of an executive summary is to present an overview of a longer report to people who may not have time to read the entire document. Generally, an executive summary is prepared by the author of the report. However, occasionally you may be asked to write an executive summary of a published report or article written by someone else. In either case you will probably do the following:

- **Summarize key points.** Your goal is to summarize the important points including the purpose of the report; the problem addressed; and the findings, conclusions, and recommendations. You might also summarize the research methods, if they can be stated concisely.
- **Look for strategic words and sentences.** Read the completed report carefully. Pay special attention to the first and last sentences of paragraphs, which often contain summary statements. Look for words that enumerate (*first, next, finally*) and words that express causation (*therefore, as a result*). Also look for words that signal essentials (*basically, central, leading, principal, major*) and words that contrast ideas (*however, consequently*).
- **Prepare an outline with headings.** At a minimum, include headings for the purpose, findings, and conclusions/recommendations. What kernels of information would your reader want to know about these topics?
- **Fill in your outline.** Some writers use their computers to cut and paste important parts of the text. Then they condense with careful editing. Others find it more efficient to create new sentences as they prepare the executive summary.

- **Begin with the purpose.** The easiest way to begin an executive summary is with the words *The purpose of this report is to . . . .* Experienced writers may be more creative.
- **Follow the report sequence.** Present all your information in the order in which it is found in the report.
- **Eliminate nonessential details.** Include only main points. Do not include anything not in the original report. Use minimal technical language.
- **Control the length.** An executive summary is usually no longer than 10 percent of the original document. Thus, a 100-page report might require a 10-page summary. A 10-page report might need only a 1-page summary—or no summary at all. The executive summary for a long report may also include graphics to adequately highlight main points.

To see a representative executive summary, look at Figure 13.4 on page 442. Although it is only one page long, this executive summary includes headings to help the reader see the main divisions immediately. Let your organization's practices guide you in determining the length and form of an executive summary.

What is the role of the introduction to a formal report?

Introduction. Formal reports begin with an introduction that sets the scene and announces the subject. Because they contain many parts serving different purposes, formal reports are somewhat redundant. The same information may be included in the letter of transmittal, summary, and introduction. To avoid sounding repetitious, try to present the data slightly differently. However, do not skip the introduction because you have included some of its information elsewhere. You cannot be sure that your reader saw the information earlier. A good report introduction typically covers the following elements, although not necessarily in this order:

- **Background.** Describe events leading up to the problem or need.
- **Problem or purpose.** Explain the report topic and specify the problem or need that motivated the report.
- **Significance.** Tell why the topic is important. You may wish to quote experts or cite newspapers, journals, books, Web resources, and other secondary sources to establish the importance of the topic.
- **Scope.** Clarify the boundaries of the report, defining what will be included or excluded.
- **Organization.** Orient readers by giving them a road map that previews the structure of the report.

Beyond these minimal introductory elements, consider adding any of the following information that is relevant to your readers:

- **Authorization.** Identify who commissioned the report. If no letter of transmittal is included, also tell why, when, by whom, and to whom the report was written.
- **Literature review.** Summarize what other authors and researchers have published on this topic, especially for academic and scientific reports.
- **Sources and methods.** Describe your secondary sources (periodicals, books, databases). Also explain how you collected primary data, including survey size, sample design, and statistical programs used.
- **Definitions of key terms.** Define words that may be unfamiliar to the audience. Also define terms with special meanings, such as *small business* when it specifically means businesses with fewer than 30 employees.

LEARNING OBJECTIVE 5

Describe the body and back matter of formal business reports and how they serve the purpose of your report.

Body and Back Matter Components of Formal Business Reports

The body of a formal business report is the "meat" of the document. In this longest and most substantive section of the text, the author or team discusses the problem and findings, before reaching conclusions and making recommendations. Extensive and bulky materials that don't fit in the text belong in the appendix. Although some very long reports may have additional components, the back matter usually concludes with a list of sources. The body and back matter of formal business reports are discussed in this section. Figure 13.3 shows the parts of typical reports, the order in which they appear, and elements usually found only in formal reports.

Because formal business reports can be long and complex, they usually include more sections than routine informal business reports do. These components are standard and conventional; that is, the audience expects to see them in a professional report. Documents that conform to such expectations are easier to read and deliver their message more effectively. You will find most of the components addressed here in the model report in Figure 13.4, the analytical report studying the economic impact of an industrial park on Flagstaff, Arizona.

Body. The principal section in a formal report is the body. It discusses, analyzes, interprets, and evaluates the research findings or solution to the initial problem. This is where you show the evidence that justifies your conclusions. Organize the body into main categories following your original outline or using one of the organizational methods described in Chapter 12 (i.e., time, component, importance, criteria, or convention).

Although we refer to this section as the body, it does not carry that heading. Instead, it contains clear headings that explain each major section. Headings may be functional or talking. Functional heads (such as *Results of the Survey, Analysis of Findings,* or *Discussion*) help readers identify the purpose of the section but do not reveal what is in it. Such headings are useful for routine reports or for sensitive topics that may upset readers. Talking heads (for example, *Findings Reveal Revenue and Employment Benefits*) are more informative and interesting, but they do not help readers see the organization of the report. The model report in Figure 13.4 uses combination headings; as the name suggests, they combine functional heads for organizational sections (*Introduction, Conclusions and Recommendations*) with talking heads that reveal the content. The headings divide the body into smaller parts.

Conclusions. This important section tells what the findings mean, particularly in terms of solving the original problem. Some writers prefer to intermix their conclusions with the analysis of the findings—instead of presenting the conclusions separately. Other writers place the conclusions before the body so that busy readers can examine the significant information immediately. Still others combine the conclusions and recommendations. Most writers, though, present the conclusions after the body because readers expect this structure. In long reports this section may include a summary of the findings. To improve comprehension, you may present the conclusions in a numbered or bulleted list. See Chapter 12 for more suggestions on drawing conclusions.

What is the purpose of the recommendations section of a formal report?

Recommendations. When asked, you should submit recommendations that make precise suggestions for actions to solve the report problem. Recommendations are most helpful when they are practical, reasonable, feasible, and ethical. Naturally, they should evolve from the findings and conclusions. Do not introduce new information in the conclusions or recommendations sections. As with conclusions, the position of recommendations is somewhat flexible. They may be combined with conclusions, or they may be presented before the body, especially when the audience is eager and supportive. Generally, though, in formal reports they come last.

Recommendations require an appropriate introductory sentence, such as *The findings and conclusions in this study support the following recommendations.* When making many recommendations, number them and phrase each as a command, such as *Begin an employee fitness program with a workout room available five days a week.* If appropriate, add information describing how to implement each recommendation. Some reports include a timetable describing the who, what, when, where, why, and how for putting each recommendation into operation. Chapter 12 provides more information about writing recommendations.

Appendix. Incidental or supporting materials belong in appendixes at the end of a formal report. These materials are relevant to some readers but not to all. They may also be too bulky to include in the text. Appendixes may include survey forms, copies of other reports, tables of data, large graphics, and related correspondence. If additional appendixes are necessary, they are named *Appendix A, Appendix B,* and so forth.

What does the works-cited or references section of a formal report contain?

Works Cited or References. If you use the MLA (Modern Language Association) referencing format, list all sources of information alphabetically in a section titled *Works Cited*. If you use the APA (American Psychological Association) format, your list is called *References*. Your listed sources must correspond to in-text citations in the report whenever you are borrowing words or ideas from published and unpublished resources.

Regardless of the documentation format, you must include the author, title, publication, date of publication, page number, and other significant data for all ideas or quotations used in your report. For electronic references include the preceding information plus a description of the Internet address or URL leading to the citation. Also include the retrieval date on which you located the electronic reference. To see electronic and other citations, examine the list of references at the end of Figure 13.4. Appendix C of this textbook contains additional documentation information.

LEARNING OBJECTIVE 6
Specify tips that aid writers of formal business reports.

Final Writing Tips

Formal business reports are not undertaken lightly. They involve considerable effort in all three phases of writing, beginning with analysis of the problem and anticipation of the audience (as discussed in Chapter 4). Researching the data, organizing it into a logical presentation, and composing the first draft (Chapter 5) make up the second phase of writing. Revising, proofreading, and evaluating (Chapter 6) are completed in the third phase. Although everyone approaches the writing process somewhat differently, the following tips offer advice in problem areas faced by most writers of formal reports:

- **Allow sufficient time.** The main reason given by writers who are disappointed with their reports is "I just ran out of time." Develop a realistic timetable and stick to it.
- **Finish data collection.** Do not begin writing until you have collected all the data and drawn the primary conclusions. Starting too early often means backtracking. For reports based on survey data, complete the tables and figures first.

How do smart report writers approach time management, research, and their writing task?

- **Work from a good outline.** A big project such as a formal report needs the order and direction provided by a clear outline, even if the outline has to be revised as the project unfolds.
- **Provide a proper writing environment.** You will need a quiet spot where you can spread out your materials and work without interruption. Formal reports demand blocks of concentration time.
- **Use the features of your computer wisely.** Your word processor enables you to keyboard quickly; revise easily; and check spelling, grammar, and synonyms readily. A word of warning, though: save your document often and keep backup copies on disks or memory sticks. Print out important materials so that you have a hard copy. Take these precautions to guard against the grief caused by lost files, power outages, and computer malfunctions.
- **Write rapidly; revise later.** Some experts advise writers to record their ideas quickly and save revision until after the first draft is completed. They say that quick writing avoids wasted effort spent in polishing sentences or even sections that may be cut later. Moreover, rapid writing encourages fluency and creativity. However, a quick-and-dirty first draft does not work for everyone. Many business writers prefer a more deliberate writing style, so consider this advice selectively and experiment with the method that works best for you.
- **Save difficult sections.** If some sections are harder to write than others, save them until you have developed confidence and a rhythm working on easier topics.

ETHICS CHECK
Cheater on the Team
If one of your teammates cowriting a formal report with you has been found to have plagiarized a portion of your writing project, typically the instructor will punish the entire group, assuming ownership by the entire team. After all, researchers are expected to deliver a product that they have jointly prepared. Is this fair?

When should you use the past tense, and when should you use the present tense in formal reports?

- **Be consistent in verb tense.** Use past-tense verbs to describe completed actions (for example, *the respondents said* or *the survey showed*). Use present-tense verbs, however, to explain current actions (*the purpose of the report is, this report examines, the table shows*). When citing references, use past-tense verbs (*Jones reported that*). Do not switch back and forth between present- and past-tense verbs in describing related data.

[The list of Final Writing Tips continues on page 448.]

FIGURE 13.4 Model Format Report with APA Citation Style

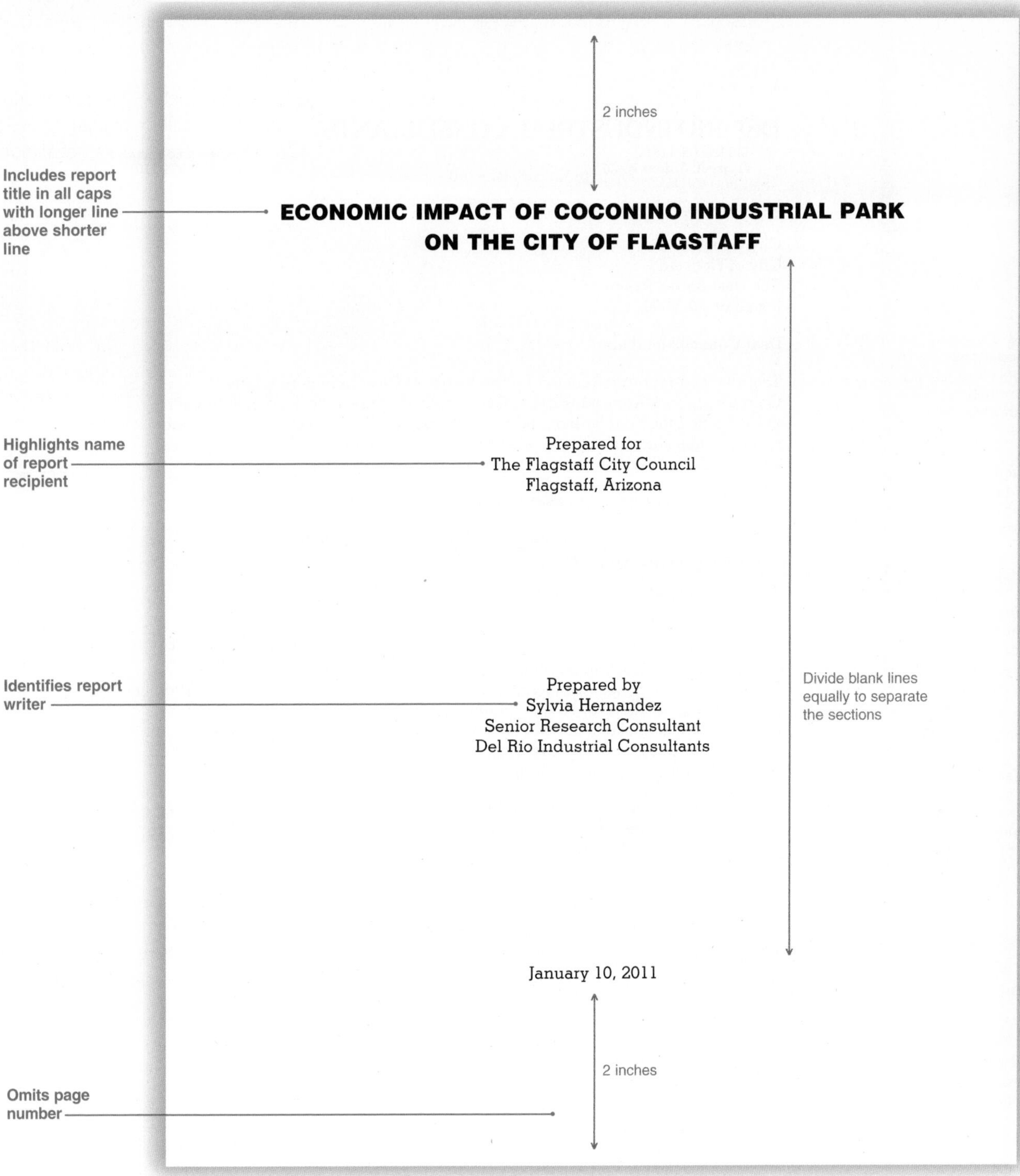

2 inches
Includes report title in all caps with longer line above shorter line
ECONOMIC IMPACT OF COCONINO INDUSTRIAL PARK
ON THE CITY OF FLAGSTAFF
Highlights name of report recipient
Prepared for
The Flagstaff City Council
Flagstaff, Arizona
Identifies report writer
Prepared by
Sylvia Hernandez
Senior Research Consultant
Del Rio Industrial Consultants
Divide blank lines equally to separate the sections
January 10, 2011
2 inches
Omits page number

The title page is usually arranged in four evenly balanced areas. If the report is to be bound on the left, move the left margin and center point ¼ inch to the right (i.e., set the left margin to 1.25 inches). Notice that no page number appears on the title page, although it counts as page i. In designing the title page, be careful to avoid anything unprofessional—such as too many type fonts, italics, oversized print, and inappropriate graphics. Keep the title page simple and professional.

This model report uses APA documentation style. However, it does not use double-spacing, the recommended format for research papers using APA style. Instead, this model uses single-spacing, which saves space and is more appropriate for business reports.

FIGURE 13.4 (Continued) Letter of Transmittal

DEL RIO INDUSTRIAL CONSULTANTS
110 West Route 66
Flagstaff, Arizona 86001

www.delrio.com
(928) 774-1101

January 12, 2011

City Council
City of Flagstaff
211 West Aspen Avenue
Flagstaff, AZ 86001

Dear Council Members:

Announces report and identifies authorization

The attached report, requested by the Flagstaff City Council in a letter to Goldman-Lyon & Associates dated October 20, describes the economic impact of Coconino Industrial Park on the city of Flagstaff. We believe you will find the results of this study useful in evaluating future development of industrial parks within the city limits.

Gives broad overview of report purposes

This study was designed to examine economic impact in three areas:

- Current and projected tax and other revenues accruing to the city from Coconino Industrial Park
- Current and projected employment generated by the park
- Indirect effects on local employment, income, and economic growth

Describes primary and secondary research

Primary research consisted of interviews with 15 Coconino Industrial Park (CIP) tenants and managers, in addition to a 2010 survey of over 5,000 CIP employees. Secondary research sources included the Annual Budget of the City of Flagstaff, county and state tax records, government publications, periodicals, books, and online resources. Results of this research, discussed more fully in this report, indicate that Coconino Industrial Park exerts a significant beneficial influence on the Flagstaff metropolitan economy.

Offers to discuss report; expresses appreciation

We would be pleased to discuss this report and its conclusions with you at your request. My firm and I thank you for your confidence in selecting our company to prepare this comprehensive report.

Sincerely,

Sylvia Hernandez

Sylvia Hernandez
Senior Research Consultant

SMH:mef
Attachment

Uses Roman numerals for prefatory pages

ii

A letter or memo of transmittal announces the report topic and explains who authorized it. It briefly describes the project and previews the conclusions, if the reader is supportive. Such messages generally close by expressing appreciation for the assignment, suggesting follow-up actions, acknowledging the help of others, or offering to answer questions. The margins for the transmittal should be the same as for the report, about 1 to 1¼ inches on all sides. The letter should be left-justified. A page number is optional.

FIGURE 13.4 (Continued) Table of Contents and List of Figures

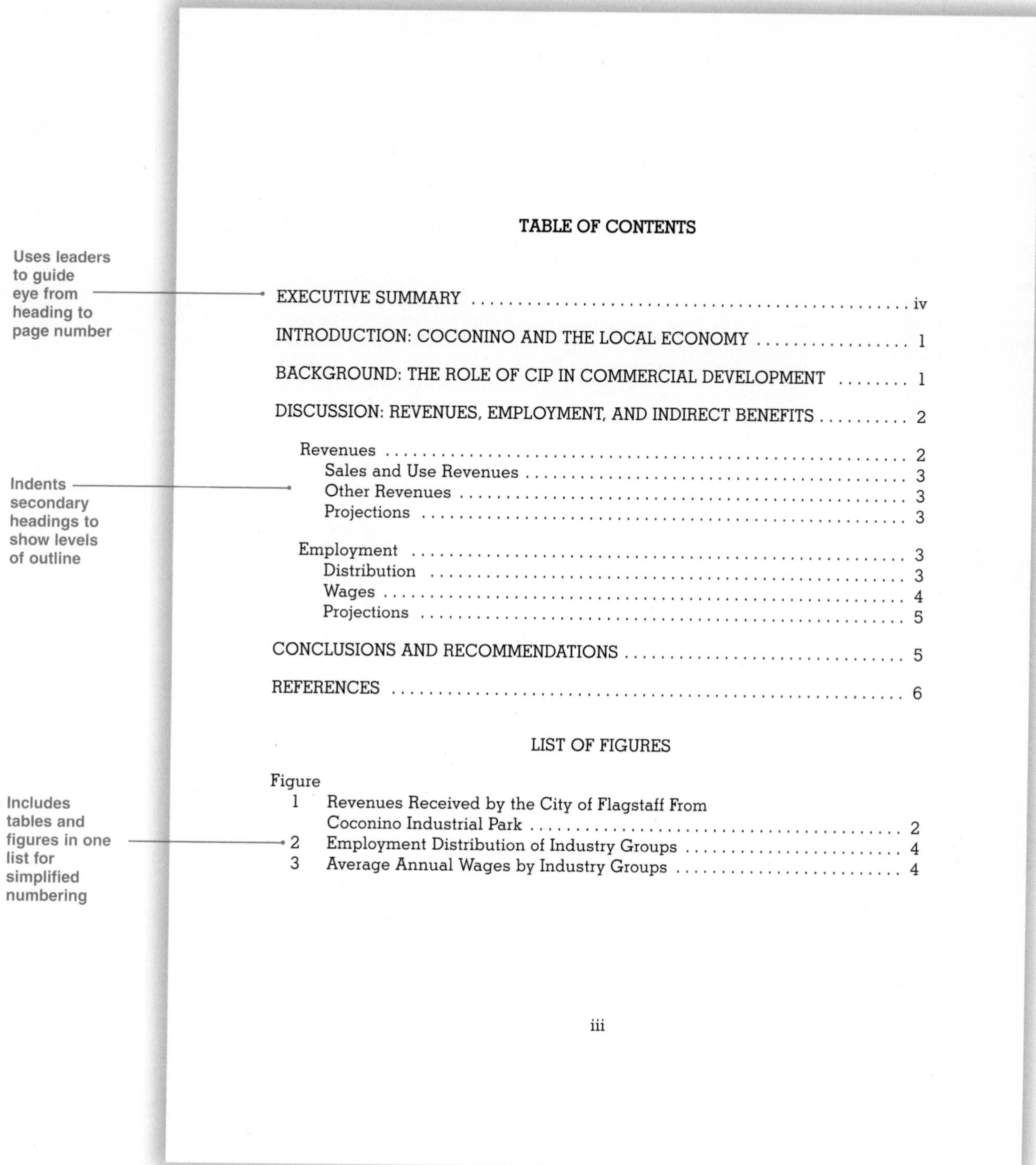
Uses leaders to guide eye from heading to page number
Indents secondary headings to show levels of outline
Includes tables and figures in one list for simplified numbering

TABLE OF CONTENTS

LIST OF FIGURES

iii

Because the table of contents and the list of figures for this report are small, they are combined on one page. Notice that the titles of major report parts are in all caps, while other headings are a combination of upper- and lowercase letters. This duplicates the style within the report. Advanced word processing capabilities enable you to generate a contents page automatically, including leaders and accurate page numbering—no matter how many times you revise. Notice that the page numbers are right-justified. Multiple-digit page numbers must line up properly (say, the number 9 under the 0 of 10).

FIGURE 13.4 (Continued) Executive Summary

EXECUTIVE SUMMARY

Opens directly with major research findings

The city of Flagstaff can benefit from the development of industrial parks like the Coconino Industrial Park. Both direct and indirect economic benefits result, as shown by this in-depth study conducted by Del Rio Industrial Consultants. The study was authorized by the Flagstaff City Council when Goldman-Lyon & Associates sought the City Council's approval for the proposed construction of a G-L industrial park. The City Council requested evidence demonstrating that an existing development could actually benefit the city.

Identifies data sources

Our conclusion that the city of Flagstaff benefits from industrial parks is based on data supplied by a survey of 5,000 Coconino Industrial Park employees, personal interviews with managers and tenants of CIP, city and state documents, and professional literature.

Summarizes organization of report

Analysis of the data revealed benefits in three areas:

- **Revenues.** The city of Flagstaff earned nearly $2 million in tax and other revenues from the Coconino Industrial Park in 2009. By 2015 this income is expected to reach $3.4 million (in constant 2009 dollars).
- **Employment.** In 2009, CIP businesses employed a total of 7,035 workers, who earned an average wage of $56,579. By 2015, CIP businesses are expected to employ directly nearly 15,000 employees who will earn salaries totaling over $998 million.
- **Indirect benefits.** Because of the multiplier effect, by 2015 Coconino Industrial Park will directly and indirectly generate a total of 38,362 jobs in the Flagstaff metropolitan area.

Condenses recommendations

On the basis of these findings, it is recommended that development of additional industrial parks be encouraged to stimulate local economic growth. The city would increase its tax revenues significantly, create much-needed jobs, and thus help stimulate the local economy in and around Flagstaff.

iv

For readers who want a quick overview of the report, the executive summary presents its most important elements. Executive summaries focus on the information the reader requires for making a decision related to the issues discussed in the report. The summary may include some or all of the following elements: purpose, scope, research methods, findings, conclusions, and recommendations. Its length depends on the report it summarizes. A 100-page report might require a 10-page summary. Shorter reports may contain one-page summaries, as shown here. Unlike letters of transmittal (which may contain personal pronouns and references to the writer), the executive summary of a long report is formal and impersonal. It uses the same margins as the body of the report. See the discussion of executive summaries in this chapter.

FIGURE 13.4 (Continued) Page 1

Uses a bulleted list for clarity and ease of reading

Lists three problem questions

Describes authorization for report and background of study

Includes APA citation with page number to help readers find reference

INTRODUCTION: COCONINO AND THE LOCAL ECONOMY

This study was designed to analyze the direct and indirect economic impact of Coconino Industrial Park on the city of Flagstaff. Specifically, the study seeks answers to these questions:

- What current tax and other revenues result directly from this park? What tax and other revenues may be expected in the future?
- How many and what kinds of jobs are directly attributable to the park? What is the employment picture for the future?
- What indirect effects has Coconino Industrial Park had on local employment, incomes, and economic growth?

BACKGROUND: THE ROLE OF CIP IN COMMERCIAL DEVELOPMENT

The development firm of Goldman-Lyon & Associates commissioned this study of Coconino Industrial Park at the request of the Flagstaff City Council. Before authorizing the development of a proposed Goldman-Lyon industrial park, the city council requested a study examining the economic effects of an existing park. Members of the city council wanted to determine to what extent industrial parks benefit the local community, and they chose Coconino Industrial Park as an example.

For those who are unfamiliar with it, Coconino Industrial Park is a 400-acre industrial park located in the city of Flagstaff about 4 miles from the center of the city. Most of the land lies within a specially designated area known as Redevelopment Project No. 2, which is under the jurisdiction of the Flagstaff Redevelopment Agency. Planning for the park began in 1994; construction started in 1996.

The original goal for Coconino Industrial Park was development for light industrial users. Land in this area was zoned for uses such as warehousing, research and development, and distribution. Like other communities, Flagstaff was eager to attract light industrial users because such businesses tend to employ a highly educated workforce, are relatively quiet, and do not pollute the environment (Cohen, 2010, p. C1). The city of Flagstaff recognized the need for light industrial users and widened an adjacent highway to accommodate trucks and facilitate travel by workers and customers coming from Flagstaff.

1

Titles for major parts of a report are centered in all caps. In this model document we show several combination headings. As the name suggests, combination heads are a mix of functional headings, such as *INTRODUCTION, BACKGROUND, DISCUSSION,* and *CONCLUSIONS,* and talking heads that reveal the content. Most business reports would use talking heads or a combination, such as *FINDINGS REVEAL REVENUE* and *EMPLOYMENT BENEFITS*. First-level headings (such as Revenues on page 2) are printed with bold upper- and lowercase letters. Second-level headings (such as Distribution on page 3) begin at the side, are bolded, and are written in upper- and lowercase letters. See Figure 12.6 for an illustration of heading formats. This business report is shown with single-spacing, although some research reports might be double-spaced. Always check with your organization to learn its preferred style.

Provides specifics for data sources

Usess combination heads

Previews organization of report

Places figure close to textual reference

The park now contains 14 building complexes with over 1.25 million square feet of completed building space. The majority of the buildings are used for office, research and development, marketing and distribution, or manufacturing uses. Approximately 50 acres of the original area are yet to be developed.

Data for this report came from a 2009 survey of over 5,000 Coconino Industrial Park employees; interviews with 15 CIP tenants and managers; the annual budget of the city of Flagstaff; county and state tax records; and current books, articles, journals, and online resources. Projections for future revenues resulted from analysis of past trends and "Estimates of Revenues for Debt Service Coverage, Redevelopment Project Area 2" (Miller, 2009, p. 79).

DISCUSSION: REVENUES, EMPLOYMENT, AND INDIRECT BENEFITS

The results of this research indicate that major direct and indirect benefits have accrued to the city of Flagstaff and surrounding metropolitan areas as a result of the development of Coconino Industrial Park. The research findings presented here fall into three categories: (a) revenues, (b) employment, and (c) indirect benefits.

Revenues

Coconino Industrial Park contributes a variety of tax and other revenues to the city of Flagstaff, as summarized in Figure 1. Current revenues are shown, along with projections to the year 2015. At a time when the economy is unstable, revenues from an industrial park such as Coconino can become a reliable income stream for the city of Flagstaff.

Figure 1

REVENUES RECEIVED BY THE CITY OF FLAGSTAFF
FROM COCONINO INDUSTRIAL PARK

Current Revenues and Projections to 2015

	2010	2015
Sales and use taxes	$ 904,140	$1,335,390
Revenues from licenses	426,265	516,396
Franchise taxes	175,518	229,424
State gas tax receipts	83,768	112,134
Licenses and permits	78,331	112,831
Other revenues	94,039	141,987
Total	$1,762,061	$2,448,162

Source: Arizona State Board of Equalization Bulletin. Phoenix: State Printing Office, 2010, p. 28.

2

Notice that this formal report is single-spaced. Many businesses prefer this space-saving format. However, some organizations prefer double-spacing, especially for preliminary drafts. If you single-space, do not indent paragraphs. If you double-space, do indent the paragraphs. Page numbers may be centered 1 inch from the bottom of the page or placed 1 inch from the upper right corner at the margin. Your word processor can insert page numbers automatically. Strive to leave a minimum of 1 inch for top, bottom, and side margins. References follow the parenthetical citation style (or in-text citation style) of the American Psychological Association (APA). Notice that the author's name, the year of publication, and page number appear in parentheses. The complete bibliographic entry for any in-text citation appears at the end of report in the references section.

FIGURE 13.4 (Continued) Page 3

Continues interpreting figures in table

Includes ample description of electronic reference

Sets stage for next topic to be discussed

Sales and Use Revenues

As shown in Figure 1, the city's largest source of revenues from CIP is the sales and use tax. Revenues from this source totaled $904,140 in 2010, according to figures provided by the Arizona State Board of Equalization (2010, p. 28). Sales and use taxes accounted for more than half of the park's total contribution to the city of $1,762,061.

Other Revenues

Other major sources of city revenues from CIP in 2010 include alcohol licenses, motor vehicle in lieu fees, trailer coach licenses ($426,265), franchise taxes ($175,518), and state gas tax receipts ($83,768). Although not shown in Figure 1, other revenues may be expected from the development of recently acquired property. The U.S. Economic Development Administration has approved a grant worth $975,000 to assist in expanding the current park eastward on an undeveloped parcel purchased last year. Revenues from leasing this property may be sizable.

Projections

Total city revenues from CIP will nearly double by 2015, producing an income of $2.45 million. This estimate is based on an annual growth rate of 0.65 percent, as projected by the Bureau of Labor Statistics and reported at the Web site of Infoplease.com ("Economic Outlook Through 2010").

Employment

One of the most important factors to consider in the overall effect of an industrial park is employment. In Coconino Industrial Park the distribution, number, and wages of people employed will change considerably in the next six years.

Distribution

A total of 7,035 employees currently work in various industry groups at Coconino Industrial Park. The distribution of employees is shown in Figure 2. The largest number of workers (58 percent) is employed in manufacturing and assembly operations. The next largest category, computer and electronics, employs 24 percent of the workers. Some overlap probably exists because electronics assembly could be included in either group. Employees also work in publishing (9 percent), warehousing and storage (5 percent), and other industries (4 percent).

Although the distribution of employees at Coconino Industrial Park shows a wide range of employment categories, it must be noted that other industrial parks would likely generate an entirely different range of job categories.

3

Only the most important research findings are interpreted and discussed for readers. The depth of discussion depends on the intended length of the report, the goal of the writer, and the expectations of the reader. Because the writer wants this report to be formal in tone, she avoids *I* and *we* in all discussions.

As you type a report, avoid widows and orphans (ending a page with the first line of a paragraph or carrying a single line of a paragraph to a new page). Strive to start and end pages with at least two lines of a paragraph, even if a slightly larger bottom margin results.

FIGURE 13.4 (Continued) Page 4

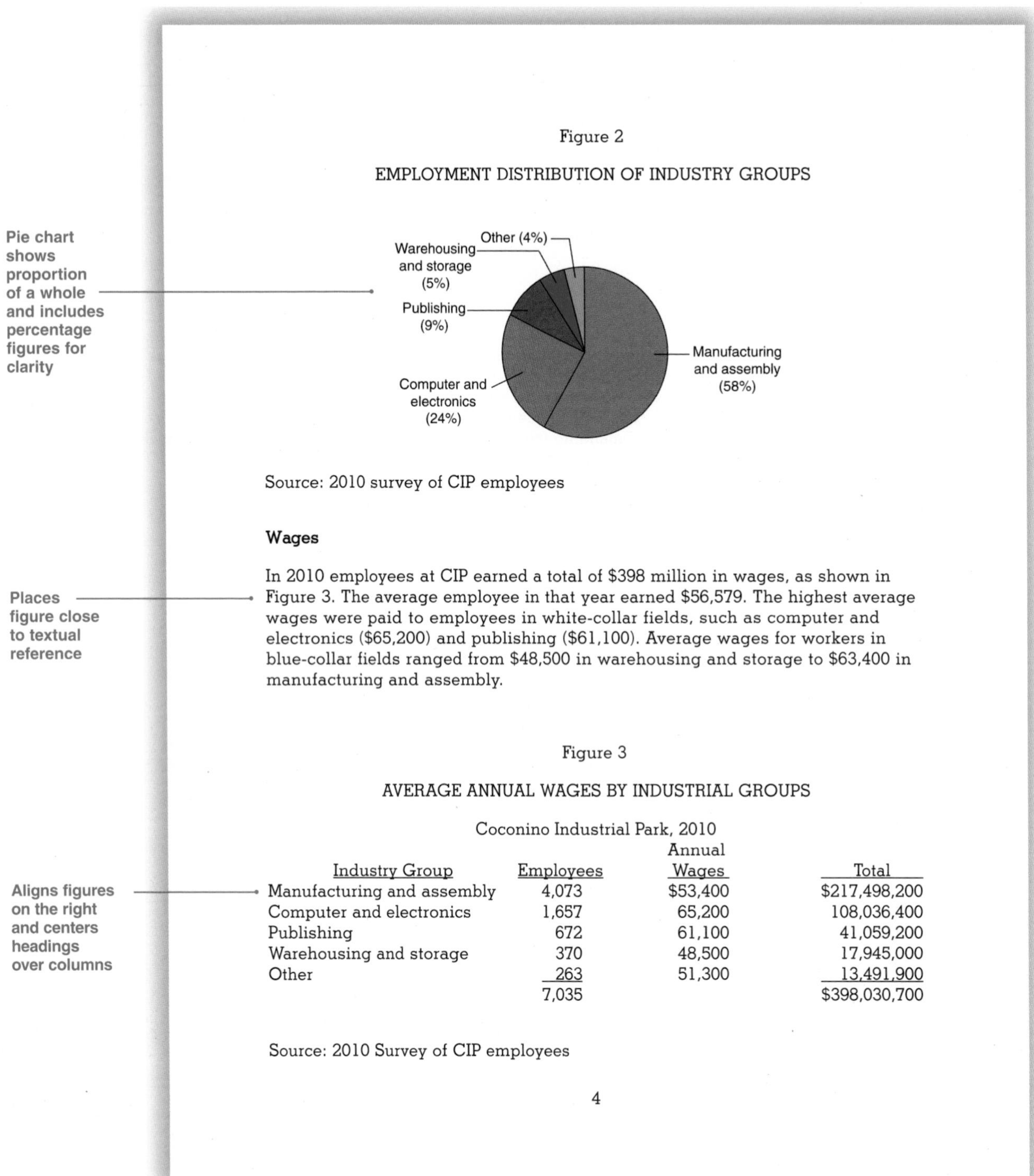

Pie chart shows proportion of a whole and includes percentage figures for clarity
Places figure close to textual reference
Aligns figures on the right and centers headings over columns
Figure 2
EMPLOYMENT DISTRIBUTION OF INDUSTRY GROUPS
Other (4%)
Warehousing and storage (5%)
Publishing (9%)
Computer and electronics (24%)
Manufacturing and assembly (58%)
Source: 2010 survey of CIP employees

Wages

In 2010 employees at CIP earned a total of $398 million in wages, as shown in Figure 3. The average employee in that year earned $56,579. The highest average wages were paid to employees in white-collar fields, such as computer and electronics ($65,200) and publishing ($61,100). Average wages for workers in blue-collar fields ranged from $48,500 in warehousing and storage to $63,400 in manufacturing and assembly.

Figure 3

AVERAGE ANNUAL WAGES BY INDUSTRIAL GROUPS

Coconino Industrial Park, 2010

Industry Group	Employees	Annual Wages	Total
Manufacturing and assembly	4,073	$53,400	$217,498,200
Computer and electronics	1,657	65,200	108,036,400
Publishing	672	61,100	41,059,200
Warehousing and storage	370	48,500	17,945,000
Other	263	51,300	13,491,900
	7,035		$398,030,700

Source: 2010 Survey of CIP employees

4

If you use figures or tables, be sure to introduce them in the text (for example, *as shown in Figure 3*). Although it is not always possible, try to place them close to the spot where they are first mentioned. To save space, you can print the title of a figure at its side. Because this report contains few tables and figures, the writer named them all "Figures" and numbered them consecutively. Graphics that serve for reference only and aren't discussed in the text belong in the appendix.

FIGURE 13.4 **(Continued) Page 5**

Clarifies information and tells what it means in relation to original research questions

Projections

By 2015 Coconino Industrial Park is expected to more than double its number of employees, bringing the total to over 15,000 workers. The total payroll in 2015 will also more than double, producing over $998 million (using constant 2010 dollars) in salaries to CIP employees. These projections are based on an 9 percent growth rate (Miller, 2009, p. 78), along with anticipated increased employment as the park reaches its capacity.

Future development in the park will influence employment and payrolls. One CIP project manager stated in an interview that much of the remaining 50 acres is planned for medium-rise office buildings, garden offices, and other structures for commercial, professional, and personal services (I. M. Novak, personal communication, November 30, 2010). Average wages for employees are expected to increase because of an anticipated shift to higher-paying white-collar jobs. Industrial parks often follow a similar pattern of evolution (Badri, 2010, p. 41). Like many industrial parks, CIP evolved from a warehousing center into a manufacturing complex.

Combines conclusions and recommendations

CONCLUSIONS AND RECOMMENDATIONS

Analysis of tax revenues, employment data, personal interviews, and professional literature leads to the following conclusions and recommendations about the economic impact of Coconino Industrial Park on the city of Flagstaff:

1. Sales tax and other revenues produced nearly $1.8 million in income to the city of Flagstaff in 2010. By 2015 sales tax and other revenues are expected to produce $2.5 million in city income.

Uses a numbered list for clarity and ease of reading

2. CIP currently employs 7,035 employees, the majority of whom are working in manufacturing and assembly. The average employee in 2010 earned $56,579.

3. By 2015 CIP is expected to employ more than 15,000 workers producing a total payroll of over $998 million.

4. Employment trends indicate that by 2015 more CIP employees will be engaged in higher-paying white-collar positions.

On the basis of these findings, we recommend that the City Council of Flagstaff authorize the development of additional industrial parks to stimulate local economic growth. The direct and indirect benefits of Coconino Industrial Park strongly suggest that future commercial development would have a positive impact on the Flagstaff community and the surrounding region as population growth and resulting greater purchasing power would trigger higher demand.

As the Coconino example shows, gains in tax revenue, job creation, and other direct and indirect benefits would follow the creation of additional industrial parks in and around Flagstaff.

5

After discussing and interpreting the research findings, the writer articulates what she considers the most important conclusions and recommendations. Longer, more complex reports may have separate sections for conclusions and resulting recommendations. In this report they are combined. Notice that it is unnecessary to start a new page for the conclusions.

FIGURE 13.4 **(Continued) Page 6 References**

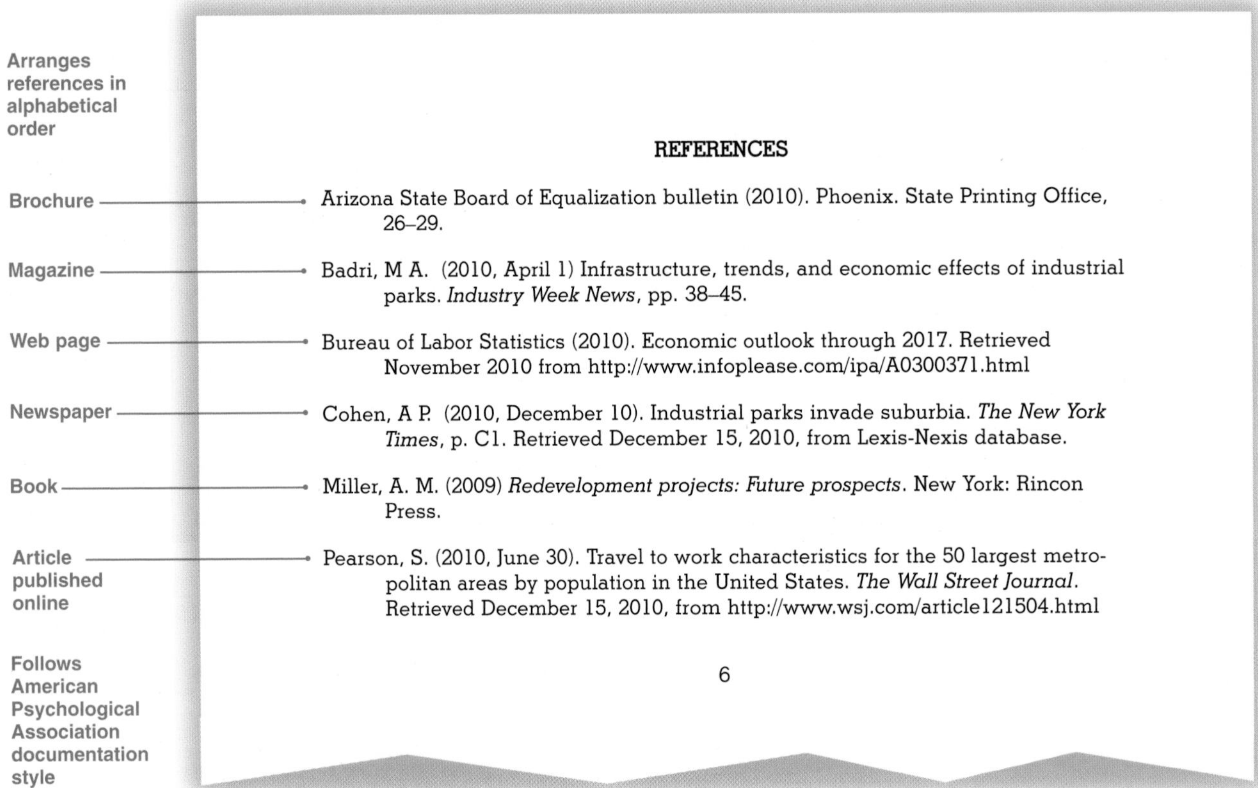

REFERENCES

Arizona State Board of Equalization bulletin (2010). Phoenix. State Printing Office, 26–29.

Badri, M A. (2010, April 1) Infrastructure, trends, and economic effects of industrial parks. *Industry Week News*, pp. 38–45.

Bureau of Labor Statistics (2010). Economic outlook through 2017. Retrieved November 2010 from http://www.infoplease.com/ipa/A0300371.html

Cohen, A P. (2010, December 10). Industrial parks invade suburbia. *The New York Times*, p. C1. Retrieved December 15, 2010, from Lexis-Nexis database.

Miller, A. M. (2009) *Redevelopment projects: Future prospects*. New York: Rincon Press.

Pearson, S. (2010, June 30). Travel to work characteristics for the 50 largest metropolitan areas by population in the United States. *The Wall Street Journal*. Retrieved December 15, 2010, from http://www.wsj.com/article121504.html

6

On this page the writer lists all references cited in the text as well as others that she examined during her research. The writer lists these citations following the APA referencing style. Notice that all entries are arranged alphabetically. Book and periodical titles are italicized, but they could be underlined. When referring to online items, she shows the full name of the citation and then identifies the URL as well as the date on which she accessed the electronic reference. This references page is shown with single-spacing, which is preferable for business reports. However, APA style recommends double-spacing for research reports, including the references page. APA style also shows "References" in upper- and lowercase letters. However, the writer preferred to use all caps to be consistent with other headings in this business report.

[Final Writing Tips continued from page 438.]

- **Generally avoid *I* and *we*.** To make formal reports seem as objective and credible as possible, most writers omit first-person pronouns. This formal style sometimes results in the overuse of passive-voice verbs (for example, *periodicals were consulted* and *the study was conducted*). Look for alternative constructions (*periodicals indicated* and *the study revealed*). It is also possible that your organization may allow first-person pronouns, so check before starting your report.
- **Let the first draft sit.** After completing the first version, put it aside for a day or two. Return to it with the expectation of revising and improving it. Do not be afraid to make major changes.
- **Revise for clarity, coherence, and conciseness.** Read a printed copy out loud. Do the sentences make sense? Do the ideas flow together naturally? Can wordiness and flabbiness be cut out? Make sure that your writing is so clear that a busy manager does not have to reread any part. See Chapter 6 for specific revision suggestions.
- **Proofread the final copy three times.** First, read a printed copy slowly for word meanings and content. Then read the copy again for spelling, punctuation, grammar, and other mechanical errors. Finally, scan the entire report to check its formatting and consistency (page numbering, indenting, spacing, headings, and so forth).

Putting It All Together

Formal reports in business generally aim to study problems and recommend solutions. Sylvia Hernandez, senior research assistant with Del Rio Industrial Consultants, was asked to study the economic impact of a local industrial park on the city of Flagstaff, Arizona, resulting in the formal report shown in Figure 13.4.

Checklist

Preparing Formal Business Reports

Report Process

- **Analyze the report and purpose.** Develop a problem question (*How is e-mail affecting productivity and security at MegaTech?*) and a purpose statement (*The purpose of this report is to investigate the use of e-mail at MegaTech and recommend policies and procedures that enhance company productivity and security*).
- **Anticipate the audience and issues.** Consider primary and secondary audiences. What do they already know? What do they need to know? Divide the major problem into subproblems for investigation.
- **Prepare a work plan.** Include problem and purpose statements, as well as a description of the sources and methods of collecting data. Prepare a tentative project outline and work schedule with anticipated dates of completion for all segments of the project.
- **Collect data.** Begin by searching secondary sources (electronic databases, books, magazines, journals, newspapers) for information on your topic. Then, if necessary, gather primary data by surveying, interviewing, observing, and experimenting.
- **Document data sources.** Establish a system for keeping track of your sources. When saving files from business databases or the Internet, be sure to record the complete publication information. Some researchers like to prepare note cards or separate sheets of paper citing all references (author, date, source, page, and quotation). Select a documentation format and use it consistently.
- **Interpret and organize the data.** Arrange the collected information in tables, grids, or outlines to help you visualize relationships and interpret meanings. Organize the data into an outline (Chapter 5).
- **Prepare graphics.** Make tables, charts, graphs, and illustrations—but only if they serve a function. Use graphics to help clarify, condense, simplify, or emphasize your data.
- **Compose the first draft.** At a computer write the first draft from your outline. Use appropriate headings as well as transitional expressions (such as *however, on the contrary,* and *in addition*) to guide the reader through the report.
- **Revise and proofread.** Revise to eliminate wordiness, ambiguity, and redundancy. Look for ways to improve readability, such as bulleted or numbered lists. Proofread three times for (a) word and content meaning, (b) grammar and mechanical errors, and (c) formatting.
- **Evaluate the product.** Examine the final report. Will it achieve its purpose? Encourage feedback so that you can learn how to improve future reports.

Report Components

- **Title page.** Balance the following lines on the title page: (a) name of the report (in all caps); (b) name, title, and organization of the individual receiving the report; (c) author's name, title, and organization; and (d) date submitted.
- **Letter of transmittal.** Announce the report topic and explain who authorized it. Briefly describe the project and preview the conclusions, if the reader is supportive. Close by expressing appreciation for the assignment, suggesting follow-up actions, acknowledging the help of others, or offering to answer questions.
- **Table of contents.** Show the beginning page number where each report heading appears in the report. Connect the page numbers and headings with leaders (spaced dots) using your word processing software. In MS Word 2007, for example, select the **Home** tab, open the **Paragraph** menu and click **Tabs** at the bottom left of the window.
- **List of illustrations.** Include a list of tables, illustrations, or figures showing the title of the item and its page number. If space permits, put these lists on the same page with the table of contents.
- **Executive summary.** Summarize the report purpose, findings, conclusions, and recommendations. Gauge the length of the summary by the length of the report and by your organization's practices.
- **Introduction.** Explain the problem motivating the report; describe its background and significance. Clarify the scope and limitations of the report. Optional items include a review of the relevant literature and a description of data sources, methods, and key terms. Close by previewing the report's organization.
- **Body.** Discuss, analyze, and interpret the research findings or the proposed solution to the problem. Arrange the findings in logical segments following your outline. Use clear, descriptive headings.
- **Conclusions and recommendations.** Explain what the findings mean in relation to the original problem. If asked, make enumerated recommendations that suggest actions for solving the problem.
- **Appendix.** Include items of interest to some, but not all, readers, such as questionnaires, transcripts of interviews, data sheets, and other information that is not essential to explain your findings, but that supports your analysis. Add large graphics—pictures, maps, figures, tables, charts, and graphs—that are not discussed directly in the text.
- **Works cited or references.** If footnotes are not provided in the text, list all references in a section called *Works Cited* or *References*.

Zooming In — YOUR TURN

Applying Your Skills at Raytheon

Proposals and reports are written, often in teams, to accomplish serious business purposes. Both require research, and sometimes resources are unavailable. Assume that you are an intern at Raytheon working with Dr. Grinyer. He has asked you to help him develop materials to improve Raytheon reports and proposals. He suggests two possible tasks:

1. A short (three to five pages) business report recommending a structured writing process to be used for team-written company documents
2. A memo evaluating several (two to four) proposal consulting companies that might be able to help Raytheon teams write good proposals when the company's proposal specialists are unavailable

Your Task

Select one of the suggested tasks. For Option 1, in a two- or three-person team, plan the required report and have each team member prepare an outline of his or her assigned section. As a team, review and improve the outlines with written comments and annotations. For Option 2, individually research, plan, and write the required one- to two-page memo for your instructor.

Want to do well on tests and excel in your course? Go to **www.meguffey.com** for helpful interactive resources.

- **Review the Chapter 13 PowerPoint slides to prepare for the first quiz.**

The city council hired the consultants to evaluate Coconino Industrial Park and to assess whether future commercial development would stimulate further economic growth. Sylvia Hernandez subdivided the economic impact into three aspects: Revenue, Employment, and Indirect Benefits. The report was compiled from survey data as well as from secondary sources that Sylvia researched.

Sylvia's report illustrates many of the points discussed in this chapter. Although it is a good example of the typical report format and style, it should not be viewed as the only way to present a report. Wide variation exists in reports.

The accompanying checklist feature on the previous page summarizes the report process and report components in one handy list.

Summary of Learning Objectives

1 Discuss the general uses and basic components of informal proposals, and grasp their audience and purpose. Although they may vary, most proposals have certain standard parts in common. Informal proposals contain the following: a persuasive introduction that explains the purpose of the proposal and qualifies the writer; background material identifying the problem and project goals; a proposal, plan, or schedule outlining the project; a section describing staff qualifications; a budget showing expected costs; and a request for approval or authorization.

2 Discuss formal proposals and their specific components. Beyond the six components generally contained in informal proposals, formal proposals may include these additional parts: a copy of the RFP (request for proposal), a letter of transmittal, an executive summary, a title page, a table of contents, a list of illustrations, and an appendix.

3 Identify the components of typical business plans, and ethically create buy-in for your business ideas. Business plans help entrepreneurs secure start-up funding and also provide a road map to follow as a business develops. Typical business plans include the following: letter of transmittal or an executive summary, table of contents, company description, product or service description, market analysis, description of operations and management, financial analysis, and appendixes. For start-up businesses seeking financial backing, the product or service description as well as the operations and management analyses are particularly important. They must promote growth potential and promise a management team capable of implementing the business plan.

Are you ready? Get more practice at **www.meguffey.com**

4 Describe the components of the front matter in formal business reports, and show how they further the purpose of your report. Formal business reports may include these beginning components: a vinyl or heavy paper cover, a title page, a letter of transmittal, a table of contents, a list of illustrations, and an executive summary. The introduction to a formal report sets the scene by discussing some or all of the following topics: background material, problem or purpose, significance of the topic, scope and organization of the report, authorization, review of relevant literature, sources and methods, and definitions of key terms.

5 Describe the body and back matter of formal business reports and how they serve the purpose of your report. The body of a report discusses, analyzes, interprets, and evaluates the research findings or solution to a problem. The conclusion states what the findings mean and how they relate to the report's purpose. The recommendations tell how to solve the report problem. The last portions of a formal report are the appendix and references or works cited.

6 Specify tips that aid writers of formal business reports. Before writing, develop a realistic timetable and collect all necessary data. During the writing process, work from a good outline, work in a quiet place, and use a computer. Also, try to write rapidly, revising later. While writing, use verb tenses consistently, and avoid *I* and *we*. A few days after completing the first draft, revise to improve clarity, coherence, and conciseness. Proofread the final copy three times.

Chapter Review

1. What purpose do proposals serve? (Objs. 1, 2)
2. Who uses requests for proposals (RFPs), and why? (Objs. 1, 2)
3. What are the six principal components of an informal letter proposal? (Obj. 1)
4. Why is the budget section in a proposal particularly important? (Obj. 2)
5. Why does an entrepreneur need to write a business plan? (Obj. 3)
6. Name eight components of typical business plans. (Obj. 3)
7. What should a business plan mission statement include, and how long should it be? (Obj. 3)
8. Why are formal reports written in business? Give an original example of a business-related formal report. (Obj. 4)
9. What is a letter or memorandum of transmittal? (Obj. 4)
10. How long should a typical executive summary be? (Obj. 4)
11. Name the steps necessary to write an executive summary in a formal business report. (Obj. 4)
12. What should be included in the introduction to a formal business report? (Obj. 4)
13. What should the writer strive to do in the body of a formal business report? (Obj. 5)
14. Why must writers list their sources and identify them in the text? (Obj. 5)
15. In your view, what are six of the most important tips for the writer of a formal report? Explain each of your choices. (Obj. 6)

Critical Thinking

1. Which category of proposal, solicited or unsolicited, is more likely to succeed, and why? (Obj. 1)
2. Compare and contrast proposals and business plans. (Objs. 1–3)
3. What is the purpose of a business plan, and what should it communicate to investors? (Obj. 3)
4. How do formal business reports differ from informal business reports? (Objs. 4–6)
5. **Ethical Issue:** How can a team of writers ensure that each member shoulders an equal or fair amount of the work on an extensive writing project, such as a formal proposal or business report?

Activities

13.1. Proposals: Solving a Workplace Problem in an Unsolicited Informal Proposal (Obj. 1)

The ability to spot problems before they turn into serious risks is prized by most managers. Draw on your internship and work experience. Can you identify a problem that could be solved with a small to moderate financial investment? Look for issues such as missing lunch or break rooms for staff; badly needed health initiatives such as gyms or sports club memberships; switching to low-gas-mileage, high-emission company vehicles; or lack of recycling efforts.

Your Task. Discuss with your instructor the workplace problem that you have identified. Make sure you choose a relatively weighty problem that can nevertheless be lessened or eliminated with a minor expenditure. Be sure to include a cost–benefit analysis. Address your unsolicited letter or memo proposal to your current or former boss and copy your instructor.

13.2 Proposals: Think Like an Entrepreneur (Obj. 1)

Web

Perhaps you have fantasized about one day owning your own company, or maybe you have already started a business. Proposals are offers to a very specific audience whose business you are soliciting. Think of a product or service that you like or know much about. On the Web or in electronic databases, research the market so that you understand going rates, prices, and costs. Search the Small Business Administration's Web site **(http://www.sba.gov)** for valuable tips on how to launch and manage a business.

Your Task. Choose a product or service you would like to offer to a particular audience, such as a window cleaning business, an online photography business, a new vehicle on the U.S. market, or a new European hair care line. Discuss products and services as well as target audiences with your instructor. Write a letter proposal promoting your chosen product or service.

13.3 Proposals: Comparing Real Proposals (Objs. 1, 2)

Web

Many new companies with services or products to offer would like to land corporate or government contracts. However, they are intimidated by the proposal (RFP process). You have been asked for help by your friend Mikayla, who has started her own designer uniform company. Her goal is to offer her colorful yet functional uniforms to hospitals and clinics. Before writing a proposal, however, she wants to see examples and learn more about the process.

Your Task. Use the Web to find at least two examples of business proposals. Do not waste time on sites that want to sell templates or books. Find actual examples. Then prepare a memo to Mikayla in which you do the following:

a. Identify two sites with sample business proposals.
b. Outline the parts of each proposal.
c. Compare the strengths and weaknesses of each proposal.
d. Draw conclusions. What can Mikayla learn from these examples?

13.4 Proposals: Medicus Associates Solicits Your Proposal (Obj. 1)

Team

In university towns, sports medicine is increasingly popular. A new medical clinic, Medicus Associates, is opening its doors in your community. A friend recommended your small business to the administrator of the clinic, and you received a letter asking you to provide information about your service. The new medical clinic specializes in sports medicine, physical therapy, and cardiac rehabilitation services. It is interested in retaining your company, rather than hiring its own employees to perform the service your company offers.

Your Task. Working in teams, first decide what service you will offer. It could be landscaping, uniform supply, laundry of uniforms, general cleaning, computerized no-paper filing systems, online medical supplies, patient transportation, supplemental hospice care, temporary office support, or food service. As a team, develop a letter proposal outlining your plan, staffing, and budget. Use persuasion to show why contracting your services is better than hiring in-house employees. In the proposal letter, request a meeting with the administrative board. In addition to a written proposal, you may be expected to make an oral presentation that includes visual aids and/or handouts. Send your proposal to Dr. Pat Leigh, Director, Medicus Associates. Supply a local address.

13.5 Proposal and Grant Writing: Learning From the Nonprofits (Objs. 1, 2)

Web

You would like to learn more about writing business proposals and especially about writing grants. Grants are written to solicit funding from institutions, foundations, or the government. You might one day even decide to become a professional grant/proposal writer. However, first you need experience.

Your Task. Volunteer your proposal or grant writing services at a local nonprofit organization, such as a United Way **(http://national.unitedway.org)** member agency, an educational institution, or your local religious community. To learn more about writing proposals and grants, use a search engine to look up *proposal*. Try categories such as *business proposal writing* and *grant proposal writing*. In the browser window, enclose the search terms in quotation marks. Your instructor may ask you to submit a preliminary memo report outlining ten or more pointers you learn about writing proposals and grants for nonprofit organizations.

13.6 Business Plans: Can Your Team Write a Winning Business Plan? (Obj. 3)

Team Web

Business plans at many schools are more than classroom writing exercises. They have won regional, national, and worldwide prizes. Although some contests are part of MBA programs, other contests are available for undergraduates. One business plan project at the University of California, Santa Barbara, resulted in the development of a portable oxygen concentrator. Three students wrote a proposal that not only won one of the school's business plan writing contests but also attracted venture capital backing of over $500,000. The trio was challenged to come up with a hypothetical business plan. One of the team members suggested making a portable oxygen device to improve the mobility and quality of life for her grandmother. The students didn't actually make the device—they just outlined the concept. Contest judges recognized the commercial potential and helped bring the device into production.[7]

As part of a business plan project, you and your team are challenged to come up with an idea for a new business or service. For example, you might want to offer a lunch service with fresh sandwiches or salads delivered to office workers' desks. You might propose building a better Web site for an organization. You might want to start a document preparation business that offers production, editing, and printing services. You might have a terrific idea for an existing business to expand with a new product or service.

Your Task. Working in teams, explore entrepreneurial ventures based on your experience and expertise. Conduct team meetings to decide on a product or service, develop a work plan, assign responsibilities, and create a schedule. Your goal is to write a business plan proposal that will convince potential investors (sometimes your own management) that you have an excellent business idea and that you can pull it off. Check out sample business plans on the Web. The two "deliverables" from your project will be your written business plan and an oral presentation. Your written report should include a cover, transmittal document (letter or memo), title page, table of contents, executive summary, proposal (including introduction, body, and conclusion), appendix items, glossary (optional), and sources. In the body of the proposal, be sure to explain your mission and vision, the market, your marketing strategy, operations, and financials. Address your business plan proposal to your instructor.

*A complete instructional module for this activity is available at **www.meguffey.com**.

13.7 Business Plans: Studying Samples and Selecting the Best (Obj. 3)

Web

As a member of a group of venture capitalists with money to invest in start-up companies, you must make a choice. Assume your group has received three business plan proposals.

Your Task. Visit either Bplans.com at **http://www.bplans.com** or the Small Business Administration site at **http://www.sba.gov/smallbusinessplanner**. Search for sample business plans. Browse the list and select three business plans to study. Analyze all parts of each plan. Then, select one that you will recommend for funding. Prepare a memo to your investor group explaining why you think this start-up business will succeed. Also comment on the organization, format, and writing style of the business plan. What are its strengths and weaknesses? Address your memo to your instructor.

13.8 Formal Business Reports: Intercultural Communication (Objs. 4–6)

Web | Intercultural | Team

U.S. businesses are expanding into foreign markets with manufacturing plants, sales offices, and branches abroad. Most Americans, however, have little knowledge of or experience with people from other cultures. To prepare for participation in the global marketplace, you are to collect information for a report focused on an Asian, Latin American, or European country where English is not regularly spoken. Before selecting the country, though, consult your campus international student program for volunteers who are willing to be interviewed. Your instructor may make advance arrangements with international student volunteers.

© imagebroker / Alamy

Your Task. In teams of three to five, collect information about your target country from electronic databases, the Web, and other sources. Then invite an international student representing your target country to be interviewed by your group. As you conduct primary and secondary research, investigate the topics listed in Figure 13.5. Confirm what you learn in your secondary research by talking with your interviewee. When you complete your research, write a report for the CEO of your company (make up a name and company). Assume that your company plans to expand its operations abroad. Your report should advise the company's executives of the social customs, family life, attitudes, religions, education, and values in the target country. Remember that your company's interests are business oriented; do not dwell on tourist information. Write your report individually or in teams.

13.9 Proposal, Business Plan, and Business Report Topics (Objs. 1–6)

Web

A list of nearly 100 report topics is available at **www.meguffey.com**. The topics are divided into the following categories: accounting, finance, personnel/human resources, marketing, information systems, management, and general business/education/campus issues. You can collect information for many of these reports by using electronic databases and the Web. Your instructor may assign them as individual or team projects. All involve critical thinking in organizing information, drawing conclusions, and making recommendations. The topics include assignments appropriate for proposals, business plans, and formal business reports. Also, a number of self-contained report activities that require no additional research are provided at the end of Chapter 12.

13.10 Executive Summary: Reviewing Articles (Objs. 4, 5)

Web | E-mail

Many managers and executives are too rushed to read long journal articles, but they are eager to stay current in their fields. Assume your boss has asked you to help him stay abreast of research in his field. He asks you to submit to him one executive summary every month on an article of interest.

Your Task. In your field of study, select a professional journal, such as the *Journal of Management*. Using ProQuest, Factiva, EBSCO, or some other database, look for articles in your target journal. Select an article that is at least five pages long and is interesting to you. Write an executive summary in a memo format. Include an introduction that might begin with *As you requested, I am submitting this executive summary of....* Identify the author, article title, journal, and date of publication. Explain what the author intended to do in the study or article. Summarize three or four of the most important findings of the study or article. Use descriptive, or "talking," headings rather than functional headings. Summarize any recommendations made. Your boss would also like a concluding statement indicating your reaction to the article. Address your memo to Marcus E. Fratelli. Alternatively, your instructor may ask you to e-mail your executive summary in the body of a properly formatted message or as an MS Word attachment in correct memo format.

13.11 Executive Summary: Locating Expert Information About Business Plans (Obj. 3)

Web | Team | E-mail

To supplement your knowledge of business plans and draw on various sources, search electronic databases to find recent articles about business plans and business models. This activity can be completed in teams, with each member contributing valuable tips and insights about business plans from an article or two.

Your Task. Using ProQuest, Factiva, EBSCO, or some other business database, search for the keywords *business plan*, and if you want more sources, for *business model*. You may also try searching *BusinessWeek Online* and similar business publications on the Internet. Select an article that is at least 1,200 words long and discusses business plans fully. Write an executive summary in memo format, or write an e-mail, if requested by your instructor. Identify the author, article title, periodical, and date of publication. Summarize the most important findings of the article. Use "talking" rather than functional headings if helpful.

13.12 Unsolicited Proposal: Requesting Funding for Your Campus Business Club (Obj. 1)

Let's say you are a member of a campus business club, such as the Society for the Advancement of Management (SAM), the American Marketing Association (AMA), the American Management Association (AMA), the Accounting Society (AS), the Finance Association (FA), or the Association of Information Technology Professionals (AITP). You have managed your finances well, and therefore, you are able to fund your monthly activities. However, membership dues are insufficient to cover any extras. Identify a need such as for a hardware or software purchase,

FIGURE 13.5 Intercultural Interview Topics and Questions

Social Customs

- How do people react to strangers? Are they friendly? Hostile? Reserved?
- How do people greet each other?
- What are the appropriate manners when you enter a room? Bow? Nod? Shake hands with everyone?
- How are names used for introductions? Is it appropriate to inquire about one's occupation or family?
- What are the attitudes toward touching?
- How does one express appreciation for an invitation to another's home? Bring a gift? Send flowers? Write a thank-you note? Are any gifts taboo?
- Are there any customs related to how or where one sits?
- Are any facial expressions or gestures considered rude?
- How close do people stand when talking?
- What is the attitude toward punctuality in social situations? In business situations?
- What are acceptable eye contact patterns?
- What gestures indicate agreement? Disagreement?

Family Life

- What is the basic unit of social organization? Basic family? Extended family?
- Do women work outside of the home? In what occupations?

Housing, Clothing, and Food

- Are there differences in the kinds of housing used by different social groups? Differences in location? Differences in furnishings?
- What occasions require special clothing?
- Are some types of clothing considered taboo?
- What is appropriate business attire for men? For women?
- How many times a day do people eat?
- What types of places, food, and drink are appropriate for business entertainment? Where is the seat of honor at a table?

Class Structure

- Into what classes is society organized?
- Do racial, religious, or economic factors determine social status?
- Are there any minority groups? What is their social standing?

Political Patterns

- Are there any immediate threats to the political survival of the country?
- How is political power manifested?
- What channels are used for expressing political opinions?
- What information media are important?
- Is it appropriate to talk politics in social situations?

Religion and Folk Beliefs

- To which religious groups do people belong? Is one predominant?
- Do religious beliefs influence daily activities?
- Which places are considered sacred? Which objects? Which events?
- How do religious holidays affect business activities?

Economic Institutions

- What are the country's principal products?
- Are workers organized in unions?
- How are businesses owned? By family units? By large public corporations? By the government?
- What is the standard work schedule?
- Is it appropriate to do business by telephone? By computer?
- How has technology affected business procedures?
- Is participatory management used?
- Are there any customs related to exchanging business cards?
- How is status shown in an organization? Private office? Secretary? Furniture?
- Are businesspeople expected to socialize before conducting business?

Value Systems

- Is competitiveness or cooperation more prized?
- Is thrift or enjoyment of the moment more valued?
- Is politeness more important than factual honesty?
- What are the attitudes toward education?
- Do women own or manage businesses? If so, how are they treated?
- What are your people's perceptions of Americans? Do Americans offend you? What has been hardest for you to adjust to in America? How could Americans make this adjustment easier for you?

a special one-time event that would benefit a great number of students, or officer training.

Your Task. Request one-time funding to cover what you need by writing an unsolicited letter or memo proposal to your assistant dean, who oversees student business clubs. Identify your need or problem, show the benefit of your request, support your claims with evidence, and provide a budget (if necessary).

13.13 Unsolicited Proposal: Thwarting Dorm Room Thievery (Objs. 1, 2)

Team | Web

As an enterprising college student, you recognized a problem as soon as you arrived on campus. Dorm rooms filled with pricey digital doodads were very attractive to thieves. Some students move in with more than $3,000 in gear, including laptop computers, flat-screen TVs, digital cameras, MP3 players, video game consoles, PDAs, and DVD players. You solved the problem by buying an extra-large steel footlocker to lock away your valuables. However, shipping the footlocker was expensive (nearly $100), and you had to wait for it to arrive from a catalog company. Your bright idea is to propose to the Associated Student Organization (ASO) that it allow you to offer these steel footlockers to students at a reduced price and with campus delivery. Your footlocker, which you found by searching the Web, is extremely durable and works great as a coffee table, nightstand, or card table. It comes with a smooth interior liner and two compartments.

Your Task. Working individually or with a team, imagine that you have made arrangements with a manufacturer to act as an intermediary selling footlockers on your campus at a reduced price. Consult the Web for manufacturers and make up your own figures. How can you get the ASO's permission to proceed? Give that organization a cut? Use your imagination in deciding how this plan might work on a college campus. Then prepare an unsolicited proposal to your ASO. Outline the problem and your goals of protecting students' valuables and providing convenience. Check the Web for statistics regarding on-campus burglaries. Such figures should help you develop one or more persuasive "hooks." Then explain your proposal, project possible sales, discuss a timetable, and describe your staffing. Submit your proposal to Billie White, president, Associated Student Organization.

Chat About It

In each chapter you will find five discussion questions related to the chapter material. Your instructor may assign these topics for you to discuss in class, in an online chat room, or on an online discussion board. Some of the discussion topics may require outside research. You may also be asked to read and respond to postings made by your classmates.

Topic 1: Why is being precise about the deliverables of a project so important?

Topic 2: Some consulting firms use experienced managers, but they also employ inexperienced, lower-paid staff to lower costs. How would you write the staffing section of a proposal with experienced managers but inexperienced staff?

Topic 3: If you managed a team of proposal-writing professionals, how would you organize the work to prepare a 200-page formal proposal? How many professionals do you think you would need? What tasks would each professional be assigned?

Topic 4: Discuss the pros and cons of the following two methods for completing the outline of the executive summary of a formal report: (a) cutting and pasting existing report sentences, or (b) creating new sentences.

Topic 5: Is it ethical for a student team to "borrow" and then substantially revise a report from a team that wrote about the same topic during the previous semester? What does your school say about such a practice?

Grammar/Mechanics C.L.U.E. Review 13

Total Review

Each of the following sentences has a total of **three** errors in grammar, punctuation, capitalization, usage, or spelling. On a separate sheet, write a correct version. Avoid adding new phrases, starting new sentences, or rewriting in your own words. When finished, compare your responses with the key beginning on page Key-3.

Example: The following 3 statistical terms frequently describe data, Mean, median, and mode.
Revision: The following three statistical terms frequently describe data: mean, median, and mode.

1. Lack of job security and high unemployment is here to stay. Even if we do our work really good.
2. Managers in 3 departments' complained that there departments were over budget for supplies.
3. After sending many e-mails to Frank and I, the client felt badly about barraging us with messages to solicit a response from our two teams'.
4. The new vice president and her decided to move up the launch to May 3rd, as a result, the software was buggy.
5. Managers of big corporations' sometimes do not know how to motivate, consequently, the executives miss an opportunity to develop their worker's.
6. The Director of marketing wanted to speak to you and I about the poor moral in our division.
7. Laura and him decided to except assistance with their proposal, therefore, they completed the project by the deadline.
8. We invited seventy-five employees to hear 2 experts disberse information about wellness.
9. Memo's usually contain four necessary parts, subject line, opening, body and action closing.
10. Darrin Jizmejian who was recently evaluated, wondered whether his formal report would be presented at the March 13th meeting?

CHAPTER 14

Business Presentations

OBJECTIVES

After studying this chapter, you should be able to

1. Discuss two important first steps in preparing effective business presentations.
2. Explain the major elements in organizing a presentation, including the introduction, body, and conclusion.
3. Identify techniques for gaining audience rapport, including (a) using effective imagery, (b) providing verbal signposts, and (c) sending appropriate nonverbal messages.
4. Discuss designing visual aids, handouts, and multimedia presentations and using presentation technology competently.
5. Specify delivery techniques for use before, during, and after a presentation, and apply reflective thinking skills.
6. Organize team-based written and oral presentations, and understand how to communicate in teams.
7. Explain effective techniques for adapting oral presentations to intercultural audiences, and demonstrate intercultural and diversity understanding.
8. List techniques for improving telephone and voice mail skills to project a positive image.

Want to do well on tests and excel in your course? Go to **www.meguffey.com** for helpful interactive resources.

- **Review the Chapter 14 PowerPoint slides to prepare for the first quiz.**

Zooming In PART 1

Apple's Steve Jobs and His Keynotes

Come January, when CEO Steve Jobs launches yet another hot new Apple product during one of his famously simple, yet striking keynote presentations, the world listens. Weeks and months of feverish preparation and secrecy precede the "Stevenote" at the annual Macworld conference. Understandably, the tech world is abuzz on the Web. The pundits weigh in with their speculations about the latest unveiling, kept tightly under wraps until Jobs announces it. Sometimes not even the name of the newest gizmo is known, as was the case with the Apple iPad, a sleek tablet device promising to revolutionize computing. Until the last moment, the technorati were guessing at its specifications and names, ranging from iSlate, iBook, and iTablet to Canvas. A few hundred industry insiders, analysts, and members of the media gathered expectantly at the Yerba Buena Center in San Francisco.

During the launch of the iPad—a large iPhone or iPod Touch look-alike—some invited guests were covering the event live in their blogs and tweets. Bobbie Johnson, technology correspondent for the UK newspaper *The Guardian*, was one of them. His readers and Twitter followers all over the world were able to witness not only the actual keynote presentation, but rumors and speculation even before the event unfolded. Steve Jobs' impressive images, passionate delivery, and nearly messianic zeal are legendary. Johnson remarked later in his first hands-on review of the iPad: "Jobs trumpeted it as exactly that, a magical device that will change the way we use computers in our everyday lives. And while playing with the iPad was not exactly a religious experience, it's not hard to see that the gadget, or at least the ideas it contains, will be with us for a long time to come."[1]

The long buildup and the secrecy are calculated communication strategies. They work to stoke excitement and fascination, as one blogger put it: "The iPhone … blew people away not only because of what it was capable of, but also because many of its features came as a complete surprise to even the most well-informed of Apple bloggers."[2] This expert also suggests that Jobs is hedging against the risk of hyping up products that are still under development. Instead of revealing unfinished devices too soon, Apple manages the public's expectations and prevents consumer disappointment. A master showman, Jobs calls himself "a big-bang guy,"[3] meaning that he likes flashy and fast launches. You will learn about the Apple executive's storied presentation techniques in Part 2 of this feature on page 467.

Breakthrough deal with AT&T
$14.99 for up to 250 MB
$29.99 for unlimited data
Free use of AT&T WiFi hotspots
Activate on iPad
No contract – cancel anytime

© Tony Avelar/Bloomberg via Getty Images

Critical Thinking

- What kinds of oral presentations might you have to make in your chosen career field?
- Why are most people fearful of making presentations?
- How do you think people become effective speakers?

http://www.apple.com/contact/

Preparing Effective Oral Presentations

LEARNING OBJECTIVE 1
Discuss two important first steps in preparing effective business presentations.

Like his archnemesis Bill Gates of Microsoft, Steve Jobs is a college dropout, but he is one who has elevated communication with the public to an art form. Few of us will ever talk to an audience of millions, whether face-to-face or mediated by technology, about a spectacular new product. At some point, however, all businesspeople have to inform others or sell an idea. Such information and persuasion are often conveyed in person and involve audiences of various sizes. If you are like most people, you have some apprehension when speaking in public. That's normal. Good speakers are made, not born. The good news is that you can conquer the fear of public speaking and hone your skills with instruction and practice.

Many future businesspeople fail to take advantage of opportunities in college to develop speaking skills. However, such skills often play an important role in a successful career. In fact, the No. 1 predictor of success and upward mobility, according to an AT&T and Stanford University study, is how much you enjoy public speaking and how effective you are at it.[4] Speaking skills are useful at every career stage. You might, for example, have to make a sales pitch before customers or speak to a professional gathering. You might need to describe your company's expansion plans to your banker, or you might need to persuade management to support your proposed marketing strategy. This chapter prepares you to use speaking skills in making oral presentations, whether alone or as part of a team.

For any presentation, you can reduce your fears and lay the foundation for a professional performance by focusing on five areas: preparation, organization, audience rapport, visual aids, and delivery.

Spotlight on Communicators

© Kim White/Bloomberg via Getty Images

How long should a PowerPoint presentation be? Business leader and venture capitalist Guy Kawasaki says that ten-slide presentations are plenty. And e-mail messages should be no more than five sentences. Why? No one wants to read *War and Peace* e-mails or sit through hour-long presentations of 50 plus slides. What you learn in schools, he asserts, is just the opposite of what happens in the real world. In school you're always worried about minimum word count and slide numbers, he says. In business, that's not the case.

Before you can prepare your business presentation, which two important pieces of information do you need?

Knowing Your Purpose

The most important part of your preparation is deciding what you want to accomplish. Do you want to sell a health care program to a prospective client? Do you want to persuade management to increase the marketing budget? Do you want to inform customer service reps of three important ways to prevent miscommunication? Whether your goal is to persuade or to inform, you must have a clear idea of where you are going. At the end of your presentation, what do you want your listeners to remember or do?

Mark Miller, a loan officer at First Fidelity Trust, faced such questions as he planned a talk for a class in small business management. Mark's former business professor had asked him to return to campus and give the class advice about borrowing money from banks in order to start new businesses. Because Mark knew so much about this topic, he found it difficult to extract a specific purpose statement for his presentation. After much thought he narrowed his purpose to this: *To inform potential entrepreneurs about three important factors that loan officers consider before granting start-up loans to launch small businesses.* His entire presentation focused on ensuring that the class members understood and remembered three principal ideas.

What are the elements of audience analysis, and how will they affect your message?

Knowing Your Audience

A second key element in preparation is analyzing your audience, anticipating its reactions, and making appropriate adaptations. Audiences may fall into four categories, as summarized in Figure 14.1. By anticipating your audience, you have a better idea of how to organize your presentation. A friendly audience, for example, will respond to humor and personal experiences. A neutral audience requires an even, controlled delivery style. The talk would probably be filled with facts, statistics, and expert opinions. An uninterested audience that is forced to attend requires a brief presentation. Such an audience might respond best to humor, cartoons, colorful visuals, and startling statistics. A hostile audience demands a calm, controlled delivery style with objective data and expert opinion.

Other elements, such as age, gender, education, experience, and the size of the audience will affect your style and message content. Analyze the following questions to help you determine your organizational pattern, delivery style, and supporting material.

- *How will this topic appeal to this audience?*
- *How can I relate this information to my listeners' needs?*
- *How can I earn respect so that they accept my message?*
- *What would be most effective in making my point? Facts? Statistics? Personal experiences? Expert opinion? Humor? Cartoons? Graphic illustrations? Demonstrations? Case histories? Analogies?*
- *What measures must I take to ensure that this audience remembers my main points?*

If you have agreed to speak to an audience with which you are unfamiliar, ask for the names of a half dozen people who will be in the audience. Contact them and learn about their backgrounds and expectations for the presentation. This information can help you answer questions about what they want to hear and how deeply you should explore the subject. You will want to thank these people when you start your speech. Doing this kind of homework will impress the audience.

Organizing the Content for a Powerful Impact

LEARNING OBJECTIVE 2

Explain the major elements in organizing a presentation, including the introduction, body, and conclusion.

Once you have determined your purpose and analyzed the audience, you are ready to collect information and organize it logically. Good organization and intentional repetition are the two most powerful keys to audience comprehension and retention. In fact, many speech experts recommend the following admittedly repetitious, but effective, plan:

- **Step 1:** Tell them what you are going to say.
- **Step 2:** Say it.
- **Step 3:** Tell them what you have just said.

FIGURE 14.1 Succeeding With Four Audience Types

Audience Members	Organizational Pattern	Delivery Style	Supporting Material
Friendly			
They like you and your topic.	Use any pattern. Try something new. Involve the audience.	Be warm, pleasant, and open. Use lots of eye contact and smiles.	Include humor, personal examples, and experiences.
Neutral			
They are calm, rational; their minds are made up, but they think they are objective.	Present both sides of the issue. Use pro/con or problem/solution patterns. Save time for audience questions.	Be controlled. Do nothing showy. Use confident, small gestures.	Use facts, statistics, expert opinion, and comparison and contrast. Avoid humor, personal stories, and flashy visuals.
Uninterested			
They have short attention spans; they may be there against their will.	Be brief—no more than three points. Avoid topical and pro/con patterns that seem lengthy to the audience.	Be dynamic and entertaining. Move around. Use large gestures.	Use humor, cartoons, colorful visuals, powerful quotations, and startling statistics.
	Avoid darkening the room, standing motionless, passing out handouts, using boring visuals, or expecting the audience to participate.		
Hostile			
They want to take charge or to ridicule the speaker; they may be defensive, emotional.	Organize using a noncontroversial pattern, such as a topical, chronological, or geographical strategy.	Be calm and controlled. Speak evenly and slowly.	Include objective data and expert opinion. Avoid anecdotes and humor.
	Avoid a question-and-answer period, if possible; otherwise, use a moderator or accept only written questions.		

In other words, repeat your main points in the introduction, body, and conclusion of your presentation. Although it seems redundant, this strategy works surprisingly well. Let's examine how to construct the three parts of an effective presentation.

Capturing Attention in the Introduction

What are some openers that grab the audience's attention?

How many times have you heard a speaker begin with, *It's a pleasure to be here.* Or, *I'm honored to be asked to speak.* Boring openings such as these get speakers off to a dull start. Avoid such banalities by striving to accomplish three goals in the introduction to your presentation:

- Capture listeners' attention and get them involved.
- Identify yourself and establish your credibility.
- Preview your main points.

If you are able to appeal to listeners and involve them in your presentation right from the start, you are more likely to hold their attention until the finish. Consider some of the same techniques that you used to open sales letters: a question, a startling fact, a joke, a story, or a quotation. Some speakers achieve involvement by opening with a question or command that requires audience members to raise their hands or stand up. Additional techniques to gain and keep audience attention are presented in the accompanying Career Coach box.

To establish your credibility, you need to describe your position, knowledge, or experience—whatever qualifies you to speak. Try also to connect with your audience. Listeners respond particularly well to speakers who reveal something of themselves and identify with them. A consultant addressing office workers might reminisce about how she started as an administrative assistant; a CEO might tell a funny story in which the joke is on himself.

After capturing attention and establishing yourself, you will want to preview the main points of your topic, perhaps with a visual aid. You may wish to put off actually writing your introduction, however, until after you have organized the rest of the presentation and crystallized your principal ideas.

CAREER COACH

The 10/20/30 Rule of PowerPoint

Would you like to pitch a business idea to one of Silicon Valley's most successful venture capitalists? If yes, you had better whip your PowerPoint skills into shape. Former Apple man Guy Kawasaki is tired of lousy pitches from would-be entrepreneurs and their endless slides laden with fuzzy jargon. An early advocate of customer evangelism in high tech, Kawasaki decided to evangelize the 10/20/30 Rule of PowerPoint: 10 slides, 20 minutes, and 30-point typeface. In his blog, Kawasaki writes that this rule applies to any presentation aiming to reach agreement:

> **Ten slides.** Ten is the optimal number of slides in a PowerPoint presentation because a normal human being cannot comprehend more than ten concepts in a meeting—and venture capitalists are very normal. (The only difference between you and a venture capitalist is that he is getting paid to gamble with someone else's money.) If you must use more than ten slides to explain your business, you probably don't have a business. The ten topics that a venture capitalist cares about are:
>
> 1. Problem
> 2. Your solution
> 3. Business model
> 4. Underlying magic/technology
> 5. Marketing and sales
> 6. Competition
> 7. Team
> 8. Projections and milestones
> 9. Status and timeline
> 10. Summary and call to action
>
> **Twenty minutes.** You should give your ten slides in twenty minutes.... [P]eople will arrive late and have to leave early. In a perfect world, you give your pitch in twenty minutes, and you have forty minutes left for discussion.
>
> **Thirty-point font.** The reason people use a small font is twofold: first, they don't know their material well enough; second, they think that more text is more convincing. Total bozosity. Force yourself to use no font smaller than thirty points. I guarantee it will make your presentations better because it requires you to find the most salient points and to know how to explain them well. If "thirty points" is too dogmatic, then I offer you an algorithm: find out the age of the oldest person in your audience and divide it by two. That's your optimal font size.

Career Application

Revise an existing PowerPoint presentation, preferably a persuasive one, based on Guy Kawasaki's 10/20/30 rule. Use one of your own presentations or peruse a few slideshows from several thousand selections on SlideShare.net. Go to the Business category. To download a presentation, you may need to register with the Web site. Which topics lend themselves the most to the 10/20/30 principle? When might this rule be difficult to follow?

To visit Guy Kawasaki's blog, go to **http://www.blog.guykawasaki.com** or follow him on Twitter: **http://twitter.com/Guykawasaki**

Take a look at Mark Miller's introduction, shown in Figure 14.2, to see how he integrated all the elements necessary for a good opening.

How does the saying "less is more" apply to oral presentations?

Organizing the Body

The biggest problem with most oral presentations is a failure to focus on a few principal ideas. This is why the body of your short presentation (20 or fewer minutes) should include a limited number of main points, say, two to four. Develop each main point with adequate, but not excessive, explanation and details. Too many details can obscure the main message, so keep your presentation simple and logical. Remember, listeners have no pages to leaf back through should they become confused.

How can you organize main ideas in a presentation?

When Mark Miller began planning his presentation, he realized immediately that he could talk for hours on his topic. He also knew that listeners are not good at separating major and minor points. Therefore, instead of submerging his listeners in a sea of information, he sorted out a few main ideas. In the banking industry, loan officers generally ask the following three questions of each applicant for a small business loan: (a) Are you ready to "hit the ground running" in starting your business? (b) Have you done your homework? and (c) Have you made realistic projections of potential sales, cash flow, and equity investment? These questions would become his main points, but Mark wanted to streamline them further so that his audience would be sure to remember them. He encapsulated the questions in three words: *experience, preparation,* and *projection.* As you can see in Figure 14.2, Mark prepared a sentence outline showing these three main ideas. Each is supported by examples and explanations.

FIGURE 14.2 **Oral Presentation Outline**

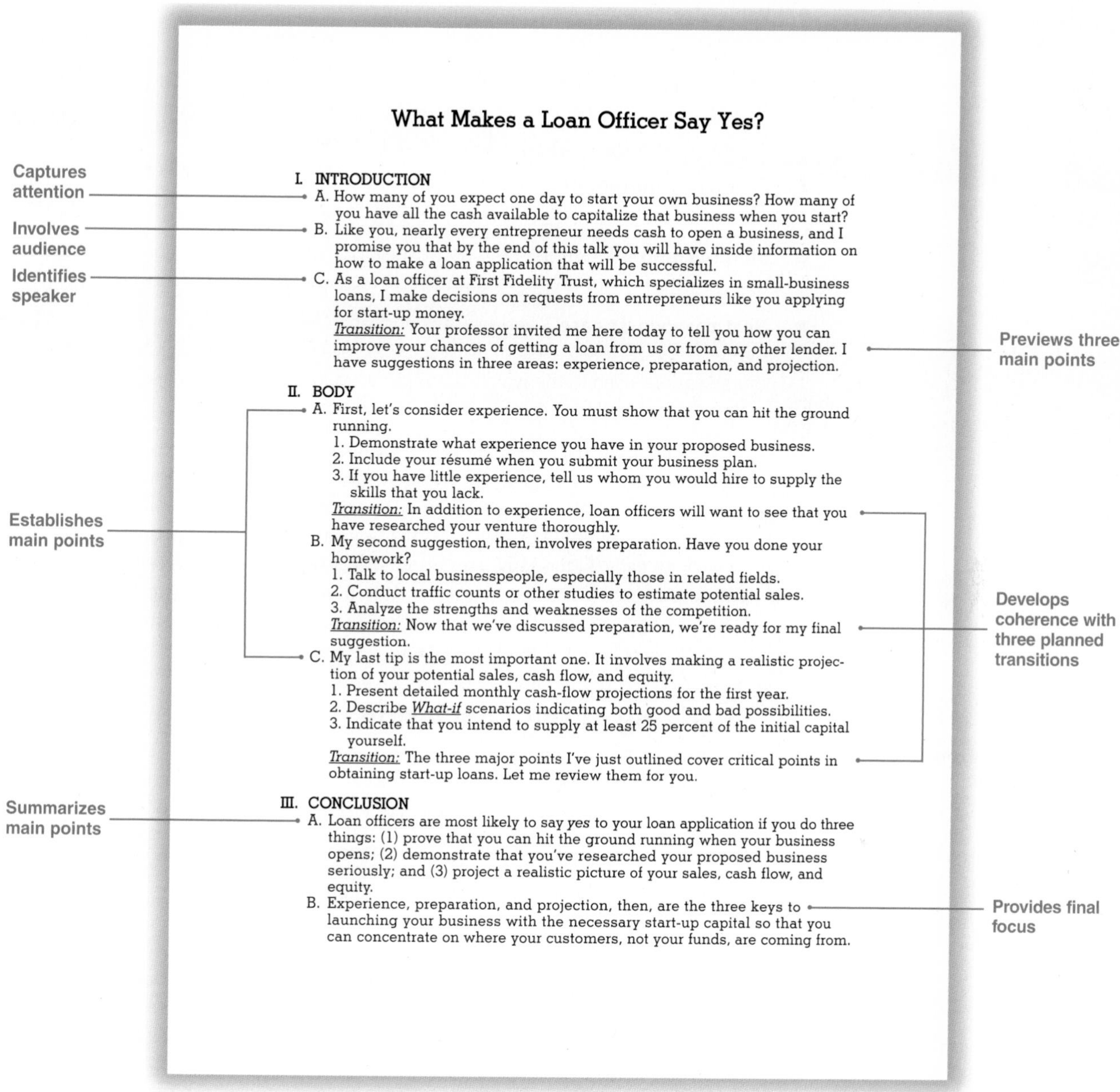
What Makes a Loan Officer Say Yes?

I. INTRODUCTION
A. How many of you expect one day to start your own business? How many of you have all the cash available to capitalize that business when you start?
B. Like you, nearly every entrepreneur needs cash to open a business, and I promise you that by the end of this talk you will have inside information on how to make a loan application that will be successful.
C. As a loan officer at First Fidelity Trust, which specializes in small-business loans, I make decisions on requests from entrepreneurs like you applying for start-up money.
Transition: Your professor invited me here today to tell you how you can improve your chances of getting a loan from us or from any other lender. I have suggestions in three areas: experience, preparation, and projection.

II. BODY
A. First, let's consider experience. You must show that you can hit the ground running.
1. Demonstrate what experience you have in your proposed business.
2. Include your résumé when you submit your business plan.
3. If you have little experience, tell us whom you would hire to supply the skills that you lack.
Transition: In addition to experience, loan officers will want to see that you have researched your venture thoroughly.
B. My second suggestion, then, involves preparation. Have you done your homework?
1. Talk to local businesspeople, especially those in related fields.
2. Conduct traffic counts or other studies to estimate potential sales.
3. Analyze the strengths and weaknesses of the competition.
Transition: Now that we've discussed preparation, we're ready for my final suggestion.
C. My last tip is the most important one. It involves making a realistic projection of your potential sales, cash flow, and equity.
1. Present detailed monthly cash-flow projections for the first year.
2. Describe What-if scenarios indicating both good and bad possibilities.
3. Indicate that you intend to supply at least 25 percent of the initial capital yourself.
Transition: The three major points I've just outlined cover critical points in obtaining start-up loans. Let me review them for you.

III. CONCLUSION
A. Loan officers are most likely to say *yes* to your loan application if you do three things: (1) prove that you can hit the ground running when your business opens; (2) demonstrate that you've researched your proposed business seriously; and (3) project a realistic picture of your sales, cash flow, and equity.
B. Experience, preparation, and projection, then, are the three keys to launching your business with the necessary start-up capital so that you can concentrate on where your customers, not your funds, are coming from.

Captures attention
Involves audience
Identifies speaker
Previews three main points
Establishes main points
Develops coherence with three planned transitions
Summarizes main points
Provides final focus

How to organize and sequence main ideas may not be immediately obvious when you begin working on a presentation. The following methods, which review and amplify those discussed in Chapter 12, provide many possible strategies and examples to help you organize a presentation:

- **Chronology.** Example: A presentation describing the history of a problem, organized from the first sign of trouble to the present.
- **Geography/space.** Example: A presentation about the changing diversity of the workforce, organized by regions in the country (East Coast, West Coast, and so forth).
- **Topic/function/conventional grouping.** Example: A report discussing mishandled airline baggage, organized by names of airlines.
- **Comparison/contrast (pro/con).** Example: A report comparing organic farming methods with those of modern industrial farming.

- **Journalistic pattern.** Example: A report describing how identity thieves can ruin your good name. Organized by *who, what, when, where, why,* and *how.*
- **Value/size.** Example: A report describing fluctuations in housing costs, organized by prices of homes.
- **Importance.** Example: A report describing five reasons a company should move its headquarters to a specific city, organized from the most important reason to the least important.
- **Problem/solution.** Example: A company faces a problem such as declining sales. A solution such as reducing the staff is offered.
- **Simple/complex.** Example: A report explaining genetic modification of plants such as corn, organized from simple seed production to complex gene introduction.
- **Best case/worst case.** Example: A report analyzing whether two companies should merge, organized by the best-case result (improved market share, profitability, employee morale) as opposed to the worst-case result (devalued stock, lost market share, employee malaise).

In the presentation shown in Figure 14.2, Mark arranged the main points by importance, placing the most important point last where it had maximum effect. When organizing any presentation, prepare a little more material than you think you will actually need. Savvy speakers always have something useful in reserve such as an extra handout, transparency, or idea—just in case they finish early. At the same time, most speakers go about 25 percent over the allotted time as opposed to their practice runs at home in front of the mirror. If your speaking time is limited, as it usually is in your classes, aim for less than the limit when rehearsing, so that you don't take time away from the next presenters.

Summarizing in the Conclusion

What do effective conclusions achieve?

Nervous speakers often rush to wrap up their presentations because they can't wait to flee the stage. However, listeners will remember the conclusion more than any other part of a speech. That's why you should spend some time to make it most effective. Strive to achieve three goals:

- Summarize the main themes of the presentation.
- Leave the audience with a specific and memorable take-away.
- Include a statement that allows you to leave the podium gracefully.

Some speakers end limply with comments such as, *I guess that's about all I have to say* or *That's it.* Such lame statements show little enthusiasm and are not the culmination of the talk that listeners expect. Skilled speakers alert the audience that they are finishing. They use phrases such as, *In conclusion, As I end this presentation*, or, *It's time for me to sum up.* Then they proceed immediately to the conclusion. Audiences become justly irritated with a speaker who announces the conclusion but then digresses with one more story or talks on for ten more minutes.

A straightforward summary should review major points and focus on what you want the listeners to do, think, or remember. You might say, *In bringing my presentation to a close, I will restate my major purpose ...*, or, *In summary, my major purpose has been to.... In support of my purpose, I have presented three major points. They are (1) ..., (2) ..., and (3) ....* Notice how Mark Miller, in the conclusion shown in Figure 14.2, summarized his three main points and provided a final focus to listeners.

If you are promoting a recommendation, you might end as follows: *In conclusion, I recommend that we retain Matrixx Marketing to conduct a telemarketing campaign beginning September 1 at a cost of X dollars. To complete this recommendation, I suggest that we (a) finance this campaign from our operations budget, (b) develop a persuasive message describing our new product, and (c) name Lisa Beck to oversee the project.*

A conclusion is akin to a punch line and must be memorable. Think of it as the high point of your presentation, a valuable kernel of information to take away. The valuable kernel of information, or take-away, should tie in with the opening or present a forward-looking idea. Avoid merely rehashing, in the same words, what you said before, but ensure that the audience will take away very specific information or benefits and a positive impression of you and your company. The take-away is the value of the presentation to the audience and the benefit audience members believe they have received. The tension that you built in the early parts of the talk now culminates in the close.

In your conclusion you might want to use an anecdote, an inspiring quotation, or a statement that ties in the opener and offers a new insight. Whatever you choose, be sure to include a closing thought that indicates you are finished. For example, *This concludes my presentation. After investigating many marketing firms, we are convinced that Matrixx is the best for our purposes. Your authorization of my recommendations will mark the beginning of a very successful campaign for our new product. Thank you.*

Building Audience Rapport Like a Pro

LEARNING OBJECTIVE 3
Identify techniques for gaining audience rapport, including (a) using effective imagery, (b) providing verbal signposts, and (c) sending appropriate nonverbal messages.

Good speakers are adept at building audience rapport. They form a bond with the audience; they entertain as well as inform. How do they do it? Based on observations of successful and unsuccessful speakers, we learn that the good ones use a number of verbal and nonverbal techniques to connect with the audience. Their helpful techniques include providing effective imagery, supplying verbal signposts, and using body language strategically.

Effective Imagery

How can you keep the audience's interest?

You will lose your audience quickly if you fill your talk with abstractions, generalities, and dry facts. To enliven your presentation and enhance comprehension, try using some of the following techniques. However, beware of exaggeration or distortion. Keep your imagery realistic and credible.

- **Analogies.** A comparison of similar traits between dissimilar things can be effective in explaining and drawing connections. For example, *Product development is similar to the process of conceiving, carrying, and delivering a baby.* Or, *Downsizing or restructuring is similar to an overweight person undergoing a regimen of dieting, habit changing, and exercising.*
- **Metaphors.** A comparison between otherwise dissimilar things without using the words *like* or *as* results in a metaphor. For example, *Our competitor's CEO is a snake when it comes to negotiating* or *My desk is a garbage dump.*
- **Similes.** A comparison that includes the words *like* or *as* is a simile. For example, *Our critics used our background report like a drunk uses a lamppost—for support rather than for illumination.* Or, *She's as happy as someone who just won the lottery.*
- **Personal anecdotes.** Nothing connects you faster or better with your audience than a good personal story. In a talk about e-mail techniques, you could reveal your own blunders that became painful learning experiences. In a talk to potential investors, the founder of a new ethnic magazine might tell a story about growing up without positive ethnic role models.
- **Personalized statistics.** Although often misused, statistics stay with people—particularly when they relate directly to the audience. A speaker discussing job searching might say, *Look around the room. Only three out of five graduates will find a job immediately after graduation.* If possible, simplify and personalize facts. For example, *The sales of Coca-Cola totaled 2 billion cases last year. That means that every man, woman, and child in the United States consumed six full cases of Coke.*
- **Worst- and best-case scenarios.** Hearing the worst that could happen can be effective in driving home a point. For example, *If we do nothing about our computer backup system now, it's just a matter of time before the entire system crashes and we lose all of our customer contact information. Can you imagine starting from scratch in building all of your customer files again? However, if we fix the system now, we can expand our customer files and actually increase sales at the same time.*

Spotlight on Communicators

© Courtesy of Dianna Booher—Booher Consultants, Inc.

Communication expert Dianna Booher tries to describe the sometimes elusive quality that permits a skillful speaker to establish a rapport with listeners: "Presence may be difficult to define, but it is easy to spot. Most people know it when they see it. It is a manner of moving and interacting that commands attention and creates confidence in the speaker and increases credibility for the content." Although, to some extent, personality may determine presence, the good news is that speaking skills can be learned. You can become an effective speaker by adopting the techniques discussed in this chapter.

How can you ensure that your audience does not get lost?

Verbal Signposts

Speakers must remember that listeners, unlike readers of a report, cannot control the rate of presentation or flip back through pages to review main points. As a result, listeners get lost easily. Knowledgeable speakers help the audience recognize the organization and main points in an oral message with verbal signposts. They keep listeners on track by including helpful previews, summaries, and transitions, such as these:

- **Previewing**

  The next segment of my talk presents three reasons for....

  Let's now consider the causes of....

- **Summarizing**

  Let me review with you the major problems I have just discussed....

  You see, then, that the most significant factors are....

- **Switching directions**

  Thus far we have talked solely about...; now let's move to....

  I have argued that... and..., but an alternate view holds that....

You can further improve any oral presentation by including appropriate transitional expressions such as *first, second, next, then, therefore, moreover, on the other hand, on the contrary,* and *in conclusion.* These transitional expressions, which you learned about in Figure 5.8 on page 156, build coherence, lend emphasis, and tell listeners where you are headed. Notice in Mark Miller's outline, in Figure 14.2, the specific transitional elements designed to help listeners recognize each new principal point.

How can your nonverbal behavior affect the success of your presentation?

Nonverbal Messages

Although what you say is most important, the nonverbal messages you send can also have a potent effect on how well your audience receives your message. How you look, how you move, and how you speak can make or break your presentation. The following suggestions focus on nonverbal tips to ensure that your verbal message is well received.

- **Look terrific!** Like it or not, you will be judged by your appearance. For everything but small in-house presentations, be sure you dress professionally. The rule of thumb is that you should dress at least as well as the best-dressed person in the audience.
- **Animate your body.** Be enthusiastic and let your body show it. Emphasize ideas to enhance points about size, number, and direction. Use a variety of gestures, but don't consciously plan them in advance.
- **Speak extemporaneously.** Do not read from notes or a manuscript, but speak freely. Use your presentation slides to guide your talk. You will come across as more competent and enthusiastic if you are not glued to your notes or manuscript. Use note cards or a paper outline only if presenting without an electronic slideshow.
- **Punctuate your words.** You can keep your audience interested by varying your tone, volume, pitch, and pace. Use pauses before and after important points. Allow the audience to take in your ideas.
- **Get out from behind the podium.** Avoid being glued to the podium. Movement makes you look natural and comfortable. You might pick a few places in the room to walk to. Even if you must stay close to your visual aids, make a point of leaving them occasionally so that the audience can see your whole body.
- **Vary your facial expression.** Begin with a smile, but change your expressions to correspond with the thoughts you are voicing. You can shake your head to show disagreement, roll your eyes to show disdain, look heavenward for guidance, or wrinkle your brow to

Spotlight on Communicators

Cisco is a worldwide leader in networking that transforms how people connect, communicate, and collaborate. When Chairman and CEO John Chambers introduces new Cisco products to a diverse audience made up of analysts, media, and consumers, he captivates his audience using persuasive communication skills. One of his strategies is to use movement and hand gestures to punctuate every sentence, allowing him to work the crowd. To maintain your listeners' attention, strive to be animated in your voice and body.

show concern or dismay. To see how speakers convey meaning without words, mute the sound on your TV and watch the facial expressions of a talk show personality.

Whenever possible, beginning presenters should have an experienced speaker watch them and give them tips as they rehearse. Your instructor is an important coach who can provide you with invaluable feedback. In the absence of helpers, tape yourself and watch your nonverbal behavior on camera.

Planning Visual Aids and Multimedia Presentations

LEARNING OBJECTIVE 4
Discuss designing visual aids, handouts, and multimedia presentations and using presentation technology competently.

Before you make a business presentation, consider this wise proverb: "Tell me, I forget. Show me, I remember. Involve me, I understand." Your goals as a speaker are to make listeners understand, remember, and act on your ideas. To get them interested and involved, include effective visual aids. Some experts say that we acquire 85 percent of all our knowledge visually: "Professionals everywhere need to know about the incredible inefficiency of text-based information and the incredible effects of images," says developmental molecular biologist John Medina.[5] Therefore, an oral presentation that incorporates visual aids is far more likely to be understood and retained than one lacking visual enhancement.

What purposes do visual aids serve?

Good visual aids have many purposes. They emphasize and clarify main points, thus improving comprehension and retention. They increase audience interest, and they make the presenter appear more professional, better prepared, and more persuasive. Well-designed visual aids illustrate and emphasize your message more effectively than words alone; therefore, they may help shorten a meeting or achieve your goal faster. Visual aids are particularly helpful for inexperienced speakers because the audience concentrates on the aid rather than on the speaker. However, experienced speakers work hard at not being eclipsed or upstaged by their slideshows. Good visuals also serve to jog the memory of a speaker, thus improving self-confidence, poise, and delivery.

Types of Visual Aids

Fortunately for today's speakers, many forms of visual media are available to enhance a presentation. Figure 14.3 describes the pros and cons of a number of visual aids that can guide you in selecting the best one for any speaking occasion. Three of the most popular visuals are multimedia slides, overhead transparencies, and handouts.

Multimedia Slides. With today's excellent software programs—such as Microsoft PowerPoint, Apple Keynote, Lotus Freelance Graphics, Corel Presentations, and Adobe Presenter or Adobe Ovation—you can create dynamic, colorful presentations with your PC. The output from these programs is generally shown on a computer monitor, a TV monitor, an LCD (liquid crystal display) panel, or a screen. With a little expertise and advanced equipment, you can create a multimedia presentation that includes stereo sound, videos, and hyperlinks, as described shortly in the discussion of multimedia presentations.

Overhead Transparencies. Some speakers still rely on the overhead projector for many reasons. Most meeting areas are equipped with projectors and screens. Moreover, acetate transparencies for the overhead are cheap, easily prepared on a computer or copier, and simple to use. Because rooms need not be darkened, a speaker using transparencies can maintain eye contact with the audience. Many experienced speakers create overhead slides in addition to their electronic slides to have a backup plan in the case of malfunctioning presentation technology. More important, though, overhead transparencies are ideal if the speaker needs to draw on the images or data using a marker. A word of caution, though, when using transparencies: stand to the side of the projector so that you don't obstruct the audience's view.

When should you distribute handouts?

Handouts. You can enhance and complement your presentations by distributing pictures, outlines, brochures, articles, charts, summaries, or other supplements. Speakers who use presentation software often prepare a set of their slides along with notes to hand

FIGURE 14.3 Pros and Cons for Visual Aid Options

Medium	Pros	Cons
Multimedia slides	Create professional appearance with many color, art, graphic, and font options. Easy to use and transport via removable storage media, Web download, or e-mail attachment. Inexpensive to update.	Present potential incompatibility issues. Require costly projection equipment and practice for smooth delivery. Tempt user to include razzle-dazzle features that may fail to add value.
Transparencies	Give professional appearance with little practice. Easy to (a) prepare, (b) update and maintain, (c) locate reliable equipment, and (d) limit information shown at one time.	Appear to some as an outdated presentation method. Hold speaker captive to the machine. Provide poor reproduction of photos and some graphics.
Handouts	Encourage audience participation. Easy to maintain and update. Enhance recall because audience keeps reference material.	Increase risk of unauthorized duplication of speaker's material. Can be difficult to transport. May cause speaker to lose audience's attention.
Flipcharts or whiteboards	Provide inexpensive option available at most sites. Easy to (a) create, (b) modify or customize on the spot, (c) record comments from the audience, and (d) combine with more high-tech visuals in the same presentation.	Require graphics talent. Difficult for larger audiences to see. Prepared flipcharts are cumbersome to transport and easily worn with use.
Video	Give an accurate representation of the content; strong indication of forethought and preparation.	Create potential for compatibility issues related to computer video formats. Expensive to create and update.
Props	Offer a realistic reinforcement of message content. Increase audience participation with close observation.	Lead to extra work and expense in transporting and replacing worn objects. Limited use with larger audiences.

out to viewers. Timing the distribution of any handout, though, is tricky. If given out during a presentation, your handouts tend to distract the audience, causing you to lose control. Therefore, you should discuss handouts during the presentation but delay distributing them until after you finish.

Speaker's Notes. You have a variety of options for printing hard-copy versions of your presentation. You can, for example, make speaker's notes, which are a wonderful aid for practicing your talk. Beneath the miniature image of each slide is space for you to key in your supporting comments for the abbreviated material in your slides. You can also include up to nine miniature versions of your slides per printed page. These miniatures are handy if you want to preview your talk to a sponsoring organization or if you want to supply the audience with a summary of your presentation. However, resist the temptation to read from your notes during the slide presentation. It might turn off your audience and make you appear insecure and incompetent.

Designing an Impressive Multimedia Presentation

How do businesspeople view PowerPoint and other presentation software?

Few corporate types or entrepreneurs would do without the razzle-dazzle of colorful images to make their points. Electronic slideshows, PowerPoint in particular, have become a staple of business presentations. However, overuse or misuse may be the downside of the ever-present multimedia slideshow. Over the two decades of the software program's existence, millions of poorly created

Apple Computer

Do you want to learn presentation secrets from the "world's greatest corporate storyteller," Steve Jobs? The Apple cofounder and CEO is the subject of a book by Carmine Gallo, in which the communication coach reveals the techniques that Jobs uses to deliver "mind-blowing keynote presentations." Jobs' keynotes, or "Stevenotes," inform, educate, and entertain. As Gallo points out, Jobs does not sell computers; he sells an experience: Apple presentations resemble a great theatrical production—a terrific script, heroes and villains, stage props, amazing visuals, and a moment meant to stun the audience.[6]

If you would like to sell your product or ideas the Steve Jobs way, study the following five elements that Gallo culled from hours of Jobs' keynotes:

1. **A headline.** Steve Jobs characterizes every product with a catch phrase that is shorter than a 140-character tweet. Even before it first hit the stores, the iPad was consistently announced as "a magical and revolutionary product at an unbelievable price." All marketing materials use this headline.
2. **A villain.** Rivalry is entertaining and suspenseful. Classic stories feature heroes fighting villains. In the Apple narrative, Microsoft plays the part of the villain, most evident in the "I'm a Mac" TV commercials. Conquering a shared enemy motivates customers and turns them into brand evangelists.
3. **A simple slide.** Jobs' slides are as uncluttered, visual, and simple as Apple products. Powerful images, not bullet points, rule. Just remember the MacBook Air being pulled out of a manila envelope. As opposed to the average 40-word PowerPoint slide, Jobs may use as few as seven words in ten slides.
4. **A demo.** The Apple CEO does not let his audience lose interest. About ten minutes into a presentation, he is demonstrating a new product or feature. His enthusiasm is infectious. Presenting the iPhone in 2007, Jobs showed off Google Maps by looking up Starbucks and just for fun pretended to order 4,000 lattes to go.

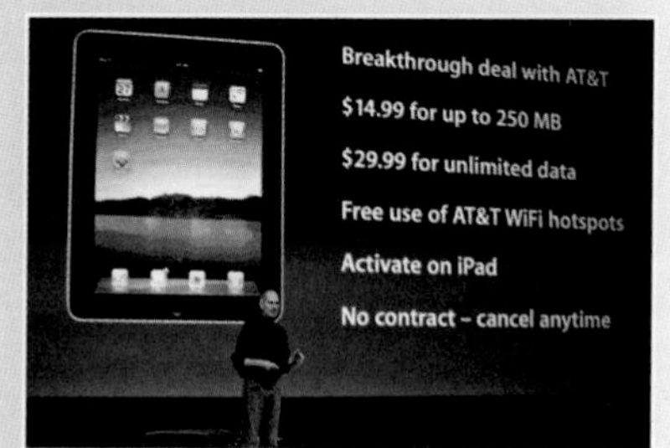
Breakthrough deal with AT&T
$14.99 for up to 250 MB
$29.99 for unlimited data
Free use of AT&T WiFi hotspots
Activate on iPad
No contract – cancel anytime
©Tony Avelar/Bloomberg via Getty Images

5. **A holy smokes moment.** Jobs creates an emotional experience that becomes truly memorable. He built drama to a crescendo when introducing three new devices, "an iPod, a phone, an Internet communicator," only to stun the audience with the surprising revelation that all three were really one, the new iPhone.

Critical Thinking

- What can you learn from the speaking style of Steve Jobs?
- Why is simplicity important in an oral presentation?
- Communication coach Carmine Gallo says that charismatic speakers such as Steve Jobs are driven by the zeal to make the world a better place and enrich people's lives. If you were an entrepreneur, what would be your sense of mission?

and badly delivered PowerPoint presentations have tarnished PowerPoint's reputation as an effective communication tool. Tools, however, are helpful only when used properly.

Imagine those who sit through the more than 30 million PowerPoint presentations that Microsoft estimates are made each day.[7] No doubt, many of them would say that this "disease" has reached epidemic proportions. As a result, PowerPoint is often ridiculed as an ineffective communication tool. PowerPoint, say its detractors, dictates the way information is structured and presented. They say that the program is turning the nation's businesspeople into a "mindless gaggle of bullet-pointed morons."[8] If you typed *death by PowerPoint* in your favorite search engine, you would score over 1 million hits. However, text-laden, amateurish slides that distract and bore audiences are the fault of their creator and not the software program itself.

In the sections that follow, you will learn to create an impressive multimedia presentation using the most widely used presentation software program, PowerPoint. With any software program, of course, gaining expertise requires an investment of time and effort. You could take a course, or you could teach yourself through an online tutorial such as that at **http://office.microsoft.com/en-us/training/default.aspx**. Another way to master PowerPoint is to read a book such as Doug Lowe's *Microsoft Office PowerPoint 2007 for Dummies.* More advanced guidebooks about effective slideshows abound. If operated by a proficient slide preparer and a skillful presenter, PowerPoint can add a distinct visual impact to any presentation.

Applying the 3-x-3 Writing Process to Slide Presentations

Some presenters prefer to create their slides first and then develop the narrative around their slides. Others prefer to prepare their content first and then create the visual component. The risk associated with the first approach is that you may be tempted to spend too much time making your slides look good and not enough time preparing your content. Remember that great-looking slides never compensate for thin content. In the following discussion, we review the three phases of the writing process and show how they help you develop a visually appealing PowerPoint presentation. In the first phase (prewriting), you analyze, anticipate, and adapt. In the second phase, you research, organize, compose, and design. In the third phase, you revise, edit, and evaluate.

How do you determine presentation content and design?

Analyzing the Situation. Making the best content and design choices for your slides depends greatly on your analysis of the presentation situation. Will your slides be used during a live presentation? Will they be part of a self-running presentation such as in a store kiosk? Will they be saved on a server so that those with Internet access can watch the presentation at their convenience? Will they be sent as a PowerPoint show or a PDF document—also sometimes called a deck—to a client instead of a hard-copy report? Are you converting PowerPoint slideshows for viewing on iPhones, video iPods,[9] or BlackBerry devices?[10]

If you are e-mailing the presentation or posting it online as a self-contained file, the slides will typically feature more text than if they were delivered orally. If, on the other hand, you are creating slides for a live presentation, your analysis will prompt you to choose powerful, telling images over boring text-laden slides.

Anticipating Your Audience. Think about how you can design your presentation to get the most positive response from your audience. Audiences respond, for example, to the colors you use. Primary ideas are generally best conveyed with bold colors such as blue, green, and purple. Because the messages that colors convey can vary from culture to culture, colors must be chosen carefully. In the United States, blue is the color of credibility, tranquility, conservatism, and trust. Therefore, it is the background color of choice for many business presentations. Green relates to interaction, growth, money, and stability. It can work well as a background or an accent color. Purple can also work as a background or accent color. It conveys spirituality, royalty, dreams, and humor.[11]

Just as you anticipate audience members' reactions to color, you can usually anticipate their reactions to special effects. Using animation and sound effects—flying objects, swirling text, clashing cymbals, and the like—only because they are available is not a good idea. Special effects distract your audience, drawing attention away from your main points. You should add animation features only if doing so helps convey your message or adds interest to the content. When your audience members leave, they should be commenting on the ideas you conveyed—not the cool swivels and sound effects.

Which handy rule can help you design effective slides and select proper background and text colors?

Adapting Text and Color Selections. Adapt the amount of text on your slide to how your audience will use the slides. As a general guideline, most graphic designers encourage the 6-x-6 rule: "Six bullets per screen, max; six words per bullet, max."[12] You may find, however, that breaking this rule is sometimes necessary, particularly when your users will be viewing the presentation on their own with no speaker assistance. For most purposes, though, strive to break free from bulleted lists whenever possible and minimize the use of text.

Adapt the colors based on where the presentation will be given. Use light text on a dark background for presentations in darkened rooms. Use dark text on a light background for presentations in lighted rooms. Avoid using a dark font on a dark background, such as red text on a dark blue background. In the same way, avoid using a light font on a light background, such as white text on a pale blue background. Dark on dark or light on light results in low contrast, making the slides difficult to read.

Researching Your PowerPoint Options. You may need to present a complicated idea and will have to learn more about PowerPoint to determine the best way to clarify and simplify its visual presentation. Besides using online tutorials and studying books on the subject, be on the lookout as you view other people's presentations to learn fresh ways to illustrate your content more effectively. Chances are you will learn the most from fellow students and team members who have truly mastered the software.

Organizing Your Slides. When you prepare your slides, translate the major headings in your presentation outline into titles for slides. Then build bullet points using short phrases. In Chapter 5 you learned to improve readability by using graphic highlighting techniques, including bullets, numbers, and headings. In preparing a PowerPoint presentation, you will use those same techniques.

The slides you create to accompany your spoken ideas can be organized with visual elements that will help your audience understand and remember what you want to communicate. Let's say, for example, that you have three points in your presentation. You can create a blueprint slide that captures the three points in a visually appealing way, and then you can use that slide several times throughout your presentation. Near the beginning, the blueprint slide provides an overview of your points. Later, it will provide transitions as you move from point to point. For transitions, you can direct your audience's attention by highlighting the next point you will be talking about. Finally, the blueprint slide can be used near the end to provide a review of your key points.

What are visual clichés, and why should you avoid them?

Working With Templates. All presentation programs require you to (a) create a template that will serve as the background for your presentation and (b) make each individual slide by selecting a layout that best conveys your message. When you craft your template, be cautious about selecting the slide templates that came with the program. They have been seen by millions and amount to what one expert has labeled "visual clichés."[13] Overused templates and even clip art that ship with PowerPoint can weary viewers who have seen them repeatedly in presentations. Instead of using a standard template, search for *PowerPoint template* in Google or your favorite search engine. You will see hundreds of template options available as free downloads. Unless your employer requires that presentations all have the same look, your audience will most likely appreciate fresh templates that complement the purpose of your presentation and provide visual variety.

Office PowerPoint 2007 presentation templates replace the **AutoContent Wizard**. They come with new as well as familiar layouts and themes that you can modify. Templates get you started quickly. They allow you to add your own images or a logo and delete or modify text. Relying only on templates, however, generally leads to text-heavy presentations that lack visual elements. Nevertheless, it's a good start for a PowerPoint newbie. With more experience, you can create backgrounds and layouts from scratch by adding your own elements to each slide.

Composing Your Slideshow. During the composition stage, many users fall into the trap of excessive formatting and programming. They fritter away precious time fine-tuning their slides. They don't spend enough time on what they are going to say and how they will say it. To avoid this trap, set a limit for how much time you will spend making your slides visually appealing. Your time limit will be based on how many "bells and whistles" (a) your audience expects and (b) your content requires to make it understandable. Remember that not every point nor every thought requires a visual. In fact, it's smart to switch off the slides occasionally and direct the focus to yourself. Darkening the screen while you discuss a point, tell a story, give an example, or involve the audience will add variety to your presentation.

Create a slide only if the slide accomplishes at least one of the following purposes:

- Generates interest in what you are saying and helps the audience follow your ideas
- Highlights points you want your audience to remember
- Introduces or reviews your key points
- Provides a transition from one major point to the next
- Illustrates and simplifies complex ideas

In a later section of this chapter, you will find very specific steps to follow as you create your presentation.

Designing for Optimal Effect. Try to avoid long, boring bulleted lists in a presentation. You can alter layouts by repositioning, resizing, or changing the fonts for the placeholders in which your title, bulleted list, organization chart, video clip, photograph, or other elements appear. Figure 14.4 illustrates two of the many layout and design options for creating your slides. The figure shows that you can make your slides visually more appealing and memorable even with relatively small changes.

Notice that the bulleted items on the first slide in Figure 14.4 are not parallel. The slide looks as if the author had been brainstorming or freewriting a first draft. The second and sixth bullet points

FIGURE 14.4 Revising and Enhancing Slides for Greater Impact

Before Revision

Reasons for Selling Online

- Your online business can grow globally.
- Customer convenience.
- Conduct business 24/7.
- No need for renting a retail store or hiring employees.
- Reduce inquiries by providing policies and a privacy statement.
- Customers can buy quickly and easily.

After Revision

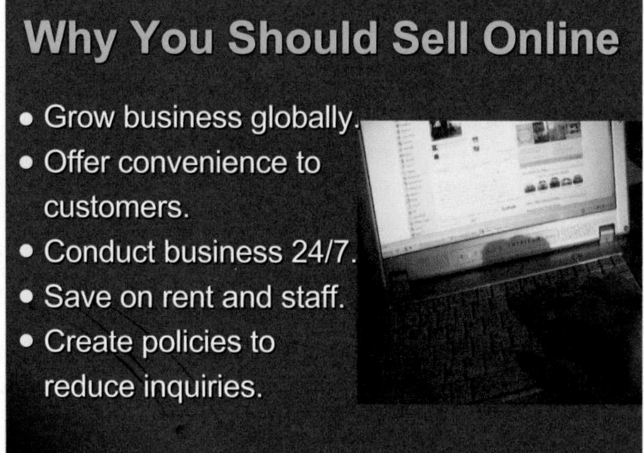

Why You Should Sell Online
• Grow business globally.
• Offer convenience to customers.
• Conduct business 24/7.
• Save on rent and staff.
• Create policies to reduce inquiries.

The slide on the left contains bullet points that are not parallel and that overlap in meaning. The second and sixth bullet points say the same thing. Moreover, some bullet points are too long. After revision, the slide on the right has a more convincing title illustrating the "you" view. The bullet points are shorter, and each begins with a verb for parallelism and an emphasis on action. The photo adds interest.

express the same thought, that shopping online is convenient and easy for customers. Some bullet points are too long. The bullets on the improved slide are very short, well within the 6-x-6 rule, although they are complete sentences. The photograph in the revised slide adds interest and illustrates the point. You may use stock photos that you can download from the Web for personal or school use without penalty, or consider taking your own pictures if you own a digital camera.

How can you add pizzazz to your slides?

Figure 14.5 shows how to add variety and pizzazz to your slides. Notice that the information that appeared as bullet points in Figure 14.4 now appears as exciting spokes radiating from the central idea: Why You Should Sell Online. This spoke diagram is just one of numerous **SmartArt graphics** in the **Illustrations** tab in PowerPoint. You can also animate each item in the diagram. Occasionally, try to convert pure text and bullet points to graphics, charts, and other images to add punch to your slideshow. This will keep your audiences interested and help them retain the information you are presenting.

FIGURE 14.5 Converting a Bulleted Slide Into a Diagram

Revised With a SmartArt Graphic

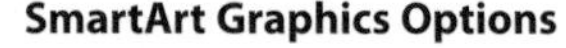

SmartArt Graphics Options

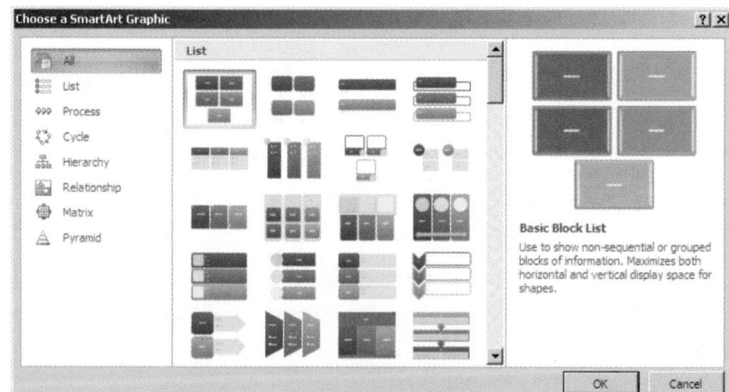

The same content that appears in the Figure 14.4 slides takes on a totally different look when arranged as spokes radiating from a central idea. Add a 3-D effect and a muted background image to the middle shape, for example, and you depart from the usual boring template look. When presenting this slide, you can animate each item and control when it is revealed, further enlivening your presentation. PowerPoint 2007 provides SmartArt graphics with many choices of diagrams and shapes for arranging information.

Revising, Proofreading, and Evaluating Your Slideshow. Use PowerPoint's **Slide Sorter** view to rearrange, insert, and delete slides during the revision process. This is the time to focus on making your presentation as clear and concise as possible. If you are listing items, be sure that all items use parallel grammatical form. Figure 14.6 shows how to revise a slide to improve it for conciseness, parallelism, and other features. Study the design tips described in the first slide and determine which suggestions were not followed. Then compare it with the revised slide.

Notice that both slides in Figure 14.6 feature a blue background, the calming blue serving as the color of choice for most business presentations. However, the background swirls on the first slide are distracting. In addition, the uppercase white font contributes to the busy look, making the slide hard to read. Inserting a transparent overlay and choosing a dark font to mute the distracting waves create a cleaner-looking slide.

As you are revising, check carefully to find spelling, grammar, punctuation, and other errors. Use the PowerPoint spell check, but don't rely on it without careful proofing, preferably from a printed copy of the slideshow. Nothing is as embarrassing as projecting errors on a huge screen in front of an audience. Also, check for consistency in how you capitalize and punctuate points throughout the presentation.

The final stage in applying the 3-x-3 writing process to developing a PowerPoint presentation involves evaluation. Consider whether you have done all you can to use the tools PowerPoint provides to communicate your message in a visually appealing way. In addition, test your slides on the equipment and in the room you will be using during your presentation. Do the colors you selected work in this new setting? Are the font styles and sizes readable from the back of the room? Figure 14.7 shows examples of slides that incorporate what you have learned in this discussion.

The dark purple background and the green and blue hues in the slideshow shown in Figure 14.7 are standard choices for many business presentations. With an unobtrusive dark background, white fonts are a good option for maximum contrast and, hence, readability. The creator of the presentation varied the slide design to break the monotony of bulleted or numbered lists. Images and animated diagrams add interest and zing to the slides.

Using PowerPoint Effectively With Your Audience

What do you have to watch out for with technology?

Many promising presentations have been sabotaged by technology glitches or by the presenter's unfamiliarity with the equipment. Fabulous slides are of value only if you can manage the technology expertly. As we have seen, Apple CEO Steve Jobs is famous for his ability to wow his audiences during his keynote addresses. A *BusinessWeek* cover story described his approach: "Jobs

FIGURE 14.6 Designing More Effective Slides

Before Revision

DESIGN TIPS FOR SLIDE TEXT

1. STRIVE TO HAVE NO MORE THAN SIX BULLETS PER SLIDE AND NO MORE THAN SIX WORDS PER BULLET.
2. IF YOU USE UPPER-AND LOWERCASE TYPE, IT IS EASIER TO READ
3. IT IS BETTER TO USE PHRASES RATHER THAN SENTENCES.
4. USING A SIMPLE, HIGH-CONTRAST TYPE FACE IS EASIER TO READ AND DOES NOT DETRACT FROM YOUR PRESENTATION
5. BE CONSISTENT IN YOUR SPACING, CAPITALIZATION, AND PUNCTUATION.

After Revision

Design Tips for Slide Text

Six bullets per slide or fewer
Six words per bullet or fewer
Upper- and lowercase type
Concise phrases, not sentences
Simple typeface
Consistent spacing, capitalization, and punctuation

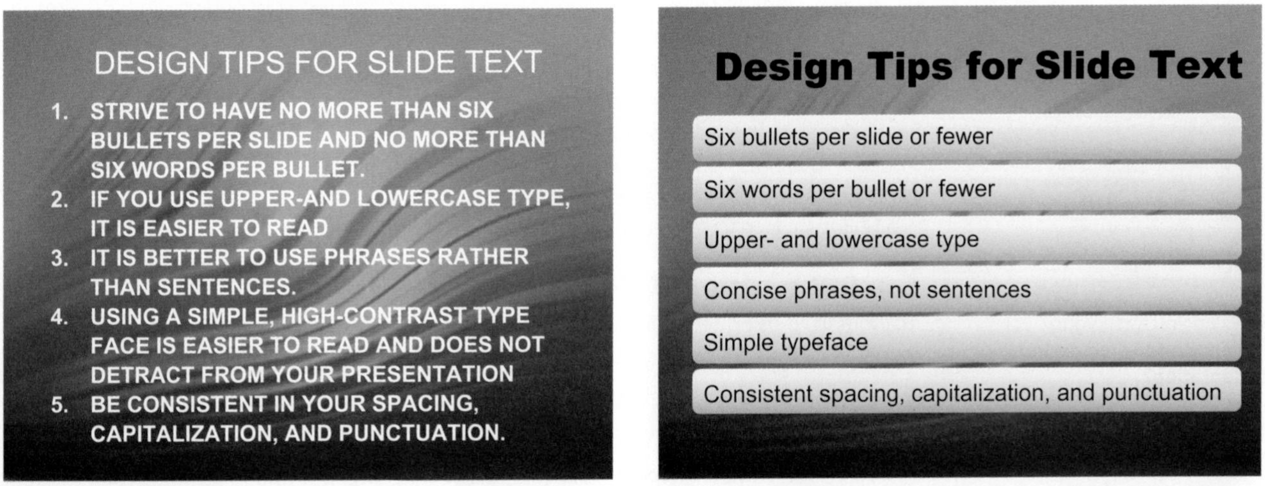

The slide on the left is difficult to read and understand because it violates many slide-making rules. How many violations can you spot? The slide on the right illustrates an improved version of the same information. Which slide do you think viewers would rather read?

FIGURE 14.7 **PowerPoint Slides That Summarize and Illustrate Multimedia Presentations**

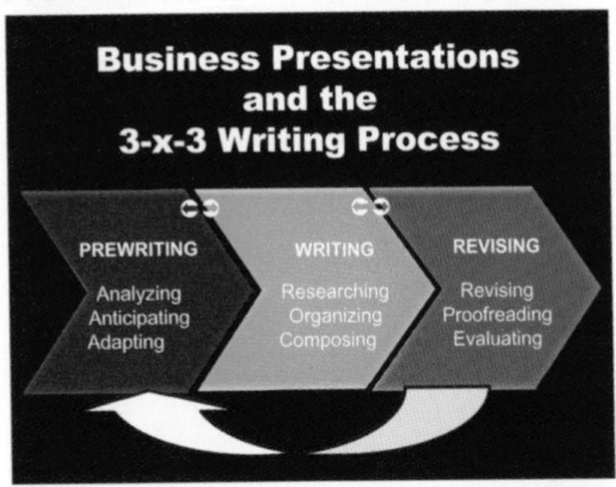

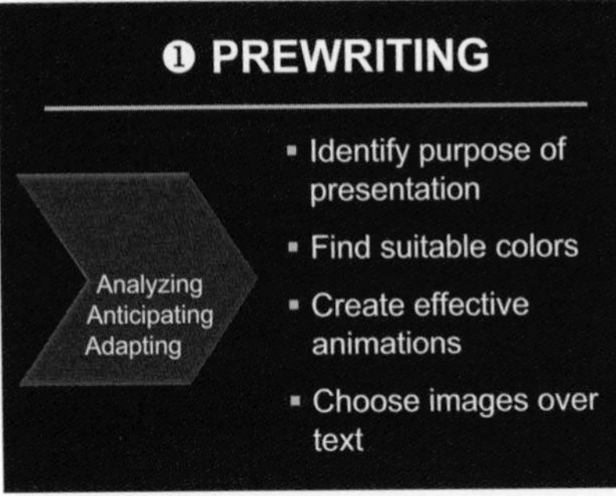

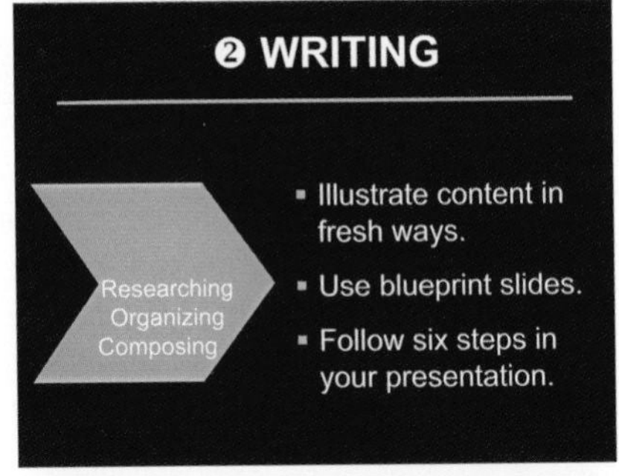

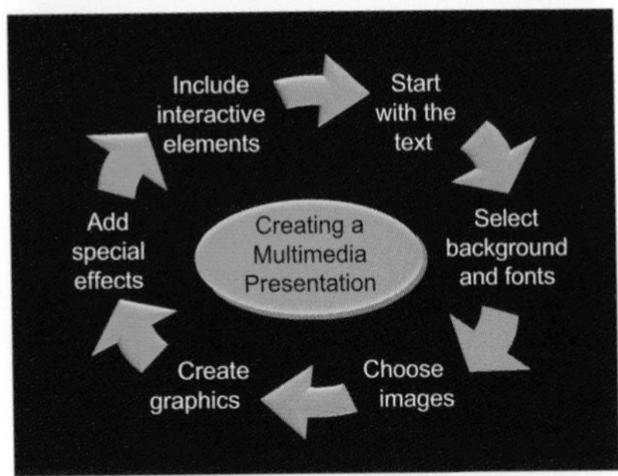

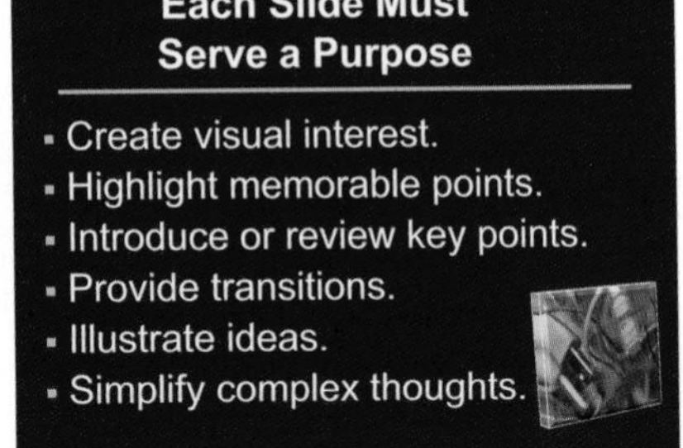

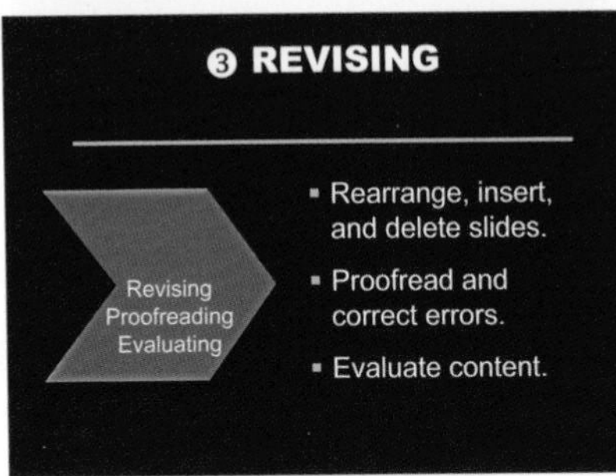

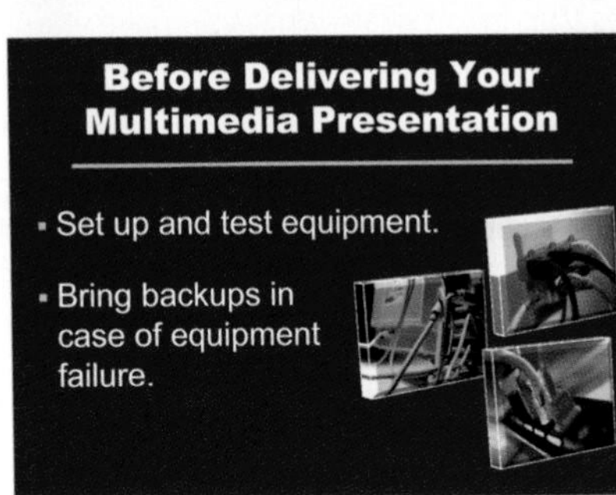

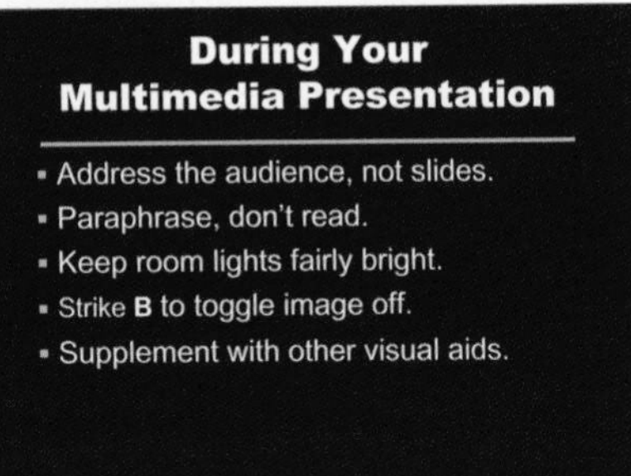

unveils Apple's latest products as if he were a particularly hip and plugged-in friend showing off inventions in your living room. Truth is, the sense of informality comes only after grueling hours of practice."[14] At one of his recent Macworld rehearsals, for example, he spent more than four hours on stage practicing and reviewing every technical and performance aspect of his product launch.

Practicing and Preparing

Allow plenty of time before your presentation to set up and test your equipment.[15] Confirm that the places you plan to stand are not in the line of the projected image. Audience members do not appreciate having part of the slide displayed on your body. Make sure that all links to videos or the Web are working and that you know how to operate all features the first time you try. No matter how much time you put into preshow setup and testing, you still have no guarantee that all will go smoothly. Therefore, you should always bring backups of your presentation. Overhead transparencies or handouts of your presentation provide good substitutes. Transferring your presentation to a CD or a USB flash drive that could run from any available notebook might prove useful as well.

How can you keep your audience interested during your presentation?

Keeping Your Audience Engaged

In addition to using technology to enhance and enrich your message, here are additional tips for performing like a professional and keeping the audience engaged:

- Know your material. This will free you to look at your audience and gaze at the screen, not your practice notes. Maintain genuine eye contact to connect with individuals in the room.
- As you show new elements on a slide, allow the audience time to absorb the information. Then paraphrase and elaborate on what the listeners have seen. Don't insult your audience's intelligence by reading verbatim from a slide.

- Leave the lights as bright as you can. Make sure the audience can see your face and eyes.
- Use a radio remote control (not infrared) so you can move freely rather than remain tethered to your computer. Radio remotes allow you to be up to 50 feet away from your laptop.
- Maintain a connection with the audience by using a laser pointer to highlight slide items to discuss. Be aware, however, that a dancing laser point in a shaky hand may make you appear nervous. Steady your hand.
- Don't leave a slide on the screen when you have finished discussing it. In **Slide Show** view on the **View** tab, strike *B* on the keyboard to turn on or off the screen image by blackening it. Pushing *W* will turn the screen white.

Some presenters allow their PowerPoint slides to steal their thunder. One expert urges speakers to "use their PowerPresence in preference to their PowerPoint."[16] Although multimedia presentations supply terrific sizzle, they cannot replace the steak. In developing a presentation, don't expect your slides to carry the show. You can avoid being upstaged by not relying totally on your slides. Help the audience visualize your points by using other techniques. For example, drawing a diagram on a white board or flipchart can be more engaging than showing slide after slide of static drawings. Demonstrating or displaying real objects or props is a welcome relief from slides. Remember that slides should be used only to help your audience understand the message and to add interest. You are still the main attraction!

Analyzing an Effective Presentation

As you are reviewing the many tips for crafting successful slide presentations, study the sample slides in Figure 14.8. The nine slides in Figure 14.8 shown in PowerPoint's **Slide Sorter** view are taken from a longer slide presentation. Corinne Livesay, a management training consultant, recently used them during a 2½-hour training session for members of the Dayton Chamber of Commerce. They provide several examples of what you have learned about creating slides.

- The photographs used on Slides 1, 5, and 8 were downloaded from Microsoft Office Online. This Web site offers a great variety of royalty-free pictures as opposed to the limited number of images and clip art that ships with the software.
- Slides 2 and 4 were designed using PowerPoint's various **Illustrations** in the **Insert** tab. Slide 2 encourages the audience to interact with the speaker and get involved in the topic of discussion. Even though you can't tell from the image of Slide 4, it is programmed using PowerPoint's **Custom Animation** feature in the **Animations** tab. The presenter brings in elements of the model as they are explained.
- Slides 3 and 6 illustrate how blueprint slides can be used to introduce your main points and later to move from point to point.
- Slide 7 illustrates interactivity with the audience by presenting a polling question. After audience members respond using their handheld devices, the pie chart follows and displays the results.
- Slide 8 illustrates interactivity with the Internet by providing links that can take the audience directly to relevant Web sites.

Eight Steps to Making a Powerful Multimedia Presentation

What is the best process for creating powerful multimedia presentations?

We have now discussed many suggestions for making effective PowerPoint presentations, but you may still be wondering how to put it all together. Here is a step-by-step process for creating a powerful multimedia presentation:

1. **Start with the text.** The text is the foundation of your presentation. Express your ideas using words that are clear, concise, and understandable. Once the entire content of your presentation is in place, you are ready to begin adding color and all the other elements that will make your slides visually appealing.
2. **Select background and fonts.** Select a template that will provide consistent font styles and sizes and a background for your slides. You can create your own template or use one included with PowerPoint. You can also download free templates or pay for templates from

FIGURE 14.8 Creating Visually Appealing Slides That Engage Your Audience

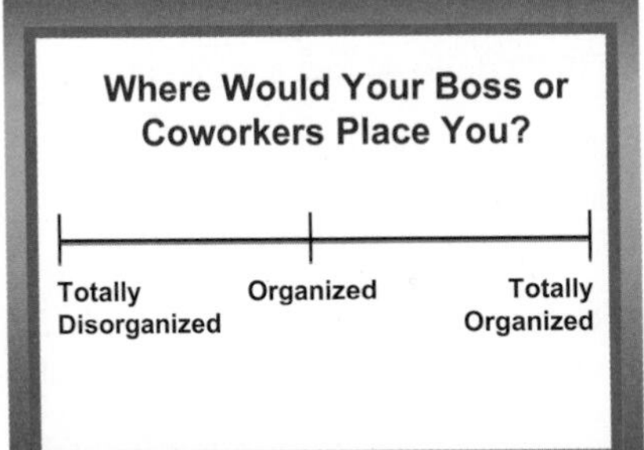

Six Organizing Guidelines

1. Select what should be organized.
2. Unclutter your life.
3. Break tasks into specific steps.
4. Establish a simple system.
5. Stay organized.
6. Prioritize and don't go overboard.

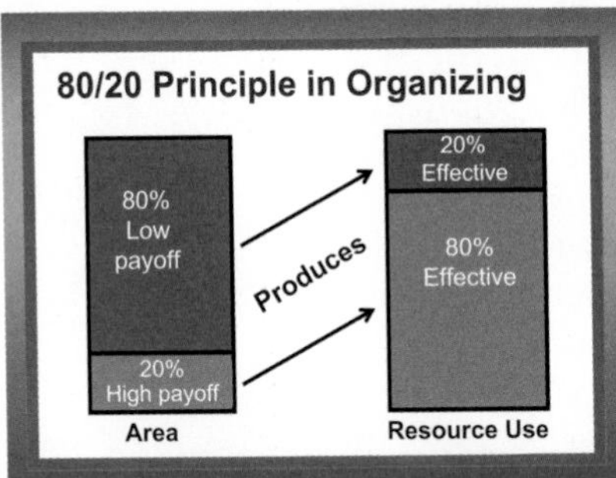

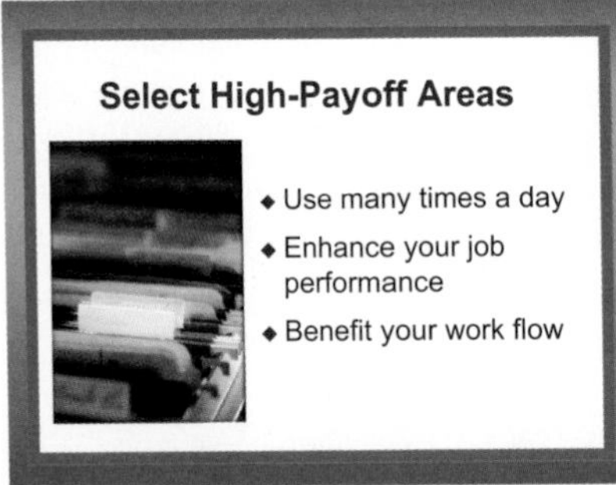

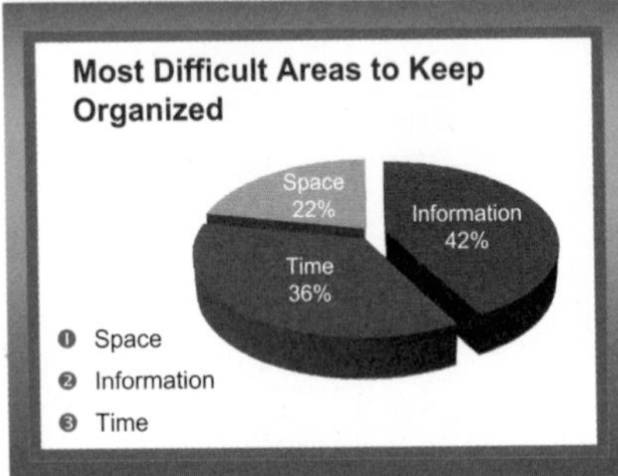

Conclusion

- Reclaim your time, space, and information.
- Increase your efficiency.
- Enhance your quality of life.
- Further your career.
- Get organized!

many online sites. You can't go wrong selecting a basic template design with an easy-to-read font, such as Times New Roman or Arial. As a general rule, use no more than two font styles in your presentation. The point size should be between 24 and 36. Title fonts should be larger than text font. The more you use PowerPoint and find out what works and doesn't work, the more you can experiment with bolder, more innovative background and font options that effectively convey your message.

3. **Choose images that help communicate your message.** Images, such as clip art, photographs, and maps, should complement the text. Never use an image that is not immediately relevant. Microsoft Office Online is accessed in PowerPoint and contains thousands of clip art images and photographs, most of which are in the public domain and require no copyright permissions. Before using images from other sources, determine whether permission from the copyright holder is required. Bear in mind that some people consider clip art amateurish, so photographs are usually preferable. In addition, clip art is available to any user, so it tends to become stale fast.

4. **Create graphics.** PowerPoint includes a variety of tools to help you simplify complex information or transform a boring bulleted list into a visually appealing graphic. You can use PowerPoint's **Illustrations** tools in the **Insert** tab to create a time line or a flowchart. The **SmartArt** graphic will help you create an organization chart or a cycle, radial, pyramid, Venn, or target diagram. With the **Chart** function, you can select over a dozen chart types including line, pie, and bar charts. All of these tools require practice before you can create effective graphics. Remember that graphics should be easy to understand without overloading your audience with unnecessary details or too much text. In fact, it's a good idea to put such details in handouts rather than cluttering your slides with them.

How can you simplify complex information?

5. **Add special effects.** To keep your audience focused on what you are discussing, use PowerPoint's **Animations** tab to control when objects or text appear on the screen. Animate points in a bulleted list to appear one at a time, for example, or the boxes in a radial diagram to appear as each is discussed. Keep in mind that the first thing your audience sees on every slide should describe the slide's content. With motion paths and other animation options, you can move objects to various positions on the slide; or to minimize clutter, you can dim or remove them once they have served their purpose.

   In addition, as you move from slide to slide in a presentation, you can select transition effects, such as *wipe down*. The animation and transition options range from subtle to flashy—choose them with care so that the visual delivery of your presentation does not distract from the content of your message. An option at this step is to purchase a PowerPoint add-in product, such as Ovation, that can add professional-looking special effects to your presentation with very little effort.[17]

6. **Create hyperlinks to approximate the Web browsing experience.** Make your presentation more interactive and intriguing by connecting your PowerPoint presentation, via hyperlinks, to other sources that provide content that will enhance your presentation. You can hyperlink to (a) other slides within the presentation or in other PowerPoint files; (b) other programs that will open a second window that displays items such as spreadsheets, documents, or videos; and (c) if you have an Internet connection, Web sites.

   Once you have finished discussing the hyperlinked source or watching the video that opened in a second window, close that window and your hyperlinked PowerPoint slide is in view. In this way, you can break up the monotony of typical linear PowerPoint presentations. Instead, your hyperlinked show approximates the viewing experience of a Web user who enters a site through a main page or portal and then navigates at will to reach second- and third-level pages.

7. **Engage your audience by asking for interaction.** When audience response and feedback are needed, interactive tools are useful. Audience response systems may be familiar to you from game shows, but they are also used for surveys and opinion polls, group decision making, voting, quizzes and tests, and many other applications. To interact with your audience, present polling questions. Audience members submit their individual or team responses using handheld devices read by a PowerPoint add-in program. The audience immediately sees a bar chart that displays the response results.[18]

© John Briggs (www.kiva.org)

When the founders of microlending upstart Kiva make business presentations around the world, audiences respond with enthusiastic applause and even tears. Kiva's online lending platform connects personal lenders with poverty-stricken individuals in developing nations, enabling villagers to start tomato farms, carpet kiosks and other small ventures that improve their lives. Kiva's presentations use heartwarming stories and videos about village entrepreneurs to show that small loans can make a big difference. *What tips can communicators use to deliver powerful, inspirational presentations?*

How can you present slideshows on the Internet?

8. **Move your presentation to the Internet.** You have a range of alternatives, from simple to complex, for moving your multimedia presentation to the Internet or your company's intranet. The simplest option is posting your slides online for others to access. Even if you are giving a face-to-face presentation, attendees appreciate these *electronic handouts* because they don't have to lug them home. The most complex option for moving your multimedia presentation to the Internet involves a Web conference or broadcast.

   Web presentations with slides, narration, and speaker control have emerged as a way for anyone who has access to the Internet to attend your presentation without leaving the office. For example, you could initiate a meeting via a conference call, narrate using a telephone, and have participants see your slides from the browsers on their computers. If you prefer, you could skip the narration and provide a prerecorded presentation. Web-based presentations have many applications, including providing access to updated training or sales data whenever needed.[19]

   Some businesses convert their PowerPoint presentations to PDF documents or send PowerPoint shows (file extension *.PPSX), which open directly in **Slide Show** view, ready to run. Both types of documents are highly suitable for e-mailing. Among their advantages are that they start immediately, can't be easily changed, and typically result in smaller, less memory-hogging files.

Polishing Your Delivery and Following Up

LEARNING OBJECTIVE 5

Specify delivery techniques for use before, during, and after a presentation, and apply reflective thinking skills.

Once you have organized your presentation and prepared visuals, you are ready to practice delivering it. You will feel more confident and appear more professional if you know more about various delivery methods and techniques to use before, during, and after your presentation.

Choosing a Delivery Method

What is extemporaneous delivery, and why is it more convincing than a memorized or read speech?

Inexperienced speakers often feel that they must memorize an entire presentation to be effective. Unless you are an experienced performer, however, you will sound wooden and unnatural. What's more, forgetting your place can be disastrous! That is why we don't recommend memorizing an entire oral presentation. However, memorizing significant parts—the introduction, the conclusion, and perhaps a meaningful quotation—can be dramatic and impressive.

If memorizing your business presentation won't work, is reading from a manuscript the best plan? Definitely not! Reading to an audience is boring and ineffective. Because reading suggests that you don't know your topic very well, the audience loses confidence in your expertise. Reading also prevents you from maintaining eye contact. You can't see audience reactions; consequently, you can't benefit from feedback.

Neither memorizing nor reading creates very convincing business presentations. The best plan, by far, is to present *extemporaneously*, especially when you are displaying an electronic slideshow such as PowerPoint. Extemporaneous delivery means speaking freely, generally without notes, after preparation and rehearsing. It means that in your talk you comment on the electronic slideshow you have prepared and rehearsed several times. Remember, PowerPoint and other presentation software have replaced traditional outlines and notes. Reading notes or a manuscript in addition to PowerPoint slides will damage your credibility.

If you give a talk without PowerPoint, however, you may use note cards or an outline containing key sentences and major ideas, but beware of reading from a script. By preparing and then practicing with your notes, you can talk to your audience in a conversational manner. Your notes should be neither entire paragraphs nor single words. Instead, they should contain a complete sentence or two to introduce each major idea. Below the topic sentence(s), outline subpoints and illustrations. Note cards will keep you on track and prompt your memory, but only if you have rehearsed the presentation thoroughly.

Combating Stage Fright

What is stage fright, and how can you control it?

Nearly everyone experiences some degree of stage fright when speaking before a group. "If you hear someone say he or she isn't nervous before a speech, you're talking either to a liar or a very boring speaker," says corporate speech consultant Dianna Booher.[20] Being afraid is quite natural

CAREER COACH

How to Avoid Stage Fright

Ever get nervous before making a presentation? Everyone does! And it's not all in your head, either. When you face something threatening or challenging, your body reacts in what psychologists call the fight-or-flight response. This physical reflex provides your body with increased energy to deal with threatening situations. It also creates those sensations—dry mouth, sweaty hands, increased heartbeat, and stomach butterflies—that we associate with stage fright. The fight-or-flight response arouses your body for action—in this case, making a presentation.

Because everyone feels some form of apprehension before speaking, it's impossible to eliminate the physiological symptoms altogether. However, you can reduce their effects with the following techniques:

- **Breathe deeply.** Use deep breathing to ease your fight-or-flight symptoms. Inhale to a count of ten, hold this breath to a count of ten, and exhale to a count of ten. Concentrate on your counting and your breathing; both activities reduce your stress.
- **Convert your fear.** Don't view your sweaty palms and dry mouth as evidence of fear. Interpret them as symptoms of exuberance, excitement, and enthusiasm to share your ideas.
- **Know your topic and come prepared.** Feel confident about your topic. Select a topic that you know well and that is relevant to your audience. Test your equipment and arrive with time to spare.
- **Use positive self-talk.** Remind yourself that you know your topic and are prepared. Tell yourself that the audience is on your side—because it is! Moreover, most speakers appear to be more confident than they feel. Make this apparent confidence work for you.
- **Take a sip of water.** Drink some water to alleviate your dry mouth and constricted voice box, especially if you're talking for more than 15 minutes.
- **Shift the spotlight to your visuals.** At least some of the time the audience will be focusing on your slides, transparencies, handouts, or whatever you have prepared—and not totally on you.
- **Ignore any stumbles.** Don't apologize or confess your nervousness. If you keep going, the audience will forget any mistakes quickly.
- **Feel proud when you finish.** You will be surprised at how good you feel when you finish. Take pride in what you have accomplished, and your audience will reward you with applause and congratulations. Your body, of course, will call off the fight-or-flight response and return to normal!

Career Application

Interview someone in your field or in another business setting who must make oral presentations. How did he or she develop speaking skills? What advice can this person suggest to reduce stage fright? When you next make a class presentation, try some or all of the techniques described here and note which are most effective for you.

and results from actual physiological changes occurring in your body. Faced with a frightening situation, your body responds with the fight-or-flight response, discussed more fully in the accompanying Career Coach box. You can learn to control and reduce stage fright, as well as to incorporate techniques for effective speaking, by using the following strategies and techniques before, during, and after your presentation.

Before Your Presentation

Speaking in front of a group will become less daunting if you allow for adequate preparation, sufficient practice, and rehearsals. Interacting with the audience and limiting surprises such as malfunctioning equipment will also add to your peace of mind. Review the following tips for a smooth start:

- **Prepare thoroughly.** One of the most effective strategies for reducing stage fright is knowing your subject thoroughly. Research your topic diligently and prepare a careful sentence outline. Those who try to "wing it" usually suffer the worst butterflies—and make the worst presentations.
- **Rehearse repeatedly.** When you rehearse, practice your entire presentation, not just the first half. In PowerPoint you may print out speaker's notes, an outline, or a handout featuring miniature slides, which are excellent for practice. If you don't use an electronic slideshow, place your outline sentences on separate note cards. You may also wish to include transitional sentences to help you move to the next topic as you practice. Rehearse alone or before friends and family. Also try an audio or video recording of your rehearsals so that you can evaluate your effectiveness.
- **Time yourself.** Most audiences tend to get restless during longer talks. Therefore, try to complete your presentation in no more than 20 minutes. Set a simple kitchen timer during

your rehearsal to keep track of time. Better yet, PowerPoint offers a function called **Rehearse Timings** in the **Slide Show** tab that can measure the length of your talk as you practice.

- **Check the room.** If you are using a computer, a projector, or sound equipment, be certain they are operational. Before you start, check electrical outlets and the position of the viewing screen. Ensure that the seating arrangement is appropriate to your needs.
- **Greet members of the audience.** Try to make contact with a few members of the audience when you enter the room, while you are waiting to be introduced, or when you walk to the podium. Your body language should convey friendliness, confidence, and enjoyment.
- **Practice stress reduction.** If you feel tension and fear while you are waiting your turn to speak, use stress-reduction techniques, such as deep breathing. Additional techniques to help you conquer stage fright are presented in the accompanying Career Coach box.

How can you enhance a presentation during delivery?

During Your Presentation

To stay in control during your talk, to build credibility, and to engage your audience, follow these time-tested guidelines for effective speaking:

- **Begin with a pause.** When you first approach the audience, take a moment to make yourself comfortable. Establish your control of the situation.
- **Present your first sentence from memory.** By memorizing your opening, you can immediately establish rapport with the audience through eye contact. You will also sound confident and knowledgeable.
- **Maintain eye contact.** If the size of the audience overwhelms you, pick out two individuals on the right and two on the left. Talk directly to these people. Don't ignore listeners in the back of the room.
- **Control your voice and vocabulary.** This means speaking in moderated tones but loudly enough to be heard. Eliminate verbal static, such as *ah, er, you know,* and *um.* Silence is preferable to meaningless fillers when you are thinking of your next idea.
- **Put the brakes on.** Many novice speakers talk too rapidly, displaying their nervousness and making it very difficult for audience members to understand their ideas. Slow down and listen to what you are saying.
- **Move naturally.** If you have a lectern, don't remain glued to it. Move about casually and naturally. Avoid fidgeting with your clothing, hair, or items in your pockets. Do not roll up your sleeves or put your hands in your pockets. Learn to use your body to express a point.
- **Use visual aids effectively.** You should discuss and interpret each visual aid for the audience. Move aside as you describe it so that it can be seen fully. Use a pointer if necessary, but steady your hand if it is shaking.
- **Avoid digressions.** Stick to your outline and notes. Don't suddenly include clever little anecdotes or digressions that occur to you on the spot. If it is not part of your rehearsed material, leave it out so that you can finish on time. Remember, too, that your audience may not be as enthralled with your topic as you are.
- **Summarize your main points and arrive at the high point of your talk.** Conclude your presentation by reiterating your main points or by emphasizing what you want the audience to think or do. Once you have announced your conclusion, proceed to it directly.

What tasks are best left for after the presentation?

After Your Presentation

As you are concluding your presentation, handle questions and answers competently and provide handouts if appropriate. Try the following techniques:

- **Distribute handouts.** If you prepared handouts with data the audience will need, pass them out when you finish.
- **Encourage questions.** If the situation permits a question-and-answer period, announce it at the beginning of your presentation. Then, when you finish, ask for questions. Set a time limit for questions and answers.

- **Repeat questions.** Although the speaker may hear the question, audience members often do not. Begin each answer with a repetition of the question. This also gives you thinking time. Then, direct your answer to the entire audience.
- **Reinforce your main points.** You can use your answers to restate your primary ideas (*I'm glad you brought that up because it gives me a chance to elaborate on …*). In answering questions, avoid becoming defensive or debating the questioner.
- **Keep control.** Don't allow one individual to take over. Keep the entire audience involved.
- **Avoid *Yes, but* answers.** The word *but* immediately cancels any preceding message. Try replacing it with *and*. For example, *Yes, X has been tried. And Y works even better because….*
- **End with a summary and appreciation.** To signal the end of the session before you take the last question, say something like, *We have time for just one more question.* As you answer the last question, try to work it into a summary of your main points. Then, express appreciation to the audience for the opportunity to talk with them.

Organizing Team-Based Written and Oral Presentations

LEARNING OBJECTIVE 6
Organize team-based written and oral presentations, and understand how to communicate in teams.

Companies form teams for many reasons, as discussed in Chapter 2. The goal of some teams is an oral presentation to pitch a new product or to win a high-stakes contract. Before Apple CEO Steve Jobs and his team roll out one of their hotly anticipated new electronic gadgets, you can bet that team members spend months preparing so that his "Stevenote" presentation flows smoothly.[21]

The goal of other teams is to investigate a problem and submit recommendations to decision makers in a report. At BMW, for example, nimble cross-functional teams excel at problem solving across divisions. Such teams speed innovation and the development of new products such as the electronics that now comprise about 20 percent of a new vehicle's value.[22]

The outcome of any team effort is often (a) a written report; (b) a series of self-contained electronic slides, also called a slide deck; or (c) an oral presentation delivered live. The boundaries are becoming increasingly blurred between flat, two-dimensional hard-copy reports and multimedia, hyperlinked slideshows. Both hard-copy reports and multimedia presentations are delivered to clients in business today. This is why team writing and speaking appear side by side in this chapter.

Whether your team's project produces written reports, slide decks, or oral presentations, you generally have considerable control over how the project is organized and completed. If you have been part of any team efforts before, you also know that such projects can be very frustrating—particularly when some team members don't carry their weight or when members cannot resolve conflict. On the other hand, team projects can be harmonious and productive when members establish ground rules and follow guidelines related to preparing, planning, collecting information for, organizing, rehearsing, and evaluating team projects.

Preparing to Work Together

How can teams prepare for a fruitful and smooth collaboration?

Before any group begins to talk about a specific project, members should get together and establish basic ground rules. One of the first tasks is naming a meeting leader to conduct meetings, a recorder to keep a record of group decisions, and an evaluator to determine whether the group is on target and meeting its goals. The group should decide whether it will be governed by consensus (everyone must agree), by majority rule, or by some other method.

The most successful teams make meetings a top priority. They compare schedules to set up the best meeting times, and they meet often. They avoid other responsibilities that might disrupt these meetings.

When teams first organize, they should consider the value of conflict. By bringing conflict into the open and encouraging confrontation, teams can prevent personal resentment and group dysfunction. Confrontation can actually create better final products by promoting new ideas and avoiding groupthink. Conflict is most beneficial when team members can air their views fully. Another important topic to discuss during team formation is how to deal with team members who are not pulling their share of the load. Teams should decide whether they will "fire" members who are not contributing or take some other action in dealing with slackers.

Planning the Document or Presentation

Once teams have established ground rules, members are ready to discuss the target document or presentation. During these discussions, they must be sure to keep a record of all decisions. They should establish the specific purpose for the document or presentation and identify the main issues involved. They must decide on the final format. For a collaborative business report, they should determine what parts it will include, such as an executive summary, figures, and an appendix. They should consider how the report or presentation will be delivered—in person, online, or by e-mail. For a team oral presentation, they should decide on its parts, length, and graphics. For either written or oral projects, they should profile the audience and focus on the questions audience members would want answered. If the report or presentation involves persuasion, they must decide what appeals would achieve the team's purpose.

When work groups plan a team document or presentation, what steps should they follow?

Next the team should develop a work plan (see Chapter 11), assign jobs, and set deadlines. If time is short, members should work backward from the due date. For oral presentations, teams must schedule time for content and creative development as well as for a series of rehearsals. The best-planned presentations can fall apart if they are poorly rehearsed.

For oral presentations, all team members should have written assignments. These assignments should detail each member's specific responsibilities for researching content, producing visuals, developing handout materials, building transitions between segments, and showing up for rehearsals. For written reports, members must decide how the final document will be composed: individuals working separately on assigned portions, one person writing the first draft, the entire group writing the complete document together, or some other method.

Why must facts in reports and presentations be correct?

Collecting Information

One of the most challenging jobs for team projects is generating and collecting information. Unless facts are accurate, the most beautiful report or the most high-powered presentation will fail. As you brainstorm ideas, consider cluster diagramming (see Figure 5.2 on page 140 in Chapter 5). Assign topics and decide who will be responsible for gathering what information. Establishing deadlines for collecting information is important if a team is to remain on schedule. Team members should also discuss ways to ensure the accuracy of the information collected.

Organizing, Writing, and Revising

When a project progresses into the organizing and writing stages, a team may need to modify some of its earlier decisions. Team members may review the proposed organization of the final document or presentation and adjust it if necessary. In composing the first draft of a written report or presentation, team members will probably write separate segments. As they work on these segments, they should use the same version of a word processing or presentation graphics program to facilitate combining files.

Why should teams assign one person to coordinate all the parts of the project?

As individuals work on separate parts of a written report, the team should decide on one person (probably the best writer) to coordinate all the parts. The writer strives for a consistent style, format, and feel in the final product. For oral presentations, team members must try to make logical connections between segments. Each presenter builds a bridge to the next member's topic to create a smooth transition. Team members should also agree to use the same template, and they should allow only one person to make global changes in color, font, and other formatting on the slide and title masters.

Editing, Rehearsing, and Evaluating

The last stage in a collaborative project involves editing, rehearsing, and evaluating. For a written report, one person should assume the task of merging the various files, running a spell checker, and examining the entire document for consistency of design, format, and vocabulary. That person is responsible for finding and correcting grammatical and mechanical errors. Then the entire group meets as a whole to evaluate the final document. Does it fulfill its purpose and meet the needs of the audience?

For oral presentations, one person should also merge all the files and be certain that they are consistent in design, format, and vocabulary. Teams making presentations should practice together several times. If that is not feasible, experts say that teams must schedule at least one full real-time rehearsal with the entire group.[23] Whenever possible, practice in a room that is similar to the location of your talk. Consider video recording one of the rehearsals so that each presenter can critique his or her own performance. Schedule a dress rehearsal with an audience at least two days before the actual presentation. Practice fielding questions.

Successful group documents emerge from thoughtful preparation, clear definitions of contributors' roles, commitment to a group-approved plan, and a willingness to take responsibility for the final product. More information about writing business reports appeared in previous chapters of this book.

Adapting Presentations to Intercultural Audiences

LEARNING OBJECTIVE 7

Explain effective techniques for adapting oral presentations to intercultural audiences, and demonstrate intercultural and diversity understanding.

Every good speaker adapts to the audience, and intercultural presentations call for special adjustments and sensitivity. Most people understand that they must speak slowly, choose simple English, avoid jargon and clichés, use short sentences, and pause frequently when communicating with nonnative speakers of English.

Beyond these basic language adaptations, however, more fundamental sensitivity is often necessary. In organizing a presentation for an intercultural audience, you may need to anticipate and adapt to different speaking conventions, values, and nonverbal behavior. You may also need to contend with limited language skills and a certain reluctance to voice opinions openly.

Understanding Different Values and Nonverbal Behavior

What must you consider when addressing intercultural audiences?

In addressing intercultural audiences, anticipate expectations and perceptions that may differ significantly from what you may consider normal. Remember, for example, that the North American emphasis on getting to the point quickly is not equally prized across the globe. Therefore, think twice about delivering your main idea up front. Many people (notably those in Japanese, Latin American, and Arabic cultures) consider such directness to be brash and inappropriate. Remember that others may not share our cultural emphasis on straightforwardness.[24]

When working with an interpreter or speaking before individuals whose English is limited, you must be very careful about your language. For example, you will need to express ideas in small chunks to give the interpreter time to translate. You may need to slow down as you speak and stop after each thought to allow time for the translation that will follow. Even if your presentation or speech is being translated simultaneously, remember to speak slowly and to pause after each sentence to ensure that your message is rendered correctly in the target language.

The same advice is useful in organizing presentations. Consider breaking your presentation into short, discrete segments. You may want to divide your talk into distinct topics, developing each separately and encouraging discussion periods after each. Such organization enables participants to ask questions and digest what has been presented. This technique is especially effective in cultures where people communicate in "loops." In the Middle East, for example, Arab speakers "mix circuitous, irrelevant (by American standards) conversations with short dashes of information that go directly to the point." Presenters who are patient, tolerant, and "mature" (in the eyes of the audience) will make the sale or win the contract.[25]

Match your presentation and your nonverbal messages to the expectations of your audience. In Germany, for instance, successful presentations tend to be dense with facts and precise statistics. Americans might say "around 30 percent" whereas a German presenter might say "30.4271 percent." Similarly, constant smiling is not as valued in Europe as it is in North America. Many Europeans distrust a speaker who is cracking jokes, smiling, or laughing in a business presentation. Their expectation is of a rational—that is, "serious"—fact-based delivery. American-style enthusiasm is often interpreted abroad as hyperbolic exaggeration or, worse, as dishonesty and can lead to misunderstandings. If an American says "Great job!" to offer praise, a Spanish counterpart might believe the American has approved the project. "When Europeans

ETHICS CHECK

The Robot Presenter

In one of your courses, you are witnessing a PowerPoint presentation, during which it becomes obvious that the speaker has completely memorized her talk. However, she stumbles badly a few times, struggling to remember her lines. Worse yet, you perceive her accent as nearly impenetrable. How should the instructor and the class handle the evaluation of such a presentation?

realize there's no commitment implied," warned an intercultural consultant, "they might feel deceived or that the American is being superficial."[26]

Remember, too, that some cultures prefer greater formality than Americans exercise. Instead of first names, use only honorifics (*Mr.* or *Ms.*) and last names, as well as academic or business titles—such as *Doctor* or *Director*. Writing on a flipchart or transparency seems natural and spontaneous in this country. Abroad, though, such informal techniques may suggest that the speaker does not value the audience enough to prepare proper visual aids in advance.[27]

Adjusting Visual Aids to Intercultural Audiences

Although you may have to exercise greater caution with culturally diverse audiences, you still want to use visual aids to help communicate your message. Find out from your international contact whether you can present in English or will need an interpreter. In many countries listeners are too polite to speak up when they don't understand you. One expert advises explaining important concepts in several ways using different words and then requesting

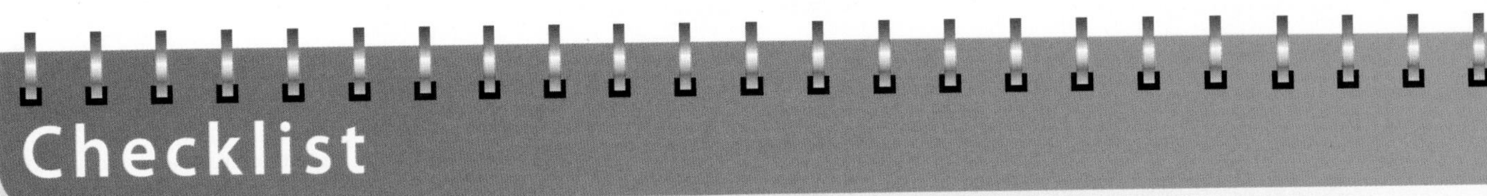

Preparing and Organizing Oral Presentations

Getting Ready to Speak

- **Identify your purpose.** Decide what you want your audience to believe, remember, or do when you finish. Aim all parts of your talk toward this purpose.
- **Analyze the audience.** Consider how to adapt your message (its organization, appeals, and examples) to your audience's knowledge and needs.

Organizing the Introduction

- **Get the audience involved.** Capture the audience's attention by opening with a promise, story, startling fact, question, quote, relevant problem, or self-effacing joke.
- **Establish yourself.** Demonstrate your credibility by identifying your position, expertise, knowledge, or qualifications.
- **Preview your main points.** Introduce your topic and summarize its principal parts.

Organizing the Body

- **Develop two to four main points.** Streamline your topic so that you can concentrate on its major issues.
- **Arrange the points logically.** Sequence your points chronologically, from most important to least important, by comparison and contrast, or by some other strategy.
- **Prepare transitions.** Between major points write "bridge" statements that connect the previous item to the next one. Use transitional expressions as verbal signposts (*first, second, then, however, consequently, on the contrary,* and so forth).
- **Have extra material ready.** Be prepared with more information and visuals in case you have additional time to fill.

Organizing the Conclusion

- **Review your main points.** Emphasize your main ideas in your closing so that your audience will remember them.
- **Provide a strong, final focus.** Tell how your listeners can use this information, why you have spoken, or what you want them to do. As the culmination of your talk, end with a specific audience benefit or thought-provoking final thought (a take-away), not just a lame rehash.

Designing Visual Aids

- **Select your medium carefully.** Consider the pros and cons of each alternative.
- **Highlight main ideas.** Use visual aids to illustrate major concepts only. Keep them brief and simple.
- **Try to replace bullets whenever possible.** Use flowcharts, diagrams, time lines, and so forth, to substitute for bulleted lists when suitable.
- **Use aids skillfully.** Talk to the audience, not to the visuals. Paraphrase their contents.

Developing Multimedia Presentations

- **Learn to use your software program.** Study template and slide layout designs to see how you can adapt them to your purposes.
- **Select colors based on the light level in the room.** Consider how mixing light and dark fonts and backgrounds affects their visibility. Use templates and preset slide layouts if you are new to PowerPoint.
- **Use bulleted points for major ideas.** Make sure your points are all parallel, and observe the 6-x-6 rule.
- **Include multimedia options that will help you convey your message.** Use moderate animation features and hyperlinks to make your talk more interesting and to link to files with related content in the same document, in other documents, or on the Internet.
- **Make speaker's notes.** Jot down the narrative supporting each slide, and use these notes to practice your presentation. Do not read from notes while speaking to an audience, however.
- **Maintain control.** Don't let your slides upstage you. Engage your audience by using additional techniques to help them visualize your points.

members of the audience to relay their understanding of what you have just said back to you. Another expert suggests packing more text on PowerPoint slides and staying closer to its literal meaning. After all, most nonnative speakers of English understand written text much better than they comprehend spoken English. In the United States presenters may spend 90 seconds on a slide, whereas in other countries they may need to slow down to two minutes per slide.[28]

To ensure clarity and show courtesy, provide handouts in English and the target language. Never use numbers without projecting or writing them out for all to see. If possible, say numbers in both languages, but only if you can pronounce or even speak the target language well enough to avoid embarrassment. Distribute translated handouts, summarizing your important information, when you finish.

Spotlight on Communicators

© Nancy Friedman President Telephone Doctor Customer Service Trainer

Instead of commanding telephone callers to "Hold, please," ask politely whether the caller is *able* to hold, advises Telephone Doctor Nancy Friedman. She helps companies improve their employees' telephone skills. One phrase she prohibits is "I don't know." It's better to say, "I will find out." She also recommends that people smile *before* they answer the phone. That prevents "emotional leakage," taking personal frustration out on a caller.

Whether you are speaking to familiar or intercultural audiences, your presentation requires attention to content and strategy. The checklist on the previous page summarizes suggestions for preparing, organizing, and illustrating oral presentations.

Improving Telephone and Voice Mail Skills

LEARNING OBJECTIVE 8

List techniques for improving telephone and voice mail skills to project a positive image.

One form of business presentation involves presenting yourself on the telephone, a skill that is still very important in today's workplace. Despite the heavy reliance on e-mail, the telephone remains an extremely important piece of equipment in offices. With the addition of today's wireless technology, it doesn't matter whether you are in or out of the office. You can always be reached by phone. This section focuses on traditional telephone techniques and voice mail—both opportunities for making a good impression. As a business communicator, you can be more productive, efficient, and professional by following some simple suggestions.

How can telephone and voice mail use promote goodwill and increase productivity?

Making Telephone Calls Efficiently

Before making a telephone call, decide whether the intended call is really necessary. Could you find the information yourself? If you wait a while, will the problem resolve itself? Perhaps your message could be delivered more efficiently by some other means. Some companies have found that telephone calls are often less important than the work they interrupt. Alternatives to telephone calls include instant messaging, texting, e-mail, memos, and calls to automated voice mail systems. If you must make a telephone call, consider using the following suggestions to make it fully productive:

How can you make productive telephone calls?

- **Plan a mini-agenda.** Have you ever been embarrassed when you had to make a second telephone call because you forgot an important point the first time? Before placing a call, jot down notes regarding all the topics you need to discuss. Following an agenda guarantees not only a complete call but also a quick one. You will be less likely to wander from the business at hand while rummaging through your mind trying to remember everything.
- **Use a three-point introduction.** When placing a call, immediately (a) name the person you are calling, (b) identify yourself and your affiliation, and (c) give a brief explanation of your reason for calling. For example: *May I speak to Larry Lopez? This is Hillary Dahl of Sebastian Enterprises, and I'm seeking information about a software program called Power Presentations.* This kind of introduction enables the receiving individual to respond immediately without asking further questions.
- **Be brisk if you are rushed.** For business calls when your time is limited, avoid questions such as *How are you?* Instead, say, *Lisa, I knew you would be the only one who could answer these two questions for me.* Another efficient strategy is to set a contract with the caller: *Look, Lisa, I have only ten minutes, but I really wanted to get back to you.*
- **Be cheerful and accurate.** Let your voice show the same kind of animation that you radiate when you greet people in person. In your mind try to envision the individual

answering the telephone. A smile can certainly affect the tone of your voice, so smile at that person. Keep your voice and throat relaxed by keeping your head straight. Don't squeeze the phone between your shoulder and your ear. Obviously, don't eat food or chew gum while on the phone. Moreover, be accurate about what you say. *Hang on a second; I will be right back* rarely is true. It is better to say, *It may take me two or three minutes to get that information. Would you prefer to hold or have me call you back?*

- **Bring it to a close.** The responsibility for ending a call lies with the caller. This is sometimes difficult to do if the other person rambles on. You may need to use suggestive closing language, such as the following: (a) *I have certainly enjoyed talking with you;* (b) *I have learned what I needed to know, and now I can proceed with my work;* (c) *Thanks for your help;* (d) *I must go now, but may I call you again in the future if I need . . .?* or (e) *Should we talk again in a few weeks?*
- **Avoid telephone tag.** If you call someone who's not in, ask when it would be best to call again. State that you will call at a specific time—and do it. If you ask a person to call you, give a time when you can be reached—and then be sure you are in at that time.
- **Leave complete voice mail messages.** Remember that there is no need to rush when you are leaving a voice mail message. Always enunciate clearly and speak slowly when giving your telephone number or spelling your name. Be sure to provide a complete message, including your name, telephone number, and the time and date of your call. Explain your purpose so that the receiver can be ready with the required information when returning your call.

Receiving Telephone Calls Professionally

How do professionals ensure that the telephone calls they receive are productive?

With a little forethought you can project a professional image and make your telephone a productive, efficient work tool. Developing good telephone manners and techniques, such as the following, will also reflect well on you and on your organization.

- **Identify yourself immediately.** In answering your telephone or someone else's, provide your name, title or affiliation, and, possibly, a greeting. For example, *Larry Lopez, Proteus Software. How may I help you?* Force yourself to speak clearly and slowly. Remember that the caller may be unfamiliar with what you are saying and fail to recognize slurred syllables.
- **Be responsive and helpful.** If you are in a support role, be sympathetic to callers' needs. Instead of *I don't know*, try *That's a good question; let me investigate.* Instead of *We can't do that,* try *That's a tough one; let's see what we can do.* Avoid *No* at the beginning of a sentence. It sounds especially abrasive and displeasing because it suggests total rejection.
- **Practice telephone confidentiality.** When answering calls for others, be courteous and helpful, but don't give out confidential information. Better to say, *She's away from her desk* or *He's out of the office* than to report a colleague's exact whereabouts. Also, be tight-lipped about sharing company information with strangers. Security experts insist that employees answering telephones must become guardians of company information.[29]
- **Take messages carefully.** Few things are as frustrating as receiving a potentially important phone message that is illegible. Repeat the spelling of names and verify telephone numbers. Write messages legibly and record their time and date. Promise to give the messages to intended recipients, but don't guarantee return calls.
- **Explain what you are doing when transferring calls.** Give a reason for transferring, and indicate the extension to which you are directing the call in case the caller is disconnected.

ETHICS CHECK

Telling White Lies

Obviously, you wouldn't want to tell callers that your colleague went to the restroom or that your boss is responding to e-mail from a golf course in Hilo, Hawaii. But what about people who, for instance, hide behind voice mail and want you to lie about it? When is it acceptable to tell white lies on the phone to maintain confidentiality and decorum, and when is lying for others wrong?

Making the Best Use of Voice Mail

What are the advantages of voice mail?

Because telephone calls can be disruptive, many businesspeople are making extensive use of voice mail to intercept and screen incoming calls. Voice mail links a telephone system to a computer that digitizes and stores incoming messages. Some systems also provide functions such as automated attendant menus, allowing callers to reach any associated extension by pushing specific buttons.

Voice mail is quite efficient for message storage. Because as many as half of all business calls require no discussion or feedback, the messaging capabilities of voice mail can mean huge savings for businesses. Incoming information is delivered without interrupting potential receivers and without all the niceties that most two-way conversations require. Stripped of superfluous chitchat, voice mail messages allow communicators to focus on essentials. Voice mail also eliminates telephone tag, inaccurate message taking, and time zone barriers.

However, voice mail should not be overused. Individuals who screen all incoming calls cause irritation, resentment, and needless telephone tag. Here are some ways to make voice mail work most effectively for you:

- **Announce your voice mail.** If you rely principally on a voice mail message system, identify it on your business stationery and cards. Then, when people call, they will be ready to leave a message.
- **Prepare a warm and informative greeting.** Make your mechanical greeting sound warm and inviting, both in tone and content. Identify yourself and your organization so that callers know they have reached the right number. Thank the caller and briefly explain that you are unavailable. Invite the caller to leave a message or, if appropriate, call back. Here's a typical voice mail greeting: *Hi! This is Larry Lopez of Proteus Software, and I appreciate your call. You have reached my voice mailbox because I'm either working with customers or talking on another line at the moment. Please leave your name, number, and reason for calling so that I can be prepared when I return your call.* Give callers an idea of when you will be available, such as, *I will be back at 2:30;* or, *I will be out of my office until Wednesday, May 20.* If you screen your calls as a time-management technique, try this message: *I'm not near my phone right now, but I should be able to return calls after 3:30.*
- **Test your message.** Call your number and assess your message. Does it sound inviting? Sincere? Understandable? Are you pleased with your tone? If not, says one consultant, have someone else, perhaps a professional, record a message for you.

This chapter has provided valuable tips for preparing and delivering first-rate oral presentations. You have also learned effective techniques for adapting oral presentations to intercultural audiences. Finally, we illustrated techniques for improving telephone and voice mail skills. All of these techniques and tips can help you be a successful business communicator in an increasingly challenging workplace.

Want to do well on tests and excel in your course? Go to **www.meguffey.com** for helpful interactive resources.

- **Review the Chapter 14 PowerPoint slides to prepare for the first quiz.**

Zooming In — YOUR TURN

Applying Your Skills at Apple Computer

When Steve Jobs unveiled the iPad tablet computer amid much fanfare and hype stoked by months of secrecy, the tech world seemed skeptical at first. Many bloggers were wondering what purpose the "oversized iPhone" would serve or what gap in the Apple product mix and crowded consumer electronics field it would fill. Much derision was leveled at the name of the device for its supposed reference to feminine hygiene products. Marketing experts, however, predicted a huge success for the iPad and argued that the name would have no impact on its wide adoption.

Some of the criticism was aimed at the iPad's technical features. Battery life, compatibility with Adobe's Flash software, and Wi-Fi versus 3G capability ranked high among the hotly debated subjects. The price of the new gadget and Apple's continued exclusive alliance with AT&T in the United States were also discussed.

Your Task

Steve Jobs asks you and other Apple interns to research and monitor the buzz surrounding the company's latest hot gadget. The Apple CEO wants you to monitor traditional news and opinion outlets, but also blogs, tweets, forums, and social media sites. Prepare an outline of your findings. Then use the outline as the basis for creating a simple, image-driven PowerPoint presentation to inform Steve of your findings.

Breakthrough deal with AT&T
$14.99 for up to 250 MB
$29.99 for unlimited data
Free use of AT&T WiFi hotspots
Activate on iPad
No contract – cancel anytime

© Tony Avelar/Bloomberg via Getty Images

Summary of Learning Objectives

1 Discuss two important first steps in preparing effective business presentations. First, identify what your purpose is and what you want the audience to believe or do so that you can aim the entire presentation toward your goal. Second, know your audience so that you can adjust your message and style to its knowledge and needs.

2 Explain the major elements in organizing a presentation, including the introduction, body, and conclusion. The introduction of a good presentation should capture the listener's attention, identify the speaker, establish credibility, and preview the main points. The body should discuss two to four main points, with appropriate explanations, details, and verbal signposts to guide listeners. The conclusion should review the main points, provide a final focus or take-away, and allow the speaker to leave the podium gracefully.

3 Identify techniques for gaining audience rapport, including (a) using effective imagery, (b) providing verbal signposts, and (c) sending appropriate nonverbal messages. You can improve audience rapport by using effective imagery including analogies, metaphors, similes, personal anecdotes, statistics, and worst case/best-case scenarios. Rapport is also gained by including verbal signposts that tell the audience when you are previewing, summarizing, and switching directions. Nonverbal messages have a powerful effect on the way your message is received. You should look terrific, animate your body, punctuate your words, get out from behind the podium, and vary your facial expressions.

4 Discuss designing and using effective visual aids, handouts, and multimedia presentations and using presentation technology competently. Use simple, easily understood visual aids to emphasize and clarify main points. Choose multimedia slides, transparencies, flipcharts, or other visuals. Generally, it is best to distribute handouts after a presentation. Speakers employing a program such as PowerPoint use templates, layout designs, and bullet points to produce effective slides. A presentation may be enhanced with slide transitions, hyperlinks, sound, animation, video elements, and other multimedia effects. Speaker's notes and handouts may be generated from slides. Web-based presentations allow speakers to narrate and show slides without leaving their home bases. Increasing numbers of speakers are using the Internet to e-mail or post their slides as electronic shows or report deliverables instead of generating paper copies.

5 Specify delivery techniques for use before, during, and after a presentation, and apply reflective thinking skills. Before your talk, prepare a sentence outline on note cards or speaker's notes and rehearse repeatedly. Check the room, lectern, and equipment. During the presentation, consider beginning with a pause and presenting your first sentence from memory. Speak freely and extemporaneously, commenting on your PowerPoint slides but using no other notes. Make eye contact, control your voice, speak and move naturally, and avoid digressions. After your talk, distribute handouts and answer questions. End gracefully and express appreciation.

6 Organize team-based written and oral presentations, and understand how to communicate in teams. In preparing to work together, teams should name a leader and decide how they will make decisions (by consensus, majority rule, or some other method). They should work out a schedule, discuss the benefits of conflict, and determine how they will deal with members who fail to pull their share. They should decide on the purpose, form, and procedures for preparing the final document or presentation. They must brainstorm ideas, assign topics, and establish deadlines. In composing the first draft of a report or presentation, they should use the same software version and meet to discuss the drafts and rehearsals. For written reports, one person should probably compose the final draft, and the group should evaluate it. For group presentations, team members need to work for consistency of design, format, and wording. Several rehearsals, one of which should be videotaped, will enhance the final presentation.

7 Explain effective techniques for adapting oral presentations to intercultural audiences, and demonstrate intercultural and diversity understanding. In presentations before groups whose English is limited, speak slowly, use simple English, avoid jargon and clichés, and opt for short sentences. Pause often to allow an interpreter to keep up with you. Consider building up to your main idea rather than announcing it immediately. Also, consider breaking the presentation into short segments to allow participants to ask questions and digest small parts separately. Beware of appearing too spontaneous and informal. Use visual aids to help communicate your message, but also distribute translated handouts summarizing the most important information.

8 List techniques for improving telephone and voice mail skills to project a positive image. You can improve your telephone calls by planning a mini-agenda and using a three-point introduction (name, affiliation, and purpose). Be cheerful and responsive, and use closing language to end a conversation. Avoid telephone tag by leaving complete messages. In answering calls, identify yourself immediately, avoid giving out confidential information when answering for others, and take careful messages. For your own message, prepare a warm and informative greeting. Tell when you will be available. Evaluate your message by calling it yourself.

Chapter Review

1. Can speaking skills be improved, or do we have to be "born" communicators? (Obj. 1)
2. Why are analyzing an audience and anticipating its reactions particularly important before business presentations, and how would you adapt to the four categories of listeners? (Obj. 1)
3. In preparing an oral presentation, you can reduce your fears and lay a foundation for a professional performance by focusing on what five areas? (Obj. 1)
4. In the introduction of an oral presentation, you can establish your credibility by using what two methods? (Obj. 2)
5. What is Guy Kawasaki's 10/20/30 rule, and what is it good for? (Obj. 2)
6. List six techniques for creating effective imagery in a presentation. Be prepared to discuss each. (Obj. 3)
7. List suggestions that would ensure that your nonverbal messages reinforce your verbal messages effectively. (Obj. 3)
8. What is the picture superiority effect? (Obj. 4)
9. Name specific advantages and disadvantages of multimedia presentation software. (Obj. 4)
10. How is the 6-x-6 rule applied in preparing bulleted points? (Obj. 4)
11. What delivery method is most effective for speakers? (Obj. 5)
12. Why should speakers deliver the first sentence from memory? (Obj. 5)
13. What five issues should be resolved before a team can collaborate productively? (Obj. 6)
14. How might presentations before intercultural audiences be altered to be most effective? (Obj. 7)
15. How can you avoid telephone tag? (Obj. 8)

Critical Thinking

1. Why should even practiced speakers plan their presentations when addressing a business audience instead of just "winging it"? (Obj. 3)
2. "Communicate—don't decorate." This principle is one of 20 rules that graphic designer and educator Timothy Samara discusses in his 2007 book *Design Elements: A Graphic Style Manual*. How could you apply this principle to the design of your PowerPoint presentations? (Obj. 4)
3. How can speakers prevent multimedia presentation software from stealing their thunder? (Obj. 4)
4. Discuss effective techniques for reducing stage fright. (Obj. 5)
5. **Ethical Issue:** Critics of PowerPoint claim that flashy graphics, sound effects, and animation often conceal thin content. Consider, for example, the findings regarding the space shuttle *Challenger* accident that killed seven astronauts. Report authors charged that NASA scientists had used PowerPoint presentations to make it look as though they had done analyses that they hadn't. Overreliance on presentations instead of analysis may have contributed to the shuttle disaster.[30] What lessons about ethical responsibilities when using PowerPoint can be learned from this catastrophe in communication? (Objs. 1, 2, and 4)

Activities

14.1 Critiquing a Speech (Objs. 1–4)

Your Task. Search online or your library for a speech that was delivered by a significant businessperson or a well-known political figure. Consider watching Steve Jobs' excellent 15-minute "Stay Hungry, Stay Foolish" commencement speech at Stanford on YouTube. Transcripts of that well-known speech are also available online. Write a memo report to your instructor critiquing the speech in terms of the following:

a. Effectiveness of the introduction, body, and conclusion
b. Evidence of effective overall organization
c. Use of verbal signposts to create coherence
d. Emphasis of two to four main points
e. Effectiveness of supporting facts (use of examples, statistics, quotations, and so forth)

14.2 Knowing Your Audience (Objs. 1, 2)

Your Task. Select a recent issue of *Fortune, Fast Company, BusinessWeek,* or another business periodical approved by your instructor. Based on an analysis of your classmates, select an article that will appeal to them and that you can relate to their needs. Submit to your instructor a one-page summary that includes (a) the author, article title, source, issue date, and page reference; (b) a one-paragraph article summary; (c) a description of why you believe the article will appeal to your classmates; and (d) a summary of how you can relate the article to their needs.

14.3 Overcoming Stage Fright (Obj. 5)

Team

What makes you most nervous when making a presentation before class? Being afraid of becoming tongue-tied? Having all eyes on you? Messing up? Forgetting your ideas and looking silly?

Your Task. Discuss the previous questions as a class. Then, in groups of three or four, talk about ways to overcome these fears. Your instructor may ask you to write a memo, an e-mail, or a discussion board post (individually or collectively) summarizing your suggestions, or you may break out of your small groups and report your best ideas to the entire class.

14.4 Investigating Oral Communication in Your Field (Objs. 1, 5)

Your Task. Interview one or two individuals in your professional field. How is oral communication important in this profession? Does the need for oral skills change as one advances? What suggestions can these people make to newcomers to the field for developing proficient oral communication skills? Discuss your findings with your class.

14.5 Outlining an Oral Presentation (Objs. 1, 2)

One of the hardest parts of preparing an oral presentation is developing the outline.

Your Task. Select an oral presentation topic from the list in **Activity 14.14**, or suggest an original topic. Prepare an outline for your presentation using the format starting at the top of the next column:

Title	
Purpose	
	I. INTRODUCTION
State your name	A.
Gain attention and involve audience	B.
Establish credibility	C.
Preview main points	D.
Transition	
	II. BODY
Main point	A.
Illustrate, clarify, contrast	1.
	2.
	3.
Transition	
Main point	B.
Illustrate, clarify, contrast	1.
	2.
	3.
Transition	
	C.
Main point	1.
Illustrate, clarify, contrast	2.
	3.
Transition	
	III. CONCLUSION
Summarize main points	A.
Provide final focus or take-away	B.
Encourage questions	C.

14.6 Critiquing a Satirical Clip Lampooning PowerPoint (Objs. 1–4)

Watch Don McMillan's now famous YouTube hit "Life After Death by PowerPoint" from 2008 or the expanded version "Life After Death by PowerPoint 2010." Which specific PowerPoint ills is McMillan satirizing? Write a brief summary of the short clips for discussion in class. With your peers discuss whether the bad habits the YouTube videos parody correspond with design principles introduced in this chapter.

14.7 Evaluating and Outlining Podcasts of Apple Keynotes (Objs. 1–4)

To learn from the presentation skills of one of the best corporate speakers today, visit iTunes and watch one or more of the Apple keynotes posted there. They mostly cover Steve Jobs' famous product launches, including that of the iPad, and other important announcements.

Your Task. Download iTunes if you don't yet have a copy of the software and search for *apple keynotes,* or in your browser go to **http://itunes.apple.com/us/podcast/apple-keynotes/id275834665**.

If your instructor directs, watch one of the keynotes and outline it. You may also be asked to critique Steve Jobs' presentation techniques based on the guidelines you have studied in this chapter. Jot down your observations either as notes for a classroom discussion or to serve as a basis for an informative memo or e-mail.

14.8 Creating an Oral Presentation: Outline Your Job Duties (Objs. 1–4)

What if you had to create a presentation for your classmates and instructor, or perhaps a potential recruiter, that describes the multiple tasks you perform at work? Could you do it in a five-minute PowerPoint presentation?

Your instructor, for example, may wear many hats. Most academics (a) teach; (b) conduct research to publish; and (c) provide service to the department, college, university, and the community. Can you see how those aspects of their profession lend themselves to an outline of primary slides (teaching, publishing, service) and second-level slides (instructing undergraduate and graduate classes, presenting workshops, and giving lectures under the *teaching* label)?

Your Task. Now it's your turn to introduce the duties of a current position or a past job, volunteer activity, or internship in a brief, simple, yet well-designed PowerPoint presentation. Your goal is to inform your audience of your job duties in a three- to five-minute talk. Use animation features and graphics where appropriate. Your instructor may show you a completed example of this project.

14.9 Creating an Oral Presentation: Pitch to Guy Kawasaki (Objs. 1–4)

Could you interest an angel investor such as Guy Kawasaki in your business idea? The venture capitalist believes that if you must use more than ten slides to explain your business, you probably don't have one. Furthermore, Kawasaki claims that the ten topics a venture capitalist cares about are the following:

1. Problem
2. Your solution
3. Business model
4. Underlying magic/technology
5. Marketing and sales
6. Competition
7. Team
8. Projections and milestones
9. Status and time line
10. Summary and call to action

Your Task. Dust off that start-up fantasy you may have, and get to work. Prepare a slideshow that would satisfy Kawasaki's 10/20/30 rule: In ten slides and a presentation of no more than 20 minutes, address the ten topics that venture capitalists care about. Make sure that the fonts on your slides are at least 30 points in size. You may want to peek at the coverage of business plans in Chapter 13.

14.10 Delivering an Impromptu Elevator Speech (Objs. 1–4)

"Can you pass the elevator test?" asks presentation whiz Garr Reynolds in a new twist on the familiar scenario.[31] He suggests this technique as an aid in sharpening your core message. In this exercise you need to pitch your idea in a few brief moments instead of the 20 minutes you had been granted with your vice president of product marketing. You arrive at her door for your appointment as she is leaving, coat and briefcase in hand. Something has come up. This meeting is a huge opportunity for you if you want to get the OK from the executive team. Could you sell your idea during the elevator ride and the walk to the parking lot? Reynolds asks. Although this scenario may never happen, you will possibly be asked to shorten a presentation, say, from an hour to 30 minutes or from 20 minutes to 5 minutes. Could you make your message tighter and clearer?

Your Task. Take a business idea you may have, a familiar business topic you care about, or a promotion or raise you wish to request in a time of tight budgets. Create a spontaneous two- to five-minute speech making a good case for your core message. Even though you won't have much time to think about the details of your speech, you should be sufficiently familiar with the topic to boil it down and yet be persuasive.

14.11 Self-Contained Multimedia Activity: Creating a PowerPoint Presentation (No additional research required) (Objs. 2, 3)

You are a consultant who has been hired to improve the effectiveness of corporate trainers. These trainers frequently make presentations to employees on topics such as conflict management, teamwork, time management, problem solving, performance appraisals, and employment interviewing. Your goal is to teach these trainers how to make better presentations.

Your Task. Create six visually appealing slides.* Base the slides on the following content, which will be spoken during the presentation titled Effective Employee Training. The comments shown here are only a portion of a longer presentation.

> Trainers have two options when they make presentations. The first option is to use one-way communication: the trainer basically dumps the information on the employees and leaves. The second option is to use a two-way audience involvement approach. The two-way approach can accomplish many purposes, such as connecting the trainer with the employees, reinforcing key points, increasing employees' retention rates, changing the pace, and adding variety. The two-way approach also encourages employees to get to know each other better. Because today's employees demand more than just a "talking head," trainers must engage their audiences by involving them in a dialogue.
>
> When you include interactivity in your training sessions, choose approaches that suit your delivery style. Also, think about which options your employees would be likely to respond to most positively. Let's consider some interactivity approaches now. Realize, though, that these ideas are presented to help you get your creative juices flowing. After I present the list, we will think about situations in which these options might be effective. We will also brainstorm to come up with creative ideas we can add to this list.

- Ask employees to guess at statistics before revealing them.
- Ask an employee to share examples or experiences.
- Ask a volunteer to help you demonstrate something.
- Ask the audience to complete a questionnaire or worksheet.
- Ask the audience to brainstorm or list something as fast as possible.
- Ask a variety of question types to achieve different purposes.
- Invite the audience to work through a process or examine an object.
- Survey the audience.
- Pause to let the audience members read something to themselves.
- Divide the audience into small groups to discuss an issue.

14.12 Improving the Design and Content of PowerPoint Slides (Objs. 2, 3)

Your Task. Identify ways to improve the design and content of the three slides presented in Figure 14.9. Classify your comments under the following categories: (a) color choices, (b) font choice including style and point size, (c) 6-x-6 rule, (d) listings in parallel grammatical form,

*See the Instructor's Manual and the Instructor's Resource CD.

FIGURE 14.9 PowerPoint Slides Needing Revision

Webcasting Basics

- Hold meetings inexpensively.
- Broadcast via one of many options.
- Include Q&A sessions and live polls.
- Access meetings via Internet.
- View stored presentations when convenient.

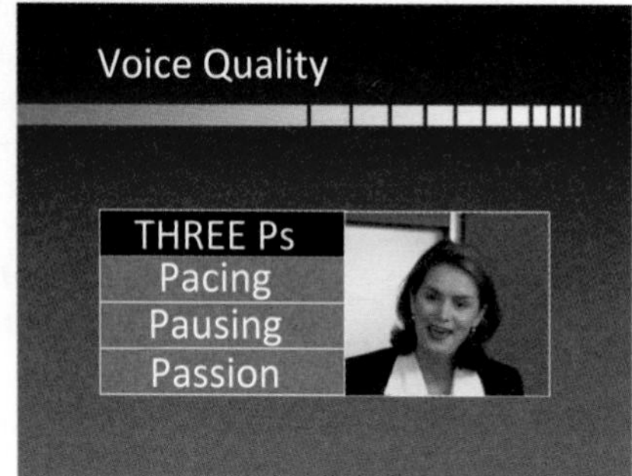

Webcasting Pointers

- Engage audience with personal stories.
- Stand to add energy to your voice.
- Remember that smiles are audible.
- Change slides frequently.
- Conclude with summary after Q&A session.

(e) consistent capitalization and punctuation, and (f) graphics and images. Identify what needs to be improved and exactly how you would improve it. For example, if you identify category (d) as an area needing improvement, your answer would include a revision of the listing. When you finish, your instructor may show you a revised set of slides.*

14.13 Researching *Fortune* List Information (Objs. 1–5)

Web

Your Task. Using an electronic database, perform a search to learn how *Fortune* magazine determines which companies make its annual lists. Research the following lists. Then organize and present a five- to ten-minute informative talk to your class.

a. Fortune 500
b. Global 500
c. 100 Best Companies to Work For
d. America's Most Admired Companies
e. Global Most Admired Companies

14.14 Choosing a Topic for an Oral Presentation (Objs. 1–6)

Team

Your Task. Select a topic from the following list or from the report topics in the activities at the ends of Chapters 11 and 12. For an expanded list of report topics, go to **www.meguffey.com.** Individually or as a team, prepare a five- to ten-minute oral presentation. Consider yourself an expert or a team of experts called in to explain some aspect of the topic before a group of interested people. Because your time is limited, prepare a concise yet forceful presentation with effective visual aids.

If this is a group presentation, form a team of three or four members and conduct thorough research on one of the following topics, as directed by your instructor. Follow the tips on team presentations in this chapter. Divide the tasks fairly, meet for discussions and rehearsals, and crown your achievement with a 15- to 20-minute presentation to your class. Make your PowerPoint presentation interesting and dynamic.

a. Is PowerPoint evil, as Yale professor emeritus Edward Tufte has claimed in his now famous essay? Consider this excerpt: "At a minimum, a presentation format should do no harm. Yet the PowerPoint style routinely disrupts, dominates, and trivializes content. Thus PowerPoint presentations too often resemble a school play—very loud, very slow, and very simple."
b. What information and tools are available at Web job banks to college students searching for full-time employment after graduation? Consider Monster.com and other job banks.
c. How could your peers (in college or in your workplace) be persuaded to make healthful food choices?
d. What simple computer security tips can your company employ to avoid problems?
e. What is telecommuting, and for what kind of workers is it an appropriate work alternative?
f. How could your company use Facebook or Twitter to advantage?
g. How can consumers protect themselves against identity theft?
h. What is the economic outlook for a given product, such as domestic cars, laptop computers, digital cameras, fitness equipment, or a product of your choice?
i. How can your organization or institution improve its image?
j. What are the Webby Awards, and what criteria do the judges use to evaluate Web sites?
k. What brand and model of computer and printer represent the best buy for college students today?
l. What franchise would offer the best investment opportunity for an entrepreneur in your area?
m. What are the differences among casual, business casual, and business formal attire?
n. Which smartphone on the market today offers the best features for businesspeople?
o. Are internships worth the effort?
p. What risks are involved for companies without written policies for e-mail, instant messaging, texting, and social media Web sites?
q. Where should your organization hold its next convention?
r. What is your opinion of the statement "Advertising steals our time, defaces the landscape, and degrades the dignity of public institutions"?[32]
s. What are the advantages and disadvantages of fractional ownership, say, of corporate jets or yachts?
t. What is the outlook for real estate (commercial or residential) investment in your area?
u. What are the pros and cons of videoconferencing for [name an organization]?
v. What do the personal assistants for celebrities do, and how does one become a personal assistant? (Investigate the Association of Celebrity Personal Assistants.)
w. Can a small or midsized company reduce its telephone costs by using Internet phone service?
x. What scams are on the Federal Trade Commission's List of Top 10 Consumer Scams, and how can consumers avoid falling for them?
y. What is fair trade coffee (or cocoa), and why should U.S. businesses such as Starbucks purchase it?
z. Should employees be allowed to use computers in a work environment for anything other than work-related business?

*See the Instructor's Manual and the Instructor's Resource CD.

14.15 Consumer: Will Maxing Out My Credit Cards Improve My Credit Rating? (Objs. 1–5)

Consumer | Web

The program chair for the campus business club has asked you to present a talk to the group about consumer credit. He saw a newspaper article saying that only 10 percent of Americans know their credit scores. Many consumers, including students, have dangerous misconceptions about their scores. Not knowing your score could result in a denial of credit as well as difficulty obtaining needed services and even a job.

Your Task. Using electronic databases and the Web, learn more about credit scores and typical misconceptions. For example, is a higher or lower credit score better? Can you improve your credit score by marrying well? If you earn more money, will you improve your score? If you have a low score, is it impossible to raise it? Can you raise your score by maxing out all your credit cards? (One survey reported that 28 percent of consumers believed the latter statement was true!) Prepare an oral presentation appropriate for a student audience. Conclude with appropriate recommendations.

14.16 Improving Telephone Skills by Role-Playing (Obj. 8)

Your Task. Your instructor will divide the class into pairs. For each scenario take a moment to read and rehearse your role silently. Then play the role with your partner. If time permits, repeat the scenarios, changing roles.

Partner 1	Partner 2
a. You are the personnel manager of Datatronics, Inc. Call Elizabeth Franklin, office manager at Computers Plus. Inquire about a job applicant, Chelsea Chavez, who listed Ms. Franklin as a reference. Respond to Partner 2.	a. You are the receptionist for Computers Plus. The caller asks for Elizabeth Franklin, who is home sick today. You don't know when she will be able to return. Answer the call appropriately.
b. Call Ms. Franklin again the following day to inquire about the same job applicant, Chelsea Chavez. Ms. Franklin answers today, but she talks on and on, describing the applicant in great detail. Tactfully close the conversation.	b. You are now Ms. Franklin, office manager. Describe Chelsea Chavez, an imaginary employee. Think of someone with whom you have worked. Include many details, such as her ability to work with others, her appearance, her skills at computing, her schooling, her ambition, and so forth.
c. You are now the receptionist for Tom Wing, of Wing Imports. Answer a call for Mr. Wing, who is working in another office, at Extension 134, where he will accept calls.	c. You are now an administrative assistant for attorney Michael Murphy. Call Tom Wing to verify a meeting date Mr. Murphy has with Mr. Wing. Use your own name in identifying yourself.
d. You are now Tom Wing, owner of Wing Imports. Call your attorney, Michael Murphy, about a legal problem. Leave a brief, incomplete message.	d. You are now the receptionist for attorney Michael Murphy. Mr. Murphy is skiing in Aspen and will return in two days, but he doesn't want his clients to know where he is. Take a message.
e. Call Mr. Murphy again. Leave a message that will prevent telephone tag.	e. Take a message again as the receptionist for attorney Michael Murphy.

14.17 Presenting Yourself Professionally on the Telephone and in Voice Mail (Obj. 8)

Practice the phone skills you learned in this chapter. Leave your instructor a professional voice mail message. Prepare a mini-agenda before you call. Introduce yourself. If necessary, spell your name and indicate the course and section. Speak slowly and clearly, especially when leaving your phone number. Think of a comment you could make about an intriguing fact, a peer discussion, or your business communication class.

14.18 Presenting Yourself as a Professional When Texting (Obj. 8)

Your phone skills extend not only to voice mail but also to the brief text messages you send to your boss and coworkers. Such *professional* texts are often markedly different in style and tone from the messages you may be exchanging with friends.

Your Task. Send a professional text message to your instructor or to another designated partner in class responding to one of the following scenarios: (a) Explain why you must be late to an important meeting; (b) request permission to purchase a piece of important equipment for the office; or (c) briefly summarize what you have learned in your latest staff development seminar (use a key concept from one of your business classes). Use the recipient's e-mail address to send your text. Do not use abbreviations or smiley faces.

Video Resource

Video Library 1, Effective On-the-Job Oral Presentations

In this video you see Ramon and Sarah in the planning stages of an oral presentation to the board of directors for Integrity Investments. Ramon must persuade the directors that a paid time-off plan makes sense for Integrity employees. Ramon and Sarah brainstorm ideas in the prewriting stage of the writing process. Notice how they apply the 3-x-3 writing process by anticipating the audience and focusing on a purpose. We see Ramon and Sarah go through all three phases of the process, including Ramon's successful presentation.

As you watch the film, be prepared to answer the following questions:

- How is the writing process useful in preparing an oral presentation?
- What techniques can a speaker employ to overcome fear?
- Should every business presentation use PowerPoint? Why or why not?

Are you ready? Get more practice at **www.meguffey.com**

Chat About It

In each chapter you will find five discussion questions related to the chapter material. Your instructor may assign these topics for you to discuss in class, in an online chat room, or on an online discussion board. Some of the discussion topics may require outside research. You may also be asked to read and respond to postings made by your classmates.

Topic 1: How would you classify your classmates as an audience to student presentations: friendly, neutral, uninterested, or hostile? Why?
Topic 2: Why do some presenters avoid making steady eye contact? What might these individuals do to correct this problem?
Topic 3: When might slides with an absolute minimum of text and a maximum of images not be effective?
Topic 4: Do some research to determine what made the "I Have a Dream" speech by Dr. Martin Luther King Jr. so memorable.
Topic 5: When is it acceptable not to return a call when a callback was requested?

Grammar and Mechanics C.L.U.E. Review 14

Total Review

Each of the following sentences has a total of **three** errors in grammar, punctuation, capitalization, usage, or spelling. On a separate sheet, write a correct version. Avoid adding new phrases, starting new sentences, or rewriting in your own words. When finished, compare your responses with the key beginning on page Key-1.

Example: She said that a list of our customers names and addresses were all ready available.
Revision: She said that a list of our **customers'** names and addresses **was already** available.

1. If you are planning a short presentation you should focus on about 3 main points and limit yourself to twenty minutes.
2. Because he was President of the company Mr. Yost made at least 6 major presentations every year.
3. The companys CPA asked me to explain the principle ways we planned to finance the thirty-year mortgage.
4. My accountant and me are greatful to be able to give a short presentation, however, we may not be able to cover the entire budget.
5. The introduction to a presentation should accomplish three goals, (a) Capture attention, (b) establish credibility, and (3) preview main points.
6. Steven wondered whether focusing on what the audience is to remember, and summarizing main points was equally important?
7. A list of suggestions for a speakers ideas are found in the article titled "How To Improve Your Listening Skills."
8. The appearance and mannerisms of a speaker definately effects a listeners evaluation of the message.
9. Melody Hobson, who is an expert speaker said that reading from slides is the Kiss of Death in a presentation.
10. In a poll of three thousand workers only one third felt that there companies valued their opinions.

UNIT 5

Employment Communication

Chapter 15
The Job Search, Résumés, and Cover Letters

Chapter 16
Interviewing and Following Up

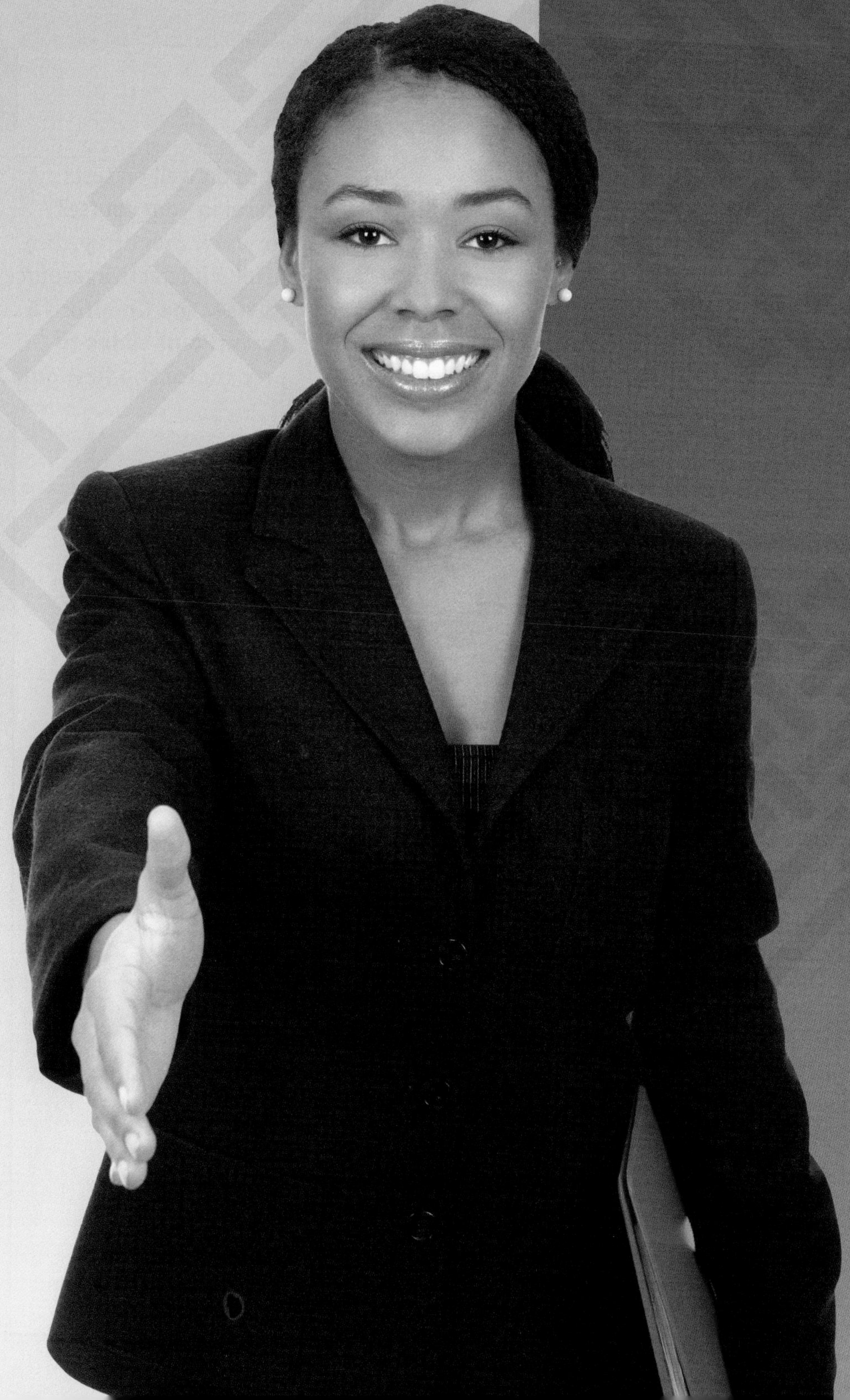

© Kurhan/Shutterstock.com

CHAPTER 15

The Job Search, Résumés, and Cover Letters

OBJECTIVES

After studying this chapter, you should be able to

1. Prepare for a successful job search by identifying your interests, evaluating your assets, recognizing the changing nature of jobs, and choosing a career path.
2. Apply both online and traditional job search techniques.
3. Appreciate the need to customize your résumé, and know whether to choose a chronological or a functional résumé style.
4. Organize your qualifications and information into effective résumé segments.
5. Describe techniques that optimize a résumé for today's technologies, including preparing a scannable résumé, a plain-text résumé, and an e-portfolio.
6. Write a customized cover letter to accompany a résumé.

Want to do well on tests and excel in your course? Go to **www.meguffey.com** for helpful interactive resources.

- **Review the Chapter 15 PowerPoint slides to prepare for the first quiz.**

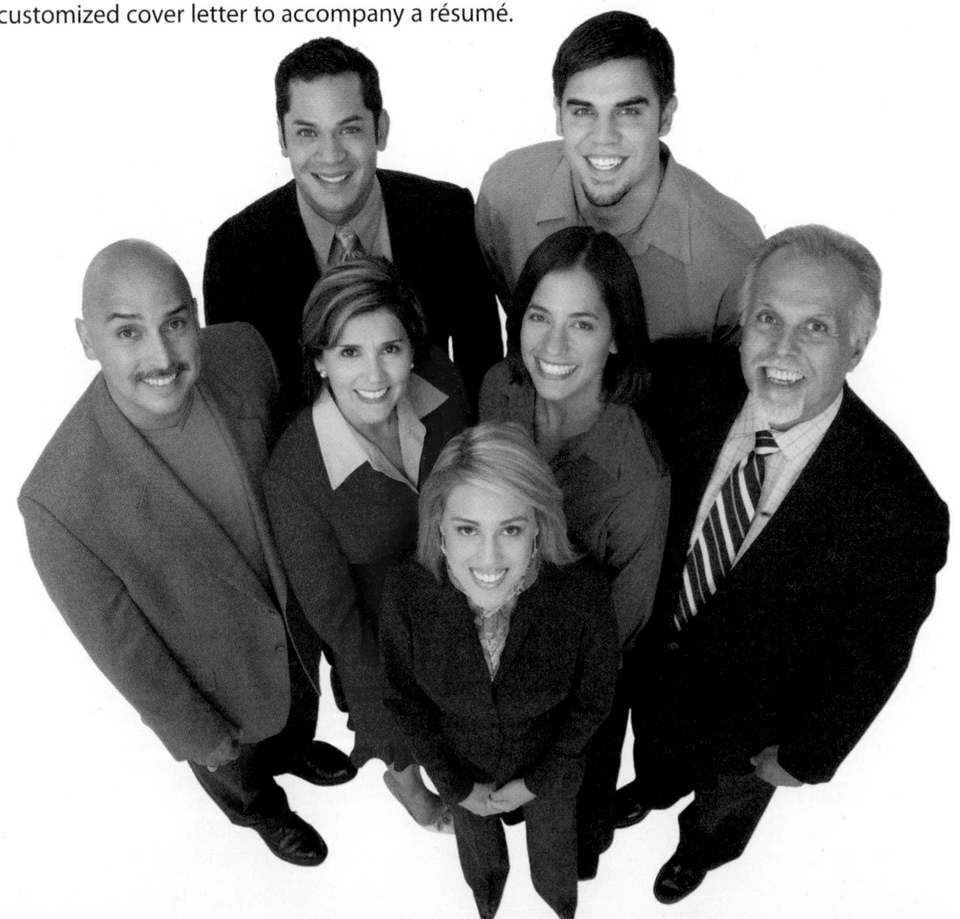

© Jack Hollingsworth/Photodisc/Getty Images

Zooming In — PART 1

Career and Workplace Expert Liz Ryan Helps Job Seekers Be Competitive

Job candidates should not spend more than one hour a day searching for jobs online, says career and workplace expert Liz Ryan. A former Fortune 500 human resources executive, Liz Ryan is a leader in contemporary job searching. She maintains several blogs, writes articles for online forums, delivers speeches internationally, provides career coaching, and is a columnist for *BusinessWeek Online*.

The Web has made job searching easier, acknowledges Ryan, but it also can sidetrack candidates who devote their energies to online searching, while ignoring other methods that could help them. Instead of spending all their time online, job seekers should develop their own personal networks of friends and acquaintances.[1] Job seekers also have to realize that positions in today's workplace tend to open and close at lightning speed. "These days," says Ryan, "you've got to jump on job openings when you hear about them. If you wait a couple of weeks to send a résumé in response to a job you're interested in, the window of opportunity may already have slammed shut."[2] Ryan recommends that job seekers have people in their personal networks help in the job search process by keeping their eyes and ears open for available positions.

In today's workplace, Ryan observes, what constitutes a strong résumé has also changed. Years ago it was acceptable to include common phrases such as *team player* and *strong work ethic* on résumés. However, warns Ryan, "Stodgy boilerplate phrases in your résumé today mark you as uncreative and vocabulary challenged."[3] She recommends making a résumé more persuasive by replacing boring phrases such as *results-oriented professional* and *excellent communication skills* with more conversational, human-sounding phrases.

Finally, in today's competitive employment market, job seekers must be memorable. According to Ryan, too many job seekers who are highly skilled never get called back for a second interview because they are not dynamic enough during the first interview. Ryan asserts, "This may be the biggest problem job seekers face in the interview setting: They can worry so much about saying the wrong thing that they say nothing of substance at all."[4] How can you make yourself memorable during the job search? According to Ryan, "You have to believe that you're meant to be there, in that room, talking about that job. You have to be fully present." Memorable job seekers are confident in themselves and communicate that confidence to employers at every stage of the job search.

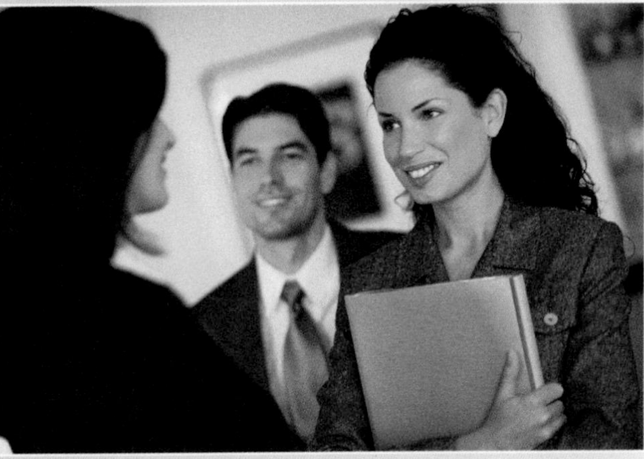

© PhotoAlto/Eric Audras/Getty Images

Critical Thinking

- Why is searching for a job both exhilarating and intimidating? How can you overcome feelings of intimidation?
- Is it easier to search for a job by visiting online job boards or by networking? Which method do you think is more successful?
- Why is it important to be memorable during the job search? What techniques would you use to make yourself memorable?

http://www.asklizryan.com

Preparing for a Successful Job Search

LEARNING OBJECTIVE 1

Prepare for a successful job search by identifying your interests, evaluating your assets, recognizing the changing nature of jobs, and choosing a career path.

The Web has changed the way we look for jobs today. As workplace expert Liz Ryan pointed out in the opening case study, the Web has made job searching easier but also more challenging. Because hundreds and perhaps thousands of candidates may be applying for an advertised position, you must do everything possible to be noticed and to outshine the competition. You must also look beyond the Web.

The better prepared you are, the more confident you will feel during your search. This chapter provides expert current advice in preparing for a job search, searching the job market, writing a customized résumé, and developing an effective cover letter. What you learn here can lead to a successful job search and maybe even your dream job.

You may think that the first step in finding a job is writing a résumé. Wrong! The job search process actually begins long before you are ready to prepare your résumé. Regardless of the kind of employment you seek, you must invest time and effort getting ready. You can't hope to find the position of your dreams without (a) knowing yourself, (b) knowing the job market, and (c) knowing the employment process.

FIGURE 15.1 The Employment Search

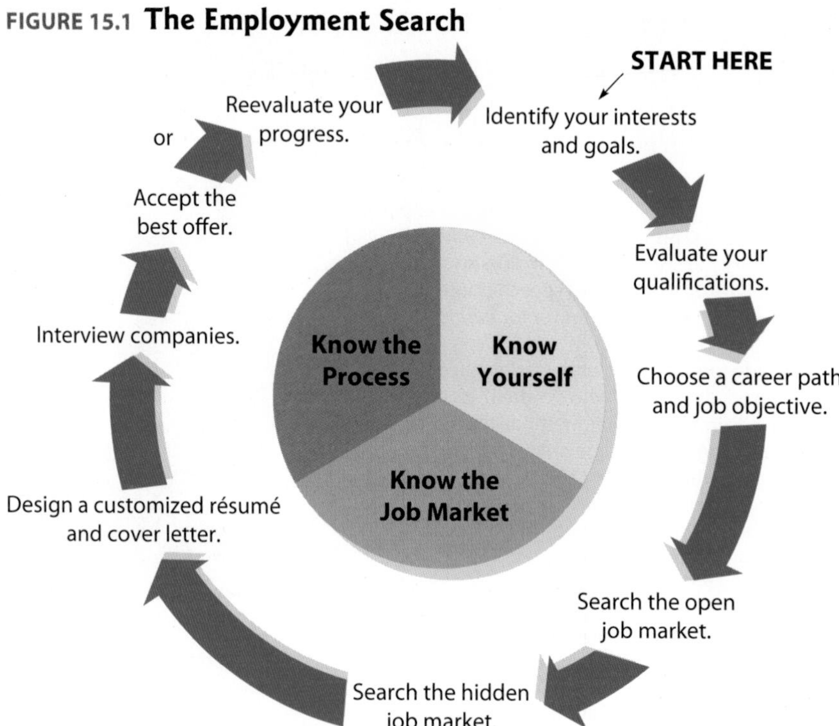

What steps can you take to find a satisfying career?

Begin the job search process by identifying your interests and goals and evaluating your qualifications. This self-evaluation will help you choose a suitable career path and job objective. At the same time, you should be studying the job market and becoming aware of significant changes in the workplace and hiring techniques. You will want to understand how to use the latest Web resources in your job search. Use these Web resources and traditional resources to search the open and hidden job markets for positions. Once you know what jobs are available in your field, you will need to design a résumé and cover letter that you can customize for small businesses as well as for larger organizations. Following these steps, summarized in Figure 15.1 and described in this chapter, gives you a master plan for securing a job you really want.

Identifying Your Interests and Goals

Why is it important to analyze your likes and dislikes at the beginning of your job search?

Buddha once said, "Your work is to discover your work and then with all your heart to give yourself to it." Following this ancient wisdom, you should begin the employment process with introspection. This means looking inside yourself to analyze what you like and dislike so that you can make good employment choices. Career counselors charge large sums for helping individuals learn about themselves. You can do the same kind of self-examination—without spending a dime. For guidance in choosing a career that eventually proves to be satisfying, answer the following questions. If you have already chosen a career path, think carefully about how your answers relate to that choice.

What questions can you ask that will help you choose a career path?

- *What are you passionate about? Can you turn this passion into a career?*
- *Do you enjoy working with people, data, or things?*
- *Would you like to work for someone else or be your own boss?*
- *How important are salary, benefits, technology support, and job stability?*
- *How important are working environment, colleagues, and job stimulation?*
- *Would you rather work for a large or small company?*

- *Must you work in a specific city, geographical area, or climate?*
- *Are you looking for security, travel opportunities, money, power, or prestige?*
- *How would you describe the perfect job, boss, and coworkers?*

Spotlight on Communicators

© AFP PHOTO/FILES/Vladimir Kmet/Newscom

Computer mogul and entrepreneur Michael Dell says that he learned one lesson early: Don't hire someone based on the company's immediate job needs. Because the nature of jobs is changing constantly, Dell prefers to hire a candidate based on that person's potential to grow and develop. He works hard to sustain a culture of "thought leadership" within his company, saying, "As leaders, we need to be willing and open to empowering a culture of entrepreneurship. This means listening very carefully to our employees to ensure we are capturing all the innovative, creative thinking that enables us to better serve our customers while driving our own next wave of growth."

Evaluating Your Qualifications

In addition to your interests and goals, assess your qualifications. Employers today want to know what assets you have to offer them. Your responses to the following questions will target your thinking as well as prepare a foundation for your résumé. Remember, though, that employers seek more than empty assurances; they will want proof of your qualifications.

- *What technology skills can you offer?* Employers are often interested in specific software programs, Web experience, and social media skills.
- *What other skills have you acquired in school, on the job, or through activities?* How can you demonstrate these skills?
- *Do you work well with people? Do you enjoy teamwork?* What proof can you offer? Consider extracurricular activities, clubs, class projects, and jobs.
- *Are you a leader, self-starter, or manager?* What evidence can you offer? What leadership roles have you held?
- *Do you speak, write, or understand another language?* In today's global economy, being able to communicate in more than one language is an asset.
- *Do you learn quickly? Are you creative?* How can you demonstrate these characteristics?
- *Do you communicate well in speech and in writing?* How can you verify these talents?
- *What are the unique qualifications you can offer that will make you stand out among other candidates?* Think about what you offer that will make you memorable during your job search.

Recognizing Employment Trends in Today's Workplace

As you learned in Chapter 1, the nature of the workplace is changing. One of the most significant changes involves the concept of the "job." Following the downsizing of corporations and the outsourcing and offshoring of jobs in recent years, companies are employing fewer people in permanent positions.

Other forms of employment are replacing traditional jobs. In many companies teams complete special projects and then disband. Work may also be outsourced to a group that is not even part of the organization. Because new technologies can spring up overnight making today's skills obsolete, employers are less willing to hire people into jobs with narrow descriptions. Instead, they are hiring contingency employees who work temporarily and then leave. What's more, big companies are no longer the main employers. People work for smaller companies, or they are starting their own businesses. According to the Small Business Administration, small companies employ over half of all private sector employees, and that number is expected to grow over the next decade.[5]

What employment trends can you expect in the new workplace?

What do these changes mean for you? For one thing, you should probably forget about a lifelong career with a single company. Don't count on regular pay raises, promotions, and a comfortable retirement income. You should also become keenly aware that a career that relies on yesterday's skills is headed for trouble. You are going to need updated, marketable skills that serve you well as you move from job to job. Technology skills will become increasing important over the next decade as more than 2 million new technology-related jobs are expected to be created by 2018, according to the Bureau of Labor Statistics.[6] This means that upgrading your skills and retraining yourself constantly are the best career strategies for the twenty-first century. People who learn quickly and adapt to change will always be in demand even in a climate of surging change.

Choosing a Career Path

Where can you go to find useful career information during your job search?

The job picture in the United States is extraordinarily dynamic and flexible. On average, workers between ages 18 and 38 in the United States will have ten different employers, and job tenure averages 6.6 years.[7] Although you may be frequently changing jobs in the future (especially before you reach forty), you still need to train for a specific career area now. In choosing an area, you will make the best decisions when you can match your interests and qualifications with the requirements and rewards in specific careers. Where can you find the best career data? Here are some suggestions:

- **Visit your campus career center.** Most campus career centers have literature, inventories, career-related software programs, and employment or internship databases that allow you to investigate such fields as accounting, finance, office technology, information systems, hotel management, and so forth. Some have well-trained job counselors who can tailor their resources to your needs. They may also offer career exploration workshops, job skills seminars, career days with visiting companies, assistance with résumé preparation, and mock interviews.
- **Search the Web.** Many job search sites on the Web offer career-planning information and resources. You will learn about some of the best career sites in the next section.
- **Use your library.** Print and online resources in your library are especially helpful. Consult *O*NET Occupational Information Network, Dictionary of Occupational Titles, Occupational Outlook Handbook,* and *Jobs Rated Almanac* for information about career duties, qualifications, salaries, and employment trends.

What are the benefits of taking summer jobs, part-time employment, and internships in your field?

- **Take a summer job, internship, or part-time position in your field.** Nothing is better than trying out a career by actually working in it or in a related area. Many companies offer internships and temporary or part-time jobs to begin training college students and to develop relationships with them. Experts commonly believe that at least 60 percent of these relations result in permanent positions.
- **Interview someone in your chosen field.** People are usually flattered when asked to describe their careers. Inquire about needed skills, required courses, financial and other rewards, benefits, working conditions, future trends, and entry requirements.
- **Volunteer with a nonprofit organization.** Many colleges and universities encourage service learning opportunities. In volunteering their services, students gain valuable experience and nonprofits appreciate the expertise and fresh ideas that students bring.
- **Monitor the classified ads.** Early in your college career, begin monitoring want ads and Web sites of companies in your career area. Check job availability, qualifications sought, duties, and salary range. Don't wait until you are about to graduate to see how the job market looks.
- **Join professional and student organizations in your field.** Frequently, professional organizations offer student membership status and reduced rates. You will receive inside information on issues, career news, and possibly jobs. Student business clubs and organizations such as Phi Beta Lambda can also provide leadership development, career tips, and networking opportunities.

Conducting a Successful Job Search

LEARNING OBJECTIVE 2

Apply both online and traditional job search techniques.

Searching for a job today is vastly different than it used to be as a result of the Web. Until fairly recently a job seeker browsed the local classified ads, found a likely-sounding job listing, prepared an elegant résumé on bond paper, and sent it out by U.S. mail. All that has changed because of the Web. The challenge today is realizing how to use the Web to your advantage, while realizing that traditional job search techniques can still be effective. Like other smart job seekers, you can combine both online and traditional job search tactics to land the job of your dreams.

Searching for a Job Online

Searching for a job online has become a common, but not always fruitful, approach. With all the publicity given to Web-based job boards and career sites, you might think that online job searching has totally replaced traditional methods. Not so! Although Web sites such as CareerJournal.com, and Monster.com, shown in Figure 15.2, list millions of jobs, actually landing a job is much harder than just clicking a mouse. In addition, these job boards now face competition from social networking sites such as LinkedIn, Facebook, and Twitter.[8]

What are some of the negatives of using online job boards?

Both recruiters and job seekers complain about online job boards. Corporate recruiters say that the big job boards bring a flood of candidates, many of whom are not suited for the listed jobs. Workplace experts estimate that the average Fortune 500 company is inundated with 2,000 résumés a day.[9] Job candidates grumble that listings are frequently outdated and fail to produce leads. Some career advisors call these sites black holes,[10] into which résumés vanish without a trace. Applicants worry about the privacy of information posted at big boards. Most important, a recent study has shown that the percentage of external hires resulting from job boards is astonishingly low—3.95 percent at CareerBuilder.com, 3.14 percent at Monster.com, and 1.35 percent at HotJobs.com.[11] As workplace expert Liz Ryan says in the opening case study, don't count on finding a job by devoting all your energy to searching online job boards.

What kind of information can you find on the large online job boards?

Despite these gloomy prospects, many job seekers use job boards to gather job search information, such as résumé, interviewing, and salary tips. Job boards also serve as a jumping-off point in most searches. They can inform you about the kinds of jobs that are available and the skill sets required. With tens of thousands of job boards and employment Web sites deluging the Internet, it is hard to know where to start. We have listed a few of the best-known online job sites here:[12]

FIGURE 15.2 Using the Web to Search for a Job

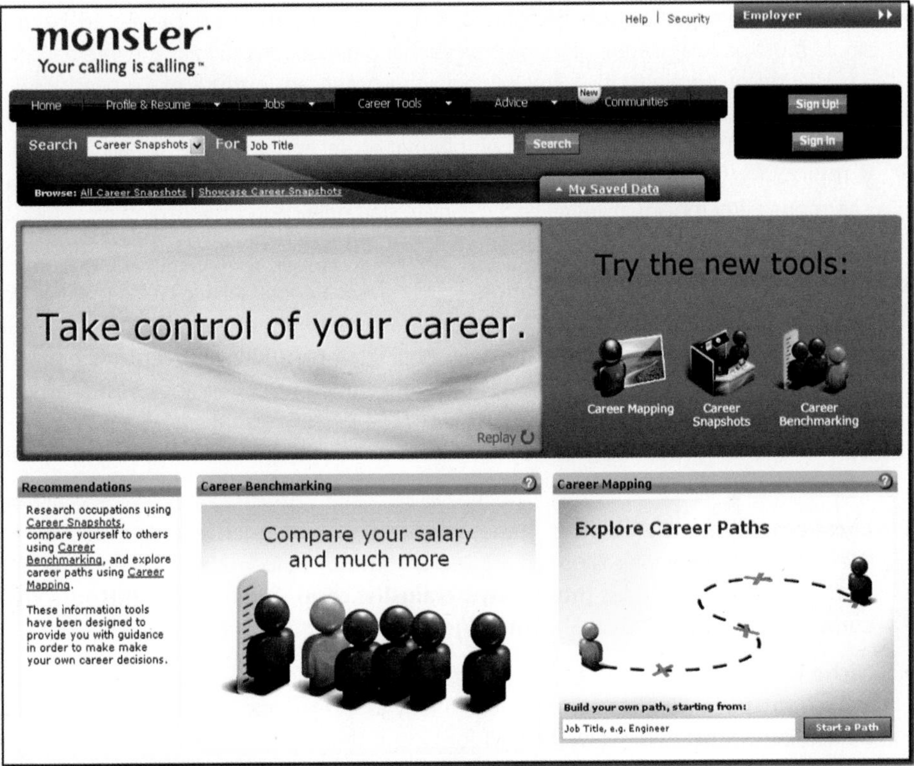

Courtesy of Monster Worldwide

Monster.com is one of many popular Web sites that allow you to search for jobs but also provide excellent tips for conducting job searches, writing résumés, organizing cover letters, preparing for job interviews, and planning careers.

- **CareerBuilder (http://www.careerbuilder.com)** claims to be the nation's largest employment network. Users can search for millions of jobs by job category, geographic location, keyword, industry, or type of job (full-time, part-time, internship, and so on).
- **Indeed (http://www.indeed.com)** is one of the newest and fastest growing job search sites on the Web. Indeed.com is a metasearch engine that uses a Google-like interface to search the entire Web for jobs.
- **Monster (http://www.monster.com)** offers access to information on millions of jobs worldwide. With the recent acquisition of Yahoo HotJobs, this figure will grow even larger. Monster.com uses a search technology called 6Sense to match applicants with the best job opportunities. Because of this cutting-edge search system, many consider Monster.com to be the Web's premier job site.
- **CollegeGrad (http://www.collegegrad.com)** describes itself as the "number one entry-level job site" for students and graduates. In addition to searching for entry-level jobs, users can also search for undergraduate and graduate degree programs to help them become more marketable.
- **CareerJournal (http://www.careerjournal.com)**, which is part of *The Wall Street Journal*, focuses on listing high-level executive and finance positions.

In addition to the big online job boards, where can you look online for job postings and career information?

Beyond the Big Online Job Boards. Disillusioned job seekers may turn their backs on job boards but not on online job-searching tactics. Savvy candidates know how to use their computers to search for jobs at Web sites such as the following:

- **Company Web sites.** Probably the best way to find a job online is at a company's own Web site. Many companies now post job openings only on their own Web sites to avoid being inundated by the volume of applicants that respond to postings on online job boards. Many job seekers also find that they are more likely to obtain an interview if they post their résumés on company sites. In addition to finding a more direct route to decision makers, job seekers find that they can keep their job searches more private than at big board sites.
- **Professional organization Web sites.** Online job listings have proved to be the single-most popular feature of many professional organizations such as the International Association of Administrative Professionals, the American Institute of Certified Public Accountants, the National Association of Sales Professionals, the National Association of Legal Assistants, and the Association of Information Technology Professionals. Although you pay a fee, the benefits of joining a professional association in your career field are enormous. Remember that it is never too early to start networking. If you join a professional organization while you are still in college, you will jump-start your professional connections.
- **JobCentral National Labor Exchange.** JobCentral is a public service Web site provided by the DirectEmployers Association, a nonprofit consortium of Fortune 500 and other leading U.S. corporations. Many companies now use **http://www.jobcentral.com** as a gateway to job listings at their own Web sites, advertising millions of jobs. Best of all, this service is free, bypassing the big commercial job boards. You can enter a job description or job title, and a list of openings pops up. When you click one, you are taken straight to the company's Web site, where you can apply.
- **Local employment Web sites.** Although many of the big job boards allow you to search for jobs geographically, many job seekers have more luck using local employment Web sites such as Craigslist **(http://www.craigslist.com)**, Cumulus Jobs **(http://www.cumulusjobs.com/)**, and JobStar **(http://jobstar.org)**.
- **Niche Web sites.** If you want a job in a specialized field, look for a niche Web site, such as Dice **(http://www.dice.com)** for technology jobs, Advance for Health Care **(http://health-care-jobs.advanceweb.com/)** for jobs in the medical field, and Accountemps **(http://www.accountemps.com/)** for accounting positions. Niche Web sites also exist for job seekers with special backgrounds or needs, such as the disabled **(http://www.gettinghired.com/)** and older workers **(http://www.workforce50.com/)**.

- **Social media sites.** Perhaps you use sites such as Facebook or Google Buzz to communicate with family and friends. However, users are increasingly tapping into social media sites to prospect for jobs; and recruiters also use these sites to find potential employees. LinkedIn is currently the top site for job seekers, with over 42 million users, including job seekers and recruiters. Other popular sites include Facebook, Plaxo, TheLadders, BlueSteps, and Jobster.[13] Twitter has created a job search engine called TwitJobSearch **(http://www.twitjobsearch.com/)**, and many companies now post recruitment videos on YouTube. Savvy job seekers use these tools to network and to search for available positions. Of course, the most successful job seekers understand the necessity of maintaining a professional online appearance at all times.

What can you do to ensure a safe and effective online job search?

You need to be aware of the dangers associated with using online job boards and other employment sites. Your current boss might see your résumé posted online, or a fraudster could use the information in your résumé to steal your identity. The following tips can help you conduct a safe, effective Web job search:

- **Use reputable sites.** Stick to the well-known, reputable job boards. Never use a site that makes you pay to post your résumé.
- **Be selective.** Limit the number of sites on which you post your résumé. Employers dislike "résumé spammers."
- **Use a dedicated e-mail address.** Set up a separate e-mail account with a professional-sounding e-mail address for your job search.
- **Limit personal information.** Never include your social security or other identification numbers on your résumé. Consider omitting your home address and home phone number to protect your privacy.
- **Post privately.** If given an option, choose to post your résumé privately. Doing so means that you can control who has access to your e-mail address and other contact information.
- **Count the days.** Renew your résumé posting every 14 days. If you keep it up longer, it will look as if employers have no interest in you. If you haven't received a response in 45 days, pull your résumé from the site and post it somewhere else.
- **Keep careful records.** Keep a record of every site on which you post your résumé. At the end of your job search, remove all posted résumés.
- **Protect your references.** If you post your résumé online, don't include your references. It is unethical for job seekers to post their references' personal contact information online without their knowledge.
- **Don't respond to a "blind" job posting.** Respond only to job postings that include a company name and contact information. It is unfortunate that many scammers use online job boards to post fake job ads as a way to gather your personal information.

Despite these dangers, job seekers use online sites to search millions of openings. The harsh reality, however, is that landing a job still depends largely on personal contacts. Stanford sociologist Mark Granovetter found that 70 percent of jobs are discovered through networking.[14] One employment expert believes that overreliance on technology may have made job seekers lazy: "At the end of the day, the job hunt is largely about people and it is about networking—looking at who you know and where they work."[15]

Searching for a Job Using Traditional Techniques

What steps can you take to launch an aggressive, proactive job search campaign?

Finding the perfect job requires an early start and a determined effort. One study of college graduates revealed that those with proactive personalities were the most successful in securing interviews and jobs. Successful candidates were not passive; they were driven to "make things happen."[16]

Whether you use traditional or online job search techniques, you should be prepared to launch an aggressive campaign—and you can't start too early. Some universities now require first- and second-year students to take an employment seminar called Reality 101. Students are told early on that a college degree alone doesn't guarantee a job. They are cautioned that grade point averages make a difference to employers.[17] They are also advised of the importance of experience, such as internships. Traditional job search techniques, such as those described here, continue to be critical in landing jobs.

- **Check classified ads in local and national newspapers.** Classified job ads can be found in print or online versions of newspapers. Be aware, though, that classified ads are only one small source of jobs, as discussed in the accompanying Career Coach box.

CAREER COACH

Network Your Way to a Job in the Hidden Market

According to Cornell University Career Services, the "hidden" job market accounts for up to 80 percent of all positions available.[19] Companies do not always announce openings publicly because interviewing all the applicants, many of whom aren't qualified, is time consuming. What's more, even when a job is advertised, companies dislike hiring "strangers." The key to finding a good job, then, is converting yourself from a "stranger" into a known quantity through networking. This can take time. As Walter Kraft, vice president for communications for Eastern Michigan University, reminds us, "Finding a job is a full-time job. It is far more than making a phone call and sending out a resume." Here are traditional and online resources for tapping into the hidden job market:[20]

Traditional Networking

- **Develop a list.** Make a list of anyone who would be willing to talk with you about finding a job. List your friends, relatives, former employers, former coworkers, members of your professional organization, members of your church, people in social and athletic clubs, present and former teachers, neighbors, and friends of your parents, even if you haven't talked with them in years. Also consider asking your campus career center for alumni contacts who will talk with students.
- **Make contacts.** Call the people on your list, or even better, try to meet with them in person. To set up a meeting, say, *Hi, Aunt Martha! I'm looking for a job and I wonder if you could help me out. When could I come over to talk about it?* During your visit be friendly, well organized, polite, and interested in what your contact has to say. Provide a copy of your résumé, and try to keep the conversation centered on your job search area. Your goal is to get two or more referrals. In pinpointing your request, ask, *Do you know of anyone who might have an opening for a person with my skills?* If the person does not, ask, *Do you know of anyone else who might know of someone who would?*
- **Follow up on your referrals.** Call the people whose names are on your referral list. You might say something like, *Hello. I'm Eric Rivera, a friend of Meredith Medcalf. She suggested that I call and ask you for help. I'm looking for a position as a marketing trainee, and she thought you might be willing to spare a few minutes and steer me in the right direction.* Don't ask for a job. During your referral interview, ask how the individual got started in this line of work, what he or she likes best (or least) about the work, what career paths exist in the field, and what problems must be overcome by a newcomer. Most important, ask how a person with your background and skills might get started in the field. Send an informal thank-you note to anyone who helps you in your job search, and stay in touch with the most promising contacts. Ask whether you may call every three weeks or so during your job search.

Online Networking

- **Join a career networking group.** Build your own professional network by joining one or more of the following: **http://www.linkedin.com/**, **http://www.networkingforprofessionals.com/**, **http://www.facebook.com/**, and **http://www.ziggs.com/**. You can also sign up for a universal address book at **http://www.plaxo.com** to help you keep your network contacts organized. Typically, joining a network requires creating a password, filling in your profile, and adding your business contacts. Once you connect with an individual, the content of your discussions and the follow-up is similar to that of traditional networking.
- **Participate in a discussion group or mailing list.** Two especially good discussion group resources for beginners are Yahoo Groups **(http://groups.yahoo.com)** and Google Groups **(http://groups.google.com/)**. You may choose from groups in a variety of fields including business and computer technology.
- **Locate a relevant blog.** Blogs are the latest trend for networking and sharing information. A quick Web search reveals hundreds of career-related blogs and blogs in your field of study. Many companies, such as Microsoft, also maintain employment-related blogs. A good list of career-related blogs can be found at **http://www.quintcareers.com/career-related_blogs.html**. You can also search a worldwide blog directory at **http://www.blogcatalog.com/**. Once you locate a relevant blog, you can read recent postings, search archives, and reply to postings.
- **Start tweeting.** Set up an account at **http://twitter.com** so that you can start marketing yourself, following employers, and getting updates from recruiters. According to Miriam Salpeter from Keppie Careers, "With over 3 million users, Twitter offers an unparalleled opportunity to create an extended network."[21]

Career Application

Begin developing your network. Conduct at least one referral interview, or join one online networking group. Record the results you experienced and the information you learned from the networking option you chose. Report to the class your reactions and findings.

- **Check announcements in publications of professional organizations.** If you do not have a student membership, ask your instructors to share current copies of professional journals, newsletters, and so on. Your college library is another good source.
- **Contact companies in which you are interested, even if you know of no current opening.** Write an unsolicited letter and include your résumé. Follow up with a telephone call. Check the company's Web site for employment possibilities and procedures. To learn immediately of job openings, use Twitter to follow companies where you would like to work.
- **Sign up for campus interviews with visiting company representatives.** Campus recruiters may open your eyes to exciting jobs and locations. They may also help you prepare by offering mock interviews.
- **Attend career fairs.** Job fairs are invaluable in your quest to learn about specific companies and your future career options. Recruiters say that the more you know about the company and its representatives, the more comfortable you will be in an interview.[18]
- **Ask for advice from your instructors.** Your teachers often have contacts and ideas for conducting and expanding your job search.
- **Develop your own network of contacts.** Networking still accounts for most of the jobs found by candidates. Therefore, plan to spend a considerable portion of your job search time developing a personal network. The accompanying Career Coach box gives you advice for traditional networking as well as suggestions for online networking.

Creating a Customized Résumé

LEARNING OBJECTIVE 3
Appreciate the need to customize your résumé, and know whether to choose a chronological or a functional résumé style.

After using both traditional and online resources to learn about the employment market and to develop job leads, you will focus on writing a customized résumé. This means you will prepare a special résumé for every position you want. The competition is so stiff today that you cannot get by with a generic, all-purpose résumé. Although you can start with a basic résumé, you should customize it to fit each company and position if you want your résumé to stand out from the crowd. Include many keywords that describe the skills, traits, tasks, and job titles associated with your targeted job. You will learn more about keywords shortly.

The Web has made it so easy to apply that recruiters are swamped with applications. As a job seeker, you have about five seconds to catch the recruiter's eye—if your résumé is even read by a person. Many companies use computer scanning technologies to weed out unqualified candidates. Your goal is to make your résumé fit the targeted position and be noticed. Such a résumé does more than merely list your qualifications. It packages your assets into a convincing advertisement that sells you for a specific job.

What is the ultimate goal of a customized résumé?

The goal of a résumé is winning an interview. Even if you are not in the job market at this moment, preparing a résumé now has advantages. Having a current résumé makes you look well organized and professional should an unexpected employment opportunity arise. Moreover, preparing a résumé early can help you recognize weak areas and give you time to bolster them. Even after you have accepted a position, it is a good idea to keep your résumé up-to-date. You never know when an opportunity might come along!

Choosing a Résumé Style

Résumés usually fall into two categories: chronological and functional. In this section we present basic information as well as insider tips on how to choose an appropriate résumé style, how to determine its length, and how to arrange its parts. You will also learn about adding a summary of qualifications, which busy recruiters increasingly want to see. Models of the résumés in the following discussion are shown in our comprehensive Résumé Gallery beginning on page 511.

How do chronological and functional résumés differ?

Chronological. The most popular résumé format is the chronological résumé, shown in Figures 15.6 through 15.9 in our Résumé Gallery. It lists work history job by job, starting with the most recent position. Recruiters favor the chronological format because it quickly reveals a candidate's education and experience record. Recruiters are familiar with the chronological résumé, and a recent research study showed that 75 percent of employers prefer to see a candidate's résumé in this format. The chronological style works well for candidates who have experience in their field of employment and for those who show steady career growth, but it is less appropriate for people who have changed jobs frequently or who have gaps in their employment records. For college students and others who lack extensive experience, the functional résumé format may be preferable.

What types of job seekers can benefit from using the functional résumé format?

Functional. The functional résumé, shown in Figure 15.10 on page 515, focuses on a candidate's skills rather than on past employment. Like a chronological résumé, the functional résumé begins with the candidate's name, contact information, job objective, and education. Instead of listing jobs, though, the functional résumé groups skills and accomplishments in special categories, such as *Supervisory and Management Skills* or *Retailing and Marketing Experience.* This résumé style highlights accomplishments and can de-emphasize a negative employment history. People who have changed jobs frequently, who have gaps in their employment records, or who are entering an entirely different field may prefer the functional résumé. Recent graduates with little or no related employment experience often find the functional résumé useful. Older job seekers who want to downplay a long job history and job hunters who are afraid of appearing overqualified may also prefer the functional format. Be aware, though, that online job boards may insist on the chronological format. In addition, some recruiters are suspicious of functional résumés, thinking the candidate is hiding something.

Deciding on Length

How long should your résumé be?

Experts simply do not agree on how long a résumé should be. Conventional wisdom has always held that recruiters prefer one-page résumés. A recent survey of 150 senior executives, however, revealed that 52 percent of executives polled believe a single page is the ideal length for a staff-level résumé, but 44 percent said they prefer two pages. Nearly one third of those surveyed (31 percent) also said that three pages is ideal for executive positions.[22] Recruiters who are serious about candidates often prefer the kind of details that can be provided in a two-page or longer résumé. On the other hand, many recruiters are said to be extremely busy and prefer concise résumés.

Perhaps the best advice is to make your résumé as long as needed to sell your skills to recruiters and hiring managers. Individuals with more experience will naturally have longer résumés. Those with fewer than ten years of experience, those making a major career change, and those who have had only one or two employers will likely have one-page résumés. Those with ten years or more of related experience may have two-page résumés. Finally, some senior-level managers and executives with a lengthy history of major accomplishments might have résumés that are three pages or longer. [23]

Organizing Your Information Into Effective Résumé Categories

LEARNING OBJECTIVE 4

Organize your qualifications and information into effective résumé segments.

Although résumés have standard categories, their arrangement and content should be strategically planned. A customized résumé emphasizes skills and achievements aimed at a particular job or company. It shows a candidate's most important qualifications first, and it de-emphasizes any weaknesses. In organizing your qualifications and information, try to create as few headings as possible; more than six generally looks cluttered. No two résumés are ever exactly alike, but most writers consider including all or some of these categories: main heading, career objective, summary of qualifications, education, experience, capabilities and skills, awards and activities, personal information, and references.

Main Heading

Your résumé, whether it is chronological or functional, should start with a main heading that is as uncluttered and simple as possible. The first line of the main heading should always be your name; add your middle initial for an even more professional look. Format your name so that it stands out on the page. Following your name, list your contact information, including your complete address, area code and phone number, and e-mail address. Be sure to include a telephone number where you can receive messages. The outgoing message at this number should be in your voice, it should mention your full name, and it should be concise and professional. If you include your cell phone number and are expecting an important call from a recruiter, pick up only when you are in a quiet environment and can concentrate.

For your e-mail address, be sure it sounds professional instead of something like *toosexy4you@hotmail.com* or *sixpackguy@yahoo.com.* Also be sure that you are using a personal e-mail address. Putting your work e-mail address on your résumé announces to prospective employers that you are using your current employer's resources to look for another job. If you have a Web site where an e-portfolio or samples of your work can be viewed, include the address in the main heading.

Career Objective

When should you include a career objective on your résumé?

Opinion is divided about the effect of including a career objective on a résumé. Recruiters think such statements indicate that a candidate has made a commitment to a career and is sure about what he or she wants to do. Career objectives, of course, make the recruiter's life easier by quickly classifying the résumé. Such declarations, however, can also disqualify a candidate if the stated objective doesn't match a company's job description.[24] A well-written objective—customized for the job opening—can add value to either a chronological or a functional résumé.

A person applying for an auditor position might include the following objective: *Seeking an auditor position in an internal corporate accounting department where my accounting skills, computer experience, knowledge of GAAP, and attention to detail will help the company run efficiently and ensure that its records are kept accurately.*

Your objective should also focus on the employer's needs. Therefore, it should be written from the employer's perspective, not your own. Focus on how you can contribute to the organization, not on what the organization can do for you. A typical self-serving objective is *To obtain a meaningful and rewarding position that enables me to learn more about the graphic design field and allows for advancement.* Instead, show how you will add value to the organization with an objective such as *Position with advertising firm designing Web sites, publications, logos, and promotional displays for clients, where creativity, software knowledge, and proven communication skills can be used to build client base and expand operations.* As Rick Saia, a certified professional résumé writer, advises, these days, "the company is really not as interested in what they can do for you as in what you can do for them."[25]

Also be careful that your career objective doesn't downplay your talents. For example, some consultants warn against using the words *entry-level* in your objective, as these words emphasize lack of experience or show poor self-confidence. Finally, your objective should be concise. Try to limit your objective to no more than three lines. Avoid using complete sentences and the pronoun *I*.

If you choose to omit the career objective, be sure to discuss your objectives and goals in your cover letter. Savvy job seekers are also incorporating their objectives into a summary of qualifications, which is discussed next.

Summary of Qualifications

What is the purpose of a summary of qualifications section on a résumé?

"The biggest change in résumés over the last decade has been a switch from an objective to a summary at the top," says career expert Wendy Enelow.[26] Recruiters are busy, and smart job seekers add a summary of qualifications to their résumés to save the time of recruiters and hiring managers. Once a job is advertised, a hiring manager may get hundreds or even thousands of résumés in response. A summary at the top of your résumé makes it easier to read and ensures that your most impressive qualifications are not overlooked by a recruiter, who skims résumés quickly. Job applicants must often capture a recruiter's attention in 20 to 30 seconds. A well-written summary of qualifications, therefore, motivates the recruiter to read further.

A summary of qualifications (also called *career profile, job summary*, or *professional highlights*) should include three to eight bulleted statements that prove you are the ideal candidate for the position. When formulating these statements, consider your experience in the field, your education, your unique skills, awards you have won, certifications, and any other accomplishments that you want to highlight. Include numbers wherever possible. Target the most important qualifications an employer will be looking for in the person hired for this position. Examples of summaries of qualifications appear in Figures 15.6, 15.7, 15.8, 15.9, and 15.11 in the résumé models found in our Résumé Gallery.

What information should be included in the education section of a résumé?

Education

The next component in a chronological résumé is your education—if it is more noteworthy than your work experience. In this section you should include the name and location of schools, dates of attendance, major fields of study, and degrees received. By the way, once you have attended college, you don't need to list high school information on your résumé.

Your grade point average and/or class ranking may be important to prospective employers. In a recent study, the National Association of Colleges and Employers found that 66 percent of employers screen candidates by GPA, and 58 percent of those surveyed said they would be much less likely to hire applicants with college GPAs of less than 3.0.[27] One way to enhance your GPA is to calculate it in your major courses only (for example, *3.6/4.0 in major*). It is not unethical to showcase your GPA in your major—as long as you clearly indicate what you are doing. Although some hiring managers may think that applicants are hiding something if they omit a poor record of grades, consultant Terese Corey Blanck suggests leaving out a poor GPA. Instead, she advises that students try to excel in internships, show extracurricular leadership, and target smaller, lesser-known companies to offset low grades.[28] Remember, however, that many employers will assume your GPA is lower than a 3.0 if you omit it.[29]

Under *Education* you might be tempted to list all the courses you took, but such a list makes for very dull reading and uses valuable space. Refer to courses only if you can relate them to the position sought. When relevant, include certificates earned, seminars attended, workshops completed, scholarships awarded, and honors earned. If your education is incomplete, include such statements as *BS degree expected 6/14* or *80 units completed in 120-unit program.* Title this section *Education, Academic Preparation,* or *Professional Training.* If you are preparing a functional résumé, you will probably put the education section below your skills summaries, as Kevin Touhy has done in Figure 15.10.

What information should be included in the work experience section of a résumé?

Work Experience or Employment History

When your work experience is significant and relevant to the position sought, this information should appear before education. List your most recent employment first and work backward, including only those jobs that you think will help you win the targeted position. A job application form may demand a full employment history, but your résumé may be selective. Be aware,

© AP Images/Joe Raymond

Résumés should always be accurate, never misleading or inflated. The consequences of falsifying personal information were illustrated dramatically when George O'Leary was forced to resign from his position as head football coach of Notre Dame University only one week after he started. He submitted his resignation after it was discovered that he had lied about his academic background and athletic experience. This situation was an embarrassment not only to O'Leary but also to the entire Notre Dame football program. *What is the right way to portray limited education and experience on résumés?*

though, that time gaps in your employment history will probably be questioned in the interview. For each position show the following:

- Employer's name, city, and state
- Dates of employment (month and year)
- Most important job title
- Significant duties, activities, accomplishments, and promotions

Describe your employment achievements concisely but concretely to make what résumé consultants call "a strong value proposition."[30] Avoid generalities such as *Worked with customers.* Be more specific, with statements such as *Served 40 or more retail customers a day; Successfully resolved problems about custom stationery orders;* or *Acted as intermediary among customers, printers, and suppliers.* If possible, quantify your accomplishments, such as *Conducted study of equipment needs of 100 small businesses in Houston; Personally generated orders for sales of $90,000 annually;* or *Keyed all the production models for a 250-page employee procedures manual.* One professional recruiter said, "I spend a half hour every day screening 50 résumés or more, and if I don't spot some [quantifiable] results in the first 10 seconds, the résumé is history."[31]

How can you make your achievements stand out on a résumé?

Your employment achievements and job duties will be easier to read if you place them in a bulleted list. When writing these bullet points, don't try to list every single thing you have done on the job; instead, customize your information so that it relates to the target job. Make sure your list of job duties shows what you have to contribute and how you are qualified for the position you are applying for. Don't make your bullet points complete sentences, and avoid using personal pronouns (*I, me, my*). If you have performed the same duties for multiple employers, you don't have to repeat them.

In addition to technical skills, employers seek individuals with communication, management, and interpersonal capabilities. This means you will want to select work experiences and achievements that illustrate your initiative, dependability, responsibility, resourcefulness, flexibility, and leadership. Employers also want people who can work in teams. Thus, include statements such as *Collaborated with interdepartmental task force in developing ten-page handbook for temporary workers* and *Headed student government team that conducted most successful voter registration in campus history.*

Statements describing your work experience can be made forceful and persuasive by using action verbs, such as those listed in Figure 15.3 and illustrated in Figure 15.4. Starting each of your bullet points with an action verb will help ensure that your bulleted lists are parallel.

Capabilities and Skills

What special skills and capabilities should you add to your résumé to make yourself more marketable?

Recruiters want to know specifically what you can do for their companies. Therefore, list your special skills, such as *Proficient in preparing federal, state, and local payroll tax returns as well as franchise and personal property tax returns.* Include your ability to use the Web, software programs, social media, office equipment, and communication technology tools. If you speak a foreign language or use sign language, include it on your résumé. Describe proficiencies you have acquired through training and experience, such as *Certified in computer graphics and Web design through an intensive 350-hour classroom program.* Use expressions such as *competent in, skilled in, proficient with, experienced in,* and *ability to;* for example, *Competent in writing, editing, and proofreading reports, tables, letters, memos, manuscripts, and business forms.*

You will also want to highlight exceptional aptitudes, such as working well under stress, learning computer programs quickly, and interacting with customers. If possible, provide details and evidence that back up your assertions; for example, *Mastered PhotoShop in 25 hours with little instruction.* Include examples of your writing, speaking, management, organizational, and interpersonal skills—particularly those talents that are relevant to your targeted job. For recent graduates, this section can be used to give recruiters evidence of your potential. Instead of *Capabilities,* the section might be called *Skills and Abilities.*

Those job hunters preparing a functional résumé will place more focus on skills than on any other section. A well-written functional résumé groups skills into categories such as *Accounting/Finance Skills, Management/Leadership Skills, Communication/Teamwork Skills,* and *Computer/Technology Skills.* Each skills category includes a bulleted list of achievements and experience that demonstrate the skill, including specific numbers whenever possible. These skills categories

FIGURE 15.3 Action Verbs for Powerful Résumés

The **underlined** words are especially good for pointing out accomplishments.

Communication Skills
arbitrated, arranged, authored, clarified, collaborated, convinced, corresponded, defined, developed, directed, drafted, edited, enlisted, explained, formulated, influenced, integrated, interpreted, mediated, moderated, negotiated, participated, persuaded, promoted, publicized, reconciled, recruited, resolved, spoke, specified, suggested, summarized, translated, wrote

Teamwork, Supervision Skills
adapted, advised, assessed, assisted, clarified, coached, collaborated (with), communicated, coordinated, counseled, demonstrated, demystified, developed, enabled, encouraged, evaluated, expedited, explained, facilitated, guided, informed, instructed, motivated, persuaded, set goals, stimulated, teamed (with), trained

Management, Leadership Skills
administered, analyzed, assigned, attained, authorized, chaired, consolidated, contracted, coordinated, delegated, developed, directed, evaluated, executed, handled, headed, implemented, improved, increased, led, modeled, organized, oversaw, planned, prioritized, produced, recommended, reorganized, reviewed, scheduled, strengthened, supervised, trained

Research Skills
analyzed, clarified, collected, critiqued, diagnosed, evaluated, examined, experimented, extracted, formulated, gathered, identified, informed, inspected, interpreted, interviewed, invented, investigated, located, measured, observed, organized, researched, reviewed, searched, solved, studied, summarized, surveyed, systematized

Clerical, Detail Skills
activated, approved, arranged, catalogued, classified, collected, compiled, edited, executed, generated, implemented, inspected, logged, maintained, monitored, operated, organized, prepared, processed, proofread, purchased, recorded, retrieved, screened, specified, streamlined, systematized, tabulated, updated, validated

Creative Skills
acted, conceptualized, created, customized, designed, developed, directed, established, fashioned, founded, illustrated, initiated, instituted, integrated, introduced, invented, originated, performed, planned, revitalized, shaped

Technical Skills
assembled, built, calculated, computed, configured, designed, devised, engineered, fabricated, installed, maintained, operated, overhauled, performed, troubleshooting, programmed, remodeled, repaired, retrieved, solved, upgraded

Financial Skills
administered, allocated, analyzed, appraised, audited, balanced, budgeted, calculated, computed, developed, forecast, managed, marketed, planned, projected, researched

More Accomplishment Verbs
achieved, expanded, improved, pioneered, reduced (losses), resolved (problems), restored, revamped, spearheaded, transformed

Revised and updated from Yana Parker, *The Damn Good Résumé Guide*. (Berkeley, CA: Ten Speed Press). Reprinted with permission.

should be placed at the beginning of the résumé, where they will be highlighted, followed by education and work experience. The action verbs shown in Figures 15.3 and 15.4 can also be used when constructing a functional résumé.

What types of awards, honors, and activities should be included on a résumé?

Awards, Honors, and Activities

If you have three or more awards or honors, highlight them by listing them under a separate heading. If not, put them in the education or work experience section if appropriate. Include awards, scholarships (financial and other), fellowships, dean's list, honors, recognition, commendations, and certificates. Be sure to identify items clearly. Your reader may be unfamiliar, for example, with Greek organizations, honoraries, and awards; tell what they mean. Instead

FIGURE 15.4 **Use Action Verbs in Statements That Quantify Achievements**

Identified weaknesses in internships and **researched** five alternate programs
Reduced delivery delays by an average of three days per order
Streamlined filing system, thus reducing 400-item backlog to zero
Organized holiday awards program for 1,200 attendees and 140 workers
Designed three pages in HTML for company Web site
Represented 2,500 students on committee involving university policies and procedures
Calculated shipping charges for overseas deliveries and **recommended** most economical rates
Managed 24-station computer network linking data in three departments
Distributed and **explained** voter registration forms to over 500 prospective voters
Praised by top management for enthusiastic teamwork and achievement
Secured national recognition from National Arbor Foundation for tree project

of saying *Recipient of Star award,* give more details: *Recipient of Star award given by Pepperdine University to outstanding graduates who combine academic excellence and extracurricular activities.*

It is also appropriate to include school, community, volunteer, and professional activities. Employers are interested in evidence that you are a well-rounded person. This section provides an opportunity to demonstrate leadership and interpersonal skills. Strive to use action statements. For example, instead of saying *Treasurer of business club,* explain more fully: *Collected dues, kept financial records, and paid bills while serving as treasurer of 35-member business management club.*

Personal Data

What personal data should be omitted from a résumé? Why?

Today's résumés omit personal data, such as birth date, marital status, height, weight, national origin, health, disabilities, and religious affiliation. Such information doesn't relate to genuine occupational qualifications, and recruiters are legally barred from asking for such information. Some job seekers do, however, include hobbies or interests (such as skiing or photography) that might grab the recruiter's attention or serve as conversation starters. For example, let's say you learn that your hiring manager enjoys distance running. If you have run a marathon, you may want to mention it. Many executives practice tennis or golf, two sports highly suitable for networking. You could also indicate your willingness to travel or to relocate since many companies will be interested.

References

Should references be included on your résumé? Why or why not?

Listing references directly on a résumé takes up valuable space. Moreover, references are not normally instrumental in securing an interview—few companies check them before the interview. Instead, recruiters prefer that you bring to the interview a list of individuals willing to discuss your qualifications. Therefore, you should prepare a separate list, such as that in Figure 15.5, when you begin your job search. Ask three to five individuals—instructors, your current employer or previous employers, colleagues or subordinates, and other professional contacts—whether they would be willing to answer inquiries regarding your qualifications for employment. Be sure, however, to provide them with an opportunity to refuse. No reference is better than a negative one. Better yet, to avoid rejection and embarrassment, ask only those contacts who will give you a glowing endorsement.

Do not include personal or character references, such as friends, family, or neighbors, because recruiters rarely consult them. Companies are more interested in the opinions of objective individuals who know how you perform professionally and academically. One final note: most recruiters see little reason for including the statement *References furnished upon request.* It is unnecessary and takes up precious space.

In Figures 15.6 through 15.11 beginning on page 510, you will find our Résumé Gallery, which contains models of chronological and functional résumés. Use these models to help you organize the content and format of your own persuasive résumé.

FIGURE 15.5 **Sample Reference List**

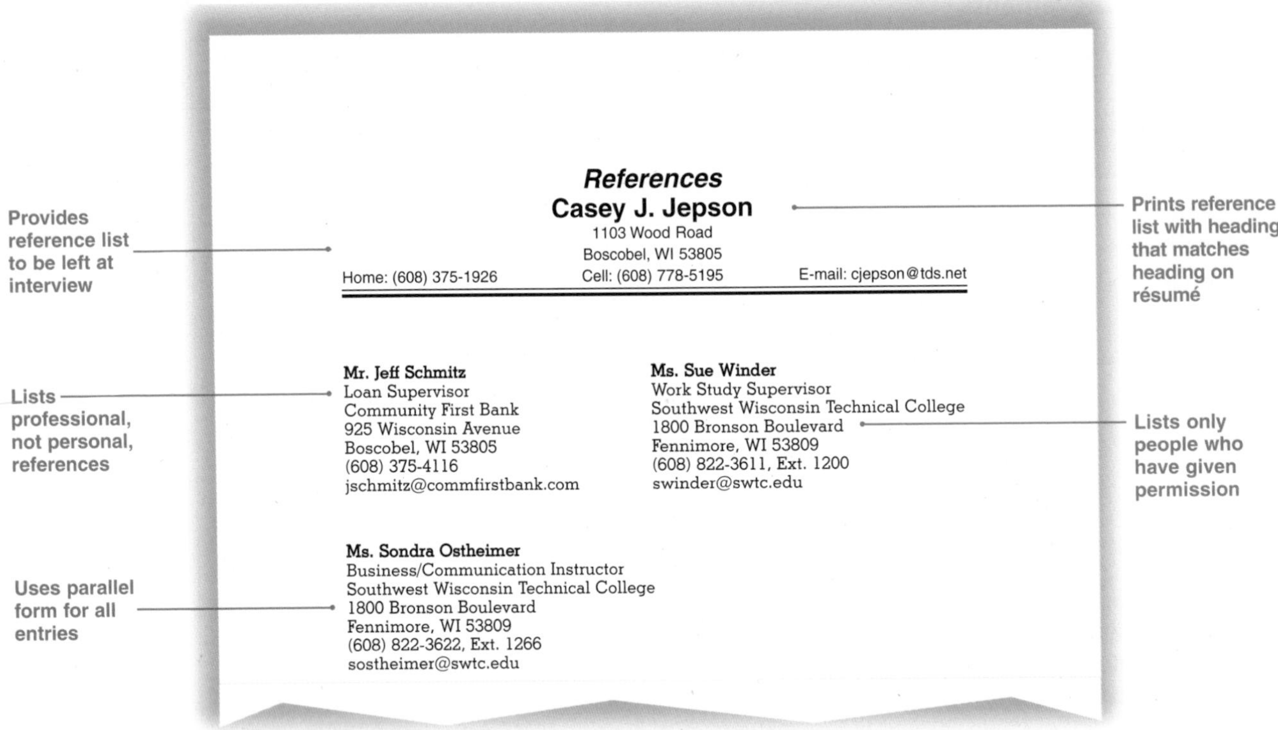

References
Casey J. Jepson
1103 Wood Road
Boscobel, WI 53805
Home: (608) 375-1926
Cell: (608) 778-5195
E-mail: cjepson@tds.net
Mr. Jeff Schmitz
Loan Supervisor
Community First Bank
925 Wisconsin Avenue
Boscobel, WI 53805
(608) 375-4116
jschmitz@commfirstbank.com
Ms. Sue Winder
Work Study Supervisor
Southwest Wisconsin Technical College
1800 Bronson Boulevard
Fennimore, WI 53809
(608) 822-3611, Ext. 1200
swinder@swtc.edu
Ms. Sondra Ostheimer
Business/Communication Instructor
Southwest Wisconsin Technical College
1800 Bronson Boulevard
Fennimore, WI 53809
(608) 822-3622, Ext. 1266
sostheimer@swtc.edu
Provides reference list to be left at interview
Lists professional, not personal, references
Uses parallel form for all entries
Prints reference list with heading that matches heading on résumé
Lists only people who have given permission

Zooming In PART 2

Career and Workplace Expert Liz Ryan Helps Job Seekers Be Competitive

When asked about the biggest mistakes job seekers make, career and workplace expert Liz Ryan says that people applying online tend to "go long." That is, they don't make an effort to be concise because they think that online space is unlimited. Recruiters, however, don't want to read pages and pages of text. Ryan advises keeping your résumé, cover letter, and other messages brief and snappy. Does this mean you should use the abbreviated style of instant messages? Absolutely not! she responds. Use appropriate business language—no abbreviations, no all caps or all lowercase, and no strings of exclamation points.

One big mistake new grads make online is that they fail to look beyond the big boards. She encourages job candidates to focus on smaller, local sites. Examples include such sites as BayAreaJobs **(http://www.bajobs.com)** and JobStar **(http://jobstar.org)**. Also check company Web sites because jobs are often listed there before they are posted on the big boards. Even if you don't see exactly the job you want at a company site, you can get a feel for the kinds of positions available. If your skill set doesn't match a particular opening, use that channel to respond. You can say, "I'm not exactly right for this job, but I have this, this, and this, and if something comes along that fits my skills, I'm available."[32]

Ryan encourages job candidates to join e-mail discussion groups such as Craigslist **(http://sfbay.craigslist.org/)**. Groups carry job listings and allow members to post their own messages letting employers and fellow members know they are job hunting.

Another mistake of candidates is not reading job listings carefully. If an ad says, "no phone calls," that means no calls. Some ads say, "When you respond, please comment on our newsletter at this link."[33] Ryan emphasizes that following the directions in the ad is critical.

© PhotoAlto/Eric Audras/Getty Images

Critical Thinking

- Compare the advantages and disadvantages of searching for jobs at big online job boards, such as Monster.com, with searching at company Web sites.
- Why would companies ask job applicants to comment on their newsletter?
- If recruiters are so pressed for time, why don't they appreciate résumés and cover letters written in the abbreviated style of instant messaging?

Résumé Gallery

FIGURE 15.6 Chronological Résumé: Recent College Graduate With Related Experience

Courtney Castro used a chronological résumé to highlight her work experience, most of which is related directly to the position she seeks. Although she is a recent graduate, she has accumulated experience in two part-time jobs and one full-time job. She included a summary of qualifications to highlight her skills, experience, and interpersonal traits aimed at a specific position.

Notice that Courtney designed her résumé in two columns with five major categories listed in the left column. In the right column she included bulleted items for each of the five categories. Conciseness and parallelism are important in writing an effective résumé. In the *Experience* category, she started each item with an active verb, which improved readability and parallel form.

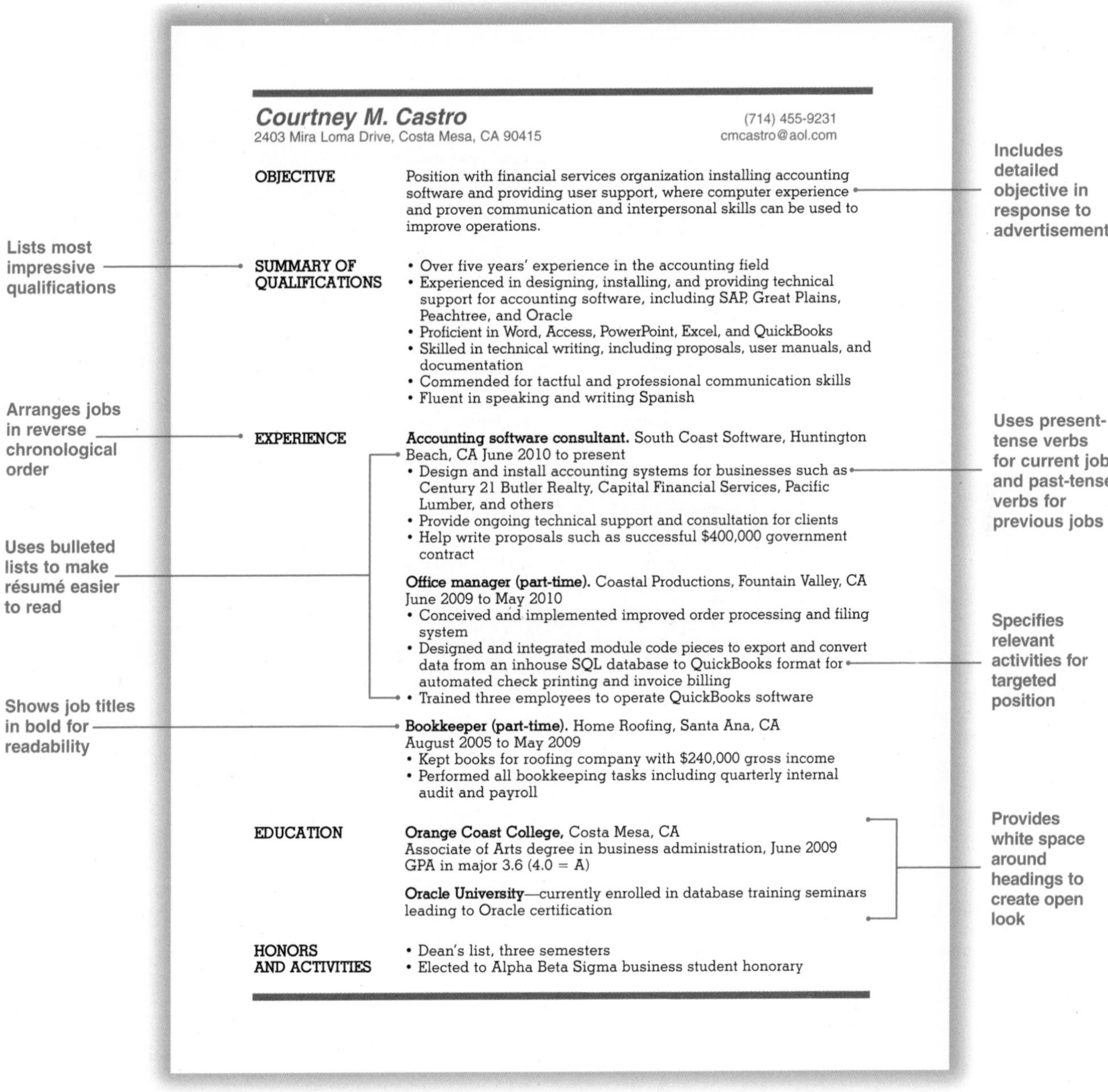

Courtney M. Castro
2403 Mira Loma Drive, Costa Mesa, CA 90415
(714) 455-9231
cmcastro@aol.com

OBJECTIVE
Position with financial services organization installing accounting software and providing user support, where computer experience and proven communication and interpersonal skills can be used to improve operations.

SUMMARY OF QUALIFICATIONS
- Over five years' experience in the accounting field
- Experienced in designing, installing, and providing technical support for accounting software, including SAP, Great Plains, Peachtree, and Oracle
- Proficient in Word, Access, PowerPoint, Excel, and QuickBooks
- Skilled in technical writing, including proposals, user manuals, and documentation
- Commended for tactful and professional communication skills
- Fluent in speaking and writing Spanish

EXPERIENCE
Accounting software consultant. South Coast Software, Huntington Beach, CA June 2010 to present
- Design and install accounting systems for businesses such as Century 21 Butler Realty, Capital Financial Services, Pacific Lumber, and others
- Provide ongoing technical support and consultation for clients
- Help write proposals such as successful $400,000 government contract

Office manager (part-time). Coastal Productions, Fountain Valley, CA June 2009 to May 2010
- Conceived and implemented improved order processing and filing system
- Designed and integrated module code pieces to export and convert data from an inhouse SQL database to QuickBooks format for automated check printing and invoice billing
- Trained three employees to operate QuickBooks software

Bookkeeper (part-time). Home Roofing, Santa Ana, CA
August 2005 to May 2009
- Kept books for roofing company with $240,000 gross income
- Performed all bookkeeping tasks including quarterly internal audit and payroll

EDUCATION
Orange Coast College, Costa Mesa, CA
Associate of Arts degree in business administration, June 2009
GPA in major 3.6 (4.0 = A)

Oracle University—currently enrolled in database training seminars leading to Oracle certification

HONORS AND ACTIVITIES
- Dean's list, three semesters
- Elected to Alpha Beta Sigma business student honorary

Includes detailed objective in response to advertisement
Lists most impressive qualifications
Arranges jobs in reverse chronological order
Uses present-tense verbs for current job and past-tense verbs for previous jobs
Uses bulleted lists to make résumé easier to read
Specifies relevant activities for targeted position
Shows job titles in bold for readability
Provides white space around headings to create open look

FIGURE 15.7 Chronological Résumé: Current College Student With Limited Experience

To highlight her skills and capabilities, Casey placed them in the summary of qualifications at the top of her résumé. She used the tables feature of her word processing program to help her format. Because she wanted to describe her skills and experience fully, she used two pages.

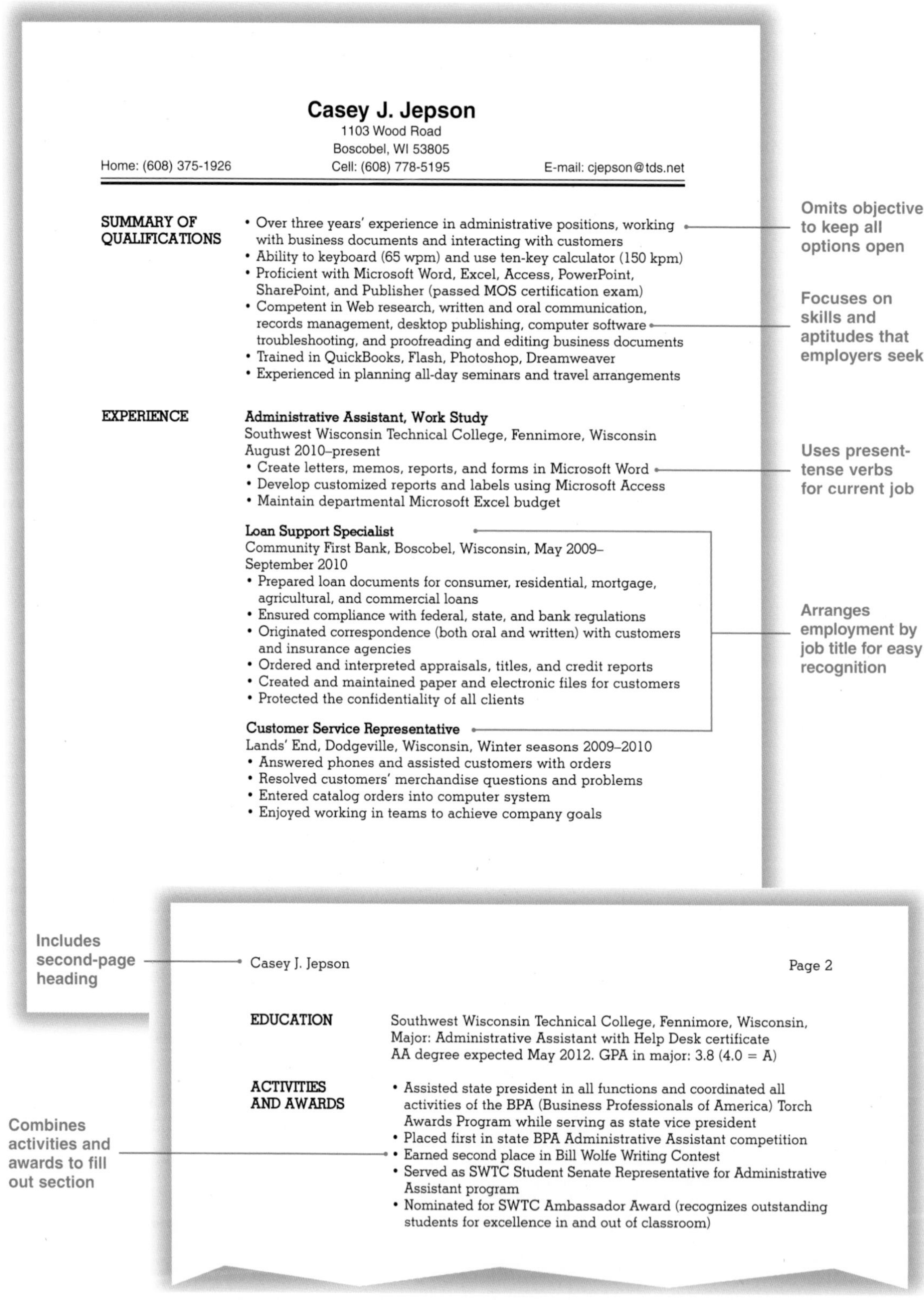

Casey J. Jepson
1103 Wood Road
Boscobel, WI 53805
Home: (608) 375-1926 | Cell: (608) 778-5195 | E-mail: cjepson@tds.net

SUMMARY OF QUALIFICATIONS

- Over three years' experience in administrative positions, working with business documents and interacting with customers
- Ability to keyboard (65 wpm) and use ten-key calculator (150 kpm)
- Proficient with Microsoft Word, Excel, Access, PowerPoint, SharePoint, and Publisher (passed MOS certification exam)
- Competent in Web research, written and oral communication, records management, desktop publishing, computer software troubleshooting, and proofreading and editing business documents
- Trained in QuickBooks, Flash, Photoshop, Dreamweaver
- Experienced in planning all-day seminars and travel arrangements

EXPERIENCE

Administrative Assistant, Work Study
Southwest Wisconsin Technical College, Fennimore, Wisconsin
August 2010–present
- Create letters, memos, reports, and forms in Microsoft Word
- Develop customized reports and labels using Microsoft Access
- Maintain departmental Microsoft Excel budget

Loan Support Specialist
Community First Bank, Boscobel, Wisconsin, May 2009–September 2010
- Prepared loan documents for consumer, residential, mortgage, agricultural, and commercial loans
- Ensured compliance with federal, state, and bank regulations
- Originated correspondence (both oral and written) with customers and insurance agencies
- Ordered and interpreted appraisals, titles, and credit reports
- Created and maintained paper and electronic files for customers
- Protected the confidentiality of all clients

Customer Service Representative
Lands' End, Dodgeville, Wisconsin, Winter seasons 2009–2010
- Answered phones and assisted customers with orders
- Resolved customers' merchandise questions and problems
- Entered catalog orders into computer system
- Enjoyed working in teams to achieve company goals

Casey J. Jepson | Page 2

EDUCATION

Southwest Wisconsin Technical College, Fennimore, Wisconsin,
Major: Administrative Assistant with Help Desk certificate
AA degree expected May 2012. GPA in major: 3.8 (4.0 = A)

ACTIVITIES AND AWARDS

- Assisted state president in all functions and coordinated all activities of the BPA (Business Professionals of America) Torch Awards Program while serving as state vice president
- Placed first in state BPA Administrative Assistant competition
- Earned second place in Bill Wolfe Writing Contest
- Served as SWTC Student Senate Representative for Administrative Assistant program
- Nominated for SWTC Ambassador Award (recognizes outstanding students for excellence in and out of classroom)

Omits objective to keep all options open
Focuses on skills and aptitudes that employers seek
Uses present-tense verbs for current job
Arranges employment by job title for easy recognition
Includes second-page heading
Combines activities and awards to fill out section

FIGURE 15.8 Chronological Résumé: Current University Student With Limited Relevant Experience

Eric used MS Word to design a traditional chronological print-based résumé that he plans to give to recruiters at campus job fairs or during interviews. Although Eric has work experience not related to his future employment, his résumé looks impressive because he has transferable skills. His internship is related to his future career, and his language skills and study abroad experience will help him score points when in competition with other applicants. Eric's volunteer experience is also attractive because it shows him as a well-rounded, compassionate individual. Because his experience in his future field is limited, he omitted a summary of qualifications.

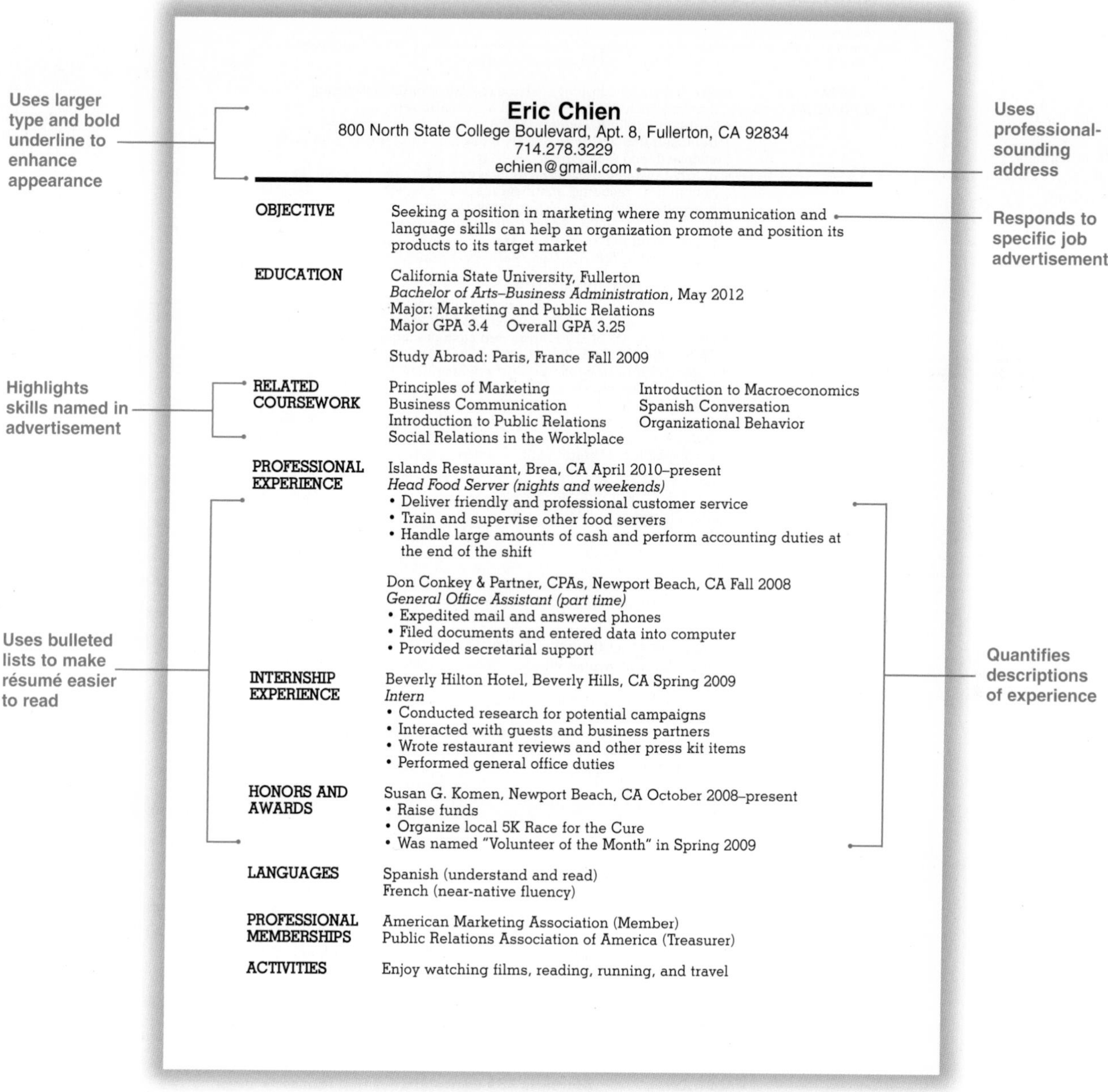

Eric Chien
800 North State College Boulevard, Apt. 8, Fullerton, CA 92834
714.278.3229
echien@gmail.com

OBJECTIVE Seeking a position in marketing where my communication and language skills can help an organization promote and position its products to its target market

EDUCATION California State University, Fullerton
Bachelor of Arts–Business Administration, May 2012
Major: Marketing and Public Relations
Major GPA 3.4 Overall GPA 3.25

Study Abroad: Paris, France Fall 2009

RELATED COURSEWORK
Principles of Marketing
Business Communication
Introduction to Public Relations
Social Relations in the Worklplace
Introduction to Macroeconomics
Spanish Conversation
Organizational Behavior

PROFESSIONAL EXPERIENCE Islands Restaurant, Brea, CA April 2010–present
Head Food Server (nights and weekends)
- Deliver friendly and professional customer service
- Train and supervise other food servers
- Handle large amounts of cash and perform accounting duties at the end of the shift

Don Conkey & Partner, CPAs, Newport Beach, CA Fall 2008
General Office Assistant (part time)
- Expedited mail and answered phones
- Filed documents and entered data into computer
- Provided secretarial support

INTERNSHIP EXPERIENCE Beverly Hilton Hotel, Beverly Hills, CA Spring 2009
Intern
- Conducted research for potential campaigns
- Interacted with guests and business partners
- Wrote restaurant reviews and other press kit items
- Performed general office duties

HONORS AND AWARDS Susan G. Komen, Newport Beach, CA October 2008–present
- Raise funds
- Organize local 5K Race for the Cure
- Was named "Volunteer of the Month" in Spring 2009

LANGUAGES Spanish (understand and read)
French (near-native fluency)

PROFESSIONAL MEMBERSHIPS American Marketing Association (Member)
Public Relations Association of America (Treasurer)

ACTIVITIES Enjoy watching films, reading, running, and travel

Uses larger type and bold underline to enhance appearance
Uses professional-sounding address
Responds to specific job advertisement
Highlights skills named in advertisement
Uses bulleted lists to make résumé easier to read
Quantifies descriptions of experience

FIGURE 15.9 Chronological Résumé: University Graduate With Substantial Experience

Because Rachel has many years of experience and seeks executive-level employment, she highlighted her experience by placing it before her education. Her summary of qualifications highlighted her most impressive experience and skills. This chronological two-page résumé shows the steady progression of her career to executive positions, a movement that impresses and reassures recruiters.

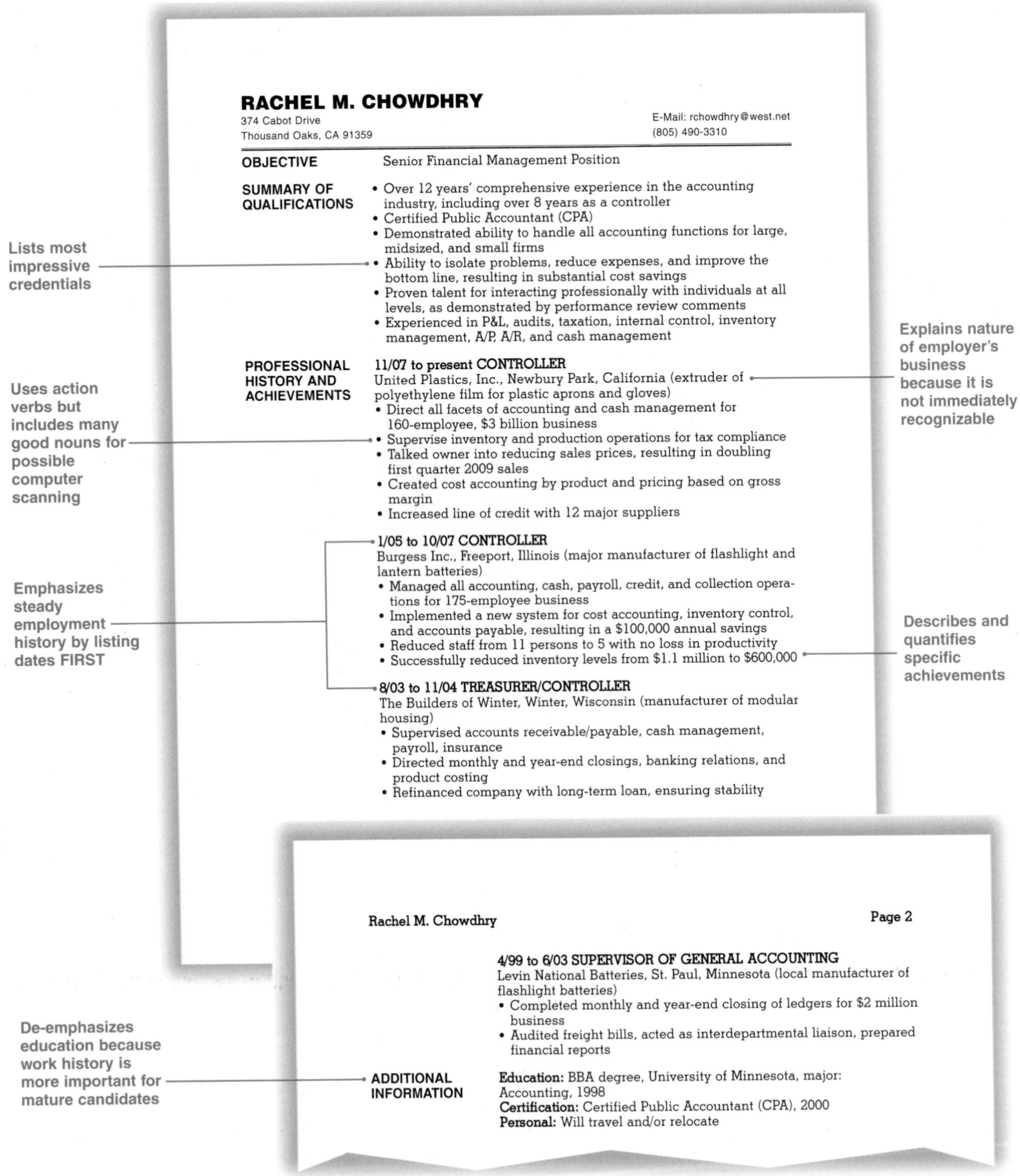
RACHEL M. CHOWDHRY
374 Cabot Drive
Thousand Oaks, CA 91359
E-Mail: rchowdhry@west.net
(805) 490-3310

OBJECTIVE Senior Financial Management Position

SUMMARY OF QUALIFICATIONS
- Over 12 years' comprehensive experience in the accounting industry, including over 8 years as a controller
- Certified Public Accountant (CPA)
- Demonstrated ability to handle all accounting functions for large, midsized, and small firms
- Ability to isolate problems, reduce expenses, and improve the bottom line, resulting in substantial cost savings
- Proven talent for interacting professionally with individuals at all levels, as demonstrated by performance review comments
- Experienced in P&L, audits, taxation, internal control, inventory management, A/P, A/R, and cash management

PROFESSIONAL HISTORY AND ACHIEVEMENTS

11/07 to present CONTROLLER
United Plastics, Inc., Newbury Park, California (extruder of polyethylene film for plastic aprons and gloves)
- Direct all facets of accounting and cash management for 160-employee, $3 billion business
- Supervise inventory and production operations for tax compliance
- Talked owner into reducing sales prices, resulting in doubling first quarter 2009 sales
- Created cost accounting by product and pricing based on gross margin
- Increased line of credit with 12 major suppliers

1/05 to 10/07 CONTROLLER
Burgess Inc., Freeport, Illinois (major manufacturer of flashlight and lantern batteries)
- Managed all accounting, cash, payroll, credit, and collection operations for 175-employee business
- Implemented a new system for cost accounting, inventory control, and accounts payable, resulting in a $100,000 annual savings
- Reduced staff from 11 persons to 5 with no loss in productivity
- Successfully reduced inventory levels from $1.1 million to $600,000

8/03 to 11/04 TREASURER/CONTROLLER
The Builders of Winter, Winter, Wisconsin (manufacturer of modular housing)
- Supervised accounts receivable/payable, cash management, payroll, insurance
- Directed monthly and year-end closings, banking relations, and product costing
- Refinanced company with long-term loan, ensuring stability

Rachel M. Chowdhry Page 2

4/99 to 6/03 SUPERVISOR OF GENERAL ACCOUNTING
Levin National Batteries, St. Paul, Minnesota (local manufacturer of flashlight batteries)
- Completed monthly and year-end closing of ledgers for $2 million business
- Audited freight bills, acted as interdepartmental liaison, prepared financial reports

ADDITIONAL INFORMATION
Education: BBA degree, University of Minnesota, major: Accounting, 1998
Certification: Certified Public Accountant (CPA), 2000
Personal: Will travel and/or relocate

Lists most impressive credentials
Explains nature of employer's business because it is not immediately recognizable
Uses action verbs but includes many good nouns for possible computer scanning
Emphasizes steady employment history by listing dates FIRST
Describes and quantifies specific achievements
De-emphasizes education because work history is more important for mature candidates

FIGURE 15.10 **Functional Résumé: Recent College Graduate With Unrelated Part-Time Experience**

Recent graduate Kevin Touhy chose this functional format to de-emphasize his meager work experience and emphasize his potential in sales and marketing. This version of his résumé is more generic than one targeted for a specific position. Yet, it emphasizes his strong points with specific achievements and includes an employment section to satisfy recruiters.

The functional format presents ability-focused topics. It illustrates what the job seeker can do for the employer instead of narrating a history of previous jobs. Although recruiters prefer chronological résumés, the functional format is a good choice for new graduates, career changers, and those with employment gaps.

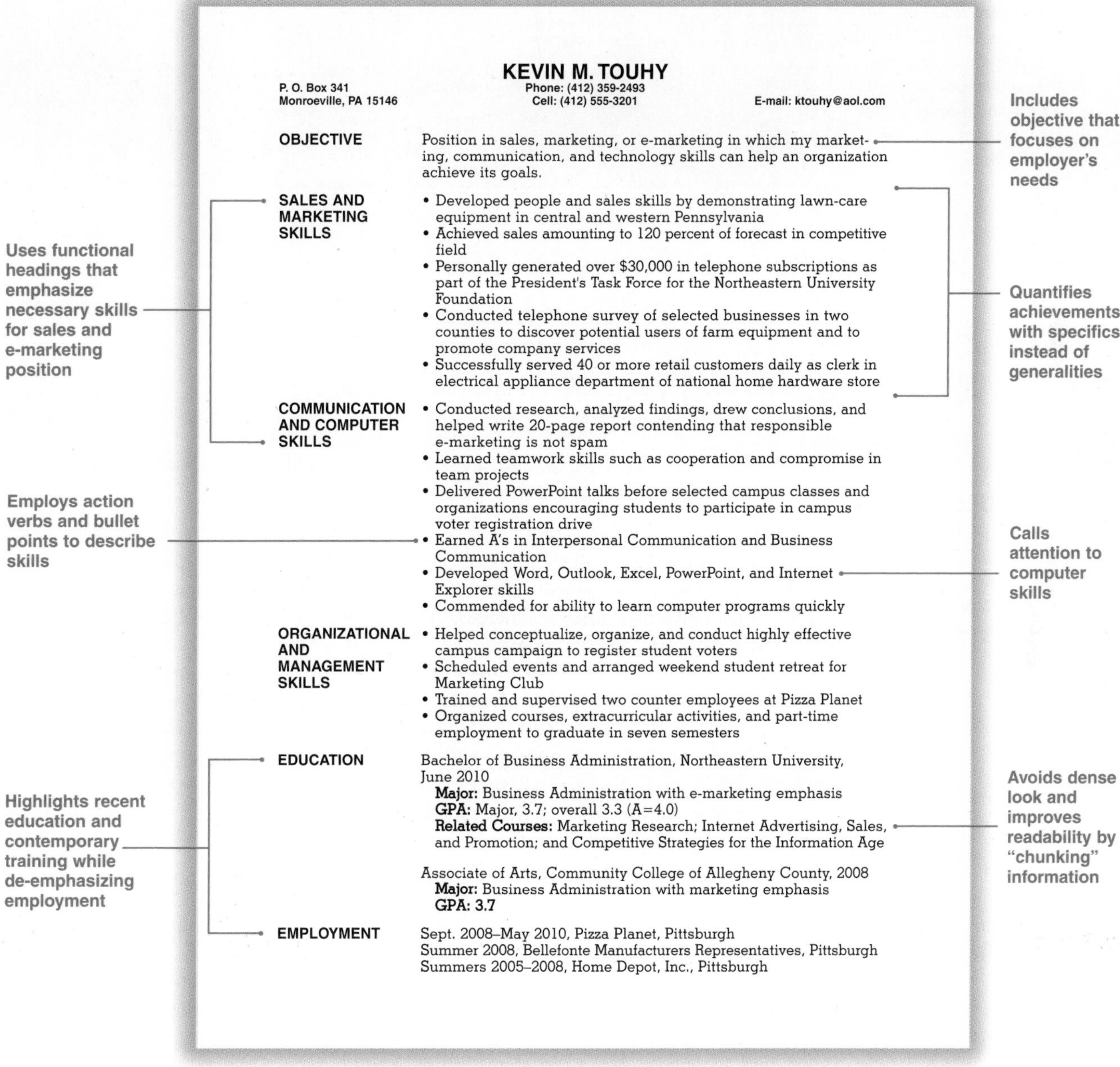

KEVIN M. TOUHY

P. O. Box 341
Monroeville, PA 15146

Phone: (412) 359-2493
Cell: (412) 555-3201

E-mail: ktouhy@aol.com

OBJECTIVE — Position in sales, marketing, or e-marketing in which my marketing, communication, and technology skills can help an organization achieve its goals.

SALES AND MARKETING SKILLS
- Developed people and sales skills by demonstrating lawn-care equipment in central and western Pennsylvania
- Achieved sales amounting to 120 percent of forecast in competitive field
- Personally generated over $30,000 in telephone subscriptions as part of the President's Task Force for the Northeastern University Foundation
- Conducted telephone survey of selected businesses in two counties to discover potential users of farm equipment and to promote company services
- Successfully served 40 or more retail customers daily as clerk in electrical appliance department of national home hardware store

COMMUNICATION AND COMPUTER SKILLS
- Conducted research, analyzed findings, drew conclusions, and helped write 20-page report contending that responsible e-marketing is not spam
- Learned teamwork skills such as cooperation and compromise in team projects
- Delivered PowerPoint talks before selected campus classes and organizations encouraging students to participate in campus voter registration drive
- Earned A's in Interpersonal Communication and Business Communication
- Developed Word, Outlook, Excel, PowerPoint, and Internet Explorer skills
- Commended for ability to learn computer programs quickly

ORGANIZATIONAL AND MANAGEMENT SKILLS
- Helped conceptualize, organize, and conduct highly effective campus campaign to register student voters
- Scheduled events and arranged weekend student retreat for Marketing Club
- Trained and supervised two counter employees at Pizza Planet
- Organized courses, extracurricular activities, and part-time employment to graduate in seven semesters

EDUCATION
Bachelor of Business Administration, Northeastern University, June 2010
Major: Business Administration with e-marketing emphasis
GPA: Major, 3.7; overall 3.3 (A=4.0)
Related Courses: Marketing Research; Internet Advertising, Sales, and Promotion; and Competitive Strategies for the Information Age

Associate of Arts, Community College of Allegheny County, 2008
Major: Business Administration with marketing emphasis
GPA: 3.7

EMPLOYMENT
Sept. 2008–May 2010, Pizza Planet, Pittsburgh
Summer 2008, Bellefonte Manufacturers Representatives, Pittsburgh
Summers 2005–2008, Home Depot, Inc., Pittsburgh

Includes objective that focuses on employer's needs
Uses functional headings that emphasize necessary skills for sales and e-marketing position
Quantifies achievements with specifics instead of generalities
Employs action verbs and bullet points to describe skills
Calls attention to computer skills
Highlights recent education and contemporary training while de-emphasizing employment
Avoids dense look and improves readability by "chunking" information

Online job boards, e-portfolios, and online videos are making it easier than ever for job seekers and employers to connect. For applicants, uploading video résumés to YouTube, Alumwire, or other recruiting sites is an effective way to supplement traditional print résumés. For employers, viewing video résumés streamlines the interview selection process, saving time and money. *What are the pros and cons of adding a video component to your résumé submission?*

© AFP PHOTO/ROBYN BECK/Newscom

Optimizing Your Résumé for Today's Technologies

LEARNING OBJECTIVE 5
Describe techniques that optimize a résumé for today's technologies, including preparing a scannable résumé, a plain-text résumé, and an e-portfolio.

Thus far we have aimed our résumé advice at human readers. However, the first reader of your résumé may well be a computer. Hiring organizations today use a variety of methods to process incoming résumés. Some organizations still welcome traditional print-based résumés that may include attractive formatting. Larger organizations, however, must deal with thousands of incoming résumés. Increasingly, they are placing those résumés directly into searchable databases. To optimize your chances, you may need three versions of your résumé: (a) a traditional print-based résumé, (b) a scannable résumé, and (c) a plain-text résumé for e-mailing and online posting. This does not mean that you have to write different résumés. You are merely preparing different versions of your traditional résumé. With all versions, you should also be aware of the significant role of résumé keywords. You may decide to create an e-portfolio to showcase your qualifications. You may also decide to prepare a professional video résumé to describe your skills. However, a video résumé is generally used as a supplement to, not a substitute for, a traditional résumé.

What three versions of résumés do you need today, and why?

Designing a Print-Based Résumé

Print-based résumés (also called *presentation résumés*) are attractively formatted to maximize readability. You can create a professional-looking résumé by using your word processing program to highlight your qualifications. The Résumé Gallery in this chapter provides ideas for simple layouts that are easily duplicated. You can also examine résumé templates for design and format ideas. Their inflexibility, however, may lead to frustration as you try to force your skills and experience into a predetermined template sequence. What's more, recruiters who read hundreds of résumés can usually spot a template-based résumé. Instead, create your own original résumé that fits your unique qualifications.

When is a print-based résumé needed?

Your print-based résumé should follow an outline format with headings and bullet points to present information in an orderly, uncluttered, easy-to-read format. An attractive print-based résumé is necessary (a) when you are competing for a job that does not require electronic submission, (b) to present in addition to an electronic submission, and (c) to bring with you to job interviews. Even if a résumé is submitted electronically, nearly every job candidate will want to have an attractive printed résumé handy for human readers.

Preparing a Scannable Résumé

A scannable résumé is one that is printed on plain white paper and scanned by a computer. According to Pat Kendall, president of the National Resume Writers' Association, more than 80 percent of résumés are scanned by companies using automated applicant-tracking software.[34] These systems scan an incoming résumé with optical character recognition (OCR) looking for keywords or keyword phrases. The most sophisticated programs enable recruiters and hiring managers to rank résumés based on the number of "hits" and generate reports. Information from your résumé is stored, usually from six months to a year.

What is a scannable résumé, and how does is differ from a traditional print-based résumé?

Before sending your résumé, find out whether the recipient uses scanning software. If you can't tell from the job announcement, call the company to ask whether it scans résumés electronically. If you have even the slightest suspicion that your résumé might be read electronically, you will be smart to prepare a plain, scannable version as shown in Figure 15.11. Although current scanning software can read a résumé in any format, many companies still use older versions that have difficulty with complex fonts and formatting. Therefore, it pays to follow these tips for maximizing scannability and "hits."

Tips for Maximizing Scannability. A scannable résumé must sacrifice many of the graphic enhancements you might have used to make your print résumé attractive. To maximize scannability:

What can you do to maximize scannability of your résumé?

- **Use 10- to 14-point type.** Use a well-known font such as Times New Roman or Arial. The font size in the body of your résumé should be 10-, 11-, or 12-point, and headings should be no larger than 14-point.
- **Avoid fancy formatting.** Don't use underlining, italics, borders, shading, or other graphics to highlight text. These features don't scan well. Most applicant-tracking programs, however, can accurately read bold print, solid bullets, and asterisks.
- **Place your name on the first line.** Reports generated by applicant-tracking software usually assume that the first line of a résumé contains the applicant's name.
- **List each phone number on its own line.** Your landline and cell phone numbers should appear on separate lines to improve recognition.
- **Avoid double columns.** When listing job duties, skills, and so forth, don't tabulate items into two- or three-column lists. Scanners read across and may convert tables into nonsensical output.
- **Take care when printing and mailing.** When printing your scannable résumé for mailing, use smooth white paper and black ink and print it on a quality printer. Mail your résumé in a large envelope to avoid folding it. If your résumé is longer than one page, do not staple it.

Tips for Maximizing "Hits." In addition to paying attention to the physical appearance of your résumé, you must also be concerned with keywords or keyword phrases that produce "hits," or recognition by the scanner. The following tips will help you maximize hits:

What are keyword? What can you do to maximize "hits" of keywords and keyword phrases on your résumé?

- **Focus on specific keywords or keyword phrases.** Study carefully any advertisements and job descriptions for the position you want. Describe your experience, education, and qualifications in terms associated with the job advertisement or job description for this position. Select keywords or phrases that describe specific skills, traits, expertise, tasks, and job titles.
- **Use accurate names.** Spell out complete names of schools, degrees, and dates. Include specific names of companies, products, and services as appropriate.
- **Be careful of abbreviations and acronyms.** Spell out unfamiliar abbreviations and acronyms, but maximize easily recognized abbreviations and acronyms—especially those within your field, such as CAD, JPG, or JIT.
- **Describe interpersonal traits and attitudes.** Hiring managers look for keywords and phrases that describe interpersonal traits and attitudes that are related to the specific position.

FIGURE 15.11 Scannable Résumé

Leticia P. Lopez prepared this plain résumé free of graphics and fancy formatting so that it would scan well if read by a computer. Within the résumé, she included many job titles, skills, traits, and other descriptive keywords that scanners are programmed to recognize. To improve accurate scanning, she avoided bullets, italics, underlining, and columns. If she had had more information to include, she could have gone on to a second page since a résumé to be scanned need not be restricted to one page.

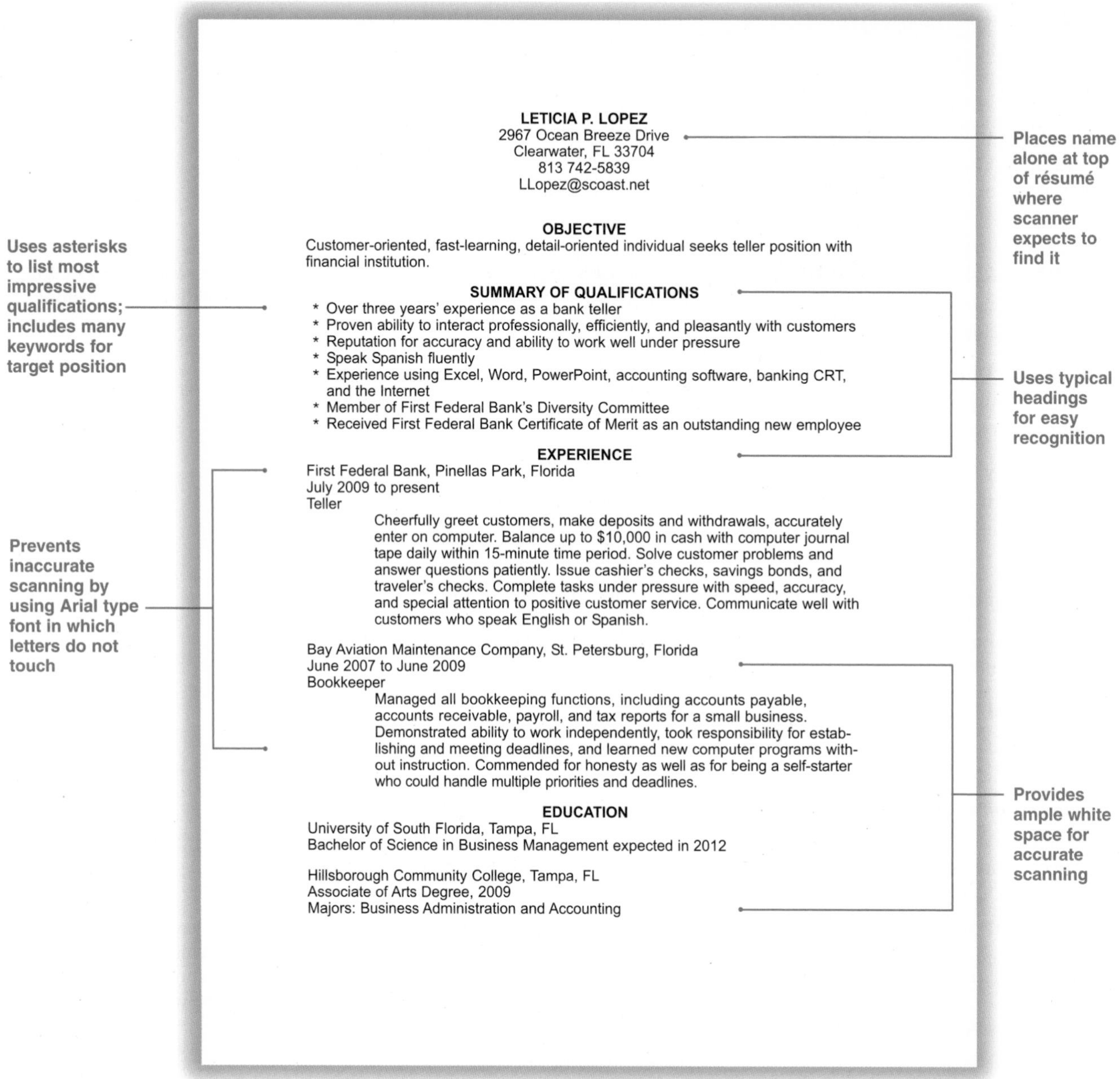

LETICIA P. LOPEZ
2967 Ocean Breeze Drive
Clearwater, FL 33704
813 742-5839
LLopez@scoast.net

OBJECTIVE

Customer-oriented, fast-learning, detail-oriented individual seeks teller position with financial institution.

SUMMARY OF QUALIFICATIONS

* Over three years' experience as a bank teller
* Proven ability to interact professionally, efficiently, and pleasantly with customers
* Reputation for accuracy and ability to work well under pressure
* Speak Spanish fluently
* Experience using Excel, Word, PowerPoint, accounting software, banking CRT, and the Internet
* Member of First Federal Bank's Diversity Committee
* Received First Federal Bank Certificate of Merit as an outstanding new employee

EXPERIENCE

First Federal Bank, Pinellas Park, Florida
July 2009 to present
Teller

Cheerfully greet customers, make deposits and withdrawals, accurately enter on computer. Balance up to $10,000 in cash with computer journal tape daily within 15-minute time period. Solve customer problems and answer questions patiently. Issue cashier's checks, savings bonds, and traveler's checks. Complete tasks under pressure with speed, accuracy, and special attention to positive customer service. Communicate well with customers who speak English or Spanish.

Bay Aviation Maintenance Company, St. Petersburg, Florida
June 2007 to June 2009
Bookkeeper

Managed all bookkeeping functions, including accounts payable, accounts receivable, payroll, and tax reports for a small business. Demonstrated ability to work independently, took responsibility for establishing and meeting deadlines, and learned new computer programs without instruction. Commended for honesty as well as for being a self-starter who could handle multiple priorities and deadlines.

EDUCATION

University of South Florida, Tampa, FL
Bachelor of Science in Business Management expected in 2012

Hillsborough Community College, Tampa, FL
Associate of Arts Degree, 2009
Majors: Business Administration and Accounting

Places name alone at top of résumé where scanner expects to find it
Uses asterisks to list most impressive qualifications; includes many keywords for target position
Uses typical headings for easy recognition
Prevents inaccurate scanning by using Arial type font in which letters do not touch
Provides ample white space for accurate scanning

Preparing a Plain-Text Résumé

Why do many employers prefer that a résumé be included in the body of an e-mail message rather than attached to it?

A plain-text résumé is an electronic version suitable for e-mailing or pasting into online résumé bank submission forms. Employers prefer plain-text résumés because they avoid possible e-mail viruses and word processing incompatibilities. Usually included in the body of an e-mail message, a plain-text résumé, shown in Figure 15.12, is immediately searchable. You should prepare a plain-text résumé if you want the fastest and most reliable way to contact potential employers. To create a plain-text résumé, follow these suggestions:

- **Observe all the tips for a scannable résumé.** A plain-text résumé requires the same attention to content, formatting, and keywords as that recommended for a scannable résumé.

FIGURE 15.12 Plain-Text Résumé

To be sure her résumé would transmit well when embedded within an e-mail message. Leticia prepared a special version with all lines starting at the left margin. She used a 4-inch line length to avoid awkward line breaks. To set off her major headings, she used the tilde character on her keyboard. She saved the document as a text file (.txt or .rtf) so that it could be read by various computers. At the end she included a statement saying that an attractive. Fully formatted hard copy of her résumé was available on request.

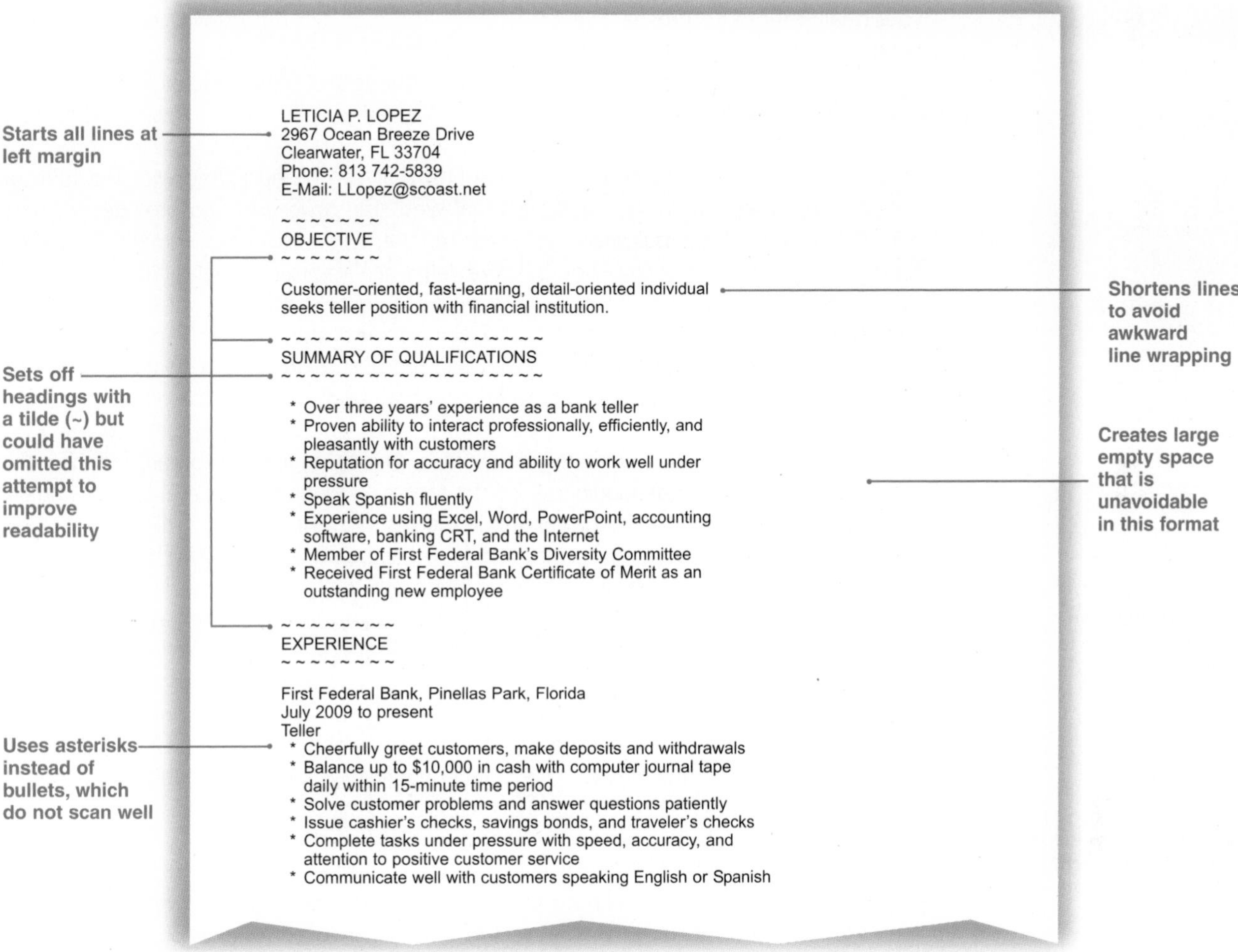

Starts all lines at left margin
Sets off headings with a tilde (~) but could have omitted this attempt to improve readability
Uses asterisks instead of bullets, which do not scan well
Shortens lines to avoid awkward line wrapping
Creates large empty space that is unavoidable in this format
LETICIA P. LOPEZ
2967 Ocean Breeze Drive
Clearwater, FL 33704
Phone: 813 742-5839
E-Mail: LLopez@scoast.net
~ ~ ~ ~ ~ ~ ~
OBJECTIVE
~ ~ ~ ~ ~ ~ ~
Customer-oriented, fast-learning, detail-oriented individual seeks teller position with financial institution.
~ ~ ~ ~ ~ ~ ~ ~ ~ ~ ~ ~ ~ ~ ~ ~ ~ ~ ~
SUMMARY OF QUALIFICATIONS
~ ~ ~ ~ ~ ~ ~ ~ ~ ~ ~ ~ ~ ~ ~ ~ ~ ~ ~
* Over three years' experience as a bank teller
* Proven ability to interact professionally, efficiently, and pleasantly with customers
* Reputation for accuracy and ability to work well under pressure
* Speak Spanish fluently
* Experience using Excel, Word, PowerPoint, accounting software, banking CRT, and the Internet
* Member of First Federal Bank's Diversity Committee
* Received First Federal Bank Certificate of Merit as an outstanding new employee
~ ~ ~ ~ ~ ~ ~ ~
EXPERIENCE
~ ~ ~ ~ ~ ~ ~ ~
First Federal Bank, Pinellas Park, Florida
July 2009 to present
Teller
* Cheerfully greet customers, make deposits and withdrawals
* Balance up to $10,000 in cash with computer journal tape daily within 15-minute time period
* Solve customer problems and answer questions patiently
* Issue cashier's checks, savings bonds, and traveler's checks
* Complete tasks under pressure with speed, accuracy, and attention to positive customer service
* Communicate well with customers speaking English or Spanish

- **Reformat with shorter lines.** Many e-mail programs wrap lines longer than 65 characters. To avoid having your résumé look as if a chain saw attacked it, use short lines.
- **Think about using keyboard characters to enhance format.** In addition to using capital letters and asterisks, you might use spaced equals signs (= = =) and tildes (~ ~ ~) to create lines that separate résumé categories.
- **Move all text to the left.** Do not center items; start all text at the left margin. Remove tabs.
- **Save your résumé in plain-text (.txt) or rich text format (.rtf).** Saving your résumé in one of these formats will ensure that it can be read when pasted into an e-mail message.
- **Test your résumé before sending it to an employer.** After preparing and saving your résumé, copy and paste a copy of it into an e-mail message and send it to yourself to make sure that it looks professional. Make any necessary changes.

When sending a plain-text résumé to an employer, be sure that your subject line clearly describes the purpose of your message.

Showcasing Your Qualifications in an E-Portfolio or a Video Résumé

What is an e-portfolio, and how can it benefit you?

As the workplace becomes increasingly digital, you have yet another way to display your qualifications to prospective employers—the digitized e-portfolio. Resourceful job candidates in certain fields—writers, models, artists, and graphic artists—have been creating print portfolios to illustrate their qualifications and achievements for some time. Now business and professional job candidates are using electronic portfolios to show off their talents.

An e-portfolio is a collection of digital files that can be navigated with the help of menus and hyperlinks much like a personal Web site. An e-portfolio provides viewers with a snapshot of a candidate's performance, talents, and accomplishments. A digital portfolio may include a copy of your résumé, reference letters, commendations for special achievements, awards, certificates, work samples, a complete list of your courses, thank-you letters, and anything else that touts your accomplishments. An e-portfolio might include links to digital copies of your artwork, film projects, videos, blueprints, documents, photographs, multimedia files, and blog entries that might otherwise be difficult to share with potential employers.

E-portfolios are generally accessed at Web sites, where they are available around the clock to employers. Some colleges and universities not only make Web site space available for student e-portfolios, but also provide instruction and resources for scanning photos, digitizing images, and preparing graphics. E-portfolios may also be burned onto CDs and DVDs to be mailed to prospective employers.

How can you make an e-portfolio available to potential employers?

E-portfolios have many advantages. On Web sites they can be viewed at an employer's convenience. Let's say you are talking on the phone with an employer in another city who wants to see a copy of your résumé. You can simply refer the employer to the Web address where your résumé resides. E-portfolios can also be seen by many individuals in an organization without circulating a paper copy. But the real reason for preparing an e-portfolio is that it shows off your talents and qualifications more thoroughly than a print résumé does.

How can you use a video résumé during your job search?

Tech-savvy applicants even use videos to profile their skills. A professional-grade video résumé may open doors and secure an interview when other techniques have failed.[35] However, some recruiters are skeptical about digital or video portfolios because they fear that such applications will take more time to view than paper-based résumés do. Nontraditional applications may end up at the bottom of the pile or be ignored. Worse yet, lack of judgment can lead to embarrassment. In a now-legendary case, Aleksey Vayner's video résumé somehow ended up on YouTube in late 2006, causing him to be widely ridiculed. The Yale senior and budding investment banker concocted a six-minute video titled "Impossible Is Nothing," showing him boisterously lifting weights, ballroom dancing, and playing tennis, all the while engaging in shameless puffery.[36]

Experts agree that the new medium will need to mature before smart guidelines can be established. You can learn more about video résumés by searching the Web.

Applying the Final Touches to Your Résumé

Because your résumé is probably the most important message you will ever write, you will revise it many times. With so much information in concentrated form and with so much riding on its outcome, your résumé demands careful polishing, proofreading, and critiquing.

As you revise, be certain to verify all the facts, particularly those involving your previous employment and education. Don't be caught in a mistake, or worse, a distortion of previous jobs and dates of employment. These items likely will be checked, and the consequences of puffing up a résumé with deception or flat-out lies are simply not worth the risk. The Ethical Insights box on page 523 outlines dangerous areas to avoid.

Polishing Your Résumé

What steps should you take to improve your résumé?

While you continue revising, look for other ways to improve your résumé. For example, consider consolidating headings. By condensing your information into as few headings as possible, you will produce a clean, professional-looking document. Study other résumés for valuable formatting ideas. Ask yourself what graphic highlighting techniques you can use to improve readability: capitalization, underlining, indenting, and bulleting. Experiment with headings and styles to achieve a pleasing, easy-to-read message. Moreover, look for ways to eliminate wordiness. For example, instead of *Supervised two employees who worked at the counter*, try *Supervised two counter employees*. Review Chapter 5 for more tips on writing concisely.

In addition to making your résumé concise, make sure that you haven't included any of the following information, which doesn't belong on a résumé:

- Any basis for discrimination (age, marital status, gender, national origin, religion, race, number of children, disability)
- A photograph
- Reasons for leaving previous jobs
- The word *résumé*
- Social security number
- Salary history or requirements
- High school information
- References
- Full addresses of schools or employers (include city and state only)

Above all, make sure your print-based résumé looks professional. Avoid anything humorous or "cute," such as a help-wanted poster with your name or picture inside. Eliminate the personal pronoun *I* to ensure an objective style. Use high-quality paper in a professional color, such as white, off-white, or light gray. Print your résumé using a first-rate printer. Be prepared with a résumé for people to read as well as versions for computer scanning, sending by e-mail, and posting to Web sites.

ETHICS CHECK

Résumé Fibbing

Insecure entry-level workers are not the only job seekers who sometimes feel tempted to fudge the facts. RadioShack's CEO David Edmondson had to resign after it was found that he had incorrectly claimed to have two academic degrees. Are such lies always wrong, or can you imagine extenuating circumstances, such as when the dishonest employee or executive is highly effective?

Proofreading Your Résumé

Why is it so important to proofread your résumé until it is perfect?

After revising, you must proofread, proofread, and proofread again for spelling, grammar, mechanics, content, and format. Then have a knowledgeable friend or relative proofread it yet again. This is one document that must be perfect. Because the job market is so competitive, one typo, misspelled word, or grammatical error could eliminate you from consideration.

By now you may be thinking that you'd like to hire someone to write your résumé. Don't! First, you know yourself better than anyone else could know you. Second, you will end up with either a generic or a one-time résumé. A generic résumé in today's highly competitive job market will lose out to a customized résumé nine times out of ten. Equally useless is a one-time résumé aimed at a single job. What if you don't get that job? Because you will need to revise your résumé many times as you seek a variety of jobs, be prepared to write (and rewrite) it yourself.

Submitting Your Résumé

What are some popular ways of submitting résumés to employers?

If you are responding to a job advertisement, be sure to read the listing carefully to make sure you know how the employer wants you to submit your résumé. Not following the prospective employer's instructions can eliminate you from consideration before your résumé is even reviewed. Employers will probably ask you to submit your résumé as a Word, plain-text, or PDF document. You may also be asked to submit it in the company database or by fax.

- **Word document.** Recruiters may still ask candidates to send their résumés and cover letters by surface mail. They may also allow applicants to attach their résumés as MS Word documents to e-mail messages, despite the fear of viruses.
- **Plain-text document.** As discussed earlier, some employers expect applicants to submit résumés and cover letters as plain-text documents. This format is widely used for posting to an online job board or for sending by e-mail. Plain-text résumés may be embedded within or attached to e-mail messages.

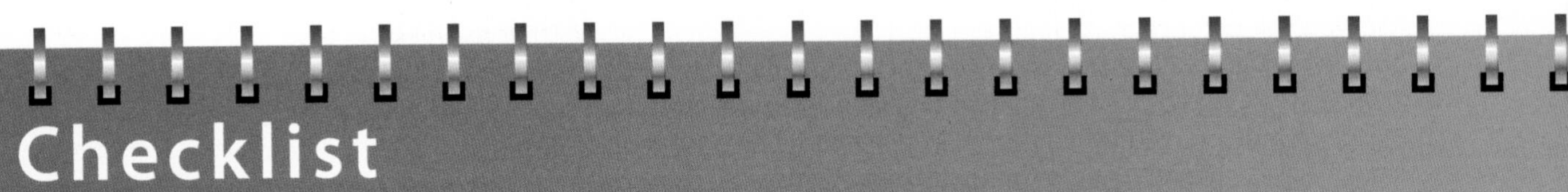

Checklist

Preparing for Employment and Submitting a Customized Résumé

Preparation

- **Research the job market.** Learn about available jobs, common qualifications, and potential employers. The best résumés are customized for specific jobs with specific companies.
- **Analyze your strengths.** Determine what aspects of your education, experience, and personal characteristics will be assets to prospective employers.
- **Study models.** Look at other résumés for formatting and element placement ideas. Experiment with headings and styles to achieve a creative, readable product.

Heading, Objective, and Summary

- **Identify yourself.** List your name, address, telephone number, and e-mail address.
- **Include a career objective for a targeted job.** Use an objective only if it is intended for a specific job (*Objective: Junior cost accountant position in the petroleum industry*).
- **Prepare a summary of qualifications.** Include a list of three to eight bulleted statements that prove you are the ideal candidate for the position.

Education

- **Name your degree, date of graduation, and institution.** Emphasize your education if your experience is limited.
- **List your major and GPA.** Give information about your studies, but don't inventory all your courses.

Work Experience

- **Itemize your jobs.** Start with your most recent job. Give the employer's name and city, dates of employment (month, year), and most significant job title.
- **Describe your experience.** Use action verbs to summarize achievements and skills relevant to your targeted job.
- **Promote your "soft" skills.** Give evidence of communication, management, and interpersonal talents. Employers want more than empty assurances; try to quantify your skills and accomplishments (*Developed teamwork skills while collaborating with six-member task force in producing 20-page mission statement*).

Special Skills, Achievements, and Awards

- **Highlight your technology skills.** Remember that nearly all employers seek employees who are proficient in using the Web, e-mail, word processing, databases, spreadsheets, and presentation programs.
- **Show that you are a well-rounded individual.** List awards, experiences, and extracurricular activities—particularly if they demonstrate leadership, teamwork, reliability, loyalty, industry, initiative, efficiency, and self-sufficiency.

Final Tips

- **Look for ways to condense your data.** Omit all street addresses except your own. Consolidate your headings. Study models and experiment with formats to find the most readable and efficient groupings.
- **Double-check for parallel phrasing.** Be sure that all entries have balanced construction, such as similar verb forms (*Organized files, trained assistants, scheduled events*).
- **Make your résumé computer friendly.** If there's a chance your résumé will be read by a computer, be sure to remove graphics and emphasize keywords.
- **Consider omitting references.** Have a list of references available for the interview, but don't include them or refer to them on your résumé unless you have a specific reason to do so.
- **Project professionalism and quality.** Avoid personal pronouns and humor. Use quality paper and a high-performance printer.
- **Resist the urge to inflate your qualifications.** Be accurate in listing your education, grades, honors, job titles, employment dates, and job experience.
- **Proofread, proofread, proofread!** Make this important document perfect by proofreading at least three times. Ask a friend to check it, too.

Submitting

- **Follow instructions for submitting.** Learn whether the employer wants candidates to send a print résumé, a plain-text version, a PDF file, or a fax.
- **Practice sending plain-text résumés.** Before submitting a plain-text résumé, try sending it to yourself or friends. Perfect your skill in achieving an attractive format.

- **PDF document.** For safety reasons, many employers prefer PDF (portable document format) files. A PDF résumé will look exactly like the original and cannot be altered. Most computers have Adobe Acrobat Reader installed for easy reading of PDF files. Converting your résumé to a PDF file, however, requires Adobe software.

ETHICAL INSIGHT

Are Inflated Résumés Worth the Risk?

A résumé is expected to showcase a candidate's strengths and minimize weaknesses. For this reason, recruiters expect a certain degree of self-promotion. Some résumé writers, however, step over the line that separates honest self-marketing from deceptive half-truths and flat-out lies. Distorting facts on a résumé is unethical; lying is illegal. Most important, either practice can destroy a career.

Given the competitive job market, it might be tempting to puff up your résumé. You would not be alone in telling fibs or outright whoppers. A recent survey of 8,700 workers found that only 8 percent admitted to lying on their résumés; however, the same study found that of the 3,100 hiring managers surveyed, 49 percent caught a job applicant lying on some part of his or her résumé. And 57 percent of employers will automatically dismiss applicants who lie on any part of their résumés. According to Rosemary Haefner, vice president of Human Resources for CareerBuilder.com, "Even the slightest embellishment can come back to haunt you and ruin your credibility. If you're concerned about gaps in employment, your academic background or skill sets, invention is not the answer."[37] Although recruiters can't check everything, most will verify previous employment and education before hiring candidates. Over half will require official transcripts.

After hiring, the checking process may continue. If hiring officials find a discrepancy in GPA or prior experience and the error is an honest mistake, they meet with the new-hire to hear an explanation. If the discrepancy wasn't a mistake, they will likely fire the person immediately. No job seeker wants to be in the unhappy position of explaining résumé errors or defending misrepresentation. Avoiding the following problems can keep you off the hot seat:

- **Inflated education, grades, or honors.** Some job candidates claim degrees from colleges or universities when in fact they merely attended classes. Others increase their grade point averages or claim fictitious honors. Any such dishonest reporting is grounds for dismissal when discovered.
- **Enhanced job titles.** Wishing to elevate their status, some applicants misrepresent their titles. For example, one technician called himself a programmer when he had actually programmed only one project for his boss. A mail clerk who assumed added responsibilities conferred upon herself the title of supervisor. Even when the description seems accurate, it is unethical to list any title not officially granted.
- **Puffed-up accomplishments.** Some job seekers inflate their employment experience or achievements. One clerk, eager to make her photocopying duties sound more important, said that she assisted the *vice president in communicating and distributing employee directives.* An Ivy League graduate who spent the better part of six months watching rented videos on his DVD player described the activity as *Independent Film Study.* The latter statement may have helped win an interview, but it lost him the job. In addition to avoiding puffery, guard against taking sole credit for achievements that required many people. When recruiters suspect dubious claims on résumés, they nail applicants with specific—and often embarrassing—questions during their interviews.
- **Altered employment dates.** Some candidates extend the dates of employment to hide unimpressive jobs or to cover up periods of unemployment and illness. Let's say that several years ago Cindy was unemployed for 14 months between working for Company A and being hired by Company B. To make her employment history look better, she adds seven months to her tenure with Company A and seven months to Company B. Now her employment history has no gaps, but her résumé is dishonest and represents a potential booby trap for her.
- **Hidden keywords.** One of the latest sneaky tricks involves inserting invisible keywords into electronic résumés. To fool scanning programs into ranking their résumés higher, some job hunters use white type on a white background, or they use Web coding to pack their résumés with target keywords. However, newer recruiter search tools detect such mischief, and those résumés are tossed.[38]

If your honest qualifications aren't good enough to get you the job you want, start working now to improve them. No job seeker should want to be hired based on lies.

Career Application

As a class, discuss the ethics of writing résumés. What's the difference between honest self-marketing and deception? What are some examples from your experience? Where could college students go wrong in preparing their résumés? Is a new employee "home free" if an inflated résumé is not detected in the hiring process? Are job candidates obligated to describe every previous job on a résumé? How can candidates improve an unimpressive résumé without resorting to "puffing it up"?

- **Company database.** Some organizations prefer that you complete an online form with your résumé information. This enables them to plug your data into their formats for rapid searching. You might be able to cut and paste your information into the form.
- **Fax.** Although still a popular way of sending résumés, faxing presents problems such as blurry text and lost information. If you must fax your résumé, use at least 12-point font to improve readability. Thinner fonts—such as Times, Palatino, New Century Schoolbook, Arial, and Bookman—are clearer than thicker ones. Avoid underlines, which may look broken or choppy when faxed. Follow up with your polished, printed résumé.

Creating a Customized, Persuasive Cover Letter

LEARNING OBJECTIVE 6
Write a customized cover letter to accompany a résumé.

Job candidates often labor over their résumés but treat the cover letter as an afterthought. Some send out résumés without including a cover letter at all. These critical mistakes could destroy a job search. Even if an advertisement doesn't request one, be sure to distinguish your application with a customized cover letter (also called a *letter of application*). Some hiring managers won't even look at a résumé if it is not accompanied by a cover letter. A cover letter has three purposes: (a) introducing the résumé, (b) highlighting your strengths in terms of benefits to the reader, and (c) gaining an interview. In many ways your cover letter is a sales letter; it sells your talent and tries to beat the competition. It will, accordingly, include many of the techniques you learned for sales letters in Chapter 10, especially if your letter is unsolicited.

Recruiting professionals disagree about how long to make a cover letter. Many prefer short letters with no more than three paragraphs. Others desire longer letters that supply more information, thus giving them a better opportunity to evaluate a candidate's qualifications. These recruiters argue that hiring and training new employees is expensive and time consuming; therefore, they welcome extra data to guide them in making the best choice the first time. Follow your judgment in writing a brief or a longer cover letter. If you feel, for example, that you need space to explain in more detail what you can do for a prospective employer, do so.

How can you gain attention in the opening of a cover letter?

Regardless of its length, a cover letter should have three primary parts: (a) an opening that captures attention, introduces the message, and identifies the position; (b) a body that sells the candidate and focuses on the employer's needs; and (c) a closing that requests an interview and motivates action. When putting your cover letter together, remember that the biggest mistake job seekers make when writing cover letters is making them sound too generic. You should, therefore, write a personalized, customized cover letter for every position you apply for.

Spotlight on Communicators

Courtesy of Liz Ryan

How can you find a contact person in your targeted company? Career expert Liz Ryan suggests doing the following: (a) Use LinkedIn or another networking site and search for the target company name to find people who work there. (b) Search Google with a string such as *Apex+Foods+marketing+director.* (c) Use Google's blog search function to locate people in your target organization. (d) Check the online archive for the local business paper in the city where the company is located. (e) Search the archives at Yahoogroups.com. (f) Study the target company's Web site for the names of staffers involved in community and charity work. (g) Search the database of your school's alumni site for graduates who might be employed at the target company.

Gaining Attention in the Opening

Your cover letter will be more appealing, and will more likely be read, if it begins by addressing the reader by name. Rather than sending your letter to the *Hiring Manager* or *Human Resources Department*, try to identify the name of the appropriate individual. Kelly Renz, vice president for a recruiting outsourcing firm, says that savvy job seekers "take control of their application's destiny." She suggests looking on the company's Web site, doing an Internet search for a name, or calling the human resources department and asking the receptionist the name of the person in charge of hiring. Ms. Renz also suggests using professional networking sites such as LinkedIn to find someone working in the same department as the posted job. This person may know the name of the hiring manager.[39] See the accompanying Spotlight feature for additional ways to locate contacts within your target company. If you still cannot find the name of any person to address, you might replace the salutation of your letter with a descriptive subject line such as *Application for Marketing Specialist Position.*

How you open your cover letter depends largely on whether the application is solicited or unsolicited. If an employment position has been announced and applicants are being solicited, you can use a direct approach. If you do not know whether a position is open and you are prospecting for a job, use an indirect approach. Whether direct or indirect, the opening should attract the attention of the reader. Strive for openings that are more imaginative than *Please consider this letter an application for the position of . . .* or *I would like to apply for. . . .*

Openings for Solicited Jobs. When applying for a job that has been announced, consider some of the following techniques to open your cover letter:

How can you effectively open a cover letter that is written for a solicited job?

- **Refer to the name of an employee in the company.** Remember that employers always hope to hire known quantities rather than complete strangers.

  Mitchell Sims, a member of your Customer Service Department, told me that IntriPlex is seeking an experienced customer service representative. The enclosed summary of my qualifications demonstrates my preparation for this position.

  At the suggestion of Ms. Jennifer Larson of your Human Resources Department, I submit my qualifications for the position of staffing coordinator.

- **Refer to the source of your information precisely.** If you are answering an advertisement, include the exact position advertised and the name and date of the publication. If you are responding to a position listed on an online job board, include the Web site name and the date the position was posted:

  Your advertisement in Section C-3 of the June 1 Daily News for an accounting administrator greatly appeals to me. With my accounting training and computer experience, I am confident I could serve Quad Graphics well.

  From your company's Web site, I learned about your need for a sales representative for the Ohio, Indiana, and Illinois regions. I am very interested in this position and am confident that my education and experience are appropriate for the opening.

  Susan Butler, placement director at Sierra University, told me that DataTech has an opening for a technical writer with knowledge of Web design and graphics.

  My talent for interacting with people, coupled with more than five years of customer service experience, make me an ideal candidate for the director of customer relations position you advertised on the CareerJournal.com Web site on August 3.

- **Refer to the job title and describe how your qualifications fit the requirements.** Hiring managers are looking for a match between an applicant's credentials and the job needs:

  Will an honors graduate with a degree in recreation and two years of part-time experience organizing social activities for a convalescent hospital qualify for your position of activity director?

  Because of my specialized training in finance and accounting at Boise State University, I am confident that I have the qualifications you described in your advertisement for a staff accountant trainee.

How should you begin a cover letter written for an unsolicited job?

Openings for Unsolicited Jobs. If you are unsure whether a position actually exists, you might use a more persuasive opening. Because your goal is to convince this person to read on, try one of the following techniques:

- **Demonstrate an interest in and knowledge of the reader's business.** Show the hiring manager that you have done your research and that this organization is more than a mere name to you:

  Because Signa HealthNet, Inc., is organizing a new information management team for its recently established group insurance division, could you use the services of a well-trained information systems graduate who seeks to become a professional systems analyst?

- **Show how your special talents and background will benefit the company.** Human resources managers need to be convinced that you can do something for them:

  Could your rapidly expanding publications division use the services of an editorial assistant who offers exceptional language skills, an honors degree from the University of Maine, and two years' experience in producing a campus literary publication?

Do recruiters really read cover letters? Although some hiring managers ignore them, others read them carefully. Given the stiff competition for jobs today, making an effort to write a cover letter and to customize it for the position makes sense. Crafting a letter specifically for a job opening enables the job seeker to stand out from all those who skip this important step.

In applying for an advertised job, Kendra Hawkins wrote the solicited cover letter shown in Figure 15.13. Notice that her opening identifies the position and the newspaper completely so that the reader knows exactly what advertisement Kendra means. Using features on her word processing program, Kendra designed her own letterhead that uses her name and looks like professionally printed letterhead paper.

FIGURE 15.13 Solicited Cover Letter

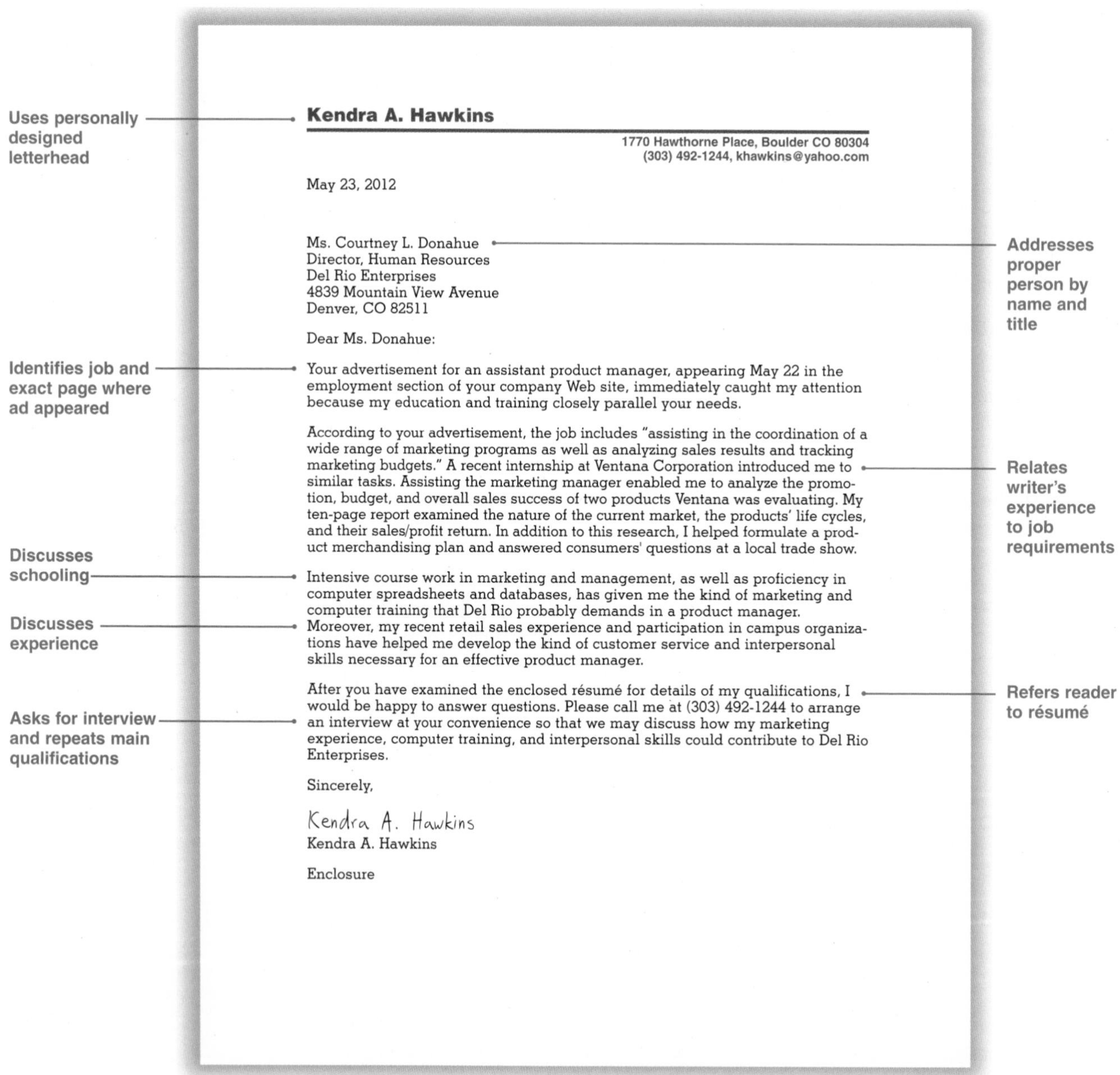

Kendra A. Hawkins

1770 Hawthorne Place, Boulder CO 80304
(303) 492-1244, khawkins@yahoo.com

May 23, 2012

Ms. Courtney L. Donahue
Director, Human Resources
Del Rio Enterprises
4839 Mountain View Avenue
Denver, CO 82511

Dear Ms. Donahue:

Your advertisement for an assistant product manager, appearing May 22 in the employment section of your company Web site, immediately caught my attention because my education and training closely parallel your needs.

According to your advertisement, the job includes "assisting in the coordination of a wide range of marketing programs as well as analyzing sales results and tracking marketing budgets." A recent internship at Ventana Corporation introduced me to similar tasks. Assisting the marketing manager enabled me to analyze the promotion, budget, and overall sales success of two products Ventana was evaluating. My ten-page report examined the nature of the current market, the products' life cycles, and their sales/profit return. In addition to this research, I helped formulate a product merchandising plan and answered consumers' questions at a local trade show.

Intensive course work in marketing and management, as well as proficiency in computer spreadsheets and databases, has given me the kind of marketing and computer training that Del Rio probably demands in a product manager. Moreover, my recent retail sales experience and participation in campus organizations have helped me develop the kind of customer service and interpersonal skills necessary for an effective product manager.

After you have examined the enclosed résumé for details of my qualifications, I would be happy to answer questions. Please call me at (303) 492-1244 to arrange an interview at your convenience so that we may discuss how my marketing experience, computer training, and interpersonal skills could contribute to Del Rio Enterprises.

Sincerely,

Kendra A. Hawkins

Kendra A. Hawkins

Enclosure

FIGURE 15.14 Unsolicited Cover Letter

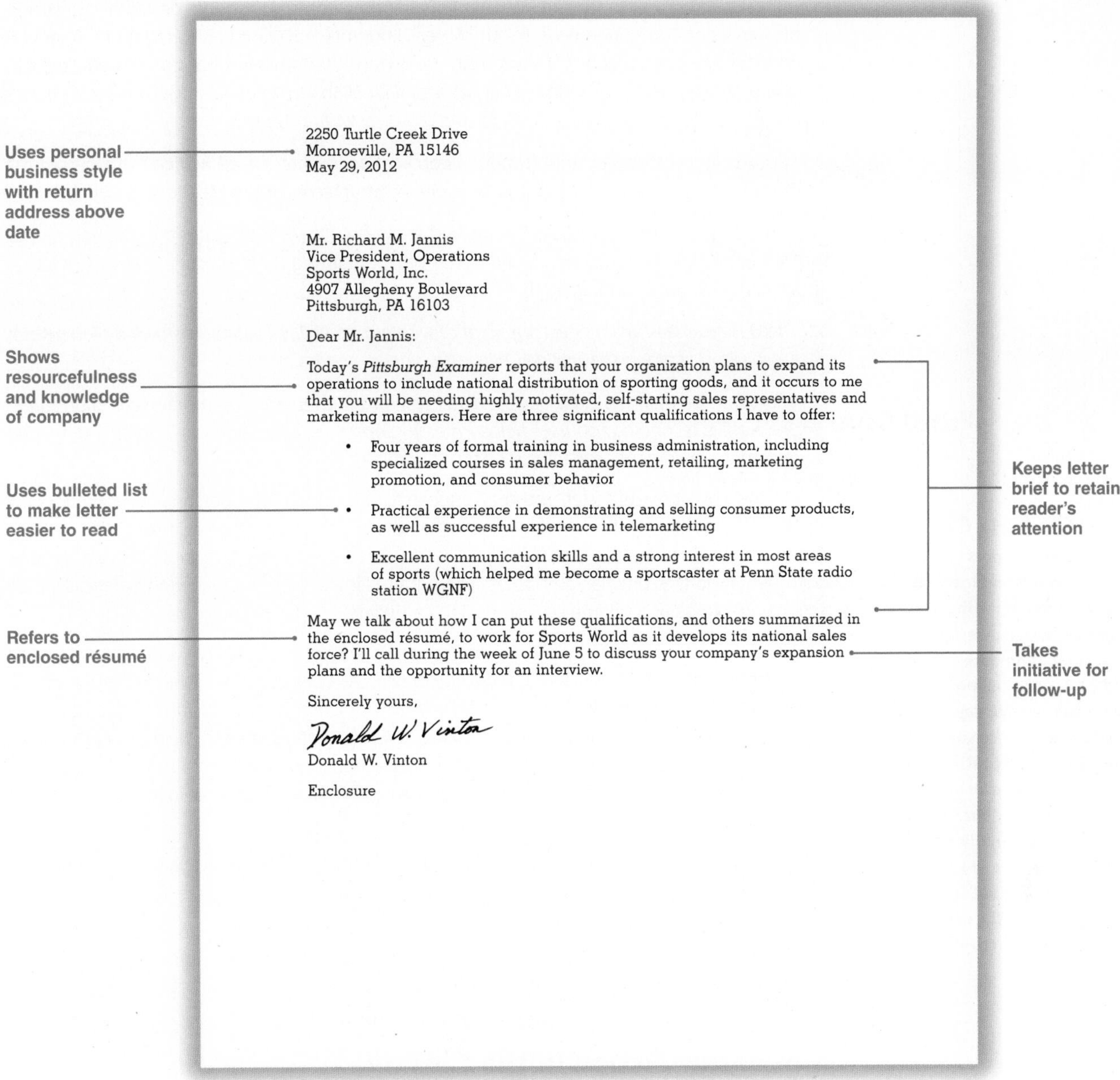
Uses personal business style with return address above date
Shows resourcefulness and knowledge of company
Uses bulleted list to make letter easier to read
Refers to enclosed résumé
Keeps letter brief to retain reader's attention
Takes initiative for follow-up

2250 Turtle Creek Drive
Monroeville, PA 15146
May 29, 2012

Mr. Richard M. Jannis
Vice President, Operations
Sports World, Inc.
4907 Allegheny Boulevard
Pittsburgh, PA 16103

Dear Mr. Jannis:

Today's *Pittsburgh Examiner* reports that your organization plans to expand its operations to include national distribution of sporting goods, and it occurs to me that you will be needing highly motivated, self-starting sales representatives and marketing managers. Here are three significant qualifications I have to offer:

- Four years of formal training in business administration, including specialized courses in sales management, retailing, marketing promotion, and consumer behavior
- Practical experience in demonstrating and selling consumer products, as well as successful experience in telemarketing
- Excellent communication skills and a strong interest in most areas of sports (which helped me become a sportscaster at Penn State radio station WGNF)

May we talk about how I can put these qualifications, and others summarized in the enclosed résumé, to work for Sports World as it develops its national sales force? I'll call during the week of June 5 to discuss your company's expansion plans and the opportunity for an interview.

Sincerely yours,

Donald W. Vinton

Donald W. Vinton

Enclosure

More challenging are unsolicited cover letters, such as Donald Vinton's shown in Figure 15.14. Because he hopes to discover or create a job, his opening must grab the reader's attention immediately. To do that, he capitalizes on company information appearing in an online article. Donald purposely kept his cover letter short and to the point because he anticipated that a busy executive would be unwilling to read a long, detailed letter. Donald's unsolicited letter "prospects" for a job. Some job candidates feel that such letters may be even more productive than efforts to secure advertised jobs, since prospecting candidates face less competition and show initiative. Notice that Donald's letter uses a personal business letter format with his return address above the date.

Selling Your Strengths in the Body

Once you have captured the attention of the reader and identified your purpose in the letter opening, you should use the body of the letter to promote your qualifications for this position. If you are responding to an advertisement, you will want to explain how your preparation and experience fill the stated requirements. If you are prospecting for a job, you may not know the

What information should be included in the body of a cover letter?

exact requirements. Your employment research and knowledge of your field, however, should give you a reasonably good idea of what is expected for this position.

It is also important to stress reader benefits. In other words, you should describe your strong points in relation to the needs of the employer. Hiring officers want you to tell them what you can do for their organizations. This is more important than telling what courses you took in college or what duties you performed in your previous jobs. Instead of *I have completed courses in business communication, report writing, and technical writing,* try this:

> *Courses in business communication, report writing, and technical writing have helped me develop the research and writing skills required of your technical writers.*

Choose your strongest qualifications and show how they fit the targeted job. Remember that students with little experience are better off spotlighting their education and its practical applications, as these candidates did:

> *Because you seek an architect's apprentice with proven ability, I submit a drawing of mine that won second place in the Sinclair College drafting contest last year.*

> *Composing e-mail messages, business letters, memos, and reports in my business communication and office technology courses helped me develop the writing, language, proofreading, and computer skills mentioned in your ad for an administrative assistant.*

ETHICS CHECK

Cover Letter Bloopers

Advice columns and Internet blogs are teeming with cover letter bloopers. Downright lies aside, some candidates simply need a lesson in selling: *P.S. I haven't taken a sick day in years; I don't get sick.* Or consider this candid job board posting: *I live in _______. I have a lot of customer service experience, but I am willing to do just about anything. I am in a lot of debt and need a good solid job to help me get out of it.* After reading this chapter, what advice would you give such job seekers?

In the body of your letter, you may choose to discuss relevant personal traits. Employers are looking for candidates who, among other things, are team players, take responsibility, show initiative, and learn easily. Don't just list several personal traits, though; instead, include documentation that proves you possess these traits. Notice how the following paragraph uses action verbs to paint a picture of a promising candidate:

> *In addition to developing technical and academic skills at Mid-State University, I have gained interpersonal, leadership, and organizational skills. As vice president of the business students' organization, Gamma Alpha, I helped organize and supervise two successful fund-raising events. These activities involved conceptualizing the tasks, motivating others to help, scheduling work sessions, and coordinating the efforts of 35 diverse students in reaching our goal. I enjoyed my success with these activities and look forward to applying such experience in your management trainee program.*

Finally, in this section or the next, you should refer the reader to your résumé. Do so directly or as part of another statement, as shown here:

> *As you will notice from my enclosed résumé, I will graduate in June with a bachelor's degree in business administration. Please refer to the attached résumé for additional information regarding my education, experience, and references.*

Motivating Action in the Closing

What is the purpose of the closing paragraph of a cover letter?

After presenting your case, you should conclude by asking confidently for an interview. Don't ask for the job. To do so would be presumptuous and naïve. In requesting an interview, you might suggest reader benefits or review your strongest points. Sound sincere and appreciative. Remember to make it easy for the reader to agree by supplying your telephone number and the best times to call you. In addition, keep in mind that some hiring officers prefer that you take the initiative to call them. Avoid expressions such as *I hope*, which will weaken your closing. Here are possible endings:

> *This brief description of my qualifications and the additional information on my résumé demonstrate my genuine desire to put my skills in accounting to work for McLellan and Associates. Please call me at (405) 488-2291 before 10 a.m. or after 3 p.m. to arrange an interview.*

> *To add to your staff an industrious, well-trained administrative assistant with proven word processing and communication skills, call me at (350) 492-1433 to arrange an interview. I look forward to meeting with you to further discuss my qualifications.*

> *I look forward to the opportunity to discuss my qualifications for the financial analyst position more fully in an interview. I can be reached at (213) 458-4030. Next week, after you have examined the enclosed résumé, I will call you to discuss the possibility of arranging an interview.*

FIGURE 15.15 E-Mail Cover Letter

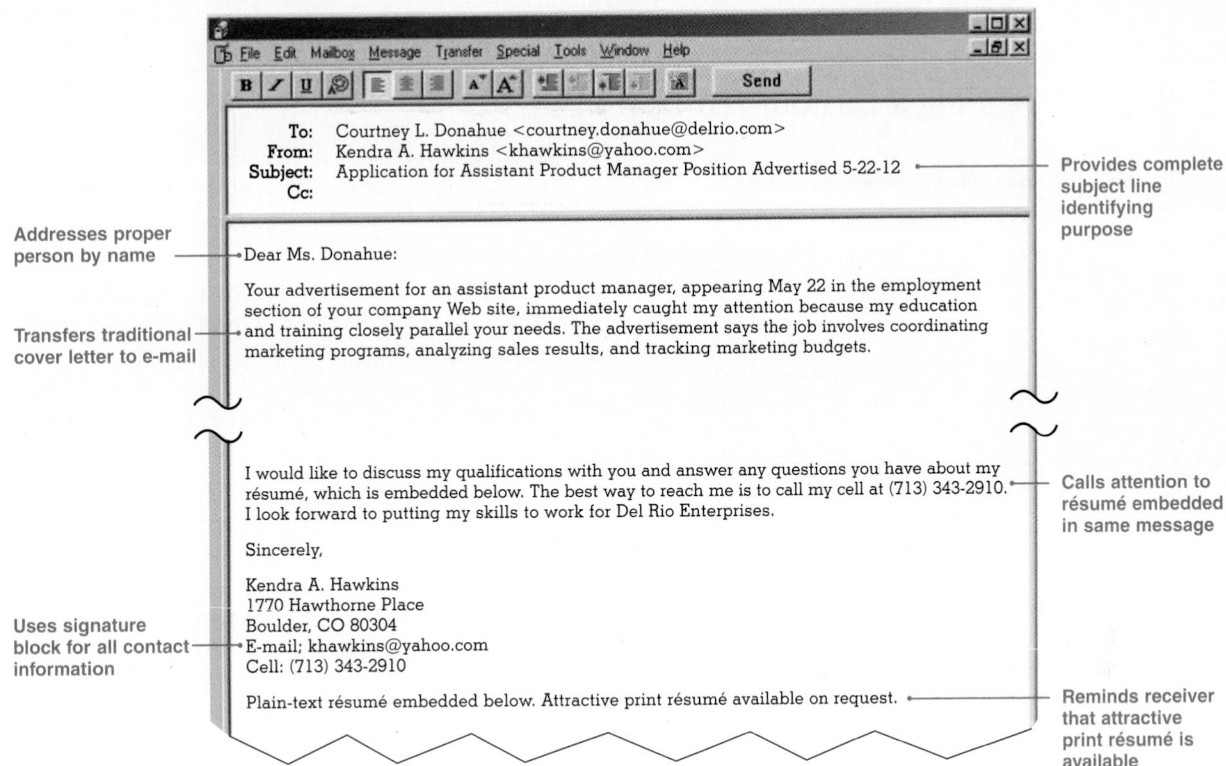
To: Courtney L. Donahue <courtney.donahue@delrio.com>
From: Kendra A. Hawkins <khawkins@yahoo.com>
Subject: Application for Assistant Product Manager Position Advertised 5-22-12
Cc:

Dear Ms. Donahue:

Your advertisement for an assistant product manager, appearing May 22 in the employment section of your company Web site, immediately caught my attention because my education and training closely parallel your needs. The advertisement says the job involves coordinating marketing programs, analyzing sales results, and tracking marketing budgets.

I would like to discuss my qualifications with you and answer any questions you have about my résumé, which is embedded below. The best way to reach me is to call my cell at (713) 343-2910. I look forward to putting my skills to work for Del Rio Enterprises.

Sincerely,

Kendra A. Hawkins
1770 Hawthorne Place
Boulder, CO 80304
E-mail; khawkins@yahoo.com
Cell: (713) 343-2910

Plain-text résumé embedded below. Attractive print résumé available on request.

File Edit Mailbox Message Transfer Special Tools Window Help
Send
Provides complete subject line identifying purpose
Addresses proper person by name
Transfers traditional cover letter to e-mail
Calls attention to résumé embedded in same message
Uses signature block for all contact information
Reminds receiver that attractive print résumé is available

Sending Your Cover Letter

More than 90 percent of résumés at Fortune 500 companies arrive by e-mail or are submitted through the corporate Web site.[40] Many applicants using technology make the mistake of not including cover letters with their résumés submitted by e-mail or by fax. A résumé that arrives without a cover letter makes the receiver wonder what it is and why it was sent. Recruiters want you to introduce yourself, and they also are eager to see some evidence that you can write. Some candidates either skip the cover letter or think they can get by with one-line cover letters such as this: *Please see attached résumé, and thanks for your consideration.*

Should a cover letter always accompany a résumé? Why or why not?

If you are serious about landing the job, take the time to prepare a professional cover letter. If you are sending your résumé via e-mail, you may use the same cover letter you would send by surface mail but shorten it a bit. As illustrated in Figure 15.15, an inside address is unnecessary for an e-mail recipient. Also, move your return address from the top of the letter to just below your name. Include your e-mail address and phone number. Remove tabs, bullets, underlining, and italics that might be problematic in e-mail messages. If you are submitting your résumé by fax, send the same cover letter you would send by surface mail. If you are submitting your résumé as a PDF file, do the same for your cover letter.

Final Tips for Successful Cover Letters

As you revise your cover letter, notice how many sentences begin with *I*. Although it is impossible to talk about yourself without using *I*, you can reduce "I" domination with this writing technique. Make activities and outcomes, and not yourself, the subjects of sentences. For example, rather than *I took classes in business communication and computer applications,* say *Classes in business communication and computer applications prepared me to....* Instead of *I enjoyed helping customers,* say *Helping customers was a real pleasure.*

Because the beginning of a sentence is a prominent position, avoid starting sentences with *I* whenever possible. Use the "you" view (*You are looking for a hardworking team player*), or

Checklist

Preparing and Sending a Customized Cover Letter

Opening

- **Use the receiver's name.** Whenever possible, address the proper individual by name.
- **Identify your information source, if appropriate.** In responding to an advertisement, specify the position advertised as well as the date and publication name. If someone referred you, name that person.
- **Gain the reader's attention.** Use one of these techniques: (a) tell how your qualifications fit the job specifications, (b) show knowledge of the reader's business, (c) describe how your special talents will be assets to the company, or (d) use an original and relevant expression.

Body

- **Describe what you can do for the reader.** Demonstrate how your background and training fill the job requirements.
- **Highlight your strengths.** Summarize your principal assets in terms of education, experience, and special skills. Avoid repeating specific data from your résumé.
- **Refer to your résumé.** In this section or the closing, direct the reader to the attached résumé. Do so directly or incidentally as part of another statement.

Closing

- **Ask for an interview.** Also consider reviewing your strongest points or suggesting how your assets will benefit the company.
- **Make it easy to respond.** Tell when you can be reached during office hours, or announce when you will call the reader. Note that some recruiters prefer that you call them.

Sending

- **Include a cover letter with your résumé.** Send your cover letter along with your résumé as a Word attachment, embedded in an e-mail message, as a plain-text attachment, or as a PDF file.
- **If you e-mail your cover letter, put your contact information in the signature area.** Move your return address from the top of the letter to the signature block. Include your phone number and e-mail address.

try opening with phrases that de-emphasize you, the writer—for example, *All through college, I worked full time at. . . .* Above all, strive for a comfortable style. In your effort to avoid sounding self-centered, however, don't write unnaturally.

Like the résumé, your cover letter must look professional and suggest quality. This means using a traditional letter style, such as block or modified block. Also, be sure to print it on the same quality paper as your résumé. As with your résumé, proofread it several times yourself; then have a friend read it for content and mechanics. Don't rely on spell check to find all the errors. Just like your résumé, your cover letter must be perfect.

Zooming In — YOUR TURN

Applying Your Skills With Liz Ryan

As an intern working with Liz Ryan, you are expected to help her prepare advice articles and interesting blog items. She plans to write an article in the near future about students searching for jobs. She wants you to give her firsthand information. These are some questions she posed:

- What do students fear the most in job searching? Do you have any ideas for overcoming those fears?
- Where would most of your friends go first when they begin a job search?
- How can students begin networking? What would you and your friends do?
- How would you and your friends use the Web for job searching?

Your Task

In a well-organized e-mail or memo, prepare a short informational report answering the questions listed here. Add any other information or advice that you think would be helpful to students looking for jobs. Arrange your memo or e-mail as an informational report, which was covered in Chapter 12.

© PhotoAlto/Eric Audras/Getty Images

Summary of Learning Objectives

1 **Prepare for a successful job search by identifying your interests, evaluating your assets, recognizing the changing nature of jobs, and choosing a career path.** The employment process begins with an analysis of your preferences and your qualifications. Because the nature of jobs is changing, your future work may include flexible work assignments, multiple employers, and constant retraining. You can learn more about career opportunities through your campus career center, the Web, your library, internships, part-time jobs, interviews, classified ads, and professional organizations.

2 **Apply both online and traditional job search techniques.** Online job search techniques include visiting the big commercial sites (such as Monster, Career Builder, and CollegeGrad) as well as corporations' sites, professional organizations' sites, and niche sites. To establish online networking, job seekers are joining social media sites such as LinkedIn and Facebook. Traditional job search techniques include checking classified ads, studying announcements of professional organizations, contacting companies directly, signing up for campus interviews, attending career fairs, asking for advice from instructors, and developing a personal network of contacts.

3 **Appreciate the need to customize your résumé, and know whether to choose a chronological or a functional résumé style.** Because of intense competition, you must customize your résumé for every position you seek. Chronological résumés, listing work and education by dates, rank highest with recruiters. Functional résumés, highlighting skills instead of jobs, appeal to people changing careers or those having negative employment histories. Functional résumés are also effective for recent graduates who have little work experience.

4 **Organize your qualifications and information into effective résumé segments.** In preparing a résumé, organize your skills and achievements so that they aim at a particular job or company. Study models to arrange most effectively your main heading, career objective (optional), summary of qualifications, education, work experience, capabilities, awards and activities, personal data (optional), and references (optional). Use action verbs to show how your assets will help the target organization.

5 **Describe techniques that optimize a résumé for today's technologies, including preparing a scannable résumé, a plain-text résumé, and an e-portfolio.** You should consider preparing a scannable résumé that limits line length, avoids fancy formatting, and emphasizes keywords and keyword phrases. Keywords are nouns that an employer might use to describe a position and its requirements. Plain-text résumés are stripped of all formatting and prepared as text files so that they may be embedded within e-mail messages or submitted online. An e-portfolio is a collection of digitized materials that illustrate your performance, talents, and accomplishments. E-portfolios may be posted at Web sites or burned onto CDs or DVDs.

6 **Write a customized cover letter to accompany a résumé.** Gain attention in the opening of a cover letter by addressing the receiver by name and mentioning the job or a person who referred you. Build interest in the body by stressing your strengths in relation to the stated requirements. Explain what you can do for the targeted company. Refer to your résumé, request an interview, and make it easy for the receiver to reach you. If you send your cover letter by e-mail, shorten it a bit and include complete contact information in the signature block. Remove tabs, bullets, underlining, and italics that could be problematic in e-mail.

Chapter Review

1. You are about to begin your job search. What should you do first? (Obj. 1)
2. What employment trends are occurring in today's workplace? (Obj. 1)
3. What sources can you use to help you determine a career path? (Obj. 1)
4. Using the Web, where should you look in addition to searching the big job board sites? (Obj. 2)

5. What are some tips you should follow to ensure a safe and effective online job search? (Obj. 2)
6. Even with the popularity of online job search sites, traditional job search techniques are still important. What are some traditional sources for finding jobs? (Obj. 2)
7. What is a customized résumé, and why should you have one? (Obj. 3)
8. What is a chronological résumé, and what are its advantages and disadvantages? How does it differ from a functional résumé? (Obj. 3)
9. Describe a summary of qualifications, and explain why it is increasingly popular on résumés. (Obj. 4)
10. What personal information should be included, and what should be omitted, on a résumé? (Obj. 4)
11. To optimize your résumé for today's technologies, how many versions of your résumé should you expect to make? What are they? (Obj. 5)
12. What is an e-portfolio? How can having one benefit you? (Obj. 5)
13. What are the three purposes of a cover letter? (Obj. 6)
14. What information goes in the body of a cover letter? (Obj. 6)
15. Why is it important to include a cover letter with all résumés you send, even if you send them by e-mail or fax? (Obj. 6)

Critical Thinking

1. How has the Web changed job searching for individuals and recruiters? Has the change had a positive or a negative effect? Why? (Obj. 1)
2. In regard to hiring, conventional wisdom holds that it's all about whom you know. How can job candidates find an insider to refer them for a job opening? (Obj. 2)
3. Discuss the advantages and disadvantages of unconventional job applications that use gimmicks such as video résumés to get noticed. (Obj. 5)
4. Some job candidates think that applying for unsolicited jobs can be more fruitful than applying for advertised openings. Discuss the advantages and disadvantages of letters that "prospect" for jobs. (Obj. 6)
5. **Ethical Issue:** Job candidate Karen is an older job seeker who is worried that her age will hurt her during her job search. While preparing her résumé, she has decided to omit the year she graduated from college and to leave off several positions she held earlier in her career so that she will appear younger to recruiters. Is what she is doing unethical?

Activities

15.1 Document for Analysis: Résumé (Obj. 4)

One effective way to improve your writing skills is to critique and edit the résumé of someone else.

Your Task. Analyze the following poorly organized résumé. List its weaknesses. Your instructor may ask you to revise sections of this résumé before showing you an improved version.

Résumé
Janet P. Garza
530 N. Comanche St., Apt. B
San Marcos, TX 78666
Phone 396-5182
E-Mail: Hotchilibabe08@gmail.com

OBJECTIVE

I would love to find a first job in the "real world" with a big accounting company that will help me get ahead in the accounting field

SKILLS

Word processing, Internet browsers (Explorer and Google), Powerpoint, Excel, type 30 wpm, databases, spreadsheets; great composure in stressful situations; 3 years as leader and supervisor and 4 years in customer service

EDUCATION

Austin Community College Lamar Center. San Marcos, Texas. AA degree Fall 2009

Now I am pursuing a BA in Accounting at TSU-San Marcos, majoring in Accounting; my minor is Finance. Expected degree date is June 2011; I recieved a Certificate of Completion in Entry Level Accounting in June 2009

I went to Scranton High School, Scranton, PA. I graduated in June 2006.

Highlights:

- Named Line Manger of the Month at Home Depot, 09/2006 and 08/2005
- Obtained a Certificate in Entry Level Accounting, June 2009
- Chair of Accounting Society, Spring and fall 2009
- Dean's Honor List, Fall 2010
- Financial advisor training completed through Primerica (May 2010)
- Webmaster for M.E.Ch.A., Spring 2011

Part-Time Employment

Financial Consultant, 2010 to present
I worked only part-time (January 2010-present) for Primerica Financial Services, San Marcos, TX to assist clients in obtaining a mortgage or consolidating a current mortgage loan and also to advice clients in assessing their need for life insurance.

Home Depot, Kyle, TX. As line manager, from September 2004–March 2008, I supervised 50 cashiers and front-end associates. I helped to write schedules, disciplinary action notices, and performance appraisals. I also kept track of change drawer and money exchanges; occasionally was manager on duty for entire store.

Penn Foster Career School-Scranton, PA where I taught flower design, I supervised 15 florists, made floral arrangements, sent them to customers, and restocked flowers.

15.2 Document for Analysis: Cover Letter (Obj. 6)

The following cover letter accompanies Janet Garza's résumé (**Activity 15.1**).

Your Task. Analyze each section of the following cover letter written by Janet and list its weaknesses. Your instructor may ask you to revise this letter before showing you an improved version.

To Whom It May Concern:

I saw your internship position yesterday and would like to apply right away. It would be so exiting to work for your esteemed firm! An internship would really give me much needed real-world experience and help my career.

I have all the qualifications you require in your add and more. I am a junior at Texas State University-San Marcos and an Accounting major (with a minor in Finance). Accounting and Finance are my passion and I want to become a CPA and a financial advisor. I have taken Intermediate I and II and now work as a financial advisor with Primerica Financial Services in San Marcos. I should also tell you that I was at Home Depot for four years. I learned alot, but my heart is in accounting and finance.

I am a team player, a born leader, motivated, reliable, and I show excellent composure in stressful situation, for example, when customers complain. I put myself through school and always carry at least 15 units while working part time.

You will probably agree that I am a good candidate for your internship position, which should start July 1. I feel that my motivation, passion, and strong people skills will serve your company well.

Best regards,

List at least six weaknesses in the cover letter.

15.3 Identifying Your Employment Interests and Goals (Obj. 1)

E-mail

Your Task. In an e-mail or a memo addressed to your instructor, answer the questions in the section "Identifying Your Interests and Goals" at the beginning of the chapter. Draw a conclusion from your answers. What kind of career, company, position, and location seem to fit your self-analysis?

15.4 Evaluating Your Qualifications (Objs. 1, 2, and 3)

Your Task. Prepare four worksheets that inventory your qualifications in these areas: employment, education, capabilities and skills, and honors and activities. Use active verbs when appropriate.

a. **Employment.** Begin with your most recent job or internship. For each position list the following information: employer; job title; dates of employment; and three to five duties, activities, or accomplishments. Emphasize activities related to your job goal. Strive to quantify your achievements.
b. **Education.** List degrees, certificates, and training accomplishments. Include courses, seminars, and skills that are relevant to your job goal. Calculate your grade point average in your major.
c. **Capabilities and skills.** List all capabilities and skills that recommend you for the job you seek. Use words and phrases such as *skilled, competent, trained, experienced*, and *ability to*. Also list five or more qualities or interpersonal skills necessary for success in your chosen field. Write action statements demonstrating that you possess some of these qualities. Empty assurances aren't good enough; try to show evidence (*Developed teamwork skills by working with a committee of eight to produce a* ...).
d. **Awards, honors, and activities.** Explain any awards so that the reader will understand them. List campus, community, and professional activities that suggest you are a well-rounded individual or possess traits relevant to your target job.

15.5 Choosing a Career Path (Obj. 1)

Web

Many people know amazingly little about the work done in various occupations and the training requirements.

Your Task. Use the online *Occupational Outlook Handbook* at **http://www.bls.gov/OCO**, prepared by the Bureau of Labor Statistics, to learn more about an occupation of your choice. Find the description of a position for which you could apply in two to five years. Learn about what workers do on the job, working conditions, training and education needed, earnings, and expected job prospects. Print the pages from the *Occupational Outlook Handbook* that describe employment in the area in which you are interested. If your instructor directs, attach these copies to the cover letter you will write in **Activity 15.10**.

15.6 Locating Salary Information (Obj. 1)

Web

What salary can you expect in your chosen career?

Your Task. Visit America's Career InfoNet at **http://www.acinet.org** or **Salary.com** at **http://www.salary.com** and select an occupation based on the kind of employment you are seeking now or will be seeking after you graduate. Use your current geographic area or the location where you would like to work after graduation. What wages can you expect in this occupation? Click to learn more about this occupation. Take notes on three or four interesting bits of information you uncovered about this career. Bring a printout of the wage information to class and be prepared to discuss what you learned.

15.7 Searching the Job Market (Obj. 1)

Web

Where are the jobs? Even though you may not be in the market at the moment, become familiar with the kinds of available positions because job awareness should become an important part of your education.

Your Task. Clip or print a job advertisement or announcement from (a) the classified section of a newspaper, (b) a job board on the Web, (c) a company Web site, or (d) a professional association listing. Select an advertisement or announcement describing the kind of employment you are seeking now or plan to seek when you graduate. Save this advertisement or announcement to attach to the résumé you will write in **Activity 15.9.**

15.8 Posting a Résumé on the Web (Obj. 2)

Web

Learn about the procedure for posting résumés at job boards on the Web.

Your Task. Prepare a list of three Web sites where you could post your résumé. Describe the procedure involved in posting a résumé and the advantages for each site.

15.9 Writing Your Résumé (Obj. 4)

Your Task. Using the data you developed in **Activity 15.4**, write your résumé. Aim it at a full-time job, part-time position, or internship. Attach a job listing for a specific position (from **Activity 15.7**). Also prepare a list of references. Revise your résumé until it is perfect.

15.10 Preparing Your Cover Letter (Obj. 6)

Your Task. Using the job listing you found for **Activity 15.7**, write a cover letter introducing your résumé. Again, revise until it is perfect.

15.11 Using Social Media in the Job Search (Obj. 2)

One of the fastest-growing trends in employment is using social media sites during the job search.

Your Task. Locate one social media site and set up an account. Explore the site to discover how job seekers can use it to search for a job and how employers can use it to find job candidates. Be prepared to share your findings in class.

15.12 E-Portfolios: Job Hunting in the Twenty-First Century (Obj. 5)

Team | Web

In high-tech fields, digital portfolios have been steadily gaining in popularity and now seem to be going mainstream as universities are providing space for student job seekers to profile their qualifications in e-portfolios online. Although digital portfolios are unlikely to become widely used very soon, you would do well to learn about them by viewing many samples—good and bad.

Your Task. Conduct a Google search using the search term *student e-portfolios* or *student digital portfolios*. You will see long lists of hits, some of which will be actual digital document samples on the Web or instructions for creating an e-portfolio. Your instructor may assign you individually or as a team to visit specific digital portfolio sites and summarize your findings in a memo or a brief oral presentation. You could focus on the composition of the site, page layout, links provided, colors used, types of documents included, and so forth. A fine site that offers many useful links is maintained by the Center for Excellence in Teaching (CET) at the University of Southern California. Visit **http://www.usc.edu** and type *student e-portfolios* to search the USC Web pages. Click the link to the CET site.

Alternatively, teams or the whole class could study sites that provide how-to instructions, and then combine the advice of the best among them to create practical tips for making a digital portfolio. This option lends itself to team writing; consider using a wiki, collaborative software, or a document-sharing tool such as Google Docs.

Video Resource

Video Library 1, The Job Search

At Clifton-Harding Associates (CHA), owner Ella Clifton realizes that she needs another employee to help run the business. She places a "blind" advertisement, to which her current employee, Stephanie, responds. Ella interviews a promising candidate, Yolanda. She also learns that Stephanie has lied on the résumé she posted to the job site. Not knowing she was applying to her own employer, Stephanie enhanced her qualifications." In addition to the ethical dilemma, you observe good and bad job search and résumé techniques for both candidates. After viewing the film, be prepared to discuss these questions:

- What action should Ella and co-owner Rob take after learning that Stephanie lied on her résumé?
- Yolanda prepared a functional résumé to de-emphasize her limited work experience and promote her unique skills and potential for success in the new position. Which résumé format is best for you—the functional or the chronological? Why?
- Yolanda customized her résumé to best match the needs of the organization and the open position. She adjusted the career goal and emphasized her foreign language skills to make her résumé stand out from the others. Describe the advantages of customizing a résumé instead of sending the same one to all potential employers.

Chat About It

In each chapter you will find five discussion questions related to the chapter material. Your instructor may assign these topics for you to discuss in class, in an online chat room, or on an online discussion board. Some of the discussion topics may require outside research. You may also be asked to read and respond to postings made by your classmates.

Topic 1: What is your one favorite source for finding information about choosing a career path? Choose a traditional or online source, and share it with your classmates. Why did you choose this source? How can it benefit one's career path exploration?

Topic 2: What do you think are more effective, online or traditional job search techniques? Why? Share your thoughts and personal job search experience with your classmates.

Topic 3: Why do you think it is so important to customize your résumé for each employer and job for which you apply? How do you think employers will respond to a customized résumé versus a generic résumé? Is creating a customized résumé for each position worth your time and effort? Share your opinions with your classmates.

Topic 4: Assume you will prepare a video résumé to apply for positions. What would you say and do in the video? What would you wear? What steps would you take in the video to impress potential employers? Share your ideas with your classmates.

Topic 5: Many employers will not even look at a résumé unless it is accompanied by a cover letter. Why do you think cover letters are so important to potential employers? What would you include in a cover letter to impress employers? Share your thoughts and ideas with your classmates.

Grammar and Mechanics C.L.U.E. Review 15

Total Review

Each of the following sentences has a total of **three** errors in grammar, punctuation, capitalization, usage, or spelling. On a separate sheet, write a correct version. Avoid adding new phrases or rewriting sentences in your own words. When finished, compare your responses with the key beginning on page Key-1.

Example: One West coast company found that e-mail consumed about 24% of staff members workdays.
Revision: One West **Coast** company found that e-mail consumed about 24 **percent** of staff **members'** workdays.

1. Many employers use sights like Facebook to learn about potential employees. Which mean job seekers must maintain a professional online presence.
2. To conduct a safe online job search, you must: (a) Use only reputable job boards, (2) keep careful records, and (c) limit the number of sites on which you post your résumé.
3. When Melissas job search was complete she had received 4 job offers.
4. If you loose your job dont become discouraged by the thought of having to find another.
5. Joseph wondered whether it was alright to ask his professor for employment advise?
6. At last months staff meeting team members examined several candidates résumés.
7. Rather then schedule face to face interviews the team investigated videoconferencing.
8. 12 applicants will be interviewed on April 10th, consequently, we may need to work late to accommodate them.
9. Professional e-mail manners reflects on you and your company, however, to few employees are trained properly.
10. In the last issue of *Newsweek* did you see the article titled "Should a résumé include a Career Objective?"

CHAPTER 16

Interviewing and Following Up

OBJECTIVES

After studying this chapter, you should be able to

1. Understand the importance of a job interview, its purposes, and its forms, including screening, hiring/placement, one-on-one, panel, group, sequential, stress, and online interviews.
2. Describe what to do before an in-person or online interview, including researching the target company, rehearsing success stories, practicing answers to possible questions, and cleaning up digital dirt.
3. Explain what occurs the day of your interview, including traveling to and arriving at the interview, performing effectively during the interview, sending positive nonverbal messages, and using good techniques in answering questions.
4. Describe how to answer typical interview questions such as those that seek to get acquainted, gauge your interest, probe your experience, explore your accomplishments, look to the future, and inquire about salary expectations.
5. Understand how to close an interview positively, including asking meaningful questions.
6. Outline the activities that take place after an interview, including thanking the interviewer and contacting references.
7. Understand how to complete employment applications and write résumé follow-up, rejection follow-up, job acceptance, and job rejection messages.

Want to do well on tests and excel in your course? Go to **www.meguffey.com** for helpful interactive resources.

- **Review the Chapter 16 PowerPoint slides to prepare for the first quiz.**

Zooming In PART 1

Googling for Jobs

Résumés from thousands of prospective Nooglers (new Google employees) arrive at Google's Mountain View, California, headquarters every day. Admired for its technological excellence and nontraditional corporate culture, Google is one of the top ranked on *Fortune's* list of America's 100 Best Companies to Work For. Its growth had been so rapid that Google's employee roster soared from about 1,600 in 2003 to well over 20,000 now. With major offices worldwide, the company typically hires several Nooglers a day. It looks for talented, passionate people from a variety of backgrounds. Ann Pellegrini, people programs specialist with Google, gives this advice to prospective employees: "What we want most is for a candidate to be himself or herself. Candidates should bring their whole selves to the interview and not try to fit some mold that they think Google wants. We encourage you to be candid and active in your interview. Clearly articulate what skills you bring and how a role at Google fits into your broader career path."[1]

Hiring and retaining the best people are central to Google's continuing success and growth. "It's no accident that my title is Vice-President of People Operations, and not the more traditional description of 'human resources,'" said Laszlo Bock, "People are our most vital competitive asset. . . . Our strategy is simple: We hire great people and encourage them to make their dreams a reality."[2]

The uniqueness of the Mountain View Googleplex contributes to employee satisfaction and keeps turnover low—just 4 to 5 percent. Its informal, collaborative work environment has been compared to a university setting. Employees work in small teams that promote creativity and an open exchange of ideas. As the leading Internet search site and advertising giant, Google values out-of-the-box thinking. Managers encourage employees to work on special projects and expand their responsibilities well beyond their original job descriptions.

In addition to encouraging a high-energy atmosphere, Google supports its employees with an exceptional list of benefits. Gourmet meals and snacks, haircuts, car washes and oil changes, gym facilities, sports, language lessons, personal concierge services, day care, running trails, medical and dental care—all these and more are available at the Googleplex.

© AP Images/Paul Sakuma

Google's high growth rate places intense pressure on Google's recruiters to fill its many open positions. "As we get bigger, we find it harder and harder to find enough people," said Vice President Bock.[3] Many senior managers were devoting almost one third of their time to interviewing candidates. As a result, one of Mr. Bock's first initiatives was to streamline Google's rigorous hiring processes—while still striking "the right balance between letting candidates get to know Google, letting us get to know them, and moving quickly."[4]

Critical Thinking

- Before you apply for a job, why must you investigate carefully the company's background?
- What types of skills and background do you think Google recruiters look for in a candidate?
- How would you craft a résumé and cover letter so that it would stand out when it arrives at Google?

http://www.google.com

The Job Interview: Understanding Its Importance, Purposes, and Types

LEARNING OBJECTIVE 1

Understand the importance of a job interview, its purposes, and its forms, including screening, hiring/placement, one-on-one, panel, group, sequential, stress, and online interviews.

A job interview, whether at Google or anywhere else, can change your life. Because employment is a major part of everyone's life, the job interview takes on enormous importance. Interviewing is equally significant whether you are completing your education and searching for your first serious position or whether you are in the workforce and striving to change jobs.

Everyone agrees that job interviews are extremely stressful. However, the more you learn about the process and the more prepared you are, the less stress you will feel. It is also important to realize that a job interview is a two-way street. It is not just about being judged by the employer. You, the applicant, will be using the job interview to evaluate the employer. Do you really want to work for this organization?

This chapter will increase your interviewing effectiveness and confidence by explaining the purposes and kinds of interviews and how to prepare for them. You will learn how to project a professional image throughout the interview process, gather information about an employer, and reduce nervousness. You will receive advice on how to send positive nonverbal messages that will help you stay in control during your interview. You will pick up tips for responding to recruiters' favorite questions and learn how to cope with illegal questions and salary matters. Moreover, you will receive pointers on significant questions you can ask during an interview. Finally, you will learn what you should do as a successful follow-up to an interview.

Yes, job interviews can be intimidating and stressful. However, you can expect to ace an interview when you know what's coming and when you prepare thoroughly. Remember, preparation often determines who gets the job. First, though, you need to know the purposes of employment interviews and what types of interviews you might encounter in your job search.

Purposes of Employment Interviews

What three things should you try to achieve during a job interview?

An interview has several purposes for you as a job candidate. It is an opportunity to (a) convince the employer of your potential, (b) find out more about the job and the company, and (c) expand on the information in your résumé. This is the time for you to gather information about whether you would fit into the company culture. You should also be thinking about whether this job suits your career goals.

From the employer's perspective, the interview is an opportunity to (a) assess your abilities in relation to the requirements for the position; (b) discuss your training, experience, knowledge, and abilities in more detail; (c) see what drives and motivates you; and (d) decide whether you would fit into the organization.

Types of Employment Interviews

Job applicants generally face two kinds of interviews: screening interviews and hiring/placement interviews. You must succeed in the first to proceed to the second. Once you make it to the hiring/placement interview, you will find a variety of interview styles, including one-on-one, panel, group, sequential, stress, and online interviews. You will be better prepared if you know what to expect in each type of interview.

What is the purpose of screening interviews?

Screening Interviews. Screening interviews do just that—they screen candidates to eliminate those who fail to meet minimum requirements. Companies use screening interviews to save time and money by eliminating lesser-qualified candidates before scheduling face-to-face interviews. Although some screening interviews are conducted during job fairs or on campuses, many screening interviews take place on the telephone, and some take place online. For example, Lowe's Home Improvement has applicants access a Web site where they answer a series of ethics-related questions, and Wal-Mart screens cashiers, stockers, and customer service representatives with a multiple-choice questionnaire that applicants answer by pushing buttons on a phone keypad.[5] Even more cutting-edge, some employers such as Hewlett-Packard, Microsoft, and Verizon are using Second Life, an online virtual community, to hold virtual job fairs and to screen job applicants.[6]

During a screening interview, you will likely be asked to provide details about the education and experience listed on your résumé; therefore, you must be prepared to sell your qualifications. Remember that the person conducting the screening interview is trying to determine whether you should move on to the next step in the interview process.

A screening interview may be as short as five minutes. Even though it may be short, don't treat it casually. If you don't perform well during the screening interview, it may be your last interview with that organization. You can use the tips that follow in this chapter to succeed during the screening process.

What do recruiters try to learn about candidates during hiring/placement interviews?

Hiring/Placement Interviews. The most promising candidates selected from screening interviews are invited to hiring/placement interviews. Hiring managers want to learn whether candidates are motivated, qualified, and a good fit for the position. Their goal is to learn how the candidate would fit into their organization. Conducted in depth, hiring/placement interviews may take many forms.

One-on-One Interviews. In one-on-one interviews, which are the most common type, you can expect to sit down with a company representative and talk about the job and your qualifications. If the representative is the hiring manager, questions will be specific and job related. If the representative is from human resources, the questions will probably be more general.

Panel Interviews. Panel interviews are usually conducted by people who will be your supervisors and colleagues. Usually seated around a table, interviewers take turns asking questions. Panel interviews are advantageous because they save the company time and money, and they show you how the staff works together. When answering questions, keep eye contact with the questioner as well as with the others.[7] Try to take notes during the interview so that you can remember each person's questions and what was important to that individual.

What kinds of hiring interviews might you encounter?

Group Interviews. Group interviews occur when a company interviews several candidates for the same position at the same time. Some employers use this technique to measure leadership skills and communication styles. During a group interview, stay focused on the interviewer, and treat the other candidates with respect. Even if you are nervous, try to remain calm, take your time when responding, and express yourself clearly. The key during a group interview is to make yourself stand out from the other candidates in a positive way.[8]

Sequential Interviews. In a sequential interview, you meet individually with two or more interviewers on a one-on-one basis over the course of several hours or days. You must listen carefully and respond positively to all interviewers. Sell your qualifications to each one; don't assume that any interviewer knows what was said in a previous interview. Keep your responses fresh, even when repeating yourself many times over. Subsequent interviews also tend to be more in-depth than first interviews, which means that you need to be even more prepared and know even more about the company. According to Chantal Verbeek-Vingerhoed, head of enterprise talent for ING, during subsequent interviews, "They dig deeper into your technical skills, and make connections about how you'd add value and solve issues in the department. If you know the exact job requirements and expectations, you can really shine."[9]

Stress Interviews. Stress interviews are meant to test your reactions during nerve-wracking situations and are usually used for jobs in which you will face significant stress. You may be forced to wait a long time before being greeted by the interviewer, you may be given a test with an impossible time limit, or you may be treated rudely by one or more of the interviewers. Another stress interview technique is to have interviewers ask questions at a rapid rate. If asked rapid-fire questions from many directions, take the time to slow things down. For example, you might say, *I would be happy to answer your question, Ms. X, but first I must finish responding to Mr. Z.* If greeted with silence (another stress technique), you might say, *Would you like me to begin the interview? Let me tell you about myself.* Or ask a question such as, *Can you give me more information about the position?* One career expert says, "The key to surviving stress interviews is to remain calm, keep a sense of humor, and avoid getting angry or defensive."[10]

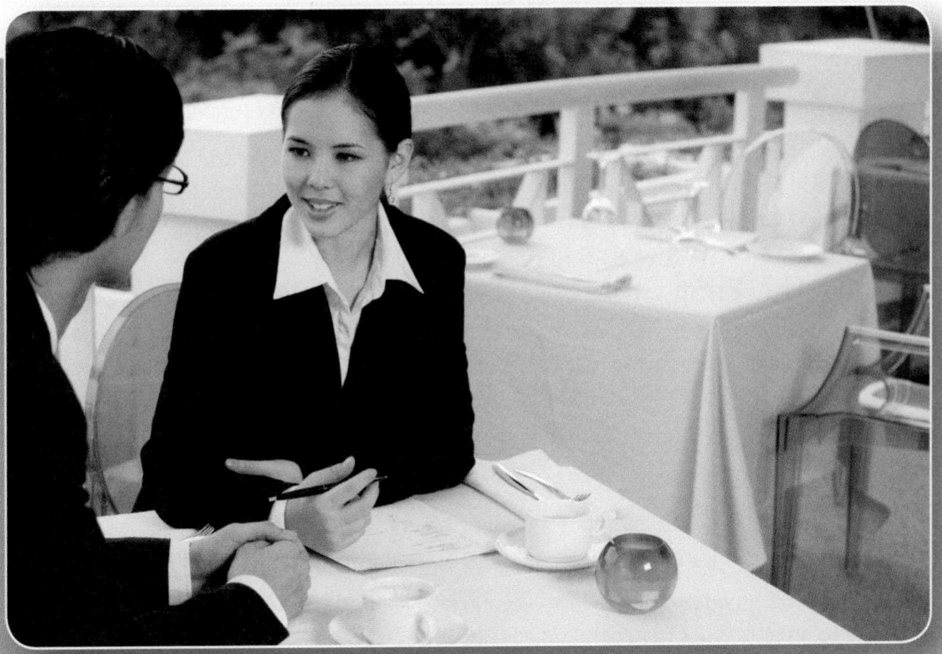

You might find that your job interview takes place over a meal. Meal interviews are especially common for positions in which the employee will interact frequently with clients. Employers want to make sure that candidates for these types of jobs have good manners and follow proper dining etiquette. During a meal interview, order food that is easy to eat and avoid alcohol, even if the interviewer orders a drink. Above all, try to relax, listen carefully, and take part in the conversation. *What would you do to impress a potential employer favorably during a meal interview?*

Online Interviews. Many companies today use technology to interview job candidates from a distance. Although conference call interviews have long been used, today's savvy companies such as Zappos.com use webcams to conduct interviews. If an applicant doesn't have a webcam, Zappos sends one with a return label.[11] Webcam interviews save job applicants and companies time and money, especially when applicants are not in the same geographic location as the company. Even though your interview may be online via a webcam, don't take it any less seriously than a face-to-face interview.

No matter what interview structure you encounter, you will feel more comfortable and be better prepared if you know what to do before, during, and after the interview.

Before the Interview

LEARNING OBJECTIVE 2
Describe what to do before an in-person or online interview, including researching the target company, rehearsing success stories, practicing answers to possible questions, and cleaning up digital dirt.

Once you have sent out at least one résumé or filled out at least one job application, you must consider yourself an active job seeker. Being active in the job market means that you should be prepared to be contacted by potential employers. As discussed earlier, employers often use screening interviews to narrow the list of candidates. If you do well in the screening interview, you will be invited to an in-person or online job interview.

Ensuring Professional Phone Techniques

Even with the popularity of e-mail, most employers contact job applicants by phone to set up interviews. Employers can judge how well applicants communicate by hearing their voices and expressions over the phone. Therefore, once you are actively looking for a job, anytime the phone rings, it could be a potential employer. Don't make the mistake of letting an unprofessional voice mail message or a lazy roommate ruin your chances. To make the best impression, try these tips:

- Invest in a good answering machine or voice mail service. Make sure that your outgoing message is concise and professional, with no distracting background sounds. It should be in your own voice and include your full name for clarity. You will find more tips for creating professional outgoing messages in Chapter 14.
- Tell those who might answer your phone at home about your job search. Explain to them the importance of acting professionally and taking complete messages. Family members or roommates can affect the first impression an employer has of you.
- If you have children, prevent them from answering the phone during your job search. Children of all ages are not known for taking good messages!
- If you have put your cell phone number on your résumé, don't answer it unless you are in a good location to carry on a conversation with an employer. It is hard to pay close attention when you are driving down the highway or eating in a noisy restaurant!
- Use voice mail to screen calls. By screening incoming calls, you can be totally in control when you return a prospective employer's call. Organize your materials and ready yourself psychologically for the conversation.

How can you make a good first impression when a potential employer contacts you by phone?

Making the First Conversation Impressive

Whether you answer the phone directly or return an employer's call, make sure you are prepared for the conversation. Remember that this is the first time the employer has heard your voice. How you conduct yourself on the phone will create a lasting impression. To make that first impression a positive one, follow these tips:

- Keep a list near the telephone of positions for which you have applied.
- Treat any call from an employer just like an interview. Use a professional tone and businesslike language. Be polite and enthusiastic, and sell your qualifications.
- If caught off guard by the call, ask whether you can call back in a few minutes. Take that time to organize your materials and yourself.

- Have a copy of your résumé available so that you can answer any questions that come up. Also have your list of references, a calendar, and a notepad handy.
- Be prepared for a screening interview. As discussed earlier, this might occur during the first phone call.
- Take good notes during the phone conversation. Obtain accurate directions, and verify the spelling of your interviewer's name. If you will be interviewed by more than one person, get all of their names.
- Before you hang up, reconfirm the date and time of your interview. You could say something like *I look forward to meeting with you next Wednesday at 2 p.m.*

Researching the Target Company

What should you find out about a company prior to an interview?

Once you have scheduled an in-person or online interview, it is time to start preparing for it. One of the most important steps in effective interviewing is gathering detailed information about a prospective employer. Never enter an interview cold. Recruiters are impressed by candidates who have done their homework. In an OfficeTeam survey, 47 percent of executives polled said that the most common mistake job seekers make during interviews is having little or no knowledge about the potential employer.[12]

Visit the library, explore your campus career center, or search the Web for information and articles about the target company or its field, service, or product. Visit the company's Web site and read everything. Call the company to request annual reports, catalogs, or brochures. Ask about the organization and possibly the interviewer. Learn something about the company's history, mission and goals, size, geographic locations, number of employees, customers, competitors, culture, management structure, names of leaders, reputation in the community, financial condition, strengths and weaknesses, and future plans. Also learn what you can about the industry in which the company operates.

Analyze the company's advertising, including sales and marketing brochures. One candidate, a marketing major, spent a great deal of time poring over brochures from an aerospace contractor. During his initial interview, he shocked and impressed the recruiter with his knowledge of the company's guidance systems. The candidate had, in fact, relieved the interviewer of his least favorite task—explaining the company's complicated technology.

Talking with company employees is always a good idea, if you can manage it. They are probably the best source of inside information. Try to be introduced to someone who is currently employed—but not working in the immediate area where you wish to be hired. Be sure to seek out someone who is discreet.

What can you learn about a company on blogs or social network sites?

Blogs are also good sources for company research. Many employees maintain both formal and informal blogs, where they share anecdotes and information about their employers. You can use these blogs to learn about a company's culture, its current happenings, and its future plans. Many job seekers find that they can get a more realistic picture of a company's day-to-day culture by reading blogs than they would by reading news articles or company Web site information.[13] Also join the company's Facebook page, and start following the company on Twitter to gather even more information prior to your interview.

In learning about a company, you may uncover information that convinces you that this is not the company for you. It is always better to learn about negatives early in the process. More likely, though, the information you collect will help you tailor your interview responses to the organization's needs. You know how flattered you feel when an employer knows about you and your background. That feeling works both ways. Employers are pleased when job candidates take an interest in them. Be ready to put in plenty of effort in investigating a target employer because this effort really pays off at interview time.

Preparing and Practicing

After you have learned about the target organization, study the job description or job listing. Knowing as much as you and about the position enables you to practice your best response strategies prior to the interview.

The most successful job candidates never go into interviews unprepared. They rehearse success stories and practice answers to typical questions. They also clean up digital dirt and plan their responses to any problem areas on their résumés. As part of their preparation before the interview, they decide what to wear, and they gather the items they plan to take with them.

What is the purpose of a success story during a job interview?

Rehearse Success Stories. To feel confident and be able to sell your qualifications, prepare and practice success stories. These stories are specific examples of your educational and work-related experience that demonstrate your qualifications and achievements. Look over the job description and your résumé to determine what skills, training, personal characteristics, and experience you want to emphasize during the interview. Then prepare a success story for each one. Incorporate numbers, such as dollars saved or percentage of sales increase, whenever possible. Your success stories should be detailed but brief. Think of them as 30-second sound bites.

Practice telling your success stories until they fluently roll off your tongue and sound natural. Then in the interview be certain to find places to insert them. Tell stories about (a) dealing with a crisis, (b) handling a tough interpersonal situation, (c) successfully juggling many priorities, (d) changing course to deal with changed circumstances, (e) learning from a mistake, (f) working on a team, and (g) going above and beyond expectations.[14]

Why is practicing answers to possible job interview questions important?

Practice Answers to Possible Questions. Imagine the kinds of questions you may be asked and work out sample answers. Although you can't anticipate precise questions, you can expect to be asked about your education, skills, experience, salary expectations, and availability. Recite answers to typical interview questions in front of a mirror, with a friend, while driving in your car, or in spare moments. Keep practicing until you have the best responses down pat. Consider recording a practice session to see and hear how you answer questions. Do you look and sound enthusiastic?

Why should you make sure that what you post online is professional and positive?

Clean Up Any Digital Dirt. A recent survey shows that 45 percent of employers now screen job candidates using Google and social networking sites such as Facebook, LinkedIn, MySpace, and Twitter. Even more important, 35 percent of those employers found something online that caused them not to hire a candidate. The top reasons cited for not considering an applicant after an online search were that the candidate (a) posted provocative or inappropriate photographs or information; (b) posted content about drinking or doing drugs; (c) talked negatively about current or previous employers, colleagues, or clients; (d) exhibited poor communication skills; (e) made discriminatory comments; (f) lied about qualifications; or (g) revealed a current or previous employer's confidential information.[15]

For example, the president of a small consulting company in Chicago was about to hire a summer intern when he discovered the student's Facebook page. The candidate described his interests as "smokin' blunts [cigars hollowed out and stuffed with marijuana], shooting people and obsessive sex."[16] The executive quickly lost interest in this candidate. Even if the applicant was merely posturing, it showed poor judgment. Teasing photographs and provocative comments about drinking, drug use, and sexual exploits make job applicants look immature and unprofessional. You should, therefore, follow these steps to clean up your online presence:

- **Remove questionable content.** Remove any incriminating, provocative, or distasteful photos, content, and links that could make you look unprofessional to potential employers.
- **Stay positive.** Don't complain about things in your professional or personal life online. Even negative reviews you have written on sites such as Amazon.com can turn employers off.
- **Be selective about who is on your list of friends.** You don't want to miss out on an opportunity because you seem to associate with negative, immature, or unprofessional people. Your best bet is to make your personal social networking pages private.
- **Avoid joining groups or fan pages that may be viewed negatively.** Remember that online searches can turn up your online activities, including group membership, blog postings, and so on. If you think any activity you are involved in might show poor judgment, remove yourself immediately.
- **Don't discuss your job search if you are still employed.** Employees can find themselves in trouble with their current employers by writing status updates or sending tweets about their job search.

- **Set up a professional social networking page.** Use Facebook, LinkedIn, or other social networking sites to create a professional page. Many employers actually find information during their online searches that convinces them to hire candidates. Make sure your professional page demonstrates creativity, strong communication skills, and well-roundedness.[17]

Expect to Explain Problem Areas on Your Résumé. Interviewers are certain to question you about problem areas on your résumé. If you have little or no experience, you might emphasize your recent training and up-to-date skills. If you have gaps in your résumé, be prepared to answer questions about them positively and truthfully. If you were fired from a job, accept some responsibility for what happened and explain what you gained from the experience. Don't criticize a previous employer, and don't hide the real reasons. If you received low grades for one term, explain why and point to your improved grades in subsequent terms.

Decide How to Dress. What you wear to a job interview still matters. Even if some employees in the organization dress casually, you should look qualified, competent, and successful. One young applicant complained to his girlfriend about having to wear a suit for an interview when everyone at the company dressed casually. She replied, "You don't get to wear the uniform, though, until you make the team!" Avoid loud colors; strive for a coordinated, natural appearance. Favorite "power colors" for interviews are gray and dark blue. Cover tattoos and conceal body piercings; these can be a turnoff for many interviewers. Don't overdo jewelry, and make sure that what you do wear is clean, pressed, odor-free, and lint-free. Shoes should be polished and scuff-free. Forget about flip-flops. To summarize, ensure that what you wear projects professionalism and shows your respect for the interview situation.

Gather Items to Bring. Decide what you should bring with you to the interview, and get everything ready the night before. You should plan to bring copies of your résumé and your reference list, a notebook and pen, money for parking and tolls, and samples of your work, if appropriate. Place everything in a businesslike briefcase to add that final professional touch to your look.

Ethics Check

Just Looking!

Like all relationships, the job search process is about two parties looking to find a good match. Filling a position is costly for employers, and candidates likewise invest time and money in their job hunts. Under the circumstances, is it ethical for a job seeker to accept on-site interviews when not genuinely interested in the prospective employer?

What should you wear to a job interview?

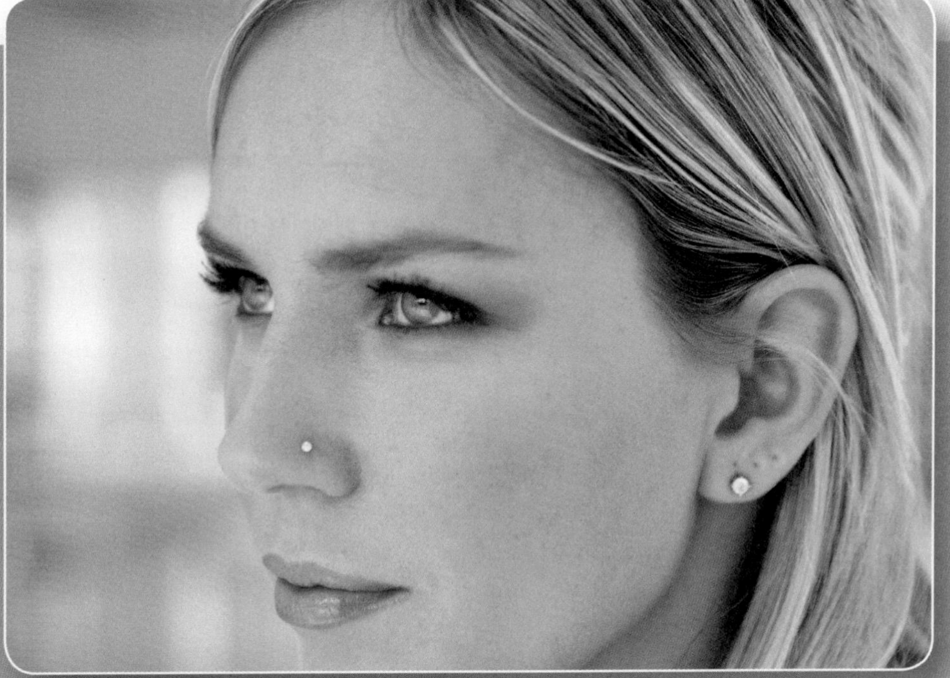

No longer adornments restricted to sailors, bikers, Goths, and ruffians, tattoos and piercings have gained popularity with celebrities, pro athletes, fashion models, and everyday people of all ages. The proliferation of the body art trend has meant that tattoos and piercings are increasingly showing up in the white-collar world of business executives, accountants, and lawyers. Despite their "cool factor" within the broader culture, tattoos and piercings present unique challenges for job seekers who want to know how to dress properly for interviews. *How should individuals with tattoos and piercings dress for success during the job interview and in the workplace?*

Traveling to and Arriving at Your Interview

LEARNING OBJECTIVE 3

Explain what occurs the day of your interview, including traveling to and arriving at the interview, performing effectively during the interview, sending positive nonverbal messages, and using good techniques in answering questions.

The big day has arrived! Ideally you are fully prepared for your interview. Now you need to make sure that everything goes smoothly. That means making sure the trip to the potential employer's office goes smoothly and that you arrive on time. The accompanying Career Coach box provides tips for fighting fear on the day of your interview.

On the morning of your interview, give yourself plenty of time to groom and dress. Then make sure you can arrive at the employer's office without being rushed. If something unexpected happens that will to cause you to be late, such as an accident or bridge closure, call the interviewer right away to explain what is happening. Most interviewers will be understanding, and your call will show that you are responsible. On the way to the interview, don't smoke, don't eat anything messy or smelly, and don't load up on perfume or cologne. Arrive at the interview five or ten minutes early. If possible, check your appearance before going in.

When you enter the office, be courteous and congenial to everyone. Remember that you are being judged not only by the interviewer but by the receptionist and anyone else who sees you before and after the interview. They will notice how you sit, what you read, and how you look. Introduce yourself to the receptionist, and wait to be invited to sit. You may be asked to fill out a job application while you are waiting. You will find tips for doing this effectively later in this chapter.

Greet the interviewer confidently, and don't be afraid to initiate a handshake. Doing so exhibits professionalism and confidence. Extend your hand, look the interviewer directly in the eye, smile pleasantly, and say, *I'm pleased to meet you, Mr. Thomas. I am Constance Ferraro.* In this culture a firm, not crushing, handshake sends a nonverbal message of poise and assurance. Once introductions have taken place, wait for the interviewer to offer you a chair. Make small talk with upbeat comments, such as *This is a beautiful headquarters* or *I'm very impressed with the facilities you have here.* Don't immediately begin rummaging in your briefcase for your résumé. Being at ease and unrushed suggest that you are self-confident.

CAREER COACH

Fighting Fear During Your Job Interview

Expect to be nervous before and during the interview. It is natural! Other than public speaking, employment interviews are the most dreaded events in people's lives. One of the best ways to overcome fear is to know what happens in a typical interview. You can further reduce your fears by following these suggestions:

- **Practice interviewing.** Try to get as much interviewing practice as you can—especially with real companies. The more times you experience the interview situation, the less nervous you will be. If offered, campus mock interviews also provide excellent practice, and the interviewers offer tips for improvement.
- **Prepare thoroughly.** Research the company. Know how you will answer the most frequently asked questions. Be ready with success stories. Rehearse your closing statement. One of the best ways to reduce anxiety is to know that you have done all you can to be ready for the interview.
- **Understand the process.** Find out ahead of time how the interview will be structured. Will you be meeting with an individual, or will you be interviewed by a panel? Is this the first of a series of interviews? Don't be afraid to ask about these details before the interview so that you won't be caught off guard.
- **Dress professionally.** If you know you look sharp, you will feel more confident.
- **Breathe deeply.** Take deep breaths, particularly if you feel anxious while waiting for the interviewer. Deep breathing makes you concentrate on something other than the interview and also provides much-needed oxygen.
- **Know that you are not alone.** Everyone feels some level of anxiety during a job interview. Interviewers expect some nervousness, and a skilled interviewer will try to put you at ease.
- **Remember that an interview is a two-way street.** The interviewer isn't the only one who is gleaning information. You have come to learn about the job and the company. In fact, during some parts of the interview, you will be in charge. This should give you courage.

Career Application

In small groups discuss other techniques for fighting fear during the job interview. Share your findings with the class.

During the Interview

Throughout the interview you will be answering questions and asking your own questions. Your demeanor, body language, and other nonverbal cues will also be on display. The interviewer will be trying to learn more about you, and you should be learning more about the job and the organization. Although you may be asked some unique questions, many interviewers ask standard, time-proven questions, which means that you can prepare your answers ahead of time.

Sending Positive Nonverbal Messages and Acting Professionally

How can you send positive nonverbal messages during your job interview?

You have already sent nonverbal messages to your interviewer by arriving on time, being courteous, dressing professionally, and greeting the receptionist and interviewer confidently. You will continue to send nonverbal messages throughout the interview. Remember that what comes out of your mouth and what is written on your résumé are not the only messages an interviewer receives from you. Nonverbal messages also create powerful impressions on people. Here are suggestions that will help you send the right nonverbal messages during face-to-face and online interviews:

- **Control your body movements.** Keep your hands, arms, and elbows to yourself. Don't lean on a desk. Keep your feet on the floor. Don't cross your arms in front of you. Keep your hands out of your pockets.
- **Exhibit good posture.** Sit erect, leaning forward slightly. Don't slouch in your chair; at the same time, don't look too stiff and uncomfortable. Good posture demonstrates confidence and interest.
- **Practice appropriate eye contact.** A direct eye gaze, at least in North America, suggests interest and trustworthiness. If you are being interviewed by a panel, remember to maintain eye contact with all interviewers.
- **Use gestures effectively.** Nod to show agreement and interest. Gestures should be used as needed, but don't overdo it.
- **Smile enough to convey a positive attitude.** Have a friend give you honest feedback on whether you generally smile too much or not enough.
- **Listen attentively.** Show the interviewer you are interested and attentive by listening carefully to the questions being asked. This will also help you answer questions appropriately.
- **Turn off your cell phone or other electronic devices.** Avoid the embarrassment of having your cell phone ring or your BlackBerry buzz during an interview by turning it completely off, not just switching it to vibrate.
- **Don't chew gum.** Chewing gum during an interview is distracting and unprofessional.
- **Sound enthusiastic and interested—but sincere.** The tone of your voice has an enormous effect on the words you say. Avoid sounding bored, frustrated, or sarcastic during an interview. Employers want employees who are enthusiastic and interested.
- **Avoid empty words.** Filling your answers with verbal pauses such as *um*, *uh*, *like*, and *basically* communicates that you are unprepared. Also avoid annoying distractions such as clearing your throat repeatedly or sighing deeply.

Remember that the way you answer questions can be almost as important as what you say. Use the interviewer's name and title from time to time when you answer. *Ms. Lyon, I would be pleased to tell you about....* People like to hear their own names. Be sure you are pronouncing the name correctly, and don't overuse this technique. Avoid answering questions with a simple *yes* or *no*; elaborate on your answers to better sell yourself. Keep your answers positive; don't criticize anything or anyone.

During the interview it may be necessary to occasionally refocus and clarify vague questions. Some interviewers are inexperienced and ill at ease in the role. You may even have to ask your own question to understand what was asked, *By _____, do you mean _____?* Consider

FIGURE 16.1 Twelve Interview Actions to Avoid

1. **Don't be late or too early.** Arrive five to ten minutes before your scheduled interview.
2. **Don't be rude.** Treat everyone you come into contact with warmly and respectfully.
3. **Don't ask for the job.** Asking for the job is naïve, undignified, and unprofessional. Wait to see how the interview develops.
4. **Don't criticize anyone or anything.** Don't criticize your current or previous employer, supervisors, colleagues, or job. The tendency is for interviewers to wonder whether you would speak about their companies similarly.
5. **Don't be a threat to the interviewer.** Avoid suggesting directly or indirectly that your goal is to become head honcho, a path that might include the interviewer's job.
6. **Don't act unprofessionally.** Don't discuss controversial subjects, and don't use profanity. Don't talk too much.
7. **Don't emphasize salary or benefits.** Don't bring up salary, vacation, or benefits early in an interview. Leave this up to the interviewer.
8. **Don't focus on your imperfections.** Never dwell on your liabilities or talk negatively about yourself.
9. **Don't interrupt.** Interrupting is not only impolite but also prevents you from hearing a complete question or remark.
10. **Don't bring someone along.** Don't bring a friend or relative with you to the interview. If someone must drive you, ask that person to drop you off and come back later.
11. **Don't appear impatient.** Your entire focus should be on the interview. Don't glance at your watch, which can imply that you are late for another appointment.
12. **Don't act desperate.** A sure way to turn off an interviewer is to act too desperate. Don't focus on why you *need* the job; focus on how you will add value to the organization.

closing out some of your responses with *Does that answer your question?* or *Would you like me to elaborate on any particular experience?*

Always aim your answers at the key characteristics interviewers seek: expertise, competence, motivation, interpersonal skills, decision-making skills, enthusiasm for the company and the job, and a pleasing personality. Remember to stay focused on your strengths. Don't reveal weaknesses, even if you think they make you look human. You won't be hired for your weaknesses, only for your strengths.

Be sure to use good English and enunciate clearly. Avoid slurred words such as *gonna* and *din't*, as well as slangy expressions such as *yeah, like,* and *ya know.* As you practice answering expected interview questions, it is always a good idea to make a recording or to ask a trusted friend for feedback. Is your speech filled with verbal static?

You cannot expect to be perfect in an employment interview. No one is. However, you can avert sure disaster by avoiding certain topics and behaviors such as those described in Figure 16.1.

Answering Typical Interview Questions

LEARNING OBJECTIVE 4

Describe how to answer typical interview questions such as those that seek to get acquainted, gauge your interest, probe your experience, explore your accomplishments, look to the future, and inquire about salary expectations.

Employment interviews are all about questions, and many of the questions interviewers ask are not new. You can anticipate a large percentage of questions that will be asked before you ever walk into an interview room. Although you cannot anticipate every question, you can prepare for different types.

This section presents questions that may be asked during employment interviews. Some questions are meant to help the interviewer become acquainted with you. Others are aimed at measuring your interest, experience, and accomplishments. Still others will probe your future plans and challenge your reactions. Some will inquire about your salary expectations. Your interviewer may use situational or behavioral questions and may even occasionally ask an illegal question. To get you thinking about how to respond, we have provided an answer for, or a discussion of, one or more of the questions in each of the following groups. As you read the remaining questions in each group, think about how you could respond most effectively. For additional questions, contact your campus career center, or consult one of the career Web sites mentioned in Chapter 15.

Questions to Get Acquainted

After opening introductions, recruiters generally try to start the interview with personal questions designed to put you at ease. They are also striving to gain an overview to see whether you will fit into the organization's culture. When answering these questions, keep the employer's needs in mind and try to incorporate your success stories.

1. Tell me about yourself.

   Experts agree that you must keep this answer short (one to two minutes tops) but on target. Use this chance to promote yourself. Stick to educational, professional, or business-related strengths; avoid personal or humorous references. Be ready with at least three success stories illustrating characteristics important to this job. Demonstrate responsibility you have been given; describe how you contributed as a team player. Try practicing this formula: *I have completed a ______ degree with a major in ____. Recently I worked for ______ as a ______. Before that I worked for ______ as a _____. My strengths are ________* (interpersonal) *and* ________ (technical). Try rehearsing your response in 30-second segments devoted to your education, work experience, qualifications, and skills.

2. What are your greatest strengths?

   Stress your strengths that are related to the position, such as, *I am well organized, thorough, and attentive to detail.* Tell success stories and give examples that illustrate these qualities: *My supervisor says that my research is exceptionally thorough. For example, I recently worked on a research project in which I. . . .*

3. Do you prefer to work by yourself or with others? Why?

   This question can be tricky. Provide a middle-of-the-road answer that not only suggests your interpersonal qualities but also reflects an ability to make independent decisions and work without supervision.

4. What was your major in college, and why did you choose it?
5. What are some things you do in your spare time?

Questions to Gauge Your Interest

Interviewers want to understand your motivation for applying for a position. Although they will realize that you are probably interviewing for other positions, they still want to know why you are interested in this particular position with this organization. These types of questions help them determine your level of interest.

How can you convince the interviewer that you are interested in working for his or her organization?

1. Why do you want to work for (name of company)?

   Questions like this illustrate why you must research an organization thoroughly before the interview. The answer to this question must prove that you understand the company and its culture. This is the perfect place to bring up the company research you did before the interview. Show what you know about the company, and discuss why you want to become a part of this organization. Describe your desire to work for this organization not only from your perspective but also from its point of view. What do you have to offer that will benefit the organization?

2. Why are you interested in this position?
3. What do you know about our company?
4. Why do you want to work in the ______________ industry?
5. What interests you about our products (or services)?

Questions About Your Experience and Accomplishments

After questions about your background and education and questions that measure your interest, the interview generally becomes more specific with questions about your experience and accomplishments. Remember to show confidence when you answer these questions. If you are not confident in your abilities, why should an employer be?

How can you convince an interviewer to hire you, even if you have less experience and fewer accomplishments than other applicants?

Zooming In PART 2

Googling for Jobs

Although Google has improved the efficiency and timeliness of its hiring efforts, the process is still demanding. To sort through the huge volume of résumés quickly without missing qualified applicants, the company developed an online survey with questions about attitudes, work habits, personality, and past experiences. Recruiters use search techniques to identify suitable candidates for particular jobs. Then they conduct one or more screening interviews by telephone to get more background on applicants.

Candidates who meet the hiring criteria then spend a day at the company participating in interviews with at least four people, including managers and potential colleagues. "They'll meet the hiring manager, of course, but also a few peers and a few people who would be senior to them, but not direct supervisors," said Judy Gilbert, director of staffing programs.[18] Some interviewees are asked to perform job-related tasks during the visit.

Interviewers give their feedback to a hiring committee, which evaluates the applicant's skills for the position as well as his or her overall fit into Google's culture and potential future contributions. All hiring decisions at Google are made by consensus, which can take up to two weeks. At Google the opinions of all employees involved in the hiring process count, which ensures a fair hiring process that maintains Google's high standards as the company grows.[19]

© AP Images/Paul Sakuma

Critical Thinking

- Why are online questionnaires and screening interviews useful tools for Google's recruiters?
- How does thorough preparation help a candidate reduce the stress and butterflies that most people feel during an interview?
- How can you prepare in advance for behavioral interview questions?

1. Why should we hire you when we have applicants with more experience or better credentials?

   In answering this question, remember that employers often hire people who present themselves well instead of others with better credentials. Emphasize your personal strengths that could be an advantage with this employer. Are you a hard worker? How can you demonstrate it? Have you had recent training? Some people have had more years of experience but actually have less knowledge because they have done the same thing over and over. Stress your experience using the latest methods and equipment. Be sure to mention your computer training and use of the Web. Tell success stories. Emphasize that you are open to new ideas and learn quickly. Above all, show that you are confident in your abilities.
2. Describe the most rewarding experience of your career so far.
3. How have your education and professional experiences prepared you for this position?
4. What were your major accomplishments in each of your past jobs?
5. What was a typical workday like?
6. What job functions did you enjoy most? Least? Why?
7. Tell me about your computer skills.
8. Who was the toughest boss you ever worked for and why?
9. What were your major achievements in college?
10. Why did you leave your last position? *OR:* Why are you leaving your current position?

What should you focus on when answering questions about the future?

Questions About the Future

Questions that look into the future tend to stump some candidates, especially those who have not prepared adequately. Employers ask these questions to see whether you are goal oriented and to determine whether your goals are realistic.

1. Where do you expect to be five (or ten) years from now?

   Formulate a realistic plan with respect to your present age and situation. The important thing is to be prepared for this question. It is a sure kiss of death to respond that you would like to have the interviewer's job! Instead, show an interest in the current job and in making a contribution to the organization. Talk about the levels of responsibility you would like to achieve. One employment counselor suggests showing ambition but not committing to a specific job title. Suggest that you hope to have learned enough to have progressed to a position in which you will continue to grow. Keep your answer focused on educational and professional goals, not personal goals.

2. If you got this position, what would you do to be sure you fit in?
3. This is a large (or small) organization. Do you think you would like that environment?
4. Do you plan to continue your education?
5. What do you predict for the future of the ______________ industry?
6. How do you think you can contribute to this company?
7. What would you most like to accomplish were you to get this position?
8. How do you keep current with what is happening in your profession?

Challenging Questions

How can you turn a discussion of your weaknesses into one that shows your strengths?

The following questions may make you uncomfortable, but the important thing to remember is to answer truthfully without dwelling on your weaknesses. As quickly as possible, convert any negative response into a discussion of your strengths.

1. What is your greatest weakness?

   It is amazing how many candidates knock themselves out of the competition by answering this question poorly. Actually, you have many choices. You can present a strength as a weakness (*Some people complain that I'm a workaholic or too attentive to details*). You can mention a corrected weakness (*Because I needed to learn about designing Web sites, I took a course*). You could cite an unrelated skill (*I really need to brush up on my Spanish*). You can cite a learning objective (*One of my long-term goals is to learn more about international management. Does your company have any plans to expand overseas?*). Another possibility is to reaffirm your qualifications (*I have no weaknesses that affect my ability to do this job*). Be careful that your answer doesn't sound too cliché (*I tend to be a perfectionist*) and instead shows careful analysis of your abilities.

2. What type of people do you have no patience for?

   Avoid letting yourself fall into the trap of sounding overly critical. One possible response is, *I have always gotten along well with others. But I confess that I can be irritated by complainers who don't accept responsibility.*

3. If you could live your life over, what would you change and why?
4. How would your former (or current) supervisor describe you as an employee?
5. What do you want the most from your job?
6. What is your grade point average, and does it accurately reflect your abilities?
7. Have you ever used drugs?
8. Who in your life has influenced you the most and why?
9. What are you reading right now?
10. Describe your ideal work environment.
11. Is the customer always right?
12. How do you define success?

How can you prepare to answer questions about salary?

Questions About Salary

Remember that nearly all salaries are negotiable, depending on your qualifications. Knowing the typical salary range for the target position helps. The recruiter can tell you the salary ranges—but you will have to ask. If you have had little experience, you will probably be offered a salary somewhere between the low point and the midpoint in the range. With more experience, you can negotiate for a higher figure. A word of caution, though. One personnel manager warns that candidates who emphasize money are suspect because they may leave if offered a few thousand dollars more elsewhere. See the accompanying Career Coach box for dos and don'ts in negotiating a starting salary. Here are some typical salary-related questions:

1. What salary are you looking for?

   One way to handle salary questions is to ask politely to defer the discussion until it is clear that a job will be offered to you (*I'm sure when the time comes, we will be able to work out a fair compensation package. Right now, I'd rather focus on whether we have a match*). Another possible response is to reply candidly that you can't know what to ask until you know more about the position and the company. If you continue to be pressed for a dollar figure, give a salary range with an annual dollar amount. Be sure to do research before the interview so that you know what similar jobs are paying in your geographic region. For example, check a Web site such as **http://www.salary.com**. When citing salary expectations, you will sound more professional if you cite an annual salary range rather than a dollar-per-hour amount.

2. How much are you presently earning?
3. How much do you think you're worth?
4. How much money do you expect to earn within the next ten years?
5. Are you willing to take a pay cut from your current (or previous) job?

CAREER COACH

Let's Talk Money: Salary Negotiation Dos and Don'ts

Nearly all salaries are negotiable. The following dos and don'ts can guide you to a better starting salary.

- **Do** make sure you have done your research on the salary you should expect for the position you are seeking. **Do** understand how geographic location affects salary ranges.
- **Don't** bring up salary before the employer does. **Do** delay salary negotiation until you know exactly what the position entails.
- **Do** be aware of your strengths and achievements. **Do** be sure to demonstrate the value you will bring to the employer.
- **Don't** tell the employer the salary you need to pay your bills or meet personal obligations.
- **Do** let the employer make the first salary offer. **Do**, if asked, say you expect a salary that is competitive with the market, or give a salary range that you find acceptable.
- **Don't** inflate your current earnings just to get a higher salary offer.
- **Don't** feel obligated to accept the first salary offer. **Do** negotiate salary if the offer made is inadequate.
- **Do** thank the employer for the offer when it is made. **Don't** try to negotiate right after the offer is made. **Do** take the time to consider all factors before making any job offer decisions.
- **Don't** be overly aggressive in negotiating the salary you want.
- **Don't** focus solely on salary. **Do** consider the entire compensation package.
- **Do** try to obtain other concessions (shorter review time, better title, better workspace) or benefits (bonuses, vacation time) if you aren't successful at negotiating a salary you want.
- **Don't** enter salary negotiations as part of an ego trip or game.
- **Don't** agree to the first acceptable salary offer you receive if you are not sure about the job or the company.
- **Do** get the offer in writing.

Career Application

Role-play a situation in which a hiring manager offers a candidate a starting salary of $42,500. The candidate wants $45,000 to start. The candidate responds to preliminary questions and negotiates the salary offer.

Situational Questions

Questions related to situations help employers test your thought processes and logical thinking. When using situational questions, interviewers describe a hypothetical situation and ask how you would handle it. Situational questions differ based on the type of position for which you are interviewing. Knowledge of the position and the company culture will help you respond favorably to these questions. Even if the situation sounds negative, keep your response positive. Here are just a few examples:

What are the purposes of situational and behavioral interview questions?

1. You receive a call from an irate customer who complains about the service she received last night at your restaurant. She is demanding her money back. How would you handle the situation?
2. If you were aware that a coworker was falsifying data, what would you do?
3. Your supervisor has just told you that she is dissatisfied with your work, but you think it is acceptable. How would you resolve the conflict?
4. Your supervisor has told you to do something a certain way, and you think that way is wrong and that you know a far better way to complete the task. What would you do?
5. Assume that you are hired for this position. You soon learn that one of the staff is extremely resentful because she applied for your position and was turned down. As a result, she is being unhelpful and obstructive. How would you handle the situation?
6. A colleague has told you in confidence that she suspects another colleague of stealing. What would your actions be?
7. You have noticed that communication between upper management and first-level employees is eroding. How would you solve this problem?

Behavioral Questions

Instead of traditional interview questions, you may be asked to tell stories. The interviewer may say, *Describe a time when* … or *Tell me about a time when* … . To respond effectively, learn to use the storytelling, or STAR, technique. Ask yourself, what the **S**ituation or **T**ask was, what **A**ction you took, and what the **R**esults were.[20] Practice using this method to recall specific examples of your skills and accomplishments. To be fully prepared, develop a coherent and articulate STAR narrative for every bullet point on your résumé. When answering behavioral questions, describe only educational and work-related situations or tasks, and try to keep them as current as possible. Here are a few examples of behavioral questions:

When answering behavioral questions, what types of situations or tasks should you discuss?

1. Tell me about a time when you solved a difficult problem.

   Tell a concise story explaining the situation or task, what you did, and the result. For example, *When I was at Ace Products, we continually had a problem of excessive back orders. After analyzing the situation, I discovered that orders went through many unnecessary steps. I suggested that we eliminate much paperwork. As a result, we reduced back orders by 30 percent.* Go on to emphasize what you learned and how you can apply that learning to this job. Practice your success stories in advance so that you will be ready.

2. Describe a situation in which you were able to use persuasion to successfully convince someone to see things your way.

   The recruiter is interested in your leadership and teamwork skills. You might respond, *I have learned to appreciate the fact that the way you present an idea is just as important as the idea itself. When trying to influence people, I put myself in their shoes and find some way to frame my idea from their perspective. I remember when I.…*

3. Describe a time when you had to analyze information and make a recommendation.
4. Describe a time that you worked successfully as part of a team.

Spotlight on Communicators

Employers today increasingly rely on behavioral interviews to select the right candidate. Instead of traditional questions, you may be asked to "describe a time when…." Career consultant Daisy Wright advises using the storytelling, or STAR, technique when responding. Ask yourself what the **S**ituation or **T**ask was, what **A**ction you took, and what the **R**esults were. This method helps you recall specific job-related examples of your skills and accomplishments. Be sure to focus on the successful role you played.

5. Tell me about a time when you dealt with confidential information.
6. Give me an example of a time when you were under stress to meet a deadline.
7. Tell me about a time when you had to go above and beyond the call of duty to get a job done.
8. Tell me about a time you were able to deal with another person successfully even though that person did not like you personally (or vice versa).
9. Give me an example of when you showed initiative and took the lead.
10. Tell me about a recent situation in which you had to deal with an upset customer or coworker.

What is the best way to handle an illegal interview question?

Illegal and Inappropriate Questions

Federal laws prohibit employment discrimination based on gender, age, religion, color, race, national origin, and disability. In addition, many state and city laws prohibit employment discrimination based on such factors as sexual orientation.[21] Therefore, it is inappropriate for interviewers to ask any question related to these areas. These questions become illegal, though, only when a court of law determines that the employer is asking them with the intent to discriminate.[22] Most illegal interview questions are asked innocently by inexperienced interviewers. Some are only trying to be friendly when they inquire about your personal life or family. Regardless of the intent, how should you react?

If you find the question harmless and if you want the job, go ahead and answer it. If you think that answering it would damage your chance to be hired, try to deflect the question tactfully with a response such as, *Could you tell me how my marital status relates to the responsibilities of this position?* or, *I prefer to keep my personal and professional lives separate.* If you are uncomfortable answering a question, try to determine the reason behind it; you might answer, *I don't let my personal life interfere with my ability to do my job,* or, *Are you concerned with my availability to work overtime?* Another option, of course, is to respond to any inappropriate or illegal question by confronting the interviewer and threatening a lawsuit or refusing to answer. However, you could not expect to be hired under these circumstances. In any case, you might wish to reconsider working for an organization that sanctions such procedures.

Here are some inappropriate and illegal questions that you may or may not want to answer:[23]

1. What is your marital status? Are you married? Do you live with anyone? Do you have a boyfriend (or girlfriend)? (However, employers can ask your marital status after hiring for tax and insurance forms.)
2. Do you have any disabilities? Have you had any recent illnesses? (But it is legal to ask if the person can perform specific job duties, such as, *Can you carry a 50-pound sack up a 10-foot ladder five times daily?)*
3. I notice you have an accent. Where are you from? What is the origin of your last name? What is your native language? (However, it is legal to ask what languages you speak fluently if language ability is related to the job.)
4. Have you ever filed a workers' compensation claim or been injured on the job?
5. Have you ever had a drinking problem or been addicted to drugs? (But it is legal to ask if a person uses illegal drugs.)
6. Have you ever been arrested? (But it is legal to ask, *Have you ever been convicted of ____________?* when the crime is related to the job.)
7. How old are you? What is your date of birth? When did you graduate from high school? (But it is legal to ask, *Are you 16 years (or 18 years or 21 years) old or older?* depending on the age requirements for the position.)
8. Of what country are you a citizen? Where were you born? (But it is legal to ask, *Are you a citizen of the United States?* or, *Can you legally work in the United States?)*
9. What is your maiden name? (But it is legal to ask, *What is your full name?* or, *Have you worked under another name?)*

Ethics Check

Jack and Suzy Welch: Human Resources Must Get Firing Right

Former General Electric CEO Jack Welch and his business journalist wife, Suzy M believe that human resources must execute layoffs fairly: First, the Welches recommend that pink slips be delivered "face-to-face, eyeball-to-eyeball" by the employee's manager, not a stranger. Second, HR must handle severance arrangements evenhandedly. Last, HR has to provide genuine consolation and assist with the transition, the Welches suggest. Do you believe that such attempts at making downsizing more humane are effective?

10. Do you have any religious beliefs that would prevent you from working weekends or holidays? (An employer can, however, ask if you are available to work weekends and holidays.)
11. Do you have children? Do you plan to have children? Do you have adequate child care arrangements? (However, employers can ask for dependent information for tax and insurance purposes after you are hired.)
12. How much do you weigh? How tall are you? (However, employers can ask you about your height and weight if minimum standards are necessary to safely perform a job.)

Closing the Interview

LEARNING OBJECTIVE 5

Understand how to close an interview positively, including asking meaningful questions.

Once the interview nears conclusion, start thinking about how to end on a positive note. It is easy to become flustered after a challenging interview, so be sure to practice questions that you plan to ask. Also, focus on how to leave a lasting positive impression.

Asking Your Own Questions

At some point in the interview, usually near the end, you will be asked whether you have any questions. The worst thing you can do is say *No,* which suggests that you are not interested in the position. Instead, ask questions that will help you gain information and will impress the interviewer with your thoughtfulness and interest in the position. Remember that this interview is a two-way street. You must be happy with the prospect of working for this organization. You want a position for which your skills and personality are matched. Use this opportunity to learn whether this job is right for you. Be aware that you don't have to wait for the interviewer to ask you for questions. You can ask your own questions throughout the interview to learn more about the company and position. Here are some questions you might ask:

What are some good questions for you to ask at the end of the job interview?

1. What will my duties be (if not already discussed)?
2. Tell me what it's like working here in terms of the people, management practices, workloads, expected performance, and rewards.
3. What training programs are available from this organization? What specific training will be given for this position?
4. Who would be my immediate supervisor?
5. What is the organizational structure, and where does this position fit in?
6. Is travel required in this position?
7. How is job performance evaluated?
8. Assuming my work is excellent, where do you see me in five years?
9. How long do employees generally stay with this organization?
10. What are the major challenges for a person in this position?
11. What do you see in the future of this organization?
12. What do you like best about working for this organization?
13. May I have a tour of the facilities?
14. When do you expect to make a decision?

Do not ask about salary or benefits, especially during the first interview. It is best to let the interviewer bring those topics up first.

Ending Positively

What can you do to end the interview positively?

After you have asked your questions, the interviewer will signal the end of the interview, usually by standing up or by expressing appreciation that you came. If not addressed earlier, you should at this time find out what action will follow. Demonstrate your interest in the position by asking when it will be filled or what the next step will be. Too many candidates leave the interview without knowing their status or when they will hear from the recruiter. Don't be afraid to say that you want the job!

Before you leave, summarize your strongest qualifications, show your enthusiasm for obtaining this position, and thank the interviewer for a constructive interview and for considering you for the position. Ask the interviewer for a business card, which will provide the information you need to write a thank-you letter, which is discussed later. Shake the interviewer's hand with confidence, and acknowledge anyone else you see on the way out. Be sure to thank the receptionist. Leaving the interview gracefully and enthusiastically will leave a lasting impression on those responsible for making the final hiring decision.

After the Interview

LEARNING OBJECTIVE 6

Outline the activities that take place after an interview, including thanking the interviewer and contacting references.

After leaving the interview, immediately make notes of what was said in case you are called back for a second interview. Write down key points that were discussed, the names of people you spoke with, and other details of the interview. Ask yourself what went really well and what could have been improved. Note your strengths and weaknesses during the interview so that you can work to improve in future interviews. Next, write down your follow-up plans. To whom should you send thank-you letters? Will you contact the employer by phone? If so, when? Then be sure to follow up on those plans, beginning with writing a thank-you letter and contacting your references.

Thanking Your Interviewer

Why is it important to send a thank-you message after a job interview?

After a job interview, you should always send a thank-you message, also called a follow-up message. This courtesy sets you apart from other applicants, most of whom will not bother. Your message also reminds the interviewer of your visit as well as suggesting your good manners and genuine enthusiasm for the job.

Follow-up messages are most effective if sent immediately after the interview. Experts believe that a thoughtful follow-up message carries as much weight as the cover letter does. Almost nine out of ten senior executives admit that in their evaluation of a job candidate they are swayed by a written thank-you.[24] In your thank-you message, refer to the date of the interview, the exact job title for which you were interviewed, and specific topics discussed. "An effective thank-you message should hit every one of the employer's hot buttons," author and career consultant Wendy Enelow says.[25] Avoid worn-out phrases, such as *Thank you for taking the time to interview me.* Be careful, too, about overusing *I*, especially to begin sentences. Most important, show that you really want the job and that you are qualified for it. Notice how the thank-you message in Figure 16.2 conveys enthusiasm and confidence.

If you have been interviewed by more than one person, send a separate thank-you message to each interviewer. It is also a good idea to send a thank-you message to the receptionist and to the person who set up the interview. Your thank-you message will probably make more of an impact if prepared in proper business letter format and sent by regular mail. However, if you know the decision will be made quickly, send your follow-up message by e-mail. Make sure that your e-mail message is written using professional language, standard capitalization, and proper punctuation. One job candidate now makes a follow-up e-mail a practice. She summarizes what was discussed during the face-to-face interview and adds information that she had not thought to mention during the interview.[26]

Contacting Your References

Why should you contact your references after a job interview?

Once you have thanked your interviewer, it is time to alert your references that they may be contacted by the employer. You might also have to request a letter of recommendation to be sent to the employer by a certain date. As discussed in Chapter 15, you should have already asked permission to use these individuals as references, and you should have supplied them with a copy of your résumé and information about the types of positions you are seeking.

To provide the best possible recommendation, your references need information. What position have you applied for with what company? What should they stress to the prospective

FIGURE 16.2 Interview Follow-Up Message

Christopher D. Wiley
3592 Channel Islands Boulevard, Ventura, CA 90630
(805) 483-6734, cwiley@yahoo.com

May 31, 2012

Mr. Eric C. Nielsen
Comstock Images & Technology
3201 State Street
Santa Barbara, CA 93104

Dear Mr. Nielsen:

Talking with you Wednesday, May 30, about the graphic designer position was both informative and interesting.

Thanks for describing the position in such detail and for introducing me to Ms. Ouchi, the senior designer. Her current project designing an annual report in four colors sounds fascinating as well as quite challenging.

Now that I've learned in greater detail the specific tasks of your graphic designers, I'm more than ever convinced that my computer and creative skills can make a genuine contribution to your graphic productions. My training in design and layout using Photoshop, Illustrator, and InDesign ensures that I could be immediately productive on your staff.

You will find me an enthusiastic and hardworking member of any team effort. As you requested, I'm enclosing additional samples of my work. I'm eager to join the graphics staff at your Santa Barbara headquarters, and I look forward to hearing from you soon.

Sincerely,

Christopher D. Wiley
Christopher D. Wiley

Enclosures

Uses customized letterhead but could have merely typed street and city address above dateline

Mentions the interview date and specific job title

Personalizes the message by referring to topics discussed in the interview

Highlights specific skills for the job

Shows good manners, appreciation, and perseverance—traits that recruiters value

Reminds reader of interpersonal skills as well as enthusiasm and eagerness for the job

employer? Let's say you are applying for a specific job that requires a letter of recommendation. Professor Orenstein has already agreed to be a reference for you. To get the best letter of recommendation from Professor Orenstein, help her out. Write an e-mail message or letter telling her about the position, its requirements, and the recommendation deadline. Include copies of your résumé and college transcript. You might remind her of a positive experience with you that she could use in the recommendation. Remember that recommenders need evidence to support generalizations. Give them appropriate ammunition, as the student has done in the following request:

Dear Professor Orenstein:

Recently I interviewed for the position of administrative assistant in the Human Resources Department of Host International. Because you kindly agreed to help me, I am now asking you to write a letter of recommendation to Host.

In a reference request letter, tell immediately why you are writing. Identify the target position and company.

Checklist

Performing Effectively Before, During, and After a Job Interview

Before the Interview

- **Expect to be screened by telephone.** Near your telephone, keep your résumé, a list of references, a calendar, and a notepad. Also have a list of companies where you applied.
- **Research the target company.** Once an interview is scheduled, conduct in-depth research about the company's history, mission and goals, size, geographic locations, number of employees, customers, competitors, culture, management structure, names of leaders, reputation in the community, financial condition, strengths and weaknesses, and future plans. Talk to company employees if possible.
- **Prepare success stories.** Organize and practice many success stories with specific examples of your educational and work-related experiences that demonstrate your accomplishments and achievements. Be ready to recite them in 30-second sound bites.
- **Practice answers to possible questions.** Recite answers to typical questions in a mirror, with a friend, or in spare moments. Consider recording a practice session to evaluate your performance. Be ready to explain problem areas on your résumé.
- **Clean up your digital dirt.** Remove any incriminating, provocative, or distasteful photos, contents, and links that could make you look unprofessional to potential employers.
- **Get ready.** Take a trial trip to locate the employer. Select professional-looking clothes for the interview. Gather items to take with you: copies of your résumé and reference list, a notebook and pen, money for parking and tolls, and work samples, if appropriate. Use a presentable briefcase to carry your items.

During the Interview

- **Send positive nonverbal messages.** Control your body movements; use good posture; maintain appropriate eye contact; use gestures effectively; smile enough to convey a positive attitude; listen attentively; turn off your cell phone or other electronic devices; don't chew gum; sound enthusiastic and interested; and avoid empty words such as *um, uh, like,* and *ya know.*
- **Fight fear.** Remind yourself that you are thoroughly prepared, breathe deeply, know that your fear is typical, and remember that the interviewer has to please you as well.
- **Be confident.** Use the interviewer's name, refocus and clarify vague questions, and aim your answers at key characteristics interviewers seek.
- **Incorporate your success stories.** As you answer questions, work in your success stories that emphasize your skills and accomplishments. Keep in mind the employer's needs for this particular position.
- **Express enthusiasm for working for this company.** Show what you know about the company and explain why you want to become part of this organization.

Closing the Interview

- **Ask your own questions.** Be prepared with meaningful, thoughtful questions to help you determine whether this job is right for you.
- **End the interview positively.** Summarize your strongest qualifications, show your enthusiasm for the job, and thank the interviewer. Ask for the interviewer's business card. Shake hands, and acknowledge anyone else on the way out.

After the Interview

- **Make notes.** Immediately record key points, and note what you could improve for your next interview.
- **Send a thank-you message.** Thank the interviewer in a message that notes the date of the interview, the exact title of the position, and specific topics discussed. Express your enthusiasm for the job, and thank the interviewer for sharing information about the position and the organization. E-mail messages are increasingly acceptable.
- **Contact your references.** Alert your references that they may be contacted by the employer. Provide any additional information that will help them make supportive statements.

Specify the job requirements so that the recommender knows what to stress.

The position calls for good organizational, interpersonal, and writing skills, as well as computer experience. To help you review my skills and training, I enclose my résumé. As you may recall, I earned an A in your business communication class; and you commended my long report for its clarity and organization.

Provide a stamped, addressed envelope.

Please send your letter to Mr. James Jenkins at Host International before July 1 in the enclosed stamped, addressed envelope. I'm grateful for your support, and I promise to let you know the results of my job search.

Sincerely,

Following Up

If you don't hear from the interviewer within five days, or at the specified time, call him or her. Practice saying something like, *I'm wondering what else I can do to convince you that I'm the right person for this job*, or, *I'm calling to find out the status of your search to fill the ____________ position.* You could also e-mail the interviewer to find out how the decision process is going. When following up, it is important to sound professional and courteous. Sounding desperate, angry, or frustrated that you have not been contacted can ruin your chances. The following follow-up e-mail message would impress the interviewer:

Dear Ms. Jamison:

I enjoyed my interview with you last Thursday for the receptionist position. You should know that I'm very interested in this opportunity with Coastal Enterprises. Because you mentioned that you might have an answer this week, I'm eager to know how your decision process is coming along. I look forward to hearing from you.

Sincerely,

Depending on the response you get to your first follow-up request, you may have to follow up additional times. Keep in mind, though, that some employers will not tell you about their hiring decision unless you are the one hired. Don't harass the interviewer, and don't force a decision. If you don't hear back from an employer within several weeks after following up, it is best to assume that you didn't get the job and to continue with your job search.

To review the important actions you can take to perform effectively before, during, and after a job interview, see the checklist on page 556.

When should you call or send a follow-up e-mail message to a potential employer?

ETHICS CHECK

Halfhearted

Assume that you have been offered a job. However, you have gone to several other interviews that seemed to have gone very well, and now you are emboldened by your success and want to wait for a better offer. Is it ethical to accept the present offer while you are waiting, and later turn it down if something better comes along?

Other Employment Documents and Follow-Up Messages

LEARNING OBJECTIVE 7

Understand how to complete employment applications and write résumé follow-up, rejection follow-up, job acceptance, and job rejection messages.

Although the résumé and cover letter are your major tasks, other important documents and messages are often required during the employment process. You may need to complete an employment application form and write follow-up letters. You might also have to write a letter of resignation when leaving a job. Because each of these tasks reveals something about you and your communication skills, you will want to put your best foot forward. These documents often subtly influence company officials to offer a job.

Application Form

Some organizations require job candidates to fill out job application forms instead of, or in addition to, submitting résumés. This practice permits them to gather and store standardized data about each applicant. Whether the application is on paper or online, follow the directions carefully and provide accurate information. The following suggestions can help you be prepared:

- Carry a card summarizing vital statistics not included on your résumé. If you are asked to fill out an application form in an employer's office, you will need a handy reference to the following data: graduation dates, beginning and ending dates of all employment; salary history; full names, titles, and present work addresses of former supervisors; full addresses and phone numbers of current and previous employers; and full names, occupational titles, occupational addresses, and telephone numbers of people who have agreed to serve as references.
- Look over all the questions before starting.
- Fill out the form neatly, using blue or black ink. Many career counselors recommend printing your responses; cursive handwriting can be difficult to read.
- Answer all questions honestly. Write *Not applicable* or *N/A* if appropriate. Don't leave any sections blank.

- Use accurate spelling, grammar, capitalization, and punctuation.
- If asked which position you desire, give a specific job title or type of position. Don't say, *Anything* or *Open*. These answers make you look unfocused; moreover, they make it difficult for employers to know what you are qualified for or interested in.
- Be prepared for a salary question. Unless you know what comparable employees are earning in the company, the best strategy is to suggest a salary range or to write *Negotiable* or *Open*.
- Be prepared to explain the reasons for leaving previous positions. Use positive or neutral phrases such as *Relocation, Seasonal, To accept a position with more responsibility, Temporary position, To continue education*, or *Career change*. Avoid words or phrases such as *Fired, Quit, Didn't get along with supervisor*, or *Pregnant*.
- Look over the application before submitting to make sure it is complete and that you have followed all instructions. Sign and date the application.

Application or Résumé Follow-Up Letter

If your résumé or application generates no response within a reasonable time, you may decide to send a short follow-up letter such as the following. Doing so (a) jogs the memory of the personnel officer, (b) demonstrates your serious interest, and (c) allows you to emphasize your qualifications or to add new information.

Dear Ms. Lopez:

Open by reminding the reader of your interest.

Please know I am still interested in becoming an administrative support specialist with Quad, Inc.

Review your strengths or add new qualifications.

Since I submitted an application [or résumé] in May, I have completed my degree and have been employed as a summer replacement for office workers in several downtown offices. This experience has honed my word processing and communication skills. It has also introduced me to a wide range of office procedures.

Close positively; avoid accusations that make the reader defensive.

Please keep my application in your active file and let me know when I may put my formal training, technical skills, and practical experience to work for you.

Sincerely,

Rejection Follow-Up Letter

If you didn't get the job and you think it was perfect for you, don't give up. Employment specialists encourage applicants to respond to a rejection. The candidate who was offered the position may decline, or other positions may open up. In a rejection follow-up letter, it is OK to admit you are disappointed. Be sure to add, however, that you are still interested and will contact the company again in a month in case a job opens up. Then follow through for a couple of months—but don't overdo it. You should be professional and persistent, but not a pest. Here's an example of an effective rejection follow-up letter:

Dear Mr. O'Neal:

Subordinate your disappointment to your appreciation at being notified promptly and courteously.

Although I am disappointed that someone else was selected for your accounting position, I appreciate your promptness and courtesy in notifying me.

Emphasize your continuing interest.

Because I am confident that I have the technical and interpersonal skills needed to work in your fast-paced environment, I encourage you to keep my résumé in your active file. My desire to become a productive member of your Transamerica staff remains strong.

Refer to specifics of your interview.

I enjoyed our interview, and I especially appreciate the time you and Ms. Goldstein spent describing your company's expansion into international markets. To enhance my qualifications, I have enrolled in a course in international accounting at CSU.

Should you have an opening for which I am qualified, you may reach me at (818) 719-3901. In the meantime, I will call you in a month to discuss employment possibilities.

Take the initiative; tell when you will call for an update.

Sincerely,

Job Acceptance and Rejection Letters

When all your hard work pays off, you will be offered the position you want. Although you will likely accept the position over the phone, it is a good idea to follow up with an acceptance letter to confirm the details and to formalize the acceptance. Your acceptance letter might look like this:

Dear Ms. Scarborough:

It was a pleasure talking with you earlier today. As I mentioned, I am delighted to accept the position of Web designer with Innovative Creations, Inc., in your Seattle office. I look forward to becoming part of the IC team and to starting work on a variety of exciting and innovative projects.

Confirm your acceptance of the position with enthusiasm.

As we agreed, my starting salary will be $46,000, with a full benefits package including health and life insurance, retirement plan, stock options, and three weeks of vacation per year.

Review salary and benefits details.

I look forward to starting my position with Innovative Creations on September 15, 2012. Before that date I will send you the completed tax and insurance forms you need. Thanks again for everything, Ms. Scarborough.

Include the specific starting date.

Sincerely,

If you must turn down a job offer, show your professionalism by writing a sincere letter. This letter should thank the employer for the job offer and explain briefly that you are turning it down. Taking the time to extend this courtesy could help you in the future if this employer has a position you really want. Here is an example of a job rejection letter:

Dear Mr. Opperman:

Thank you very much for offering me the position of sales representative with Bendall Pharmaceuticals. It was a difficult decision to make, but I have accepted a position with another company.

Thank the employer for the job offer and decline the offer without giving specifics.

I appreciate your taking the time to interview me, and I wish Bendall much success in the future.

Express gratitude and best wishes for the future.

Sincerely,

Resignation Letter

After you have been in a position for a period of time, you may find it necessary to leave. Perhaps you have been offered a better position, or maybe you have decided to return to school full-time. Whatever the reason, you should leave your position gracefully and tactfully. Although you will likely discuss your resignation in person with your supervisor, it is a good idea to document your resignation by writing a formal letter. Some resignation letters are brief, while others contain great detail. Remember that many resignation letters are placed in personnel files; therefore, you should format and write yours using the professional business letter–writing techniques you learned earlier. Here is an example of a basic letter of resignation:

Dear Ms. Patrick:

This letter serves as formal notice of my resignation from Allied Corporation, effective Friday, August 17. I have enjoyed serving as your office assistant for the past two years, and I am grateful for everything I have learned during my employment with Allied.

Confirm exact date of resignation. Remind employer of your contributions.

Zooming In — YOUR TURN

Applying Your Skills at Google

With your passion for marketing and technology, you were excited to find a posting for a sales internship on the Google Web site. Interns work on a sales team and assist with industry research, data analysis, advertising strategy, sales administration, and related responsibilities. The requirements for the internship included good organizational and analytical skills, detail orientation, problem-solving abilities, and excellent written and verbal communication skills. You decided to apply for the Google internship, and you sent a cover letter and résumé and filled out the online questionnaire.

Several weeks later, a recruiter called you to chat about your qualifications for the job. You were pleased with how well the screening interview went. The recruiter was too, and she invited you to spend a day at the Googleplex.

Your Task

Using the techniques and resources described in this chapter, prepare for your visit to Google's corporate headquarters. Research the company and prepare a summary of the company's business philosophy, corporate culture, products, and other topics you consider relevant to the sales internship. Then develop a "cheat sheet" to help you highlight your skills as you answer typical interview questions. (See **Activity 16.10** to learn about cheat sheets.) Include questions that you would like to ask the interviewers. Submit your cheat sheet to your instructor.

© AP Images/Paul Sakuma

Offer assistance to prepare for your resignation.	*Please let me know what I can do over the next two weeks to help you prepare for my departure. I would be happy to help with finding and training my replacement.*
Offer thanks and end with a forward-looking statement.	*Thanks again for providing such a positive employment experience. I will long remember my time here.*

Sincerely,

Want to do well on tests and excel in your course? Go to **www.meguffey.com** for helpful interactive resources.

- **Review the Chapter 16 PowerPoint slides to prepare for the first quiz.**

Although the employee who wrote the preceding resignation letter gave the standard two-week notice, you may find that a longer notice is necessary. The higher your position and the greater your responsibility, the longer the notice you give your employer should be. You should, however, always give some notice as a courtesy.

Writing job acceptance, job rejection, and resignation letters requires effort. That effort, however, is worth it because you are building bridges that may transport you to even better jobs in the future.

Summary of Learning Objectives

1 Understand the importance of a job interview, its purposes, and its forms, including screening, hiring/placement, one-on-one, panel, group, sequential, stress, and online interviews. Job interviews are extremely important because they can change your life. As a job candidate, you have the following purposes in an interview: (a) convince the employer of your potential, (b) find out more about the job and the company, and (c) expand on the information in your résumé. From the employer's perspective, the interview is an opportunity to (a) assess your abilities in relation to the requirements for the position; (b) discuss your training, experience, knowledge, and abilities in more detail; (c) see what drives and motives you; and (d) decide whether you would fit into the organization. Screening interviews seek to eliminate less qualified candidates. Hiring/placement interviews may be one-on-one, panel, group, sequential, stress, or online.

Are you ready? Get more practice at **www.meguffey.com**

2 Describe what to do before an in-person or online interview, including researching the target company, rehearsing success stories, practicing answers to possible questions, and cleaning up digital dirt. If you are lucky enough to be selected for an interview, either in person or online, you should research the target company by learning about its products, mission, customers, competitors, and finances. Before your interview prepare 30-second success stories that demonstrate your qualifications and achievements. Practice answers to typical interview questions. Clean up any digital dirt. Expect to explain any problem areas on your résumé. If you are not sure where the employer is located, take a trial trip the day before your interview. Decide how to dress so that you will look qualified, competent, and professional. On the day of your interview, make sure you arrive on time and make a good first impression.

3 Explain what occurs the day of your interview, including traveling to and arriving at the interview, performing effectively during the interview, sending positive nonverbal messages, and using good techniques in answering questions. During your interview send positive nonverbal messages by controlling body movements, showing good posture, maintaining eye contact, using gestures effectively, and smiling enough to convey a positive attitude. Listen attentively, turn off your cell phone or other electronic devices, don't chew gum, and sound enthusiastic and sincere. If you feel nervous, breathe deeply and remind yourself that you are well prepared. Remember that you control part of this interview and that interviews are a two-way street.

4 Describe how to answer typical interview questions such as those that seek to get acquainted, gauge your interest, probe your experience, explore your accomplishments, look to the future, and inquire about salary expectations. Interviewers often ask the same types of questions. Be prepared to respond to inquiries such as, *Tell me about yourself.* Practice answering questions about why you want to work for the organization, why you should be hired, how your education and experience have prepared you for the position, where you expect to be in five or ten years, what your greatest weaknesses are, and how much money you expect to earn. Be ready for situational questions that ask you to respond to hypothetical situations. Expect behavioral questions that begin with *Tell me about a time when you . . . .* Think about how you would respond to illegal or inappropriate questions.

5 Understand how to close an interview positively, including asking meaningful questions. Toward the end of an interview, you should be prepared to ask your own questions, such as, *What will my duties be?* and, *When do you expect to make a decision?* After asking your questions and the interviewer signals the end of the meeting, find out what action will follow. Summarize your strongest qualifications, show your enthusiasm for obtaining this position, and thank the interviewer. Ask for the interviewer's business card. Shake the interviewer's hand with confidence, and acknowledge anyone else you see on the way out.

6 Outline the activities that take place after an interview, including thanking the interviewer and contacting references. After leaving the interview, immediately make notes of the key points discussed. Note your strengths and weaknesses during the interview so that you can work to improve in future interviews. Write a thank-you letter including the date of the interview, the exact job title for which you were interviewed, and specific topics discussed. Show that you really want the job. Alert your references that they may be contacted.

7 Understand how to complete employment applications and write résumé follow-up, rejection follow-up, job acceptance, and job rejection messages. If you don't hear from the interviewer within five days, or at the specified time, call him or her. You could also e-mail to learn how the decision process is going. Sound professional, not desperate, angry, or frustrated. If asked to fill out an application form, look over all the questions before starting. If asked for a salary figure, provide a salary range or write *Negotiable* or *Open*. If you don't get the job, consider writing a letter that expresses your disappointment but your desire to be contacted in case a job opens up. If you are offered a job, write a letter that confirms the details and formalizes your acceptance. If you decide not to accept a position, write a sincere letter to turn down the job offer. Upon resigning from a position, write a letter that confirms the date of resignation, offers assistance to prepare for your resignation, and expresses thanks.

Are you ready? Get more practice at **www.meguffey.com**

Chapter Review

1. How are the main purposes of a job interview different for the job candidate and for the employer? (Obj. 1)
2. What is a screening interview, and why is it so important? (Obj. 1)
3. Briefly describe the types of hiring/placement interviews you may encounter. (Obj. 1)
4. You have scheduled an interview with a large local company. What kind of information should you seek about this company, and where can you expect to find it? (Obj. 2)
5. What are success stories, and how can you use them during a job interview? (Obj. 2)
6. What is digital dirt, and what should you do to clean it up during the employment process? (Obj. 2)
7. How can you address problem areas on your résumé such as lack of experience, getting fired, or earning low grades? (Obj. 2)
8. What is your greatest fear of what you might do or what might happen to you during an employment interview? How can you overcome your fears? (Obj. 2)
9. Name at least six interviewing behaviors you can exhibit that send positive nonverbal messages during the job interview. (Obj. 3)
10. Should you be candid with an interviewer when asked about your weaknesses? (Obj. 4)
11. What should you do if asked a salary question early in an interview? (Obj. 4)
12. How should you respond to questions you feel are inappropriate or illegal? (Obj. 4)
13. What kinds of questions should you ask during an interview? (Obj. 5)
14. List the steps you should take immediately following your job interview. (Obj. 6)
15. If you are offered a position, why is it important to write an acceptance letter, and what should it include? (Obj. 7)

Critical Thinking

1. What can you do to appear professional when a potential employer contacts you by phone for a screening interview or to schedule a job interview? (Obj. 2)
2. Why do you think so many employers search for information about job applicants online using Google, Facebook, Twitter, and other online tools? Do you think these kinds of searches are ethical or appropriate? Isn't this similar to snooping? (Obj. 2)
3. Do you think behavioral questions (such as, *Tell me about a business problem you had, and how you solved it*) are more effective than traditional questions (such as, *Tell me what you are good at*)? Why? (Obj. 4)
4. If you are asked an illegal interview question, why is it important to first assess the intentions of the interviewer? (Obj. 4)
5. **Ethical Issue:** When asked about his previous salary in a job interview, Jeremy boosts his salary a bit. He reasons that he was about to get a raise, and he also felt that he deserved to be paid more than he was actually earning. Even his supervisor said that he was worth more than his salary. Is Jeremy justified in inflating his previous salary? (Obj. 4)

Activities

16.1 Researching an Organization (Obj. 2)

Web

An important part of your preparation for an interview is finding out about the target company.

Your Task. Select an organization where you would like to be employed. Assume you have been selected for an interview. Using resources described in this chapter, locate information about the organization's leaders and their business philosophies. Learn about the organization's history, accomplishments, setbacks, finances, products, customers, competition, and advertising. Prepare a summary report documenting your findings.

16.2 Learning What Jobs Are Really About Through Blogs, Facebook, and Twitter (Obj. 2)

Web

Blogs and social media sites such as Facebook and Twitter are becoming important tools in the employment search process. By accessing blogs, company Facebook pages, and Twitter feeds, job seekers can learn additional information about a company's culture and day-to-day activities.

Your Task. Using the Web, locate a blog that is maintained by an employee of a company where you would like to work. Monitor the blog for at least a week. Also access the company's Facebook page and monitor Twitter feeds for at least a week. Prepare a short report summarizing what you learned about the company through reading the blog postings, status updates, and tweets. Include a statement of whether this information would be valuable during your job search.

16.3 Taking a Look at Corporate Web Videos (Obj. 2)

Web

Would you like to know what it is like to work for the company that interests you? Check out Web videos posted by companies on their career pages, job boards, and even YouTube. Currently about 7,000 corporate videos await you on Jobing.com, a job board that lists openings in specific geographic regions.

Your Task. Search company recruiting Web sites, YouTube, or Jobing.com for videos featuring two or three companies in your chosen industry. Compare how the employers introduce themselves, which aspects they emphasize about their organizations, how they present their employees, what they offer potential applicants, and so forth. Write a short report addressed to your instructor comparing and contrasting the corporate Web videos you examined.

16.4 Building Interview Skills (Obj. 2)

Successful interviews require diligent preparation and repeated practice. To be well prepared, you need to know what skills are required for your targeted position. In addition to computer and communication skills, employers generally want to know whether a candidate works well with a team, accepts responsibility, solves problems, is efficient, meets deadlines, shows leadership, saves time and money, and is a hard worker.

Your Task. Consider a position for which you are eligible now or one for which you will be eligible when you complete your education. Identify the skills and traits necessary for this position. If you prepared a résumé in Chapter 15, be sure that it addresses these targeted areas. Now prepare interview worksheets listing at least ten technical and other skills or traits you think a recruiter will want to discuss in an interview for your targeted position.

16.5 Preparing Success Stories (Obj. 2)

You can best showcase your talents by being ready with your own success stories that show how you have developed the skills or traits required for your targeted position.

Your Task. Using the worksheets you prepared in **Activity 16.4**, prepare success stories that highlight the required skills or traits. Select three to five stories to develop into answers to potential interview questions. For example, here is a typical question: *How does your background relate to the position we have open?* A possible response: *As you know, I have just completed an intensive training program in _____________. In addition, I have over three years of part-time work experience in a variety of business settings. In one position I was selected to manage a small business in the absence of the owner. I developed responsibility and customer service skills in filling orders efficiently, resolving shipping problems, and monitoring key accounts. I also inventoried and organized products worth over $200,000. When the owner returned from a vacation to Florida, I was commended for increasing sales and was given a bonus in recognition of my efforts.* People relate to and remember stories. Try to shape your answers into memorable stories.

16.6 Exploring Appropriate Interview Attire (Obj. 2)

Web

As you prepare for your interview by learning about the company and the industry, don't forget a key component of interview success: creating a favorable first impression by wearing appropriate business attire. Job seekers often have nebulous ideas about proper interview wear. Some wardrobe mishaps include choosing a conservative "power suit" but accessorizing it with beat-up casual shoes or a shabby bag. Grooming glitches include dandruff on dark suit fabric, dirty fingernails, or mothball odor. Women sometimes wrongly assume that any black clothing items are acceptable, even if they are too tight, revealing, sheer, or made of low-end fabrics. Most image consultants agree that a workplace wardrobe has three main categories: business formal, business casual, and casual. Only business formal is considered proper interview apparel.

Your Task. To prepare for your big day, search the Web for descriptions and images of *business formal*. You may research *business casual* and *casual* styles, but once you interview, always dress on the side of caution—conservatively. Compare prices and look for suit sales to buy one or two attractive interview outfits. Share your findings (notes, images, and price ranges for suits, solid shoes, and accessories) with the class and your instructor.

16.7 Polishing Answers to Interview Questions (Obj. 4)

Practice makes perfect in interviewing. The more often you rehearse responses to typical interview questions, the closer you are to getting the job.

Your Task. Select three questions from each of these question categories discussed in this chapter: Questions to Get Acquainted, Questions to Gauge Your Interest, Questions About Your Experience and Accomplishments, Questions About the Future, and Challenging Questions. Write your answers to each set of questions. Try to incorporate skills and traits required for the targeted position, and include success stories where appropriate. Polish these answers and your delivery technique by practicing in front of a mirror or by making an audio or video recording.

16.8 Learning to Answer Situational Interview Questions (Obj. 4)

Team | Web

Situational interview questions can vary widely from position to position. You should know enough about a position to understand some of the typical situations you would encounter on a regular basis.

Your Task. Use your favorite search tool to locate typical job descriptions of a position in which you are interested. Based on these descriptions, develop a list of six to eight typical situations someone in this position would face; then write situational interview questions for each of these scenarios. In pairs, role-play interviewer and interviewee, alternating with your listed questions.

16.9 Developing Skill With Behavioral Interview Questions (Obj. 4)

Team | Web

Behavioral interview questions are increasingly popular, and you will need a little practice before you can answer them easily.

Your Task. Use your favorite search tool to locate lists of behavioral questions on the Web. Select five skill areas such as communication, teamwork, and decision making. For each skill area, find three behavioral questions that you think would be effective in an interview. In pairs, role-play interviewer and interviewee, alternating with your listed questions. You goal is to answer effectively in one or two minutes. Remember to use the STAR method when answering.

16.10 Creating an Interview Cheat Sheet (Objs. 2–5)

Even the best-rehearsed applicants sometimes forget to ask the questions they prepared, or they fail to stress their major accomplishments in job interviews. Sometimes applicants are so rattled they even forget the interviewer's name. To help you keep your wits during an interview, make a cheat sheet that summarizes key facts, answers, and questions. Review it before the interview and again as the interview is ending to be sure you have covered everything that is critical.

Your Task. Prepare a cheat sheet with the following information:

Day and time of interview:
Meeting with: (name of interviewer[s], title, company, city, state, zip, telephone, cell, fax, e-mail)
Major accomplishments: (four to six)
Management or work style: (four to six)
Things you need to know about me: (three or four items)
Reason I left my last job:
Answers to difficult questions: (four or five answers)
Questions to ask interviewer:
Things I can do for you:

16.11 Handling Inappropriate and Illegal Interview Questions (Obj. 4)

Although some questions are considered inappropriate and potentially illegal by the government, many interviewers will ask them anyway—whether intentionally or unknowingly. Being prepared is important.

Your Task. How would you respond in the following scenario? Assume you are being interviewed at one of the top companies on your list of potential employers. The interviewing committee consists of a human resources manager and the supervising manager of the department where you would work. At various times during the interview, the supervising manager asks questions that make you feel uncomfortable. For example, he asks whether you are married. You know this question is inappropriate, but you see no harm in answering it. But then he asks how old you are. Because you started college early and graduated in three and a half years, you are worried that you may not be considered mature enough for this position. However, you have most of the other qualifications required, and you are convinced you could succeed on the job. How should you answer this question?

16.12 Knowing What to Ask (Obj. 5)

When it is your turn to ask questions during the interview process, be ready.

Your Task. Decide on three to five questions that you would like to ask during an interview. Write these questions out and practice asking them so that you sound confident and sincere.

16.13 Role-Playing in a Mock Interview (Objs. 3,4)

Team

One of the best ways to understand interview dynamics and to develop confidence is to role-play the parts of interviewer and candidate in a mock interview.

Your Task. Choose a partner for this activity. Each partner makes a list of two interview questions for each of the nine interview question categories presented in this chapter. In team sessions you and your partner will role-play an actual interview. One acts as interviewer; the other is the candidate. Prior to the interview, the candidate tells the interviewer the job he or she is applying for and the name of the company. For the interview, the interviewer and candidate should dress appropriately and sit in chairs facing each other. The interviewer greets the candidate and makes the candidate comfortable. The candidate gives the interviewer a copy of his or her résumé. The interviewer asks three (or more depending on your instructor's time schedule) questions from the candidate's list. The interviewer may also ask follow-up questions if appropriate. When finished, the interviewer ends the meeting graciously. After one interview, reverse roles and repeat.

16.14 Recording an Interview (Objs. 3–6)

Seeing how you look and hearing how you sound during an interview can help you improve your body language and presentation style. Your instructor may act as an interviewer, or an outside businessperson may be asked to conduct mock interviews in your classroom.

Your Task. Engage a student or campus specialist to prepare a video or audio recording of your interview. Review your performance and critique it looking for ways to improve. Your instructor may ask class members to offer comments and suggestions on your interview.

16.15 Saying Thanks for the Interview (Obj. 6)

You have just completed an exciting employment interview, and you want the interviewer to remember you.

Your Task. Write a follow-up thank-you letter to Ronald T. Ranson, Human Resources Development, Electronic Data Sources, 1328 Peachtree Plaza, Atlanta, GA 30314 (or a company of your choice). Make up any details needed.

16.16 Requesting a Reference (Obj. 6)

Your favorite professor has agreed to be one of your references. You have just arrived home from a job interview that went well, and you must ask your professor to write a letter of recommendation.

Your Task. Write to the professor requesting that a letter of recommendation be sent to the company where you interviewed. Explain that the interviewer asked that the letter be sent directly to him. Provide data about the job description and about yourself so that the professor can target its content.

16.17 Following Up After Submitting Your Résumé (Obj. 6)

A month has passed since you sent your résumé and cover letter in response to a job advertisement. You are still interested in the position and would like to find out whether you still have a chance.

Your Task. Write a follow-up letter to an employer of your choice that does not offend the reader or damage your chances of employment.

16.18 Refusing to Take *No* for an Answer (Obj. 7)

After an excellent interview with Electronic Data Sources (or a company of your choice), you are disappointed to learn that someone else was hired. However, you really want to work for EDS.

Your Task. Write a follow-up letter to Ronald T. Ranson, Human Resources Development, Electronic Data Sources, 1328 Peachtree Plaza, Atlanta, GA 30314 (or a company of your choice). Indicate that you are disappointed but still interested.

16.19 Saying *Yes* to a Job Offer (Obj. 7)

Your dream has come true: you have just been offered an excellent position. Although you accepted the position on the phone, you want to send a formal acceptance letter.

Your Task. Write a job acceptance letter to an employer of your choice. Include the specific job title, your starting date, and details about your compensation package. Make up any necessary details.

16.20 Searching for Advice (Objs. 1–7)

Web E-mail

You can find wonderful, free, and sometimes entertaining information about job search strategies and career tips, as well as interview advice, on the Web.

Your Task. Use the Web to locate articles or links to sites with job search, résumé, and interview information. Make a list of at least five good interview pointers—ones that were not covered in this chapter. Send an e-mail to your instructor describing your findings, or post your findings to a class discussion board to share with your classmates.

16.21 Evaluating Your Course

Your boss has paid your tuition for this course. As you complete the course, he (or she) asks you for a letter about your experience in the course.

Your Task. Write a letter to a boss in a real or imaginary organization explaining how this course made you more valuable to the organization.

Video Resource

Video Library 1, Sharpening Your Interview Skills

In the video titled *Sharpening Your Interview Skills*, you see the job search and employment interview of a recent college graduate, Betsy Chan. We follow Betsy as she finds a job advertisement and prepares for a job interview. The strength of this video lies in the interchange between the company interviewer and Betsy, a typical applicant. You catch an inside look at how an actual interview takes place. It also gives you a chance to see how both the interviewer and Betsy herself critique the interview. As you watch the video interview, be prepared to answer these questions:

- What did Betsy do well in her interview?
- What could she have improved?
- How can a candidate prepare for an interview?
- How can a candidate prepare for and respond to behavioral and situational questions?

Chat About It

In each chapter you will find five discussion questions related to the chapter material. Your instructor may assign these topics for you to discuss in class, in an online chat room, or on an online discussion board. Some of the discussion topics may require outside research. You may also be asked to read and respond to postings made by your classmates.

Topic 1: Now that you have had a chance to learn about resources that can help you during the job search, find one Web site not mentioned in the book that would be helpful for job seekers. Share the following information about the reference with the class: complete title of Web site, Web site address (URL), brief description of the Web site and why you chose it, and an explanation of how you would use it during the job search.

Topic 2: What company do you want to work for most? Why? How would you tailor your résumé to land an interview at this company?

Topic 3: What's the worst thing that has happened to you before, during, or after a job interview? What did you learn from that experience?

Topic 4: What was the most difficult interview question you have had to answer (or a question you anticipate would be the most difficult to answer)? How did you respond to the question (or how would you respond)?

Topic 5: How do you feel about the trend of employers doing Google searches on, and checking MySpace and Facebook pages of, potential employees? Is this kind of online background check justified? Why or why not?

Grammar and Mechanics C.L.U.E. Review 16

Total Review

Each of the following sentences has a total of **three** errors in grammar, punctuation, capitalization, usage, or spelling. On a separate sheet, write a correct version. Avoid adding new phrases, starting new sentences, or rewriting in your own words. When finished, compare your responses with the key beginning on page Key-1.

1. Before going to a job interview you should do the following—research the company, practice answering questions, rehearse success stories and choose appropriate clothing.
2. I wonder how many companys go online to find out more about candidates backgrounds?
3. Even with the popularity of e-mail most employers' contact job applicants by telephone to set up there interviews.
4. Initial contacts by employers are usualy made by telephone, therefore, insure that you keep important information nearby.
5. If you have gaps in your employment history explain what you did during this time, and how you kept up to date in your field.
6. Interviewees should not criticise anyone or anything and they should not focus on there imperfections.
7. Evan was asked whether he had a bachelors degree, and whether he had five years experience.
8. If you are hopping to create a good impression be sure to write a thank you message after a job interview.
9. When Robins interview was over she told friends that she had done good.
10. Robin was already to send a thank-you message, when she realized she could not spell the interviewers name.

Grammar and Mechanics Guide

APPENDIX A

Competent Language Usage Essentials (C.L.U.E.)

In the business world, people are often judged by the way they speak and write. Using the language competently can mean the difference between success and failure. Often a speaker sounds accomplished; but when that same individual puts ideas in print, errors in language usage destroy his or her credibility. One student observed, "When I talk, I get by on my personality; but when I write, the flaws in my communication show through. That's why I'm in this class."

How This Grammar and Mechanics Guide Can Help You

This grammar and mechanics guide contains 50 guidelines covering sentence structure, grammar, usage, punctuation, capitalization, and number style. These guidelines focus on the most frequently used—and abused—language elements. Frequent checkpoint exercises enable you to try your skills immediately. In addition to the 50 language guides in this appendix, you will find a list of 160 frequently misspelled words plus a quick review of selected confusing words.

The concentrated materials in this guide help novice business communicators focus on the major areas of language use. The guide is not meant to teach or review *all* the principles of English grammar and punctuation. It focuses on a limited number of language guidelines and troublesome words. Your objective should be mastery of these language principles and words, which represent a majority of the problems typically encountered by business writers.

How to Use This Grammar and Mechanics Guide

Your instructor may give you the short C.L.U.E. language diagnostic test (located in the Instructor's Manual) to help you assess your competency. A longer self-administered diagnostic test is available as part of Your Personal Language Trainer at **www.meguffey.com**. Either test will give you an idea of your language competence. After taking either diagnostic test, read and work your way through the 50 guidelines. You should also use the self-teaching Trainer exercises, all of which correlate with this Grammar and Mechanics Guide. Concentrate on areas in which you are weak. Memorize the spellings and definitions of the confusing words at the end of this appendix.

In this text you will find two kinds of exercises for your practice. (1) *Checkpoints,* located in this appendix, focus on a small group of language guidelines. Use them to test your comprehension as you complete each section. (2) *Review exercises,* located at the end of each chapter, help reinforce your language skills at the same time you are learning about the processes and products of business communication.

Many students want all the help they can get in improving their language skills. For additional assistance with grammar and language fundamentals, *Business Communication: Process and Product,* 7e, offers you unparalleled interactive and print resources:

- **Your Personal Language Trainer.** This self-paced learning tool is located at **www.meguffey.com.** Dr. Guffey acts as your personal trainer in helping you pump up your language muscles. Your Personal Language Trainer provides the rules plus hundreds of sentence applications so that you can test your knowledge and build your skills with immediate feedback and explanations.

- **Speak Right!,** found at **www.meguffey.com,** reviews frequently mispronounced words. You will hear correct pronunciations from Dr. Guffey so that you will never be embarrassed by mispronouncing these terms.
- **Spell Right!,** found at **www.meguffey.com**, presents frequently misspelled words along with exercises to help you improve your spelling.
- **Reference Books.** A more comprehensive treatment of grammar and punctuation guidelines can be found in Clark and Clark's *A Handbook for Office Workers* and Guffey's *Business English.*

Grammar and Mechanics Guidelines

Sentence Structure

GUIDE 1: Avoid sentence fragments. A fragment is an incomplete sentence. You can recognize a complete sentence because it (a) includes a subject (a noun or pronoun that interacts with a verb), (b) includes a verb (a word expressing action or describing a condition), and (c) makes sense (comes to a closure). A complete sentence is an independent clause. One of the most serious errors a writer can make is punctuating a fragment as if it were a complete sentence.

Fragment	Improved
Because 90 percent of all business transactions involve written messages. Good writing skills are critical.	Because 90 percent of all business transactions involve written messages, good writing skills are critical.
The recruiter requested a writing sample. Even though the candidate seemed to communicate well.	The recruiter requested a writing sample, even though the candidate seemed to communicate well.

Tip. Fragments often can be identified by the words that introduce them—words such as *although, as, because, even, except, for example, if, instead of, since, so, such as, that, which,* and *when.* These words introduce dependent clauses. Make sure such clauses are always connected to independent clauses.

DEPENDENT CLAUSE INDEPENDENT CLAUSE

Since she became supervisor, she had to write more memos and reports.

GUIDE 2: Avoid run-on (fused) sentences. A sentence with two independent clauses must be joined by a coordinating conjunction *(and, or, nor, but)* or by a semicolon (;). Without a conjunction or a semicolon, a run-on sentence results.

Run-on	Improved
Ramon visited resorts of the rich and the famous he also dropped in on luxury spas.	Ramon visited resorts of the rich and famous, and he also dropped in on luxury spas.
	Ramon visited resorts of the rich and famous; he also dropped in on luxury spas.

GUIDE 3: Avoid comma-splice sentences. A comma splice results when a writer joins (splices together) two independent clauses—without using a coordinating conjunction *(and, or, nor, but).*

Comma Splice	Improved
Disney World operates in Orlando, EuroDisney serves Paris.	Disney World operates in Orlando; EuroDisney serves Paris.
	Disney World operates in Orlando, and EuroDisney serves Paris.
Visitors wanted a resort vacation, however they were disappointed.	Visitors wanted a resort vacation; however, they were disappointed.

Tip. In joining independent clauses, beware of using a comma and words such as *consequently, furthermore, however, therefore, then, thus,* and so on. These conjunctive adverbs require semicolons.

Note: Sentence structure is also covered in Chapter 5.

✓ *Checkpoint*

Revise the following to rectify sentence fragments, comma splices, and run-ons.

1. Although it began as a side business for Disney. Destination weddings now represent a major income source.
2. About 2,000 weddings are held yearly. Which is twice the number just ten years ago.
3. Weddings may take place in less than one hour, however the cost may be as much as $5,000.
4. Limousines line up outside Disney's wedding pavilion, they are scheduled in two-hour intervals.
5. Most couples prefer a traditional wedding, others request a fantasy experience.

For all the Checkpoint sentences, compare your responses with the answers at the end of Appendix A.

Grammar

Verb Tense

GUIDE 4: Use present tense, past tense, and past participle verb forms correctly.

Present Tense	Past Tense	Past Participle
Today I______)	(Yesterday I_____)	(I have_____)
am	was	been
begin	began	begun
break	broke	broken
bring	brought	brought
choose	chose	chosen
come	came	come
do	did	done
give	gave	given
go	went	gone
know	knew	known
pay	paid	paid
see	saw	seen
steal	stole	stolen
take	took	taken
write	wrote	written

The package *came* yesterday, and Kevin *knew* what it contained.

If I *had seen* the shipper's bill, I *would have paid* it immediately.

I *know* the answer now; I wish I *had known* it yesterday.

Tip. Probably the most frequent mistake in tenses results from substituting the past-participle form for the past tense. Notice that the past-participle tense requires auxiliary verbs such as *has, had, have, would have,* and *could have.*

Faulty	**Correct**
When he *come* over last night, he *brung* pizza.	When he *came* over last night, he *brought* pizza.
If he *had came* earlier, we *could have saw* the video.	If he *had come* earlier, we *could have seen* the video.

Verb Mood

GUIDE 5: Use the subjunctive mood to express hypothetical (untrue) ideas. The most frequent misuse of the subjunctive mood involves using *was* instead of *were* in clauses introduced by *if* and *as though* or containing *wish.*

If I *were* (not *was*) you, I would take a business writing course.

Sometimes I wish I *were* (not *was*) the manager of this department.

He acts as though he *were* (not *was*) in charge of this department.

Tip. If the statement could possibly be true, use *was.*

If I *was* to blame, I accept the consequences.

✓ *Checkpoint*

Correct faults in verb tenses and mood.

6. If I was you, I would have went to the ten o'clock meeting.
7. The manager could have wrote a better report if he had began earlier.
8. When the vice president seen the report, he immediately come to my office.
9. I wish the vice president was in your shoes for just one day.
10. If the manager had knew all that we do, I'm sure he would have gave us better reviews.

Verb Voice

For a discussion of active- and passive-voice verbs, see pages 151–152 in Chapter 5.

Verb Agreement

GUIDE 6: Make subjects agree with verbs despite intervening phrases and clauses. Become a detective in locating *true* subjects. Don't be deceived by prepositional phrases and parenthetic words that often disguise the true subject.

Our study of annual budgets, five-year plans, and sales proposals *is* (not *are*) progressing on schedule. (The true subject is *study.*)

The budgeted item, despite additions proposed yesterday, *remains* (not *remain*) as submitted. (The true subject is *item.*)

A vendor's evaluation of the prospects for a sale, together with plans for follow-up action, *is* (not *are*) what we need. (The true subject is *evaluation.*)

Tip. Subjects are nouns or pronouns that control verbs. To find subjects, cross out prepositional phrases beginning with words such as *about, at, by, for, from, of,* and *to.* Subjects of verbs are not found in prepositional phrases. Also, don't be tricked by expressions introduced by *together with, in addition to,* and *along with.*

GUIDE 7: Subjects joined by *and* require plural verbs. Watch for true subjects joined by the conjunction *and.* They require plural verbs.

The CEO and one of his assistants *have* (not *has*) ordered a limo.

Considerable time and money *were* (not *was*) spent on remodeling.

Exercising in the gym and jogging every day *are* (not *is*) how he keeps fit.

GUIDE 8: Subjects joined by *or* or *nor* may require singular or plural verbs. The verb should agree with the closer subject.

Either the software or the printer *is* (not *are*) causing the glitch. (The verb is controlled by the closer subject, *printer.*)

Neither St. Louis nor Chicago *has* (not *have*) a chance of winning. (The verb is controlled by *Chicago.*)

Tip. In joining singular and plural subjects with *or* or *nor,* place the plural subject closer to the verb. Then, the plural verb sounds natural. For example, *Either the manufacturer or the distributors are responsible.*

GUIDE 9: Use singular verbs for most indefinite pronouns. The following pronouns all take singular verbs: *anyone, anybody, anything, each, either, every, everyone, everybody, everything, neither, nobody, nothing, someone, somebody,* and *something.*

Everyone in both offices *was* (not *were*) given a bonus.

Each of the employees *is* (not *are*) being interviewed.

GUIDE 10: Use singular or plural verbs for collective nouns, depending on whether the members of the group are operating as a unit or individually. Words such as *faculty, administration, class, crowd,* and *committee* are considered *collective* nouns. If the members of the collective are acting as a unit, treat them as singular subjects. If they are acting individually, it is usually better to add the word *members* and use a plural verb.

Correct

The Finance Committee *is* working harmoniously. (*Committee* is singular because its action is unified.)

The Planning Committee *are* having difficulty agreeing. (*Committee* is plural because its members are acting individually.)

Improved

The Planning Committee members *are* having difficulty agreeing. (Add the word *members* if a plural meaning is intended.)

Tip. In the United States collective nouns are generally considered singular. In Britain these collective nouns are generally considered plural.

✓ *Checkpoint*

Correct the errors in subject–verb agreement.

11. The agency's time and talent was spent trying to develop a blockbuster ad campaign.

12. Your e-mail message, along with both of its attachments, were not delivered to my computer.

13. Each of the Fortune 500 companies are being sent a survey regarding women in management.

14. A full list of names and addresses are necessary before we can begin.

15. Either the judge or the attorney have asked for a recess.

Pronoun Case

GUIDE 11: Learn the three cases of pronouns and how each is used. Pronouns are substitutes for nouns. Every business writer must know the following pronoun cases.

Subjective (Nominative) Case	Objective Case	Possessive Case
Used for subjects of verbs and subject complements	Used for objects of prepositions and objects of verbs	Used to show possession
I	me	my, mine
we	us	our, ours
you	you	you, yours
he	him	his
she	her	her, hers

Subjective (Nominative) Case	Objective Case	Possessive Case
Used for subjects of verbs and subject complements	Used for objects of prepositions and objects of verbs	Used to show possession
it	it	its
they	them	their, theirs
who, whoever	whom, whomever	whose

GUIDE 12: Use subjective-case pronouns as subjects of verbs and as complements. Complements are words that follow linking verbs (such as *am, is, are, was, were, be, being,* and *been)* and rename the words to which they refer.

She and *I* (not *her* and *me*) are looking for entry-level jobs. (Use subjective-case pronouns as the subjects of the verb phrase *are looking.*)

We hope that Marci and *he* (not *him*) will be hired. (Use a subjective-case pronoun as the subject of the verb phrase *will be hired.*)

It must have been *she* (not *her*) who called last night. (Use a subjective-case pronoun as a subject complement.)

Tip. If you feel awkward using subjective pronouns after linking verbs, rephrase the sentence to avoid the dilemma. Instead of *It is she who is the boss,* say, *She is the boss.*

GUIDE 13: Use objective-case pronouns as objects of prepositions and verbs.

Send the e-mail to *her* and *me* (not *she* and *I*). (The pronouns *her* and *me* are objects of the preposition *to.*)

The CEO appointed Rick and *him* (not *he*) to the committee. (The pronoun *him* is the object of the verb *appointed.*)

Tip. When a pronoun appears in combination with a noun or another pronoun, ignore the extra noun or pronoun and its conjunction. Then, the case of the pronoun becomes more obvious.

Jason asked Jennifer and *me* (not *I*) to lunch. (Ignore *Jennifer and.*)

The waiter brought hamburgers to Jason and *me* (not *I*). (Ignore *Jason and.*)

Tip. Be especially alert to the following prepositions: *except, between, but,* and *like.* Be sure to use objective pronouns as their objects.

Just between you and *me* (not *I*), that mineral water comes from the tap.

Everyone except Robert and *him* (not *he*) responded to the invitation.

GUIDE 14: Use possessive pronouns to show ownership. Possessive pronouns (such as *hers, yours, whose, ours, theirs,* and *its)* require no apostrophes.

All reports except *yours* (not *your's*) have to be rewritten.

The apartment and *its* (not *it's*) contents are *hers* (not *her's*) until June.

Tip. Don't confuse possessive pronouns and contractions. Contractions are shortened forms of subject–verb phrases (such as *it's* for *it is, there's* for *there is, who's* for *who is,* and *they're* for *they are).*

✓ *Checkpoint*

Correct errors in pronoun case.

16. My partner and me have looked at many apartments, but your's has the best location.

17. We thought the car was her's, but it's license plate does not match.

18. Just between you and I, do you think there printer is working?

19. Theres not much the boss or me can do if its broken, but its condition should have been reported to him or I earlier.

20. We received several applications, but your's and her's were missing

GUIDE 15: Use pronouns ending in *self* only when they refer to previously mentioned nouns or pronouns.

The president *himself* ate all the M&Ms.

Send the package to Mike or *me* (not *myself*).

Tip. Trying to sound less egocentric, some radio and TV announcers incorrectly substitute *myself* when they should use *I*. For example, "Jerry and *myself* (should be *I*) are cohosting the telethon."

GUIDE 16: Use *who* or *whoever* for subjective-case constructions and *whom* or *whomever* for objective-case constructions. In determining the correct choice, it is helpful to substitute *he* for *who* or *whoever* and *him* for *whom* or *whomever.*

For *whom* was this software ordered? (The software was ordered for *him.*)

Who did you say called? (You did say *he* called?)

Give the supplies to *whoever* asked for them. (In this sentence the clause *whoever asked for them* functions as the object of the preposition *to.* Within the clause *whoever* is the subject of the verb *asked.* Again, try substituting *he: he asked for them.*)

✓ *Checkpoint*

Correct any errors in the use of *self*-ending pronouns and *who/whom.*

21. The boss herself is willing to call whoever we decide to honor.

22. Who have you asked to develop ads for our new products?

23. I have a pizza for whomever placed the telephone order.

24. The meeting is set for Wednesday; however, Matt and myself cannot attend.

25. Incident reports must be submitted by whomever experiences a personnel problem.

Pronoun Reference

GUIDE 17: Make pronouns agree in number and gender with the words to which they refer (their antecedents).

When the gender of the antecedent is obvious, pronoun references are simple.

> One of the boys lost *his* (not *their*) new tennis shoes. (The singular pronoun *his* refers to the singular *One.*)
>
> Each of the female nurses was escorted to *her car* (not *their cars*). (The singular pronoun *her* and singular noun *car* are necessary because they refer to the singular subject *Each.*)
>
> Somebody on the girls' team left *her* (not *their*) headlights on.

When the gender of the antecedent could be male or female, sensitive writers today have a number of options.

Faulty	Improved
Every employee should receive *their* check Friday. (The plural pronoun *their* does not agree with its singular antecedent *employee.*)	All employees should receive *their* checks Friday. (Make the subject plural so that the plural pronoun *their* is acceptable. This option is preferred by many writers today.)
	All employees should receive checks Friday. (Omit the possessive pronoun entirely.)
	Every employee should receive *a* check Friday. (Substitute *a* for a pronoun.)
	Every employee should receive *his or her* check Friday. (Use the combination *his or her.* However, this option is wordy and should be avoided.)

GUIDE 18: Be sure that pronouns such as *it, which, this,* and *that* refer to clear antecedents.

Vague pronouns confuse the reader because they have no clear single antecedent. The most troublesome are *it, which, this,* and *that.* Replace vague pronouns with concrete nouns, or provide these pronouns with clear antecedents.

Faulty	Improved
Our office recycles as much paper as possible because *it* helps the environment. (Does *it* refer to *paper, recycling,* or *office?*)	Our office recycles as much paper as possible because *such efforts* help the environment. (Replace *it* with *such efforts.*)
The disadvantages of local area networks can offset their advantages. That merits further evaluation. (What merits evaluation: advantages, disadvantages, or the offsetting of one by the other?)	The disadvantages of local area networks can offset their advantages. That fact merits further evaluation. (*Fact* supplies a concrete noun for the vague pronoun *that.*)
Negotiators announced an expanded health care plan, reductions in dental coverage, and a proposal of on-site child care facilities. *This* caused employee protests. (What exactly caused employee protests?)	Negotiators announced an expanded health care plan, reductions in dental coverage, and a proposal of on-site child care facilities. *This* reduction in child care facilities caused employee protests. (The pronoun *This* now has a clear reference.)

Tip. Whenever you use the words *this, that, these,* and *those* by themselves, a red flag should pop up. These words are dangerous when they stand alone. Inexperienced writers often use them to refer to an entire previous idea, rather than to a specific antecedent, as shown in the preceding examples. You can usually solve the problem by adding another idea to the pronoun (such as *this reduction).*

✓ Checkpoint

Correct the faulty and vague pronoun references in the following sentences. Numerous remedies exist.

26. Every employee must wear their picture identification badge.

27. Flexible working hours may mean slower career advancement, but it appeals to many workers.

28. Any renter must pay his rent by the first of the month.

29. Someone in this office reported that his computer had a virus.

30. Obtaining agreement on job standards, listening to coworkers, and encouraging employee suggestions all helped to open lines of communication. This is particularly important in team projects.

Adjectives and Adverbs

GUIDE 19: Use adverbs, not adjectives, to describe or limit the action of verbs. Use adjectives after linking verbs.

Andrew said he did *well* (not *good*) on the exam. (The adverb *well* describes how he did.)

After its tune-up, the engine is running *smoothly* (not *smooth*). (The adverb *smoothly* describes the verb *is running.*)

Don't take the manager's criticism *personally* (not *personal*). (The adverb *personally* tells how to take the criticism.)

She finished her homework *more quickly* (not *quicker*) than expected. (The adverb *more quickly*) explains how she finished her homework.)

Liam felt bad (not badly) after he heard the news. (The adjective *bad* follows the linking verb *felt.*)

GUIDE 20: Hyphenate two or more adjectives that are joined to create a compound modifier before a noun.

Follow the *step-by-step* instructions to construct the *low-cost* bookshelves.

A *well-designed* keyboard is part of this *state-of-the-art* equipment.

Tip. Don't confuse adverbs ending in *-ly* with compound adjectives: *newly enacted* law and *highly regarded* CEO would not be hyphenated.

✓ Checkpoint

Correct any problems in the use of pronouns, adjectives, and adverbs.

31. My manager and me could not resist the once in a lifetime opportunity.

32. Because John and him finished their task so quick, they made a fast trip to the recently opened snack bar.

33. If I do good on the exam, I qualify for many part time jobs and a few full time positions.

34. The vice president told him and I not to take the announcement personal.

35. In the not too distant future, we may enjoy more practical uses of robots.

Punctuation

GUIDE 21: Use commas to separate three or more items (words, phrases, or short clauses) in a series. (CmSer)

Downward communication delivers job instructions, procedures, and appraisals.

In preparing your résumé, try to keep it brief, make it easy to read, and include only job-related information.

The new ice cream flavors include cookie dough, chocolate raspberry truffle, cappuccino, and almond amaretto.

Tip. Some professional writers omit the comma before *and*. However, most business writers prefer to retain that comma because it prevents misreading the last two items as one item. Notice in the previous example how the final two ice cream flavors could have been misread if the comma had been omitted.

GUIDE 22: Use commas to separate introductory clauses and certain phrases from independent clauses. (CmIntro) This guideline describes the comma most often omitted by business writers. Sentences that open with dependent clauses (frequently introduced by words such as *since, when, if, as, although,* and *because)* require commas to separate them from the main idea. The comma helps readers recognize where the introduction ends and the big idea begins. Introductory phrases of four or more words or phrases containing verbal elements also require commas.

If you recognize introductory clauses, you will have no trouble placing the comma. (A comma separates the introductory dependent clause from the main clause.)

When you have mastered this rule, half the battle with commas will be won.

As expected, additional explanations are necessary. (Use a comma even if the introductory clause omits the understood subject: *As we expected.*)

In the spring of last year, we opened our franchise. (Use a comma after a phrase containing four or more words.)

Having considered several alternatives, we decided to invest. (Use a comma after an introductory verbal phrase.)

To invest, we needed $100,000. (Use a comma after an introductory verbal phrase, regardless of its length.)

Tip. Short introductory prepositional phrases (three or fewer words) require no commas. Don't clutter your writing with unnecessary commas after introductory phrases such as *by 2012, in the fall* or *at this time.*

GUIDE 23: Use a comma before the coordinating conjunction in a compound sentence. (CmConj) The most common coordinating conjunctions are *and, or, nor,* and *but.* Occasionally, *for, yet,* and *so* may also function as coordinating conjunctions. When coordinating conjunctions join two independent clauses, commas are needed.

The investment sounded too good to be true, *and* many investors were dubious about it. (Use a comma before the coordinating conjunction *and* in a compound sentence.)

Southern California is the financial fraud capital of the world, *but* some investors refuse to heed warning signs.

Tip. Before inserting a comma, test the two clauses. Can each of them stand alone as a complete sentence? If either is incomplete, skip the comma.

Promoters said the investment offer was for a limited time and could not be extended even one day. (Omit a comma before *and* because the second part of the sentence is not a complete independent clause.)

Lease payments are based largely on your down payment and on the value of the car at the end of the lease. (Omit a comma before *and* because the second half of the sentence is not a complete clause.)

✓ Checkpoint

Add appropriate commas.

36. Before she enrolled in this class Erin used to sprinkle her writing with commas semicolons and dashes.

37. After studying punctuation she learned to use commas more carefully and to reduce her reliance on dashes.

38. At this time Erin is engaged in a serious yoga program but she also finds time to enlighten her mind.

39. Next fall Erin may enroll in communication and merchandising or she may work for a semester to earn money.

40. When she completes her junior year she plans to apply for an internship in Los Angeles Burbank or Long Beach.

GUIDE 24: Use commas appropriately in dates, addresses, geographical names, degrees, and long numbers. (CmDate)

September 30, 1963, is his birthday. (For dates use commas before and after the year.)

Send the application to James Kirby, 20045 45th Avenue, Lynnwood, WA 98036, as soon as possible. (For addresses use commas to separate all units except the two-letter state abbreviation and the zip code.)

Lisa expects to move from Cupertino, California, to Sonoma, Arizona, next fall. (For geographical areas use commas to enclose the second element)

Karen Munson, CPA, and Richard B. Larsen, PhD, were the speakers. (For professional designations and academic degrees following names, use commas to enclose each item.)

The latest census figures show the city's population to be 342,000. (In figures use commas to separate every three digits, counting from the right.)

GUIDE 25: Use commas to set off internal sentence interrupters. (CmIn)

Sentence interrupters may be verbal phrases, dependent clauses, contrasting elements, or parenthetical expressions (also called transitional phrases). These interrupters often provide information that is not grammatically essential.

Harvard researchers, working steadily for 18 months, developed a new cancer therapy. (Use commas to set off an internal interrupting verbal phrase.)

The new therapy, which applies a genetically engineered virus, raises hopes among cancer specialists. (Use commas to set off nonessential dependent clauses.)

Dr. James C. Morrison, who is one of the researchers, made the announcement. (Use commas to set off nonessential dependent clauses.)

It was Dr. Morrison, not Dr. Arturo, who led the team effort. (Use commas to set off a contrasting element.)

This new therapy, by the way, was developed from a herpes virus. (Use commas to set off a parenthetical expression.)

Tip. Parenthetical (transitional) expressions are helpful words that guide the reader from one thought to the next. Here are typical parenthetical expressions that require commas:

As a matter of fact	in addition	of course
As a result	in the meantime	on the other hand
Consequently	nevertheless	therefore
for example		

Tip. Always use *two* commas to set off an interrupter, unless it begins or ends a sentence.

✓ *Checkpoint*

Insert necessary commas.

41. James listed 1805 Martin Luther King Street San Antonio Texas 78220 as his forwarding address.

42. This report is not however one that must be classified.

43. Employment of paralegals which is expected to increase 32 percent next year is growing rapidly because of the expanding legal services industry.

44. The contract was signed May 15 2009 and remains in effect until May 15 2015.

45. As a matter of fact the average American drinks enough coffee to require 12 pounds of coffee beans annually.

GUIDE 26: Avoid unnecessary commas. Do not use commas between sentence elements that belong together. Do not automatically insert commas before every *and* or at points where your voice might drop if you were saying the sentence out loud.

Faulty

Growth will be spurred by the increasing complexity of business operations, and by large employment gains in trade and services. (A comma unnecessarily precedes *and.*)

All students with high grades, are eligible for the honor society. (A comma unnecessarily separates the subject and verb.)

One of the reasons for the success of the business honor society is, that it is very active. (A comma unnecessarily separates the verb and its complement.)

Our honor society has, at this time, over 50 members. (Commas unnecessarily separate a prepositional phrase from the sentence.)

✓ *Checkpoint*

Remove unnecessary commas. Add necessary ones.

46. Car companies promote leasing because it brings customers back into their showrooms sooner, and gives dealers a steady supply of late-model used cars.

47. When shopping for a car you may be offered a fantastic leasing deal.

48. The trouble with many leases is, that the value of the car at the end of the lease may be less than expected.

49. We think on the other hand, that you should compare the costs of leasing and buying, and that you should talk to a tax adviser.

50. American and Japanese automakers are, at this time, offering intriguing lease deals.

Semicolons, Colons

GUIDE 27: Use a semicolon to join closely related independent clauses. Experienced writers use semicolons to show readers that two thoughts are closely associated. If the ideas are not related, they should be expressed in separate sentences. Often, but not always, the second independent clause contains a conjunctive adverb (such as *however, consequently, therefore,* or *furthermore)* to show the relation between the two clauses. Use a semicolon before a conjunctive adverb of two or more syllables (such as *however, consequently, therefore*, or *furthermore*) and a comma after it.

> Learning history is easy; learning its lessons is almost impossible. (A semicolon joins two independent clauses.)

> He was determined to complete his degree; consequently, he studied diligently. (A semicolon precedes the conjunctive adverb, and a comma follows it.)

> Serena wanted a luxury apartment located near campus; however, she couldn't afford the rent. (A semicolon precedes the conjunctive adverb, and a comma follows it.)

Tip. Don't use a semicolon unless each clause is truly independent. Try the sentence test. Omit the semicolon if each clause could not stand alone as a complete sentence.

Faulty	**Improved**
There is no point in speaking; unless you can improve on silence. (The second half of the sentence is a dependent clause. It could not stand alone as a sentence.)	There is no point in speaking unless you can improve on silence.
Although I cannot change the direction of the wind; I can adjust my sails to reach my destination. (The first clause could not stand alone.)	Although I cannot change the direction of the wind, I can adjust my sails to reach my destination.

GUIDE 28: Use a semicolon to separate items in a series when one or more of the items contains internal commas.

> Representatives from as far away as Blue Bell, Pennsylvania; Bowling Green, Ohio; and Phoenix, Arizona, attended the conference.

> Stories circulated about Henry Ford, founder, Ford Motor Company; Lee Iacocca, former CEO, Chrysler Motor Company; and Shoichiro Toyoda, founder, Toyota Motor Company.

GUIDE 29: Use a colon after a complete thought that introduces a list of items. Words such as *these, the following,* and *as follows* may introduce the list or they may be implied.

> The following cities are on the tour: Louisville, Memphis, and New Orleans.

> An alternate tour includes several West Coast cities: Seattle, San Francisco, and San Diego.

Tip. Be sure that the statement before a colon is grammatically complete. An introductory statement that ends with a preposition (such as *by, for, at,* and *to)* or a verb (such as *is, are,* or *were)* is incomplete. The list following a preposition or a verb actually functions as an object or as a complement to finish the sentence.

Faulty	**Improved**
Three Big Macs were ordered by: Pam, Jim, and Lee. (Do not use a colon after an incomplete statement.)	Three Big Macs were ordered by Pam, Jim, and Lee.
Other items that they ordered were: fries, Cokes, and salads. (Do not use a colon after an incomplete statement)	Other items that they ordered were fries, Cokes, and salads.

GUIDE 30: Use a colon after business letter salutations and to introduce long quotations.

Dear Mr. Duran: Dear Lisa:

The Asian consultant bluntly said: "Americans tend to be too blabby, too impatient, and too informal for Asian tastes. To succeed in trade with Pacific Rim countries, Americans must become more willing to adapt to native cultures."

Tip. Use a comma to introduce short quotations. Use a colon to introduce long one-sentence quotations and quotations of two or more sentences.

✓ *Checkpoint*

Add appropriate semicolons and colons.

51. Marco's short-term goal is an entry-level job his long-term goal however is a management position.

52. Speakers included the following professors Rebecca Hilbrink University of Alaska Lora Lindsey Ohio University and Michael Malone Central Florida College.

53. The recruiter was looking for three qualities loyalty initiative and enthusiasm.

54. Microsoft seeks experienced individuals however it will hire recent graduates who are skilled.

55. South Florida is an expanding region therefore many business opportunities are available.

Apostrophe

GUIDE 31: Add an apostrophe plus *s* to an ownership word that does not end in an *s* sound.

We hope to show a profit in one year's time. (Add *'s* because the ownership word *year* does not end in *s*.)

The company's assets rose in value. (Add *'s* because the ownership word *company* does not end in *s*.)

All the women's votes were counted. (Add *'s* because the ownership word *women* does not end in *s*.)

GUIDE 32: Add only an apostrophe to an ownership word that ends in an *s* sound—unless an extra syllable can be pronounced easily.

Some workers' benefits will cost more. (Add only an apostrophe because the ownership word *workers* ends in *s*.)

Several months' rent are now due. (Add only an apostrophe because the ownership word *months* ends in *s*.)

The boss's son got the job. (Add *'s* because an extra syllable can be pronounced easily.)

Tip. To determine whether an ownership word ends in *'s*, use it in an *of* phrase. For example, *one month's salary* becomes *the salary of one month*. By isolating the ownership word without its apostrophe, you can decide whether it ends in *s*.

GUIDE 33: Use a possessive pronoun or add 's to make a noun possessive when it precedes a gerund (a verb form used as a noun).

We all protested *Laura's* (not *Laura*) smoking. (Add *'s* to the noun preceding the gerund.)

His (not *Him*) talking on his cell phone angered moviegoers. (Use a possessive pronoun before the gerund.)

I appreciate *your* (not *you*) answering the telephone while I was gone. (Use a possessive pronoun before the gerund.)

✓ *Checkpoint*

Correct any problems with possessives.

56. Both companies executives received huge bonuses, even when employees salaries were falling.

57. In just one weeks time, we promise to verify all members names and addresses.

58. The manager and I certainly appreciate you bringing this matter to our CPAs attention.

59. All beneficiaries names must be revealed when insurance companies write policies.

60. Is your sister-in-laws job downtown?

Other Punctuation

GUIDE 34: Use one period to end a statement, command, indirect question, or polite request. Never use two periods.

Matt worked at BioTech, Inc. (Statement. Use only one period.)

Deliver it before 5 p.m. (Command. Use only one period.)

Stacy asked whether she could use the car next weekend. (Indirect question)

Will you please send me an employment application. (Polite request)

Tip. Polite requests often sound like questions. To determine the punctuation, apply the action test. If the request prompts an action, use a period. If it prompts a verbal response, use a question mark.

Faulty	**Improved**
Could you please correct the balance on my next statement? (This polite request prompts an action rather than a verbal response.)	Could you please correct the balance on my next statement.

Tip. To avoid the punctuation dilemma with polite requests, do not phrase the request as a question. Phrase it as a command: *Please correct the balance on my next statement.* It still sounds polite, and the punctuation problem disappears.

GUIDE 35: Use a question mark after a direct question and after statements with questions appended.

Are they hiring at BioTech, Inc.?

Most of their training is in-house, isn't it?

GUIDE 36: Use a dash to (a) set off parenthetical elements containing internal commas, (b) emphasize a sentence interruption, or (c) separate an introductory list from a summarizing statement. The dash has legitimate uses. However, some writers use it whenever they know that punctuation is necessary, but they are not sure exactly what. The dash can be very effective, if not misused.

Three top students—Gene Engle, Donna Hersh, and Mika Sato—won awards. (Use dashes to set off elements with internal commas.)

Executives at IBM—despite rampant rumors in the stock market—remained quiet regarding dividend earnings. (Use dashes to emphasize a sentence interruption.)

Japan, Taiwan, and Turkey—these were areas hit by recent earthquakes. (Use a dash to separate an introductory list from a summarizing statement.)

GUIDE 37: Use parentheses to set off nonessential sentence elements, such as explanations, directions, questions, or references.

Researchers find that the office grapevine (see Chapter 1 for more discussion) carries surprisingly accurate information.

Only two dates (February 15 and March 1) are suitable for the meeting.

Tip. Careful writers use parentheses to de-emphasize and the dash to emphasize parenthetical information. One expert said, "Dashes shout the news; parentheses whisper it."

GUIDE 38: Use quotation marks to (a) enclose the exact words of a speaker or writer; (b) distinguish words used in a special sense, such as slang; or (c) enclose titles of articles, chapters, or other short works.

"If you make your job important," said the consultant, "it's quite likely to return the favor."

The recruiter said that she was looking for candidates with good communication skills. (Omit quotation marks because the exact words of the speaker are not quoted.)

This office discourages "rad" hair styles and clothing. (Use quotes for slang.)

In *BusinessWeek* I saw an article titled "Communication for Global Markets." (Use quotation marks around the title of an article; use all caps, underlines, or italics for the name of the publication.)

Tip. Never use quotation marks arbitrarily, as in *Our "spring" sale starts April 1.*

✓ *Checkpoint*

Add appropriate punctuation.

61. Will you please send your print catalog as soon as possible

62. (Direct quotation) Our Super Bowl promotion said the CEO will cost nearly $500,000

63. (De-emphasize) Two kinds of batteries see page 16 of the instruction booklet may be used in this camera

64. Tim wondered whether sentences could end with two periods

65. All computers have virus protection don't they

Capitalization

GUIDE 39: Capitalize proper nouns and proper adjectives. Capitalize the *specific* names of persons, places, institutions, buildings, religions, holidays, months, organizations, laws, races, languages, and so forth. Do not capitalize seasons, and do not capitalize common nouns that make *general* references.

Proper Nouns	**Common Nouns**
Michelle Deluca	the manufacturer's rep
Everglades National Park	the wilderness park
College of the Redwoods	the community college
Empire State Building	the downtown building
Environmental Protection Agency	the federal agency
Persian, Armenian, Hindi	modern foreign languages
Annual Spring Festival	in the spring
Proper Adjectives	
Hispanic markets	Italian dressing
Xerox copy	Japanese executives
Swiss chocolates	Reagan economics

GUIDE 40: Capitalize only specific academic courses and degrees.

Professor Donna Howard, PhD, will teach Accounting 121 next spring.

James Barker, who holds bachelor's and master's degrees, teaches marketing.

Jessica enrolled in classes in management, English, and business law.

GUIDE 41: Capitalize courtesy, professional, religious, government, family, and business titles when they precede names.

Mr. Jameson, Mrs. Alvarez, and Ms. Robinson (Courtesy titles)

Professor Andrews, Dr. Lee (Professional titles)

Rabbi Cohen, Pastor Williams, Pope Benedict (Religious titles)

Senator Tom Harrison, Mayor Jackson (Government titles)

Uncle Edward, Mother Teresa, Cousin Vinney (Family titles)

Vice President Morris, Budget Director Lopez (Business titles)

Do not capitalize a title when it is followed by an appositive (that is, when the title is followed by a noun that renames or explains it).

Only one professor, Jonathan Marcus, favored a tuition hike.

Local candidates counted on their governor, Lee Jones, to help raise funds.

Do not capitalize titles following names unless they are part of an address:

Mark Yoder, president of Yoder Enterprises, hired all employees.

Paula Beech, director of Human Resources, interviewed all candidates.

Send the package to Amanda Harr, Advertising Manager, Cambridge Publishers, 20 Park Plaza, Boston, MA 02116.

Generally, do not capitalize a title that replaces a person's name.

Only the president, his chief of staff, and one senator made the trip.

The director of marketing and the sales manager will meet at 1 p.m.

Do not capitalize family titles used with possessive pronouns.

my mother, his father, your cousin

GUIDE 42: Capitalize the main words in titles, subject lines, and headings. *Main* words are all words except (a) the articles *a, an,* and *the;* (b) the conjunctions *and, but, or,* and *nor,* (c) prepositions containing two or three letters (e.g., *of, for, in, on, by*); (d) the word *to* in infinitives (such as *to work, to write,* and *to talk*); (e) the word *as*—unless any of these words are the first or last words in the title, subject line, or heading.

I enjoyed the book *A Customer Is More Than a Name.* (Book title)

Team Meeting to Discuss Deadlines Rescheduled for Friday (Subject line)

We liked the article titled "Advice From a Pro: How to Say It With Pictures." (Article)

Check the Advice and Resources link at the *CareerBuilder* Web site.

(Note that the titles of books are underlined or italicized but the titles of articles are enclosed in quotation marks.)

GUIDE 43: Capitalize names of geographic locations. Capitalize *north, south, east, west,* and their derivatives only when they represent specific geographical regions.

from the Pacific Northwest	heading northwest on the highway
living in the West	west of the city
Midwesterners, Southerners	western Oregon, southern Ohio
peace in the Middle East	a location east of the middle of the city

GUIDE 44: Capitalize the main words in the specific names of departments, divisions, or committees within business organizations. Do not capitalize general references.

All forms are available from our Department of Human Resources.

The Consumer Electronics Division launched an upbeat marketing campaign.

We volunteered for the Employee Social Responsibility Committee.

You might send an application to their personnel department.

GUIDE 45: Capitalize product names only when they refer to trademarked items. Do not capitalize the common names following manufacturers' names.

Dell laptop computer	Skippy peanut butter	NordicTrack treadmill
Eveready Energizer	Norelco razor	Kodak color copier
Coca-Cola	Panasonic plasma television	Big Mac sandwich

GUIDE 46: Capitalize most nouns followed by numbers or letters (except in page, paragraph, line, and verse references).

Room 14	Exhibit A	Flight 12, Gate 43
Figure 2.1	Plan No. 1	Model Z2010

Checkpoint

Capitalize all appropriate words.

66. vice president moore bought a new nokia cell phone before leaving for the east coast.

67. when you come on tuesday, travel west on highway 5 and exit at mt. mckinley street.

68. The director of our human resources department called a meeting of the company's building security committee.

69. our manager and president are flying on american airlines flight 34 leaving from gate 69 at the las vegas international airport.

70. my father read a businessweek article titled can you build loyalty with bricks and mortar?

Number Usage

GUIDE 47: Use word form to express (a) numbers *ten* and under and (b) numbers beginning sentences. General references to numbers *ten* and under should be expressed in word form. Also use word form for numbers that begin sentences. If the resulting number involves more than two words, however, recast the sentence so that the number does not fall at the beginning.

We answered *six* telephone calls for the *four* sales reps.

Fifteen customers responded to the *three* advertisements today.

A total of 155 cameras were awarded as prizes. (Avoid beginning the sentence with a long number such as *one hundred fifty-five.*)

GUIDE 48: Use figures to express most references to numbers 11 and over.

Over *150* people from *53* companies attended the two-day workshop.

A four-ounce serving of Haagen-Dazs toffee crunch ice cream contains *300* calories and *19* grams of fat.

GUIDE 49: Use figures to express money, dates, clock time, decimals, and percents.

One item costs only *$1.95*; most, however, were priced between *$10* and *$35*. (Omit the decimals and zeros in even sums of money.)

We scheduled a meeting for May 12. (Notice that we do *not* write May 12th.)

We expect deliveries at 10:15 a.m. and again at 4 p.m. (Use lowercase *a.m.* and *p.m.*)

All packages must be ready by 4 o'clock. (Do *not* write 4:00 o'clock.)

When U.S. sales dropped *4.7* percent, net income fell *9.8* percent. (In contextual material use the word *percent* instead of the symbol %.)

GUIDE 50: Use a combination of words and figures to express sums of 1 million and over. Use words for small fractions.

Orion lost *$62.9 million* in the latest fiscal year on revenues of *$584 million*. (Use a combination of words and figures for sums of 1 million and over.)

Only one half of the registered voters turned out. (Use words for small fractions.)

Tip. To ease your memory load, concentrate on the numbers normally expressed in words: numbers *ten* and under, numbers at the beginning of a sentence, and small fractions. Nearly everything else in business is generally written with figures.

✓ *Checkpoint*

Correct any inappropriate expression of numbers.

71. Although he budgeted fifty dollars, Jake spent 94 dollars and 34 cents for supplies.

72. Is the meeting on November 7th or November 14th?

73. UPS deliveries arrive at nine AM and again at four fifteen PM.

74. The company applied for a fifty thousand dollar loan at six%.

75. The U.S. population is just over 300,000,000, and the world population is estimated to be nearly 6,500,000,000.

Key to Grammar and Mechanics Checkpoint Exercises in Appendix A

This key shows all corrections. If you marked anything else, double-check the appropriate guideline.

1. Disney, destination

2. yearly, which

3. hour; however,

4. pavilion;

5. wedding;

6. If I *were* you, I would have *gone* ....

7. could have *written* ... had *begun* earlier.

8. vice president *saw* ... immediately *came*

9. vice president *were*

10. manager had *known* ... would have *given*

11. time and talent *were* spent (Note that two subjects require a plural verb.)

12. attachments, *was* (Note that the subject is *message*.)

13. Each of ... companies *is* (Note that the subject is *Each*.)

14. list of names and addresses *is* (Note that the subject is *list*.)
15. attorney *has*
16. My partner and *I* .... but *yours*
17. was *hers*, but *its*
18. you and *me* ... *their* printer
19. *There's* not much the boss or *I* can do if *it's* broken, ... reported to him or *me* earlier.
20. but *yours* and *hers*
21. *whomever*
22. *Whom* have you asked ....
23. for *whoever*
24. Matt and *I*
25. by *whoever*
26. Every employee must wear *a* picture identification badge, *OR: All employees* must wear *picture identification badges*.
27. slower career advancement, but *flexible scheduling* appeals to many workers. (Revise to avoid the vague pronoun *it*.)
28. Any renter must pay *the* rent .... *OR: All renters* must pay *their* rent ....
29. reported that *a* computer ... *OR*: reported that *his or her* computer ....
30. communication. *These techniques are* particularly important (Revise to avoid the vague pronoun *This*.)
31. My manager and *I* could not resist the *once-in-a-lifetime* opportunity.
32. John and *he* finished their task so *quickly* (Do not hyphenate *recently opened*.)
33. do *well* ... *part-time* jobs and a few *full-time*
34. told him and *me* ... *personally*.
35. *not-too-distant* future
36. class, Erin ... with commas, semicolons,
37. studying punctuation,
38. program,
39. merchandising,
40. junior year, ... in Los Angeles, Burbank,
41. Street, San Antonio, Texas 78220,
42. not, however,
43. paralegals, ... next year,
44. May 15, 2009, ... May 15, 2015.
45. fact,
46. sooner [delete comma]
47. car,
48. is [delete comma]
49. think, on the other hand, ... buying [delete comma]
50. automakers are [delete comma] at this time [delete comma]
51. entry-level job; his long-term goal, however,
52. professors: Rebecca Hilbrink, University of Alaska; Lora Lindsey, Ohio University; and Michael Malone, Central Florida College.
53. qualities: loyalty, initiative,
54. individuals; however,
55. region; therefore,
56. companies' ... employees'
57. one week's time, ... members'
58. appreciate *your* ... CPA's
59. beneficiaries'
60. sister-in-law's
61. possible.
62. "Our Super Bowl promotion," said the CEO, "will cost nearly $500,000."
63. Two kinds of batteries (see page 16 of the instruction booklet)
64. two periods.
65. protection, don't they?
66. Vice President Moore ... Nokia ... East Coast
67. When ...Tuesday, ... Highway 5 ... Mt. McKinley Street.
68. Human Resources Department ... Building Security Committee
69. Our ... American Airlines Flight 34 ... Gate 69 at the Las Vegas International Airport
70. My ... *BusinessWeek* article titled "Can You Build Loyalty With Bricks and Mortar?"
71. $50 ... $94.34
72. November 7 or November 14 [delete *th*]
73. 9 a.m.... 4:15 p.m. (Note only one period at the end of the sentence.)
74. $50,000 ... 6 percent.
75. 300 million ... 6.5 billion

Confusing Words

accede:	to agree or consent
exceed:	over a limit
accept:	to receive
except:	to exclude; (prep) but
adverse:	opposing; antagonistic
averse:	unwilling; reluctant
advice:	suggestion, opinion
advise:	to counsel or recommend
affect:	to influence
effect:	(n) outcome, result; (v) to bring about, to create
all ready:	prepared
already:	by this time
all right:	satisfactory
alright:	unacceptable variant spelling
altar:	structure for worship
alter:	to change
appraise:	to estimate
apprise:	to inform
ascent:	(n) rising or going up
assent:	(v) to agree or consent
assure:	to promise
ensure:	to make certain
insure:	to protect from loss
capital:	(n) city that is seat of government; wealth of an individual; (adj) chief
capitol:	building that houses state or national lawmakers
cereal:	breakfast food
serial:	arranged in sequence
cite:	to quote; to summon
site:	location
sight:	a view; to see
coarse:	rough texture
course:	a route; part of a meal; a unit of learning
complement:	that which completes
compliment:	(n) praise or flattery; (v) to praise or flatter
conscience:	regard for fairness
conscious:	aware
council:	governing body
counsel:	(n) advice, attorney, consultant; (v) to give advice
credible:	believable
creditable:	good enough for praise or esteem; reliable
desert:	(n) arid land; (v) to abandon
dessert:	sweet food
device:	invention or mechanism
devise:	to design or arrange
disburse:	to pay out
disperse:	to scatter widely
elicit:	to draw out
illicit:	unlawful
envelop:	(v) to wrap, surround, or conceal
envelope:	(n) a container for a written message
every day:	each single day
everyday:	ordinary
farther:	a greater distance
further:	additional
formally:	in a formal manner
formerly:	in the past
grate:	(v) to reduce to small particles; to cause irritation; (n) a frame of crossed bars blocking a passage
great:	(adj) large in size; numerous; eminent or distinguished
hole:	an opening
whole:	complete
imply:	to suggest indirectly
infer:	to reach a conclusion
lean:	(v) to rest against; (adj) not fat
lien:	(n) legal right or claim to property
liable:	legally responsible
libel:	damaging written statement
loose:	not fastened
lose:	to misplace
miner:	person working in a mine
minor:	(adj) lesser; (n) person under age
patience:	calm perseverance
patients:	people receiving medical treatment
personal:	private, individual
personnel:	employees
plaintiff:	(n) one who initiates a lawsuit
plaintive:	(adj) expressive of suffering or woe
populace:	(n) the masses; population of a place
populous:	(adj) densely populated
precede:	to go before
proceed:	to continue
precedence:	priority
precedents:	events used as an example
principal:	(n) capital sum; school official; (adj) chief

principle:	rule of action
stationary:	immovable
stationery:	writing material
than:	conjunction showing comparison
then:	adverb meaning "at that time"
their:	possessive form of *they*
there:	at that place or point
they're:	contraction of *they are*
to:	a preposition; the sign of the infinitive
too:	an adverb meaning "also" or "to an excessive extent"
two:	a number
waiver:	abandonment of a claim
waver:	to shake or fluctuate

160 Frequently Misspelled Words

absence
accommodate
achieve
acknowledgment
across
adequate
advisable
analyze
annually
appointment
argument
automatically
bankruptcy
becoming
beneficial
budget
business
calendar
canceled
catalog
changeable
column
committee
congratulate
conscience
conscious
consecutive
consensus
consistent
control
convenient
correspondence
courteous
criticize
decision
deductible
defendant
definitely
dependent
describe
desirable
destroy
development
disappoint
dissatisfied
division
efficient
embarrass
emphasis
emphasize
employee
envelope
equipped
especially
evidently
exaggerate
excellent
exempt
existence
extraordinary
familiar
fascinate
feasible
February
fiscal
foreign
forty
fourth
friend
genuine
government
grammar
grateful
guarantee
harass
height
hoping
immediate
incidentally
incredible
independent
indispensable
interrupt
irrelevant
itinerary
judgment
knowledge
legitimate
library
license
maintenance
manageable
manufacturer
mileage
miscellaneous
mortgage
necessary
nevertheless
ninety
ninth
noticeable
occasionally
occurred
offered
omission
omitted
opportunity
opposite
ordinarily
paid
pamphlet
permanent
permitted
pleasant
practical
prevalent
privilege
probably
procedure
profited
prominent
quality
quantity
questionnaire
receipt
receive
recognize
recommendation
referred
regarding
remittance
representative
restaurant
schedule
secretary
separate
similar
sincerely
software
succeed
sufficient
supervisor
surprise
tenant
therefore
thorough
though
through
truly
undoubtedly
unnecessarily
usable
usage
using
usually
valuable
volume
weekday
writing
yield

Document Format Guide

APPENDIX B

Business communicators produce numerous documents that have standardized formats. Becoming familiar with these formats is important because business documents actually carry two kinds of messages. Verbal messages are conveyed by the words chosen to express the writer's ideas. Nonverbal messages are conveyed largely by the appearance of a document and its adherence to recognized formats. To ensure that your documents carry favorable nonverbal messages about you and your organization, you will want to give special attention to the appearance and formatting of your e-mails, letters, envelopes, and fax cover sheets.

E-Mail

E-mails are sent by computers through networks. After reading e-mails, receivers may print, store, or delete them. E-mail is an appropriate channel for *short* messages. E-mails should not replace business letters or memos that are lengthy, require permanent records, or transmit confidential or sensitive information. Chapter 7 presented guidelines for preparing e-mails. This section provides additional information on formats and usage. The following suggestions, illustrated in Figure B.1 and also in Figure 7.1 on page 194, may guide you in setting up the parts of any e-mail. Always check, however, with your organization so that you can follow its practices.

FIGURE B.1 E-Mail

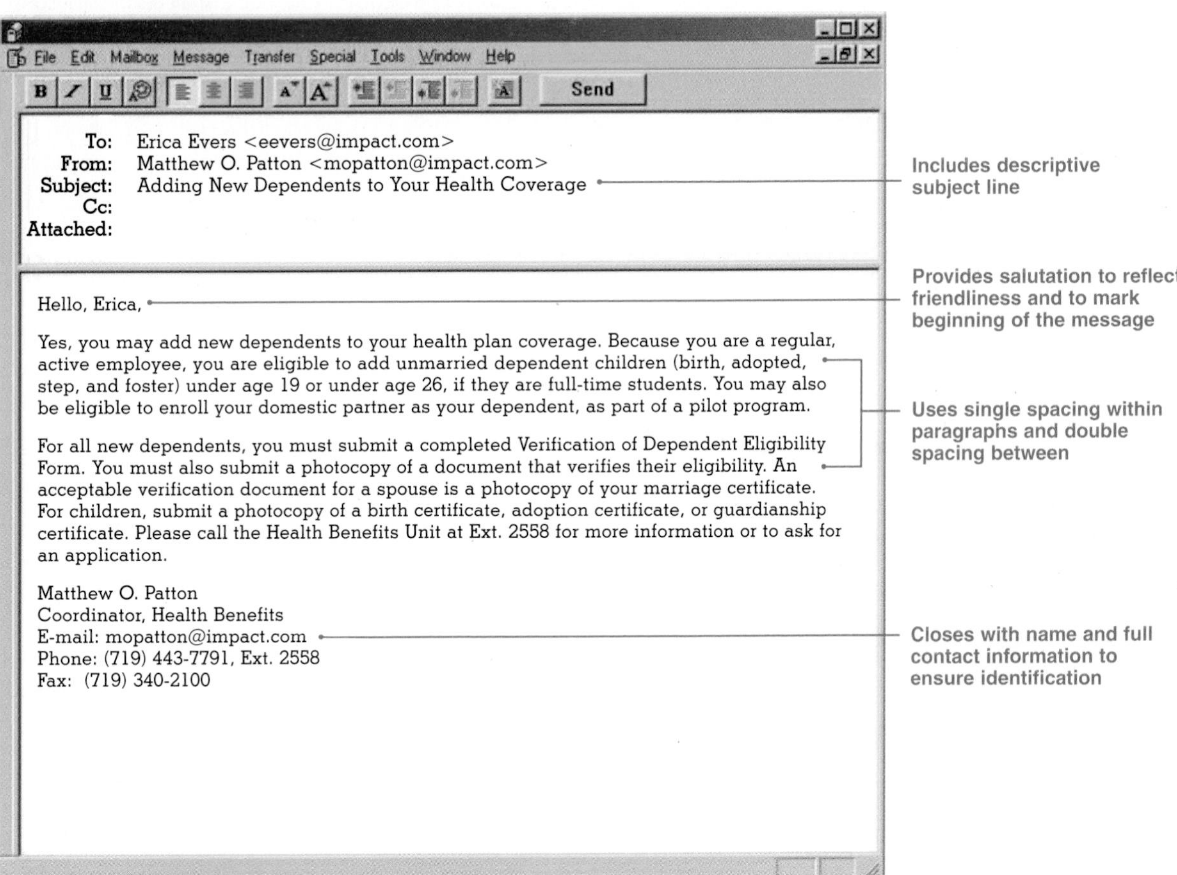

To: Erica Evers <eevers@impact.com>
From: Matthew O. Patton <mopatton@impact.com>
Subject: Adding New Dependents to Your Health Coverage
Cc:
Attached:

Hello, Erica,

Yes, you may add new dependents to your health plan coverage. Because you are a regular, active employee, you are eligible to add unmarried dependent children (birth, adopted, step, and foster) under age 19 or under age 26, if they are full-time students. You may also be eligible to enroll your domestic partner as your dependent, as part of a pilot program.

For all new dependents, you must submit a completed Verification of Dependent Eligibility Form. You must also submit a photocopy of a document that verifies their eligibility. An acceptable verification document for a spouse is a photocopy of your marriage certificate. For children, submit a photocopy of a birth certificate, adoption certificate, or guardianship certificate. Please call the Health Benefits Unit at Ext. 2558 for more information or to ask for an application.

Matthew O. Patton
Coordinator, Health Benefits
E-mail: mopatton@impact.com
Phone: (719) 443-7791, Ext. 2558
Fax: (719) 340-2100

_To_ Line. Include the receiver's e-mail address after *To.* If the receiver's address is recorded in your address book, you just have to click on it. Be sure to enter all addresses very carefully since one mistyped letter prevents delivery.

From Line. Most mail programs automatically include your name and e-mail address after *From.*

_Cc_ and _Bcc_. Insert the e-mail address of anyone who is to receive a copy of the message. *Cc* stands for carbon copy or courtesy copy. Don't be tempted, though, to send needless copies just because it is easy. *Bcc* stands for blind carbon copy. Some writers use *bcc* to send a copy of the message without the addressee's knowledge. Writers also use the *bcc* line for mailing lists. When a message is sent to a number of people and their e-mail addresses should not be revealed, the *bcc* line works well to conceal the names and addresses of all receivers.

Subject. Identify the subject of the e-mail with a brief but descriptive summary of the topic. Be sure to include enough information to be clear and compelling. Capitalize the initial letters of main words. Main words are all words except (a) the articles *a, an,* and *the*; (b) prepositions containing two or three letters (such as *at, to, on, by, for*); (c) the word *to* in an infinitive (*to work, to write*); and (d) the word *as*—unless any of these words are the first or last word in the subject line.

Salutation. Include a brief greeting, if you like. Some writers use a salutation such as *Dear Erica* followed by a comma or a colon. Others are more informal with *Hi, Erica; Hello, Erica; Good morning*; or *Greetings*. See Chapter 7 for additional discussion of e-mail greetings.

Message. Cover just one topic in your message, and try to keep your total message under three screens in length. Single-space and be sure to use both upper- and lowercase letters. Double-space between paragraphs.

Closing. Conclude an e-mail, if you like, with *Cheers, Best wishes,* or *Warm regards,* followed by your name and complete contact information. Some people omit their e-mail address because they think it is provided automatically. However, programs and routers do not always transmit the address. Therefore, always include it along with other identifying information in the closing.

Attachment. Use the attachment window or button to select the path and file name of any file you wish to send with your e-mail. You can also attach a Web page to your message.

Business Letters

Business communicators write business letters primarily to correspond with people outside the organization. Letters may go to customers, vendors, other businesses, and the government, as discussed in Chapters 8, 9, and 10. The following information will help you format your letters following conventional guidelines.

Spacing and Punctuation

For some time typists left two spaces after end punctuation (periods, question marks, and so forth). This practice was necessary, it was thought, because typewriters did not have proportional spacing and sentences were easier to read if two spaces separated them. Professional typesetters, however, never followed this practice because they used proportional spacing, and readability was not a problem. Influenced by the look of typeset publications, many writers now leave only one space after end punctuation. As a practical matter, however, it is not wrong to use two spaces.

Letter Placement and Line Endings

The easiest way to place letters on the page is to use the defaults of your word processing program. In Microsoft Word 2003, default side margins are set at 1¼ inch; in Word 2007 they are set at 1 inch. Many companies today find these margins acceptable. If you want to adjust your margins to better balance shorter letters, use the following chart:

Words in Body of Letter	Margin Settings	Blank Lines After Date
Under 200	1½ inches	4 to 10
Over 200	1 inch	2 to 3

Experts say that a ragged-right margin is easier to read than a justified (even) margin. You might want to turn off the justification feature of your word processing program if it automatically justifies the right margin.

Business Letter Parts

Professional-looking business letters are arranged in a conventional sequence with standard parts. Following is a discussion of how to use these letter parts properly. Figure B.2 illustrates the parts of a block style letter. See Chapter 8 for additional discussion of letters and their parts.

Letterhead. Most business organizations use 8½ × 11-inch paper printed with a letterhead displaying their official name, street address, Web address, e-mail address, and telephone and fax numbers. The letterhead may also include a logo and an advertising message.

Dateline. On letterhead paper you should place the date one blank line below the last line of the letterhead or 2 inches from the top edge of the paper (line 13). On plain paper place the date immediately below your return address. Because the date goes on line 13, start the return address an appropriate number of lines above it. The most common dateline format is as follows: *June 9, 2012*. Don't use *th* (or *rd, nd* or *st*) when the date is written this way. For European or military correspondence, use the following dateline format: *9 June 2012*. Notice that no commas are used.

Addressee and Delivery Notations. Delivery notations such as *FAX TRANSMISSION, FEDEX, MESSENGER DELIVERY, CONFIDENTIAL,* or *CERTIFIED MAIL* are typed in all capital letters two blank lines above the inside address.

Inside Address. Type the inside address—that is, the address of the organization or person receiving the letter—single-spaced, starting at the left margin. The number of lines between the dateline and the inside address depends on the size of the letter body, the type size (point or pitch size), and the length of the typing lines. Generally, one to nine blank lines are appropriate.

Be careful to duplicate the exact wording and spelling of the recipient's name and address on your documents. Usually, you can copy this information from the letterhead of the correspondence you are answering. If, for example, you are responding to *Jackson & Perkins Company*, do not address your letter to *Jackson and Perkins Corp.*

Always be sure to include a courtesy title such as *Mr., Ms., Mrs., Dr.,* or *Professor* before a person's name in the inside address—for both the letter and the envelope. Although many women in business today favor *Ms.*, you should use whatever title the addressee prefers.

In general, avoid abbreviations such as *Ave.* or *Co.* unless they appear in the printed letterhead of the document being answered.

Attention Line. An attention line allows you to send your message officially to an organization but to direct it to a specific individual, officer, or department. However, if you know an individual's complete name, it is always better to use it as the first line of the inside address and avoid an attention line. Two common formats for attention lines follow:

The MultiMedia Company
931 Calkins Avenue
Rochester, NY 14301

ATTENTION MARKETING DIRECTOR

The MultiMedia Company
Attention: Marketing Director
931 Calkins Avenue
Rochester, NY 14301

FIGURE B.2 **Block and Modified Block Letter Styles**

Letterhead — **Island Graphics**
893 Dillingham Boulevard
Honolulu, HI 96817-8817
(808) 493-2310
http://www.islandgraphics.com

↓ Dateline is 2 inches from the top or 1 blank line below letterhead

Dateline — September 13, 2012

↓ 1 to 9 blank lines

Inside address — Mr. T. M. Wilson, President
Visual Concept Enterprises
1901 Kaumualii Highway
Lihue, HI 96766

↓ 1 blank line

Salutation — Dear Mr. Wilson:

↓ 1 blank line

Subject line — Subject: Block Letter Style

↓ 1 blank line

This letter illustrates block letter style, about which you asked. All typed lines begin at the left margin. The date is usually placed 2 inches from the top edge of the paper or one blank line below the last line of the letterhead, whichever position is lower.

Body — This letter also shows mixed punctuation. A colon follows the salutation, and a comma follows the complimentary close. Open punctuation requires no colon after the salutation and no comma following the close; however, open punctuation is seldom seen today.

If a subject line is included, it appears one blank line below the salutation. The word *SUBJECT* is optional. Most readers will recognize a statement in this position as the subject without an identifying label. The complimentary close appears one blank line below the end of the last paragraph.

↓ 1 blank line

Complimentary close — Sincerely,

↓ 3 blank lines

Mark H. Wong

Signature block — Mark H. Wong
Graphic Designer

↓ 1 blank line

Reference initials — MHW:pil

Modified block style, Mixed punctuation

In the modified block style letter shown at the left, the date is centered or aligned with the complimentary close and signature block, which start at the center. Mixed punctuation includes a colon after the salutation and a comma after the complimentary close, as shown above and at the left.

Attention lines may be typed in all caps or with upper- and lowercase letters. The colon following *Attention* is optional. Notice that an attention line may be placed one blank line below the address block or printed as the second line of the inside address. Use the latter format so that you may copy the address block to the envelope and the attention line will not interfere with the last-line placement of the zip code. Mail can be sorted more easily if the zip code appears in the last line of a typed address. Whenever possible, use a person's name as the first line of an address instead of putting that name in an attention line.

Salutation. For most letter styles, place the letter greeting, or salutation, one blank line below the last line of the inside address or the attention line (if used). If the letter is addressed to an individual, use that person's courtesy title and last name (*Dear Mr. Lanham*). Even if you are on a first-name basis (*Dear Leslie*), be sure to add a colon (not a comma or a semicolon) after the salutation. Do not use an individual's full name in the salutation (not *Dear Mr. Leslie Lanham*) unless you are unsure of gender (*Dear Leslie Lanham*).

For letters with attention lines or those addressed to organizations, the selection of an appropriate salutation has become more difficult. Formerly, writers used *Gentlemen* generically for all organizations. With increasing numbers of women in business management today, however, *Gentlemen* is problematic. Because no universally acceptable salutation has emerged as yet, you could use *Ladies and Gentlemen* or *Gentlemen and Ladies.*

Subject and Reference Lines. Although experts suggest placing the subject line one blank line below the salutation, many businesses actually place it above the salutation. Use whatever style your organization prefers. Reference lines often show policy or file numbers; they generally appear one blank line above the salutation. Use initial capital letters for the main words or all capital letters.

Body. Most business letters and memorandums are single-spaced, with double-spacing between paragraphs. Very short messages may be double-spaced with indented paragraphs.

Complimentary Close. Typed one blank line below the last line of the letter, the complimentary close may be formal (*Very truly yours*) or informal (*Sincerely* or *Cordially*).

Signature Block. In most letter styles, the writer's typed name and optional identification appear three or four blank lines below the complimentary close. The combination of name, title, and organization information should be arranged to achieve a balanced look. The name and title may appear on the same line or on separate lines, depending on the length of each. Use commas to separate categories within the same line, but not to conclude a line.

Sincerely yours,

Jeremy M. Wood

Jeremy M. Wood, Manager
Technical Sales and Services

Cordially yours,

Casandra Baker-Murillo

Casandra Baker-Murillo
Executive Vice President

Some organizations include their names in the signature block. In such cases the organization name appears in all caps one blank line below the complimentary close, as shown here:

Cordially,

LIPTON COMPUTER SERVICES

Shelina A. Simpson

Shelina A. Simpson
Executive Assistant

FIGURE B.3 Second-Page Heading

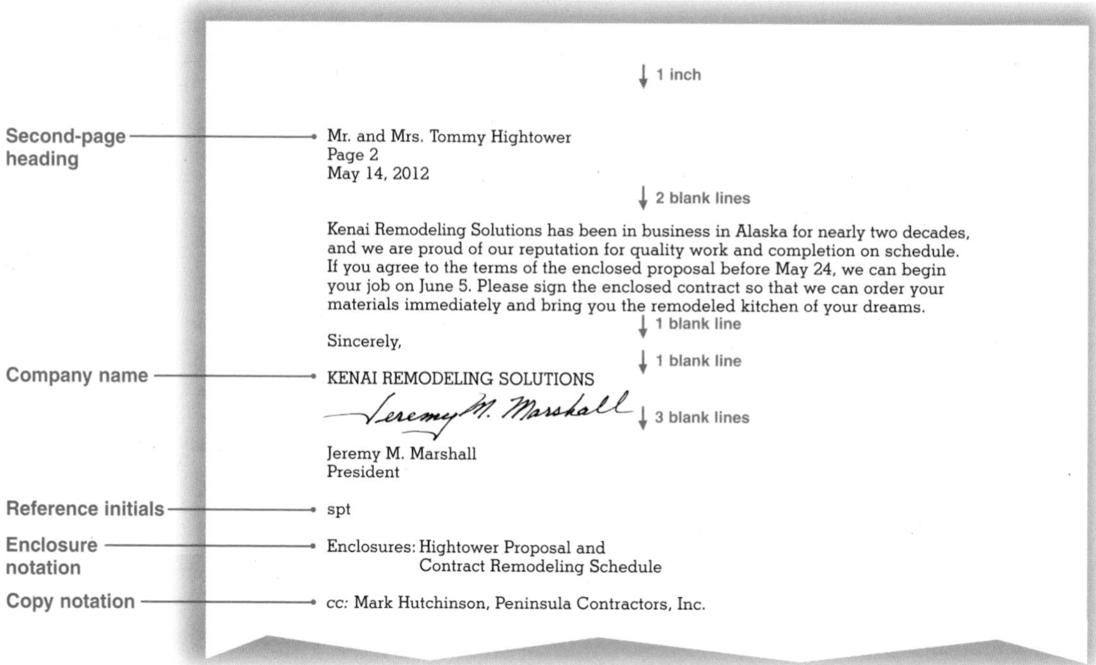

Mr. and Mrs. Tommy Hightower
Page 2
May 14, 2012

Kenai Remodeling Solutions has been in business in Alaska for nearly two decades, and we are proud of our reputation for quality work and completion on schedule. If you agree to the terms of the enclosed proposal before May 24, we can begin your job on June 5. Please sign the enclosed contract so that we can order your materials immediately and bring you the remodeled kitchen of your dreams.

Sincerely,

KENAI REMODELING SOLUTIONS

Jeremy M. Marshall

Jeremy M. Marshall
President

spt

Enclosures: Hightower Proposal and
Contract Remodeling Schedule

cc: Mark Hutchinson, Peninsula Contractors, Inc.

Reference Initials. If used, the initials of the typist and writer are typed one blank line below the writer's name and title. Generally, the writer's initials are capitalized and the typist's are lowercased, but this format varies.

Enclosure Notation. When an enclosure or attachment accompanies a document, a notation to that effect appears one blank line below the reference initials. This notation reminds the typist to insert the enclosure in the envelope, and it reminds the recipient to look for the enclosure or attachment. The notation may be spelled out (*Enclosure, Attachment*), or it may be abbreviated (*Enc., Att.*). It may indicate the number of enclosures or attachments, and it may also identify a specific enclosure (*Enclosure: Form 1099*).

Copy Notation. If you make copies of correspondence for other individuals, you may use *cc* to indicate courtesy copy, *pc* to indicate photocopy, or merely *c* for any kind of copy. A colon following the initial(s) is optional.

Second-Page Heading. When a letter extends beyond one page, use plain paper of the same quality and color as the first page. Identify the second and succeeding pages with a heading consisting of the name of the addressee, the page number, and the date. Use the following format or the one shown in Figure B.3:

Ms. Sara Hendricks	2	May 3, 2012

Both headings appear six blank lines (1 inch) from the top edge of the paper followed by two blank lines to separate them from the continuing text. Avoid using a second page if you have only one line or the complimentary close and signature block to fill that page.

Plain-Paper Return Address. If you prepare a personal or business letter on plain paper, place your address immediately above the date as shown at the top of the next page. Do not include your name; you will type (and sign) your name at the end of your letter. If your return address contains two lines, begin typing so that the date appears 2 inches from the top. Avoid abbreviations except for a two-letter state abbreviation.

580 East Leffels Street
Springfield, OH 45501
December 14, 2012

Ms. Ellen Siemens
Escrow Department
TransOhio First Federal
1220 Wooster Boulevard
Columbus, OH 43218-2900

Dear Ms. Siemens:

The above return address and inside address illustrate the personal business style. For letters in the block style, type the return address at the left margin. For modified block style letters, start the return address at the center to align with the complimentary close.

Letter and Punctuation Styles

Most business letters today are prepared in either block or modified block style, and they generally use mixed punctuation.

Block Style. In the block style, shown in Figure B.2 on page B-4, all lines begin at the left margin. This style is a favorite because it is easy to format.

Modified Block Style. The modified block style differs from block style in that the date and closing lines appear in the center, as shown at the bottom of Figure B.2. The date may be (a) centered, (b) begun at the center of the page (to align with the closing lines), or (c) backspaced from the right margin. The signature block—including the complimentary close, writer's name and title, or organization identification—begins at the center. The first line of each paragraph may begin at the left margin or may be indented five or ten spaces. All other lines begin at the left margin.

Mixed Punctuation Style. Most businesses today use mixed punctuation, shown in Figure B.2. It requires a colon after the salutation and a comma after the complimentary close. Even when the salutation is a first name, a colon is appropriate.

Envelopes

An envelope should be of the same quality and color of stationery as the letter it carries. Because the envelope introduces your message and makes the first impression, you need to be especially careful in addressing it. Moreover, how you fold the letter is important.

Return Address. The return address is usually printed in the upper left corner of an envelope, as shown in Figure B.4 on the next page. In large companies some form of identification (the writer's initials, name, or location) may be typed above the company name and address. This identification helps return the letter to the sender in case of nondelivery.

On an envelope without a printed return address, single-space the return address in the upper left corner. Beginning on line 3 on the fourth space (½ inch) from the left edge, type the writer's name, title, company, and mailing address. On a word processor, select the appropriate envelope size and make adjustments to approximate this return address location.

Mailing Address. On legal-sized No. 10 envelopes (4⅛ x 9½ inches), begin the address on line 13 about 4¼ inches from the left edge, as shown in Figure B.4. For small envelopes (3⅝ x 6½ inches), begin typing on line 12 about 2½ inches from the left edge. On a word processor, select the correct envelope size and check to be sure your address falls in the desired location.

The U.S. Postal Service recommends that addresses be typed in all caps without any punctuation. This Postal Service style, shown in the small envelope in Figure B.4, was originally developed to facilitate scanning by optical character readers. Today's OCRs, however, are so sophisticated that they scan upper- and lowercase letters easily. Many companies today do not follow the Postal Service format because they prefer to use the same format for the envelope as for the inside address. If the same format is used, writers can take advantage of word processing programs to copy the inside address to the envelope, thus saving keystrokes and reducing errors. Having the same format on both the inside address and the envelope also looks more professional and consistent. For those reasons you may choose to use the familiar upper- and lowercase combination format. But you will want to check with your organization to learn its preference.

In addressing your envelopes for delivery in this country or in Canada, use the two-letter state and province abbreviations shown in Figure B.5. Notice that these abbreviations are in capital letters without periods.

Folding. The way a letter is folded and inserted into an envelope sends additional nonverbal messages about a writer's professionalism and carefulness. Most businesspeople follow the procedures shown here, which produce the least number of creases to distract readers.

For large No. 10 envelopes, begin with the letter face up. Fold slightly less than one third of the sheet toward the top, as shown in the following diagram. Then fold down the top third to within ⅛ inch of the bottom fold. Insert the letter into the envelope with the last fold toward the bottom of the envelope.

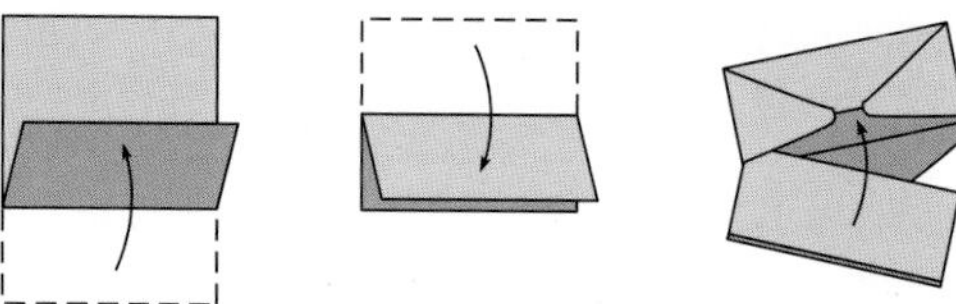

For small No. 6¾ envelopes, begin by folding the bottom up to within ⅛ inch of the top edge. Then fold the right third over to the left. Fold the left third to within ⅛ inch of the last fold. Insert the last fold into the envelope first.

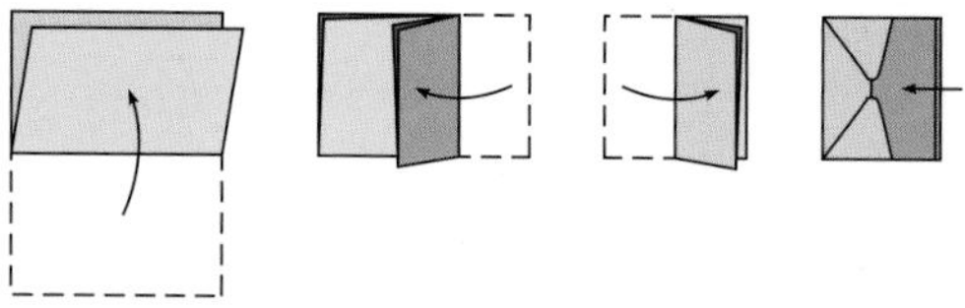

FIGURE B.4 **Envelope Formats**

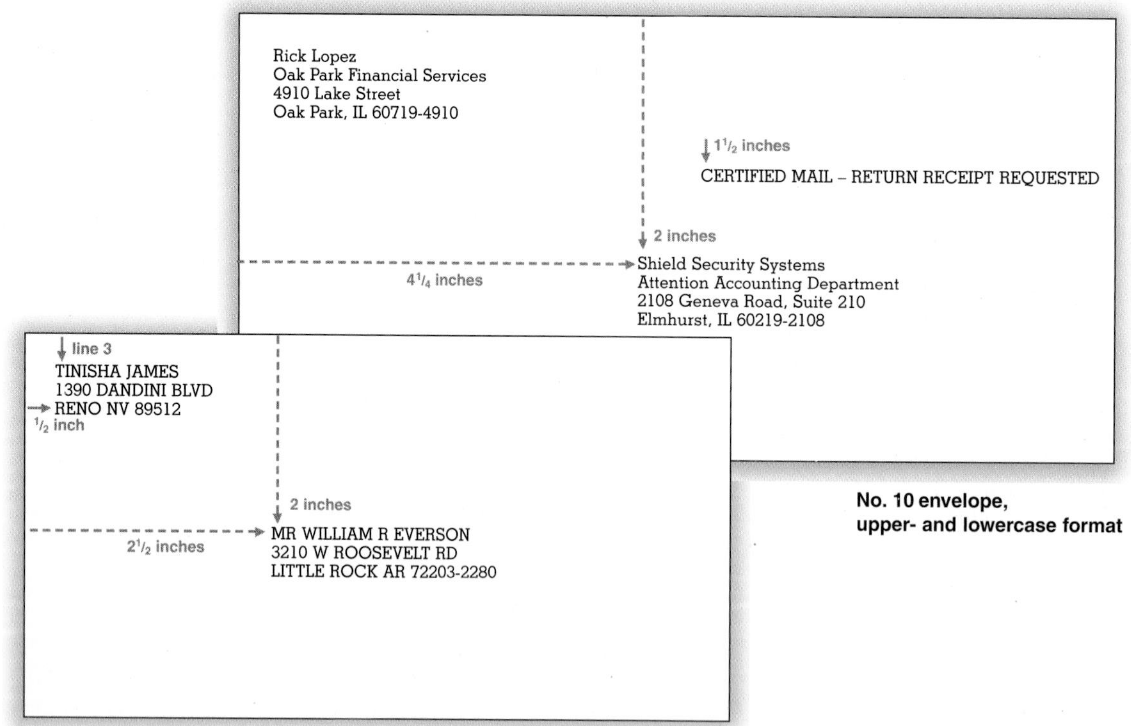

No. 10 envelope, upper- and lowercase format

No. 6¾ envelope, Postal Service uppercase format

FIGURE B.5 Abbreviations of States, Territories, and Provinces

State or Territory	Two-Letter Abbreviation	State or Territory	Two-Letter Abbreviation
Alabama	AL	North Carolina	NC
Alaska	AK	North Dakota	ND
Arizona	AZ	Ohio	OH
Arkansas	AR	Oklahoma	OK
California	CA	Oregon	OR
Canal Zone	CZ	Pennsylvania	PA
Colorado	CO	Puerto Rico	PR
Connecticut	CT	Rhode Island	RI
Delaware	DE	South Carolina	SC
District of Columbia	DC	South Dakota	SD
Florida	FL	Tennessee	TN
Georgia	GA	Texas	TX
Guam	GU	Utah	UT
Hawaii	HI	Vermont	VT
Idaho	ID	Virgin Islands	VI
Illinois	IL	Virginia	VA
Indiana	IN	Washington	WA
Iowa	IA	West Virginia	WV
Kansas	KS	Wisconsin	WI
Kentucky	KY	Wyoming	WY
Louisiana	LA	**Canadian Province**	
Maine	ME	Alberta	AB
Maryland	MD	British Columbia	BC
Massachusetts	MA	Labrador	LB
Michigan	MI	Manitoba	MB
Minnesota	MN	New Brunswick	NB
Mississippi	MS	Newfoundland	NF
Missouri	MO	Northwest Territories	NT
Montana	MT	Nova Scotia	NS
Nebraska	NE	Ontario	ON
Nevada	NV	Prince Edward Island	PE
New Hampshire	NH	Quebec	PQ
New Jersey	NJ	Saskatchewan	SK
New Mexico	NM	Yukon Territory	YT
New York	NY		

Fax Cover Sheet

Documents transmitted by fax are usually introduced by a cover sheet, such as that shown in Figure B.6. As with memos, the format varies considerably. Important items to include are (a) the name and fax number of the receiver, (b) the name and fax number of the sender, (c) the number of pages being sent, and (d) the name and telephone number of the person to notify in case of unsatisfactory transmission.

When the document being transmitted requires little explanation, you may prefer to attach an adhesive note (such as a Post-it fax transmittal form) instead of a full cover sheet. These notes carry essentially the same information as shown in our printed fax cover sheet. They are perfectly acceptable in most business organizations and can save considerable paper and transmission costs.

FIGURE B.6 Fax Cover Sheet

FAX TRANSMISSION

DATE: ______________________

TO: ______________________ FAX NUMBER: ______________________

____

____

FROM: ______________________ FAX NUMBER: ______________________

____

____

NUMBER OF PAGES TRANSMITTED INCLUDING THIS COVER SHEET: ______________________

MESSAGE:

If any part of this fax transmission is missing or not clearly received, please call:

NAME: ______________________

PHONE: ______________________

Documentation Guide

APPENDIX C

For many reasons business writers are careful to properly document report data. Citing sources strengthens a writer's argument, as you learned in Chapter 11. Acknowledging sources also shields writers from charges of plagiarism. Moreover, good references help readers pursue further research.

Before we discuss specific documentation formats, you must understand the difference between *source* notes and *content* notes. Source notes identify quotations, paraphrased passages, and author references. They lead readers to the sources of cited information, and they must follow a consistent format. Content notes, on the other hand, enable writers to add comments, explain information not directly related to the text, or refer readers to other sections of a report. Because content notes are generally infrequent, most writers identify them in the text with a raised asterisk (*). At the bottom of the page, the asterisk is repeated with the content note following. If two content notes appear on one page, a double asterisk identifies the second reference.

Your real concern will be with source notes. These identify quotations or paraphrased ideas in the text, and they direct readers to a complete list of references (a bibliography) at the end of your report. Researchers have struggled for years to develop the perfect documentation system, one that is efficient for the writer and crystal clear to the reader. As a result, many systems exist, each with its advantages. The important thing for you is to adopt one system and use it consistently.

Students frequently ask, "But what documentation system is most used in business?" Actually, no one method dominates. Many businesses have developed their own hybrid systems. These companies generally supply guidelines illustrating their in-house style to employees. Before starting any research project on the job, you will want to inquire about your organization's preferred documentation style. You can also look in the files for examples of previous reports.

References are usually cited in two places: (a) a brief citation appears in the text, and (b) a complete citation appears in a bibliography at the end of the report. The two most common formats for citations and bibliographies in academic work are those of the Modern Language Association (MLA) and the American Psychological Association (APA). Each has its own style for textual references and bibliography lists. The citations in this textbook are based on the APA style, which is increasingly the standard in business communication.

Modern Language Association Format

Writers in the humanities and liberal arts frequently use the MLA format, which is illustrated in Figure C.1. In parentheses close to the textual reference appears the author's name and page cited. If no author is known, a shortened version of the source title is used. At the end of the report, the writer lists alphabetically all references in a bibliography called "Works Cited." The MLA no longer requires the use of URLs in Web citations because Web addresses change and most readers can find Web addresses by using a Web browser and searching for the publication title. In another recent change, MLA style now requires identification of the publication medium, such as *Print* or *Web.* For more information consult *MLA Handbook for Writers of Research Papers*, 7e (New York: The Modern Language Association of America, 2009) or Rossiter's *The MLA Pocket Handbook* (DW Publishing).

MLA In-Text Format. In-text citations generally appear close to the point where the reference is mentioned or at the end of the sentence inside the closing period. Follow these guidelines:

- Include the last name of the author(s) and the page number. Do not use a comma, as (Smith 310).

FIGURE C.1 Portions of MLA Text Page and Works Cited

Peanut butter was first delivered to the world by a St. Louis physician in 1890. As discussed at the Peanut Advisory Board's Web site, peanut butter was originally promoted as a protein substitute for elderly patients ("History"). However, it was the 1905 Universal Exposition in St. Louis that truly launched peanut butter. Since then, annual peanut butter consumption has zoomed to 3.3 pounds a person in the United States (Barrons).

America's farmers produce 1.6 million tons of peanuts annually, about half of which is used for oil, nuts, and candy. Lisa Gibbons, executive secretary of the Peanut Advisory Board, says that "peanuts in some form are in the top four candies: Snickers, Reese's Peanut Butter Cups, Peanut M & Ms, and Butterfingers" (Meadows 32).

Works Cited

Barrons, Elizabeth Ruth. "A Comparison of Domestic and International Consumption of Legumes." *Journal of Economic Agriculture* 23 (2010): 45–49. Print.

"History of Peanut Butter." *Peanut Advisory Board.* Alabama Peanut Producers Association. (n.d.) Web. Retrieved 19 Jan. 2011.

Meadows, Mark Allen. "Peanut Crop Is Anything but Peanuts at Home and Overseas." *Business Monthly* May 2011: 31–34. Print.

- If the author's name is mentioned in the text, cite only the page number in parentheses. Do not include either the word *page* or the abbreviations *p.* or *pp.*
- If no author is known, refer to the document title or a shortened version of it, as ("Facts at Fingertips" 102).

MLA Bibliographic Format. In the "Works Cited" bibliography, list all references cited in a report. Some writers include all works consulted. A portion of an MLA bibliography is shown in Figure C.1. A more complete list of model references appears in Figure C.2. Following are selected guidelines summarizing important points regarding MLA bibliographic format:

- Use italics for the titles of books, magazines, newspapers, journals, and Web sites. Capitalize all main words.
- Enclose the titles of magazine, newspaper, and journal articles in quotation marks. Include volume and issue numbers for journals only.
- Use the following sequence for electronic sources: author; article name in quotation marks; title of Web site, project, or book in italics; name of institution, organization, or publisher affiliated with the site; page numbers if available; URL (only if necessary for retrieval); and publication medium (such as *Web, Print,* or *PDF*); and access date.

American Psychological Association Format

Popular in the social and physical sciences, the American Psychological Association (APA) documentation style uses parenthetic citations. That is, each author reference is shown in parentheses when cited in the text, as shown in Figure C.3. At the end of the report, all references are listed alphabetically in a bibliography called "References." Because online materials can change, APA now recommends providing a digital object identifier (DOI) when available rather than the URL. In another departure from previous advice, APA style no longer requires the date of retrieval. For more information about APA formats, see the *Publication Manual of the American Psychological Association*, 6e (Washington, DC: American Psychological Association, 2009) or Rossiter's *The APA Pocket Handbook* (DW Publishing).

FIGURE C.2 **MLA Sample Works Cited**

Works Cited

American Airlines. *2011 Annual Report.* Fort Worth, TX: AMR Corporation. Print.	Annual report, print
Atamian, Richard A., and Ellen Ferranto. *Driving Market Forces.* New York: HarperCollins, 2010. Print.	Book, two authors, print
"Audio Conferencing." *Encyclopaedia Britannica*. 2010. *Britannica.com*. Web. 19 Oct. 2010.	Encyclopedia, Web
Austin, Anthony. Personal interview. 16 Jan. 2012.	Interview
Balcazar, Saul. "The Future of Investing," *Fortune* 1 Mar. 2010: 62–67. *ABI/Inform*. Web. 15 Mar. 2010.	Magazine article, Web database
Berss, Marcia. "Protein Man," *Forbes* 24 Oct. 2011: 65–66. Print.	Magazine article, print
Cantrell, Mark R., and Hilary Watson. "Violence in Today's Workplace." *Office Review* 10 Jan. 2010: 24–27. PDF file. 23 May 2011.	Magazine article, PDF file
"Globalization Often Means That the Fast Track Leads Overseas." *The Washington Post* 16 June 2011: A1, A4. Print.	Newspaper article, no author, print
Grover, Hal. "When Taking a Tip From a Job Network, Proceed With Caution." *The Wall Street Journal* 7 Feb. 2011: B1. Print.	Newspaper article, one author, print
Gutzman, Debra. "Corporate Ghostwriting," *Financial Times* 14 Apr. 2011: n.pag. *FT.com*. Web. 20 Apr. 2011.	Newspaper article, Web, no page
Lynch, Diane. "Wired Women: Gender in High-Tech Workplace." *abcnews.go.com Technology*. n.d. Web. 24 Apr. 2011.	Web document without print version
U.S. Dept. of Labor. *Child Care as a Workforce Issue*. Washington: Government Printing Office, 2010. Print.	Government publication
Vitalari, Nicholas P., James C. Patton, and Andrew Milner. "Key Trends in Systems Development in Europe and North America." *Journal of Global Information Management* 3.2 (2010): 5–20. Print. [*3.2* signifies volume 3, issue 2]	Journal article with volume and issue numbers, print
Walker, Robyn C., and Jolanta Aritz. "Cognitive Organization and Identity Maintenance in Multicultural Teams," *Journal of Business Communication* 47.1 (2010): 20–41. Business Source Complete database. Web. 15 Mar. 2011.	Journal, electronic database
"Writing With Inferential Statistics." *The OWL at Purdue*. Purdue University Online Writing Lab, n.d. Web. 20 Feb. 2011.	Web document, no author, no date
Yellin, Mike. "Re: Managing Managers and Cell Phones." 9 Sept. 2011. *Yahoo Groups*. E-commerce. Web. 15 Sept. 2011.	Listserv, discussion group, blog posting

Note 1: MLA style no longer recommends listing URLs for Web sites.

Note 2: To prevent confusion, you might add the words *Accessed* or *Retrieved* preceding the date you accessed the online source.

Note 3: Although MLA style prescribes double-spacing for the works sited, we show single spacing to conserve space and to represent preferred business usage.

APA In-Text Format. Within the text, document each specific textual source with a short description in parentheses. Following are selected guidelines summarizing important elements of APA style:

- For a direct quotation, include the last name of the author(s), date of publication, and page number, as (Jones, 2010, p. 36). Use *n.d.* if no date is available.
- If no author is known, refer to the first few words of the reference list entry and the year, as (Computer Privacy, 2011).
- Include page numbers only for direct quotations.

APA Reference Format. List all citations alphabetically in a section called "References." A portion of an APA reference page is shown in Figure C.3. A more complete list of model references appears in Figure C.4. APA style requires specific capitalization and sequencing guidelines, some of which are summarized here:

- Include an author's name with the last name first followed by initials, such as *Smith, M. A.* First and middle names are not used.
- Show the date of publication in parentheses immediately after the author's name, as *Smith, M. A. (2011, March 2).*
- Italicize the titles of books. Use "sentence-style" capitalization. This means capitalize only the first word of a title, proper nouns, and the first word after an internal colon.
- Do not italicize or underscore the titles of magazine and journal articles. Use sentence-style capitalization for article titles.
- Italicize the names of magazines, newspapers, and journals. Capitalize the initial letters of all main words.
- Include the document object identifier (DOI) when available for online periodicals. If no DOI is available, include the URL but no date of retrieval.
- For an online periodical that also appears in a printed version, include *Electronic version* in brackets after the article's title. Do not include a URL.
- For articles easily obtained from an online database (such as that in a school library), provide print information. The database need not be identified. You may include an accession number in parentheses at the end, but APA style does not require it.

FIGURE C.3 Portions of APA Text Page and References

Peanut butter was first delivered to the world by a St. Louis physician in 1890. As discussed at the Peanut Advisory Board's Web site, peanut butter was originally promoted as a protein substitute for elderly patients (History, n.d.). However, it was the 1905 Universal Exposition in St. Louis that truly launched peanut butter. Since then, annual peanut butter consumption has zoomed to 3.3 pounds a person in the United States (Barrons, 2010, p. 46).

America's farmers produce 1.6 million tons of peanuts annually, about half of which is used for oil, nuts, and candy. Lisa Gibbons, executive secretary of the Peanut Advisory Board, says that "peanuts in some form are in the top four candies: Snickers, Reese's Peanut Butter Cups, Peanut M & Ms, and Butterfingers" (Meadows, 2011, p. 32).

References

Barrons, E. R. (2010, November). A comparison of domestic and international consumption of legumes. *Journal of Economic Agriculture*, *23*(3), 45–49.

History of peanut butter. (n.d.). Peanut Advisory Board. Alabama Peanut Producers Association. Retrieved from http://www.alpeanuts.com/consumer_interest/articles.phtml?articleID=102

Meadows, M. A. (2011, May). Peanut crop is anything but peanuts at home and overseas. *Business Monthly*, 31–34.

FIGURE C.4 APA Sample References

References

American Airlines. (2011). *2011 Annual Report.* Fort Worth, TX: AMR Corporation. — **Annual report**

Atamian, R. A., & Ferranto, E. (2010). *Driving market forces.* New York: HarperCollins. — **Book, two authors**

Audio conferencing. (2010). In *Encyclopaedia Britannica*. Retrieved October 19, 2011, from Encyclopaedia Britannica Online: http//www.britannica.com/eb/article-61669 — **Encyclopedia, online**

Balcazar, S. (2010, March 1). The future of investing. [Electronic version]. *Fortune*, 62–67. — **Magazine article, online, without DOI, print version available**

Beardsley, E. (2011, April 6). Building gone wild in China. [Electronic version]. Asia Today, 102, pp. 42–44. doi: 10.1090/14733300410001676403 — **Magazine article, with DOI**

Berss, M. (2008, October 24). Protein man. *Forbes*, 65–66. — **Magazine article, print**

Clay, R. (2008, June). Science vs. ideology: Psychologists fight back about the misuse of research. *Monitor on Psychology*, 39(6). Retrieved from http://www.apa.org.monitor/ — **Magazine article, online**

Globalization often means that the fast track leads overseas. (2011, June 16). *The Washington Post*, pp. A1, A4. — **Newspaper article, no author, print**

Guzman, D. (2011, April 20). Corporate ghostwriting. *Financial Times*. Retrieved from http://www.ft.com — **Newspaper article, online**

U.S. Department of Health and Human Services, National Institutes of Health, National Heart, Lung, and Blood Institute. (2003). *Managing asthma: A guide for schools* (NIH Publication No. 02-2650). Retrieved from http://www.nhlbi.nih.gov/health/prof/lung/asthma/asth_sch.pdf — **Government report**

Varma, P., Sivakumaran, B., and Marshall, R. (2010, March). Impulse buying and variety seeking: A trait-correlates perspective. *Journal of Business Research, 63*(3), 276–283. [*63*(3) signifies volume 63, series or issue 3] — **Journal article from database** (see Note 1 below)

Vitalari, N. P., Patton, J. C., & Milner, A. (2010, May). Key trends in systems development in Europe and North America. *Journal of Global Information Management, 3*(2), 5–20. — **Journal article without DOI**

Walker, R. D., & Aritz, J. (2010, January). Cognitive organization and identity maintenance in multicultural teams. [Electronic version]. *Journal of Business Communication*, 47(1): 20–41. doi: 10.1177/0021943609340669 — **Journal article with DOI**

Writing with inferential statistics. (n.d.). *The OWL at Purdue*. Retrieved from http://owl.english.purdue.edu/owl/resource/672/06/ — **Web document, no author, no date**

Yerkes, J. (2010, February 24). Re: Emerging business models [Online forum comment]. Retrieved from http://www1.wipo.int:8080/roller/trackback/ipisforum/Weblog/theme_nine_emerging_business_models — **Web posting to newsgroup, online forum, or discussion group**

Note 1: Database identification is unnecessary if the article is easily located through its primary publication.

Note 2: Do not include retrieval dates unless the source material may change over time (e.g., wikis).

Note 3: Although APA style prescribes double-spacing for the References page, we show single spacing to conserve space and to represent preferred business usage.

Correction Symbols

APPENDIX D

In marking your papers, your instructor may use the following symbols or abbreviations to indicate writing or formatting weaknesses. You will find that studying these symbols and suggestions will help you understand your instructor's remarks. Knowing this information can also help you evaluate and improve your own letters, memos, e-mail messages, reports, and other writing. To improve your command of grammar and mechanics, please review the guides in the Grammar and Mechanics Guide in Appendix A. You can also build your skills by completing the exercises in Your Personal Language Trainer at **www.meguffey.com**.

Grammar and Mechanics

Act Use active-voice verbs.

Apos Use apostrophe correctly.

Art Use a correct article (*a, an,* or *the).*

Cap Correct capitalization error.

Cm Insert a comma.

CmConj Use a comma before a coordinating conjunction (*and, or, nor, but*) that joins independent clauses.

CmIntr Use a comma after an introductory clause or a long phrase.

CmSer Insert commas to separate items in a series.

CS Correct a comma splice by separating clauses with a period or a semicolon.

DM Correct a misplaced or dangling modifier by moving the modifier closer to the word it describes or by supplying a clear subject.

Exp Eliminate expletives (*there is, there are,* and *it is*)

Frag Revise sentence fragment to express a complete thought.

Num Express numbers in appropriate word or figure form.

ProAgr Make pronoun agree in number with its antecedent.

ProCase Use appropriate nominative, objective, or possessive case.

Ref Correct vague pronoun reference. Avoid pronoun that refers to a phrase, clause, sentence, or paragraph.

RO Revise run-on or fused sentence by adding a period or a semicolon to separate independent clauses.

Sp Correct spelling error.

S/V Make verbs agree with their subjects.

Vb Use correct verb tense.

V/Shift Avoid unnecessary shifts in verb tense.

UnCm Eliminate unnecessary comma.

Content, Organization, and Style

Asgn	Follow assignment instructions.
Awk	Recast to avoid awkward expression.
Ch	Use longer sentences to avoid choppiness. Vary sentence patterns.
Cl	Improve clarity of ideas or expression.
Coh	Develop coherence between ideas. Repeat key ideas, use pronouns, or add transitional expression.
Cop	Avoid copying textbook examples or wording.
DirSt	Start directly with the main idea.
Exp	Expand or explain an incomplete idea.
IS	Use indirect strategy by explaining before introducing main idea.
Log	Reconsider faulty logic.
Neg	Revise negative expression with more positive view.
Ob	Avoid stating the obvious.
Org	Improve organization by grouping similar ideas.
Par	Express ideas in parallel form.
Redun	Avoid redundant expression.
Tone	Use conversational, positive tone that promotes goodwill.
You	Emphasize the "you" view.
WC	Improve word choice.

Format

DS	Insert a double space.
F	Choose an appropriate format for this document.
GH	Use graphic highlighting (bullets, lists, indentions, or headings) to enhance readability.
Mar	Improve margins to fit document attractively on the page.
SS	Insert a single space.
TS	Insert a triple space.

Key to Grammar and Mechanics C.L.U.E. Exercises

Chapter 1

1. Whether you are already working or about to enter today's **workplace, communication** skills are critical to your career success. [Guide 1, Fragment]
2. Surveys of employers consistently show that communication skills are important to job **success; job** advertisements often request excellent oral and written communication skills. [Use a semicolon or start a new sentence with "Job." Guide 3, Comma splice]
3. C.
4. We cannot predict future **jobs;** however, they will undoubtedly require brainpower and education. [Guide 3, Comma splice]
5. Face-to-face conversations have many **advantages even** though they produce no written record and sometimes waste time. [No punctuation required. Guide 1, Fragment]
6. A vital part of the communication process is **feedback. It** helps the sender know that the message was received and understood. [Start a new sentence or join clauses with a semicolon. Guide 3, Comma splice]
7. Knowledge workers must be critical **thinkers. They** must be able to make decisions and communicate those decisions. [Start a new sentence or join clauses with a semicolon. Guide 2, Run-on sentence]
8. Management uses many methods to distribute information **downward such** as newsletters, announcements, meetings, videos, and company intranets. [No additional punctuation is required. Guide 1, Fragment]
9. C.
10. You may be expected to agree to a company's code of **ethics. You** will also be expected to know the laws applying to your job. [Guide 3, Comma splice]

Chapter 2

1. Our recruiter must **choose** from among four strong candidates. [Guide 4]
2. The use of smartphones and laptops during meetings **is** prohibited. [Guide 6]
3. If I **were** you, I would finish my degree program. [Guide 5]
4. Considerable time and money **were** spent on communication training for employees. [Guide 7]
5. Neither the president nor the operations manager **has** read the complete report. [Guide 8]
6. Disagreement and dissension **are** normal and should be expected in team interactions. [Guide 7]
7. Everything in the meeting minutes and company reports **is** open to public view. [Guide 9]
8. A committee of three employees and two managers **is** working to establish office priorities.[Guide 10]
9. Greg said that he **saw** the report before it was distributed to management. [Guide 4]
10. Each of the office divisions **is** expected to work together to create common procedures. [Guide 9]

Chapter 3

1. Direct the visitors to my boss and **me**; she and I will give them a tour of our facility. [Guide 13]
2. Judging by you and **me** alone, this department will be the most productive one in the company. [Guide 13]
3. The team knew that **its** project was doomed once the funding was cut. [Guide 14]
4. You and **I** did the work of three; she only did hers and poorly so. [Guide 12]
5. The shift manager and I will work overtime tonight, so please direct all calls to him or **me**. [Guide 15]
6. Each new job candidate must be accompanied to **his or her** interview by a staff member.

   OR: All new job candidates must be accompanied to **their** interviews by a staff member. [Guide 17]
7. Please deliver the printer supplies to **whoever** ordered them. [Guide 16]
8. Most applications arrived on time, but **yours** and **hers** were not received. [Guide 14]
9. *C* [Guide 13]
10. **Who** did you say left messages for Connie and me? [Guide 16]

Chapter 4

1. Business writers strive to use **easy-to-understand** language and familiar words. [Guide 20]
2. Luis said he did **well** in his employment interview. [Guide 19]
3. Having prepared for months, we won the contract **easily**. [Guide 19]
4. Collaboration on **team-written** documents is necessary for big projects. [Guide 20]
5. Jenna felt **bad** when her team project was completed. [Guide 19]
6. The 3-x-3 writing plan provides **step-by-step** instructions for writing messages. [Guide 20]
7. Our **recently revised** office handbook outlined all recommended document formats. [Guide 20]
8. The project ran **smoothly** after Maria organized the team. [Guide 19]
9. **Locally installed** online collaboration tools are **easy to use** and work well. [Guide 20]
10. **Well-written** safety messages include short, familiar words. [Guide 20]

Chapter 5

1. The 3-x-3 writing process includes prewriting, **writing,** and revising. [Guide 21, CmSer]
2. Before asking others for **information,** see what you can find yourself. [Guide 22, CmIntr]
3. Formal research methods include accessing electronically, searching **manually,** and investigating primary sources. [Guide 21, CmSer]
4. If a project is **complex,** consider organizing it by outlining the major points. [Guide 22, CmIntr]
5. Careful writers define the main **topic,** and they divide it into three to five components. [Guide 23, CmConj]
6. We decided that Jill **Hawkins,** who is the best writer on the **team,** should prepare the final draft. [Guide 25, CmIn]
7. The company's executives expected new office construction to be finished by September 1, **2012,** in **Boulder,** Colorado. [Guide 24, CmDate]
8. Grammar **checkers,** by the **way,** often highlight passive voice as a grammar fault. [Guide 25, CmIn]
9. When you must be tactful and avoid naming the doer of an **action,** the passive voice can be helpful. [Guide 22, CmIntr]
10. *C* [Guide 26]

Chapter 6

1. Successful product names may appear to have been named by **magic; however,** the naming process is methodical and deliberate. [Guide 27]
2. Choosing the right name and tagline is **critical; consequently,** companies are eager to hire specialists. [Guide 27]
3. Naming is a costly **endeavor;** fees may range up to $70,000 for a global name. [Guide 27]
4. Expanding markets are in **Paris, France; Beijing, China;** and **Dubai City,** United Arab Emirates. [Guide 28]
5. As she was about to name a fashion product, Rachel Hermes **said:** "If I am launching a new fashion label, the task becomes very difficult. I have to find a name that communicates the creative style that the brand is to embody." [Guide 30]
6. For a new unisex perfume, Hermes considered the following **names:** Declaration, Serenity, and Earth. [Guide 29]
7. Naming is not a problem for small **companies; however,** it is a big problem for global brands. [Guide 27]
8. Hermes started with a thorough competitive **analysis;** it included quantifying the tone and strength of competing names. [Guide 27]
9. Attending the naming sessions were James Harper, marketing **director;** Reva Cruz, product **manager;** and Cheryl Chang, vice president. [Guide 28]
10. Distribution of goods has become **global; therefore,** names have to be registered in many countries. [Guide 27]

Chapter 7

1. Facebook **users'** accounts will be suspended if the members don't abide by the **site's** policies. [Guides 32, 31]
2. **James's** performance review was outstanding again. [Guide 32]
3. Would you please give me directions to your downtown headquarters. [Use period, not question mark. Guide 34]
4. The shipping supervisor resented **Barbara's** being late almost every morning. [Guide 33]
5. Is it true that the CEO decided to write a weekly blog. [Guide 34]
6. You must replace the ink cartridge **(see** page 8 in the **manual)** before printing. [Guide 37]
7. Justin wondered whether all the sales **managers'** databases needed to be updated. [Guide 32]
8. (Direct quotation) "**Health** care **costs,"** said the CEO, "**will** increase substantially this **year."** [Guide 38]
9. In just two **months'** time, we expect to interview five candidates for the opening. [Guide 32]
10. The meeting starts at 10 a.m. sharp, doesn't **it?** [Guide 35]

Chapter 8

1. Once the **management team** and the **union** members finally agreed, **Mayor Knox** signed the **agreement.** [Guides 39, 41]
2. All **Delta Airlines** passengers must exit the **plane** at **Gate** 14 when they reach **Los Angeles International Airport.** [Guides 39, 46]
3. The vice president of the **United States** urged members of the **European Union** to continue to seek peace in the **Middle East**. [Guides 39, 43]
4. My **uncle**, who lives in the **South**, has Skippy **peanut butter** and **Coca-Cola** for **breakfast**. [Guides 41, 43, 45]
5. Our **marketing manager** and **director** of **sales** thought that the **company** should purchase BlackBerry **smartphones** for all **sales reps**. [Guides 41, 45]
6. Personal **tax rates** for **Japanese** citizens are low by **international** standards, according to **Professor Yamaguchi** at **Osaka University**. [Guides 39, 41]
7. Jinhee Kim, who heads our **Customer Communication Division**, has a **master's degree** in social psychology from the **University** of **New Mexico**. [Guides 44, 40, 39]
8. Please consult **Figure** 4.5 in **Chapter** 4 to obtain **U.S. Census Bureau** population figures for the **Pacific Northwest.** [Guides 46, 39, 43]
9. Last **fall** did you see the article titled "The **Global Consequences** of **Using Crops** for **Fuel**"? [Guides 39, 42]
10. Toby plans to take courses in **marketing, business law,** and **English** in the **spring**. [Guides 40, 39]

Chapter 9

1. Included in her bad-news message were a **compliment** and valuable **advice**.
2. His **principal** reason for declining the invitation was his busy **calendar**.
3. In her damage-control message, the manager made a **conscious** effort to regain the customer's confidence.
4. In your **everyday** business affairs, you must show **patience** even when irritated.
5. Before you **proceed** with the report, please check those **embarrassing** statistics.
6. Although we will look into this matter **further**, I am not **surprised** at your report.
7. The judge declared that the comments of **their** attorneys were **irrelevant** to the case at hand.
8. Because the property was **too** difficult to **appraise**, its value was unrecorded.
9. Meredith hoped to **elicit** advice from her counselor, but she was **disappointed**.
10. The manager **recommended** that we switch to an annual **maintenance** schedule.

Chapter 10

1. Susan showed me **five** different customer messages with the same **two** complaints. [Guide 47]
2. **Twenty-eight** employees indicated they would change their health benefits. [Guide 47]

3. Did Mike request **$300** to attend the **one**-day seminar? [Guides 49, 47]
4. Most deliveries arrive before **10 a.m.** [Guide 49]
5. Personal income tax returns must be mailed by April **15**. [Guide 49]
6. We earned 2.5 **percent** dividends on our **$3,000** investment. [Guide 49]
7. Our company applied for a **$100,000** loan at **6 percent**. [Guide 49]
8. Average attendance at Major League Baseball games totaled **80 million** in the United States and Canada. [Guide 50]
9. I bought the item on eBay for **$1.50** and sold it for **$15.** [Guide 49]
10. That store offers a **30**-day customer satisfaction return policy. [Guide 48]

Chapter 11

1. The recruiter cited **studies** showing that **managers** leave [delete comma] when they lose their autonomy.
2. As they work more than **40 hours** a week without overtime pay, most **professionals** today are wondering **whether** their jobs can survive the recession.
3. One organization paid **$3,000** each for **12** employees to attend a **one-week** workshop in communication training.
4. My company **spends $500** on ink cartridges every month, but the cost doesn't worry my partner and **me** because our printed materials look sharp and professional.
5. If you find **an** open document on a colleague's computer **screen**, [add comma] **it's** inappropriate to peek.
6. **Today's** workers should brush up their marketable **skills; otherwise,** they may not find another job after being laid off.
7. On June **1** our company **president** revealed a **$4 million** drop in profits, which was bad news for everyone.
8. Most of us prefer to be let down **gently** [delete comma] when we are being refused **something;** that is why the **reasons-before-refusal** pattern is effective.
9. Between you and **me,** if we **were** to share a ride each **morning**, [insert comma] we would save a lot of money.
10. Despite the recent economic **downturn**, [insert comma] our **president** and CEO gave an optimistic assessment of the **company's** outlook.

Chapter 12

1. Toyota, the best-selling **Japanese** carmaker, has enjoyed a strong favorable perception of high **quality; therefore,** it long remained unharmed by a string of much-publicized recalls.
2. The **auditor's** report, which my boss and **I** read very closely, featured the following three main **flaws:** factual inaccuracies, omissions, and incomprehensible language.
3. **Eight** of the 20 workers in my department were **fired;** as a result, we had to work much harder to **achieve** our objectives.
4. As a matter of **principle**, we offer some form of financial support to more than **60** percent of our current MBA **candidates, which** proves our commitment to executive education.
5. To post easily to your blog on the **Web,** you could use Mozilla's **Web** browser **Firefox** and an add-on called ScribeFire.
6. **Peter's** presentation for a nonprofit group on advanced Internet marketing netted him only **$200**, a fifth of his usual **honorarium,** but he believes in pro bono work.
7. The old company manual covers the basics **of** [delete colon] searching, **selecting, interpreting,** and organizing data.
8. Our latest press **release,** which was written in our Corporate Communication **Department,** announces the opening of **three** Canadian offices.
9. Letter reports **usually have** side margins of **1¼** inches.
10. The CEO and **manager,** who had **gone** to a meeting in the West, delivered a report to Jeff and **me** when they returned.

Chapter 13

1. Lack of job security and high unemployment **are** here to **stay** [delete period] even if we do our work **well**.
2. Managers in **three departments** complained that **their** departments were over budget for supplies.
3. After sending many e-mails to Frank and **me**, the client felt **bad** about barraging us with messages to solicit a response from our two **teams**.
4. The new vice president and **she** decided to move up the launch to **May 3;** as a result, the software was buggy.
5. Managers of big **corporations** sometimes do not know how to **motivate;** consequently, the executives miss an opportunity to develop their **workers**.
6. The **director** of marketing wanted to speak to you and **me** about the poor **morale** in our division.
7. Laura and **he** decided to **accept** assistance with their **proposal;** therefore, they completed the project by the deadline.
8. We invited **75** employees to hear **two** experts **disperse** information about wellness.
9. **Memos** usually contain four necessary **parts:** subject line, opening, **body,** and action closing.
10. Darrin **Jizmejian,** who was recently evaluated, wondered whether his formal report would be presented at the **March 13 meeting.**

Chapter 14

1. If you are planning a short **presentation,** you should focus on about **three** main points and limit yourself to **20** minutes.
2. Because he was **president** of the **company,** Mr. Yost made at least **six** major presentations every year.
3. The **company's** CPA asked me to explain the **principal** ways we planned to finance the **30**-year mortgage.
4. My accountant and **I** are **grateful** to be able to give a short **presentation;** however, we may not be able to cover the entire budget.
5. The introduction to a presentation should accomplish three **goals:** (a) **capture** attention, (b) establish credibility, and (**c**) preview main points.
6. Steven wondered whether focusing on what the audience is to **remember** [delete comma] and summarizing main points **were** equally **important.** [delete question mark]
7. A list of suggestions for a **speaker's** ideas **is** found in the article titled "How **to** Improve Your Listening Skills."
8. The appearance and mannerisms of a speaker **definitely affect** a **listener's** evaluation of the message.
9. Melody Hobson, who is an expert **speaker,** said that reading from slides is the **kiss** of **death** in a presentation.
10. In a poll of **3,000 workers,** only one third felt that **their** companies valued their opinions.

Chapter 15

1. Many employers use **sites** like Facebook to learn about potential employees**, which means** job seekers must maintain a professional online presence.
2. To conduct a safe online job search, you **must** [delete colon] (a) **use** only reputable job boards, **(b)** keep careful records, and (c) limit the number of sites on which you post your résumé.
3. When **Melissa's** job search was **complete,** she had received **four** job offers.
4. If you **lose** your **job, don't** be discouraged by the thought of having to find another.
5. Joseph wondered whether it was **all right** to ask his professor for employment **advice.** [change question mark to period]

6. At last **month's** staff **meeting,** team members examined several **candidates'** résumés.
7. Rather **than** schedule **face-to-face interviews,** the team investigated videoconferencing.
8. **Twelve** applicants will be interviewed on **April 10;** consequently, we may need to work late to accommodate them.
9. Professional e-mail manners **reflect** on you and your **company;** however, **too** few employees are trained properly.
10. In the last issue of ***Newsweek,*** did you see the article titled "Should a **Résumé Include** a Career Objective?"

Chapter 16

1. Before going to a job **interview,** you should do the **following:** [delete hyphen] research the company, practice answering questions, rehearse success **stories,** and choose appropriate clothing.
2. I wonder how many **companies** go online to find out more about **candidates' backgrounds.** [delete question mark]
3. Even with the popularity of **e-mail,** most **employers** [delete apostrophe] contact job applicants by telephone to set up **their** interviews.
4. Initial contacts by employers are **usually** made by **telephone;** therefore, **ensure** that you keep important information nearby.
5. If you have gaps in your employment **history,** explain what you did during this **time** [delete comma] and how you stayed **up-to-date** in your field.
6. Interviewees should not **criticize** anyone or **anything,** and they should not focus on **their** imperfections.
7. Evan was asked whether he had a **bachelor's degree** [delete comma] and whether he had five **years'** experience.
8. If you are **hoping** to create a good **impression,** be sure to write a **thank-you** message after a job interview.
9. When **Robin's** interview was **over,** she told friends that she had done **well**.
10. Robin was **all ready** to send a thank-you **message** [delete comma] when she realized she could not spell the **interviewer's** name.

Notes

Chapter 1

[1] PepsiCo's Indian icon. (2001, January 8). *Business India*. Retrieved March 23, 2009, from http://www.answers.com/topic/indra-nooyi. See also Brady, D. (2007, June 11). Keeping cool in hot water. *BusinessWeek*. Retrieved March 20, 2009, from http://www.businessweek.com; and Useem, M. (2008, December 1–8). New ideas for this Pepsi generation. *U.S. News & World Report*, p. 49.

[2] Kinsman, M. (2004, February 1). Are poor writing skills holding back your career? *California Job Journal*. Retrieved April 24, 2009, from http://www.jobjournal.com; Tucker, M. L., & McCarthy, A. M. (2001, Summer). Presentation self-efficacy: Increasing communication skills through service-learning. *Journal of Managerial Issues*, 227–244; Cohen, A. (1999). The right stuff. *Sales and Marketing Management*, p. 151; and Messmer, M. (1999, August). Skills for a new millennium. *Strategic Finance*, pp. 10–12.

[3] Koncz, A. (2009, January 29). Employers cite qualities, attributes of "perfect" job candidate. National Association of Colleges and Employers. Press release retrieved April 24, 2009, from http://www.naceweb.org

[4] Moody, J., Stewart, B., & Bolt-Lee, C. (2002, March). Showcasing the skilled business graduate: Expanding the tool kit. *Business Communication Quarterly, 65*(1), 23.

[5] Vance, E. (2007, February 2). College graduates lack key skills, report says. *The Chronicle of Higher Education*, p. A30.

[6] Communication skills—Start here! (n.d.). *MindTools*. Retrieved April 24, 2009, from http://www.mindtools.com

[7] Schwartz, E. (2006, June 29). Brushing up on your soft skills. *InfoWorld*. Retrieved April 24, 2009, from http://www.infoworld.com

[8] The National Commission on Writing. [press release] (2004, September 14). Writing skills necessary for employment, says big business. Retrieved April 24, 2009, from http://www.writingcommission.org/pr/writing_for_employ.html

[9] Ibid.

[10] Daniels, C. (2004, June 28). 50 best companies for minorities. *Fortune*, p. 136.

[11] Anderson, R. (2009, April 26). He wants subjects, verbs and objects. *The New York Times*, p. 2 BU Y.

[12] Drucker, P. (1989, May). New realities, new ways of managing. *Business Month*, pp. 50–51.

[13] Schadler, T. (2009). A day in the life of a U.S. information worker. Forrester Research. Retrieved October 31, 2009, from http://www.forrester.com. See also Grimes, A. (2002, June 27). Techno talk. *The Wall Street Journal*, p. B4.

[14] Haag, S., Cummings, M., & Phillips, A. (2003). *Management information systems for the information age* (3rd ed.). New York: McGraw-Hill Higher Education.

[15] Thinking for a living. (2006, January 21). *The Economist* (U.S.). Retrieved May 14, 2009, from InfoTrac College Edition database.

[16] O'Toole, J. & Lawler, E. E., III. (2006, July). *The new American workplace*. New York: Palgrave Macmillan, p. 17.

[17] Koncz, A. (2009, January 29). Employers cite qualities, attributes of "perfect" job candidate. NACE Web Press Release. Retrieved April 26, 2009, from http://www.naceweb.org

[18] Jargon, J. (2008, May 1) Kraft reformulates Oreo, scores in China. *The Wall Street Journal*, p. B1.

[19] Welcome to McDonald's Russia. (n.d.). Retrieved April 26, 2009, from http://www.mcdonalds.com/countries/russia.html; see also Arvedlund, E. E. (2005, March 17). McDonald's commands a real estate empire in Russia. *The New York Times*, p. C5.

[20] Heller, L. (2006, August 7). Customer experience evolves in China. *Retailing Today, 45*(14), 42. Retrieved May 29, 2009, from InfoTrac database.

[21] Balfour, F., & Kiley, D. (2005, April 25). Ad agencies unchained. *BusinessWeek*, p. 51.

[22] Friedman, T. L. (2005). *The world is flat*. New York: Farrar, Straus and Giroux, pp. 178–179.

[23] Malone, T. W. (2004). *The future of work*. Cambridge: Harvard Business School Press, p. 32.

[24] Weintraub, A. (2007, June 18). J & J's new baby. *BusinessWeek*, p. 48.

[25] Miller, C. C. (2008, June 2). Higher office. *Forbes*, p. 62. See also Shinkle, K. (2008, March 10). Running an office by wiki and e-mail. *U.S. News & World Report*, p. 50.

[26] Holland, K. (2008, September 28). The anywhere, anytime office. *The New York Times*, p. 14 BU Y.

[27] Telework trendlines (2009, February). Retrieved April 16, 2009, from Worldatwork, http://www.workingfromanywhere.org/news/Trendlines_2009.pdf

[28] Holland, K. (2008, September 28). The anywhere, anytime office. *The New York Times*, p. 14 BU Y.

[29] About Google Wave. Google Web site. Retrieved January 2, 2010, from http://wave.google.com/help/wave/about.html

[30] Karoly, L. A., & Panis, C. W. A. (2004). *The 21st century at work*. Santa Monica, CA: Rand Corporation, pp. 36–39.

[31] Shifting workplace demographics and delayed retirement. (2002, May). *Monthly Labor Review*. Retrieved October 11, 2006, from http://www.microsoft.com/enable/aging/references.aspx

[32] DeMars, N. (2008, April). Office ethics: News from the front lines. *OfficePro*, p. 28.

[33] Hamilton, C., & Parker, C. (1996). *Communicating for results* (6th ed.). Belmont, CA: Wadsworth, p. 7.

[34] Sullivan, J., Karmeda, N., & Nobu, T. (1992, January/February). Bypassing in managerial communication. *Business Horizons, 34*(1), 72.

[35] Brewer, E., & Holmes, T. (2009, October). Obfuscating the obvious: Miscommunication issues in the interpretation of common terms. *Journal of Business Communication, 46*(4), 480–496.

[36] McGirt, E. (2006, March 20). Getting out from under: Beset by interruptions, information overload, and irksome technology, knowledge workers need help: A survival guide. *Fortune*, p. 88.

[37] Drucker, P. (1990). *Managing the non-profit organization: Practices and principles*. New York: HarperCollins, p. 46.

[38] E-mail becoming crime's new smoking gun. (2005). *USA Today*. Retrieved May 14, 2009, from http://www.usatoday.com/tech/news/2002-08-15-email-evidence_x.htm

[39] Sims, R. R., Veres, J. G., III, Jackson, K. A., & Facteau, C. L. (2001). *The challenge of front-line management*. Westport, CT: Quorum, p. 10.

[40] Steelcase Inc. (2007, August 9). Steelcase Workplace Index Survey examines 'water cooler' conversations at work. Retrieved May 4, 2009, from http://www.prnewswire.com

[41] Ibid.

[42] Useem, M. (2008, December 8). New ideas for this Pepsi generation. *U.S. News & World Report*, p. 49.

[43] PepsiCo releases sustainable development report. (2009, January 6). PepsiCo press release. Retrieved March 21, 2009, from http://ca.csrwire.com

[44] Steelcase Inc., ibid. See also Karathanos, P., & Auriemmo, A. (1999, March-April). Care and feeding of the organizational grapevine. *Industrial Management, 41*(2), 26. Retrieved May 4, 2009, from InfoTrac College Edition database.

[45] Goman, C. K. (2006, June). I heard it through the grapevine. Paper presented at the International Association of Business Communicators, Vancouver, Canada. Retrieved October 22, 2006, from http://common.iabc.com/employee/2006/06

[46] Zimmermann, S., Davenport, B., & Haas, J. W. (1996, April). A communication metamyth in the workplace: The assumption that more is better. *Journal of Business Communication, 33*(2), 185–204.

[47] DeMars, N. (2008). What you can do when you're the latest topic on the rumor mill. Retrieved May 4, 2009, from http://www.office-ethics.com/columns/gossip.html

[48] Gentile, M. C. (2009, February 5). Business schools: A failing grade on ethics. *BusinessWeek*. Retrieved March 29, 2009, from http://www.businessweek.com

[49] Gardiner, B. (2009, March 26). B-schools rethink curricula amid crisis. Wall Street Journal Online. Retrieved April 1, 2009, from http://online.wsj.com

[50] DeMars, N. (2008, April). Office ethics: News from the front lines. *OfficePro*, p. 28.

[51] Pfanner, E. (2009, April 18). Four convicted in Internet piracy case. *The New York Times*, p. B1.

[52] Campbell, A. (2003, November 25). More women starting businesses. Small business trends. Retrieved April 15, 2009, from http://smallbiztrends.com

[53] Trudel, R., & Cotte, J. (2008, May 12). Does being ethical pay? *The Wall Street Journal*, p. R4.

[54] O'Connell, V. (2009, January 7). Test for dwindling retail jobs spawns a culture of cheating. *The Wall Street Journal*, p. A1.

[55] Henriques, D. (2009, June 29). Madoff Is Sentenced to 150 Years for Ponzi Scheme. *New York Times*. Retrieved December 19, 2009, from http://www.nytimes.com/2009/06/30/business/30madoff.html

[56] Nooyi, I. (n.d.). Meritocracy. Cornell University eClips. Video transcript. Retrieved March 24, 2009, from http://eclips.cornell.edu/clip.do?id=12279&tab=TabClipPage

[57] Do your reps' writing skills need a refresher? (2002, February). *Customer Contact Management Report*, p. 7.

[58] Sandberg, J. (2008, January 19). Global-market woes are more personality than nationality. *The Wall Street Journal*, p. B1.

[59] Sandberg, J. (2006, September 18). What exactly was it that the boss said? You can only imagine. *The Wall Street Journal*, p. B1.

[60] Ahmad, A. (2006, May). To the manner born at the workplace. *The Economic Times*. Retrieved January 7, 2007, from InfoTrac College Edition database.

[61] Armour, S. (2007, September 7). Did you hear the real story about office gossip? *USA Today*, p. 1B.

[62] The Wall Street Journal ethics quiz. (1999, October 21). *The Wall Street Journal*, p. B1.

[63] El Pollo Loco. (n.d.) Healthier dining. Retrieved May 15, 2009, from http://www.elpolloloco.com/menu/healthydinning.html

[64] Jargon, J. (2008, May 9). Rival chicken chain calls out KFC. *USA Today*, p. B5.

Chapter 2

[1] Thomas, D., senior manager, Sales Development and Education, FedEx Office (personal communication with Mary Ellen Guffey, November 11, 2009).

[2] Brent, P. (2006, November). Soft skills speak volumes. *CA Magazine, 139*, 112. Retrieved June 3, 2009, from InfoTrac College Edition database.

[3] O'Toole, J., & Lawler, E. E., III. (2005). *The new American workplace*. New York: Palgrave Macmillan, p. 20.

[4] Mueller, F., Procter, S., & Buchanan, D. (2000, November). Teamworking in its context(s): Antecedents, nature and dimensions. *Human Relations, 53*, 1387. Retrieved June 3, 2009, from Business Source Complete database.

[5] DiSanza, J. R., & Legge, N. J. (2000). *Business and professional communication*. Boston: Allyn and Bacon, p. 98.

[6] Coutu, D., & Beschloss, M. (2009, May). Why teams don't work. *Harvard Business Review, (87)*, 5, 98-105. Retrieved June 1, 2009, from Business Source Complete database.

[7] Hymowitz, C. (2006, February 13). Rewarding competitors over collaborators no longer makes sense. *The Wall Street Journal*, p. B1.

[8] Ennen, S. (2003, April). Red baron soars with teamwork. *Food Processing, 64*, 40. Retrieved June 3, 2009, from http://www.foodprocessing.com/articles/2003/141.html

[9] Edmondson, G. (2006, October 16). BMW's dream factory. *BusinessWeek*, p. 80.

[10] Katzenbach, J. R., & Smith, K. (1994). *The wisdom of teams*. New York: HarperBusiness, pp. 68–69.

[11] Crash course in managing a virtual team. (2007, September 3). *Management Today*. Retrieved June 3, 2009, from InfoTrac College Edition database.

[12] Lipnack, J., & Stamps, J. (2000). *Virtual teams: People working across boundaries with technology* (2nd ed.). New York: Wiley, p. 18.

[13] Kiger, P. J. (2006, September 25). Flexibility to the fullest: Throwing out the rules of work—Part 1 of 2. *Workforce Management, 85*(18), 1. See also Holland, K. (2006, December 3).When work time isn't face time. *The New York Times*, p. BU 3.

[14] Cutler, G. (2007, January-February). Mike leads his first virtual team. *Research-Technology Management, 50*(1), 66. Retrieved June 3, 2009, from InfoTrac College Edition database.

[15] Miculka, J. H. (2007). *Speaking for success* (2nd ed.). Cincinnati, OH: South-Western, pp. 96–97.

[16] Janis, I. L. (1982). *Groupthink: Psychological studies on policy decisions and fiascoes*. Boston: Houghton Mifflin. See also Miranda, S. M., & Saunders, C. (1995, Summer). Group support systems: An organization development intervention to combat groupthink. *Public Administration Quarterly, 19*, 193–216. Retrieved June 1, 2009, from Business Source Complete database.

[17] Amason, A. C., Hochwarter, W. A., Thompson, K. R., & Harrison, A. W. (1995, Autumn). Conflict: An important dimension in successful management teams. *Organizational Dynamics, 24*, 1. Retrieved June 2, 2009, from InfoTrac College Edition database.

[18] Parnell, C. (1996, November 1). Teamwork: Not a new idea, but it's transforming the workplace. *Executive Speeches, 63*, 46. Retrieved December 11, 2006, from InfoTrac College Edition database.

[19] Katzenbach & Smith. (1994). *Wisdom of teams*. New York: HarperBusiness, p. 45.

[20] Makower, J. (1995, Winter). Managing diversity in the workplace. *Business & Society Review*, 48. Retrieved June 2, 2009, from Business Source Complete database.

[21] Bayot, J. (2000, November 8). Developers bet on theaters in glutted L.A. *The Wall Street Journal*, Eastern edition, p. C1.

[22] Callahan, D. (2009, April 21). Breaking the ice; success through teamwork and partnerships. Retrieved June 1, 2009, from Your Great Lakes Coast Guard blog at http://uscgd9.blogspot.com

[23] Survey finds workers average only three productive days per week. (2005, March 15). Microsoft survey retrieved June 8, 2009, from http://www.microsoft.com. See also Herring, H. B. (2006, June 18). Endless meetings: The black holes of the workday. *The New York Times*. Retrieved June 4, 2009, from http://www.nytimes.com

[24] Loechner, J. (2009, May 12). Meeting optimization too. Retrieved June 4, 2009, from http://www.mediapost.com

[25] Herring, H. B. (2006, June 18). Endless meetings: The black holes of the workday. *The New York Times*. Retrieved June 4, 2009, from http://www.nytimes.com

[26] Lancaster, H. (1998, May 26). Learning some ways to make meetings less awful. *The Wall Street Journal*, p. B1.

[27] Maher, K. (2004, January 13). The jungle. *The Wall Street Journal*, p. B6.

[28] Bruening, J. C. (1996, July). There's good news about meetings. *Managing Office Technology, 41*, 24–25. Retrieved December 4, 2006, from InfoTrac College Edition database.

[29] Marquis, C. (2003, July). Doing well and doing good. *The New York Times*, p. BU2.

[30] Schabacker, K. (1991, June). A short, snappy guide to meaningful meetings. *Working Women*, 73.

[31] Based on the following: Master the meeting madness. (2008). *Briefings Bonus*, Communication Briefings; and Egan, M. (2006, March 13). Meetings can make or break your career. *Insurance Advocate, 117*, 24.

[32] Lohr, S. (2008, July 22). As travel costs rise, more meetings go virtual. *The New York Times*. Retrieved June 4, 2009, from http://www.nytimes.com

[33] Bulkeley, W. M. (2006, September 28). Better virtual meetings. *The Wall Street Journal*, p. B1.

[34] Lohr, S. (2008, July 22). As travel costs rise, more meetings go virtual. *The New York Times*. Retrieved June 5, 2009, from http://www.nytimes.com

[35] Yu, R. (2009, June 23). Videoconferencing eyes growth spurt. *USA Today*, p. 3B.

[36] Lohr, S. (2008, July 22). As travel costs rise, more meetings go virtual. *The New York Times*. Retrieved June 5, 2009, from http://www.nytimes.com

[37] Schindler, E. (2008, February 15). Running an effective teleconference or virtual meeting. *CIO*. Retrieved June 5, 2009, from www.cio.com. See also Brenowitz, Randi S. (2004, May). Virtual meeting etiquette. Article 601, *Innovative Leader*. Retrieved June 5, 2009, from http://www.winstonbrill.com

[38] Ibid.

[39] Robbins, H., & Finley, M. (1995). *Why teams don't work*. Princeton, NJ: Peterson's/Pacesetter Books, p. 123.

[40] Pellet, J. (2003, April). Anatomy of a turnaround guru. *Chief Executive*, 41; Mounter, P. (2003). Global internal communication: A model. *Journal of Communication Management, 3*, 265; Feiertag, H. (2002, July 15). Listening skills, enthusiasm top list of salespeople's best traits. *Hotel and Motel Management*, 20; Goby, V. P., & Lewis, J. H. (2000, June). The key role of listening in business: A study of the Singapore insurance industry. *Business Communication Quarterly, 63*, 41–51; Cooper, L. O. (1997, December). Listening competency in the workplace: A model for training. *Business Communication Quarterly, 60*, 75–84; and Penley, L. E., Alexander, E. R., Jerigan, I. E., & Henwood, C. I. (1997). Communication abilities of managers: The relationship to performance. *Journal of Management, 17*, 57–76.

[41] Awang, F., Anderson, M. A., & Baker, C. J. (2003, Winter). Entry-level information services and support personnel: Needed workplace and technology skills. *The Delta Pi Epsilon Journal*, 48; and American Management Association. (1999, August). The challenges facing workers in the future. *HR Focus*, 6.

[42] Harris, T. W. (1989, June). Listen carefully. *Nation's Business*, 78.

[43] Steil, L. K., Barker, L. I., & Watson, K. W. (1983). *Effective listening: Key to your success* Reading, MA: Addison-Wesley; and Harris, J. A. (1998, August). Hear what's really being said. *New Zealand Management, 45*, 18.

[44] Nelson, E., & Gypen, J. (1979, September/October). The subordinate's predicament. *Harvard Business Review*, 133.

[45] International Listening Association. (2009). Listening and speech rates. Retrieved June 20, 2009, from http://www.listen.org

[46] Wolvin, A., & Coakley, C. G. (1996). *Listening* (5th ed.). New York: McGraw-Hill, pp. 136–137.

[47] Effective communication. (1994, November). *Training Tomorrow*, 32–33.

[48] Wood, J. T. (2003). *Gendered lives: Communication, gender, and culture* (5th ed.). Belmont, CA: Wadsworth, pp. 119–120; Anderson, K. J., & Leaper, C. (1998, August). Meta-analyses of gender effects on conversational interruption: Who, what, when, where, and how. *Sex Roles: A Journal of Research*, 225; and Booth-Butterfield, M. (1984). She hears: What they hear and why. *Personnel Journal, 44*, 39.

[49] Tear. J. (1995, November 20). They just don't understand gender dynamics. *The Wall Street Journal*, p. A12; and Wolfe, A. (1994, December 12). She just doesn't understand. *New Republic*, 26–34.

[50] Burgoon, J., Coker, D., & Coker, R. (1986). Communication explanations. *Human Communication Research*, 463–494.

[51] Tarsala, M. (1997, November 7). Remec's Ronald Ragland: Drawing rivals to his team by making their concerns his. *Investor's Business Daily*, A1.

[52] Birdwhistel, R. (1970). *Kinesics and context*. Philadelphia: University of Pennsylvania Press.

[53] What's A-O.K. in the U.S.A. is lewd and worthless beyond. (1996, August 18). *The New York Times*, p. E7.

[54] Zielinski, D. (2001, April). Body language. *Presentations*, 15, 36–42. Retrieved July 1, 2009, from InfoTrac College Edition database.

[55] Body speak: What are you saying? (2000, October). *Successful Meetings*, 49–51.

[56] Finney, P. (2007, October 23). Redefining business casual. *The New York Times*. Retrieved June 10, 2009, from InfoTrac College Edition database. See also Osterman, R. (2006, March 20). Casual loses its cool in business: More employers are trying to tighten up workplace clothing standards. *Sacramento Bee*. Retrieved June 10, 2009, from InfoTrac College Edition database; and Business casual: Out of style? (2005, May). *HR Focus*, 9. Retrieved June 10, 2009, from InfoTrac College Edition database.

[57] Wilkie, H. (2003, Fall). Professional presence. *The Canadian Manager*, 14; and Kaplan-Leiserson, L. (2000, November). Casual dress/back to business attire. *Training & Development*, 38–39.

[58] Kennedy, M. M. (1997, September–October). Is business casual here to stay? *Executive Female*, 31.

[59] Wood, N., & Benitez, T. (2003, April). Does the suit fit? *Incentive*, 31.

[60] Business casual out of style. (2005, May). *HR Focus, 82*, 16. Retrieved December 16, 2006, from InfoTrac database; Egodigwe, L. (2003, March). Here come the suits. *Black Enterprise, 33*, 59. Retrieved June 4, 2009, from InfoTrac College Edition database; and Summerson, C. (2002, November 18). The suit is back in business. *BusinessWeek*, 130.

[61] Chao, L. (2006, January 17). Not-so-nice costs. *The Wall Street Journal*, p. B1.

[62] Workplace rudeness is common and costly. (2002, May). *USA Today Magazine*, 9.

[63] Coutu, D., & Beschloss, M. (2009, May). Why teams don't work. *Harvard Business Review, (87)*, 5, 98–105.

Retrieved June 1, 2009, from Business Source Complete database.

[64] Maturo, D. (2007, Winter). Being a technician is not enough: Develop leadership and communication skills. *The Pennsylvania CPA Journal*. Retrieved June 4, 2009, from http://www.picpa.org/asp/Journal/journal_article_details.asp?action=Normal&ID=1294

[65] Horovitz, B. (2008, May 23). Denny's wants to rock 'n' roll all night long. *USA Today*, p. 3B.

[66] Arrien, A. (2003, March–April). Geese teach lessons on teamwork. *Motion Systems Distributor, 17*, 32. Retrieved June 15, 2009, from InfoTrac College Edition database; and Flying like the geese. (2001, December). *Design Engineering*, 9. Retrieved June 15, 2009, from InfoTrac College Edition database.

[67] Office Team poll. (2008, June 23). Meetings and productivity. Graphic appearing in *USA Today*, p. 1.

[68] What's the universal hand sign for "I goofed"? (1996, December 16). *Santa Barbara News-Press*, p. D2.

[69] Bell, A. H. (1999, September). Using nonverbal cues. *Incentive, 173*, 162. Retrieved June 5, 2009, from Business Source Complete database.

[70] McCarty, M. (2007, January/February). Tattoos: Not just for sailors anymore. *OfficePro*, 26.

[71] Williams, A. (2008, June 24). At meetings, it's mind your BlackBerry or mind your manners. *The New York Times*, pp. A1, A3.

Chapter 3

[1] Landler, M., & Barbaro, M. (2006, August 2). No, not always. *New York Times*, p. 1. Retrieved July 23, 2009, from http://www.nytimes.com

[2] Metro's chief executive, Hans-Joachim Koerber, in Hall, A., & Bawden, T. (2006, July 29). Wal-Mart pulls out of Germany at cost of $1bn. *The Times Online*. Retrieved July 7, 2009, from http://business.timesonline.co.uk/tol/business/industry_sectors/retailing/article694345.ece

[3] Landler, M., & Barbaro, M. (2006, August 2). No, not always. *New York Times*, p. 1. Retrieved July 23, 2009, from http://www.nytimes.com

[4] Ibid.

[5] David Rogers, president of DSR Marketing Systems, Deerfield, Illinois, quoted in Davis, G. (2008, May 26). World vision (Walmart). *Supermarket News, 56*(21). Retrieved July 7, 2009, from Factiva database.

[6] Holstein, W. (2007). Why Wal-Mart can't find happiness in Japan. *Fortune, 156*(3), pp. 73-78. Retrieved July 23, 2009, from ProQuest database.

[7] Smith, J. (2007). The perils of prediction. *World Trade, 20*(1), 39-44. Retrieved July 20, 2009, from Business Source Premier database.

[8] Flannery, R. (2004, May 10). China is a big prize. *Forbes, 173*(10), p. 163. Retrieved July 25, 2009, from ProQuest database.

[9] Sewell, D. (2009, June 10). Report: P&G's McDonald to succeed Lafley. *USAToday.com*. Retrieved July 25, 2009, from http://www.usatoday.com/money/industries/manufacturing/2009-06-09-pg-ceo_N.htm

[10] Seven-Eleven Japan (2007). Retrieved July 25, 2009, from http://www.sej.co.jp/english/company/g_stores.html

[11] Flannery, R. (2004, May 10). China is a big prize. *Forbes, 173*(10), p. 163. Retrieved July 25, 2009, from ProQuest database.

[12] Holmes, S. (2003, July 21). The real Nike news is happening abroad. *BusinessWeek*, p. 30; Ronaldo decisivo. (2009, March 26). Nike Futebol. Retrieved July 25, 2009, from http://inside.nike.com/blogs/nikefootball-pt_BR/tags/v%C3%ADdeo?view=all

[13] Browning, E. S. (1992, April 23). In pursuit of the elusive Euroconsumer. *The Wall Street Journal*, p. B1. Retrieved July 25, 2009, from ProQuest database; and Wheatley, M. (1995). The branding of Europe. *Management Today*, 66. Retrieved July 25, 2009, from ProQuest database.

[14] Stern, G. (1992, November 21). Heinz aims to export taste for ketchup. *The Wall Street Journal*, p. B1. Retrieved July 25, 2009, from ProQuest database.

[15] International Specialty Regional Toppings. (2008). Inside Domino's. Retrieved July 25, 2009, from http://www.dominos.com/

[16] Brooks, S. (2006, December). Tomorrow, the world. *Restaurant Business, 105*(12), pp. 26–32. Retrieved July 25, 2009, from Wilson Web database.

[17] Adamy, J. (2007, January 17). Dunkin' begins new push into China. *The Wall Street Journal*, p. A4. Retrieved July 25, 2009, from ProQuest database.

[18] Creative jobs destruction. (2004, January 6). *The Wall Street Journal*, p. A18. Retrieved July 25, 2009, from ProQuest database.

[19] Glater, J. D. (2004, January 3). Offshore services grow in lean times. *The New York Times*, p. B1. Retrieved July 25, 2009, from Business Full Text (Wilson) database.

[20] Kalin, S. (1997, June 9). Global net knits East to West at Liz Claiborne. *Computerworld*, G4-G6. Retrieved July 25, 2009, from ProQuest database.

[21] U.S. Department of Labor. (2007). Futurework: Trends and challenges for work in the 21st century. Retrieved July 25, 2009, from http://www.dol.gov/oasam/programs/history/herman/reports/futurework/report/chapter1/main.htm#1b

[22] Gleckman, H. (1998, August). A rich stew in the melting pot. *BusinessWeek*, p. 76.

[23] Pollack, A. (1996, December 22). Barbie's journey in Japan. *The New York Times*, p. E3. Retrieved July 25, 2009, from http://www.nytimes.com/1996/12/22/weekinreview/barbie-s-journey-in-japan.html

[24] Hall, E. T., & Hall, M. R. (1990). *Understanding cultural differences*. Yarmouth, ME: Intercultural Press, pp. 183–184.

[25] Chaney, L. H., & Martin, J. S. (2000). *Intercultural business communication* (2nd ed.). Upper Saddle River, NJ: Prentice Hall, p. 83.

[26] Zunker, V. (2008). Career, work, and mental health. Thousand Oaks, CA: Sage Publications, p. 140; see also Reardon, K. K. (1987). *Where minds meet*. Belmont, CA: Wadsworth, p. 199.

[27] Sheer, V. C., & Chen, L. (2003, January). Successful Sino-Western business negotiation: Participants' accounts of national and professional cultures. *The Journal of Business Communication, 40*(1), 62; see also Luk, L., Patel, M., & White, K. (1990, December). Personal attributes of American and Chinese business associates. *The Bulletin of the Association for Business Communication*, 67.

[28] Gallois, C., & Callan, V. (1997). *Communication and culture*. New York: Wiley, p. 24.

[29] Jarvis, S. S. (1990, June). Preparing employees to work south of the border. *Personnel*, p. 763. Retrieved July 25, 2009, from Business Full Text (Wilson) database; Murtagh, B. (2008, August 22). Working south of the border. Pittsburgh Business Times. Retrieved July 25, 2009, from http://pittsburgh.bizjournals.com/pittsburgh/stories/2008/08/25/focus1.html?page=2

[30] Gallois, C., & Callan, V. (1997). *Communication and culture*. New York: Wiley, p. 29.

[31] Copeland, L., & Griggs, L. (1985). *Going international*. New York: Penguin, p. 94.

[32] Ibid., p. 108.

[33] Ibid., p. 12.

[34] Copeland, J. (1990, December 15). Stare less, listen more. American Airlines: *American Way*, p. 32.

[35] Chen, G. M., & Starosta, W. J. (1998). *Foundations of intercultural communication*. Boston: Allyn and Bacon, p. 40.

[36] Varner, I., & Beamer, L. (2001). *Intercultural communication in the global workplace*. Boston: McGraw-Hill Irwin, p. 18.

[37] Browning, E. S. (1994, May 3). Computer chip project brings rivals together, but the cultures clash. *The Wall Street Journal*, pp. A1, A11. Retrieved July 25, 2009, from ProQuest database.

[38] Holstein, W. (2007). Why Wal-Mart can't find happiness in Japan. *Fortune, 156*(3), pp. 73–78. Retrieved July 23, 2009, from ProQuest database.

[39] Based on McGee, S. (2007, June 29). What's on the shelves in China's Wal-Marts? *MSN Money*. Retrieved July 8, 2009, from http://moneycentral.msn.com/home.asp

[40] Martin, J. S., & Chaney, L. H. (2006). *Global business etiquette*. Westport, CT: Praeger, p. 69.

[41] Hammer, M. R. (1993). Quoted in Chen and Starosta's *Foundations of intercultural communication*, p. 247.

[42] Chaney, L. H., & Martin, J. S. (1995). *Intercultural business communication*. Englewood Cliffs, NJ: Prentice Hall Career and Technology, p. 67.

[43] Weber, G. (2004, May). English rules. *Workforce Management*, 47–50; Desai, D. (2008). Globalization and the English skills gap. *Chief Learning Officer, 7*(6), 62–63. Retrieved July 25, 2009, from Business Source Premier (EBSCO) database; and Dvorak, P. (2007, November 5). Plain English gets harder in global era. *Wall Street Journal*. Retrieved July 25, 2009, from ProQuest database.

[44] Axtell, R. E. (Ed.). (1990). *Do's and taboos around the world* (2nd ed.) New York: Wiley, p. 7l.

[45] Martin, J. S., & Chaney, L. H. (2006). *Global business etiquette*. Westport, CT: Praeger, p. 36.

[46] Ibid., p. 191.

[47] Finney, P. B. (2005, May 17). Shaking hands, greasing palms. *The New York Times*, p. C1.

[48] Berenbeim, R. (2000, May). Global ethics. *Executive Excellence*, p. 7.

[49] Kimes, M. (2009, February 16). Fluor's corporate crime fighter. *Fortune*, p. 26. Retrieved July 7, 2009, from Academic Search Premier database.

[50] Dorroh, J. (2003, June). Stay out of the shadows: Mexican companies, government move to improve business ethics and values. *Business Mexico, 13*(6), p. 42. Retrieved July 25, 2009, from ProQuest database.

[51] Schubert, S., & Miller, T. C. (2008, December 21). Where bribery was just a line item. *New York Times*, p. BU1. Retrieved July 23, 2009, from ProQuest Newspapers database.

[52] Going after Chiquita. (2008, March 24). *BusinessWeek*, p. 10.

[53] Finney, P. B. (2005, May 17). Shaking hands, greasing palms. *The New York Times*, p. C1.

[54] Wei, S-J. (2003, March 12). Corruption in developing countries. *Global Economics*. Retrieved July 23, 2009, from http://brookings.org/views/speeches/wei/20030312.htm

[55] Bush, J. (2009, July 2). Why IKEA is fed up with Russia. *BusinessWeek.com*. Retrieved August 4, 2009, from http://www.businessweek.com/magazine/content/09_28/b4139033326721.htm

[56] Alvarez, S. (2006, December). Global integrity: Transparency International's David Nussbaum is fighting for a world that is free of bribery and corruption. *Internal Auditor, 63*(6), 53. Retrieved July 23, 2009, from Factiva database.

[57] Hodgson, K. (1992, May). Adapting ethical decisions to a global marketplace. *Management Review*, 56. Retrieved July 23, 2009, from Factiva database. See also Digh, P. (1997, April). Shades of gray in the global marketplace. *HR Magazine*, p. 42. Retrieved July 23, 2009, from Business Full Text (Wilson) database.

[58] Solomon, C. M. (1996, January). Put your ethics to a global test. *Personnel Journal*, 66–74. See also Smeltzer, L. R., & Jennings, M. M. (1998, January). Why an international code of business ethics would be good for business. *Journal of Business Ethics*, 57–66. See also Barker, T. S., & Cobb, S. L. (2000). A survey of ethics and cultural dimensions of MNCs [Multinational companies]. *Competitiveness Review, 10*(2), 123. Retrieved July 23, 2009, from Academic Search Premier database.

[59] Hodgson, K. (1992, May). Adapting ethical decisions to a global marketplace. *Management Review*, 54. Retrieved July 23, 2009, from Factiva database. See also Franke, G. R. (2008, March). Culture, economic development, and national ethical attitudes. *Journal of Business Research, 61*(3). Retrieved July 23, 2009, from Business Source Premier database.

[60] Based on 2000 U.S. Census figures, as reported by Little, J. S., & Triest, R. K. (2001). Proceedings from the Federal Reserve Bank of Boston Conference

Series. The impact of demographic change on U.S. labor markets. *Seismic shifts: The economic impact of demographic change*. Retrieved July 23, 2009, from http://www.bos.frb.org/economic/conf/conf46/conf46a.pdf

[61] Hansen, F. (2003, April). Tracing the value of diversity programs. *Workforce*, p. 31.

[62] Carbone, J. (2005, August 11). IBM says diverse suppliers are good for business. *Purchasing*, p. 27. Retrieved July 25, 2009, from Business Full Text (Wilson) database.

[63] Neff, J. (1998, February 16). Diversity. *Advertising Age*, p. S1.

[64] Terhune, C. (2005, April 19). Pepsi, vowing diversity isn't just image polish, seeks inclusive culture. *The Wall Street Journal*, p. B4.

[65] Andre, R. (1995, June). Diversity stress as morality stress. *Journal of Business Ethics*, 489–496.

[66] Ibid.

[67] Schwartz, J., & Wald, M. L. (2003, March 9). Smart people working collectively can be dumber than the sum of their brains. Appeared originally in *The New York Times*. Retrieved July 25, 2009, from http://www.mindfully.org/Reform/2003/Smart-People-Dumber9mar03.htm

[68] Capowski, G. (1996, June). Managing diversity. *Management Review*, p. 16.

[69] Makower, J. (1995, Winter). Managing diversity in the workplace. *Business and Society Review*, pp. 48–54.

[70] White, M. D. (2002). *A short course in international marketing blunders*. Novato, CA: World Trade Press, p. 46.

[71] Based on Walmart Brazil mobilizes suppliers and announces sustainability pact. (2009, June 23). *Facts & News/Walmart.com*. Retrieved July 23, 2009, from http://walmartstores.com/FactsNews/NewsRoom/9223.aspx; Winston, A. (2009, July 14). Wal-Mart Brazil thinks green. *BusinessWeek/Harvard Business Online*. Retrieved July 23, 2009, from http://www.businessweek.com; and Aston, A. (2009, May 14). Wal-Mart: Making its suppliers go green. *BusinessWeek Online*. Retrieved July 23, 2009, from http://www.businessweek.com/magazine/content/09_21/b4132044814736.htm

[72] Winston, A. (2009, July 14). Wal-Mart Brazil thinks green. *BusinessWeek/Harvard Business Online*. Retrieved July 23, 2009, from http://www.businessweek.com

[73] Rothrock, V. (2004, July 16). Culture clash. Retrieved July 23, 2009, from Business Source Premier database.

[74] Špaček, L. (2008). *Nová velká kniha etikety*. Prague: Mladá Fronta, p. 260.

[75] Cottrill, K. (2000, November 6). The world according to Hollywood. *Traffic World*, p. 15.

[76] Conlin, M. (2007, April 23). Go-go-going to pieces in China. *BusinessWeek*, p. 88.

[77] Nasr, O. (2009, June 15). Tear gas and Twitter: Iranians take their protests online. *CNN.com*. Retrieved July 20, 2009, from http://edition.cnn.com/2009/WORLD/meast/06/14/iran.protests.twitter/; Grossman, L. (2009, June 17). Iran protests: Twitter, the medium of the movement. *Time.com*. Retrieved July 18, 2009, from http://www.time.com/time/world/article/0,8599,1905125,00.html; and Sarno, D. (2009, March 6). Twittergates: Twitter's @billgates isn't really Bill Gates. *Los Angeles Times.com*. Retrieved July 20, 2009, from http://latimesblogs.latimes.com/technology/2009/03/latest-twitter.html

[78] Thapanachai, S. (2003, October 6). Awareness narrows cross-cultural gap in Thai management training courses. *Bangkok Post*. Retrieved July 21, 2009, from Factiva database.

[79] Dawson, D. (2005, March 1). At the top and still climbing. *High performance composites*. Retrieved January 22, 2007, from http://www.compositesworld.com/articles/at-the-top-and-still-climbing.aspx; and Wucker, M. (1998, December/January). Keep on trekking. *Working Woman*, pp. 32–36.

[80] Smith, J. (2008, July 29). Tracking Facebook's 2008 international growth by country. Inside Facebook. Retrieved July 22, 2009, from http://www.insidefacebook.com/2008/07/29/tracking-facebooks-2008-international-growth-by-country/

[81] Based on Knotts, R., & Thibodeaux, M. S. (1992). Verbal skills in cross-culture managerial communication. *European Business Review, 92*(2), pp. v–vii.

[82] Martin, K., & Walsh, S. M. (1996, October). Beware the Foreign Corrupt Practices Act. *International Commercial Litigation*, 25–27; and Lay-person's guide to Foreign Corrupt Practices Act (FCPA). (n.d.). United States Department of Justice. Retrieved July 21, 2009, from http://www.usdoj.gov/criminal/fraud/fcpa/

[83] Kellner, T. (2002, March 18). Insert foot. *Forbes*. Retrieved July 21, 2009, from Business Sources Premier database.

[84] Daniels, C. (2004, June 28). 50 best companies for minorities. *Fortune*, p. 138.

Chapter 4

[1] Welch, S. (2009, May 11). Suze Orman. *Time*, p. 67; and Fabrikant, G. (2006, March 5). Cleaning up messages, friend to friend [Suze Orman]. *The New York Times*, p. BU5. Retrieved July 13, 2009, from InfoTrac College Edition database.

[2] Grainger, D. (2003, June 16). The Suze Orman show. *Fortune*, pp. 82-88. Retrieved July 12, 2009, from Business Source Complete database.

[3] Erler, S. (2005, March 31). Suze Orman spills, signs books. *Times* (Munster, Indiana). Retrieved March 7, 2007, from InfoTrac College Edition database.

[4] Gallo, C. (2001, June). Best presentations. Suze Orman. *BusinessWeek Online*. Retrieved July 1, 2009, from http://images.businessweek.com/ss/06/01/best_communicators/index_01.htm

[5] Arnold, V. (1986, August). Benjamin Franklin on writing well. *Personnel Journal*, p. 17.

[6] Bacon, M. (1988, April). Quoted in Business writing: One-on-one speaks best to the masses. *Training*, p. 95. See also Effective communication: Remember to pack your writing with reader focus. (2009, March 22). *Sales Insider*. p. 4. Retrieved July 1, 2009, from Business Source Premier database; and Danziger, E. (1998, February). Communicate up. *Journal of Accountancy*, p. 67.

[7] Wallis, C., & Steptoe, S. (2006, January 26). The case for doing one thing at a time. *Time South Pacific* (Australia/New Zealand edition), issue 2, p. 50. Retrieved July 16, 2009, from Business Source Complete database.

[8] Ibid.

[9] Be positive. (2009, March). *Communication Briefings*, p. 5. Adapted from Brandi, J. *Winning at customer retention* at http://www.customercarecoach.com

[10] Based on Fichter, D. (2005, July/August). The many forms of e-collaboration: Blogs, wikis, portals, groupware, discussion boards, and instant messaging. *Online*, pp. 48-50. Retrieved July 15, 2009, from Business Source Complete database.

[11] Dahl, D. (2009, June). Connecting the dots: How to choose the right collaboration software for your company. *Inc.*, p. 103. Retrieved July 19, 2009, from InfoTrac College Edition database.

[12] Iwata, E. (2007, January 5). Diet pill sellers fined $25M. *USA Today*, p. B1.

[13] Woolever, K. (1990, June 2). Corporate language and the law: Avoiding liability in corporate communications. *IEE Transactions on Professional Communication*, pp. 95-98.

[14] Ibid.

[15] Newark, N. A. (2005). Avoiding an "implied" employment contract or drafting a favorable one: A primer. *FindLaw*. Retrieved July 14, 2009, from http://library.findlaw.com/2005/Mar/2/157726.html; see also Jenner, L. (1994, March). Employment-at-will liability: How protected are you? *HR Focus*, p. 11.

[16] Walter, R., & Sleeper, B. (2002, Spring). Employee recruitment and retention: When company inducements trigger liability. *Review of Business*, pp. 17–23.

[17] Pickens, J. (1985, August). Communication: Terms of equality: A guide to bias-free language. *Personnel Journal*, p. 5.

[18] Armour, S. (2005, June 14). Warning: Your clever little blog could get you fired. *USA Today*. Retrieved July 16, 2009, from http://www.usatoday.com/money/workplace/2005-06-14-worker-blogs-usat_x.htm

[19] Ziobro, P. (2009, July 14). Burger King scraps plans for $1 burger. *The Wall Street Journal*, p. B6.

[20] Templeton, B. (2004, October). 10 big myths about copyright explained. Retrieved February 24, 2007, from http://www.templetons.com/brad/copymyths.html

Chapter 5

[1] O'Donnell, J., & Fetterman, M. (2007, January 24). Can Gap be saved? *USA Today*, p. B1.

[2] Ibid.

[3] The misnomer of specialty apparel. (2009, February). *Chain Store Age*, p. 2. Retrieved January 5, 2010, from Business Source Complete database.

[4] Sutton, R. I. (2006, September 5). The truth about brainstorming. *BusinessWeek*, p. 17. Retrieved January 2, 2010, from InfoTrac College Edition database.

[5] Heslin, P. (2009, March). Better than brainstorming? *Journal of Occupational & Organizational Psychology, 82*(2), 129–145. Retrieved January 4, 2010, from Business Source Complete database.

[6] Harris, A., Finkelstein, D., et al. (2009, July 9). BRW Twitter Homepage. *BRW Magazine*, p. 7. Retrieved January 2, 2010, from Business Source Complete database.

[7] Based on information retrieved February 7, 2007, from http://www.gapinc.com

[8] Rindegard, J. (1999, November 22). Use clear writing to show you mean business. *InfoWorld*, p. 78.

[9] Working with factories. (2007). Gap Inc. Retrieved February 6, 2007, from http://www.gapinc.com/public/SocialResponsibility/sr_fac_wwf.shtml

[10] Factory approval process. (2007). Gap Inc. Retrieved February 6, 2007, from http://www.gapinc.com/public/SocialResponsibility/sr_fac_wwf_fap.shtml. See also Merrick, A. (2004, May 12). Gap offers unusual look at factory conditions. *The Wall Street Journal*, p. A1.

[11] Goddard, R. W. (1989, April). Communication: Use language effectively. *Personnel Journal*, 32.

[12] Toffler, B. L. quoted in Schmitt, R. B. (2002, November 5). Companies add ethics training; will it work? *The Wall Street Journal*, p. Bl.

[13] Mannes, G. (2006, September). Earning a degree in debt. *Money*, pp. 98–105. Retrieved August 3, 2009, from http://www.mutualofamerica.com/articles/Money/2006September/money2.asp. See also Kristof, K. M. (2003, September 14). More grads struggling to repay loans. *Los Angeles Times*, p. C3.

[14] United Press International. (2009, July 20). Programs seek to ease student loan debt. Retrieved January 4, 2010, from InfoTrac College Edition database.

Chapter 6

[1] Yum! brands recognized in corporate responsibility officer magazine's "100 best corporate citizens" list. (2009, March 25). *Biotech Week*, p. 4400. Retrieved January 2, 2010, from Business Source Complete database.

[2] Lockyer, S. E. (2006, December 18). Yum to expand Taco Bell breakfast test. *Nation's Restaurant News, 40*(51), 3. Retrieved January 3, 2010, from InfoTrac College Edition database.

[3] Yum Brands: Taco Bell to expand. (2009, January). *MarketWatch: Food*, p. 16. Retrieved January 3, 2010, from Business Source Complete database.

[4] Brumback, N. (1998, September 1). Yo quiero Mexican food. *Restaurant Business*, pp. 43–44.

[5] Elbow, P. (1998). *Writing with power: Techniques for mastering the writing process.* Oxford, UK: Oxford University Press, p. 30.

[6] Cook, C. K. (1985). *Line by line.* Boston: Houghton Mifflin, p. 17.

[7] van Roon, Ilja. (2006, May 23). Quoted in Sorry, no more excuses for bad business writing. *PR Newswire.* Retrieved January 4, 2010, from InfoTrac College Edition database.

Chapter 7

[1] Colker, D. (2009, August 13). CEO's wife tweets during childbirth. *Los Angeles Times*, p. B3.

[2] Hof, R. (2009, August 17). Betting on the real-time Web. *BusinessWeek*, p. 46.

[3] Ibid., p. 47.

[4] Ladaga, L. (2009, July 23). TMT: Too much Twitter? *Yahoo News*. Retrieved January 18, 2010, from http://news.yahoo.com

[5] Sandberg, J. (2006, September 26). Employees forsake dreaded email for the beloved phone. *The Wall Street Journal*, p. B1.

[6] Wikipedia. (2009, October 24). *Wikipedia, the free encyclopedia*. Retrieved February 24, 2010, from http://en.wikipedia.org/wiki/Wikipedia

[7] Tschabitscher, H. (2009). How many emails are sent every day? *About.com: Email*. Retrieved January 29, 2010, from http://email.about.com/od/emailtrivia/f/emails_per_day.htm

[8] Maney, K. (2003, July 24). How the big names tame e-mail. *USA Today*, p. 2A.

[9] American Management Association & The ePolicy Institute. (2004). Workplace e-mail and IM survey. *ePolicy Institute.com*. Retrieved January 28, 2010, from http://www.epolicyinstitute.com/

[10] E-mail becoming crime's new smoking gun. (2002, August 15). *USA Today.com*. Retrieved January 28, 2010, from http://www.usatoday.com/tech/news/2002-08-15-email-evidence_x.htm

[11] Revkin, A. C. (2009, November 20). Hacked e-mail is new fodder for climate dispute. *New York Times*. Retrieved January 28, 2010, from http://www.nytimes.com/2009/11/21/science/earth/21climate.html

[12] Goldsmith, M. (2007, May 16). Understanding the perils of e-mail. *BusinessWeek*. Retrieved January 20, 2010, from http://www.businessweek.com/careers/content/may2007/ca20070516_392697.htm?chan=rss_topEmailedStories_ssi_5

[13] Sanati, C. (2008, June 20). Dealbook extra: E-crimination. *The New York Times*, p. C6. Retrieved January 29, 2010, from LexisNexis Academic database; and Goldsmith, M. (2007, May 17). Understanding the perils of e-mail. *BusinessWeek Online*, p. 31. Retrieved January 19, 2010, from Academic Search Premier database.

[14] Living the fast, young life in Asia. (2008, April). *Change Agent*. Retrieved January 24, 2010, from http://www.synovate.com/changeagent/index.php/site/full_story/living_the_fast_living_young_in_asia/

[15] 5 ways Twitter can get you fired. (2009, October 8). *Applicant.com*. Retrieved January 28, 2010, from http://applicant.com/5-ways-twitter-can-get-you-fired/

[16] Baker, S., & Green, H. (2009, June 2). Beyond blogs. *BusinessWeek*, p. 49.

[17] Fortune 500 business blogging wiki. (2009, October 1). *Socialtext.net*. Retrieved January 14, 2010, from http://www.socialtext.net/bizblogs/index.cgi

[18] Beutler, W. (2007, April 10). Yes, but how many blogs are there really? Blog, P. I. Retrieved January 6, 2010, from http://www.blogpi.net/yes-but-how-many-blogs-are-there-really

[19] Baker, S., & Green, H. (2008, May 22). Beyond blogs: What business needs to know. *BusinessWeek Online*. Retrieved January 6, 2010, from http://www.businessweek.com/magazine/ content/08_22/b4086044617865.htm?chan=search

[20] Ibid.

[21] Reality check: State of the media democracy survey. (2008). Retrieved January 3, 2010, from www.deloitte.com/us/realitycheck

[22] Baker, S., & Green, H. (2008, June 2). Beyond blogs: What business needs to know. *BusinessWeek Online*. Retrieved January 6, 2010, from http://www.businessweek.com/magazine/ content/08_22/b4086044617865.htm?chan=search

[23] Taking cues from Facebook. (n.d.). *About McDonald's*. Retrieved January 14, 2010, from http://www.aboutmcdonalds.com/mcd/students/did_you_know/taking_cues_from_facebook.html?DCSext.destination=http://www.aboutmcdonalds.com/mcd/students/did_you_know/taking_cues_from_facebook.html

[24] Conlin, M., & MacMillan, D. (2009, June 1). Managing the tweets. *BusinessWeek*, p. 21.

[25] Baker, S., & Green, H. (2008, June 2). Beyond blogs. *BusinessWeek*, pp. 46, 48.

[26] Conlin, M., & MacMillan, D. (2009, June 1). Managing the tweets. *BusinessWeek*, p. 20.

[27] Ibid., pp. 20–21.

[28] Irvine, M. (2009, July 12). Young workers push employers for wider Web access. *USA Today*. Retrieved January 14, 2010, from http://www.usatoday.com/tech/webguide/internetlife/2009-07-13-blocked-internet_N.htm

[29] Ibid.

[30] Villano, M. (2009, April 26). The online divide between work and play. *The New York Times*. Retrieved February 14, 2010, from http://www.nytimes.com

[31] Ibid.

[32] Ibid.

[33] Ibid.

[34] Dougherty, C. cited in Hiring pros share insights about social networking. (2009). *Yahoo! Hotjobs*. Retrieved January 3, 2010, from http://hotjobs.yahoo.com/career-articles-hiring_pros_share_insights_about_social_networking_sites-1030

[35] Searcey, D. (2009, November 24). Some courts raise bar on reading employee email. *The Wall Street Journal*, p. A31. Retrieved January 28, 2010, from http://online.wsj.com/article/SB125859862658454923.html; and Na, G. (2006, October 17). Employee e-mail use: Big brother may be watching. *Mondaq Business Briefing*. Retrieved January 28, 2010, from Factiva database.

[36] Klein, K. E. (2009, December 1). Putting a fair Internet use policy in place. *BusinessWeek.com*. Retrieved January 28, 2010, from http://www.businessweek.com/smallbiz/content/dec2009/sb2009121_245449.htm

[37] Zetter, K. (2006, October). Employers crack down on personal net use: Misusing e-mail or browsing the wrong sites can cost you your job. *PC World*, p. 26. Retrieved January 28, 2010, from Factiva database.

[38] Breaton, S. (2007, January/February). Blogging: Priceless? *CA Magazine*, p. 13. Retrieved January 28, 2010, from Business Source Premier (EBSCO) database.

[39] Gardner, T. (2009, September 13). It may pay to Twitter. *Los Angeles Times*, p. L8.

[40] Needleman, S. E. (2009, August 4). For companies, a Tweet in time can avert PR mess. *The Wall Street Journal*. Retrieved February 4, 2010, from http://online.wsj.com

[41] Garvey, M. (2009, October 31). Fifth years of simplicity as style. *The Wall Street Journal*, p. A19.

[42] Greene, D. (Host). (2009, July 2). Twitter music reviews: Criticism as haiku. *Morning Edition*. Washington, DC: National Public Radio. Retrieved January 31, 2010, from http://www.npr.org/templates/story/story.php?storyId=106178234

[43] Ibid.

Chapter 8

[1] Based on Clark, N. (2009, August 12). The cold wars. *Marketing*. Retrieved January 20, 2010, from InfoTrac College Edition database; Ethical Companies. (2009, April 9), *Marketing Week*, p. 18. Retrieved January 19, 2010, from InfoTrac College Edition database; Ben & Jerry's Mission. (n.d.). Retrieved January 15, 2010, from http://www.benjerry.com/activism/mission-statement; Brown, K. (2004, April 15). Chilling at Ben & Jerry's: Cleaner, greener. *The Wall Street Journal*, p. B1; Arnold, M. (2001, May 3). Is Ben & Jerry's losing its Bohemian appeal? *Marketing*, p. 17; and Ben & Jerry's goes cage-free and expands fair trade. (2006, October 20). *Ice Cream Reporter*, p. 4. Retrieved January 20, 2010, from InfoTrac College Edition database.

[2] Messmer, M. (2001, January). Enhancing your writing skills. *Strategic Finance*, pp. 8–10. Retrieved January 15, 2010, from Business Source Complete database.

[3] Blachly, A., Ben & Jerry's (personal communication with Mary Ellen Guffey, January 12, 1993).

[4] Zhu, Y., and White, C. (2009, September). Practitioners' views about the use of business email within organizational settings: Implications for developing student generic competence. *Business Communication Quarterly, 72*(3), 292.

[5] Fallows, J. (2005, June 12). Enough keyword searches. Just answer my question. *The New York Times*, p. BU3.

[6] Quinley, K. (2008, May). Apology programs. *Claims*, pp. 14-16. Retrieved January 22, 2010, from Business Source Premier database. See also Runnels, M. (2009, Winter). Apologies all around: Advocating federal protection for the full apology in civil cases. *San Diego Law Review,46*(1), 137–160. Retrieved February 1, 2010, from Business Source Premier database.

[7] Davidow, M. (2003, February). Organizational responses to customer complaints: What works and what doesn't. *Journal of Service Research, 5*(3), 225. Retrieved February 2, 2010, from Business Source Premier database; Blackburn-Brockman, E., & Belanger, K. (1993, June). You-attitude and positive emphasis: Testing received wisdom in business communication. *The Bulletin of the Association for Business Communication*, 1–5; Mascolini, M. (1994, June). Another look at teaching the external negative message. *The Bulletin of the Association for Business Communication*, 46.

[8] Liao, H. (2007, March). Do it right this time: The role of employee service recovery performance in customer-perceived justice and customer loyalty after service failures. *Journal of Applied Psychology, 92*(2), 475. Retrieved January 25, 2010, from Business Source Premier database; Gilbert, P. (1996, December). Two words that can help a business thrive. *The Wall Street Journal*, p. A12.

[9] Martin, J. S., & Chaney, L. H. (2006). *Global business etiquette.* Westport, CT: Praeger, p. 150.

[10] Haneda, S., & Hirosuke, S. (1982). Japanese communication behavior as reflected in letter writing. *The Journal of Business Communication (1)*, 29. See also Varner, I., & Beamer, L. (2001). *Intercultural Communication*. Chicago: McGraw-Hill Irwin, pp. 131–132.

[11] Martin, J. S., & Chaney, L. H. (2006). *Global business etiquette.* Praeger: Westport, CT, p. 159.

[12] Loewy, D., German interpreter (personal communication with Mary Ellen Guffey, July 2007).

[13] Luciani-Samec, A., French instructor, & Samec, P. French businessman (personal communication with Mary Ellen Guffey, May 1995).

[14] Fallows, J. (2005, June 12). Enough keyword searches. Just answer my question. *The New York Times*, p. BU3.

[15] Based on Scarp, M. J. (1995, October 28). Hotel to cease pigeon poisoning. *Scottsdale Tribune.*

Chapter 9

[1] Southwest Airlines confirms passengers are not superstitious. (2009, November 13). *PR Newswire*. Retrieved January 4, 2010, from http://www.southwest.com

[2] Less baggage. (2008, June 12). *The Tampa Tribune* (Tampa, FL), p. 1.

[3] Edwards, J. (2008, September 22). Sour tweets get sweet results. *Brandweek*. Retrieved January 4, 2010, from InfoTrac College Edition database.

[4] Bailey, J. (2007, March 18). Airlines learn to fly on a wing and an apology. *The New York Times*, p. 1.1. Retrieved January 3, 2010, from http://www.nytimes.com; and Taylor, F. (2008, January 23, March 5). Being proactive—The next generation of customer service. Message posted to Nuts About Southwest blog. Retrieved January 3, 2010, from http://www.blogsouthwest.com/

[5] Mintz, J. (2009, February 23). Microsoft: Laid-off can keep extra pay after all. *USA Today*. Retrieved January 3, 2010, from http://www.usatoday.com/tech/news/2009-02-23-microsoft-layoffs_N.htm

[6] Greenwald, J. (2009, June 1). Layoffs may spark defamation suits. *Business Insurance*. Retrieved January 13, 2009, from Business Source Complete database.

[7] American Management Association. 2004 Survey on workplace e-mail and IM reveals unmanaged risks. (2004). Retrieved June 10, 2007, from http://www.amanet.org/press/amanews/im_survey.htm

[8] McCord, E. A. (1991, April). The business writer, the law, and routine business communication: A legal and rhetorical analysis. *Journal of Business and Technical Communication*, 183.

[9] Ibid.

[10] Shuit, D. P. (2003, September). Do it right or risk getting burned. *Workforce Management*, p. 80.

[11] Brodkin, J. (2007, March 19). Corporate apologies don't mean much. *Networkworld, 24*(11), p. 8. Retrieved January 4, 2010, from Business Source Complete database.

[12] Schweitzer, M. (2006, December). Wise negotiators know when to say "I'm sorry." *Negotiation*, 4. Retrieved January 4, 2010, from Business Source Complete database.

[13] Brodkin, J. (2007, March 19). Rating apologies. *Networkworld, 24*(11), p. 14. Retrieved January 3, 2010, from Business Source Complete database.

[14] Neeleman, D. (2007). An apology from David Neeleman. Retrieved January 4, 2010, from http://www.jetblue.com/about/ourcompany/apology/index.html

[15] Letters to Lands' End. (1991, February). 1991 Lands' End Catalog. Dodgeville, WI: Lands' End, p. 100.

[16] Mowatt, J. (2002, February). Breaking bad news to customers. *Agency Sales*, 30; and Dorn, E. M. (1999, March). Case method instruction in the business writing classroom. *Business Communication Quarterly, 62*(1), 51–52.

[17] Forbes, M. (1999). How to write a business letter. In K. Harty (Ed.), *Strategies for business and technical writing*. Boston: Allyn and Bacon, p. 108.

[18] Harris, D. (2004, July 5). Court: Dealerships need not repeat a lender's credit rejection notice. *Automotive News*, , p. 18. Retrieved January 5, 2010, from InfoTrac College Edition database.

[19] Mainz, C. (2005, June). Southwest Star of the Month: Fred Taylor. *Spirit*. Retrieved January 6, 2010, from http://www.fredtaylorjr.com/1894/10001.html; McGregor, J., Jespersen, F., Tucker, M., & Foust, D. (2007, March 5). Customer service champs. Retrieved January 6, 2010, from http://www.businessweek.com/magazine/content/07_10/b4024001.htm

[20] Browning, M. (2003, November 24). Work dilemma: Delivering bad news a good way. *Government Computer News*, p. 41; and Mowatt, J. (2002, February). Breaking bad news to customers. *Agency Sales*, p. 30.

[21] Ensall, S. (2007, January 30). Delivering bad news. *Personnel Today*, p. 31. Retrieved January 5, 2010, from Business Source Premier database; and Lewis, B. (1999, September 13). To be an effective leader, you need to perfect the art of delivering bad news. *InfoWorld*, p. 124.

[22] Gilsdorf, J. W. (1997, June). Metacommunication effects on international business negotiating in China. *Business Communication Quarterly, 60*(2), 27.

[23] Beamer, L., & Varner, I. (2001). *Intercultural communication in the global workplace*. New York: McGraw-Hill/Irwin, p. 141.

[24] Conaway, R. N., & Wardrope, W. J. (2004, December). Communication in Latin America. *Business Communication Quarterly, 67*(4), 472.

[25] Bristol-Smith, D. (2003, November). Quoted in Need to deliver bad news? How & why to tell it like it is. *HR Focus*, p. 3. Retrieved January 5, 2010, from InfoTrac College Edition database.

[26] Gartner identifies top ten disruptive technologies for 2008-2012. (n.d.) Press release. Retrieved January 5, 2010, from http://www.gartner.com/it/page.jsp?id=68117

[27] Based on Lee, L. (2007, June 11). A smoothie you can chew on. *BusinessWeek*, p. 64.

[28] Hines announces HinesGO sustainability tool to green office space. (2009, November 2). Retrieved January 5, 2010, from http://www.immo-news.net/Hines-announces-HinesGO-sustainability-tool-to-green-office-space_a5733.html

[29] Based on Sloan, G. (1996, November 29). Under 21? Carnival says cruise is off. *USA Today*; Sieder, J. (1995, October 16). Full steam ahead: Carnival Cruise Line makes boatloads of money by selling fun. *U.S. News & World Report*, p. 72; and About Carnival Cruise Line. Retrieved July 27, 2004, from http://www.cruisecritic./reviews/cruiseline.cfm?CruiseLineID=9

[30] Based on Burbank, L. (2007, June 8). Personal items can be swept away between flights. *USA Today*, p. 3D.

[31] Kucher, K. (2009, March 31). UCSD email erroneously welcomes all who applied. Retrieved January 10, 2010, from http://www3signonsandiego.com/stories/2009/mar31/bn31letter114447/

[32] Sorkin, A. R. (1999, November). J. Crew web goof results in discount. *The New York Times*, p. D3.

[33] Mishory, J. (2008, June). Don't shoot the messenger: How to deliver bad news and still keep customers satisfied. *Sales and Marketing Management*, 18.

[34] Based on Harari, O. (1999, July–August). The power of complaints. *Management Review*, p. 31.

[35] Based on SUV surprise. (2004, June 15). *The Wall Street Journal*, p. W7.

Chapter 10

[1] Betancourt, C. M. (1999, November 28). Head of Make-A-Wish chapter is a man with many missions. *The Miami Herald*, p. B1.

[2] Morris, P., president and CEO, Hands on Miami (personal communication with Mary Ellen Guffey, August 2, 2006).

[3] Hamilton, C. (2005). *Communicating for results* (7th ed.). Mason, OH: Wadsworth/Thomson, p. 334.

[4] Hoar, R. (2005, March 1). Be more persuasive. *Management Today*, 56.

[5] Cialdini, R. B. (1993). *Influence: The power of persuasion*. New York: Quill, William Morrow, p. 238.

[6] Fracaro, K. E. (2004, August). Managing by persuasion. *Contract Management, 44*(8), 4. Retrieved January 29, 2010, from InfoTrac College Edition database.

[7] Conde, C. (2010, January 17). Structure? The flatter the better. *The New York Times*, p. BU2.

[8] Newman, R. (2006, September 25). Lessons from the rule breakers. *U.S. News & World Report*, Executive Edition, p. 4. Retrieved January 30, 2010, from InfoTrac College Edition database.

[9] Pollock, T. (2003, June). How to sell an idea. *Supervision*, p. 15. Retrieved January 29, 2010, from InfoTrac College Edition database.

[10] Communicating with the boss. (2006, May). *Communication Briefings*, p. 8.

[11] Friesen, P. (2003, October). Customer testimonials. *Target Marketing*, p. 137.

[12] McLaughlin, K. (1990, October). Words of wisdom. *Entrepreneur*, 101. See also Wastphal, L. (2001, October). Empathy in sales letters. *Direct Marketing*, 55.

[13] Consumer complaints about Vital Basics—Focus Factor. Retrieved September 17, 2006, from http://www.consumeraffairs.com/nutrition/vital.html; see also Clifford, S. (2009, November 22). Are ads true? New lawsuits ask for proof. *The New York Times*, p. 1.

[14] Singer, N. (2009, February 11). A pill that promised too much. *The New York Times*, B1.

[15] Clifford, S. (2009, November 22). Are ads true? New lawsuits ask for proof. *The New York Times*, p. 1.

[16] Loathing of mail and Web activity on rise. (2006, April 28). *Precision Marketing*, p. 2.

[17] Howard, T. (2008, November 28). E-mail grows as direct-marketing tool. *USA Today*, p. 5B.

[18] Suited for employment. (2005, July 15). *The Chronicle of Higher Education*, p. A8.

[19] Based on Fritscher-Porter, K. (2003, June/July). Don't be duped by office supply scam artists. *OfficePro*, 9–10.

[20] Yancey, K. B. (2006, September 2). Hotels give guests a hand with GPS. *USA Today*, p. 1D.

[21] Based on Yu, R. (2009, 13 March). Hotels take action to pare down food, restaurant expenses. *USA Today*, p. 3D.

[22] Zbar, J. D. (2001, March). Training to telework. *Home Office Computing*, p. 72.

[23] Based on Marquez, J. (2006, January 16). On-site blood testing raises privacy issues. *Workplace Management*, p. 10.

[24] Based on DuFrene, D. D., & Lehman, C. M. (2002, March). Persuasive appeal for clean language. *Business Communication Quarterly, 65*(1), 48–55.

[25] Belluck, P. (2010, January 14). After a longtime rise, obesity rates in U.S. level off, data suggest. *The New York Times*, p. A20(L). Retrieved January 28, 2010, from InfoTrac College Edition database.

[26] Know the true cost of obesity: Related lost productivity. (2008, April 1). *Occupational Health Management*. Retrieved January 27, 2010, from InfoTrac College Edition database.

[27] Based on Yunxia, Z. (2000, December). Building knowledge structures in teaching cross-cultural sales genres. *Business Communication Quarterly, 63*(4), 66–67.

Chapter 11

[1] Flying with companion animals: Protect your precious "cargo." (n.d.). *HelpingAnimals.com*. Retrieved January 15, 2010, from http://www.helpinganimals.com/Travel_cargo.asp

[2] 2009/2010 National Pet Owners Survey cited by American Pet Products Association. (2010). *APPA.com*. Retrieved January 15, 2010, from http://www.americanpetproducts.org/press_industrytrends.asp

[3] Questions for David McCullough. (2006, July 7). *Workforce Management*, p. 9.

[4] Cohen, J. S. (2009, December 28). Top 10 favorite foods preferred by college students. *Chicago Tribune*. Retrieved January 22, 2010, from http://www.inyork.com/ci_14080691?source=most_viewed

[5] Giorgetti, D., & Sebastiani, F. (2003, December). Automating survey coding by multiclass text categories. *Journal of the American Society for Information Science and Technology, 54*(14), 1269. Retrieved January 22, 2010, from ABI/INFORM Global database; and Brennan, M., & Holdershaw, J. (1999). The effect of question tone and form on responses to open-ended questions: Further data. *Marketing Bulletin*, 57-64.

[6] Goldsmith, B. (2002, June). The awesome power of asking the right questions. *OfficeSolutions*, 52; and Bracey, G. W. (2001, November). Research-question authority. *Phi Delta Kappan*, 191.

[7] Berfield, S. (2009, August 17). Howard Schultz versus Howard Schultz. *BusinessWeek*, p. 31.

[8] Lenhart, A. (2009, October 8). The democratization of online social networks. *Pew Internet & American Life Project*, slide 4. Retrieved January 22, 2010, from http://www.pewinternet.org/Presentations/2009/41--The-Democratization-of-Online-Social-Networks.aspx

[9] Netcraft, Ltd. (n.d.) *January 2010 Web Server Survey*. Retrieved January 22, 2010, from http://news.netcraft.com/archives/web_server_survey.html

[10] Alpert, J., & Hajaj, N. (2008, July 25). We knew the Web was big . . . *The Official Google Blog*. Retrieved January 22, 2010, from http://googleblog.blogspot.com/2008/07/we-knew-web-was-big.html

[11] Little, L. (2006, March 7). Using a multiple search. *The Wall Street Journal*, p. D1. Retrieved January 23, 2010, from Factiva database.

[12] Vincent, J. (n.d.). Write or wrong: Thoughts on plagiarism. *Helium.com*. Retrieved January 22, 2010, from http://www.helium.com/items/982257-thoughts-on-plagiarism

[13] Arenson, K. W., & Gootman, E. (2008, February 21). Columbia cites plagiarism by a professor. *The New York Times*. Retrieved January 22, 2010, from http://www.nytimes.com/2008/02/21/education/21prof.html; and Bartlett, T. (2006, September 8). Professor faces firing for plagiarism. *Chronicle of Higher Education*, p. 11. Retrieved January 22, 2010, from Academic Search Elite database.

[14] Writing Tutorial Services, Indiana University. *Plagiarism: What it is and how to recognize and avoid it*. Retrieved January 22, 2010, from http://www.indiana.edu/~wts/pamphlets/plagiarism.shtml

[15] Brady, D. (2006, December 4). *!#?@ the e-mail. Can we talk? *BusinessWeek*, p. 109.

[16] Berfield, S. (2009, August 17). Howard Schultz versus Howard Schultz. *BusinessWeek*, p. 33.

[17] Spake, A. (2003, November 17). Hey kids! We've got sugar and toys. *U.S. News & World Report*, p. 62.

[18] Reena, J. (2006, October 16). Enough with the shoot-'em-ups. *BusinessWeek*, p. 92.

[19] Hibbard, J. (2006, October 9). How Yahoo! gave itself a face-lift. *BusinessWeek*, p. 77.

[20] Goldman, A. (2006, December 1). Wal-Mart limps into the holidays. *Los Angeles Times*, p. C4.

[21] 2010 College food trends: Students crave global, national and regional comfort food with a twist. (2009, December 14). *SodexoUSA.com*. Retrieved February 5, 2010, from http://www.sodexousa.com/usen/newsroom/press/press09/2010collegefoodtrends.asp

[22] Teens more "normal" than you think regarding media usage. (2009, June 25). *Nielsenwire*. Retrieved February 5, 2010, from http://blog.nielsen.com/nielsenwire/consumer/teens-more-normal-than-you-think-regarding-media-usage/

[23] Edwards, C., & Ihlwan, M. (2006, December 4). Upward mobility. *BusinessWeek*, pp. 68–82.

[24] World Internet usage and population statistics. (2009, September 30). *Internet World Stats*. Retrieved February 5, 2010, from http://www.internetworldstats.com/stats.htm

[25] Naughton, K. (2006, July 3). Corporate giant. *Newsweek*, p. 74. Retrieved February 4, 2010, from Business Source Premier (EBSCO) database.

[26] How undergraduate students use credit cards. (2009). *Sallie Mae*. Retrieved February 5, 2010, from http://www.salliemae.com/NR/rdonlyres/0BD600F1-9377-46EA-AB1F-6061FC763246/10744/SLMCreditCardUsageStudy41309FINAL2.pdf

Chapter 12

[1] Case based on Berfield, S. (2009, August 17). Howard Schultz versus Howard Schultz. *BusinessWeek*, pp. 28-33; Temkin, B. (2010, January 25). Starbucks brews a comeback with purpose. *BusinessExchange*. Retrieved February 15, 2010, from http://bx.businessweek.com/starbucks; Starbucks brews up instant coffee line. (2009, February 18). *The Boston Globe*. Retrieved February 15, 2010, from http://www.boston.com/business/articles/2009/02/18/starbucks_brews_up_instant_coffee_line; and Bramhall, J. (2007, January 1). Starbucks. *Hoover's Company Records*, 15745. Retrieved January 9, 2010, from ProQuest database.

[2] Ewing, J. (2007, May 4). First mover in mobile: How Nokia is selling cell phones to the developing world. *BusinessWeek Online*. Retrieved February 20, 2010, from http://www.businessweek.com

[3] Temkin, B. (2010, January 25). Starbucks brews a comeback with purpose. *Business Exchange*. Retrieved February 20, 2010, from http://bx.businessweek.com/starbucks/

[4] Groom, N., & Baertlein, L. (2008, April 24). Starbucks steps back from music business. *Business Exchange*. Retrieved February 15, 2010, from http://bx.businessweek.com/starbucks; and Van Riper, T. (2007, February 27). Dunkin' Donuts edges Starbucks. *Forbes.com*. Retrieved February 15, 2010, from http://www.forbes.com/2007/02/26/starbucks-dunkin-donuts-biz-cx_tvr_0227starbucks.html

[5] Toyo sets tire recall. (2010, February 23). *Tire Review*. Retrieved February 23, 2010, from http://www.tirereview.com/Article/71180/toyo_sets_tire_recall.aspx; and Aeppel, T. (2000, November 20). Firestone recall fuels interest in "smart" tires. *The Wall Street Journal*, p. B1.

[6] Cornish, A. (Writer). (2006, July 18). Nissan workers make Tennessee move. [Radio Broadcast episode]. In M. Block (Host). *All Things Considered*. Washington, DC: National Public Radio; Halcomb, R. (2005, October 20). Nissan may move its U.S. headquarters. *Autoblog*. Retrieved February 20, 2010, from http://www.autoblog.com/2005/10/20/nissan-may-move-its-u-s-headquarters; and Halcomb, R. (2005, November 3). Nissan to move headquarters to Tennessee. *Autoblog*. Retrieved February 20, 2010, from http://www.autoblog.com/2005/11/03/nissan-to-move-headquaters-to-tennessee/

[7] Berfield, S. (2009, August 17). Howard Schultz versus Howard Schultz. *BusinessWeek*, p. 33.

[8] Red light camera reform. (2003, May/June). *WestWays*, 19.

[9] Roberts, D., Engardio, P., Bernstein, A., Holmes, S., & Ji, X. (2006, November 27). Secrets, lies, and sweatshops. *BusinessWeek Online*. Retrieved February 20, 2010, from http://www.businessweek.com

Chapter 13

[1] Based on Grinyer, M., Raytheon proposal consultant (personal communication with Mary Ellen Guffey, July 23, 2007).

[2] City of Las Vegas. (2010, January 4). RFP for public private partnership parking initiative. *Onvia DemandStar*. Retrieved March 4, 2010, from http://www.lasvegasnevada.gov/Business/5990.htm?ID

[3] Buck Institute for Age Research. (n.d.). Architecture. Retrieved February 5, 2010, from http://www.buckinstitute.org/TheInstitute/architecture.asp

[4] Sant, T. (2004). Persuasive business proposals. New York: AMACOM, pp. 99–100.

[5] MasterPlans: Professional Business Plan Writers. (n.d.). Rapid development cycle. Retrieved March 5, 2010, from MasterPlans Web site: http://www.masterplans.com

[6] Turner, M. L. (2007). Guide to business plan consultants: Hiring help is the next best thing to writing your plan yourself. *Work.com*. Retrieved March 5, 2010, from http://www.work.com/business-plan-consultants-880/

[7] Nelson, F. (2004, September 5). Device from UCSB trio ready to take its first breath. *Santa Barbara News-Press*, p. F1.

Chapter 14

[1] Johnson, B. (2010, January 27). Apple iPad: The first review. *Guardian.co.uk*. Retrieved March 28, 2010, from http://www.guardian.co.uk/technology/2010/jan/27/apple-ipad-tablet-first-review

[2] Steve Jobs' obsession with secrecy and the "big-bang." (2009, December 8). *Edible Apple Blog*. Retrieved March 28, 2010, from http://www.edibleapple.com/steve-jobs-obsession-with-secrecy-and-the-big-bang/

[3] Ibid.

[4] Joy, D. (2007, April 26). Blog post: Do public speaking skills affect your technology career success? *Jobing.com*. Retrieved March 30, 2010, from http://glendale.jobing.com/blog_post.asp?post=4221

[5] Dr. John J. Medina as quoted by Reynolds, G. (2010). *Presentation zen design*. Berkeley, CA: New Riders, p. 97.

[6] Gallo, C. (2009, October 6). Uncovering Steve Jobs' presentation secrets. *BusinessWeek*. Retrieved March 28, 2010, from http://www.businessweek.com/smallbiz/content/oct2009/sb2009106_706829.htm

[7] Lewis, A. (2005, July 5). So many meetings, so little point, *The Denver Post*, p. C1. Retrieved March 20, 2010, from LexisNexis database; and Paradi, D. (2003). Are we wasting $250 million per day due to bad PowerPoint? *Think Outside The Slide*. Retrieved March 28, 2010, from http://www.thinkoutsidetheslide.com/articles/wasting_250M_bad_ppt.htm

[8] Stanford communication professor Clifford Nass quoted in Simons, T. (2001, July). When was the last time PowerPoint made you sing? *Presentations*, p. 6. See also Geoffrey Nunberg, G. (1999, December 20). The trouble with PowerPoint. *Fortune*, pp. 330–334.

[9] ThinkFree Office 3 and PodPresenter now available online. (2006, March 27). *ThinkFree Corporation*. Retrieved March 26, 2010, from http://company.thinkfree.com/views/jsp/user/company/articleList.jsp?currentPage=91&seq=33&type=&lang_type=en

[10] Bajaj, G. (2009, February 28). Impatica ShowMate. Retrieved March 28, 2010, from http://www.indezine.com/products/powerpoint/hardware/impaticashowmate.html

[11] Booher, D. (2003). *Speak with confidence: Powerful presentations that inform, inspire, and persuade*. New York: McGraw-Hill Professional, p. 126; Paradi, D. (2009, March 3). Choosing colors for your presentation slides. Retrieved March 26, 2010, from http://www.indezine.com/ideas/prescolors.html

[12] Bates, S. (2005). *Speak like a CEO: Secrets for commanding attention and getting results*. New York: McGraw-Hill Professional, p. 113.

[13] Bergells, L. (2007, May 2). Top nine visual clichés. Maniactive.com Blog. Retrieved March 15, 2010, from http://www.maniactive.com/states/2007/05/top-nine-visual-cliches.html; See also: How to avoid the 7 deadly sins of PowerPoint. (2004, July 30). *Yearbook of Experts News Release Wire*, Retrieved March 15, 2010, from LexisNexis Academic database.

[14] Burrows, P., Grover, R., & Green, H. (2006, February 6). Steve Jobs' magic kingdom. *BusinessWeek*, p. 62. Retrieved March 26, 2010, from http://www.businessweek.com; Gallo, C. (2006, April 6). How to wow 'em like Steve Jobs. *BusinessWeek*. Retrieved March 26, 2010, from http://www.businessweek.com

[15] See the PowerPoint preshow checklist at http://www.tlccreative.com/images/tutorials/PreShowChecklist.pdf

[16] Ellwood, J. (2004, August 4). Less PowerPoint, more powerful points, *The Times (London)*, p. 6.

[17] Ozer, J. (2006, January 11). Ovation for PowerPoint. *PC Magazine*. Retrieved March 26, 2010, from http://www.pcmag.com/article2/0,1759,1921436,00.asp; See more information at http://www.adobe.com/products/ovation/

[18] For more information, go to http://www.turningtechnologies.com, http://www.audienceresponse.com, or http://www.optiontechnologies.com

[19] Boeri, R. J. (2002, March). Fear of flying? Or the mail? Try the Web conferencing cure. *Emedia Magazine*, p. 49.

[20] Booher, D. (2003). *Speak with confidence*. New York: McGraw-Hill Professional, p. 14; and Booher, D. (1991). *Executive's portfolio of model speeches for all occasions*. Englewood Cliffs, NJ: Prentice Hall, p. 259.

[21] Gallo, C. (2006, July 6). Steve Jobs' greatest presentation. *BusinessWeek Online*. Retrieved March 26, 2010, from http://www.businessweek.com; and

Evangelist, M. (2006, January 5). Behind the magic curtain. *The Guardian*. Retrieved March 26, 2010, from http://technology.guardian.co.uk

[22] Edmondson, G. (2006, October 16). The secret of BMW's success. *BusinessWeek Online*. Retrieved March 26, 2010, from http://www.businessweek.com/magazine/content/06_42/b4005078.htm

[23] Peterson, R. (n.d.). Presentations: Are you getting paid for overtime? *Presentation Coaching Institute*. Retrieved March 20, 2010, from http://www.passociates.com/getting_paid_for_overtime.shtml; The sales presentation: The bottom line is selling. (2001, March 14). *Marken Communications*. Retrieved March 20, 2010, from http://www.markencom.com/docs/01mar14.htm

[24] Schneider, P. (2001, August 12). Scenes from a marriage: Observations on the Daimler-Chrysler merger from a German living in America. *The New York Times Magazine*, p. 47.

[25] Wunderle, W. (2007, March/April). How to negotiate in the Middle East. *The U.S. Army Professional Writing Collection, 5*(7). Retrieved March 20, 2010, from http://www.army.mil/professionalwriting/volumes/volume5/july_2007/7_07_4.html; see also Marks, S. J. (2001, September). Nurturing global workplace connections. *Workforce*, p. 76.

[26] Brandel, M. (2006, February 20). Sidebar: Don't be the ugly American. *Computerworld*. Retrieved March 20, 2010, from http://www.computerworld.com/s/article/108772/Sidebar_Don_t_Be_the_Ugly_American

[27] Dulek, R. E., Fielden, J. S., & Hill, J. S. (1991, January/February). International communication: An executive primer. *Business Horizons*, p. 22.

[28] Davidson, R., & Rosen, M. Cited in Brandel, M. (2006, February 20). Sidebar: Don't be the ugly American. *Computerworld*. Retrieved March 20, 2010, from http://www.computerworld.com/s/article/108772/Sidebar_Don_t_Be_the_Ugly_American

[29] Burge, J. (2002, June). Telephone safety protocol for today. *The National Public Accountant*, p. 35.

[30] Vergano, D. (2004, August 31). Computers: Scientific friend or foe? *USA Today*, p. D6.

[31] Reynolds, G. (2008). *Presentation zen*. Berkeley, CA: New Riders, pp. 64ff.

[32] Jackson, M., quoted in Garbage In, Garbage Out. (1992, December). *Consumer Reports*, p. 755.

Chapter 15

[1] Ryan, L. (2007). Online job searching. *BusinessWeek Online*. Video interview retrieved February 12, 2010, from http://feedroom.businessweek.com/?fr_story=5e1ec1bacf73ae689d381f30e80dfea30cd52108&rf=sitemap

[2] Ryan, L. (2009). Five ways to grow your job-search army. *Yahoo HotJobs Articles*. Retrieved February 12, 2010, from http://ca.hotjobs.yahoo.com/career-experts-5_ways_to_grow_your_job_search_army-95

[3] Ryan, L. (2009). Ten boilerplate phrases that kill résumés. Retrieved February 12, 2010, from LizRyan.com at http://www.asklizryan.com/lizarticles/tenboilerplatephrasesthatkillsresumes.html

[4] Ryan, L. (2010). Job Seeker, Are you memorable? *Yahoo HotJobs Articles*. Retrieved February 12, 2010, from http://hotjobs.yahoo.com/career-experts-job_seeker_are_you_memorable-74

[5] U.S. Small Business Administration. FAQs: Frequently Asked Questions. Retrieved February 12, 2010, from http://web.sba.gov/faqs/

[6] Middleton, D. (2009, December 28). Landing a job of the future takes a two-track mind. *CareerJournal*. Retrieved February 12, 2010, from http://online.wsj.com/article/SB10001424052748703278604574624392641425278.html?mod=WSJ_WSJ_Careers_NewsTrends_4

[7] Kimmitt, R. M. (2007, January 23). Why job churn is good. *The Washington Post*, p. A17. Retrieved February 12, 2010, from http://www.washingtonpost.com/wp-dyn/content/article/2007/01/22/AR2007012201089.html

[8] Levy, R (2010). How to use social media in your job search. *About.com*. Retrieved February 12, 2010, from http://jobsearch.about.com/od/networking/a/socialmedia.htm

[9] Korkki, P. (2007, July 1). So easy to apply, so hard to be noticed. *The New York Times*. Retrieved July 8, 2008, from LexisNexis database.

[10] Marquardt, K. (2008, February 21). 5 tips on finding a new job. *U.S. News & World Report*. Retrieved February 16, 2010, from http://www.usnews.com/articles/business/careers/2008/02/21/5-tips-on-finding-a-new-job.html

[11] Crispin, G., & Mehler, M. (2009, February). CareerXroads 8th Annual Source of Hire Study. *CareerXroads.com*. Retrieved February 12, 2010, from http://www.careerxroads.com/news/SourcesOfHire09.pdf

[12] The top ten other job web sites for job-seekers. (2010). *QuintCareers.com*. Retrieved February 12, 2010, from http://www.quintcareers.com/top_10_sites.html

[13] Boyle, M. (2009, June 25). Recruiting: Enough to make a monster tremble. *BusinessWeek*. Retrieved February 17, 2010, from http://www.businessweek.com/magazine/content/09_27/b4138043180664.htm; and Shawbel, D. (2009, February 24). Top ten social sites for finding a job. *Mashable: The Social Media Guide*. Retrieved February 12, 2010, from http://mashable.com/2009/02/24/top-10-social-sites-for- finding-a-job/

[14] McConnon, A. (2007, August 30). Social networking graduates and hits the job market. *BusinessWeek*. Retrieved February 15, 2010, from http://www.businessweek.com/innovate/content/aug2007/id20070830_886412.htm?chan=search

[15] Cheeseman, J., quoted by Wolgemuth, L. (2008, February 25). Using the Web to search for a job. *U.S. News & World Report*. Retrieved February 15, 2010, from http://www.usnews.com/articles/business/careers/2008/02/25/using-the-web-to-search-for-a-job.html

[16] Brown, J., Cober, R. T., Kane, K., Levy, P. E., & Shalhoop, J. (2006). Proactive personality and the successful job search: A field investigation with college graduates. *Journal of Applied Psychology, 91*(3), 717–726. Retrieved July 15, 2007, from Business Source Premier (EBSCO) database.

[17] Koeppel, D. (2006, December 31). Those low grades in college may haunt your job search. *The New York Times*, p. 1. Retrieved February 15, 2010, from http://www.nytimes.com/2006/12/31/jobs/31gpa.html

[18] Black, D., quoted by Brandon, E. (2007, January 31). Tips for getting that first job. *U.S. News & World Report*. Retrieved February 15, 2010, from http://www.usnews.com/usnews/biztech/articles/070131/31firstjob.htm

[19] Gabbard, D. (2009, June 12). Unlocking the hidden job market. *Examiner.com Washington DC*. Retrieved February 15, 2010, from http://www.examiner.com/x-/x-11194-Cleveland-Unemployment-Examiner~y2009m6d12-Unlocking-the-hidden-job-market

[20] Borney, N. (2010, February 16). 10 ways to crack Michigan's hidden job market. *AnnArbor.com*. Retrieved February 17, 2010, from http://www.annarbor.com/business-review/ann-arbor-human-resources-experts-offer-tips-how-to-get-hired-in-2010/

[21] Salpeter, M. (2010). Leverage Twitter for your job search. *Twitip.com*. Retrieved February 15, 2010, from http://www.twitip.com/leverage-twitter-for-your-job-search/

[22] Résumés inching up. (2009, March 20). *Accountemps*. Retrieved February 15, 2010, from http://accountemps.rhi.mediaroom.com/index.php?s=189&item=210

[23] Isaacs, K. (2007). How to decide on résumé length. Retrieved February 15, 2010, from http://www.resumepower.com/resume-length.html

[24] Hansen, K. (2007). Should you use a career objective on your résumé? Retrieved February 15, 2010, from http://www.quintcareers.com/resume_objectives.html

[25] Coombes, A. (2010, February 7). First aid for your résumé. *The Wall Street Journal*. Retrieved February 15, 2010, from http://online.wsj.com/article/SB126550131743542087.html

[26] Korkki, P. (2007, July 1). So easy to apply, so hard to be noticed. *The New York Times*. Retrieved February 15, 2010, from http://www.nytimes.com/2007/07/01/business/yourmoney/01career.html

[27] Koeppel, D. (2006, December 31). Those low grades in college may haunt your job search. *The New York Times*, p. 1. Retrieved February 15, 2010, from http://www.nytimes.com/2006/12/31/jobs/31gpa.html

[28] Ibid.

[29] Build the résumé employers want. (n.d.). Retrieved July 21, 2007, from http://www.jobweb.com/resources/library/Interviews

[30] Locke, A. (2008, June 18). Is your resume telling the wrong story? *The Ladders.com*. Retrieved February 15, 2010, from http://www.theladders.com/career-advice/Is-Your-Resume-Telling-the-Wrong-Story

[31] Washington, T. (2007). Effective résumés bring results to life. Retrieved July 21, 2007, from http://www.careerjournal.com/jobhunting/resumes/20000913-washington.html

[32] Ryan, L. (2007). Online job searching. *BusinessWeek Online*. Video interview retrieved February 15, 2010, from http://feedroom.businessweek.com/?fr_story=5e1ec1bacf73ae689d381f30e80dfea30cd52108&rf=rss

[33] Ibid.

[34] Hansen, K. (2010). Tapping the power of keywords to enhance your résumé's effectiveness. *QuintCareers.com*. Retrieved February 16, 2010, from http://www.quintcareers.com/resume_keywords.html

[35] The video resume technique. (2007). Retrieved February 16, 2010, from http://www.collegegrad.com/jobsearch/guerrilla-insider-techniques/the-video-resume-technique/

[36] McGrath, B. (2006, October 23). Aleksey the Great. *New Yorker*. Retrieved February 16, 2010, from http://www.newyorker.com/archive/2006/10/23/061023ta_talk_mcgrath

[37] Zupek, R. (2008). Honesty is the best policy in résumés and interviews. Retrieved February 16, 2010, from http://www.careerbuilder.com/Article/CB-1180-Cover-Letters-and-Resumes-Honesty-is-the-Best-Policy-in-R%c3%a9sum%c3%a9s-and-Interviews/

[38] Needleman, S. E. (2007, March 6). Why sneaky tactics may not help résumé. *The Wall Street Journal*, p. B8.

[39] Korkki, P. (2009, July 18). Where, oh where, has my application gone? *The New York Times*. Retrieved February 16, 2010, from http://www.nytimes.com/2009/07/19/jobs/19career.html?_r=1&scp=1&sq=Where,%20oh%20where,%20has%20my%20application%20gone&st=cse

[40] Korkki, P. (2007, July 1). So easy to apply, so hard to be noticed. *The New York Times*. Retrieved February 16, 2010, from http://www.nytimes.com/2007/07/01/business/yourmoney/01career.html

Chapter 16

[1] Jones, E. (January 25, 2010). They're hiring! *CNNMoney.com*. Retrieved March 8, 2010, from http://money.cnn.com/galleries/2010/fortune/1001/gallery.bestcompanies_mosthiring.fortune/index.html

[2] Bock, L. (2007, June 6). Testimony of Google's Laszlo Bock, House Judiciary Subcommittee on Immigration, Citizenship, Refugees, Border Security, and International Law. *BusinessWeek Online*. Retrieved February 22, 2010, from http://www.businessweek.com/bwdaily/dnflash/content/jun2007/db20070606_682422.htm

[3] Hansell, S. (2007, January 3). Google answer to filling jobs is an algorithm. *The New York Times*. Retrieved February 22, 2010, from http://www.nytimes.com/2007/01/03/technology/03google.html

[4] Delaney, K. (2006, October 23). Google adjusts hiring process as needs grow. *The Wall Street Journal*, p. B1.

[5] Wilmott, N. (n.d.). Interviewing styles: Tips for interview approaches. *About.com: Human Resources*. Retrieved February 22, 2010, from http://humanresources.about.com/cs/selectionstaffing/a/interviews.htm

[6] Athavaley, A. (2007, June 20). A job interview you don't have to show up for. *The Wall Street Journal*. Retrieved February 22, 2010, from http://online.wsj.com/article/SB118229876637841321.html#articleTabs%3Darticle

[7] Ziebarth, B. (2009, December 10). Tips to ace your panel job interview. *Associated Content, Inc.* Retrieved February 22, 2010, from http://www.associatedcontent.com/article/2470148/tips_to_ace_your_panel_job_interview.html?cat=31

[8] Cristante, D. (2009, June 15). How to succeed in a group interview. *CareerFAQs*. Retrieved February 22, 2010, from http://www.careerfaqs.com.au/job-interview-tips/1116/How-to-succeed-in-a-group-interview

[9] Weiss, T. (2009, May 12). Going on the second interview. *Forbes*. Retrieved February 22, 2010, from http://www.forbes.com/2009/05/12/second-interview-advice-leadership-careers-basics.html

[10] Hansen, R. (2010). Situational interviews and stress interviews: What to make of them and how to succeed in them. *QuintCareers*. Retrieved February 22, 2010, from http://www.quintcareers.com/situational_stress_interviews.html

[11] Bergey, B. (2009, December 10). Online job interviews becoming more popular. *WKOWTV*. Retrieved February 22, 2010, from http://www.wkowtv.com/Global/story.asp?S=11655389

[12] Domeyer, D. (2007, January/February). *OfficePro*, p. 5.

[13] Maher, K. (2004, October 5). Job seekers and recruiters pay more attention to blogs. Retrieved August 12, 2007, from http://www.careerjournal.com/jobhunting/usingnet/20041005-maher.html

[14] Ryan, L. (2007, May 6). Job seekers: Prepare your stories. Retrieved February 22, 2010, from http://ezinearticles.com/?Job-Seekers:-Prepare-Your-Stories&id=142327

[15] Haefner, R. (2009, June 10). More employer screen candidates via social networking sites. *CareerBuilder*. Retrieved February 22, 2010, from http://www.careerbuilder.com/Article/CB-1337-Getting-Hired-More-Employers-Screening-Candidates-via-Social-Networking-Sites/

[16] Finder, A. (2006, June 11). For some, online persona undermines a résumé. *The New York Times*. Retrieved February 22, 2010, from http://www.nytimes.com/2006/06/11/us/11recruit.html?ex=1307678400&en=ddfbe1e3b386090b&ei=5090

[17] Haefner, R. (2009, June 10). More employer screen candidates via social networking sites. *CareerBuilder*. Retrieved February 22, 2010, from http://www.careerbuilder.com/Article/CB-1337-Getting-Hired-More-Employers-Screening-Candidates-via-Social-Networking-Sites/

[18] Mahoney, S. (2006, September 4). Finding postmodern marketers. *Advertising Age*. Retrieved March 2, 2010, from http://findarticles.com/p/articles/mi_hb6398/is_200609/ai_n25579339/

[19] Hiring process. (2010). *Google.com*. Retrieved March 13, 2010, from http://www.google.com/intl/en/jobs/joininggoogle/hiringprocess/

[20] Wright, D. (2004, August/September). Tell stories, get hired. *OfficePro*, pp. 32–33.

[21] FAQs about interview questions. (2009). Retrieved February 25, 2010, from University of Wisconsin-Eau Claire Career Center at http://www.uwec.edu/career/Online_Library/illegal_ques.htm

[22] Doyle, A. (n.d.). Illegal interview questions. *About.com*. Retrieved February 25, 2010, from http://jobsearchtech.about.com/od/interview/l/aa022403.htm

[23] Anten, T. (2008, October 15). How to handle illegal interview questions. Retrieved February 25, 2010, from http://www.careerservices.calpoly.edu/students/interviewing/illegal.htm; Illegal interview questions. (2010). Retrieved February 25, 2010, from http://www.jobinterviewquestions.org/questions/illegal-questions.asp; and Illegal interview questions. (2007). *FindLaw.com*. Retrieved February 25, 2010, from http://employment.findlaw.com/employment/employment-employee-hiring/employment-employee-hiring-interview-questions.html

[24] Lublin, J. S. (2008, February 5). Notes to interviewers should go beyond a simple thank you. *The Wall Street Journal*, p. B1. Retrieved February 25, 2010, from http://online.wsj.com/public/article_print/SB120215930971242053.html

[25] Ibid.

[26] Needleman, S. E. (2006, February 7). Be prepared when opportunity calls. *The Wall Street Journal*. Retrieved March 2, 2010, from http://online.wsj.com/article/SB113927577768966742.html

Acknowledgments

Chapter 1

p. 3 Opening case study based on Useem, M. (2008, December 8). New ideas for this Pepsi generation. *U.S. News & World Report*, p. 49; Indra K. Nooyi biography. (n.d.). Retrieved March 21, 2009, from http://www.notablebiographies.com; Brady, D. (2007, June 11). Keeping cool in hot water. Retrieved July 10, 2007, from Business Source Premier database; PepsiCo touts water, energy savings from 2007 (n.d.). Retrieved March 21, 2009, from http://www.greenbiz.com; and Nooyi, I. (n.d.). The best advice I ever got. Retrieved March 27, 2009, from www.cnnmoney.com.

p. 4 Spotlight (Aylwin Lewis) based on Berner, R. (2005, October 31). At Sears, a great communicator. *BusinessWeek*, p. 50.

p. 6 Spotlight (Oren Harari) based on Harari, O. (1997, November). Flood your organization with knowledge. *Management Review*, p. 33; and Harari, O (2006). *Break from the pack: How to compete in a copycat economy*. Upper Saddle River, NJ: FT Press.

p. 9 Photo essay about Google Wave. Google Web site. Retrieved January 2, 2010, from http://wave.google.com/help/wave/about.html

p. 12 Figure 1.3 based on U.S. 2001 Bureau of the Census figures appearing in Karoly, L. A., & Paris, C. W. A. *The 21st century at work*. Santa Monica, CA: Rand Corporation, pp. 36–39.

p. 14 Ethics Check (Bypassing or False Advertising?) based on Burnsed, B. BTW. (2009, June 29). *BusinessWeek*, p. 019.

p. 28 Photo essay based on Henriques, D. (2009, June 29). Madoff Is Sentenced to 150 Years for Ponzi Scheme. *New York Times*. Retrieved December 19, 2009, from http://www.nytimes.com/2009/06/30/business/30madoff.html

Chapter 2

p. 40 Photo essay based on Wilson, M., & Baker, A. (2009, January 15). A Quick Rescue Kept Death Toll at Zero. *The New York Times*. Retrieved December 21, 2009, from http://www.nytimes.com/2009/01/16/nyregion/16rescue.html

p. 42 Plugged In based on Schindler, E. (2008, February 15). Running an effective teleconference or virtual meeting. *CIO*. Retrieved June 28, 2009, from http://www.cio.com; Gordon, J. (2005, June). Do your virtual teams deliver only virtual performance? *Training*, 20; Brown-Johnston, N. (2005, January–February). Virtual teamwork: Smart business leaders are building high-performance virtual teams. *Detroiter*, 55; Managing virtual teams. (2004, March 16). *Info-Tech Advisor Newsletter*; Snyder, B. (2003, May). Teams that span time zones face new work rules. *Stanford Business Magazine*. Retrieved April 15, 2007, from http://www.gsb.stanford.edu/news/bmag/sbsm0305/feature_virtual_teams.shtml; Loudin, K. H. (2003, June). Building bridges: Virtual teamwork in the 21st century. *Contract Management*; and Armstrong, D. (2000, March). Building teams across borders. *Executive Excellence*, 10.

p. 43 Figure 2.1 adapted from Robbins, H. A., and Finley, M. (1995). *Why Teams Don't Work*. Princeton, NJ: Peterson's/Pacesetter Books, Chapters 5 to 16.

p. 43 Discussion of Tuckman's model based on Robbins, H. A., & Finley, M. (1995). *Why teams don't work*. Princeton, NJ: Peterson's/Pacesetter Books, Chapter 22.

pp. 44–45 Discussion of conflict and groupthink based on Toledo, R. (2008, June). Conflict is everywhere. *PM Network*. Retrieved June 28, 2009, from Business Source Complete database; McNamara, P. (2003, August/September). Conflict resolution strategies. *OfficePro*, p. 25; Weiss, W. (2002, November). Building and managing teams. *SuperVision*, p. 19; Eisenhardt, K. (1997, July/August). How management teams can have a good fight. *Harvard Business Review*, pp. 77–85; Brockmann, E. (1996, May). Removing the paradox of conflict from group decisions. *Academy of Management Executives*, pp. 61–62; and Beebe, S., & Masterson, J. (1999). *Communicating in small groups*. New York: Longman, pp. 198–200.

p. 45 Spotlight (Steve Ballmer) based on the following: CEO job was surprisingly different. (2007, April 30). *USA Today*, p. B2.

p. 46 Ethical Insights based on Wilson, G. (1996). *Groups in context*. New York: McGraw-Hill, pp. 24–27; and Robbins, H., & Finley, M. (1995). *Why teams don't work*. Princeton, NJ: Peterson's/Pacesetter Books, pp. 88–89.

p. 49 Spotlight (Reid Hastie) based on Hastie, R. (2009, January 18). Meetings are a matter of precious time. *The New York Times*, p. BU2.

p. 53 Figure 2.6 Courtesy of MeetingSense Software Corporation, http://www.meetingsense.com.

p. 61 Career Coach box (Listening to Nonnative Speakers) based on Marshall, T., & Vincent, J. Improving listening skills: Methods, activities, and resources; Instructor's Manual, *Business communication: Process and product*, 6e; Varner, I., & Beamer, L. (1995). *Intercultural communication in the global workplace*. (Boston: Irwin, McGraw-Hill), p. 37; and Lee, C. (1993, January). How to deal with the foreign accent. *Training*, pp. 72, 75.

p. 62 Spotlight (Oprah Winfrey) based on Marshall, L. (1998, November). The intentional Oprah. *InStyle*, p. 341.

Chapter 3

p. 81 Figure 3.1 based on Bellman, E. (2009, June 30). McDonald's to expand in India. *The Wall Street Journal*. Retrieved July 7, 2009, from http://online.wsj.com; Adams, B. (2007, July 19). McDonald's strange menu around the world. Retrieved July 7, 2009, from www.trifter.com; Adamy, J. (2007, October 16). As burgers boom in Russia, McDonald's touts discipline. *The Wall Street Journal*. Retrieved July 14, 2009, from http://online.wsj.com; and Steinberger, M. (2009, June 25). How McDonald's conquered France. *Slate*. Retrieved July 14, 2009, from http://www.slate.com/id/2221246/pagenum/all/

p. 82 Plugged In (Greenland and Iceland: The Most Connected Countries in the World?) based on the following: Internet usage statistics: The Internet big picture. (2009). *Internet World Stats*. Retrieved July 16, 2009, from http://www.internetworldstats.com/stats.htm

p. 85 Figure 3.2 based on Chaney, L. H., & Martin, J. S. (2000). *Intercultural business communication*, 2e. Upper Saddle River, NJ: Prentice Hall, Chapter 5; J. Chung's analysis appearing in Chen, G. M., & Starosta, W. J. *Foundations of intercultural communication*. Boston: Allyn and Bacon, 1998, p. 51; and O'Hara-Devereaux, M. & Johansen, R. (1994). *Globalwork: Bridging distance, culture, and time*. San Francisco: Jossey-Bass, p. 55.

p. 88 Ethical Insights based on Saslow, E. (2009, June 3). As the myths abound, so does Islamic outreach. *The Washington Post*, p. C1. Retrieved July 8, 2009, from Factiva database.

p. 89 Ethics Check (The World's Worst Tourists) based on Tandy, J., & Mackenzie, J. (2009, July 9). French tourists seen as world's worst: Survey. *Reuters.com*. Retrieved July 9, 2009, from http://www.reuters.com/

p. 91 Figure 3.3 based on Ostheimer, S. (1995, February). Internationalize yourself. *Business Education Forum*, p. 45. Reprinted with permission of Sondra Ostheimer, Southwest Wisconsin Technical College.

p. 93 Figure 3.4 based on Horwitz, S. (2002). Why the crazy dates? *PSA Journal*, 68(7), 11. Retrieved July 20, 2009, from Academic Search Premier database; and Horton, W. (1993, Fourth Quarter). The almost universal language: Graphics for international documents. *Technical Communication*, p. 690.

p. 96 Spotlight (International Perp Walk: Siemens Busted for Bribery) based on Schubert, S., & Miller, T. C. (2008, December 21). Where bribery was just a line item. *New York Times*, p. BU1. Retrieved July 23, 2009, from ProQuest Newspapers database.

p. 97 Figure 3.7 based on The 2008 Corruption Perceptions Index, Transparency International. Retrieved July 9, 2009, from http://www.transparency.org/policy_research/surveys_indices/cpi

p. 99 Spotlight (Ursula Burns) based on Byrnes, N., & Crockett, R. O. (2009, May 28). Ursula Burns: An historic succession at Xerox. *BusinessWeek.com*. Retrieved August 4, 2009, from http://www.businessweek.com/magazine/content/09_23/b4134018712853_page_3.htm

p. 100 Photo essay based on UPS Corporate Responsibility Web site. (2009). UPS Supplier Diversity Guidelines. Retrieved December 26, 2009, from http://www.community.ups.com/docs/UPS_Supplier_Diversity_Guidelines.pdf

p. 101 Spotlight (Andrea Jung) based on Adler, S. J. (2006, February 6). Avon, the Net, and glass ceilings: A conversation with Andrea Jung. *BusinessWeek.com*. Retrieved August 4, 2009, from http://www.businessweek.com/magazine/content/06_06/b3970143.htm; On the call: Avon Products CEO Andrea Jung. (2009, July 30). *Associated Press/BusinessWeek.com*. Retrieved August 4, 2009, from http://www.businessweek.com/ap/financialnews/D99OSFVO1.htm; and Jones, D. (2009, June 14). Avon's Andrea Jung: CEOs need to reinvent themselves. *USAToday*. Retrieved July 15, 2009, from http://www.usatoday.com/money/companies/management/advice/2009-06-14-jung-ceo-avon_N.htm

p. 101 Career Coach (He Said, She Said) based on Basow, S. A., & Rubenfeld, K. (2003, February). Troubles talk: Effects of gender and gender-typing. *Sex Roles: A Journal of Research*, 183. Retrieved July 23, 2009, from http://www.springerlink.com/content/rm75xx843786037q/fulltext.pdf; Wood, J. T. (2002).

Gendered lives. Belmont, CA: Wadsworth, p. 119; Tear, J. (1995, November 20). They just don't understand gender dynamics. *The Wall Street Journal*, p. A12. Retrieved July 23, 2009, from Factiva database; Roiphe, A. (1994, October). Talking trouble. *Working Woman*, pp. 28–31; Stuart, C. (1994, February). Why can't a woman be more like a man? *Training Tomorrow*, pp. 22–24; and Wolfe, A. (1994, December 12). She just doesn't understand. *New Republic, 211*(24), pp. 26–34.

Chapter 4

p. 114 Ethics Check (Cramster) based on Foderaro, L. S. (2009, May 18). Psst! Need the answer to No. 7? Just click here. *The New York Times*, p. A17.

p. 117 Spotlight (Warren Buffett) based on the following: *A Plain English Handbook*, Preface. (1997). Retrieved August 12, 2009, from http://www.sec.gov/pdf/handbook.pdf

p. 120 Spotlight (John H. Johnson) based on the following: How he went from a tin-roof shack to the Forbes 400. (1998, March 26). *Investor's Business Daily*, p. 1.

p. 127 Photo essay based on Dahl, D. (2009, June 1). How to Choose the Right Collaboration Software. *Inc.* magazine. Retrieved December 28, 2009, from http://www.inc.com/magazine/20090601/how-to-choose-theright-collaboration-software.html

p. 128 Discussion of online collaboration tools based on the following: Beyond Google Docs: 7 Web-based collaboration tools. (2009, July 6). *Information Week*. Retrieved July 19, 2009, from InfoTrac College Edition database; Dahl, D. (2009, June). Connecting the dots: How to choose the right collaboration software for your company. *Inc.*, p. 103. Retrieved July 19, 2009, from InfoTrac College Edition database; and Fichter, D. (2005, July/August). The many forms of e-collaboration: Blogs, wikis, portals, groupware, discussion boards, and instant messaging. *Online*, pp. 48–50. Retrieved July 18, 2009, from Business Source Complete database.

p. 130 Ethics Check (Shepard Fairey) based on Crovitz, L. G. (2009, March 16). The fine art of copyright. *The Wall Street Journal*, p. A17.

Chapter 5

p. 141 Spotlight (Chris Heatherly and Len Mazzocco) based on Damian, J. (2009, July 2). Inside Disney's toy factory. *BusinessWeek Online*. Retrieved August 7, 2009, from Business Source Complete database.

p. 146 Ethics Check (How Sweet It Is) based on Lerner, I. (2009, May 25). Sweet nothings. *ICIS Chemical Business*. Retrieved August 18, 2009, from Business Source Complete database.

p. 152 Spotlight (Bob Knight) based on Knight, B. (2007, February). Guard against five common mistakes. *Writing That Works*, p. 2.

p. 154 Ethics Check (Blogging for Pay) Based on Frazier, M. (2006, October 30). Want to build up blog buzz? *Advertising Age*. Retrieved August 7, 2009, from InfoTrac College Edition.

Chapter 6

p. 163 Opening case study based on Lockyer, S. E. (2009, August 12). Yum lays out plans for Taco Bell. *Nation's Restaurant News*. Retrieved August 17, 2009, from Business Source Complete database; Lockyer, S. E. (2008, February 18). Yum readies menu tweaks aimed at boosting soft U.S. sales. *Nation's Restaurant News*. Retrieved August 19, 2009, from Business Source Complete database; Lockyer, S. E. (2006, December 18). Yum to expand Taco Bell breakfast test: Potential rollout anchors company's plan to boost core chains' flagging U.S. sales. *Nation's Restaurant News*. Retrieved August 18, 2009, from InfoTrac College Edition database; Analysis of Yum! Brands Inc. (2007, February 13). *M2 Presswire*. Retrieved April 17, 2007, from InfoTrac College Edition database; Wheaton, K. (2007, March 5). Yum Brands has a rat problem, but it will have customers, too. *Advertising Age*, p. 4. Retrieved April 7, 2007, from Business Source Premier database; and Sharma, S. (2007, January 10). Brand should not get trapped in low-price bracket. *The Economic Times*. Retrieved April 7, 2007, from InfoTrac College Edition database.

p. 169 Spotlight (Colin Powell) based on Powell, C. (1996, December). Quotations from Chairman Powell: A leadership primer. *Management Review*, p. 36.

p. 172 Spotlight (Arthur Levitt) based on Nielan, C. (2000, November). Arthur Levitt and the SEC: Promoting plain English. *Intercom*, p. 17. Retrieved August 19, 2009, from Business Source Complete database.

p. 173 Ethics Check (Costly Writing) based on Duffy, S. P. (2007, April 23). Attorney hit with $6.6 million malpractice verdict. *The Legal Intelligencer*. Retrieved August 16, 2009, from http://www.law.com.

p. 173 Spotlight (William Raspberry) based on Raspberry, W. (1998, April). Words to the wise on students' speech. *Writing Concepts*, p. 3.

p. 184 Activity 6.18 based on Pomerenke, P. J. (1998, December). Teaching ethics with apartment leases. *Business Communication Quarterly, 61*(4), 119.

Chapter 7

p. 193 Spotlight (James E. Gaskin) based on Gaskin, J. E. (2009, August 19). Three tips for more effective e-mailing. *Network World*. Retrieved January 29, 2010, from http://www.networkworld.com/columnists/2009/090819-gaskin.html

p. 199 Spotlight (Nancy Flynn) based on Irvine, M. (2009, July 12). Young workers push employers for wider Web access. *Associated Press*. Retrieved January 13, 2010, from http://hosted.ap.org/dynamic/stories/U/US_TEC_BLOCKED_OFFICE_INTERNET?SITE=VTBEN&SECTION=HOME&TEMPLATE=DEFAULT

p. 200 Zooming In Part 2 (Got Something to Tweet About at Work? Think Again) based on 5 ways Twitter can get you fired. (2009, October 8). *Applicant.com*. Retrieved January 28, 2010, from http://applicant.com/5-ways-twitter-can-get-you-fired/

p. 201 Spotlight (Donagh Herlihy) based on Hamm, S. (2009, June 15). Cloud computing's big bang for business. *BusinessWeek*, pp. 42–44.

p. 201 Plugged In box (Cloud Computing) based on Hamm, S. (2009, June 15). Cloud computing's big bang for business. *BusinessWeek*, pp. 43–44; Wildstrom, S. H. (2009, April 6). What to entrust to the cloud. *BusinessWeek*, pp. 89–90; Burrows, P. (2009, August 17). Apple and Google: Another step apart. *BusinessWeek*, pp. 24–25; and Hamm, S. (2009, April 6). IBM reaches for the clouds. *BusinessWeek*, p. 34.

p. 204 Tips for Creating a Professional Blog based on Wuorio, J. (n.d.). Blogging for business: 7 tips for getting started. Microsoft Small Business Center. Retrieved January 14, 2010, from http://www.microsoft.com/smallbusiness/resources/marketing/online-marketing/small-business-blog.aspx#Smallbusinessblog

p. 204 Ethics Check (Fired for Blogging) based on Palan, E. (2008, May 29). Seven people fired for blogging. *Mental Floss*. Retrieved January 31, 2010, from http://www.mentalfloss.com/blogs/archives/15329

p. 205 The five main uses of wikis based on Nations, D. (2009). The business wiki. About.com: Web Trends. Retrieved February 13, 2010, from http://webtrends.about.com/od/wiki/a/business-wiki.htm

p. 208 Ethics Check (Social Media Help Spread Errors Like Wildfire) based on Anderson, M. (2009, August 12). Best Buy $9.99 TV offer was too good to be true. *Yahoo News*. Retrieved December 16, 2009, from http://news.yahoo.com; and Pricing blunder: Ecommerce. (2003, November 11.) *Webmaster World*. Retrieved December 16, 2009, from http://www.webmasterworld.com/forum22/1310.htm

p. 211 Spotlight (Scott Townsend) based on Karpinski, R. (2009, April 6). B-to-b followers flock to Twitter. *B to B*. Retrieved December 17, 2009, from ProQuest database.

Chapter 8

p. 223 Spotlight (Peggy Foran) based on Levitt, A. (2002). *Take on the street*. New York: Pantheon Books, p. 226.

p. 234 Ethics Check (Renting or Buying?) based on the following: An eagle eye on retail scams. (2005, August 8). *BusinessWeek*. Retrieved September 21, 2009, from http://www.businessweek.com

p. 234 Photo essay based on Zimmermann, S. (2007, June 24). The fixer: Honeymoon glitch—cruising to a solution. *The Chicago Sun-Times*. Retrieved June 29, 2007, from http://www.suntimes.com/news/zimmermann/440955,CST-NWS-fixer24.article

p. 240 Spotlight (Andrew S. Grove) based on the following: The fine art of feedback. (1992, February). *Working Woman*, p. 26.

p. 236–240 Discussion of claim and adjustment letters based on A new take on complaints. (2009, October). *Communication Briefings*, p. 4; McCartney, S. (2007, March 20). What airlines do when you complain. *The Wall Street Journal*, p. D5; Liao, H. (2007, March). Do it right this time: The role of employee service recovery performance in customer-perceived justice and customer loyalty after service failures. *Journal of Applied Psychology, 92*(2), 475. Retrieved January 22, 2010, from Business Source Premier database; Davidow, M. (2003, February). Organizational responses to customer complaints: What works and what doesn't. *Journal of Service Research, 5*(3) 31. Retrieved January 20, 2010, from Business Source Premier database; Michelson, M. W., Jr. (2003, December). Turning complaints into cash. *The American Salesman*, p. 22; Torp, J. R. (2003, March/April). In person, by phone, by mail, or online: Managing customer complaints. *ABA Bank Compliance*, p. 10; Kim, C., Kim, S., Im, S., & Shin, S. (2003). The effect of attitude and perception on consumer complaint intentions. *The Journal of Consumer Marketing, 20*, 352; and David, D., & Baker, M. A. (1994). Rereading bad news: Compliance-gaining features in management memos. *The Journal of Business Communications*, 267–290.

Chapter 9

p. 264 Ethics Check based on Nifong issues apology to ex-lacrosse players. (2007, April 12). Retrieved January 19, 2010, from http://www.wral.com/news/local/story/1270348/?d_full_comments=1&d_comments_page=2

p. 264 Spotlight (Marshall Goldsmith) based on Goldsmith, M., & Reiter, M. (2007). *What got you here won't get you there*. New York: Hyperion Books. Excerpt retrieved January 20, 2010, from http://www.businessweek.com

p. 265 Spotlight (Malcolm Forbes) based on Forbes, M. (1999). How to write a business letter. In K. Harty (Ed.), *Strategies for business and technical writing*. Boston: Allyn and Bacon, p. 108.

p. 271 Spotlight (Jeff Bezos) based on Milliot, J. (2009, July 27). Cracks in Amazon's e-book empire. Retrieved January 11, 2010, from www.publishersweekly.com/article/CA6673024.html

p. 273 Plugged In box based on Weber, H. R. (2009, October 13). Social sites new conduits for customer service. Retrieved January 21, 2010, from, http://www.crmbuyer.com; Social networking and customer service. (n.d.) Retrieved January 21, 2010, from http://www.allthingscrm.com; Baker, L. (2008, July 24). How to combat complaints sites in Google. Retrieved January 21, 2010, from http://www.searchenginejournal.com; Whitehead, J. (2009, December 9). Are customer complaints on Twitter good for brands? Retrieved January 22, 2010, from http://www.brandrepublic.com; and Miles, S. (2009, October 26). Complain, complain, complain. Retrieved January 22, 2010, from http://www.recessionwire.com

p. 279 Ethics Check based on RadioShack uses e-mail to fire employees. (2006, August 30). Associated Press. Retrieved January 21, 2009, from http://www.sfgate.com/cgi-bin/article.cgi?f=/n/a/2006/08/30/financial/f131351D00.DTL

Chapter 10

p. 299 Spotlight (Irene Rosenfeld) based on Berfield, S., & Arndt, M. (2010, January 25). Kraft's sugar rush. *Bloomberg BusinessWeek*, p. 37.

p. 302 Ethical Insights box based on Troyka, L. Q. (2005). *Simon & Schuster handbook for writers* (7th ed.). Upper Saddle River, NJ: Prentice Hall, pp. 142–145; Crews, F. (1987). *The Random House Handbook.* New York: Random House, pp. 76–78; and Downes, S. (n.d.). Stephen's guide to the logical fallacies. Retrieved January 28, 2010, from http://onegoodmove.org/fallacy/

p. 312 Spotlight (Herb Kelleher) based on Krames, J. A. (2003, November). Performance culture. *Executive Excellence*, 16; and Kelleher, K. (1992). Beware the impossible guarantee. *Inc.*, p. 30.

p. 319 Figure 10.8. Letter adapted from Yunxia, Z. (2000, December). Building knowledge structures in teaching cross-cultural sales genres, Appendix B. *Business Communication Quarterly, 63*(4), 67–68. Permission to reprint granted by Association for Business Communication. Chinese characters provided by Dr. Bertha Du-Babcock.

p. 326 Activity 10.6. Sales letter adapted from Yunxia, Z. (2000, December). Building knowledge structures in teaching cross-cultural sales genres, Appendix A. *Business Communication Quarterly, 63*(4), 66–67. Permission to reprint granted by Association for Business Communication.

Chapter 11

p. 347 Zooming In, Part 2, based on Shah, D. (2006, October 16). Six interesting stats about startup success. *OnStartups.com.* Retrieved January 28, 2010, from http://onstartups.com/tabid/3339/bid/79/Six-Interesting-Stats-About-Startup-Success.aspx; and Kehrer, D. (2006). Upping the odds of startup success. *Business.com.* Retrieved January 28, 2010, from http://www.business.com/directory/advice/startup/getting-started-basics/upping-the-odds-of-startup-success/

p. 351 Figure 11.7's image published with permission of ProQuest. Further reproduction is prohibited without permission. Image produced by ProQuest. Inquires may be made to: ProQuest, P.O. Box 1346, 789 E. Eisenhower Parkway, Ann Arbor, MI 48106-1346 USA. Telephone (734) 761-7400; E-mail: info@proquest.com; Web-page: www.proquest.com

p. 354 Spotlight (Tom Peters) based on Peters, T. (1991). *Thriving on chaos.* New York: Knopf, pp. 230–231.

p. 356 Spotlight (Eric Dezenhall) based on Conlin, M. (2007, April 16). Web attack. *BusinessWeek*, p. 54.

p. 357 Figure 11.9 based on Search Engine Watch (2009, September 15). Top search providers for August 2009. SearchEngineWatch.com. Retrieved January 29, 2010, from http://searchenginewatch.com/3634991; Sullivan, D. (2006, August 21). ComScore media metrix search engine ratings. Retrieved January 28, 2010, from http://searchenginewatch.com/reports/article.php/2156431

p. 361 Spotlight (Jim Berkowitz) based on Jones, D. (2006, August 1). Authorship gets lost on Web: Some bloggers don't give credit where it's due. *USA Today*, p. B3. Retrieved January 22, 2010, from ProQuest database.

Chapter 12

p. 395 Spotlight (Relmond Van Daniker) based on Mosquera, M. (2008, February 20). Government accountants: Taxpayers distrust federal financial reporting. *Federal Computer Week.* Retrieved February 23, 2010, from http://fcw.com/Articles/2008/02/20/Government-accountants-Taxpayers-distrust-federal-financial-reporting.aspx?Page=1

p. 396 Career Coach box based on Booher, D. (2001, April). E-writing. *Executive Excellence*, p. 16; Bernstel, J. B., & Thomases, H. (2001, March). Writing words for the Web. *Bank Marketing*, pp. 16–21; and Graves, P. R., & Murry, J. E. (1990, Summer). Enhancing communication with effective page design and typography. *Delta Pi Epsilon* Instructional Strategies Series.

p. 402 Ethics Check based on Neuman, W. (2010, February 25). Hidden ingredient: The sweetener. *The New York Times*, pp. B1, B5.

p. 421 Activity 12.28 Feasibility Report: Can Rainbow Precision Instruments Afford a Children's Center? is based on a case study, "Excel Industries, Inc." by James S. O'Rourke, IV, and is used by permission. Copyright: 1995. Revised: 2005. University of Notre Dame. All rights reserved.

Chapter 13

p. 430 Spotlight (Michael Asner) based on Bellett, G. (2009, July 24). Expert on government contracts sees a winning bid as a work of art. *ProposalWorks.com.* Retrieved March 5, 2010, from http://www.proposalworks.com/articles/work-of-art.asp

p. 432 Spotlight (Tim Berry) based on Berry, T. (2009, November 1). Common business plan mistakes. *Bplans.com.* Retrieved March 9, 2010, from http://articles.bplans.com/writing-a-business-plan/common-business-plan-mistakes/31

p. 454 Figure 13.5 based on Sokuvitz, S., & George, A. M. (2003, June). Teaching culture: The challenges and opportunities of international public relations. *Business Communication Quarterly*, 97; Koh, A. C. (2003). Teaching understanding cultural differences for business in an Internet-based economy. *Journal of Teaching in International Business, 15*(2), 27; and Sterkel, K. S. (1988, September). Integrating intercultural communication and report writing in the communication class. *The Bulletin of the Association for Business Communication*, 13–16.

Chapter 14

p. 457 Zooming In Part 1 based on Johnson, B., & Arthur, C. (2010, January 27). Apple iPad launch: Live coverage. *Guardian.co.uk.* Retrieved March 28, 2010, from http://www.guardian.co.uk/technology/blog/2010/jan/27/apple-tablet-launch-live-coverage; Steve Jobs' obsession with secrecy and the "big-bang." (2009, December 8). *Edible Apple Blog.* Retrieved March 28, 2010, from http://www.edibleapple.com/steve-jobs-obsession-with-secrecy-and-the-big-bang/

p. 458 Spotlight (Guy Kawasaki) based on Bryant, A. (2010, March 21). Just give him 5 sentences, not "War and Peace." *The New York Times*, p. BU 2. Retrieved March 29, 2010, from http://www.nytimes.com/2010/03/21/business/21corner.html

p. 459 Figure 14.1 based on Elsea, J. G. (1985, September). Strategies for effective presentations. *Personnel Journal*, pp. 31–33 in Hamilton, C. (2001). *Communicating for results.* Belmont, CA: Wadsworth/Thomson Learning, p. 340.

p. 460 Career Coach (Guy Kawasaki) based on Kawasaki, G. (2005, December 30). The 10/20/30 rule of PowerPoint. *How to Change the World.* Retrieved March 20, 2010, from http://blog.guykawasaki.com/2005/12/the_102030_rule.html and on personal communication by e-mail on April 8, 2010.

p. 463 Spotlight (Dianna Booher) based on Booher, D. (2003). *Speak with confidence.* New York: McGraw-Hill Professional, p. 13.

p. 464 Spotlight (John Chambers) based on Gallo, C. (2007, January 4). The camera doesn't lie. *BusinessWeek Online.* Retrieved August 3, 2007, from http://www.businessweek.com/smallbiz/content/jan2007/sb20070103_877305.htm?chan=search

p. 466 Figure 14.3 based on Booher, D. (2003). *Speak with confidence.* New York: McGraw-Hill Professional, pp. 131–143; U.S. Department of Labor. (1996, May). Presenting effective presentations with visual aids. Retrieved March 26, 2010, from http://www.osha.gov/doc/outreachtraining/htmlfiles/traintec.html; and McConnon, S. (2002). *Presenting with power.* Oxford: How To Books, pp. 38–43.

p. 467 Zooming In Part 2 based on Gallo, C. (2009, October 6). Uncovering Steve Jobs' presentation secrets. *BusinessWeek.* Retrieved March 28, 2010, from http://www.businessweek.com/smallbiz/content/oct2009/sb2009106_706829.htm

p. 475 Photo essay based on Fisher, A. (2009, August 24). 50 Best Websites 2009: Kiva. *Time.* Retrieved April 10, 2010, from http://www.time.com; Schonfeld, E. (2009, November 1). Four years after founding, Kiva hits $100 million in microloans. *TechCrunch.* Retrieved April 10, 2010, from http://techcrunch.com

p. 483 Spotlight (Patrick Forsyth) based on Forsyth, P. (2000). *Telephone skills.* London: Management Shapers, pp. 21–23.

p. 489 Activity 14.11 based on Booher, D. (2003). *Speak with confidence.* New York: McGraw-Hill Professional, pp. 167–172.

Chapter 15

p. 497 Spotlight (Michael Dell) based on Dell Press Release (2010, January 25). Michael Dell shares vision for role of IT, entrepreneurialism in driving sustainable competitiveness. Retrieved February 25, 2010, from http://content.dell.com/us/en/corp/d/press-releases/2010-1-25-Michael-Dell-Speaks-at-GCF.aspx; Batelle, J., & Dell, M. (2004, May). Still giving 'em Dell twenty years in, Michael Dell's hair is a little grayer—but his taste for beating the competition remains as strong as ever. *Business2.0*, 99; and Turner, N. (1999, March 1). Entrepreneur Michael Dell. *Investor's Business Daily*, p. A8.

p. 502 Career Coach (networking) partially based on Gabbard, D. (2009, June 12). Unlocking the hidden job market. *Examiner.com Washington DC.* Retrieved February 15, 2010, from http://www.examiner.com/x-/x-11194-Cleveland-Unemployment-Examiner~y2009m6d12-Unlocking-the-hidden-job-market; Salpeter, M. (2010). Leverage Twitter for your job search. *Twitip.com.* Retrieved February 15, 2010, from http://www.twitip.com/leverage-twitter-for-your-job-search/; Dickler, J. (2009, June 10) The hidden job market. *CNNMoney.com.* Retrieved February 17, 2010, from http://money.cnn.com/2009/06/09/news/economy/hidden_jobs/; and Borney, N. (2010, February 16). 10 ways to crack Michigan's hidden job market. *AnnArbor.com.* Retrieved February 17, 2010, from http://www.annarbor.com/business-review/ann-arbor-human-resources-experts-offer-tips-how-to-get-hired-in-2010/

p. 506 Photo essay (George O'Leary) based on Di Meglio, F. (2009, June 8). The temptation to lie on your résumé. *BusinessWeek.* Retrieved February 19, 2010, from http://www.businessweek.com/bschools/blogs/mba_admissions/archives/2009/06/the_temptation.html; Zupek, R. (2007, September 24). Infamous résumé lies. *MSN.Careers.* Retrieved February 19, 2010, from http://msn.careerbuilder.com/Article/MSN-1154-Cover-Letters-Resumes-Infamous-R%c3%a9sum%c3%a9-Lies/?ArticleID=1154&cbRecursionCnt=1&cbsid=89a54a8c9fa14c02a47d88d64c184c64-319896364-R1-4

p. 516 Photo essay (video résumés) based on Athavaley, A. (2006, December 7). Posting your résumé on YouTube to stand out from the competition. *CareerJournal.com.* Retrieved July 31, 2007, from http://www.careerjournal.com/jobhunting/usingnet/20061207-athavaley.html

p. 524 Spotlight (Liz Ryan) based on Ryan, L. (2007). For job-hunters: How to find a contact name inside a target company. Retrieved July 2, 2007, from http://ezinearticles.com/?For-Job-Hunters:-How-to-Find-a-Contact-Name-Inside-a-Target-Company&id=101910

Chapter 16

p. 539 Photo essay (meal interview) based on Doyle, A. (2010). Interview etiquette: Manners, meals, and interviews. *About.com Guide.* Retrieved February 22, 2010, from http://jobsearch.about.com/cs/interviews/a/interviewdining.htm

p. 543 Photo essay (tattoos and piercings) based on Borlik, J. (2009, December 2). Tattoos still not overlooked in job search. *Central Michigan Life.* Retrieved March 8, 2010, from http://www.cm-life.com/2009/12/02/tattoos-still-not-overlooked-in-job-search/

p. 550 Career Coach (Let's Talk Money) based on Hansen, R. S. (2007). Salary negotiation do's and don'ts. Reprinted with permission of Quintessential Careers. Retrieved March 2, 2010, from http://www.quintcareers.com/salary-dos-donts.html

p. 551 Spotlight (Daisy Wright) based on Wright, D. (2004, August/September). Tell stories, get hired. *OfficePro*, pp. 32–33.

Index

B

C

D

E

J

K

L

M

N

O

P

Q

R

T

U

V

W

X

Y

Z